Sarada Ramakrishna Vivekananda
Associations

*Setting the feet of humanity
on the path of Universal Truth*

Footfalls of the Indian Rishis

Charting the Scriptures of Sacred Mother India

Babaji Bob Kindler

For further information contact:

SRV Associations
P.O. Box 1364
Honoka'a, HI 96727 USA
        or
P.O. Box 380
Paauilo, HI., 96776 USA

srvinfo@srv.org

www.srv.org

Cover Art — Subhavrata Chandra.

All color charts appearing in this book were created by Babaji Bob Kindler.

All copyrights of artwork utilized in this book remain the property of their respective copyright
holders. Special thanks to Rama Nand Tiwari for his permission to use many selections from his
personal collection of Indian art for the production of these dharma art wisdom charts.

The first printing of this book was made possible by funding from Mahesh Madhav.

Printed in the United States of America
ISBN: 978-1-891893-27-8

Table of Contents

List of Illustrations/Charts 7

Introduction 11

Chapter 1 The Baby Steps of Authentic Spirituality 17
    False Superimposition and the Five Sheaths

Chapter 2 The Swaggering Strut of Individuation 29
    Space, Time, Causation, Involution, and Divine Reflection

Chapter 3 Matching Strides with the Seers 58
    Spiritual Self-effort, Qualification, the Preceptor, the Aspirant, Purification, Mantra, and The Word

Chapter 4 Beating the Old Familiar Path 160
    Karma, Reincarnation, Samskaras, and Desire

Chapter 5 Walking Backwards 218
    Impediments and Obstacles on the Path: gunas, passions, fetters, ignorance

Chapter 6 Running a Race in a Dream 259
    Maya and Mahamaya, Sankalpa and Vikalpa, Action and Inaction

Chapter 7 Giant Steps — The Gait of the Gods 313
    Cosmology, Darshanas, and the Wisdom Pathways - 7 stages of knowledge, 4 yogas, 4 noble truths

Chapter 8 The Locomotion of Devotion 464
    Bhakti, Shraddha, Yajna, and the Path of Love

Chapter 9 Treading a Trail of Translucent Teachings 499
    Kundalini, Meditation, Brahmajnana, Moksha, Nirvana (Buddhism)

Chapter 10 The Ever-Stationary Self 673
    Brahman, Atman, Advaita, Samadhi, Shakti, Divine Reality

All Footfalls Charts Alphabetized 776

Sanskrit Glossary 782

Dedication

This dharmic testament is dedicated to You,

along with the reminder that if You should ever forget that Thou art That,

all You need to do is to open the pages of this book to see the many blessed Wisdom Teachings

that illustrate the truth of this fact.

May Peace be unto You.

List of Illustrations/Charts

≈ Chapter One: The Baby Steps of Spirituality

The Five Koshas of the Adhara System...19
The Five Sheaths and their Properties 21

≈ Chapter Two: Retracing the Strut of Individuation

Akasha — The Five Atmospheres...30
From Atomic to Atmic Particles..33
Kalpa — The Concept of Time in Vedic Cosmology...39
Time and Enlightenment 41
The Stainless Cause of the Universe 45
Causality, Origins, and Reincarnation 47
Chidabhasa — The Reflection of Brahman in the Cosmos 56

≈ Chapter Three: Matching Stride With the Seers

The Seven Qualifications and Seven Victories of a Tantric Aspirant...................59
The Four Treasures and Six Jewels 65
The Eight Limbs of Patanjali's Yoga 69
Precepts, Points, Practice, and Process of the Vajrayana Path...........................84
The Four Levels of Knowers of Brahman..88
The Ten Conditions of the Guru/Shishya Relationship 91
Sri Ramakrishna's Radiant Road to Self-Realization 103
Fourteen Qualities of a World Teacher 106
Waves in the Ocean of Mature Universalism 109
The Five Eternal Questions 116
Shuddha, Ashuddha, and Shuddhashuddha Tattvas...119
Chit Shuddhi, Kriya Shuddhi, and Dravya Shuddhi — The Three Kinds of Purity 122
Golden Rules for Sadhana and Transformation of Mind 125
Fundamental Facts about the Mantra 131
Sacred Bijas of Mantra Science 133
Twenty-one Points of Mantra Practice..135
The Four Stages of Mantra Practice 140
Transformation of Mind in Mantra Practice 142
Om and Hrim — The Two Great Bijas 144
The Three Matras of AUM in the Mandukyopanisad 146
The 3 States, 7 Limbs, and 19 Mouths of the Individual 149
Yogic Connections and Correlations in Meditation Practice 151
Four Stages of Knowledge and Four Phases of the Word...................................154
Nine Step Process of Meditation on AUM 157

≈ Chapter Four: Beating the Old Familiar Path

The Three Bodies Comprising the Nonself 161
The Process of Embodiment..164
Samskaras in the Human Mind 167
The Makeup of a Samskara and a Samskaraskandha 170
Cause and Effect in the Mind 172
The Nine Ways of Dealing With Desire 176
The Two Main Forms of Desire 180
Desire, Karma, Sanskaras, and Rebirth 184

Rebirth and the Refinement of Consciousness..186
The Sevenfold Road to Ruination 189
Teachings on the Bardo States 190
The Chain of Rebirth and its Twelve Links (nidanas) in Buddhism 192
The Appearance of the Puryastaka Body..194
The Mind's Release from Rebirth 197
The Illusory Ego's Projection via Rebirth 200
Varnashrama — The Four Castes of Life 202
Dharmashrama — The Four Stages of Life 204
Granthis — Knots in the Body/Mind Mechanism 206
The Four Types of Karma 210
The Dynamics of Karma Yoga...213
Karma Yoga — The Philosophy of Work 216

≈ Chapter Five: Walking Backwards

The Three Stages, Three Plateaus, and Three Obstacles...................................219
The Three Gunas of Maya According to Shankara 221
The Binding and Liberating Nature of the Three Gunas of Prakriti 223
Transcending the Six Billows and Six Transformations 225
Sri Ramachandra's Discourse of Divine Discontent 227
The Truth of the Existence of Suffering (Four Noble Truths & Eightfold Path) 229
Trividham Dukham — The Threefold Sorrows of Existence 231
The Origin and Perpetuation of Disease 233
The Destruction of Disease 235
The Three Dispositions of Living Beings 237
The Five Cosmic Bondages and Three Great Desires 240
The Six Passions, Six Transformations, Six Billows, and Eight Fetters 247
The Three Enemies of Reason, The Three Stupefactions, and The Four Deadly Traps.....249
The Six Illusory Bodies...251
The Seven Descending Steps of Negligence of Brahman 253
The Nine Obstacles (Vikshepas/Antarayas) to Yoga 255

≈ Chapter Six: Running a Race In a Dream

Vedantic and Conventional Views of Birth and Death 260
Vedanta, Theology, and Science 262
Aparinama — The Principle of Nontransformation 265
The Three Levels of Sankalpa/Vikalpa 267
Atmic and Mayic Sankalpa 269
"Lead Us from Lower Truth to Higher Truth" 271
Pratibha — Power of Intelligence 272
The Tree of Samsara 275
The Sword of Discrimination...276
The Evolutes, Characteristics, and Limiting Factors of Maya...........................279
Prakasha Shakti — The Revealing Power 293
False Assumptions about the Atman 294
King Svotta's Sankalpa City 297
The Three Types of Bondage and the Three Types of Liberation 299
The Nine Steps to Perfection 303
The Three Gunas of Nature 307
The Nine Complacencies and The Eight Great Accomplishments......................309

≈ Chapter Seven: Giant Steps — The Gait of the Gods

The Natural Unity of Vedic Religion and Philosophy.................................315

India's Sanatana Dharma.................................317

Manifested and Unmanifested Prakriti.................................321

Omkara — The Great Cause.................................323

The Five Akashas of Vedanta Philosophy.................................327

Dasabhumikas — The Ten Pure Lands.................................329

The Seven Stages of Spiritual Progress in Seven Systems.................................333

The Seven Stages of Knowledge in Yoga Vasishtha.................................335

The Fourteen Stages of Upper and Lower Knowledge.................................337

Knowledge, Knower, and That Which is to be Known.................................339

Brahmapada: How Brahman, Divine Reality, Disports Itself.................................341

Supreme Pathway to the Eternal Moksha.................................343

The Four Sentinels and the Three Great Sources.................................345

The Twenty-Four Cosmic Principles of Sankhya Philosophy.................................349

The Ten Fundamental Tenets of Sankhya.................................351

The Five Types of Minds and Intellects in Action.................................353

The Threefold Fruits, Threefold Causes, and Five Incitements to Action in the Gita.................................355

Thirty-Two Points of the Immortal Dharma.................................357

The Thirty-Six Cosmic Principles of Shaivism.................................359

The Twelve Higher Spandas of Shaivism.................................360

The Hierarchy of Existence in Shavism.................................363

The Purusharthas — The Four Fruits of Life.................................365

The Four Boons and The Four Fruits of Life.................................367

Siva's Two Shaktis, Four Padas, and Five Functions.................................369

The Eight Subtle and Eight Visible Forms of Siva.................................371

Triloka — The Three Worlds.................................373

The Seven Spheres, Seven Worlds, Seven Chakras, and Five Koshas.................................375

The Three Eternal Gateways.................................377

The Three Stages of Indian Philosophy.................................379

Vedantic Secrets of the Scriptures.................................381

The Synchronicity of Iti Iti and Neti Neti.................................383

The Seven Levels of Higher Knowledge in Those Fitted for the Brahman State.................................385

The Fourfold Presence and Other Gita Teachings.................................387

The Twelve Levels of Vairagya, Detachment.................................389

The Precipitous Ascent into Higher Awareness.................................391

The Seven Methods for Mastering Awareness.................................393

Some Obstacles and Solutions in Spiritual Life.................................396

The Yamas and Niyamas of Patanjali's Yoga.................................399

The Twenty Yamas and Niyamas of Tantra.................................403

Patanjali's Kriya Yoga and the Three Treasures of Patanjala.................................407

Patanjali's Nine Levels of Awareness in Aspirants.................................409

Viveka, Vairagya, Abhyasa, and Sthiti.................................411

The Seven Steps to Attainment of Kaivalya.................................413

Shankara's Doorways to Yoga.................................415

Controlling the Five Senses in Yoga.................................417

The Insinuation of the Five Kleshas on Spiritual Life.................................419

Controlling the Chitta-vrttis in Yoga.................................421

The Four Clarities of Spiritual Life.................................423

Patanjali's and Shankara's Yoga of the Mind 425
The Paths of Action and Inaction 427
The Two Complementary Paths 429
Chaturdasya Yoga — The Four Yogas 431
The Four Yogas and Their Synthesis 433
The Ocean of Awareness and its Yogic Waves 435
The Attainment of Rare Jnana 439
King Janaka's Song of Victory 441
Prescribed Pathways to Quiescence of Mind 443
Jujukai — The Ten Basic Precepts of Buddhism 445
Ahimsa in Jainism 447
Early Sankhya Acharyas 449
The Ancient Chest of Consciousness 451
The Three Bodies and the Five Sheaths 453
Sangai-Yui-Isshin — Three Worlds, One Mind 455
Brahmachakra — The Grand Vedic Wheel 457
The Mighty River of the Manifest Brahman 459
Quintessential Quintuplications 461
Srsti Rahasya — Tantra's Secret of Creation 463

≈ Chapter Eight: The Locomotion of Devotion

The Imminent and Transcendent Reality 465
The Four Parts and Eight Glories of Ishvari/Ishvara 467
The Four Types of Love According to Sri Ramakrishna 469
Pancha Bhava — The Five Worshipful Attitudes 471
The Four Forms of Liberation & The Five Divine Moods 473
The Eight Devotional Aids of Narada 475
Narada's Eight Devotional Aids 476
The Four Sensitivities, Four Beneficial Attitudes, & Four Perfections of the Heart 479
The Two Yogas of the Matri Avatar 481
Mother Kali, The Adyashakti 483
The Six Treasures & Six Divine Powers of God 485
The Unique Features of Sri Ramakrishna's Descent, Part 1 489
The Unique Features of Sri Ramakrishna's Descent, Part 2 490
The Fivefold Strata of Sacrifice (Yajna) 493
The Five Kinds & Twelves Types of Sacrifices 495
The Nine Limbs of Bhakti According to Sri Ram 497

≈ Chapter Nine: Treading a Trail of Translucent Teachings

Jnana Matra, Atom of Wisdom 501
Dissolving the Mindstream 503
Two Forms and Eight Main Types of Meditation 505
Nirguna and Saguna Brahman 507
Meditation and Prayer 509
Stages of Dissolution of the Mind in Yoga 511
Dissolved and Crystallized Mind 513
Walker of the Skies 515
Daigo-Tettei, Grounds of Satori 517
Fashioning a Pure and Buoyant Mind 519
Mother India's Revealed Scriptures on Earth 522

The 108 Upanisads 524

Shankara's Vivekachudamani Siddhanta 526

The Seer, The Seen, The Unseen, & The Obscene..529

The Sacred Doctrine of Conjunctions...531

The Four Celebrated Mystical Utterances...533

Inward Ascension of the Free Soul 535

Phases and Permutations of the All-Pervasive Prana 536

The Four States & The Vital Breath...539

The Singular Prana & Its Five Forms 541

Prana and the Illusion of Death...543

Manahpranasambandha, Connecting the Living Prana to the Luminous Mind.....545

Lokas, Nadis, and the Transmigration of Souls..548

Curtain of Nescience/Cloud of Unknowing..550

Jnana Chakshu — The Wisdom Eye 553

Mahashakti — The Supporting Force 555

The Ten Divine Articles of Sri Durga..557

Meditation on the Goddess 559

Preliminary Practices to Mantra and Meditation..561

Sadhana For Purification 564

The Disappearance of Ignorance 569

Progress Towards True Freedom 571

Spiritual Awakening by Stages...572

Phases of the Soul in Relativity...575

Lack of Spiritual Success & Its Causes 577

Qualification is King...578

Food and Brahman..581

Asana and Pranayama in Tantric Yoga 583

The Role of Food & Prana in Self-Realization..584

The Seven Centers & Planes of Awareness and Existence......................................587

The Seven Causes & Ten Impediments in Kundalini Yoga.....................................589

Palace with Seven Gates 591

The Seven Sat Chakras of Kundalini Yoga 593

The Six Ways of Attaining Brahmajnana in Tantra...595

The Four Plateaus for Approaching Brahman..597

Natural Renunciation in Four Phases...598

Para & Aparavidya 600

The Seven Great Universal Ideals..603

Principles of Brahman According to the Upanisads...604

Points About Brahman According to the Upanisads..607

The Course of Atmic Realization 609

Vedic Triputis and Quintuplications 611

The Five States of the Mind Field in Yoga 612

The Palette of Conscious Future Lives 614

Lord Brahma's Universal Projection 617

The Four Main Aspects of Kundalini Shakti 619

The Four Main Aspects of Kundalini Shakti 2 621

The Five Ways to Perfection According to Sri Ramakrishna 622

Omkara: The Silent Call of the Hamsa 624

The Different Types of Diksha, Spiritual Initiation...626

The Inner Meaning of the Mala 629

The Meaning of the Gayatri Mantra...630

Shakti Mantra, Kamakala, and the Unity of Siva and Shakti.........................633

Echelons of Fire 635

The Process of Neti Neti Leading to Nirvikalpa...636

Illumination of the Jiva — How the Sharirin Informs the Sharira 638

The Great Actor, The Great Enjoyer, and The Great Renouncer 641

The True Meaning of Perfection — Siddhi 642

Kundalini Yoga as Mahayoga 645

Mahamudra — The Great Seal 647

Zen Principles and Distractions 649

Zen Buddhist and Advaita Vedanta Correlations...651

The Meaning of Objects 652

The Meaning of Maya..654

Cutting Through Clouds of False Superimposition 657

The Ten Major Knots in the Rope of Human Bondage 659

Occult Powers & the Raincloud of Virtues 660

The Four Noble & Mighty Combats...662

The Three Main Factors in the Attainment of Enlightenment........................665

The Three Pillars of Zen Practice 666

Jugyu-No-Zu: The Ten Stages of Ox-Herding 669

Astika & Nastika 670

≈ Chapter Ten: The Ever Stationary Self

The Integral Constitution of the Luminaries...675

Mahavakyas of the World's Avatars 677

Daivi Vak — Divine Sayings 679

Shaktadvaitavada — Divine Mother Nonduality...680

Tantra's Siva and Shakti 683

Transmuting the Poison of Relativity Into the Nectar of Immortality.............685

The True Meaning of Moksha/Mukti 686

The State and Characteristics of a Jivanmukta 689

Advaita Vedanta's Pillar of Axioms 691

The Process of Samprajnata to Asamprajnata Samadhi 693

The Seeded Samadhis of Patanjala 697

Paravairagya & Aparavairagya 698

The Seven Earmarks of Self-Realization...701

The Four Ways of Perceiving God in Indian Darshanas..................................703

The Four Levels of Brahman's Subtleties 705

The Six Complements & Ten Immutables of Paramatman 706

Five Eternal & Essential Facts of Nondual Indian Philosophy........................709

The Four States of Consciousness & Seven Attributes of Turiya....................711

The Four Stages of Absorption & The Four Stages of Formlessness................712

The Six-fold Process of Immersion in Brahman..715

The Divisions of the Atman, from the Sri Rama Hrydayam 716

The Spiritual Art of Mental Asana 719

Mental Postures that Bind 721

Christ the Sannyasin: The Key Renunciation Teachings of Jesus of Nazareth 723

Wisdom Facets from the Garland of Universality 724

Asparsha Yoga — The "Nontouch" Yoga, According to Gaudapada's Karika............727

The Province of the Enlightened: Three Types of Knowledge Samadhis in Advaita Vedanta 728
Guide to Gaudapada's Karika 731
Inscrutable Epithets of Brahman 732
The Thirteen Inherent Characteristics of Atman...735
The Five Modes of the Divine Experiencer (and Their Five Corresponding Kanchukas) 737
The Six Proofs of Purusha 739
Tathagatagarbha / Atman — Transparency of the Self..740
Ri-Bi — Zen Buddhist Truth Principles 743
The Incomparable Views of an Advaita Vedantist 744
Ajativada: Nonorigination 746
India's "Mind Only School" Perspective 749
Vivartopadana / Adhyasa Astitva 751
All Hail, Surya Narayan!...752
Signs of Battle: Maintaining Spiritual Life in the World 755
The Corrosion of Human Consciousness...756
Mahavakyas of the World's Avatars II...759
The Six Esoteric Yogic Gateways: Yoga's Secret of Transcendence 761
Cosmic Involution and Scientific Evolution 762
The Kundalini Shakti and Her Chakras...765
Spiritual Transmission and the Goddess 766
Six Proofs of Reality in Advaita Vedanta 773

Sanskrit Glossary..782

Internal Reference Guide for All Charts and Their Respective Subjects
See Pages 767 - 774

INTRODUCTION

Footfalls of the Indian Rishis
Charting the Scriptures of Mother India

Several millennia before the more recent "Christ Era," a society of spiritually oriented wisdom knowers lived on the subcontinent of Bharat, now known as India, subsiding in a natural mode of existence called *dharma* — divine life. They managed this peaceful, blissful mode of awareness by transcending the cosmic laws via the extraordinary abilities which they had gleaned from practicing specialized austerities amidst the ever-changing world of name and form, which they ingeniously termed *"maya."* Their early appearance in history, centered and focused along the sacred banks of the now peaceful, now surging, *Indus* river, eventually earned them the name of Hindus, an affectionate title which brings to mind the benign, nonviolent culture they represented and the rich spiritual legacy that they left behind for the highest good of all struggling souls. For their arduous, sincere, and heartily sustained austerities (*sadhana*) had taught and trained them well about the limitations of relative existence in the mutable and transitory sweep of *nama-rupa* — name and form. They became aware over the expanse of this well-spent time of inward self-effort that the many-tiered worlds of name and form, all based upon the triple principle of *Desha, Kala, Nimitta* (space, time, and causality), posed a considerable conundrum to the human mind, seeming contrary to the indivisible principle of Absolute Reality, or *Brahman,* which they had glimpsed and realized in their deepest contemplations. In other words, after purifying the fourfold mind (dual mind, thought, ego, and intellect) and the five senses (hearing, seeing, tasting, touching, and smelling), and coming to perceive the nature of Reality as imminently nondual (*advaita*), the problem of the changing and variegated exterior realm of the five elements (earth, water, fire, air, ether) presented itself in full force, begging a study and a resolution.

Based upon two main principles — the phenomena of changefulness and the obscuring power of form — the incomparable Indian philosophy, known now mainly as *Vedanta* (with its *Sankhya, Yoga, Tantra* and *Buddhistic* components), sprung forth and developed over ages. The spiritual ingenuity of Mother India and her auspicious parade of illumined souls lies partly in the fact that they uncovered or espied *maya* to begin with, and designated it with a word. Other religious approaches, both up to that time and after, strove to live harmoniously, mostly via morals and ethics, side by side with nature. But this was not enough for the Indian *Rishi*. To transcend nature and the host of bodies produced by it, based upon both its ephemeral nature and its host of suffering-laden problems, had to be added into the quotient, for the fallacious assumption of lasting happiness amidst constant change was, to them, a fundamental misunderstanding of the nature of relativity.

With such rare and astute understanding of both Reality and relativity in hand, a host of enlightened beings, the likes of which has never been seen in history, sprang forth from Mother India's infinitely productive essence (*Shakti*). Not limited to just one prophet and one scripture, the spiritually prolific generative force of Mother India, ancient and contemporary, brought forth a series of divine incarnations, *rishis,* seers, *yogis,* sages, and saints who then contributed to this most worthy cause a plethora of revealed scriptures of all types of authenticity. *Shruti,* the primary or non-dual scriptures, *Smriti,* the secondary or recollected traditional scriptures, *Itihasa,* the poetic sagas of legendary beings, and even scriptures around the codes and laws which must govern the social behavior of mankind and society — all of these were gifted forth from the hearts and minds of these realized beings titled *"rishis."*

Over time, and out of this marvelous sweep of spiritually-based philosophy in practice, a collection of *darshanas,* ways of clear seeing, were formulated by certain high-souled personages. Lord Kapila donated the *Sankhya* system, from which *Vedanta, Shaivism,* and *Buddhism* (to name a few) still derive authority and gratitude, even today. Patanjali came forth with the *Yoga Sutras*, giving birth, or clarity and crystallization, to the eight-limbed system which was to bear his name (*Patanjala*, or *Yoga*). Along this unprecedented philosophical trajectory, the *Tantra* was always present, adding into the *Vedic* tendency of transcendentalism its copious gifts of knowledge, earthly experience, deity worship, and deification of all name and form, possibly itself a pathway which was indigenous to the very soil of Mother India, present in some form even previous to the great Aryan incursion. And then there was the mature evolution of true religion that Lord Buddha contributed by his coming and presence on earth, bestowing upon aspiring souls the sure and certain knowledge that, as far as relative life in *maya* is concerned, "Suffering Is."

Given all of this, then, how was it possible that the insidious and covertly underlying presence of *maya* could fail to be detected? And so it was that another four-letter word was added into the chaotic press of temporal existence, this time in *Sanskrit* or *Devabhasya* — the language of the Gods. *Maya's* invisible stultifying presence was thus revealed. All that remained, then, was to scrutinize it from a distance, after removing oneself from it. And this the *Tantricists* and *Vedantists* did, most thoroughly, adding to the world's esoteric knowledge considerably and, more importantly, giving suffering and aspiring beings a new way of rising above the vicissitudes, vanities, and vagaries of the world of name and form. And soon they came to know, as Swami Vivekananda has stated in more modern times, that *maya* is not mere illusion. It is the ability of consciousness to fabricate worlds of name and form in time and space based upon causality. Further, this magical and mesmerizing *maya* seemed so real, but ultimately was unreal.

The problem with scrutinizing *maya*, then, and as Sri Ramakrishna has stated, is that upon being studied, it tends to draw the examiner into its many flexuous folds. This is a statement which begs examination itself so as to perceptively pit the path of worldliness *(pravritti/bhogamarga)* against the wise way of spirituality *(nivritti/jnanamarga)* in order to eke out a clear and beneficial comparison. In these contemporary times, a case could be made that Western science, by examining *maya* (without really knowing what it is) i.e., everything from the vastness of physical space to the tiniest increment of material particles in nano-measurements, is only wrapping itself further into the impermeable plan of *maya* which causes beings — even intelligent beings — to believe in what is only mere appearance. Further, science, based upon its premature conclusions founded in the invisible *maya*, will then sally forth and pose to society a matter-oriented, object-owning, health and wealth seeking, pleasure-loving lifestyle — even though beings like Jesus warned seriously against such pursuits, advising *"storing up thy treasures in Heaven,"* instead (note: the *Vedantist* interprets the word "Heaven" in this context to mean nondual Reality, not a subtle world in space and time).

This belief in appearances, this fallacious assumption that forms are real and abiding, despite proof otherwise, is the diaphanous fabric upon which *maya*, as illusion, proceeds to operate and exert its chimerical influence. That is, as if name and form was not vexing enough to the human mind seeking transcendental answers, a further superimposition of *mayic* metamorphosis begins to take place. In other words, there is sort of naturalness about nature producing worlds of name and form out of the five elements, but when the mind gets obsessed and thereby confused by *maya's* maelstrom and melange of illusory legerdemain, then delusion replaces discrimination and things like covetousness, greed, anger, hatred, and war get on the march, causing suffering which is undue and unnecessary to even *maya's* comparatively harmless plan.

This is another great contribution to philosophy, what to speak of mental clarity. The ancient *rishis* found out that *maya* was insentient. This is one of the ten characteristics of *maya*, revealing the fallaciousness of the statement that "there is a devil out to get you," as they say. Rather, and as Jesus inferred when he declared, *"Resist not evil,"* it is more that evil, like *maya*, has no real and abiding substance. That is, to the mind under their influence, or that cognizes them as real, evil and suffering become real when essentially they are not. And it is thus that the true healers of men's souls have always worked to break down the misconceptions in the mind of deluded beings rather than shoring up such deceptions, and thereby do adeptly lead souls up and out of darkness instead of instigating fear of darkness. The fog bank, for instance, has no substance; its only power is that of covering or obscuration. But leave its confines and climb a nearby hill and one will find out everything about its workings, what to speak of its dissolution under the presence of the midday sun. This has always been the way that the Indian *rishi* or luminary has proceeded, even up until the present day, when current day teachers are presently bringing light to a Western culture that is floundering in outdated, outmoded modes of fundamentalism.

To repeat and proceed, then, changefulness, called *Parinama,* and the power of obscuration, called *Avarana Shakti,* are two main points of Indian philosophy, without which the presence of *maya* would never have been uncovered. That all things here are constantly in a state of flux (like the various phases of the particle of matter), and that the formless Reality — call it Almighty Father, Allah, *Prajnaparam,* or *Brahman,* just so — is being covered over by a host and series of causes or superimpositions, each one locked secretly inside of the other like a set of oriental wooden dolls, both belies the desirability of ordinary life in the physical universe and causes the rise of a pure desire to transcend it. Perhaps this is what Jesus meant when he talked of birds and foxes having nests and holes, while man is left wanting a home on earth.

In the case of mankind, however, this is thankful wanting, since an apt examination of *maya* will reveal the presence of a thousand ills, better avoided. Of course, developing character is always and better done via the vehicles of the various trials and challenges that come upon human beings in the course of conscious everyday living, but that law only holds true for the sincere seekers and aspirants, not for the worldly-minded. For the devotees of Divine Reality, even sporting in the playground of the universe leaves much to be desired. What kind of a playground is it, after all? asks the discriminating child of God, if my playmates are lust, anger, greed, delusion, envy, and vanity; if my companions are hatred, shame, regret, fear, secrecy, grief, and pride; if my playthings are birth, growth, disease, old age, decay, and death; if my modes of sport are egotism, intolerance, narrowness, worldliness, insensitivity, and jadedness. In such a school, how much fun can I have at recess?

And so, piercing through all forms takes prominence among the truth-seekers. *Vivarta,* or false superimposition of name and form over Reality, reveals not only the above short list of *mayic* foibles, but also conceals That which is the nature of true Existence, profound Knowledge, and ecstatic Bliss. Peace, three times — on the outside, on the inside, and transcendent — also accompanies the penetration of *maya* by the nondual mind. With so much at stake, then, it is no wonder that the wise soul not only leans towards purification via self-effort, but wastes no time here on earth, in the body, in developing a strong and resilient love for Truth that can withstand everything that *maya* levels at it.

In the pages of this book, offered with both the highest of intentions and heartfelt apologies for any discrepancies or omissions inadvertently committed in its presentation, will be found a copious set of charts or philosophical storyboards which ought to give the student of Eastern spiritual thought a deep insight into how the Indian *rishi* birthed and formulated his or her (there were many Indian woman *rishis* of great acumen) astute thinking around both Reality (*Brahman*) and relativity (*maya/samsara*). The reader should keep in mind that the entire collection of charts come from some seven categories which represent a cross-section of the more major modes of Indian spiritual understanding. *Vedanta,* of course, coming from Veda and *Upanisad,* the primary scriptures, is first, followed by the ever-present *Tantra* and the still somewhat prevalent *Yoga* system. I have also included in this book of charts, each one which is a footfall of some Indian *rishi* of the past, the categories of *Sankhya Yoga* of Kapila and the teachings of Lord Vasishtha, both with their incomparable ways of clarifying the mind and performing purificatory *sadhana.* In addition, and after years of devout study of the *Bhagavad Gita,* it became apparent that a series of charts on Sri Krishna's ever valuable teachings should also be included. To the above mentioned six *darshanas* I have added in some few representations of Buddhist teachings, drawn mainly from both Indian *Buddhism* and *Tibetan Buddhism,* to which I have a close affiliation.

As a quick aside, and in relation to the *Patanjala* System, the term "Yoga" here, of course, means Patanjali's eight-limbed *Yoga* of Meditation leading to *Samadhi* which leans definitively towards the *Jnanamarga* (path of knowledge) and away from the currently popular but potentially detrimental path of physical postures and breathing exercises called *hatha yoga*. In our way of thinking, and on record with many of the great *rishis* — from Lord Vasishtha to Sri Ramakrishna — one should not give a materially-oriented society, already attached to the body and prone to nonstop activity, the *yoga* of physical postures only. This would be somewhat like giving money to a drug addict in front of his dealer's dwelling place. What is needed is that which will curtail attachment and addiction, not fan its flames indiscriminately. Therefore, Patanjali's *Raja Yoga*, also called *Ashtanga Yoga* is prescribed and represented, one of the most effective and highly detailed spiritual pathways available.

Obviously, much more could be presented, and possibly will be in the future, but this much will suffice in ushering any interested student into the spiritual wonders of this superlative culture and its wide and catholic philosophical and religious understanding. I must also add here that a few of these charts have sprung from what we nowadays call the Neo-*Vedanta* category, meaning a more contemporary reckoning and offering of the *Vedanta* teachings of India, Here I have taken license and gathered, in Vedavyasa style, certain smatterings of spiritual teachings and principles seldom or never presented together in their current form. That is, whereas I do believe in the old adage, *"There is nothing new under the sun,"* nevertheless all material, some of it remaining long-hidden or under-emphasized until recently, has been culled, brought forth, and transmitted to today's peoples in the light of a fresh interpretation.

The charts themselves, besides being representations on paper of certain key spiritual teachings, are accompanied by quotes and words from a host of different luminaries, not all of them hailing from India. Thus, inclusion of the spirit of Universalism has been contributed, in order that we come to know that there is no such thing as a "foreign religion," since all religion, coming from the one God, nondual Reality, is indigenous to our very soul.

Finally, these charts, being in creation since 2006, have been presented to audiences over the past few years at SRV's weekly discourses and spiritual retreats. As this process went forward, and a small demand for them in book form came to be, it became obvious that each one ought to be accompanied with its own commentary which would briefly explain the parameters and teachings contained therein. In most instances I have kept these individual commentaries brief but concentrated, except where more teaching is needed. In addition, I am relying upon the student and the reader to seek qualification in the fundamentals of *Vedanta*, and to attend classes and retreats where these teachings are being explained and expanded upon. For, authentic spiritual life is based upon the Three Great Sources, namely *Guru Anushashana* (the acceptance of a teacher); *Vidya Shastra* (the study of the revealed scriptures), and *Aparokshanubhuti* (ones own direct experience via personal *sadhana* and insight).

To explain, the world can be likened to a dense forest full of dangers, and the soul, one beset by amnesia. If one were to suddenly awaken in that world-forest (as happens with ones birth as an infant) the first thing one would do is to seek out either a path or a guide. As it so happens, some come to the path first, finding the guide later, sitting beside it. Others, making their way through the dense undergrowth, come upon the guide first, who then points to the path. In both cases,, the way of spirituality proceeds. What is to be avoided is getting lost and suffering thereby, and to fall into the jaws of lurking dangers, unawares.

With all of this said, may this collection of charts, symbolizing the many fortunate footfalls of the Indian seers, go a long way towards dissolving the hidden confusions and delusions lurking in the embodied soul's conditioned awareness. And further, may the young children of interested parents and devotees receive these teachings at an early age, thereby exposing the world-bewitching *maya* before it has an opportunity to sink roots and take up residence in the human mind.

Footfalls of the Indian Rishis
— Chapter One —

The Baby Steps of Authentic Spirituality

It is a singular and unique moment in a baby's young life, for both child and parents, when it manages its first steps from mother to father. All those who have witnessed this have had that occasion indelibly imprinted on the mind's memory, never to be erased, even in succeeding lifetimes. It is a primal impression representing a significant advance in mankind's attainment and facility, and is destined to open up the many worlds of experience that now lie within ready access, spread out like a living carpet in front of that anxious and precocious infant.

Similar, and by way of analogy, but of much more profound import, are the first steps of an aspiring soul's spiritual life, when he or she discovers that there is a kingdom lying within oneself that transcends space and time and remains ever uninhibited by restrictions reactions which inundate the physical world and its frustrating labyrinth of limiting laws. Like a baby stretching out its tiny but ambitious hand to attempt to naively pluck the moon from nocturnal skies, so too does the novitiate of religious life educe, then err, in turns, while attempting to access and draw out that wonderful spiritual wealth within — only to find out, again and again, that invisible veils and forces are resisting the possession of that superlative treasure.

Vivarta — False Superimposition of Form over Reality

Ironically, it is this predicament of revelation and resistance that constitutes the infantile steps towards authentic spirituality. Placed in another perspective, and vernacular, the aspiring soul has stumbled upon, still unknowingly, the principle of *vivarta*, or *adhyasa*, which in *Vedic* speak means a subtle yet natural covering that impedes and thereby obfuscates the mind's perception of higher truth. In English, the term "false superimposition" is utilized, in order to convey a double-edged universal fact, a relative law which must be accepted and comprehended before any appreciable spiritual progress can be made. The first edge of this law states that any form — physical, mental, or cosmic — obscures the formless nature of Reality by its mere presence and appearance. The second and accompanying edge declares avidly that the presence of name and form over the formless Reality does not in the least change, transform, or affect said Reality in the least, and that Reality always remains immutable despite the many overlays which seem to collect over It. Thus the term, "false" superimposition.

At this juncture it would be helpful to state that the cause of these muzzy masking devices of *maya* is ignorance, called *avidya* in *Sanskrit*. In Indian philosophy, ignorance is an insentient force, not an incarnate evil, and is present in the human mind by the mute and complacent allowance of the individual lost in *maya* — a word we will also explore at length in this book. Further, these overlays of mental ignorance, strewn recklessly and carelessly across the otherwise glabrous surface of an unchanging Reality which *Vedanta* reverently titles *Brahman,* occur in three modes: individual *(vyasti);* collective *(samasti);* and cosmic *(vyapti).* That is, in brief, that ignorance appears and wreaks its havoc in the individual mind, the collective mind, and the cosmic mind, simultaneously, causing a "cloud of unknowing" to descend and hamper all of life, dampening its truer expression. Happily, the first mode, ones own ignorance, can be done away with by spiritual knowledge *(vidya)* transmitted by an illumined soul, combined with self-effort *(sadhana)* and meditation *(dhyana).* The second mode, collective consciousness, involves myriad of souls embodying out of ignorance, and fully ensconced in it to the extent that few would ever venture away from it, what to speak of even see the need for leaving it behind. It needs transcending, as does the third mode, the cosmic, where ignorance is at its subtlest. Such is the power of the mind in *maya* under the influence of *avidya* — a double helping of primal deception stored under three indiscernible layers. It is here where the lonely spiritual aspirant begins to realize the singular nature of the journey and its steep and precipitous ascent. That is okay. *"Grant unto Caesar what is Caesar's, but take unto thyself what is the Lord's."* In other words, misery may love company, but so does peace and bliss. A multitude of saints, seers, sages, and saviors, and other holy company, all await the seeker of the highest Truth.

The Five *Koshas* — Coverings and Containers

Vivarta, false superimposition, concerning both human life and cosmology, is described in terms of those containers, *koshas*, or sheaths/coverings, *upadhis*, (some key words in *Sanskrit*, the ancient language of spiritual realization), that are most obvious to us and which, when looked at in the light of revelatory wisdom, will proffer us a sense of innate freedom. This freedom (*moksha* in *Vedanta; kaivalya* in *Yoga, satori* or *kensho* in *Zen*, etc) is ever-present and unalterable in spite of the presence, or seeming presence, of ignorance and its offspring, like confusion, sorrow, suffering, and evil. This freedom, call it *mukti* as well, must be consciously maintained in memory and rendered sacrosanct by the mind throughout every stage having to do with the spiritual path — awakening, striving, attaining, arriving, and abiding. As we will find out later via a series of far-reaching examples, explorations, and explanations, this freedom is not of the personal, political, sensual, or religious kind. It is not a matter of production, practice, purification, or transformation. It does not originate, evolve, formulate, or develop. It is the very nature and essence *(svarupa)* of true Existence, beyond all origins.

There are five *koshas* (containers) or *upadhis* (sheaths) which make up the human being:

Annamaya-kosha — Sheath of food/matter (body with flesh, fat, bone, muscle, etc.)
Pranamaya-kosha — Sheath of energy (life-force and its five main functions)
Manomaya-kosha — Sheath of mind (dual mind posited in pairs of opposites)
Vijnanamaya-kosha — Sheath of intellect (thought, mentation, conception, etc.)
Anandamaya-kosha — Sheath of bliss (sense of separate self/ego-based happiness and joy)

These five are called "sheaths" or "coverings" (*upadhis*) when they are seen from the standpoint of transcendence, and "containers" (*koshas*) when seen from the standpoint of expression. That is, when they are perceived by the aspiring soul as coverings that limit existence, it is best if he or she immediately practices detachment from and transcendence of them in meditation. But after realization has dawned, these same five can be acknowledged as containers which the Lord, as Divine Consciousness, puts on like a five piece suit and utilizes for various pastimes beneficial to embodied beings. This echoes the "body is the temple for the spirit" teaching. However, this teaching has been used pretentiously as an excuse for committing any and all manner of transgressions. But it will be seen via the wisdom under study herein that *Vedanta* does not allow this, and undermines such fallacies by recommending a thorough analysis of the body *(annamayakosha)* and all other sheaths/containers to ensure purity of act, thought, and deed. After coming to know the nature of these coverings over Reality, the pathway to freedom will be an assured acquisition.

The nature of the *koshas/upadhis* can be summed up in one word: mutable *(parinama)*. In Indian philosophy, if an object, thing, concept, or situation changes it cannot be assigned to the same incomparable status as that of the immutable *Brahman*. This acid test for Truth has long stood the test of time, leaving India as the main country which hosted seers *(rishis)* who were able to both perceive and describe the imperceptible and the indescribable. By recognizing the difference between Spirit and Matter (God and Mammon), and deftly detaching from the latter and seeking realization of the former, the ancient *rishis* arrived at Truth. The system of the five *koshas* provided an excellent start to this process. On the opposite page is a chart which illustrates this *"Adhara"* system.

THE FIVE KOSHAS OF THE ADHARA SYSTEM

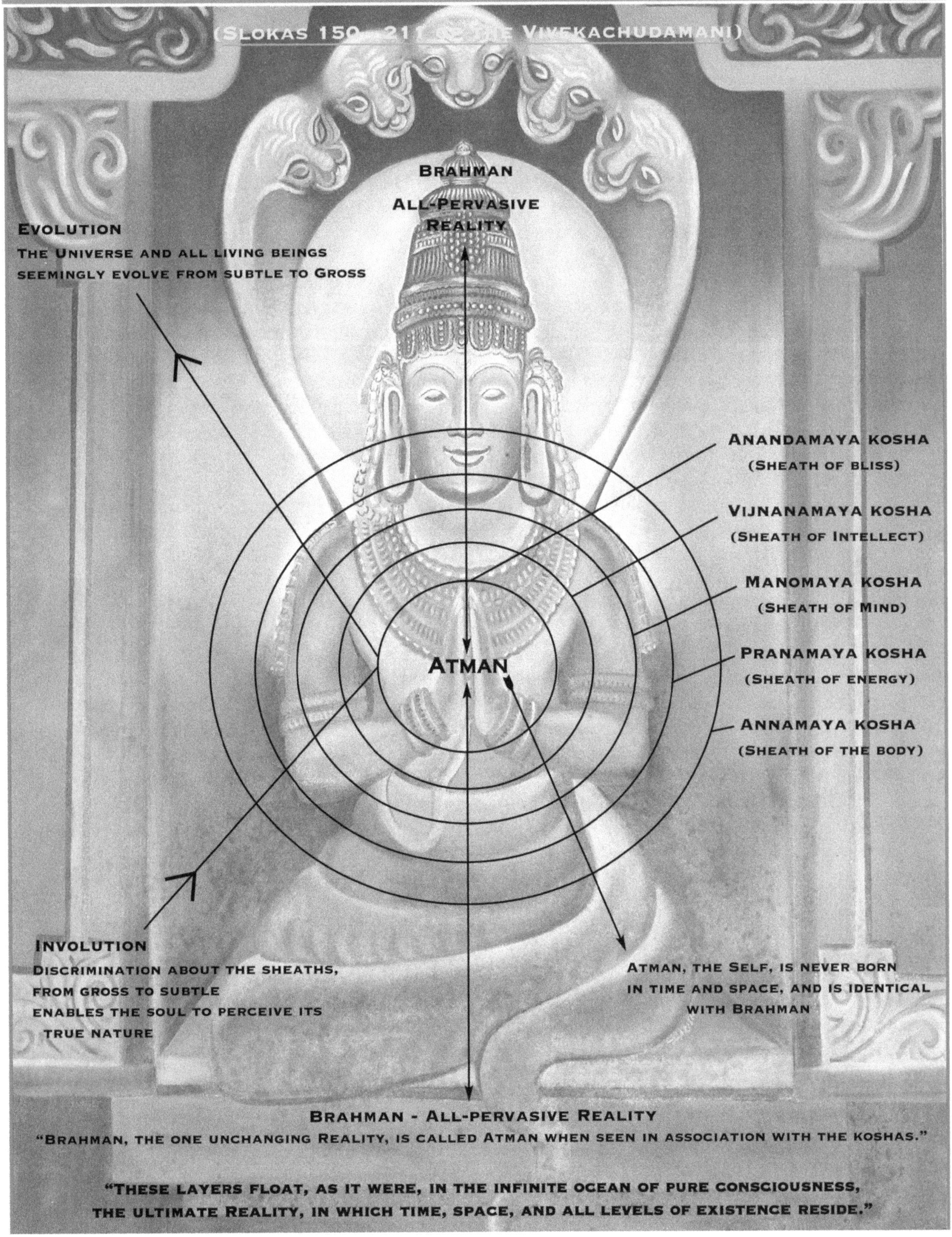

(SLOKAS 150 - 211 OF THE VIVEKACHUDAMANI)

EVOLUTION
THE UNIVERSE AND ALL LIVING BEINGS
SEEMINGLY EVOLVE FROM SUBTLE TO GROSS

**BRAHMAN
ALL-PERVASIVE
REALITY**

ANANDAMAYA KOSHA
(SHEATH OF BLISS)

VIJNANAMAYA KOSHA
(SHEATH OF INTELLECT)

MANOMAYA KOSHA
(SHEATH OF MIND)

PRANAMAYA KOSHA
(SHEATH OF ENERGY)

ANNAMAYA KOSHA
(SHEATH OF THE BODY)

ATMAN

INVOLUTION
DISCRIMINATION ABOUT THE SHEATHS,
FROM GROSS TO SUBTLE
ENABLES THE SOUL TO PERCEIVE ITS
TRUE NATURE

**ATMAN, THE SELF, IS NEVER BORN
IN TIME AND SPACE, AND IS IDENTICAL
WITH BRAHMAN**

BRAHMAN - ALL-PERVASIVE REALITY
"BRAHMAN, THE ONE UNCHANGING REALITY, IS CALLED ATMAN WHEN SEEN IN ASSOCIATION WITH THE KOSHAS."

"THESE LAYERS FLOAT, AS IT WERE, IN THE INFINITE OCEAN OF PURE CONSCIOUSNESS,
THE ULTIMATE REALITY, IN WHICH TIME, SPACE, AND ALL LEVELS OF EXISTENCE RESIDE."

In *slokas* 150 through 211 of the famed scripture, *Vivekachudamani,* Shankara, one of the most enlightened of nondualists in recent memory, reads the riot act on the problem of the superimposition of the changing layers (*koshas/upadhis*) of *maya* over Absolute Reality. The point is to galvanize the human mind in order to awaken it to its habitually sleepy predicament; for falling asleep in *maya* due to thinking the sheaths to be ones true self is akin to forgetting, maybe for lifetimes, ones changeless, blissful nature, called *Atman.*

This brings up a subtle point and key teaching with regard to the problem of false superimposition, a point that even many modern *Vedantists* do not properly ascertain. The point revolves around the distinction between *Brahman* and *Atman.* Faced with hearing the statement that *Atman* and *Brahman* are one, many get confused. If there is, as *Advaita Vedanta* confirms, just one Reality, and it is indivisible, then why call it by two names? The answer comes by way of the following clarification: When Reality is seen/known from the singular station of perfect perception, i.e., the nondual state, then that Reality is called *Brahman.* However, when that same Reality is seen/known from the perspective of the containers or sheaths (*koshas/upadhis*), called "body/mind mechanism" or "psycho-physical being" in *Vedanta,* then Reality is termed *Atman.* In other words, and quoting from the chart on the previous page, *"Brahman, the one unchanging Reality, is called Atman when seen in association with the koshas."* As long as the human being is in *maya,* and trying to comprehend *maya* with a mind that gets formed in *maya,* so long must he/she render accessible and utilize this great aid of dividing the Indivisible into two distinctive but interrelated high-minded perspectives. This very ability, developed over time, is exactly the same facility which will assist the aspirant later on along the spiritual path in taking on and integrating the various systems and philosophies of world religions. For, just like the truths of Nonorigination (*Ajativada*) and Nontransformation (*aparinama*), Universality is a preferred and supreme acquisition in authentic spiritual life. There will be much more to say about these three nondual pillars in the forthcoming chapters.

The containers or coverings called *annamayakosha, pranamayakosha, manomayakosha, vijnanamayakosha,* and *anandamayakosha* — five very long words — can be reduced into easy English for quick understanding. They are thus termed the sheath of food, the sheath of energy, the sheath of mind, the sheath of intellect, and the sheath of separate self or ego, respectively. Right away, several important teachings surface around these definitions in order to further our understanding of the system and keep the mind free of misperceptions. The first applies to the sheath of energy.

Modern man, especially Western man, does not know much about any type of energy other than kinetic, electric, etc. Even in medical circles, and among botanists and biologists, the energy called "life force" goes mostly uncomprehended. In several of the Eastern schools, especially *Tantra* and *Yoga,* we find a more thorough definition, and even exploration, of life force, called *Prana* in *Sanskrit.* But even in these systems it is mostly only the *prana* associated with the five senses and the five elements that gets presented, while the psychic *prana* remains unexplained for the most part.

But as regards to the elements and the senses, we find that *prana* is a subtle carrier of unseen forces to the various forms and functions within. The five *pranas* in one form, as Swami Vivekananda calls them, effect such "vital" functions as the digestion of food, distribution of nourishment through the blood to the organs, animation of the lungs and their triple-phased breathing process, evacuation of perspiration and bodily waste, and even the all-important aspiration of the mind towards higher thoughts. Thus, when discovered as such, it is no wonder that the *prana* takes on foremost importance in the healing arts, and in other advanced medical arenas which look beyond the mere effect of disease and its external treatment with chemicals, and towards its fundamental cause. This means that man does not live by bread alone, but by its subtle constituent.

The sheath of ego is also a very interesting principle to ponder, though its rumination will necessarily confer philosophical ramifications rather than physical ones. The individual ego is often perceived as a spoiler, insinuating itself on all areas of life with a negative influence. But what lies beneath or behind it can lead the seeker away from the reflection and to the original. We can explore this via another chart — a complementary "footfall" of the seer, Shankara, on the facing page.

The Five Sheaths and their Properties
(From Slokas 149-211 of the Vivekachudamani)

Pupil: "I do not understand. You ask me to do away with these five sheaths, and when I do then I see nothing but the void remains. What is to be known there?" (sloka 213)

Teacher: "If you can do away with these five sheaths through the instructions of the scriptures, what remains? It is the Witness, Consciousness, the Atman, thine own Self." (sloka 211)

Anandamayakosha - The Sheath of Bliss

It is a reflection of Bliss, but is reflected in the Tamas of Maya
It appears and is felt only in favorable conditions and circumstances
It has a cause, for it requires good actions to be operative
It is not to be mistaken for the Atman, as it is dependent on something else
It is experienced in deep sleep, glimpsed in waking and dreaming upon the fulfillment of desires
It always remains with the body, under the control of the gunas

Vijnanamayakosha - The Sheath of Intelligence

It consists of the buddhi, the organs of feeling, and the sense of "I am the doer"
It reflects Consciousness, but is a transformation of nature — prakriti
It works, feels, and says "I am the doer, the seer. engaging in works and enjoying their results
It holds within it the three states of Consciousness, and pleasure and pain
It is the upadhi of the Atman, and very near to It, and reflects It best
The Atman uses mind and intellect for Its appearance

Manomayakosha - The Sheath of Mind

It consists of the organs of feeling and the mind
infills the other two sheaths and thinks itself separate from others
It depends on the five senses for its knowledge, and is thus limited
It retains its existence and interest via sense-life, objects, and desire
It is the very home of ignorance and the cause of all bondage
It causes the universe to appear and disappear by its projecting power
Binds the soul to body and objects via attachment, and frees it from them via non-attachment
Gets itself purified by resort to discrimination and detachment/renunciation
Deludes itself by creating objects, varieties, distinctions, qualities, and belief in them
It undergoes change, has a beginning and an end, suffers pain, and is not the seer

Pranamayakosha - The Sheath of Vital Energy

Consists of the five organs of action and the five vital forces
Dwelling in and permeating the Annamayakosha, it engages beings in all works
It moves like the wind, inside and out, so is not immutable like the Atman
It has no knowledge, is insentient, and knows no difference between good and bad

Annamayakosha - The Sheath of Food/Matter

The body sheath is a transformation of food. lives by food, and dies without it
Being skin, bone, flesh and marrow, etc, it cannot be the Atman which is unchanging
It is insentient, an object for the senses, and is a non-enjoyer
It is material, undergoes change, borrows its life, has various attributes, and is controlled
It has a cause, and itself causes ignorance and identification with the unreal

"Being enveloped by the five sheaths the Atman does not manifest. If these sheaths are taken away, the Atman manifests — ever-pure, eternal bliss, unchangeable, direct, and self-luminous." Adishankaracharya

As we learn the crucial teaching of the five sheaths, and as we soak in all the information associated with it, the luminaries encourage us to keep in mind the one most important facet of this teaching, and of all knowledge: changing things, whether they are constituted of matter, energy, thought, or conception, are not Reality. *Brahman/Atman*, only, is That, being the one unchanging and totally sentient verity in Existence. In the *Upanisads*, the seer, Svetasvatara, puts this in pre-eminent terms for our cogent comprehension: *"Practicing the method of meditation, they realized that divine Being (devatmashakti) who is the God of religion, the Self of philosophy, and the Energy of Science; who exists as the self-luminous power in everyone; who is the source of the intellect, emotions, and will; who is one without a second; who presides over all the causes listed as Cosmology, beginning with time and ending with the individual soul; and who had been previously incomprehensible because of the limitations of their own intellects."* It will be seen, then, that a study of the sheaths is not mainly for intellectual achievements, or the mere gathering of knowledge, but for making a distinction between the changing and the unchanging — what *Vedanta* calls the "real and the unreal." Once this act of inner discrimination is achieved, Reality will stand forth naturally of Its own accord.

With that stated, and duly emphasized, we can take up the two previous charts for further exploration. On the previous page, the quote at the bottom infers that if the five sheathes are allowed to take over the mind's pristine Awareness, then the *Atman* cannot manifest fully in life. It remains, nevertheless, fully complete and perfect, unchanged for eternity, Its infinite potential only waiting on realization. Thus we are reminded again of the dangerous presence of *mula-avidya* — root ignorance. Additionally, we can begin to perceive the real cause of suffering and, in full awareness of that, all the problems of the world. Ironically, while all the world's beings are running about for eons in cycles, trying to solve its many problems, it is the forgetfulness of ones already perfect nature that is at the very root of them all. This is why the worldly stay worldly for lifetimes, and only the saints and seers solve their issues and get free — helping other get free as well.

Referring back many a time to the two charts presented already, let us now take up a *kosha* by *kosha* study of these perplexing but marvelous mechanisms, whose power of allurement, albeit insentient, has thrown all of humanity — with a comparatively few rare exceptions — into long-standing delusion.

First comes the strange power of the *annamayakosha*, called the body, the sheath of food/matter. Just look and see what it consists of: flesh, bone, nails, nerves, marrow, blood, bile, phlegm, excrement. None of these elements of themselves hold any great attraction; some even repel. But put together as a whole and animated by the next two coverings, *prana* and mind (*manas*), it is indeed a marvelous mechanism. And let it be so! After all it is, at best, a temple for the Spirit. But taken otherwise, what the *Tantric*ists have called *Dehadhyasahamkara* — taking the body to be the *Atman* — major problems ensue. As Sri Ramakrishna has said, *"Just look what mischief man gets into, clothed in this body measuring but two and a half cubits tall!"* The implications of this observation are obvious. *Atman* has gotten into the body, as it were (in the all-pervasive sense), but being left unrealized, there is only hell to pay for it. Taking the body to be the soul is the first evolute of mind-bewitching *maya*.

What is more — and another tense situation for the seeker who strives to disidentify with the body for purposes of spiritual realization — is the fact that the body sheath lives by food. This ushers in the survival side of existence. That is, whereas mankind ought to be able to live on very little, and also needs to have leisure time in which to figure out a way to master and even transcend matter, he instead is forced to forage like *"the birds and beasts of the fields"* for his mere subsistence. Eventually this ultimatum on physical life, if left unchecked and devoid of spiritual influence, will bring about heaviness. This weigh of matter begins as competition for what nourishment is available, leading to outright violence and bloodshed for the sake of a few morsels of food. Later on, when "civilization" kicks in, the whims and pleasures of the palate dictate the field, and mankind begins to resemble a mere caricature of his real self, called a sensualist or a hedonist, "living to eat rather than eating to live." The fourth and fifth sheaths, the intellect and ego, have a connection here as well, but we will take them up in more depth later on.

We have pointed out the physical side of the first sheath, inferring its relationship with decay and death, and we have noted and observed its relationship with food. Philosophically speaking, for those wanting higher explanations than those based in matter, the phenomenon of transformation should be brought to the fore. Here is where the Buddhists and the *Vedantists* talk about *Sadurmi*, the six transformations, also referred to as the Six Billows or Clouds of Temporal Existence. Living beings of today should come to know, that the scientists and physicists are not the only ones who have been gathering information. For ages the Indian luminaries, blessings be upon them first and foremost, have sacrificed their own peaceful repose in the Spirit to embody right alongside ignorant and sleeping souls to find and point out a way to get free of bondage. In this context, *Sadurmi*, the Six Transformations, may as well equate to bondage (please refer to the chart on the six transformations on page 225). The body, the *annamayakosha*, is all too familiar with these six henchmen of despondency and death, the strangest part of this familiarity being that the soul, though experiencing them again and again throughout lifetimes, will not leave off from identification with the body even though it suffers immensely at their behest.

Jayati (birth), *asti* (growth), *vardhate* (disease), *jara* (old age), *kshara* (decay), and *mara* (death) constitute the Six Transformations. Rather than get into in-depth examinations of them (see chart on page 227), it is best to state, and from a nondual standpoint, the following double-faceted conclusion with regards to them: the Soul, *Atman*, does not go through transformation and, secondly, *Atman* is the only Reality. Placing these two facts about the nature of true Existence (*Sat*, Truth) in juxtaposition with the sobering teaching above, we can conclude that 1) these infringements on peaceful, blissful existence are unreal or ultimately nonactual and 2) they are meant to be dispensed with, either via forbearance or by transcendence. A third conclusion can be drawn as well, being that they are intended to be, or are naturally inherent in life, i.e., endemic to the soil of relativity. This conclusion follows closely on the teachings of *Yoga*, wherein the aspiring *yogi* or *yogini* faces off against the vicissitudes present in the worlds of embodiment and learns the sweet art of forbearance — what the *Vedantists* call *titiksha*. Ordinary souls take two other methods in this regard, either suffering the ills of relativity in ignorance of the laws of cause and effect (please see chart on page 231), or attempting to run away from all of these unwanted insinuations — what are called *karmic* repercussions — completely. Neither of these "methods" last for long or provide any final or fitting solution. The piper must be paid when recompense is due. In brief, *karma* is the God of the physical universe. It may as well be God here in this world, for the real God, *Brahman*, is transcendent of the world.

This aspect or principle, called transformation, will eventually fuel some of the final inner ruminations of the apt and advanced meditator. That is, everything in form is subject to transformation, or apparently so. If that is the fact, however lamentable at first, why not use it to monitor everything in the realm of name and form in order to uncover all — any little thing — that does not transform? This was the thinking of the ancient *rishis*, whose footfalls grace every page and word of this literary offering. And in fact, historically speaking, this became the main criteria for the proof of Truth for the Indian *rishis*, what people nowadays call the "theory" of God's existence.

If we place this "*Brahman* barometer" of changefulness, meant for searching out or divining the Divine, on the teaching at hand, namely the five *koshas*, it will be seen that every one of the coverings, and every little thing about them, is always and ever subject to change. Again, that word, "mutable," stands out boldly. From the body, through to the mind, and on up to the ego, everything here is in constant flux. That is why no real peace of mind can occur to the person attached to or obsessed with the body/mind mechanism that these five sheaths represent. Just as science has seen that the objective world is filled with objects that consist of countless swirling particles, all changing at a billionth of a second, so too, the spiritual luminary sees that both the mind and the intellect that behold the illusory objects through the five senses are also constantly in flux. This realization caused Jesus to proclaim that man cannot build his house on the sand of matter, but must seek out the bedrock of the Spirit. May all beings learn to do so.

Enough has been said about the *annamayakosha*, the covering of the body over the Spirit, though more will inevitably come up in the course of these incomparable teachings (*dharma*). Before moving on to take up the *pranamayakosha* once more, it will help to place Swami Vivekananda's words about preoccupation with the body in modern times here before us. This statement from a truth-knowing, wandering free soul, who visited and saw our country in the late 1800's, is telling, and in a sobering way: *"The Americans are drunk with new wine. But a hundred waves of prosperity have come and gone over my country. We have learned the lesson which no child can understand: It is vanity, this hideous world is maya. So renounce and be happy. Give up the idea of sex and possession. There is no other bond. Marriage and sex and money are the only living devils. All earthly love proceeds from the body."*

The physical side of *prana* has been introduced in its five phases. The task of explaining the psychic *prana* is much more daunting, which is why it has not been broached adequately, either in the scriptures or even in conversations with illumined souls. As well, its workings are lightning bolt swift, another of its facets that helps it elude discovery. It is in conjunction with mind and intelligence, however, that it gets exposed in a better light, for it acts to bring thought and conception into manifestation from realms of subtle and causal vibrations where human capabilities such as senses and intuition cannot go. In other words, the trickle down effect of Consciousness, stage by stage, into intellect, mind, life, senses, and body, is carried on via the speedy and efficient auspices of the vital force called psychic *prana*, which is more connected with *shakti* than with physical *prana*. To better understand this, a *Vedic* analogy can be utilized.

In the *Upanisads*, the example is used of the spider which can project its web and construct it into its own little world. It can also then gad about on that web, and even has the ability of drawing this sticky-stranded substance back into itself. This is analogous to the Divine Mother *Shakti* and Her force of *prana*. What is more, once the spider's web has been constructed, its sensitivity can detect every little current of vibration, movement, etc., that passes within the vast proximity of the web itself. This symbolizes the fact that Divine Reality, herein called *Shakti*, notices every little thing about Her intricately woven creation. This is all-knowingness. Thus, I have termed it the Three Oms — Omniscience, Omnipotence, and Omnipresence.

In the light of *Vedic* teachings, then, there is no more need of people remaining in the dark around the workings of Divine Reality, certainly not by the triple excuses of ignorance, fear, and inaccessibility to right knowledge. The teaching of *prana* and its all-pervasiveness quells all such impositions, and reveals how everything comes in and out of manifestation. Speculations by persons of superficial imagination, holding half-digested knowledge, also get defused and become defunct in the light of this revelation. There is no supposing, for example, that *prana* has a will, or even a whim. It is an insentient power, and no one can or should assign any mystery of occult ramifications to it. Those doing so risk turning life force, and thus life itself, into a circus side-show where *pranic* tricks are placed on display to both excite and befuddle human minds — usually for the sake of illicit monetary gain and undue fame. This is a liable on life itself. The prana must be kept pure and natural.

Prana stretches upwards, or inwards, from the ebb and flow of the five elements to the realm of the Cosmic Trinity. As far as the most astute separate observer (witness) can tell, it disappears into the Primal Word, *AUM*, but returns full force, carrying everything that is held in formless potential therein outwards into manifestation by stages. And just like the spider's web, beings can get stuck on it, or in it in this case. In other words, life force is addicting, and the vaunted and much lauded *"thirst for life"* that Vivekananda says *"drags from birth to death and death to birth the soul,"* claims votaries on a level much greater than the lord of death, *Yama*. For the seeker, then, it is better to observe *prana*'s workings from a detached witness standpoint, watching it course inward and outward and utilizing its flow, but never falling victim to either its alluring forces or its attempted possession. Like any other form of magical proportions, it is ultimately unreal. Reality awaits at a much higher and more aware level than *prana*.

The *manomayakosha*, the sheath of mind, explains many mysteries as well, in addition to cogently laying out a host of clarifying facts about this mechanism and its various functions. When arriving at something as complex as the human brain, what to speak of the mind (Indian philosophy makes a distinction between the two), it is helpful to relegate the matter into the three aforementioned subdivisions: individual (*vyasti*), collective (*samasti*), and cosmic (*vyapi*). Each *kosha*, then should be ascertained through this triple lens. For instance, the sheath of the body, when referred to in the individual sense, is the physical organism with all its personal characteristics, i.e., contents, makeup, features, looks, etc. When this same sheath is seen from the standpoint of the collective aspect, it takes on the proportions of the collective body of humanity, i.e., all bodies as a conglomerate whole and their entire field of action. And when the cosmic aspect of this *kosha* is considered, the entire collection of bodies, including gods, celestials, ancestors, elementals, even plants and animals, ought to be included — what to speak of the "All-pervading One."

In this evaluation, the *pranamayakosha* has already been explained. Suffice to say that the individual aspect of the *prana* would be its association with the five elements, the human body and breath, its functions, etc. The collective aspect of the *prana* sheath would get assigned to the subtle energy of the entire human race, bringing into inclusion the overall life force of beings across the planet. This would be seen, basically, as all beings waking, dreaming, sleeping, breathing, acting, and living as one unit. The cosmic aspect of the *pranamayakosha* would be its coursing inward to make connections to the subtle and causal worlds and all principles and beings residing there. This would have more to do with deities and their subtle powers than with human affairs alone.

With this point introduced, we can take up *manomayakosha*, the sheath of the mind, on all three of these levels. The individual mind is what is called the brain. Besides its access to knowledge, the main function of the brain has to do with its memory facility, for knowledge is not real knowledge if it cannot get effectively stored and utilized. It is this consideration that allows for the idea and implementation of higher mind, for the fact that storage and access function at all, leads the soul to consider what has occurred before — not just in one lifetime, but in past lifetimes as well. A seer or *yogi* is one who has seen past lifetimes and thus is operating under an expanded view not yet possible for ordinary beings. And here, in part, is where the mind on the collective level applies. The being who has access to the collective mind has perceived a rare universal perspective wherein activity taken up for the higher good of humanity is manifesting. The possibilities at this level are endless, and many will receive their introduction to the cosmic mind (*Mahat*) via this open doorway.

The cosmic mind is wonderful, most *sattvic*, most pure. Much more will come to the fore on it as this study proceeds. The *manomayakosha* must verily include the cosmic in its vast sweep, since the human mind, or brain, has the ability to access it and, if the truth be told, is just a spark off of the same fire. This gets understood better by studying the fourth *kosha*, the *vijnanamayakosha*, the sheath of intellect. But first, and referring back to the chart under study on page 21, with its cosmic bondages that include and effect the mind, it will be seen that the mental sheath has a host of limitations to overcome before it can aspire to the collective and unite with the cosmic (the word "cosmic," here, indicates subtle worlds within, not outer space or the "cosmos").

According to Shankara and other luminaries, the human brain and its generally impeded force of memory also stores such problematic things as sensations and emotions (like in the bondages of *linga, kama,* and *karma*). Interestingly enough, then, and contrary to what modern beings believe, the heart is the mind. That is, if one is thinking that feelings, sentiments, and passions are harbored somewhere in the heart, the enlightened ones beg to differ. The heart, as heart, is a mere organ, destined for decay and dissolution like all other physical things. It does not even have the function of memory like the brain does. All these feelings and the like are stored in the brain, more specifically, in the mind. The proof of this, if any is needed, is in the purification of the mind (see chart on page 519). When this marvelous act is completed, feelings are equalized, emotions are pacified, and passions are brought swiftly under control. They all must have been lodged in the mental body, then. So the heart, the real heart, is what the seers refer to as *Atman*. There is nothing out of order there, and so no need for purification, equalization, transformation, or control.

The brain/mind complex, what we are calling the *manomayakosha* at this point, has other amazing functions as well, deserving of exploration and study. The coming and going of the human soul in and out of the body takes place by way of the mind and its thinking processes. The Western thinker might aver that all this takes place in space, but the wonderful fact revealed by the *advaitic* seers is that all of space exists in the mind/soul of mankind. Space in an idea. According to Western philosophers like Descartes, he averred that *"I think, therefore I am,"* but the *Vedic* seers conclusion is, "I am, therefore I think." "I am" is the declaration of realization by the nondualist and the root and essence of the highest thinking, beyond thinking. But more on that later. The point under study at present takes into consideration what we have learned previously about the *koshas*. Videlicet (in other words), the *koshas* are not independent of one another, though embodied consciousness identifying with one to the exclusion of the others may assume so. They are interdependent, and here, with the mention of the soul's transmigration, is a good place for explication of this point.

First, when the body drops and the soul "moves on," it is the *prana* that facilitates said movement — inwardly *("The Kingdom of Heaven lies within you")*. But the actual movement, if the expression can be allowed (since all movement is dreamlike); *Brahman* is static, immovable), takes place in the mind and intellectual sheaths. Time and space are concepts in the mind, and the mind is fully capable of projecting them outwardly and inwardly. Life heavens, intermediate realms, higher *lokas* — these are all dreams at the cosmic and collective levels of mind, involving deities of preternatural proportions. This in-depth and very interesting cosmology will be taken up at great length in the succeeding pages of this book. For now, however, in order to facilitate a greater understanding later, the interconnected nature of the five *koshas* should be contemplated. In brief, the human soul is a complex, not just a body, and it has many layers to it, all deserving of study and consideration. Some beings are busy, no doubt, utilizing the intellect and its relative marvels. But we can see by the explanation above that they are really accessing only the individual level of the *manomayakosha*, while the collective and cosmic strata remain mostly unseen and unencountered.

This fact creates a convenient insertion point for the fourth *kosha*, the intellect, or *vijnanamayakosha*. The word *vijnana* generally denotes higher intelligence, lending this *kosha* a special facet that is most desirable of attainment and usage. But as the teachings reveal, the intellect, like the body, *prana,* and mind, is weighed down with its stark limitations too. That is to say, if left uncultivated, the sheath of intelligence will not only place stodgy impediments in the way of true progress, but can also distort, like a shorted circuit board, causing confusions and sufferings untold. A full refining and upkeep of this precious sheath of humanity, on its individual, collective, and cosmic levels, is therefore advised. In other words, *sadhana*, self-discipline/purification/refinement, is needed.

In the *Vivekachudamani* (recommended reading for this powerful subject), Shankara both cautions about and praises the *vijnanamayakosha* of the aspiring human being. His praise revolves around the fact that this refined intellectual faculty of mankind is the best reflector of Consciousness (see chart on page 56). To understand this principle of reflection, called *abhasa* in *Sanskrit* (one of some five meanings for this word), a simple illustration of Sri Ramakrishna can be shared. Placing this teaching in accessible terms, He said, *"Light reflects poorly off of a stone, faintly off of a leaf, better off of a lake, but best of all in a mirror."* This could easily and effectively be applied to the five *koshas* as well, in that the Light of pure, conscious Awareness does not emanate in the body very well, and is only a bit more prominent in the life-force called *prana*. In mind, more of that radiant Light comes through, especially in a scholar or a genius, while in the refined and matured intellect, say, like in that of the luminary, a positively halcyon glow shines forth.

But the great ones are quick to point out that reflection is not imminence or direct presence. The moon shines, but it does so via borrowed light. The sun has its own light, so is self-effulgent — *svayam-jyoti*. This means, and importantly, that all manifest phenomena perceived under the mind and intellect's supervision is only a reflection, not the original. This truth applies to ordinary perceptions, clever inventions, intellectual realizations, scriptural revelations — even the visions of the saints and seers. Moses seeing the burning bush, the resurrection of Jesus — do such phenomena really occur? It hardly matters, for it is all *chidabhasa* — the reflection of the Light of Reality upon the surface of the awakened soul's sheath of intelligence. Only, this surface has to be calm, not restless or dull, in order to have a vision of Reality — a temporary and apparent formulation of the eternally unformed *Brahman*. The roiling waters of an ocean at night, like a rock, do not make for good reflectors, and the mind is no stranger to commotion.

There is another aspect of the *vijnanamayakosha* that should be acknowledged, for it is responsible for a host of mighty errors in human judgment. It also hangs close on the tail of the fifth sheath, the *anandamayakosha*, or sheath of bliss. As our previous chart (page 21) declares, the intellect is very keen upon the sense of doer-ship. Ideas of "I am the agent of my action," and "It is I who will enjoy the fruits," though held in tandem with the ego sheath, are lodged deeply in this *kosha*. This is so because the success and failure that adheres to the thought process is held in check in the intellectual sheath. In other words, the ego sheath suffers this duality, but the intellect is responsible for it. Shankara also mentions that it is the intellect which courts the idea of going from one realm to another, like from heaven to earth to hell, while the ego only enjoys and suffers as a result.

Obviously, then, there is a close relationship and connection between these last two *koshas*, and a very subtle one at that. And what is at stake here, from the standpoint of the individual soul, is happiness or relative bliss. The ego sheath takes its very name from this precept, being called the *anandamaykosha*. Ananda is the *Sanskrit* word for bliss. A distinction is to be drawn here, albeit a temporal one, between the bliss of the ego and the Bliss of the Self. That is, at the level of cosmic mind and ripened ego, the difference between principles like man and God, creature and Creator, nature and Spirit, the ego and the Self, become paper thin. Another way of putting this is that as the five sheaths level less and less influence upon the aspiring soul the more the *Atman* and "Witness Consciousness," come to the fore. In simple terms, this equates to the human being's loss of attachment to body, senses, and their objects, to begin with. Later, even the pleasures and attainments of mind and intellect become insipid. This, what the seers have noted as "world-weariness," is a grand sign of renunciation, and if acted upon in the company of the adept and able preceptor, will lead to Enlightenment, even in this very lifetime. In this regard, some of the aspects of the ego mechanism should be examined.

Our chart presently under study states off the top that the *anandamayakosha*, if it is attached to form, *Linga*, has bliss. But its bliss is only a reflection of true Bliss — the Bliss of the *Atman*. As all sincere and advanced aspirants who have done their inner homework can tell you, the acid test for this statement is that the bliss of the ego waxes and wanes, and when it does, our little self (*ahamkara*) enjoys and suffers accordingly. The ups and downs are too much for the frail ego-self to bear, and it falls victim, like an immature person, to fits of merriment and insouciance side by side with ensuing disappointment and depression in the end. And by comparison, the Bliss of the Self, the *Atman*, never increases or decreases, as is instanced by the perfect equanimity of mind that every true sage and seer possesses, even under duress, even under the threat of death.

All of the five sheaths possess one great defect other than that of mutability: that is dependency. To be really free is to be wholly independent. This is the real meaning behind the statement *"Thou shalt have no other God before Me."* If the ego is unripe, and only stares outward and downward toward the territories of the intellect, mind, *prana*, and body, then a host of other gods, all vying for attention within those constricted realms, will rise and seek worship. Pandemonium will then ensue, a life disoriented and out of balance. But if this selfsame ego is ripe, i.e., rendered non-invasive and transparent by spiritual practices and self-surrender, the *Atman* suddenly emerges out of hiding and all the sheaths swiftly turn transparent. This is precisely why the great incarnations like Krishna, Buddha, Christ, and Ramakrishna were seen by their apostles to have palpable light emanating out of them. Even their physical bodies, the *annamayakosha*, were as if see-through, translucent to the extent that the Light of Consciousness was seeping out of their very pores, like starlight beaming out of the darkness of space.

This brings out another salient fact about the five sheaths. Their contemplation, even their very presence, opens up the relative law of evolution and involution for scrutiny. As the astronomers tell us, we are looking back in time when we stare into the night skies and see the light of stars. Similarly, if we meditate upon the five *koshas*, from gross to subtle, we are actually retracing the steps (the strut of individuation; see chapter two) we took when we decided to separate ourselves from the Formless Essence and take on a human birth in time.

To this date even knowledgeable philosophers are missing the real point of involution, relegating it to time and space only, and to matter. Involution is not the disappearance of matter into energy, and energy into the void. Involution is the decisive and effective putting away of mental concepts like time, space, matter, and energy into the formless vault of the Primal Word from which they all sprang, like a housewife laying piles of freshly folded clothes neatly into a huge chest of drawers, shutting it up and walking away (see chart on page 451). Verily, and from the standpoint of Reality, the five *koshas* are not needed anymore; they have had their facility and their play. Certainly, the sheath of food and matter, the *annamayakosha* and all that it entails, gets dropped efficiently and perfunctorily every time the desire, need, or will for freedom's advent suggests itself to the aspiring soul. Embodiment is bondage, any way one cuts it. Conscious transcendence is freedom, fully unimpeded. As the exceedingly lucid *Svetasvataropanisad* puts it, *"Matter is perishable, but Brahman is imperishable. That, the indivisible Reality, rules over perishable nature and individual souls. By meditating on That, by uniting with That, via Oneness with That, there is a cessation to these rounds of creation and destruction in the end."*

To the embodied being, and one who is inordinately attached to the body as the self, the idea of involution never occurs. This body, this world, this one lifetime is all there is. This type of thinking, or not-thinking, is called root ignorance in India, and was seen as such from time out of mind. But whatever the case may be, and despite the heaviness and grossness of the deluded brain, there comes an initial awakening when all beings seek liberation from the trammels and vicissitudes of the world. All struggle, on all levels of life, is really a sign of this internal push for Freedom.

The teaching of the five *koshas*, *Panchakosha*, is meant to avail these still sleepy but stirring souls with the information necessary to return to their Source. The way outward has been exceedingly long, combined lethargically with the often dense and demeaning dream of evolution. Exempt, as yet, from knowing the truth of nonorigination and nontransformation — *advaita* — the attempt at espying and following the way of involution is the only recourse for most souls. Having fallen into the sleep of matter, it will be preponderately difficult to extract the soul from its dalliance with decay and death and return it to the state of *"Yogic* Insomnia." As the poet-sage, Ramprasad sings in one of his devotional hymns to the Mother of the Universe, *"To be born in this body composed of earth is a heavy burden for the soaring soul. To incarnate again and again across the face of this vast planetary realm can never slake our burning thirst. The aspiring soul who sings this song proclaims: 'No more birth for me from the womb of matter; only emanation from my Divine Mother.'"*

Much more will naturally be presented in accord with the five *upadhis* or *koshas*, coverings or containers, in the forthcoming pages of this book. But the subject of involution, along with space, time, and causation, has now been effectively broached. This adequately outlines the study, the quest, the task at hand for humanity in the present age or *yuga*. Of course, *Vedanta* will meet and present this challenge with characteristic detachment, using nondualism as its first weapon of choice. For those with the cotton of materialism and the wax of fundamentalism lodged deep within their ears, some other techniques will have to be applied. For, the crying need here is not a mere imitation of the Christ and other luminaries, but to consciously become "one with the Father." As the *rishi*, Svetasvatara, has stated, after omnisciently glancing back into past ages: *"By first harnessing the power of the mind and senses, and with a view to realizing the Truth they had intuited, and then having brought out the Light from within them, evolving souls successfully brought the Self out of all wayward contact with the earth and the gross realm of matter."*

Retracing the Strut of Individuation
The Myth and Benefit of Evolution and Involution

Advaita Vedanta, the polestar of nondual philosophy and the revivifier of true Religion from age to age, avidly states that the soul of mankind is unborn and undying. This is not a case of rising out of a fall from grace, or repairing a failed relationship with an angry God. It does not involve a fear-inspired assumption of original sin, or require a moral reprieve leading to a post-mortem emancipation. This truth of the innate perfection of mankind epitomizes the natural and spontaneous life of the acreate Soul.

As must be admitted, the view from this profound and lofty philosophical position is incomparable (see chart on page 744). Therefore, the seers of different religious traditions deeply desire to share it with all other beings. If this were possible, what might be the result or reaction? The analogy of a deaf and dumb man trying to explain his first taste of ice cream comes to mind here, or the attempt at trying to explain the conjugal happiness of a newly married woman to a five-year-old girl. But if well comprehended, and when taught by an illumined teacher, this "good news" of *Vedanta* will allow for a full transformation of the human mind, rendering it fit for the *Brahman* state (see chart on page 385). With this statement, the *Vedantist* confirms a very important point for all spiritual seekers: that it is the mind (*manas*) which needs transforming, while the Soul (*Atman*) of mankind remains ever-pure and ever-perfect. All spiritual practice and attainment, then, ought to be accomplished under the direct influence of this inspiring axiom.

And it is on that sterling note that the subjects of space, time, and causality can be taken up, what were called *desha*, *kala*, and *nimitta* by the ancient *rishis* (knowers of Truth). That is, the *rishis* of India spent most all of their time meditating upon and discoursing about *Brahman*, the Absolute Reality. That is why, to this day, the *Upanisads* and *Bhagavad Gita*, among other scriptures, emanate the truth of Reality in Its naturally formless condition like no other. But when these unique souls came out of *samadhi* long enough to breathe and act, they duly placed their attention upon two other related areas: the problems of life and the practices that would remove them.

Therefore, it was meet that *desha*, *kala*, and *nimitta* came to the fore of their minds, since all problems and their solutions require space, time, and causation to exist — which is a very good reason why they kept their minds on *Brahman* to begin with, since these three relative imperatives do not exist in the nondual state. And as they contemplated the realm of *nama-rupa*, name and form, they espied a numbered sequence to these three. This was based upon the fact that space must exist in order for time to proceed, and activity goes forth when time is operative. With this fundamental criterion perceived, the principle of space was taken up and dissected, resulting in realizations which, to this day, are among the most important of all discoveries pertaining to the cosmos, albeit going unrecognized by most beings of the present time.

Desha — Space

The first fact to be made broadcast was the existence of five layers of space, which these profound thinkers termed *akashas*. Most beings think in terms of one dimension in this regard, which is physical space alone. The condition of rank materialism oozes up from this narrow perspective, whereas the universally-minded beings come to know of four other *akashas*. The following chart illustrates this.

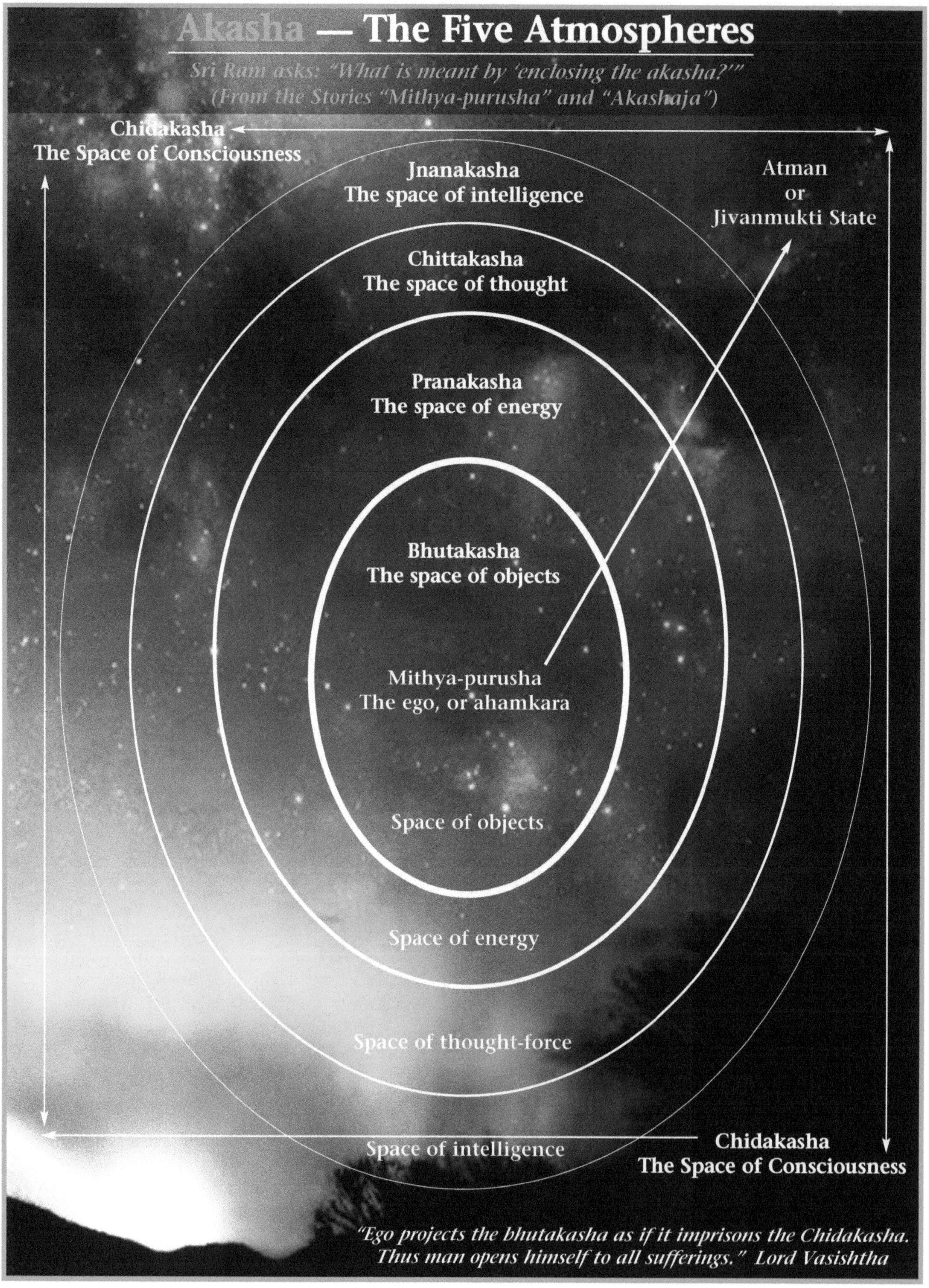

Akasha — The Five Atmospheres

Sri Ram asks: "What is meant by 'enclosing the akasha?'"
(From the Stories "Mithya-purusha" and "Akashaja")

Chidakasha
The Space of Consciousness

Jnanakasha
The space of intelligence

Atman
or
Jivanmukti State

Chittakasha
The space of thought

Pranakasha
The space of energy

Bhutakasha
The space of objects

Mithya-purusha
The ego, or ahamkara

Space of objects

Space of energy

Space of thought-force

Space of intelligence

Chidakasha
The Space of Consciousness

"Ego projects the bhutakasha as if it imprisons the Chidakasha. Thus man opens himself to all sufferings." Lord Vasishtha

As can be seen by this simple rendering, the five *akashas* run from gross to subtle, each layer of space being intimately related to the other four. That is, they read gross to subtle from the standpoint of the physical worlds, which are contained inside the *Bhutakasha,* the space of *bhutas,* or objects. Here, the word "object" means everything from stalks and stones, to human bodies, to planets spinning through space. The *bhutas* also include the realm of animals and plants, and even the realm of disembodied spirits who have lost their way. All that is physical by nature, and limited to the gross level of name and form, are found in the *Bhutakasha.*

Lying up close to the *Bhutakasha,* and unbeknownst to most living beings, is the *Pranakasha,* the space of subtle energy, or life-force. This animating power is responsible for everything from the lifting of ones arm to the transference of thought to higher mind. To detect and perceive the realm of *prana* is to effectively be able to transcend physical space. When this occurs, one cognizes all that is beyond the particles of matter that make up the physical universe. Perhaps the very first line of one of Swami Vivekananda's profound poems says it best: *"We shall crush the stars to atoms; we will unhinge the universe..."* This is what the *yogi* accomplishes in deep meditation, and also what the stuff of various types of *samadhis* are made of. The mind, usually so accustomed to playing with and amidst fields of gross atoms, and to such an extent that a narrow habit forms around the relationship with them, deftly graduates to a finer level of perception and beholds the realm of *pranic* particles. This is a lower *samadhi,* no doubt, but is nevertheless key to the deeper levels of Consciousness that await.

An interesting and ameliorating fact is applicable here, signifying what *pranic* particles really represent. We know that atomic particles and their host of smaller concomitants make up objects. The Dalai Lama has pointed out, for instance, that the tree we are looking at has three dimensions: first, there is the appearance tree; second, there is the actual tree — which is a mass of swirling particles; and third, there is the Buddha Nature tree, or Essence tree (see chart on page 652). So the tree everyone thinks of as a tree is not the real tree at all, but just an appearance. And just as there are objects consisting of physical particles in the *Bhutakasha,* there are also forms in the *Pranakasha.* And in fact, these forms are the forms of beings who have left the physical realm and taken up residence in the *Pranakasha,* in short, the "departed," what people think of and call their ancestors. The *Pranakasha,* then, holds a direct correlation to the heavens talked about in the respective cosmologies of various world religions.

Another fact about the *pranic* realms, or *lokas,* is that they are gradated. That is, there is a denser form of *prana* which would correspond to the lower heavens of the ancestors, and finer *pranic* particles/realms pertinent to the intermediate and higher heavens. This is where beings such as celestials and demigods abide and reign. The inner traveler, the one taking the path of involution, would necessarily course through these *lokas* when leaving the surface of Awareness, diving deeper and deeper into the ocean of Consciousness called *Brahman.* Thus, this knowledge, albeit quite esoteric for this earth and for conventional human beings, not only goes a long way towards bridging the gap between science and theology, but also provides the key for understanding the real import of the statement, *"The kingdom of heaven is within you."* When Christ declared *"My Father's Mansion has many chambers,"* we are to understand that He saw them and entered into them in his deepest contemplations. Leaving the body and senses aside, like adept meditators can do, the realms of subtle form next come into view. This occurs to ordinary people as well when they go to sleep, but ignorance and lack of spiritual awareness renders these worlds hazy and unstable. This is called the dream state (*svapna*). *Prana* plays a huge role in the inward ascension of the human soul, then, and more of this will come to light in the forthcoming pages of this chapter.

The *Chitakasha,* the third level of space, is the subtle space of mind. Most beings think of their brain as their mind. But the brain is a mere organ which decays upon death. Mind goes on forever, stretching back inside oneself and containing all the realms of name and form within its vast territories. From the standpoint of the subtle mind, the entire universe of worlds and beings is beheld — all heavens, all earths, all hells. Here, the power of thought, *chitta,* is king. The abilities of the mind to conceive, project, imagine, dream, fantasize, etc., is legion, is unlimited. In the time of the *rishis,* the *Sanskrit* words describing all this mental activity were *sankalpa* and *vikalpa,* meaning "various imaginings in cycles of time." Thus, earth's living beings, all laboring under the idea that they live once and then die, have very little idea of how potent and productive their own mind is, capable of creating numbers of bodies and countless worlds without limits over infinite stretches of time. But more on time, later. We must first continue to course through inner space.

Closely linked to the *Chitakasha,* but even more powerful in a subtle sense, is the space of intelligence, the *Jnanakasha.* It could easily be conceived of as the *Chitakasha,* the space of thought-force, but is more potent in its power. For, there is a difference between thought and wisdom, and that is precisely the distinction here. *Jnana* is a form of knowledge that is spiritually based, and so is higher and more refined than intellectual acumen (see chart on page 600). It is coveted and adored by sages and seers, and these same beings use it on earth to fashion the holy scriptures of different religions. At the extreme end of *jnana,* that is, moving away from the earth and its pull, it is this same knowledge, now wisdom, that will dissolve the mind of the one who is desirous of merging completely into Divine Reality. Thus is seen the dissolution of the mind into pure wisdom, which will take the inner traveler through the *Chitakasha* into the *Jnanakasha,* then into the *Chidakasha.*

The *Chidakasha* is the space of pure Consciousness. Really, this is only an expression, for Consciousness has no restricted space. It is hard enough for the mind to determine the disappearance of atomic particles into *pranic* particles, but is wholly beyond the mind to figure its own dissolution. But this describes and defines the distinct and unequaled quality of the enlightened soul as compared to the earth-bound being. The latter is afraid of death, and can barely conceive of, let alone uncover and acknowledge, the fact of life after death. The former has gotten over both death and afterlife. He has long since given up the habit of consuming matter with the mind and senses and is now imbibing the "nectar of nondual wisdom" penultimate to formless *samadhi.*

The ordinary soul's penchant, then, is for recklessly and unknowingly restricting the boundless soul to the space of matter, the *Bhutakasha.* Lord Vasishtha states this in answer to Sri Ram's question, as indicated on the previous chart (page 30). If the reader will remember, or look back on the first chapter of this book, the five *koshas* correspond fairly readily to these five atmospheres, except that the fifth *kosha,* the ego sheath, does not match up well with the fifth *akasha.* And in fact it is this ego self which, according to Lord Vasishtha in his quote, projects physical space as if to somehow trap and imprison the limitless Spirit. And this ruse works....for a time. As long as the desire-based soul is busy playing in the *"fields of the Lord,"* so long will such distractions pin him, like a moth, to the painful corkboard of the atomic world alone. What he does not know, however, is that *"the fields of the Lord"* are not just physical ones; they reach, as we have seen thus far, ever inward towards the Infinite Being. It is therefore that higher knowledge, only, will truly satisfy.

In the chart presently under study it is seen that the *Chidakasha* pervades and permeates all the other levels of space. This explains nicely and lends clarity to the *Vedantic* Dictum (*Vedanta Dindima*), *"All is Brahman."* Another facet of the chart observes the position of the *Mithya-purusha,* or false self, as contrasted to the *Atman,* or real Self. The two are as if in entirely different territories. But the reflection of the moon in a mud puddle, despite its poor imitation of the real thing, nevertheless causes the observer to look skyward and behold the original. The same can be said for this false self. It is like a wax apple which, though tasteless, makes the mouth water just by the thought of the real thing. The false self, a petty potentate, only needs to be dethroned, and the real sovereign installed in its place. Then the entire world will become nothing other than the *Chidakasha.*

With the principle of *desha,* space, now in place, and transcending the dwarfed idea that physical space alone is real, a more in-depth study can be made of this rich and galvanizing topic. The following chart coalesces these five *akashas* with their corresponding realms, all placed in the context of the refinement of particles. This is a "new" particle theory which mediates between the views of science and theology. Man, the divine being, is at the center of this process, with the teaching couched in terms of evolution and involution only for the sake of higher comprehension.

From Atomic Particles to "Atmic" Particles

> "Verily, that one indivisible Consciousness is the indwelling Essence in all things.
> Fire is Its head, the sun and moon Its two eyes, and the unstruck sound, Om, Its ears.
> The revelation of scripture is Its cosmic mind, the many-tiered universe of name and form,
> from gross to subtle, Its heart, and Its arms and legs, the four directions. Truth is Its voice,
> the wind is Its breath, and from Its feet the verdant earth has originated." *Mundakopanisad*

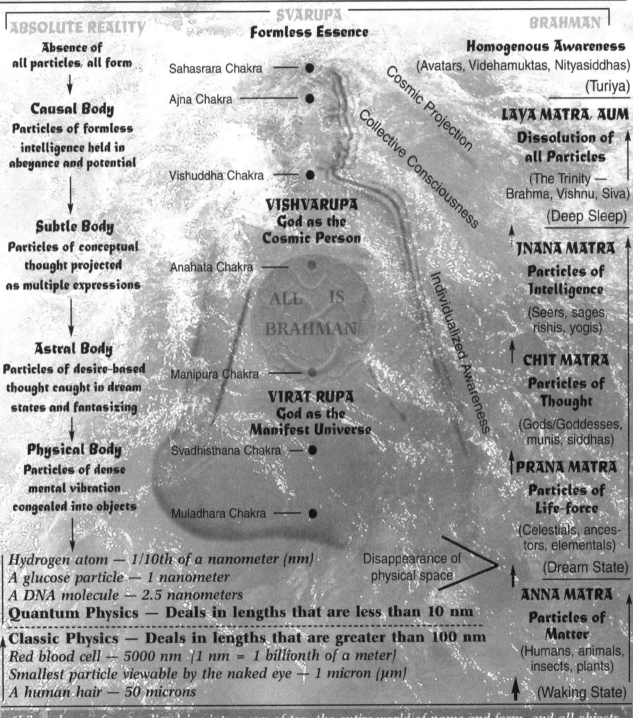

SVARUPA
Formless Essence

ABSOLUTE REALITY

Absence of all particles, all form

↓

Causal Body
Particles of formless intelligence held in abeyance and potential

↓

Subtle Body
Particles of conceptual thought projected as multiple expressions

↓

Astral Body
Particles of desire-based thought caught in dream states and fantasizing

↓

Physical Body
Particles of dense mental vibration congealed into objects

↓

Sahasrara Chakra — ●

Ajna Chakra — ●

Vishuddha Chakra — ●

VISHVARUPA
God as the Cosmic Person

Anahata Chakra —

ALL IS BRAHMAN

Manipura Chakra —

VIRAT RUPA
God as the Manifest Universe

Svadhisthana Chakra — ●

Muladhara Chakra — ●

Cosmic Projection

Collective Consciousness

Individualized Awareness

BRAHMAN

Homogenous Awareness
(Avatars, Videhamuktas, Nityasiddhas)

(Turiya)

LAYA MATRA, AUM
Dissolution of all Particles
(The Trinity — Brahma, Vishnu, Siva)

(Deep Sleep)

JNANA MATRA
Particles of Intelligence
(Seers, sages, rishis, yogis)

CHIT MATRA
Particles of Thought
(Gods/Goddesses, munis, siddhas)

PRANA MATRA
Particles of Life-force
(Celestials, ancestors, elementals)

(Dream State)

ANNA MATRA
Particles of Matter
(Humans, animals, insects, plants)

(Waking State)

Disappearance of physical space

Hydrogen atom — 1/10th of a nanometer (nm)
A glucose particle — 1 nanometer
A DNA molecule — 2.5 nanometers
Quantum Physics — Deals in lengths that are less than 10 nm
- -
Classic Physics — Deals in lengths that are greater than 100 nm
Red blood cell — 5000 nm (1 nm = 1 billionth of a meter)
Smallest particle viewable by the naked eye — 1 micron (µm)
A human hair — 50 microns

> "Like a lump of sugar dissolving into a cup of tea, the entire world of name and form, and all objects,
> merge into Brahman, the Ultimate Reality, at the end of a cosmic cycle. All manifested things
> are soluble into the supremely unmanifested Brahman."   *Sri Ramakrishna Paramahamsa*

This new chart up for study (page 33), created on Christmas Day of 2009 as a gift to all students and devotees, is aptly named, "From Atomic Particles to *'Atmic'* Particles." Beginning its inward march in the realm of classic physics, and using the old standard measurement of a micron, it is stated that this tiny amount of physical space is equal to the smallest thing the human eye can see. Of course, the eye can see a human hair, which measures some 50 microns. But a red blood cell is not discernible by the naked eye, and must be calculated by a much smaller measuring device called the nanometer. Here, Quantum Physics enters the fray, and cites the miniscule scale of tiny bits of matter like the DNA molecule, the glucose particle, and the hydrogen atom. Place some ten of these latter elfin structures side by side and you will know how small a nanometer is.

The question might well be asked at this point, what is the point of all this? That is, after the fundamental fact of a universe consisting of particles has been established, and as scientific determination of points of matter reaches such microscopic proportions, where does it end? Where does it all go? This is precisely what the ancient *rishis* examined, only they did not have or need an electron microscope to figure it out. In short, one does not have to create a particle accelerating or decelerating chamber for the simple reason that the mind is already that. As mentioned earlier, through the acquired ability of focused Awareness to abandon at will the body and senses, the meditator enters into rarefied realms of finer particles, incomprehensible to others, and beholds what the *Tantric*ists of ancient times called *Sristhi Rahasya,* the "Secret of Creation." (see chart on page 463).

This secret really consists of the fact that creation and evolution are both a myth, that all these worlds, inner to outer, are being continually and spontaneously projected by the mind's Awareness. In this regard, Holy Mother, Sri Sarada Devi, has stated: *"Objects are just thought made manifest."* Placed in *Buddhist* terms, the whole world, all worlds, are nothing but the *"void illuminating mind."* They are "void" because they consist of nothing but vibrating particles changing at a billionth of a second. They are "illuminating" due to the mind's intrinsic connection to the source of origins, the Word (see chart on page 144), the Light of *Brahman.* But again, more on this later.

So this is where all of this measuring of matter is headed, or should be headed. If Western science, psychology, and religion would indeed become so open-minded, then the next step in Physics should not be to merely render the phenomena of this universe into material particles only; and the next step in Psychology and Medicine should not be to relegate the human condition to a collection of neuropeptides, etc., in the brain; and the next step of Religion should not be to remain fixated with the fictitious separation between God and mankind. A step should be a profound footfall, it must leave an impression. The impression we must be left with, both as human beings and as truth-seekers, is one of the formless nature of Existence — the *Nirvana* of the Buddha, the Beatific Vision of Christ in the Wilderness, the *Samadhi* of Sri Ramakrishna in modern times. Only this will permanently mark life as truly meaningful and worthwhile, everything else being constant flux and change — including our modern advancements, with no purchase point and no final place of arrival.

These statements are emphasized in the chart under study (page 33) by the expression, "the disappearance of physical space." This is the beginning of formlessness, because it signals the absence of matter in tandem with the still existing presence of the observer. This is why it is likened to the dream state, wherein objects are evanescent, while the participant is still sporting among them. Additionally, all the objects experienced within are definitely projected by the dreamer, which is another key. Better yet is the example of deep sleep (*sushupti*), where all forms are gone, but a waking presence is still potential. These three states of existence — waking, dreaming, and deep sleep — are essential to *Vedantic* understanding, and will be taken up in forthcoming chapters.

Here, we pick up the right hand side of the chart, moving upwards. The disappearance of physical particles, as has been mentioned earlier, allows for the revelation of *prana* and, therefore, the worlds of the ancestors. So many cultures, so many religions, worship the ancestors. Their world lies hand in glove next to ours, and we always feel their influence and presence as a result of that intimate proximity. Most souls who are born here on earth are coming forth from that realm of the forefathers, as that is the pool (beyond gene pools) out of which these "formless" souls, who still have desires for earthly pleasures, emerge. There is no need for the physicist to draw back here due to the lack of sensual perception and its "proofs," for the metaphysician is born out of the insights that spring from studying this particular level of science. Unfortunately, occultists, clairvoyants, and other opportunists huddle around this thin veneer of a realm, many of them exacting both superficial preoccupation and a shady living from its shiny surface. Sensationalists, *hatha* yogis, shamans, and others of that ilk also gravitate to this area of existence, some fixated on the energy of life force and the various and alluring "tricks of *prana*" it demonstrates, and others desirous of merely learning and going on.

To further explain the space of *prana*, or *pranamayakosha*, and the realm of the ancestors in relation to the principle of reincarnation (see chart on page 327), a teaching on the process of dying (see chart on page 190) can be given. A word must be said here, that *Vedanta* does not emphasize the mortality aspect of dying, or even the vaunted "art of dying," but rather the transcendence of the very idea of death — because it is illusory. If one thinks in terms of nothingness after death, then it must be seen that even Western science, what to speak of the world's enlightened sages, have sufficiently demonstrated that "nothing" does not exist (i.e., even matter only converts to energy). If one believes in a life after death, a post-mortem emancipation after earthly life ends, then read on.

Some beings may have heard of the "silver thread," or that subtle cord that connects the soul to the body (the word "soul" in *Vedanta* means the mental complex, not the real Self). Over the period of an ordinary man's life, how he thinks and acts leaves a series of impressions called *samskaras* (see charts on page 167 & 170) on his mind. Those get stored up, not just as habits and complexes which he formulates and holds in his brain's subconscious memory in this lifetime alone, but as definite directive forces that will predicate his future movements in terms of rebirth.

When a man leaves his body, then, the previously accented and unresolved contents of his mind empty up and out of the mind through the silver cord under the auspice of *prana* and its powers of transference. Those subtle contents, holding all that is in store for him in the future, are deposited into a *pranic* container, resembling an invisible bubble, called a spirit body by some, which then goes looking for another host. Measuring in increments of time, this process could take about a hundred earth years as the ordinary earthbound soul "rests" and "plans." Importantly, the real Self, *Atman*, which is never subject to either movement (since It is all-pervasive) or transmigration (since It is ever-stationary), looks on from a detached witness standpoint. Of course, if this mind/soul has practiced identification with the Witness/*Atman* (*sakshi bhutam*, the witness of all phenomena), it no longer undergoes this dreamlike metamorphosis, and can even skirt the realms of the ancestors, celestials, and the gods, to arrive at a much finer place of existence — can even merge in the Absolute, *"like a hailstone falling into an ocean."*

The analogy of the camel who eats thorny bushes, mentioned by Sri Ramakrishna, is helpful here. We may have often wondered, under the surface of our daily lives, why there are so many camels, so many cows, so many humans. It is all based upon desire. Holy Mother, Sri Sarada Devi, has told us that the creation (projection) is going on because so many beings have not fulfilled their desires (see chart on page 164). A camel is certainly one of these beings. The Great Master has said, *"A camel eats thorny bushes until its gums bleed from laceration and blood gushes from its mouth; but still it goes on eating."*

Taking this observation to a deeper level, the desire for eating thorny bushes lodges deeply in the brain of the camel, forming a *samskara* or mental impression there. When the camel body dies, the contents of its brain empty into the *pranic* sheath and, due to its prevalent desire for the taste of thorny greenery, it seeks for a host that will provide it with just such a repast. The camel parents, of which there are many, are available in great numbers — much to the delight of the camel driver.

A further note could be added here in terms of the refinement of consciousness. We have mentioned that a human soul has the potential to rise up and out of lower realms of existence. The animals are also effecting such a rise by degrees. Take for instance a cow. It does not pain itself with thorny bushes, but rather quietly grazes on soft grasses, even giving milk to others via that process. This is a sign of evolution, not only on the level of gradation of species, but also through the subtle operations of a benign presence overseeing the growth and sustenance of all creatures.

And so we see the import of that refined awareness that remains after atomic particles dissolve. It is all one all-pervasive Awareness, no doubt, but beings devoid of cognizance of It adapt It to various qualified and limited usages (see chart on page 294). This is rather like blowing bubbles out of one uniform body of soapy liquid. The air within the bubble is the empty ego, and the membrane itself is the body and brain complex. But who is the one doing the blowing? One gets closer to That along the trajectory of this dreamlike ascension into formlessness.

As the mind/soul refines itself (chart on page 33), *pranic* particles give way to particles of thought, called *chit*. The *Sanskrit* word for particle is *matra*. Therefore, particles of food or matter are called *anna matra*, of *prana*, *prana matra*, and of thought, *chit matra*. It was mentioned earlier that the cross-section of *pranic* realms hold within them lower, intermediate, and higher heavens. The ancestors occupy the lowest heavens, the angels and celestials the next rungs of the ladder, and the gods and goddesses (signifying greater manifestations of divinity) take up residence and dominance in the higher *pranic* plateaus. On the cusp of this high heaven is where the *Chit matra* becomes so fine that the soul, coursing along in involution, finds some very profound personages there — *munis, siddhas, devas, and devis.* Some of these beings are so profound that merely making their acquaintance results in the ability to refrain from taking birth in lower realms, ever again.

In this regard, Swami Vivekananda has stated, *"The gods and goddesses are just big men and women,"* indicating, among other things, that some great souls who have transcended earthly life have taken a more prominent position in the sweep of worlds and are now presiding over millions of souls in their subtle bodies, much like a religious leader would do so here on earth. This also clarifies that recurring phenomena called the conqueror, world leader, genius, etc., who are great souls in the realm of higher mind but who, in order to realize their higher Self, take up a birth in the world of gross matter in another human form. Thus, there are an infinite amount of possibilities in the *"....fields of the Lord,"* and one should remain open to them and study them as well.

As we course up the ladder of the present chart under study (page 33), the realm of the spiritual luminary appears, especially and expressly to those who are blessed enough to perceive it. This is where the particles of existence become so rarefied that even subtle forms are all but absent. This is why the word "causal" must be applied. The particle of intelligence, the *jnana matra*, is a shining verity, packed with power that is not merely atomic, but *Atmic* in nature. Power for destruction became all the "rage" back on earth, in the realm of matter, with the splitting of the atom. Such discoveries as this — with their promise of granting greater wealth, greater fame, greater power over others — caused scientists, politicians, and businessmen to run about for decades in a vociferous frenzy, like hens cackling at the manifestation of a fresh hatching of insects on the barnyard floor. Meanwhile, beyond even the very idea of destruction, seers, sages, *raja* yogis, and other luminaries focused instead in deep meditation upon the *jnana matra* and, piercing that, released a benign force for the highest good of all beings in all realms — if they would but accept and release it.

The word "causal" has been brought up. The realm of the spiritually illumined ones is interwoven inextricably with the realmless realm of *AUM*, the primal Word into which all dissolves, and out of which all emerges. The chart under study cites this as *"laya matra."* The word *"laya"* signifies what has undergone dissolution. So here, finally, is the dissolution of all particles. It is the realm of formlessness where all bodies, whether gross, or subtle, are rendered free, emancipated. It is the causal state, like deep sleep, since it is the origin of all things which partake of form. The saying of Christ to John takes on greater significance and makes more sense here: *"In the beginning was the Word, and the Word was with God, and the Word was God."*

Taking up this saying in the incomparable light of *Vedanta*, in the realm of the *jnana matra*, all this can be safely and cogently unwrapped. To begin, God, Reality, has no beginnings, so Its Word must supply that. The Word is the servant of all cause for that which is Causeless. *Brahman* cannot be a cause for anything, being ever pure. So this is the meaning of *"the Word was with God."* It is inseparable from the Lord, but has the potential for appearing separate. This is why one sometimes hears that God and His Word are one and the same, while at other times, the distinction of God from His Word is proclaimed. Further, *"the Word was with God"* is meant to convey that, while the Word can appear separate, and is responsible for formulating all the worlds of name and form in time and space, it nevertheless remains always unified with God.

In conclusion, Reality (God) is free of origins and beginnings (see chart on page 746); Its Word is the seat of all manifestation, and all expression resulting in apparently separate worlds that appear distinct from Reality is contained essentially within It. It is in this sense that even the subtlest of dualities, like birth and death, bondage and liberation, form and formlessness, are rendered nonactual, or apparent only. Reality is one indivisible and homogenous whole, despite all appearances otherwise or to the contrary. This is the "stuff" that spiritual realization is made of, and it will become more discernible as deep and concentrated studies of this nature go forth.

More will be stated about knowledge, wisdom, and its essential role in God-realization. Suffice to say that after the *jnana matra* has dissolved into *AUM*, the only step to make from there is an extremely subtle one. Swami Brahmananda has stated that this is where true spiritual life actually begins. The chart under study has assigned several names to that uppermost spiritual strata, like *Brahman*, *Svarupa* (Essence), and Absolute Reality. The greatest beings, like the Divine Incarnations, are most conversant with It, but this applies only upon departing from It and taking on a form. In other words, these luminaries can, at will, take on a form while still remaining conscious of *Brahman* as their true nature, as their Eternal Abode. Others fall victim to forgetfulness, to ignorance. As Sri Ramakrishna has so aptly related, *"The more lives that people live in ignorance, the more they come to believe that birth and death are real, and that God is not."*

The divine memory of the luminaries is a most amazing thing. The left hand side of the chart (page 33) shows the process of assuming form, of gradually lowering oneself into the bath of subtle and grosser particles, like getting into hot water a bit at a time. Further, the assumption of form can be done either in ignorance, or in consciousness. That is, the unillumined soul is *"dragged from birth to death and death to birth,"* as Swami Vivekananda states, by what Sri Krishna calls *trishna*, desire. Such benighted souls hanker after the unreal and substanceless things of the worlds, and will take births in matter again and again in order to enjoy them. This is rather like feasting on marshmallows and cotton candy to gain nutrition. And the circus of this world will be only too glad to false and force-feed the transmigrating soul in this fashion. But the illumined ones never stray from their connection to *Brahman*, and if they take on embodiment in the various worlds at all, it is due to fulfilling some divinely guided and oriented mission.

Tracing the left hand side of the chart presently under study, now from top to bottom, we see how the conscious soul takes on the always difficult prospect of form. Unconscious souls never know themselves, so are unaware of the splendors which exist in subtle and causal realms. This is much like remaining uncognizant during the deep sleep phase. But conscious souls have, as Sri Aurobindo has stated, *"....traveled up and down the amber stairs of birth and death"* so often, that they know the way. They have known the Truth, and the Truth has set them free.

Out of the causal body, then — called *AUM*, *Hiranyagarbha*, Lord *Brahma*, Cosmic Mind, *Mahat*, etc., — higher Awareness, now putting on the garb of an individual soul, seeks to gravitate into the subtle realm where the powers of mental projection are encountered. Following the present theme of our teaching — the miniscule particle — the conscious soul desirous of embodiment is now effectively congealing particles — from causal to subtle to gross — into denser forms, in similar fashion, opposite of what was done previously when dropping all forms and merging into *Brahman*.

The taking on of the physical body, the final and most concrete form, is a careful undertaking for such a soul. Whereas others are as if on a roulette wheel, gambling and hoping for the best circumstances, the luminary (as we have read in the Tibetan Book of the Dead and in other salient sources) is busy choosing country, parents, gender, and many other fine points of life in order to facilitate the optimum chances of success for his or her divine mission. The role of past *karmas* here (see charts on pages 210, 213), or lack thereof, determines so much of this process. As has been related earlier, what a man thought of and acted upon in previous lifetimes is now imminent and ready for fructification. If he was wicked, violent, careless, callous, stubborn, etc., he can hardly stop himself from being *"born in ignorant wombs,"* as Sri Krishna has stated in the *Bhagavad Gita*. But the illumined soul is like an excellent archer who hits the intended mark perfectly due to his wealth of spiritual experience. The world, even in all its ignorance, welcomes this great one into its fold, grateful for such a compassionate being on earth. The *prana* vibrates in rare and unusual ways when such an event occurs, and other sincere souls are already making their way, consciously or unconsciously, towards the location of this special soul's birth.

In the center of this chart under study on page 33 is the image of God in human form. The upper strata, where the finer particles hum with all-penetrating wisdom, is called *Visvarupa,* the Cosmic Person, and the lower strata, where the gross particles congeal, is called *Viratrupa,* the universal soul. It is all *Brahman,* as the *Mahavakya* (Great Saying) at the center of his being declares, but as the ancient *rishis* proclaimed, *Brahman* is with form and beyond form as well. Its formless essence is *nirguna,* free of all attributes and overlays, and Its appearance in form is s*aguna,* a taking on of qualities for the express purpose of manifestation (see chart on page 507).

This chart also incorporates aspects of the *Kundalini Yoga* system. Noted at several pivotal points along the expanse of this divine form are the names of the *chakras,* or spiritual vortexes, centers of divine energy where Reality sports in the human form via awakened intelligence, or *Shakti* power. The three aspects of individual, collective, and cosmic consciousness are also indicated, signifying yet another way of both classifying and explaining the inscrutable miracles and movements of Divine Reality. As the *Mundakopanisad* quote at the top relates, the entire universe, its many aspects, and universes unseen, make up The Lord's all-pervasive form.

It is clear that the ancient seers beheld the Lord and Mother in everything, and everything in Them. To experience this Divine Couple is possible and encouraged for all (see chart on page 683), the necessary element in this undertaking being a firm grasp of ones divine nature as Consciousness. Departing the chart on page 33, Sri Ramakrishna's quote at the bottom intimates that the mind has the ability to dissolve itself into its Source, *Brahman*. Those atomic particles, like the fused granules of a sugar cube, then melt away by degrees in rapt and focused meditation, sweetening life immeasurably in the process. If there be any purpose for this pretended game of evolution and involution, the secret lies here, and space, *desha*, in its five forms, plays a major role.

Kala — Time

Kala, time, also exerts a profound influence over all processes. When considering space, the makeup and study of particles naturally comes to mind. When contemplating time, the prospect of Enlightenment comes to the fore. This chapter concerns itself with the appearance and phenomenon of the individual as he/she transmigrates from one mode of existence to the other. Unique to Indian philosophy and religion, this process, called evolution and involution, is not restricted to earth and physical space as in Western science, or even limited to heaven, earth, and hell like in Christian theology. It takes in the entire sweep of the many-tiered *"House of God"* with all its *"many Mansions."* And the all-important spiritual element finds its rightful and necessary place here via *Vedic* truth and culture as well. This is true wholism, authentic spirituality, as well as authentic universality.

Before taking up the subject of Enlightenment in relation to time, a fundamental overview of the Hindu concept of time can be given, all in a very simple chart which appears on the next page. As the definition at the top of this chart relates, the illusoriness of time is illustrated well in the *Sanskrit* word, *"kalpanika."* *Kalpanika* means an imagination in time, and everything which gets imagined in this linear span is ultimately unreal, however real it may seem at the "time." Lord Vasishtha, our revered guide in this often disconcerting topic, declares that *"This miraculous legerdemain is enacted by mind, and by mind alone."* One of the earliest adherents of what were later to be titled the "mind only schools," this mind-born son of *Brahma* opened avenues to Enlightenment for many aspiring beings desirous of escaping time. Let us look at this marvelous sweep called time.

Kalpa — The Concept of Time in Vedic Cosmology

(From the Story of the Siddhi and King Lavana)

(Definition: kalpana; imagination of the mind; kalpanika; false imaginings in time)

Brahman — Timeless, Deathless Awareness

**Shiva/Kala
— the Witness of all Phenomena in Time**

**100 Kalpas
(Para - A Lifetime of Lord Brahma)**

**One Kalpa - A Day of Brahma
(14 Manvantaras, or Svetavarahakalpa)
(4,320,000,000 Years)**

**One Manvantara
(71 Mahayugas)**

**One Mahayuga
(1200 Celestial Years)**

**One Celestial Year
(320 Human Years)**

**Brahman Pervading
Throughout**

"Through the force of the mind, a Kalpa is reckoned by it as a mere moment in time. Time, space, and the multifarious legerdemain of the world is enacted by mind, and mind alone." Lord Vasishtha

The declaration of *Brahman* as timeless, deathless Reality on this chart is a fitting appellation, and goes well with our forthcoming study of time. *Vedanta*, and all of the Indian *darshanas*, differ in their conception of time and creation from Western science and theology (see chart on pages 262). Whereas theology sticks doggedly with the idea of a seven day creation theory by a Creator God, and science looks towards a billions of years evolutionary scheme on the physical level only, Indian seers perceived both the illusory nature of time and its appearance in cycles, in that order, and only then taught about time.

Utilizing the human year as an incremental measuring device, the *rishis*, early on, fashioned a system that sees beyond conventional thinking and is more fitting for the noble facade of time that *Maya* has conjured up. In this system, three-hundred and twenty human years equals one year in the celestial regions, and twelve-hundred of these celestial years was reckoned as a *Mahayuga* (a *Mahayuga* also gets divided into four *Yugas*, called *satya, treta, dvapara,* and *kali*). Seventy-one *Mahayugas* form a *Manvantara*. Fourteen of these *Manvantaras* are a *Kalpa*, which is said to be one day of Lord *Brahma's* life. And that *Kalpa* is four billion, three-hundred and twenty million earth years.

Further, if we take one-hundred of these *Kalpas* and put them together, we can reckon Lord *Brahma's* (Lord of Creation) entire lifetime, which gives a clue into how long any given extended cycle of manifestation will last before *Pralaya*, which is the dissolution of all name and form into a timeless condition until the next cycle begins anew. The life of the Trinity of *Brahma, Vishnu,* and *Siva*, then, responsible for overseeing one grand cycle of creation, preservation, and destruction, lasts a very long time. This fact acquaints the individual mind with the Cosmic Mind and some of its ramifications. Some have heard of the Cosmic Mind of God in the West, or God's Mind. In Eastern conception, many facets of it have been introduced to humanity, allowing for a closer relationship with this Lord as the Supreme Personality. More of this will be encountered in this book with the study of *Sankhya* and other *darshanas* (philosophies/clear ways of seeing).

Before moving along other trajectories of this new chart, it would be wise to repeat that when the *Vedanta* speaks about the phenomenon of creation, preservation, and destruction, and the Trinity that oversees it, what is really being stated is projection, sustenance, and dissolution. To give a simple analogy, waves rise up, sport a moment, then fall back into the ocean. Millions of them are doing so all of the time, ad infinitum. But the remarkable fact is not the sportive play so much as the fact that both ocean and water remain the same and retain their inherent nature in all this constant motion. By all appearances, form is getting assumed and released, but all forms are drawn out of one indivisible liquid with one essence. Whereas this analogy applies well to embodying souls and *Brahman*, it also pertains to waves of time. The Cosmic Mind does not "create" them out of nothing, it projects them out of the ocean of potential lying within the Great Mind Itself. The mathematical sign for infinity and the snake swallowing its own tail have been used as symbols for this illimitable principle.

The fact that *Brahman* pervades all cycles of time also shows time up to be illusory. The condition of a man resting in the deep sleep state (*sushupti*) illustrates the disappearance of the concept of time. There he is "lost to the world," as the saying goes. No family, job, or location, much less any worry about time, belabors him there. And besides the *Brahman* state, wherein no separate observer exists, there is a witness of time. Listed on the chart, its name, *Sivakala*, lends itself to many connotations, including destroyer of time, victorious over death, witness of phenomena, etc. He destroys the illusion of time so that the sincere seeker can realize his or her timeless, deathless nature and receive, acknowledge, and enjoy the enlightened state of pure Awareness. As we have mentioned earlier, this is the living liberated condition called *jivanmukti*.

And it is that, after having pondered the immensely extended cycles of time in Hindu cosmology, that we take up in our further study of time in conjunction to enlightenment — called by such illustrious names as *mukti, moksha, samadhi, nirvana, kaivalya, satori, prajna-param,* and others. In this rendering, however, we will retain the *Sanskrit* word, *mukti*.

Time and Enlightenment

"'Here I shall dwell in the rainy season, and there during the snowy winter, and some place distant during the hot summer months.' Thus does the witless fool muse, never imagining what suffering and danger may befall him during that vast, all-consuming, and seemingly unending season called Time." Lord Buddha

SARVAMUKTI
PERPETUAL
ENLIGHTENMENT

Perceiving Brahman everywhere, in everything

"The great souls are no more subject to rebirth, which is the abode of pain, for they reach the highest perfection."

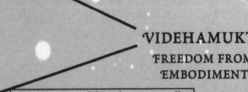

Absorption in Absolute Reality

Equanimity and unified vision

"The holy ones worship Me, for they would stay clear of the joyless, transient worlds."

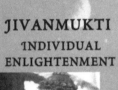

VIDEHAMUKTI
FREEDOM FROM
EMBODIMENT

Attainment of formless samadhi

Selfless service with mature compassion

JIVANMUKTI
INDIVIDUAL
ENLIGHTENMENT

Study of the nondual scriptures and practice of meditation

Gaining holy company and adherence to dharma

Pursuit of the rational and practical mind

Observance of morals and ethics

"Once hearing of the Essence, all tasks will be accomplished, and all confusion will end."

"My Father's mansion has many chambers."

KRAMAMUKTI
GRADUAL
ENLIGHTENMENT

The Seven Realms

Attachment to physical objects for gross enjoyment and possession

False identification with the physical body and the senses

Belief in the actual existence of matter & energy

Projection of the worlds in space & time

Assumption of the human ego

SAMSARA
DREAM TRANSMIGRATION
IN ASSUMED BONDAGE

Illusory Dimensions of Mayic Variety

Brahma/Satyaloka - realm of the Trinity

Taparloka - realm of Vairajas, Saptarishis

Janaloka - realm of Prajapati and Manus

Maharloka - realm of the Sages and

Svarloka - realm of Indra and the Gods

Bhuvarloka - realm of the Munis, Siddhas

Bhurloka - realm of Humans and Animals

Patalas - realm of the disembodied Spirits

In this chart, and in typical *Vedantic* fashion, we learn how time is both helpful towards an enlightened end and, as already stated, ultimately illusory. To introduce the finer points of this enthralling subject is to court freedom itself, which is a state completely unfettered by time. The ordinary mind, however, is not aware of this, especially at the outset of its incarnation. It must be trained, over time, about time, in order to make the best use of time — all so that it can transcend time. As Sri Ramchandra has stated, *"Enlightenment dawns on the mind in stages."* With this in mind, we explore the topic of time via a clear visual aid (facing page) and some pertinent words.

According to Hindu cosmology, the gradation of *lokas*, or realms, is broken into seven upper and seven lower, with each subdivision holding countless worlds of its own. All of them are, of course, projected by the mind, never created out of nothing. A creation out of nothing is an obvious impossibility. There is always something existing; it is just a matter of whether worlds and their objects are in a state of manifestation or nonmanifestation. When all is in a state of nonmanifestation, worlds, beings, and objects, simply do not appear. They are nevertheless held in abeyance, or in potential, in seed *(bijams)* form. This is where the Word, *AUM*, comes into play (see charts from pages 144-157). All "beginnings" are in the Word, and even these are nonactual, only apparent.

When this fact is understood, further realizations such as nontransformation and the nonexistence of birth and death can dawn. To make this cosmological assertion clearer is to state simply that what human beings on earth perceive of as a void is actually only a period of nonmanifestation. Realizations such as this will put to rest such theories like the "big bang" and what happened before it, or concerns like the extinction of a species or a race, etc. Basically, nothing gets born, i.e., gets created, and nothing dies, i.e., gets destroyed. Existence Itself, call It by any name, is eternal. All that comes out of It — like *lokas*, universes, planets, worlds, people, bodies, objects — are equally eternal. The only distinction to make is between the sentient and the insentient. Both categories are unborn, but one seems to change while the other remains completely static and immutable. The *Svetasvataropanisad* states: *"The ever-conscious subject and the unconscious object, the master and the dependent, both are unborn."* This immutability is called *Aparinama* in *Sanskrit* (see chart on page 265), or nontransformation. The illusion or absence of birth and death is called *Ajativada,* or the Path of the unborn. These two all-important axioms, though introduced several times thus far, will be both focused upon and brought to the fore later in certain sections of this book.

The seven upper worlds of the Hindu cosmological system contain three which constitute the worlds of return, and four which, though they are not subject to rebirth, nevertheless lie in the realm of form, albeit very subtle form. These worlds, listed on the chart at the bottom right, are *Bhurloka, Bhuvarloka, Svarloka, Maharloka, Janaloka, Taparloka,* and *Brahmaloka* (also called *Satyaloka*). Amazingly enough, all seven are categorized as to fall under the heading of *Maya* (see chart on page 654). This gives us a more thorough definition of this perplexing word. *Maya* is simply the worlds of name and form in time and space based upon causation. This makes sense, since the definition of Reality, or *Brahman*, is that it is essentially formless.

Thus, the chart shows the realm of *Maya*, a cube of multiple overlapping dimensions, as containing the seven upper and lower worlds (see chart on page 337). Additionally, the lower worlds are called *patalas,* roughly translated as "sunken grounds," and are where lost, confused, and demented minds take up their residence based upon their own darkened state — in turn based upon the actions they perpetrated in life on earth. Thus earth, the *Bhurloka*, is a pivotal one, for there the human soul makes or breaks itself with regards to bondage and liberation.

As pertaining to all worlds — lower, intermediate, higher; gross, subtle, and causal — they are not actual locations. They are mental projections fashioned at the behest of the cosmic, collective, and individual mind, combined. All worlds exist in Consciousness, then, while Consciousness does not exist in the worlds. That is, Consciousness, pure and indivisible, cannot be made to inhabit a world or a form. As one philosopher put it, *"The body is not a location for the Soul."* Rather, the unawakened mind, with the help of the insentient *Maya*, fashions the worlds and then imagines itself sporting there. This is rather like a wizard who conjures up an enchanting world with his magic wand, then, fascinated by his own design, enters into it to play, leaving the wand outside. Once therein, however, he forgets that he created said world and thereby gets trapped therein. This is similar to the condition of the benighted soul, dreaming and in forgetfulness of his birthless, deathless, timeless, spaceless, causeless, divine nature. It now becomes clear, and in perfect context to this subject, why Sri Ramakrishna has said: *"The mind is both the doorway to heaven and the gateway to hell."* His divine consort, Sri Sarada Devi, followed that up by stating: *"One must make a friend of it."*

Another word for *Maya* is *Samsara*, though *Samsara* has its own connotations as well. And though the word has been defined as "rounds of birth and death in ignorance based upon *karma* and suffering," a more complete rendering might state "a dream transmigration in assumed bondage based upon the relative laws of *karma* leading to unreal suffering." Whatever the case may be, the benighted soul's feigned journey, which seems real enough to it, begins here, as indicated at the lower left hand side of the chart (page 41).

Contrary to other perspectives, *Vedanta* avers that the entire idea of time is really so that beings can work their way out of this falsely superimposed separation from Reality that they themselves have created. And soberingly enough, no god will help them do this, and no devil will keep them from it, for both god and devil are dubious concepts that have been hammered out in this self-same furnace of the mind over countless eons. This is not to say that god and devil do not exist; it means that they exist in the mind of mankind, like all other ideas — including space and time. If the objection is raised that God cannot be limited to the mind, that is exactly the point. God, Reality, cannot be limited. The idea of god and devil that one has in ones mind, being an idea, is not Reality. Reality is formless, as has already been stated, transcendent of ideas and concepts. Thus, Swami Vivekananda says, *"There is no God, there is no Devil; there is only the Great Self."* Now, one can call this Great Self by the word "God" if one wants, but it would be better to keep Reality both nameless and formless, as It is. Lord Buddha was not an atheist, as some would opine. When asked if there was a God, he said, *"Did I say there was a God?"* When asked, next, if there was no God, then, he stated, *"Did I say there was no God?"* This noncommittal attitude is beneficial at times, for many of us have seen what a confused mess fundamentalist religion and name and fame-based theology has made of the otherwise honorable principle of the personal God (see chart on page 467).

As beings work their way to realization of a freedom that is ever within them, this march over time culminates in unity with Reality. Christ defined this via the nondual statement, *"I and my Father are One."* Freedom of this ultimate type was called *Mukti* in *Sanskrit* by the ancient *rishis*. However, as one scours the scriptures, and takes in the stories, teachings, and experiences of the saints and seers, the existence of a few conditioned types of *mukti* are noticed as well. In terms of the transmigrating soul (mind) of the *jiva* (embodied being), the entire matter is about *kramamukti*, or gradual enlightenment — what my *guru* used to call a "post-mortem emancipation." Though not the best case scenario, it nevertheless applies to beings who are as yet unable to cognize their stainless, birthless, Self, *Atman* — impervious to both evolution and involution.

Kramamukti can be likened to a sleeper who, though awakened in the morning, falls back asleep, then is awakened again later. Even when he is up and around he is still sleepy-headed, and does not come into full awareness until late afternoon. Perhaps he really "lives" only at night. Whatever the case may be, our chart under study reveals what criteria are to be satisfied for *Kramamukti*, but placed in the perspective of what the soul is laboring under that keeps it from seeking freedom. The unripe ego, participation in deluded thinking, obsession with matter, identification with the physical form, and running after material objects for the sake of fleeting pleasure, make up this list in part. But as our happy and good fortune-conferring elephant-headed god, Ganesha, points out: *"Once hearing of the Essence, all tasks will be accomplished and all confusions will end."* This describes well the fortuitous occurrence of *Kramamukti*, for when all facets of the aforementioned list are seen as projections of the spiritually unawakened mind in *Maya*, the prospect of a noble and blissful freedom becomes desirable and enters the realm of possibility.

The next stage of Enlightenment is the wonder of *Jivanmukti*. Great souls have spoken of it, from the ancient Lord Vasishtha to the more recent Shankara, and on up to the contemporary divine personage, Swami Vivekananda. The path to its attainment is paved at the outset by such practice as the observance of morality and the calming and centering of the intellectual mind. Later, the boon of holy company is gained, which compels the aspirant after freedom to pick up the scriptures and study them, while clarifying their points and principles with an illumined *guru*.

Jivanmukti, as elevated as it is, begs that all beings be free. That is, individual freedom is both unsatisfactory and implausible, for the *Jivanmukta* is aware that so long as even a single person suffers in the darkness of ignorance, no real freedom is possible. Here, the vow of a *Bodhisattva* in *Buddhism* correlates, which strives for the removal of suffering in all souls. *Jivanmukti* has at least one great advantage over *Kramamukti* in that the worlds of name and form are rendered insipid and undesirable. No "falling from grace" happens to a *Jivanmukta*. This is instanced in the quote by Sri Krishna stating: *"The holy ones worship Me, for they would stay clear of the joyless, transient worlds."* *"Asukham anityam,"* as the *Sanskrit* evinces so convincingly, characterize this world of matter. If it were not for the overall ignorance of society in general, more people might come to know this. But societies run after the objects of their desires, gross or subtle, not knowing that they are empty. This emptiness is called *shunyata* in *Buddhism*.

Emptiness contains two teachings, two spiritual laws about objects (see chart on page 652). And we can borrow from Western Science and Christianity to understand them both. First, objects are substanceless. Science has revealed this, showing how tiny particles which make up objects are both constantly in motion and changing at a billionth of a second. No further proof of emptiness need be offered in this regard. Secondly, emptiness means that the object does not have, nor can it confer, any ability to fulfill its possessor. Here, and where the word *shunyata* is a *Buddhist* contribution, the Christ gave us ultimatums such as *"You cannot worship God and Mammon at the same time,"* and, *"Store up your riches in heaven and not on earth,"* and, *"All fulfillment is in the Lord, sayeth the Lord."*

Taking this double-edged sword of spiritual discrimination, then (see chart on page 276), the *Jivanmukta* cuts through his confusion regarding the objective world seen only by the senses, as easily as a mid-wife cuts an umbilical cord. Free from nature and its six transformations (see chart on page 225), the soul can now know itself as Sentiency Itself. This is *Kaivalya* in Lord Patanjali's *Yoga* (see chart on page 413), and peace of mind and Self-realization are soon to follow.

The expanse of time that it takes an embodied soul to get free of the trammels of nature and *maya* depends upon how adept that soul is at comprehending truth, and how many previous *karmas* exist. Going to assumed death with a confused mind will only deposit one back, prefunctorily and unceremoniously, in the worlds of name and form. That is why the *Jivanmukta* will look long and longingly at that upper echelon of Enlightenment called *Videhamukti*, freedom from all types of bodies. For, as the scheme of the seven upper worlds has related, freedom from birth in the *bhurloka* (earth), in the *bhuvarloka* (intermediary heavens), and in *svarloka* (higher heaven) does not mean that name and form have now become dissolved into *Aum* (*Omkaravrittidhyan*), or into *Brahman* (*Brahmakaravrittidhyan*). These four upper worlds have form too. (see chart on page 505)

To make this clearer we can again consult the Buddha, who once stated: *"Architect of the worlds, I have seen thee! I will now cease to build any more houses — houses made of wood or brick, houses made of flesh and bone, or houses made of thought and wise conception."* In *Vedic* terms, the Buddha, the awakened one, perceived the world-bewitching *maya* in his deepest contemplations, and having achieved that striking revelation, vowed to transcend all bodies, gross or subtle.

As the chart then concludes, the only *mukti* left after the happy abandonment of all bodies, all forms, is *Sarvamukti*, the All-Enlightened state. Living in this state beyond all states is indescribable, for all beings are seen as nothing less than the Light of *Brahman*, whether in form or not. Thus, all beings are Ever-Enlightened, and all ideas of bondage and suffering are mere superimpositions.

There is no cause for *mukti*, it being an ever-present perfection. But there is a cause for bondage. The following two charts will adequately introduce us to causality on both a basic and an advanced level.

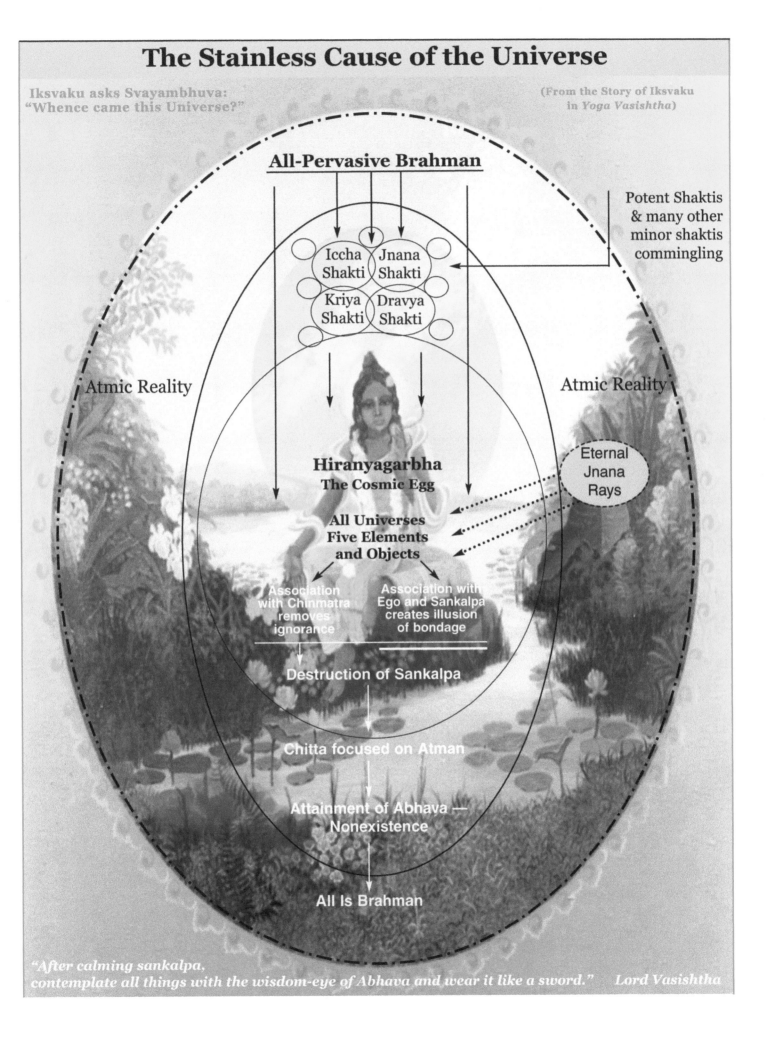

The Stainless Cause of the Universe

Iksvaku asks Svayambhuva:
"Whence came this Universe?"

(From the Story of Iksvaku
in *Yoga Vasishtha*)

All-Pervasive Brahman

Potent Shaktis
& many other
minor shaktis
commingling

Iccha
Shakti

Jnana
Shakti

Kriya
Shakti

Dravya
Shakti

Atmic Reality

Atmic Reality

Hiranyagarbha
The Cosmic Egg

Eternal
Jnana
Rays

All Universes
Five Elements
and Objects

Association
with Chinmatra
removes
ignorance

Association with
Ego and Sankalpa
creates illusion
of bondage

Destruction of Sankalpa

Chitta focused on Atman

Attainment of Abhava —
Nonexistence

All Is Brahman

"After calming sankalpa,
contemplate all things with the wisdom-eye of Abhava and wear it like a sword."   *Lord Vasishtha*

Nimitta — Causation

Coming as a gift from Lord Vasishtha, teachings on the origins of the universe and the origin-less nature of the *Atman* abound in the profound scripture, *Yoga Vasishtha*. Combined within a chart called "The Stainless Cause of the Universe" (page 45), the idea comes across that Reality, called *Brahman* in *Vedanta*, unlike everything else, depends upon nothing — either inside, outside, or beyond the universe. Such appellations as the "Causeless Cause" would apply here; or if thinking in terms of human destiny, the "Unmoved Mover"; or if acknowledging the role of vibration in the cosmic process, "The Unstruck Sound"; or if considering by way of activities, the "Inactive Agent." Many such titles can be given (see chart on page 732), each illustrating the distinct and singular nature of Reality as contrasted to all other things — objects, senses, worlds, beings, concepts, etc.

In the realm of causality, then, the first chart (on page 45) demonstrates a trickle down effect like no other. Given by way of *tattvas*, or eternal principles, we find at the outset that, as Sri Ramakrishna has stated, *"Brahman and Shakti are one."* That is, the first thing out the gate in terms of subtle manifestation is *Mahashakti*, the Lord's Dynamic Power. *Shakti's* minions are by the hundreds, but four main forces take up the lead in facilitating what is to come. They are the Mother's force of Wisdom (*jnana*), Will, (*iccha*), Spontaneity (*kriya*), and Production (*dravya*). In brief, using all the potential stored in Her Wisdom Word, She wills everything into animation while manifesting all the products (like ether, air, fire, water, and earth) needed for their sport and sustenance. The aforementioned minor *shaktis*, permeating everything, carry out the rest. For instance, a shipyard bustling with activity at wartime, or a handful of soil, are all filled with many *shaktis*. And *Atmic* Reality, as the chart illustrates, is all about awareness of *Shakti*. She is the Soul's Sovereign, and Its boundless regions as well. Great beings abide in Her, radiating the Light of Consciousness like She does. These are Wisdom Rays, shown penetrating the denser areas of mind and matter by degrees (refer ahead to the chart on page 56).

Mahashakti also facilitates and tenders the Cosmic Egg, called *Hiranyagarbha* in ancient language. It is also known as the Cosmic Mind, or Mind of God, where the Wisdom Word, *AUM*, hums blissfully and eternally with neither increase nor decrease, neither expansion nor contraction. That Great Mind, manifesting the Ten *Manus* or Great Minds that emanate from it, oversee the functions of the cosmos and the doings of gods, goddesses, men, women, and all beings right on down to that proverbial "blade of grass." All universes, as the chart relates, including the five elements and the various objects of the senses, rise and fall in proper order, despite periods of chaos, under the bright auspices of these overseers, some lesser and some greater in endowment of *Shakti* power.

And an important fact gets deftly revealed in this harmonious sequence of manifesting Awareness. All beings, if they would steer clear of the negative effects of *maya*, must remain conscious of Consciousness, aware of Awareness. *Chinmatra*, particles of living awareness, permeate everything, even matter. That selfsame thought force helped to fashion matter. Therefore, remaining aware of it while sporting in the worlds of matter will provide a safety net against forgetfulness and root ignorance.

On the other hand, giving in to forgetfulness by association with the false self, ego, or *ahamkara*, leads to a preoccupation with the mind's base desires and the resultant conjuring up of a force which indulges unwisely in the manufacture of whims and fancies which are detrimental to ones innate spirituality. Here, the *Sanskrit* words *Sankalpa* and *Vikalpa* come to the fore for inspection (see chart on page 267). These are powers of projection that the mind possesses. If these forces are controlled by this very same mind's focused concentration on the *Atman*, the bliss of freedom from mental projection and limiting desires is achieved. This important stage of renunciation, called *Abhava*, reminds the mind of its Source, *Brahman*, where objects and the desire for them are nonexistent. Only Light abides there, completely fulfilling on Its own.

With this basic look at the natural efflorescence of Divine Consciousness, like a boundless ocean breaking into waves, a more detailed examination of the relative laws of causation can be taken up. The next chart (on page 47) places this subject into broad cross-sections for our perusal.

Causality, Origins & Reincarnation

⏭ **Causality, Origins & Reincarnation** ⏮

"The ability to project worlds of name and form, seemingly actual, in space and time, furthers the circle of influence of cause and effect. With the curbing of the unruly mind's penchant for mayic manufacturing comes instant freedom from the trammels of relativity. This liberating process is facilitated by tracing origins." King Janaka

Causeless Cause

Brahman   **Shakti**

🕉

Remote Cause

Ishvara
AUM
Mahaprakrti
Mahat

> *Primordial Soul*
> *Unstruck Sound/Word*
> *Unmanifest Nature*
> *Cosmic Mind*

"Inner analysis brings the first real glimmerings of spirituality. In that light the soul perceives the assumed happenstance of cause and effect. In a series of deep recollections it scrutinizes life, even to infanthood, and glimpses past lifetimes. By perceiving its origin it courts freedom." Vasishtha

"Differentiation between jiva and Ishvara is right if one is a dualist. But for Advaitans this notion of jiva as distinct from God is the cause of bondage." Swami Vivekananda

Cosmic Cause

Maya
Vidya
Kala, Desha, Nimitta
Niyati, Kalas, Raga
Purusha

Evolution

> *Form & Formlessness*
> *Higher Cognizance*
> *Time, Space, Causation*
> *Cosmic Laws, Phases,*
> *Attraction Individual Soul*

"The very moment that cause and effect comes to an end one realizes God. That is one's last birth. This, plus the practice of spiritual discipline, and time, are the main factors in the full attainment of spiritual knowledge." Sri Sarada Devi

Subtle Cause

Buddhi
Ahamkara
Chitta
Manas
Kama
Karma

> *Intelligence*
> *Projected Self/Ego*
> *Thought*
> *Mind*
> *Desire for Life*
> *Desire for Activity*

"Souls embody to enact an array of karmas which place them under the influence of the unforgiving laws of cause and effect. Not all of these lifetimes, these dream-streams of conditioned awareness, are founded in negativity. Many there are, masters of mental projection, who wrap themselves in the fabric of maya to merely enjoy ephemeral pleasure." Queen Chudala

Primordial Cause

Pancha Tanmatras → *5 Subtle Elements* → Audibility, Tangibility, Visibility, Flavor, Odor
Prana - Pancha Vayus → *5 Life Forces* → Prana, Apana, Vyana, Udana, Samana

(Inhalation, Exhalation, Digestion, Aspiration, Circulation)

Efficient Cause

Prakrti & 3 Gunas → *Nature/Gunas* → Tamas, Rajas, Sattva (inertia, activity, balance)
Pancha Mahabhutas → *5 Elements* → Earth, Water, Fire, Air, Ether

Material Cause

Antahkarana
Pancha Jnanendriyas
Pancha Karmendriyas
Deha
Maharaja
Sukra
Mukhyaprana
Annam

Involution

> *Human Brain*
> *5 Cognitive Senses* → Hearing, Seeing, Touching, Tasting, Smelling
> *5 Active Senses* → Speaking, Moving, Handling, Procreating, Excreting
> *Physical Body*
> *Ovum*
> *Sperm*
> *Vital Energy*
> *Food*

"If higher knowledge is not already in the soul, then rebirth continues and there will be no other recourse than to suffer cause and effect. Even striving for light will not bestow any real benefit, for to seek enlightenment without the mantra, the teachings, and the guru, is like trying to grow crops only at night." Vasishtha

What is the cause? This question has been the source of constant confusion ever since mankind started utilizing his God-given intelligence. But this same question, when placed in a spiritually inquisitive setting, has led aspiring beings on to comprehension of all that lies beyond the ken of the five senses. For, when one thinks in terms of causation, one must necessarily consider the subject of origins. The ancient *rishis*, whose footfalls we are presently tracing in this book as origins of wisdom, had searched inside of themselves for centuries for that barely discernable path leading Godward, and had finally found a trail of subtle bread crumbs left undisturbed by the pesky birds of ignorance and forgetfulness. Of course, the esoteric topic of reincarnation also got a thorough investigation, coming up, as it did, in the interim of this exacting search.

Importantly, when Indian philosophy broaches the subject of origins, it does so with ripe and mature acknowledgment that Reality, called *Brahman*, is originless. In this way it begins on a footing which is already solid, lofty and well-determined, giving it an advantage over many other systems which always try to put Reality in terms of human thinking or, even worse, matter alone. According to Swami Vivekananda, *Brahman* is "acreate," placing It in a superlative category all Its own. In Sri Ramakrishna's words, *"Brahman is untouched and intrinsically ever-pure, and the only thing which has never been defiled by the tongue or mind of man."*

With this sterling principle in place and intact, this chart (on page 47) in particular is offered. In formulating it I have stretched the traditional terminology pertaining to the term and principle of causality to afford a wider and deeper view of the subject. Nothing particularly new has been added in this process, for all this wisdom is to be either found or inferred in the *Vedic* scriptures. I have only arranged it under headings that expand present usage. For instance, the terms "material cause" and "efficient cause" are well know to the orthodox *darshanas*, the six philosophical schools of India, the former pertaining to nature and the latter to *Brahman* and its dynamic power, *Shakti*.

But deeper thinking on this matter reveals that *Brahman* cannot be a cause for anything, for if It was, It would necessarily have to enter in and involve Itself with divine, celestial, and human affairs, what to speak of lordship, guidance, *karma*, and cosmological and planetary matters. If the truth be known, however, *Brahman's Shakti* and Her sons and daughters fulfill this set of onerous duties, the key word here being *Ishvara* or *Ishvari* — the highest manifestation of God with form that the human mind can comprehend, envision, or conceive of. Again, Reality is formless, must remain sacrosanct; It should be left alone in its ivory tower — a fact that both conventional religion and living beings would be wise to finally accept and adhere to.

In the wider spirit of honoring and remaining true to the tradition, and of bringing out what is only inferred, sometimes cryptically, in the Indian scriptures, I have thereby layered this chart of cause and effect, complete with the outward and inward directions of evolution and involution, so as to lay out a trail of bread crumbs that will lead the seeker after Truth from one superimposed strata of relativity to the next, the purpose being several fold.

First, the riddle of cause and effect can more easily be worked out after such a teaching transmission is gained. In this regard, it ought to be stated outright that the benighted or spiritually unawakened soul is enmeshed in the diaphanous and impermeable net of *maya*, a flexuous and mesmerizing labyrinth of worlds, chimerical in nature, which are the invention of the omnifarious mind given over unreservedly to unbridled imaginative desire (*sankalpa* and *vikalpa*). Such a mass of actions, such a series of *karmas*, has been wrought over endless cycles of time by multitudes of beings, that it will take some mighty deeds of purification and transcendence for the freedom-seeking soul to see its way clear of it all.

A second reason for offering such esoteric wisdom to the people at large is to generate a healthy hunger for cosmology, both in religion and in everyday life. Who among us that is caring and concerned has not rued the disappearance of ancient and primitive cultures, and regretted watching their store of knowledge die to the character-obliterating sweep of this modern and technological age. To bring back, restore, or even solidify one of the great world cultures in the contemporary mind's memory would be a feat well worthwhile, and a great benefit to all of humanity.

For what is good is called cosmology; what is better is called philosophy; and what is best is called spirituality. The three are innately interconnected, each dependent on the other in the overall and total scheme of things. The study of a culture's cosmology via a visual like this chart (page 47) reveals the deep richness of such a system, demonstrating, among other things, the presence of God as a living Verity — for such creative genius cannot but have an extremely profound Source.

In order to effectively introduce this chart, several ways are possible. Whereas the most intelligible way would be to start from the top down, the bottom up method is also very helpful, beginning as it does on the same level which most beings on Earth are presently operating at. The reader can see by the wealth of strata and ingredients that the subject of "causation" has been drawn into several headings, all with their pertinent concomitants. Quotes from the luminaries and the scriptures have also been applied here and there, fleshing out the possibility for greater understanding. These I leave to the reader to contemplate and fathom. For, causation is an esoteric topic, and one that, due to the prevalent customs and opinions of the day, does not get aired anywhere except for the rare and occasional spiritual circle of *guru* and sangha. Even there, the subject is seldom presented so as to bring it into the clear and proper light of day.

The Material Cause

Referring to the chart, we can now look at the many-tiered strata of the causation ladder. It begins with the Material Cause, rises to the Efficient Cause, enters into the Primordial Cause, brooks the Subtle Cause, meets the Cosmic Cause, and then merges into the Remote Cause, or *AUM* — The Word. What lies beyond that is causeless, *Brahman*. If one prefers to start with the one and only singular Reality, which is most sensible and understandable, then from *Brahman* down the chart can be traced. This would reveal how everything effloresces out of The Word, with *Brahman* as the Eternal Substratum, and how all then burgeons into manifestation. But let us start, in earnest, from the bottom, where mankind is presently trying to ponder his situation (we hope) based upon the triple principles of *desha*, *kala*, and *nimitta* — space, time, and causation.

It is not just in the Hindu scriptures that food is considered foundational; all of life is based upon food. As the line of one scripture states, *"Everything here is just food. Beings come into being by way of food. They sustain their lives by way of food. Going to death, their bodies then become food for others — insects, animals, fire, etc."* This reasoning is practical enough. Food is also a way of life and society for all cultures, all nations. And it is for these good reasons and more that it is placed at the foundation of the category called the Material Cause. Coursing onward, when food is eaten it fosters vital energy and gets converted into sperm. Then it is given reverently to the future mother for purposes of conception. The fetus is then born from the mother's womb and, over time, the physical body develops wherein the five active and five cognitive senses mature. All along the way, the human brain is growing, and that rare and valued commodity called intelligence may then visit it.

Two very remarkable things can be said about the Material Cause: first, the fact that the brain is not the mind becomes more evident here; and second, that the entire contemporary world, and many cultures and races throughout time, believe the Material Cause to be all of life — end of story. That is, beings believe that nothing exists beyond matter, despite the presence of intelligence. A detached observer can readily see how an origins theory which proposes that man is created out of nothing, or dust, and a scientific mind-set which avers that it took billions of years to evolve the gross universe, came into being and vogue. Whatever the case may be, both of these points will be brought up for exploration in the course of this particular study.

The Efficient Cause

The Efficient Cause is nature. How can we forget nature? Though some look upon it as Reality, it is insentient, so it cannot be "That." There is also nothing mystical about it, though primeval man, via his ignorance and superstition, attempted to make it so. Still, most would agree that nature is an obvious sign of a Creator, what with its fascinating show of earth, water, fire, air, and ether. But there is more to nature than meets the eye. There is, of course, what is called unmanifested nature, but we will study more about that when we broach the subject of the Remote Cause. What is being referred to here is that unseen and unheralded trio called the Three *Gunas,* namely *Tamas, Rajas,* and *Sattva* (see charts on pages 221, 223, 307). The three *gunas,* in a subtler form, are actually already present in the Cosmic Cause amongst a plethora of macrocosmic laws. But they appear more readily and concretely here in manifest nature, solidified nature. In a similar way that the pumping of the lungs infers the presence of a hidden life force, so too do the qualities and attributes of the five elements intimate the subtle presence of the three gunas. On Earth, *tamas* is inertia; *rajas* is energy; *sattva* is stasis. In the mind, *tamas* is sloth, *rajas* is restlessness, and *sattva* is balance.

To clarify the *gunas* via example, water, when still and stagnant, like a swamp, is under the predominance of *tamas.* Water, when it is flowing furiously, like a raging river, is under the influence of *rajas.* Water, when it is still but clear, like a mountain lake, partakes of the *sattva guna.* Interestingly enough, when we take the three *gunas* into the arena of potential called the human mind, similar analogies are available. The mind that is dull and slothful is suffering the *tama guna.* The mind that is frenetic and restless is laboring under the *raja guna.* The mind that is balanced is *sattvic.* Even among the animal kingdom, the astute observer can see the three *gunas* at work. A dog, for instance, may be seen lying flat on its side, tongue lolling out and flies alighting there. That dog is definitely in a *tamasic* mood at that time. But just wait! Soon it is up and on its four legs, running around barking and threatening other dogs, the fear of every fire-hydrant in the neighborhood — *rajasic.* But most wonderful indeed is that same dog transformed, sitting regally in the sun, neither lazy nor restless — *sattvic.* Everyone cherishes the peace and balance of *sattva* most highly.

The three *gunas* are a powerful and revealing subject treated at length in other sections of this book, the detection of which is tantamount to one of the most profound "footfalls" that the Indian *rishis* has ever gifted to mankind.

The Primordial Cause

As we encounter more rarefied levels of causation in the inward sweep towards Divine Reality, we come upon one that is obscure but pivotal as far as man's present spiritual understanding is concerned. This has been mentioned already in our treating of the chart on Atomic and *Atmic* particles (refer to chart on page 33), as well as in the section on the five sheaths or *koshas* of our psycho-physical being. It is the *prana* that is being cited here again, that subtle life force which, though so obvious and connected as the inner cause of what people think and do, is never given any thought or credit whatsoever along those lines. The Primordial Cause, then, as it is being entitled here, is the flow of vital force on both gross and subtle levels of existence. That is, on gross levels it courses through the elements, animates the senses, operates the bodily functions, etc. And all of this deserves some individual inspection.

As pertaining to the life functions, and has been already mentioned earlier, the heart beats, the blood circulates, the lungs inflate and deflate, the body's waste gets evacuated, the senses operate, and the mind thinks — all under the facilitating auspices of *prana.* And as to how this pertains further to the five senses and the brain, these "six" senses (five senses and mind) owe a great allegiance to the *pranic* force. Relative to this, there is one story in the *Upanisads* wherein the gods of the mind and senses, the gods of the five elements, and the gods of other various functions in the heavens and on earth, all got together one day to debate on who was the greatest amongst them. Every one of them got up and spoke most convincingly on how he or she was the greatest power in the universe. But the god of *prana* only *sat* and waited, silently. When all had taken their turn and had their say, then *prana* stood up and said, "I am most definitely the greatest among you, and I can prove it!" Speaking thus, and before anyone could object, *prana* thereby and immediately vacated the premises, whereas all the lesser gods and goddesses present there fell down lifeless. No further argument was given, was even possible.

The presence of life force, then, is undeniable, yet most beings, even intelligent ones, fail to acknowledge it. What is more, beings who do espy it see its inner workings and thus keep the mental picture clear. That is, people are always and ever attributing their actions and thoughts, and what happens to them on a daily basis, to God. "God made me do it," "God granted me this boon," "God took away my child or loved one," "God helped me win the battle, or the war" — these are common exclamations, heard often enough. But we have already stated that God, *Brahman*, is actionless and free of any intention or motive for beings or their lives — these lives (except in the case of the illumined souls) being assumed by the decision of their own selfish egos and lived under the force of their own personal *karmas*. Practically speaking, *prana* animates the body and senses, *prana* brings the forces of repercussion to bear on everyday life, and *prana*, again, causes the thoughts to rise and fall, advance and retard, aspire and fall down. *Prana* even facilitates life and death. Knowing this, beings should refrain from blaming God for matters not pertaining to God, and instead bring the forces of *prana* under their personal control so as to live a *dharmic* life — like the luminaries do.

On the subtle level, *prana* holds sway too. This has already been inferred by indicating the mind and its thoughts. These are presided over by what is called the psychic *prana*, which differs from the gross *prana* just as gross thought differs from refined thought. And here is the bridge to rudimentary spirituality. If a physicist once detected the *prana*, and became sure of it like the yogis are, he would soon become a metaphysicist. This epitomizes entrance into the subtler worlds which lie back in the recesses of the mind, as in the Christ's saying that *"The kingdom of heaven lies within you."* Here, in this refined region, called a *loka*, the *prana* works in lightning swift fashion to bring thoughts, insights, and realizations to bear on the now and newly awakened mind. This teaching actually reveals the distinction between brain and mind, the former which decays and dissolves, and the latter which stretches beyond matter and senses, remaining operative in what religion calls the "afterlife."

To complete this overall description of the Primordial Cause, a mention of what the yogis call "the five *tanmatras*" is required. Listed on the chart under study as the "five subtle elements," they are another unseen and missing bit of knowledge in our present day understanding. Knowing about them will inform and connect us to the world of vital forces on so many levels which are important to our lives — scientifically, religiously, spiritually, and medically — to mention a few.

To explain this from the root up, the world, the senses, and the life forces are not to be taken for granted or left disconnected in the human mind. Through focused and quiescent meditation, like that which the ancient *rishis* taught their children, the nature of each *tattva* (mutable principle) is to be examined and known, and connected consciously back into the Self/*Atman*. In brief, after separate meditations are accomplished on each *tattva*, then this liberating process of internal connections can be undertaken. This art of introspection is mostly missing in our Western science and education due to a preoccupation with appearances perceived only by the senses. What underlies appearances, seen by the single eye of meditation, is far more real and thus, important.

And so, and as a part of the meditative process, the seeker after all that is subtle consciously brings together the element earth with the sense of smell, then water with tasting, fire with seeing, air with feeling, and ether with listening. When this work is complete, in full awareness, and the five elements have been linked to the five senses, the allocation of the elements and the senses to the subtle elements (*tanmatras*) comes next, i.e., earth and smell with the principle of odor/solidity, water and taste with the principle of flavor/liquidity, fire and seeing with the principle of visibility, air and touch with the principle of tangibility, and hearing and ether with the principle of audibility. In other words, the principle of a thing/object is distinct and subtler than the thing itself, and also subtler than the senses which behold or experience it. This, in a nutshell, is the thorough examination of the world and its causes and effects on the fundamental *yogic* level, and how to look beneath appearances, or *maya*, to behold subtler causes.

It may be asked how the connecting process described above can really help us. The answer has several facets. First, if external life is left unconnected, and all the elements of our existence are allowed to exist in a random and unordered fashion, the mind itself soon becomes fragmented. Then complaints inevitably begin to surface, oft repeated in this day and time, like "I do not see any purpose to my life," "I am bored and listless," "Life does not make any sense," and "What is the purpose of living," etc. Here, zest and verve for life are lost, and the inner mystery of existence overlooked — those very things which are epitomized by *prana* itself. When a person is listless, then, he has literally lost hold of or control of his vital energy, his *prana*.

And here is a second reason for the integration of physical elements to their primordial counterparts, that being that one can consciously gain control of the vital force, using it for revivification of body, life, and mind. This is called wholistic health in this day and age, though both higher intelligence and pure spirituality are really left out of the quotient thus far due to contemporary man's preoccupation with food and bodily health. Besides the fact that we have never seen nor heard of a bored or listless luminary (this adage could be added to the famous list of impossible and illusory things in *Vedanta*, like the "son of a barren woman"), the control of vital energy will allow the inner wayfarer to access what is subtler still. That is, if the gaining of control over the gross *prana* can bring good health and energy, and the acknowledgment and facility around the subtler level of *prana* can open one up to the secrets of where our ancestors have gone and are abiding, then the gaining of the manipulation of the psychic level of *prana* can throw open the doors of the all-powerful mind, and introduce the aspirant to the Subtle Cause.

The Subtle Cause

Higher intelligence has already been mentioned. In spiritual systems and circles, higher intelligence does not mean knowledge of intellectual subjects. As the study of the five *koshas* and other systems should have already related to us, intellect is different from intelligence. The former is a sheath (*upadhi*) or container (*kosha*), and the latter is a free-flowing verity (partly due to *prana*) which shines with the Light of Consciousness Itself. The distinction between brain and mind also applies here. Suffice to say, however, that the Subtle Cause is the realm of Mind per say, and intelligence plays the most important part in that realm.

In the chart under examination (on page 47) are found the concomitants of the Subtle Cause or Subtle Body (see chart on page 161), consisting of *karma, kama, manas, chitta, ahamkara,* and *buddhi.* Taking the last four of these elements and placing them into one complex, we have what the ancient *rishis* called the *antahkarana,* or inner cause. Just this very name alone informs us as to what the luminaries of that time knew to be the cause of the universe. It is mind. Everything spills out of it like a ripe harvest from a cornucopia. Where does mind get it all? We will have to look to subtler causes than the *antahkarana* for that answer, and will do so in due time.

Getting back to the elements of the Subtle Cause, by *karma* and *kama* is meant the innate drive of the human being to satisfy the thirst for life in the mode of separation. That is, few know the bliss of oneness with Divine Reality, or having overlooked it in the exciting sweep and prospect of physical manifestation and expression, decided or preferred to attempt to slake the thirst for worldly existence instead. This is like overlooking the value of land for the sake of its resources.

On a related note here, the *prana,* or life force, is probably the greatest addiction there is. A great hunger for what it can confer is at the root of most being's drive for satiation in the realms of name and form. And the mind will lose itself and give itself into that *pranic* fire of potential passion with a thirst and hunger that far surpasses obsessions with the various allurements of the world. Here is another reason why the yogis strive to control *prana* and not give free reign to it via the desire-driven mind. *"Freedom from the senses, not freedom to the senses,"* is how my *guru,* Swami Aseshananda, always put it.

In addition to desire, *kama,* there may be hell to pay in the form of *karma.* The Subtle Cause predicates that all actions require a reaction. This law is not just a physical one applying only to matter and energy, but is an ethical one as well, applying to the mind and its thinking process. "What a man thinks, so he becomes." *"This is so true,"* said the Holy Mother, Sri Sarada Devi. Further, *"A ship passing in front of a magnetic hill has its screws pulled out and sinks in the ocean,"* stated Sri Ramakrishna. While this story can be applied to the realized soul's body under the influence of divine passion, it can also be applied to the ignorant man under the press of worldly passion, as over time his *karmas* tend to pull apart his common sense, practicality, and his very ability to reason. So, that *karma* and *kama* are innate parts of the mental body, and that body is the cause for all that has been listed up to this point, is telling, to say the least. It means that everything here in the realm of name and form has the seal or the impress of dual mind (*manas*) upon it.

That dual mind, called *manas*, along with the ego (*ahamkara*), are the potentially dangerous parts of the human mind, though thought (*chitta*) and intellect (*buddhi*), if given a dark turn, can wreak havoc on life as well. But *manas* is dual by nature, whereas the other three elements of the *Antahkarana* are said to be open to transformation. When *manas* is said to be dual by nature, it means that it willingly and constantly throws up propositions without number for the consideration (and distraction) of *buddhi* and *ahamkara*, the intellect and the ego. Good and bad, virtue and vice, pleasure and suffering, praise and blame, birth and death, bondage and liberation — these and many other dualities accost the mind minute to minute, year to year, lifetime to lifetime. The mind that develops a habit of dual thinking becomes worldly and superficial, and rendered ineffective in reaching any higher moral, intellectual, or spiritual ground. What is more, later it can become fragmented, retarded, randomly dispersed and scattered, thereby subjecting itself to be born in conditions which are unsavory and undesirable.

This overt penchant for dualities is what Sri Krishna warns about in the *Bhagavad Gita*. The dualities themselves are termed *"...the deluding pairs of opposites,"* or *dvanda mohena* in *Sanskrit*. But this selfsame mind, if brought under control by subjection to purificatory exercises and disciplines, can become a portal in the opposite direction, opening to a realm of light that is peaceful, blissful, and liberating. Here, the thoughts, or *chitta*, come into play. If charged up with this positive light, they naturally become buoyant, like a hot air balloon. But if left brooding on the deluding pairs of opposites they sink like a ship's anchor, gravitating to the lowest position possible, like rainwater flowing into sewage drains in the streets. Such are the dangers, and the import, of mind and its thoughts.

As for the other couple of the *Antahkarana*, they are intellect and ego. Much like their companions they are troublesome if left fallow and unattended by higher awareness. The inflated ego alone is notorious for causing much of the problems in the world, but its opposite, the ripened and refined ego, is responsible for compassionate goodness. As Sri Ramakrishna has stated, *"In front of the mansion of God there is a great stump. One must jump over it or go around it to enter there."* This great stump is the rascal ego. Not only will it stir up countless problems in the world, it also acts as a potential barrier between the transmigrating soul and its union (*samadhi*) with the Divine.

As was stated earlier, the intellect is really a key for the door leading into higher mind. It is most luminous, capable of holding and exuding the light of *Brahman*. If the mind is rendered nondual (*"If thine eye be single thou shalt know the truth."*), the thoughts charged up with inspiration, and the ego diminished so as to step out of the way, then the light of intelligence can shine, naturally and spontaneously, illuminating the very ground leading to the "Sky of Awareness." The soul seeking involution then knows which way to go, and is lost no longer. Even the secrets of the causal realms are now open and accessible to it.

The Cosmic Cause

Lying between the fourfold mind mechanism (*antahkarana*) and the most diaphanous realms of name and form is the Cosmic Cause, consisting of the witness soul, the various cosmic laws, the principle of wisdom, and the subtlemost *maya* itself. Regarding the soul, when the ego element of the *antahkarana* gets refined, the sense of individuality begins to evaporate like fog and mist under the advancing noonday sun. What takes its place is *sakshi*, or witness. Some systems call this the *Purusha*, which may be called the authentic individual soul, much different in nature and more real than the projected self, or ego. Even on earth, among embodied beings, there are cases of beings transcending their ego and becoming transparent, living in a completely different state or condition of mind than others. This *Purusha* is splendid and radiant with burgeoning Self-awareness. Only the fact that it still retains a slight sense of separation from *Brahman* — a residue of the distinction between the observer and the observed — differentiates it from *Atman*, its ultimate destination.

The *Purusha* looks in upon the causal worlds of cosmic law and sees the workings and the secrets of the cosmic process. The true origins of space, time, and causation themselves, under study in this chapter, form a part of those worlds of higher thought. The question is, whose thought is it? It belongs to the *Mahat*, the Great Mind, a subtle strata soon to be examined. And other laws, far beyond human ones, are present there as well, including the inexorable art of the passage of time in expanded cycles (*kalas*) and the alluring power of attraction between entities (*raga*). All beings, all things, even insentient ones, fall under the press of *raga*, the power of close adhesion based upon irresistible attraction. Far distant, at the universal and atomic level, the effects of this law cause planets to spin on their axis and circumambulate stars, and atoms and molecules to adhere to set patterns in their own tiny spheres of rotation. On the intrapersonal level, the attraction of child to mother, and the divine attraction of the soul for Reality, ever partakes of the enthralling and congenial qualities of *raga*. In short, the realm of the Cosmic Cause is rife with abundant light emitting off of these and other more specialized elements of Divine Reality (see chart on page 359).

Vidya, intelligence, is inherent in the Cosmic Cause as well. Our chart under study calls it higher intelligence, and the seeker after Truth has been tracking it for lifetimes. In it, and in the refined *buddhi* that shines with it, the *Atman*, pure Awareness, reflects best of all. Further, its connection with the Primal Word, *AUM*, is indivisible, as we will see as this study progresses.

Puzzling, but also revealing, is the presence of *maya* at this lofty strata. Most beings who have heard of the word *maya* define it as "illusion." But *maya* is mainly only the worlds of name and form in time and space based upon causation. Reality is formless, so anything that covers It, namely the urge towards form in general, is of the nature of *maya*. Thus, if one looks at this chart (page 47) from the Cosmic Cause downwards, more in evolution style rather than by way of involution as we are studying it here, the entire sweep of *maya*'s domain is seen. As Shankara has put it in his *Vivekachudamani*, the Crest Jewel of Discrimination, *"Everything from avyaktam (the indiscernible unmanifest nature) on down to the five elements, is the nonself."*

The term "not-self" refers to what is insentient and mutable. The distinction, then, and a liberating one at that, divides the changing from the Unchanging, the nonessence from the Essence, *maya* from *Brahman*. And conventional religious wisdom takes a step in the right direction when it states that one needs to *"separate the wheat from the chaff"* in order to get the grain. But this does not pertain to food and commerce, or worldly matters and their concerns. Spiritual food, grains of truth, need to be gleaned, and this act of mental discrimination that separates insentient nature from the Sentient Soul is crucial for Self-realization. Once that step has been concluded one can see that *maya* is in *Brahman*, as Sri Ramakrishna has pointed out, *"like poison is in the snake."* The realization of "All Is *Brahman*" is then not far off.

The chart defines *maya* as form and formlessness, which brings up another subtle distinction to be made. That is, as has been told, there is manifest nature and there is unmanifest nature; then there is the Supremely Unmanifested Nature as well, *Brahman*. To understand this is to become aware that when all manifest things disappear — as in decay, destruction, and death — it is only their outer form that dissolves, while the inner substance simply moves into seed form, or potential. This has to do, in part, with abiding memory of them in the mind, but has more to do with their unoriginated nature as subtle seeds always lying in ready potential. This is why knowing the Essence, *Brahman*, is so important, for then one will not fall into the fallacious assumption that birth and death, and creation and destruction, are real or actual; they are merely transitional. When a baby is born, it simply appears out of the unmanifested state it went into before, and when an old person dies, he or she only passes back into that selfsame unmanifested condition. Thus, it is less a matter of *"ashes to ashes, dust to dust,"* and more a matter of visible seed to invisible seed. All the while nothing has actually happened; no transformation has taken place. This principle is called *Aparinama* (see chart on page 265), which will be taken up for study in succeeding pages. Importantly, the Supreme Unmanifest stands by, unaffected, but acting as the underlying and quiescent substratum for all that seems to pass from state to state under *maya*'s domain.

The Remote Cause

To comprehend more fully the apparent transformation of things, objects, worlds, and beings from one state of relative awareness to another, the Remote Cause needs to be fathomed, at least to a degree. This could also be called the Causal Cause. It has been likened to the deep sleep state wherein man is fully immersed in a naturally formless condition, but is, as of yet, unaware of it, there being a veil of nescience over his cognizance. To be perceptive in this pure realm would be to awaken to inner wisdom, behold all that unmanifested nature holds, hear the unstruck sound of *Om*, and come face to face with *Ishvara* — the highest conception of God with form that the human mind can comprehend or envision. One might be tempted to disclose that all four living principles listed here — *Mahat, Mahaprakriti, AUM*, and *Ishvara* — are one and the same, only seen from four different picture windows of the soul. *Mahat*, the Cosmic Mind, fulfills the cosmological view; *Mahaprakriti*, the purveyor of all the principles of nature, fulfills the philosophical wisdom view; *AUM*, the Primal Word/Vibration, fulfills the mystical view; and *Ishvara*, the Chosen Ideal, fulfills the theistic and anthropomorphical view. Other appellations for Divine Awareness, such as the Cosmic Egg (*Hiranyagarbha*), the Firstborn, the Primeval Soul, and more, also fit in here, in this very broad, very transcendent category.

The Remote Cause, or Causal Cause, is that transcendental location in Consciousness where everything resides, and from whence everything springs. All of this can be put in terms of wisdom — living liberating wisdom. The coruscating Light of *Brahman*, the silent Sound of *Om*, the Divine Body of *Ishvara* and Its incarnations — they are all just wisdom: Mother Wisdom. This Mother is the *Shakti* of *Brahman*, She who fashions everything out of *Brahman*-potential or, She who fragments Indivisible Consciousness into many parts. The dichotomy of this is that something that is indivisible cannot be fragmented. Yet there it is, the various universes of names and forms and the mass of individualized souls that inhabit them. This segues nicely into a description, however rudimentary, of The Causeless Cause, which is the ultimate point of any study of cause and effect, of involution, of this stratified chart, and of our very existence.

The Causeless Cause

The collection of citations and quotes gathered on this chart (page 47) pertain specifically to the various strata of causes stacked one atop the other in layered form. Of all of them, perhaps King Janaka's astute saying at the top heads the row, pertaining most directly to the actual march of cause and effect, and emphasizing the need for aspiring beings to transcend it. And this brings to the fore the Highest, the Foremost, the Perfect, the Ever-free — that which lies far beyond even the most remote of causes, yet which infills them all completely. This is Reality Itself, untainted by any and all causes and effects, therefore being nondependent upon anything other than Itself. This is *Brahman* and Its *Shakti*.

Intrinsically and inseparably unified, like fire and heat, whiteness and snow, wetness and water, a diamond and its radiance, *Brahman* and *Shakti* are the twin aspects of one singular and indivisible Absolute Reality. The fact that They are rarely even distinguishable from one another has earned Them the name, "The Two who are One." Like a snake and its wriggling motion, *Brahman* and *Shakti* are the preternatural Essence in all things, sentient or insentient. Known also as *Akandha Satchidananda* — pure Existence, pure Wisdom, and pure Bliss — they are also referred to as pure Consciousness, or timeless, deathless Awareness, and Absolute Reality. Though fundamentally immovable, it is nevertheless Their quiet presence that animates all things, all worlds, all beings — even the gods and goddesses in the highest spheres. And though there are several layers of causality between Them and all other principles — cosmic mind, intellect, mind, *prana*, senses, nature, etc. — They nevertheless remain constant and immediate, and intimately available to all the sincere practitioners who deeply desire to know and see Them. Like sweetness in sugarcane juice, They appear everywhere as the true and essential nature existing in everything, sentient and insentient. The chart on the next page, page 56, will illustrate this aptly, as it takes up the often puzzling but always interesting facet of existence known as "reflected awareness" in *Vedic* philosophical circles.

Chidabhasa — The Reflection of Brahman in the Cosmos

"God is not in the universe; the universe is in God."   Swami Vivekananda

BRAHMAN — ABSOLUTE REALITY

(Maha Shakti)

Direct Emanation of Pure, Conscious Awareness
(Atman)   (Unmanifest Prakriti)

BUDDHI — COSMIC INTELLIGENCE

Chidabhasa

Reflected Consciousness

Brahmajnan Appearing as Various Principles

Prana & Akasha

Subtle Energy,
The Subtle Worlds,
Higher Gradated Beings

Human Ego-Mind Complex

Thought, Conceptualization,
Visions, Imagination,
Projection, Invention, Desire

"The One remains, the many change and pass; Heaven's light forever
shines, Earth's shadows fly; Life, like a dome of many-colored glass,
stains the white radiance of Eternity...."

Time & Space

Five Subtle Elements,
Five Gross Elements.
Physical Universe,
Flow of Events, Karma

Human Embodiment

The Body,
Five Senses of Knowledge,
Five Senses of Action

"The embodied being is none other than an emanation of the Jnana-wisdom of Brahman.
The hosts of myriad worlds and objects appearing within endless cycles of time duly shine
as the objective vision and ideation of its inherent Consciousness. Thus, it is the
one, all-pervading Atman which assumes the name of 'Jiva,' materializing
with the intelligent force of its own innate Awareness."   Lord Vasishtha

The term *"Chidabhasa,"* mentioned earlier as well, indicates the reflection of Divine Reality in all things. Though used unknowingly by most all beings to cite or explain the presence of God in the world, certain questions come up around this principle. That is, as the quote from Swami Vivekananda states at the top of this chart, *"God is not in the universe; the universe is in God."* This clarification, among other things, relates that God can never be a form. Further, forms do not reflect in God, they reflect in Mind — cosmic, collective, and individual. To understand this on a deep level is to see all manifestation as reflection, leaving Reality to be the one, ever-pure, original Verity that It is. An analogy will help us to comprehend this.

In the case of a sun reflecting in a pool of water, there are three things involved: there is the reflected sun; there is the pool; and there is the original sun in the sky. The reflected sun stands for all objects; the pool represents the mind; and the original sun in the sky is *Brahman*, which is self-effulgent, shining by its own light. And there can be said to be a fourth element as well — the rays of the sun. They symbolize *Chidabhasa*. And what are these rays made up of? They are the Light of *Brahman*, rays of wisdom-intelligence emanating off of Divine Reality, like fragrance off of a mature sandalwood tree. (see chart on page 716)

Taking the chart opposite for reference, we can see how these rays of conscious living Light waft off of *Brahman* and, via the force of the *Mahashakti*, stream down to invest *Buddhi*/Mind (cosmic, collective, and individual) with its most prized asset, Consciousness. From there it is a matter of a trickle down effect, as has been cited earlier. This Wisdom-principle, now called *Brahmajnan*, permeates all atmospheres, all *tattvas*, all concepts, all beings, and all things.

The mention of "things" here means objects which, as we have already discussed, have no creation, have no existence separate from *Brahman* — because they are nothing more or less than *Brahman*'s wisdom rays in a solid state. Obviously, objects are not aware, are less animate; but as distant emanations of wisdom their true purpose is to point the way back to *Brahman*. If taken as objects for their own sake, as in for pleasure, possession, power, preoccupation, etc., they only lead beings into bondage in *maya*. But when meditated upon as to their origins, their appearance as elements of the gross Material Cause will get transformed into representatives of nothing other than the subtlemost Causeless Cause, rendering everything into *Brahman* — *"Sarvam Khalvidam Brahma."*

This is a great secret, and epitomizes the Wisdom Way of spiritual alchemy that transforms the world of name and form into the nameless, formless Reality. Therefore, the enigmatic saying, *"Form is emptiness and emptiness is form"* from the *Diamond Sutra,* is not a statement on the unreality of the world, but rather a declaration on the all-pervasiveness of Reality. In other words, beyond the stage of emptiness lies fullness, a fullness that speaks in terms of all-inclusiveness based upon all-pervasiveness.

To make this even clearer, and as mentioned earlier, Sri Ramakrishna has given the analogy of sunlight which reflects poorly off of a rock, a little better off of a leaf, better still on the surface of a lake, and best of all on a mirror. The rock represents inanimate elements such as objects, bodies, etc.; the leaf could be insects, animals, the five senses, and the like; the lake is ordinary human mind and its thinking process; and the mirror, the illumined mind. None of these are *Brahman* from the standpoint of their respective forms, but from the perspective of how much light they possess they all fall closer (*shuddha*) or more distant (*shuddhashuddha*) to *Brahman*, as the case may be.

And so the spiritual aspirant's inward journey must include using inherent wisdom to uncover the Truth of Existence. Space, time, and causality — *desha, kala,* and *nimitta* — lie open and exposed for those who would caringly and lovingly court their own divine nature as the quintessential Verity in all the worlds, and beyond the worlds. As the *Tantras* so convincingly declare, *"You, your own true Self, is the precious darling of your own devout worship."* Or as the Sufis are wont to say, *"When I reached up to pluck the fruit of religious attainment from the branch of intense spiritual practice, I found that the entire tree was within myself!"* This tree of realization of *Brahman*, with its branches of space, time, and causation, is to be climbed, and its fruits gathered along the way in order to benefit all sentient beings — awakened, striving, suffering, and sleeping.

Matching Strides With the Seers
The Saving Grace of Sadhana — Spiritual Self-effort

There are certain crucial elements to the art of self-effort in *Vedic* culture and religion which have been laid down in no uncertain terms, which always thought in terms of integrating practice with philosophy, not alienating them from one another. First, and importantly, the necessity of qualifying oneself for receiving the teachings is paramount. A great cause for failure in religious and spiritual life is due to the lack of qualification and/or purification in the aspirant, a fact that has gradually given true religion a bad name over the centuries and distanced it ever farther from the ken of ordinary beings. Secondly, the need for a teacher stands out, and this is especially out of balance in the West, where taking a teacher for worldly subjects is acknowledged by all, while accepting a guide in spiritual life is both unpopular and carelessly overlooked. Third, is the practice itself, and the need for both maintaining it and intensifying it. The practices of worship, study, *japa*, and meditation stand out here as most necessary. Finally, the need for perceiving both ones shortcomings and ones past deeds in tandem with the presence of desires, *karma*, and reincarnation, will benefit ones spiritual life immensely. These four elements of a healthy and well-informed *sadhana* will get examined in this chapter, accompanied by a host of helpful charts.

Qualification and Purification

Although a good teacher will make lessons available for one and all, regardless of the level of aptitude in any given group of students, there is no doubting that a special bond forms when adept preceptor and able pupil meet. In terms of the contemporary human mind, and in accordance with subjects of a religious and spiritual nature, there is an obvious absence of substance in today's potential aspirants, what to speak of a lack of interest and a general overall indeterminacy. When examining the classic case of devout practitioner, however, the presence of character and substance stands out, particularly alongside those having little or none. What is missing, to use an important *Sanskrit* word, are positive *samskaras* (see charts on pages 165, 167), mental impressions from the past. These mental impressions are most often talked about in terms of negative *samskaras* which impede and bind living beings, but equally important of note are those positive ones which awaken, unshackle, and liberate. If the teacher, called a *guru* in India, perceives this positive *samskaric* material in the mind of the aspirant, called a *shishya*, then he knows that much of the work has been done already. In short, it is much easier to awaken latent impressions than it is to create them from nothing. Sri Ramakrishna told a story that is applicable here: Once, a farmer, coming to survey a new field he had just purchased, was walking about the land, exploring his acquisition, when his foot accidently brushed against a partially buried pipe. Immediately water began gushing out. The farmer was overjoyed to see this, for he had just been saved days of work in digging irrigation ditches. In just this way are both the *guru* and the disciple saved laborious work if the student's mind contains *samskaras* for spiritual life that were planted there and tended in previous existences.

Today, *samskaras* of spirituality are either missing in humanity or buried very deep, and in fact and lamentably, short of creating *samskaras* for practice, for attainment, for nondualism, etc., there is much mental de-programming to do. The question naturally arises, then, what was required of the student in ancient times. The following chart shows what a *Tantric* aspirant must know before committing to this comprehensive path.

The Seven Qualifications & Seven Victories
Of A Tantrik Aspirant

Tantra-Shastra-Adhikari – The Well-Rounded Tantrik Aspirant

Daksha
Intelligent

Dvaitadita
A Nondualist

Shuchi
Pure of Heart

Astika
Devotion to
Scriptures

Jitendriya
Sense Mastery

Brahmanistha,
Brahmavadi,
Brahmaparayana
Faith, Path & Refuge
in God

Sarvahimsa Vinirmukta
Peaceful, Nonviolent

The Seven Victories of Involution

Bhuta Jaya,
mastery of the five elements

Indriya Jaya,
control of mind and senses

Prakrti Jaya,
control of all creative principles

Manojavittvam,
mastery of the mind's powers

Vikarana Bhava,
perception without the senses

Pradhana Jaya,
control of the primal principle

Sattva Purusha Nytakhyati, knowing soul & matter to be different

Complaints abound from seekers of the day around how difficult spiritual life is. The sincere and knowledgeable aspirant comes to know right away that the feigned bliss of a "pie in the sky" spiritual existence is a lie, a hollow promise proceeding from the lips of charlatans and pretenders of the pseudo-spiritual arena. Realistically, the oft-repeated adage of a razor's edged path is more apropos to authentic spiritual striving. In the beginning real practice is, as one swami once stated, *"one percent inspiration and ninety-nine percent perspiration."* Over decades of hard inner work this formula may change, and the balance shift a bit, but there is no replacement for *sadhana* since the pervasiveness of suffering in relativity goes on unabated, regardless.

For the *tantric sadhika* sincere striving is a part of the quotient, and is expected at the outset and along the way of any authentic path he or she undertakes. As Sri Krishna has advised in the *Bhagavad Gita*, one of the three most important of Indian scriptures, *"Beware of what is sweet in the beginning, for it turns sour at the end. On the other hand, look to that which is sour in the beginning, for it often turns sweet later on."* Such a declaration pertains so readily and directly to the singular mode of self-effort the gurus and preceptors call *sadhana*, spiritual discipline.

The Seven Qualifications of a Tantric Aspirant are an indication of what a seeker of Truth must do to set the ground for realization. Tellingly, they are as applicable today as they were millennia ago. First, the aspirant must be *daksha*, intelligent. Why are some born intelligent and others arrive on earth with a dull mind? Is God partial? No, but *karma* certainly is. It is agent specific. Those who sow must reap accordingly. A person's intelligence, or lack thereof, points directly to his or her *samskaras*, those all-important and telling mental impressions from previous existences. So, one is not born intelligent due to chance, luck, good fortune, or as a gift from God. This attribute, like all others, is earned, and was developed in a past lifetime.

Then again, there are persons who, though intelligent, fail to draw that precious commodity out of the mind, dust it off, and apply it in this life. This is due to laziness and complacency, or procrastination. Whatever the case may be, intelligence does form the ground upon which authentic spirituality will eventually appear and mature. And this quality is not the same in all beings either. The intelligence of some is practical. For others, it is devotional in nature. Suffice to say, however, that "intellectualism" is not what is being cited here, for that attribute often masks some of the darkest and densest ignorance in the world. For instance, Sri Ramakrishna has stated that *"Knowing many things is ignorance; knowing one thing is knowledge."* As one *rishi* in the *Upanisads* asked, *"Sir: show me that one thing by which knowing all else will be known."*

Therefore, it is something special indeed that the aspirant seeks in the form of intelligence, which shows up as a terrible void in the minds of others. This specialized intelligence allows the aspirant to walk the right path, fulfill life's *dharmic* requisites, recognize holy company, comprehend the scriptures, and fully understand the message of the *guru* and the luminaries. All other matters, of earthly concern, are easily dispatched by it. A deep mental and spiritual relationship with living wisdom, insights and profound realizations — realization itself — also comes on account of this subtle intelligence — also called, fittingly, *buddhi*. Yet all of this remains lost to the one who fails to develop it. As Ramprasad sings in his hymns to the Divine Mother of the Universe, *"That stubborn and lazy child who fails to complete his studies is spanked soundly and put to bed without his supper."*

The second quality sought after by the seeker, and looked for by the *guru* in the aspirant as well, is called *shuchi*, purity, known also as *saucha* and *shuddhi* (see chart on page 122). Humility, reverence, chastity, balance, etc., are all associated with purity. But what is really meant by the word is absolute fealty to the Ideal. One-pointed devotion to the Chosen Ideal (*Ishtam*) is looked upon as purity by the wise, because everything else will come naturally if it is gained. Purity of heart is really purity of mind, and what the *rishis* call purity of mind is the highest and best of all purities.

Jitendriya, control of the senses, is also sought after by the *tantric* aspirant, though it is advised and coveted by all the Indian *darshanas*. The idea here is that each of the five senses has a great power contained within it. The word, *Indriya*, also refers to the Lord of gods. Therefore, each of the senses is a little god. The problem with owning a set of senses is that the human being most often misuses them, even abuses them, which leads to gluttony, ill health, lack of vigor, and eventually, mental imbalance. In other words, the natural power in the senses gets squandered, wasted, frittered away, with laziness and lethargy being the regrettable result. A marked difference is noticed in the one who reserves this precious energy, however, resisting the outward going impetus of the senses and instead storing up the force that lies inherent within them. This is *jitendriya,* and its secret has been known for ages by the dispensers and purveyors of spirituality among human beings.

Dear to all true human beings who are sensitive and empathetic by nature is the principle of *ahimsa,* nonviolence. It is therefore that *Sarvahimsa Vinirmukta* is one of the seven main requisites for the *Tantric* path. And here one must be *sarvahimsa,* all peaceful — nonviolent in thought, word, and deed, as they say.

But it would be very good to realize that authentic nonviolence is beyond these three movements in relativity. Even beyond refraining from hurting others, going to war, turning the other cheek, etc., *ahimsa* is an inflexible law of Truth Itself, in accordance with both the principles of Nontransformation and Nonorigination. That is, ultimately it is impossible to harm anything, since everything is nothing less than the indestructible *Brahman* in essence. As has been outlined previously, everything exists at all times. Sri Krishna relates this fact to the warrior, Arjuna, on the battlefield of *Kurushektra,* stating: *"Those warriors, princes, and kings that you see lined up across the battlefield before us, Dhananjaya — there was never a time, nor will there ever come a time, when they will not exist."* In other words, we must not relegate the Eternal *Brahman* to an ephemeral form. Therefore, knowing that "All is *Brahman,*" and that "Everything is," constitutes real nonviolence. All other forms of *ahimsa* fall under, after, and behind that stainless and immutable law.

And speaking of immutability, the fifth requisite that a *tantric* aspirant must covet is to be a lover of and adherent to nonduality, *Advaita. Dvaitahina* strongly suggests that though *dvaita,* duality, is going to be the position that most beings gravitate to, being most manageable by the general sweep of humanity, nonduality will become the new standard for those seeking higher Truth. It is said of the great Adishankaracharya that, after the decline of *Buddhism* in the early centuries after Christ's passing, he came to resurrect the *Advaita Vedanta.* Remarkably, he did so by first moving into towns and villages to reconstruct temples. Then he called together the Brahmin priests and together with them reinstalled the images of the deities which the Buddhists of the time had removed. After this was done, he invited the common people back to worship and thereby "spun the *dharma* wheel" in a positive direction. Finally, he then set himself up in the courtyard outside the temple and taught nonduality to those who were not moved to enter the temples. Thus did duality, qualified nonduality, and nonduality go on, as was natural, in the daily life of pious human beings.

A fine mention of this religious principle in other traditions was made by Swami Vivekananda as well. Speaking of the Christ, Swamiji pointed out that when Christ said *"Pray to the Father who art in Heaven,"* he was talking to the dualists (*dvaitists*); when he stated *"I am the vine and you are the branches,"* he was speaking to his qualified nondualistic followers; but when he declared *"I and my Father are One,"* he was affirming and advising nonduality among His most advanced apostles. These three stages of religion and philosophy are interconnected and are not to be seen as mutually exclusive, for it is one single and indivisible Reality that all are speaking of (see chart on page 379). As the great swami also said, if one is going towards the sun in a spaceship and takes pictures along the way, upon returning, the sun looks different in each one of them. But it is the same sun nevertheless. Similarly, the one Reality seems different to the differing perspectives of various votaries depending upon the philosophical angle from which they are looking.

Even given all this, the *tantric* aspirant seeking the highest wants the best vantagepoint possible, and the perspective of *"I and my Father are one"* most decidedly affords this. Additionally, this lofty height even sweetens all the more the acceptable views of authentic duality and qualified nonduality, bringing all to a unified perspective much more swiftly and easily.

Astika, devotion to the scriptures, is the sixth qualification in *Tantra.* It is crucially important in *Yoga, Vedanta, Sankhya* and other great pathways as well, and in all the religions of the world. And it stands to reason that if the *tantric* aspirant has dedicated him or herself to nonduality, *dvaitahina,* then the scriptures under inspection will also have to be nondual in nature. This is why great luminaries from Lord Vasishtha (thousands of years B.C.) to Shankara (800 A.D.) have all recommended that the "revealed" scriptures take up much of the time of the devout seeker's *sadhana.* (see chart on pages 437, 522). An exhaustive list could be compiled (see chart on page 522), some of it subject to personal preference and opinion, but suffice to say that if the teachings under study speak in terms of the union of the apparently individualized soul with the Supreme Soul, then it is a sure bet that the testament is nondual and thereby fully trustworthy.

Further, if *jnana,* nondual wisdom, is being shared under the above mentioned caption, all the better. This is primary. Secondarily, what can be allowed are those pithy sayings, aphorisms, and stories which relate to nondual truths, which support the *dharma,* and that enforce morals and ethics. On the other hand, what is best avoided are empty and watered down simperings about religious conventions, worldly affairs, and especially the constant harping on sin and evil. There is enough of this latter infesting the tomes of literature of the world so that people are already made well-enough aware of it. All of that worldliness, and the darksome intrigue that attends upon it, are best left there, in books and novels, and left out of the scriptures — which should have to do only with Divine Reality, its modes and teachings, and the practices that lead beings to realization of It. More will be said about revealed scripture over the vast sweep of this book.

The seventh and final qualification listed on the present chart under study is threefold. Faith, path, and refuge — all of these ought to be directed towards and culminated in *Brahman,* the Reality. *Nistha* is a *Sanskrit* world, unlike any other in that it pleads and endears itself unto the devotee for attaining one-pointed love and dedication. *Ishta-nistha,* one-pointed devotion to the Ideal, is a famous principle in Hinduism, and one that is seen, even today, deeply-rooted in the culture. Its teaching applies more than ever in this time as well, since there is so much of spiritual menu-tasting going on, and precious little of dedication to a single path and ideal.

When referring to the incomparable principle of Universality, the Truth of all Religions, what the seers of this wondrous perspective want to convey is not that all religions be practiced simultaneously, but that they all be accepted as valid while the aspirant chooses one to practice. Digging many shallow wells never uncovered water, never slaked ones thirst. One deep well is best. Choosing one excellent Ideal in spiritual life will suffice perfectly in leading one to enlightenment, whereas crossing back and forth between or mixing up a host of ideals will only dilute ones energies and even confuse the mind in the end. This is why the devotee's faith, his pathway, and his overall and final refuge must always be in God, in the formless nondual *Brahman.* And it is not only a matter of good practical sense; it is also a matter of well-guided intuition. The homing pigeon for instance, once released, knows which direction to fly in order to get home. All souls, unless lost or disoriented in *maya,* are much like this.

Along with the Seven Qualifications, the Seven Victories are also very worthy of mention. This is involution *Tantra* style, running many of the same routes that our earlier explorations of the subject traversed, but having some unique features of its own.

First, *Bhuta Jaya* urges the seeker on towards transcendence of the five elements of earth, water, fire, air, and ether. The emphasis in the early stages of Patanjali's *Yoga* as we know, or will find out (see chart on pages 693), is to meditate upon the five elements (and other *tattvas*) as "alambanas," supports for meditation, in order to know them in all their modes and aspects. For instance, water slakes thirst; it also drowns. Knowing this via inner contemplation will give the meditator a healthy respect for and detachment from water, and this knowledge will allow mastery of water forevermore. Water will never daunt one, or attract one inordinately, again. This is mastery over one element.

In *Tantra,* this salient way also occurs, but the emphasis seems to be more on the experiential than the meditative. That is, experiences are gained in nature in order to be able to transcend any given *tattva* or principle. This is different than the way of repetitive everyday experiences that worldly and spiritually unawakened persons tread. Their experiences are random, unconnected, sought for pleasure, and often had unconsciously. There is no connecting point or ground beneath this flow of experiences by which to lend them continuity and meaning. The *tantric* aspirant wants to know everything, have every experience, but will never be satisfied with or taken off course by experiences alone. This is because the highest experience, called *samadhi*, is not an experience at all, but a state of perpetual Existence. The sincere seeker wants that alone.

And this is why, when *Bhuta Jaya* is attained, the *tantric* acolyte courses onwards to master the five senses. This is termed *Indriya Jaya*. Since *Tantra* and *Yoga* are so interconnected, and similar in so many ways, a reference again to *Yoga* here is pertinent, especially *Raja Yoga*. In this highly respected system the senses are to be joined, in consciousness, to the elements. Earth joins with the sense of smell, water with taste, fire with sight, air with touch, and ether with hearing. The fact that ordinary people do not consciously perform this consummate marriage, in consciousness, is a cause for the disjointedness of life and confusion of the mind, what to speak of alienation from nature. What is wanted in the goal of realization is not alienation, but mastery over nature, then isolation from it, which can then be followed by a proper and beneficial relationship with it based upon enlightenment rather than on bondage.

And so, whatever pathway one takes, the five elements and the ten senses take on a prominent import, at least in the beginning. And this process, whatever form it takes, is what is meant by the purification of the senses. That is, for this one does not take out an eyeball and wash and polish it, or scrub the ears, inside and out, with a washcloth. Inner impurities are of a different nature, and require inner work. One must take out the dullness of sense enjoyment from the eyes, and wash away the overlay of ignorance from the ears. Then the human being will *"see what is good and spiritual and hear what is noble and uplifting,"* as one of the seven Peace Chants states (i.e., *bhadram karnebih srinuyama devah*, etc.). In other words, these same senses, with this endeavor achieved, will be instrumental in facilitating the forthcoming stages leading to enlightenment of mind.

Therefore, the role of the mind in the purification process must be taken into account. In this regard the mind is called the "sixth sense," and is seen as the "grand central station" where all the senses and the nerve endings meet. Later, in the fourth level of mastery, mind takes on other ramifications, more subtle and more powerful. This is similar to what was studied earlier in accord with the difference between brain and mind. But here, in this second level of mastery, mind, with its valuable component of fundamental will, must take the initiative to gather the senses together after calling them away from their desired objects. In *Yoga* this is called *pratyahara*, the fifth limb of *Patanjala*, and in *Vedanta* it is referred to as *Vairagya*, or detachment.

But since *Tantra's* way includes seeking after experiences while remaining free of bondage, its detachment will necessarily be of a somewhat different or distinct character. The mind will perform its purificatory function, no doubt, but the unique ingredient of spontaneous deification will form a part of the process as well. One might say that the truth of "All is *Brahman*" is being proclaimed all along the way of the *tantric* path, whereas in other more staunch and stern pathways this most sacrosanct of proclamations will be reserved for the consummate arrival. This is much like the old comparison of the slow scenic route of the *bhakti* path (devotion) in contrast to the swift and focused way of *jnana* (wisdom). Whatever the case may be, the dual mind's willing participation in it all is of paramount importance. And so, the *tantric* aspirant strives to bring it under his or her complete control.

And when this is actuated, *Prakriti Jaya*, the third of seven potential masteries, appears on the horizon of advancing practice. Here, we must look back and remember that the word "nature" in *Vedic* religion and philosophy does not apply to the five elements only, but to all that is contained in the realms of name and form. Gross objects, for instance, are a combination of the five elements; a primal and anterior quintuplication process has formulated them. And so, after mastering the five elements, the sincere *tantric* aspirant has a good start at viewing the world of objects with a mind to fully master them. In the cases of most people, the objects have mastered them. They are slaves to their bodies, to their cars, to their houses, to their televisions, etc. It is an old story. Without hands-on knowledge of the five elements, then, and conscious experiences with them via the five senses in nature, nature in its creative mode and the world of objects consisting of earth, water, fire, air, and ether, will never be known for what they are (mere appearances), and will impose an influence, albeit insentient, to enslave the embodied soul out of his or her own ignorance.

But with knowledge of the elements, mastery over the senses, and the willing involvement of the controlled and one-pointed mind, this potential calamity will not manifest. What will occur instead is an insight into the creative principle itself, what can be called the primordial workings of nature. This was termed *Pradhana* in the *Sankhya* philosophy in very early times, and was so impressive to the thinkers of that antediluvian period that it was said to be independent of God, possessing its own separate reality. Whatever the case may have been, recognizing and mastering it formed a major accomplishment in the spiritual life, the main facet of this achievement being the perception of the subtlest secrets of nature — what some *yogins* would term inchoate or incipient nature. That is, the final products of the universe have not yet completely formulated, presenting a rare look into the origins of the subtlemost building blocks of nature. This could be likened to seeing the process of inception and development of the fetus in the mother's womb, day by day, thus looking at the burgeoning of life itself.

With this deed under ones belt, it is no wonder that *Manojavittvam* is the next strata of victory. Defined as the inconceivable speed of the mind, the vast expanse of the inner terrain of the burgeoning soul can be fully explored, for once the primal manifestation of nature is overseen, the mind feels freer than ever before. This segues nicely into the fifth victory too, called *Vikarana Bhava,* wherein the seeker comes to know that his consciousness exists even beyond the dropping of the body and the senses. This truism usually only occurs to the human mind in two unconscious states: deep sleep and death. But few have the depth and capabilities to ponder these phenomena. It is only when two other conscious states, meditation and *samadhi*, are experienced, that the idea of an eternally existing Awareness dawns on the mind. When that condition matures, the seeker, now a mature meditator, will spend long hours in the Light of Consciousness, abandoning the body and senses as easily as the wind leaves the sails of a sinking ship.

The penultimate victory for a *tantric* adept to attain has to do with nature again, only, what is called "unmanifested" nature. This is *Pradhana Jaya,* the control over the very first creative principle of nature. Earlier, in the third victory, the honed awareness of the adept perceived and pierced through primordial nature. But this was the inception of the gross form of nature, the beginnings of *prakriti* on the sub-elemental and gross elemental levels. Now, the expression of creativity is much more conscious — is so aware as to be given the name of Lord *Brahma*, the Deity of the creative process. Coming face to face with this aspect of the Divine Trinity is a very rare experience that most never have. At that time, the adept *tantric* practitioner offers back to Lord *Brahma* all that was given at the time of inception — life itself, relative existence — and repairs further inwards from that high realm to merge into the primal Word. This is tantamount to handing creation itself, and all it represents, back to the gods, so as to have nothing more to do with it.

And this brings about what *Yoga* calls *Kaivalya,* the separation of Spirit from Matter. *Sattva Purusha Nytakhyati,* the full knowledge of the separateness of *Atman* from all other principles (*tattvas*) is Self-realization in *Tantra.* For the consummate *tantric* adept it all amounts to this: recognition is simultaneous to realization. Through the full experience of life and all that it had to offer, the soul has reached anew the pinnacle of all attainments, and now rests in *Brahman* forever.

The *Tantric* qualifications and victories have thus been generally laid out in this informative chart, along with condensed descriptions of each practice. As a comparison, and due to its profound import in *Vedanta* in the realm of qualification, the Four Treasures and Six Jewels are now presented for study.

The Four Treasures and Six Jewels of Vedanta Philosophy

"The sages have spoken of four qualifications for spiritual attainment: deep discrimination between the eternal and the noneternal; renunciation of the fruits of action; acquiring the six jewels; and longing for liberation. When these four are present devotion to Reality succeeds. When they are absent it will fail."

Shankaracharya

1. Cognizing the Distinction between the Real and the Unreal

Viveka

"Dejection due to loss, and disappointment at not gaining the objects of one's desire are only stepping stones to Viveka and Vairagya — clear discernment about the unreal nature of the world and the acquisition of indifference to it. Together these conduce to the quiescent state of mind leading to Brahman." Vishvamitra

"Seek not to store up thy treasures on earth, but rather store them up in Heaven." Jesus of Nazareth

Adhyaropa
Recognizing False Superimposition

Apavada
Refutation of Misconception

2. Rejecting the Unreal and Accepting the Real

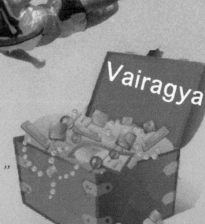
Vairagya

3. Locating and Manifesting The Six Jewels

Sama — Inner Peace

Shat-sampati

Titiksha — Forbearance

Dama — Self Control

Samadhana — Concentration

Uparati — Self-Settledness

Shraddha — Faith

4. Developing a Sincere Yearning for Liberation

Mumuk-shutvam

"If the desire for wealth is abandoned through asceticism, then ajnana, ignorance, will persist. But if such desire be transcended through Viveka, it will disappear." *Queen Chudala*

"The study of Atma-jnan books, the grace of a guru, ceaseless practice of Vairagyam, and freeing oneself from desires for the world — when all these are attained and meditation on Brahman is engaged in, prana and mind will more readily come under control." *Vasishtha*

"Your country is the incomparable state of Moksha. You, Atmic Reality, are the King residing there. Your minister is the cosmic intelligence, and the way to this radiant land is via the pathways of Viveka and Vairagya and the Wisdom that proceeds from them." *Virochana*

"Advance towards liberation is the worthiest gain of mankind. May you speedily attain to freedom, and help others attain it!" *Vivekananda*

Sadhanachatushtaya, the four precious treasures of *Vedantic* practice, is one of the few indications of any system of self-effort in *Vedanta.* For it seems that *bhakti,* or devotion, forms the general mode of practice for souls on dualistic levels, while the nondualistic level, if realized, scarcely brooks or needs any practice at all. Still, for the discerning aspirant, the one who feels the deep urge to purify and perfect to the 'nth degree, a practice, however transparent and transcendent, is wanted and sought after. The Four Treasures and their Six Jewels certainly fill this need, being, as they are, works to be accomplished on the internal level, with the discerning mind.

Basically, *Viveka* and *Vairagya* head the bill, meaning that the first wise move on the part of any *Vedantic* seeker after truth is to draw a subtle but definite line of distinction between the real and the unreal — words that relate to the difference between the essential and the nonessential, the substantial and the insubstantial, i.e., *Brahman* and Nature. After that line has been established, and what is purely actual has been espied and perceived as distinct in character from the apparent, then a gradual and smooth withdrawal from the nonactual is pursued. This completed, the six jewels of inner peace, self-control, contentedness, forbearance, concentration, and faith can be claimed, and this brings into possession a desire for freedom that is sincere and unwavering, called *Mumukshutvam.* Let us examine each one of these in brief, along with their concomitant aids.

The *Sanskrit* term, *Nityanityavastuviveka,* describes this system of *Sadhanachatushtaya* briefly and best of all. *Nitya* is what is real; *anitya,* what is unreal: v*astu* mean the difference between, and *viveka* means spiritual discrimination (or discernment). Thus, the realization of truth along the *jnana-marga,* the path of wisdom, is to cogently discern the difference between the real and the unreal using the subtle discriminatory power of the awakened mind and intellect. Put in a few pregnant words, *Brahman satya, jagad mithya; "Brahman is real, the world is unreal."* But beings attached to the world are not going to perceive this, or believe this. Only the seeker after truth will go in this unconventional direction, plunging very far or deep into such uncharted regions. One would needs be a veritable Sherlock Holmes of the Spirit to detect, what to speak of uncover, the melange of unfathomable workings of *maya.*

To do so, the art of *viveka* is of foremost importance in ones esoteric education. As the chart indicates, two aids will be brought into play to afford any success in this critical area. Of these two, *adhyaropa* is simultaneously a statement on the obscuring power of name and form, and a challenge to remove all such coverings using the power of the controlled and focused mind. Its counterpart, *apavada,* is the ability to do away with this invisible but troublesome blanket of ignorance so that pure knowledge can visit the mind, followed thereafter by a host of desirable qualities. The reader is asked to view and contemplate the *rishi* Visvamitra's pellucid quote on this chart, so as to assess and glean the true value of these first two treasures and their aids.

It is clear that *viveka* and *vairagya* — "the two v's that are the two d's" (discrimination and detachment) — form the one-two punch that knocks the opponent of ignorance to the mat for all time. This is why *Vedanta* is called the finishing school of spirituality among those highest of knowers, for it cuts at the throat and puts to death fallacy and untruth for all time. One famous song of modern India avers that *viveka* and *vairagya* are the only two belongings in the shoulder bag of the wandering holy man. The quality of *viveka,* discrimination between the real and the unreal, is so valued and coveted by the wise ones that Swami Vivekananda took it for his monastic name.

A few words about the word "unreal" would be well-placed here, especially for all those who will decide to stay in the world but be not of the world, as the saying goes. When *Vedanta* declares the world to be "unreal," this refers to its changing nature. That is, the world is not unreal like water in a mirage; it is not merely illusory, as some immature beings might say. The world has a certain abidance, a temporary reality at least. But compared to *Brahman,* the unchanging Reality, it is unreal — passing, ephemeral, transitory, fleeting, unstable, unreliable. A firm conviction of this fact, a final and determinate decision in this regard, is mature *apavada.* From there it is only a matter of time before the precious six jewels verily fall into the hands of the sincere seeker.

The six jewels themselves are more than just proof that the early stages of discernment have been put into place; they are both qualities and practices at once. They fall into couples which work together, each to usher in the presence and maturity of the next. *Sama* and *Dama* are first, called inner peace and self-control. How is one possible of attainment without the other? Still, it is peace of mind which all wise beings seek, for from that quiescent platform of blissful balance all other attainments are possible; not otherwise. This marks the difference in quality between the words calm and peace, stillness and peace, quietude and peace. That is, there may be lapses in and short-comings to marital peace, familial peace, political peace, national or world peace, but spiritual peace harbors no such inconsistencies. That is why the word *"Shanti"* in *Sanskrit* is so widely used and understood. Everyone knows it pertains to a specifically spiritual peace, what Jesus Christ called a *"Peace which passeth all understanding."* This is the case with *sama* too, for it ushers in the possibility for a thorough self-control, namely *dama*.

The benefits of a human being who has controlled the self, consisting of body, senses, energy, moods, etc., are legion. *Dama*, then, is a quality seen in realized souls and advanced aspirants which acts as an influential example to humanity. It is as if a sign were held up saying "You, too, can control yourself." The fruits of such self-control are both obvious and inspiring. What is more, *dama* sets the stage for the next *Vedantic* jewel, *uparati*, called self-settledness or contentment. It and its partner, *titiksha*, are pivotal attributes of spiritual life which not only expand individual capacity for practice and attainment, but assure that no falling back into *maya* is ever going to take place again. For *titiksha* means forbearance. The conclusion is, then, that a man who is "content with any-thing," as Sri Krishna advises, and who can forbear all that the embodied condition can dish out and level at him, is literally self-made and perfected. He has no desire and can withstand pain and pleasure both. He can also thereby wait out and work towards annulment of all residues of *karma* still present on his mental record of reincarnation and rebirth.

Inner peace, self-control, contentment, and forbearance — and their requisites of discrimination and detachment — all of these make up what *Vedic* religion calls faith (*shraddha*). So these are the constituents of *Vedantic* faith. If any adherent of another religion approaches the nonviolent and contented *Vedantist* and asks, "What does your faith consist of, pray tell," the *Vedantist* can readily answer. In other words, true faith is not blind, nor does it waffle or change at the slightest threat, nor does it inflate with pride when presented, or react with anger when challenged. It does not attempt or need to proselytize or convert. It does not conflict with higher reason either — all of this because it contains inner peace, self-control, contentment and forbearance as eternal supports.

And faith has one other attribute that is coveted by all beings seeker higher truth. That is called concentration. And this type of concentration, called *samadhana*, is special; it is not of the regular kind, however helpful that may be at the outset of life. *Samadhana* is a rare variety of focus which allows the meditator to zero in on Reality alone, to the exclusion of all other points or principles. All competitors for the throne of total Freedom will be reduced to nothing in the light of that pure and unadulterated concentration that *samadhana* evinces. Besides, it stands on the ground of qualities like peace, contentment, and forbearance. What can disturb its base, then? Once put into operation, the contemplations which ensue will be deep and long, easily devoid of both shallowness and distraction. For instance, forbearance alone will stand concentration in good stead, for when hardships or obstacles are encountered in meditation, the inner traveler will simply fall back on his or her tolerance and endurance gleaned during the acquisition of the six jewels of *Vedanta*. This is the power and content of pure concentration.

As the chart under study reveals, there is still a fourth treasure to encounter. We have found that *viveka* is the first, *vairagya* the second, and the third treasure is sixfold, called the six jewels. These are precious gems kept inside the vast and gleaming caskets of the first two treasures. But the fourth treasure is dear indeed, incomparable and priceless. Its *Sanskrit* name, *Mumukshutvam*, contains reference to the word *"mukti"* within it, reflective of an emancipation that is most conducive to unbounded freedom.

Of all the words in any language, it is a fair bet that, given a choice, the *Vedantist*, the *Yogi*, the *Tantric*ist, the *Buddhist*, and many others would declare the word "Freedom" to be the most important. It is synonymous with words like Truth and Love. It is also Bliss, for Bliss in its unalloyed condition would not be possible without it. King Virochana's quote included on this chart deserves special mention here, for he likens the human being to a sovereign who has everything he could possibly want, need, or desire. His vast lands are freedom themselves, and the roads, paths, and byways which crisscross its verdant expanse are all of discrimination and dispassion. Further, he himself is the *Atman*, pure Sentience, and even if there should arise some unforeseeable dispute among the peoples of his land — body, senses, *prana*, mind, intellect, thought, and ego — his very own astute advisor is none other than Cosmic Intelligence (*Mahat*) itself. Possibly, this is what it feels like to be entirely free, with no possible fears or worries concerning interlopers like disease, decay, and death. For this freedom, *mumukshutvam*, is entirely spiritual in nature, having transcended any attachment to or belief in what is finite and changing, long ago.

With this brief mention and estimation of one of *Vedanta's* superlative systems, an initial idea of mankind's infinite potential can be perceived. Though there are many charts on *Vedantic* subjects and teachings in this book, the system of the Four Treasures and Six Jewels is most foundational, as if puts forth both a list of highest attainments essential to enlightenment, and casts a broad and scintillating light on the path and the practice. What is more, it outlines the goal as well.

And another note can be sounded here about the fourth treasure called *mumukshutvam*. It is defined as "a sincere desire for Freedom," inferring that Freedom itself is still to be realized. A way of explaining this surfaces in the example of the weak aspirations of the people of this day and time. It is a well-known fact that religious life and the attainment of spiritual qualities are not priorities among the masses today. Instead, a sort of half-conscious reliance upon the occasional occurrence of some passing dream or vision tends to make up the contemporary person's store of religious experience, accompanied by an on-again, off-again, luke warm sporadic practice. All of this forms a weak call to spiritual arms at best. In brief, a sincere echo of true freedom — what is referred to as a "clarion call" — has not yet sounded in the human heart, generally speaking.

And so the *rishis* of India clearly revealed what a true call to freedom consists of, which can only be trusted as authentic after attaining the first three treasures with their incomparable six jewels. In other words, there is no more pretending that "God spoke to me," or that "I heard an inner voice," as they say. Either you have the requisites or you don't, and they have been laid out from earliest times for all aspiring beings to see, assess, acknowledge, and attain.

To summate for now, the real test of spirituality is *sadhana*, spiritual practices. And the system of *Sadhanachatushtaya*, outlined here, leaves no doubt as to what is required in order to possess what it takes to gain enlightenment. True religion consists of this — not posturing, pretending, prevarication, or pontification. Even ethics and morals will not win this prize, what to speak of intellectualism alone. One, a group of people were in a boat crossing a river. One of them was bragging about his philosophical knowledge "Do you know the *Vedanta?*" he said to one man. "No," came the reply. "Do you know anything about *Yoga?*" he asked again. "No," the man admitted. Suddenly the boat began to sink and all the passengers started to jump into the river. The egoist cried out, "Help! I can't swim." The man he had been talking down too simply replied, "I may not know your *Vedanta* and *Yoga*, but I do know how to swim." Mere intellectualism devoid of hands on practice will not help one to navigate the problems of life, or save one in the end from the threat of death.

We have now studied two systems of Indian thought which prescribe ways of qualifying oneself for spiritual life. The Seven Qualifications of a Tantric Aspirant and the Four Treasures and Six Jewels of Vedanta epitomize the essential requirements for this most crucial refinement process, which is missing in so many aspirants. Lack of qualification stymies one in reaching the higher levels of spiritual attainment, such as *samadhi*. Mention of *samadhi* naturally brings up the famous system called *Yoga*, more specifically *Raja Yoga*, or *Patanjala*, also termed *Ashtanga Yoga*, the Eight-limbed *Yoga*. Though more will be said about this *darshana* later, the next chart shows the tree of *Yoga* with its eight limbs and crucial roots — the *Yamas* and *Niyamas*, being our present concern.

The Eight Limbs of Patanjali's Yoga

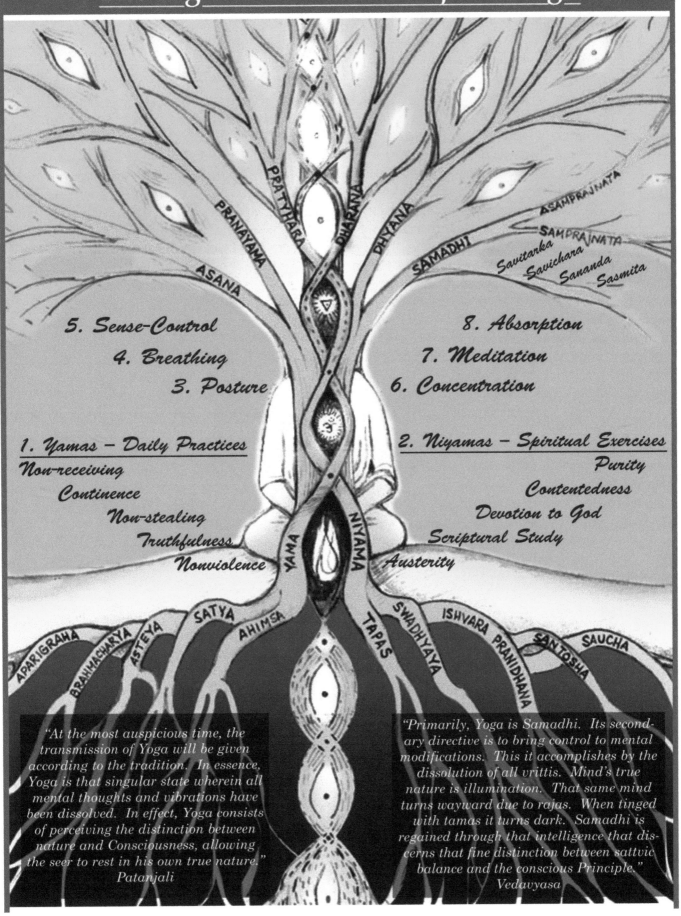

ASAMPRAJNATA

SAMPRAJNATA

Savitarka *Savichara* *Sananda* *Sasmita*

PRATYHARA
DHARANA
DHYANA
SAMADHI
PRANAYAMA
ASANA

5. *Sense-Control*

4. *Breathing*

3. *Posture*

8. *Absorption*

7. *Meditation*

6. *Concentration*

1. *Yamas – Daily Practices*

Non-receiving

Continence

Non-stealing

Truthfulness

Nonviolence

2. *Niyamas – Spiritual Exercises*

Purity

Contentedness

Devotion to God

Scriptural Study

Austerity

YAMA

NIYAMA

APARIGRAHA BRAHMACHARYA ASTEYA SATYA AHIMSA TAPAS SWADHYAYA ISHVARA PRANIDHANA SANTOSHA SAUCHA

"At the most auspicious time, the transmission of Yoga will be given according to the tradition. In essence, Yoga is that singular state wherein all mental thoughts and vibrations have been dissolved. In effect, Yoga consists of perceiving the distinction between nature and Consciousness, allowing the seer to rest in his own true nature."
Patanjali

"Primarily, Yoga is Samadhi. Its secondary directive is to bring control to mental modifications. This it accomplishes by the dissolution of all vrittis. Mind's true nature is illumination. That same mind turns wayward due to rajas. When tinged with tamas it turns dark. Samadhi is regained through that intelligence that discerns that fine distinction between sattvic balance and the conscious Principle."
Vedavyasa

Possibly of all the lists regarding the early qualification of the student for authentic spiritual life, Patanjali's *yamas* and *niyamas* are best known. Ironically, however, they are also the most overlooked list of requisites. In this day and time this is due to the penchant of living beings to focus on the body, and on matter/objects over and above every other concern. Perhaps Sri Ramakrishna's observation keys into this unfortunate fact, citing the age we are in. The Great Master states: *"In this age, the Kali Yuga, man's life is wholly dependent upon food."* This present age may be the most technologically advanced we have seen, but it is also the most spiritually benighted one as well. Food faddism and catering to the body is practically a religion in itself, and has more devout adherents than any religion of the past has ever seen.

How this relates to *Raja Yoga darshana* is instanced in the fact that many aspirants entirely forego the important *yamas* and *niyamas* and head straight for the third limb of *asana*, physical postures. But the Father of *Raja Yoga*, Patanjali, laid out the divine plan in a masterful way, placing for our initial consideration and practice some ten requisites designed to prepare the human instrument — what *Vedanta* calls the psycho/physical being — for spiritual heights yet to come. In this regard, another story by Ramakrishna Paramahamsa can be told, to illustrate the import of preparation.

Once, there was a man who, upon walking through a well-to-do neighborhood, saw a rooftop that would afford a beautiful view. Desiring to climb on top of the house, he began to search for a way of doing so. But he soon found out that there were many obstacles. The property was gated, so he needed to contact the owner for permission for his strange request. After that, he found that the roof was exceedingly steep, and one could easily lose his footing. So he consulted a climber who had experience in these matters. The climber then had to teach him the use of traction devices and ropes and pulleys, which took more time. Eventually he was ready for the ascent. Probably, by this time, the owner had changed his mind and the police were on the scene.

This story explains the difficulty of approaching an undertaking without the proper method, teacher, experience, and expertise — plus patience. The upper limbs of *Yoga* can be likened to this steep roof, and the *yamas* and *niyamas* to the basics of climbing and the permission of the teacher to ascend. Those who think they can jump steps on this particular journey and still court success have another thing coming down the line. Falls from the path of *Yoga* are countless, while successful ascents to the upper reaches of *samadhi* are rare indeed. With a brief exposition on the *yamas* and *niyamas*, perhaps this fact and its import will be rendered additionally clear.

The bottom half of the chart presently under scrutiny shows the five *yamas* and the five *niyamas* as the roots of the tree of *Yoga*. They are struck and run deep in the soil of root *shakti* power, Mother *Kundalini's* subterranean force of pure dynamism. A closer look shows them to be the principles of a thoroughly practical spirituality, five of them covering the subject of ethical observances and five steeped in the realm of daily practice.

Namely, the *yamas* are *ahimsa* (nonviolence), *satya* (truthfulness), *asteya* (noncovetousness), moderation (*brahmachari*), and nonreceiving (*aparigraha*). The *niyamas* are *tapas* (austerities), *svadhyaya* (study of scripture), *ishvara-pranidhana* (devotion to God), *santosha* (contentedness), and *saucha* (purity). These ten are both principles and practices simultaneously, and work together to fashion the moral life of a beginner into a strong foundation for spiritual advancement. These two sets of quintuplets represent the infant stage of *Yoga*. They are crucial to success in spiritual life, forming the basis upon which succeeding limbs can thrive. In a sense, these are the nutrients in the soil of the soul which nourish the roots of formal meditation posture and the flow of life force (*prana*).

To enter into *Yogic* practice without first learning and implementing these prerequisites, what to speak of mastering them, is foolhardy. What is being advised, then, is that a student who would qualify for the practice of *Yoga* must be established in nonviolence or nonharming of living things, attached to Truth in all its moral, scriptural, and nondual forms, free of coveting the possessions of others, pure in physical relations, and unattached to objects of the senses. Via practice, the potential *yogi* and *yogini* will also undergo healthy austerities that strengthen body, expand the mind, ennoble the spirit. They will study daily with a *guru* sporting a view to comprehend the revealed scriptures, maintain inner and outer cleanliness, strive for peace and equanimity, and offer heartfelt devotions to God with form. Further, if the student, being sincere and devout, perseveres in the practice of these ten golden rules of *Yoga* with resolve and alacrity, certain results will emerge.

In relation to the five *yamas,* and according to Patanjali:

From the steady stance of nonviolence in thought, word, and deed proceeds the cessation of all enmities in the *yogi*'s presence, whether springing from animals, humans, and from ones own mind.

By maintaining truthfulness, all *karmas* will fructify, carrying with them the highest and most beneficial results.

By refusing to give in to the temptation of taking what belongs to others springs forth the receiving of all wealth from the Goddess of Wealth Herself, as well as the knowledge of how best to utilize said abundance.

By sublimating sexual energy instead of squandering it, the *yogi* stores up great power for the realization of the Self.

And through nonattachment to goods, wealth, and gifts, the *yogi* gains access to a heretofore hidden power of memory that confers the knowledge of past lifetimes. These ultimate fruits of *yama* practice will be discussed in greater length hereafter.

As for the resultant fruits of *niyama* practice, they are:

By undergoing austerities, the practitioner of *yoga* destroys impurities that persist in the mind, thus paving the way to illumination of mind while freeing up any restricted flow of *prana* that causes illness in the body.

By undergoing study of scriptures with an enlightened preceptor, all previously transmitted instructions along the spiritual path come to fruition, and the *mantra* given at the time of initiation successfully reveals the vision of ones chosen deity — the *Ishtam.*

When outer and inner purity is achieved and maintained, a wonderful freedom from bodily concerns and detachment from matter occurs, resulting in general overall cheerfulness and the ability to concentrate.

When the desire for contentment is strengthened, a happiness of the lasting variety visits the mind, heralding the advent of that state of Peace, Peace, Peace so valued by spiritual luminaries.

Finally, and last but far from least, is possibly the most important prerequisite of all, devotion to *Ishvara,* which when practiced and achieved, leads to the ultimate fruit of *Yoga,* called *samadhi.*

Placed in a prominent position among the daily observances in *Yogic* practice, *ahimsa* is not only prescribed, it is also popular among many noble-minded people of the day. This positive principle has both a moral and an absolute value, the former being associated with demonstrating to the world the efficacy and preferability of peaceful living (free of karmas), while the latter applies on the level of realization and transcendence. About the moral implications, much has been written and spoken on the subject. Mahatma Gandhi, for instance, has successfully demonstrated the dynamics of *ahimsa* in recent times before the eyes of the world. Suffice to say that it is far past time for human beings to learn the art of nonviolence with regard to one another — as individuals aspiring for fulfillment, as human beings attempting successful cohabitation of the planet, and as nations striving for peaceful coexistence free of imperious trespass and intransigent domination.

Whereas it must be admitted that struggle and strife is as much a part of life on earth as peace and well-being, the embodied being must not use this as a convenient excuse to fall from the triple ideal of honesty, justice, and meritorious action. Deceit, injustice, and wrong doing form the road to ruin, and learning this lesson through trial and error demands a dear price in terms of human suffering. Once learned, however, the lesson must become an inherent and inseparable part of our very being, and one with its moral fabric.

And here is where *ahimsa*, on the level of the prerequisites in *Yoga*, has its prime efficacy. As so often noted, nonviolence must be of thought, word, and deed, rather than restricted only to ones actions. Though it is good to restrain oneself so as not to commit physical harm on others, the root of anger still lies untended and unresolved in the mind's subtle regions. It comes forth in our daily language, first of all. Though many people refrain from actually committing harm, their words often perpetrate an unending string of harm and abuse. This verbal vilification is a definite type of violence which goes unchecked for the most part, and behind it often lies the intention to hurt, to harm, to aggravate, to belittle, to manipulate, etc. The *yogi* or *yogini* practicing *ahimsa* is impervious to this and other forms of harmful behavior while remaining firm in their vow to not harm others in any way. As Sri Ramakrishna states, "*When a thunderbolt hits a house, the heavy things inside may not be affected, but the windowpanes rattle.*" This means that the worldliness, abusive behavior, and fowl language found rampant in the conventional world may strike the eardrums, but they cannot shake the internal attributes of a true devotee of God, or deter him or her from the set course of nonviolence.

With this in mind, it becomes obvious that at the root of successful nonviolence — and subtler than it ramifications regarding the word or the deed — is peaceful thought, or freedom from violence within the thinking process. A peaceful mind gives rise to positive thinking, which in turn, when maintained for some length of time, allows for an actual peaceful existence free of the encroachments of detrimental thought forms. For, negative thoughts, called *aklista vrittis* by the Father of *Yoga*, store up erratic energy which then forms undesirable impressions in the subconscious mind. These impressions, called *samskaras* in *Sanskrit*, if left unresolved, lead to complexes of *samskaras* (*samskaraskandhas*) which then manifest as aberrant acts of violence and various atrocities. Thus, the way out of this particular hell is not via a mere moral stance of "I will not do bad acts," but rather a complete and thorough cleansing of the mental apparatus resulting in purification of the mind on all its levels. This is facilitated by spiritual practice, called *sadhana* in *Yoga*, and here is where *ahimsa*, and all other preliminaries to an enlightened state of mind, transcend mere ethical considerations and take their rightful place as purificatory mechanisms which transform rather than hide or cover up.

Therefore, beyond the moral implications of the practice of nonviolence, transcendent and purifying even of its triune levels of thought, word, and deed, and even more important than its effects in social life, are the spiritual implications and benefits of this timeless quality. Since the world consists of the many pairs of opposites that underlie its very appearance as a supposed reality, it is foolish and fanciful to think that there will ever be an end to violence on earth. This being the case, the aspirant, through intense spiritual self-effort leading to enlightenment, goes beyond the station of a dreamer, an altruist, or a social reformer, and realizes Truth based upon Absolute Reality alone.

It is here that *ahimsa* reveals its true colors, its unique intensity, for what was once a practice engaged in for personal and social betterment now transforms into an internal instrument which affords a view of the nature of Reality Itself. That view is of nondual implications which reveals that *ahimsa*, in reality, is perfect freedom from fear, based upon the fact that there is no arbiter, no enemy, and actually no second person, place, or thing through which threat or harm can occur. This is not just the ultimate perspective; it is the ultimate protection as well, for the singular fact emerges that "seeing other" — perceiving difference where none should exist in the first place — was the tool of trouble, tension, torsion and terror all along. Thus it is that the ancient *Upanishads* state, "*Those who recognize only difference and distinction here, and thereby cause a rift in consciousness by constantly perceiving this and that, here and there, they go through repeated births and deaths in ignorance. There is no peace for them.*"

Living beings must therefore implement *ahimsa* into life itself. This is where *ahimsa* as a daily observance is helpful. It is a strange fact that, due to the influence of *Maya*, beings cannot see the end in view. Therefore, they must utilize the *yamas* and *niyamas* — the tools of the trade of Truth — until deeper realization dawns. One cannot project oneself hopefully into enlightenment, but must awaken there via direct experience based upon self-effort. Grace will dawn thereby, and nonviolence will become more than a hope, an effort, or a technique for bettering life on earth. It will stand out as the truth of Oneness that boldly proclaims the essential oneness of all creation, and the absolute union in identity of the apparently individualized soul with Supreme Reality.

The second *yama*, truthfulness, just like the freedom from violent thoughts and actions, has its relative and absolute levels of operation as well. As a *yama*, a day to day observance, its presence graces everyday conversations and activities, while its absence turns the same into *karma*-producing, pain-bearing mechanisms. Like *ahimsa*, truth is applicable to thought, word, and deed and, in fact, truth and *ahimsa* are one and the same. For anything that does not hold up to truth is antagonistic to human existence and is therefore violent in nature. In other words, all that is violent, committed with mind, speech, or body, is devoid of truth's sanction.

Yet, this brings up the classic question, the ultimate dilemma. If truth cannot sanction any form of violence, then what about the natural defense of a nation against invaders, or the protection from immediate violence that a man must provide for his family? Further, even the scriptures admit to violence and the bending of the truth, like in Sri Krishna's exhortation to Arjuna to fight in the great war of *Kurukshetra*. It may be stated here that truth, in its ultimate form, is transcendent of these situations. For instance, we must remember that Sri Krishna did everything possible to avoid the war between the Pandava and Kaurava clans. His encouragement of Arjuna to fight came only after all else was decided and no other recourse was left. Even then His decree was given in the face of a potential cowardice that might have allowed the evil Kaurava clan to win the day and plunge the earth into a dark age again. It was a matter of proper and obvious choice, then. Truth was already well out the door, abandoned by the evil doers who commanded the situation. And most importantly, and often overlooked, was the fact that Sri Krishna had access to ultimate Truth all along, and knew what was to happen by the will of the Lord, since the end of an age was approaching.

All of this brings out truth's unique stature and design. It is ultimately beyond both right and wrong, for many an apparently positive situation in this day and age has for its underpinnings a horrible set of lies, while oft times the seemingly worst sets of circumstances, painful to the pampered sensibilities of mankind, are really being played out for the sake of honesty and integrity. Therefore, fools and children talk about "my truth" and "your truth." There is only one Truth, and human beings must raise their ideals and efforts to the highest level to perceive It. Thus, even in the practice phase, *satya* provides the backbone to *Yoga*, without which no union with God — the epitome of Truth Absolute — will ever take place. Thus does the Great Master say that, *"Even if one follows only truth and no other practice, he will reach God, for truth is the austerity of the age."*

As was declared earlier, on the *yama* level, *satya* means telling no lies, refraining from wrong doing, thinking no untoward thoughts. This, as a day to day practice, trains the mind, counsels and ego, and hones the intellect so that higher truth can eventually come into view. Otherwise, man resides comfortably but uneasily in the dim, opaque land of mundane human convention, or lives a life based upon false premises and outright lies. *"An elephant's tusks must come out,"* states Sri Ramakrishna, *"but they must not turn and go back in."* He is referring to the predicament of a rogue elephant who has been driven mad by a returning circular tusk piercing into its skull bone, causing it to run amuck and kill due to the intense pain. The metaphor is as effective and sobering as the vision it conjures up. Man becomes as violent and bestial as a mad elephant running rampant when truth is forsaken. This fact can be verified everyday by merely picking up a newspaper.

But sweet, clear, and refreshing is the advent of ultimate Truth from on high. After the practice of truthfulness has been adhered to, the scene is set for God-realization. The Lord's very atmosphere, the *"House in which He dwelleth,"* is built upon Truth. This Truth is nondual, and it has for its foundation knowledge and wisdom. They who seek and find the twin tiers of knowledge and wisdom, moving from secular knowledge to scriptural knowledge, and from that to higher wisdom via direct experience, understand the nature of Truth. All others only repeat the word like a parrot.

The back to back principles of *ahimsa* and *satya* are placed into test mode in the case of the remaining three *yamas*. Via the practice of *asteya*, noncoveting of others' goods or possessions, man learns not to take what does not belong to him. This may seem to be a very obvious lesson, but besides the presence of greed in the human mind, even deeper shades of *asteya* are eventually revealed to him, revealing that he need not covet anything, nor want for anything. This is because *asteya* is akin to the deeper qualities of *vairagya*, detachment, and *tyaga*, renunciation. This secret is hidden from most novitiates and practitioners, because they are narrowly focused at first upon the moral scope of fundamental practice and fail to comprehend the deeper implications. Perhaps they did not take a *guru*, and so do not benefit from the profound experience available to them there.

Whatever the case may be, refraining from stealing, and also from plotting to gain by stealth, is an early exercise in ethics that can only result in awakenings applicable to a gradually maturing spiritual life, wherein rewards such as contentment, peace of mind, bliss, and devotion for the Lord transform human nature gradually, if not completely, and lead naturally to complete nonattachment. Here, noncoveting transfigures into non-desiring, and non-desiring mystically transforms into the deep-rooted urge of *sharanagata*, selfless sacrifice — to give away all and everything to others in the service of God. Marvelously, then, somewhere along that veiled inner pathway, discrimination dawns, detachment ripens and matures, and renunciation bursts upon the scene, proclaiming nobly, "This is the true nature of mankind, free and unencumbered!"

Given this profound connection of *asteya* with renunciation, the authentic luminaries do not at all underestimate or undervalue this basic and simple *yama*. In the very first *sloka* of the *Ishavasyopanisad* is written, "*Whatever there is in this changeful universe, all is permeated by and contained in Brahman. By renunciation of the world do thou become free. Do not covet the wealth of any being.*" They knew, unlike ordinary souls who have forgotten, that true existence is based upon generosity and giving, that it proceeds via honesty and fairness, and that it reaches culmination through renunciation of all that is temporal and transient. Thus, those victorious ones of ancient times, called *rishis*, stated conclusively, "*Having realized this Self, the illumined give up the desire for sons, the desire for wealth, the desire for the worlds, and lead the life of religious mendicants.*" This "giving up," which is ennobling rather than unnerving, salubrious rather than slavish, is the supreme renunciation that has its humble but vital beginnings with *asteya*, the simple practice of "*hands off,*" to quote Swami Vivekananda.

To put it in another way, and relative to basic practice, taking to the self flies in the face of a divinely intentioned life. To give is the law of life, and this sets mankind apart from the other occupants of the material loka, the *Bhurloka* or *Bhutakasha* (see chart on page 327), many of whom follow the natural law of balance via beneficial exchange and mutual protection anyway. For instance, dogs fight if table scraps are thrown among them, but crows often call out to others of their kind to come share in the bounty. But even this way of action that both man and animals pursue is ultimately counterproductive, is not conducive to a divine life and its singular way. Mankind, by now, thousands of years into evolution, should have long since graduated to the ideal station where giving away replaces gathering, hoarding, and guarding. Based upon this tendency of selfish clinging inherent in the problem of covetousness, nations, organizations, even friends and family members "*...turn each other out for the sake of a few coins or a clod of earth,*" to quote the Holy Mother, Sri Sarada Devi. It is unconscionable.

But here is where the practices of *satya* and *ahimsa* are put to the test by the aspiring student of *Yoga*. Such a being realizes that taking from others is a type of violence. And to convince others to give out of personal desire or individual greed is a form of lying. Even receiving from others by way of presents or gifts, called *parigraha*, is potentially riddled with problems, as will be seen relative to the fifth *yama*, *aparigraha*, to be explored later. Thus, all the *yamas*, and surely the *niyamas*, are intrinsically connected. Taken cohesively they can be counted upon to support one another in a finely tuned system leading to spiritual perfection, but betrayal of even one of these ten constituents will cause the downfall of ones entire *yogic* practice, along with its excellent lifestyle and its radiant consummation in *samadhi*. This reveals, strikingly, both the innate dependence of the *yamas* and *niyamas* upon each other, and the crucial importance of all of them to *Yoga* in general.

Observing the genius of Patanjali's system, then, what is to be said for those who, for the sake of monetary gain, health, and "feeling good," reduce the ennobling system of authentic *Yoga* to a regimen of mere postures and breathing exercises; or of those who, having the opportunity of introducing the eight-limbed *Yoga* to beginning practitioners, fail to present the *yamas* and *niyamas* first as prerequisite practices before *asana* and *pranayam* are even mentioned? As a result, however, and judging by the "sweaty" climate of so-called *Yoga* in the West in present times, the *Patanjala* system, like so many other *darshanas* of India before it, is fading away before it gets a chance to offer the profound and beneficial merit that it contains. If this system were adhered to according to traditional form, the *yama* of *asteya* would play a huge part in ushering in purity of mind, the kind of which is to be found in the fourth *yama*, *Brahmacharya*.

A traditional rendering of the practice of *brahmacharya*, so crucial to *yoga* practice, would have to include in its regimen periods of abstinence from sexual activity. In a materialistic and pleasure oriented society, this will not be a popular idea. Possibly this is one reason why the *yamas* and *niyamas* are ignored by present day *hatha yoga* adherents, and by beings futilely seeking quick success in spiritual life, free of properly oriented self-effort. The problem here is threefold, the first being worldliness, the second being impure mind, and the third being habit. To free oneself in the spiritual sense is to refrain from all of these insidious inhibitors, and in order to accomplish that, mundane convention, perverse thinking and habitual laziness will have to go.

Here, and relative to *brahmacharya*, the very force that potentially corrupts a man is the same force that will rouse and free him. That is, the poison present in the primal sexual force in terms of lust, anger, power, and the like is actually superimposed over it by the human mind. This false attribution is the work of the three aforementioned problems above. In short, raised in a worldly setting devoid of spiritual teachings like the *yamas* and *niyamas*, mankind is encouraged to engage, compete, dominate, and dictate, and thus becomes imbued with a mind distorted by unbridled passions and obsessed with the darksome feelings arising from them (see chart on page 247, 249). This condition, a form of mental illness that is quietly permitted by society, becomes habitual, the result being a world founded on, oriented towards, and operating under the binding laws of root ignorance (*avidya*). It does not stop here. This deluded and precarious existence forms the basis for *Samsara* — cyclic rounds of birth and death in ignorance of ones true Self, *Atman*. Thus, by way of detrimental preoccupation, as Sri Ramakrishna states, *"Human beings resemble the camel who eats thorny bushes all the time, even though its gums bleed painfully and profusely."*

With a purified mental process, however, the base component present in the sexual force, if it be there to begin with, can be transformed and turned for higher purposes. Examples of this refined power are seen in the good children of pious parents, the great works of fine artists, the original discoveries of scientific minds, and other forms of pure genius. Where the sexual energy is completely sublimated, the result is seen in the wondrous workings and teachings of the sages, seers, saints and saviors of the various religious traditions of the world. Thus, there is no need to shut down the primal force in living beings, but rather a need to refine it and use it for life's higher purposes, resulting in great benefit for all.

However, the *yama* of *brahmacharya* should not be relegated only to sexuality and its concerns. This practice is really about fidelity to a single purpose, in this case, desire for enlightenment. Thus, *brahmacharya* is both a harbinger and a stabilizer of that rare and sought after quality of *Ishta-nistha*, devotion to a single and cherished "Chosen Ideal." Abstinence from sexual activity, especially at a young age, allows for the building up of spiritual power that will later be utilized in achieving such great attainments.

Many of the ancient *rishis* and other great seers of Truth were married and had families. *Brahmacharya* was valued by them as a means to sublimate and refine human potential, even in the context of family life. The misnomer that only those who retain lifelong celibacy can achieve liberation is therefore disproved, as stated by Lord Kapila in his *Tattva Samasa Sutras*. In this way, all sense of superiority adopted by anyone practicing celibacy is false and prideful. On the other hand, those who hedonistically engage in sensual pastimes, ignoring and wasting the potential for physical, mental, and spiritual purification residing in them, are foolish and headstrong. In short, the practice of *brahmacharya*, rightly guided, is enjoined by the wise as a practice suitable and beneficial for all beings, but it is not meant to be a lifetime vow for the many. In the same way that a village dog, rolling in the ashes of the holy fire, does not become holy thereby, similarly, adherence to abstinence from sexual activity alone does not conduce to spiritual perfection. Grace, combined with sincerity and self-effort, is the consummate formula for enlightenment, generally speaking. All other practices are meant as aids, and as such must be implemented to the extent that they lead to that ultimate goal.

The practice of *brahmacharya* is best engaged in with a mind bent on attaining purity. The attainment of purity, especially where the mind is concerned, cannot be understated. Since purity, *saucha*, is one of the *niyamas*, it will be dealt with later. But suffice to say that the connection between *brahmacharya* and *saucha* is a very close one. Basically, *brahmacharya* is akin to and conducive of purity, and the latter would not be fully attainable if not for it. For, essentially, the aspirant needs very much to feel devotion to one Ideal. This singular devotion, the kind of which a child feels for its parents, a married women feels for her husband, and a young lover feels for his paramour, is galvanizing, inspiring, all-attracting, and, ultimately purifying. There is no force quite like it in human life. It is both a product of and a precursor to the divine quality of Divine Love, Love of God first and foremost. It is seen, then, that the boundless estate of God's Love is built upon the corner stones and support beams of such qualities as purity and devotion, which in turn owe their presence and stability to the foundational concrete slabs of *yama* and *niyama*.

Some have said that the seemingly enigmatic practice of *aparigraha*, the nonreceiving of gifts, is really an ancient observance undertaken by beings invested with the vows of nonownership and renunciation. The implication is that, nowadays, it is obsolete, and thereby need not be taken seriously. This would certainly agree with the preferences of most human beings today, especially around that time of year called Christmas. But that aside for now, this view, prematurely accepted, diminishes the potency of *Yoga* in general and flies in the face of traditional interpretations of *Yoga* coming from the likes of Vedavyas and other revered commentators of *Patanjala*. The practice of *aparigraha* is crucial, then, for both its reasons and its results are thoroughly cogent and fully in harmony with the overall tenets of *Yoga*.

Before proceeding to explore *aparigraha*, it can be said that every *yama* studied previously to this point is laced strongly, through and through, with detachment and renunciation. *Ahimsa* wants you to give up violence; *satya* asks you to forsake falsehood; *asteya* demands that you not desire the wealth or possessions of others; and *brahmacharya* asks you to sacrifice both the pleasure of sexual relations and your fealty to a host of secondary ideals. It is all a giving up and letting go, then, all for the sake of spiritual life and its highly prized and advised attainments.

Aparigraha is not different in this respect either, for it seeks to free one by simplifying life. The many seductive forces that living beings succumb to in this life — forces of nature, of ego, of other beings, of cosmic powers — all come to bear on life and mind due to accepting gifts and favors. Opening to these and other forces to receive what is desired leaves one defenseless against energies that are both tainted and binding. And it is here that *asteya* and *aparigraha* become a team of *yogic* helpers. The former leads the practitioner to freedom by ensuring that he does not seek after what belongs to others, and the latter keeps him free by making sure that he does not even accept what is given, especially if it be saturated with desire and overshadowed with shades of secret motive, as most gifts usually are. In this way, beings bind themselves; no one else does that to them. Whether they are lured, encouraged, driven by desire, or are even forced into a trap, they undertake these wayward routes by their own naive or selfish design. Thankfully, they can also free themselves when any particular bondage becomes unbearable.

But the bait that throws the intricate mechanism of mental immurement into motion is most always some acquirement, some possession, some gain — whether ill-gotten or freely given — it makes little difference. And deeper of note, subtler by far: it is not the thing itself that binds, but the association with it. And thus comes the need for and the benefit of *aparigraha*, which keeps the wiser arm from impulsively extending, closes the grasping palm, and slaps the impetuous hand that would only grasp at endless troubles.

To understand the subtleties of this is to perceive the fine nature of energy. Energy is of various types, but the one that most directly pertains here is of subtle, often devious design. Of itself it is neither good nor bad, positive nor negative, but as a vehicle for transferring force and influence from one party to another, it is very powerful. Motive, intention, desire — these are some of the subtle mechanisms through which this energy passes, taking on the specific vibration there and transferring it into the next point of arrival. In the force of motive, intention, or desire, there resides such selfish ends as ill-will, desire for manipulation, or even just a mere curiosity for outcomes. In this way, an offering or gift, whether it be an object, a wish, or a boon, is not the real stumbling block. Rather, it is the energy tied to it that binds, and this is where ordinary souls fall foolishly into cycles of trouble and its contribution to *karmic* accrual (see charts on pages 184, 210, 213).

To explain this enigma better, the example of food can be used. By the time food comes to the mouth it has already seen several shades and levels of energy. First, it has defects in it from lack of nutrients in the soil, and perhaps from scarcity of water as it was growing and forming. Perhaps the farmer sprayed it with poisons, and insects invaded it nonetheless. Then, it is imbued with questionable energy from the hand that picked it. At the market or processing plant, many hands touched it and it got subjected to various dyes, chemicals, germs, and other contaminants. Then it passed through the hands of the preparer and cook, and the establishment that offered it for sale and consumption. Finally, the server carried it to the table, and other beings stared at it before it was taken into the mouth to be eaten (see chart on page 423). Along this winding and hardly winsome way, then, so many types of energies have entered into it, so many vibrations have passed through it. Whatever mood the various people who saw or handled it were in at the time, affected its makeup. It is hardly difficult to comprehend, then, why sensitive, spiritual people bless their food before taking it. Some may think that it is out of gratitude to God that this is done, but does God need to be thanked? God is the food, the partaker of the food, the act of taking the food, the sustaining power in the food, and even the articles on which the food is placed. Does God thank God for feeding God? This is all well and good, if that is what is wanted. But the deeper need and purpose is in the acts of purification, for food carries with it all power for satisfying or disappointing, for replenishing or for depleting, for invigorating or for devitalizing, for healing or for rendering ill — even for creating anew and destroying as well.

With this example given, one can more completely comprehend the nature of the energy that attends upon food, objects, gifts, and the many other things that are transferred from being to being. And here is where the close discrimination of a spiritual aspirant saves and protects him or her from the many dangers associated with such acts and objects. If a gift is given by one person to another, and the giving is tainted by a desire or motivation that is bent upon gaining favor, controlling, manipulating, or binding the person to some sort of personal or individual allegiance or obligation, all for some highly desired selfish end, then the whole affair is tainted and an entire cycle of repercussive *karmas* are set into motion. This occurs in contemporary politics all of the time, for instance, and is even accepted across the board as the thing to do. What to speak of political putrefaction, friends and neighbors bind each other with a thousand invisible bonds of *karma* into unseen traps of motive-based inclination all the time. Relatives and family indulge and engage in this often insidious transference of motive-based energy continually, plying the trade of tit for tat and this for that, all in the name of making an impression, gaining a favor, or getting something in return.

Ironically, all rue the many sins and transgressions that occur in human society that are obvious, grievous, and there on the surface for all to see and condemn, but the personal and ongoing sin of "quid pro quo" is conveniently overlooked. For, if it were not, a strange sense of lack would creep over people's minds and an unwanted hole would get bored into the very heart of social custom —

a fearsome void spreading over the mountain of conventional living, dealing a brutal blow to the insidious religion of materialism. What is most lamentable in all this, is that few beings involved in life ever see the simple solution for the mind's pervasive but unnecessary sense of loss. But those who are detached, renounced, and surrendered to God, they joyfully see, and their great joy is due to that auspicious day when they took to *yogic* practice and came to fully understand the *yama* of *aparigraha* — nonreceiving of gifts.

To conclude the teaching of *aparigraha*, many people talk about the power of "Yes" in this day and age, but few comprehend the power of "No." "No," said the political candidate, rejecting a bribe and keeping his integrity intact. "No," said the young beauty to the rogue, narrowly escaping a life of dire servitude. "No," exclaimed the employee to the manipulative boss, accepting less money over dishonest jobs and wages. "No," said the nephew to the distant uncle, remaining free of future obligations. The peoples of the world, on both sides of the moral fence, are all too familiar with these tedious scenes and dangerous situations. The practice of *aparigraha* means "No" on many levels, and thus wisely helps one to escape the potential sufferings inherent in human interactions. And what of the power of "Yes" — the free offerings, motiveless gifts, unselfish acts of giving? If there truly be such marvels, they, too, are to be examined for the energy contained within them. And the practices of *ahimsa*, *satya*, *asteya*, *brahmacharya*, and *aparigraha*, will assist adeptly in such crucial internal examinations.

With the five *yamas* presented, making up the very first limb of *Raja Yoga*, the *niyamas* can be considered. As was stated, whereas the *yamas* are daily observances which the spiritual aspirant needs to maintain, the *niyamas* are purificatory practices which will connect the seeker to deeper levels of *yogic* attainment. As the chart under study illustrates, the *niyamas*, making up the second limb of *Raja Yoga*, consist of *tapas* (austerity), *svadhyaya* (study of scriptures), *ishvara-pranidhana* (devotion to God), *santosha* (contentedness), and *saucha* (purity). Importantly, Patanjali himself has indicated three of these as the makeup of the original *Kriya Yoga* system, a special practice whereby the inner spiritual power inherent in the human being is awakened and caused to ascend towards the realm of enlightenment. Therefore, the first three *niyamas* take on great import at this second phase of *Yoga*, and will be taken up as a trio for study.

As has been mentioned already, the *Ashtanga Yoga* System, called *Patanjala*, *Raja Yoga*, or just *Yoga* proper, consists of eight limbs of advancement which include ten prerequisite practices and observances that are crucial for ongoing spiritual progress. Unfortunately, these requisites are overlooked by most students, both by way of acknowledgement and practice. Even many of those calling themselves *Yoga* teachers ignore or pass over these crucial ten in their haste to indulge in and teach a series of body-oriented exercises called *asanas* which are not even a part of Patanjali's original *Yoga*. What is *Yoga*, then?

"Yoga is samadhi," states Vedavyasa, the Father of *Vedanta* and the quintessential commentator on *Yoga*, and by this he does not mean *samadhi* of the body — that aesthetic pleasure-based *pranic* high that proceeds from the daily winding up of the physical frame and nervous system through exercises. Body attachment is one of the first obstacles to overcome in *Yoga*, and in any authentic spiritual path. If one wants to speak purely in terms of the health of the body, that is referred to in the *Yoga* Sutras in conjunction with overcoming the distraction *(vikshepa)* of *vyadhi* (disease), imbalance in the *dhatus* (blood, flesh, bones, air, bile, phlegm, etc.), in the *rasas* (hormones, gastric and other fluids) and in the *karanas* (active, cognitive senses and the mind). The means of overcoming *vyadhi* and other *vikshepas* is ultimately through the powers of the mind, because all problems have their origin therein, including diseases (see charts on pages 233, 235). Proper diet, moderate exercise, and moral living are complements to *yogic* attainment, whereas body-orientation is a detriment.

Patanjali proceeds to outline his regimen of *yogic* purification not based upon physical exercises, then, but aimed along the lines of meditation upon the twenty-four *alambanas*, or universal factors. This involves scrutinizing the sixteen *visheshas* (five elements, five active senses, five cognitive senses and mind), the subtler *avisheshas* (*tanmatras* and ego) the *Mahat* (Cosmic Mind), and *Prakriti* (manifest and unmanifest nature) with an eye to knowing them, detaching from them, and thus transcending their influence to gain *kaivalya*, spiritual liberation. Nowhere in his great system is there provision or allowance made for exercises that risk the danger of attachment to the physical condition, especially given that this gives rise to attendant dangers as well.

In modern times, human beings are predominantly sense-oriented and worldly-minded. This is due mainly to two factors: the decline of higher awareness and the beneficial practices that reveal the spiritual nature of existence; and the burgeoning increase of opportunities for material gain that quite often only foster desire, greed, and selfish clinging. This ease of acquisition, plus an aversion to intense self-effort, contribute to that habit of stagnation or spiritual complacency which duly overwhelms the mind, dulls the nervous system, and inflicts life with a numbing spiritual paralysis. If any regimen for intellectual or spiritual progress is instituted by society, it is one based on catering to the body, and even here the motivation is not so much to benefit the human condition as to attract a following, achieve personal monetary success, and to increase ones possessions and the pleasures they bring.

There is a way out of the prison house of desire, attachment, complacency, and the suffering that arises from them. To insure that life vibrates with balance and equipoise, with the ability to control the negative propensities and increase the positive spiritual potential of the human condition, Eastern philosophy proclaims the practice of *Yoga* with its many tools and techniques. Among them, and buried in the treasure chest of *Yogic* wealth, is the gem of *Kriyayoga* — the combination of austerity, intellectual attainment, and devotional development (see chart on page 407). These three will surely make short work of the weakness and ignorance that assails the human mind in its journey through relativity. They are part and parcel of the ten aforementioned prerequisite practices (*yamas* and *niyamas*) advised by Patanjali and intended by him to be well-mastered before progressing on to the subsequent limbs of practice in *Yoga*. With regards to *Kriyayoga*, Patanjali places a spotlight upon three of these ten — the *niyamas* of austerity, study of the scriptures, and devotion to God.

Tapas, defined as austerity, is somewhat a thing of the past with relation to the original. Defined in *Sanskrit* dictionaries with a wide variety of connotations, it is listed as purificatory practice, self-denial, mortification, penance, and other meanings. Suffice to say that its initial purpose as a practice is to release the mind from attachment to pleasures, luxuries, and objects of the senses which distract it from concentration. This is not a popular endeavor in a materialistic age, nor is the need for concentration consciously recognized, especially with regard to spirituality. The discomfort that *tapas* causes, as well as the dedication it demands, is for a great purpose, however, and beings seeking to uncover the truth of their existence take to it with relish and depend willingly upon the regimen it dictates and the attainment it requires and accomplishes.

In *Sanskrit*, the word *"tapana"* means "to heat." Heat is a purifier, even on the physical level, and within the territory of spiritual discipline it is no less effective for that end. One who practices *tapas* is called a *tapasvin* and is usually an ascetic who desires to purge the body/mind mechanism of all dross and limitation. In toto, this means that effort must be made to transcend what is known as the *Tapatraya*, the three kinds of sufferings common to embodied existence. *Tapatraya* consists of *Adhyatmika*, *Adhibhaudika* and *Adhidaivika* — suffering coming from ones own body and mind, from contact with other creatures and external circumstances, and from cosmic beings in subtler realms (see chart on pages 231).

True *tapas* is not based upon mortification of the flesh, but rather purification of the mind and its ideas about the body and embodied existence. A *tapasvin* of a high order does not engage in austerity for purposes of attaining bodily strength or occult powers such as lasting health and longevity, for these are not only distractions to *samadhi*, they are even contradictory terms. Matter decays and dies, while the Soul undergoes no real transformation and is eternal. But it is not that the world is an evil place, or that people and objects are to be avoided. The entire principle of austerity revolves around making the psycho/physical being fit for the reception of higher Awareness and the vision of Ultimate Reality. In this regard, *tapas* is a preparatory practice, an observance that not only purifies but also sustains the aspirant in the atmosphere of meditation and *samadhi* even while inhabiting a body and living in a terrestrial realm. It also is a way of life, for the realm of austere practice and abidance is sublime, appealing especially to the seeker who possesses a pure heart and a freedom-loving mind.

Tapas, as viewed by most, is of a physical variety and is indulged in for immediate results to the human body and its basic life-force. In that regard, exercises like physical postures, breathing, fasting, and other more popular forms of discipline are utilized for health, longevity, and access to energy. But *Yoga*, from which is drawn the triple tenet of *Kriyayoga*, emphasizes a single posture rather than multiple positions, and that is for the purpose of facilitating long periods of meditation that will enable the aspirant to transcend bondage to the limiting effects of the elements, nature, mind, and intellect. Stability of the body as a foundation allows stillness of the mind in meditation.

With regard to purification of the nervous system and its connection to both the body and the mind, the illumined teachers prescribe *japa mantra* — repetition of the sacred formula and its seed syllable (*bijam*). Patanjali advises practice of the *mantra*, then, stating that the repetition of *Aum* along with knowledge of Its meaning is needed so that attachment to thoughts and the *samskaras* that form in the mind due to them can be dissolved. *Japa* of the *mantra* is actually established in *ishvara-pranidhana*, and is thus conducive to intimacy with Divine Reality. Vyasa states that the *yogi* who engages in *japa* succeeds in making the mind one-pointed. Further, he states: *"Japa of the mantra along with the study of scriptures leads to liberation."*

Therefore, *japa* of the *mantra* that is given in sacred ceremony by the initiatory *guru* will purify the mind and cleanse the body and nervous system much more effectively than breathing exercises. It will also reduce the potential dangers of both mental imbalance and an unhealthy attachment to the transitory bliss of rushing blood and a pumping heart. In point of fact, it is a slowing of the pumping of the heart that conduces to a quiet and calm state of mind, which then facilitates a deeper, more effective meditation. If the mind is called back to the body again and again due to pains, or the restless inclination to always move about or shift positions, the crucial act and practice of meditation is upset. This is referred to as *vyuntthana* by Patanjali, the urge to always change postures or get up and leave the seat of meditation once it has been established. It leads to the succumbing of the mind to the problem of restlessness. Notions that the assuming of more *asanas* will somehow help this condition are mistaken, for shifting about continually only creates *vrittis* (thought-forms) in the mind associated with the desire to move. This causes the aspirant to seek both aid and relief through motion associated with various *hatha*-based postures. Soon, an imposing *samskara* (mind impression) follows, and no calmness of mind or body is possible. Thus, in most cases, those who are teaching only a physically-based *yoga* run the risk of injuring the spiritual life of students and aspirants and distorting or compromising the purity of authentic *Ashtanga Yoga*.

With regards to *asana*, the authentic teachers advise and illustrate one posture (*ekasana*), cross-legged, with straight back and regulated breathing (*pranayama*). For old or ailing bodies, sitting in a chair with a straight posture is adequate. For beginners, practice of one posture, simple breathing, and focused mind, all demonstrated and guided by the *guru*, is far better than learning various asanas which most often only distract the seeker and seduce him or her into a world of glamour and obsession with health that is alien to authentic *Yoga*. It can be stated in this context that nowhere in the system is success in *Yoga* predicated on seated posture alone, and never upon many postures. Many have attained gradual success sitting in a chair with a straight back, studying the *Yoga Sutras*, and following the instructions of the *guru* with faith and perseverance.

The issue of fasting is also put into perspective in *Yoga*. In the *Bhagavad Gita*, the Lord of *Yoga*, Sri Krishna, states that *"Yoga is not for those who eat too much or fast to much."* And in fact, sensitivity around what one eats, how food is taken, and the offering of it as sanctified food is much more important than denying the body what it needs for strength in order that it can support intense spiritual striving (such as *tapas*). Those who make a fad out of fasting, thinking it to be somehow crucial to Self-realization, miss the boat entirely. As Swami Vivekananda so astutely states: *"No food or drink can taint that noble Self which knows Itself."* The *Atman* is ever-perfect and transcendent of the physical. It is to be realized, and both the overfeeding of the body and the lack of feeding the body are detrimental to this process. The body as a fit instrument is a different matter, however, and proper diet, exercise, and moderate appetites will accomplish that. Fasting for reasons of health and increased awareness are both possible and allowable if the main aim of such exercises are conducive and in step with the purpose of living a spiritual life.

What constitutes authentic and properly oriented *tapasya*, then? Sri Krishna informs us that love of lonely study, heartfelt devotions to God, and the selfless service of *guru*, devotees, and the world's peoples, rank among the highest. There are also the taking and completion of vows, the expanding of ones ability to endure hardship with equanimity, and the cultivation of compassion and other virtues. It is no wonder, then, that we find in *Kriyayoga* all of these high disciplines.

And *svadhyaya* is one of these elite practices as well. It entails study of the scriptures, examination of the inner self, repetition of the inspirational *slokas* found in the *Vedas* and other texts, and chanting of the ancient divine hymns. Of all the important practices in *Yoga*, and in spiritual life in general, it is the one that is most often ignored. This is because it takes time and effort, and requires a clear and resilient mind and intellect. It also demands a *guru*, an adept in uncovering and revealing the often abstruse truths of the scriptures, and one who can also demonstrate how to implement those important teachings and principles into daily life. This is no small undertaking. Those who seek for an illumined guide, and who strive to expand the mind and intellect to accommodate higher truth, must have fortitude and perseverance.

The scriptures are the most crucial link to God that human beings have recourse to, aside from their own inherent divinity. But in a world where spiritual values are not so highly valued, and the true nature of humanity not only goes unacknowledged but is forgotten completely, a reminder of the divinity of mankind and the sacred boon and the purpose of life is essential. There was a time when *svajatiyavrittipravaha* — the continuous thought of ones divine nature — inhabited the minds of all beings, and their joy was without bounds. But in today's arid religious climate, the pursuit of fame, the accumulation of wealth, the attainment of pleasure, and the wielding of power over others are taken as ultimate goals. When God has been forgotten and materialism is the religion of choice, it is good to know that somewhere in this vast sweep of time and space there exists a record of all that the best of humanity has aspired to and attained, an accurate reading of the illumined minds and devoted hearts of the saints, sages, and luminaries of all the religious traditions of the world. Herein lies the key to both a return to true knowledge, and an abidance in Truth eternal, what to speak of an openness to the descent of divinity into the human condition, as was always intended before the immature individual and perverted collective ego gained control of the world.

About *svadhyaya* and its close concomitants, Vedavyasa, the noble father of *Vedanta*, states: *"Establishing one posture, remaining firm in yoga, and repeating the truths of the scriptures, let the divine Self within radiate forth with all resplendence."* Thus, *svadhyaya* helps fill the criteria for establishment in *Yoga* by illumining the human mind, which is both the cause of bondage and the gateway to liberation. It is the thinking mind that gets uplifted, wherein the *buddhi* (intellect) gets convinced of its inherent connection with the *Atman* and dissolves into the higher realization that the true Self within is not a material principle, but an eternal spiritual verity.

How does *svadhyaya* accomplish all this? Through study, through repetition, and through the power vested in the Divine Word. When the mind is poised and ready to hear about its divine Source, the scriptures cast brilliant light upon it, and all its previously darkened recesses become illumined. The clarity that ensues, the peaceful state of *samprasad*, changes forever the relationship between the mind and the world. The mind, the mind's thoughts, the intellect, and even the ego, turn away from ignorance and delusion and face towards the resplendent sun of wisdom that has no equal. Such a vision of Truth can only bring about the birth of true devotion and the boon of pure love, which is what *ishvara-pranidhana* is all about.

Some define the word "*pranidhana*" as self-surrender, humility, or prostration before God.

Others interpret it as "coming close" as in approaching divinity, or even "pushing away," as in renunciation of the world. Whatever the differing shades of meaning, Patanjali states that *samadhi* can be attained swiftly and effectively through *ishvara-pranidhana*. By focusing the mind's thoughts on God, in whatever form the devotee prefers, the Lord's grace falls quickly upon him/her and the experience of intense communion is known at last. It is no wonder, then, that this important tenet of *Bhakti Yoga* is prescribed and advised by all who know of the spiritual path.

The word "*Ishvara*" is of extreme importance as well. *Ishvara* is said by some to be none other than *Brahman* Itself inhabiting a special form, and by others to be equal to *Saguna Brahman*, the personal God who presides over the universe. In either case, proximity to the Divine Being will always be purifying and uplifting. The presence and power of *Ishvara* will be discussed at length in succeeding chapters.

In *Kriya*yoga's triple element, it is not just each element taken alone, but all three practiced and performed simultaneously, that brings the most powerful results. Imagine the immense force for realization that could be mustered and utilized in one who practices austerities, studies hard the teachings from the *guru* and the scriptures, and has intense devotion for *Ishvara* coupled with a deep-rooted desire to realize *Brahman*. Such a *yogi* is rare indeed, and this is made all the more evident by Patanjali's assertion that those who accomplish austerities and meditation are far above those questionable *yogis* who, not able to gain realization due to weakness and complacency, instead take recourse to the imbibing of herbs and elixirs in order to simulate the mere feeling of being illumined through physical intoxication (see chart on page 407). This is not only an unfortunate situation based upon self-deception, it also creates *samskaras* that persist well into subsequent lifetimes. As Sri Sarada Devi noted, the Himalayan regions are full of so-called *yogis* who sit idle all day, smoking their pipes and pretending to be spiritual in front of others. Sri Ramakrishna gives this fact a humorous turn by stating, *"False yogis lay around inebriated, doing various simple preoccupations. When one approaches them, however, they put away their knitting needles and sit up straight in cross-legged position!"* That somnolent state which enslaves lazy humanity is itself certainly not funny, however, and bespeaks of the quality of *tamas* more than of *sattva* — or even *rajas*.

There are some who have attempted to modernize *Kriya*yoga by giving it a persona geared towards attracting the public and making it popular. This is, no doubt, a money-making technique designed to bring name and fame as well. It is a telling characteristic of glory-seeking and sensationalism, but it only results in pride, and in further deluding the masses as to the nature of authentic *Yoga*. This pretentious type of *Kriya* Yoga is a system that prescribes various breathing exercises and a callow and misguided preoccupation with the gross nerves in the human body. But Patanjali and Vedavyasa are clear as to the nature of what constitutes both beneficial purification conducive to spiritual practice, and meditation leading to Self-realization. Based upon the firm edifice of *Sankhya Yoga*, for instance, the decree comes forth that all of creation is to be known, from the five elements on inwards to the Cosmic Mind (*Mahat*), and all for the one crucial realization that the true Self of mankind, called *Purusha* or *Atman*, is essentially different from body, life-force, and thought. It is, in fact, the only truly living Essence in existence. Knowing this salient fact, beings will be able to disidentify from material principles and no longer suffer the ignoble whips of pain arising from a sense-bound life of worldliness lived in ignorance.

With the triple tenet of *Kriya Yoga* defined and illustrated, which forms the first three *niyamas* of *Yoga's* second limb, the other two practices of contentment and purity can be taken up. *Santosha*, contentedness, sometimes referred to as self-settledness, is not only a *niyama* of *Yoga*, but is also one of the four sentinels (see chart on page 345) given by the revered Lord Vasishtha in the scripture, *Yoga Vasishtha*. It also has its correlation with the *Vedantic* jewel of *uparati*, discussed earlier (see page 65). Additionally, it is also sometimes likened to peace of mind, though that quality may come later along the inward *yogic* trajectory. Suffice to say, that without the mind's and soul's contentment there could be no forward progress made in any type of existence, and if the truth be told, it would be ideal if the seeker after realization would come to the teacher with *santosha* already in hand. For, with *santosha* present, the act and art of meditation would be practically at hand as well. Who can meditate with a restless mind? Restlessness, according to Patanjali's *Yoga*, appears as *styana* (fickleness) of the body and *pramada* (heedlessness) of the mind. It fosters *bhrantidarshana* (misconception) in the intellect, and causes *anavasthitatvani* (unsettledness) in the spirit (see chart on page 255). With all of this to deal with, it is no wonder that the realized souls both value and recommend the practice and attainment of *santosha* in the aspiring mind.

Saucha, purity, has been brought up many times in the earlier pages of this book. Again, and as always, the consummate spiritual observer looks at a quality such as this from both dual and nondual perspectives. From the dual standpoint, that of practice rather than philosophy, purity is a coveted possession which will literally clear obstacles from the path of itself, such is its power. Persons devoid of intellectual acumen have realized the Goal via the approach of purity and pure mind. That makes the *niyama* of purity a special kind of intelligence, valued particularly by the *"salt of the earth,"* and *"the meek and humble who will inherent the earth."*

On the nondual level, *saucha* is the inborn essence which dwells naturally and spontaneously in the minds of saints and seers prior to coming into the embodied condition. In terms of relativity, then, this valued asset was practiced and perfected in a previous lifetime by these illumined souls. Sri Ramakrishna has a very excellent story that illustrates this. He told it in this fashion: *"Once, a mahut (elephant handler) took an elephant out of its stall to give it a bath. When the bath was accomplished, the mahut no sooner turned his back then the elephant dropped down and rolled in the dirt, getting all muddy. The mahut then bathed the elephant again and immediately put the animal in its stall thereafter, thus avoiding an unwanted repeat of the tiring incident."*

The Great Master's story is not about elephant management. He means to convey that some souls come out of the "stall" of rebirth dirty, with many mental problems and animalistic habits. If a great soul then washes them in the "bath" of wisdom teachings, they only drop onto the "ground" of old habit later on and roll in the "mud" of worldliness. But some worthy souls are taken from the stall of rebirth by their *"mahut-gurus"* already clean, and so need no bath of wisdom before taking up their life's mission. In terms of purity, then, it is an attribute already at hand for those illumined souls who take up the body for the sake of others.

As to both *santosha* and *saucha*, they will receive more attention within the spotlight of different systems as the pages of this book get turned in due time. Suffice to say that these two sterling attributes, like other dynamic duos, work together to both empower one another and clear the path for future insights and progress. *Santosha*, contentment with everything as it is, settles the mind into periods of silence and quietude, allowing time for *saucha*, purity, to both manifest itself and inundate the deeper recess of the mind with clarity and illumination. As the Holy Mother, Sri Sarada Devi, has said, *"People may talk glibly about the realization of God, but one must remember that the mind is everything. One gets everything when the mind becomes pure and steady."*

We have looked closely at the need for qualification in the noble systems of *Tantra*, *Vedanta*, and *Yoga*. It would be valuable to inspect the same criteria in another wisdom tradition of Mother India, one with its own unique way of expressing itself. Understandably, when the subject of *Buddhism* comes up today, thoughts of China, Japan, Ceylon, Burma, and Tibet arise in the mind. But just as Christ was not a Caucasian man, just so, Lord Buddha was not Chinese or Japanese. He was an Indian *rishi* who was well aware of the *Vedas* and who based much of what he taught upon them. As Swami Vivekananda has stated, *"Buddhism is just a contemporary extension of the Vedanta."* With this in mind, we can take up for consideration all forms of *Buddhism* in Indian Philosophy.

Buddhism expects a very high level of commitment and self-effort from its acolytes. Its votaries are spread over a vast expanse of *dharmic* territories, classified generally in Hinayana, Mahayana, and Vajrayana divisions. In the Tibetan form of Vajrayana philosophy, there exists what is termed as the Precepts, Points, Practice, and Process of the well laid out path. These act, among other things, to prepare and qualify the aspirant for realization of Buddha Nature, so rare and highly anticipated by all sincere aspirants. The following chart reveals this basic system.

Precepts, Points, Practice, & Process of the Vajrayana Path

Empowerment, Effort, Insight, and Transcendence

I. Guru Yoga and Empowerment
   a) Seek and Develop a Relationship with the Guru
   b) Qualify for Empowerment and Gain the Wisdom Transmission

> ### *Four Points Concerning the Process*
> *1) Meditate three times a day with faith and devotion*
> *2) Practice holding the mind in an unmodified state*
> *3) Realize that whatever appears comes from one's own mind*
> *4) Meditate constantly until conceptualization disappears*

II. Vajrayana Practice (Shamata, or Dwelling in Peace)
   a) Receive and Observe the Vows of the Tantric Vehicle
   b) Purify the Nadis and Centers for the Flow of Prana
   c) Worship Vajra Vahini, Embodiment of Wisdom; see all Women as Her
   d) Visualize and Meditate on the Herukas/Dakinis to Penetrate the World
   e) Establish a Relationship with one Chosen Deity (Yidam) & Merge in It
   f) Realize the Voidness of both the Deity and the World
   g) Gain Realization of Trikaya — The Three Bodies

> The Three Bodies ———→ *1) Dharmakaya, or Dharma Body (Buddha Nature & Dharma)*
> *Confers the knowledge that all thoughts and phenomena are devoid of any independent identity*
> ———→ *2) Sambhogakaya, or Enjoyment Body (Buddha Fields)*
> *Confers the means by which the practitioner communicates with other practitioners in meditation*
> ———→ *3) Nirmanakaya, or Emanation Body (Buddha Incarnations)*
> *Confers the pure force of will, transcending karma, which the yogi uses to benefit all sentient beings*

III. Process of Gaining Quiescence and Insight
   a) Accrue Merit via Offerings and Prayers so as to Clear Subtle Karmas
   b) Meditation on the 100 Syllable Vajrasattva Mantra
   c) Constantly Strive for Deeper Insight

> ### *Mental Process of Attaining Quiescence*
> *Overcome Mental Sluggishness; Calm all Mental Tendencies;*
> *Gain Detachment from Names and Forms; Develop Analytic Insight;*
> *Attain Transcendent Wisdom*

IV. Direct Perception of Voidness
   a) Refine Mental Readiness via Analysis and Formless Concentration
   b) Dissolve Ordinary Concepts/Perceptions by Perceiving their Voidness
   c) Realize Voidness in all Stages of Life
   d) Develop the Mental Agility Necessary to Attain Mahamudra

The four overall stages that aspirants of the *Vajrayana* path utilize for preparation are well-thought and comprehensive. Initially, a *guru* is sought out, for no aspirant would be so careless and unthinking as to attempt the subtlemost of all journies without the aid of a preceptor. There are far too many twists and turns along this precipitous road to Reality, and the *guru* has familiarized himself with them after consciously coursing back and forth between the realms of form and formlessness numbers of times. It is this vexing torsion in the fabric of the spiritual struggle that Sri Ramakrishna describes when He states, *"A magician holds up a string with many knots tied into it, shakes them once, and they all disappear. Another man tries hard to do this, but only makes the knots tighter."* Attempting to untie the knots of ignorance, worldliness, passions, attachments, mental complexes, fears, *karmas*, and the like, often only "tighten" these very formations if one does not know where to look, what to find, how to proceed, what tools to use, and how to know if any given obstacle has actually been destroyed for good. Yet, the Great Master also observed that people take doctors for an illness, and lawyers for a court case, but they will not go to the *guru* when it is time to seek and realize God.

The path called *Guruyoga* is a sensitive one, no doubt. Not only are there many type of teachers — higher, lower, older, younger, traditional, unorthodox, adept, inept — but the seekers are of many types and levels as well. The qualities of humility and dedication will be necessary in order to gain any success with the enigmatic spiritual figure called a *guru*. As our chart under study declares, a relationship must be developed so that "empowerment" can be transmitted. That is, when the *guru* is satisfied that the student is both sincere and serious, he can begin to transmit the teachings into the mind of the aspirant. Just as a farmer will first fertilize the soil before planting, so too will the wise preceptor transfer some of his or her stored up power to the beginner so as to help form a foundation upon which further growth can take place.

Along the windy and often precarious outset of the *Guruyoga* way, there are four points about which the *guru* instructs that will stand a seeker in good stead. They speak to the basic stance of the mind. Bodily postures have been mentioned and explored earlier, but the all-important mental posture is much more crucial to progress in authentic spiritual life.

The importance of building up and sustaining a meditation practice comes first in the *Vajrayana dharma*, followed close on the heels with establishing the proper mental attitude of seizing and securing the mind within the parameters of a formless state. For the preceptor has noticed how many seekers only sit and repeat all the habits of their earlier life in their minds, helplessly running trains of thoughts continually. The practitioner may look perfectly still on the outside, but in the mind there is constant turmoil going on, and this can go on for years, unabated, due to the lack of initial training. In this regard it is important, for instance, to train the child in meditation, and not wait until middle age or even teenage years to set in. The sooner one can master this *"holding of the mind in an unmodified state,"* the better both earthly life and spiritual life will proceed. As an example, hasty and often regrettable reactions springing from the errant ego will be curtailed if the mind is habitually calm and controlled, and this can save dozens of unwanted repercussions — including that one fatal and unforeseen one that may set back or even ruin an entire lifetime.

After the habit of meditation and the stance of contemplativeness have been established, the devotee must correct the mind's misconceptions and maintain the practice until the habit of conceptualization weakens and ends. That is, the meditator begins to perceive the darksome and distorted bends and tendencies in the mind over a period of time, which would never have been even guessed at without the help of the *guru* and the contemplative practice. And one of the key realizations which will come naturally forward over the dedicated span of ones practice is the fact that the manifest universe exists in the mind, not in space. Later on, the adept will see that matter is not a location for consciousness, but obversely, that matter emerges from modified consciousness via the mind's powers of projection. But prior to the mind's clarification on such matters, it will continue to conjure up the universe and its beings and objects as if they were separate entities, somehow unrelated to it. Without the key inner connections that meditation practice facilitates, mind will only continue to throw up *"all such queer creatures of our fancy as man, woman, child, body, mind, earth, sun, moon, stars, the world, love, hate, property, wealth, etc.; also ghosts, devils, angels, and gods, God, etc.,"* as Swami Vivekananda has stated. This conceptualization process will disappear in the light of a burgeoning realization which proceeds from observing the mind in meditation. And it all got facilitated by encountering and engaging the four points of *Vajrayana* process.

All that has gotten transmitted by *Guruyoga* and its empowerment finds a fuller maturation in actual *Vajrayana* practice. Amazingly, what has gone before, as involved as it has been, proceeded under the auspices of training and qualification, not actual hands on practice. Remarkably, practice in many schools of *Buddhism* is not undertaken with the idea of undue effort, but rather as a matter of uncovering what is ever-present via patience and perseverance. This is calm abiding, called *Shamata,* not frantic striving out of fear of failure, or a personal sense of agency. Vows become important to the Buddhist at this point in time, as if they could not be taken seriously earlier for fear of breaching them before an initial and proper start was made. This is both important and admirable, for the vows of an ordinary person or a novice are often seen to be a matter of hollow pretense ill-fated to end in prevarication. The "straw on fire" syndrome is applicable here — much show in the beginning, but no stamina in the end. Taking a vow, *vrata,* is a serious matter, then, and the *guru* is instrumental here as well.

As yet another requisite of spiritual life is satisfied, the acolyte moves on to the level of practice known in most paths as purification. As in classic *Yoga, Buddhist Yoga* sees the necessity of working with the body, the breath, and the energies of the human body/mind mechanism before proceeding on to more refined levels of being. The emphasis in the *Vajrayana dharma* is decidedly devotional here, though it may not come off looking like it on the outside. Worship of the Goddess, meditation on minor deities, selecting an *Ishtam* or Ideal — these are all elements of the devotional path.

And this only goes to show how well-integrated is the way of the *Vajrayana,* the "Diamond Vehicle," for aspects of *Jnana Yoga, Kundalini Yoga,* and nondual *Advaita* also permeate this practice. Purifying the subtle nervous system so that *prana* can flow more readily is a *tantric* practice associated with the awakening of *shakti* power. Penetration through the appearances and overlays of form to realize the emptiness behind all forms is a classically *Buddhist* way of proceeding, but is shared in common with all pathways which seek to merge with the formless, nondual Reality, whether one calls it *Atman* or *Prajnaparam.*

But the wisdom element of this practice really shines through in the search after cognition and attainment of the Three Bodies of the Buddha. The realization of the insubstantiality of all phenomena alone is a wisdom aspect which will take the seeker far beyond the ordinary ken of conventional religious observance and understanding, opening up windows of insight and clarity scarcely even thought of by moralists and reformers. And the first Buddha Body (*dharmakaya*) will, in turn, connect the practitioner to the presence of other meditating minds of transcendent nature, existing in rarefied atmospheres too subtle for mere believers to perceive. Such inner relationships tend to contribute power and energy to the already aspiring devotee, increasing spiritual strength and knowhow by which he or she can dispel residual *karmas* and rid the mind of other impeding blockages, no matter how subtle.

After the practice phase towards *Shamata* is instigated, and the basic ability of dwelling in peace is gained, the process phase can get under way. For there is still much insight to be gleaned from the inner stores of the revelatory mind, and a total and overall quiescence to be accessed and put to good use. The indwelling intelligence will also come to the fore of the picture, as the advancing and adept practitioner begins to realize more and more that his practice and efforts are not only for himself, but for the higher good of all sentient beings. As the chart reflects, all traces of sluggishness and torpor in the mind must be solved, and all attachment to form that is still clinging in the desire body must go. The power of the intellect to properly analyze and rightly resolve takes on a great importance as well. All of this will be facilitated in the phase of ongoing process with the help of prayers, prostrations, offerings, and *mantras,* recited consciously and with full concentration of mind. Here, the prize of transcendent wisdom is both potentially at hand and, possibly, at stake. A thorough inspection and purification will allow the adept to become instrumental in the full awakening and thorough enlightenment of all suffering and aspiring beings.

The "Direct Perception of Voidness" is a classic term in *Buddhism*, referring to the natural condition of Original Mind before (in the case of sleeping/dreaming beings) it took on the conditionings and modifications of form via ignorance. In similar fashion to that of *Advaita Vedanta*, the practices and processes which are recommended by spiritual preceptors are necessary to undertake from the standpoint of an already accruing ignorance of mind, which nevertheless has never effected or influenced Original Mind whatsoever, despite misleading appearances. *"Good and bad smells on the wind do not effect the air, which only carries them temporarily"* says Sri Ramakrishna, meaning that the dualities which the diseased, misguided, and conventional mind hold on to as if they were real never change ones pure nature, or *Buddha* Mind. Smoke may stain a window, but not a screen. Therefore the human mind seeking freedom must become a flow-through mechanism that allows both the pleasant and disgusting smells of relativity to pass, leaving no trace and no consequence.

In mature *Buddhism*, the term "voidness," like the term "unreal" in *Vedanta*, refers to changing phenomena that are empty of abiding substance, but not of underlying Essence. An object, for instance, is not to be coveted of itself or for its own sake, because it lacks the ability to fulfill; only Buddha Nature, or *Atman*, can confer that. That is, the object goes through too many changes and mutations. It can get lost, it can get stolen, it can get damaged, it can decay, it can get destroyed, and lastly, as is the case with even wealth, one can get bored with it. These good reasons and more cause the wise person to loose their hold on relativity and attempt to secure a better hold on Reality. This, too, will be difficult, because of the "void nature of being" which persists there as well. In other words, both objects and the lack of objects will stultify human beings, who will find no purchase point whatsoever if what they are looking for is satisfaction — a satisfaction which is only present in their own true nature. *"The musk dear runs about frantically,"* says Sri Ramakrishna humorously, *"searching for that sweet scent in the air, all the while never suspecting that this heady aroma is emitting from its own navel."*

This reveals the hustle and bustle of beings in relativity who are searching for happiness amongst empty and unreal things, scarcely ever sitting to consult the all-blissful Self within them — or a wise *guru*. This is why the path prescribes seeing through both the apparent fullness of objects, and the fear of emptiness or voidness beyond them. The peace and bliss of freedom from sensual perception and mental conceptualization must be experienced, for then the true fullness and inherent completeness of spiritual realization can be duly attained. In *Vajrayana* this means attaining *Mahamudra,* or the Supreme Position (see chart on page 647). More will be written on this later.

In the meantime, mental facility and agility are needed. Striving for such abilities will both require and bring forth deeper insights into the path and its goal. Through it all, learning the precepts, noting the points, performing the practice, and coursing through all processes, the aspirant will observe and become convinced that all phases such as these are inherently empty, that every stage of life, being a movement of the mind alone, is void of abiding substance. The equality and equanimity of mind which such realizations allow will stand the seeker in good stead for *Nirvana*.

Having gazed into four different *dharmic* windows for qualification (the four points on the chart on page 84), the subjects of *Guru* and *Mantra* can be taken up. Taking birth in this world is often likened to a man waking up out of a deep and benighted sleep and finding himself in an impenetrable forest. Worst of all, he has developed amnesia and knows nothing of the past or the future. The first thing this forlorn being must do is to sally forth to find a proper direction. For that he will need assistance. In short, he is looking for either a path or a person, i.e., a way or a guide, a goal ands a *guru*. Some will find the path first; others will locate the guide first. It all depends on the karmas of previous lifetimes. Whatever the order of detection, both of these prime ingredients of the spiritual path are sorely needed, and are inseparably interconnected. The following charts will suffice to illustrate this well.

THE FOUR LEVELS OF KNOWERS OF BRAHMAN

The Four Qualities of an Authentic Spiritual Teacher
Akamahata — Devoid of selfish motives
Shrotriya — Transmits the essence of the scriptures
Avrigina — Leads a pure and simple life
Brahmavid — Is a knower of Brahman

The Four Levels of a Knower of Brahman

Level 1	Level 2	Level 3	Level 4
Brahmavit	*Brahmavidvara*	*Brahmavidvariya*	*Brahmavidvarishtha*

Seven Levels of Higher Knowledge (*Jnana-Bhumikas*)

Shubhecha	Shubhecha	Shubhecha	Shubhecha
Vicharana	Vicharana	Vicharana	Vicharana
Tanumanasa	Tanumanasa	Tanumanasa	Tanumanasa
Sattvapati	Sattvapati	Sattvapati	Sattvapati
	Asamshakti	Asamshakti	Asamshakti
		Padartha-bhavana	Padartha-bhavana
			Turiya

Shubhecha — Right Aspiration: possesses detachment, knowledge of scriptures, and wisdom
Vicharana — Proper Inquiry: gains all virtues, knows the nature of maya, contemplates Atman
Tanumanasa — Peaceful Mind: is free of desire, masters concentration, transcends mind
Sattvapati — Illumined Intelligence: attains renunciation, equality of vision, & nondual Truth
Asamshakti — Nonattachment: transcends gunas, becomes jivanmukta, merges in Atman
Padartha-bhavana — Grasp of Truth: identifies with Consciousness, sees God in all
Turiya — Abidance in the Self: immerses in Brahman, and rest in the disembodied state

"The painful rounds of birth and death in ignorance will never cease until one has reached the first level of jnana-wisdom. To attain that, seek virtue and develop indifference to the world. Then take recourse to the spiritual teachings transmitted by an illumined preceptor." Lord Vasishtha

Guru, The Spiritual Preceptor

As my own spiritual teacher, Swami Aseshananda, often stated, speaking from the podium on *Advaita Vedanta*, *"Guru is a principle, not a personality."* If more people in these contemporary times knew this fact, a host of unnecessary sufferings would be alleviated, even nipped in the bud before they started. This is true because of four other salient facts which go unknown for the most part, called the Four Qualities of an Authentic Spiritual Teacher. Such teachings stop the pretender, the charlatan, and the opportunist of the spiritual marketplace dead in their tracks by informing all potential aspirants of the dangers of following spurious teachers. Of course, it must be mentioned that there are as many paths and teachers as there are seekers, just as there are various levels in grade school, high school, and college. The intensity, naivete, or outright insincerity of the aspirant — as the case may be — figures in here too, since many beings will select teachers based upon their own desires — gross, refined, or swiftly dissipating.

But this obstacle aside for now, the merit and proof of an authentic, sincere, and adept preceptor is most important, and the Four Qualities gives these out in no uncertain terms. In other words, just as the aspirant will need to have qualification in order to walk the spiritual path, just so, the preceptor will need to have developed qualities that authorize him or her to teach about it and guide others along its winsome way. The wise ones say that these qualities are extremely specialized, that they were forged in the furnace of direct hands-on experience with suffering and aspiring humanity, thus earned, then applied, in a rarefied atmosphere that is specific to illumined souls alone. In brief, the spiritual teacher has to qualify himself or herself as well, but these credentials are of a more exceptional and particularized variety than that of a student or adept.

The ideal spiritual preceptor is wondrous indeed, and since few have met such a being he remains an unsought and unheralded phenomena on this earth. As fraudulent teachers go, such as the sensationalist, the opportunist, and the occultist, these types are well known to beings in both worldly and spiritual circles. The unfortunate fact in this regard, however, is that those who follow a worldly path both put up with and join forces with such questionable personages, creating *karmic* situations that are unconscionable to sincere teachers and seekers, and giving religion a bad name. But in the end this only results in helping the true *dharmic* teacher to stand out so that those who are actual seekers of the path and goal can come to him of her, unimpeded.

The first thing an honest and observant student will notice about an authentic teacher is the quality of *akamahata,* the lack of any selfish interests or motives. Of course, the luminary will not have any desires for himself in this regard, so what is meant here is that the teacher will not have the slightest interest in manipulating the student in any undue way. Whereas questionable teachers that the student may have encountered earlier (hopefully not) have wanted money, notoriety, or praise, the lack of such motives in the true *dharma* teacher will endear him to the novice and thereby inaugurate the noble journey of spirituality along the spiritual path on a solid footing. *Kama* means desire, so *akama* refers to the absence of desire. This is one sure sign that the teacher whom one is considering is of rare and exalted character.

Shrotriya comes next, and is the special quality of the *dharma* teacher to transmit the teachings and the scriptures to the disciple so that sure and gradual understanding will dawn. It is the essence of the teachings which will come through here, not just the letter of the law. The type of text-torturing, interpolation, and misinterpretation that is present in less qualified teachers will be absent in the illumined preceptor who has the quality of *shrotriya,* and only the pure transmission will be given. As Sri Ramakrishna has said in this regard, *"A true teacher is like the honest fish-mongerer who cuts off the head and the tail of the fish and sells only the body."*

This ability of teaching-transmission is present only in those who have studied the scriptures themselves, having contemplated them deeply while coming to sure and solid conclusions which are in tune with the luminaries of the past. If the teacher under consideration has this rare and special ability, the aspirant can humbly and without any misgivings bow down at this *guru's* feet and ask for discipleship. As the *Ashtavakra Samhita* puts it, *"As to the teacher, if he be young or old, male or female, learned or illiterate, none of these need be considered. One should acknowledge only the essence, meaning whether or not the teachings can be transmitted."*

Avrijina is third on this list of credentials for the teacher, which has to do with the lifestyle such a being conducts and sustains. A simple, pure, and unostentatious life is best, exemplifying moderation in all appetites. A strong love of austerities (*tapas*) is also a sure sign of authenticity, revealing that the teacher has undergone the practices which he now advises for all his students. The presence of peace and its pursuit rounds out the picture, illustrating the attainment and importance of equanimity of mind. When quiescence of mind is perceived in the teacher, the student feels confident that the Lord is present there as well, and the process of transmission can go forward with full trust and sweet communion.

Lastly, and acting as a gateway into the related teaching listed on this chart, is the quality of *Brahmavid*. The spiritual preceptor must be a knower of *Brahman*. This is a hard thing to detect and rightly assess. As Narada relates in his *Bhakti Sutras*, *"It is hard to attain the grace of a great soul, because it is hard to recognize such a one."* Or as Sri Ramakrishna used to put it, *"It takes a jeweler to recognize the value of a diamond."* On the other hand, *Brahmavid* is not completely undetectable, especially under the auspice of the three other qualities of a true teacher. If these are taken into consideration, an apt conclusion may be drawn based upon ensuing spiritual depth.

If a *Brahmavid* is hard to recognize, the three succeeding levels of a *Brahmavid* will be more difficult of recognition. Therefore the seers of several different philosophical systems have collaborated to create a list called the Seven Levels of Higher Knowledge, what to speak of the Fourteen Levels of Upper and Lower Wisdom (see charts on pages 331, 335, 337). On the chart presently under study, the upper seven are displayed, giving us a good look into the subtle differences in the four levels of knowers of God.

A *Brahmavid* has attained the first four of the seven levels of higher knowledge, namely, right aspiration, proper inquiry, peaceful mind, and illumined intelligence. This is an amazing achievement, and one that few in this world ever manage to attain. One can scarcely imagine, then, what the deeper levels of knowers are like, called *Brahmavidvara*, *Brahmavidvariya*, and *Brahmavidvaristha*. As the chart under inspection shows, the second level of knower adds another superlative quality to the four he had mastered previously, and gains a strata of nonattachment which allows for individual freedom, called *jivanmukti*. This level of knower transcends the three *gunas* of nature and is able to merge in the *Atman* again and again, almost at will. Thus does the *Brahmavidvara* penetrate deep into the nature of Reality, experiencing a period of internal communion that leads beyond the world of name and form and into the indivisible Self.

The *Brahmavidvariya*, however, climbs another and very subtle rung of this spiritual ladder and attains a sixth quality called *Padartha-bhavana*. Short of going in and out of *atmic* experiences, the *Brahmavidvariya* tends to stay close to "Home" and just abides in Consciousness. Wonderfully enough, this level of knower identifies with nondual Awareness, all the while seeing it everywhere else as well, permeating everything. And this can only lead, inexorably and ultimately, to an eternally disembodied state, which is the province of the *Brahmavidvarishtha*. Like some rare bird that many have heard of but none have ever seen, this highest knower of *Brahman* frequents only the unfathomable heights of nondual Awareness, seldom coming down to rest on the cliffs of refined wisdom — what to speak of the treetops of intellectualism.

This brief sojourn into the world of knowers of *Brahman* will act as an enticement of what is to come, though it demonstrates that there are gradations to the world of qualification for both aspirant and teacher. And more will be explored in relation to the Seven Stages of Higher Knowledge as well, in addition to the stages of Lower Knowledge. And all of this segues nicely into the meeting ground of teacher and student as the next chart up for study (page 91) illustrates. According to the highest knowers of *Brahman*, particularly those who maintain a form so as to teach spirituality to others, there are conditions to satisfy in the relationship between teacher and student. The blessed Sri Ram, in his early days, learned these from Lord Vasishtha, and we can learn them now.

The Ten Conditions of the Guru/Shishya Relationship

"By worshiping the embodied guru devoutly, the disciple learns to follow the dictates of the infallible Guru Principle within. Knowing that the Lord is present in the universe of name and form as the eternal companion in sport, and as the compassionate guide in all trials and tribulations, lends a sense of peace and equanimity to the disciple's existence. From this calm, detached, and contented state of mind proceeds clear vision...."

From "Guru Tattva"
in — The Avadhut

2. Yukti
Ability to Contemplate
the Truth

1. Shruti
Strong Desire to
Hear the Truth

3. Anubhava
Striving to Realize
the Truth

4. Atma Vichara
Close Scrutiny
of Reality

5. Vivarta Nirodha
Detachment from
the Unreal

6. Mithya-Tyagi
Renunciation of
the Unreal

7. Brahma Shuddhi
Meditation on
Brahman

8. Brahmajnana
Acquiring
Nondual Wisdom

9. Vinasha Samskara
Destroying Subtle
Mental Impressions

10. Sthiti Samadhi
Merging and Remaining
in Steady Samadhi

"Where the authentic guru is present and the disciple is completely sincere, there occurs an implosion of such subtle and profound ramifications that it turns the course of the aspirant's entire existence, changing it forever. This amazing process happens swiftly or more slowly according to the practitioner's capacity and inherent karmas."

From "Guru Tattva"
in — The Avadhut

Guru Tattva (*Guru* Principle), the very principle of wisdom transmission in the universe, and *Guru Yoga*, adherence to the instructions of the beloved guide with surrender, self-effort, and devotion, lead the student to a deeper understanding of just who the *Guru* is and what the *Guru* represents. Moreover, one uncovers and recognizes that selfsame eternal presence in oneself and learns to follow the dictates of the infallible *Guru* principle within, spoken of by all great luminaries. This conduces to peace and bliss. For, knowing that the Lord is present in the universe of name and form as an eternal companion in earthly sport, and as compassionate guide through all the trials and tribulations of life, a sense of subtle joy and calm equanimity descends on the devotee's mind. Then, from a calm, detached, and contented state of mind, clear vision proceeds. Applying that clarity to the presence of God as *Guru*, one then gleans many valuable lessons that had since been forgotten or overlooked in the polluted religious climate of conventional living.

The problems facing the world today with regards to spiritual life — which the great luminaries believe to be the solution to all of life's obstacles — are legion. According to the system of *Guru Tattva*, they can be classed into two basic subdivisions. First, there is the problem of worldliness, a term used to denote materialism, complacency, jadedness, insensitivity, mundane convention, and a whole host of other descriptive sayings. All this is classified under the *Vyavaharika* path spoken of by *Vedanta* teachers, and is the way followed by most beings in this day and age. It is also referred to as the *Bhogamarga*, or path of enjoyment. In it, there is little or no room for God, unless God is seen as secondary to pleasure-seeking, the search for security, and pressing individual desires and concerns. For the most part, this path and its adherents perceive the physical universe along with the present lifetime as the only Reality, disregarding any thought about past or future existences, subtler realms, or higher states of awareness.

Secondly, there is the problem of the outright antagonism of egocentric beings full of pride and lust for power. These *asuric* (demonic) beings, temporarily under the destructive influence of negativity, eschew what is good and spiritual and go out of their way to cause havoc among the ranks of those who are engendering peace, love, and goodwill in themselves and in others. *Guru Tattva* is, to them, an evil that must be either destroyed, or held at bay for as long as possible in order to enjoy personal dominion over the world of name and form.

Strangely enough, though anything is possible in this age of spiritual slumber, these two paths are not so clear cut or distinct from one another as they might seem. The former seems to be comprised of beings who simply prefer to live their lives without acknowledging a creator or a divine presence. They merely ensconce themselves in all that the material world has to offer with no deep thought for the morrow, and have little desire to contemplate a profound meaning or purpose to life. The beings following the other way, that of negativity, have similar characteristics, but have an actual aversion to the idea of God and *Guru*.

Where these two paths blend, an intermingling of disturbing patterns manifest, which undermine much of the potential good that spiritual teachers attempt to accomplish for living beings. Present day world leaders, for instance, are mostly adherents of the *Bhogamarga*, having little or nothing to do with anything resembling spiritual life as the illumined see it. They may profess to be pious or "God-fearing" but their lives and actions reflect a sad condition that is spiritually undernourished and religiously immature. Even if dualistic religion were enough to sustain a healthy spiritual life, which, as practiced today, it is not, these beings would not be able to live up to the relative truths and practices contained therein and would simply continue to involve themselves with fame, power, money, and sensual satisfaction for personal or ulterior motives.

Even more deplorable is the wayward tendency of such beings, placed in positions of power, to be seduced by the dangerous enticements of relative existence so that, in actuality, they unknowingly become exponents of the negative path. In other words, they are not just worldly beings pursuing material comforts and benefits in simple and naive fashion, but become habitually obsessed with such things and begin to grasp after them. Covetousness (*asteya*), then, becomes the law of their lives. At the level of world affairs, this undesirable transformation creates beings who, though they outwardly profess to be law-abiding and moralistic members of society, are in actuality nothing less than negative forces acting for selfish and corrupt purposes.

This pretension, being an effective facade that covers all nefarious doings, is a most dangerous deception. From positions of power which are operative in both church and state, beings of deceived and demonic influence, masquerading as beneficent leaders in religion and government, can effectively control the pulse and pace of all that influences public life in general. These unwitting deceivers also distort and deter specialized or esoteric information destined to be given to the masses for their earthly and spiritual benefit. Some of this information is actually spiritual transmission in the form of subtle vibration which is a well-informed mental composite of all that illumined beings have accomplished and realized in life.

It may be asked how these *asuric* beings resist the positive forces of beneficent beings and effectively obscure the presence and emanation of subtle spiritual vibrations. These negative powers, like the *asuras* of ancient *Vedic* religion, have mixed qualities. Unlike an independent and incarnate evil proposed by contemporary fundamentalist Christians, the *asuras* are possessed of some good attributes as well. Since they have focused their awareness on certain attainments, this very concentration has brought them certain abilities which they use for selfish purposes. These abilities are called occult powers (*siddhis*) in spiritual circles (see charts on pages 642, 660), and their effects have a distorting influence on individualized awareness. Politics, military, corporate business, high society — these arenas of worldly existence provide fit vehicles for the amassing of power and wealth and are therefore perfect arenas for the exercising of an *asuric* being's powers. These powers are detrimental to the way of spirituality taught by the *Guru*. Therefore, a profound difference is noticed between the *Guru* principle, which is the force of Mother-wisdom manifesting through dedicated human teachers, and so-called world leaders and secular teachers.

Before delving deeper into the eternal and ever-blessed subject of *Guru*, a few more mentions should be made about God and the world. In essence, the two are not different. In the *Sanatana Dharma* of the ancient *rishis*, the eternal and illustrious pathway to Divine Life and Ultimate Reality, we find some definite answers to the problem of duality or relativity in all its aspects. The *rishis* of ancient India held two ideals simultaneously: one, that of the common good of all living beings with regards to material well-being and bodily and mental health; and the other, admittedly the most prominent and of the utmost importance, the realization of *Atman* and Its intrinsic connection with *Brahman*. The Peace Invocations of the *Vedas* are replete with profound sacred assertions to this effect.

There is peace in the sky, there is peace on earth.
There is peace in the heavens, there is peace in the world.
There is peace in the waters, there is peace on land.
There is peace with the plants, animals, flowers, insects and herbs.
There is peace with men, and peace with women and children.
There is peace with the gods and peace with the goddesses.
May this all-pervading peace enter into us and permeate us to the very core of our being.
Om peace, peace, peace.

O gods, may we hear with our ears hear what is noble and uplifting.
May we see with our eyes what is auspiciousness and spiritual
And may we, while praising the gods with healthy minds and bodies,
live a life that is beneficial to ourselves and to all others.
Om peace, peace, peace.

May we chant in praise of sacrifice and sing in praise of the Lord of sacrifice.
May divine blessings be upon us.
May peace be unto the whole human race.

> *May healing, well-being and prosperity abide among us.*
> *Om peace, peace, peace.*
>
> *May all the gods and the all-pervading Vishnu*
> *be propitious to us and grant us earthly welfare and spiritual bliss.*
> *Reverent prostrations to Brahman,*
> *and to Vayu, who is verily the perceptible Brahman.*
> *Thou art what is right, what is true, what is best.*
> *May the Universal One preserve me.*
> *May that One preserve my teacher.*
> *May Brahman protect me, and my guru.*
> *Om peace, peace, peace.*
>
> *O Supreme One, grace my limbs with strength.*
> *May my speech, vital force, eyes, ears and all my senses expand in capacity.*
> *The Upanisads rightly declare that all existence is Brahman.*
> *May I never deny Brahman and may Brahman never deny me.*
> *Let there be no rejection of Brahman by me, ever.*
> *May all the virtues cited in the Upanishads reside within me,*
> *I who am devoted to the Atman.*
> *Om peace, peace, peace.*

It is encouraging and inspiring to know that there was a period in human history where these two ideals — earthly success and spiritual attainment — were both realized and seen as one. We should not, however, make the mistake of thinking that it was easy of attainment. The foundation of this twin ideal was based upon living a spiritual life in the world. This requires *sadhana*, spiritual practice and mental discipline, and the *rishis* exerted such self-effort for hundreds of years in order to purify the mind and realize That which is eternal. Here, an interesting and crucial distinction comes to light.

The physical universe, relatively speaking, is not eternal, but passes through changes and upheavals that mark it as a transitory and ephemeral realm. What is more, it is insentient, not imbued with Consciousness. Instead, it is a derivative of Consciousness. What is eternal, then, according to those who have effected *sadhana* and come to realize the nature of all things, is *Brahman* alone — Pure Consciousness, Absolute. As a reflection is not different than the medium that it is reflected in, but is nonetheless a passing phase of that, so too is the universe a reflection of and a superimposition over the Brahmic Reality, and one with It.

In the final evaluation, then, the universe has its own semblance of reality. It is real only as a facet of *Brahman*, a finite expression of Its infinite expanse. The Peace Invocation before the *Ishavasyopanishad* clarifies and explains this nicely:

> *What is visible, though finite in nature, is infinite.*
> *What is invisible is also infinite.*
> *Out of the infinite, the finite has come,*
> *yet being infinite, only infinite remains.*
> *Om peace, peace, peace.*

Knowing all of this in proper perspective provides an important key for opening the diverse and multidimensional doors of homogenous existence. At every door there is a guide, and a guard, all of which are expressions of one, all-pervasive *Guru* Principle. The universe would have neither sentiency nor order without the inherent presence of *Guru* in and throughout everything. The person or persons that deny this principle suffer in body and mind, going round the wheel of birth and death inexorably in ignorance of their true nature, and unaware of their underlying and essential relationship with *Brahman*, Absolute Reality.

This is, of course, their choice. In a world where relative free will is operational, and where the sense of separation from God is strong in human beings due to the prominence and pervasiveness of the unripe and immature ego, beings go forth into life uneducated and uninformed about the *Guru* Principle within. As a result, the maladies of life, many of them wrapped up with the seed-forms contained within the sprouting layers of the unillumined mind (see charts on pages 167, 170, 172), emerge and cause havoc and suffering. The manner in which unenlightened beings, both individually and collectively, as a society and its members, deal with these unwanted problems, often creates more distortion, compounding an already volatile situation. Far from finding solutions to the original root discrepancy and ending its repetitive cycle, most beings waste precious time fighting an unending series of secondary and related problems. Instead of the divinely oriented existence that God intended, then, human beings experience a caricature of true life. Thus does a mundane worldly life gain prominence over a wise and noble spiritual life in the minds of living beings.

The divinely intended life mentioned here proceeds under the guidance of *Guru*, always and ever. Even those who are spiritually oriented, if they denounce *Guru* and opt to follow their own way, are still dependent on the inner guide which is simply *Guru* in another form. *Guru* is not merely a person of extraordinary capabilities, or even just God in human form. *Guru* is not found only in *Ishvara*, the Cosmic Being, either, unless one defines *Ishvara* as the totality of all souls.

In actuality, *Guru* is present from the inception of the creation, and is anterior to it as well. As the energy that guides and facilitates — God's own presence in subtle form — *Guru* is there in the seed of a tree, guiding it to its fullest growth and expression. A flower opens at the proper time and with all inherent portions intact and operable due to *Guru*'s guidance and overseership. What to speak of these minute elements of the creation, the cosmic laws themselves are put in place and rendered functional because of *Guru*. Even without parents, a baby would eventually walk on its own, and that is due to *Guru* dwelling within the child as its own *Atman*. Nevertheless, *Guru* is there in the parents too.

With these few examples, though more could be cited ad infinitum, the next directive is to find out what obscures or alienates the awareness of this blessed *Guru* Principle within us. Due to the prominence and popularity of the two paths of this earthly realm listed earlier — the worldly and the demoniacal — this pristine principle gets apparently tarnished and misused. Charlatans and opportunists abound in religious life, as well as in government and business. Since *Guru* can never truly be sullied or destroyed, being an eternal principle, it only gets submerged under the dense covering of egocentric motive and action. The deep waters of *samsara* are a fit place to enact the forgetfulness of ones inner guide — that which God placed in the human heart and in everything, sentient and insentient, from the "beginning" of time. Even this submersion, though, is only apparent. Acting in every aspect of life, *Guru* witnesses the entire drama in all its phases, from the corrupt on up the exalted. The harshest of lessons as well as the most sublime boons are bestowed by *Guru*. In short, balance is maintained by *Guru*; chaos is loosed and kept in check by the same principle.

It is helpful to look into that aspect of *Guru* which manifests as a human being. A stone contains powerful *Guru* principle, being the best example of still and silent meditation one can find. A silent lake is inspiring as well, but it cannot explain the intricacies of the human heart and mind. Thus, those who take nature as their teacher make some progress, but when it comes to dealing with the world in all its phases, and in particular that semi-divine and bittersweet drama called human life and existence, nature remains as if aloof, unable to assist. Herein we find the human *guru* on the scene, and if such is authentic — i.e., unattached to name and fame, above desire for power and its manipulation, and not attracted by wealth, lucre and personal gain — there is hardly a more worthy and beneficial ideal to be found.

In this day and age, *Guru* is not popular. Nevertheless, It permeates every aspect of life. Whereas the most traditional and classical approaches to religious life place *Guru* on a par with God

Itself, humanity will not accept the presence of divinity in its midst. There is little wonder in this, for when beings realize that they are in dire need of a guide, either due to their own lack of direction and insight or because of the untimely fructification of their distressing and incapacitating negative *karmas*, they turn to that guide that most suits their own level of understanding, especially with regards to motive. If the intention is to supplicate the Divine for all manner of selfish ends, the teacher that is in accord with the substance of such a lowly motive appears before them and, together, they play the game of victor and victimized. After the fallacy of such interaction is realized, there is little chance that *Guru* will be sought after again, at least for some time. Thus do false prophets act as despoilers for attaining the highest good in life.

In the case of those whose intentions are somewhat sincere, and whose motives are of a higher caliber, there are a host of teachers ready to guide and direct. These, like the aspirants that attend upon them, are of a mixed nature and reflect limited facets of the ultimate *Guru*. Some growth can be attained here, though the attraction towards occult powers and sensationalism often persists amongst these, and some of this gets passed on to the disciple — if it did not already attract the student in the first place. In short, like attracts like, and one gets what is in line with what one desires and seeks after.

It is only amidst the pure teachers, rare as they are, that true spirituality is found. They are rare because they do not seek accolades or notoriety as others do. This keeps them invisible to those who seek after the sensational rather than the spiritual, and thereby endears them to those of pure motive. Due to this, the two — bona fide *guru* and sincere disciple (*shishya*) — easily recognize one another, while others seek elsewhere according to a more inhibited capacity and limited insight based upon impure or mixed motives. This crucial moment in spiritual life represents the very height of all human relationships. Suffice to say that where the authentic *guru* is present and the disciple is completely sincere, there occurs an implosion of such subtle and powerful ramifications that it turns the course of the aspirant's entire existence, changing it forever. Instead of the usual evolution in time and space, the disciple's direction reverses and involution occurs, entirely independent of the world, its creatures, and the cyclic trajectory along which they are heading. This amazing process happens swiftly or more slowly according to the practitioner's capacity and inherent *karmas*, and here again, where worthy teachers are concerned, guidance is both patient and infallible.

Many of the salient attributes of the *Satguru*, the authentic world teacher, emerge as we take a look at the famous *Guru/Shishya Dashangika* — the ten conditions of the teacher/ disciple relationship mentioned by Shankaracharya (from chart on page 91).

The first condition to be satisfied in the spiritual aspirant's earnest drive to attain enlightenment is *Sruti/Shravana*. The seeker needs to hear the fundamental truths stated in the sacred scriptures from the lips of an illumined soul. Hearing lower knowledge from friends, parents, or secular teachers will never make the impression that is required. This is the all-important tenet of holy company mentioned by saints and sages in every sacred religious tradition of the world, and must be accomplished both in one-on-one communion between instructor and instructed, and in classes and discourses given by the teacher among those of like mind. Thus, the Truth is heard and understood through the medium of a direct transmission that carries with it not only the original revelatory power of the ancient seers, but also the inherent comprehension and realization of the living *Guru*. Such profound spiritual weight impresses the intrinsic meaning of the teachings deep into the devotee's thought processes where it will gradually release both intellectual and intuitive forces. These destroy ignorance and delusion and prepare the heart and mind of the student for the advent of the incomparable light of pure conscious Awareness. Therefore, the crucial nature of hearing the precious truths of the scriptures through the personage of the preceptor is of the utmost import.

Further, the truths which are initially conveyed are, at the root, the essential messages of nonduality, which form the basis for all authentic spiritual transmission. The truth of the indivisibility of Consciousness, Its eternal and undying nature, Its all-pervasive presence, and Its pure and taintless condition, count as the most important. In addition, the *guru* reveals the secret of the presence of the *Atman*, the Immortal Soul existing within the inmost being of the seeker, and affirms Its identity with the infinite expanse of conscious Awareness called *Brahman* or Absolute Reality beyond name, form, time, space and creation. This welcome news immediately awakens a strong and intense inner desire for freedom, and compels the aspirant to embark upon the transformation of human nature that will eventually culminate in total illumination.

All of this proceeds from the rare and precious boon of holy company which itself is a blessing that comes about through ones good thoughts, virtuous deeds, and spiritual practices from previous lifetimes. These positive effects arise and get combined with the gracious concern and compassion of the Blessed Lord and Divine Mother of the Universe, called *Shiva* and *Shakti* — who are none other than the *Atman* within, the *Antaryami* — the Inner Ruler Immortal enshrined within the heart. The *Guru's* presence and bestowal of teachings are extremely efficacious, then, and amount to nothing less than beholding the Divine Being face-to-face and receiving immeasurable Grace. Therefore, hearing the Truth from an enlightened being, *Sruti/Shravana*, is not to be underestimated. From spiritual transmission, that one intrinsically real moment in time, while abiding in the precariously balanced medium of the tiny human frame, there will proceed such power as will transform forever ones various broodings on mortality into revelations of the Immortal Self within.

Yukti/Manana is the second condition of this special relationship. Here, it is up to the student to put forth effort, both in the form of quiet study and inner reflection, as well as in daily actions, moment-to-moment thoughts, conversations, and in service of others. This alternating combination of inward contemplation of spiritual truths and careful application of them into everyday existence plays a key role in fusing all aspects of life together into one healthy and cohesive divine expression. This is where the Four Yogas — the paths of knowledge, devotion, action and meditation (see chart on page 433) — begin to become successfully integrated, which in turn leads the aspiring seeker to a peaceful and joyful existence.

It is crucial that the disciple spend time reflecting on the transmission from the *Guru*. Not to do so is likened to the difference between merely looking at food and actually consuming and digesting it. Ongoing nourishment of ones spiritual practice is the result of the latter, while weakness, stagnancy, and confusion in alternating cycles is the outcome otherwise. It can therefore be said that being near the *Guru* is one form of receiving, hearing the *Guru* speak is another, while acting on the *Guru's* instructions insure the optimum result. The three together comprise the highest wisdom-level transmission to the student.

It is at this juncture that the aspirant begins to feel the movements of inner intuition and hears the subtle spiritual voice of the higher element of mind and intelligence. It does not take long for the powerful elixir of Truth and its acid-like effect to penetrate deep into subconscious layers of the mind. Purification on this deep level leads to the uncovering of That which the disciple has been searching for. Spending time in contemplation upon what has been given by the *Guru* — that esoteric knowledge that few in the world are fit to hear and act upon — the aspiring student begins to understand that all knowledge lies within his/her own consciousness. The meanings to all the teachings, as well as the solutions to all problems, then lie within reach and are accessible to the calm and reflective mind that gains this inner vision. With open, single eye, the seeker observes the mutable nature of all phenomena while simultaneously beholding That which is changeless and eternal. It is also through such deep contemplation on spiritual matters that one rids the mind of the habit of brooding, which causes the mind to become heavy and despondent, and lose its natural spiritual buoyancy.

Anubhava/Nididhysana, the third condition of the *guru*/disciple relationship, brings multifaceted experiences to bear on life and mind. Initial realization occurs at this auspicious level, for the student has fulfilled the twin prerequisites of approaching the teacher and listening closely to spiritual instruction. Through a thorough reasoning-out process that utilizes logic and rationale, the aspirant approaches the pinnacle of the illumined intellect where, with specific meditation instruction given by the adept guide, the light-filled nature of the spiritualized mind rises spontaneously and naturally, giving birth to various sublime experiences. Thus, the infinite nature of Awareness is introduced, intimately, upon the aspirant's mind.

One important occurrence that emerges during this phase of spiritual experience is the knowledge that the *Atman* is different from the universe of name and form. The astute and persevering aspirant is then able to perceive the distinction between what is mutable and what is immutable, and this wisdom both increases inspiration and heightens the desire to behold the Eternal Being face to face. Coming to know that even the intellect is different from the Immortal Self within, and that it only reflects a minute portion of that ineffable Verity, the aspirant places more attention and concentration on the *Atman*, seeking the source of that great wonder. This gives rise to the fourth stage of *guru*/disciple relationship.

The well-known principle of *Atma Vichara* — inquiry into the nature of the *Atman* — is the fourth step along the *Brahman* way, and the *Guru* still plays an important part. It is nothing less than the essence of Reality that is being encountered in this process, but first, the devotee must complete the discrimination process that matures the ability to clearly perceive what is real and what is unreal, what is eternal and what is transitory. In addition, this selfsame devotee must then learn to live in that transcendent essence of Pure Being, to abide in Absolute Reality more and more, and this is to be accomplished in the midst of life and in the company of others who may or may not be awakened or empathetic to such inner realizations.

All the while that this internal analysis is taking place, the mind is receiving an intense makeover of the most exacting degree. Subconscious and unconscious layers of mind, with their recurring thought patterns, preferences and aversions, concepts, old habits, and even hidden and latent impressions, are gradually becoming exposed to the light of Awareness radiating from the still seemingly distant *Atman*. Recollections of past existences surface in the mind's memory at this time as well, and the devotee is amazed to see the record of such lifetimes and notice their effects. Realization takes on a twofold significance here, for along with the comprehension of something subtle, eternal, and sublime existing within, comes the additional realization that much inner work must be accomplished before the radiant sun of *Atman* will fully emerge from behind the clouds and shadows of the curtain-like nature of the mind in *maya*.

As the process of inquiry into the nature of the *Atman* goes on, the devotee feels more and more that the *Atman* is a completely distinct Reality from life and mind, and he or she begins to realize Its eternal nature. It is noticed that as the various elements of the mind, such as ego-sense, variegation, apprehension, and the phases of the thinking process rise and fall, the *Atman* remains still and constant. While the changing attributes of the mind such as perception, awareness, intelligence, and determination dance within the inner vision of the awakening aspirant, the *Atman* remains stationary and all-pervasive. Also, when the cognitive powers of the mind perceive the five elements through the five senses, and react outwardly to their stimuli, the *Atman* stays detached and aloof, uninvolved in the play of life and death, poised magisterially above all dualities.

As the devotee moves nearer to this undying Source of pure Existence, the *Atman's* all-supportive yet transcendent nature fascinates and inspires all the more. Keenly aware of the basic difference between created things and That which is, as Swami Vivekananda has stated in his writings, "acreate," consummate Wisdom, which is beyond the triple distinction of knower, knowing and that which is known, dawns on the aspirant's mind. Then, an experience of union beyond all diversity permeates existence, and a clear view of Reality is attained. This ushers in the fifth stage of this rare and sacred relationship.

In the fifth stage, called *Vivarta Nirodha* — the destruction of what is unreal — the seeker comes to know without a doubt that Ultimate Reality is different from the Universe and all created things. The *Guru* affirms this truth by continuing to guide the aspirant into deeper levels of communion with the *Atman*, while leading the student around and through various obstacles and impediments that crop up due to the mind's negative propensities and inconsistencies.

Vivarta, false superimposition, the projection of appearances, coverings, or secondary realities over *Brahman*, is the result of the illusory power of *maya* which veils Reality (see charts on pages 221, 279). *Maya* is neither good nor evil, neither positive nor negative, neither real nor unreal, nor both real and unreal. Yet, it is a fact of existence whose very presence indicates the possibility for creation and expression. Through its tenuous though pervasive substance, the universe appears and the march of time and events go forward. With its force it projects coverings over the *Atman* which obscure Its nondual radiance. This projection is called *vivarta*. Body, life-force, mind, intelligence and ego — these are some of the obscurations that veil Reality from view. From mind, in the cosmic sense, proceed other concealing elements such as thought, whose conceptual vibrations produce time, space, the three gunas, nature, the five senses, and other phenomenal principles. Much of this has already been described in the early chapters of this book, and more will come.

All manifestation is ultimately an appearance, a phantasmagoria projected by the inherent power in *Brahman* called *Shakti*, who wields the power of *maya* in a similar way that a magician enchants an audience with various optical illusions. Thus, the aspirant who has seen the glory of the *Atman* seeks to shatter this illusion completely, see through the play of universal manifestation, and go beyond name and form. As Swami Vivekananda has expressed it, *"We will crush the stars to atoms; we will unhinge the universe."* Great *Gurus* like he, though rare, demonstrate in their own lives, in plain view for all to see, that the destruction of such appearances is not only possible, but extremely desirable, for it is only by this powerful act of internal *sadhana* and austerity that *maya* will recede, enlightenment will dawn, and Freedom will be regained.

As has been presented already, discrimination and detachment and the twin modes of *adhyaropa* and *apavada* help the seeker after Truth to reveal the presence of cosmic illusion and individual delusion. The aspirant, under the recondite but inestimable guidance of the illumined preceptor, tears away the superimpositions from in front of Reality and achieves a vision of the Absolute. Such a glimpse changes the mind forever, and brings about the ultimate renunciation that is so often mentioned by illumined beings. Such renunciation often penetrates outward as well, and the aspiring devotee becomes indifferent to externals such as home, family, food, and worldly attainments. This heralds the sixth level of the *guru/shishya* relationship.

Mithya-Tyagi, the sixth stage of the interaction between *Guru* and disciple, compels the aspirant to relinquish social formalities and human conventions. Personal habits, as well, get a transformation. Seeing the *Guru* and other illumined beings living a life of equanimity and balance, unattached to self-motivated works and undisturbed by rounds of distracting activities that take precious time and energy away from the true goal of human existence, the seeker follows suit and gradually or all at once gives up the desire, both factitious and fictitious, for satisfaction in the world. This wise observance is for all, not just for monastics and ascetics. Having come to know that the world is only a temporary state of existence, in actuality a projection of the mind, the aspirant no longer hungers after sensual pleasures or the allurements of name, fame, and power in it. To abide continually at the highest level of purified awareness, with Its bliss, peace, and all-attracting light, is far more appealing, even irresistible.

Ironically, it is at this stage of renunciation that the disciple begins to lose the sense of separation from others, and from all created phenomena. All manifest phenomena now become friendly portions of one indivisible Reality. Even the *Guru* is seen as nothing less than the Self in all. Therefore, and oddly enough, it is while finally giving up all attachments to the external world and its various beings that one finds ultimate union with them. This is because when beings are preoccupied with their individual egos, they are selfish, no matter how kind and loving they might appear. But in the sublime state of oneness that the devotee experiences, there is none to love and none to hate, for all are part and parcel of the true Self, which is one and inseparable. It is not hard to imagine, then, how bliss comes upon the aspirant, leaving him or her with a profound and lasting sense of peace.

Though some find it difficult to conceive of, after beholding the *Atman*, external objects and the stimulations they produce begin to feel insipid. It is not that one becomes lifeless and devoid of drive and passion. It is rather that all energies, desires, and ambitions get fused into one force that gets directed towards the ultimate attainment of God-realization. What joy to behold the Source of all, and what relief to be free from the limitations of creation, which includes in its sweep the pains of birth and death, as well as life. Renunciation finds its fullest expression here, in the perfectly natural and fully mature atmosphere of one-pointed focus upon the *Atman*. What follows such singular concentration is equally blissful.

In the seventh stage of the *Guru/Shishya* relationship, called *Brahma-Shuddhi*, the devotee becomes pure by meditation on *Brahman*. The *Upanisads* state, *"Taking as bow that mighty weapon furnished by the nondual scriptures, fasten to it the mind made sharpened by thoughts of Brahman alone."* Perceiving the *Atman* within via study and contemplation gives way to entering into It fully and tracing Its pathway to the formless *Brahman*, the Ultimate Reality. As longer periods of immersion into that radiant effulgence ensue, more and more of the deeply buried impressions of the mind (*samskaras*) get unearthed and purified. As this process goes on, the mind is transformed into something other than mind, for all of its contents get emptied and what is left over gets thoroughly cleansed. This is why Sri Ramakrishna stated that *"Pure mind is God."*

At this wonderful plateau of spiritual experience, meditation per se finally gets defined. Here, it is no more a withdrawal of the mind from externals through self-effort, or a mere attempt at concentration with varied results. Steady and constant, the mind focuses naturally and easily, like the cobra upon a snake-charmer's music. What is more, the devotee begins to meditate in all that he or she does. Whether eyes are closed or wide open, the Reality is nonetheless ever-present and all-pervasive. This Reality is not merely apparent either, like the realms of *maya*, but is obvious and thrilling to behold. All of life gets transformed in Its peerless presence.

Atma-Jnana, direct experience of the true Self, comes next. In the previous stage, as well as in this one, the *Guru* has melted into boundless light. That is, though the provisional *guru* may still be present and accessible, the eternal *Guru*, the *Atman* within, is so brilliant and arresting that one naturally refrains from seeing that omniscient principle of guidance in any one location. In truth, there is nothing but *Guru* all around and within. *Guru-bhakti* becomes, as it were, a contradiction in terms, for where there is only one effulgent radiance lighting the way, what becomes of darkness and of losing the way? In addition, who is there that is distinct from oneself, towards which one may exercise any form of devotion?

Atma-Jnana has been described by many as the ultimate stage of realization, but the mind and its impressions from many past lives, as well as the ego sense that occupies it, struggle to stay alive up until the very last moment. Relative consciousness, which is in the habit of perceiving duality everywhere, and that has accumulated many fear-laden impressions, is tenacious and stubborn. Doubts, though subtle at this stage, continue to rise, and must be effaced completely. The penultimate stage sees the destruction of these subtle impediments.

Vinasha Samskara, the ninth stage, involves the detection and dissolution of very subtle detrimental impressions in the mind. Here, the aspirant faces and does away with the final vestiges of seed desires which hamper final immersion into *Brahman*. As the consummate vision of the Absolute presents itself, trepidation born of tiny residual waves left over from past desires and fears interrupt the flow of conscious Awareness towards its intended goal. By proximity to *Brahman* alone, and through elongated periods of meditation along with encouragement from the *Guru*, the devotee finally succeeds in transcending the fear of leaving behind temporal existence and moves beyond both attachment to joy and refined pleasure and the desire for conditional bliss in an individualized state of consciousness. The portals of relative existence are then broken down, and all boundaries are destroyed. The illusion of separation from *Brahman* fades away, and one, boundless ocean of Light-filled Awareness, remains.

The final stage of the precious communion between teacher and disciple culminates in an uninterrupted experience of union with *Brahman*, called *Sthiti Samadhi*. This steady and balanced conditionless condition is peace-filled, bliss-filled, and full of Truth and Wisdom. Freedom is Its atmosphere, and Consciousness its only substance. *Guru* and *shishya* are merged in It. All distinctions are effaced, all boundaries and divisions, dissolved. Eternity, infinity, and indivisibility are natural to It. All is Peace, Peace, Peace.

To those four types of beings who have accepted the spiritual preceptor's timely assistance — the suffering, the seeking, the aspiring, and the liberated — the attributes of *Guru* are well-known and appreciated. To the rest, it is a moot point. And this brings up another issue for consideration. To the illumined ones, *Guru* is within. Seeking outwardly, the uninitiated and the unenlightened never understand *Guru* with any clarity or precision. The condition of most seekers, those of mixed or impure motive, is such that the principle of *Guru* becomes a fad, a sensation, and something to be bantered about and gossiped about. What is worse, many who title themselves *gurus* are, more often than not, deceitful, pretentious, or deluded about their own spiritual status, and this makes for more confusion among the masses.

A secret emerges due to this, however. The realization of God is, as the saying goes, *"The Pearl of Great Price."* It is neither cognizable nor attainable to those of immature intellect and insincere devotion. The truth of this fact is a natural safeguard against all who would "defile the temple," so to speak, for God, the very essence of purity and excellence, is accessible only to those who are themselves pure and of excellent character. That is why, in this day and age, one finds so few authentic teachers and aspirants. Rare are those who are willing to follow the true teacher's instructions, what to speak of taking the considerable effort needed in finding and recognizing such a being in the first place. As Sri Ramakrishna has stated, *"It takes a jeweler to recognize the value of a diamond."*

Besides this important point, there are several other insights which figure into the picture. Personality worship, for example, is best left amidst the exponents of the *Vyavaharika* path, among those who seek entertainment, pleasures, fun, glamour, sensationalism, and the like. The constituents of this worldly path mimic the words and actions of others who, having forsaken the true purpose of life, leave the field of the soul untended and instead seek name, fame, and wealth — that which is of no lasting value or benefit. Speaking about the worldly-minded, the poet/saint, Ramprasad sings, *"Seeking for answers amidst friends, family, and society provides no profound solution. Don't you know that all are lost here? Everyone lives in pallid imitation of everyone else."*

In the spiritual realm, that is, where true spirituality is fostered and appreciated, the personality, rather than being the point and essence of existence, is eschewed for the most part. Egolessness is the ideal. It is not that the personality is not appreciated, for many of the saints and sages of the past were great characters. But in spiritual life it is the Divine Being which takes prominence, and those who have been seeking That for lifetimes take this as a welcome change. The Divine Being is not without personality either. Its ultimate nature is formless, but where the universe of names and forms is concerned, and where the spiritual well-being of precious sincere seekers is at stake, It assumes the form of its own nature and appears before the world's awestruck eyes as *Avatar*, the messenger of *Ishvara*. Those who have the great good fortune to behold this auspicious manifestation of Divinity experience transcendence of what is usual or normal in mundane life, and perceive the Lord sporting in the universe for the good of all beings. This is an especially powerful aspect of *Guru* Principle.

The personality of a man or woman of lesser stature, however, can only reflect so much of this form-effacing divinity. This truth is a direct indication as well as a dead giveaway. That is, it reveals those whom the Lord would make His true representatives, and betrays those who hide behind the facade of opportunism and pretension. If a person pretends to be spiritual, the ego-oriented tendency there will emerge in stark contrast to the pure and humble condition that a holy being exudes. Conversely, if someone wants to ascertain if another is holy, an examination of the person's character under all conditions of life will bring this to light, for the lack of certain known distortions found in the egocentric person will be noticed, and noted, in the seer. Therefore, one of the accepted and crucial practices a seeker undertakes is the intense scrutiny and examination of the teacher, which leaves by the wayside all doubts pertinent to the subject. One who does not apply this practice deserves the teacher he or she accepts and, as a result, suffers the consequences.

All legitimate preceptors point towards the formless *Guru* within. They do not, unless to effect certain beneficial ends, position themselves in such a manner as to appear as the only teacher or the ultimate *Guru*. Still, those who have realized the inner guide cannot but reflect what It entails and begin to radiate those excellent qualities associated with that Eternal Principle. Such mysteries are known only by those who experience the blessing of intimacy between *Guru* and disciple.

Along with the absence of ego and the lack of desire for worldly goods and attainments, the true preceptor takes seriously the charge of helping others out of the darkness of ignorance and delusion. Whereas fakes and frauds put on a show and enjoy all that comes from being worshipped and admired, the true spiritual teacher works hard, quite often behind the scenes, for the benefit of the students, showing them how to remove certain blocks that are in the way of spiritual advancement and realization of the *Atman* within. This is a lifetime's preoccupation with them, and it is difficult terrain wherein only patience, perseverance, and reliance on God prevail. The prospect of such austerity would cause the charlatan to "run away with the money," and many fraudulent teachers in this day and age have been caught doing just that. Such aberrations occur often in today's spiritual marketplace, but it does not open the eyes of the deluded. They remain duped, as dull as ever, and accept the imitation while overlooking or denying the original.

One can only stand, bow, and lovingly salute the true *Guru*. Soon, after certain disciplines have been exercised, the *Atman* chooses to reveal Itself, both in the preceptor and in the disciple. This is the point and purpose of all life, both worldly and spiritual. This moment is brought to bear by the presence of *Guru*. With reverence mixed with awe, the beholder of such inner radiance and excellence can only prostrate and praise the human *guru*, seeing that one as nothing less than the Ultimate Reality manifested in a form. In this realization there is much less aggrandizement, adulation, personality worship, and the like, and much more of reverence, appreciation, and love instead. It is with this in mind that the *Kularnava Tantra* states:

> *Following the instructions of Guru is more beneficial*
> *than study, knowledge, offerings, sacrifices, charity, or worship.*
> *Guru is higher than friends and family, and more efficacious than mantra.*
> *Meditation is, itself, the form of Guru, and by Guru is liberation gained.*
> *All holy actions are facilitated by Guru, and all fulfillment granted thereby.*
> *Fear, distress, grief, and other pains disappear through Guru's Grace.*
> *Wandering in the trackless wastes of Samsara is brought to an end by Guru.*
> *When Guru gives himself to the disciple, sins drop away and peace descends.*
> *Brahma, Vishnu, and Shiva bestow their Grace when Guru is pleased.*
> *Through Guru's direction alone, karmas are transcended and freedom is attained.*

To illustrate all of the above in a fun and friendly manner, the next chart presents the long and winding road of moving from ignorance to illumination, or as Swami Vivekananda has so kindly put it, *"...moving from lower truth to higher Truth."* At this point it will be beneficial to take one of contemporary time's most authentic and beloved of Gurus, Sri Ramakrishna Paramahamsa, and lay out His Radiant Road to Reality as epitomized by both His life and His teachings. For *Guru Tattva*, or *Guru* Principle, has never been so clearly expressed, especially in current times, as in an exemplary life such as His. From compassionately assisting fallen, lowly, and suffering beings, to experiencing a plethora of various *samadhis*, and all that lies in between these wide and disparate strata of existence, Sri Ramakrishna Deva did it all. To read about, know about, and meditate upon such a being in this day and age is an incomparable boon, emphasized all the more by what great beings like Sri Aurobindo, Mahatma Gandhi, and Swami Vivekananda have said about Him. In the following chart, based on the Great Master's many fine stories, we can see the path clearly laid out.

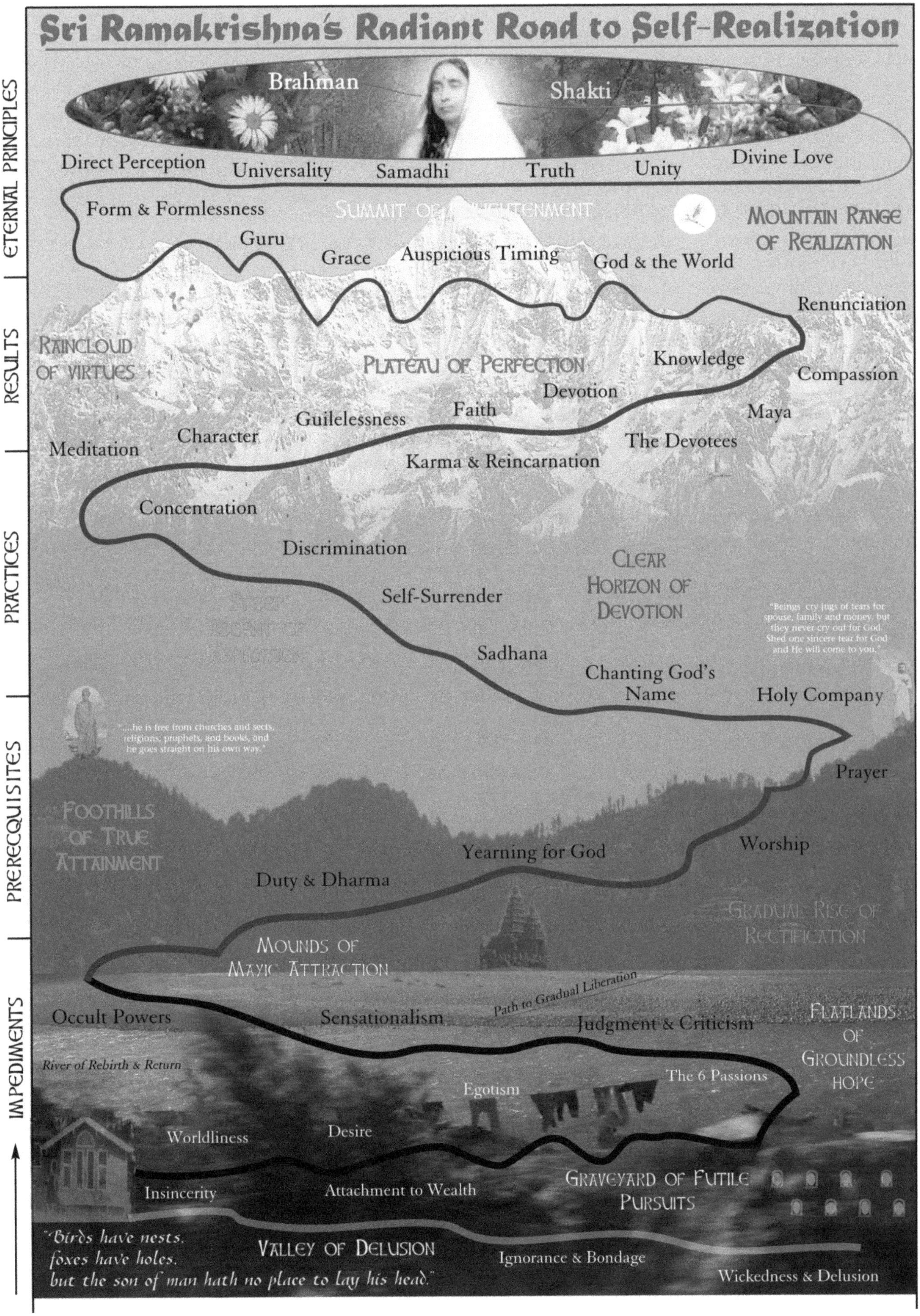

Sri Ramakrishna's Radiant Road to Self-Realization

ETERNAL PRINCIPLES

Brahman — Shakti

Direct Perception — Universality — Samadhi — Truth — Unity — Divine Love

Form & Formlessness — SUMMIT OF ENLIGHTENMENT — MOUNTAIN RANGE OF REALIZATION

Guru

Grace — Auspicious Timing — God & the World

RESULTS

RAINCLOUD OF VIRTUES

Renunciation

PLATEAU OF PERFECTION — Knowledge — Compassion

Devotion — Maya

Guilelessness — Faith

Character — The Devotees

Meditation — Karma & Reincarnation

PRACTICES

Concentration

Discrimination — CLEAR HORIZON OF DEVOTION

Self-Surrender

"Beings cry jugs of tears for spouse, family and money, but they never cry out for God. Shed one sincere tear for God and He will come to you."

Sadhana

Chanting God's Name — Holy Company

PREREQUISITES

"...he is free from churches and sects, religions, prophets, and books, and he goes straight on his own way."

Prayer

FOOTHILLS OF TRUE ATTAINMENT

Yearning for God — Worship

Duty & Dharma

GRADUAL RISE OF RECTIFICATION

MOUNDS OF MAYIC ATTRACTION

IMPEDIMENTS

Path to Gradual Liberation

Occult Powers — Sensationalism — Judgment & Criticism — FLATLANDS OF GROUNDLESS HOPE

River of Rebirth & Return — The 6 Passions

Egotism

Worldliness — Desire

Insincerity — Attachment to Wealth — GRAVEYARD OF FUTILE PURSUITS

"Birds have nests, foxes have holes, but the son of man hath no place to lay his head." — VALLEY OF DELUSION — Ignorance & Bondage

Wickedness & Delusion

Stretching out as far as the eye can see, from the all too friendly doorway which exists in the earthly home of conventional living, to the all too familiar valley of delusion, darkness, despair, and death, is the vast realm of *maya* with its truculent traps and omnifarious opportunities. Both of these paths — the conventional and the darksome — spoken of by such luminaries as Sri Krishna, lie within easy access of those hopeful and often ill-considered footfalls that humanity considers lifetime to lifetime. The wayward way, as reflected in our chart (page 103), is paved with insincerity and attachment to ephemeral wealth and pleasure, and leads on through the graveyard of empty and futile pursuits. The conventional path, trodden by so many, leads one to enticements which, even if attained, are often better left alone. To quote the wise, mankind hath no place to lay his head here, in either realm, even though he tries so hard, again and again, to do so.

But a more unique type of living soul sees a different way when coming fresh from the womb of the earthly mother, as is also revealed by the chart presently under study. Far-seeing, these souls gaze long and hard at the tired and tawdry goods which worldly beings seek, all set along the conventional path of desire, egotism, and passion, and abjures. This way only leads to the flatlands of groundless hope, and so the avid seeker only passes by and thus pierces through this land and its paltry offerings to encounter what at first seems worthy of attainment. But upon closer inspection, this mountain of hope only disappoints further, showing itself up as a few mere mounds of *mayic* attainment where beings get lost in the specious allurements of sensationalism and occult powers, and habitual pastimes like criticism and fault-finding.

But at least, from here, the particular and perspicacious seeker of truth can glimpse the foothills of true attainment looming in the distance, and wastes no time in making haste for their welcome precincts. Upon arrival there, due to this soul's sincerity, the fiery sun of worldly duty falling upon his shoulders begins to feel like the warmth of drudgery-dispelling *dharma* wherein the distinct desire for God-realization makes itself known. This is the yearning for communion with Divine Reality, a rare mood which comes over the devotee after the workaday world has shown itself up to be nothing more than a temporal condition. This uncommon inclination towards God has one particular benefit in that it will guide one, unerringly and in due time, to that unique and rarefied atmosphere referred to as "holy company" among the knowers of *Brahman*. From there, the dizzying steep rise of the ascent to true aspiration, the steppes leading to the highlands of authentic spirituality, can be accessed. Therefore, all sincere aspirants go for refuge there.

The ascent of aspiration begins with practice, or self-effort, called *sadhana* by the Indian *rishis* who prescribed it for their devotees. Having passed through the vacuous valleys, gruesome graveyards, feckless flatlands, and the mocking mounds of *maya*, the authentic aspirant is anxious to encounter and test him or herself along the steep slopes of *sadhana*. For this, the adherents of holy company will prescribe such practices as worship, prayer, and the chanting of the names of the Lord, all done under the capacious canvas of self-surrender in order to render it successful.

In this first phase of *sadhana*, the callow side of man's ego is being attenuated, allowing for a more open-minded stance. Going forward dauntlessly, and with characteristic "elan," the razor's-edged practices of intellectual discrimination, mental concentration, and spiritual meditation are met with, meant to temper and refine the proud and passionate side of the ego, making it calm and pure. These are the foothills of true attainment where Lord Siva dances blissfully under the illuminating sunlight of wisdom and its profound transmission. If the devotee can round the corner of this lofty and dizzying spiritual altitude, the mountain range of realization comes into view.

But before these mountains of deep spirituality are encountered, the natural building of character, the guilelessness of a child, and deep faith must increase and manifest, For, it is only with the development of sterling qualities like these that devotion and knowledge, called the two wings of the bird, will come under the aspirant's possession (see charts on pages 427, 429). When a man has these for his own, the entire world becomes his. But it is not the world of objects that belongs to him, nor does he want that. As the chart reflects, devotion and wisdom, together, culminate in renunciation. Ironically, true love and authentic wisdom tend to cause the mind to let go of ephemeral things like wealth and worldly concerns. This happens at a level of spiritual realization.

From the mountaintops of spiritual realization, many things, heretofore unbeknownst to mankind, become revealed. The distinctions between God and the world, as well as their connections, are perceived. Secrets like auspicious timing, the workings of grace, and knowledge of the *Guru* principle all occur here as well. Here is where spiritual teachers are made, or awakened to their true mission. And rounding this particular corner, like a mountain path affording the most marvelous views, eternal principles such as the workings of form and formlessness, the subtlest of dualities, are understood, as are immutable truths like the axiom of Universality and the harmony, even unity, of all religions. Sublime mysteries such as these are barely known, even to saints and sages, who quite often know, follow, and teach just their own singular approach to Reality. The specialized knowledge which brings to the fore the truths of all religions is definitely acquired and held by that most superb of all qualities called direct perception, or *aparokshanubhuti* (see chart on page 345). Decades of devout practice, even lifetimes of self-effort, adept guidance, and personal experience, are needed for such rare spiritual proficiency.

The Radiant Road to Reality contains even more than this fine host of attributes and accomplishments as well, as attested to in the exemplary lives of Sri Ramakrishna, His divine consort, Sri Sarada Devi, and His direct disciple, Swami Vivekananda. The experience of *samadhi*, if it could be called that, was a special characteristic of the Great Master's life, since He blissfully received so many different types of *samadhi* within His slight and tender frame — *jada, unmana, chetana, sthiti, savikalpa, samprajnata,* even *Asamprajnata* or *Nirvikalpa*, the nondual state, pervaded Him thoroughly on many occasions. Thus we have, on recent historical record and in plain view of contemporary humanity, a divine being who demonstrated to the people of this modern world the true condition of a human being. He was therefore a natural human being — what one should look and be like. Gazing at such a soul we can see just how far we have fallen from our divine heritage in this age.

Samadhi paves the way for the incomparable glories of Truth, Unity, and Divine Love as well, which are infrequent, even unprecedented signs, seen at the very summit of Enlightenment. At this most elevated or inward of rarefied atmospheres, where Consciousness Itself is the very air that is breathed, only the divine Couple, *Brahman* and *Shakti*, abide. *Brahman*, of course, is the underlying subject of everything in this book. *Shakti*, extremely precious, also underlaying everything, will be allocated entire chapters and sections herein, in order to convey a bit of Her comprehensive role.

The Radiant Road presented here is found inherent in the Great Master and all He taught. The storyboard itself came about by simply placing some 700 stories which He told into categories, thus tracing the passage which any sincere and intrepid spiritual wayfarer will traverse on his or her way to Enlightenment. The Great Master invites us to it, pleads with us to set foot upon it, and challenges us to conquer it — all for our own best good, and the highest good of all living beings.

Sri Ramakrishna's chief disciple, Swami Vivekananda, will also be heard from, and about, throughout the pages of this book. As a contemporary Indian *rishi*, he plays an extremely important part in the re-introduction of authentic spirituality into the modern and mechanized world. He, and beings such as Ramana Maharshi, along with a few important others, could be cited as the best representatives of world leaders that have come out of Mother India in recent times. And when the term "world leader" is used here, it refers to a being who is not just honored in political arenas amidst people who are worried about world affairs having to do with only their own countries and concerns, but a leader of religious, spiritual, and divine standards — a being so much more mature, with so much more capacity for both amelioration and transformation that far surpasses the likes of beings involved in terrestrial affairs alone. Working with even-mindedness at levels of degradation, reformation, transformation, and realization, such a being leaves a huge impression upon the collective memory of humanity for ages at a time. In the next chart up for consideration, which uses Swami Vivekananda for its superlative example, the qualities of a true world teacher and leader on the cosmic and divine levels is put forward for review, in contrast to what people today think of as a world leader.

"You may go and knock your head against the four corners of the world, seek in the Himalayas, the Alps, the Caucasus, the desert of Gobi or Sahara, or the bottom of the sea, but perfection will not come until you find a Teacher." Swami Vivekananda

1 Atma-Jnana — Self-realization A true world teacher/leader must:
a) possess spirituality; b) strive to help the suffering c) free the oppressed d) inspire the masses

2) Mantra Drashta — Sagehood/Rishihood A true world teacher/leader has:
a) Purity and holiness b) the ability to transmit spirituality c) a desire to benefit all beings

3) Abhaya Pratistha — Fearlessness A true world teacher/leader is:
a) undaunted in the face of struggle, work, or adversity b) willing to take on the karma of others
c) a direct channel of the Divine whose counsels and decisions are transformative

4) Shakti-Sanchara — Spiritual Dynamism A true world teacher/leader possesses:
a) the power of a warrior, the dedication of a servant, the practicality of a merchant, and the insight of a savior b) knowledge of the ancient scriptures and knowledge of the needs of the time

5) Shraddha — Faith A true world teacher/leader is able to:
a) retain pure faith in God, Seers, and Self b) see the good in others c) exude an aura of assurance d) inspire others to take up the work e)remove obstacles and gain success based upon faith

6) Krypa — Power of Grace A true world teacher/leader demonstrates:
a) the spirit of selflessness b) the ability to release others from suffering c) the power to awaken others from ignorance d) the quality of selflessness e) the fact that excellence avoids competition

7) Prema-Seva — Service through Love A true world teacher/leader perceives:
a) the unity of all beings and things b) the need to help the lowly c) the importance of sacrifice

8) Utsaha — Positivity and Enthusiasm A true world teacher/leader:
a) changes the hearts and minds of others b) transforms enemies into friends c) compels beings to act without any thought of reward d) causes introspection in others e) demonstrates divinity

9) Chitprasadana — Practicality/Clarity of Mind A true world teacher/leader:
a) works with right attitude and proper means b) places equal attention on all levels of endeavor
c) fulfills duty with detachment to work and its outcome d) directs all towards the highest good

10) Moksha cha Tulya — Freedom and Equality A true world teacher/leader strives:
a) to bring equality to the underprivileged b) to give all a desire for and taste of freedom
c) to convince the well-to-do to serve and work for the amelioration of the masses

11) Jnana-Vijnana — Knowledge and Wisdom A true world teacher/leader wields:
a) worldly wisdom, scientific knowledge, and scriptural truth b) the ability to make decisions based upon comprehension understanding c) both God's presence and personal experience

12) Parama-Drk — Supreme Vision A true world teacher/leader envisions:
a) the future of mankind b) the need to bring out the potential in all beings/nations c) Reality

13) Niskama Karma — Victory in Action A true world teacher/leader imbues:
a) all beings with the nobility of works b) all beings with the desire to better the world in God

14) Alaya Vijnana — Wise Integration A true world teacher/leader reveals:
a) that peace is superior to power b) that internal excellence predicates external excellence
c) adept guidance to those seeking spiritual evolvement while embodied on earth

1. *Atmajnan*, a term utilized many times in the pages of this copious work on Indian religion and philosophy, is the singlemost indispensable element in life. And it is as important to earthly life as it is to spiritual life, for it is in the press of its absence that beings run afoul of *maya* and enter into so many conjured up realms of suffering, called hell in conventional religion. From the hallowed station of authentic spiritual life, however, this simply does not occur, for those possessing *Atmajnan* have long ago realized, due to its cleansing and clarifying effects, that all worlds in space and time are transitory, even illusory from the standpoint of nondual *samadhi*. What hell could persist, and what heaven would beckon in the heights of such an illumined state? This is why my teacher, Swami Aseshananda, used to state adamantly that *"The Vedantist does not care for a post-mortem emancipation,"* and *"is not interested in heaven."*

For our purposes here, it is enough to call *Atmajnan* "spirituality." All citizens of the *Bhurloka* (physical worlds) must attempt to secure it, while the true world leader already possesses it. With this innate spirituality realized and intact, such a select soul can go forward, as this chart indicates page 106), to help suffering beings, inspire the masses, and even free oppressed peoples. It should be noted that all this is not accomplished merely on the political and cultural level, which is the thin veneer of a domain presided over by leaders devoid of *Atmajnan*. Their attraction to money, power, and fame spoils them for authentic selfless service. The true world leader is interested more in the transmission of highest wisdom into the hearts and minds of living beings — a feat which only such a superlative soul can accomplish. This will purify the thinking process, destroy residual *karmas*, and bring about the sought after spiritual transition on the physical plane over time.

Each of these directives — removing suffering, inspiring the masses, and freeing the oppressed — requires a singular mind-set. The consummate world leader does not think like ordinary leaders, like altruists and politicians, nor will he or she fall into the many false assumptions like they do. For instance, ideas of utopia have been shorn away from such a mind, for he sees that suffering is in the nature of embodied existence. The statement, "Suffering is," may as well be the first noble truth of embodied existence, then, and knowing it as such, the true leader of humanity will refrain from the attempt to remove the suffering that is part and parcel of relativity, for it is crucial to the healing process. All his salubrious energies will become focused upon those types of suffering which are unnecessary. What people suffer due to narrowness of mind, lowness of spirit, weakness of heart, and ignorance of *dharma* — those things will get the lion's share of the authentic world teacher's attention — while the ordinary leader focuses on the outer symptoms only.

As for the oppressed, they need an ideal, and the world leader is there to point one out. With the death of authentic religion in people's hearts and minds comes forgetfulness of God with Form, or *Ishvara/Ishvari*. *Ishvara* is not that tired and monotonous God of the conventional church, who seems to love only the rich and successful and forget the fallen and lowly ones. *Ishvara* does not condemn or forgive the sinner, nor sacrifice for the redemption of the lost. *Ishvara* does not forgive the lost soul, but serves and worships it, and thus causes remembrance of its innate divinity to rise up in those who suffer the most. This is reflected in one of Swami Vivekananda's unique sayings: *"May I be born again and again, and suffer thousands of miseries, so that I may worship the only God that exists, the only God I believe in, the sum total of all souls — and above all my God the wicked, my God the miserable, my God the poor of all races, of all species, is the special object of my worship."*

Such a superlative attitude sets the world leader apart from all other pretenders to the throne, and reveals him to be far above the ken of the gods of various religious institutions. These latter, whether good or assumed good, look at human beings as if they were evil, and judge their suffering under the narrow scope of moral judgment. But the true world teacher sees on a very different level. Another of Swami Vivekananda's amazing statements demonstrates this distinction: *"Again, I have heard that if one does not see the evil round him, he cannot do good work — he lapses into a sort of fatalism. I do not see that. On the other hand, my power of work is immensely increasing and becoming immensely effective. Some days I get into a sort of ecstasy. I feel that I must bless everyone, everything, love and embrace everything, and I do see that evil is a delusion."*

Seeing and penetrating through the illusory front of evil and suffering is unique to the world teacher, then. Few others would even dare to imagine on this level. Even the occasional genius is a mere infant when it comes to spiritual truths of this lofty caliber. Armed with divine missiles such as these, the illumined teacher can easily rouse and inspire the masses, moving them to return, as a collective whole, to that path of transcendent righteousness called *svadharma*. For the great teacher knows that life is not a matter of unity; it is a matter of harmony. What lies beyond the embodied condition — that smacks of unity. Formlessness is unity, but form, i.e., life, must strive for harmony. The world teacher possesses this secret and is ready to bestow it as a special gift upon certain qualified souls who want to transcend desire and fear. Thus, the world teacher epitomizes the consummate divine warrior, armed with an inconceivable collection of convincing weapons. More about *Atmajnan* will occur throughout the pages of this book.

2. The second quality of note which the world teacher possesses is sagehood, called *Mantra Drashta* on the chart under study. This is an attainment which is precious, and which can never be diminished or taken away. A strict and prolonged school of trials and challenges, even hard knocks, has fashioned the awakened soul into a *rishi*, or a seer of truth. The holiness and purity that he possesses is both hard won and authentic. Few know what such a soul has undergone in order to create and instill such depth and intensity into the heart and mind. But graciously, along with these two qualities has come the ability to transmit spirituality to others. This is not a common person who gives advice, or counsels with a few kind words, or absolves one of sins by recommending penances and the like. With a gaze or a word this superlative soul can inject his or her own divinity straight into the soul of another, whether worthy or not. This is accomplished not for credit or praise, but comes as a result of the sincere desire to be of deepest and highest benefit to all beings.

3. The third quality listed in our chart under study is the rare boon of fearlessness, *Abhaya Pratistha*. Some of us have heard the wonderful poem, *Abhaya Pratistham* (a state of steady fearlessness), by Swami Vivekananda, written to one of his English disciples during a time of her great need. Even the first few lines are enough to inspire deeply: *"We shall crush the stars to atoms. We shall unhinge the universe. Don't you know who we are? We are the children of Sri Ramakrishna...."* The ability to transcend the realms of name and form results in such fearlessness. Of course, freedom from the fear of death comes to mind immediately. As the many teachings contained in this book will attest to, the real condition of the human being is birthless and deathless (see chart on page 746), what is termed *ajati*, or "nonorigination" by the nondualists. Full identification with the *Atman*, rather than the body, has brought this power to bear in the mind of the luminary.

Knowing the principle of nonorigination (*ajativada*) inside and out, and thereby being beyond the reach of fear of any kind, the world teacher works unstintingly for the highest good of the world's creatures, but also remains *"undaunted in the face of struggles, work, and adversity,"* as the chart under study reflects. This fearlessness extends even to the realm of people's personal problems, since the illumined soul holds within him the rare ability to neutralize the *karmas* of others, taking their poisonous effects onto himself. These he works out in a manner all his own, unbeknownst to others. And even in the midst of this, the world teacher goes on guiding and directing, on individual, collective, and cosmic levels of existence, selflessly. Nothing in existence quite matches the wonder and outright marvel of God manifesting and expressing through the fully illumined soul.

4. Spiritual dynamism, *Shakti Sanchara*, is a striking property of the illumined soul as well, and in the hands of the world teacher, the *Jagad Guru*, manifests the combined force of *"the power of a warrior, the dedication of a servant, the practicality of a merchant, and the insight of a savior."* A long and loving relationship with sacred scriptures has much to do with this type of flexibility. Studying the ancient *darshanas* of the world, the illumined soul has developed both nondual wisdom and the power of integration. Far beyond one-sided savants, scholars, and religionists, this incomparable soul has seen and experienced the ingrained truth in all wisdom traditions, and has thereby founded his greater comprehension on the unalterable principle of Universality. A brief deviation from the chart under study can be taken here, to reveal the uniqueness of Universality as compared to other views:

"I have practiced the disciplines of all paths, each for a few days. Otherwise I would have had no peace of mind. I respect the Shaktas, the Vaishnavas, the Vedantists, and also the modern Brahmajnanis. Therefore, people of all sects come to me. And everyone of them think that I belong to his school." Sri Ramakrishna

Universalism

universalism / n: a principle corresponding to reality and its essence which declares that all beings will be saved based upon a truth that is comprehensively broad and versatile, existent and operative everywhere and under all conditions, that embraces the totality of mankind without limits or exceptions regardless of religious differences, and that is easily adaptable or adjustable to meet the varied philosophical requirements of all of humanity.

Ecumenism

ecumenism / n: of or relating to an entire body of churches, particularly of one religious tradition.

Eclecticism

eclecticism / n: to select what appears to be best from a number of various doctrines or methods.

"I have gathered the many different religions of the world and fashioned a bouquet of them, offering it at the Fearless Feet of the Universal Wisdom-Mother." Ramakrishna

Fundamentalism

fundamentalism / n: a movement of 20th century Protestantism stressing the literal interpretation of the Bible as the only truth.

"We reject none, neither theist, pantheist, monist, polytheist, agnostic, nor atheist; the only condition of being a disciple is modeling a character at once the broadest and most intense. We leave everybody free to know, select, and follow whatever suits and helps him."
Swami Vivekananda

Atheism

atheism / n: the doctrine which proposes a basic disbelief in the existence of God or deity.

Agnosticism

agnosticism / n: the doctrine which espouses the belief that God is unknown and unknowable.

Intellectualism

intellectualism / n: devotion to the exercise of the intellect and to rational intellectual pursuits.

"Dry knowledge is like cheap fireworks, or a rocket that bursts into a few sparks and dies away. But spiritual knowledge is like an expensive rocket that showers different colors, stops, then bursts forth again many times. Yet, the minds of pundits and scholars are fixed on dry knowledge, like the eyes of a vulture fixed on the carrion pit." Ramakrishna

Secularism

secularism / n: indifference to or rejection or exclusion of religion and religious considerations.

Materialism

materialism / n: preoccupation with matter to the exclusion of intellectual and spiritual considerations based upon the belief that matter is the only reality.

"There once was a man who owned a dye-tub. Such was its wonderful property that people could dye their clothes any color they desired by merely dipping them into it. Observing this unusual phenomena, one clever man approached the owner of the tub and said, 'Sir, please dye my cloth the color of the dye in your tub.'" Sri Ramakrishna

This chart (page 109) has been created by utilizing the English dictionary in order to define some of these common and not so common secular and religious terms that get bandied about by people operating mentally, intellectually, and religiously at differing levels of the mind's understanding. The particular juxtaposition shown here is comprehensive, placing side by side, and according to accepted definitions, several adopted perspectives on the chain of ascension, from secular to religious to spiritual to transcendent. The chart is self-explanatory, and all the definitions should be studied and taken in by the reader for a well synthesized consideration.

What we have here are nine main views, if the term may be used, espoused by people at differing levels of their evolution and understanding. These are: materialism, secularism, intellectualism, agnosticism, atheism, fundamentalism, eclecticism, ecumenism, and universalism. Hearkening back to our previous chart (page 106), still under inspection, a world teacher is aware of all of these, having come upon countless souls over many lifetimes who hail from all of these widely adapted and multifarious opinions or persuasions. Of course, the "opinion" of this book, and its inspection of the various Indian philosophies which have established themselves throughout history, is distinctly spiritual. The crowning achievement of Mother India, culturally and religiously speaking, has to be Her universal acceptance of all religions, which goes well beyond the idea of mere tolerance. This acceptance is unprecedented among the world's people and cultures.

In Her earliest and most important scriptures, namely the *Upanisads*, we find this excellent confirmation of the truth of all religions: *"Ekam sat viprah bahudha vadanti — Truth is one; sages call it by various names,"* sometimes also translated more compactly as *"Truth is one, paths are many."* Again, there is another *upanisadic sloka* which declares that all the religions of the world are like so many rivers, all flowing to the sea. Sri Ramakrishna, whose image graces this chart, has also used the element of water in the analogy of many kinds of beings coming to a lake, at different landings, and drawing the same water into differing vessels while calling it by various names — the Hindu calling it jal, the Muslim, pani, the Englishman, water, the Greek man, aqua, etc. So this idea, or principle, is in the very lifeblood of India's thinking process, the very essence of its spirituality.

This chart has been constructed in plateaus which represent three main strata of human thinking: the spiritual, the religious, and the secular. The secular holds all that is intellectual by nature, whose proponents rest either in the lofty skies of wise conception, on the fixed and dry ground of worldliness, or in the stunted basement of limited, even rank, materialism. It is interesting to note what a great soul like Sri Ramakrishna has to say about the tendency of restricting life and mind to this quotidian strata, and what he points out about the pundits and scholars who make their constricted home here. Again, the quotes on the chart are to be examined by the reader.

Next in order of ascension is the religious level. It is often hard to determine whether the souls who take to this level of thinking are higher or lower than the intellectuals. It was Swami Vivekananda who once said that he had met many atheists in his day who seemed better people than those who professed religion. But this raises a good point. One who has a problem with religion has nevertheless necessarily contemplated it, one way or another, and so must be classed among those who have considered its ideals.

At this point it is interesting to observe the difference between atheism and agnosticism. Everyone is aware of the narrow views of the fundamentalists, and many are seeing through their often impractical and unreasonable claims in this day and time, but the difference between someone who rejects the existence of God as opposed to one who simply has no opinion one way or another is telling. And actually, according to the dictionary's definition of agnosticism, such a soul sounds a bit like a nondualist, or a believer in formlessness. This perspective does not necessarily indicate someone who believes in a void, like a nihilist, either. That "God is unknown and unknowable" sounds much like a statement belonging to a higher wisdom school.

Whatever the case may be, the real teachings of this chart begin at the level of spirituality, where all rejections and resistances are thankfully thrown to the four winds. Here, it is interesting to note that there is no word in the *Sanskrit* language of Mother India for the term "atheist." The closest the seers could come to defining such a person was to call him *"one of deluded understanding."* This relates that the illumined beings hailing from ancient India, on top of being universalists, were also people of faith. Consciousness *(chaitanya)* was their real God, thought of in the nondual sense, and Consciousness is, obviously, everywhere; signs of it pervade all levels of human existence. From here it all becomes a matter of realizing Consciousness, a journey which has many plateaus and valleys, as well as many problems and impediments. But more on that later, in the chapters on *sadhana* and *maya*.

Comparing the terms eclecticism and ecumenism brings out an interesting distinction. The "bad rap" on eclecticism has always been its penchant for accepting all and everything before verifying any of it via modes of practice. In other words, a certain lack of discriminative wisdom is noted in the case of the one who espouses to be eclectic. It is the "I have accepted every religion as true but have never practiced a single one of them" syndrome that is objectionable. On the other hand, the ecumenicist runs the risk of criticism as well, for the term is oft used by so-called open-minded persons who attempt to bring together the views of various churches and lineages for the sake of some vaunted unity. The problem with this, however, is that all the factions sought for the act of uniting belong to just one religion, like Christianity. In this scenario, all the other religions get perfunctorily left out in the cold, forsaken, not even considered in the sweep of religion itself! This is unconscionable.

Still, there is general trend towards religious inclusion in the use of the term ecumenism. The Dalai Lama has utilized the term in the sense of a Buddhist-Christian understanding which brings India's great *rishi*, Gautama Buddha, together with the also thoroughly Eastern Christ. This works well considering that these two spiritual giants lived only some 500 years apart. And whatever the outcome, the narrow confines of fundamentalism may be broken asunder by such inroads, or at least struck a blow for the higher good of aspiring souls.

After all is said and done, however, it is in the superlative principle of Universalism that all religions get their due. As the definition on the chart relates, broad and versatile, operative everywhere and under all conditions, embracing all of mankind without exceptions, easily adaptable — who would not want a religion such as this? Further, the main exponent of this grand Truth, Sri Ramakrishna Paramahamsa, has come amongst us already in this day and age, exemplifying its loftiest tenets for all to see and sowing the seeds for its inception into collective humanity's heart and mind. A quick reading of the two quotes on the chart by this incomparable past master should be enough to convey the depth and profundity of his vision. Recognition of the desirability of Universalism, and placing its principles into practice, can swiftly follow thereafter.

5. Returning to our previous chart, involving the fourteen qualities of a world teacher (page 106), we next explore the attribute of faith, *Shraddha*. The five subheadings here describe the makeup of a perfected soul. First of all, his/her faith in the Lord, and in the seers and sages (and *gurus*), is unshakable. Since their positive influence has formed an important part of his life, he can pass such inspiration on to others, compelling them to take up the mantle of selfless service to God dwelling in all living beings. The saying is that faith can move mountains. The subtle but considerable mountains of doubt, fear, delusion, and the like are not only moved at the great teacher's command, they are converted into examples for others watching nearby, revealing the irresistible force of a mind that is focused upon Divine Reality. Here we can repeat one *Sanskrit sloka* that advises: *"Fashion the scriptures into a mighty bow, and fasten the mind, made sharpened by thoughts of Reality alone, into an arrow. With those two, aim, release and hit the mark — the Imperishable Brahman."*

6. Grace, *Krypa*, is an unfigurable element in the prime quotient of spiritual life. With it, all obstacles fall easily to their demise. The world teacher, humble yet powerful, possessing grace, charges the spirits of others with the quality of selfless service, and thereby helps others destroy all vestiges of ignorance in the mind. Avoiding old and stale methods of conventionally-conceived growth, such as pitting one faction against the other, the competitive spirit thus either dies outright, replaced by a higher standard, or gets transformed into a sense of spiritual comradery. Perhaps the

song of Lord Chaitanya says it best when it states: *"Give all praise to others, take all blame to yourself."* Through this kind of self-effacing attitude, undue pride — which is the antithesis of welcome and ready Grace — gets destroyed forever.

7. We have mentioned earlier that *Ishvara/Ishvari*, the highest God with Form, is not characterized by the sacrifice of suffering alone. Otherwise ones God becomes a matter of morbidity. He becomes a doormat upon which the transgressor wipes the feet of justification for sins. The sacrifice of love, *Prema-Seva*, more specifically characterizes *Ishvara*. It is not out of empathy, or pity, or even compassion that the Lord offers succor to suffering and aspiring souls, but rather out of pure Love — *Prema*. This is because Love is Its nature. The Lord, the Mother, wants to share this ecstatic Love with all Her children. This is bliss. This bliss is to be shared by all because all beings are really one Soul, the Great Self. Swami Vivekananda explains this sacred act and its dynamic in another of his great sayings: *"When you serve an embodied soul with the idea that he is a jiva, embodied soul, it is daya, compassion, and not prema, love; but when you serve him with the idea that he is the Self, Atman, that is prema. That the Atman is the one objective of love is known from shruti, smriti, and anubhava. Bhagavan Chaitanya was right when He said: 'Love to God, compassion to the jiva.' This conclusion of the Bhagavan, intimating differentiation between Jiva and Ishvara was right, as He was a dualist. But for us, Advaitans, this notion of jiva as distinct from God is the cause of bondage. Our principle should be, therefore, love and not compassion. The application of the word compassion even to jiva seems to me to be rash and vain. For us, it is not to pity, but to serve. Ours is not the feeling of compassion but of love, and the feeling of Self in all."* And such realizations are nothing less than the Grace of the Lord.

8. The *Sanskrit* word, *Utsaha*, means enthusiasm. What is meant here is not to be confused with the word "zeal," at least in the conventional religious sense, for many beings are all too familiar with the likes of those proselytizers who emanate religious zeal for purposes of conversion. But the point of religion is altogether stymied by the concept of conversion. All beings are really one Great Soul, and that real Soul has no denominational markings on it. Beings should follow their inmost hearts, and as such find a wealth of wisdom existing in all religions. The world teacher knows this incontrovertible fact, and thereby changes the hearts and minds of beings — not in the sense of jumping from one religion to another in confusion, but by showing the means for purification of mind leading to Enlightenment. Then, even beings who were once enemies become great friends, confused souls take to sweet inward contemplation, and those who were once selfish convert not their religious beliefs, but rather their mode and attitude around selfless service to all souls. As Vivekananda states in his famous poem, *Song of the Sanyasin: "Say peace to all, from me no danger be to ought that lives. From those who dwell on high, to those who lowly creep, I am the Self in all...."*

9. In the Indian scriptures, purity is talked about at four levels: purity of food; purity of mood/thought; purity of mind; and purity of Self. It is purity of mood which is spoken of here — *Chittaprasadana*. It is a great secret, and a great boon upon all, to work free of both design and desire, and to do so with a pure attitude. The mind is so powerful, and the world is its vibrational field. All that it undertakes and enacts it permeates. Its thoughts, as projections, sink deep into the fabric of the world, into matter, objects, food, etc. Knowing this, and in conjunction with *utsaha*, enthusiasm, the world teacher ensures that all he says and does, as well as his thoughts, maintain a standard of high integrity. In works, this means utilizing the wonderful combination of such seemingly contrasting mediums as detachment and attention to detail. Endeavor free of restlessness, satisfied in the mere doing, is the telling result — a result which most beings have never witnessed before, since the members of conventional society demonstrate an entirely different way of operations, one that is frenetically restless and personally self-centered. The higher good is never satisfied in this latter scenario, so the true world leader brings something new and fresh to the table in this regard.

10. Freedom and equality, *Moksha cha Tulya*, has become a tired term in today's arid political and conventional climate. In today's democratically-based nations it means the freedom and equality to be able to gain wealth and status for oneself, often irrespective of the rights and needs of oth-

ers. This is injustice masquerading as justice. Rather than trying to convince deluded and devious souls to mend their ways via morality and ethics, the world teacher instead *"grants unto Caesar"* what Caesar most wants, and instead works to instill into the masses the desire for a freedom based upon transcendence. At the same time, the world teacher has a practical side, and does not ignore those *dharmic* individuals who have gained the grace of the goddess of wealth and acquired riches by legitimate means. These he will convince to use their honestly earned wealth to benefit others who are in need. *Mahat Seva*, service of the great souls, is thus one of the great boons of a householder's life, through which he can perfectly justify his life and living and exonerate himself and his family of all distortions which may come from handling and owning wealth. All of this also acts to present a great example to others as to how they too can purify all actions perpetrated in the atmosphere of the world and its various modes and avenues. *Dharma* first, then *moksha* — liberation. This seems to be the especial modus operandi of the illumined soul in his dealings with the more sensitive souls of this earthly plane.

11. Whereas most beings live in *ajnana*, the lack of discriminative wisdom of the spiritual kind, the world leader will blend knowledge and Truth, *Jnana-Vijnana*, into a comprehensive tool for uplifting the masses. This upliftment will occur where it is really needed — at the spiritual level. People think that their worldly knowledge will save them and, acting under this misconception, they set up their lives in preconceived and conventionally-figured ways that leave little room for either change or spontaneity. Even intellectual knowledge stands little chance against the ravages of time and the irreversible onslaught of death. Thus, ignorance and worldly knowledge (which are much the same thing) correspond to earthly existence. It is Wisdom and Truth which relate specifically to spiritual life, and these latter give one both personal spiritual experience and the boon of God's presence (also roughly the same thing). Via the tool of detached observation, the spiritual seeker can come to see clearly that most of the decisions made by worldly people, like scientists, politicians, businessmen, etc., are short-sighted and lacking in true perception, and thus are subject to constant error. Placing faith in the *Guru*, the seer, the Chosen Ideal and, especially, the world teacher, the spiritual practitioner selects knowledge over ignorance, wisdom over conventional thinking, and Truth over all. In brief, the decisions of the world teacher are based in God and in Truth. They are infallible, despite temporary appearances to the contrary.

12. Similar to the dynamics of knowledge and wisdom, the quality of vision, *Parama-Drk*, is a main attribute in the world teacher's arsenal of illusion-destroying weapons. An important distinction between several types of visions is to be drawn here. There is the vision of the altruist; the vision of the occultist; and then there is the supreme vision of the luminary. Of course there is the vision of the worldly man, but that is completely short-sighted, based upon moment to moment gains and losses and accompanied, always, by fear and trepidation.

Leaving aside the latter, then, one takes a look at the well-intentioned vision of the altruist. It is external, founded on hopes for a better society and world on the physical plane only. As relatively helpful as it can be at times, it disregards the constant changes and upheavals which occur in both matter and mind. The fickle human mind itself is a great danger to any altruistic plan. Without constancy of mind, which only comes via *Atmajnan* and higher wisdom, no plan, however well-conceived, can be trusted to mature and manifest itself. The energy of restlessness in the mind which formulated the plan, or in those who strive to work it out, will bring about its failure in the end. Or it will transmorph into something entirely unintended and unrecognizable. As the old story goes, the sculptor enthusiastically sets forth to create a masterpiece in stone, but only ends up with the statue of a monkey! The lack of forward, even intuitive or precognitive vision, is at fault here. The world remains much the same in the end, regardless — a fact that few altruists are able or willing to recognize.

The vision of the occultist is both more authentic and possibly more suspect than that of the altruist, for the occultists vision is an inward one closely akin to spiritual matters. Since this is the case, being that the vision is not purely spiritual in nature, a certain dangerous energy accompanies it, one which tempts the sensation-mongerer to use this rarer perception for personal gains or power over others. The tendency towards spiritual showboating, with its harmful offshoot of religious vanity and spiritual ego, thus insinuates itself, spoiling the overall vision and its effects, both. To put a finer point on it, a vision of this kind is based in *prana* (see chart on page 536), and thus its mere reflection from the source, as well as its imprint on the desiring mind, render it unreliable. Beyond the *pranic* level lies the realm of wisdom and spirituality, or the strata of the purified mind and intellect, whose vision is both clear and long-lived.

And it is this vibration, pure and eternal, from which the world leader gathers his or her singular and salutary visions. He does so for the purpose of drawing out the highest divine expression in all beings — whatever they are capable of at the present time. This is practicality on the spiritual level, a rare thing to behold in any age. The intended and final result will be the possibility of *moksha*, Enlightenment, for all beings, regardless of station or abilities. As Swami Vivekananda wrote, "*All beings from Brahma down to a clump of grass will attain liberation-in-life in course of time, and our duty lies in helping all to reach that state. This help is called religion — the rest is irreligion. To advance oneself towards freedom, physical, mental, and spiritual, and help others to do so is the supreme prize of man. Those social rules which stand in the way of unfoldment of this freedom are injurious, and steps should be taken to destroy them speedily. Those institutions should be encouraged by which men advance in the path of freedom.*"

We can see by this glowing statement of a true world teacher, that both building up the true *dharmic* foundation and tearing down old outmoded belief systems form a part of his divine plan. A well-constructed approach based on perfect vision, *parama-drk*, will thus place all beings in an excellent position to perceive Reality, in this lifetime or in a better future one. Otherwise, all plans will only get grounded in relativity, as they most often do, and the grinding wheels of *samsara* will have their sway, as they most often do as well — grist for the mill of *maya*. In this vein, the great Swami declares: "*Although I am in full sympathy with the various branches of religious and social work, I find specialization of work absolutely necessary. Our special branch is to preach Vedanta. Helping in other work should be subservient to that one ideal. As soon as human beings perceive the glory of the Vedanta, all abracadabras fall off of themselves. This has been my uniform experience. Whenever mankind attains a higher vision, the lower vision disappears of itself.*"

13. Until this better world, based in a more profound and comprehensive vision and plan, can manifest itself, modes of work and activity must be undergone. But the world leader is unique in this field as well, declaring, unlike most other types of leaders, that all work should be done as worship, as sacrifice, and as service — *Niskama Karma*. The latter of this magnificent trio, service, must be selfless, he declares. If it is, a certain nobility will return to the field of action, an abstemious quality which has been long missing due to the corrupting influences of personal gain. All and sundry these days speak deploringly about the state of the world and the condition of the environment. It is all just talk. Until beings begin to realize that the world cannot be made a better place, mainly because it is not a world, but *Brahman*, and can only be improved by realizing *Brahman* or, until then, seeing it as *Brahman*'s expression through the cosmic, collective, and individual mind, then no appreciable change for the better will be enjoyed. As our world leader presently under inspection says: "*A good world,' 'a happy world,' and 'social progress,' are all terms equally intelligible with 'hot ice' or 'dark light.' If it were good, it would not be the world. The soul foolishly thinks of manifesting the Infinite in finite matter, intelligence through gross particles; but at last it finds out its error and tries to escape. This going-back is the beginning of religion, and its method, destruction of self, that is love.*"

"Destruction of the self" is not as bad a thing as it sounds, for selfishness is the cause of so much suffering. And selflessness is the remedy. Via *niskama karma* (desire-free works), not *sakama karma* (desire-based works), the present world situation, presently so undesirable and productive of stress and harm, will right itself. The world teacher, while in the body, encourages more and more souls to take up this ideal. Through such subtle divine influence true change takes place, going on beneath the scene, and unbeknownst to most.

14. As the world is an eternally cyclic realm, moving inexorably through the relative principles of time and space via the power of *sankalpa*, mental projection, the world teacher is always searching for ways of synthesizing a host of viable and volatile elements for the highest good of living beings. Therefore he becomes known as the greatest integrator, revealing *Alaya Vijnana* in the realm of name and form. Not only actions, races, cultures, and people are brought together in a uniquely ameliorating way, but even religions are smoothly integrated as well. This is the way of the peaceful warrior, as the saying goes. For the world leader both emphasizes and exemplifies the fact that, ultimately, peace is greater than power. This is why *ahimsa*, or nonviolence, has long been the ideal of Mother India and Her religions. But the West has shown a different face over time. As my teacher, Swami Aseshananda, was often heard to say, *"The West has split the atom, releasing a great power for the potential destruction of mankind. But Sri Ramakrishna has split the curtain of maya, opening the way for aspiring souls and their release into absolute freedom."* Peace over power, knowledge over ignorance, spiritual truth over conventional wisdom — this is the way of proceeding which distinguishes the world teacher and true leader of mankind from ordinary souls.

The aspiring souls who are precious to the luminary, who are very dear to the world teacher, it is not that they are held above other souls by way of preference, but that they are either prepared for the journey or keep themselves poised in readiness over their series of physical embodiments. Releasing souls from the illusion of finitude is thus one of the great functions of the illumined being who guides the world on the spiritual level. Not physical evolution, which is an outright illusion, but spiritual evolution, a much more useful illusion, is the world teacher's concern. In short, the luminary knows, unlike most others, that human beings are souls, not evolving animals. In other words, one does not go to see ones ancestors in a zoo as my illumined *guru* said, and as Science would have it, but rather in ones Self, in the ever-present unchanging, nonevolving *Atman*. That is the true nature of mankind, a fact which the world teacher and leader wishes to reveal and instill in the minds of living beings so that their embodied existence will be both justified and fulfilled.

Over and throughout the inspection of this chart, with its fourteen points, we have been both broaching and entering into the subject of the need for an illumined teacher in spiritual life. The present chapter, which will end up being a long and healthy one, has begun by showing the need for qualifying oneself so as to enable one to secure a path, a *guru*, and a redeeming practice. Regarding the spiritual teacher, or preceptor, that soul is different from ordinary teachers, be they secular, intellectual, or religious. On the pertinent subject of the wisdom teacher, we began by presenting the Four Levels of Knowers of *Brahman*, then revealed Sri Ramakrishna's Radiant Road to Reality. His chief disciple, Swami Vivekananda, was then placed under the illuminating spotlight of rapt inspection by citing fourteen divine qualities that a world teacher possesses in order to be called such.

In and throughout the presentation thus far, the need for qualification has been cited and examined, for both the aspirant and the *guru*. And before we leave this important subject and visit the abundance of gifts which the teacher bestows on the devotee, it would be helpful to summate what it is that the seeker is searching for when a teacher is approached. It can be asserted that a valuable asset of a sincere seeker is the nature of his or her questions. In other words, not only the intensity and veracity of the query is to be examined, but also the content. When disciples approach an authentic teacher, possibly after having consulted questionable teachers who also present themselves in this arena, they also divide themselves into category by the nature of the questions they propose. Some ask about home, life, and the world. Others propose queries based upon the emotional states which they pass through day to day. Still others are all excited about the few and oft-times paltry spiritual experiences they have felt, and which they want everyone else to know about.

But a few stand out above these kinds of seekers. Perhaps Sri Krishna puts it most succinctly when he states, *"The sincere student approaches the illumined preceptor via prostration, service, and questioning. Then the wise one initiates him into the highest Truth."* Humility first, then, followed by being of service or "being there." After this useful formula is carefully set into place, the all-important line of questioning ensues. The following chart illustrates the nature of this conscious agenda.

The Five Eternal Questions

"There are five eternal questions which come to a seeker in the due course of life, called the five W's. If a man asks 'What?' he is limited to the realm of name and form; if he asks 'Where?' he relegates himself to space; if he asks 'When?' he gets restricted to time; if he asks 'Why?' he finds himself confined in the world of causation. It is only when he asks the fine question, 'Who?' that he begins to release himself from self-imposed bondage." *Babaji Bob Kindler*

"O Blissful Mother, You alone can discern who I am and who You are. Is there any real distinction?" *Ramprasad*

What?
— Objects, Name, and Form
"The total insensitivity of the mind to external objects on account of bliss is Nirvikalpa. When the meditator becomes indifferent to objects and sounds, he then gets absorbed in the realization of the bliss of the Self." *Shankara*

Where?
— Space, Worlds
"There is no world in the Atman, and even when it is seen, it is seen through ignorance. It is our delusion that superimposes the world over Brahman. When the mind is absorbed in the Supreme Being, the world of appearances vanishes." *Shankara*

When?
— Time, Cycles
"We have been trying to realize God from time without beginning in the objective and in the attempt throwing up such queer creatures of our fancy. But herein lies the secret. When a man rejects all the superhuman powers, then he attains the raincloud of virtues." *Vivekananda*

Who?

Why?
— Cause and Effect, Phenomena
"Mental cognition is always conditioned by cause and effect; otherwise there would be no seer and seen. On account of the destruction in time of all that is dual, and the ongoing experiences of afflictions, beings harbor the false notion that objects are real." *Gaudapada*

"If there is this unreality of entities and objects in the waking and dreaming states, who then is the cogniser of these things, and who, again, is their imaginer? It is the shining Atman who imagines himself by himself, through his Maya. It is That alone that cognises entities, say the Upanisads." *Gaudapada*

The Modes and Makeup of a Seeker

Whatever the grade of questioning, and the caliber of questioner, most queries which proceed from the minds and mouths of various seekers fall under the auspice of time, space, objects, and the cause and effect phenomena which results in coming in contact with them. Of course, the realm of objects, name and form, so to speak, is a vast realm, containing everything from solid objects, to more subtle objects like bodies and thought-forms. It is therefore that the seers have come up with a teaching called the Five Eternal Questions, which have to do with the four categories just listed above — plus one. The additional question, one that a more intense and committed disciple might broach and contemplate, has to do with the nature of oneself or, more properly, ones Self. The seeker usually comes to know of this especial consideration in spiritual life by the adage, "Who am I?" All stages leading up to that superlative one are penultimate to the great question "Who," and propose instead asking it instead of what?, where?, when?, and why?"

This process, which goes on under the *guru*'s watchful eyes and sensitive ears, is geared to unwrap some of the riddles of spiritual awakening and launch the seeker into deeper and more profound levels of inquiry. Spiritual inquiry proper is called *Atma-vichara*, and is famous as a superlative method of enlightenment throughout the three worlds. It will lead to *Atmajnan*, that prime spiritual principle of discriminative wisdom which we examined previously, and which will come up again. In the meantime, questions beginning with "what" have to do with name, form, or objects, as has been related. Queries starting with "where" obviously correspond to space. The question, "when," involves itself with time and its cycles. Finally, the question, "why," relates to cause and effect. Within the dotted ovals on our present chart (facing page) lie four quotes, gleaned from the scriptures and the minds of the seers. Taking the time to read and absorb these will contribute a heady weight to what is being conveyed here.

To explain further, the questions of the greater percentage of seekers will naturally revolve around these first four "w's — "What is happening now?," "Where am I?," "When did this all come about?," and "Why did this happen to me?" Questions like these pour out of the minds and mouths of those who have not yet either heard about or even stumbled upon the superlative question, "Who?" Coming into the rarefied atmosphere of an illumined soul, however, answers questions based in the four w's swiftly and naturally, and also introduces the aspiring soul, gradually and by capacity and preparedness, to *Atma-vichara*, or Self-analysis.

Self-analysis is not as simple as it sounds. There are teachers of lesser quality who carelessly opine that one only need ask the question, "Who am I," and enlightenment will suddenly flower forth! But *Atma-vichara* is based upon deep inspection of the essence within oneself, and in order to know what that true nature is, one will necessarily have to find out what one is not. *Vedanta*, under whose vast and deep mantle of wisdom the *Atma-vichara* system has come forth and flourished, and even before the query "Who am I" is conjectured, proposes first the pondering of a few great preliminary declarations, such as, *"Brahman satya, Jagad mithya — Brahman is real, the world is unreal"*; and *"Nityanityavastuviveka — one must know the difference between the real and the unreal."* A host of persistent problems in spiritual life and seeking will more easily be disposed of when such mainstays are contemplated and implemented early on.

Relatedly, the same is true in the practice of meditation. There are beings who can sit for hours a day in meditation, and who have been doing so for years, yet they are making little appreciable progress towards realization. They may as well be worldly people, except that they have the right resolve. But they are missing discriminative wisdom. All the great *darshanas* of India advise the attainment of this requisite. Lord Kapila's ancient and influential *Sankhya* philosophy, Patanjali's authentic eight-limbed *Yoga*, the patient and engrossing system of *Tantra* — all require of the aspirant that he/she root out attachment to objects, renounce illegitimate desires, quell the vital passions, and purify the mind of brooding and false projections. All of these are unreal. If they are not rooted out at the outset of spiritual practice, before meditation starts in earnest and, certainly, before one merely parrots the question, "Who am I?, then progress will be of a mixed and indeterminate kind?

This, then, is the profound modern message to the contemporary practitioner of these times. It proposes to communicate that there is no easy way, no short cut, no quick fix or instant gratification in authentic spiritual life. The work — our homework in the school for aspiring souls — is to know the field inside out and thus become perfectly aware. The *guru*, the guide who holds the Truth and its message, is here to help all souls, but perks up when a qualified soul enters the fray. "Qualified" means one who has already done most of the work and is, through self-effort of his/her own, perfectly perched, verily teetering on the precipice of nondual realization.

One of Sri Ramakrishna's great stories, told for the sake of illustrating spiritual life alone, tells of the farmer who buys a piece of land which he intends to plant. But first he must undertake the onerous job of laboriously and painstakingly digging irrigation ditches across and around the whole field. On his first day on the job, as he was tinkering around prior to beginning his task, his foot accidently bumped against a hidden pipe just under the surface of the earth and water immediately flowed forth in gushes! Imagine his joy and relief! How much toil and effort he was spared! This story reminds us of the qualified aspirant. The water of his realization lies just under the surface, and is brought to the surface by the merit of his self-effort which he had accomplished previously. The *guru* only needs to say a few words, or make a few gestures on his or her behalf, and the aspirant gains swift understanding and goes into deep states of bliss and meditation. As Vivekananda has stated, previously, *"Ah, for a few ounces of self-effort."*

Such is the beauty of preparation, as rare as it is. For the rest, the matter is not quite so straight forward, but not all that bleak either. Inquiry into the nature of space, time, worlds, objects, and causation — much of which has been covered at the beginning of this book — will set these less intense seekers up for imbibing higher teachings which will eventually burn their way, like acid, through the preponderant weights and limitations of the mind in *maya*. The special seeker must be willing to see through these relative principles, and not treat them as actual or as real.

Among the above mentioned, this latter subject, causality, is one of the final impediments to tackle and gain triumph over. The "why" of things may act as a doorway into deeper introspection, but that passage may lead to the land of mere mentation and intellectualism, what to speak of fatalism, cynicism, and other undesirable dead-ends. Even in religion, asking "why" only relegates God, or Divine Reality, to the relative position of an adjudicator, or a granter of wishes and prayers. In other words, Reality is beyond cause and effect, and the sooner the astute questioner finds this out, the more mature will his or her spiritual understanding become.

Pondering the fifth great question, "Who," is most effective, as it cuts through the layers, or sheaths (see charts on pages 19, 21, & 638) which the soul has thrown over itself and identified with. When the subtlemost sheath is encountered, called the *anandamayakosha*, or ego, a deeper inquiry of the absolute nature of "Who am I?" will reveal the Truth and show up both the futility and undesirability of keeping company with the ego personality. Next to the Light of Consciousness, which is boundless and limitless, the ego will pale to insignificance and its influence over life and mind will finally be shorn away. This is why the realized souls are so humble. Their egos have been effaced. This is why Sri Ramakrishna used to point to his body and say, *"Just a pillowcase."* Great souls have made the journey inward, and have seen the ruse of *maya* and its penchant for covering and distorting. Along the way, the great question, "Who am I?", has galvanized them, and shown them the emptiness and insubstantiality of the illusory ego and its falsely-assumed mode of separate existence.

As the seeker ponders these five great categories of questions, abilities for spiritual life and living increase. Gross and subtle veils, formally considered to be permanent black marks on the soul, simply fade away, like fog under the direct heat of the sun. It may be said, then, that whereas some may feel progress along the spiritual path as a steady increase of qualification for higher attainment in them, others feel it as purification. The word for purity in *Sanskrit*, *shuddha*, makes for an interesting and informative study, for in Eastern religion and philosophy it has less to do with evil, sin, and corruption, and more to do with greater or lesser distance from the Source. In the following two charts we will take a closer look at purity and purification in the view of Mother India.

Shuddha, Ashuddha & Shuddhashuddha Tattvas
Principles of Purity, Impurity & Admixture

"In Indian Philosophy, the terms pure and the impure do not necessarily correspond to morality and immorality. Here, the word 'impure' does not mean dirty or corrupt, but rather what is distant from Reality, which is Ever-Pure. Therefore, mind and its ego-tainted knowledge, energy in constant flux and change, and dense matter — these are considered impure, being that they are conditioned and limited. Beyond them, and transcendent of time and space, is pristine Awareness."

Babaji Bob Kindler

Shuddha — Inherently Pure by Nature

Brahman — Absolute Reality, or Original Awareness

Mahashakti/Kundalini — The Dynamic Power of Brahman

Kutastha — Brahman as the Substratum for all Manifestation

Sakshi — Brahman as Witness of all Phenomena (Ishvara-prana)

Atman — Brahman appearing via Association with the Five Sheaths

Ishvara/Antaryami — Primeval or Firstborn Soul seated in the Heart

---

Shuddhashuddha —
Mixed Pure & Impure Tattvas

Ashuddha —
Impure Tattvas

Maya

Niyati

Antahkarana

Tanmatras

Raga

Indriyas   *Kama*

Vidya

Mahabhutas

Purusha

Kala

Deha

Nama Rupa

Maya - Formless substance of the worlds
Kala - Concept of Time, phases of time
Vidya - Knowledge in differentiation
Niyati - Cosmic laws and natural order
Raga - Power of attraction, involvement
Purusha - Individual sentient soul

Antahkarana - Fourfold Mind
Tanmatras - 5 elements in a subtle state
Indriyas - 10 senses connected to mind
Kama - Force of desire and attachment
Deha - Physical body and constituents
Mahabhutas - 5 elements in a gross state

In the ancient *Sanskrit* language, termed *Devabhasya* — the language of spirituality — by the wise, there are several inscrutable yet irrefutably crucial words which have penetrated modern language and established themselves there. Words such as *guru, karma, dharma, nirvana, samadhi,* and others grace modern language with an appealing and revealing element that has been lost over the long efflux of time and its destructive cycles. Words such as *maya,* for instance, fill a gap in the contemporary thinker's mind, providing both a means to explain the inexplicable, and increasing his mode of expression and explication around matters which, otherwise, remain beyond intellectual grasp. Expressed in another way, there is no word in the English language which so readily and directly indicates the pervasive yet undetectable presence of some deluding force which deftly obscures higher wisdom and its easy understanding. Therefore, mention the word *"maya"* in spiritual circles and eyes widen, lips close, and heads nod knowingly in their assent to something which no mind can really fathom, but which everyone present there is aware of. The reader is encouraged to take advantage of the copious *Sanskrit* Glossary at the end of this book.

The *Sanskrit* word, *"tattva,"* is another candidate for inclusion into our day-to-day speech. It indicates a subtle wisdom principle which is, at once, operative and eternal, an unseen vibratory sphere that holds keys to both inner life and deeper comprehension. A close equivalent to the word *tattva* is the English word, "principle." It is a salient point or outstanding feature of existence. The only thing is, is that there are principles of nature and science, and then there are principles of philosophy and spirituality. These latter are the eternal and unchanging ones, and the ones whose subtle and living vibrations point inward towards realms of vibrant life which go totally overlooked by those masses of worldly minds living only on the surface of existence.

With this brief but glowing testament to the power and meaning of *tattva,* the spiritual aspirant on an inner journey can be made ready for encountering these living vibratory spheres, called *spandas* in *Tantra* (see chart on page 360). When the grosser vibrations of the ordinary mind die away, usually by purificatory exercises like conscious breathing, *japa,* and meditation, *dhyanam,* these wisdom principles open beautifully, exposing their core essence for the mind's taking. Thus, and in the devotional wisdom songs and spiritual poems of this tradition, the seeker of Truth feels and gets likened to a bee exploring many fragrant flowers, joyfully sipping the nectar in each.

Tattvas are gross and subtle. The element earth, for instance, is a *tattva,* as are its four companions of water, fire, air, and ether. Many beings, seen or unseen, from insects to fish to birds and planets, inhabit these conceptual worlds. But *tattvas* extend inward as well as outwards or upwards. One could say that "The Word" spoken of by Jesus to John, and which the Vedic tradition speaks of as *"Om* Eternal," is the deepest and subtlest of all *tattvas.* Importantly, however, there are many things lying hidden which have their existence between the realm of the five elements and The Word. This is what is termed as cosmology (see charts on pages 349 & 359) — all the life heavens, as they are sometimes called, stretching inwards towards our Source of Existence.

Our chart presently under study on the previous page (page 119), concerning the three qualities of purity, demonstrates some of the levels of *tattva* which lie in nondual Awareness, It being the all-pervasive, truly living, and sentient Principle of principles in all. In this radiant realm of Consciousness, various wisdom *tattvas* vibrate scintillatingly, each possessing more or less of the Essence of conscious Light emanating off of The Word (see chart on page 501). In keeping with the subject at hand, those *tattvas* which fall close to this "Home of Truth" are considered most pure, while those lying far off are thought of as impure, containing less of the Light of Consciousness. To use a simple analogy, light reflects well off of a mirror, but less off of a leaf. A rock hardly shines at all. In this way, gross *tattvas,* like the five elements, possess very little of Consciousness, while realms which lie concealed deep within us verily pulsate with that Light — the Light of pure, conscious Awareness. This is why those realms are of interest to the seers of all religious traditions.

Definitions for the *tattvas* shown on this chart, some of them *Tantric* in nature, have been listed at the bottom, to help with the aspirant's understanding of the same. What is inexplicable, however, is the category called *Shuddha,* for here, innate purity is intrinsic by nature. Only some esoteric and majestic words like *Brahman, Shakti, Kutastha, Sakshi, Atman,* and *Ishvara* are left to somehow reflect for us the utter transcendence of Divine Reality (see chart on page 733). In terms of *spandas,* or vibrating spheres, there is little or no vibration there; even wisdom principles have been rendered silent. Still, they are all held in potential within that highest purity, *Shuddha.*

Entering into the realm of subtle or causal vibration, we find the category of mixed pure and impure *tattvas.* They have a gradation to them. The subtle material of creation, the very idea of time and its cycles, higher knowledge and its potential for manifestation, the power of attraction, and even the individual soul of man, all have their true homes here. Yet, the pure Consciousness which was dwelling, untouched and indivisible, at the *shuddha* state, has somehow gotten modified here at the *shuddhashuddha* levels — not in and of Itself, but by the mechanisms, or *tattvas,* which absorb and reflect It. Thus we can more fully understand what *Vedanta* is speaking about when it talks in terms of conditioned awareness, or modified consciousness, or limiting adjuncts, which cover and apparently distort Reality. On the level of human understanding, for instance (may it be awakened and illumined), we can see and better comprehend the primal error of the individualized soul *(purusha)* if it involves itself in the projected worlds of becoming (lower *tattvas*) and forgets its true nature as pure Being. In brief, the *tattvas* are to be contemplated and gleaned as wisdom principles, not as Reality. That, Reality, is sacrosanct, beyond vibration, no matter how fine such movement is. Like a bee sipping nectar from flowers, then, the soul should course along its blissful way, stopping to imbibe wisdom-nectar from the flowers in the garden of Wisdom, but never forgetting the gardener *(Shakti)* and the owner of the garden *(Brahman).*

The impure *tattvas, ashuddha,* are, as we said, not corrupt or degraded, but far flung from their source. Here, the mind has become the brain, forgetting all the worlds back within it. The five subtle elements which are the components of the five gross elements (solidity and earth, liquidity and water, luminosity and fire, homogeneity and air, all-pervasiveness and ether), are overlooked in lieu of the brain's burning desire to have physical contact with gross objects via the ten senses (see chart on page 349). What else are we to call this realm but "impure," for the soul has become mad with material wealth and pleasure-seeking, and has thereby forgotten its true Home. And in fact, preoccupation with *deha,* the physical body, has taken over the brain's attention completely. As Vivekananda has written, *"To the people of the West, ministering to the body is a great thing: they would trim and polish and give their whole attention to that. A thousand instruments for paring nails, ten thousand for hair-cutting, and who can count the varieties of dress and toilet and perfumery. They are a good-natured people, kind and truthful. All is right with them but that enjoyment is their God. It is a country where money flows like rivers, with beauty as its ripple, and learning its waves, and which rolls in luxury."*

With this powerful and quite handy set of teachings, what the *Vedic rishis* called "The Three Worlds" open up to us — immanent, transcendent, and absolute (see charts on pages 373, 455). The imminent world is the physical universe, a far distant echo of pure Consciousness, vibrating densely, so densely that conceptualization has become stone, as it were, and thought has turned into objects. It is *ashuddha,* impure, in that it has become scattered and worked its way out and out to the farthest reaches, where the physical universe presents itself, fallaciously, to the mind and senses, as an independent world separate from Reality. The transcendent world is the mind, subtle, and beyond the ken of the senses. Consciousness is humming here, more identified with knowledge than with matter. Thus it is termed *shuddhashuddha,* mixed pure and impure, for knowledge is not yet Truth. Its vibration is subtle, for sure, but what is more pure, called causal, is yet to be encountered. The third world, the absolute, has this en toto, and more. It is *shuddha,* pure, and vibration has all but quelled itself, dissolving into Peace, Peace, Peace — *"The Peace which Passeth all understanding."*

If one is not interested in relegating the kingdom of the soul to bodies and matter, what then? The *Vedic* seers have proposed ways for those who would undergo the necessary purification of mind needed to return to the natural mode of spirituality once again. For, if the mind becomes impure, the world follows suit; for the mind is the projector of the worlds of name and form. The following chart on the three levels of purity leads us through this wisdom *tattva* and its related concomitants:

Chit Shuddhi, Kriya Shuddhi, & Dravya Shuddhi
The Three Modes of Purity

Chit Shuddhi ⟶ **Prema Bhakti**

Purity of Mind
and Intellect

"But one cannot realize God without prema bhakti. When one has such love one does not get attracted to the maya of wife, children, relatives, and friends. One retains only compassion for them." Sri Ramakrishna

Kriya Shuddhi ⟶ **Raga Bhakti**

Purity of Act
and Deed

"Vaidhi bhakti is like moving a fan to create a breeze. But the fan is set aside when the south wind blows by itself. This is like raga bhakti, wherein one feels love and attachment to God naturally." Sri Ramakrishna

Dravya Shuddhi ⟶ **Vaidhi Bhakti**

Purity of Location
and Atmosphere

"Repeating the name of God a fixed number of times, fasting, making pilgrimages, worship with offerings, doing sacrifices — by continuing on in this path for a time one gradually attains raga bhakti." Sri Ramakrishna

- **Practice of Formless Meditation**
- **Study of Nondual Scriptures**
- **Increasing Devotion to God**
- **Sacrifice of Selfless Service**
- **Observance of Austerities**
- **Offering of Prayer and Charities**
- **Receiving of Mantra Diksha**
- **Chanting the Names of the Lord**
- **Performance of Puja and Arati**

The Threefold Level of Dispersion of Pure Food & Water

"The scriptures state that if one does not eat for ten days he becomes a nonseer, a nonthinker, a nonhearer, a nondoer, and a nonknower. And so the great statement comes, 'anne hidam sarvam prathistham' — all here is supported by food. Life-force, mukhyaprana, nourished by the ingestion of pure food, supports the organs and maintains life and body." Lord Vasishtha

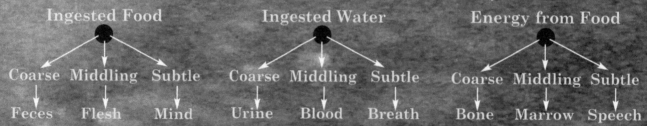

Ingested Food			Ingested Water			Energy from Food		
Coarse	Middling	Subtle	Coarse	Middling	Subtle	Coarse	Middling	Subtle
Feces	Flesh	Mind	Urine	Blood	Breath	Bone	Marrow	Speech

"In ancient days, my Lord, the heroic lad, Svetaketu, placed his attention on the subject and fasted for fifteen days. After this experiment, being faint and weak, he accepted the testament of the scriptures and his father's statements on the role of food in spiritual life." Vasishtha

According to beings of spiritual attainment and mastery, the human mind, responsible for both the appearance of the worlds and all that occurs there, is to be analyzed in order to ferret out the presence of ignorance and be purged of the same. This is called *sadhana* in *Vedanta*, spiritual self-effort. It requires of the practitioner, the *sadhika,* that he/she be open and willing to undergo mental disciplines which are considered as requisites to the mind's complete and overall mastery.

For those seekers who are not yet capable of entering into the atmosphere of mental discipline, the levels of purification around action and location are to be considered. Each of these three levels — *chit shuddhi, kriya shuddhi,* and *dravya shuddhi* — correspond more or less with three types of devotion noted by the seers: outer worship in accord with location; inner worship with relation to acts and deeds; and transcendent worship relative to the thoughts of the mind. The chart shown here juxtaposes these two sets of three side by side, in order to bring about higher comprehension of the teachings, and to afford utilization of them in *sadhana.* For *sadhana* is the only true and effective self-help; all other systems, especially conventional ones based upon money-making, are ultimately ineffectual for the main aim and end of human existence. In other words, and using words which everyone can understand, *"God helps those who help themselves."*

In order to benefit by *sadhana,* spiritual practice, two great points are to be reflected upon at the outset. First, it is helpful to know that spiritual practice will not net one freedom, or enlightenment, for enlightenment is more a matter of grace married to right timing. Freedom is indigenous to the Soul. Thus, transformation is of the mind, not the true Self, which does not require any regimen of purification. Second, all effort is to be accomplished as a mental practice first and foremost, rather than as a mere physical effort, since the origins of delusion lie in the mind, not in the body.

In regard to the first point above, the proper attitude is paramount to said transformation of mind. That all manner of ills — mistakes, errors in judgement, sins, transgressions, oversights, etc. — take place at the unfortunate behest of the uninformed, misinformed, and ill-informed mind is a fact that ought to be accepted outright from the start. Nothing — no pretentious justification, no deceitful shifting of the blame to any outer agent, no assigning of fault to any deity (God, gods, demons, or devil), no vague or foggy belief in the randomness or serendipitous nature of things and events, no excuses or citing of the occurrence of bad luck with regard to the outcomes of ones life — none of these, in addition to a host of other falsely-assumed defaults which people take temporary refuge in, will confer any real benefit in the end. And anything ending in negativity must necessarily have been dependent upon misconceptions which were held in the mind along the way.

Therefore, assuming the right attitude is crucial to all of life, but most of all to this unique area or inner arena called spiritual practice. The one who embarks upon a well-planned and thought out regimen of spiritual discipline, transmitted to him via an illumined preceptor, is to think in his or her mind that this is the moment in a series of lifetimes that everything has been headed for. All attainments, all successes, and even and especially all sufferings, have brought the seeker to this one fortunate life and its potential revelation. Holding such positive thoughts in mind will turn the mental field (thoughts, intellect, and ego) into a fertile ground where rarefied practices and realizations can flower side by side. But first, the purifications.

Assuming that the seeker is new to spiritual life, a start must be made. Such an auspicious beginning is not to be squandered upon the pursuit of *sattvic* pleasures, like bliss and visions, etc. These come as a matter of course later, and even then are to be observed from a wise station of detachment. As Holy Mother, Sri Sarada Devi, has told us, visions and such are the by-products of spiritual practice. The building of character is the essence of spiritual life.

The auspicious beginning referred to here is at the level of *dravya shuddhi.* In other words, one must make sure initially that both the location one inhabits and the atmosphere associated with it are pure. For instance, one would not intricately prepare a sumptuous repast and then eat it in the bathroom, or meditate in the bedroom. The vibration is not right, not pure, and therefore not conducive to right living (*dharma*). And here is where *Vaidhi Bhakti,* sometimes referred to as *Gauna Bhakti,* external worship, has its facility. The sincere worshiper, wishing to make connection with the deities within, and the Self, will set up a place of worship where the necessary practices can be engaged in. In that consecrated space, where pictures, candles, incense, flowers, and other accoutrements have been installed (again, with the proper attitude and religious etiquette), prayer, worship, study of scriptures, and meditation can and should go forth, adding even more sacredness to the area. A healthy, even a refined and subtle atmosphere, will then be created, and those practices performed — chanting, puja, and recitation of the *mantra* — will be conducive to spiritual progress.

After a period of external worship is engaged in, spiritual energy begins to get stored up within the soul due to all the devotional intensities which are taking place. *Raga Bhakti* is the result. It is as if the altar which was located outside in the physical atmosphere now reveals itself as a holy place within oneself. In conjunction with this, all the divine energy within begins to exude outwardly, irrepressibly, and the devotee feels the need to express the spirituality he or she is feeling. This is the connection between inward *bhakti* and outer activity. In this fresh urge of integration, a new type of sacred commerce with the field of activity is engendered, and act and deed take on a whole new meaning for the devotee. Abilities such as performance of austerity, prayer for the higher good of all, and charity — all done in the spirit of selfless service — take hold. In brief, the vibration of the mind has been changed from harsh and uneven, to smooth and balanced. This is precisely what is intended, for it ushers in the possibility of purifying the mind itself — *chit shuddhi*.

The greatest increase of devotion to Divine Reality is found in the state of *Prema Bhakti*, at the level of pure mind. Such unimaginable and immeasurable love, according to Sri Ramakrishna, the king of the devotees in this age, is so intense that it causes one to forget the body, the king of objects that is most dear to people. In the press of this divine emotion the mind cannot help but surrender all its reservations and limitations, as the living Light of pure, conscious Awareness infills its every nook and cranny. Such a mind, once saturated, is called *Buddha* Mind in the *Buddhist* tradition. To quote Sri Ramakrishna, *"Pure Mind is God."*

What is most notable about such a mind, at least from the outside, is its absolute command of all the *Yogas*. Ready knowledge of the sacred scriptures, particularly those of nondual content, expresses itself therein. The ability to enter into formless meditation is also available, as is the intention, willingness, and facility for transmitting the art of spiritual life and living to others. And as the quote on the chart by the incomparable Paramahamsa relates, in the lofty state of *Prema Bhakti*, where thoughts are always bright and buoyant, the world and its offerings and allures seem to pale to insignificance next to the realm of pure mind. One loses base attachment for living beings, too, yet retains compassion for their sufferings, and works for their highest spiritual and earthly good.

We have now taken a deep glimpse at the attribute of purity, both from the standpoint of wisdom principles (*tattvas*), and that of the individual mind and soul. The conclusion which was drawn by the *Vedic* seers is that the word, purity, is tantamount to degrees of realization itself, while impurity correlates with all that has evolved away from the Source. Even human intelligence, once so akin to *Brahman*, distances itself by recklessly taking on the many weights of superimposition and mental overlays via root-ignorance and the delusion it causes. The lesson of such a teaching, this particular *triputi*, is thus brought home to the aspiring mind, which will consequently save itself from much suffering in the interim of life and spiritual search.

It would be helpful for the aspiring novitiate, the sincere one who longingly desires to get to the root of the mind's host of unwholesome problems, to inspect the category of *chit shuddhi* more thoroughly — "with a fine tooth comb," as the saying goes. Otherwise, the idea of purification of mind may get passed off as something akin to relieving oneself of mere bad habits If this were the case, humanity may begin to confer the otherwise hard-won appellations of saint and seer upon those who merely give up caffeine and nicotine and go to church every Sunday. And actually, this is not far from what is occurring in religion in this day and age. But that aside for now, what does the particular and enterprising devotee of the Lord, the seeker after Truth, search for and encounter along the precipitous mountain path to authentic spirituality and realization? The chart on the opposite page will tell us, in part, as will the following commentary on it:

Golden Rules for Sadhana & Transformation of Mind

"In order to benefit by sadhana, spiritual practice, two great points are to be reflected upon at the outset. First, it is helpful to know that spiritual practice will not net one freedom, or enlightenment, which is more a matter of grace married to right timing. Freedom is indigenous to the Soul. Thus, transformation is in and of the mind, not the true Self, which does not require any regimen of purification. Second, all effort is to be accomplished as a mental practice first and foremost, rather than merely physically, since the origins of delusion lie in the mind."   Babaji Bob Kindler

Samyag-darshana — Proper and Preeminent View & Attitude

√   *Sandilya-vidya* — **Identification with the Source while keeping relations with the world**

√   *Artha-shunya* — **Clear comprehension of the nature of motiveless practice**

√   *Samasti-chitta* — **Grounded and unalterable stance of open-mindedness**

√   *Alaya-vijnana* — **Positive and natural idea of universality**

√   *Prayojana* — **Profound underlying sense of ultimate purpose**

√   *Autsukya-puraka* — **Ready store of interest and inspiration**

<u>Sentinels at the Gate</u>:
- no pretensions, justifications, or complaints about one's status
- no shifting of blame to any external circumstance or outer agent
- no assigning of fault to any deity such as god, gods, demons, or devil
- no citing of the occurrence of luck with regard to the outcomes of one's life
- no vague or foggy belief in the random or serendipitous nature of things and events
- no excuses or inadvertence around one's inadequacy for accomplishing sadhana
- no false refuge in ignorance, unpreparedness, unworthiness, or poor upbringing

Chit-shuddhi — Initial Purification/Transformation of Mind

Δ *Anya-samskara-pratibandhin* — **Willingness to perceive and remove the subtle barriers which block the formation of positive mental samskaras**

Δ *Smriti-shuddha* — **Effort to awaken and reveal the memory so as to bring about recollection of all divine traits**

Δ *Buddhehparatah* — **Ability to transcend logic to gain intuition in order to engender spiritual experience**

Δ *Utpaya-pratyaya* — **Irrepressible determination to ensure arrival at the goal**

Δ *Yataman* — **Firm control over all desires, emotions, thoughts, and ego**

Δ *Kala-shakti* — **Development of skill in sacred sound and scripture**

Δ *Utsaha* — **Constant alertness with regard to spiritual exertions**

Δ *Upeksha-ananyata* — **Equanimity and single-mindedness**

Δ *Dhriti* — **Spiritual patience that knows no bounds**

Δ *Samatva* — **Steadiness and even composure**

Δ *Titiksha* — **Forbearance of all dualities**

"My children, the secret of religion lies not in theories, but in practice. Doctrines have been expounded enough. There are books by the millions. Oh, for an ounce of practice!"
Swami Vivekananda

As was mentioned earlier, and in accord with the right attitude to adopt when approaching the spiritual path — what Lord Buddha spoke of in three stages of his system of the Four Noble Truths and the Eightfold Path (see chart on page 229) — the sincere seeker's mental and intellectual view must be clear and free of distortions. Shankara mentions this in his teachings, stating: *"The mind must be like a mirror, polished daily, affording the most perfect reflection of Reality possible."* This sentence is pregnant with esoteric meaning. First of all, it reminds us that the mind is not the Soul, or Self *(Atman)*, but rather a reflector of the Light of the Self. The indivisible Self is not an apparently independent entity like the ego, but the all-pervading Essence in all things, all beings, thought of as *Prajnaparam,* or *Tathagatagarbha,* by Lord Buddha. In other words, *Buddha* nature and *Atman* are one and the same. And in order to realize that identical Essence, some polishing, called *sadhana* or spiritual self-effort, is necessary. Only when the reflector, the human mind, is wiped clean by inner and outer disciplines, or *sadhana,* will the Light of pure, conscious Awareness reflect perfectly, transforming life and mind completely.

As in any school of Philosophy, taking up a resolve to acquire such a perfect view via spiritual education begins with the citing and practice of several golden rules. On the chart under study we can see not only the impurities which the aspirant is beginning to purge himself of, but also the requisites which, once having been implemented, will help him or her remove, for all time, these pernicious intruders which spoil the perfect peace and bliss of the naturally enlightened state.

Initially, a correct view will demand proper orientation, and *sandilya-vidya* confers just that and more. Put in another way, those who do not have their feet on the ground while their heads are in the air are headed for a fall. One must start from where one is, and not prematurely pull all present structures out from under ones feet before the right time arrives. Denying the embodied state and holding aversion for the world is much different than renouncing the world while maintaining the necessary relations with it. Still, one must always identify with the Source of Existence, for failing to do so results in losing the way and running the risk of *samsaric* suffering. But in the interim, until enlightenment is a given and realization a fact, the seeker will do well to consider all the gifted tools — the body, the earth, the mind, the teachers, etc. — as aids and supports, rather than as crutches or dependencies. Thus, *sandilya-vidya* is a crucial part of a mature spiritual beginning afforded the seeker who holds the "Preeminent View."

Most crucial, yet found wanting in most beginners on the path, is *artha-shunya,* the precognitive understanding that spiritual practice will not grant Enlightenment. As Sri Ramakrishna has said, *"A man has barely set foot on the lowest branch of the tree, yet he is already coveting that cluster of fruit which he sees ripening on its uppermost limbs."* Such is the excited anticipation of the novice who is devoid of patience and the willingness to seek, step by step, the fruits of spiritual practice — especially that ultimate Fruit called *Moksha* (see charts on pages 343, 365, 680). Practice free of motive, however rare and unthinkable, is a valuable key to success in spiritual life. The eyes must be on the prize, no doubt, but a part of the gaze has to be fixed upon the feet as they follow in the "footfalls of the *rishis,"* watchful of the impediments which could harm or stymie spiritual growth and progress.

The following twin qualities on the chart under investigation are also rare of perception. In most religious circles, a kind of narrowness is both prescribed and avowed. But the noble man seeking nondual Truth rather than mundane religious convention has a broad and universal outlook which both accepts all religious preferences and honors them as well. Thus, open-mindedness and a universal outlook, when adopted at the outset of spiritual practice, will make for a more substantial realization in the long run. This is in conjunction with what was shown earlier on the superlative tenets of Universality, and more on this will appear in the succeeding pages of this book.

With these four main elements of the Preeminent View listed and studied, the sincere seeker of Truth need only keep sacrosanct that sense of ultimate purpose which drew him to the path in the first place. Backsliding and complacency only create impressions of failure in the mind, making it most difficult to mount a second attack on its castle-like fortress of root ignorance. Therefore, the aspirant must keep a ready store of interest and inspiration always at hand, bringing it forth on every possible occasion to bolster up any signs of flagging spirit with regard to this most important of human endeavors. Otherwise, people are well-aware of the downside of failed self-effort, with its prevarication and procrastination. Many of these are listed on the chart as sentinels at the gate, and were mentioned in earlier pages of this book.

As for the bottom half of our chart under study, we now see some of the tools which the spiritual mechanic must procure, learn to apply, and operate to, for instance, facilitate that most desirous of mental states called *chit shuddhi*. This list is, admittedly, a fairly esoteric one, citing practices which are not specifically handed out in today's religious circles. To be more specific, it takes a student who is willing to go deep into the recesses of the mind, both subconscious and unconscious, to find the hidden barriers to spiritual progress, many of them fabricated and placed there lifetimes ago by the transmigrating ego complex. And finding them lurking there, as one might do in a therapy session of today, is far different than having the tools available to facilitate further processing or purification. And a far cry from availability is the ability to work these tools and bring about the destruction, or even neutralization, of said impediments, many of them being very illusive and hard to pin down. Mere advice and pills will not do it. A well-guided *sadhana* is what is needed.

For those who, in the far distant past, found their way out of *maya* to arrive in the sweet Light of pure Awareness, their fealty lies with the preceptor who guided them and the spiritual resources which were given to them in sacred trust. Along with what has been stated previously about the *guru* in this chapter, this can be added. For, true spiritual work, along with its related progress, begins when the solution of *anya-samskara-pratibandhin* comes to light. To explain, the subtle mental impressions which inhabit the recesses of the mental body (*manomayakosha*) are not just problems of the moment, as difficult as those can be. As long as they remain undetected and are allowed to lie fallow, they restrict the formation of positive mental impressions, thus stymie spiritual progress. This may sound rather obvious, but if that is so, then why are people striving in the first place, since all that they seek to attain is actually being blocked by these insentient despoilers which retard forward motion or, worse, masquerade as advancement along the path. This latter phenomenon is most insidious, for it waylays the sincere seeker's hard and honest efforts, and turns the weaker and as yet inexperienced aspirant into a mere fool and pretender. And it is therefore that we encounter so many persons in Western cultures who are either seriously striving but never really attaining, or are only making a show of *sadhana* and getting nowhere.

The solution, then, is not the therapist's couch, or a shot or pill given by a doctor, or dancing mindlessly or pretentiously at an occasional local sing-along event, or even attending a 30-day meditation retreat with no chosen path, guide, or routine of sadhana in place. To sit still in focused meditation, diving deep into ones own mind, making it the specific object of *yogic* inspection and, with the tools given by the *guru* and the scriptures, scouring it, top to bottom, like one would an old house that has been deserted for decades, is far better. Let us see further what such a spiritual spring-cleaning and religious renovation might consist of, and what resources need to be on hand for it.

A valuable but seldom considered ability called *smriti-shuddha* is next on our list. The mind has so many realms back within it. The kingdoms of heaven, as well as earth and causal realms, all exist within it. But as well as locations in time, there exist pat and independent divisions to the mind as well, like intellect, ego, thoughts, etc. One of these divisions or properties is called the memory. This beloved element of the mind is most often associated with recollections of the past, a past that has been relegated to a one lifetime scenario only. If one could access and purify the deeper levels of *smriti*, causal memory, one would perceive a host of lifetimes that the transmigrating ego lived previously and forgot about, and also an infinite storehouse of personal attainments and divine attributes. This is what the *yogi* espies in the pure atmospheres of deep and dedicated *yogic* practice.

The memory, like the mind, has individual, collective, and cosmic proportions and ramifications. To think of it, and especially to contemplate it from the standpoint of spiritual life and practice, is to begin to notice that everything which one now knows has sprung from there. It is a storehouse, as was just pointed out, and souls entering into the realm of embodiment unknowingly draw everything that they seek and aspire for from that ready and recondite repository. When embodied beings strive for wealth, education, knowledge, and merit, they are really attempting to draw it forth from within themselves. If embodied beings knew this fact, without a doubt, like the luminary does, for instance, problems such as fear of want and selfish grasping would become things of the past.

Purifying the memory, then, is a matter of contemplating it, but with an eye to remove subtle (and not so subtle) layers from its doorway. For example, if the memory is assigned the position of merely calling forth people and events from the past, and the mutable present, its efficacy is greatly undermined and no appreciable insight, what to speak of the heights of revelation, will be experienced. That is, the appearance and flow of feelings, emotions, desires, reminiscences, and the like, flitting across the mind's memory, purely fleeting as they are, only transforms the memory into a static reflective screen. It then only produces a mere television sitcom of ones own grey study of a life, hypnotizing the soul with thoughts and worries of the past. This is why the seers have advised detachment in the first place, so as to help the soul to withdraw from the shallows of consciousness reflected across the ordinary mind's wide but thin surface. And in fact, the word, *"smriti,"* in *Sanskrit* does not just refer to a person's memory, but more directly to the scriptures and what they contain. The idea is that by contemplating something deeper, day after day, not only will the ordinary mind remake itself and gain depth and insight again, but it will also begin to remember the ocean of wisdom that all proceeded from, and begin to make wise use of it again — for the highest good of beings.

Purifying the memory by contemplating it also calls up the recollection of something much more profound and beneficial than a tearful trip or two down memory lane. Ones series of lifetimes also lies in the inmost reaches of the memory. This is akin to what, among the occultists, has come to be called the *"akashic* record." Gaining access to this cosmic reckoning of the actions and results of all beings throughout time gives the aspiring *yogi* or *yogini* a glimpse of all that has gone forth in the past. As far as the personality is concerned, and its succession of projections over time, this is helpful — especially to the seeker who is attempting more and more to identify with Divine Reality and de-emphasize the import of the individual mind/ego complex. As Sri Sarada Devi once said, *"Remembering your true Self, forget the personality."*

In new age circles, among fanciful people given to *vikalpic* sport, the pretense is to "recall" all the famous persons one has been in the past. Ironically, there is no mention among them of anyone having lived the life of an impoverished soul, a slave, or a mentally imbalanced person. Whatever the case may be there, for the sedulous and sincere seeker, the point of remembering ones series of lifetimes is to bring about realization of the truth of who one really is and always was throughout this parade of masquerading names and forms — namely, the *Atman,* the nameless, formless Essence. Enlightenment consists of realizations such as this, not posing and posturing as this ego and that personality, which are essentially empty of substance. Otherwise, these insentient mechanisms would not change and pass, to be forgotten at the approach of the next assumed identity.

To finalize this teaching on *smriti-shuddha* is to stress the importance of study of scripture combined with meditation. The combination of *jnana* and *dhyana* acts as a corrosive acid upon the obscuring layers which cover the mind's memory. Again, coming to know who one is not, is tantamount to remembering who one truly is, which is a step towards realizing the *Atman.*

Arrival at the art of *Buddhehparatah* represents a major shift which transforms the tendency of a man to live only in his individual intelligence, into the ability of a spiritual luminary to abide near to the Source. The classic scene, not often enacted, unfortunately, is the transition from intellect to intuition to direct knowing. In other words, and put succinctly, the evolving man eventually puts down his works of literary accomplishments, picks up the scriptures, contemplates them, places their wisdom into practice, and gains *samadhi.* Real purification occurs in this sequence — of mind, of memory, of intelligence, and of heart. Sri Ramakrishna explains this by saying that if one has a thorn lodged in ones flesh, he must take another thorn from the same bush and use it to extract the painful thorn. Ignorance is the thorn lodged in ones flesh, and knowledge is the thorn which removes it. But when the process is complete, one simply discards both thorns. This is realization, where both knowledge and ignorance pay deference. With enough time spent in such a state, even if on and off, this duality and all others begin to fade away, leaving the mind in a blissful state.

The three tools/signs of purification of mind just related herein (chart on page 25) are most subtle, esoteric, and efficacious. What comes next are teachings which most beings have heard of, though they are still of a crucial nature. *Utpaya-pratyaya* is a watchdog for the spiritual aspirant, ensuring that the ultimate goal, *Paragatam,* is keep in sight. For, it is one of the dangers of spiritual striving that the seeker forgets that changeless and perfect nature that he is by falling victim to involvement in the acts and concerns of attainment. This is why we are taking pains to disseminate the golden rules of *sadhana* in these pages, the foremost of which is that practice cannot itself directly net one realization. Termed *Advaita Vedanta Sadhana* by the knowers of *Brahman,* the art of spirituality is to retain cognizance of eternal perfection of the Soul, both in the press of striving for merit and in the midst of everyday trials and tribulations. One can thus see the great advantage of keeping *utpaya-pratyaya* as a tool for ensuring a consummate arrival into the Source of ones Being.

Yataman, inferred earlier, allows full control over all the distractions which may and probably will arise in the course of daily *sadhana.* There are few spiritual distractions which so effectively skew the mind and swerve the seeker off the path of *sadhana* than desires and emotions. Many beings previously committed to the path, once daunted, have simply given up striving altogether due to lack of control over some little traumatic experiences that came upon them. One might say, then, that the opposite of *yataman* is weakness, pure and simple. So, and to play with words, *yataman* is penultimate to "*Atman.*" Here, the English *mantra* "get over it" is applicable. Spiritual progress will never come amidst the atmosphere of depleting desires and enervating emotions. So give these up.

Of great aid along the path of spiritual striving is the development of a healthy regard and assessment for the benefits of sound. In the realm of sound there are inferior *mantras,* mediocre *mantras,* and superior *mantras.* More about this will be stated in the forthcoming section on *mantras* and The Word. But as an introduction to the topic, the principle of *kala-shakti* is of meritorious note here, since it indicates a facility or even a thorough mastery over all that interests and inspires (note *autsukya-puraka* on previous pages). This is more a matter of didactics, wherein sound is used to teach rather than for mere entertainment, as worldly people use it for. Further, the teaching mentioned herein is not for purposes of fattening up the intellect either, reminiscent of our previous study of *buddhehparatah.* Sacred sound, like devotional music, and transmission in the form of wisdom words, are more to the point. Thus, we become aware of the area and efficacy of spiritual arts.

Utsaha, upeksha-ananyata, dhriti, samatva, and *titiksha* — alertness, equanimity, patience, steadiness, and forbearance — are well known to spiritual aspirants, and even to adherents of conventional wisdom and its soothsayers. Thus they need little commentary here. Suffice to say that, individuality to consider, they build up the arsenal of weapons which a spiritual seeker will eventually bring forth and brandish against the demon hoards of ignorance. But placed together, as an integrated whole, this fine host of attributes represent the rare and magnanimous ability to remain poised in what the *rishis* of India referred to as "Abidance in the *Atman.*" That is, after attainment of the goal of human existence, namely *moksha* or liberation, there is still the wondrous facility of attempting to remain steady in that realization, imperturbable under any influence which the world and the embodied state may throw up. Such freedom (*jivanmukti*) leads inexorably to an easy abidance in formlessness (*videhamukti*).

The import of correct view, along with keen observance and adroit practice of the tools utilized by the wise in the pursuit of transformation of mind, have been presented accordingly. The ground has thus been set for both comprehending and implementing the sacred art of *mantra.* In truth, everything, in all the worlds of form, consists of particles of intelligence. It may seem to the uninformed that there is nothing but material particles, but that is due to the inability of the tactile senses and the ordinary mind to see beyond what is apparent only. Through the study of The Word, and the many *mantras* which constantly stream mellifluously from It, an entirely new and fresh outlook will inhabit the mind, requisitioning it for higher purposes.

Mantra and its Semipiternal Seeds

Intrinsically connected to the *guru*, permeated by the vibration of wisdom, and corresponding directly with the quality of purity as well, the spiritual art of *mantra* combines both the consummate school of devotion and the sententious science of sound. My *Paramaguru* (*guru* of my *guru*), Sri Sarada Devi, was a past master at this most effective principle and practice. In honor of Her, then, a series of explanatory charts has been created which will be taken up for study in the forthcoming pages, charts which will assist and benefit the aspirant in further comprehending the subtle and often enigmatic nature of these rarefied spiritual formulas. Related deeply with *mantra*, the *bijam* (seed) *AUM*, must be taken up and studied as well. But first, some fundamental facts about the *mantra* can be explored.

Referring to the chart on the opposite page, we find listed a dozen important facts about *mantra*. The fact around *mantra* being a science of cosmic sound has already been stated, but what does it mean? That is, there are physical sounds, and there are sounds that are inaudible to the human ear; this much is known. But the phrase, "cosmic sound," refers to subtle vibrations which originate in the Great Mind, or *Mahat*, and are thus beyond audibility and inaudibility. Called "the Mind of God" in some traditions, what is intimated here is pure, ever-sentient Intelligence which is always in existence in causal form. It is most balanced and most refined among manifest principles, and in fact is the hub of manifestation itself. Its sound is the internal humming of Consciousness when it desires to express Itself, and its mediums for expression are all manifest phenomena (i.e., like *tattvas*). This primal vibration is so powerful as to establish whole realms of existence which last in and of themselves for eons.

But all of this is in reference to manifestation that is flowing outwards from within. The real efficacy of *mantra* is that it is able to turn the tide of this outward direction and route consciousness back toward its source of origin. This is what is meant by Holy Mother's quote in reference to "awakening the *Kundalini*" (see chart on page 619). There are certain seed words, ancient and impacted with subtle power, which when utilized in an adept and well-guided fashion, serve to arouse the hidden power of spirituality in those rare beings who are sensitive to internal suggestion and ready for realization. Therefore, and where it may be true that "a picture is worth a thousand words," in the realm of *mantra* there are certain words which encompass all the pictures ever imagined by the human mind.

Coming to know the power for transformation that these seed words, called *bijams*, possessed, the *rishis* of India turned within to unlock this irrepressible force and use it for spiritual purposes. These notable beings observed the effect that combinations of seed words had upon human minds and nature, and soon were fast at work breaking down the barriers of *maya* with these penetrating vibratory condensations called *mantras*. When light is intensified it reaches laser proportions and can cut through dense matter. Similarly, but on an internal level, when sound is intensified, it transforms into an intense vibratory medium which can pierce through barriers which veil the Light of Consciousness.

The secret of *mantra* science, shared by the *Tantric*ists and the *Vedantins*, could not be contained in one country, by one race, and verily swept across the world so that many beings, and religions, were soon in possession of this priceless boon. This unique form of practice became the friend of all types of aspirants, from high to low, from adept to inexperienced. All found in it a welcome way to feel the presence of God, no matter their level of realization, or lack thereof. The *mantra* welcomed all these beings into the realm of spirituality by rendering their bodies pure immediately. Thus, beings could leave the ground of the ordinary and keep company with the holy, and walk among men and women of the Spirit.

But for the deeper ramifications of *mantras* to have their salient and salubrious effects, sensitive aspirants came to know that the *mantra* was most effective when transmitted by a sage or seer who had realized its inner meaning. Such a being has seen through *maya*'s veils, and has done so from the Ground of Awareness, or *Bodhi* Mind. *Bodhi* Mind is the very form of concentrated intel-

Fundamental Facts About The Mantra

"God cannot be realized through japa, worship, and meditation. God is only realized through His Grace. Nonetheless, one must perform japa and meditation, for they can remove the impurities of one's mind. God's Grace then becomes revealed." Sri Sarada Devi

MANTRA.... ⟶ **Is the Science of Cosmic Sound**

"Through the science of mantra the Kundalini will awaken. Repetition of God's name will lead to the goal."

Is Vedic in Origin

"The rishis of ancient Vedic times practiced mantra and other austerities to realize God."

Is Unique among Spiritual Practices

"Such is the power of the mantra that, in addition to the mind, it also purifies the body."

Is a Universal Mode of Practice

"People in other countries are also repeating recitation of the Lord's Holy Names."

Is Effective as Repetition

"Even if your mind does not awaken, you must repeat the mantra thousands of times."

Originates in the Bodhi Mind

"After attaining true wisdom one sees that gods and deities are all Maya."

Grants Knowledge of Unity

Provides Protection during Practice

"God's name protects. Instead of losing a leg, one might merely suffer a thorn of the foot."

Clears the Subconscious Mind

"Man becomes pure and the mind still, by repeating the mantra of God."

1/4 of the Mantra is given by the Guru at time of Initiation

"The purpose of initiation is to try to realize God through sincere effort."

3/4 of the Mantra is Hidden as Mother's Form

"When a pure soul repeats the mantra, the holy name bubbles up from within."

Mantras are Associated with Deities and are Innumerable

"Man achieves the highest goal through the practice of japa. God has given us fingers that we might be blessed by repeating His Name. Be content under all circumstances and repeat His Name."

"The Master gave me mantras possessing great power, and all of them are associated with the deities. They are imbued with the power of renunciation."

ligence, almost vibrationless, and therefore free of the realms of gods, and other deities. The knower of *Brahman* has a place which is transcendent of the various realms of the gods, for he has coursed through them via knowledge of the mantras and seed words of power under which the gods perform their very functions. And this knowledge is the knowledge of the unity of all things, their innate connection with one another.

When the *mantra* is transmitted by the *guru*, many elements come into play, and are at work immediately. At the threat of the possibility of enlightenment, it is as if every dense and earthbound creature and circumstance comes running to thwart the aspirant's best intentions. To counteract this, the *mantra* hoists a net of protection around the novitiate so that he or she can practice, in peace, and with relative assurance of safety and success. All that the seeker need do is to maintain the practice and forbear all the effects that crop up in the interim. For what is occurring, as well as protection, is the unwinding of *karmas*, *karmas* which have acted as a blindfold around the soul, or the "third eye," for the entire duration of ones life, maybe even for lifetimes. Thus, good and bad *karmas* surface at the behest of the recited *mantra*, and this is why one must repeat it many times, regardless of the mind's strongest objections and the world's harshest reactions. As illustrated by one of Holy Mother's quotes on the chart at hand, ones karma may dictate that a disastrous event may be headed ones direction, but by remaining wrapped in recitation of the *mantra*, this occurrence may be diverted or greatly diminished as a result. Thus, the protection of the *mantra* holds true, even in the most trying of times and under the direst of circumstances.

And all along the way, the subconscious mind is getting penetrated and purified. This is the most positive force of the *mantra*. The dredging up of *karmas* would have been avoided had the aspirant not accumulated them in the first place. This is why some take to the *mantra* so easily, while others have to struggle. Some make swift and immediate progress, and others seem to plod along. Whatever the case, the same end result is in store for the devotee who maintains steady and resolute practice of the recitation of the *mantra*, or *japa* practice. When the subconscious mind finally offers up all it resistances, then the *mantra* becomes, as the seers say, a bubbling spring of ambrosia, causing inner bliss to rise to the surface. So these three phases — protection, purification, and revelation of inner bliss — can be cited as the inner dynamics of *mantra* practice.

The aspirant after Truth should not fall into the misconception that what the *guru* gives at the time of initiation, called *mantra-diksha* in the tradition, is the end of the matter. The mystics say that only a third of the meaning of the *mantra* is transmitted at the time of initiation, and that the other two thirds await the seeker's discovery, in meditation. Thus, by steady practice, deep contemplation, and through phases of well utilized time, the inner meaning and force of the *mantra* gets unwrapped.

Further, when it does, the aspirant gets introduced, in a very real way, to the various deities residing within. Calling out the name of a friend will cause that friend to turn and look. In the same way, reciting the names of the deities in conjunction with the *bijams* brings the force of divine attention upon the newly awakened seeker. Thus, we come full circle, like in the *mala* itself, for all deities and the aspirant himself have their existence nowhere else but in *Kundalini Shakti* Herself.

In order to engender understanding of what is meant by seed words, *bijams,* and to convey a subtle sense of the power that they contain, the following chart on the facing page is offered for inspection. This teaching could be reserved for a later stage of presentation, but it may benefit the reader to have some advance awareness of the import which Indian philosophy places in certain root words. Therefore, six of the most prevalent and relevant *bijams* are presented here, all contained in Mother Sarasvati's *mala*, or "rosary." The chart's concise explanations of what these powerful seed words represent is in keeping with the fact that they are practically impossible to define. Thus, no commentary will be undertaken. Suffice to say that the interested seeker must approach a wise preceptor who is knowledgeable in the art of *mantra* science. When the *mantra* is earned via the *guru's* grace and boon, direct experience of the *bijams* will become more accessible. In line with verbal formulas of power, this chart also shows the Four *Mahavakyas*, which are great statements meant to be stated once, rather than mantras which require multiple recitations over time.

Sacred Bijams of Mantra Science

Bija of Transcendence

* Representative of Timeless Awareness
* Medium for the Absolute and Relative

AUM

Bija of Transformation

* Impetus for revolution
* Weapon of regeneration

KLIM

Bija of Wisdom

* Herald of spiritual wisdom
* Subtle key of creation

AIM

Bija of Purification

* Implement of refinement
* Neutralizer of negativity

HRIM

KRIM

Bija of Abundance

* Harbinger of quality and quantity
* Bestower of mature fulfillment

SHRIM

Bija of Insight

* Oracle of infallible omniscience
* Revealer of eternal perfection

Do you know that the Master Himself taught me these mantras and bijams, and how they connect to the deities?....

....He gave me mantras possessing great power. They are imbued with the pure force of renunciation.
Sri Sarada Devi, The Holy Mother

The Four Major Mahavakyas

Tat Tvam
Asi

"Thou Art That"

Ayamatma
Brahma

*"This Self
is Brahman"*

Prajnanam
Brahma

*"The Self is pure
Consciousness"*

Aham
Brahmasmi

"I am Brahman"

The next chart up for inspection, on the facing page, shows us a complete and in-depth sequence of the order of *mantra* practice. These twenty-one points fall in four stages, thought of as the Four Stages of the Word in *Vedic* tradition. Several charts involving that teaching will follow soon hereafter, which will demonstrate how concepts, thoughts, realms, worlds, and much more burgeon into manifestation from a single primordial principle. Though the interested reader can trace the twenty-one points of *mantra* practice via this chart, some added commentary will undoubtedly be useful, consisting of a few things to relate about each of these from the standpoint of both the aspiring practitioner, and the adept holder of the *mantra* tradition. And it is this latter which first deserves extra mention.

The practitioner of spirituality, at least in this day and time, is seldom prepared for *sadhana*, either by way of requisite qualifications, the capacity for intense forms of austerity which will need to be undergone, or appreciation for the wisdom preceptor. About the latter, few can assess or properly evaluate the true greatness of their selected *guru* until much later, and even if they can, the assessment is based upon hearsay or grandiose proclamations from others. As the *Avadhuta Gita* states, *"Of the teacher — even if he be young, illiterate, or addicted to enjoyment of the sense objects, even if he be a servant or a householder — none of these should be considered. Does anyone shun a gem fallen in an impure place? In such a case one should not consider even the quality of scholarship. A worthy disciple should recognize only the essence, and if it can be transmitted. For, does not a boat, though devoid of beauty and vermillion paint, nevertheless ferry passengers to the other side?"* Or, to repeat what Sri Ramakrishna was wont to say in this regard, *"It takes a jeweler to estimate the value of a diamond."* Therefore, the seeker after Truth must prepare the mind to acquire the power of proper evaluation. And as this power dawns, more and more, true gratitude and reverence, for both God and *guru*, will dawn alongside of it.

And, for many aspirants, this most often comes about through recitation of the *mantra* given by the illumined preceptor. Just as God and His Word are one and the same, so too are the *guru* and the traditional lineage of *mantra* realization which he holds identical with one another. And this brings up an important but scarcely accepted fact: *mantra*, in order to be effective, is transmitted, not selected from a book, or picked up from a saying on a tea bag. Furthermore, it is not something to be passed around by ordinary people, or through inexperienced and unqualified mediums — people who boast and posture but have accomplished no inner or outer practice. Only the preceptor can instill *mantra's* true power into a sincere devotee, and this is due to the *guru* once being a disciple himself. Having devoutly received the *mantra*, or *mantras*, from an adept *mantra* master, it being passed down from his teacher, he has recited it in deep meditation for many years, even lifetimes. Having studied its meaning and realized its subtle power, then and then only will this qualified luminary pass it on to aspiring souls desirous of gaining freedom from worldliness and relativity. In other words, he has brought forth, honed and polished the *mantra's* inner force by his own sweat and tears — the sweat of inner aspiration and the tears of intense devotion. We can call this noble effort, then, a quintessential part of the dynamics of spiritual transmission.

This first point on the chart may be the most crucial of all these twenty-one points, for without its implementation the entire process will run askew, or peter out — as is instanced in the cases of so many wayward and unsuccessful beings who give up spiritual life altogether when the *mantra* fails to have any effect, or to live up to their usually unrealistic expectations. This brings forth yet another point to consider here, that of what the *mantra* is really supposed to accomplish. This will become clearer as the commentary on this chart unfolds, starting with point number two.

Initially, the practitioner needs to "animate the *chitta*," which means taking the *mantra* into the mind's inner regions in order to charge and bolster up all mental vibrations. The *mantra* is a pure vibration, or series of condensed vibrations itself, so it enters into the field of erratic vibrations and quells them accordingly. This inner phenomena has been likened to a huge tidal wave which sucks up all other waves into it as it mounts up. Ideally then, the mind ought to be left with one mighty principle to contemplate, which the *mantra* itself (with *Ishtam*) represents most perfectly.

The Twenty-One Points of Mantra Practice

In Four Stages

Vaihkari — Early Stage
Madhyama — Middle Stage

Pasyanti — Subtle Stage
Para — Supreme Stage

V A I H K A R A

1 Receive the Mantra from a Guru

2 Animate the Chitta

3 Awaken Mind to the Antaryami

4 Anahata Sound is Detected

5 Thoughts Dissolve

6 Intensification of Awareness

7 Breath Becomes Equalized

8 Kundalini Awakens and Rises

9 Sounds and Visions Occur

10 Perception of Inner Realms

11 Nada is Clearly Heard

21 Everything is seen as Mantra/Word

20 Rishi-hood is Attained

19 The Vak Devi Resides

18 Experience of Pure, Conscious Awareness

17 Witness Consciousness Develops

16 Nada Reveals Jyoti

15 Aspirant Stays Detached from Bliss

14 Aspirant Rejects Occult Powers

13 Resistance to Inner Worlds

12 Awareness Focuses on AUM

P A R A

P A S Y A N T I

— MADHYAMA —

"Uttering the sacred bija, AUM, the wise mentally practice mantra and recite the Upanisads. Realizing the Truth in this manner, they are the truly enlightened ones who become supremely qualified to guide others along the spiritual path."   *Aruneyi Upanisad, 1.5*

Another way of looking at this animation process is by thinking in terms of negative and positive thoughts. In *Yoga*, for instance, Lord Patanjali, its best exemplar, speaks in terms of *klistha* and *aklistha vrittis*. *Klistha*, in *Sanskrit*, means "pain-bearing." Such thoughts have a soporific effect on the mind, tending to dull consciousness rather than ignite it. This is why, bereft of spiritual education by uninformed parents and uneducated societies, the youth of our day are found to suffer from boredom and listlessness, then routed towards habitual work with restless minds. Spiritual practice and recitation of the *mantra* will counteract all this, while regimens of secular education, social events, medications, and the like often only make things worse. A secondary meaning of the word *"klistha"* is *"a thought which leads one to favor an attraction."* Thus, the mind's attraction to changing events and objects will net it nothing but pain in the end.

Aklistha vrittis, on the other hand, are thought vibrations that confer more favorable results. The idea is to neutralize the negative thoughts with favorable thoughts so as to be able to eventually reach a transcendent state beyond this and other dualities. Thus we have meditation, which is the penultimate aim of *Yoga* and other Indian *darshanas*. So, animation of the thoughts will be of utmost facility in the practice of *mantra* — it and its sempiternal seeds being the most powerful thought concept of all. As Sri Ramakrishna put it: *"A hot air balloon will not rise if it is weighed down by so many sandbags. Cast a few of them out and ascension is assured. In the same way, do away with heavy thoughts which only weigh the mind down to worldliness and mundane matters."*

The *mantra* has bijams, as we have seen, but it also contains the "Names of the Lord." This tells us two primary things about *mantra*: first, it is a tool for helping the mind concentrate on and uncover God with form; secondly, devotion is going to play a major part in this process, for it is said that one waters the seed of the *mantra* with the tears of ones inner longing for Truth and freedom. And for those who prefer the formless reality to God with Form, it can be stated here that the tree which sprouts and grows from the watered seed of the *mantra* is that selfsame formless Reality — God beyond Form. The two are not separate, so why fallaciously make them so in ones mind? This would amount to delusion at the spiritual level.

The famous and well-liked saying/*mantra* from the Diamond *Sutra* declares that *"Form is emptiness and emptiness is form."* Why would one deny one to get to the other? One should rather utilize one to get to the next, and back again as well! *"One gets to the Father through the Son,"* as Jesus said. And for the many, and for many different reasons, beings need to get back into form as well, once having had the formless experience. All this is directed towards those who have some issue with God with Form and the path of devotion. Where it is true that great beings like Lord Buddha and Patanjali inferred that it is not necessary to believe in God with Form in order to gain Enlightenment, they also averred that qualities like love, compassion, and faith make the difficult ascent into formless Reality much smoother and more accessible.

Our inner journey is not one of mere emptiness, either. The *Sanskrit* word, *Antaryami*, signifies the imperative existence of an *"inner ruler Immortal seated in the heart."* We can call this Nondual Awareness, the Witness, the Guide, or a guiding angel; it is all much the same. It is no doubt essentially formless, but it speaks to everything in the realms of name and form nonetheless, especially to those who have the ears to hear. And persons reciting the *mantra* are in the process of developing such subtle capacities of inner hearing. They will eventually meet this most empyrean of benign controllers, because by reciting the *mantra* silently within they are doing nothing less than calling out His, or Her, name.

The Name of the Lord and Mother of the Universe is an eternal principle, and one that has awakened and freed souls for time out of mind. And truly speaking, the more refined the practice of *japa* becomes, the more the *mantra* begins to take on its essential form. Its essential form is reflected most accurately in its primary seed or *bijam*, namely *AUM*. This primeval sound, or unstruck sound as it is called, is what the meditator begins to hear within as his practice deepens. When that sound is detected, it is then that the ordinary thoughts begin to break down, and when they do, the practitioner can actually perceive his or her own Awareness existing as the underlying substratum of all create things. This occurs in fits and starts initially, or in glimpses, but the result is salubrious. Therefore, points three through six of this chart (page 135) happen simultaneously, and lead to what the seers both encourage and entitle "an authentic inner life." That is, nothing much can really happen in religion, philosophy, or spiritual striving without these signs of spiritual advancement.

With the vision and intensification of ones inner awareness comes the difficulty of having to adjust to it. So many problems and dangers are possible at this stage of *mantra* practice. That is why ones spiritual studies and a gracious preceptor must be kept close at hand, so that these barriers, once they arise, can be virtually destroyed at the outset. Bad habits haunt spiritual life just as readily as they do earthly and ethical life, and one must be on guard in order to counteract them early on. But the adepts and luminaries have also noted that a conscious practice of evening out the breathing process has a profound effect on the aspirant who is already at the intermediate stage of *mantra* practice. That is, addiction to breathing exercises is one of the dangers that body-oriented beginners face on the path of authentic spiritual effort, but at the intermediate level it affords one greater facility in cognizing and expanding the mind's capacity for inner experience via pure *prana*.

And, marvelously, it is less of a breath or breathing exercise at this level of practice, than a kind of relaxing into the expansiveness of ones own inner being. As the yogis tell us, it is really equalization of breath, its inward *(puraka)*, suspended *(kumbhaka)*, and outward *(rechaka)* movements. Many teachings, called *triputis*, associated with these three *pranic* movements, come forth here, but they will be dealt with via the charts on *AUM* which are forthcoming. A more esoteric teaching can be handed out here. With regard to *mantra* practice, the in-breath represents its recitation, the retained breath accords with contemplation of its meaning, and the outbreath symbolizes the dissolution of the *mantra* into formlessness. Such a practice, when enacted consciously, will more swiftly and effectively awaken Mother *Kundalini* and the visions and experiences corresponding with Her. This consummates the first phase of *mantra* practice, called *Vaikhari* (initial), and ushers in the second phase, called *Madhyama* (intermediate). Please note this on the chart presently under study (page 135).

The next five steps to *mantra* practice transport the inner space traveler into *"the kingdom of heaven within."* This is pure inner cosmology. The exploration of outer space, being the inspection of constant change *(maya)* by constantly changing minds *(samsaris)*, is ultimately unreal and insubstantial. Therefore, perception of the real existence of worlds, called *lokas* in *Sanskrit*, existing back inside one, begins this phase of *mantra* practice and realization. Objects consist of material particles. Words consist of intelligent particles (refer again to chart on page 501). The *mantra* is formed of concentrated intelligence, where particles are almost completely dissolved. This fine and fecund formula brooks immersion in The Word, *AUM*, so naturally it must course through the subtle worlds on its way inwards towards ones essential "Home of Peace." *(Atman)*

And as the opened inner eye of the fast developing mind of the aspirant views and observes the workings of The Word, he is also connecting all things, all events, and all beings, to it. In other words, he understands that everything, even what he left behind in the physical worlds, is made up of pure intelligence, or *AUM*. As the *Mandukyopanisad* states powerfully, in its very first *sloka*: *"All this world is the syllable AUM. Its further explanation is this: The past, the present, and the future — everything is just AUM. And whatever transcends the three divisions of time — that, too, is just AUM."*

And in accordance with that realization, steps ten through twelve revolve around *AUM*, or what is called *nada* in the tradition, and *shabda*. But here, in this middling state, called *madhyama*, the emphasis is mainly upon intuiting that blissful sound within and bringing it into clear focus via ones own consciousness. The danger here is that this focus of the practitioner might deviate and begin to gaze, rather hypnotically, upon what the *nada* is manifesting, rather than what it signifies. Its facile puissance spontaneously manifests the worlds of name and form in time and space merely as a natural effect of its all-pervasive presence, but what it signifies is its role as a direct indicator of the formless Essence, *Brahman*. This is much like the case of pure sunlight in which all manner of beings make their appearance — germs, insects, even specks of dust. But why would one overlook the sweet light and its source to obsess over insignificant objects and creatures? Why indeed? Yet it happens, such is the power of attraction interfering with the aspirant's inward journey.

To put a finer point on this subject, sincere aspirants will overlook the various visions which arise in individual awareness as they behold the subtle worlds, like heavens, resting there within. At first it is natural to gaze a while in wonder, which is why beings having their first real spiritual experience of this nature experience "stunned consciousness," called *jada samadhi*. Since one had forgotten the infinite worlds within when one embraced limitation in the physical world and body, the shock of becoming cosmically aware again stultifies the mind for a time, rendering it static.

But recovering from this temporary state, the empowered practitioner, the one who has *utpaya-pratyaya*, for instance (review chart on page 125), will not forget the supreme Goal. And not only will the worlds, like jewels laying there in internal awareness, need to be transcended, but also the considerable powers which come at this stage will need to be renounced. These are called "occult powers," or *astabala-siddhis*, (see chart on page 660), which according to the great ones — from Sri Krishna to Sri Ramakrishna — pose great obstacles in spiritual growth and realization. Inferior teachers and sensation-mongerers play with and advise the acquisition of these, but the one seeking spiritual emancipation pass them by as if they were *"...crow droppings by the side of the road."*

There is one more impediment to reaching the higher stages of *mantra* practice and its most excellent attainments. Point number fifteen illustrates it well. In brief, and understandably, great joy will overtake the aspirant, newly freed from limitation into the subtle worlds or heavenly realms. This limited bliss can also act as a retardant to spiritual advancement, for it is only a reflection of the real Bliss, *Ananda* as it is called, which awaits the soul at the doorway to formless Reality. And even back here in the body, where consciousness returns after it has broken free and experienced inner life, this rule holds true. That is, and as Patanjali states in his *Yoga Sutras*, there are four main obstacles to meditation — the last and most alluring being attachment to subtle bliss.

Mantra and inner life is a sacred and esoteric art scarcely known by a greater percentage of embodied beings. And even among those who hear of it, and give it a try, many of these never comprehend what an amazing and beneficial boon they have stumbled upon in this lifetime. And of those who only go half way, this *madhyama* stage explains, among other things, their inability or reticence to move onwards, instead getting stuck in phenomena, much the same way that those attached to matter become obsessed with the physical realm, never knowing anything higher. Yet throughout this middling stage the Unstruck Sound is shining, emanating, attracting the soul beyond lesser lights and distant glares to the hub of Awareness Itself. This becomes fully evident in the third stage of *mantra* practice, called *Pasyanti*.

There are basically two types of souls when it comes to inner life. There is the one attracted to sound and the one attracted to light. The former is more mystically oriented, and the latter more visionary-based. Here, at the *pasyanti* stage, that sacred all-attracting inner hum, *AUM*, transforms into Light, called *Jyoti* in *Sanskrit*. This is the Light of Consciousness. When it is seen within, the practitioner can know with certitude that the *mantra* practice is fructifying, and the *mantra* itself is unfolding another part of its three part internal essence *(Tripura-sundari)*. And actually, it is the Goddess of the Word who is doing the unfolding. But more on this later. Suffice to say, that when this Light of pure Awareness reveals Itself, and for an extended period of timeless time, the practitioner, now no longer a novice or intermediate, sees the Soul, or *Atman*, and begins to detach from name and form completely. This is called the maturation of Witness Consciousness, or *Sakshi-bhutam*. The word *"bhuta"* in *Sanskrit* refers to anything with a form, but particularly all that is found in the physical universe. Even ghosts or disembodied spirits are called *bhutas*. They are in the physical universe as well, but lying "below" it, in the *patalas*. Whatever the case may be, the adept seeker now sees all from a witness standpoint, which is like a true individual Self as opposed to a false ego-self. The word *Purusha* comes into play here as an effective description.

But the hierarchy of relative consciousness is not yet through with the *Purusha*. Witness Consciousness, as pure as it is, has not yet seen or experienced nondual Awareness per se. There are other and very subtle levels to Consciousness (see chart on page 705). We shall come to those in due time. For now, and in keeping with the translucent topic of *mantra* practice — which is not a goal in itself, but a superlative practice — the adept enjoys for a time some glimpses of pure Consciousness *(chaitanya)*, until the third stage of *mantra* practice is satisfied. It is here that the *Para* stage dawns mellifluously.

From the *Para*, or supreme stage, the aspirant accesses and enjoys an unimaginable vista which stretches upward towards Nondual Awareness *(Brahman)* and outward towards the three worlds lying "below," as it were. This fortunate soul can now look back from a high perch on the uppermost branch of the Eternal Tree of Spiritual Life and perceive all vibrating with the Light or Sound of pure conscious Awareness. And mainly, this great Witness, now a soul of *rishi*-like proportions, can behold how The Word has become everything, and how the *mantras* are its various subtle ways of expression, infilling all worlds, all beings, all things. This vision is seen as a gift, now; for from the standpoint of the bliss of his own Consciousness, this great and grateful being finally perceives the Mother of the Word and Her multitudinous ways of expression. She, the *Vak Devi*, is the singular sentient principle abiding in all beings. As the wisdom songs of India proclaim, *"Even great saints and sages seldomly behold Her, even in their deepest meditations!"*

And therefore, the *Para* stage culminates all that *mantra* practice was intended to transmit. Possessing the key to the secret door of creationism, or projectionism as the *Vedic* seers would call it, the illumined soul is ready to enter into the vast reaches of nondual *samadhi*, or *nirvana*. It only remains to be seen how much of his own sweet time he will take in making this most subtle of transitions, and if, once having immersed in the boundless and eternal depths of pure Being, whether or not he will return again into the worlds manifested by The Word. For, as Sri Ramakrishna has said, *"I had to come down a long way from Nondual Awareness to get to AUM."*

This reveals that *Brahman* (God), and His Word *(AUM)*, however intrinsically connected, are only one in the sense of the continuity of Consciousness, not in the sense of the subtlemost strata. Further revelation comes that The Word is a means of expression and manifestation, while *Brahman* remains beyond all that — "acreate," as Swami Vivekananda stated. This is all the more reason that the aspiring soul ought to prepare for the experiences of inner ascension, and be ready to go beyond all signs and traces of form — not out of any coercion by religious adherents, or desperation due to guilt, or a sense of escapism within the fearful mind, or feelings of aversion on the part of the as yet immature soul — but in order to know the Truth which will finally and irrevocably set it free for all time, beyond time.

In accordance with the four stages of *mantra* practice and their twenty-one points to ponder and act upon, the next chart summates what has just been studied, but by way of brief description rather than in-depth enumeration. Viewed from top to bottom and in circular order, it is hoped that these condensed explanations will proffer an effective conclusion to this study, rendering it fruitful and ready of implementation.

The quote at the head of this chart (page 140) is particularly helpful in putting together any mental pieces which have not fallen into place. Mention of the *maya-shakti*, the force which covers all true meaning — of life, of embodiment, of words and ideas, of thoughts — is brought forth here, helping us to understand, in part, why people fall victim to self-imposed limitation and let themselves in for endless suffering. And importantly, the practice of *mantra* is held up by Sri Sarada Devi and others as the easiest, most direct, and most effective means of realizing the Self, starting with the detection of root-ignorance, proceeding on to the acquisition of secular and religious knowledge, and culminating in the attainment of higher spiritual wisdom that is indispensable for the gaining of illumination, or Enlightenment. As She Herself has explained to us in recent times, *"Perhaps one practices japa and austerity in this life. In the next life one intensifies that spiritual mood, and in the following advances it further, and thus spiritual evolution goes on. Then, the moment ones karma comes to an end one realizes God. That is ones last birth. This, plus the practice of spiritual disciplines and time, are the factors in the attainment of spiritual knowledge."* (see chart on page 665).

The Four Stages of Mantra Practice

"All the alphabets and their corresponding fractions, and the mantras comprised of them, are all intrinsically connected with the Self. Due to the influence of neiscience, the maya-shakti covers their true meaning and function and the eternal Self takes on a sense of individuality and assumes atomic proportions. Recitation of the mantra awakens the power inherent in the Word and restores meaning, thus wisdom."

Vaikhari

The fourth stage, Vaikhari, represents the articulate form of sound at which stage the mantra charges and purifies the mind, revealing the presence of the Antaryami. The Sound-Brahman is then perceived, one's awareness intensifies, the breathing stills, Kundalini rises, and inner visions occur.

The initial state beyond stages, Para represents the primordial hub of potentiality and divine emanation and expression, including worlds, beings, words, and their fractions manifest as atomic centers of consciousness. Para is the unity existing in all diversity, directly realizable through the awakening and upward ascent of Kundalini power. Shiva, Chit-shakti, and Prana-shakti are all associated with the Paravaka.

Para

Madhyama

Madhyama stage, which acts as an intermediary between Vaikhari and Pasyanti, represents the third and slightly gross form of sound. Here, the seeker perceives the interior realms but remains clear of them, accesses occult powers yet resists them, and feels bliss but rises above it.

Pasyanti represents the subtle and second stage of sound. Om, perceived earlier, now turns to Light, or Jyoti. An indrawn state of Witness is prevalent here, and the soul experiences pure Awareness beyond bliss. Pasyanti-vak is divine vision, the supreme speech of the Vak-Devi, unmanifest and full of Spirit. The seers and gods use it for envisioning everything. Pervading all, it extends from Muladhara up to Sahasrara.

Pasyanti

"I give you initiation because you show signs of being a noble soul. See that you do not betray me. You are perfectly satisfied if you get the sacred mantra, but you never think of the consequence." Sri Sarada Devi

The principle and practice of *mantra* science is shared equally by both *Tantra* and *Vedanta*. Many religions of the world also prescribe and utilize it, making it, as was mentioned earlier, a universal practice. Now that we have studied some salient facts about the *mantra*, and scrutinized the twenty-one point, four stage process of the dynamics of the *mantra*, and even briefly looked at the presence and meaning of certain seed words of power, called *bijams*, it would be enlightening to demonstrate, as far as words and images can convey, just how the mind gets transformed via this tried and true method. And in order for that to effectively register in the mind, some advance knowledge of terms will help, terms which are borrowed from the time-tested *Tantric* tradition.

The following alphabetized list of *Tantric* words and phrases is a brief rendering that conveys, in part, the incredible depth of understanding of Divine Reality which the *rishis* of Mother India possessed and passed on over time. It will help the reader and the aspirant to better understand the following chart (page 142), and also to comprehend the host of charts on *Tantric* wisdom and principles which will appear in the succeeding pages of this book. Definitions given here are specific to *Tantra*:

Abhava Yoga — The *yoga* of negation wherein God is perceived of as emptiness or voidness.
Avarana-shakti — *Maya*'s subtle power of covering or obscuration; *tamas*.
Bhuvana — Planes of existence made up of *tattvas*, or wisdom principles.
Bija — A seed word of inner power which activates and empowers the *mantra*.
Bindu — The timeless, spaceless point where all wisdom principles reside.
Chakras — Spiritual vortexes through which *Kundalini Shakti* rises.
Chid-jyoti — Infinite Ocean of Intelligent Light.
Jivas — Embodied souls.
Kala — The concept of time on the Cosmic level.
Kalas — Phases of time.
Kamakala — *Shiva* and *Shakti* in Union.
Laya — Dissolution – of objects, worlds, thought-forms, conceptions.
Mahamaya — The Divine Mother of the Universe, the controller of *maya*.
Mahayoga — The *yoga* of blissful communion wherein the Self and God are seen as one.
Mantra — Sacred saying used to purify the mind; science of sound which reveals the unseen Truth.
Matrika — Alphabets, words, letters, and their subtle power which formulates the worlds.
Maya — The worlds of name and form in time and space based in causality.
Nada — The inchoate sound, or Unstruck Sound; *AUM or Om*.
Niyati — Cosmic Laws.
Pada — The construction of letters and words into profound statements.
Prakasha-shakti — *Maya*'s subtle power of revelation, or unveiling; pure *sattva*.
Purusha — Real individual soul, as opposed to *ahamkara*, or ego.
Raga — The force of divine attraction.
Spanda — A vibratory realm; a philosophical system of Shaivism
Sristi Rahasya — Secret of Creation, which reveals that all comes into being by mental projection.
Svatantriya — Unbounded freedom in unbridled expression.
Tattva — A wisdom principle experienced by awakened consciousness.
Varna — The science of alphabets, called the garland of letters, or *Varna-mala*.
Vichikirsa — The Will of the Divine (*Shiva/Shakti*) to set the creative process in motion.
Vikshepa-shakti — *Maya*'s subtle power of distortion; *rajas*.

With this short list of terms, plus what will be given and translated in the following pages, a general working knowledge may be gleaned which will enable the reader to begin to fathom the mystic and rather esoteric teachings of *Tantra*. With regard to Indian philosophy, *Tantra* is the heart, *Vedanta*, the brain; *Sankhya* is the body, and *Yoga* is the energy and way of proceeding. With this in mind, the next chart, involving the mind's awakening via the *mantra*, is offered:

Transformation of Mind in Mantra Practice

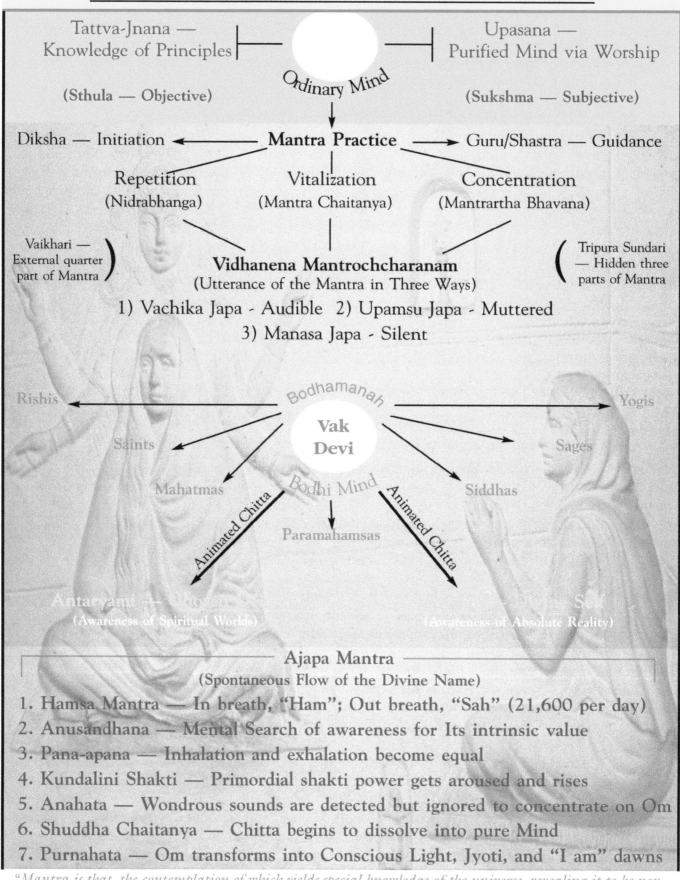

Tattva-Jnana —
Knowledge of Principles
(Sthula — Objective)

Ordinary Mind

Upasana —
Purified Mind via Worship
(Sukshma — Subjective)

Diksha — Initiation ← **Mantra Practice** → Guru/Shastra — Guidance

Repetition
(Nidrabhanga)

Vitalization
(Mantra Chaitanya)

Concentration
(Mantrartha Bhavana)

Vaikhari —
External quarter
part of Mantra

Vidhanena Mantrochcharanam
(Utterance of the Mantra in Three Ways)

Tripura Sundari
— Hidden three
parts of Mantra

1) Vachika Japa - Audible 2) Upamsu Japa - Muttered
3) Manasa Japa - Silent

Rishis

Bodhamanah

Yogis

**Vak
Devi**

Saints

Sages

Mahatmas

Bodhi Mind

Siddhas

Animated Chitta

Paramahamsas

Animated Chitta

Antaryami —
(Awareness of Spiritual Worlds)

Self
(Awareness of Absolute Reality)

—— **Ajapa Mantra** ——
(Spontaneous Flow of the Divine Name)

1. Hamsa Mantra — In breath, "Ham"; Out breath, "Sah" (21,600 per day)
2. Anusandhana — Mental Search of awareness for Its intrinsic value
3. Pana-apana — Inhalation and exhalation become equal
4. Kundalini Shakti — Primordial shakti power gets aroused and rises
5. Anahata — Wondrous sounds are detected but ignored to concentrate on Om
6. Shuddha Chaitanya — Chitta begins to dissolve into pure Mind
7. Purnahata — Om transforms into Conscious Light, Jyoti, and "I am" dawns

"Mantra is that, the contemplation of which yields special knowledge of the universe, revealing it to be non-distinct from Brahman; in other words, the universe is full of Brahman." Sri Ramakrishna Paramahamsa

It is very difficult for anyone to explain what happens to the heart and soul of a man or woman who takes to spiritual life, and an even more onerous task to reveal the mind's transformation under the purifying press of an intense individual *sadhana* like *japa*. Suffice to say, that the ordinary mind has two main routes or courses it can follow, called in *Tantra, Tattva-jnan* and *Upasana.* Generally, in wide connotation, the former proceeds by sedulously imbibing wisdom principles via the mind/intellect complex, and the latter progresses via worship of the powers or deities whose presence makes up the various strata of human consciousness. Whereas many aspirants take to one or the other, the comprehensive devotee places the mind between them both and, in vice-like fashion, verily presses ignorance out of the thinking process forever. It is as the old *Vedic* saying relates, *"Wisdom tells me I am nothing; Love tells me I am everything. Between the two my life flows."* This kind of wise synthesis of pathways which becomes accessible to the fortunate seeker is highly advisable and most commendable. About it, Swami Vivekananda states: *"Would to God that all men were so constituted that in their minds all of these elements — philosophy, mysticism, emotion, and work — were equally present in full! That is the ideal of a perfect man. Everyone who has only one or two of these elements I consider one-sided, and the world is almost full of such one-sided men, with knowledge of that one road only in which they move."*

With this beautiful sense of universality in practice in mind, we can consult the chart which shows the ordinary mind of mankind being exposed, at long last, to these two mighty *Tantric* paths. Here, the best of the objective and subjective worlds are harmonized, and all that is left to accomplish thereafter is to add into the quotient the two revolutionary elements of the spiritual preceptor and the sacred *mantra*. And so *diksha,* spiritual initiation by the *guru*, and guidance in the form of the scriptures, *shastras,* are brought to bear on the mind. Now it is up to the practitioner to repeat the *mantra* with devotion and constancy, vitalize it with the quest for inner knowledge, and enter into states of deep concentration along the avenues via which the *mantra* leads.

As the four stages of *mantra* practice, with their twenty-one points, kick in (as explained in the preceding pages), *manas,* or ordinary dual mind, swiftly transforms into *bodhamanah.* This means that *bodhi,* or subtle inner intelligence of the mind, is brought out from hiding, much like sesame oil is produced from squeezing a sesame seed, or patina rises magically out of a penny. The transformed mind, now opened to a host of amazing possibilities, gets freed from mundane, superficial thoughts and conventions, and joins the ranks of the many types of luminaries, as listed on the chart. And with this animated *chitta,* the soul catches glimpses of the *Antaryami,* the Chosen Ideal, and comes to behold the true Self within. The entire process has been facilitated mainly by the *mantra,* the Wisdom Word principle, married to a little self-effort. Thus, the adage, *"Knock and it shall be opened unto thee"* is a fitting description, for the *mantra* holds several doors within it, behind which reside the Divine Mother Herself, the *Shaktiman.* She is the power and its holder. When the mind is ready to proceed on its inner journey back to its source, She is the infallible Guide.

The study of the most natural flow of all *mantras,* namely the breathing process, takes up the remaining portion of this chart. It is applicable here as a study, since it reveals more inner dynamics of this pristine process. The idea is, since we breathe in and out some 21,600 times a day, we may as well become aware of that fact and use it to awaken our consciousness. Thus, the intrepid spiritual traveler examines Awareness in order to assess its true value and power. This inner inspection brings about the awakening of Mother *Kundalini*, with unimaginable results. Meditating upon Her in the form of Intelligent Sound and Living Light, the mind easily accomplishes the dissolution of its limitations, including the liquidation of its crystallized mental impressions, and the removal of its self-imposed barriers of separation. Snapping the chain of rebirth is the result.

More will be written and communicated about the superlative subject of Mother *Kundalini*. But the promise has been made to bring about the study of *AUM,* the Word of God, which has a deep connection to the *mantra,* being the single most important of all *bijams.* In the following chart we are afforded the opportunity of taking this Wisdom Word apart in order to see what it signifies. Once knowing that, our practice will be immeasurably enriched for all time:

Om & Hrim — The Two Great Bijas

"One should go into the region where there is no speech or thing spoken, absolutely free from dualities — Akhanda Satchitananda. There, with Aum, meditate on that Highest Flame of Consciousness. In this rare meditation great beings have destroyed ignorance, realized their perfect Nature, and established identity of the Jiva with Brahman. This is My Highest Self!"
Srimad Devi Bhagavatam

Aum — Brahman

"From Adyashakti issues the first letter, "A," and it produces "U" and expands."

Static — Potential

Formless Reality

"After shravana, manana, and nididhyasana, my devotee becomes fit for absorption in the Spirit after understanding the meanings of the separate letters discovered in the seed mantra of Mahamaya."

A	U	M
Brahma	Vishnu	Shiva
Imminent	Transcendent	Absolute
Waking	Dreaming	Deep Sleep
Speech	Life-Force	Mind
Mother	Father	Guru
Feminine	Masculine	Neuter
Activity	Balance	Inertia
Past	Present	Future
Gross Form	Subtle Form	Causal Form

Hrim — Shakti

".....where Iccha Shakti, Jnana Shakti, and Kriya Shakti all meet and merge."

Dynamic — Expressed

Assumption of Form

Other Important Bijas

ऐं	श्री	क्ली
Aim	Krim	Klim

HA	RA	I
Gross Form (Vaishvanara)	Subtle Form (Taijasa)	Causal Form (Prajna)
Five Elements	Fourfold Mind	Formlessness
Physical Body	Five	Nonvibration
Active Organs	Tanmatras	Equilibrium
	Cog. Organs	
	Five Pranas	

"After balancing the breath via pranayama, and cognizing the differentiated states of the bija-mantra and what they signify, meditate on that bija and mentally dissolve the gross body into the subtle body, the subtle body into the causal body, and the causal body into the Turiya state of Hrim symbolized by the matra M. And before entering Samadhi, focus upon Me, the Supreme Deity, the luminous, Self-effulgent Goddess who is one with Brahman."
Srimad Devi Bhagavatam

Om Sweet *Om* — Our Real Home

The greatest facility of this chart lies in its closer examination of the *bijams*, with the accent upon The Word, or Word of God. The Word, *Om*, or *AUM* as we will spell it in this teaching, is the Word of God because, of all things within the realm of comprehension and conceptualization, it represents formless Reality the best. This assertion is not based on philosophical speculation, either, but upon both rational and experiential conclusion. That is, the seers have entered into the luminescent realm of *AUM*, and found there all the potential for expression and manifestation. This is why, throughout time, and in the various *darshanas* which Mother India has authored, one finds correlations to it. The ancient *Sanskrit* word, *Hiranyagarbha,* for instance, means Cosmic Egg, and was seen as the hub or source of all things entering into form. Lord *Brahma*, of the Hindu Trinity, also corresponds with *AUM*, He being the "creator" god out of which all the *lokas* and their various beings spring. Then there is the principle of Unmanifested *Prakriti* in *Sankhya*, a most interesting subject for meditation. More will be written about it in this book, but modern peoples, even with all their knowledge, seldom know of it, never contemplate it. Is it coincidence that all things spring into manifestation? Is it a matter of creating something out of nothing? Or would it be better to assume that what we are experiencing with mind and senses is only the outer show of something much more subtle which forms the basis for form, much like the formless ether holds millions of solid planets.

And this *AUM*, this cosmic egg, this unmanifested nature, is not a physical element like ether. One would have to go very deep within to find it, and to uncover its considerable secrets. It is detected, as we have read, in meditation, as the humming of Consciousness Itself. Like a man moving over sand dune after sand dune in order to find the source of that roaring sound in the distance, finally to break over the last dune to behold the vast ocean — this is the fitting analogy for the meditator who sits quietly, enrapt, focusing upon that mystic sound which has risen out of his very depths.

In the most definitive of Divine Mother scriptures, the *Srimad Devi Bhagavatam*, we find references to *Aum* sprinkled throughout its many pages. Not content with mere verbal teachings, this scripture takes apart its *matras,* or units, to help the seeker begin to comprehend just what is being uttered. As the first box on the chart relates, the three *matras* of *AUM* designate a whole host of triple teachings, called *triputis.* The first three of these sets of three are the most important, for they pertain to the devotional, cosmological, and psycho/spiritual levels of our being. And so, for the practitioner who is devout, connecting up the three *matras* of *AUM* with *Brahma, Vishnu*, and *Shiva* is going to facilitate his or her highest aim, while the seeker of knowledge will benefit by contemplating the three worlds and their origins — imminent, transcendent, and absolute. For the meditator searching for the doorway into Formlessness, cognition of the three states of human consciousness is an indispensable teaching. Such a being will connect "A" to the waking state, "U" to the dream state, and "M" to the deep sleep state. More on this will be related in our next chart up for inspection, which will further demonstrate the profound power of *AUM*.

The *bijam, AUM,* also corresponds to the three bodies of humanity, often called gross, subtle and causal, but also termed individual, collective, and cosmic. The principle of time is stretched out across the boundless expanse of this great Word, as past, present, and future all correspond to its three *matras*. It is no wonder, then, that *"In the beginning was the Word."* Cosmic principles like activity, balance, and inertia get represented by *AUM* as well, showing its immeasurable facility on all levels. As the *Mandukhya Upanisad* states, *"Everything is just AUM."*

In conjunction with *AUM* is the *bijam, Hrim*. This is Mother's Word of transformation, and designates the irrepressible force of *Shakti, Brahman's* dynamic power. As *AUM* represents all the potential lying in Formlessness, *Hrim* reveals everything in the realms of form. And the two bijams are one, inextricable from one another. *Brahman*, the essential Consciousness, lies in *AUM*. *Jnana* (Wisdom), *Iccha* (Will), and *Kriya* (activity) *Shaktis* lie in *Hrim*. Put the two together in the *mantra* and you have the most powerful subtle force for transformation and realization possible.

In order to communicate a modicum of what lies in even one of these *triputis* of The Word, an explanation of mankind's divine nature follows. For this, please study the next chart:

The Three Matras of AUM in the Mandukyopanisad

"There is one Paramatman, who is all-pervading, which associates with Its projections in different ways and in different states. What is considered enjoyable in these three abodes, and the enjoyer present in these abodes, they who know these two as distinct from each other, though they enjoy, are never contaminated thereby."   *Gaudapada*

The Three Avasthas – Realms of Existence

Jagrat, Waking	Svapna, Dreaming	Sushupti, Deep Sleep
"Waking is for those who mistake matter for Reality."	"Dreaming is for those who perceive Reality otherwise."	"Sleep is for those who do not know Reality at all."

 A   *Quality of pervading*   **U**   *Quality of being*   **M**   *Quality of merging*

1. Vishva
Cognizer of the External

"Residing in the right eye, it experiences the gross world by means of the mind and sense organs in the waking state."

3. Prajna
Cognition Amassed

"Residing in the heart, it experiences the bliss of prajna in deep sleep."

"The nonperception of duality is common to both prajna and Turiya. Prajna, though, is bound in deep sleep, which does not exist in Turiya."

2. Taijasa
Cognizer of the Internal

"Residing in the mind, it enjoys subtle realms in the dream state."

Turiya
Pure Awareness

"The syllable A leads to Vishva; U leads to Taijasa M leads to Prajna. There is no course for that which has no syllabic portions. When the adorable seer knows the three abiding qualities in these three abodes, that great sage enters Turiya and becomes worthy of worship."

Gaudapada's Process of Meditation on the Pranava, Om

- Know that to comprehend the Pranava, Om, is to attain Brahman.
- Envision the Pranava as the beginning, middle, and end of everything.
- Contemplate Om, quarter by quarter; and then meditate upon nothing else.
- Fix the mind unwaveringly on the blessed syllable, Om, and then destroy all fear.
- Come to know the Pranava as the Lord set in the heart of all, then grieve no more.
- Know Om, the Pranava, as the lower Brahman, and the Atman as the higher Brahman.
- Perceive the Pranava as being devoid of both inside and outside, as unique and immutable.
- To know Om as portionless, yet possessed of infinite portions, is what is known as realization.

One of the most endearing elements of the teaching illustrated on this particular chart is the connection, even identity, of mankind with God — the *Jivatman* with *Paramatman*. Early on in the pages of this book we studied the system of the five sheaths (see charts on pages 19, 21) to find out that these coverings were insentient without Consciousness behind them. The body decays, the *prana* ebbs and flows, the mind broods and obsesses with objects and dualities, the intellect categorizes knowledge, and the empty ego surreptitiously takes it all for itself. Amidst all the change of this quintuplication process, the true Self of mankind, called *Atman*, remains hidden. To the noble and aspiring human soul, this is not acceptable. Herein enters the Word. The Word and its understanding both represent the oneness between man and God, and acts as a truth-teaching to reestablish said connection, once and for all. For, and as my teacher, Swami Aseshananda, used to repeat often in his discourses, quoting from the *Vivekachudamani*, *"Those who imagine that there is a distinction between God and Man, Creature and Creator, Nature and Spirit, are deluded."* False superimposition is at work here, which is the first ruse of *maya* that the intelligent seeker strives to unravel.

Armed with *AUM* and what it signifies, the adamant seeker is on the path to Truth. When the *guru* reveals that the three *matras* of *AUM* stand for the three stages of his ones consciousness, a new element is introduced into the realm of seeking itself. First, waking, dreaming, and deep sleep become defined, or pointed out. Then they become objects for meditation. In this meditation a witness or observer appears, heretofore unseen and unknown. Life in the body/mind mechanism now seems dreamlike itself, neither good nor bad; only indifferent. This indifference is where peace and calm comes from. And whereas, previously, the three stages of consciousness were all broken up and disconnected, they now seem as one homogenous whole. Thus, calm turns to subtle bliss — the bliss of Knowing. This is the knowing of intrinsic identity with Reality, called *"I and my Father are One,"* in Christ's words.

One point which comes forth in the study of this teaching is that usage of The Word is not so much mysticism as it is natural awakening. All the "abracadabras" of *maya* fall away, as Vivekananda has stated, and the soul perceives its innate unity with all. And yes, that unity is with nature as well as with God. But now there is no confusion about the difference and the Source; that is, that nature is insentient and God is pure Sentiency, and is thereby the Source. And that Source is the Self which is one with God. When the soul (mind/intelligence/ego complex) finds out that nature does not exist either outwardly or independently, it sees all in the Self. At this moment the self-imposed game of *maya* that the mind is playing is over — if it ever really truly existed in the first place.

The terms on this chart are not necessarily for the layman, but English equivalents have been provided to ease and hasten the comprehension process. For what is crucial to know is that the three states of ones consciousness are gateways moving inward, not just life (waking), dreams (dream state), and nescience (deep sleep). This is why the aspirant on a *Vedic*-based path, for instance, is not interested in finding out what dreams mean (there is no aim in *maya*!), but rather where they have come from. By tracing the dream one had the previous night, in a contemplative meditation, one might deftly locate the first vibration or initial picture of that dream sequence that issued forth from the deep sleep state. This is tantamount to perceiving the deep sleep state itself, which is equivalent to seeing the Cosmic Mind, or *AUM*. Gaining a glimpse of this with the mind's open and single eye of rapt concentration, a profound sense of unity pervades the mind, transforming it forever.

Some of the dynamics of this transformation are the linking of the waking state to the A of *AUM*. When spiritually awake, the aspirant can now think of himself as conscious cognizer of all the externals worlds When he sees and links the dream state to the U of *AUM*, again, consciously, he becomes aware that the entire inner terrain of his mind, and all its realms of possibility, are his to experience as well. When he successfully links the M of *AUM* to *AUM*, he understands, possibly for the first time in a series of embodiments, that he is essentially formless, and can dissolve all vibrations, things, events, at will. And there is no fear in this, as before. Perhaps this short description will relay why an illumined being, like Sri Ramakrishna for instance, is always plunged in bliss, even showing signs of it on his very person.

But the real import of The Word is what it signifies over and above an embodied being's three states of consciousness. That, called *samadhi* in *Vedanta,* and *Nirvana* in *Buddhism,* is called simply *Turiya* in *Advaita Vedanta,* which means "the Fourth." The *svara* on the insignia of *AUM,* which I like to call the "one-eyed smile," represents that, and it is seen to rest independent from the rest of the letter. Experimentally, if one would fashion this *AUM* sign out of standing dominos, and then push the end domino so that all would come crashing down, the *svara* alone would remain standing. So this *Turiya* state is pure and free, as Gaudapada states, devoid of syllabic portions like A, U, and M. And that is formless Reality, unthinkable and indescribable, because the mind and senses have all become inactive there. It is here that *"....and the Word was God,"* as Jesus concluded.

And speaking of the great *Advaitin,* Gaudapada, he has left behind a profound reckoning of the devotee's process of "Meditation on the *Pranava, AUM,*" listed for viewing and study at the bottom of the previous chart. First of all, one has to resolutely establish the faith that attaining knowledge of The Word is equivalent to attaining *Brahman.* This is an *advaitic* or nondual stance, which always separates the religious novice from the spiritual adept. Once this fact of higher wisdom is verily installed in the heart and mind, The Word then becomes the end all and be all of the aspirant's practice. Day by day, he or she meditates on nothing else, having deep devotion and absolute fealty to *AUM,* and nothing else. Moving inwards and outwards along the subtle stairway that leads from A to U to M, rendering his waking, dreaming, and deep sleep states alive and aware, he dissolves impeding ideas like the presence of beginnings, middles, and ends completely, loosing their hold on his mind forever. At this stage he is practicing the nondual axiom of *Aparinama,* the removal of the illusion of transformations of all kinds (see chart on page 265).

Following this intense form of practice — the purification of one-pointedness — his mind settles upon The Word as a tired bird perches on the mast of a sailing ship, far from land. Focused in this unique and intense way, the mind completely still for hours at a time, a vision of pure Awareness appears. It is the *Antaryami,* or *Ishvara,* the final vestige of subtle form seen before immersion into formless Reality takes place. All fear and grief, if there was any left, now vanish completely, and the soul sees itself as *Atman,* and the *Atman* as *Brahman.* The *jiva* has merged in *Siva.* Separate states, portions or *matras,* inner and outer, bondage and liberation — all such thoughts come to an end, and full illumination of mind is experienced. Now, it is up to the sweet will of the luminary, presently in full conjunction and identity with the Supreme Will, as to whether to return to form or not.

As a further and deeper study of the connections made via contemplation of The Word of God, the following chart demonstrates how this highest Awareness works Its way out into relativity via the form of mankind, all without ever moving or going anywhere. As Sri Krishna states in the *Uddhava Gita,* "Of all the many-legged cities in my creation — thousand-legged, hundred-legged, six and four-legged, etc., the two-legged form is my favorite sporting place." And as Swami Vivekananda has declared, "Mankind is just God walking around on two legs. Have you seen any other God here in the universe?"

But in order to realize this, the deification process has to get under way. At present, man's divinity is a caricature of itself, especially in today's religions. But where even religion loses its way, The Word of God never changes. Contemplating the levels of his own existence in an introspective manner, that sense of nobility that a human being possesses, though remote at times, returns to work its salutary effect on life and mind. Here, what to speak of life and mind, even the senses and the body become fit vehicles for expressing divinity.

And it is in the *Mandukyopanisad,* again, that the teaching of *AUM,* scarcely equaled in any other written source, brings forth a transmission on the level of man's very form. Herein, the limbs and mouth of man transfigure and become vehicles of divine expression, revealing, as well, a being of individual, collective, and divine proportions whose head is the fire of creation, whose two eyes are the sun and moon, whose body represents all the ethers or divine atmospheres, filled with pure, conscious Awareness. Even the elements form his lower extremities, and the fertile earth has come from his very feet. The following chart expresses this further:

The 3 States, 7 Limbs & 19 Mouths of the Individual

*"The first quarter is Vaishvanara, outwardly cognitive, with the waking state as his field;
and the second quarter is Taijasa, inwardly cognitive, with the dream state for his field.
Both are seven-limbed and have nineteen mouths for enjoying gross and subtle objects.
The third quarter is prajna, the intellectual, with deep sleep as its field, unified, full of bliss,
and forming the gateway to all definite cognitions."*   *Mandukyopanisad*

His Seven Limbs

"His head is the heavens..."

"...the sun, his two eyes..."

"...the air and wind, his breath..."

"...the skies, his body..."

"...water, his lower organ..."

"...and the earth, his feet..."

His Nineteen Mouths
"Through these he enjoys the worlds."

Antahkarana —
Fourfold Mind

Intellect
Ego
Mind
Thoughts

Jnanendriyas —
5 Cognitive Senses

Hearing (sound)
Feeling (touch)
Seeing (form)
Tasting (taste)
Smelling (smell)

Karmendriyas —
5 Active Senses

Speaking (speaking)
Handling (acting)
Locomotion (moving)
Procreating (sexuality)
Excreting (eliminating)

Panchamahabhutas —
5 Elements

Ether
Air
Fire
Water
Earth

*"All things existing without and within are products of imagination, their differentiation being
due to association with the senses. The Lord verily imagines the Jivas, the entities of various
sorts - external (objective), internal (subjective); as one cognizes, so one remembers."*
Gaudapada

The divinity of mankind is a wondrous thing, but one long forgotten by the masses. That this truth, self-evident to the seers, has survived even as a teaching, serves as a saving grace for the all-important areas of religion, philosophy, and spirituality alike. Through the descent of sacred lineages over spans of time, the knowledge of Truth, Wisdom, and The Word, have persisted in men's minds. This is a testament to the presence of God in the human being — the real Soul, rather than the mere ego or personality.

This presence of God in mankind, what is Real, called Reality, subsists despite the many seemingly antagonistic and contrary limitations and overlays beings encounter in search of It. And ironically, the very things which point to limitation in the embodied condition, and on the physical plane, of which God would never partake, are to blame for human beings giving up on this exceptional and singular truth of God in mankind. These are the senses, the physical elements, and the worldly or ordinary mind. Yet these very principles take in and reflect nothing other than the Light of Consciousness, even if in a limited sense. It is in that regard that the *rishis* have seen through to a hidden Source, and given us the superlative teaching arranged on the chart on the previous page.

The three *matras* of *AUM*, which we have just studied, have, in addition to their correlation with the states of awareness (*jagrat*, waking; *svapna*, dreaming; and *sushupti*, deep sleep), an assignment for the condition of the individual at each level. That is, the human being, despite all appearances to the contrary, and the self-imposed veils he/she drops over the Truth, is really *Vishva* or *Vaishvanara*, the lord of all that is surveyed in the waking state — the A of *AUM* (see chart on page 146). His nineteen mouths consisting of the five elements, the ten senses (active and cognitive), and the fourfold mind are engaged in taking in all that exists in the objective realm. Few beings ever think of this. Who is the enjoyer here? Is it man, or is it the presence of God, the Real. Are not the five elements, the ten senses, and fourfold mind — including the ego — all insentient, passing and ephemeral? How can they hold this massive amount of bliss-filled experience? Are they its source? Then who is experiencing?

The U of *Aum* represents the dream state. At this stage of awareness a man is called *Taijasa*. Though the field of his experience has changed shape from gross to subtle, he nevertheless enjoys the same things he did in waking, utilizing the subtle equivalents of those same nineteen mouths. Even the gross earth has taken on a dream-world type of vision and atmosphere, as has water and fire, etc. Thus, in both waking and dream states, the nineteen limbs are working, as are the seven limbs — his head, his two eyes, his breath, his organs, his body, and his feet. Gross and subtle objects are thus being enjoyed by a man in both of his identities of *Vishva* and *Taijasa*.

But the individual also has his deep sleep state, mystic and non-ordinary, maybe even extraordinary, because all else vanishes there and one experiences profound rest. The individual's name here is *Prajna*, inferring that wisdom in potential is more his true nature. The limbs have become motionless, the mouths, closed and inactive. The most profound ramification of this, even beyond God sporting through mankind, is the revelatory presence of the Source of all cognitions, espied through the doorway of all cognitions — the deep sleep state of *sushupti*. This *"cognition amassed"* changes the perceptions of man, both at the levels of nescient formlessness (deep sleep) and sentient Formlessness (*Brahman*). One begins to understand that it is the Lord, or Divine Reality, that infills all states, even going so far as to project the *jivas*, the embodied beings. *Atmic Sankalpa*, *Chit-shakti*, and other names for this, all come to the fore, understood now from the unique perspective of ones direct spiritual experience. God, mankind, deities, living beings, worlds, elements — all now have their assigned place as manifestations of the one Consciousness. And more than that, the divisions between them, which are the work of ignorance, are now gone, and existence has transformed into an indivisible ocean of pure, conscious Awareness. God and mankind are one and the same.

As this superlative experience is a matter of ones own direct realization, some additional information regarding the dynamics of this level of enlightenment would be helpful. As a matter of practice, the *yogi* or *yogini*, both striving for union with Divine Reality, take to certain exercises which connect the outer world with the inner realms, as the chart on the next page (page 151) demonstrates:

Yogic Connections and Correlations in Meditation Practice

"Utilizing the supports (alambanas), the yogi stabilizes the mind-field by meditating upon them all, from the grossest magnitude inward to the subtlest principles. Let the yogi focus upon what is agreeable, then, observing it all in waking, dreaming, and deep sleep states with detachment."

Vedavyasa

Alambanas, in Order of Meditation

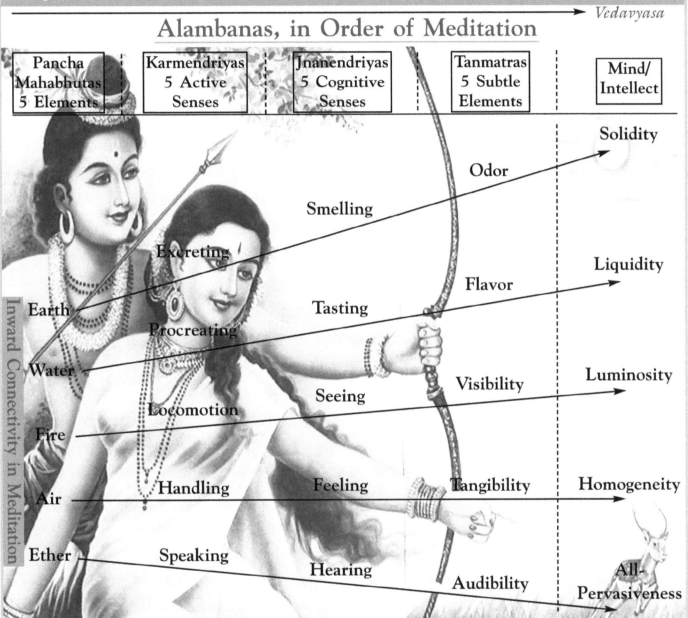

Pancha Mahabhutas 5 Elements	Karmendriyas 5 Active Senses	Jnanendriyas 5 Cognitive Senses	Tanmatras 5 Subtle Elements	Mind/ Intellect
			Odor	Solidity
		Smelling		
	Excreting		Flavor	Liquidity
Earth		Tasting		
	Procreating		Visibility	Luminosity
Water		Seeing		
Fire	Locomotion			
	Handling	Feeling	Tangibility	Homogeneity
Air				
Ether	Speaking	Hearing	Audibility	All-Pervasiveness

Inward Connectivity in Meditation

* The Three Origins *

Ahamkara, Ego ⟶ Buddhi, Determinative Intelligence ⟶ Mahat, Cosmic Mind

Meditate Upon Each Via

- its origin
- its qualities, attributes, characteristics
- its consistency and content
- its appearance in waking and dream
- its changing nature
- its place in the mind and thoughts
- its power and hold over the mind
- its disappearance in deep sleep

"Wisdom samadhi occurs via the process of gross thought to subtle thought, culminating in the indescribable state of 'I-am-ness.' In Abhava Yoga and Mahayoga, wherein one begins to see the blissful Self, the alambanas are absent. Thus, they are to be transcended in deep meditation."

In today's world, authentic and authoritative religion and philosophy are hard put for survival, what to speak of the supreme art of spirituality. Over the passing centuries human beings have divorced themselves from Reality more and more, and have taken refuge in relativity, so much so that nature has 1) become a mere resource for covetousness and enjoyment and 2) has come to be perceived as an exterior world separate from man. Whereas the independent person, tired of the ills of the conventional world, profit-oriented business, etc., may envision a desired return to the Source to be a kind of "getting back to the land," and the like, the spiritual aspirant sees it as getting back to the laws governing *dharmic* living, and thus a return to the eternal principles of spiritual life, i.e., true Religion. For the aspiring *yogi* or *yogini*, it all begins with the internal act of interconnectivity to all which he or she has become divorced from, maybe for lifetimes. That is, the "building blocks of nature" have become scattered about in the wayward recesses of the inattentive mind, and they need to be gathered up and placed into a configuration which is both conducive to harmonious living, and commensurate with the truth of innate Unity. This, the aspirant facilitates by a process of connecting the dots — not on a game puzzle, but in the puzzled human mind. In short, nature, all that is seemingly outside of him, is really within him, has come forth of him. Benighted modes and systems of conventional thinking, encrusted with age-old coverings of ignorance, have foisted upon his mind their twisted and backwards ways of perception. It is time to recover the luminous lands and terrains of wisdom which reside within him. This, the sincere *yogi* and *yogini* sets off to do.

The basic *yogic* teaching in this regard concerns the *alambanas*, as shown in the chart on the previous page (151). An *alambana* is a "support" for meditation. Everything visible, and many things invisible to the eye, are simply that — vehicles which, when the mind is geared to this particular wisdom perspective, will carry the soul to harmonious communion with both the nonself (*prakriti*) and the true Self (*atman*). The entire beginning focuses around the will and ability to connect the five elements to the five senses; this, at least, is a good start. In other words, and for example, the element of earth is intrinsically linked to the sense of smell. If the spectacle of this earth beheld by the soul contains no sense of analytic inspection or, accordingly, if ones sense of smell is working but is only a vehicle for isolated pleasure; and if both of these are left unexplored and taken for granted, then a form of disconnection or alienation has already taken place. Put another way, the five elements and the five senses all have a deeper meaning and function than just surface experience.

And this becomes more obvious when the meditator links in the active senses and the subtle elements, as shown in the chart. Taking water as the example, one perceives its connection to procreation (seminal fluid), the act of tasting, the characteristic of flavor, and finally, in the subtlemost link in the mind — as the very thought or concept of liquidity. Performing this connection mentally, in practice, via introspective visualization, with knowledge and observer intact, some powerful realizations come to bear upon the mind. For one, the meditator comes to know that the thought precedes the object, that the idea of liquidity is present in the "Mind of God," (*Mahat, AUM*, etc.,) long before the element of water actually manifests physically. In other words, the entire cosmos is present in subtle form, always and ever, before it manifests outwardly or, to put a finer point on it, *"Anterior to life and mind is the Atman,"* to quote the *Mundakopanisad*.

So, *Brahman* first (the Uncaused Cause), then *AUM* (Cosmic Mind or Unmanifested *Prakriti*) next. After that, all the principles spring forth in sequence over time, time itself being one of them. If one finds oneself embodied in a physical world, devoid of the knowledge of where one comes from, and in possession of a hefty spiritual curiosity, a system such as this will afford a way to trace the origins, in order, of every manifest thing — including the individual self/ego. Thus, the connection of fire to activity to seeing to sight leads to the knowledge of the presence of the very idea of revelatory wisdom. Just as the sun provides light so that beings can move about unhindered in their daily path, so too, on a subtler level, does the light of intelligence, representing the luminosity of Consciousness, reveal wisdom principles for human involution. Therefore, to the visionary, the light of a billion suns radiating in the nocturnal skies is an outer symbol of the infinite Light of Awareness which illuminates the three worlds, lending all those suns their ability to shine. Thus comes forth the *Katho Upanisad*'s famous *sloka* on true Light: *"There, deep within the limitless depths of all living beings, the sun does not shine, nor the moon, nor fire, nor stars, nor lightning — much less this tiny mortal flame (prana). That one Light shining, all else shines; by It's radiance all else is made luminous. May that one Light of pure, conscious Awareness enter into us and permeate us to the very core of our being."*

In the case of air, and particularly, ether, the connections are most intriguing. These two atmospheres, overlooked due to their invisibility, provide connections that, when studied, open up many hidden secrets for inner life. Of course, without meditation practice, these secrets remain obscured, and people only touch the outermost significance of nature and consciousness in this case. Eating, sex life, daily activities, sensual contact, and worldly talk, then make up all of life, restricting the scope of living beings to a mere surface existence, devoid of any inner meaning.

Therefore, the striving soul places him or herself in a position where he/she is definitely "marching to the beat of a different drummer." The twenty-four cosmic principles (see chart on page 349) and all their many connections and interrelations form one of Mother India's most precious contributions to philosophy, linking it to spiritual practice. Even beyond a deep study of these principles, a practice which demonstrates how to relate them with one another is key to an inner life, and to a wholesome and fulfilling outer life as well. It is an ennobling undertaking, afforded us by one of the most comprehensive and well-thought out philosophical lists ever conceived of. The five elements, (*panchamahabhutas*), the five active senses (*karmendriyas*), the five cognitive senses (*jnanendriyas*), the five subtle elements (*tanmatras*), and the fourfold mind (*antahkarana*, or "inner cause" of all) complete any cosmological and philosophical picture, and provide a copious map of a triple terrain (physical, subtle, and causal) which all beings will, at one time or another, have to course through, back and forth, on their imaginary dream-journies of soul transmigration.

As for the "how to do's" of this practice, a spiritual guide is recommended. This excellent soul will advise as to how to contemplate the various qualities and attributes of all these principles. As a fundamental road map, however, at the bottom of the chart under study (page 151) is listed an eight-part instruction manual, to be utilized in meditation. The avid spiritual seeker will take the time to perceive the inner qualities of all that is without and within. In earlier times, when beings were more in possession of their rightful inner wisdom, this represented how life was to be encountered, confronted on its own ground and forced to give up its secrets. The sedulous aspirant, then, will find not only spiritual secrets coming to the fore of consciousness via such practices, but will also uncover and destroy a host of hidden impediments (*karmas*) which have been impeding inner progress, and even hampering earthly life, possibly for lifetimes. What relief to be free of these!

As an example, everything, from fear of water due to drowning in a past life, to the presence of mental phobias and anxieties, will be culled out and systematically done away with by an inward practice of this intensive and revealing nature. This is really what the word "fearlessness" is meant to convey. And when this particular mode of practice is further connected to The Word and what it signifies, not only will physical and mental well-being be secured, but the incomparable boon of seership will also manifest. Then, the three states of waking, dreaming, and deep sleep will be rendered lucid, and the aspiring soul will come to know himself (body, mind, intellect, and ego) and all else he surveys as vibrational manifestations springing from The Word. Reaching The Word, the vision of nondual Reality will appear. Much more on That will come later.

We have now studied a host of significances regarding *AUM*, The Word of God, the *bijam* of Formlessness. Along this comprehensive course of study a mention of the Four Stages of The Word has been made. These are titled *Para, Pashyanti, Madhyama,* and *Vaikhari,* which correlate to a supreme state, a state of undifferentiated unity, a state of subtle conceptualization, and a state of gross manifestation. A chart showing this sequence has been placed next for consideration, so as to contribute further to our intellectual knowledge of that which is, admittedly, beyond intellect, but very much one with Intelligence, Itself. This chart also combines the principle of knowledge with The Word in its four stages, illustrating that knowledge, in its essence, solidifies by degrees into all manifest things, from causal to subtle to gross.

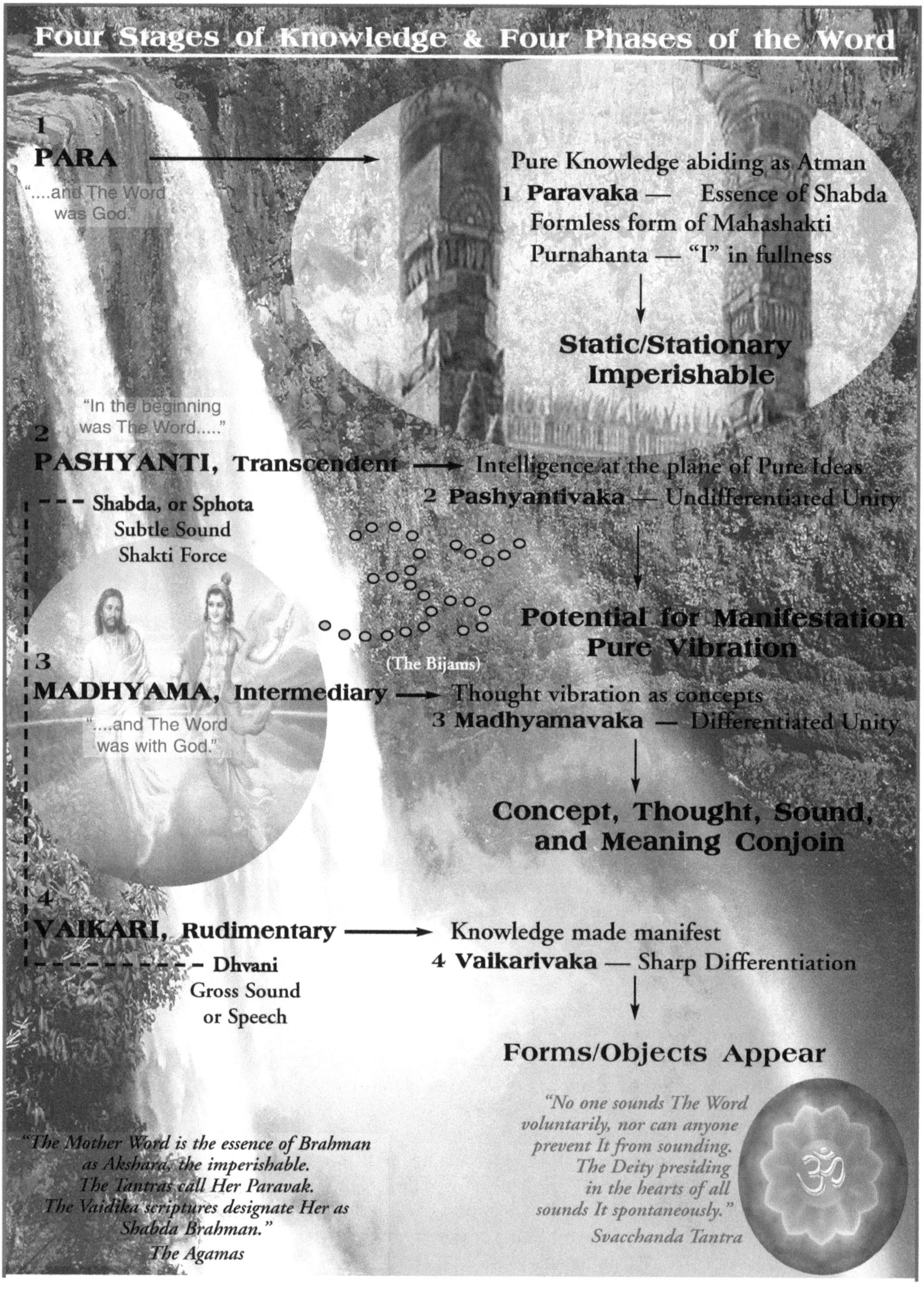

Four Stages of Knowledge & Four Phases of the Word

1
PARA
"....and The Word was God."

Pure Knowledge abiding as Atman
1 Paravaka — Essence of Shabda
Formless form of Mahashakti
Purnahanta — "I" in fullness

**Static/Stationary
Imperishable**

"In the beginning was The Word....."

2
PASHYANTI, Transcendent
Intelligence at the plane of Pure Ideas
2 Pashyantivaka — Undifferentiated Unity

- - - **Shabda, or Sphota**
Subtle Sound
Shakti Force

(The Bijams)

**Potential for Manifestation
Pure Vibration**

3
MADHYAMA, Intermediary
Thought vibration as concepts
3 Madhyamavaka — Differentiated Unity

"....and The Word was with God."

**Concept, Thought, Sound,
and Meaning Conjoin**

4
VAIKARI, Rudimentary
Knowledge made manifest
4 Vaikarivaka — Sharp Differentiation

- - - - - - - **Dhvani**
Gross Sound
or Speech

Forms/Objects Appear

*"The Mother Word is the essence of Brahman
as Akshara, the imperishable.
The Tantras call Her Paravak.
The Vaidika scriptures designate Her as
Shabda Brahman."*
The Agamas

*"No one sounds The Word
voluntarily, nor can anyone
prevent It from sounding.
The Deity presiding
in the hearts of all
sounds It spontaneously."*
Svacchanda Tantra

In spiritual circles — at least those high-minded ones where *jnana yoga* is being brought forth, studied, inquired about, and discoursed upon — the teaching of the Four Phases of the Word is often brought up for consideration and contemplation. Being raised between the "rock and a hard place" of conventional religion and modern science, beings living in present times and Westernized cultures have little recourse other than to depend meekly upon the teaching of a vaunted creator god, or even abandon all that for a temporary refuge in a physics-based, materially-oriented scientific view. Unfortunately, the former path risks fashioning a man into a person who is dependent upon all the whimsies of a misinformed fundamentalist pseudo-religion, while the latter reduces him to a soul-less entity dependent upon the senses and the elements, with no more point to his life than a few transient decades of toil and bodily existence. Neither pathway, even considering any relative good lies in them, will suffice to help him attain his true goal in life and the reason for his being here — to realize his birthless, deathless nature under the most challenging and trying of circumstances.

It is in the tepid and tenuous atmosphere related above that teachings like the Four Phases of the Word confer their utmost benefit. To come to find, as it is conveyed in such a revelation, that all material objects are nothing less than manifestations of ones own intelligence, is character-forming and courage-building — is true "man-making," to quote Swami Vivekananda. In brief, when the mind (cosmic, collective, and individual) vibrates, all the worlds burgeon, and when it ceases to vibrate, there is dissolution thereof, followed by a phase of voidness. And this is what is occurring, temporarily but continually, in a human being's ongoing states of waking, dreaming, and deep sleep. To a *yogi*, this is what his philosophy or credo should be telling him, deftly proven by the presence and occurrence of these selfsame states of his consciousness. That is, conventional wisdom tries to tell him that all this is real rather than merely phenomenal, coincidental rather than predestined, or fashioned out of nothing by a creator god rather than naturally springing from his own imaginative awareness. Further, all this imagination (*vikalpa*), once let loose and difficult of control, can be withdrawn by the very force of awareness that unleashed it. This teaching-tenet, along with the twin principles of *karma* and reincarnation, are most important of understanding for Western consciousness in general — at least if humanity is going to develop any cognition whatsoever of an ongoing internal life more specific to its fundamental core.

The Four Phases of the Word, in accordance with the Four Stages of Knowledge, should proceed by way of explanation from top to bottom, or from the absolute, to the causal, to the subtle, to the apparent (see chart on facing page). Before any hint or residue of conceptualization is present, in a state which is more like an all-pervasive homogeneity rather than a condition, and wherein The Word Itself, with all its potential, is held in complete abeyance — there is *Para,* the Essential, consisting of pure Intelligence. It is the Essence of *Shabda*, The Word, and is also seen as the Divine Mother (*Mahashakti*) of all the Worlds, abiding in Formlessness. There is hardly anything to say about It, and no way of really describing It. When the soul is merged into It, everything makes perfect sense; otherwise, it is only something to be looked up to and aspired for, never to be comprehended by the mind operating at lower levels of *samadhi*, what to speak of ordinary states. But what can be said is that "It Is"; otherwise how can all of this, the appearance of the Three Worlds in space and time, be possible? Thus, and in accordance with personal realization, the seers speak of this subtlemost Reality as *Purnahanta,* or *"I in fullness."* It is not to be imagined or theorized about as being sterile, unreachable, or merely "impersonal." To think so would be to overlook the intense experiences of It that hundreds and thousands of souls have been recipients of over vast ages.

The second Stage of Knowledge/Phase of The Word, though still formless and nearly incomprehensible, tenderly offers forth the barest possibility of conceptualization and its eventual manifestation as all forms. Speaking poetically, as the *rishis* often did, it is like a slight and unexpected movement in a windless forest, or the sudden appearance of a tiny ripple forming on dark, still waters. The only problem with this imagery is that it is external in its presentation, whereas the *Pasyanti* stage of Awareness is unfathomably subtle. And, in fact, this is where we come upon the word "causal" in this tradition, which is used to signify an eternal principle that is subtler than subtle. A *Sanskrit* word has to be borrowed in this regard, namely *Anoraniyan* — the subtlemost of the subtle. As the chart relates, this is pure intelligence, "departing" absolute *Atmic* abidance and arriving at the plane of potential ideas, ideas that are not formulated yet, but are in the process of doing so. It is a kind of cosmic incubation period for massive but as yet imponderable concepts.

Here, at the *Pashyanti* stage, and in order to convey some sort of inkling of what is there, the sages talk about what is undifferentiated, meaning also undiversified, invariable, and nonvibrational. The Word is more Itself here, closest to its true nature. The word *bijam*, related and inspected in earlier pages of this chapter, comes further into play here, for the *bijams* are something like the atoms of *AUM*, both representing and facilitating its interpenetrating power. This is demonstrated on the chart in the little illustration. Power *bijams* like *Hrim, Aim, Shrim, Krim* and the like (refer back to the chart on page 133), abide quietly, but with amazing force, in this crucial stage, all shot through and through with wisdom-power — *"like sweetness in sugar-cane juice."* They only need to be pricked or perked in order for all manner of possibility to burgeon forth — which is the intention and province of the *Shakti* force. This stage, *Pashyanti*, describes the esoteric principle of Unmanifested *Prakriti* to a tee, at least in its rarest or most refined form. Everything that was ever thought of, or is yet to be thought of, abides here in subtle form, deathless, eternal, and untouched by decay.

Though marvelously untouched by decay, the *Shakti* force touches this stage in another way — with Her incomparable animating power. Here, the stage of *Madhyama* has begun. Beautifully, and whereas all these mediums were heretofore and apparently disconnected and seemingly far flung from one another, concept, thought, sound, and meaning now all join together. This is called a stage of differentiated unity, which gives a hint into the deeper secrets of what dualistic religions erroneously call "creation," but which the *rishis* and luminaries of Mother India more wisely refer to as "projection." In other words, and to utilize the wisdom transmitted in the earlier pages of this book, vibration rises up to form the *tattvas*, all animated and projected by the *Chit-Shakti* via Her various levels of deities. The human mind which is open to this flow of inward wisdom through its various mediums benefits immensely. The rest, those as yet unawakened, do not — at least not consciously. Knowledge of subtle concepts, sound, vibration, meaning, etc., escape them, and all they see is the object, remaining completely unaware of where it proceeded from and what its meaning and secrets are. To quote a song from India's store of devotional music, *"With eyes wide open and fully functioning, they remain completely blind!"*

It is at the fourth level or phase of The Word that objects appear, which is also the fourth stage of knowledge. There they are, everywhere, consisting of the five elements. If they are examined outwardly they are matter, but they are really just concretized thought — *"mind made manifest."* This is a simple secret, but it is cognized by so few. The power of the outgoing senses is just far too convincing. The tangible wins out over the intangible or, as Sri Ramakrishna used to say, *"Avidya-shakti (power of ignorance) is far more powerful than vidya-shakti (power of knowledge)."* Whatever the case may be, beings still have and are attracted by what the senses afford them. For, there is a difference between the eye and its power to see, or sight. And this proves doubly true for the ear and its power to hear. The *Dhvani,* or gross arena of sound, has its attractions, like music and speech. These two are exceedingly alluring, which should act as a key to their being doorways into subtler worlds. But the overall and prevailing mode of procedure here, at the *Vaikari* stage, is attachment and selfish grasping. This is a world of "sharp differentiation" wherein all the real and beneficial connections have been lost to the mind, and it believes only in what the senses can perceive and enjoy. And at this level, The Word, too, has been stripped of its real power — the power to convey the Truth — and gets used as a common tool for conventional and superficial, even banal, expression.

The Word and its inherent Knowledge is more than a mere teaching; it is a pathway leading back within to the radiant reality of the Self. To close this healthy section on The Word, *AUM*, and all that it contains and infers, the next chart reveals a form of meditation in nine steps wherein the aspirant can practice the art of involution and consummate the spiritual path and its aims:

The chart on the facing page (157) is taken from teachings in Shankara's works, but has quotes

Nine Step Process of Meditation on AUM

1) Ekasana — Single Posture

" The real posture is that one in which meditation flows spontaneously and unceasingly. Absorption in the uniform Brahman should be known as the equipoise of the limbs...."   Shankaracharya

2) Japa — Recitation of AUM & Contemplating Its Meaning

" The first letter, A, is the root sound, the key, pronounced without touching any part of the tongue or palate; M represents the last sound in the series, being produced by the closed lips, and U rolls from the very root to the end of the sounding board of the mouth. Repetition of Aum, and meditating on its meaning is the way."   Swami Vivekananda

3) Manana — Silent Repetition of AUM in the Mind

" Uttering the mono-syllabled Aum, Brahman, thinking of Me, that one who departs, transcending the body, attains the Supreme Goal."   Sri Krishna

4) Nischaya-dardhyam — Inner Affirmation

" I compare Aum to the sound of a bell that dissolves in silence. The relative universe dissolves in the imperishable Absolute — the Great Silence. I have experienced this infinite ocean of Bliss and Consciousness; and Mother has shown me how innumerabl worlds issue from It and return to It."   Sri Ramakrishna

5) Ekagrata — Freedom from Distractions

" Aum, the mystic sound, is the bow, the Self within is the arrow; and Brahman is the target. One should hit that mark with an undistracted mind."   Mundakopanisad

6) Anasaktih — Detachment from Objects

" That one who meditates upon the Supreme Purusha with the sacred word, Aum, is freed from all concerns, even as a snake is freed from its slough."   Prasnopanisad

7) Nava-samskara Sunyata — Extinction of Samskaras

" The force of past impressions continue to create a physical reality, such as illness, health of the body, and other regular operations, until the force of the new impressions of samadhi being created on the mind burn these out completely."   Lord Patanjali

8) Purva-samskara Saksitvam — Witnessing Past Samskaras

" It is the self-effulgent Witness of all who is manifested in the sheath of intellect. Keeping in view that which is separate from the manifested and the unmanifested, by one undivided thought think of That always."   Shankaracharya

9) Atmanistha — Dwelling in the Self

" After traveling the path of Aum, the silent Source is reached and the Yogi becomes a realized sage, dwelling in the one Reality."   Lex Hixon — Ramakrishnadas Baul

gleaned from some of the greatest sources in Indian religion and philosophy. The reader, and especially the practitioner, are encouraged to use this chart as both a guide and an experiment — better yet, as a practice — in order to deepen the content, quality, and scope of meditation in general. Actual meditation on *AUM* is the final and most beneficial action that study of The Word can afford us. As a sort of guide in this "experiment," the following words can be offered:

An obvious and telling fact that every advanced spiritual aspirant is aware of, but which escapes the novice and pretender entirely, is that the real point and essence of spiritual practice is not physical, but mental. The mental territories of the human soul has as its concomitants the intellectual, philosophical, and cosmological elements which make up the path leading to spirituality per se. For this reason, and assuming that we are sincere and noble seekers, Shankara begins his meditation on *AUM* with an easy and most natural assumption of a basic sitting posture. Calling it *ekasana* (*eka* means one in *Sanskrit*), the gist is twofold: first, he infers that to get into meditation proper, the meditator must be motionless; second, the urge to shift into other positions (*asanas*) is counterproductive, for this will rail against the object of meditation — which is not to gain health, longevity, or occult powers as the *hatha* yogis desire, but to merge in *samadhi* as superior yogis do. Shankara, in his well-crafted scriptures and commentaries, states that a single and well-adjusted sitting position is crucial to the process of meditation over expanses of time. Otherwise, he avers, that *"the straightening and posturing of the body merely results in the condition of that of a dried up tree."* Similarly, about breathing exercises, the he states, *"Drawing every breath in the knowledge of Brahman is the point of pranayama. All else is just mere torture of the lungs and the nasal passages."* Here, it is as if the limbs and lungs, too, need to meditate, and gain their own and independent equipoise.

With this in mind, and placed into practice, the principle of *japa* gets initiated. Reciting the *mantra* audibly, *vachika* (see chart on page 143), and in one long chant, *dirgha-pranava*, is described well by the quote on the chart (page 157) by Swami Vivekananda. Intoning it, contemplating its meaning, and attempting to merge into it *(Omkaralayavritti-dhyan)* will all become very deep and successful if prior studies, like the ones offered in previous pages of this book, are well considered and digested. Then the experience assumes profound dimensions, as if chanting the Word out into the physical atmosphere is tantamount to actually calling on the Lord and Mother of the Universe.

And it is here that the third stage of our meditation engages, as the seeker undertakes silent repetition, *manasa japa*. Such refined practice vaults the mind beyond itself. The body, senses, even ones familiar surroundings, tend to fade naturally to the background. The practitioner can easily spend many hours in this sweet and subtle condition, getting the mind used to inner transcendental climes and thus setting it up for a more complete dissolution into *Brahman* (*nirvikalpa samadhi*. (see charts on pages 503, 511).

All of the aforementioned stages really culminate in *nischaya-dardhyam*, which can only be described as the soul's outright assurance that "Existence Is," for it has now beheld the source of name and form, and even intuited what lies beyond, mainly Formlessness. Like the striking of a bell, its sustaining tone, and the tone's fading away from the realm of vibration, so too do the worlds conjured by the mind rise, play, and subside, continually, without end — like an ocean's waves. But, as the maturing spiritual aspirant discovers, being the witness of these playful waves of conditioned awareness is much more peaceful and blissful than being tossed about on the surface by them, since they all contain the potential for suffering as well as sport. And so, the meditator observes from a distance, gradually coming to know and adamantly confirm (*nischaya*) that the Self is unique, being distinct from the manifestation of name and form and all their changes.

The aforementioned *Sanskrit* word, *eka*, comes forth again in the next stage of our meditative experiment on the Word within us. In this instance it is not posture that is being inferred, but rather mental flow. That is, the thinking process itself has to come under complete subjection to Divine Reality, burying itself deeply like an arrow into the center of a target. As the growing ability to do this proceeds, the old world of distractions merely fades away, no more to insinuate itself and interfere with the important matters of everyday life — the higher goals and aspirations of *dharmic* life and spiritual realization. This alone contributes substantially to the aspirant's well-being, and adds a measure of subtle bliss to existence as well. The spiritual art of meditation has even been taken by intermediate level souls for this end alone. But there is much more to come, as the Word will demonstrate if we only give it our attention.

There is a basic level of detachment from objects which occurs very early in spiritual practice. And, in fact, fundamental detachment even begins to suggest itself to the mind which lives long enough in the body to find out that all is not as its appears to be. Of the twelve levels of detachment that *Vedanta* outlines for the seeker (see chart on page 359), this one is most rudimentary. But *Anasaktih* is not just that. This is a type of nonattachment which demonstrates freedom from even the thought forms which are aligned so intrinsically with objects. In other words, there is a primal attachment which beings hold and covet for worlds, forms, concepts, etc. Imagine the sense of freedom which might dawn on the mind that had penetrated through even these veils, leaving it radiant and ready to scale the highest levels of Existence. Slipping easily out of the old snakeskin of previous ignorance, the newborn adept rejoices in an unusual and heretofore undiscovered sense of emancipation, wholly unknown to the greater masses of souls involved in the embodied condition.

And it is here that some very subtle impressions surface, exposing themselves to the fires of inner concentration, like the embers of a fire finally being reduced to ashes. This phenomenon bespeaks of two things: the first is how subtle the imperfections of the mind are, and therefore how much inner work it will take to even locate them, what to speak of disintegrate them forever. The second points to the reason why most beings who take up religion and the spiritual path, seldom get enlightenment: they do not know and cannot even imagine at the outset just how deep their mental impressions reach — lifetimes deep, to be clear. It is therefore that the sixth and seventh stage of our meditation on The Word contains another word of import, namely the *Sanskrit* word, *samskara*. All of our experiences — small and great, pleasurable and painful, demeaning or inspiring, positive or negative or mixed — have left their subtle imprint in the stuff of our minds (*chitta*), and continue to influence and impact all that we do in life, what to speak of in successive lifetimes. This mental residue reveals, by its very discovery, everything that science, psychology, medicine, history, biology evolution, and conventional religion and philosophy, to name a few, fail to explain. And so our practice and our guide are both telling us to perceive them all as *shunyata*, empty of substance, as they truly are.

Once this is effectively done, and the danger of holding these *samskaras* in secret or ignorantly has passed, the adept meditator can now simply witness them as they exit the mind, "like rats leaving a sinking ship," as they say. This becomes an essential view (*purva*), like a ritual, which the mind, from here on out, will adopt with regard to all phenomena and their appearances. The *Vedantic* adage, "I am not the world," describes this very well, while the resulting realization, "I am *Brahman*," crowns that conclusion. The ultimate arrival, then, is reached — that of abiding in the Self, *Atmanistha*, a conditionless state that The Word has so perfectly drawn us into.

Chapter one of this book has focused on the "baby steps" of authentic philosophy, as in the false superimpositions of cosmic *maya* and the coveted misconceptions of the human mind, as well as the coverings, gross to subtle to causal, that souls take on when they embody. Chapter two concentrated on the overlays of evolution and involution, and the three cosmic laws of space, time, and causation — all posited there by the "individual ego's staggering strut." In chapter three, in order to "match strides with the seers," we explored the crying need for spiritual discipline, called *sadhana*, in this day and time, and the need for qualifying oneself, further coursing through some of India's greatest offerings and pathways, such as The Word, and the *mantras* which spring from it.

In chapter four the perplexing but extremely important and explanatory principles of *karma* and reincarnation can be taken up, which will greatly clarify more of the axioms and truisms which lie buried within the mind at its various levels. These are relative laws, no doubt, but play an important part in removing ignorance from the minds of embodied beings who are temporarily occupying the realms of name and form in time and space based in cause and effect.

Beating the Old Familiar Path
The Relative Laws of Karma and Reincarnation

The considerable problems which human beings face in life can all be solved to a great extent by the mind's close inspection and understanding of the relative principles of *karma* and reincarnation. They are termed "relative" since they only apply on the planes of name and form, where *maya* conjoined with the root-ignorance (*mulavidya*) has its dissembling power and its discombobulating influence. Still, if their attributes and dynamics are studied pertinent to the relative planes upon which they are operational, a massive amount of benefit can be accrued. In addition, this intense scrutiny avails the soul of another and most crucial bit of esoteric information, that being that Divine Reality — God, *Brahman*, Allah, *Prajnaparam*, Yah-weh, Almighty Father — is not subject to these two laws, which causes aspiring beings to strive for communion with that one, singular, eternal, and ever-pure Consciousness. Thus, these two laws hold vast significance for embodied souls who are trying to uncover the true meaning of their lives, and to make sense out of the stultifying maze of *maya* which they find themselves in upon opening their eyes on this outer universe.

When presenting these two theories, or principles, to the general populace, one is bound to encounter obstacles. There is, unfortunately, the overall apathy of a materially-oriented, pleasure-seeking culture; then there is the expected incredulity overall. Ironically, the teacher who moves to present the sacred over the secular does not seek the credulous person or the incredulous person, for the latter will merely deny all proposals out of hand and never get to the teachings, while the former will be all too willing to believe, and thus fail to analyze and question properly.

And here is a huge problem that plagues many of these cogent philosophical offerings, that being the lack of a few questioners who can proceed with the correct perspective and present the most pertinent queries. And what is the correct perspective and the cogent line of questioning? It is not to ask whether reincarnation is true or false, but rather to ask questions such as "Who is reincarnating?" "What is reincarnating?" and "Where are the reincarnated coming from and going to?" Questions such as these broach the real point, so the wise welcome questioners such as these. The others only run the already divided mind into further fragmentation and thus stand no chance of uncovering true wisdom — the kind which attends upon seers, sages, saints and other luminaries.

Whatever the case or scenario, it is not that the wisdom teacher will refrain from taking a chance on an incredulous person at times, for the awakened being knows that memories of past lifetimes and past deeds lie just below the surface of consciousness. Striving souls may have an opening to inner understanding during a period which is less impeded by fructifying *karmas*, and thereby make some advancement along the spiritual path. Possibly an auspicious occurrence, or a "chance" meeting with a great soul, or even a powerful dream, will galvanize this being, and life will vibrate in a more harmonious way for a time. It is a rather common occurrence. And actually, this is how the Wisdom Mother plants seeds in us, which will sprout auspiciously in the future.

This most intriguing line of questioning that the far-seeing student follows leads the spiritual preceptor to prepare the qualified aspirant for a consummate understanding. The wise *guru* is not content to have the sincere student follow mere hearsay, or to take the teachings from a book alone. A fuller, richer explanation is deserved. So, what or who is it that reincarnates? The wise ones are ready to answer such specific questions, as instanced on the charts that follow:

The Three Bodies Comprising the Nonself

"Now I will state what you need to know — discrimination between the real and the unreal, between matter and spirit. Listen carefully and then decide in your own mind." Shankaracharya

Karana/Linga Sharira — The Causal Body

Avyaktam — It is undifferentiated
Buddhi-vrittih — Where the intellect ceases to vibrate
Bijatmanah-vasthitir — Is mind existing in its subtle state
Tri-gunam — Where the three gunas rest in equilibrium

- Sushupti, deep sleep, belongs to the causal body
- Pre-exists the physical worlds
- It is the cause of both the gross and subtle bodies

Sukshma Sharira — The Subtle Body

Antahkarana — The Inner Organ
Consisting of Buddhi (intellect), Ahamkara (ego), Chitta (thought), and Manas (dual mind)

Pancha Tanmatras — The Five Subtle Elements:
called audibility, tangibility, visibility, flavor, and odor

Pancha Jnanendriyas — The Five Senses of Knowledge:
called Ghranendriya (smelling)
Rasanendriya (tasting)
Chakshurindriya (seeing)
Sparshendriya (feeling)
and Shravenindriya (hearing)

Pancha Pranas — The Five Modes of Life-force:
called Prana (inhalation), Apana (exhalation/excretory), Vyana (circulatory), Udana (upward moving/ascension), and Samana (digestive/distributive)

Avidya — Ignorance/Nescience
Kama and Karma — Desire and Action

≈Characteristics≈
Conceptualization, happiness, misery, blindness, deafness, dumbness, breathing, yawning, hunger, thirst, secretion, arriving and departing the body, etc.

- Svapna, the dream state, belongs to the subtle body
- Is the source of all activity
- Is possessed of desire due to ignorance of the Atman
- It befriends the three gunas
- Contains latent impressions
- Is the cause of Stula Sharira

Stula Sharira — The Gross Body

Pancha Mahabhutas — The Five Elements:
called Ksiti (earth), Ap (water), Teja (fire), Marut (air), and Vyoma (heaven/ether), that combine to create the sense objects

Deha — The Body:
composed of the seven ingredients called marrow, bones, fat, flesh, blood, skin, and nails

Pancha Karmendriyas — The Five Organs of Action:
called Vagendriya (speaking), Hastendriya (handling), Padendriya (locomotion), Payuindriya (excreting), and Upasthendriya (procreation)

≈Characteristics≈
Existence, birth, growth, change, disease, decay, death, caste, color, creed, ignorance and learning, corpulence and thinness, respect and insult, etc.

- Jagrat, the waking state, belongs to the gross body
- Facilitates states of waking, dreaming, and deep sleep
- Is the house of the Purusha
- Is created by past actions
- Is the medium for personal experience

"The body, organs, pranas, mind, ego; the modifications and objects of the senses and the pleasure and pain they usher in; the five elements, the universe, and Unmanifested Nature — all these constitute the nonself. It is all Maya, from Avyaktam down to the gross body." Shankaracharya

Unbeknownst to most beings, although they carry this knowledge within them in an unrealized form, is the fact that human beings have not just one body, but three. And here is where the terminology surrounding references to gross, subtle, and causal really comes to the fore for study and utilization. The teaching of the Three Bodies of the Nonself is both ancient and eternal. It makes an excellent study on the level of cosmology, but the focal point here is to use it to answer the query regarding reincarnation, and to identify and trace the actual content or presence of that which is actually returning. For this purpose we turn to the chart (on page 161) for a closer examination.

The greatest key in this teaching, which really answers the question before we get started, is readily given in the title of this chart. It all revolves around the term "nonself." If the student has already heard from the preceptor that the true Self of mankind is birthless and deathless, and accepted this as a point of fact, then it will not be hard to transition into the mind-set that everything which changes and passes belongs to the realm of *maya*, or the nonself. Still, to prove this to the mind beyond a shadow of a doubt, a complete rendering of the constituents of the nonself is undertaken.

The gross body is well-known to most people, since they think of that as their true self and scarcely try to see otherwise. In the *Vivekachudamani* of Shankara, as well as in Lord Kapila's *Sankhya Yoga* system — two systems whose footfalls span several millennia — the ingredients of the three bodies are presented, outlined specifically for purposes of transcending all that changes and passes so as to perceive the underlying substratum behind them. In the case of the physical body, or gross self, termed *Stula Sharira*, the five elements, the five organs of action, and the body make up the list. On the chart, and for our convenience, some of the characteristics of this gross body are listed, along with its connection to the waking state and its relationship with *karma* in the form of past and present actions. This is hardly fresh news, but seeing it in this particular form has a clarifying effect on the often disconnected and drowsy human mind, waking it up to some obvious truths.

The subtle body is where it all gets more interesting. It, too, is partially cognized by living beings, but they hardly think of it as anything different than their physical body because they are focusing in on the brain rather than the mind, on intellect rather than on intelligence. It is a beautiful distinction to separate these pairs, and a great teaching that allows for it. The brain is a fleshy organ which merely follows the decaying body after death, but the mind is the holder of myriad inner worlds and, when awakened to its potential, facilitates a free and open commerce among these realms, and even a pat transcendence of them. Thinking of the mind, or subtle body — *sukshma sharira* — in this original way, already answers the question that we posed earlier. In other words, it is the mind that transmigrates from place to place, not the body and, certainly, not the *Atman*. This brings up the teaching of mental projection, or *sankalpa*, which we will study later in this chapter.

The *sukshma sharira* is made up of much different substances than the physical sheath, if they could even be called substances. As the list on the chart illustrates, there is *kama*, the seat of desire, and *karma*, the will for self-motivated action. These two alone could effectively propel a thinking body, and in the case of dense minds, actually do. But there is more to be considered, like the presence of root-ignorance. This ignorance even causes the mind to fail to perceive mind as mind, as mentioned above, but rather ignorantly imputes it as a part of the physical body. How is that for insidious? But genius would have it otherwise, as would sagehood and seership. Great beings live freely in their subtle bodies, and this can and does occur whether the physical body is living or not.

The rest of the subtle body consists of the five modes of life-force, the five senses of knowledge, the five subtle elements, and the fourfold mind itself. Each of these form a teaching and a support for meditation each of its own. Since we have studied these principles (see charts on pages 21, 47, and 119) already, we can trim this commentary down to a few essentials only. They pertain to what is referred to here as the "Inner Organ," the *Antahkarana*. The very word in *Sanskrit* provides so much crucial information, even short of its study, both in life and in meditation. *Antahkarana* translates as inner cause, which means that this highly refined mechanism, which most think rather drolly of as mere mind (or brain), stands at the apex of all that bursts upon the scene in the form of infinite manifestation, and it is also responsible for its appearance. As has been mentioned earlier, the *Vedanta*, or *Vedic*-based wisdom, does not assign the act or acts of creation to God, but to the mind at cosmic, collective, and individual levels of existence. This will be helpful to know when the teachings of *karma* are taken up; for as will be seen, the Indian philosophies wisely refrain from assigning cause and effect to God as well, thereby escaping the various traps which moralistically-based religions fall into. This will become more evident as the deeper levels of *Vedic* wisdom are gleaned. For now, and pertinent to the subtle body, a study of the characteristics and points of interest on the chart under inspection is advised.

But where does this subtle body, this inner cause of phenomena, draw from? For this bit of esoteric wisdom the seers look towards the *karana sharira*, the causal body of mankind. Its existence is inferred by the state of deep sleep which beings enter into periodically. Therefore, it is most difficult of ascertainment, what to speak of actual cognition. Substantial reference to it, or information on it, even in the scriptures, is scarce. For now, and until meditation on formlessness deepens, it is enough to know of its existence. Ironically, the seers indicate its presence by its lack; that is, where there is no vibration of the mind and intellect, and where most beings enter a void and befriend an empty nescience, there, the wise know, is the potential for all of manifestation. In the earliest *Vedic darshanas*, like *Sankhya*, it was referred to as *Mahat*, the Great Mind, or unmanifested nature *(Prakriti/Pradhana)*, or the Cosmic Egg *(Hiranyagarbha)*. Therefore, in Indian philosophy, there is no ultimate void or emptiness, a philosophical trap that the atheist and even great thinkers fall into. Something always exists or, put another way, "nothing doesn't exist." Even our present day quantum physics may be figuring this one out, though only on the physical level, as of yet.

The two most important points pertinent to the *karana sharira* are that it pre-exists the physical worlds, and that both the subtle and gross bodies come out of it. This suggests, among other intriguing facts, that it must be very close to the Source of Existence, which in turn must be formless — more formless than the causal body itself is. Thus, where the causal body is formless, the Source is Formless. And this is proven clearly by the profound effect that the deep sleep state confers upon the other two bodies. For, waking and dreaming can be extremely tiring and stressful, full of anxieties and worries. But deep sleep, even if experienced for a few minutes, is wonderfully refreshing. Where did ones consciousness, previously associated with waking and dreaming, go during that sojourn? This question is intimately associated with those presently under examination.

These three bodies have an existence all their own, and though they are intrinsically connected, that connection can be broken in several scenarios. Death is certainly one of these; *samadhi* is another But it should be clear from India's basic teachings that death is an illusion, an outright fallacy. And this courts the answer to our question again, "What transmigrates and reincarnates?" When human beings see a baby come into the world and, on the other hand, watch their grandparents pass away, they are really seeing the temporary abandonment of the physical frame and a return to the subtle body, in most cases. It is a bi-location of the mind's limited and conditioned awareness. The mind's contents, with the help of the hidden life-force called *prana*, is being emptied into the subtle body, the *sukshma sharira*, where all the worlds beyond the physical universe exist. In other cases, the soul (mind's crystalized awareness) will dissolve into the *karana sharira*, or causal body, and a period of deep and profound rest will ensue. And depending on the unresolved *karmas* which are also present in the subtle body (mind), an interruption to that peaceful repose may be imminent. The ejection of the fetus from the womb is an apt example of that, and the general cloud of unknowing which accompanies it. Importantly, when the transmigrating soul desires true freedom from this sporadic process of cyclic existence, it will seek a way beyond the subtle and causal body — which is what has happened in the case of enlightened souls. This is referred to, even in songs and *stotrams*, as "snapping the chains of birth and death" in *Vedic* tradition.

Leaving the realm of philosophical explanation, the next chart illustrates a more personal and thus more satisfying solution to our cosmological curiosity. The Holy Mother, Sri Sarada Devi, made many references to rebirth in Her recent blessed lifetime, and thus constructed a beacon of guiding light for all who seek freedom from the darkness of mental ignorance.

The Process of Embodiment

"After a birth in a human body, some attain salvation in this life, whereas others may take inferior births to reap the results of their karmas. Not everyone can be free from desire. The creation is going on because all cannot be free from desires. However, that indeed is the last birth in which one gets rid of desires completely. One will not have to come again."

Sri Sarada Devi

"Many a time a man takes birth and passes, again and again, in a certain family due to his karma. One should not blame God for this. Everyone reaps the effects of their own individual actions. And though one might have to take on a new body again, one does not necessarily lose spiritual consciousness if one retains one's karmic merits from previous births."

Absolute World	**Transcendent World**	**Imminent World**
Atman (True Being)	**Causal Body** **Subtle Body**	**Primal Body** **Physical Body**
"Only those who belong to a high spiritual category can be renunciates and gain liberation from all kinds of fetters. I bless you so that you may attain liberation in this life. Birth and death are extremely painful. May you not suffer from them anymore."	"All people, excepting some highly advanced souls, live in a spirit body for a year after death. The spirit body can be likened to a body made of air."	"People with desires take their births again and again. Afterwards they go to other planes and experience pleasure and pain and in course of time are born again in human form."

Causal Body

An undifferentiated state

Intellect ceases to vibrate

Mind exists in a subtle state

Gunas rest in equilibrium

The condition of deep sleep

Pre-exists the physical worlds

Is the cause of the
Gross and Subtle Bodies

Subtle Body

Intellect, Ego, Thought, Mind

Five Subtle Elements
Audibility, Tangibility, Visibility, Flavor, Odor

Five Senses of Knowledge
Smelling, Tasting, Seeing, Feeling, Hearing

Five Modes of Life-force
Inhalation, Exhalation, Circulatory, Ascending, Digestive/Distributive

Gross Body

Five Elements
Earth, Water, Fire, Air, Ether

The Body
Composed of Marrow, Bones, Fat, Flesh, Blood, Skin, Nails

Five Organs of Action
Speaking, Handling, Locomotion, Excreting, Procreating

"Following the 'maya of knowledge,' step by step, one attains the Knowledge of Brahman. This maya of knowledge can be likened to the last few steps of a stairway; next is the roof. Some, after reaching the roof, go up and down the stairs, which is to say that they keep the ego of knowledge for helping others, tasting divine bliss, and sporting with the devotees."

Sri Ramakrishna

For our personal edification and satisfaction, the Mother of the Universe speaks to this esoteric subject of rebirth and its causes, most crucial to higher understanding. In general, it is all well and good to gather and retain knowledge about the contents of our triple body and its states of awareness, but it is a great relief to finally comprehend the whys and wherefores of the process — mainly so that we can put an end to it, these cycles of birth and death in ignorance.

Conveniently enough, this chart bears a short list of the constituents of the three bodies for easy reference. With that under our gaze for instant clarification, this chart places these multiple ingredients and the condensed headings of the three bodies in terms of the often painful transmigration which occurs to those many souls who are still restless, roaming, or searching; who are still seeking experiences, are unresolved, imbalanced, or suffering the pleasurable, harsh, or dead ends of their accumulated *karmas*. This chart also provides for and reveals the abilities of more advanced souls who, as Sri Aurobindo has written in his epic poem, *Savitri, "...course up and down the amber steps of birth and death"* with an ease that escapes and amazes less versatile souls. Therefore, while looking with compassion upon those who are caught up in a game of their own devising — this game of mental projection, or *sankalpa/vikalpa* (see charts on pages 267, 269) — we also need to look long and hard at the capacious facility of the illumined soul and its mastery over all things cyclic. This able and flexible ability is due to their attainment of and conversance with innate spirituality.

If we make a swift inspection of some of the quotes of the Holy Mother, it becomes evident that souls take different courses after dropping the body at the time of departure. They also enter different phases of time and soul-evolution. Some reincarnate rather quickly, as if there is either some ongoing work to take up (like in the case of an enlightened soul) or a crying need to enter embodiment again (like in the case of an inexperienced or lost soul, out of desire or outright helplessness). Still others may take some one-hundred years of earth time to rest before embodying again, or commune with souls in the realm of the ancestors and celestials (heaven), etc. Advanced souls may forego rebirth all together, which points to the esoteric fact that transcendence of name and form is not only possible, but is most — if the word can be allowed here — desirable.

Another fact makes its self known in this regard as well, and that is that all reincarnation taking place in all worlds (and there are many), from gross to subtle, is really nonactual or, a product of mental projection. Using other terms, it is a fabrication of forms and worlds out of ones own interior thought-force. This is where the expression "dream-life" comes in, for life in all realms is really a matter of mass collective mental dreaming. This dream-force is based in desire (see charts on pages 176, 180, 184 & 240), and that is why Sri Sarada Devi states here that, *"That is indeed the last lifetime when one gets rid of desires completely. One will not have to come again."*

A third point to consider here is the *krama mukti* perspective studied earlier, wherein souls gather merit via good actions and gradually work their way beyond the need to be reborn. In this effect, She states, *"One does not necessarily lose spiritual consciousness if one has ones merit credits from previous births."* This brings up an interesting area of contemplation for the aspiring embodied soul. For one thing, it explains why some beings are born in possession of considerable innate spirituality and take easily to meditation and scriptural studies, while others are as a blank slate in that regard. In other words, *karma* from past lives explains why some beings are born qualified while others emerge on the field of activity more or less clueless. Conventional wisdom — principles such as genealogy, heredity, upbringing, instinct, habit, and the like — falls short of any apt explanation for this phenomenon, for they grossly overlook the principle of reincarnation. In one of India's many devotional wisdom songs, Ramprasad Sen of Bengal juxtaposes the occupation of worldly shopkeeping and accounting side by side with a burgeoning awareness of *karmic* accrual from past lives:

O mind that constantly forgets Reality, you have no idea how to keep accounts.
When you were born, you received the vast credit of pure awareness,
but every day since then you have plunged into debt.
If only you could balance your spiritual receipts and your worldly expenses,
there would be no tension in your being,

but your expenditures from the capitol of Divine Grace
far exceed your sparse income from personal efforts.
You alone are accountable for this imbalance, which must be explained in full.
This helpless child of the Mother exclaims in despair:
'O mind, why such obsession to account for credits and debits?
Just imbue your entire being with the One Who is utterly unaccountable, counting only Kali, Kali, Kali.'

And so we find that the overall condition of embodied souls — physical, vital, mental, psychological, intellectual, philosophical, and spiritual — is predicated on circumstances that predate their present existence (see chart on pages 194, 197 & 200). If this gets accepted, then it stands to further reason that the soul can modify or attenuate future conditions via actions instigated on its behalf in the present lifetime. But these actions must be conscious, well-chosen, and well-directed. For right exertion in this most crucial and esoteric of fields, called spirituality, the wise recommend self-discipline, or spiritual self effort (*sadhana*), as noted, in part, in the previous chapter of this book. Another of India's devotional wisdom songs demonstrates this subtle art in excellent fashion:

O my lazy mind, clearly you do not know how to farm.
You allow your own fertile expanse to lie fallow.
Under proper cultivation, the land of awareness becomes golden with the harvest of illumination.
Sow seeds with every breath.
Protect the precious field of your soul with the fiery fence of Mother Kali's name,
so the fruit of your dedicated effort will not be stolen by the egocentric world.

Impenetrable is the fiery fence of Kali Kali Kali! Even death dares not approach it.
Be utterly confident, O simple-minded poet.
Encircled by this powerful resonance, your meditations in song will remain fruitful
for many hundred years.

The soul is the field of free decision.
Dedicate yourself to constant cultivation for the sake of all conscious beings,
and the harvest will be without limit.
Your spiritual guide has given you the mystic syllable of Mother Essence as potent seed to sow.
Water for irrigation flows abundantly through the heart as pure love and tender devotion.

This dusty troubadour wandering through open fields now pleads with everyone:
"If you find farming difficult, please bring my poems with you."

Having broached the subject of *sadhana* in the last chapter — *sadhana* being defined mainly as study of scripture, worship of the deities, recitation of the *mantra*, meditation on Reality, and serving all beings selflessly — the next areas of elucidation in relation to the subject of *karma* must be mental impressions and the force of desire. These two are intrinsically connected, as is *karma* from previous existences. In *Sanskrit*, and in Mother India, the topic of mental impressions is indicated by the word "*samskara.*" A *samskara* is not restricted to memories of actions done in this lifetime alone, but stretches beyond into the unknown past of a living being correlated with births in other bodies. Much of the reason why Western psychology, science, philosophy and religion have fallen short in explaining and alleviating the problems of relative existence, both for the individual and for society, is due to overlooking this most important and clarifying principle of *samskaras* in relation to reincarnation. The following charts will show that the human mind harbors many unseen tendencies which are subtler than habits, instincts, and present life memories, and which also explain their content, or makeup.

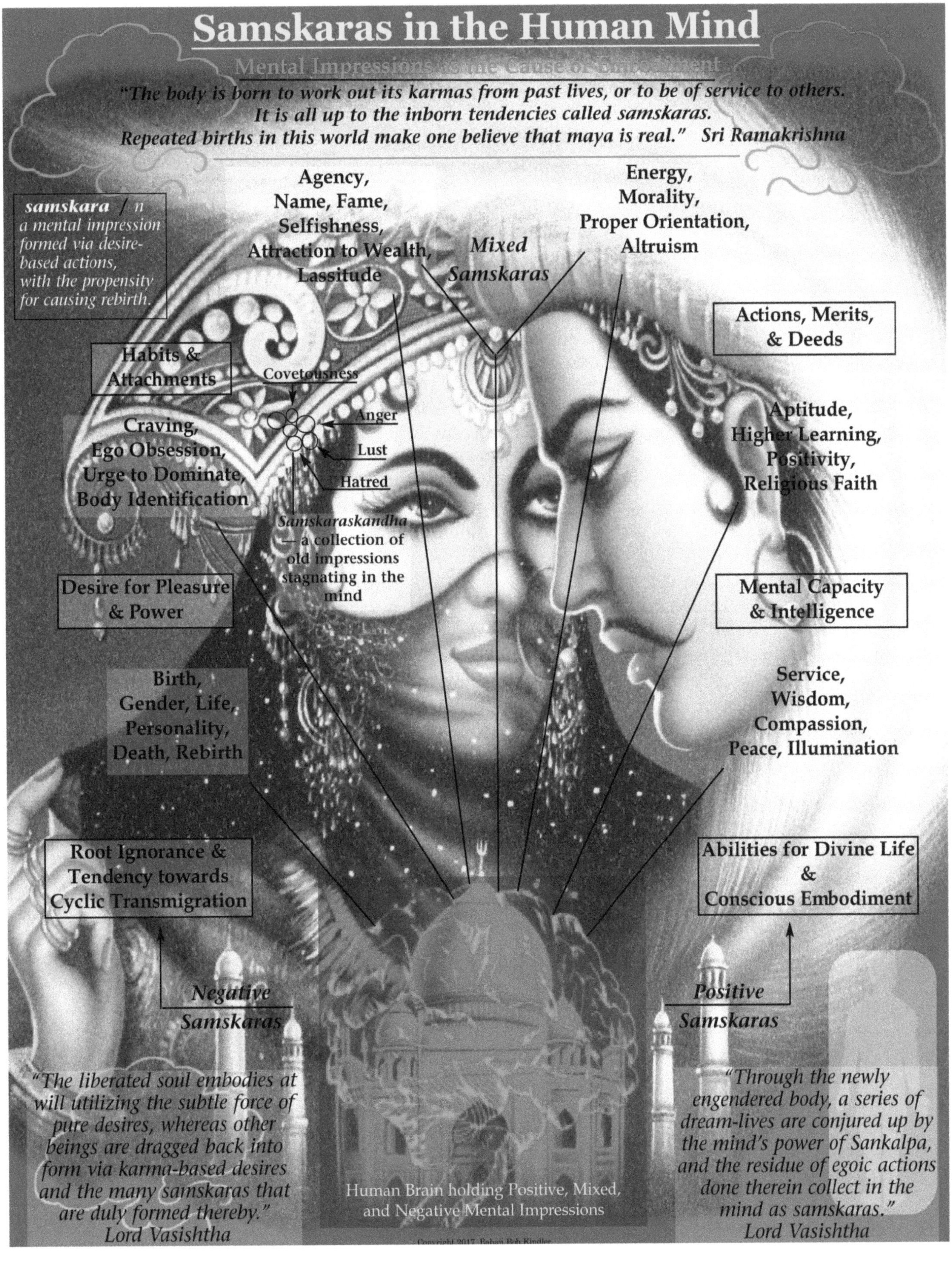

Samskaras in the Human Mind

Mental Impressions as the Cause of Embodiment

*"The body is born to work out its karmas from past lives, or to be of service to others.
It is all up to the inborn tendencies called samskaras.
Repeated births in this world make one believe that maya is real."* **Sri Ramakrishna**

samskara / *n*
*a mental impression
formed via desire-
based actions,
with the propensity
for causing rebirth.*

Agency,
Name, Fame,
Selfishness,
Attraction to Wealth,
Lassitude

*Mixed
Samskaras*

Energy,
Morality,
Proper Orientation,
Altruism

**Habits &
Attachments**

Covetousness

Anger

Lust

Hatred

**Actions, Merits,
& Deeds**

Craving,
Ego Obsession,
Urge to Dominate,
Body Identification

*Samskaraskandha
— a collection of
old impressions
stagnating in the
mind*

Aptitude,
Higher Learning,
Positivity,
Religious Faith

**Desire for Pleasure
& Power**

**Mental Capacity
& Intelligence**

Birth,
Gender, Life,
Personality,
Death, Rebirth

Service,
Wisdom,
Compassion,
Peace, Illumination

**Root Ignorance &
Tendency towards
Cyclic Transmigration**

**Abilities for Divine Life
&
Conscious Embodiment**

*Negative
Samskaras*

*Positive
Samskaras*

*"The liberated soul embodies at
will utilizing the subtle force of
pure desires, whereas other
beings are dragged back into
form via karma-based desires
and the many samskaras that
are duly formed thereby."*
Lord Vasishtha

Human Brain holding Positive, Mixed,
and Negative Mental Impressions

*"Through the newly
engendered body, a series of
dream-lives are conjured up by
the mind's power of Sankalpa,
and the residue of egoic actions
done therein collect in the
mind as samskaras."*
Lord Vasishtha

In relation to the internal and eternal vehicle of *karma* and reincarnation, and the subtle impressions which drive it, the quote from Sri Ramakrishna Paramahamsa at the head of the chart under inspection says it all. But the Great Master adds a line that is, if contemplated deeply, conducive of another dimension, and a crucial one. He states that if a human being experiences rebirth in ignorance again and again, then such a soul, or souls, begin to look upon the world, birth, death, suffering, and all its concomitants as being real in and of themselves. Short of a naive soul who simply suffers and enjoys in turns, the mind-set of a realist or a fatalist surfaces here. Such beings, finding themselves in a body, and not knowing the reasons why, simply decide to take the good with the bad and chalk the entirety up to the nature of things. And though this is a practical way of living, the seers and sages have espied and recommended another path, one of transcendence of the cycles of transmigration, or what Lord Buddha called the *kalachakra*, the wheel of birth and death.

Herein enters the spiritual luminary, and the host of aspirants who follow such souls. This unique soul inspects Consciousness for its intrinsic value, distinct from the overlays of name, form, causality, *karma*, etc., and once having merged in That as the Essence that It is, from that stable platform begins to inspect the human mind for all its tendencies, discrepancies, idiosyncrasies, and inadequacies. Herein is born the science of *samskaras*, for this intimate examination of the mind by pure and transcendent Consciousness associating with mind reveals and calls forth the causes for birth and subsequent rebirth, life and the desire for life, death and the fear of death, bondage and the fall into bondage, and a whole host of other facets around the subject.

Human behavior is one of these facets, for the human mind is so much more capable of expressing mankind's essential Awareness than any other element, force, or mechanism in the world. And due to its fine capabilities the mind is also prone to incertitude and malfunction so as to become the cause of everything from unreasoned confusion to outright depravity, along with the countless miseries which come as a matter of course. Sri Sarada Devi observed this eccentric and unpredictable behavior in Her lifetime, saying: *"Did you notice the other day how one man forcibly did more spiritual practice than he could stand, and got his mind deranged? If the mind is gone, what remains? It is like the thread of a screw. If the threads are loose the fellow becomes mad or falls into the trap of Mahamaya and thinks himself very clever. On the other hand, if it is tightened the right way, one goes along the correct path and obtains peace and bliss."*

Her words above usher in some understanding of the dual nature of mind, called *manas* in *Sanskrit*. If connected to the other three constituents of the fourfold mind mechanism (*antahkarana* - see charts on pages 349, 359), namely thought (*chitta*), intellect (*buddhi*), and ego (*ahamkara*), the human being gains the opportunity to truly live life as intended, even transform ordinary or conventional life into *dharmic* life or divine existence. If the mind remains scattered, however, and "disconnect" is the order of things, not only will this opportunity be lost, but a descent into an overall woebegone mode of living will be the result.

But the hidden details are what we want to uncover and view here, since many beings already know the effects of unconscious worldly life but few are cognizant of the causes. The chart under inspection displays a typical human brain filled with all the subtle potentials for both a *dharmic* life and a deplorable life. The cloud-like images on the chart depict *samskaras* in the human mind. They have been fabricated and placed there due to various thoughts and actions performed in previous lifetimes. Starting from the lower left-hand corner of the chart and proceeding upwards, the reader can see, both generally and specifically, many of the factors and tendencies that crowd and infill the mind of an average person. *Samskaras*, along with their roots and causes, are now revealed and can be acknowledged, the only business yet to finish being the wise and subtle perception that many of these root impressions are primal. That is, they are not readily detected in the ordinary awareness of an average man, but are ready of recognition and recollection for the one who examines his own consciousness (like in meditation).

Human beings have many *samskaras*, without which the act of re-embodying would not be probable. The case of animals coming back as animals, and trees appearing again as trees, are cases in point that help in informing our understanding of the process of reincarnation. But whereas it is a relatively simple process that produces another tree, or another camel, the re-appearance of a human being is quite involved. Even the rebirth of an ignorant being is a matter of great complexity. If we look again at the physical cause alone (see chart on page 49), that process is already very intricate, i.e., food, to sperm, to egg, to fetus, to body, to growth, to development of the brain. But the subtle cause, unknown to most beings and not accepted by the modern intelligencia, is intricate indeed.

Through an in-depth look at the chart under study on page 67, we can see that elements like desire, pleasure, power, fame, accumulation of wealth, and personal agency are prime factors in re-embodiment. These drives call the human soul back again and again into the physical frame, into the realm of gross matter. Religious lineages, political hierarchies, royal houses, scions of war, industrial family lines, descendants of scientists, educationalists, artisans, craftsmen, musicians, doctors, lawyers — all of these are stamped with the *samskaras* of their previous incarnations. Like pods of whales in a vast ocean, groups of souls reincarnate together, almost helplessly, tied together by acts of love, hate, marriage, murder, selfishness, sacrifice, learning, competition, success, failure, and a whole host of forces and ambitions. As Sri Krishna points out in the *Bhagavad Gita*, *"Animating my Prakriti, I send forth again and again all this multitude of beings, helpless under the regime of Prakriti."* Elsewhere in the *Gita*, He states: *"This multitude of beings, coming forth again and again, merge in spite of themselves at the approach of night, and manifest themselves at the approach of day. Yet beyond this manifest and unmanifest movement there is yet another Unmanifested Eternal Existence which does not perish when all these existences perish."* There is an overseer of all this wash of phenomena, then, called *Ishvara*, which we shall take up in a succeeding chapter.

Thus far we have concentrated on the left hand side of this chart, where *samskaras* of negative and mixed propensities are listed. This makes for a good study, both for understanding the human race and for pegging what ones own mind is dealing with in this present lifetime. But where all are headed stands revealed on the right hand side of the chart, where *samskaras* of positive potential are laid out. Meritorious actions, a wise leaning towards the intellect and its intelligence, developing a yen for selfless service of God in mankind, and especially the gleaning of spiritual qualities and attributes, are the welcome gateways here. The entire process ends in an ability to do everything consciously, including embodiment. This brings up a most apt comparison, and a powerful alternative.

It must have become evident by now that the act of embodiment is neither desirable nor undesirable. In other words, those who enter into it unconsciously risk locking themselves away in a prison that is nearly inescapable, while those who learn the art of conscious rebirth are able to, as Swami Vivekananda has said, *"...squeeze every drop of juice from their orange."* Metaphorically speaking, juxtaposing these two types of wayfarers side by side is like comparing a bird that flies through the air without leaving a trace, to a slug that crawls across a lettuce leaf leaving behind it a thick slime. As the quote on this chart declares, the slug-like soul is dragged back into embodied existence via *karma*-based desires, and the many *samskaras* that have formed as a result, whereas the illumined soul utilizes subtle desires to posit himself back into the body for higher purposes. As Sri Krishna says in that most unique of scriptures, the *Bhagavad Gita*: *"From age to age I embody myself forth, for the protection of the weak, the establishment of dharma, and to reveal myself in form to my devotees."* So, even the unfortunate souls, as yet still unaware of the art of conscious embodiment, have a savior through which to learn this most precious teaching.

In the next chart we will scour the teachings for clues to refining our awareness, of purifying the mind of all dross so as to afford the highest and best of outcomes. For this end we will take apart a *samskara* to see what exactly it contains. That is, there must be multiple elements to one of these ingrained tendencies, which if perceived and comprehended, could unlock secrets that will allow for the complete dissolution of all negativities in the mind. Krishna, Buddha, and Christ were in possession of this exceedingly pure mind, and therefore must have succeeded in neutralizing *samskaras*.

The Makeup of a Samskara & Samskaraskandha

"The discerning person straightens the mind, which is fickle, unsteady, and difficult to restrain, as the skilled fletcher straightens the shaft of the arrow." **Lord Buddha**

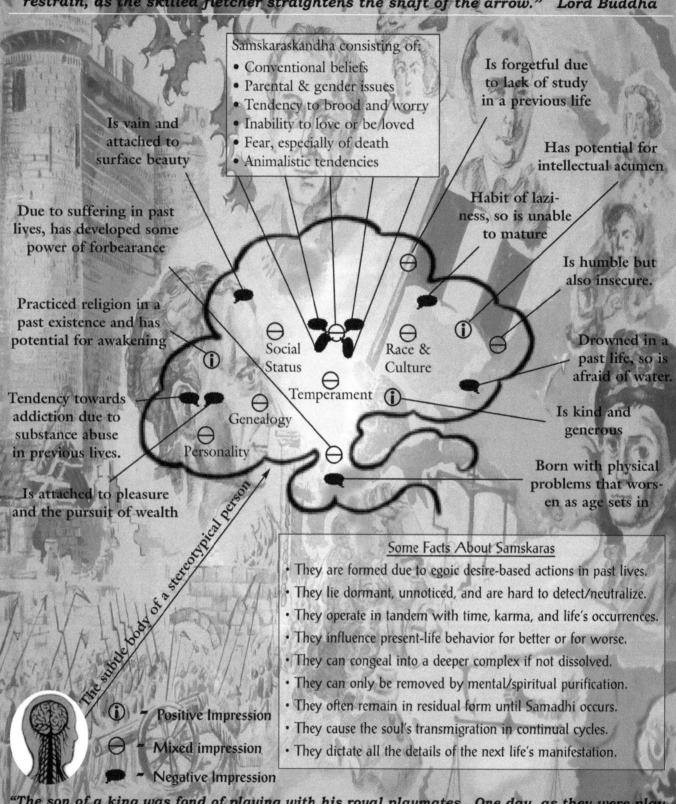

Samskaraskandha consisting of:
- Conventional beliefs
- Parental & gender issues
- Tendency to brood and worry
- Inability to love or be loved
- Fear, especially of death
- Animalistic tendencies

Is vain and attached to surface beauty

Is forgetful due to lack of study in a previous life

Has potential for intellectual acumen

Due to suffering in past lives, has developed some power of forbearance

Habit of laziness, so is unable to mature

Is humble but also insecure.

Practiced religion in a past existence and has potential for awakening

Social Status

Race & Culture

Temperament

Genealogy

Personality

Drowned in a past life, so is afraid of water.

Tendency towards addiction due to substance abuse in previous lives.

Is kind and generous

Is attached to pleasure and the pursuit of wealth

Born with physical problems that worsen as age sets in

The subtle body of a stereotypical person

ⓘ − Positive Impression

⊖ − Mixed impression

⬤ − Negative Impression

Some Facts About Samskaras
- They are formed due to egoic desire-based actions in past lives.
- They lie dormant, unnoticed, and are hard to detect/neutralize.
- They operate in tandem with time, karma, and life's occurrences.
- They influence present-life behavior for better or for worse.
- They can congeal into a deeper complex if not dissolved.
- They can only be removed by mental/spiritual purification.
- They often remain in residual form until Samadhi occurs.
- They cause the soul's transmigration in continual cycles.
- They dictate all the details of the next life's manifestation.

"The son of a king was fond of playing with his royal playmates. One day, as they were playing swords, the prince suddenly said, 'I want to play a new game. I'll lay down and all you must beat me over the back with these cloths and robes, making a swishing sound as you do.' You see, in his last lifetime the prince had been the son of a washerman." **Sri Ramakrishna**

One of the most cogent and implicit analogies about *samskaras* on record is that most excellent story told by Sri Ramakrishna of the herd of cows who, moving back and forth from the barn to the field day by day, multiple times a day, eventually wear a trail in the earth over time. At first the trail is hoof deep, but soon wears so deep as to reach towards the knee bone. The cows, however, are still habitually prone to take this trail every day, even though it restricts their overall movement, thus freedom. The Great Master is certainly not talking about mere cow-tending here, but has some other end in mind. He is describing people, or embodied souls, and their constricted behaviors based upon subtle impressions in their minds formed by repeated actions. And we now have a fitting word for those impressions, namely *samskaras*. In this world, it seems, we must name it to know it. And when we have a name for it we can believe in its existence and study it. Thus, the superstitions of the past, along with the stodgy ignorance that supported them, will be destroyed.

If, like utilizing micro-surgery for tiny incisions and removals in the body, we could extract a *samskara* from the subconscious layers of the mind, what would we find? The chart under study shows us what the makeup of a *samskara* is all about. Examining beyond the measurement of a micron, even a nanometer, we would discover an unseen conglomerate that heretofore escaped our awareness. The ancient word in the primal *Sanskrit* language for this mental germ is *"skandha."* It is where a subtle net of unwanted leftover residue, collected due to base and dull actions of the past, has coalesced into a nasty bit of negativity, lodged deeply in the mind-stuff. It is much like cancer and, in fact, is the real source and cause of diseases which may later manifest in the physical frame. Elsewhere it has been described by using the analogy of a bucket of nails left out in the rain for weeks, finally fusing together into an inseparable mass of rusty iron pieces. Taken to a microcosmic level, this is an adequate description of a *samskaraskandha*.

Lodged in that invisible mind-complex are mental particles knit together with one another, consisting of weighty and unsavory blends of passion, fear, doubt, remorse, guilt, hope, failure, expectation, and a host of other unseemly elements. To separate such a host would be to bring a laser into the mind and dissolve, one by one, each cancerous layer. But the wise say that encountering and breaking apart the *samskara* itself will go a long way towards breaking up a *skandha* that has formed around it. With the laser-like light of intense concentration and meditation, cultivated constantly, and overseen by a wise preceptor, these perplexing complexes will shatter. And when they do, the tiny bubbles that are *skandhas* that are clinging to them will scatter as well. Having no main support, they will therefore cease to influence or impede life and its higher aims.

The author here calls into attention the list of some nine facts about *samskaras* which appear on this chart (on page 170). A study, and even memorization, of these bullet-points will suffice to prepare the aspirant for a journey inwards to affect the purification process. Importantly, "watering the flowers and not the weeds" is one method whose efficacy should not be overlooked. In other words, the attainment of *samadhi* is a surefire way of eliminating unwanted *samskaras* from the mind. The problem here is that *samadhi* will not likely occur until at least a substantial degree of mental purification is accomplished. Thus, and as every well-informed seeker knows, self-effort and grace must go hand in hand.

The art of reading *samskaras* provides so many clues to both the behavior and the conditions of this present life. As one element of a *samskara* in this chart reveals, the fear of water presupposes that the soul drowned in a previous lifetime. No more need to ask why, then, only to face the fear and remove it promptly with knowledge-based action. For it was ignorance-based activity that formed the *samskaras* in the first place. One must therefore cease all actions performed in ignorance and engage only in acts accomplished with purity of mind — what Sri Krishna cites as *"scripturely-ordained works"* in the *Bhagavad Gita*. A balance of life will then kick in naturally, which in and of itself will lead to *dharmic* existence.

While the present subject of *karma* and reincarnation is still being undertaken via the concern of mental complexes, and prior to taking up the types of *karma* as *Yoga* philosophy presents them, it would be fitting to take a look at the outer ramifications of *samskaric* influence.

Cause and Effect in the Mind

Categories of Collective Mind

Effects of Ignor...

Spiritual

- Deposits subtle samskaras
- Undermines the truth of fo...
- Promotes religious narrowne...
- Resists the soul's turn towar...

Philosophical

- Stymies crucial ideological conclusions
- Seeds doubt and indifference in the mind
- Enforces a false belief in relativity
- Divides and weakens one's convictions

Intellectual

- Contributes to pride of knowledge
- Allows for the birth of misconceptions
- Fosters the ego's notion of doer/agency
- Hampers the need and desire for study

Psychological

- Fixes awareness on mind rather than Soul
- Plays upon false hopes and hidden fears
- Advances curiosity in the occult powers
- Invites dalliance with illusory perceptions

Mental

- Strengthens the bond of...
- Exacerbates the problems...
- Increases mental imbalance...
- Causes obsession...and objects

Emotional

- Increases the tendency of oversensitivity
- Heightens a false sense of security
- Breeds attachment to weakness and pity
- Ignites anger and the other passions

Karma has been understood in present day society to be a matter of cause and effect. But as the quote at the top of this chart on the facing page reveals, *karma* is not to be confused with or limited to the kind of cause and effect that takes place in the material world, or in the realm of physics, since it has a realm all its own. Even to relegate it to a moral law only, as in "good for good and bad for bad," fails to define it properly. If the truth be known, mankind would be better off to rightly determine for all time that, as one wise saying says, "Thought is father to the deed." Even beyond this conventional wisdom saying, and as we say in *Vedantic* circles, the adage "I think therefore I am" is not quite correct. "I am therefore I think" is much more accurate. But that aside for now, and with regard to actions, if they are well thought out they will be less likely to cause unwanted effects. Otherwise, like the proverbial camel who gradually sneaks his entire body into the nomad's tent over the course of an evening, effects from poorly determined thinking will continually enter into life and insinuate themselves into the field of activity, uninvited.

Therefore, the consummate spiritual aspirant — the one who, among other things, wants unalloyed and uninterrupted bliss — must scour the mind for the causes of ignorant actions, for these instigators only repercuss and appear in the mind-stuff again later, causing a cycle of almost irresistible force that mars true life and detracts from the attempt at balanced living. This effort at uncovering what most beings only allow to lie fallow in the mind defines the enterprising and intrepid spirit of the true aspirant, and represents the cutting edge of a fresh and effective contemporary practice in spiritual life.

Examination of the chart under study will illustrate that the human mind has at least six different levels to it. A minimum of four different bullet-points have been entered under these six categories in order to give an idea of how actions performed on the physical plane ricochet and circle back to complicate or exacerbate daily circumstances and situations. The points of contention under examination are all concerned with current day problems, then, which most beings have had experience with and may still be dealing with, daily. And not to forget, the invisible formation of *samskaras*, too, is implied by the constant and nagging presence of this list of circumstances, especially if they be left unresolved.

One helpful saying of Swami Vivekananda pertains here perfectly, wherein he states that the more spiritually advanced that souls are, the quicker their *karmas* come back on them. Turned in the opposite direction, we can conclude that people who are as yet spiritually immature are having to wait for extended periods of time before their *karmas* return to them. This would pertain to both positive and negative *karmas* as well. It is not hard to imagine, then, why indolent and apathetic people are always caught off guard by repercussive *karma*, and are unable to connect the effect and its sufferings to an action done in the past — since the act is so old, even forgotten. But the enthusiastic and spontaneous seeker encounters, acknowledges, and dissolves all *karmas* on the spot, as soon as they arise, thus escaping any accrual of negativity that later on may snap back and upset the already precarious balance of life (and eventually form *samskaraskandhas*).

The chart on the facing page brings into focus the many problems that beings of this day and age face on emotional, mental, psychological, intellectual, philosophical, and spiritual levels of existence. But importantly, these have a cause, and their manifestations will appear as effects with other causes if they are not destroyed at the root. For instance, there is hardly a more potentially volatile area of life and relations than human emotions. The human ego, until it is matured or ripened (self-surrendered), reacts violently to any and every prompting that it considers a threat to its nervously guarded sense of well-being. Thus, oversensitivity and attachment to a vaunted security — which really may turn out to be a false sense of security if examined deeply — is a major cause of upheaval, causing anger and its undesirable effects.

And the nightmare does not end here, but daisy-chains onward with ramifications that run in and out of the emotionally charged mind, forming *karmas* that thereafter hide in the unseen corridors of the mind, wreaking havoc on life and health. Resisting anger, reducing attachment, and strengthening the will, is the way out of the prisonhouse of base emotions, but an inspection of the damage already present in the subconscious mind will have to be undertaken. Otherwise a resurfacing of past *karmas*, like silt bubbling to the surface of a clear mountain lake, will occur. And this cause and effect scenario happens not only in daily life, but from lifetime to lifetime as well. There is therefore ample reason why so many people are born with unsettled emotions. They went to their death in a previous existence with unsettled emotions and unresolved *karmas*. What else? Are we going to place the blame for their condition on a jealous and capricious God? On an evil-intentioned demon or devil? This is superstitious thinking. It is not only far outdated, but never was of much good to anyone anyway, in any period of time.

The mental level of human existence is also potentially unstable. Few are the souls who have stability of mind, and those that do are admired overall by humanity. Controlling the mind is as hard to do as controlling the wind, as Arjuna states in the *Bhagavad Gita*. Cause and effect in the mind, springing from past actions done in ignorance, finds a ripe field for planting and harvest within the *antahkarana* mechanism. Perceiving and believing in twoness, or duality of mind, is basically at the root of all this. Leaving continual room for two and many instead of keeping the mind unified leads to obsession with things unreal, which in turn fosters confusion and delusion. Soon thereafter the soul becomes greedy and pharisaical, and a train of unwholesome manifestations begin to drive impressions into the mind-stuff (*chitta*), causing the mind to think in narrow and ignominious ways. A pattern emerges from this, and the soul carries the weights of distorted thinking into its final moments, even to states beyond death — and certainly into rebirth in ignorance. *"Oh mind,"* sings Ramprasad, *"you have not yet purified your thinking process. If you had, how sweet would be your series of births in consciousness."* For those who have cleared their minds of base cause and effect, the case is much different. There are at least two options for them: first, to live successive lives conducive to more and more light; second, to transcend the questionable occupation of embodiment altogether. Rumi, the Sufi saint, speaks to both these ways when he sings: *"When I die to this body you will find me with the angels. When I die to the angels you will never find me in form again."*

At the psychological level of mind (chart on page 172) is where the entire cause and effect process becomes much more subtle. There are people living now who are a product of their past-life preoccupation with the sensational, with the phenomenal, and with the occult. They cling to a life of mystery-mongering. Because of the investment of their thought and its energy into such nebulous affairs, they are marked with a penchant for and even an obsession with the tricks of *prana*, or life-force. Some of these turn their abilities to a positive end and learn the art of healing. Among this group some follow impossible dreams via impractical goals, like that of curing all diseases, while others, more authentic, simply serve humanity and attempt to lessen its sufferings.

Whatever the case may be, if the focus of the human mind shifts away from the Absolute to the relative, from Essence to energy, then subtle changes in the mind-stuff take place which dictate a lower path and deter the soul from higher attainments. For by the word "Spirit" is mainly meant Unchanging Consciousness, while the connotation of words like "spiritualist" and "spiritualism" usually pertain to such questionable elements as palm reading, playing with cards, hypnotization, crystal balls, seances, and the like. Unlike meditation on Reality, all of this only brings out the hidden hopes, fears, and desires of living beings, those very things which keep them bound in ignorant cycles of rebirth. A person who caters to this type of activity, who supports it in others, is causing impressions in the minds of others which will emerge in time as a sort of dependence on illusory phenomena. What to speak of ghosts and departed souls, a preoccupation with the ancestors will develop, which is where the constricting stream of cause and effect has one of its main feeding grounds. Curiosity about the occult and a desire for heavenly existence; these two have ever been close partners. A dimmed-down, dumbed-down mental perception accompanies them both.

When ill-considered actions eventually repercuss at the intellectual level of the mind, a host of misconceptions get planted there. These new growths develop roots which sink their tendrils deep into the soil of the human thinking process. False knowledge and, possibly worse, mixed knowledge, are the result, and their effect influences the mind adversely, schooling it in the dubious art of pride and arrogance. A man then thinks that he can do anything and, what is worse, imagines that he is the final agent of all his actions. Among other problems, this removes the possibility of him ever becoming aware of his Witness Consciousness, what the illumined souls come to know of in their deepest meditations as an Overseer of all human life and activity. Along with this spiritual deficiency, his mind gets thwarted from one of the most beneficial aids that life can afford — the boon of sacred study. Being devoid of all counsel save of his own ego, his intellect gets marred and a plethora of misconceptions around both earthly existence and spiritual life formulate. This wreaks havoc on his potentially burgeoning philosophical life, without which he is left without any higher ideal and is thereby summarily stripped of a path through *maya*.

What the human being does not need is a false belief in the ultimate reality of the world. When even science has demonstrated the ephemeral nature of matter, wherein the foundation of the universe is perceived to be founded on an infinite play of miniscule particles that change every billionth of a second, a positive conclusion must be drawn wherein the embodied soul can come to rest in a peaceful condition. Cause and effect from past actions, especially as they begin to manifest in life, tend to alter the mind's perception in undesirable ways. Inadvertent thoughts, immature conceptions, incomplete conclusions, and the like lead to actions which are reticent and noncommittal. Such actions create a hazy internal atmosphere that is accompanied by incertitude. A sort of whimsical mind-set then grows up, which, when it is not dealing with solicitousness, gets enmeshed in fantasy and imagination. This wastes the mind's potential for higher thought and noble endeavor.

And no where is this lack more keenly felt than at the often deprived level of a human being's spirituality. Without peace based upon wise and settled philosophical conclusion, Truth will not dawn. And all actions accomplished in such a tepid mental atmosphere will only contribute further to the complexes and *samskaras* which are already growing fat with multilayered *skandhas*. A man under this tiresome regime remains both philosophically uninformed and spiritually unattained, resulting in a loss of understanding of the essentially formless nature of Reality. With the principle of formlessness a blank in his mind, he falters, then falls back on his own religion, if indeed he has any, often centering narrowly on its fundamentalist surface teachings. The real goal of universal understanding is thus stymied, and spirituality becomes a matter of disbelief or derision. Future lifetimes also reflect this hypocritical thinking, where a free breath of truly spiritual air is never enjoyed or sought after.

Whereas people usually stand and stare in disbelief at the often devastating effects that occur in everyday life amidst family, friends, society, and in nature, few catch the inner vision or make the connection around the effects of action in the mind. And atop this pile of ongoing action and reaction, a tangled web of *karma* and a composite pool of mental residue is forming. Persons drawn out into the sensational scene that *karma* causes in the world, in nature, and in relationships, scarcely see this. To put a fine point on it, *samskaras* are fusing together in the mind due to this constant back and forth conflagration of thought and action, devoid of any resolution. But all of this predicates the condition of ones next lifetime. People may say, in regard to the reincarnation "theory," that they have enough to deal with in this lifetime, so why should they worry about the next? All well and good, but the point is to get down and actually deal with the present lifetime instead of just talking about it, and do so by utilizing the deeper knowledge and thinking of the illumined souls rather than mere conventionalists. One must start at the emotional level, inspect the passions, the individual ego, and the capacity to control such powerful forces. If a lack is detected, begin working right there. For future lives are attenuated and improved considerably by practice accomplished in this lifetime.

One of the elements of life that is most detrimental, and which all the religions of the world mention in their cautionary teachings, is the presence of desire. Following are two charts which take up this topic in a lucid and contemporary way, revealing some advanced teachings that will be most helpful for embodied beings to consider and implement. With some mental and moral flexibility, an aspiring soul can even use the force of desire to help transform life and mind, as we shall see.

Flowing up the left hand side of this chart (page 178) are listed the nine ways of dealing with

The Nine Ways of Dealing With Desire

"Not all can free themselves from desires. The creation is going on because all cannot be free of desires. People with desires take their births again and again. But that indeed is the last birth in which one gets rid of all desires."   **Sri Sarada Devi, the Holy Mother**

Transcending Desire – using nonreceptivity, asamvedana

Sublimating Desire – by removing poison from passion

Surrendering Desire – via the various acts of yajna, sacrifice

Destroying Desire – at the root, via tapas, austerity

Resisting Desire – through self-effort, avoiding repression

Fulfilling Desire – only through Dharma

Superior Modes
- - - - - - - - - - -
Inferior Modes

Satiating Desire

"Satiation never comes. The Infinite cannot be realized through the finite." Swami Aseshananda

Satisfying Desire

"Satisfaction of desires cannot be had through the worlds of name and form unless one has taken refuge in the dharma."
Lord Vasishtha

Enjoying Desire

"One cannot truly enjoy what does not exist, and what gets taken away from others in the process."
Babaji Bob Kindler

Labels within the diagram:

Formless Transcendence

Brahmaloka
Tapoloka
Janaloka
Maharloka

Direct Perception — Attaining Path/Guru
Yearning
Cycles of Dharma and Sadhana
Mahamaya's Twin Wheel of Transformation
Meditation
Vows & Precepts
Dharmic Life
Desire for Freedom
Initial Practices
Worship and Study

Worlds of no rebirth
Worlds of rebirth
Svarloka
Bhuvarloka

Attachment to Pleasure — Birth in Heaven and on Earth
Birth in Ignorance
Avidya
Moral Life
Mundane Habitual Life
Growth in Selfishness
Maya operates via the movement of simultaneously alternating and counteractive cycles.
Maya's Twin Wheel of Transmigration
Death in Doubt and Fear
Conventional Religion
Life lived in Delusion
Observance of Ethics
Bhurloka
(The Seven Realms)

desire. As the reader can see, they are divided into inferior and superior modes. Three of them — enjoying, satisfying, and satiating desires — are classed as inferior, for they are impossible to effect; they are actually contradictions in terms. That can be explored soon. As to the other six ways of dealing with desire — fulfilling, resisting, destroying, surrendering, sublimating, and transcending them — these are superior ways, but each one has a set of criteria to follow. The ground rules for each of these can be explored briefly, but are to be implemented into daily life in order to see results.

The intention of this chart is to not only list these pathways towards freedom from desire, but simultaneously to link them up with the cycles around which they revolve. The two diagrams appearing there are both double circles, one inside the other; for, as the definition of *maya's* mode of proceeding relates, *"maya operates via the movement of simultaneously alternating and counteractive cycles."* This flexuous pair of flummoxing double wheels is part of the reason why so few, even intellectual beings, ever get free from the web of *maya*. Name and form are her very nature; time and space, her subtle products; causation, her modus operandi. Few expect that what they are beholding and experiencing as soon as they enter into a form is illusory, substanceless, and ultimately void of reality. And that is why their desire for what maya offers is really baseless and senseless. Still, they come to her by the millions — some to enjoy, some to abandon themselves, some to test themselves, still others to penetrate. All are lost in maya from the outset, as soon as they enter, but it is the remarkable ability of the illumined souls to recover from maya's influences and transcend her marvelous projections. Only these singular souls can act as guides for struggling souls.

Taking up *Maya's* Twin Wheel of Transmigration at the bottom of the chart first, we see that it tells a tale of duality as contrary as its nature and operation. The inner wheel begins with birth in ignorance; for, how many souls are in knowledge of what is happening to them during the inception of their embodiment stage. And due to the nature of this all-pervasive ignorance, termed *mula-avidya*, wherein all people gasp for breath and struggle for balance, life gets lived in an arena of selfishness wherein all beings are, by nature, out for their own satisfaction. True selflessness is reserved only for saints and seers; most others, even the well-intentioned, ultimately have only their own interest at heart.

What follows, then, is a life lived in delusion. Truth is not sought after in this world: not for its own sake. As Ramprasad sings, *"To hope for help from friends and family provides no real solution. Don't you know that all are lost here? Everyone lives in pallid imitation of everyone else."* In this cruel press, a lifetime flits by, and man goes to his death with little or nothing concrete to compensate him for all his struggles and sufferings. Ironically, he does not need to brood about the end of his time, for time has no end. As Krishna states in the *Bhagavad Gita, "That which is born, dies, and that which dies, is born again. The wise grieve not on this account."* If man knew the extent of his projecting power, and the expanse of *maya's* power to provide for that, he would begin to revel in the fact of eternity. He would eventually come to the esoteric knowledge that these wheels or cycles that he is continually finding himself on, grind away inexorably, and that his mind, energy, and succession of bodies form the fodder for the mill-wheel of *maya*.

The inner cycle of *Maya's* Twin Wheel of Transmigration opens up, as the chart demonstrates, onto its outer wheel. Death in doubt and fear is temporarily offset by the joy of entering into the subtle world that some call heaven, others, *svarloka*. This is predicated on a life lived in morality, in decency, in goodness. The usual scenario for such a soul is to discover and launch into the path of conventional religion, sometimes called dualism, which thereafter leads to fealty to a code of ethics followed by a life of ritualism, earthly and religious. The drawback here is one of abiding habit wherein no real intensity is generated, and the soul simply languishes in all that is mundane. This is termed "happiness" in this world, and happiness breeds attachment to pleasure. Still, a man's pursuit of what is good and clean over the span of a lifetime warrants him a birth among his ancestors after he passes from the body, or amidst the celestial spheres. The drawback to the heaven realms, however, as spiritual luminaries who have seen these will tell you, is that they form a return doorway back into the gross physical realm. This is due to the soul's unsatisfied penchant for desire, for pleasure, and for more experience in the individual ego/body mechanism via the selfish mode of separation. Thus is the appearance of the first half of this chart on desire for our inspection, so that the transmigrating soul might have a glimpse of the dynamics of reincarnation — courtesy of the good graces of the Indian saints, sages and seers.

Before we take up the upper wheel — *Mahamaya's* Twin Wheel of Transformation — attention should be called to the list of worlds ascending the right hand side of this chart (page 176). The system of the Seven *Lokas*, or realms of existence (see chart on page 548), reveal that not only is the physical realm not the only world, but that it is key and foundational for the realms, or Five *akashas* (see chart on page 327), that envelope it. The smart saying of Jesus wherein He mentions *"My Father's Mansion has many chambers"* figures in here, and He was not talking about lower heaven only.

The Indian system, very well figured and defined by the adept spiritual travelers who "kept their wits" about them after death, reveals that *Bhur* (earth), *Bhuvar* (intermediary heaven), and *Svahar* (heaven proper) — which form the first three utterances of the famous *Gayatri mantra* — are interconnected, in that souls who are not yet spiritually percipient or are unable to maintain their awareness as they transmigrate from world to world, course up and down these three *lokas* constantly, pulled here and there by the force of their unresolved *karmas* and *samskaras*. This connection to *samskaras* places us back in the realm of self-effort in this life, so that no residue will persist in the mind as it approaches the body's inevitable demise.

Important of note here are the finer *lokas* shown in the upper right hand corner of the chart, which correlate with the wheel of *dharma* and *sadhana* that we are about to explore. These four subtler *lokas* — from *Maharloka* to *Brahmaloka* (also called *Satyaloka*) — are famous for their boon of the transcendence of the rebirth process. That is, if a soul can pierce beyond these realms of the ancestors and celestials, and leave off his desire for heavenly existence and the joy it offers (which equates to departing the twin wheel of transmigration which we have just studied), he discards for all time the need to embody again in the physical realm, which is the painful realm of disease, decay, and death. In accord with this wise movement of inner evolution, let us scrutinize *Mahamaya's* Twin wheel of Transformation, for transmigration and transformation make for good comparisons.

As was mentioned, the aspiring soul, now "akamai" (Hawaiian word for "in the know") to the goings on in the Divine Mother's vast set of *lokas*, has managed to pierce the subtle veil between *Svarloka* and *Maharloka*, and has done so by transcending the transmigratory wheel and mounting the *dharma* wheel. By searching the chart we can observe that this has been initiated by the attainment of yearning for God, or for Truth, or Freedom, if one prefers. Sincere yearning for God is the main prerequisite for beginning true religious life. Prior to its appearance in the human heart, the soul had barely maintained itself on the dualistic worship that earthly conventional religion offered. This, plus the tired old standard that the world held up in the form of duty, became boring, and failed to deliver the vital level of authentic spirituality that transforms a human being into a devotee and seeker of Truth.

And so it is that the need for higher and more meaningful demands comes upon the yearning soul. This gets provided via a host of vows and precepts that present themselves as a matter of course in the seeker's life. Rejection of committing harm to living beings, renunciation of owning or coveting wealth and goods, the tendency towards serving God in humanity — these and other promptings are requisites to *dharmic* living so necessary for the aspiring soul. Thus, *dharmic* life gets into full swing and conventional religion is left behind, for dualism and its penchant for worldly happiness and heavenly existence is, as we have stated, a relatively lower ideal to the sincere and spiritually awakened Truth-seeker. The desire for freedom, so different from the development of a distant relationship with the conceptual God, is now upon the aspirant, and life will never be the same again.

But there is a defining moment in *dharmic* life where the seeker feels an intense inward impulse that forces him to realize that he and he alone must make himself into the image of the Spirit. He understands, finally, that no God will help, and that no devil will hinder this unique calling of his. It is his highest destiny, and has been waiting for him, possibly for lifetimes. As Sri Krishna tells His beloved disciple, Arjuna, *"You must go beyond all dharmas and come to Me, the svadharma — the ultimate Dharma."* It is at this juncture that the turning of the *dharma* wheel slides, almost imperceptibly, into a new phase and angle, and the aspirant seeking full enlightenment finds himself mounting the wheel of *sadhana* — disciplined spiritual self-effort.

For the sincere and sedulous seeker of Truth, *sadhana* is the cutting edge in religious and spiritual life. Nothing experienced previously — no worldly occupation, earthly endeavor, physical regimen, religious ministry, psychological therapy, and the like — can touch spiritual self-effort as far as its outright ability to confer upon the devout disciple the boon of liberation. Success and salvation pale to insignificance next to the towering possibility of spiritual emancipation that *sadhana* promises and delivers. In other words, salvation and liberation are two different things, two qualitatively different principles of existence. The former pertains to the attainment and enjoyment of heavenly existence in the realms of name and form. The latter equates to transcendence of dualities altogether, and the complete merging of all sense of separation into Brahman, resulting in absolute Peace and incomprehensible Bliss. Words such as *Shanti*, *Moksha*, and *Ananda* come to mind here, for which there are no equivalent meanings in the English language.

The circle of *sadhana* usually begins its auspicious turning based upon a timely meeting of the minds. The prepared and potential disciple actually calls the qualified teacher to him or her by that very act of preparation itself. This rule is a hard and fast one in spiritual life, depending upon qualification. If one sites the fact that unprepared disciples also bring teachers to them, this is true. But one only has to look at the poor quality of the teacher that the unprepared disciple summons to understand the deeper implications of this rule. "Like attracts like" applies here, or as Sri Ramakrishna humorously puts it in one of His wonderful stories: *"When a cobra swallows a frog, the entire meal is over in a few swift swallows and a couple of croaks. But when the mere watersnake swallows a frog, it gets stuck in the snake's throat halfway down, causing much suffering to both parties."* May all who sincerely desire Truth and Freedom get seized by a "cobra" teacher, not a "watersnake."

The *guru* reveals the path or, in some cases, the path reveals the *guru*. Either way, these two wisdom principles work in conjunction with one another to facilitate the most marvelous and beneficial process in the Three Worlds, and the most valuable and precious relationship therein as well. And the real meaning of this relationship is twofold: the making of the novitiate into an initiate so he/she can get free; and the simultaneous boost that the *guru* gives the student along the chosen path. The precious initiation mentioned here both purifies the body to make it fit for holy company, and empowers the aspirant to undertake certain choice spiritual disciplines that will both strengthen him and endow him with higher wisdom. This is why worship and study make up the next angle of the wheel of *sadhana*. (chart on page 176) Gaining a set of practices from the *guru* is likened metaphorically to receiving a gymnasium full of equipment to work out on. Worship and study, then, transforms one into a master gymnast. The real practice and the true austerity — study of scripture, recitation of the *mantras/slokas*, worship of the deities and the Chosen Ideal, and meditation upon nondual Reality — is here, in the *sadhana* wheel of spiritual life; everything else that came prior to it was just fluff or, the nocturnal strugglings of the soul still trapped in ignorance.

Next on the chart comes meditation, the essence of spiritual life, and the last element in it to fully mature. It is penultimate to the direct perception of God/Reality. An entire section of a forthcoming chapter will be given to it. Though *mantra* meditation has already been thoroughly outlined in a previous practice, formless meditation is a distinct and supremely qualifying level of spiritual attainment. It ushers in *samadhi*, a rare absorption that will also get studied.

Before taking up the balance of this chart, i.e., the Nine Ways of Dealing with Desire, an accompanying chart on desire is presented. This is because the mind of the average person may need some purificatory practices prior to actually dealing with his or her desires. And since desires are hard to even acknowledge, the wise *gurus* have given certain advice which will aid in the effort.

This simple chart (on the next page) is an easy gathering of some of Sri Sarada Devi's sayings

The Two Main Forms of Desire

"There are two kinds of desires: one that stimulates enjoyment, and the other that quickens dispassion." Sri Sarada Devi, The Holy Mother

1 **Desire That Quickens Dispassion**	2 **Desire That Stimulates Enjoyment**
Desire for: God-Realization	**Desire for: Matter**
"The aim of life is to realize God. But do not worry; only strive. The desires of your mind — you must fulfill them. Later on you will attain to Eternal Peace."	
Spiritual Wisdom	**Worldly Knowledge**
"A man of knowledge does not commit any indiscretion. It is only the ignorant people, devoid of wisdom, who commit sins and are thereby seized with fear."	
The Well-Being of Others	**Wealth & Possessions**
"The worldly crave for money only. Never have they prayed for knowledge or devotion, even mistakenly. My children try to remove suffering of this world."	
Unalloyed Spiritual Bliss	**Pleasure via the Sense-Objects**
"The loose screw of the mind craves objects of enjoyment. On the other hand, if this screw gets tightened properly one follows the correct path and obtains peace."	
Increasing Devotion to God	**Power Over Beings/Nature**
"The worldly and wicked do not feel the Divine Presence in the image. The deity disappears before them. Only he who prays to God eagerly will really see Him."	
Serving God in Humanity	**Ego-Gratification & Selfishness**
"Selfishness, well, that persists as long as a person is self-assertive, and disappears when it is overcome. But we have come here together to serve all beings."	
Leading a Spiritual Life	**Leading a Worldly Life**
"A palm frond easily drops to the ground when it turns brown, but if it is pulled off when it is still green, the tree gets damaged." Sri Ramakrishna	

"Love for the sake of Divine Love is not possible as long as a man has any desire. Desire is at the root of all sorrows, is the cause of repeated births and deaths, and is the main obstacle on the path of liberation." Sri Sarada Devi, The Holy Mother

and teachings on the subject of desire, gleaned during Her auspicious lifetime. Sri Ramakrishna's own way of teaching about desire is unique, demonstrating as it did the difference between the moral and ethical level of a problem such as desire, and the more edifying level of *sadhana* and purification. Part of this distinction has to do with the particular mind-set that an aspirant begins with when encountering the arena of his own desires. If the emphasis of the past has been on the concept of sin and damnation, for instance, then the guilt and remorse that has already colored the thinking process of the seeker is severe, and is under a negative press that will make it difficult to move through the proposed or presumed errors of the past.

In this regard it may already have been mentioned that the *Tantric* system of India takes a much different look at the arena of sin and transgressions than westernized religion does. The word for transgression in that *darshana* is termed *mala*, which is an imperfection or limitation that the soul has consciously taken on previous to embodiment, and that he/she brings into life with a view to working it out and neutralizing it. Interestingly enough, however, the transgression, or *mala*, is not a black mark on the soul, or even an error that has some permanent taint associated with it (unless it goes unneutralized). Rather, the *mala* is a weight that, when shed, propels the seeker with all the more impetus towards the goal of the vision and realization of the Self. It is something like the case of a fruit that, when ripe, falls off of the tree naturally, in its own pre-predicated time. Imperfections, then, are self-intended overlays that give the soul more forward motion in spiritual life.

This new frame of mind is precisely what the aspirant needs in order to deal with internal limitations. Well-informed by this innovation in *sadhana*, continual progress rather than constant regress is attained. Not only is this positive method superior to other ways of encountering human desires, it is a slap in the face to those methods that shame the individual into a state of doubt and fear, and which then take away any chance of making spiritual headway in life. With all of this presented, let us take up a few of the teachings on this helpful new chart (facing page).

The chart is broken into two columns. The column on the right presents desires that only stimulate enjoyment, while the column on the left lists desires which quicken realization. Holy Mother's unique teachings on this subject are designed to show the striving human soul the difference, for when seekers entering into spiritual life and practice hear about the impediment of desire, many automatically assume that all desires are detrimental to progress. Therefore, it is very refreshing, and relieving, to hear that some of the wants and needs that are close to our heart are legitimate, and usually only need a turn towards the positive in order that they add impetus to our progress along the path. Sri Sarada then contrasts this helpful desire, to the desire for matter, which not only fails to fulfill the soul, but which also binds it outright to objects, feelings, and resultant attachments that only culminate in pain and suffering. The reader is welcome to study this list of comparisons for greater edification about the difference between freeing and limiting desires. The desire for wisdom rather than mere worldly knowledge, for spiritual bliss instead of earthly happiness, for serving God instead of the catering to the ego, all give much to think about and ponder. Even matter is brought into the purification process, when one finds out that the material well-being of others is more important than ones own wealth and well-being.

So this is the unique mind-set of the illumined soul who, from age to age, returns to the world and teaches humanity certain spiritual truths. And at the bottom of this chart we find an example of positive thinking around potentially knotty problems such as human desire. By consulting such perspectives the seeker duly learns, among other things, of the dangers involved in trying to root out desires before it is time. This, basically, is the distinction between what the *Tantric* adepts have noted in the case of repression as opposed to sublimation. For more on this interesting comparison we should return to the chart on page 176, and finish it.

Returning now to the Nine Ways of Dealing with Desire chart on page 176, the left-hand side shows all the modes, from inferior to superior, of how human beings attempt to handle their desires. As was mentioned, the first three methods are inferior, mainly because they are impossible of actuation. As the various quotes placed under the three headings relate, to enjoy, satisfy, or satiate desire is an outright impossibility. It is rather like trying to pour gasoline on a fire in order to put it out. And the fact that desire seems to be quenched after it has been enjoyed for a time poses an even greater danger to the aspiring mind, for once man is done with such lowly things and ready to go towards higher levels of existence, the habit of pleasure for objects of desire has already set in, and attachment for them proves extremely difficult to overcome. So, this game of life in *maya* is extremely engaging, and even the wise who tread here, do so with great care and concern.

But what of life lived in the *dharma*? We can see by the twin wheels on this chart, already studied, that *maya*'s chimerical influences diminish by degrees as the soul climbs out of the denser atmospheres of matter and brain and into rarer mental climes. When ignorant life and moral/ethical strictures are seen comprehended and attained, drama turns to *dharma*, and a foretaste of real spiritual life is on the horizon.

And here is where desires are both refined and consummated. Whereas attempting to enjoy, satisfy, or satiate desire while the mind is still under the hypnotism of passion and attachment is not possible, those very same modes suddenly give themselves over to transformation under the protective umbrella of *dharma*. The practitioner observing *dharma*, with its honest vows and noble precepts, is both running out the last vestiges of his *karma* in the world, and squeezing the last drops of substantial content out of it. Wondrously, he becomes exempt from lower *maya*'s flexuous and impermeable laws. That is why the wise souls are always and ever trying to convince worldly people to renounce matter and embrace the spiritual path. One sees a *dharmic* soul getting great satisfaction from home, family, spouse, children, and wealth, even though these things, when coveted in *maya* by the ignorant soul, are the very things that bind and slay. It is all so inscrutable! Yet, there is the proof, right before our eyes. Still the worldly will not give up their preoccupation with *maya*.

But the *dharmic* person still has room to consider, as they say. Such a being still falls under the pale of the higher *maya* and could, given this excellent cycle of balance and joy that has been discovered, end up revolving around the wheel of *dharma* inexorably as well. And this noble soul has not come this far to be duped and led away from the highest of all pursuits. In other words, from the *dharmic* elevation that has been reached, he/she can survey and intuit, more than ever, the atmosphere of nondual freedom which is both the source and birthright of every conscious being.

Therefore, and as we have seen, the soul finds its way to the sublime wheel of spiritual self-effort and benefits from holy company and all that it has to offer. At this juncture it now sees the efficacy of resisting the impulse of desires. Here, the soul has found its austere side, and along with it, the much greater thrill of doing without — of giving up matter rather than gaining more of it. From here, ones pure will can be exerted in order to destroy whatever desires still persist. This is a great moment in the soul's (mind's) evolution.

One important area that surfaces here is the problem of repression. To understand the real difference between psychological therapy and *dharmic* practice is to become aware that great strength has been gained via the latter. When spiritual strength, instead of mental weakness, is the case, the threat of repression simply fails to appear. It is only in the cases of those who have not mastered the mind that desire, when repressed or pushed back into the recesses of the mind, can backfire and cause damage to life and mind. It would be well, then, for people of modern times — especially those who run in therapeutic and healing circles — to become aware that the *sadhaka* is not in need of counseling or any advice of that nature. In fact, today's "counselors" could benefit substantially by both the words and the example of the austere *sadhaka*, for he has transcended worldliness and the desires and passions that still plague beings working for money in the world.

The first three ways of effectively dealing with desire have already been laid out for inspection. The next three really correspond with varying levels of spiritual accomplishment, by temperament. The surrendering of desires is a method used by many beings, especially those of devotional temperament. Success in this mode depends upon elements such as the attainment of self-surrender, an ability for selfless service, and a knowledge of the scriptures — particularly those in which *yajna,* the art of sacrifice, is enumerated and explained (see chart on page 493, 495). The entire method proceeds on one main premise: that all acts and their results are accomplished free of any desire for personal benefit or, in other words, all is done for the "sake of the Lord." This is much more difficult than it sounds, but if it is actuated, this method is a great purifier and powerful requisite to the attainment of God-realization. This is because the human ego is entirely struck from the equation, and where there is no sense of separate self, there is no distinction between the human and the divine. And so, where then is desire? Where is there any purchase point for desire? This is a safe and consummate route for all those who can accomplish it.

The next way of dealing with desire is perhaps the most popular of all, at least upon first hearing. So many souls attempt it, but few really master it. It proceeds via the refining and ascent of the subtle energy at the base of the spine. As has been spoken about in several areas of this book, the food the practitioner takes into the body needs to be pure and sanctified. Then, when it is imbibed, it conduces to pure blood and pure energy. This energy, stored up, not squandered or spent on sensual enjoyments, transforms, with the help of spiritual practices, into a principle called *ojas*, refined energy. That energy can be sublimated, taken up the spine, and will, in course of time, transform in turn to *tejas*. *Tejas* is an intelligent light that shines out the very pores of a holy personage. In possession of that sublimated energy of spirituality an illumined soul can attract sincere students, teach scripture, serve humanity — verily transmit spirituality to those around him.

How this subtle process pertains to desire involves the impurities that naturally get dissolved under the regimen of intense purification that the *yogi* or *yogini* puts themselves through. The poisons which exist at each of the six centers (*chakras*/lotuses) of consciousness will undergo subjection to the lustral fire of *ojas* and *tejas*. Desire and pure intelligence are immiscible. In the presence of one, the other has to go. So it is the way of the practitioner of *Kundalini Yoga* to bring his or her focused consciousness to bear upon the internal impediments to realization, eventually opening the subtle internal channels for the swift and revivifying passage of a Great Light, greater than *tejas*. This *Jyoti*, or Light of Consciousness, brings Bliss, *Ananda*. It will not settle for an on-again-off-again earthly happiness, nor for an ephemeral joy that only exchanges its position with recurring sorrows.

The only downside to the sublimation of desire method, at least in this day and age, certainly must be the poor quality of practitioners who attempt it — especially in the West. Weak in detachment, inefficient in works, unable to renounce properly, mind filled with all manner of hype, pretense, and fantasy, and possessing only half or poorly digested knowledge of the spiritual path, such posers approach the realm of path and preceptor wholly unprepared for the extent and intensity of what internal and external work awaits them there. Perhaps they think that they will become great and admired spiritual beings by performing a few physical postures, or that the mere pumping of lungs in and out will net them attainment of what authentic luminaries call the "razors-edged path." This, of course, is not the case. The world is full of hosts of want-to-bes, but short on even a few will-to-bes. In other words, immense strength is needed to gain access to what the *bhaktas* call, the Holy of all Holies. Can It be obtained by a few *asanas*, breaths, and fasts? even by a few years of meditation? Fifty years of constant meditation practice may not be enough. So, what is needed — for both self-realization and successful sublimation of desire — is commitment and constancy. A good measure of subtle understanding and the grace of the *guru* will also help the process greatly.

What the seers call *asamvedana*, transmitted by such realized beings as Lord Vasishtha, is the final echelon of this nine-tier tower of neutralizing desire. The English word, "nonreceptivity," is about the only one adequate for explaining it. Here, neither effort nor the lack of effort will suffice; it demands something other. If one could somehow perceive the approach of desire before it arrived, and had the facile ability to sidestep it — get out of its way — this would be *asamvedana*. It is verily "awesome." More can be said about it, and will be inferred, in forthcoming pages and chapters.

As an adventure and a teaching both, the following chart (next page) places what we have learned thus far about desire into a hands-on form that is both practical and esoteric. It gives some nuts and bolts and some inner dynamics around the otherwise stultifying subject of *karma* and rebirth.

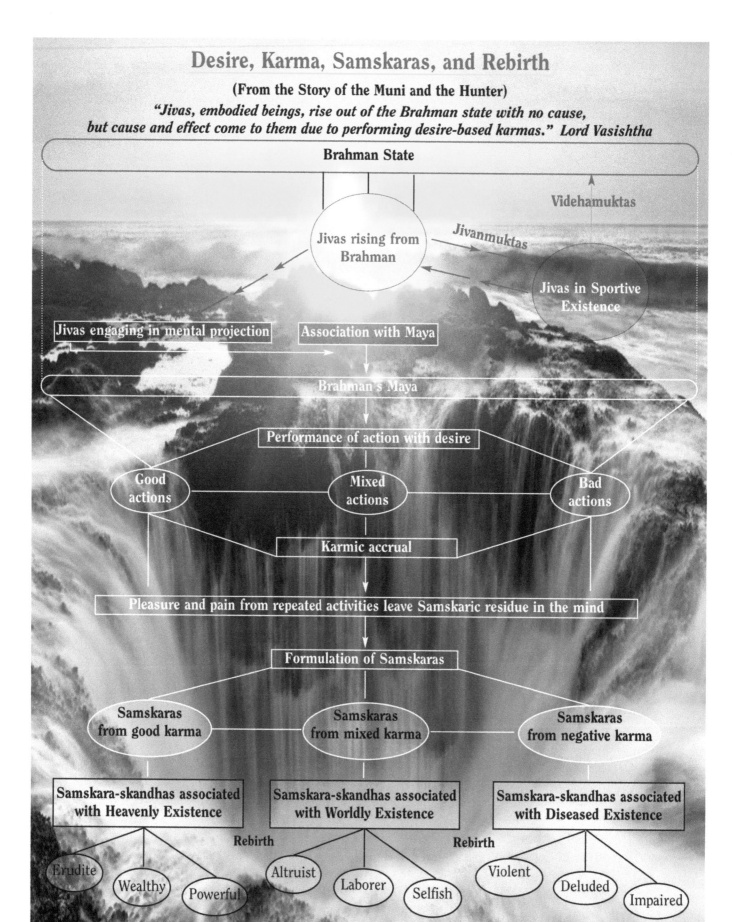

Desire, Karma, Samskaras, and Rebirth

(From the Story of the Muni and the Hunter)

*"Jivas, embodied beings, rise out of the Brahman state with no cause,
but cause and effect come to them due to performing desire-based karmas."* Lord Vasishtha

Brahman State

Videhamuktas

Jivas rising from Brahman

Jivanmuktas

Jivas in Sportive Existence

Jivas engaging in mental projection

Association with Maya

Brahman's Maya

Performance of action with desire

Good actions — **Mixed actions** — **Bad actions**

Karmic accrual

Pleasure and pain from repeated activities leave Samskaric residue in the mind

Formulation of Samskaras

Samskaras from good karma — **Samskaras from mixed karma** — **Samskaras from negative karma**

Samskara-skandhas associated with Heavenly Existence | **Samskara-skandhas associated with Worldly Existence** | **Samskara-skandhas associated with Diseased Existence**

Rebirth   Rebirth

Erudite — Wealthy — Powerful — Altruist — Laborer — Selfish — Violent — Deluded — Impaired

*"Those who long for objective existence will attain it via their own mental projections, but those who strive
for Yoga will perceive objects as being devoid of substance and will refrain from desire."*   *Lord Vasishtha*

Mention has been made about the great seer, Lord Vasishtha. In the scripture, *Yoga* Vasishtha, attributed to him, a host of stories demonstrating the truths of India's spirituality are presented. In the story of the Muni and the Hunter, wherein the hunter completely overlooks his wounded prey due to a seer's timely intervention, a copious mental map of the reincarnation process is given out. Transferring that map into a chart, we can peruse its content in order to help our *sadhana*.

Upon immediate inspection, several very cogent points come to light. The most important of them is found in Vasishtha's quote at the top of the page. In brief, there is a way of incarnating that leaves no residue of cause and effect, and the master of this mode is not pulled back into embodiment against his or her will anymore. The first graph shows that the *jivanmuktas* and the *videhamuktas* are two classes of beings who, due to their withdrawal from cause and effect-based activities, only embody once, then merge again in *Brahman*, where they came from. But let us follow the course of those who, engaging in *sankalpa* (see chart on page 269) and in association with *maya* (forgetfulness of *Brahman*) fall away from Pure Being and into the illusory worlds of becoming.

To trace this course in an effective way, the great *rishi* utilizes the proofs of desire, *karma*, and *samskaras*. As Sri Ramakrishna has said, which is worth repeating, *"The more lifetimes a man lives in ignorance, the more convinced he becomes of the reality of the world."* What happens to a soul who gets caught in the wheel of *maya* is explained by following this chart from top to bottom. And we can see that desire-based actions are the inception of bondage. Further, the pain and pleasure that rises from ones repetitive actions leaves a thick residue in the mind. Its thick haze masks the formation of *samskaras* there so that the soul has little or no idea of the predicament that is ensuing in *maya*.

Somewhat shockingly, performing good does not necessarily extract one from the cycle of *maya*. *Samskaras* are formed nevertheless. In the case of a "do-gooder," then, his or her *samskaras* lead to a life of pleasure, and thereby to a fondness for heavenly existence. Such beings, when they return to earth due to their unsatisfied penchant for pleasure, are born in the wombs of those who are capable and like-minded. Theirs' is a heavenly existence. In the case of those who commit evil acts, either knowingly or unknowingly, negative *samskaras* get formed in the mind, and their rebirth on the earth plane illicits more of the same as well, i.e., a diseased existence. Further, there are a host of beings whose activities are mixed, who are constantly and absent-mindedly performing good and bad actions in turns, almost indiscriminately. A worldly existence is the lot of such souls.

This chart and its teaching proposes that souls have a choice as to whether or not they are to be reborn in the physical body again. And it is not so cut and dried as all that. There are souls, too, who though they can merge in *Brahman* at the end of their lifetime, choose to remain in the embodied state and return for various reasons. Some of these reasons are: to help others achieve their goals on the earthly level so they can move on to better births; to finish a destined work that was instigated in a particular lifetime, but not completed in that lifetime; to expand their abilities to forbear the ills and vicissitudes of *maya* so as to become more able to aid others; to teach the truths of the scriptures and the *dharma* to aspiring souls; and finally, there are those who stay in order to help others transcend embodiment altogether; they are the highest exemplars. Of course, there are all manner of reasons why the ignorant embody as well, all too numerous to list here.

The final quote on this chart confers more esoteric knowledge upon us. Vasishtha informs us that the world is a matter of mental projection (*sankalpa*) under the auspice of the conceptual power of the mind. There will be much more on this principle in forthcoming pages. Secondly, he places another nail in the coffin of our hope for ultimate fulfillment in the world by stating, point-of-factly, that the world and its vaunted objects are void of any substance. This fact was known long before the appearance of Lord Buddha, then. Succinctly put, if the world is devoid of substance, why maintain any desire for it? Conclusion? Become a *yogi*, practice *sadhana*, perceive the hollowness of the world, and quit projecting realms from the mind while caught in the web of desire. Peace and *AUM*.

Along with the master, Lord Vasishtha, another great master, Sri Krishna, even earlier, has much to say about the subject of rebirth. Sri Krishna's demonstration of the principle of rebirth, mapped out in part on the opposite page, is both lucid and convincing. To the thoughtful and reflec-

Rebirth and The Refinement of Consciousness

"Among thousands of beings scarcely one strives for perfection, and of those who strive and succeed, scarcely one knows Me in truth." — Sri Krishna

- **Through Good Actions is Born in the Worlds of the Righteous**

"Neither in this world nor the next is there destruction for the doer of good, for my son never comes to grief."

- **Is Born into the Houses of the Pure and Prosperous**

"Having attained the realms of the righteous, and living there for countless years, one unable to reach perfection in yoga is born in the homes of the pure and prosperous."

- **Seeks Knowledge and is Born into the Families of Yogis**

"Or one is born into a family of wise yogis or rishis. A birth like this is difficult to attain in this world."

- **Strives for Higher Knowledge among Spiritual Seekers/Adepts**

"In such a birth the soul retains knowledge of its previous birth and strives harder to to attain perfection."

- **Transcends Rites and Rituals and Seeks after Yoga**

"By former attainments the soul is led on and, wishing to know of yoga, transcends religious rites and rituals and those who perform them."

- **Purifying the Mind through Many Births, Reaches Perfection**

"Thus striving with assiduity, and purified over many births, the yogi reaches the Goal Supreme."

- **Lives as an Adept Yogi, Exemplifying the Supreme Goal**

"The one established in yoga is deemed to be superior to ascetics, to men of knowledge, and to those versed in the performance of rituals. Therefore, be thou a yogi, Arjuna, steeped in yoga."

"Thus established in Yoga, even at the hour of death, they get into oneness with Brahman."

All Quotes and Teachings, Bhagavad Gita

tive person, there must be a reason why people are born in such diverse circumstances, and with so many varying qualities and attributes — and lack thereof. Coming to the aid of confused and inquisitive beings alike, the Lord of the *Bhagavad Gita* transmits a well-formulated and perspicacious manual on the art of rebirth. He begins after the march towards perfection has already begun, not reverting to the millions of reasons and conditions under which the evil and ignorant souls are taking their births.

The first ripe soul under consideration is the righteous person who, based upon goodness of heart alone, *"....never perishes or gets lost to the Lord."* This soul may still be circling amidst the lower, intermediate, and higher heavenly regions (*lokas*), but his sweet heart is accumulating good merit that will eventually allow him to burst through that level of existence and move inward to take up residence in subtler *"Chambers"* in the *"Father's Mansion."* For, *"Birds have nests, and foxes have holes, but the son of man hath no place to lay his head here."* This is the Christ's way of advising renunciation of the worlds of name and form. He knew, as well, that the *"kingdom of heaven within"* was a penultimate residence only, and that *"I and My Father are One"* was the ultimate station — namely, nonduality. Therefore, the saying, *"Seek thee the kingdom of heaven first and foremost"* was a positive push aimed at worldly people in order to galvanize them and help place them on the inward trajectory of spirituality leading to transcendence. That ladder is shown here, at the behest of Sri Krishna.

The second tier to this tower of the rebirth process indicates the soul who gains the boon of a birth with pure-hearted people. As the previous chart on dealing with desire revealed, when a soul has had enough of heavenly existence, and the yearning for something higher and sweeter surfaces, the desire for *dharma* springs forth in the heart. The practice of some form of *Yoga* is then not far behind. We should note that this level of rebirth is accompanied by the access to wealth. It is good to know that not all souls are attached and thereby trapped by wealth, that some only figure it into their lives so as to be free of having to make a living so that they can spend more time seeking ultimate Freedom. An opulent family of good-hearted souls? — this may be hard to find. But as we shall see, the search for higher births on the earthly plane gets more and more difficult as the aspiring soul reaches towards enlightenment.

And even Sri Krishna notes that the next level of ascension provides scanty support, for the soul who has reached the echelon of spiritual practice must necessarily find parents who can either teach him the *dharma*, and/or allow him free reign to seek out his higher destiny. A family of *yogis* or *rishis* fills that requisite perfectly, the only trouble being that such souls may not have that much desire for family life anymore, and may thereby choose not to have children.

This brings up a contemporary problem regarding the noble station of the "householder" in this day and time. Aspiring souls, as they become more and more enlightened as to the complexity of *maya* and *Mahamaya*, and as they reach for perfection so as to transcend the need for rebirth, will require better and more informed parents for their incarnations. Illumined souls who choose to come to earth consciously for helping others will also need the same access. It is very telling on the Western nations at this point in time that spiritually illumined souls are generally not found reincarnating there. But notice the flux of special souls who take their birth in India and Tibet, and in other countries where parents have some idea of both the need and desirability of seeking Divine Reality and getting free from ignorance and suffering. It is no wonder, given this scenario, that the Western nations are advanced in the area of materiality, but backwards in the area of spirituality, while the Eastern nations give less accent to matter, yet produce giants of the Spirit. If the Western nations are going to rise out of worldliness and acquire higher wisdom, they will need an infusion of advanced souls into their fold, and this will require at some point that the perennial teachings of the East be given out, studied, and comprehended by the householders who bear children. This key was in place in ancient India when children were raised in both recognition and knowledge of both the world's illusory nature, and the presence of the Great Self within.

If a sagacious soul is able to gain a birth among *yogis* or *rishis*, much spiritual advancement can take place for it. Then, if the supreme state is not yet attained at the end of that lifetime, the soul, due to its advanced status, will take birth among groups of families or great lineages where spiritual life is all the focus. Learning the spiritual arts such as ritual, worship, teaching the masses, priestcraft, etc., the sincere soul will advance further and rise above that cross section of beings. At the end of a succession of auspicious births of this nature, births in which spiritual striving has been the sole aim, perfection is finally reached, and the definitive *samadhi* is attained. At this point the illumined soul may merge into formlessness or descend to earth, or move into other planes of existence on order to teach and benefit others.

From the inception of spiritual striving to the consummation of spiritual attainment, and as the two quotes from Sri Krishna on this chart on the previous page evince, the true meaning for human existence finds its ultimate end. Since the body-mind mechanism was so important to the aspiring soul, it patiently searched out a way to refine that mechanism to the nth degree so as to transcend its own limitations, and those of nature (which it produced). And all the while, the Supreme Consciousness, which was the aspiring, evolving soul's true nature, dwelled in perfect equipoise, beyond movement and transformation, eternally free. But this is a subject for a later chapter.

It was mentioned at the beginning of this section that souls bereft of their innate intelligence will have to settle for the seemingly random series of births that *maya* has in store for them. Of course, their *karmas* dictate much of this, since *"You reap what you sow"* is an inscrutable and infallible law of relative existence. The chart on the facing page has been put together to show some of the causes which place negative *karmas* and their concomitant series of births in motion. This teaching is also given by Sri Krishna in the *Bhagavad Gita*, and here is fashioned into a "Sevenfold Road to Ruination." Its presentation has been supported by taking salient quotes from several of the greatest spiritual luminaries of the world, which the reader is encouraged to contemplate.

As is shown, the entire set of cautionary teachings falls under the top quote by Sri Krishna that explains the downward spiraling course of a human being's confused life, based upon succumbing to the influence of the six passions and eight fetters (see chart on page 247). That is, the root of man's problems, if a fine point is placed on the matter, is the mind's constant brooding. He broods upon matter, upon wealth, upon the opposite gender, upon career, upon suffering and sorrow, upon success and its lack, even upon happiness and its sudden disappearance. It is the game of dualities, really, which is why Sri Krishna instructs Arjuna to *"...leave off brooding on the deluding pairs of opposites,"* calling them *dvandva mohena* in Sanskrit. In short, if man could refrain from brooding on the two and the many, and begin thinking about the One and the Eternal, his life would take an entirely different course. This was stated by Jesus as well when He revealed that *"If thine eye be single, thou shalt know the Truth."* How true, this truth about Truth.

The habit of brooding gives rise to a great obsession with brooding, as well as with the subjects and objects of brooding. A human being set upon by attachment is already half gone, as they say, for when attachment increases, so does desire. We have already taken a close look at desire from several different standpoints. Suffice to say that desire is mentioned in every religious tradition of the world as being the cause of unrest and suffering. But the worst is yet to come, for anger beats everything, hands down, bringing outright violence and its resultant *karmic* accrual. It also causes forgetfulness of all the soul's good qualities, and thus ushers the soul into the deep pit called depression. From here there is no more recourse, even to that savior of depraved minds called reason. Without reason the man is mad, whether clinically or otherwise, and the world follows suit.

Though created with a comical touch, the chart just inspected here is hardly funny, especially to the suffering soul under its miserable, multi-leveled press. The sayings of Lord Patanjali, Adishankaracharya, Sri Krishna, Lord Buddha, Lord Vasishtha, and Sri Ramakrishna are all arranged under the headings specific to their topic, and each aspect is shown as a distinct but interconnected avenue linking all the others together. Thus, an expressway of error and a freeway of fear hums with the traffic of unfortunate beings who, having entered Broodway Boulevard at some point in their lifetimes, are now busy coursing their way along *maya's* thoroughfare where exits are rare indeed, and most of them even unconscious of the fact.

The Sevenfold Road to Ruination

The Mayic Map of the Brahman Bypass

"Brooding on sense objects man develops attachment to them; from attachment comes desire; from desire anger sprouts forth. From anger proceeds delusion; from delusion, confused memory; from confused memory the ruin of reason, and due to the ruin of reason he perishes." Sri Krishna, Ch. 2, Bhagavad Gita

"Mental imbalance threatens yogic equipoise and meditation. Through practice of japa and spiritual exercises the mind ceases to react and becomes impervious to brooding and depression, along with the unsteady emotional states they cause."
Lord Patanjali

"That one who is overcome by attachment, which creates entanglements in this world, his sorrows duly increase like bamboo grass in the rainy season." Lord Buddha

Broodway Blvd.
Worry Way
Lust Lane
Attachment Avenue
Oversight Overpass
Stress Street
Error Expressway
Desire Drive
Passion Place
Anger Alley
Fear Freeway
Travesty Terrace
Delusion Detour
Chaos Circle
Confusion Court
Ruination Road

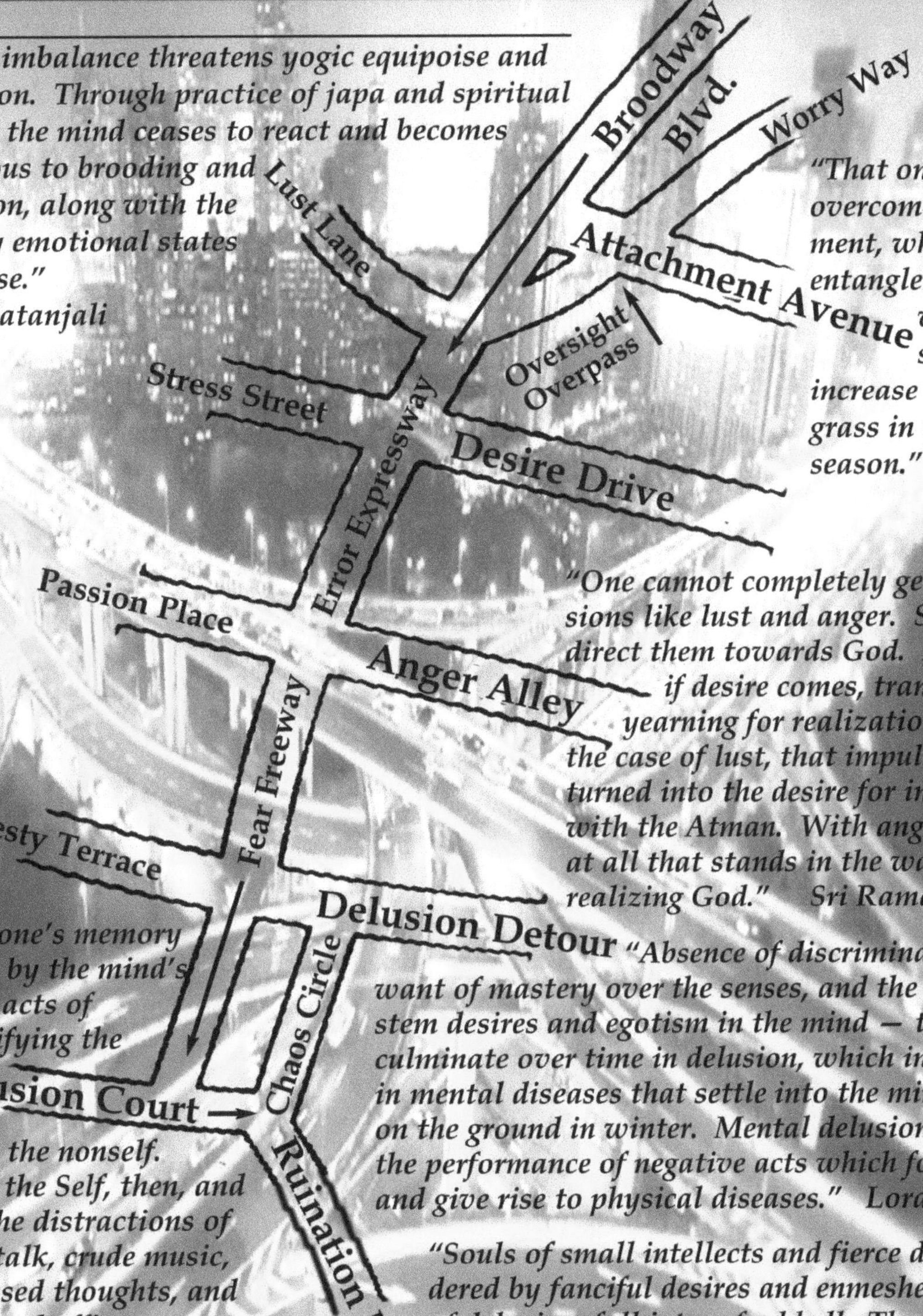

"One cannot completely get rid of passions like lust and anger. So, one must direct them towards God. For instance, if desire comes, transform it into yearning for realization of God. In the case of lust, that impulse must be turned into the desire for intercourse with the Atman. With anger, feel angry at all that stands in the way towards realizing God." Sri Ramakrishna

"Absence of discriminative wisdom, want of mastery over the senses, and the inability to stem desires and egotism in the mind — these three culminate over time in delusion, which in turn results in mental diseases that settle into the mind like snow on the ground in winter. Mental delusion results in the performance of negative acts which form karma and give rise to physical diseases." Lord Vasishtha

"Loss of one's memory is caused by the mind's constant acts of misidentifying the Self with the nonself. Focus on the Self, then, and give up the distractions of worldly talk, crude music, desire-based thoughts, and the like, and affirm your oneness with Atman."
Sri Shankara

"Souls of small intellects and fierce deeds, bewildered by fanciful desires and enmeshed in the snare of delusion, fall into a foul hell. These unfortunates get hurled into the wombs of the demonic and deluded and, reborn again and again, then fall into a condition which is lower still." Sri Krishna

Teachings on Bardo States

◊ The Bardo of Death and Rebirth ◊

"This teaching is extraordinarily important for our present day world, because today we live with widespread conditions of distraction that weaken our ability to concentrate fully upon whatever practice we are engaged in. And it is only with fearlessness that we can maintain mindfulness and awareness, free from distraction."

Jamgon Kongtrul Rinpoche

1. A duration of some 7 days

2. A duration of some 14 days

3. A duration of some 28 days

The State of Departure at the Time of Death
"....an excellent time to remember the dharma...."

The Intermediate State Between Death & Rebirth
"....an excellent time to realize Buddha Nature...."

The State of Return & Rebirth
"....an excellent time to find a teacher and strive for freedom...."

The Three Phases of the Bardo Between Death and Rebirth
"All three of these phases offer an opportunity to recognize the nature of mind and attain enlightenment."

1) The Bardo of the Moment of Death

a. Earth dissolving into Water
External Sign — Weakness
Internal Sign — Foggy Perception

b. Water dissolving into Fire
External Sign — Dryness of mouth, eyes.
Internal Sign — Dreamlike Experiences

c. Fire dissolving into Air
External Sign — Loss of warmth
Internal Sign — Consciousness is unstable

d. Air dissolving into Consciousness
External Sign — Exhalation; no inhalation
Internal Sign — Awareness is a steady light

"Those lacking training may panic here. It is important to understand that awareness is not changing, only the elements are dissolving."

"All experiences become like mirages, and moving images take on a dreamlike nature."

"Consciousness appears like a flame, but it is unsteady due to constant movement."

"Awareness becomes like a lamp that is no longer disturbed by wind."

2) The Bardo of Buddha Nature
Lights of five colors appear, associated with the five Buddhakalas and various deities.

"Deities emanating through mandalas appear in peaceful and wrathful aspects representing emptiness or clarity."

3) The Bardo of Becoming
Lights of lesser intensities appear, associated with the six modes of existence, and one relives the deeds of the past life.

"If a man fails to recognize Buddha nature then he is prepared to be reborn in one of the six realms of rebirth."

"If you practice hard enough, you can gain enlightenment in this life, and that is best. If your practice in this life was guided by a spiritual teacher, then you will experience the clear light at the time of death and recognize the nature of mind. If that does not happen, there is a possibility to do so after death. There are practices one can do at the time of death. A spiritual master can also introduce the dying person to the bardo in such a way that he or she will recognize the clear light when it occurs." **Jamgon Kongtrul Rinpoche**

"Tathagatagarbha pervades all beings in quantity as well as in quality. It is primordial Essence which is never defiled. It becomes obscured, however, when an individual engages in negative activity and accumulates karma which prevents recognition of It." **Kalu Rinpoche**

There are other profound and long-lived traditions which add immeasurable wisdom facets to any given subject around spiritual life and purified mind. And though *Buddhism* is an Indian *darshana*, its variations and departures from the paths and systems of the *Vedic* fold give it the ability to transmit a unique perspective on the subject presently at hand, mainly *karma* and rebirth. This 2500 year old, spiritually-based pathway to perfection is well known for its contribution to the topic of reincarnation, and its penchant towards describing and alleviating *karmas* via the preferred method of wholesome compassion.

In the tradition of Tibetan *Buddhism*, the process of dying and being reborn has taken the special auspice of an outright spiritual art form. One of its main teachers, Jamgon Kontrul Rinpoche, has visited the western countries and brought forth aspects of this process for the higher good and wisdom of its people. If a soul can have some cognition, even precognition, of what it is going through, or going to go through at the time of death, the result will be much more beneficial for its spiritual evolution.

Taking the chart on the opposite page, then, we can explore some of the timelines, signs, symbols, and results of the process of death and rebirth. This affords us a rare opportunity to study what one culture has been perfecting over many centuries. We should take note, then, not only out of respect for all the time and effort put into it, but also because these teachings will inform and illumine our thinking process long before the mind has to make that singular journey beyond physical existence.

And it all begins at the moment of the body's death, as instanced in the box situated in the middle of the chart. In accord with Sri Sarada Devi's teachings on time and death in one of our previous charts (see chart on page 164), we see here, similarly, but in more specific terms, the general timelines that a soul endures after death. For this particular level of soul, an initial span of seven days passes in which the experience of leaving the body is undergone. Since the soul (mind) has been associated with nature for many decades, the unwinding of its thought process from association with the five elements needs to occur in stages. The somewhat conscious soul will experience this drawing back in accord with each element, enduring a series of feelings correlative to them. From gross to subtle, i.e., from earth to water to fire to air to ether, the mind's awareness will detach. The spiritual teacher informs the dying person of the signs and stages of this, though the best case scenario would be that the dying person had taken teachings on the subject throughout his or her life, even practicing such exercises in preparation for death. It is of great import that the soul does not panic during this process, and thus lose its opportunity to exit the body consciously.

The next phase of some two weeks is taken up with visions and experiences of both light and bliss, and emptiness and trepidation. Deities appear, and it is as if a great testing of the soul to determine its real status is going on. At this stage it is important for the soul to establish itself in these realms of light, for a mere dalliance with them or just a surface enjoyment of them, will eventually leave it with no other resort than to return to earthly existence, demonstrating its inherent and unresolved *karmas*, as well as its inadvertence to seek and merge in the Light.

In this regard, and after falling back from the realms of light, a period of some 28 days passes wherein the soul examines its past lifetime and the various deeds enacted therein to determine what kind of rebirth it will require or need. The choices, many of them unfortunate births — dissimilar to the births that Sri Krishna just enumerated for us involving a more intelligent soul — will occur according to the *karmas* and other mental impressions still left unresolved in the mind's recesses. This school of philosophy believes that a birth in the form of an animal is a distinct possibility, but births in human forms are much more likely. For illumined souls, and the adepts that have practiced *dharma* for lifetimes, the realization of *Tathagatagarbha* is the aim. The reader is encouraged to study this chart, teaching by teaching, to emerge with the fullest comprehension of the subject.

Since the teachings of *Buddhism* are presently under scrutiny, another beneficial facet of wisdom is presented next. The *nidanas*, links in the chain of rebirth, make for an interesting and edifying topic, uncovering many secrets that the transmigrating soul can utilize in its bid for Freedom.

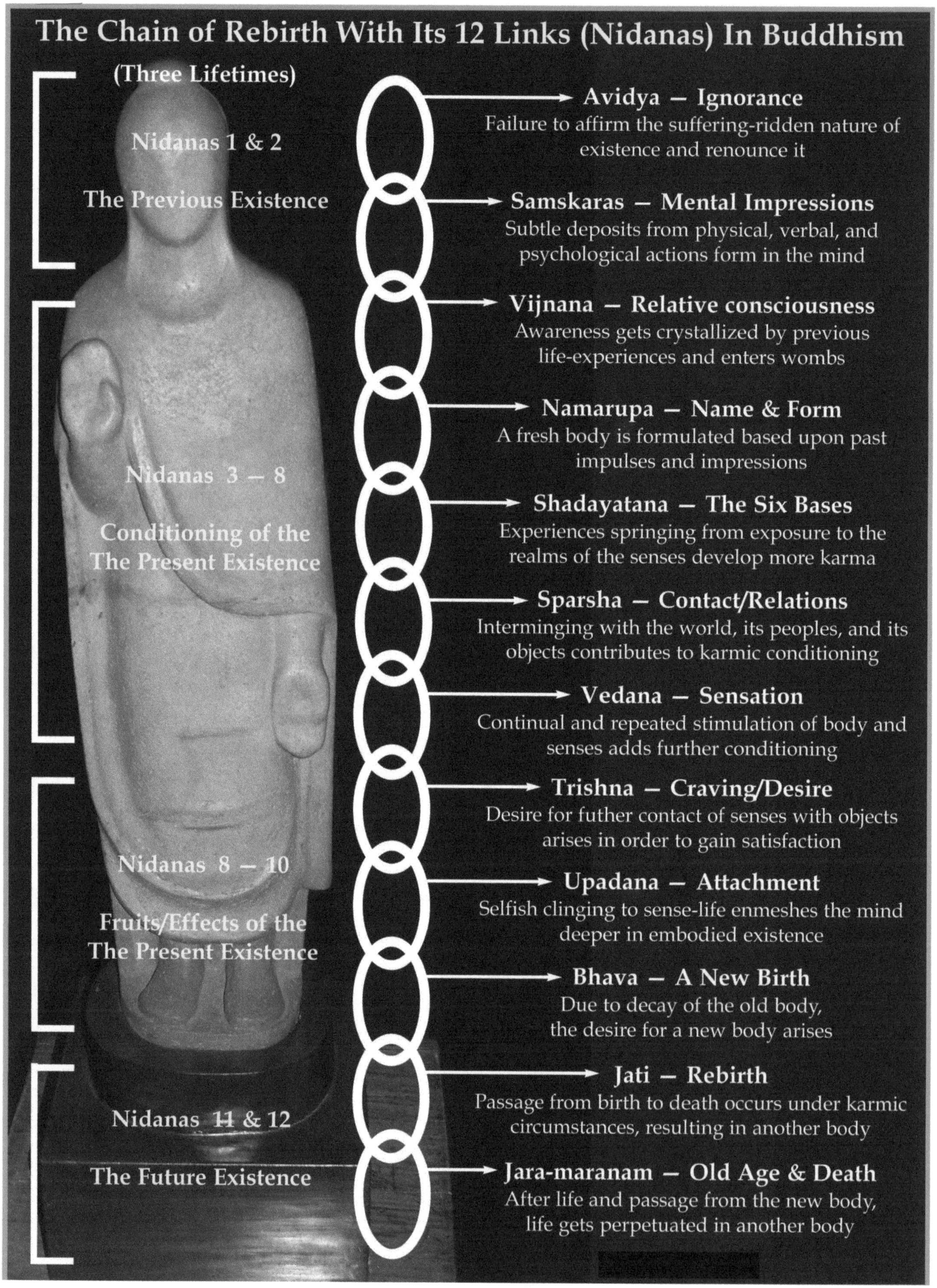

The Chain of Rebirth With Its 12 Links (Nidanas) In Buddhism

(Three Lifetimes)

Nidanas 1 & 2

The Previous Existence

Nidanas 3 — 8

**Conditioning of the
The Present Existence**

Nidanas 8 — 10

**Fruits/Effects of the
The Present Existence**

Nidanas 11 & 12

The Future Existence

Avidya — Ignorance
Failure to affirm the suffering-ridden nature of
existence and renounce it

Samskaras — Mental Impressions
Subtle deposits from physical, verbal, and
psychological actions form in the mind

Vijnana — Relative consciousness
Awareness gets crystallized by previous
life-experiences and enters wombs

Namarupa — Name & Form
A fresh body is formulated based upon past
impulses and impressions

Shadayatana — The Six Bases
Experiences springing from exposure to the
realms of the senses develop more karma

Sparsha — Contact/Relations
Interminging with the world, its peoples, and its
objects contributes to karmic conditioning

Vedana — Sensation
Continual and repeated stimulation of body and
senses adds further conditioning

Trishna — Craving/Desire
Desire for futher contact of senses with objects
arises in order to gain satisfaction

Upadana — Attachment
Selfish clinging to sense-life enmeshes the mind
deeper in embodied existence

Bhava — A New Birth
Due to decay of the old body,
the desire for a new body arises

Jati — Rebirth
Passage from birth to death occurs under karmic
circumstances, resulting in another body

Jara-maranam — Old Age & Death
After life and passage from the new body,
life gets perpetuated in another body

In ancient traditions, ample time has been utilized, and by some very intelligent and illumined beings, to plumb the depths of Reality and the various obstacles in the human mind that impede the realization of It. The solutions for such barriers, based upon finding the causes for the same, can often times be quite complex. Whatever the case may be, it is certain that knowledge of a thing, object, problem, or concept, aids the soul in overcoming it. To that end, the *Buddhist* schools have contributed the teaching of the Twelve *Nidanas*, which are links in the chain of the soul's transmigration. Following along with the chart on the opposite page, we can learn what these *nidanas* are and thereafter have a clue as to how to snap them and get free — from ignorance and suffering alike.

Identical to the *Yoga* system of Patanjali, the root of all this suffering is *avidya* — ignorance. This is not your ordinary ignorance, such as lack of knowledge of facts and figures, what people call "illiteracy." No, it is the lack of knowledge of the true Self, of who one really is. But it may not be fitting to speak of the "Self" in a *Buddhist* context, so we can use the term Buddha Nature — as in the word *Tathagatagarbha* cited in the previous chart. Whatever term one uses, awareness (knowledge) needs to become aware (act of knowing) of Awareness (the knower). That is, the mind's thinking process has to become illumined, and it can do so by concentrating on the principle of illumination Itself. As Sri Krishna states in the *Gita*, *"Ignorance veils knowledge much like smoke obscures fire, or the womb envelopes the embryo."* The womb metaphor is very fitting, considering the topic of rebirth which we are studying in this chapter. *Avidya*, then, *nidana #1*, is the first of many overlays that the embodied soul should never have assumed in the first place. Assumption of the body is hard enough. One should not identify with it, it being the very hub of pain and suffering. To the Buddha, one must admit to the existence of suffering; that is the first sign of real knowledge. And short of mere admittance, one is to see the universe as being filled with suffering — a suffering that goes away only upon recognition of ones changeless Essence. So, admittance, recognition, realization — these three form the way out of *avidya*.

Samskaras come next, *nidana #2*. We have looked into them already under the scopes of two or three different *darshana* (clear ways of seeing). Our Buddhist study here only confirms what we have already perceived. But *Buddhism* adds another key to our fuller understanding by citing that the first two *nidanas* — *avidya* and *samskaras* — together constitute the links which have formed from our previous lifetime. In simpler terms, our inability to destroy our own ignorance resulting in the formation of the effects of said ignorance have brought us here to this body, and in a state of non-awareness, still.

The links of the present lifetime are to be considered next, elements that are more comprehensible for us. The mind's limited awareness, the appearance of a fresh body, cultivation of more experiences in ignorance of our true nature (as being beyond all experiences), unbridled commerce with the many beings inhabiting relative existence with us, and the constant kindling and titillation of the five senses with regard to the sense objects — these five *nidanas* conduce to producing yet another body in the future. Thus does the cycle of *Samsara* rotate eternally. But there is more than this to the present existence and its ability to fuel rebirth. Thirst for life, selfish clinging to the body, pleasure, and the world, and the wearing out of the present body and senses all contribute mightily to an ill-considered reincarnation. That is, the body and senses lose their capacity for enjoyment long before the mind is satisfied with the same. It is an insidious process, to be sure.

The links to future existences are easy to figure. They are, simply (as the previous chart on *bardo* states has revealed), the passage from the old body at the time of death, along with all its stored up *karmas* and *samskaras*, and the production of a new body (as the three charts previous to the Bardo chart have shown). Thus, the twelve *nidanas* form links of an internal, unseen chain, which, as Vivekananda has stated in one of his poems, *"....drags from birth to death and death to birth the soul."*

The problem of *avidya* is universal, and common as an explanation to why the soul both incarnates and suffers interminably. It is easy, as well, to pair *avidya* up with *ahamkara*, egoism. In the next chart we find Sri Krishna teaching about what he calls the "*Puryastaka* body," an eightfold formation of the limited mind's own awareness and projection. It is another link in a similar chain.

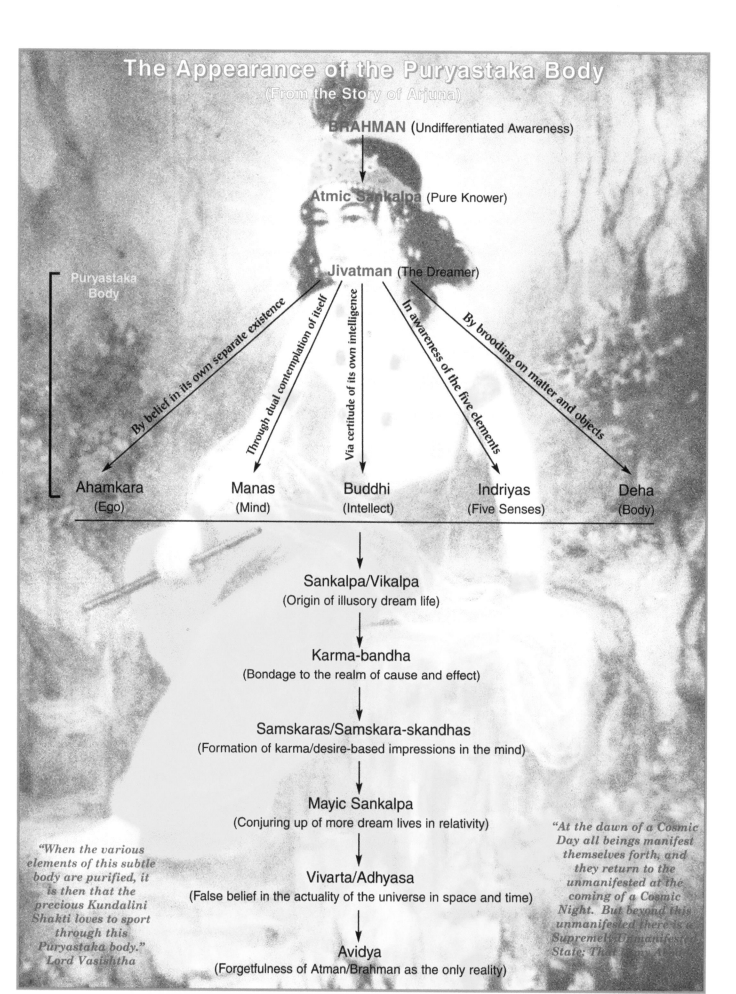

The Appearance of the Puryastaka Body
(From the Story of Arjuna)

BRAHMAN (Undifferentiated Awareness)

Atmic Sankalpa (Pure Knower)

Jivatman (The Dreamer)

Puryastaka Body

By belief in its own separate existence

Through dual contemplation of itself

Via certitude of its own intelligence

In awareness of the five elements

By brooding on matter and objects

Ahamkara (Ego)

Manas (Mind)

Buddhi (Intellect)

Indriyas (Five Senses)

Deha (Body)

Sankalpa/Vikalpa
(Origin of illusory dream life)

Karma-bandha
(Bondage to the realm of cause and effect)

Samskaras/Samskara-skandhas
(Formation of karma/desire-based impressions in the mind)

Mayic Sankalpa
(Conjuring up of more dream lives in relativity)

Vivarta/Adhyasa
(False belief in the actuality of the universe in space and time)

Avidya
(Forgetfulness of Atman/Brahman as the only reality)

"When the various elements of this subtle body are purified, it is then that the precious Kundalini Shakti loves to sport through this Puryastaka body."
Lord Vasishtha

"At the dawn of a Cosmic Day all beings manifest themselves forth, and they return to the unmanifested at the coming of a Cosmic Night. But beyond this unmanifested there is a Supremely Unmanifested State; That, when All...

In a story from the *Yoga Vasishtha* scripture we find the famous couple, Sri Krishna and His beloved disciple, Arjuna, engaged in conversation about the passing of extremely long cosmic cycles (see chart on page 39). In the interim of the conversation, Arjuna is curious to know about the appearance of the human body over the long sweep of these *yugas*. And in classic "Mind-only Schools" fashion, wherein the worlds and the various forms contained in them are seen to be projected out of the mind at their inception, or apparent inception, the Lord gives a fitting explanation. This well-documented transmission from wise *acharya* (preceptor) to devout *shishak* (disciple) was borrowed and utilized by Lord Vasishtha to school the young, still-veiled *Avatar* of the Age, Sri Ramachandra, in his time of ardent inquiry. Explaining the manifestation of the *Puryastaka* body, the eightfold mind/body complex outlined on the chart on the facing page, Lord Vasishtha stated:

"The first thing to realize dear Ram, by way of comprehension, is that the Jiva, the embodied soul, with its levels of consciousness and multi-layered bodies, is just Brahman under the power of differentiation. The idea of separateness is the business of the ego, called Ahamkara, the sense of 'I,' born by an erroneous belief in its own individual existence. With dual contemplation of itself as a separate being, then springs up the Manas, or Mind. With apprehension of Mind's own innate intelligence comes the Buddhi, the Intellect. With a burgeoning awareness of the presence of the five elements in their gross and subtle forms — the Panchromatization and the Tantaras — the five senses, called Indira, come forth. As Manas and Indira naturally go on brooding upon the Panchromatization, or in other words on matter and objects, then the physical body formulates. In short, dear Ram, Ego, plus Mind, plus Intelligence, and adding in the five senses, make up this unit called the Puryastaka body. Its powers are legion and legend. When considering it and its marvelous attributes, we must remember that when these elements are made pure, or kept pure, then the Kurilian Shakti loves to sport through this multi-faceted vehicle."

References to *Kurilian Shakti* have been made prior to this, and will be taken up in more depth in forthcoming chapters. But this very concise definition, in tandem with the process of unfolding — ego to mind to intellect to senses to body — sets a fresh precedent for how manifestation of the physical worlds, and the forms that inhabit them, come into being. Those who opine or settle for the theory of evolution are only getting a fraction of the picture, then, and are, as well, discounting the subtle role of intelligence and its fathomless and infinite nature in the overall quotient. Accounting for Intelligence spells real evolution, based on a subtle cause (in this case, the ego), as compared to evolution based on a physical cause only (see chart on page 47). Whereas there is room for both "theories" in our comprehensive conception of this grand scheme of things and events, if the mind is bereft of the knowledge of subtle beginnings (as, *"In the beginning was the Word"*), no complete rendering of the cosmic plan can be possessed. So, in order to expand on the parameters of this salient system of the *Puryastaka* body, Lord Vasishtha continues teaching his young charge:

"To explain this complexity in a deeper way, oh Ram, it all begins with the apparent shift to ahamkara, what beings think of as the ego, or small self. Here is where the indivisible One, masking Itself, as it were, takes on or assumes the idea that it is separate from Reality. The result is this divine play of multiplicity called life in relativity. You have heard how the Lord makes the impossible possible, oh Ram? Well, here is the best example of that. Ego, or ahamkara, is the primal aspect of the Puryastaka body, and all other aspects come along in turn thereafter. It is preposterous to think that Brahman can somehow separate Itself out, but It apparently does so. This happens by Its first transforming Itself into the Pure Knower with Its power to engage in Its own profound force of Attic Sankaran. By that force, the Pure Knower swiftly transforms Itself into the Puryastaka body. This means that the Witness — the Knower, the Actor, the Enjoyer — sacrifices, and takes on the appearance of the Jiva, the embodied soul, with its power to engage in limited consciousness. In this truncated awareness, dream after dream is engaged in, the experiences of which amass and ignite a whole series of existences lived under the false assumption that the physical universe and various worlds are actually real. What they call enlightenment, Ram, is finally coming to see through this massive cosmic projection."

One of the most important elements in the preceding paragraph is the apparency of change, the mere appearance of transformation, for we have stated clearly and forcefully in previous pages that Reality, in order that It be so, must be completely free of all change — immutable (*aparinama*), thus indestructible (*akshara*). Assigning change — i.e., name, form, causality, etc. — to *Brahman*, Reality, is a root error in both religion and philosophy, especially the latter. Change can be leveled at nature, at any of *maya*'s manifestations, but not at *Brahman*. As Sri Ramakrishna has said, "*Brahman* is the one principle that is untouched by the mind and tongue of man." With this reaffirmed (again and again if need be), the source of subtle and physical expression can be scrutinized, and with some critical attention as well. That is the *jiva*, the dreamer, as the chart states:

"Caught in the erroneous belief of its own difference and separateness due to formulation of the ego, the jiva next begins to contemplate, and immediately, the mind is born. Twoness has to have company, oh Ram, and that company is called diversity. And diversity must begin somewhere, and that beginning is called duality. Thus, dual mind is the perfect tool from which to project a myriad of worlds and objects. And so, mind is thereby present to help facilitate it all."

The nature of mind, *manas*, is also brought up for keen inspection here. So many of humanity's problems would be solved, outright and up front, if people, especially children, were taught that the human mind is dual by nature; that its very function is all about contrasting opposites. As Sri Krishna and Lord Vasishtha have said, brooding on the pairs of opposites, even before the worlds have sprung into being, is mind's purpose, and in that brooding the senses and the worlds are conceived. Lord Vasishtha goes on to comment on the intelligence of man.

"And with that presence comes the realization of inherent knowledge — a certitude that the mind possesses of its own inherent intelligence. This is the third aspect of the Puryastaka body, called the buddhi. After that, and via the power of thought, the five elements and the five senses with which to apprehend them all appear. That completes the eight aspects of this mentally-projected body. The physical sheath itself is only a vessel, the gross foundation for the Puryastaka form's expression, for when the ego/mind mechanism fastens itself on elements and sense-objects, it naturally fabricates a body to enjoy them. So again, Prince Ram, ego, mind, intellect, and the five senses with their corresponding elements of ether, air, fire, water, and earth compose this Puryastaka complex. In the Bhagavad Gita, Sri Krishna himself speaks of His eight-fold nature, and thereby refers to this wondrous but paradoxical form. He, the great archetypical Soul, has pointed out the path that this amazing cosmological body must tread; for all who would attain to the highest Truth."

An explanation of the lower half of the chart under study (page 194) will complete the present subject. For, once the mind/body complex is formulated, the doorways of knowledge and ignorance open up to it. The path of light and the path of darkness are two ancient alternatives for the embodied soul. The chart here lays out the latter, since embodiment itself is considered questionable. And in this "descent" we see the dubious occupation of mental projection (see chart on page 267) taking place. Much will be said about *sankalpa* and *vikalpa* in the coming pages. Suffice to say that once mental dreaming of this nature is engaged in and employed, the formation of *karmas* has already begun. And where *karma* is, *samskaras* are not far behind.

The chain of rebirth now has its main components in place, and the *mayic* curtain consisting of thousands of subsequent overlays gets fashioned in the interim. Only great souls can lift this curtain, and they manage this only for a few hundred years at a time. In the meantime the transmigrating soul revolves around the *Kalachakra*, the cyclic wheel of birth and death, inexorably. If some good *karmic* element becomes a part of this self-actuated scheme of limited existence, however, a "chance" meeting with such a soul becomes possible. The possibility that age-old and crystallized concepts might alter circumstances occurs here, providing a potential chink in the curtain of *maya*. That is, and as the closing teachings of this chart imply, the false belief that the world is actually real may get questioned, and some remembrance of an underlying Reality may thereby come forth.

In the next chart up for inspection we can see, from yet another angle, both the predicament and the hopeful possibilities of the embodied soul caught in the web of *maya*, bereft or shorn of higher wisdom as it is. This ready and available illustration was inspired from another of the powerful stories in *Yoga Vasishtha*, condensed as follows:

The Mind's Release from Rebirth

(From the Story of Manas in *Yoga Vasishtha*)

Ram's request to Vasishtha: "Please inform me as to the nature of this dual mind and inert body, and how the soul entwines itself inextricably in repeated rounds of birth and death on the wheel of Samsara."

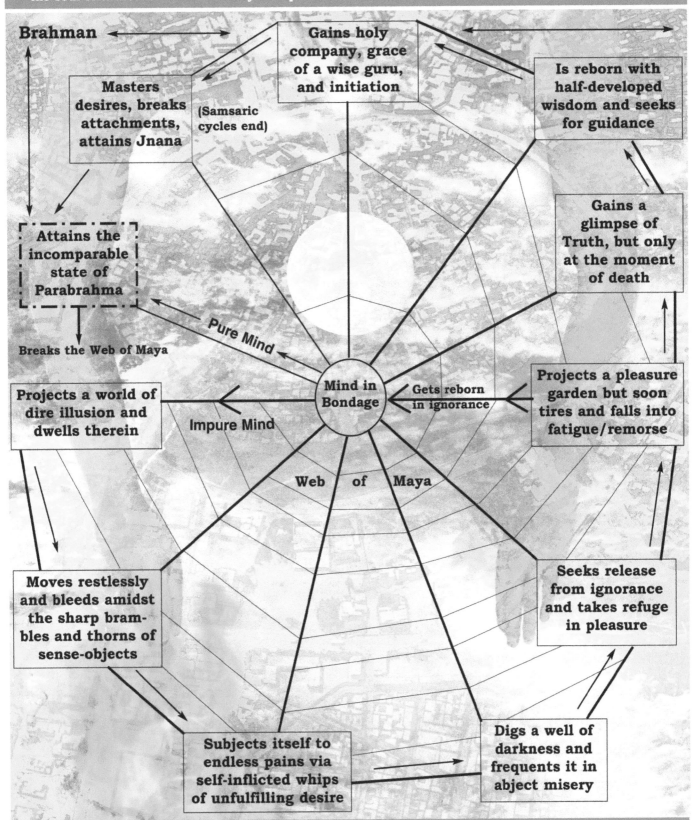

Brahman

Gains holy company, grace of a wise guru, and initiation

Is reborn with half-developed wisdom and seeks for guidance

Masters desires, breaks attachments, attains Jnana

(Samsaric cycles end)

Gains a glimpse of Truth, but only at the moment of death

Attains the incomparable state of Parabrahma

Pure Mind

Breaks the Web of Maya

Mind in Bondage

Gets reborn in ignorance

Projects a pleasure garden but soon tires and falls into fatigue/remorse

Projects a world of dire illusion and dwells therein

Impure Mind

Web of Maya

Seeks release from ignorance and takes refuge in pleasure

Moves restlessly and bleeds amidst the sharp brambles and thorns of sense-objects

Subjects itself to endless pains via self-inflicted whips of unfulfilling desire

Digs a well of darkness and frequents it in abject misery

"All become subject to bondage in a web of delusion due to desire-based, mental projections. But the bound soul can save itself via holy company, wisdom, and sadhana, rightly practiced." Lord Vasishtha

We have learned previously that the word *"manas"* is the *Sanskrit* word for the human mind. *"Mahat"* is the *Sanskrit* word for Cosmic Mind, or as some say, *"God's Mind."* The essence of these two wisdom principles is the same, but the scope is vastly different. However, when the human mind releases itself from self-imposed, time-worn limitations, it tends to lean towards Cosmic Mind and begins to borrow some of Its capacious powers and abilities for itself. The accomplishments of the seers and sages reflect this well. The human mind, besides aspiring for mastery of the cosmological, also selects a personal exemplar, a Chosen Ideal who will guide it in the best use of higher powers and unseen forces. That being is usually an incarnation, a god, or a divinely realized human being. And this was the case with a being named *Manas* in one of *Yoga* Vasishtha's stories. He was a particularly hard case and, even though his plight attracted the best of teachers — i.e., Lord Brahma and his mind-born son, Lord Vasishtha — he nevertheless showed a resilient stubbornness known only to the most reticent and unfortunate of beings.

The chart on the previous page (197) illustrates the recurring moribund state that the soul, *Manas*, got himself into. As with all human souls, no god or devil put him there, and no god or devil extracted him either. The human being plots out his/her own destiny and fate. That is both a boon and hardship. He was fortunate, however, to have attracted the attention of Lord *Brahma* — the *sattvic*, *Atmic* projector of the three worlds, replete with its seven realms and millions of *lokas* — whose great patience with *Manas* taught Lord Vasishtha a powerful lesson in both the nature of suffering and the greatness of compassion.

Holy Mother was asked one day what was the most unbelievable thing She had ever seen. She responded, *"That though people make endless mistakes, they never learn from them."* The heedless and ignorant soul, *Manas*, simply would not learn, reminiscent of masses of worldly souls who, like ostriches, bury their heads deep in the earth, i.e., matter. The two great beings mentioned here, present to help *Manas*, watched over several cycles of time as *Manas* threw himself carelessly into the deep well of trials and trammels in *maya*, with all its endless sufferings, then crawled out again in a forlorn and weary condition upon the next incarnation in *maya*, and the next. After witnessing several such cycles, Vasishtha was ready to give up on him! But Lord *Brahma* had his mind born son watch, again and again, and just observe. At one juncture in this seemingly interminable period, and at the end of one of *Manas's* horrific lives, Lord *Brahma* and Vasishtha were by his side, trying to reason with him to give up his base attachments. All of a sudden *Manas* started uttering strange things, then he gave out a loud laugh before expiring and plummeting down the well of death and rebirth again. In the Yoga Vasishtha, Lord Vasishtha describes this important incident perspicaciously:

"In the case of Manas, his strange utterances all had significance. Lord Brahma, a past master, could read them, despite their nonsensical appearance. He knew that Manas was nearing his last birth, and that his cries symbolized a death gasp that would end all embodiment forever. What a fortunate being he is who attracts Lord Brahma's most excellent assistance! Manas also laughed uncontrollably near the end. That is significant. Whereas his importunate cries indicated a state where desires were dying away, leaving no real wisdom behind, the laughter that followed signified an end to veils obscuring that knowledge, and a beginning to immersion in it. How glorious that moment, oh Ram, for that knowledge, especially in its most radiant form, puts an end to the need to produce bodies in space and time anymore. Where is the need, when living wisdom-intelligence Itself reveals Itself as everything? Still, all the many pains that Manas went through over many births had to be borne due to his ignorance of such facts. That he scourged his body and suffered only indicates that he harbored many misconceptions in his mind, for it is well-known, my son, how blissful the seers are, and that is due to the possession of a pure mind immersed in Atmajnan."

With the basics of this story in mind, a journey through the rebirth process can be taken, courtesy of the chart under study (page 197). Starting in the very middle of the chart, we see the mind in bondage. It has come to that position due to its ignorance — ignoring the presence of supreme intelligence within it, and failing to cull it out. In its ignorance, then, but nevertheless possessed of many powers, it projects a world of dire illusion and takes up residence there. Following the arrows circling down and around the web of *maya*, the elements of a worldly life in ignorance can be viewed, most of which are not unfamiliar to the minds and memories of living beings. But the real crux of the matter occurs when, after living such a life, the transmigrating soul has an opportunity to escape rebirth in ignorance. That moment is well illustrated by the last lifetime of *Manas* in our story here, indicating that an upwards turn in the soul's internal evolution (involution) is both desirable and possible. Of course, it is far better to come to some sort of understanding of relativity and Reality during ones lifetime, but at least a snapping of the chain of rebirth, which is devoid of basic knowledge, is a valuable relative goal for the soul to attain.

Instead of moving back into "darkened wombs" as has been indicated by the compassionate concerns of Sri Krishna and others, which will only land one at the center of *maya* again as our chart displays, this glimpse of Truth which the soul suddenly espies opens up a new world of potential — spiritual potential. This was accented by the recent chart on the *Bardo* states according to the *Buddhist* teachings. A chance to give up physical embodiment and attend upon subtler worlds, even merge in nondual Reality, now looms majestically on the magnificent inner horizon of the Great Mind, *Mahat*. But these alternatives are still in the offing. With this new perspective in the mind's memory, however, lodged deep therein even after entering the womb and forming another fetus, the transmigrating soul now has awareness of higher wisdom, and with that may take the foremost step towards freedom possible — the selecting of a spiritual path and illumined teacher. This is the *guru* or illumined preceptor, sprung from *Guru* Principle (see chart on page 91). Life may be attended with *upagurus*, teachers of secular and religious knowledge, but this especial *guru* teaches the esoteric wisdom of the ages. Discovering and attending upon That School and That Teacher signals an end to the transmigratory process. It is all a matter of time and intense practice, at this juncture.

Reaching the uppermost subtle strands on the web of *maya* (similar to transcending the *mayic* wheel and mounting the wheel of *dharma* shown the previous chart on fulfilling desires), the fortunate soul comes upon Holy Company and gains the grace of an illumined soul, or souls. With their help and his own increased self-effort in spiritual practice, he one by one breaks the bonds of his attachments and uncovers a different kind of well — the well of deep wisdom lying within him. This is the *"Atmajnan"* just mentioned by Lord Vasishtha in our recent story. It is awareness of the immutable, all-pervasive Self. Having discovered That, the aspiring soul wants to repossess It, and merge in It. And when this occurs at the auspicious moment in time, the incomparable state of *Parabrahman* is attained. This completely shatters the web of *maya*, like a spider's web in a hurricane-force wind. Peace and Bliss are the result, and the welcome taste of Freedom ensues.

In another story, drawn from the thirst-quenching well of wisdom that was Lord Vasishtha, we can trace this state of *Parabrahman/Atman* and also observe how it gets lost to the soul, even to great souls — such are the mesmerizing powers of *maya*. And this particular story also bridges that unspoken or overlooked area of the reincarnation "theory" which takes into account the soul's appearance in subhuman forms like animals, even insects and plants. The idea here is that if all manifestation occurs under the dream-power of the roving mind, then the soul can dream itself into any form available — consciously and unconsciously — much like a man might dream himself a bird one night during sleep. And why stop there? A series of births in the illusory flow of time, one after another in succession, might occur.

Such was the case with the noble soul Sukra who, having gotten infatuated with one particular form in Indra's high heaven — a demi-goddess named Vishvachi — left his *yogic* equipoise to sport with her and ended up getting disoriented on the journey back. What occurred in the interim was grounds for a mighty story of *Vedic* fame, an ingenious tale that shone a light upon a more advanced soul's transmigratory process. This is welcome here, especially after we have explored the many impermeable side-tracks and dark alleyways that the benighted soul laboriously traverses. But in Sukra's case he had his illumined father to watch over him, the venerable Brigu — a soul so powerful and daunting as to cause death himself, Yama, to give second thoughts to working his art.

Along with the story-line, which will be condensed in brief, a running commentary will accompany this chart so as to shed some light upon the mind's amazing powers of projection.

The Illusory Ego's Projection via Rebirth

(From the Story of Sukra)

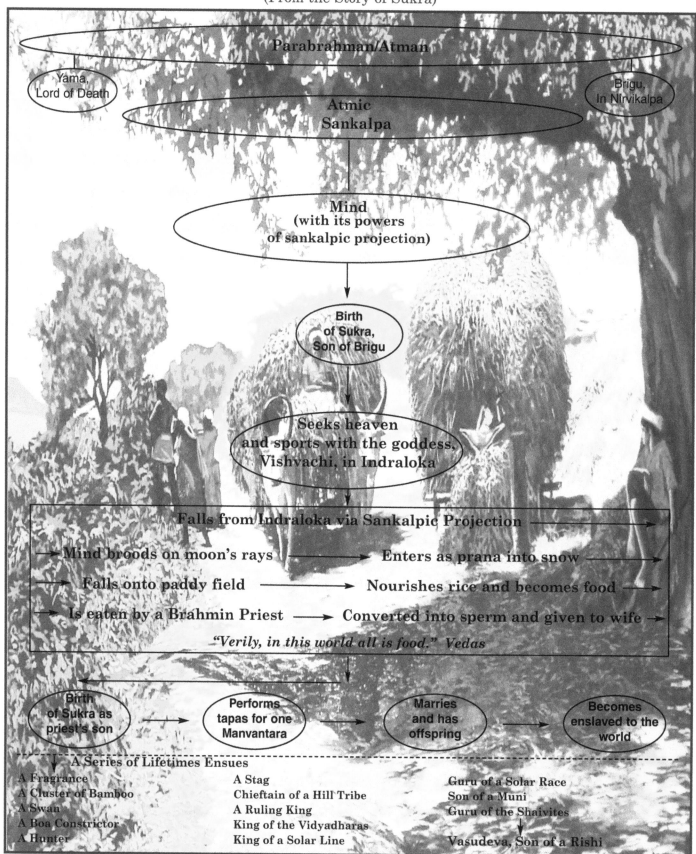

Parabrahman/Atman

Yama, Lord of Death

Brigu, In Nirvikalpa

Atmic Sankalpa

Mind (with its powers of sankalpic projection)

Birth of Sukra, Son of Brigu

Seeks heaven and sports with the goddess, Vishvachi, in Indraloka

Falls from Indraloka via Sankalpic Projection

→ Mind broods on moon's rays → Enters as prana into snow →

→ Falls onto paddy field → Nourishes rice and becomes food →

→ Is eaten by a Brahmin Priest → Converted into sperm and given to wife →

"Verily, in this world all is food." Vedas

Birth of Sukra as priest's son

Performs tapas for one Manvantara

Marries and has offspring

Becomes enslaved to the world

A Series of Lifetimes Ensues

A Fragrance
A Cluster of Bamboo
A Swan
A Boa Constrictor
A Hunter

A Stag
Chieftain of a Hill Tribe
A Ruling King
King of the Vidyadharas
King of a Solar Line

Guru of a Solar Race
Son of a Muni
Guru of the Shaivites

Vasudeva, Son of a Rishi

"Just as a stone may have many figures carved into it,
so too, in the one Brahman, all worlds and lives manifest themselves." Lord Vasishtha

Before plunging into this chart and its unusual implications, the reader is advised to take another look at the chart on page 47 — Causality, Origins, and Reincarnation. At the foot of that chart is listed the constituents of the Material Cause which, according to *Vedanta*, lies in contrast to and in humble support of the subtler causes arrayed above it. The material cause is basically what the world believes in, and to the exclusion of all other causes. Western science, psychology, society — even Westernized religion — all rest their final case with insentient matter. Even mind is a product of matter with them. The case for subtler causes, if even considered seriously, is seen as falling into the realm of postulation and conjecture alone. As far as origins go, and in the case of what the tactile senses alone can perceive and accept, people see and believe in food, vital energy, sperm, ovum, physical body, senses, and the human brain — from bottom to top.

When the superlative soul named Sukra left his formless state to sport in Indra's high heavens, he came "down" or out quite a ways to reach that relatively lower plane. When attempting to return to his eternal home via the path he had used when he externalized himself, he lost his way in the chimerical sweep of *maya* and found himself close to the earth plane, mesmerized by the sight of snowflakes falling softly on the fields of a quiet farm on a moonlit night. As the scripture says:

"This snow fell on the rice fields owned by a brahmin in the country of Dasharna. When this rice got cooked and eaten by the brahmin, it was then converted into the life-fluids of that brahmin, who then passed it into his wife in the form of sperm with an act of love for the sake of childbirth. Thus was Sukra born on earth after leaving the nondual state of meditation with his father and projecting himself into the life-heavens to sport. Taking on this earthly body, as in a dream projection, his real self still remained in deep meditation next to his father while a dream-process of incarnations began via the powers of his mind.

"Born of a brahmin, and possessed of good karma and samskaras, Sukra's projected life as the son of a priest afforded him company with seekers after enlightenment and freedom from embodiment. As a matter of course, and due to his inherent good sense, he grew attracted to tapas and began practicing austerities at an early age. But before he could complete his period of spiritual practices he became enamored of a woman, married, and gained a son. With an increasing fondness for this boy, he next forgot his earlier vow and turned his focus on the world in order to raise his child. The crucial mistake of forgetting his spiritual aims due to the insinuation of worldliness left him helpless against maya and its influences, and thus his mind fostered a growing attachment for the world and its concerns. In short, the son of Bhrgu fell from his true state and entered into a series of projected lifetimes as in a dream.

A runner in a dream actually goes nowhere, though he sees scenery going by and feels his lungs and heart pumping. In like fashion did Sukra dream himself through the experiences of being everything from a fragrance on a breeze, to the beloved son of an illumined Muni. Along the dream-way he found himself extremely restful as a forest of bamboo, floated regally on pristine mountain waters as a white swan, and slithered through a dense forest in search of prey as a huge boa constrictor. Then he moved along in the body of a hunter, killing stags and other four-legged animals in the thick woods, only to find himself incarnated as a stag, panting as he ran through the forest to escape a hunter on his tail. A powerful chief of the hill tribes was his next incarnation, then a royal king. And this royal birth and its boons gave way to the desire for several more, as the king of the Vidyadharas first, and finally a king of a solar line. And that is how he became a Shaivite Guru, and then a famed Guru of the solar line, a birth which duly ended his final desire for glory and lead him to incarnate as the son of a Muni — a birth very difficult of attainment."

The chart under study provides a visual for the process just described in the Yoga Vasishtha scripture. The reader is advised to secure this scripture and read it cover to cover, for Lord Vasishtha is one of the earliest and foremost of propounders of this unique and edifying teaching, namely the teaching of *sankalpa/vikalpa* — the projecting powers of the Mind. With the help of his father, Brigu, Sukra was able to slough off all the *karma* associated with his various rebirths and return to the state of non-dual peace and bliss — a state he never really left, and which formed the unchanging foundation for his series of dream-lives in the realm of apparent change.

Sukra's plight teaches us about the dream-power of the mind. For those under its sway, however, the dream seems real — as beings in various states of *dharmic* life can attest to.

Varnashrama — The Four Castes of Life

"He from whom is the evolution of all beings, by whom all this is pervaded. worshippimg Him with his own duty, mankind attains perfection." **Bh. Gita**

"Serenity, self-restraint, austerity, purity, forgiveness, uprightness, knowledge, realization, perception of what is beyond life and death — these are qualities of the Brahmanas..."

Brahmanas

"Agriculture, cattle-rearing, the business of trade and selling and earning based in honesty — these are some of the duties of the Vaishya, born of their own nature."

Vaishyas

Kshatriyas

Shudras

"Heroism, vigor, firmness, resourcefulness, fearlessness during encounters, generosity, and lordliness are the qualities of the Kshatriyas..."

"Selfless action consisting of service to all castes and classes is the duty of the Shudra, born of their own nature."

"Better is one's own dharma, though imperfect, than the dharma of another well-performed. That one who fulfills the duty ordained by his own nature, avoids all transgression."   **Sri Krishna**

"One should not abandon the duty to which one is born, even if it is attended with evil; for, all undertakings are fraught with imperfection, Arjuna, as fire is enveloped by smoke."   **Sri Krishna**

For those whose intelligence has been developed, and who have struggled to maintain even a semblance of higher understanding in life, the rebirth process confers upon them the station called *ashrama*. Being born into a caste, *varna*, insures not only a hold on *dharma*, but also a chance to improve themselves. *Karmas* pertinent to their station can be neutralized via works or, better, service. Therefore, and as the chart presently up for inspection on the facing page reveals, the four castes of life in India — an ancient system that was in good working order for many centuries — form a way of living in the *dharma*, and have a very deep-rooted connection with both *karma* and rebirth. As Sri Krishna infers in the quote at the top of the chart, these four castes originate from *Ishvara* and are patently confirmed in the *Vedas*. Through them mankind justifies his existence in the human body and, if each person's station is rightly maintained, then the embodied being duly propels himself into higher births in better circumstances.

The *Brahmanas*, or *Brahmin* priests, are the upper caste, for their duty is to transmit the teachings from the revealed scriptures, and even contemplate them deeply for any additional revelation that is to be had there. The *Sanskrit* root, *Brh*, to expand, and word *manas*, the mind, when placed together, infer possession and cultivation of an open and awakened mind. And in fact, if the priest class deviates from this great responsibility of preserving and conferring wisdom upon the other three castes — as has happened generally over the past two millennia in India, the consciousness of the people becomes dark and confused, superstitious and scattered.

The idea of a priest class must be based upon a group of qualified souls who are provided by society with the time necessary to meditate within themselves, thereafter coming forth with beneficial revelations. These will be used to inform a country's leaders, showing the necessary connection between spiritual life and earthly existence. Guidance — instructions for everyone from the royalty down to the common worker — will then become broadcast, and the nation can live and act in a harmonious way. Only then will *dharma* maintain itself and *adharma* be kept at bay.

The *Kshatriyas*, the warrior class, are next in the order of things. Their duty is to guard the royalty and protect the kingdom or country, no doubt, but it does not stop there. This sense of keen guardianship must extend to all peoples, ideally to those of other countries as well. Therefore, intelligence and higher vision must belong to the warrior, who will then use his strength to oversee all affairs and bring about the highest and best outcome possible.

The *Vaishyas* are the merchant class, who are responsible for the feeding and overall health of the population. Their best quality is that of honesty, and if this is missing or compromised then the society they inhabit will fall into corruption and die away. Trade and agriculture, when conducted utilizing moral principles and an eye for fairness in commerce, expand and integrate a nation substantially, making it both successful, and a fine example to other countries of how to live a *dharmic* life.

The *Sudras* are the workers, whose best quality is constancy. Seeming small and meek, they are really the greatest in strength, for the character-building lessons of humble service, self-sacrifice, and selfless works are learned best amongst the members of this caste. The upper three castes are the beneficiaries of all the labor and result which this caste produces via the credo of constant effort for little reward.

All four castes are to be taken together, and when they are, they represent the body of the Cosmic Being, called *Virat*: the *Brahmanas* are his head; the *Kshatriyas* are his heart; the *Vaishyas* are his torso and stomach; and the *Sudras* are his legs and feet. Rebirth in better and better conditions is constantly taking place in this Cosmic Being, and *karmas* peculiar to each station are getting satisfied. The secret of balance is gained via participation in this comprehensive life, then, and relative freedom from births in benighted wombs is enjoyed.

In reference to all these mentions of the principle of *dharma*, another similar system, which lies in close relation to the *Varnashrama*, is brought to the fore next. The *dharmashrama* consists of four levels as well — the renunciate; the hermit or forest dweller; the householder; and the celibate student. These are illustrated generally on the following page.

Dharmashrama — The Four Stages of Life

"Celibate student, honest merchant, retired forest dweller, and the renounced freedom-seeking soul — these four stages of life are well known among those who value dharmic living."

That initial stage of life wherein a youth receives pertinent instructions on earthly and spiritual life from parents and teachers, and strives to develop character and virtues.

Brahmacharya

The third stage of dharmic life which ensues after family life is consummated, consisting of retiring into the forest to pursue studies, devotional exercises, and meditation.

Vanaprastha

Grihastha

Sannyasa

The householder, or second stage of life, which requires marriage and the inception, rearing, and maintenance of a dharmic family, thereby fulfilling one's duty to society.

The final and highest stage of dharmic life entailing the renunciation of all earthly affairs in order to pursue moksha, spiritual emancipation.

"Whatever you do,

Whatever you sacrifice,

Whatever austerity you practice,

Thus shall you be set free

Whatever you eat,

Whatever you gift away,

Do it as an offering to Me.

From actions yielding good and bad results."

Sri Krishna

The charts on *Varnashrama* and *Dharmashrama*, with their many precious teachings, both reflect one main element — dedication, or commitment. Fealty to ones own *dharmic* duty and station of life causes life to hum with purpose. The negative forms of *maya*, it seems, have little room to exist or grow in such a society. If a world full of such societies were to be attained, the insinuation of ignorance — even around such hardships as disease and death — would cease. Thus, beings look to Mother India, who at least once on historic record has sported a golden age which consisted not only of material well-being, scholastic excellence, and refined art and culture, but a religion and philosophy that were finally worth and deserving of the title.

And examples of this great thought were also present. The *Sannyasins* of India were, and still are in present times, exemplars of what spiritual life, practice, and realization are all about. Having renounced attachment and, in most cases, affiliation with worldly matters and earthly concerns, they are free to meditate or serve as per their individual temperaments and predilections. This stage of life is not a stage, then, being transcendent of life. It is not lofty, or haughty, as some imagine, but is really free of all pretensions generally found among those who think they can heal souls, save the world, or protect the earth. Among other things, this station reveals the age-old spiritual law that to really be of aid and benefit to others, one must renounce the world outright. And so the *Sannyasins* stand at the top of the tower of life, representing what Christ called, Eternal Life.

The *Vanaprastin,* the "forest dweller," was also shining example. There are not many souls like them in present times due to the division and segmentation of land among property-owners and the disappearance of forests in which to dwell freely. But withdrawal from society has long been seen and known in India as having great merit, and suitable for that cross-section of souls who are finished with earthly concerns, such as making a living in order to raise children.

Several good teachings, helpful in this day and time, come forward upon considering the *sannyasin* and *vanaprastha* stages of life. First, it was common in Indian society to give all wealth away toward the end of ones life, for retiring into the forest and the spiritual lucubrations one practiced there would then be uninhibited by thoughts of wealth and goods. As Sri Ramakrishna has said, *"Objects kept near a mirror reflect in it constantly."* The mind is that mirror, and if one wants to keep it free of worldly thoughts for purposes of meditation, then one should take all such reflectors away. This giving away of wealth and goods was in keeping with a healthy, God-centered life, then, unlike in the West today. And that brings up a second point here, that the amassing of wealth and its enjoyment, especially for its own sake, runs counter to true freedom. Occupations such as vacations, retirement, and comfortable, secure living, seem strange to freedom-loving minds, and counterproductive. The ideals of returning to earth and going to heaven — usually left unconnected in the first place in most conventional, religious minds — are not the ideals of the *sannyasin* or *vanaprastin.* Life is too short, death too certain, and rebirth too chancy, that the lover of God, of freedom and liberation, continue to dally around with senses and objects and procrastinate about spiritual life.

In the *dharmic* picture, the other two stages of life are not that much different in outlook than the first two discussed above. The *Brahmachari,* or young student, keeps himself pure, his energy focused on studies, not so as to be a huge financial success in life, but to remain the master of mind, senses, and objects. Otherwise, wealth may enchant him and sway him from the *dharmic* circle he is so privileged to occupy during his present existence. The *Grihasthan,* the "householder,"too, keeps *dharmic* vows and precepts in daily life. He marries, raises a family, receives recompense for services rendered via his occupation, but he keeps in mind that he is heading, soon enough, for the forest-dweller stage, and maybe even a period of free wandering with nothing but God on his mind. Some beings even skip the first three phases of life and go directly, at a young age, to *sannyasi* — such is their love for and devotion to *Brahman* and Its realization.

Before looking into the principle of *karma* as philosophy to conclude this chapter, an area of life that often threatens existence on the *dharmic* wheel ought to be inspected. This entails the many impediments which arise in daily life as already discussed in part, and the crystallizations that they cause in the body/mind mechanism — subtle knots, or *granthis*, as they are called in *Sanskrit.*

Granthis – Knots in the Body/Mind Mechanism

"Granthis, complex knots congealing in one's body and energy, as well as in the emotional, mental, psychic, and spiritual bodies, impede the easy flow of spiritual force which otherwise keeps the aspiring human being strong, fit, and healthy for purposes of living a dharmic life."   Babaji Bob Kindler

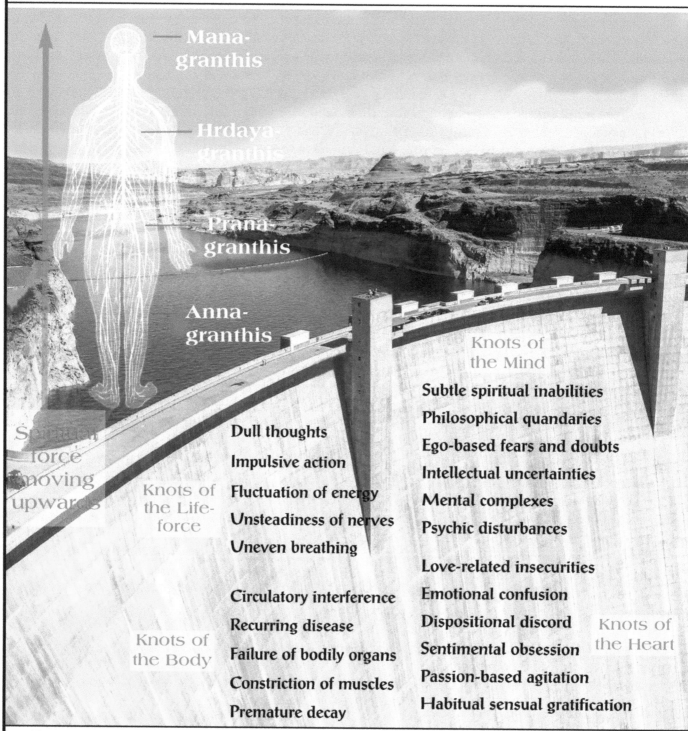

Mana-granthis

Hrdaya-granthis

Prana-granthis

Anna-granthis

Spiritual force moving upwards

Knots of the Life-force

Dull thoughts

Impulsive action

Fluctuation of energy

Unsteadiness of nerves

Uneven breathing

Knots of the Body

Circulatory interference

Recurring disease

Failure of bodily organs

Constriction of muscles

Premature decay

Knots of the Mind

Subtle spiritual inabilities

Philosophical quandaries

Ego-based fears and doubts

Intellectual uncertainties

Mental complexes

Psychic disturbances

Love-related insecurities

Emotional confusion

Dispositional discord

Sentimental obsession

Passion-based agitation

Habitual sensual gratification

Knots of the Heart

"Samadhina anena samasta-vasana granther vinasho'akhila-karma-nashah — destroy all the knots in your being caused by desire-based actions, internal and external, through the practice and attainment of samadhi."   Shankara

Granthis, knots in the psycho/physical being, play well into our subject at hand, as they cause loss of energy and, thereby, painful constriction of thought and act. All of those detrimental and intrusive events in daily life often come up due to the existence of a block, or blocks, in the human operating system. Lamentably, people end up in bad situations for lack of proper energy — physical, vital, emotional, and mental — inhibiting the strata of manifestation supporting human existence. To keep these levels of our being (the nonself) clear and running smoothly, and be able to easily conduct the various degrees of energy available to them, is a part of the art of *dharmic* living. It is very much related to the castes and stages of life which the embodied soul wants to maintain beneficial relationships with. Otherwise, a fall from grace, if the term may be used, is imminent, and the wheel of *dharma,* with its important and sacred vows and precepts, gets compromised. In other words, a step down on the ladder of spiritual evolution, being very undesirable, occurs.

At this juncture, the reader is asked to look back at the charts on pages 167 and 170, all about *samskaras,* for the *granthis* and their subtle, soporific workings can be seen therein, especially on the level of energy, working their pettish insinuations in the mind and negatively affecting future lives.

This chart is divided up into four levels. The broad arrow on the far left-hand side indicates the desired "upwards" movement of spiritual energy. Here, the spiritual seeker affirms aforehand that the body is both the temple of the spirit, and the field of the march of diseases, simultaneously. That some beings are even born with diseases already manifested, or develop them early on in life, proves the pre-existence of *granthis* and *samskaras* in the human psyche before embodiment. Otherwise, such manifestations are irrationally chocked up to happenstance, or the designs of God or the Devil. And in the case of *granthis,* the life-force — what is called *prana* in *Sanskrit* and Indian healing — is mainly and directly considered, for constriction of energy to the body, organs, and mind begins the cycles of deterioration, and *prana* is responsible for carrying this force.

Looking up the sweep of the chart from bottom to top, one can see the levels of the body/mind mechanism, the subtle levels of the mind excluded. At each level has been placed a few of the more common problems that plague the embodied being today, despite the presence of aids like exercise, pure foods, medicine, etc. It will be interesting for the avid student of holistic health to note the connections between the constriction of life-force and the effects that occur as a result. If the *pranic* flow supplying life-force to various parts of the body is stopped up, everything from shallow breathing to poor circulation to atrophied muscles takes place. The greater teaching here, beyond the issue of health and ill health, is that, as the mind suffers these maladies, it stores memory of such experiences in its deep recesses. Unlike physical diseases which can be temporarily cured, the mental residue of suffering from illness, held in the mind's memory, remains there, even after death. It coagulates there as a complex, a *samskara,* supported and fed further by the memory of the stress and pain experienced at the time of the illness. There is no cure for these complexes in ordinary life; they are irremediable. Only spiritual practice, performed consciously in the atmosphere of holy company, can dissolve them. Then they will not appear at the time of the next birth, or a future life.

Therefore, the spiritual aspirant is interested in seeking out and finding the cause of physical maladies, ones that are not necessarily based in the body nor requiring treatment via mere medicines, like drugs. These temporary cures may have their place, but a study of the upper echelons of this chart will reveal or infer another approach. That is, if the *granthis* of the mind are untied and smoothed out initially, in the present lifetime, many of the knots in the emotions, *pranic* levels, and body, will disappear and never develop in future births. This explains why some beings live lives of perfect health, while others suffer illness. And if the topic of heredity is brought up here, the strong genes found in healthy people and in long-lived family lines have formed due to *dharmic* living wherein the constant problems plaguing worldly and secular life were absent for many lifetimes.

We have seen, then, that mental problems such as guilt, nervousness, stress, and the like, are responsible for the stoppage of *pranic* flow on other levels of the psycho-physical being. These other levels include the emotional as well, an area that is particularly "knotty" in present times. The expression, *"hrdaya granthis,"* knots of the heart, is a bit contradictory. In *Vedanta* and other salient wisdom traditions, the heart is the *Atman*, the true Self of mankind, and so does not have any knots at all. As the *Upanisads* state, *"There, at the center, in the Heart, where all the subtle nerve-endings meet, like the spokes of a chariot wheel at the hub, lies the Atman."* These subtle nerves are called *nadis*, "undetectable so undissectible," and conduct the psychic *prana* much the same as the body's nerves do the gross *prana*. And *prana* has its ultimate connection in the intellect, where it refines into an energy so subtle that it carries thoughts themselves, and very lofty ones at that. It is at this sublime level that the *yogis*, meditating sententiously within, joyfully behold this most refined of all energies and meet and merge in *Shakti*, called *Chit-shakti* in Patanjali's *Yoga*. At that ultimate level it is Divine Mother's own Wisdom-force, and it permeates everything, everywhere. Her inner worlds, transcendent of the earth plane, consist of that most refined of energies.

The expression *"hrdaya granthis,"* then, refers in this context to the knots of the emotions which, though they exist in the as yet unpurified mind of spiritually unawakened beings, nevertheless are felt as painful manifestations in the human breast. And the chart under study runs down a short but familiar list of the most common but hard to break symptoms of this level. The five senses and the six passions surely make up the foundation here, where the atmosphere is continually thick with the *karma*-laden problems of humankind. Strangely enough, even though the pall of suffering rising off of this atmosphere is palpable, many beings prefer it that way, and would unwisely eschew the free and invigorating air of *dharmic* living and spirituality. Obsession, discord, and confusion are the states of mind here, however, all related to the immature ego and its ongoing dalliance with the emotions, sentiments, dramas, and disturbances of everyday quotidian life. In a telling way, everything that transpires therein is about "me," "myself," and "mine." No thought of others, what to speak of Divine Reality, crosses the minds of persons operating at this level, even by accident.

And this plays onto that precarious swinging bridge which spans the river of such emotional strife and turmoil — that of love. Here again, by the word love is not meant sincere love, or true love, or love for God, etc., but emotional love, puppy love, conditional love, temporary love, unrequited love — what Swami Vivekananda called a love involving *"fair faces and false hearts."* Since human beings did not get authentic love when they were growing up as children because their parents did not receive it from theirs, the cycle of immature, infatuated, or hate-based love only moves on. The higher *prana*, aforementioned, does not flow here, in the constricted human heart, and cannot carry such welcome dispatches as relief, forgiveness, kindness, or even self-surrender, to the soul — what to speak of outright positive qualities like contentment, peace, and aspiration for higher thought. The refined *prana* that cradles the mind's most scintillating intelligence is never experienced, then, and the human being remains, as they say, an emotional baby.

If the emotional part of ones being is resolved, however, the swinging bridge of vulnerable love is steadied and the soul crosses over into an interior land that secretly holds the source of all disturbances. This is the human mind. Fortunately, the mind also holds all solutions within it as well, though its utilization for such ends is going to require some adroit expertise and flexible knowhow. Albert Einstein noted this when he stated that problems cannot be solved at the same level of awareness that created them. This points to the various levels of the mind (see chart on page 172), and also infers that knots readily congeal at those differing levels.

Pranic knots, *granthis*, express in multifaceted ways at the gradated levels of mind. As is viewed on the chart, the mind proper, the psyche, the intellect, even the spiritual element of the mind, all get affected by the constraint of *pranic* flow due to these energy blockages. The common element in all the erroneous aspects here is doubt. Uncertainty might as well be the cause of all constriction, and it pervades the host of problems that arise in the mental mechanism. Unexplainable happenings, brooding on dualities, unfathomable intellectual complexities, impermeable philosophical quandaries, and the failure to step up and arrive at the intended goal of life — which is essentially of a spiritual nature and content — are all, in and of themselves, knots in the mind. And as was stated earlier, if solutions at this level could be successfully ferreted out and implemented, the entire system, from human emotions to vital life-force to the physical body, would even out and flow.

It could be said that the principle of *samskaras* operates more at the mental level, including its psychical, intellectual, philosophical, and spiritual strata (see chart on page 172), while the *granthis* have their play more in the areas of body and life force. But there is a profound connection between the two, and a similar one with the relative law of *karma*. That sincere seeker who is looking for causes which are at the root of all suffering and ignorance, and that escape the ordinary run of common problems and conventional solutions, will take a look at all three of these interconnecting elements, taking them as a great teaching for pondering.

The great saying from the *Vivekachudamani* by Shankara, shown at the bottom of the chart, explains how exquisitely interconnected all levels of our being are: *"Samadhina anena samasta-vasana granther vinasho'akhila-karma-nashah — Destroy all the knots in your being caused by desire-based actions, internal and external, through the practice and attainment of samadhi."* It is therefore the business of every ardent aspirant after the Truth that these various complexes which linger and stagnate at all strata of the human body/mind mechanism be located, dealt with, and destroyed. Only then will life — physical, earthly, practical, *dharmic*, spiritual, and divine — reach the illimitable potential it was intended for. If Shankara's formula listed above is accurate, then the observance and renunciation of all "desire-based action" would be a fitting starting point for the embodied soul striving for peace and freedom. And as we have already thoroughly explored the problem of desire, as well as some nine ways of attempting to deal with it, we will move on in this close inspection of *karma* and its implicit affiliates to its philosophical territories.

The Philosophy of *Karma Yoga*

As some great spiritual luminaries have told us, the relative law of *karma* is both enigmatic and inscrutable. Some of them have even opined that if one searches for God in this physical universe, one will find only *karma* instead. And as we have seen, such vast imperatives as birth and death, failure and success, virtue and vice, attainment and lack of capacity — all with their intricate complexities — are based around the ever expanding pillar of *karma*. If that is the case, then, there must needs be a science and art for *karma*, even a *yoga*, or way of union, with it. Here enters the percipient and perennial pathway called *Karma Yoga*, easy of comprehension, difficult of practice, but extremely well suited for the man or woman of active or dynamic temperament. In relation to it, it stands to reason that in a world which verily operates via interconnected masses of intense activities, the practiced and time-tested art form of *Karma Yoga* would be the most excellent way of proceeding, ingenuous in approach, obvious of conclusion, and unassailable to attack by either science or religion. One can be sure that, upon entering this fractious and factitious world of volatile cause and effect, any wise sage, seer, or any other divine worker worth his or her hard-earned merit will be fully enamored of and thoroughly well-schooled in the fine philosophy of *Karma Yoga*.

Such is the nature of the world of name and form in time and space based upon causality with which the relative principles of *karma* and reincarnation are intrinsically intertwined. The word "relative" is important to bring in at this point, since we have learned at the outset of this book, in studying some of its nondual tenets, that Reality is formless (*anama*), transformationless (*aparinama*), and beginningless (*ajati*). That means that all which is perceived to be subject to form, to cycles of change, and to birth and death, must be part and parcel of what the seers call *anitya*, noneternal, and thus *asatya*, ultimately unreal. The philosophy of *Karma*, then, is a unique and excellent system through which to both neutralize relativity and render it manageable and nonthreatening. For the worker, whether he be a worldly person, a servant, an altruist, or a divine worker, this *yoga* provides a proper pathway through the miasmic morass of otherwise unfathomable actions and their diverse effects.

With this stated out front, the following chart and its scrutiny will begin to place the art of *Karma Yoga* into classic segments for beneficial study and apt conclusion, designed to help thinking human beings come to know the inner workings of *karma* and therefore be able to overcome its negative influences and utilize its more valuable assets.

The Four Types of Karma

Sanchita (Accumulated)	Prarabdha (Operative)	Kriyamani (Imminent)	Agami (Potential)

Arrows being held in the Scabbard

(past karma)

Arrows already loosed from the bow

(present karma)

Arrows being taken from the Scabbard

(new karma)

Arrows being loaded into the bow

(future karma)

"Karma, not God, is responsible for our misery and happiness. One cannot blame God for sins committed."
Sri Sarada Devi

"Devout recitation of the Lord's Name reduces the effects of karma to almost nothing, Thus, where a sword is destined to fall, a pin must at least prick."
Sri Sarada Devi

The Four Shades of Karma

Black — negative/bad

"Bound by a hundred ties of hope, given over to lust and anger, they strive to secure by unjust means hoards of wealth for sensual enjoyment."

White — positive/good

"The world is bound by actions other than those performed for the sake of sacrifice. Do thou therefore earnestly perform action for the sake of sacrifice alone."

Black & White — mixed/good & bad

"Motivated karma is, Dhananjaya, far inferior to that performed in the equanimity of mind; take refuge in the evenness of the mind; wretched are the result seekers. Learn to do everything as an offering to Me. Thus shall you be free from the bondage of actions yielding good and bad results."

Colorless — neutral/eradicated

"That one whose intellect is unattached everywhere, who has subdued his self, from whom desire has disappeared, that one by renunciation attains the supreme state of freedom from action."

Sri Krishna, Bhagavad Gita

"The fire of knowledge destroys that which has previously been done (sanchita), and what one has yet to do (agami), but what is done (prarabdha) it cannot destroy. But those who stay close to Brahman are never affected by these three. They are Brahman without qualities."
Shankaracharya

First up under the scope of scriptural scrutiny is the teaching of the four types of *karma* — basically titled past, present, immediate, and future. Exchangeable titles which correlate respectively with these terms can also be given, which would assist the student of *Karma Yoga* in a fuller understanding of its four types, namely accumulated, operative, imminent, and potential. For the *Sanskritist,* the assignments would be *sanchita, prarabdha, kriyamani,* and *agami,* respectively. By the very mention and existence of such names and terms we can see that *Karma Yoga* concerns itself with acts done in previous lifetimes, as well as effects which are taking place in the present life, all of which, if not neutralized or transcended, could manifest and affect future lives.

Using the bow and arrow analogy, past *karma, sanchita,* can be likened to arrows which have been stored up in the scabbard, meaning actions done in past existences which, as we have seen, courtesy of several charts on recent pages, merely sit there, awaiting fructification, and crystallizing in the meantime. Importantly then, the *sadhaka* or spiritual aspirant notes that to keep the *karmic* record clean he/she must refrain from selfish and violent actions in order to reduce this type of *karma.* If this directive is adhered to there may come a lifetime in which the *karma* of past lives will be nonexistent, and a major amount of progress can then be made, free of the weights of undesirable happenings which are only the kickbacks from ill-considered actions of the past. This accumulated *karma* has been likened by seers to be like the heavy baggage that a man is burdened with as he sits on the train platform late at night. He can neither carry it away, nor go for help due to nearby thieves. Thus he merely sits with it. Mental baggage, then, is much like personal belongings. One should not accumulate more than one can easily handle — and maybe having none is best.

Prarabdha karma is operative *karma,* in effect during the present lifetime. It is a portion of the past *karma* taken up in this lifetime for neutralization. It is likened to arrows already loosed from the bow in that there can be no calling them back. One can only hope that the aim was straight, for if not, some dire effects may surface later. According to great souls like Shankara, this *karma* is the only one which cannot be neutralized by self-effort and the fire of knowledge; all the others can be attenuated, even destroyed, by *sadhana.* For *prarabdha,* then, one must needs remain in the proximity of *Brahman,* nondual Truth, for the swiftest solution to residual effects which are presently operative. In some souls, the entire *prarabdha karma* is taken up and dispelled in one lifetime. They are powerful beings. Others can only handle a portion, a bite at a time, if they can handle even that, for some beings only languish in ignorance and continue with ego-based actions that only add to the stock of *prarabdha,* which then turns into additional *sanchita* prior to the next birth.

Future *karma,* what is potential, represents arrows being loaded into the bow. There is the choice, here, of not firing these off and away. Therefore, this *karma* is the most innocuous of all, and can be relatively easy to deal with. All the aspirant needs to do is to practice spiritual disciplines so that past *karmas* will dissolve over time. With no past *karmas,* all operative *karmas* will cease to be. But this equation is difficult of actuation by ordinary souls, who see life and action as the end-all and be-all of existence. Work, activity, is all and everything to them. As has been mentioned, no thought of their formless, inactive nature, which is wonderfully Peaceful (*shanti*), ever occurs to them. With no higher idea than this, they are left at the mercy of *karma* and its dictates, scarcely knowing what blissful freedom exists within their very souls.

The old adage for this conundrum is that of oxen who, harnessed interminably to wagons, carry delicious sweets back and forth to market but can never taste them. Further, the ox is forced to keep busy for nothing, and all the while goes on developing ox *samskaras* as a result. Due to these it is born again in a similar situation. Is there any shortage of beasts of burden in this world? Just so, humans reflect their attachment to slavish labor. To break the bonds of cycles of toil and trouble and begin to taste the sweets of his own internal soul will require a human birth (see chart on page 367). Having gained this boon, he should immediately be taught the laws of *karma* in a world that is based upon cause and effect. Coming to know the whys and wherefores of his birth, and perceiving his predicament in *maya,* he can then take positive steps towards alleviating all *karmas* that brought him here in the first place, while deftly annulling all that are still left unresolved.

The fourth and final *karma* to inspect is called *kriyamani*, a word that infers something spontaneous which arises from the mind. It is a fitting title, for this *karma*, likened to arrows that are being taken from the scabbard, explains all the many little botherations of human existence that rise up and spoil or compromise a balanced life. It has been described in present times by the phrase, "all the little fires that need putting out." Other oft-heard phrases intimate and echo its presence, utterances like "I do not know the meaning of my life," and "I never got around to that," indicating that the operative *karma* (*prarabdha*) taken from the store of past *karma* (*sanchita*) which people came into the body to annul has been interrupted by the day to day *karma* (*kriyamani*) that keeps on springing up repeatedly. Can you say, "distraction?" And being devoid of spiritual capabilities such as detachment from sense-objects, concentration, and meditation, these ongoing, tiny insinuations into life's many arenas can be maddening — meaning, they drive the mind off balance into frustration.

This *karma* has fittingly been connected to what is termed "mortar and pestle" *karma* as well, pointing to the many daily activities (done unconsciously) that take place in the average household wherein many tiny organisms get destroyed. Accumulated *karma* mounts here, with its congealing body of just recompense as well. Left unresolved due to lack of spiritual practices and *dharmic* living, various stresses, strains, fights, jealousies and the like — an overall and underlying malcontent — visits the householder's life and home. As Lord Buddha has stated, *"Lack of study and recitation of scripture is the rust of monasteries; lack of spiritual self-effort is the rust of households."*

More will be said about these four types of *karma* as the path of *Karma Yoga* unfolds further in the forthcoming pages. As a familiar aside, the reader is invited to peruse the bottom half of this chart (page 210) for reminders of the four colors of *karma* — black, white, black and white (or grey), and colorless.

Negative and positive actions are understood by most beings. But the other two, grey and colorless, need some explaining. The quotes by Sri Krishna under the appropriate headings will help clarify this. But suffice to say, for now, that mixed *karma* is that dubious amalgam of the residual results of good and bad actions whose effects produce very strange outcomes, outcomes that confuse the mind and cause it to perform additional questionable acts. The modern saying, "random acts of kindness," is a good example of this senselessness, for any act done unconsciously or semi-consciously is at least suspect, and more likely liable for unexpected repercussions.

As for colorless *karma*, something about this has been explored already in these pages, and more is yet to come. It is the non-*karma* of those beings who, like a bird, fly through the sky and leave no trace behind them. This is hard to fathom and amazing to observe. That is, when an ordinary person meets a master of the art of *Karma Yoga*, it will take some time before both appreciation and comprehension of what is occurring (or not occurring in this case) will dawn in the mind. When it does, such a soul may well want to apprentice this master and learn this unique art himself. He will then find that the prerequisites for colorless *karma* are such qualities as desirelessness, detachment, and renunciation. Where this trio is present, no *karma* will dare approach. Thus, the illumined soul lives in a state of perfect balance and unruffled equanimity. As Shankara's quote says on this chart, the fire of knowledge and close proximity to *Brahman* put a final end to all vestiges of *karma* — past, present, and future. As for imminent *karma*, well, one has to deal with it.

Now that the four types of *karma* have been initially studied, and in hopes that these teachings will be memorized and implemented into the daily life of the individual, his/her family, and society in general, a further excursion into the realm of *Karma Yoga* can be undertaken. The next chart up for scrutiny (facing page) deals with the three grades of *karma* and its dynamics. That is, and in order to confer the opportunity of practicing this refined art on the field of action called everyday life, a well-defined and condensed rendering of the main points of *Karma Yoga* is given, along with the ethical structure behind it. For, many hear about the rules and requirements of *Karma Yoga* in scriptures such as the *Bhagavad Gita,* and among gracious *dharma* teachers in the know, but a condensed list of them is seldom seen. With such a list, the aspirant after truth and freedom will be afforded the necessary elements for comprehensive practice, leading to spiritual emancipation.

The Dynamics of Karma Yoga

"This vibrating castle of karma, conjured by the mind in maya, is fated to come crashing down about the ears of all and sundry. O seeker, take care; walk the rare, royal path that leads up and out of maya to the land of Enlightenment." **Sri Ram**

- Perform duty meticulously, but without laying claim to its fruits.

- Refrain from producing any fruits of karma through selfish motivation.

- Do not disregard or reject obligatory work under the pretense of inaction.

- Know that action abides with the Gunas of Prakriti, while the Purusha is Inactive.

- Execute all action fixed in yoga, being even-minded in success and failure.

- Remain steady in the face of both loss and gain, impervious to their influence.

- Do all work as worship, as an offering to the Lord dwelling in all beings.

The Three Grades of Karma

"It is needful to discriminate action, inaction, and forbidden action."

1) Vikarma — Forbidden
- Acts done out of anger to inflict violence
- Ignorant actions done at an inauspicious time
- Perverse actions committed against dharma
- Actions done out of guile and hypocrisy

2) Karma — Self-motivated
- Actions performed for selfish reasons alone
- Action done for reward or out of expectation
- Actions which are attended by attachment
- Action engaged in for glory, honor, and power
- Beneficial action abandoned due to difficulty

3) Akarma — Selfless
- Doings devoid of design and desire
- Acts successfully subjected to the fire of Yoga
- Acts engaged in while thinking 'I do nothing'
- Actions free of hope and desire for possessions
- Actions done by the mind steeped in wisdom
- Work undertaken for the sake of sacrifice

"The threefold fruits of action — good, mixed, and evil — accrue after death to all who are attached. But no karma attends those who renounce." **Sri Krishna**

Before entering into a study of the dynamics of *Karma Yoga*, the three grades of *karma* deserve a review. Again, much like the four colors of *karma* teaching, many people will not find this new, or esoteric, and others may appreciate it for the sake of review and reminder. But the way it has been laid out on this chart may uncover some heretofore hidden or forgotten wisdom, especially in the context of reincarnation which definitely is, in this day and age, esoteric in nature.

Though the quote at the top of the chart is evident, its teaching is not. Sri Krishna counsels souls who have taken on the process of embodiment by reminding them that "motivated action" brings about effects, while actions done with peace and other equanimous qualities escape such results. The merits of motiveless work will be taken up soon.

In the meantime we are to note the three grades of *karma* at the bottom, namely forbidden, self-motivated, and selfless — *vikarma*, *karma*, and *akarma* in *Sanskrit*. These three in and of themselves, if observed and followed to the letter, and for some time, will provide the arrant seeker with enough forward momentum to break free of nominal constraints and rise to higher levels of consciousness. For, if the embodied soul has steeped itself in forbidden and selfish actions for decades, even lifetimes, it will take an equal amount of time to break the habits and effects of this behavior — or at least one ought to take that attitude and begin the wise and winsome practice of selflessness in action. Forbidden and selfish actions are also much like the "grey" color of *karma* studied on the previous chart. Their unwholesome combination is responsible for both primal error in action, and the resultant confusion around all such errors.

A quick look at the bullet points of *vikarma* (chart on page 213) will reveal that it is not a good idea to act when the mind is angry, indeterminate, heedless, rebellious, or under the influence of the six passions and eight fetters. Also, the mind should be schooled in teachings on the three gunas (see charts on pages 307) by the *guru*, for if an ability to gauge the mind's moods is acquired, the art of knowing when to act and when to refrain from action begins to mature. This attribute verily epitomizes the wise sage who, refraining from sporadic and compulsive behavior, lives *karma*-free in a balanced state of mind. The triple combination of knowing when to act and when not to, knowing what acts to do and what acts to refrain from, and both of these brought about under the protective mantle of engaging in action with a quiescent mind, ensures that the *karma yogi/yogini* will not run afoul of *vikarma yoga*. Of course, the person who constantly suffers from the effects of doing otherwise is the fool who revolves on the wheel of birth and death in ignorance interminably.

Perhaps the most confusing and, "knotty" area of the *karma* problem involves what we have termed here "self-motivated" actions. Not only is the attitude difficult to work with, but so is the explanation. That is, most beings must naturally use motivation to propel them into various forms of success in works, and to keep the body/mind mechanism away from slothfulness and apathy. They will not see the sense nor the efficacy of working without motive. But motive is different from energy. It is not that energy goes away in the case of the motiveless worker, but that it gets both purified and subtly directed. The superior attitude of the selfless worker is that work must be done as worship (*karma yoga*), study undertaken as sacrifice (*jnana yoga*), duty offered as devotion (*bhakti yoga*), and all action performed as meditation (*dhyana* or *raja yoga*). These four *yogas* define the word "motiveless," wherein everything accomplished is for the Lord and Mother of the Universe, for Divine Reality, for God dwelling in living beings, knowingly or unknowingly. So, it is not just to escape recurrent *karmic* effects that the spiritually informed worker dashes his motives, but more that it is the best thing to do for all involved — including oneself.

Looking at this category from the other side, and utilizing the bullet points on the chart, in becomes evident that the worker who is "akamai" (in the know) draws back not only from doing actions in anger, greed, etc., (the faults of the *vikarmi*), but avoids performing work for any selfish reason whatsoever. Even fruits rising from actions are held at arms length, for grasping and holding to the self is contrary to the rules of *Karma Yoga*, and will bring down all manner of adverse situations on his head. These he would rather avoid, thereby "keeping the peace." For peace of mind is requisite to all higher attainments — from earthly to intellectual to spiritual. (see chart on page 443)

There is another very good reason for the *yogic* practitioner to adhere to motiveless action. The mental confusion and incertitude that always accompanies human beings in their life of desire, struggle, and attainment, will be absent in that mind which thinks only in terms of service and Self-realization. "Service while in the body, Self-realization after" seems to be his or her credo. And it is not that Enlightenment is not an ever-present verity, as we shall see in forthcoming chapters, but rather that action and Enlightenment are often at odds with one another, naturally. One may be able to act in an enlightened state, no doubt, but it will not be possible to remain in the stateless state of nondual *Samadhi* (see chart on page 427) and engage in work at the same time, for the former takes away all attention from the physical and mental levels of existence, and even vaults the soul beyond the religious, philosophical, and spiritual levels. It is conditionless, this Essence of Existence. There will be exceptional souls who can put off their experience of nondual *Samadhi* in order to serve humanity, but after the play of relativity is over there will remain no doubt as to where that soul is "heading." The entire matter revolves around whether or not the soul can reach There.

Swami Vivekananda has said that all work is only for purification of the mind, to make it fit for knowledge. Whereas the ill-informed *karmi* is out for himself, is seeking glory and fame, and gets attached to his wealth and his conquests, the *akarmi* is busy burning all his actions and their results in the fire of knowledge. His secret is "I do nothing." There is none of the ego or the glory or fame seeker in the enlightened person, then. And in fact, he makes an offering of all such things to the fire god every day, ending his night in the fine and fettle condition called peace of mind. The result is no regrets, no oversights, and no confusion — which is not the case of the selfish worker — and no loose ends left untied which might snap back later and bind him to the embodied condition once more. The *akarmi* breaks the chains of rebirth, then, by tackling the one *yoga* which, while it may not be the hardest to master, is certainly the most enigmatic to encounter and neutralize.

Though many of the dynamics of *Karma Yoga* have been touched upon by scrutinizing the bottom half on this chart, a brief condensation of all of them would be helpful. It amounts to: work done to perfection but free of selfish grasping; work performed free of the mind's tendency to have and to hold; maintenance of works that are *dharmic* and which have salutary effects on humanity; work executed with an equanimous mind which is neutral to all outcomes; steadiness in works in the face of all triumphs and failures; work done as an offering to God and as a sacrifice to humanity; and work performed in the knowledge that the true Soul of mankind is inactive. This watch-list of *Karma Yoga* directives conducts the practitioner safely along the path of action leading to purification of mind; also, the acquisition of higher knowledge, and a final and consummate understanding of the stationary and all-pervasive nature of Reality.

Some of the complexities of the *yoga* of action, taken up mainly so that the soul can both purify and transcend action, will be better placed in perspective by the following chart — a fitting testament with which to end this chapter. Through its teachings the advancing student can infer the levels, problems, and solutions that the seers espy and propose, as well as the desirability of traversing and transcending all the various levels of activity or, as *Raja Yoga* puts it, of rendering the entire field of action free of seed vibrations which may rise up and fructify in countless ways in the future. For, as Swami Abhedananda, one of Sri Ramakrishna's monastic disciples, observes (chart on page 216), the human being only simulates a mere machine by submitting to the arena of constant and countless works devoid of any inward refection, and ends up tired, disillusioned, and disappointed when no higher ends are attained through them. The purpose of human existence is not work, then. One cannot get to the Absolute through relative means. If it really wants freedom, the mind must ascend to the Spirit, not descend into matter. As Swami Vivekananda has so astutely concluded: *"Instead of materializing the Spirit, i.e., dragging the spiritual to the material plane, convert the matter into Spirit, and try to live in it day and night."* It is this which the wise and well-informed *yogi* and *yogini* attempt to do, and the wise philosophy of *Karma Yoga* is ready and able to assist.

Both serious and humorous, the images on this chart demonstrate a variety of predilections with regards to work and activity. These should be taken up so that striving human souls can begin

Karma Yoga – The Philosophy of Work

Work as Worship, Labor as Love, Service as Sacrifice

"Ordinarily, we make ourselves like machines, laboring without cessation until at last we grow weary, discouraged, and unhappy. When, however, we realize that there is within us something which transcends all activities, which is unchanging, immovable, and eternally at rest, then we accomplish our daily tasks without discouragement or loss of strength, because we have learned the great philosophy of work." — Swami Abhedananda

The Hovel of Heinous Acts

"The demonic know not what to do or what to refrain from. Bound by a hundred ties of hope, given over to lust and anger, they strive to secure by unjust means hoards of wealth for sensual enjoyment." — Sri Krishna

Exacerbated Karma

The Shanty of Selfish Works

"Once a man took up residence in an old hut. Soon, the winds began to shake it. The man remembered that Hanuman was the son of the god of the winds and so he prayed to him. Still the winds did not abate. Next, he remembered that Hanuman was the devotee of Ram whose younger brother was Lakshmana and he declared, 'This hut is Lakshmana's.' The winds continued. Finally, the man cried out, 'This is Ram's hut,' but the winds blew stronger. As the hut began to collapse, the man rushed from the hut with a curse, yelling, 'This is the devil's hut.'" — Sri Ramakrishna

Accrued Karma

The Domicile of Dire Duty

"Do not work yourself out. It is of no use. Duty is the midday sun whose fierce rays are burning the very vitals of humanity. It is necessary for a time as a discipline; beyond that it is a morbid dream." — Swami Vivekananda

Recurrent Karma

The Castle of Charitable Concerns

"Do not think lightly of merit, saying, 'It will not come to me.' By the constant fall of water drops, a pitcher is filled; likewise, the wise person, accumulating merit little by little, becomes full of merit." — Lord Buddha

Attenuated Karma

The Sanctuary of Selfless Service

"A flash of lightning is seen in a window pane, but not in the wooden shutters. Only the pure of mind can see God in others and serve Him there. In such beings spiritual power gets awakened, and liberation is attained." — Sri Sarada Devi, the Holy Mother

Neutralized Karma

The Abode of Action in Inaction

"There are two birds, closely related and very much alike, which perch on the same tree. One of them eats ripe fruits. The other, however, refrains from eating any fruits. It only watches as a spectator." — Svetashvataropanisad

Dissolved Karma

to perceive the difference between *karma* that is suffering-prone, and works which are offered as sacrifice in selfless service, and without any motive at all.

At the top of this gradated view, then, is the Hut of Heinous Acts. The image follows one of Sri Ramakrishna stories about two men who, while digging in the ground, came upon a locked wooden box buried there. Greed rose in both of their minds, despite their friendship, and a tug of war accompanied by many sulphurous oaths aimed at one another, ensued, the outcome of which saw the box splitting in two and a bunch of rusty iron spilling out on the ground. Such are heinous acts, enacted out of base passion with unfortunate results — and productive of ongoing or exacerbated *karmas*.

The Shanty of Selfish Works is not much better. By way of the illustration on the chart, a worldly man runs here and there looking for any trace of peace in the world. At home his wife is ready to swat him with a broom; on the street the loan shark is looking to beat him with a shoe; and at work the boss is waiting to threaten him with a shovel. In brief, all works that he has done have been actuated in the atmosphere of selfishness. This ground is rife with accrued *karma* which must be paid in full at some time or another. He has not yet learned to do his basic duty, what to speak of selfless actions.

The Domicile of Dire Duty is an insidious place to fall. It is the monotonous working out of constantly accruing *karma*. Habit and convention are the key words here, all suffered in the atmosphere of continually surfacing contentions. It is a lifeless land, and very mechanical. To repeat, as Swami Vivekananda has written: *"It is the tendency to bring everything down to the level of a machine that has given the West its wonderful prosperity. And it is this which has driven away all religion from its doors. Even the little that is left, the West has reduced to a systematic drill."*

It is when the soul reaches the Castle of Charitable Concerns that *karma* has a chance of being reduced. Here, the human being is thinking of others, or beginning to. He sees the desirability of contributing to the society he inhabits, even if only for reasons of practicality. As the quote from Lord Buddha under this heading relates, all that the soul does is now seen as *dharma* drops in a bucket which will soon get filled. He will be the richer and the wiser if he is generous and selfless. And this new attitude will also open up the door to freedom from the cause and effect cycle.

This freedom signals arrival at the Sanctuary of Selfless Service. There is hardly a level of existence so fine, so rarefied. The effects of actions done have become nonexistent, neutralized in the press of purification of mind and the attainment of an actual spiritual life. *Dharma* asked him to work for the good of others. Spiritual life has him serving God in others. And, as Sri Ramakrishna has said, *"If one pleases God first, then all become pleased."*

The Abode of Action in Inaction is hardly comprehendible — even to those rare few who attain and inhabit it. Difficult to perceive in its transparent and invisible workings, it is enigmatic due to its lack of any and all movement that is not performed in the nondual state of mind. This marvelous state is not only free of *karma*, but alien to its very presence, even conceptually. The soul who resides there is free, and any action he or she decides to undertake is done in full knowledge of the ultimately illusory or empty nature of work, action, and movement — and of the world.

A full rendering of rebirth, *samskaras*, desire, and *karma* has made up chapter four. In the next chapter an inspection of many of the results of these four relative laws will be undertaken, for these results are both the effects of matters left unresolved, and the cause of trials and challenges yet to come — many of them, as we shall see, wholly unnecessary.

Footfalls of the Indian Rishis:
— Chapter Five —

Walking Backwards
Ignorance and its Fractious Family of Fetters

Thus far in this collection of footfalls left by the ancient Indian *Rishis*, and to recap, we have scrutinized the three main considerations of the minds of illumined souls: *Brahman*, or divine Reality; *Maya*, or the appearance of name, form, time, space, and causation over the changeless *Brahman*; and *Atman*, the Indivisible Soul of mankind. Acknowledging these three, the conclusion must be that all beings must perceive, utilize, or deal with, as the case may be, the undeniable existence of Reality, the inscrutable presence of obscuration and distortion, and the great boon of self-effort which removes ignorance. Those who fail or refuse to do so must pay the piper in the form of twisted life-tunes like regression, backsliding, karma, and constantly impeded progress — an overall retardation of the soul, rather than the swift forward motion which was the soul's intent all along.

Walking backwards is a type of blindness, for a man's eyes are not in the back of his head. And in fact, Sri Ramakrishna Paramahamsa has said that *"The two eyes are seated in the forehead, but man's gaze is constantly cast downwards towards the lower centers of eating, drinking, and sex-life."* Nonetheless, and despite the pending ultimatum of death, there are countless souls who have made somewhat of a perverse art form of being able to walk backwards, as if they were born to suffer. In this chapter we will look at the soul's tendencies towards darkness and depravity, and the various tools which *maya* provides the misguided soul for just those lugubrious ends.

The chart on the facing page is a fitting one with which to begin our inspection of obstacles and impediments along the spiritual path, sporting, as it does, a positive message to counteract any pessimistic tendency. The first teaching is somewhat neutral, however, in that we find that the ancient *rishis* classified the human mind's progress in terms of three distinct plateaus: *Chitta-chinta*, brooding mind; *Chitta-lochana*, thinking mind; and *Chitta-bhati*, illumined mind. This summation relates that the mind visited by darkness only needs to activate its thinking powers (*pratibha*, or intelligence — see chart on page 272) and a return to Original Mind will be affected.

While the eyes pour over the aesthetics of this chart, and the image of Ganapati (Ganesha), the remover of obstacles is encountered, a rendering of the three impediments comes forth — a convenient condensation of all that ails one in the realm of spiritual practice. First of all, the obstructing presence of the sense of ownership must be removed, for *"It is easier for a camel to pass through the eye of a needle than it is for a rich man to get to heaven."* It is fine, as some contemporary practitioners are learning, to be a custodian of wealth, but any thought of owning or coveting will act as a positive detriment to the advancement of the soul along the spiritual path. (see chart on page 309) The sense of ownership also plays well with the sense of agency, as a human being's actions, particularly with the wealth he has access to, begins to develop a sense of pride in his mind. Selfishness, the old standby in this scenario, enters here, for soon, as one seer has said, a man will not think to give even a handful of rice to his starving neighbor, but will spend lavish amounts of money on mere incidentals for his daughter's wedding. Such are the signs — a few of them — of the insinuation of ownership and agency.

The sense of separation, however, is much more subtle. What is meant by this is the sense of separation from God. The disbelief in God is one form of ignorance, but the barrier which a man's mind maintains, and that acts as a line of demarcation between himself and Divine Reality, is much more subtle, and more difficult to surmount. As we have heard early on in the pages of this book,

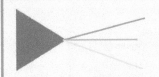

The Three Stages of Mind's Evolution
The Three Plateaus of Spiritual Evolution
The Three Obstacles to Self-Realization

The 3 Stages of Mind's Evolution

Chitta-Chinta — Brooding Mind   **Chitta-Lochana — Thinking Mind**

Chitta-Bhati — Illumined Mind

"Overcoming the mind's tendency to brood by utilizing its inherent powers of thoughtful insight augers a sure sign of spiritual evolution. Within the still and peaceful atmosphere of wisdom samadhi that results, the mind gets transported back to its original state of blissful, equanimous Awareness."
— Babaji Bob Kindler

The Three Obstacles   ### To Self-Realization

Vighna   Vinashana

Ahamta Mamata — Sense of Ownership

"I am the doer, my actions are important, I do good to others.... these are signs of the unripe ego."

Kartrtya — Sense of Agency

"Pride in one's wealth, in one's learning, and in one's possessions leave a stain on the mind."

Vibhaga — Sense of Separation

"Prahlada had two moods. Sometimes he would feel that he was God. In that mood he would say, 'Thou art verily I.' But when he was conscious of his ego, he looked upon God as his master and himself as the servant."
— Sri Ramakrishna

The 3 Plateaus of Spiritual Evolution

1

Shuddhi — Purification

"Ascetic observances, silent recitation, study of scriptures, reciting the mantra, surrender of all practices to God under the auspice of devotion — this is authentic purification."

3

Viveka-jnana — Transcendence

"The unwavering illumination of discriminatory wisdom is the way to transcendence."
— Lord Patanjal

2

Yoga-Sadhana — Transformation

"Ignorance, egotism, attachment, aversion, fear of death — afflictions like these are to be made progressively more and more subtle — reduced, and finally eliminated via meditation."

and as we will hear again towards its end, India's illumined thinkers have always counted God and mankind as one indivisible Reality, inseparable — a single and singular partless ocean of pure, homogenous, ever-conscious Awareness. This is the "good news" of *Advaita Vedanta* and other related schools. And although there are other views and plateaus, they are all ultimately figured around this singular philosophy of nondualism (see chart on page 379).

As we can see by our study of the first two thirds of this chart, correlations between the three stages and the three obstacles can be drawn. That is, when a man is caught in brooding, it is usually over matters concerning his wealth and possessions, and when he begins to think more deeply, matters of the intellect crop up for consideration. The same is true, as well, with the sense of separation and the illumined mind. Those dualities which are base, fundamental, and which are brooded over by worldly souls, are pairs like good and bad, pleasure and pain, etc. Dualities which take some thinking about fall more in the intellectual frame of reference, such as right and wrong, and virtue and vice. But at the level of the spiritually awakened mind, the pairs of opposites become subtler, as dualities like birth and death, bondage and liberation, and form and formlessness begin to foment in the finer thinking process.

Marvelously, whereas the human mind spent so much time in brooding prior to awakening, all that is soon forgotten in lieu of higher contemplation. Overall, brooding is an utter waste of time, useful only by the few who would gain control over the mind's tendencies and thereby work through them from the ground up. Its bare efficacy is over once the mind's faculty of intelligence clicks in of itself. And if a man's thinking process gets a further refinement, like when he sees the limitations of the human intellect and strives for higher wisdom, the days, years, even lifetimes of his nocturnal mental stirrings are over forever.

The lower third of this chart shows three plateaus of spiritual evolution, namely purification, transcendence, and transformation. Much has been shared about these three already. But in the rendition presently under study, another act of correlation reveals that the three plateaus correspond directly with the three stages of evolution and the three obstacles to Self-realization. To explain, when the mind is under the influence of the tendency to brood, and struggling with a false sense of ownership, it needs the power of purification to place things into proper perspective. And when thinking mind and its cohort called the sense of agency start up, *yoga-sadhana*, the power of transformation, becomes a valuable spiritual asset. And finally, when illumined mind becomes the norm, and the final sense of separation between the soul and nature and the Soul and Reality comes up, the ability for complete transcendence of even the subtlest pairs of opposites via the mind's well-honed discrimination arises. At that time the transmigrating soul (mind) brings all its stored-up internal powers to bear on life, and seeks to storm the highest citadel of Truth and Freedom called *Moksha*, or *Mukti*. (see charts on pages 343, 686)

In the previous chapter, chapter four, several mentions of the three *gunas* were made. Of all the impediments which hamper mankind's spiritual progress, and far before such progress or its impediments are even a vague idea in the mind, these three are the most difficult to detect. Both peculiar to and characteristic of Mother India's sagacious treasure house of higher wisdom, the system of the three *gunas* is not found anywhere else in religion or philosophy. Yet, when uncovered, inspected, and implemented as a tool for spiritual growth, there is hardly a more useful and powerful tool for mental, intellectual, and religious advancement.

The following two charts utilize many of the teachings found in India's blessed scriptures, while referring mainly to two of her greatest souls — Adishankara and Sri Krishna. In the first, on the opposite page, a graph appears which illustrates the three *gunas* — *tamas*, *rajas*, and *sattva*. Again, if one were to define these words in English, it could be done under the headings of both psychology and science. In the former, the mind experiences slothfulness (*tamas*), restlessness, (*rajas*), and balance (*sattva*). In terms of science, these same three can be termed inertia, energy, and stasis. Either way the meaning comes across, but for our purposes here, the former is most helpful, since the human mind can be stubborn and obstinate in its penchant for resistance and waywardness.

THE THREE GUNAS OF MAYA ACCORDING TO SHANKARA
(Vivekachudamani, Slokas 108-121)

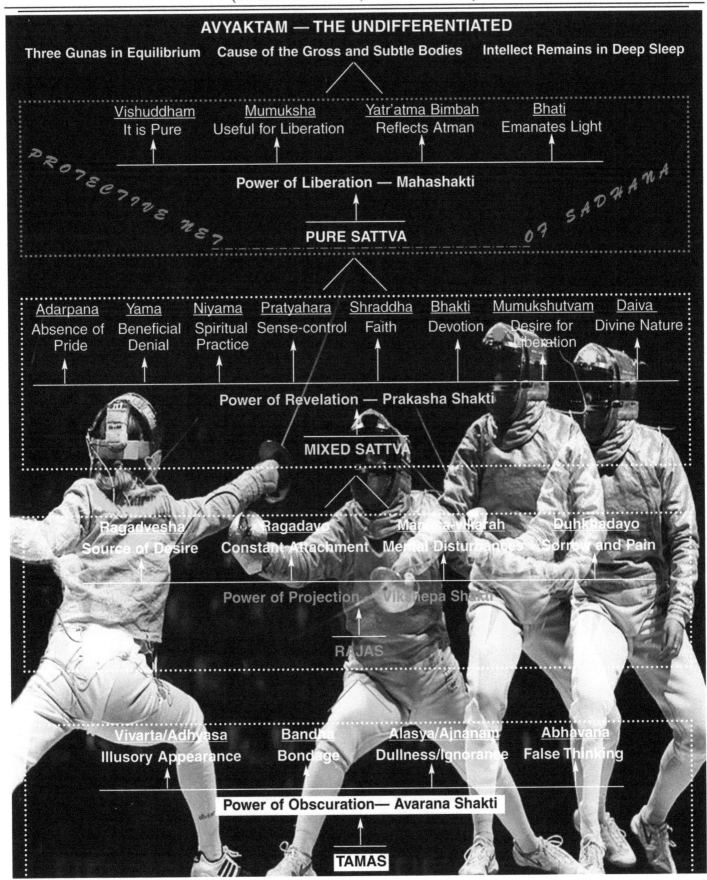

AVYAKTAM — THE UNDIFFERENTIATED

Three Gunas in Equilibrium   Cause of the Gross and Subtle Bodies   Intellect Remains in Deep Sleep

PROTECTIVE NET   *OF SADHANA*

Vishuddham	Mumuksha	Yatr'atma Bimbah	Bhati
It is Pure	Useful for Liberation	Reflects Atman	Emanates Light

Power of Liberation — Mahashakti

PURE SATTVA

Adarpana	Yama	Niyama	Pratyahara	Shraddha	Bhakti	Mumukshutvam	Daiva
Absence of Pride	Beneficial Denial	Spiritual Practice	Sense-control	Faith	Devotion	Desire for Liberation	Divine Nature

Power of Revelation — Prakasha Shakti

MIXED SATTVA

Ragadvesha	Ragadayo	Manasa-vikarah	Duhkhadayo
Source of Desire	Constant Attachment	Mental Disturbances	Sorrow and Pain

Power of Projection — Vikshepa Shakti

RAJAS

Vivarta/Adhyasa	Bandha	Alasya/Ajnanam	Abhavana
Illusory Appearance	Bondage	Dullness/Ignorance	False Thinking

Power of Obscuration— Avarana Shakti

TAMAS

And as Shankara reveals to us here in this chart under study on the previous page, that very quality may as well be termed *tamas*. It is the power of obscuration itself, called *avarana shakti* — the veiling power. When the mind comes under its influence, the characteristics which emerge are dullness, lack of clarity, an overall feeling of bondage, and the ongoing mistake of perceiving what is unreal or illusory as being true and real — and vice versa. And when the mind shifts, as in the case of an ignorant person, or when it manages to pull itself out of *tamas*, as is the case with a struggling soul, the *guna* of *rajas* becomes predominant and the soul experiences the realm of energy again. The problem with this energy is that it brings with it an overall sense of restlessness and an inability to focus. Frenetic activity is the result, and as we have learned from the previous chapter on *Karma* and *Karma Yoga*, actions done devoid of evenness of mind create negative *karmas*.

The reader is invited to study the characteristics of *rajas* as listed on the chart on the previous page. *Rajas* is the power of projection and distortion. Whereas *tamas* veils, *rajas* distorts. The mind under the influence of *tamas* has everything covered over, while with *rajas*, all is made to look other than what it really is. A detached study of the mind in even a few minutes of silent meditation will reveal the presence of both of these *gunas*, in turns. One minute a sense of gloom and lassitude will be felt, and the next, one of unease and unrest.

But a closer inspection, or better yet, concentration, will uncover the presence of the revelatory power of *sattva*, a welcome friend (although a fair-weather friend). This is *prakasha shakti*'s favorite atmosphere, and as one can see by the list on the chart, many nobler qualities come to the fore. However, Shankara notes that these qualities are of a mixed nature, not totally pure. And this is why *sattva*, until it is raised to its highest station, is a bit enigmatic still. More than that, it passes back into cycles of *tamas* and *rajas*. Further, when *sattva* is present it causes the soul to think that all is perfect — which it is not. This false sense of well-being lulls the soul into believing that he or she does not have to do their spiritual practice, and this is a subtle but fatal stroke to life overall.

Perhaps Sri Krishna's teachings will bring out more about these three *gunas*, or modes of nature, as the chart opposite (page 221) demonstrates. He couches his teaching in the setting of worlds or *lokas*, showing that when any particular *guna* gets a hold of the mind, and that mind develops a habit around said *guna*, that the outcome is birth in various worlds/wombs in accord with that *guna*. That is, there are people who are very dull and lazy, and they tend to be born together in the same locale. The same applies to the restless of mind. They gather around one another after death, as in life, and do all manner of sporadic activities with no center (like no God or Ideal) or balance. Thus he states, *"Those fixed in rajas at the time of death revolve; those fixed in tamas, fall."* These beings inhabit worlds of the blind and senseless, and worlds tainted by frenetic action, respectively.

Dissension, stagnation — what is the solution for these problems? As always, it lies right within human grasp, and under the auspice of each being's own power of self-effort. The pure worlds of the highest knowers of the cosmic process duly invite all who have mastered the mind's tendencies of slothfulness and restlessness, and who have latched on to the redeeming quality of *sattva* — balance, or equanimity. Indolence and pain are present in other worlds, but luminosity and purity are available for the *sattvic* soul. God does not dictate these choices. The problem of attachment to balance is to be considered as well, and for that we can finalize these two charts (pages 221,223).

Shankara's look at pure *sattva* decides the matter, revealing the difference between just feeling good, and being good. Pure *sattva* is the doorway to placing the three *gunas*, all modes of nature, into equilibrium. One then becomes *trigunatita*, and can enter the realm of formlessness at will. The *Mahashakti* stands as intermediary to this rare state, ushering souls into Her highest and most profound wisdom. It is here, in the unmanifested level of things, that the soul, if consciously communing there, can find the cause for his or her embodiment and neutralize it forever. Similarly, in Sri Krishna's teachings, higher *sattva* correlates with *Mahat*, the Cosmic Mind, or *AUM*, from whence interrelated but gradated realms of subtle and causal formlessness (like *Ishvara* and *Brahman*) can be accessed. A deep connection exists here, then, between *Shakti*, the dynamic power, and Divine Reality in Its highest Form (*Ishvara*) and Its pure Formless essence (*Brahman*).

The Binding and Liberating Nature of the Three Gunas of Prakrti

Ascension

"Those fixed in Sattva rise."

"They who have devoted themselves to this knowledge, having attained unity with Me, are neither born at the time of creation or disturbed at the time of dissolution." — Sri Krishna

Luminosity → Purity

Attachment to knowledge

Attachment to happiness.

Mahat/Brahma/Prakrti — Womb of the Seed-Giving Father

Brahman/Ishwara — The Seed-Giving Father

Sattva Guna

Paravidya

"From Sattva rises wisdom."

Stagnation

"Those fixed in Rajas revolve."

Pain ——→ Restlessness

Attachment to action

Attachment to desire

Kama Sangi

"The tainted worlds of attachment"

Aparavidya

"From Rajas rises greed."

Rajo Guna

Mithyajnan

"From Tamas rises error."

Descension

"Those fixed in Tamas fall."

Indolence → Slothfulness

Attachment to ignorance

Attachment to sleep

Tamasi Mudhayonishu Loka
(The blind worlds of senseless beings)

Tamo Guna

"When the seer sees no other agent than the gunas, he enters into My Being. Having crossed over these three gunas out of which the body is evolved, he is freed from birth, death, decay, and pain, and attains to eternal life." — Sri Krishna

To summate, the mind of a human being sports three modes of nature which influence it with regards to both progress and regression. These are named *tamas, rajas,* and *sattva,* and correspond directly to the *shakti*-forces of obscuration, distortion, and revelation, which in turn correlate to and dictate rebirth in the worlds (or wombs) of the indolent, nervous, and balanced souls. The first suffers false knowledge; the second receives mixed knowledge; and the last enjoys higher wisdom. Importantly, and as instanced in the two quotes by Sri Krishna, those beings who master and transcend the three *gunas* are freed from the trammels and sufferings of rebirth — a very admirable feat.

Both *Vedanta* and *Buddhism* — two very similar and complementary systems — speak of the desirability of transcending lives lived in ignorance, and with two very similar teachings. As the next chart up for study on the opposite page indicates, the *Buddhist and Vedic scriptures* refer to the six Billows and the six Transformations, or similarly, *sadurmi,* the six Waves of relativity. The constituents of all lists show many of the same principles, but the main point of the teaching is to identify the main risks of embodied existence so that they can be contemplated, comprehended, and completed for all time. In the case of most embodied beings, the presence of spiritual life and the principle of rebirth are never ruminated upon; for many they are merely a distant idea, or a theory. But beings like Lord Buddha and other confirmed luminaries have come to earth to opine differently, attempting to point out the dangers of repeated births in relativity using these teachings.

"Bear this body for the last time," comes the noble and thrilling command from the Buddha. The Holy Mother stated firmly, *"Birth and death are very painful. May you never have to suffer them again."* For, between the time-based events of birth and death exist other sobering considerations, such as disease, decay, and old age. These cause endless pain to the embodied being, leaving dire impressions on the subconscious mind. Even growth, usually so loved and lauded by all, is painful, whether it be physical, mental, intellectual, or spiritual. But do we have to experience it again and again, in constant cycles?

Then, there is the unrelenting and insatiable presence of desire-based, necessity-based elements like hunger and thirst, not only for the individual, but for the family, nation, and entire planet. Some note and mention how marvelous it is that all beings on earth get fed. It is miraculous, no doubt, especially given the overpopulated condition of the world today. But why does the Divine Mother feed all Her children? Is it just a matter of course, or for purposes of maintaining and enjoying human life? What if, instead, as the Buddha has said, that the first great truth about relative existence is that "There is suffering." Does the Mother who feeds us, then, want to perpetuate our suffering? Sri Krishna states in the *Bhagavad Gita* that, *"....in neither this world nor in the next is there happiness for those who are devoid of the practice of sacred rites,"* meaning lost to *dharmic* life and living.

It must be, then, that so long as any embodied soul procrastinates in its forward motion, hangs back and thus retards both its own salvation and liberation and that of others as well, that the Divine Mother, in Her infinite compassion, will sustain even the most rebellious and reticent of beings, sending Her sons and daughters of *dharma* again and again to attempt to raise them up and free them. And those who use the boon of food — on physical, mental, intellectual and spiritual levels (see chart on pages 423) — for purposes of living a *dharmic* life of service to others, and for gaining devotion, compassion, love, wisdom, and other divine qualities, will be freed first. They will be fed and freed! This is the art of sublimation of energy from the intake of food (see chart on page 584), taught by great teachers to their devout disciples.

But the lethargic being, the *tamasic* soul, will have to make its progress slowly, if at all, and the fruits of slow evolution are well-known to both intellectual and aspiring beings. Those who lag behind have not learned the lesson of inherent suffering yet, and have not gained the priceless possession called *viveka* — discrimination between the real and the unreal. (see chart on page 657) They are still looking at the world as if it were their oyster, as the saying goes. In this regard, it would benefit the aspirant after Truth to take a closer look at what some of the more illumined souls who have taken birth here on earth have to say about these seemingly beneficial but often times pain-bearing materials, objects, occupations, relationships, and many other elements of life.

Transcending the Six Billows & Six Transformations

"Even as the strong current of a river sweeps away reeds on its banks, so too does Mara, death, destroy all those with worldly craving again and again. These deluded souls jump from life to life, like a monkey from tree to tree. But whosoever overcomes the billows of relative existence will see their sorrows duly lifted, falling away like drops of water from a lotus leaf." Lord Buddha

← Buddhism   Vedanta →

Buddhism — The Six Billows

Mara — Death
Jara — Old Age
Bhranti — Delusion
Shoka — Grief
Pipasa — Thirst
Kshuha — Hunger

Vedanta — The Six Transformations

Mara — Death
Kshara — Decay
Jara — Old Age
Vardhata — Disease
Asti — Growth
Jayati — Birth

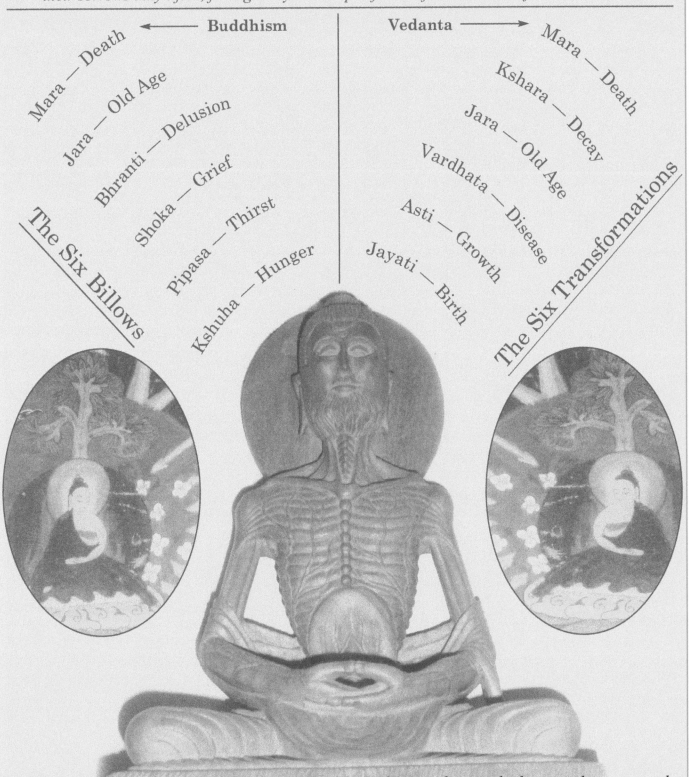

"Renounce all thirst and cravings, master philosophy and terminology, and take your place among the foremost of the sages. Bear this body for the last time. Think, 'I am the conqueror of all! I am the knower of all! I have relinquished all by the power of the Self. I am liberated.'" Lord Buddha

In the epic scripture, *Yoga Vasishtha*, it is described how the young teen-aged Ram, beloved of all beings of the kingdom, returned from his first pilgrimage to other lands very solemn and totally silent. Much like Gautama Buddha, who lived much later than Sri Ramchandra, the young Ram got a glimpse of the pervasiveness of human suffering on that journey and was stunned. In days to come he would seem entirely unlike the joyful boy whom all knew and loved so well prior to his pilgrimage. And the king, seeing his condition, and after all else had failed to galvanize Ram, sent for him with a decree to show himself at the great assembly hall one night, which was full of the citizens of the realm and many spiritual personages — including Lord Vasishtha.

What occurred as a result of this appearance was a thorough rendering of what is wrong with the world, an assessment of the drawbacks and inherent evils of the earth-plane, overall. The chart on the opposite page demonstrates, in condensed form, all that Sri Ram discoursed on during this unique event in time, including many solutions that the young but as yet unknown *Avatar* of the Age had ruminated upon since his timely encounter with *maya* on the pilgrimage. Gazing up and down the two left hand columns of the chart, those host of complaints are laid out, along with metaphors describing them and various solutions to consider. Further, but what is not shown, is that all of these dire circumstances and principles can be placed in three main categories: problems in nature; shortcomings of the mind; and cosmological imperatives, all of them difficult to transcend.

The problems in nature Ram noticed are body, infancy, youth, old age, and wealth. Mental shortcomings are ignorance, desires, ego, and mental impressions. The cosmic imperatives are such principles as *prana*, time, illusion, and false superimposition. The solutions Ram offers for bodily limitations consist of living a divine life in the world, service of others, self-effort, and the gaining of virtues at a young age — before old age sets in. Dealing with the mind's foibles would require gaining a teacher, cultivating discrimination and detachment, learning about the merits of renunciation, and performing intense *sadhana*. To deal with the cosmic level of impediments one would strive to view the world as *Brahman*, utilize ones energy for inquiring into the nature of Reality, meditate, and propitiate the Divine Mother of the Universe, the *Mahashakti*. The reader is encouraged to both read the analogies on this chart for poetic inspiration, and also contemplate the drawbacks of nature, mind, and cosmos. In addition, and for the sake of wonderment, the following excerpt from the *Yoga Vasishtha* scripture is offered, to describe a little of what happened after Ram's great discourse was given out to the fortunate group of souls gathered in the King's Hall:

"What transpired next there in the council chamber at Ayodhya is a matter of wonder indeed, and is practically unprecedented in sacred history. Out of nothingness, as it were, came forth a shower of fragrant flowers, and these began to fall on all the beings gathered there in that vast hall, to the amazement of everyone. Then, from out of the ethers above and around the hall and its inhabitants suddenly manifested the hosts of siddhas who, having been attracted by the enthralling address the young Ram had spoken forth, felt no other recourse than to immediately appear on earth and enter the great hall to pay their profound respects. The great assembly of luminaries, priests, pundits, royalty, courtiers, subjects, and servants, themselves scarcely able to breathe because of what they had just heard fall from the lips of the young Avatar to be, and all the more dumfounded at this amazing entrance of the famed and revered siddhas, immediately rushed forth to pay their respects. Visvamitra and Vasishtha were the first to pranam, followed by the king himself. And the siddhas returned these obeisances in turn.

After this reverent mutual exchange had taken place, and due to the many questions coming from the assembled group, this host of siddhas explained their rare and abrupt appearance there on earth, in that famed city, at that fortuitous moment in time.

"'We were floating in the akasha, enjoying the state of such an existence,' they proclaimed, 'yet underneath very dissatisfied with the painful separation from Brahman that our subtle state entails. The powerful wisdom-words of Sri Ram, suddenly permeating the atmospheres like so many beams of translucent light, immediately drew our attentions, simultaneously attracting us like nectar, and penetrating us like knifes. Finding that the very things that Ram was discoursing upon with such aversion — such things as birth, youth, wealth, lust, old age, time, etc. — were the very things that we were engaging with over inter-

Sri Ramachandra's Discourse of Divine Discontent – From the Vairagya Prakarana

"There is one thing that thou hast yet to do; give up the delusion of Maya that has arisen in thy mind." King Janaka to Sukadev

Tattva, or Principle	Complaint	Analogy/Metaphor	Solution
Vivarta - False super-imposition	Covers the Real with the unreal	Blue in sky, mirage in the desert	The world manifests itself in Brahman
Ajnana - Root ignorance	Source of all misery & suffering	Like a stone stuck in one's throat	An illumined teacher & holy company
Vasanas - Desires	Breeds attachment and rebirth	Like a diamond-pointed sword	Cultivate Viveka and Vairagyam
Abhimana - False identification	Causes forgetfulness of the Self	Like clouds that obscure the sun	Meditate on Atman within the heart
Prana - Life-force/Life	Is impermanent/ends in death	A drop of water falling off a leaf	Spend it engaged in Atmic Inquiry
Ahamkara - Ego	Root of worry/womb of karma	Rain for the flowers of desire	Renunciation
Manas - Mind	Root of duality/cause of objects	Wicker basket unable to hold water	Purify it and use it to gain liberation
Deha - Body	Subject to disease, age, death	A decaying house of inhabitants	Use to serve others & live a divine life
Jayate - Infancy	State of helplessness and terror	Invites the moon to come near	Transcend the need for rebirth
Vardhate - Youth	Dominated by the god of love	Like a deer falling giddily in a pit	Spend it in acquiring sterling virtues
Kama - Lust	Puts body & mind in bondage	Like dry fuel, it burns one in hell	Renunciation based on proper analysis
Apakshiyate - Old age	Renders one helpless and senile	A march of the armies of disease	Practice continence and moderation
Kala - Time	Devours all things	Like a serpent in an eagle's grasp	Engage in sadhana and meditation
Mayashakti - Illusion	Creates/destroys the 3 worlds	A tigress in a forest of delusion	Propitiate the Divine Mother
Kanchana - Wealth	Restricts true happiness/bliss	Like a ruby coated with dust	Support spirituality/dharmic family
Samskaras - Impressions	Perpetuates cycles of existence	Like many sparks rising from fire	Spiritual Practice/Self-effort

minable cycles of time, a great dispassion came upon us, and we knew we should abandon our delusion and instead seek out the eternal freedom of spiritual realization.'

"Turning their attentions on the silent Ram, who was now standing up but with his eyes lowered, the siddhas showered more flowers on him and duly proclaimed:"

"'Moreover, these unique words that this great soul has uttered today have the power of transformation within them, a power which both reveals samsara and steers the soul towards getting free of it. For, this maya that surrounds us on all sides, that even entangles the regal devas of the high heavens in the game of pleasures and possessions, is really the source of pain — whether that pain be of the type that rips through the nerve endings of the body, or that type which invades the mind and clouds the intellect in so many ways via the passions, fetters, gunas, emotions, and the like. If we had seen that Rama was entering into the enjoyment of such pleasures freely and avidly, and then embracing the various forms of pain that proceed from them, then we too would have felt fully justified in doing the same. As that is not the case, we have descended here on earth to gain true wisdom, and to discard our ignorance in maya, where it belongs.'"

In juxtaposition to Sri Ram's direct decree around human suffering, simultaneously dispassionate and compassionate, the aforementioned teachings of Lord Buddha can be brought forth. In his case an entire philosophy was created around the unwanted presence of human suffering, a very famous one called the Four Noble Truths. In the chart, appearing on the next page, the reader can take a good look at this, including its practical concomitant called the Eightfold Path.

In an enlightened rendering, the first truth of this radical system of awareness which declares "There is suffering" should better be interpreted as a decree about the nature of relativity rather than as a mere fact of existence. That is, one should not just say "I agree, it is true," and leave it at that, but ought to meditate upon the immediacy of this enlightened declaration and come to comprehend it as being part and parcel of embodied life itself. That is to say, and further, that not only should one affirm that suffering is in the nature of things, but also, that there is no ultimate happiness, joy, fame, satisfaction, or, importantly, no freedom in relativity, or in *maya*. This would tend to complete ones deepest ruminations on the subject, leaving the only thing left to do — renounce relative existence, post haste. It is not real (i.e., permanent, unchanging) anyway; only *Brahman* is real, or here, we term it Buddha Nature — *Prajnaparam, Tathagatagarbha*.

But there are other avenues of enlightenment left to explore, one being to delve into the origin of suffering itself. For, this will assist the compassionate knower of the existence of suffering to help others. An inspection of this kind will necessarily sweep one inwards towards the very first principle of creation, say, the ego. And in fact, if one would look at the eight-fold path spread out on the chart in front of us, and change the eight elements listed there to their opposites — i.e., imperfect view, imperfect resolve, imperfect speech, imperfect conduct, imperfect livelihood, imperfect effort, and imperfect concentration — one would have a perfect description of the human ego in all its suffering-laden implications. The passion of desire could be blamed for all of this, but where is desire if not lodged within the empty facade of the human ego, the self-constructed sense of "I-ness."

And so, to decrease and eventually do away completely with suffering, as the Third Noble Truth suggests, some spiritual practice must be undertaken. Note that this comes in the forms of morality first, an attempt at concentration next, and finally the gathering and possession of true insight. Along the way, freedom from fault-finding, selfless works, development of ethics, practice of the *dharma*, determinacy of mind, freedom from brooding, mindfulness of other's highest good, security in the self, absorption of mind in Reality, destruction of the mind's projections, forsaking all forms of violence, and the acquisition of mature renunciation — many of the practices, qualities, and attributes found in the other systems displayed in this book — are encountered and attained.

To conclude this brief look at the Four Noble Truths, the aspirant manned with this teaching knows what suffering consists of, i.e., the Five Aggregates of sorrow, lamentation, pain, grief, and despair, as well as what spiritual awakening consists of, i.e., the acceptance and realization of the teaching of the Four Noble Truths in ones life. All this is aspect limb of some thirty-seven other limbs found in the Buddhist path.

The Four Noble Truths and the Eightfold Path

"Recognition of the Four Noble Truths equals Spiritual Awakening; Nonrecognition equals Ignorance."

I The Truth of the Existence of Suffering —

Dukha

Sorrow   Lamentation   Pain   Grief   Despair

(The Five Aggregates)

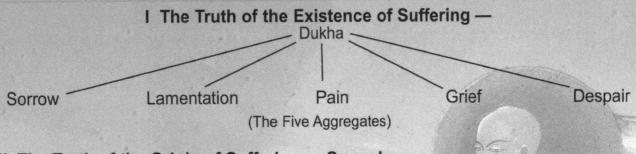

II The Truth of the Origin of Suffering — Samudaya
(Due to Craving/Desire)

III The Truth of the Cessation of Suffering — Nirodha
(Due to cessation of Craving/Desire)

IV The 8-fold Path leading to the Cessation of Suffering — Ashtangika-marga

Stage 3 **(Prajna)** Wisdom & Insight	**1 Samyag-dristi** **Perfect View**	Direct insight into the Dharmakaya Knowledge of the unity of all existence
	2 Samyak- samkalpa **Perfect Resolve**	The stilling of all mental projections Mature renunciation Goodwill to all fellow beings Absence of the desire to do harm
Stage 1 **(Shila)** Discipline & Morality	**Samyak-vak** **Perfect Speech**	Knowing the limitations of speech Refraining from lying, gossip, slander, etc.
	Samyak-karmanta **Perfect Conduct**	Abstention from profit-oriented work Conformity with ethics and morality
	Samyak-ajiva **Perfect Livelihood**	Avoidance of detrimental occupations Realization of the eternal nature of dharma
	Samyak-vyayama **Perfect Effort**	Freedom from conflicting intentions Accrual of good karma, avoiding bad karma
Stage 2 **(Samadhi)** Concentration & Meditation	**Samyak-smriti** **Perfect Mindfulness**	Freedom from vexation/brooding Sensitivity in regard to body, mind, thought
	Samyak-samadhi **Perfect Concentration**	Freedom from opinions Acquisition of the Four Absorptions of Mind

As long as apt comparisons on different systems of philosophy and religion are surfacing around the present topic of human suffering, another such system, very ancient, can also be shown here (on the facing page). The Threefold Sorrows is a teaching from the *Sankhya darshana* of Lord Kapila, very ancient, and vaguely reminiscent of Lord Buddha's Four Noble Truths shown on the previous page. And, ironically, or symbolically, Lord Buddha was born in the very birthplace of Lord Kapila, called Kapilavastu, many centuries after Kapila had lived and taught there.

There is a very good, if not rather esoteric, teaching around why the *Vedic rishis*, and Hindus today, chant *"Shanti, Shanti, Shantih"* to end their scriptural intonations. This "Peace" three times represents a deep inward prayer that blissful calm descend and remain over and throughout all the Three Worlds (*bhur, bhuvaha, svah,* also gross, subtle, causal), at all times. By examining the chart on the opposite page we can ascertain that by the term, "Three Worlds," the *rishis* meant to convey that, just as human beings have three bodies (see chart on page 161), they also occupy three general levels of existence, sometime referred to as *lokas*. It is to be known and acknowledged that each one of these three worlds contain within them countless other realms, much like planets in outer physical space, but consisting of subtler particles rather than atomic particles (see chart on page 33).

The Three Worlds envisioned by Kapila and the *Sankhya* system can be explained in easy to comprehend ways: there is the material world of external nature; the ethereal or intermediary realm of the lower deities; and then there is the realm of the mind. These are titled external, transpersonal, and intrapersonal, respectively. By noting the boxes in the upper-middle portion of the chart, the reader may view the lists which define these three worlds. And the reason why the conscious and sensitive living being wants to bring peace to these levels of existence is due to the many dangers that lurk there. From catastrophes in nature, to malevolent and wrathful internal forces, to the dangers of the uncontrolled individual mind — all these make real and lasting peace very hard to attain.

This teaching also accents the unique and sensible nondual *Vedic* perspective that all happenings in all worlds are not the doings of God. Rather, they are the doings of gods, human beings, and nature (*prakriti*). As Sri Krishna says in the *Bhagavad Gita, "The Lord does not create agency of actions for the world; He is not responsible for man's union with the fruits of action. Nature does all this."* In other words, and clearly laid out, God, Reality, is formless and inactive. "Formless" here means not found in any world or realm, and "inactive" means static and transcendent (not soul-less and sterile, for It is the Essence of blissful Awareness).

So, by *"shanti"* once, the peace-loving and sensitive soul asks for protection for all beings against natural disasters and threats from other beings occupying his world. As Sri Ramakrishna has said, *"A small germ can kill a powerful elephant."* Thus, unseen micro-organisms are also liable to cause problems. And by *"shanti"* twice, the conscious soul is shielded from designs that come from all manner of subtle forces existing in realms which fall under the jurisdiction of various deities, from mere celestials to powerful demigods and demigoddesses. Finally, by uttering *"shanti"* a third time, the man and woman of best intentions protect themselves and all others from intrapersonal dangers manifesting as diseases in the body/mind mechanism, or psycho/physical being. The invocation, *"Shanti, Shanti, Shanti"* is now revealed as to its deepest intent and purpose, covering the three worlds and conferring peace on all beings existing in them — if they will but claim it.

Since the matter of disease and its suffering has surfaced here in relation to the list of mental and physical ills listed on the chart, and though it will require a short deviation from studying the chart at hand, an important teaching regarding the origin and perpetuation of disease can be presented. This is a gift from the great Lord Vasishtha, appearing in the scripture, *Yoga Vasishtha,* mentioned and quoted from several times in this book already. Along the course of his schooling of the young teenage *Avatar,* Sri Ramachandra, Lord Vasishtha had to stop and explain to the youth the problem of disease. The divine discourse given to Ram that day was unique in that it skirted, almost entirely, all conventional thinking around this sensitive subject, focusing instead on the primal cause of all diseases, mental and physical. In Vasishtha's stunning but practical words, *"Rebirth is the cause of all disease."* The charts on pages 234 & 236 broach this subject matter.

TRIVIDHAM DUHKHAM — THE THREEFOLD SORROWS OF EXISTENCE

The Three Worlds (Triloka)

"Shanti"   "Shanti"   "Shanti"

Adhibhuta
Nature, Living Beings

1. Adhibautika
(External Dangers)

a) From Nature:
  Floods
  Earthquakes
  Plagues
  Famine

b) From Living Beings:
  Micro-organisms
  Insects
  Animals
  Human Beings

Adhidaiva
Celestial, Gods/Devas

2. Adhidaivika
(Transpersonal Dangers)

a) Lower Realms:
  Ghosts & Spirits
  Asuras
  Enemies
  Ancestors

b) Higher Realms:
  Demigods
  Siddhis
  Devas
  Devis

Adhyatma
Mental / Internal

3. Adhyatmika
(Intrapersonal Dangers)

a) Mental:
  Desire, Passion, Jealousy,
  Fear, Greed, Depression...

b) Physical Imbalances:
  Datus — Constituents
  (blood, flesh, bones, air,
  bile, phlegm)
  Rasas — Fluid essences
  (hormones, gastric, etc.)
  Karanas —Senses/Mind
  (Active & cognitive)

TRIVIDHO BANDHAH — THE THREE CAUSES OF BONDAGE

1. **Prakrtika Bandha**
(Identification with the Eight Prakrtis)

2. **Vaikrtika Bandha**
(Bondage to the Objects of the Senses)

3. **Dakshina Bandha**
(Involvement in Career, Success, & Wealth)

TRIVIDHO MOKSHA — THE THREE KINDS OF LIBERATION

1. Arising from Transcendence of
Prakrti and the Pairs of Opposites

2. Arising from the Elimination
of all Attachments

3. Arising from the Expansion
of Knowledge

ASTADHAH SIDDHIH
THE 8 GREAT ACCOMPLISHMENTS

1-3. Attaining the Three Primary Siddhis (Removal of the Threefold Sorrows)

4-8. Attaining the Five Secondary Siddhis (Means to removing the Three Sorrows)

1) Contemplation of a Traditional Religion

2) In-depth Study of the Wisdom Scriptures

3) Acquisition & Comprehension of Knowledge from the Scriptures

4) Gaining Guru, Path, & Disciples/Students/Friends/Compatriots

5) Attaining Self-Purification Leading to Self-Realization

*"May you fly to refuge in the Great Devi, who will cut the knot of this world asunder
and free you from the threefold sorrows of existence."* Srimad Devi Bhagavatam

In answer to Sri Ram's pertinent question, *"What is the origin of disease,"* asked under the sincere auspice of his deep compassion for all suffering souls, Lord Vasishtha answers concisely and directly, *"The origin of all disease begins in the mind."* For, it is the mind which goes from birth to death and back to rebirth again, as we have seen in the previous chapter, and only so long as it has not settled its desires, attachments, *karmas*, and *samskaras*. And the two categories listed on this chart signify this clearly — one as the essential cause and the other as secondary causes. The essential cause, of course, is rebirth itself. If there is no head there can be no headache, as the saying goes. So with the emergence of the body comes all manner of possibilities for *"the march of the armies of disease."*

Held back in the mind, as we have seen from earlier teachings (see charts on page 167, 170) are all the seeds of various illnesses, both mental and physical. As many healers nowadays relate, there is not one disease that has ever really been cured; they have all just left the surface of things, called the body, and either disappear only momentarily or metamorphose into another form of disease. Therefore, the seeker searching for the causes of problems needs to look under the surface for answers. This is where the second category of causes, called *samanya*, becomes interesting.

First up, and most important, is the absence of discriminative wisdom (*viveka*). This lack is the foremost of the primary causes for disease, ranking just after reincarnation itself. It is also responsible for the soul's rebirth to begin with. If this quality had been cultivated in a previous existence, either freedom from rebirth would have been won, or most of the potential manifestations of disease would be curtailed — which is the case in some rare souls we see who scarcely get sick or suffer at all. To put a finer point on this description, living beings need to be taught how to discriminate between the real and the unreal, the essential and the nonessential, at a very young age.

The continuing list makes this clearer, for next in line is the want of mastery over the senses with respects to their coveted objects. For, attachment and aversion are not just a problematic pair, but pull and twist the mind back and forth across the hot coals of indiscretion and indecision constantly. This repetitive torsion wears away the vital energy, the *prana*, which then weakens and knots up (see chart on page 206). Without the flow of *prana* to the organs through the nerves and into the muscles, etc., the possibility of illness is set in motion. Importantly, then, the immune system so often talked about in health-oriented circles of the day is not just of a physical variety, but has a subtle component that is both anterior and predominant to it. This is where to look for the subtler cause of diseases and, even more subtle, at the causal level, in the case of the absence of discriminative wisdom. And in the mind as well, as the chart shows, are these ongoing series of desires in waves, all stemming from the unripe ego and its unreasonable demands on life and mind.

From these three aforementioned direct causes spring all the results seen on the chart, along with a description of how the actual manifestation of disease rises and falls. Most important of note is how, when the thoughts of the mind turn negative due to loss of vital energy and its flow, a man's actions also turn negative due to the inability to constrain himself. This is a ripe scene for the production and fructification of various *karmas*. The reader is encouraged to study the chain of cause and effect falling under the category of *samanya*, diseases incidental to the body.

In the right hand lower corner of the chart is another list pertinent to secondary causes of disease, but even less direct than the aforementioned. These are the conventional explanations, like a mother's constant reminder to her child not to go out of the house without a jacket on in winter. Yet yogis live practically naked in high Himalayan caves in the dead of winter without getting sick. They are of a different caliber of soul than a youngster, of course, but that fact only serves to point us back to the development of discriminative wisdom. The human body/mind mechanism, when bolstered up by inner character as well as outer fiber, transcends seemingly insurmountable odds and obstacles. This character is not just of the nature of morals and ethics, either, but rather of spiritual attributes going mostly unknown to conventually-minded people of the world.

Nonetheless, an inspection of the indirect causes for disease will place them in proper perspective with the teachings of spirituality. Notably, they are all not physically based either. Many have connections to action and its role in causing disease in both body and mind. And the sincere

The Origin and Perpetuation of Disease

(From the Story of Shikidvaja)

Sri Ram asked:"What is the origin of disease?"

"The origin of all disease begins in the mind," answered Lord Vasishtha

Mind
(with inherent diseases)

Primary - Disease of the Mind

Secondary - Disease of the Body

1) Sara - Essential
Disease associated with rebirth }

"Taking a birth for the fulfillment of desires is the mind's first disease"

2) Samanya - Ordinary
Disease incidental to the body }

Direct Causes

Absence of discriminative wisdom
Want of mastery over the senses/objects
Inability to stem desires/egotism in the mind

Result

Mental delusion leading to
Mental disease leading to
Negative thoughts and actions leading to
Karmas leading to
Physical diseases

"Mental agitation caused by brooding, worry, stress, etc., weakens and breaks down the nervous system from the inside. Blockage of prana then occurs, which then flows unevenly, causing the nerves to quiver and the body to become infirm."
Lord Vasishtha

Process of Rising and Falling of Disease

Mental agitation weakens nervous system
Prana gets arrested and fails to pervade the body
Prana vibrates at an unequal rate
Nerves quiver causing body to weaken
Breathing becomes uneven and body begins to shake
Food ingested in this state turns poisonous
Energy from food is stymied and disease sets in

Indirect Causes for Physical Disease

Eating unwholesome food
Living in unhealthy conditions
Performing actions at inauspicious times
Evil desires & bad thoughts
Inflicting injuries on others
Association with evil beings
Longing for improper attainments
Distention and contraction
of the orifices of the nerves of the joints
Interruption of the prana flow in the body
Subjection to the five elements

By...ajnan married to mantra, they cease." Lord Vasishtha

...rough agit...on caused by lack of discriminative wisdom, diseases rise.

aspirant after freedom will have to study this formidable opponent called disease, and attempt to destroy it outright — bring disease to its knees. And that is what the companion chart on the facing page is all about.

In answer to Sri Ram's question of how to destroy disease, Lord Vasishtha, one of the foremost holistic healers of his time, and since, proposes cures which are of the Spirit and by the Spirit. Treating only the effect, as Western medicine is famous for in this "modern" day and age, will not go far in alleviating human suffering — something that a compassionate holistic healer has in mind first and foremost. Besides, such a being knows that there are certain types of sufferings, some of which are inherent to the embodied condition — which will never find a cure short of putting an end to reincarnation itself. Therefore, to effectively treat mankind's optional sufferings, mainly caused by weak-mindedness, is the focus.

And so, when embodiment is already upon the human soul, and these weaknesses of mind are already operational, methods involving medicines, herbs, exercise, pure food, and the like are a starting point only. Making human beings into healthy animals is a low ideal, particularly because man is not an animal, not even "an animal that thinks." Mankind is Divine, even though most beings have yet to realize this most important fact. Also, to treat a living being and then to have disease simply recur, or return in another form, is an act in futility, ultimately.

Therefore, the true holistic healer, who is also a complete luminary, will wisely instill within every "patient" the fore-knowledge of mental purification. This is primarily so that the suffering being will find a means to preempt disease before it manifests, though there are cases on record of beings actually curing themselves of disease by the inherent power of their own radiant mind alone. Whatever the case may be, this special wisdom that purifies the mind is called *Atmajnan* by the luminaries. A mind holding such diseases as confusion, depression, indecision, overindulgence, and the like — from mild to medium to virulent levels of intensity — can, before disease manifests itself, destroy them at the root, that is, in the mind, where they have their origins.

Ideally, this chart up for study (page 233) shows, top to bottom, the preferred way of dealing with illnesses. Unfortunately, this is not usually the way people proceed. They come in during different cycles, at differing angles, and with their capabilities in various stages of maturation, or lack thereof. Still, and to destroy the disease of rebirth in ignorance (*sara*, the primary cause), the consummate healer will introduce struggling souls to the presence of *Atmajnan*, the transcendent Knowledge which is intrinsic within them, so that real progress can be made in this lifetime. And as the chart indicates, where that is not yet possible, purification of thought, repetition of the *mantra*, and discerning reliance on medicines — best in that order —will be the resort.

The *mantra* and its power has been studied deeply in the previous pages of this book. Yet here is another use for it. The method here, as shown at the bottom of the chart (page 233), follows the route of securing the boon of holy company, i.e., the spiritual preceptor, and receiving the precious *mantra* in sacred ceremony. This *mantra*, besides its most important function in facilitating calmness of mind for purposes of meditation, is used to purify the food one ingests daily, at every meal. As the Holy Mother, Sri Sarada Devi stated, *"Pure food results in pure blood, and pure blood leads to pure energy, then pure thought."* With the implementation of pure thought over time, mind becomes pure, and *"Pure Mind is Brahman."* We will look at this more in depth in the following pages.

But first, there is another element or two in this process, that being the role of service and action. When recitation of the *mantra* is placed in context with service of holy beings (and commitment to a spiritual path) and the practice of performing only meritorious actions, all commingled consciously with the role of the aspirant's food intake, the result is a mind that virtually repels illness, and is thus indomitable. Coming down this ladder of true health, special knowledge of the inner Self expresses itself via pure thought, which when combined with recitation of the *mantra* results in divine life. As Lord Vasishtha states, *"Food taken in this atmosphere turns to nectar, but otherwise turns to poison in the bloodstream."*

To pursue this line of thinking further, another chart (page 235) is placed up for review:

The Destruction of Disease

(From the Story of Shikidvaja)

"The mind in its present state must be subjected to a regimen of practices that purify it of its tendency towards weakness and susceptibility." Lord Vasishtha

Mind
(with inherent diseases)

Category of Disease	Cause	Result	Cure/Solution
1) Sara - Essential Disease associated with rebirth	lack of wisdom lack of sense-control presence of desires	mental delusion, mental disease, negative actions, karmic accrual, physical disease	Atmajnana
2) Samanya - Ordinary Disease incidental to the body	negative thoughts	mental agitation physical agitation arrested prana uneven pranic vibration weak nerves and body food gets tainted energy from food poisoned	thought purification mantras medicines

Transmutation of Disease via Mantra

Mantra given by the Teacher ──→ To be utilized in life, uttered over food

Service of the wise ones ──→ Causes life to vibrate with divinity

Positive, meritorious actions ──→ Overrides negative karmas

Food taken in this beneficial state of mind conduces to perfect health

"Through mental agitation caused by lack of discriminative wisdom, diseases rise; but by Atmajnana married to mantra they cease." Lord Vasishtha

In relation to both human suffering and its end, and relative to the role of food and spiritual practice in a healthy, *dharmic* life, the following chart comes to us from another great luminary and holistic healer — Sri Krishna. Taking human temperament and disposition into account, Krishna maps out the various inclinations of living beings by category, shows what results they reap from their chosen lifestyle, and even gives a look into the differing types of austerities they perform. This is for the twofold purpose of explaining why people are the way they are, and how they might move out of slothful habits and begin to feel the peace and bliss of balance.

Using the three *gunas* (see charts on pages 221, 223, 307) as His system, Krishna reveals how beings live and grow, or stagnate, depending on their faith. The gods and goddesses, for instance, are *sattvic*, balanced. They are conscious of all that they ingest, act free of undue motive, are constantly bettering themselves and acting as examples for others to do the same, and only grant their boons in a timely way, when it will do the most good. On the other hand, those who fall into the category of weak and ignorant, called *pretas* and *bhutas,* are unconscious of what they take in, act in direct contradiction to universal laws, are violent to themselves and those around them, and if they give at all, give randomly and with evil intent, or out of complete ignorance. Somewhere in the middle, and under the auspice of frenetic activity, the proud and warlike beings take in sustenance that is pungent and acidic, do all their works under the mantle of selfish expectation, seek only that which will afford wealth and fame, and give away their gifts begrudgingly, hating to see others than themselves enjoy or benefit. To summate this section, worship, food, sacrifice, austerity, and gifts — these five categories, when examined with respect to seeing a living being as they are by temperament — communicates a full and complete story.

At the bottom of the chart under study on the facing page, another list adds to this wisdom assessment. The characteristics, attributes, effects of actions performed, and the path which they take, all transmit another aspect to the picture. The *sattvic* beings (which include men and women who have assumed god and goddess-like proportions while living), shine with the light of their own refined awareness, are happy overall in their contentment, sport knowledge without end, and always incarnate in pure worlds. Some even take their light as a gift into the impure worlds. Those beings who are violent, and who proceed through life via war and strife, verily radiate unholy passion, act continually with no pause for respite or wise consideration, have only their own ends in mind, and labor ceaselessly in the flexuous fields of futility. At the bottom of this ladder of *gunic* measurement are the clueless, ignorant beings who live in delusion, ignore the needs and benefit of others, are deluded as to the real purpose of life, and who make suffering their very lifestyle.

Can a human beings change their nature? Thankfully, they can, but only in accord with their changeless divine nature. In other words, they must become what they truly are, only having forgotten. As Lord Buddha's quote at the bottom of this chart affirms, some of the most notable and wondrous of beings have gotten free of the constraints of their base nature, and when they do, are the best examples of success in the realm of ethical and spiritual growth.

And there is a system by which these notables have managed this. It has been basically forgotten in today's work and money-oriented world. The Threefold Austerity deserves a close look by every soul who values progress on levels other than merely physical and earthly. For instance, many beings believe that any regimen of austerity for the body would involve twisting it into various postures and going on food fasts, etc. These are physical feats alone, with purely physical results. Even the mind's habitual attachment to feeling good about its healthy body is deceptively misleading. It could be called a confidence builder at one level, but if one comes to rely upon such techniques, the result is body-attachment and stagnation resulting in ignorance of higher austerities which totally remake the mental, psychological, intellectual, and spiritual levels of ones being.

With this in mind, and keeping the present materialistic Western model in mind as well, let us look back on Sri Krishna's salient advice and see what an authentic physical austerity of his time looked like. This is illustrated in the middle of the chart presently under study. And with a pleasant, if not somewhat shocking realization, we find that the real physical austerity is to use the body

The Three Dispositions of Living Beings

"The faith of embodied beings is in accordance with their natural disposition. Beings are of the nature of their faith; what their faith is, that verily they are."

Sri Krishna

	Worship	Food	Sacrifices	Austerities	Gifts
Sattvika Being	The Devas (Good/Noble)	Pure, Savory, Substantial	Motivelessness	3-Fold Austerity (**)	Selfless & timely
Rajasika Being	Yakshas & Rakshasas (Proud/Warlike)	Sour, Saline, Pungent	Expectation of of Reward	For Gain & Fame	Expectation with Grudge
Tamasika Being	Pretas/Bhutas (Dull/Fearful)	Stale, Impure, & Overcooked	Contrary to Ordinances	Self-torture & Destruction	Heedless & Insulting

** The Threefold Austerity of Sattvik Beings

Austerity of the Body	Austerity of Speech	Austerity of Mind
Worshiping the Gods	Truthful Speech	Silence of Thought
Reverence for the Wise	Beneficial Speech	Gentleness
Purity of Act	Inspiring Speech	Mental Control
Uprightness	Calming Speech	Fresh Disposition
Noninjury	Sacred Recitation	Selflessness

The Three Karmic Accruals of Living Beings

	Characteristic	Quality	Effect	Path
Sattva	Luminosity	Happiness	Knowledge	Pure Worlds
Rajas	Passion	Activity	Selfish Desire	Labor
Tamas	Ignorance	Delusion	Heedlessness	Suffering

"That one who formerly was dull and heedless, but after due consideration becomes mindful and vigilant, illumines the world like a moon set free from a cloud."

Lord Buddha

for worship of higher beings, sit it down for studies that will illumine the mind as to the body's real purpose in life, direct it in the field of action so as to avoid misconduct and acquire purity of the senses (which are a part of the body) and uprightness, and finally, and very importantly, follow the avowal of nonviolence to all living things by keeping the body in check and under ones control. If one can instigate such a regimen, then one is performing real and authentic austerity of the body.

Austerity of the faculty of speech is much easier of comprehension, though difficult of actuation. Keeping speech truthful is a beginning, and could be the only austerity of this type that one needs if followed faithfully. *"Truth is the austerity of this age,"* said Sri Ramakrishna. Once, this Great Master told someone that he was coming to his house for an event. The event got cancelled, but since the master had given his pledge, He walked a long distance to that place just to stick his head in the window and say, *"I have come."* Following the truth is more important than pleasing people, or even keeping ones word; it has a higher significance. The method of using beneficial speech to uplift others is noted here as well. This is a better perspective than saying, "Do not find fault or criticize." One can refrain from acrimonious speech, but learning the art of bolstering up the suffering, striving, and aspiring soul is much more efficacious.

And that leads us to inspiring speech. In the hands of the *guru* this is an incomparable element, as mere words become rays of light for illumination rather than just sounds of praise or encouragement. This goes hand in hand with sacred recitation, which is an aspect of the teaching which any sincere soul can engage in. One can lift oneself up via this practice, performed daily in the sacred atmosphere of the ashram or the home shrine. And then there is calming speech, useful at times when passion and excitement have entered into the otherwise peaceful mind. For, as we have seen in the recent chapter, actions done in the erratic vibration of any type of unrest or anger tend to deposit unseen *karmic* residue in the mind, which builds up over time and surfaces in the most unlikely and inauspicious of times.

This leads to what the luminaries point out as being the toughest of all austerities — purification of the mind (see chart on page 122). Before it is attempted, it would be practical to know what tools are advised for its operation and success. Silence comes first on Krishna's list, for a restless mind, constantly chattering to itself within (and outside, as well, via continual worldly talk about mundane matters), will never be able to purify itself. Of course, meditation (see chart on page 505) is recommended very highly, for it creates a habit of silence where the habit of habitual talking was present before. Also, the mind is a very complex and volatile mechanism. One must needs proceed with caution when dealing with it, which means that being gentle where necessary is best. However, where the soul is not oversensitive, and has inner strength to its credit, more direct and radical means can be implemented. This is in correlation with the ability to control the mind and place timely restraints on its tendencies towards externalization and, as a result, decentralization. More on the all-important control of the mind will be given in coming chapters of this book.

The final two elements of mental austerity are selflessness and the maintenance of a fresh disposition. Both of these are interconnected, of course, for one both supports and implies the other. Selflessness is refreshing in and of itself. It is so seldom seen that people are taken off guard and disarmed when coming into contact with it in another soul. Obviously, it is the opposite of selfishness, a simple fact which alone speaks volumes. Since it is rare of attainment and existence, it is considered an austerity of the mind, one attribute which, when missing, and despite the presence of other fine qualities, detracts from the soul's substance and effectivity. With regard to a fresh disposition, this entire chart has been about human disposition, and much has been transmitted to the thirsty soul by Sri Krishna's thorough exposition of the subject. This both explains the varying natures of embodied beings, and emits some light into these hard to encounter facts around human suffering and ignorance.

Bondages, such as the kinds characterized in the various dispositions of living beings, have an overall classification. This will be taken up next. These are termed The Five Cosmic Bondages in Vedanta.

Taking on a human body and mind has been described by the knowers of Reality as pure limitation. As we have seen in the very first chapter of this book, the act is a false superimposition of form over Formless Reality. But the body is only one element in this process. To be cast, often against ones higher will and desire, into the confines of this vast cosmic dream necessitates the acquisition of the another finely crafted instrument called *Ahamkara* in *Sanskrit*, the ego mechanism. Dubiously attended by the innate sense of possession and agency, what Sri Ramakrishna Paramahamsa often called *"I, me, and mine,"* this pervasive veil of individuality covers the knowledge of the nondual *Brahman* like a wet towel smothers fire.

To cite a brief condensation of what we have learned thus far in terms of the cosmic process and the suffering it brings, identification with *ahamkara* leads inexorably onwards to the assumption of four other coverings, each more dense by degrees, called the intellect, mind, vital energy, and physical body — the sheaths of *buddhi, manas, prana,* and *deha*. In conjunction with the five elements of earth, water, fire, air and ether, Nature thus grants and provides all that is required for the subjective and objective association of Consciousness with the realms of name and form. Equipped with the five *koshas* and availed of the five elements, the mind's thoughts, *chitta*, run along the many narrow pathways of limited and selfish desire, formulating attachments and aversions both randomly and willingly. Since the realm of name and form, indeed, all levels of the projected creation, are duly based upon cause and effect, ramifications are swift in coming, bringing with them the joys and sorrows of human existence, difficult of escape and of comprehension. Failure to effectively neutralize the results of good and bad actions performed in *maya,* and to disperse the energy accumulating from them, brings about the formation of subtle complexes that lodge in the mind's internal layers, rising periodically in the form of fructifying *karma*. It is then that what the seers call the Five Cosmic Bondages are in full operation, deftly impeding mankind's inherent freedom. The ignorant, scattered, and unfocused human mind, lost to its true inner nature, mechanically gravitates to this series of hidden calamities, and helplessly revolves there like wooden figures on a carousel.

Leading up to the chart on the next page, it is worthy of mention to state that the word "cosmic" has different definitions in Eastern and Western terminology. In Western Science it pertains to the physical universe, particularly inclusive of the vastness of space, while in the East it refers to this plus an entire realm of subtle manifestation inclusive of ancestors, celestial beings, gods and goddesses, and realms where beings maintain causal bodies. These are transcendent of matter, though connected. These are the causal realms occupied by minds that are still attended by the idea of an existence separate from Ultimate Reality. The realmless realm beyond, called *Brahman*, is without cause and effect, or individuation. It is the *Nirvikalpa* state, adorned by such appellations as the Causeless Cause, the Unmoved Mover, the Unseen Seer, the Inactive Agent, the Unmodified Modifier, the Unoriginated Originator, etc. It is sometimes described by citing the Unstruck Sound, a reference to *Shabda Brahman*, where vibrations of all types, gross and subtle, cease to echo, and Consciousness, unaltered and in its original perfection, abides as the only Existence.

Some confused Western thinkers want to assign cause and effect to *Nirvikalpa Samadhi*. But *Vedanta* is clear on this matter. In the waking and dream states cause and effect are in operation. In deep sleep cause is present, though one is not aware of the effect in the form of ideation and formulation. But *"Nir" "vikalpa,"* as the name implies, is unattended by thoughts, imaginations, fantasies, conceptualizations — mental projections of any type, or cosmic creation at any level. *Nirvikalpa* is to be seen in this light, not misinterpreted by the uninformed mind, which is ever-hopeful of life attended by various forms of individual existence and always fearful of formlessness. Those who rush to cover or alter *Brahman* only fall victim to philosophical error and misconception. This is why an inspection of the Five Cosmic Bondages is very clarifying. As the definitive chart on the forthcoming page illustrates, the embodied soul has more to deal with than mere human foibles and shortcomings. The entire construct of creation, what *Vedanta* terms "projection," has to be taken into consideration. Then only will the mind become pellucid and rid itself of unwanted and ill-considered overlays.

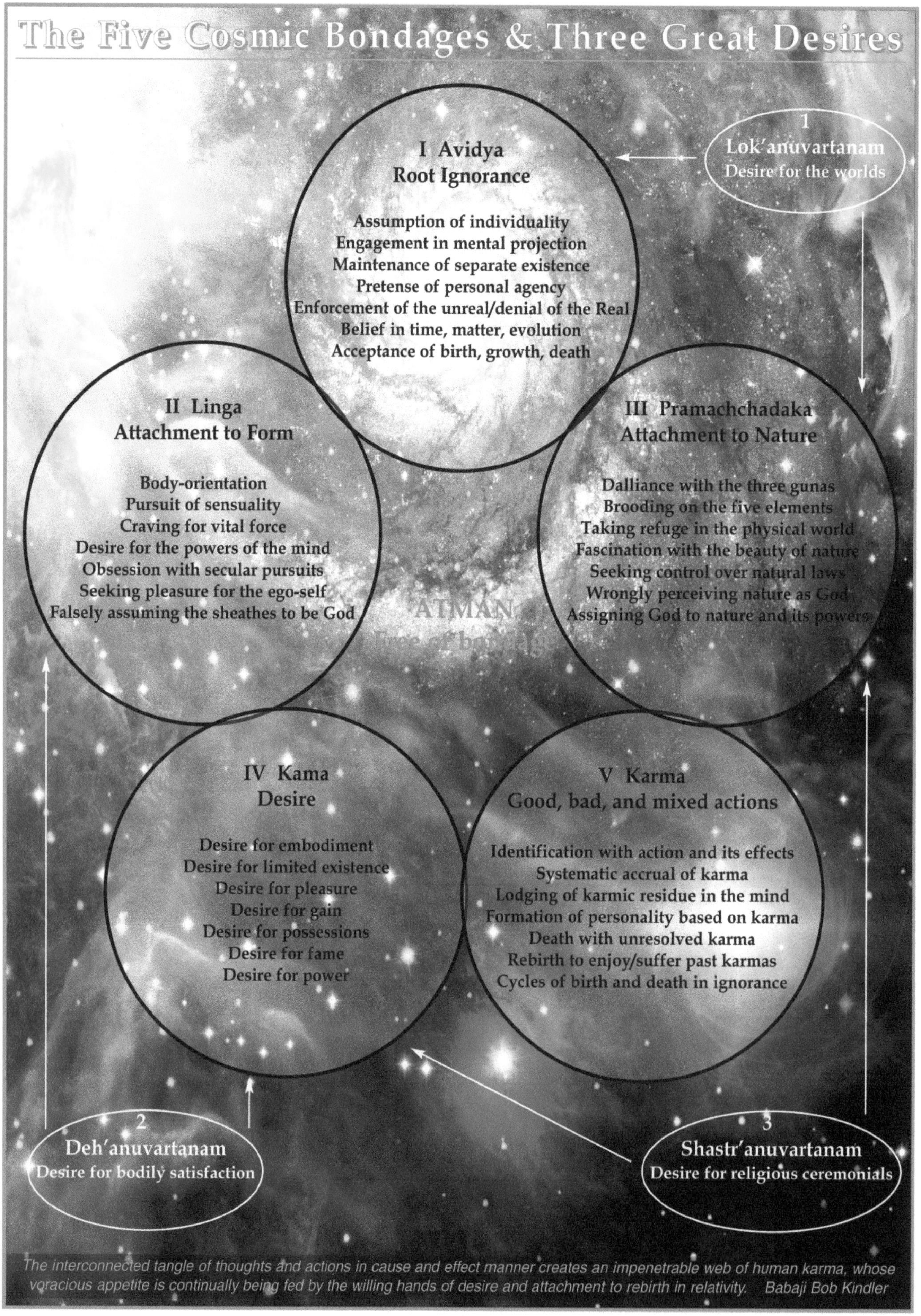

The Five Cosmic Bondages & Three Great Desires

I Avidya
Root Ignorance

Assumption of individuality
Engagement in mental projection
Maintenance of separate existence
Pretense of personal agency
Enforcement of the unreal/denial of the Real
Belief in time, matter, evolution
Acceptance of birth, growth, death

1 Lok'anuvartanam
Desire for the worlds

II Linga
Attachment to Form

Body-orientation
Pursuit of sensuality
Craving for vital force
Desire for the powers of the mind
Obsession with secular pursuits
Seeking pleasure for the ego-self
Falsely assuming the sheathes to be God

III Pramachchadaka
Attachment to Nature

Dalliance with the three gunas
Brooding on the five elements
Taking refuge in the physical world
Fascination with the beauty of nature
Seeking control over natural laws
Wrongly perceiving nature as God
Assigning God to nature and its powers

ATMAN
free of bondage

IV Kama
Desire

Desire for embodiment
Desire for limited existence
Desire for pleasure
Desire for gain
Desire for possessions
Desire for fame
Desire for power

V Karma
Good, bad, and mixed actions

Identification with action and its effects
Systematic accrual of karma
Lodging of karmic residue in the mind
Formation of personality based on karma
Death with unresolved karma
Rebirth to enjoy/suffer past karmas
Cycles of birth and death in ignorance

2 Deh'anuvartanam
Desire for bodily satisfaction

3 Shastr'anuvartanam
Desire for religious ceremonials

The interconnected tangle of thoughts and actions in cause and effect manner creates an impenetrable web of human karma, whose voracious appetite is continually being fed by the willing hands of desire and attachment to rebirth in relativity.   Babaji Bob Kindler

The five circles in the chart on the previous page might as well be subtle bubbles of cosmic, collective, and individual tendencies, which form a *samskara* in the composite mind of all beings, while the three ovals are the engines which fire and feed the entire structure. As a diatribe on name and form in time and space based in causation (*maya*), it is painful to see, but as a system utilized by a savior, seer, or *bodhisatva,* it is marvelous. It is presented here for the discerning and sobered reader and student for both reasons, seeing that such an examination should go a long way towards lifting many hidden veils and misconceptions in the contemporary mind and intellect.

Ignorance, or *avidya,* the first cosmic bondage, is a strange animal, for it facilitates the experience of individual existence while veiling the nondual *Brahman.* In its primal form, called *mula-avidya,* it designates and defines the very line of demarcation between matter and Spirit, causing an unexplainable rift in seamless Consciousness and giving rise to the appearance of the many. Aligned with the ego, it is the *"line drawn on water"* according to Sri Ramakrishna, which disappears almost as soon as it is traced with the finger, yet which momentarily parts the indivisible body of water into two seemingly individual sections. *Mahamaya* Herself, who oversees *Brahman's* power of *maya,* utilizes the ego of root ignorance deftly to project a variety of objects over a purely objectless Reality. This is called *vivarta,* or *adhyasa* — false superimposition of an apparent entity or entities over a single real and indivisible Entirety (see chart on page 751). A rope misperceived as a snake along the path at dusk is never a snake, no matter how hard the mind tries to make it one. It is an error in perception, pure and simple. Similarly, this entire manifestation of worlds is seen by the ignorant as a creation, rather than nothing less than *Brahman.*

And here, root ignorance takes another shot at the unillumined mind, attempting to convince it that unreal things are real and actual. But the Lord, Sri Krishna, the one who has made ignorance ignorant of itself, informs Arjuna in the *Bhagavad Gita* that *"The unreal never exists, and the real never ceases to be. The truth about both has been known by the seers."* As in a movie projected upon a huge screen, if *Brahman* is the backdrop and *maya* represents the various pictures playing upon it, false projection by the ignorant mind would be the various misinterpretations of the movie by its audience, and ignorance, the various misdeeds and negative thoughts arising after it is over. Something merely projected and withdrawn is thus mistakenly seen as real and, furthermore, twisted into something completely and erroneously fabricated — all when the mind is under the influence of *avidya.*

Thus we have what is actual, factual, and ephemeral — *Brahman,* Its *maya,* and the phantomlike projections of the human mind based upon desire, attachment, greed, and the rest. *Brahman* is the abiding Reality, *maya* its factual display, real for the moment, while ignorance, left unchecked and undiscriminated, creates a world of unnecessary suffering. As we have seen, *"There is suffering,"* stated by the Lord Buddha in His first of Four Noble Truths. On one level, it is all unavoidable in the embodied condition, being the nature of creation and relative existence. But the pressing and pervasive problem of compounded suffering caused by the unillumined mind is another matter entirely, and desperately needs addressing if one is to "remain uncontaminated" by the individual, collective, and cosmic overlays inherent in relative existence.

Root ignorance, *mula-avidya,* thus has its evolutes, many of them matters of misperception — what Patanjali, the father of *Yoga,* calls *Bhrantidarshana,* deluded insight. But these many evolutes — the six passions, the five fetters, the eight occult powers, and a whole host of others, soon to be displayed in this chapter, all arise from one factor: forgetfulness of ones true nature as timeless, deathless Awareness.

The Five Cosmic Bondages all group together subtly and insidiously to further compound this unconscious state, leaving the human mind lost in confusion and gasping for a breath of the everpure air of Nonduality. *Avidya* therefore veils the Infinite, while *Linga,* attachment to the body/mind mechanism, leads beings to grasp after the illusion of finitude. A further refuge or final recourse is then found in nature, *Pramachchadaka,* which finds beings further attempting to separate and concretize what is always and ever cohesive and homogenous by nature. *Kama,* desire, then easily arises and flourishes in this limited condition based upon misapprehension, a misreading of Reality as relativity, which causes attachment to take up its residence in the human heart and mind. Cause and effect, *Karma*, the fifth cosmic bondage, then kicks in, and the mechanism for cycles of birth and death in ignorance is then well-set in motion. As Gaudapada states, *"By waiting on, believing in, and brooding over birth and death, beings go to them."* On the other hand, the *Upanisads* say that *"By meditating upon the birthless, deathless Atman, the adepts and luminaries go to That."*

Avidya is also noted as the cause for suffering in other systems by other great seers of Truth. Patanjali lists it among the five obstacles to spiritual life, called *kleshas*, and it is found in *Buddhism* as well as one of the subdivisions of *"kileshas,"* associated with all unwholesome roots. To get rid of it is, unfortunately, not as easy as catching it early, for habit has already set in around it and maintains a vice-like hold on mental, psychological, emotional, conventional, and physical levels. As the *gurus* know and teach, once mustard seeds have blown out of the package they are extremely difficult to gather back in. So too, once all misdeeds and their effects proceeding from ignorance-based thought and action have been sown, what is sown must be reaped. It is *karma*, an incontrovertible law, and thus the fifth cosmic bondage, *karma*, plays right back into ignorance, the first bondage, creating a circle or wheel that rolls on inexorably.

This wheel, or *Kalachakra* as Lord Buddha called it, can be stilled. First, it must be slowed down long enough for the embodied soul to catch a glimpse of the predicament it has embroiled itself in. Such glimpses are brought about by attending upon holy company, conjoined with engagement in a strong and resolute spiritual practice. Unfortunately, many beings take these glimpses as an abnormality of the mind, an imagination, or a coincidence; such is the density of ignorance encrusted around habit and convention in this day and age. Others see them as a mere reminder of what is behind them, but fail to act upon them while the time is ripe. Yet all, except the free, complain bitterly about the ills of life, mind, and body, as if words of woe will do anything to alleviate them. Thus, Sri Ramakrishna states, that if a thorny bush pricks the flesh again and again, of what good will it be to just stand there and shout "burn bush, burn" at the plant. One must gather wood and set it ablaze. Just so does holy company and spiritual practice, rightly commingled, incinerate the weals and woes of this life.

In some schools, the term *"Linga,"* translates as a symbol of gender. In others, it refers to the three sheaths of intelligence, mind, and vital force (*sukshma-sharira*), which are particularly active in the dreaming state, fashioning complex worlds of *sankalpa* and *vikalpa* — thoughts, concepts, dreams, imaginations, fantasies, etc. This is the subtle body. Two other *linga*-bodies exist, the *karana* and the *sthula*, which equate to the causal and gross bodies respectively. Together, these three *"shariras"* constitute the coverings over *Atman*.

Finding themselves encased in this threefold psycho-physical straightjacket, beings cry out, like a baby at birth, upon the loss of unimpeded freedom and the assumption of the pervasive limitations that ensue. As Ramprasad, the poet-sage of Bengal, sings, *"Floating in the Cosmic Mother's womb all are contemplatives, but as soon as they take birth in the womb of nature, they imbibe matter instead of nectar."* This astute observation aptly describes the situation, warns as to its dangers, and should drive the temporarily embodied being to seek it Source of Being before identification with *"Linga"* becomes too fierce and deeply-rooted, and thus firmly impacted on the mental body.

Here, the shortcomings of parents, the shortsightedness of society, the inadequacy of contemporary educational systems, the narrowness of religion, and the hunger for power of various political institutions, all combine to embroil the uneducated soul further in the empirical process, making true freedom almost a veritable impossibility. It is no wonder that the seers call the way out of ignorance a *"razor's edge pathway,"* made all the sharper by the presence of the spiritual ego on the world scene in the form of charlatans, mystery-mongerers, sensationalists, occultists, and spiritual marketeers. And though much more could be revealed about *Avidya* and *Linga*, up to this point only these two Cosmic Bondages have been elucidated.

There is another allurement of the physical world which comes forward at this time, termed here *Pramachchadaka*, casting its chain of bondage over the human mind. This is the copious collection of potential sensory delights presented by Nature via the five elements. These, called the *Panchamahabhutas*, combine wondrously to portray Reality, but their constantly changing appearance holds both pleasure and pain, peace and chaos. Earth, water, fire, air, and ether are *maya's* deceptively solid playground, but as a mere molecular structure they have as their unstable basis a foundation that changes at a rate faster than a millionth of a second. In the shifting sands of this precariously vibrating world, beings attempt to build their permanent dwellings, forgetting the *Brahman*-bedrock of their true immutable and essential nature.

However, Nature is also and simultaneously a sure signboard of the presence of an underlying Reality. The five elements of Nature, when properly interpreted, speak to Reality, as does all of *maya*. The gross element, earth, represents the principle of solidity. Water, on a subtle level, is liquidity. Fire is radiance, representing the light of intelligence itself. Air equates to homogeneity, and ether to all-pervasiveness. As thought forms first, these five principles are the matrix for any creation — causal, subtle, and physical. Each have their chief quality too, with earth as sustenance, water as nourishment, fire as purification, air as transcendence, and ether as omniscience. Each element corresponds with one of the five senses (*indriyas*) as well, with earth coupled with smell, water with taste, fire with sight, air with touch, and ether with sound.

All of this, and all of the inner connections involved in it, are a marvelous and intricate weave. The soul, finding itself bereft of quintessential spiritual knowledge at birth, and anchored in the body/mind mechanism, cannot but rush to this beauteous display of Nature, engaging with a blithesome and indiscriminate abandon in all that it has to offer. Yet, if analysis as to the temporary and decaying nature of the body were properly undertaken, no attachment would form. If the constant ebb and flow of the life-force were noted, especially at death, it would be abandoned. If the ordinary mind's obsession with dualities was duly perceived, it would be swiftly controlled and dissolved. If the intellect's inability to act as the abiding light of Consciousness were revealed, it would be verily transcended. Finally, if the ego structure was perceived to be empty of any lasting substantiality, it would be promptly deflated and offered as sacrifice to the Lord and Mother of the Universe. All of nature would be transcended in order to find the one, changeless Reality.

With these three chains of *Avidya*, *Linga*, and *Pramachchadaka* ever-tightening around the indiscriminate soul, the stage is set not only for mere attraction, but also for its complete entrapment. The deer, attracted by the music of the hunter, falls into the pit and is slain. Like deer, living beings fall victim to *maya*, attracted by the cosmic and celestial "music" of bodies, senses, elements, and imaginative thought forms. These are fueled by desire, *Kama*, the fourth of the Five Cosmic Bondages, which plays its part in the perpetration of repetitive motive-laden actions resulting in mental complexes leading to recurring rebirths and deaths in ignorance. These selfish desire-based activities are *"frail crafts"* in the sea of *samsara* say the *rishis* of old, and those who man them *"fall again and again into the domain of old age and death."* As these wise ones stated in the *Upanisads*, *"Like corn the mortal ripens and falls, and like corn it is born again."* The thirst for life, then, left unbridled, is actually unquenchable amidst the many temptations found in *maya*. According to wise spiritual preceptors, that one desirous of freedom must *"....scrutinize the many worlds of deeds and become indifferent to them,"* for all that is originated cannot win Reality, which Itself is Unoriginated.

And so the spiritual aspirant learns to take a close look at the nature of desire. For those raised in contemporary Western culture, exposed to and influenced by both the fundamentalist climate of religion married to politics and military, and the secularized approach of science married to materialism, it would be wise to note that Eastern Philosophy makes a distinction between desires that bind and desires that lead towards freedom (see chart on page 180).

Before defining this distinction, however, it must be said that the basis for it rests upon whether or not the soul is resigned to the spiritual path and preceptor. In *Vedic* religion, self-surrender is one very important key which allows access into the gateway opening upon the domain of potential freedom. Conversely, actions performed in the atmosphere of willful desire, having only sensual gratification as their motive, only accrue to more of the same — like stubbornly pouring gasoline on a fire to try to put it out. Sri Sarada Devi likens this futile and detrimental process to the amassing of thread on a spool that is spinning only one way. But once the soul gains humility, commits to a spiritual path, and submits to be taught the Truth, all desires born of action, from there on out, get fulfilled, and the spool begins to spin the opposite way.

Desires, as we have seen, are of two types: the first which binds; the second which tends towards freedom. Everything that has for its main premise the negative qualities of selfishness, lust, anger, greed, attachment, and delusion — a selfish clinging to the personal self and a complete disregard for the highest good of others — is to be labeled binding in nature and is to be therefore avoided. On the other hand, when selflessness dawns on the human mind, reaching sweetly into the areas of both action and inaction, not only will higher good accrue, but lasting joy will also make its appearance in the human mind and heart.

And spiritual practice under the auspice of a watchful *guru* culminates here. This simultaneous increase of selflessness and deflation of the ego manifest through selfless action and absence of personal agency in *Karma Yoga*, through one-pointed devotion to a single ideal in *Bhakti Yoga*, through the adamant acquisition of knowledge free of possessiveness in *Jnana Yoga*, and through striving to transcend the sense of individuality and separateness in *Raja Yoga* (meditation). Desires, lower or higher, simply have no hold or ongoing existence in such an integrated setting. Transformation of mind leading to realization of the ever-pure and perfect Self is the result. But those beings who cling to selfish modes of action, who never practice disciplines, who remain bereft of devotion to God in whatever way they would see Him/Her, and who are devoid of reflection and meditation, their minds are a swamp teeming with the incubation of thousands of seed-desires, all bearing or soon to bear just ramifications.

Karma is the fifth Cosmic Bondage on the chart under study (page 240). As cause and effect, it has already been mentioned, but as a cosmic bond it has other teachings to offer. For there are aspects of *karma* which pertain outside of the realm of the individual but which nevertheless bind the human soul. These fall in the realm of collective and cosmic consciousness. That is, as a "cosmic" bondage, there is to be considered a special type of *karma* that birthed the entire realm of name and form in all its vastness and inconceivability. Enter here the cosmic level of bondage, wherein the entire idea of manifestation poses a limitation over the aspiring and freedom-loving mind of the human being. It might be somewhat easy to annul the individual *karma* that binds one simply by ceasing from negative action, engaging in positive action, and finally removing all motive from action altogether. But it is another matter entirely to heal the collective *karma* of the many who engage in a riotous array of activity on the multifaceted field of *karma*, what to speak of neutralizing that primal force which gave rise to all the fields — causal, subtle, and physical — all with their many abstractions and subdivisions.

And in fact, *karma* means action, which implies movement, and this motion extends to the mind on all its levels as well. Wherever there is thought there is motion. Only in *Nirvikalpa*, where no "*vikalpas*" are present, is there the original static condition of perfection. With this in mind, and measuring the initial creator, it is seen that transcendence of this primal urge and its personification is necessary in order for there to be true peace — an inaction appropriate to realization of the nondual Self, or *Brahman*. For motion implies a mover, a desire to move, an object to be moved, and an atmosphere to move through. Where is unconditional oneness in all of this?

Therefore, the consummate and successful spiritual aspirant must plumb the depths of existence right up to its first inception, saluting that cosmic mechanism and going beyond it into indivisible oneness. Catching sight of that original primal force in deep meditation, one must say to it, as it were: "Here is the body, the life-force, mind, intellect, and ego, along with all of nature, its five elements, and its many offerings — including the celestial worlds. Take them all back. I am through with them." This unrivaled feat, called true renunciation, is the sign of authentic spirituality. All else either fails the test, falls short, promotes compromise, or at best, provides intermediary support until the Supreme "Goal" is won.

In the same way that knowledge should be acquired before engaging in the field of action, just so, ideally, should transcendence of the cosmic process be achieved, or at least understood as a definitive end, before the task of working in the world to neutralize individual and collective *karma* is undertaken. This deep insight is really a concomitant of nondual philosophy, and comes forcefully to bear when the apparently individualized soul comes to know that nothing is ever really created and therefore can never be preserved or destroyed. With the truth of *Advaita* (the nonorigination of all objects and entities) firmly established in the receptive and purified mind, *karma* will be seen as a relative law, applicable only in the field of motivated action where beings consider cause and effect, virtue and vice, pain and pleasure, and other dualities to be real in and of themselves. In truth, the only Reality is *Brahman*, the Absolute. The luminaries tell us to *"Seek thee first"* that realm-less Kingdom, and refrain from *"serving two masters."*

The Five Cosmic Bondages is one of the most sobering and revealing systems of teaching found in any religion and philosophy, having gathered, as it has, the main reasons for both embodiment and its resultant suffering. Even if one considers a divine life on earth as the highest the human being can achieve, or the supreme mode of existence, still, the traps which might catch and impede the aspiring soul desirous of such an end are well illustrated here. Whatever the case may be, only lovers of Truth will take note of its premises, utilizing such knowledge like welcome lubricant to the rusty and frozen parts of human existence which have remained closed up for centuries, even millennia.

With such salient systems as this, given to us via the auspicious "Footfalls" of past masters, the embodied soul — either sleeping, suffering, or aspiring — can more easily and directly deliver themselves out of *maya* and attain to the highest realization. For, Truth ever triumphs. It is time to rise up and to realize It. Beyond the physical, the subtle, and the causal bodies, the seven realms of existence, and far outstripping the modes of the individual, collective, and cosmic mind, is *Brahman*, the Absolute. The wise tell us to accept no imitations, assume no limitations, be free of all permutations, and celebrate divine life and its culmination — in *Samadhi*. And in this particular rendering it is to deliver the Five Cosmic Bondages back to the fount of illusory projection and finitude from which they sprang.

To conclude this chart on the Five Cosmic Bondages, the teaching of the Three Great Desires can be pointed out (still page 240). It is a very simple matter. Beings take to *Lok'anuvartanam,* the desire for manifest worlds; *Deh'anuvartanam,* the desire for assuming and satisfying bodies and forms; and *Shastr'anuvartanam,* the desire for performing rites and rituals — religious, conventional, and otherwise. The first connects to and lives off of the cosmic bonds of Ignorance and Nature. The second thrives in the atmospheres of desire and attachment to form. The third takes its cue from nature and activity, though all three of these intermingle and play off of one another in the complex, confusing, and chimerical maelstrom of *maya*.

Inspection of the fractious family of ignorance in this chapter, so related to the pervasive problem of human suffering, must necessarily include a frank showing of some of its basic components. The next three charts, springing from the *Sankhya* and *Vedanta* philosophies, give us a close up look at what really stymies the human being on the level of his or her everyday existence. These contumacious insinuations on the embodied condition are the final results of the anterior subtle thoughts and prior lifetime activities which gave them their unseen and unwanted births, and they impede living beings throughout every day of their uninformed lives. A brief expose on them, though they are well-known to most, will prove helpful, and will accent the need to be free of them — as far as that is possible in the embodied state.

The Six Transformations and The Six Billows have already been studied in a previous chapter, though another quick look at them in a different setting can act as a good reminder of their presence and import.   The Six Passions and the Eight Fetters, shown on the chart on the facing page, however, are rather legend in *Vedanta* philosophy, being a well-culled and condensed list of all the *karma*-causing elements which the human being is party to in daily life.

Since this lachrymose list is dire of contemplation for the average person, perhaps a *Tantric* approach might prove more beneficial.   Here, it is taught that all of the six passions — lust, anger, greed, delusion, vanity, and jealousy — when harnessed properly in a consecrated atmosphere via an expertly adjusted attitude, can actually be increased to provide impetus for transcendence.   To use a famous example from the *Gospel of Sri Ramakrishna*, it was told that one of Sri Ramakrishna's monastic disciples approached the Great Master one day and asked Him how he could entirely get rid of lust.   The Master responded, *"Why try to get rid of it; increase it!"*   The monk was shocked to hear this bit of instruction and inquired after its deeper meaning.   The explanation was to turn lust towards a positive end by lusting after realization of God.   For this, the instruction is to take the poison of desire for earthly things out of the quotient and then utilize the leftover force in lust for spiritual practice.   Metaphorically speaking, this amounts to taking the poison out of a snake so that one can handle it.   For there is a great power in human passions, but it has been misused and misguided for so long that no one thinks outside of the conventional and puritanical levels anymore.   This lack of forward motion regresses into generations of guilt, and plays into centuries of intolerance — which we will see in the next chart.

This method of redirecting the force in human passion, if it works for the quality of lust, should also apply to the other five passions as well.   In that case one would increase anger by being angry that one has not realized God, increase greed by becoming greedy for God, increase jealousy by being jealous that others have realized God in the past and you have not, etc.   And we have seen, so often and in so many cases, how living beings desirous of freedom from base passion have attempted to stifle or repress it, only to have it snap back on them with double the force and twice the negative result (see chart on page 176).   A new way of dealing with this volatile area of human shortcomings is thus welcome, and the West in general needs to hear something fresh along this line in order to effect improvement.

The eight fetters are very much connected to the six passions, being an extended list of unwholesome elements which distort and constrict human life and behavior.   Illustrated here via a chain, the implication is that all eight of these despoilers receive their power from being interconnected with one another in almost inextricable fashion.   Hatred, shame, grief, pride, and fear are perhaps much better known to the human mind, whereas secrecy, pride of lineage, and pride of caste are maybe less so in Western countries.

Whatever the case may be, it is helpful for the human being — whether they be seekers who are looking to transcend their desires and passions, or ordinary beings who are presently struggling under the detrimental influence of them — to see this host of impediments displayed in one place.   Of additional assistance are the remarks of a great and timeless soul such as Sri Ramchandra, *Avatar* of the *Treta Yuga*, who summates quite nicely the sobering characteristics of the six transformations.   With a basic reading of such an excellent perspective in mind, a more careful and mature outlook on the dangers of relative existence can be had, changing the mind of the careless and impractical person for all time.   This is the stuff that transformation is made of; that is, if there is any real transformation going on at all, it is here, directly within the ever-fluctuating human mind.

And if this collection of undesirable negative presences is not enough to switch the present thinking of the worldly person to a better mode, some other tenebrous offshoots are also in the offing, as displayed on page 249 in the form of The Three Enemies of Reason, The Three Stupefactions, and the Four Deadly Traps.   Whereas the list on the facing page is rather obvious, this new list comprises elements that are more subtle, and which deserve a deeper look.

The Six Transformations, Six Passions, Six Billows, & Eight Fetters

The Six Transformations

Jayati - Birth

"Beings rush to welcome the birth of a child, overlooking serious factors like delusion and suffering which play into embodiment in Maya."

Asti - Growth

"The illusion of growth is one of the mayic elements which attaches men and women to the ever-changing realm of name and form."

Vardhate - Disease

"Outside, in the relative world, there are diseases which, though they have their origin in the subtle mind, manifest harshly in the body."

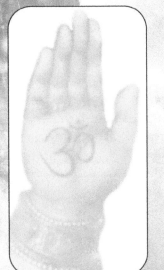

Sri Ramachandra

Jara - Old Age

"Set upon by old age, a man is hardly even able to contemplate the soul's passage to higher worlds, much less meditate upon Reality."

Kshara - Decay

"With the life-force literally squeezed out of the various human vessels, then comes the collapse and dissolution of the human frame into dust."

Mara - Death

"The grim reaper, Yama, moves among the young and aged alike, gathering heads like a farmer picking ripe melons during a seasonal harvest."

The Six Passions

Kama - Lust

Krodha - Anger

Lobha - Greed

Moha - Delusion

Mada - Vanity

Matsarya - Jealousy

The Six Billows

Kshuha - Hunger

Pipasa - Thirst

Shoka - Grief

Bhranti - Delusion

Jara - Dotage

Mrtyu - Death

The Eight Fetters

Dvesha - Hatred   Gotra - Lineage   Bhaya - Fear   Varna - Caste

Hri - Shame   Darpa - Prideful   Gopaniyata - Secrecy   Shoka - Grief

"Preoccupation with relative existence is to be transcended. When impeding factors such as the Six Transformations, the Six Passions, the Six Billows, the Eight Fetters, the Three Gunas, and the Pairs of Opposites besiege mankind at every step, all of them attended by constant change and pervasive suffering, how desirable can worldly life be?"   *Babaji Bob Kindler*

The previous chart showed us a list of basic human foibles, and ones which are intrinsically a part of human nature. But what is here before us now (facing page) may just comprise a reading of evolutes which, due to ill-considered actions, past and present, form a foundation all their own in terms of human behavior in general. That is, lust, anger, greed and the like descend upon all minds from one time to another, with obvious results, wreaking a havoc all their own. But in the case of egotism, intolerance, and narrowness — The Three Enemies of Reason — they are underground players in life, are subtle presences, devious in nature, which influence human behavior on the surface while remaining hidden themselves. The case of egotism is many-sided, so it escapes human detection via its manifold faces and movements. It is listed by great souls like Patanjali and Vedavyasa as one of the five main obstacles to spiritual life, to *Yoga*, which is reason enough to avoid it.

But the insidious underpinnings of intolerance and narrowness, like related cousins, manipulate so many of the thoughts and actions of human beings. Religious intolerance, for instance, is one of the most detrimental of negative qualities, responsible as it is for everything from alienation from society to wholesale war between nations. Even good, moral people fall victim to it, and to the hypocriticalness that always accompanies it, despite the air of appearances that they assume on their exteriors. In social and political groups it is a main cause for what has been described over time as the "lunatic fringe," wherein plans and decisions are formulated which eventually perpetrate heinous acts and deeds in the name of right wing morality. The downside of caste systems, present in every culture, is heavily weighed down by these despoilers, as egotism, intolerance, and narrowness team up in conceited individuals to cast poisonous aspersions, false judgements, injury, injustice, and a teeming nest of outright lies upon perfectly innocent people of less means and lower status. It is deplorable, this pestiferous tendency in the human mind. Worst of all is the overbearing habit which these three form, an impulse to gravitate almost exclusively to an atmosphere of fault-finding, criticism, condescension, and eventually, outright unholiness. Soon, all problems exist in others, not in oneself. Blame is placed everywhere but where it actually resides — in the individual human mind itself. Thus, any deep look at oneself, like into the true and indivisible Self of mankind, must be accompanied by an in-depth evaluation of the possible presence of these Three Enemies of Reason. For reason itself goes out the door whenever these three enter in, intended or unasked.

The latter two of the Three Stupefactions are as if underlings to the Three Enemies of Reason, and offshoots of them as well. As far as worldliness goes, however, it is ancient and, as Sri Ramakrishna has observed as recently as the 1800's, a problem worse than evil in this day and age. The idea here is that evil can easily be detected; even the evil know when they are doing evil, what to speak of the good. But worldliness is the best masquerader of all, and best suits the meaning of that mother of all four-letter words, *maya*. The meaning of *maya*, at least at its personal and most discomfiting best, is all and everything that takes up what is positive and internally wrangles it to seem negative, and vice versa. Worldliness fits this description exactly, and whole cultures, even religious traditions, are guilty of falling victim to it via tendencies like complacency, prevarication, infantilism, insouciance, conviviality, garrulousness, and a whole host of other petty pastimes. In purse-proud cultures where money is seen as the definitive measure of ones worth, it is worldliness which insinuates its odious effects, causing true human attributes such as wisdom and compassion to go unsought.

And spiritual complacency heads the bill here, wherein beings give up the finer and more intelligent pursuits in life in accord with Self-realization, Enlightenment, even higher Wisdom, to covet instead those questionable things which the Christ told us to *"grant unto Caesar."* For, enough coveting of the unreal, and the unsubstantial, then misery descends as *karmic* recompense, bringing with it the Four Deadly Traps listed on the bottom of the chart on the facing page. Enough souls suffer from these four in this day and age that no long commentary on them is necessary. Suffice to say, that when the pure teachings of Mother India come into contact with centuries of materialistic tendencies showing up in Western minds, guilt, grief, and the rest become common occurrences.

The Three Enemies of Reason, The Three Stupefactions, & The Four Deadly Traps

The Three Enemies of Reason

Garva — Egotism

Amarsha — Intolerance

Asuya — Narrowness

"This ego is the enemy of the Self, concealed like a thorn in the throat. Even after it has been cut away, if it is attended to even for a moment, it will only revive again and cause hundreds of distractions, like clouds dispersing and gathering again in the rainy season."
Sri Shankaracharya

The Three Stupefactions

Vyutthana-chitta — Worldliness

Ajanatah — Insensitivity

Ahaituka — Jadedness

"By seizing upon, possessing, and brooding over the sense objects, man desensitizes himself to the needs of others and becomes jaded."

"What? Do you mean to say that one should first save money and then seek God? The worldly man spends thousands of rupees on his family, yet all the while his neighbors are dying of starvation. He is so insensitive that he can't even give them a few morsels of rice. He says to himself, 'Let the rascals die; what do I care.' Then later one hears him talking glibly and guiltily about doing good to others." Sri Ramakrishna

The Four Deadly Traps

"The negative effects of actions done in the wrong spirit lead to a kind of remorse that is not only nonproductive, but debilitating as well. Therefore, one should steer clear of the four deadly traps of guilt, grief, depression, and lack of self-worth."

Udvega — Guilt

Shoka — Grief

Vishada — Depression

Vibhranti — Low Self-esteem

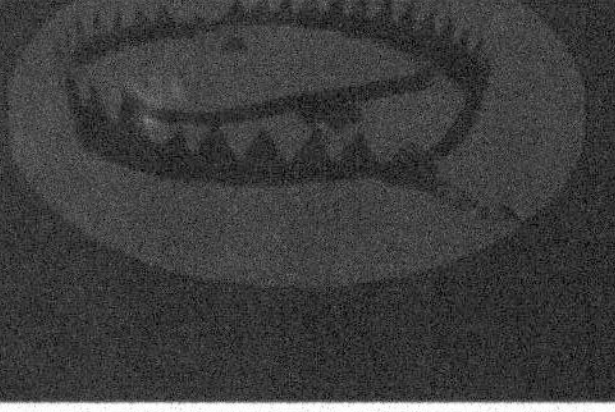

It has been mentioned that amidst the Three Enemies of Reason, and in the collection of Five Impediments to *Yoga* spoken of by Patanjali and Vedavyasa, that nemesis of good will and humility called egotism finds its home. The seers have found it abiding in the mental complex itself, the *Antahkarana* consisting of dual mind, thoughts, intellect, and ego. On the chart on the facing page we can see it among Shankara's list of illusory bodies as well, making it a very well-recognized, yet formidable, opponent for the aspirant along the spiritual path. And in this list we find it hiding well, along with five other factions to be watched for, all false assumers of Reality and pretenders to the throne of Consciousness. A devotee of Truth who wants to avoid the all too common syndrome of "walking backwards" would be well-advised to take heed of these false bodies.

In *Tantric* teachings, as well as in the *Vedanta*, the mistaking of the body for the true Self is called *Dehadhyasa*. But the matter is not all that simple, much to the aggravation of all those attached to the body yet wanting to be free. For Shankara counts at least five other bodies besides the ego-body which must be rejected — the physical body, the shadow body, the reflection body, the dream body, and the knowledge body. Each of these get subtler and subtler as they are struck from the quotient of what constitutes the real body of man — The *Atman*.

For the educated and the wise, it might seem rather elementary that bodies such as the shadow body and reflection body would even be counted among serious considerations. What fool would see his shadow, or his reflection in a pond, and mistake it for his true Self? Indeed! And though there are those on record who have fallen into such surface level hypnotization, the question really only points more directly at the fate of fools who take their physical body as the true Self. How elementary is that, the spiritually oriented person might ask? Yet there lies the mind-set of the materialist, sure and certain that his body is the Self, and bound and determined to prove this false notion to himself and everyone else in everyday life, even for lifetimes.

But it cannot be, for what courts death only gets united with death in the end, like all of nature. The real Self is Eternal, is Witness, is Observer of all that takes place in *maya*, in nature, in relativity. Just as the real individual soul (*Purusha*) returns to the world after thoroughly relinquishing the body, senses, and ego in the deep sleep state, so too does the true Individual Soul maintain its vigil as Overseer for the entire cosmic play. Unfortunately, that illusory self called the ego, which people cling to as their own, has nowhere to go except into *maya*. popping up again and again in cycles to assume its hollow existence of selfish clinging. The spiritual disciplinarian does not want this reappearance, and strives to cut it out via practices designed to eliminate it forever — or at least ripen it so as to reduce it to a mere servant.

Next to the deep sleep state, and just prior to returning to the waking state, the dream body is always making its appearance as well. More believable than the shadow body or the reflection body, it takes over the consciousness of a human being for the duration of time that it spends in this mode of wispy mental conjuring. It seems real enough, especially during a nightmare, but its life is short-lived and soon forgotten amidst the experiences of the waking state. Its lack of longevity betrays it as illusory — a finite and fugacious formulation of the mind.

There is one pretender to the throne of the true Self which poses a legitimate claim in this regard, and that is the knowledge body. And in fact, it lays claim to the waking, dreaming, and deep sleep states as its territories as well, traveling amidst them with the ego body as its willing passenger. The mental body provides the mind-scape, a series of multilayered vibrational realms which provide for plenty of hazy dreamlike experiences. The influence of this knowledge body exerts itself most powerfully on the waking state as well, where beings with intellectual capacity take it to be their very self, the provider for all that they desire and can attain in the embodied state.

One cannot own a transitory vibration, however. Trying to grasp onto a realm of vibrating atomic particles will leave one flummoxed and unsatisfied — a fact that can be attested to by countless beings who depart this earth either unfulfilled and restless, or in a state of remorse and fear about things left undone and unattained. Our next chart explores this fate of uncertainty.

The Six Illusory Bodies
Clues to the Risks and Dangers of Embodiment

"As long as one does not give up the idea of the Self as the body there is no hope of liberation. Do not take this body for the Self, just as you do not take your shadow or your reflection as real, nor the body that you see of yourself in dream, or in imagination." Shankara

"Sometimes the signs of a luminary are his clothes — sometimes precious clothes, or a deer skin, and sometimes the clothes of knowledge."

"The intellect takes bodies in different realms. Waking, dreaming, and deep sleep belong to it."

**Jnana Deha
Knowledge Body**

**Atman
Purusha**

**Anna Deha
Physical Body**

**Ahamkara Deha
Ego-Body**

"That limiting adjunct, the ego, is the shadow of the Atman that lives in the heart. It enjoys and suffers as the case may be."

"One awake in Brahman does not identify with the body, which becomes like a body seen in dreams."

**Svapna Deha
Dream Body**

**Adhyasa Deha
Reflection Body**

**Chaya Deha
Shadow Body**

"In an eclipse, when the shadow of the moon falls upon the earth, the ignorant believe the sun to be swallowed by a dragon."

"As the reflection of the moon in a puddle is not real, just so the body is not the Self."

The unfortunate fate of the entire human race throughout time, with a few genuine souls excepted, can be described by the term "negligence of *Brahman*." This is also another way of stating what was introduced earlier by the term "worldliness." In Shankara's sobering swordstroke language, however, the culprit is called brooding mind (see chart on page 219), and what other thing is most alluring for modern man to brood on than the sense objects — those conglomerates of vibrating particles just mentioned — which will never bring a man or woman happiness or fulfillment in and of themselves. Only when they are experienced by the mind poised in the *dharma* will they finally let go their hold and render up any satisfaction whatsoever. Or, when they are meditated upon (see chart on page 151) in order to find out their origin and substance — if any.

In much the same style of teaching as Sri Krishna (see chart on page 189), Shankara proposes to living beings caught in the trammels of *maya* that they give up brooding altogether, as it leads to no good and is an outright waste of time. The quote from Sri Krishna in the second chapter of the *Bhagavad Gita* gives out this unsavory sequence: *"Brooding on sense objects, man develops attachment to them; from attachment comes desire; from stymied desire anger sprouts forth. From anger proceeds delusion; from delusion, confused memory; from confused memory the ruin of reason; and due to the ruin of reason he perishes."* If one follows the descent of the stairwell on the chart on the facing page, a similar pattern emerges, a pattern that would have been avoided if the tendency of the human mind to brood on sense objects was curbed at the outset by spiritual practice. Or, if the Western society had spent time schooling their youth and culture in the wise ways of detachment, as India has done for so many millennia. But such is not the condition that we find in this day and age, so some backtracking will be necessary.

In Shankara's experience, and this was back in 700 A.D., approximately, the complex of mental brooding leads to an increased desire for sensual experience. Lord Buddha, about a millennia earlier, identified this tendency by the word *trishna* — the thirst for relative existence (review chart on the *nidanas* on page 192). Swami Vivekananda, in the early 1900's, wrote in one verse of his poem, *"Song of the Sannyasin,"* these lines which apply perfectly: *"This thirst for life, forever quench; it drags from birth to death, and death to birth, the soul."* And so a host of luminaries, well and wisely spaced throughout the flow of cycles of time, and all present on existing historical record, have agreed as to the nature of this type of detrimental mental projection.

As the bouncing ball of the worldly and conventional mind rolls down to the next lower step, falling helplessly towards the ground floor of neglect of *Brahman*, an increased thirst for enjoyment overcomes the mind. This is the gateway for most beings to enter into habitual preoccupation, for it opens the door of desire for possessions. If the mind falls into this attractive trap, as Shankara so adeptly reveals, the appearance of delusion occurs. This tendency, an ensuing habit, eventually turns into an obsession. This happens on the individual level and on the collective level both, and soon whole nations have taken to greedily grasping, coveting, owning, and enjoying mass amounts of possessions, courting them solely up until the end of their lives and fighting with others to keep them. This very collection of acts is the appearance of delusion, though its subtler dangers remain hidden behind the various masks of human passion.

And in the sweep of all this, has brooding stopped? Has satiation ever arrived? More importantly, has peace of mind ever descended? Sri Ramakrishna states in this regard that *"Objects kept near a mirror reflect therein."* This means that if one keeps the objects of the senses close at hand, and wealth and money as well, they will reflect in the mind, and as a result the mind will not be able to avoid thinking of them, constantly. This leaves no room in a soul's life for contemplating important questions pertinent to spirituality, what to speak of gaining any measure of peace of mind. What is more, bondage to nature, to insentient things, is in store, as we shall see.

The ground floor of neglect of *Brahman* is a place of base mental gravitation, but it pales in comparison to the basement of outright forgetfulness of the Self. When the mind gets used to getting what it covets, and will not practice detachment or even moderation anymore for its own good,

The Seven Descending Steps of Negligence of Brahman
(From Slokas 321-329 of the Vivekachudamani)

"For the knower, there is no greater danger than failing to remain in Brahman.
To be always in Brahman should not be neglected, for that neglect is death."

Brooding on Sense-objects

(The Bouncing Ball of the Mind)

Thirst for Enjoyment

Desire to Possess

Appearance of Delusion

Cold Ground Floor of Neglect of Brahman

Supremacy of Ego

Advent of Bondage

Copyright 2017, Babaji Bob Kindler

Freezing Basement of Forgetfulness of Self

"If the mind once forgets its own Atman it ventures far out, like a ball that, when it falls,
rolls down the stairs and does not stop until it reaches the lowest step." Adishankaracharya

then it is time for the reign of the selfish human ego. Egotism has been mentioned in previous pages as the culprit who ushers in all manner of human suffering, and thereby a host of ills on life and the world itself. Under its implacable reign — contumacious one moment and solicitous the next — no clear forward progress can be made, either in life or in spiritual life. The illusion of "going nowhere faster" enters in here, and by the time that the mind finds that its own ego component has led it so far astray, it is usually to late to escape the outcome in the form of slavery to nature. This slavishness is not the all too familiar binding of the soul to nature due to its beauty which is a comparatively harmless type of bondage, but more of a falling into depression and resultant suffering due to a combination of the loss of individual freedom and attachment to things and objects now seen and known to be empty.

The word "emptiness" has become a philosophical statement of its own in present times. A fuller understanding of the word shows its two sides, as meant by the illumined seers. First, and as applied to the world of the five senses and their objects, it means that all things are devoid of substance. Western science has already proven this for modern man, though few have brought such rare and unique conclusions to bear on life and mind yet. When an object can be stripped of its appearance of solidity and thereby shown to be a mere mass of swirling particles changing at a billionth of a second, how substantial can they really be? Secondly, objects are empty of any power to fulfill a human being. Here, we need to turn to our own practical experience over time (lifetimes, really), and to the wisdom of the seers and sages for realization. When we see that even in those who have glutted themselves on massive wealth and untold acres of lands, on an abundance of foods and drink, and on endless and constant sensual delights, that no satiation ever comes; and, when it is seen that these individuals become dull and slow, depressed, fearful of loss, subject to early illness and untimely death, then is the lesson nigh at hand with regard to both possessing and enjoying the worlds of name and form. Only death lies at the end of this road, and a woeful series of lifetimes lived in the basement of forgetfulness of the true Self of man. Thus, as Shankara declares on our chart under study (page 253), *"To be always in Brahman should not be neglected, for that neglect is death."*

Brooding, enjoyment and its loss, selfish clinging, attachment, bondage and the like all lead to different forms of depression and its close concomitants. In the chart on the facing page, we take a look at Lord Patanjali's collected observations on the impediments to *Yoga*, union with Reality. Taking the healthy universal perspective, Reality can be called by many names, like *Brahman* in the last chart, or All-mighty Father in Christianity, or *Prajnaparam* in *Buddhism*. It matters not so much how or what name It is called by, for it does not change the fact that many obstacles lie in the way of Its realization. And that very same realization will put an end to all disputes involving what It is and what to call It. Therefore, the thing is to remove the obstacles. As Sri Ramakrishna has noted in a very practical manner, *"If one wants to get ahold of the bottom book in a stack of books, one must remove all those lying on top."* God, Allah, Yahweh, or Reality, is at the bottom of everything, is the foundation for all things. But there are many overlays which must be stripped away, some of them cosmic, others historical, still others cultural, and some, personal and individual. Patanjali, the Father of *Yoga*, or its systematizer, has culled a veritable riot act of personal superimpositions that living beings have placed over Reality, a reality that he calls their very Self, or *Atman*.

Patanjali, as has been mentioned in previous pages, was a wholistically-minded luminary, catering to all levels of human existence. No doubt that he saw *Samadhi*, the nondual state of Awareness, as the Supreme Goal and the definitive end of all seeking. Nevertheless, being both practical and universal, he observed human nature with a transcendent eye and then distilled all of the major hindrances along mankind's forward moving pathway, placing them into four categories — physical, mental, intellectual, and spiritual. It is an impressive list, especially considering that so many other candidates had to be rejected in favor of these specific nine, and seeing that, if these nine are removed, all these other competing obtrusions would naturally fall away.

THE NINE OBSTACLES (VIKSHEPAS/ANTARAYAS) TO YOGA

"Beings suffer bondage to pleasure due to performing actions with attraction and aversion to matters they have assumed to be accurate based upon unstable vrittis of the mind." –Patanjali

PHYSICAL

1) VYADHI / Disease

Dhatus	Rasas	Karanas
blood, flesh, bones, air, bile, phlegm	hormones, gastric fluids, fluid essences	active &, cognitive senses, mind

"Mind reacts to illness and gets imbalanced, threatening yogic equipoise. Diet and exercise aid in retaining balance. Japa makes one impervious."

2) STYANA / Complacency, Ambivalence, Stodginess, Laziness, Procrastination, Fickleness

MENTAL

3) SAMSHAYA / Doubt, Indecision, Inadvertence, Uncertainty

4) PRAMADA / Carelessness, Resistance, Negligence, Disbelief, Heedlessness , Inattentiveness, Superficiality

5) ALASYA / Idleness, Stubbornness, Heaviness

6) AVIRATI / Immoderation, Sensuality, Incontinence

INTELLEC-TUAL

7) BHRANTIDARSHANA / Misconception, Delusion, Distortion

SPIRITUAL

8) ALABDHABHUMIKATVA / Faithlessness, Failure, Limitation

9) ANAVASTHITATVANI / Unsettledness, Inability, Stagnation, Backsliding

THE FOUR CAUSES OF DISTRACTION

DUHKHA	DAURMANASYA	ANGAMEJAYATVA	SHVASAPRASHVASAH
sorrow, pain, distress, grief, unhappiness	depression, despair, affliction, mental stress	unsteadiness, shakiness, erratic vibration	unevenness of the inbreath & outbreath

"All impediments are of three types: self-inflicted (adhyatmika), due to imbalances in the body and the world (adhibhautika), and due to genetic and cosmic defects (adhidaivika). Adherence to a single spiritual discipline, such as japa and practicing the presence of God, removes them." Patanjali

Referring to the chart under study on page 255, this copious list of "despoilers," as they have come to be known in English, can be viewed and explored. On the physical level, Patanjali has three categories for us to consider — *dhatus, rasas,* and *karanas.* Contemporary healers have marveled at the completeness and uniqueness of this listing, showing that the ancients had remarkable insight into the human system long before modern conventional medicine made its appearance. Moreover, and unlike modern medicine in some regards, this inspection on the physical level takes into account both the elements to be worked with, and the need for balance stemming from primal causes, not just secondary effects.

Paramount to all considerations, however wisely formulated, is Patanjali's deeper wisdom of a spiritual nature, that looks at disease of the body as an impediment to spiritual practice and realization rather than a mere cessation of being able to enjoy health and happiness. This becomes obvious when we read his statement under the *vyadhi* category: *"Mind reacts to illness and gets imbalanced, threatening yogic equipoise."* This revelation sets the mind on a completely different track in its healing process of the body, forcing it to realize that it is not the disease which is most important, but ones reaction to it. This insight has ramifications on all levels of the human system, especially the psychological. It reminds us that a spiritual orientation is superior to all other perspectives, that mental balance is based in an assurance on the birthless, deathless — thereby diseaseless — nature of ones very being. In the light of this salient fact, any healing which needs to take place in the body/mind mechanism is thereby and thereafter both quickened and assured, making both the transcendence of disease and its suffering, and the ongoing health of the physical instrument, a matter of natural course. Herein lies one of the ingenious facets of Patanjali's "healing" system. The rest — blood, flesh, bones, air, phlegm, hormones, gastric juices, and all other "fluid essences" — are just bits of knowledge, to be utilized by the healer and the patient almost as an afterthought.

The superlative point just mentioned connects well to the *"karana"* section of the *Vyadhi* category under inspection. The active and cognitive senses, and especially the mind, succumb to disease as well. And in fact, so much depends upon the patient's state of mind in the healing arts. This is why the second sentence in Patanjali's quote recommends the spiritual practice of *japa* to engender indifference to the onslaught of disease, i.e., *"Diet and exercise aid in retaining balance, but japa makes one impervious."* We are to think, then, that any person suffering any form of disease, if they were to come into a doctor's or healer's presence with the practice of *mantra* science already well in hand, would stand a better chance of having their illness removed swiftly and completely, than a person overcome by undue reaction followed by undue mental reaction. That is, and as the list in the proceeding *Styana* category reveals, if complacency, ambivalence, stodginess, procrastination, and the like are already weighing the mind down — as is the case with so many people suffering illness today — the healing process, should it happen at all, will be a slow and difficult one.

The physical element of Patanjali's *Yoga* system, then, is important to the foundational tenets of it, and sets up the aspiring soul for applying much the same tools to the remainder of impediments in the mind. For, it is the mental category which comes next (page 255), sporting four main encumbrances. The reader will recognize them with certitude. However, being cogently placed in such a well-thought compilation by a past master may communicate a fuller story, and give a wider picture.

Mankind's old familiar shadow known as "doubt," or *samshaya* in *Sanskrit*, is the third barrier lying in front of the aspiring soul's freedom on this daily watch list. Noted down under various other names, there can be no mistaking it when it surfaces. It causes the mind to falter, turn back, give up the fight and, most unfortunately, abandon the spiritual path and its practice. Many lukewarm practitioners of this modern day and time are guilty of allowing this restricting imposition to dictate life and action, and under its pettish and enervating influence, suddenly become devoid of all self-assurance to turn tail to run away from all that is most beneficial in their lives. The inner bounty they forfeit is astronomical, and the return of spiritual opportunity becomes rare under the memory of such ignoble past actions.

And, in fact, the fourth despoiler on Patanjali's acclaimed list enters here in interconnected fashion. It is *pramada,* called by such names as would make the sensitive person wince upon hearing them, like carelessness, inattentiveness, superficiality, and the like. Even negligence, just explored in a previous chart, is a prime translation for this *Sanskrit* word. In spiritual life, its most obvious appearance in this day and time occurs around the egoic resistance, gross ignoring, or heedless overlooking of the import of *dharma* and the *dharmic* preceptor. As Sri Ramakrishna has mentioned, almost incredulously, human beings will take all manner of guides and instructors when they need to get an education, or begin a profession, or contract a disease or malady, but they will resist seeking out a spiritual teacher when it is time to enter that most important of life's arenas.

Much of this is due to the dullness of the mind around matters subtle, or what Patanjali calls *alasya* — the fifth of these prime impedances. To convince the resistant mind to give in and begin the path — any path, earthly, religious, or spiritual — is difficult enough, but to make the obstinate mind get moving is well-nigh impossible. Thus, *pramada* combined with *alasya* makes a very tough admixture, what to speak of adding doubt, *samshaya,* into the mix. But if *alasya* can be isolated and worked with on its own, the sincere and striving aspirant desirous of a mind which flows will gradually be able to diminish its influence greatly.

However, if no spiritual power is available to the novice, or no inner substance from which to draw on (see *kundalini* chart on page 584), the ambitious prospect may fail as many times as it is attempted. This is due to the sixth barrier to *Yoga,* called *avarati,* the fourth and final problem of the mental category of despoilers. Basically, it can be termed incontinence, thus can also be indicated by the lack of the practice of celibacy. If celibacy is not possible or desirable for the individual, then moderation is another word and practice that can be considered. Whatever the case may be, too much of catering to the ego, or of indiscretion of any kind, of overall satisfaction — of body, of senses, of enjoyments, of palate, of sexuality — then little or none of this precious inner substance *(ojas)* can be acquired and maintained. Like a motor without a gas tank and a boat without a rudder, the human psycho/physical being is then devoid of any real propulsion or direction, and is left to the mercy of the *samsaric* ocean currents of desire and lack of judgement.

The more advanced practitioner, the one who perceives and perseveres, finds other recourse however. And in fact, the opposite of *avarati* is *uparati,* one of the Six Jewels of *Vedanta,* which equates to a condition of proper satiation around the senses and their objects. It culminates in what is termed "self-settledness," or contentment with what is. Further, if *avarati* is transformed into *uparati,* there may be grounds for avoiding the seventh despoiler on Patanjali's list, the single one which both occupies and aggravates at the intellectual level. It is called *bhrantidarshana,* translated as false conception. It is a type of skewed perception which both thwarts the intelligence of man via misunderstanding, and causes the results in the form of his short-sightedness to crystallize in the mind. This false seeing, or distorted perception, acts most insidiously on the philosophical level. Human beings of some high and rare intelligence fall victim to *bhrantidarshana,* failing to penetrate into the deeper mysteries of religious science and philosophy to come upon the marvels of *Paravidya* — the superlative wisdom which lies beyond relative sciences and intellectual learning *(aparavidya,* lower knowledge – see chart on page 600). Concretized attitudes such as the assumed superiority of one race over another, of one class of beings over another, of one religion over another, are classic signs of the presence of *bhrantidarshana.* Holding assumptions around mental concepts that are outdated and outmoded is also common to this impediment, which translates into stagnation of the mind overall and the unwillingness, even inability, to break through into anything original.

Given the magnitude of this soporific and intransigent despoiler, it is no surprise that the next two obstacles in the way of *Yogic* equipoise have much in common with it, and contain elements of it within them. They are listed as spiritual impediments, called by the extra long *Sanskrit* names of *alabdhabhumikatva* and *anavasthitatvani.* More difficult to render into explanation due to their being spiritual barriers, thus extremely subtle and hard to detect, their presence is nevertheless cognizable due to the effects that they wreak on human life. The first is an unseen presence in the mind which, due to past failures, causes the mind to decide that no progress or success can be made. The second is that old enemy of the progress loving individual which causes backsliding to recur, often termed as "one step forward and two steps back" in modern terminology. As a pair of twins working in conjunction, these two basically destroy the faith of a man and then render him unable to move, to gain any ground.

And where it is true that this type of stymied progress happens in all arenas of human existence, such impedance in worldly life concerning people with no religious interests is due mainly to the *gunas* and their interaction (see chart on page 223). What is meant here by way of spiritual impediments corresponds to progress which gets hampered in the areas of religious life and practice, i.e., disinterest in the scriptures, failure to repeat the *mantra*, the inability to meditate, and an overall disappointment and giving up of the vows and aspirations one once held sacred and inviolable. Those who, among other personal shortcomings, find fault with the teacher, consider the scriptures invalid or inapplicable to themselves or this age, refuse to integrate with the company of the devotees, fail to properly assess the inner merit of the holy ones, consider themselves superior to others, and the like, have most likely come upon and are suffering the subtle influence of these two despoilers. In most cases this means an end to spiritual practice and a beginning to a hazy and complacent period of languishing which is fatal to spiritual life.

To complete the informative chart on page 255, we must have a look at the Four Causes of Distraction, a few additional fractious reasons that cause the spiritual seeker to continue "walking backwards." That is, why does the mind resist and falter, and where are the causes for such weakness found? Pain is the first. It has the power of shutting down a human being's willingness to center and focus. Depression is the next, the result of brooding on the world and its imperfections rather than meditating on Divine Reality and Its innate perfection. Unsteadiness of the body and the breathing process are the final two, which are at the root of most infirmities found in beginning aspirants. With good food, right attitude, exercise, a contemplative temperament, and a loving mind given to worship and study, all four of these may be eliminated. And if they persist at all, the advancing aspirant will learn to utilize them for extra spiritual growth.

Unfortunately, suffering in general is most often allowed access into the mind, and thereafter into the body, due to ones own weaknesses. This could also be described as the inability or inadvertence to maintain the invincible shield of spiritual practice which will naturally thwart every despoiler that tries to insinuate itself upon a human being's consciousness. In other words, where is that distraction that encroaches upon the mind of the luminary? Are there any? Are they called peaceful, equanimous, unperturbed, balanced, spiritual, enlightened, and illumined for no reason? There is no devil, no evil, no hindrance or impasse for such as these. As the *Upanisads* put it, *"Peace belongs to them, and to none else."* For all others, this peace and bliss seems a long ways off. They are continually distracted by unreal concepts, preoccupations, fantasies, projections, and objects that are of their own devising. Or, as Patanjali puts it in his own inimitable way, at the top of our chart under study: *"Beings suffer via bondage to pleasure due to performing actions because of attraction and aversion to matters they have assumed to be accurate based upon unstable vrittis of the mind."* This one amazing sentence might as well include all the obstacles and distractions listed on the chart just studied, proving without a doubt that Patanjali was one of the most wholistically-minded teachers on record — and one of the most "holistically-minded" of them all as well.

Running a Race in a Dream
The Assumption of Movement and Progress; the Illusion of Change

The *Advaita Vedanta* of India holds a special place in the hearts of those who look upon, or have heard about, the existence of the world as a dream in the cosmic, collective, and individual mind. For, other theories similar to this rendering, proposed by systems which are unable to offer valid and convincing testimony, fall into the morass of confusion, which usually accompanies the wide sweep of such a suggestion — a suggestion offered as an apt alternative to the minds of a host of beings who have already formulated their beliefs around the stunning appearance of the presence of Existence — such conceptions as the four-billion year evolutionary theory and the seven-day creation theory. But as time has taught us, these systems of thought — though they may have practical, temporary use as a measure for the passage of time, the movement of planets and other bodies, and the origins of life on earth — are ultimately inadequate to the necessary task of explaining the nature and essence of Awareness. This is the definitive qualifier of them all, and without it the others only lead into materialistically-based conceptions founded on the life of the senses alone.

And so it becomes a consideration for mankind's valuable thinking process that Awareness — divine, celestial, ancestral, human, and especially Transcendent — is totally beyond the mind and senses to accurately assess and fathom, and wholly transcendent of time, space, and causation. To discover this the practitioner must contemplate more than nature; he must meditate on his true Nature. And when he does he will either eventually stumble upon or systematically and deftly unveil the fact that Awareness is all-pervasive. This is one of the most suitable words in English to describe Existence, and represents an important addition to mankind's store of knowledge. Being all-pervasive, *vyapti* in *Sanskrit*, Awareness does not require movement, nor does It exist and operate in terms of sequential progress, which also infers a type of movement. If this axiom about Awareness is accepted, then a whole host of other principles come to the fore, and a whole host of preconceived assumptions face their long overdue extinction.

An *Advaitist* does not breathe the same air that others do. The nondual air of heights, as the Chinese poet, Tufu, once wrote, is this being's favorite clime. He sees the vast expanse of space and its plenitude of planets and stars as a spacecraft hovering in the ethers might view it. As Lord Buddha related, if one sits on the banks of a river for a long enough time in rapt observation, he will notice the same object float by — meaning that the river is cyclic in nature and tends to repeat itself. Such is the case with the physical worlds in space and time. And if this expansive realm consisting of the five elements in various admixtures and combinations moves in cycles, so too will mankind and other living beings that inhabit it trail along with it.

This fact is unacceptable to a freedom-loving soul like Lord Buddha and others of his character and temperament who describe the true nature of human beings not as products of matter and the result of evolution, but as wholly independent and ever-stationary representatives of timeless, deathless Awareness. Of course, this great statement is meant to describe those who have realized such a universal condition, and who can testify to Its existence and point to Its location. But this Self of man, if it can be called such, is not found in any spatial dimension defined by breadth, depth, height and width, nor is it caught in the web of time and its apparent passage. It is not subject to causation, the like of which all material things have to endure. And herein lies the basic difference between the meditation-based thinking of India and the physics-oriented Western world.

Vedantic and Conventional Views of Birth and Death

Vedantic Superimposition/Projection	Conventional View/Creation Theory

Brahman/Atman
The One, Indivisible, All-pervasive Soul

Principle of Manifestation by Unreal Superimposition (Apparent Transformation)	**Theory of Evolution by Real Modification (Actual Transformation)**
Ajativada — Nonorigination	**Theory of Origins**
Aparinama — Nontransformation (Spirit projects matter)	**Parinama — Transformation** (Spirit "becomes" matter)
Cosmic materials are ever-present but subtle and undetected	**Cosmic materials are nonexistent and then created from "nothing"**
Principle of Thought Projection (Atmic Sankalpa)	**Principle of Creation** (Creator fashions all out of ?)
Unmanifested Prakriti projected by Mahat appears as Manifest Nature	**Nature is incepted from the Void and formed by physical force**
Consciousness assumes forms	**Souls are created from matter**
Consciousness is aware, and sports by associating with forms	**Consciousness is forgotten and the body is seen as Reality**
Prakriti rises and falls timelessly from Unmanifest Prakriti	**Nature evolves over spans of time considered to be actual**
Souls consisting of Consciousness rise and fall in and out of Brahman	**Souls give themselves to the illusion of birth and death**
Souls assume form as long as the desire to experience individuality persists	**The embodied soul lives one lifetime and then passes into heaven or hell**

"If an entity is immortal by nature, how will it change other than through artificial means or effort. Will it not remain changeless? Therefore, it should be accepted that what is known as one's nature is fully established, natural, inborn, and not manufactured artificially. One cannot ever abandon this nature. All beings are by nature free of birth and death. By waiting for birth and death, they deviate from their true nature by the very thought of them." Gaudapada

The next two charts (page 260 & 263) make a side by side comparison between the views of Theology, Science, and *Vedanta* with regards to such critical topics as the birth and death of a soul, its origins, the origins of the universe, and the origins of consciousness. In this way an idea of the propositions and conclusions of these three systems, generally speaking, can be reviewed at a glance.

Taking the chart on page 260 first, the reader can see the differences in thinking between the conventional views of the theories aforementioned, and what *Vedanta* declares about them. The charts are self-explanatory, so for purposes of posing opinions little commentary will be required. What can be explained, however, and which is of a more esoteric nature to most souls, especially in this day and time, is the unique perspective of India concerning this rare type of philosophical material, considered most serious of import by the luminaries, and beyond the reach of terrestrial subjects. If such maxims are left untended and untaught, the result is the rapid decline of religion.

India, from time out of mind, in its overall philosophy, has thought in terms of two great axioms — *Aparinama* and *Ajativada*, both interrelated. *Aparinama* means the unchanging or non-transformational nature of Existence, holding true always despite the appearances of outer phenomena. *Ajativada* is the path of those who have come to know that birth and death are illusory, or only applicable to the body/senses/brain complex, not to mind and Soul. The latter two live on after the death of the human form, the mind experiencing transmigration and the Soul (*Atman*) remaining immovable and all-pervasive as *sakshi bhutam*, the Witness of all passing and changing phenomena.

Thus, India, and especially its *Vedanta*, has perceived that name and form gets superimposed over the changeless Reality which is its backdrop. This is called "apparent transformation by unreal superimposition." In other words, the appearance and disappearance of the worlds of name and form, and the coming and going of embodied beings does not transpire in actuality, but as in a dream. This mass collective mental dream is likened to waves appearing on the surface of a boundless ocean, which itself undergoes no movement in its depths. The surface movement is both cyclic and eternally ongoing, but everything in it is fabricated and projected by the cosmic, collective, and individual mind — and this Mind in toto is contained in the changeless Reality, or *Brahman*. This "theory" is based, in part, upon the presence or absence of mental vibration. When the mind is vibrating, as in the waking and dreaming states, manifestation is projected, and when the mind ceases its vibrations, as in the deep sleep state and *samadhi* (where the breath and heart rates are nearly stilled), manifestation is withdrawn.

Contrasted to this, the conventional view of modern times, accepted by most beings, is what is termed "evolution by real modification." Those who adhere to this view believe, evidently, that the changes taking place at the atomic, molecular, chemical, material, and mental levels are actual; that all the transformations which the universe of name and form are continually undergoing on all these levels are real. But when this philosophical view is proposed, there is no provision made for an underlying substratum for this presumed change to take place upon. Even Western religion falls prey to this type of thinking, to concepts which, in India, are considered neither correct nor spiritually healthy. For instance, spirit, soul, or consciousness, then, described as being born from dust and returning to dust, is relegated in its origins to a material entity. And back to the evolutionary view, any mention or idea of an indwelling soul has to be predicated upon formulation in matter; that is, brain is the ultimate thing, yet it is nonexistent in the beginning and then has to undergo growth and transformation in the body from the stage of a fetus on to a full grown human being — all under the influence and necessity of food and education. In short, the intelligent person cannot comfortably abide with the four billion, three-hundred and twenty-million year evolutionary theory of the scientists, or get in step with the seven-day creation theory of the Western theologians — because there is no where to go between a rock and hard place.

The theory of origins lacks foresight and insight, then, whether taken in terms of science or of religion, and it labors under a lack of deeper consideration, which both the perception of God/Soul as an Unchanging Verity, and deep and long-lasting meditation upon that Verity affords. Besides the unreasonable assumption that something, say a universe or a soul, can be created out of nothing, there also must be a creator doing this impossible manufacturing. Such contradictions pose no good for the aspiring soul trying to be free. In all of this, and on the side of religion, there is very good reason to believe that Christ's teachings were not fully understood during His time, or thereafter. For instance, He never intended His nondual teachings to be based upon genesis, or origins. John's statement, evidently told him by Jesus, which declares that *"In the beginning was the Word,"* etc., was not meant to signify the "All-Mighty Father," but rather the source of all appearances. The Word in this sense is the thinking power of God's Mind, not God's Essence. Thought is father to both word and deed, but beyond thought, i.e., mental vibration, is the changeless, transformationless Reality, and upon that stationary, immutable Presence all things appear — consisting of vibration. They also disappear back into That.

And this phenomena of appearance and disappearance, called birth and death by the unknowing soul, is to the knower of Reality merely cosmic projection and withdrawal. Thought of as death by ignorant races and cultures, which even intelligent persons believe in and succumb to, it is seen as either an end to existence (Science) or a transitional mechanism into another realm (Heaven). It is never seen, as India has posited it to be, as a mere rising and falling of intelligence-driven waves of individual consciousness sporting within an undying ocean of Consciousness. This sportive play is an assumption of form, and lasts only so long as the desires which compel this passing dream of individuation are left unfulfilled. Even the substantial structure of nature, conceived and manifested out of the very idea of solidity and liquidity (see chart on page 151) in the Cosmic Mind, is in infinite supply, and never gets destroyed. It only recedes into the background at the time of dissolution, and reemerges, unchanged, at the time of another cycle of manifestation.

This is illustrated on the chart on the facing page in the first heading under the origin of Nature, Worlds, and Objects. The creation theory is proposed there under Theology, which has an advantage over science in this department which, with its death grasp on what is physical in nature only, avers that the universe is created out of energy — like the Big Bang Theory. But energy, thought, nature, mind, space, time — they are all eternal. Everyone thinks so. Certainly "God" is, unless you do not account for Him/Her/It. Whatever the case may be, if all is eternal, then there is no real origin — to any of it. Beginnings, middles, and endings are then only appearances. Then the only point to consider is the presence of cycles, also unending, which foist the false assumption of time upon the dazed mind.

Therefore, Nature, Soul, and Reality — all are unchanging, transformationless, and free of origins. What causes manifestation to seem so real is the ignorance and premature acceptance in human minds around the appearance of name and form in time and space based in causality — *maya*. As a cloud is present one minute and gone the next, yet reappears here and there across an endless expanse of infinite sky, so too does the world of name and form seem to change, seem to pass through cycles of creation and destruction, only to appear again and again.

Existence can never become nonexistent, Consciousness never becomes unconscious — not at its ultimate level, in its Essence. When It becomes delimited via the conditioned mind, that is another matter, and one which forms the very cause of false superimposition at all levels — cosmic, collective, and individual. That is, Consciousness can never be bound or limited, but the mind can make it appear so. This taking of the unlimited, eternal Consciousness, fully aware and intelligent in its very nature, and fragmenting it up into parts, parcels, and pieces, is the *mayic* game of projectionism out of which ideas such as time, space, causality, birth, life, and death emerge. It is the ruse of duality which, if left unchecked in the mind, leads to divisions and subdivisions untold, and eventually to fragmentation which is the source of distraction, confusion, depression, delusion, and the many *mayic* offshoots just explored in chapter five.

There is a single solution for the considerable problems conjured up by the mind in *maya*. The axiom of *Aparinama*, if understood correctly, leads the mind towards the contemplation of That which is immutable, and which is the ground upon which all changes, whether considered actual or not, take place. The following chart on page 265 further outlines the depth and profundity of the

Vedanta, Theology, and Science

Comparative Views of Origination, Nature, Consciousness, and Life/Death

Vedanta – Nonorigination	Theology – Genesis	Science – Evolution
— Origin of Consciousness —		
Consciousness has no origin, being anterior to life and mind	Consciousness is born in time & space; passes from state to state	Consciousness develops in nature as body & mind evolve
Consciousness is one indivisible mass, Self-aware by nature	Consciousness is divided into many separate souls	Consciousness only exists in association with the brain
Consciousness is ever-free, and transcendent of creation	Consciousness depends upon creation and a Creator	Consciousness is dependent upon matter & energy
Consciousness assumes forms but remains ever formless	Consciousness is born in form	Consciousness and form are indiscernible from one another
— Origin of Human Beings —		
All beings are non-originated and inseparable from Reality	All beings are separate from and conceived by a Creator	All beings are inseparable from nature
Human beings, who are really unborn, engage in dream-life	After conception beings live on earth, then go to heaven or hell	The lives of beings are based upon the real existence of matter
Human beings are really one birthless, deathless Soul	Human beings are so many souls, all restricted to one lifetime	Human beings are of the nature of matter, and have no soul
Intelligence is inherently spiritual, of the nature of Sentiency	Intelligence is God-given, associated with secular knowledge	Intelligence is only energy formed by experiences in matter
— Origin of Nature, Worlds, and Objects —		
Nature is an eternal, with no beginning, middle, or end	Nature is created by the Word of God via the Creation Theory	Nature is the only reality, and is formed by the force of Energy
Worlds and objects as forms are projections of the mind in maya	Worlds and objects are real, and are formed in a seven day cycle	Worlds, species, objects, evolve over a vast expanse of time
All transformation is nonactual; there is one unchanging Reality	Via transformation the Spirit becomes flesh/matter	Matter and energy are real and their permutations are actual
Nature has two modes, manifest and unmanifest; the former rises from the latter, but both are transitory. Reality transcends them.	Nature is at first nonexistent, then has a beginning when it gets created out of nothing	Matter and energy are interchangeable, and proceed out of a physical void.

"Theologians have fashioned this universe into a close knit, tidy little box. Science has rendered it into an-ever-expanding universe. Scientists think that matter is indestructible. No, matter is not indestructible; nor is it destructible. It is unoriginated."
Swami Aseshananda

absence of transformation in all of Existence. With its aid, more assurance can be gained.

The chart on the facing page is divided into *Aparinama* and *Parinama* categories — what is being proposed as nontransformation and apparent transformation, the unchanging and the apparently changing. As Gaudapada's quote on the upper half of the chart relates, a man running a race in a dream goes nowhere but his own bed. And Sri Krishna concurs, speaking the highest nondual Truth by stating that coming and going never take place in the Absolute Being. Those who fall into the misconception that change is real, then, or that Existence is subject to transformation are as beings running a race in a dream. At some point they will awaken to the fact that they themselves are projecting the dream, that they are the dreamer, and awakening will take place.

The seers of India call the results of this awakening by various names, such as *Samadhi, Nirvana, Moksha, Mukti,* and more. The appellations for those illumined souls who live in these nondual states are also many, as is instanced on the upper half of the chart under study by words like *Paramatman* and *Pratyagatman.* In brief, the Absolute and Its superlative atmosphere is not a matter for contention or argumentation; it must be experienced. "The eye sees everything but cannot see itself." This well-known saying relates to the Absolute Reality, *Brahman,* which is most subtle of detection. Suffice to say that Existence cannot be doubted. The intelligence which a man uses to argue the truth or falsity of his own existence, or the presence or absence of God, is itself that very Reality — or the most convincing sign of It. That is intelligence, not intellect.

And that brings us to the lower half of the chart under study. Since Existence is obvious, and subtlemost, it cannot be spoken or written about adequately. Thus It is called simple. Truth, God, is simple. What naturally flows off of that ever-blissful Verity is not so simple, however, and is the cause of a massive host of considerations, ponderings, wonderings, and much more — all perpetually ongoing in the mind of mankind. Perhaps that is why the *rishis* of India valued Peace so much, called *Shanti.* A stillness is required of the deep thinkers who would contemplate this mass reflection of Consciousness in the mirrors of their purified minds. Otherwise this plethora of expressions would simply overwhelm, causing the mind to give rise to multiple thought-forms, each with their own direction and effect — the result which would be forgetfulness of Consciousness Itself!

And that quiescent silence, quietude, equanimity, or inner stillness, pervades the original Consciousness. *Kutastha, Sakshi,* words listed on the top half of the chart, refer to a peaceful substratum and a witness of all phenomena which is synonymous with Reality. It is from this empyrean position that true contemplation can be both employed and enjoyed. Then one may see the emanation of pure intelligence radiating off of the Ultimate Light of unconditioned Awareness. That most primal reflection, which is the first entry under the *Parinama* half of the chart, and the first compound out of *Brahman,* is called *Chidabhasa* in *Sanskrit.* It is called a "compound" because a luminary uses it for direct perception of Reality, *Anubhava,* and since he does so it proves he is, at that time, not one with Reality, but a separate perceiver. Revelation comes forth at that stage, however, and he both intuits and notates, like some divine scribe, the wisdom which makes up the revealed scriptures — *Paravidya.* Then, to light his own way home, and to leave a sacred trail for other spiritual travelers, he next formulates his insights into capacious ideas and places them into an inner vault of divine memory. This is *Upalabdhi.*

All of these natural occurrences form the first step of the staircase of Divine Life — of Existence in seeming motion, in assumed action, in supposed change, in apparent transformation. It is the unoriginated origin of a magisterial trickle down effect springing from a divine impetus containing a terrific compulsion to overflow Itself. Simply put, it is Intelligence Absolute, the First-born, the very substance of Existence, the most ancient (timeless) of primogenitors, which emanates from the ocean of Consciousness like millions of rays from a blazing sun.

Intelligence, then, in its essential form, supersedes all other principles. As our chart relates, the mind and will complex appear next. The "race in a dream" has begun in earnest here, for evolutes such as the sense of separate self (ego), self-arrogating thought (*chitta*), and all the forms of secular intelligence (*aparavidya*) — including a brain to feed on them — make their appearance. Senses,

Aparinama — The Principle of Nontransformation

"A kind of scientific advaitism has been spreading throughout Europe ever since the theory of the conservation of energy was discovered. But all that is Parinama, evolution by real modification, as contrasted to Aparinama, progressive manifestation by unreal superimposition. Ramanuja's theory is that the bound soul has its perfections involved, and when this perfection evolves it becomes free. But the Advaitan declares that involution and evolution take place only in show. Both processes are in Maya, and so are apparent only." **Swami** *Vivekananda*

"All happenings taking place in relativity resemble the activities of a man running a race in a dream. Nothing actually transpires. Scenery, movements, race, dream — all are unreal, or apparent only. The dreamer alone is real, but he must awaken to realize this." *Gaudapada*

Brahman
Paramatman
The Nontransformational Reality

"The unreal has no existence; the Real never ceases to be. The truth about both has been realized by the seers. Coming into being and ceasing to be do not take place in the Absolute. It is unborn, eternal, constant and timeless." *Sri Krishna*

Pratyagatman
Antaryami
Kutastha
Sakshi
Aum

Aparinama
Nontransformation

Parinama
Apparent Transformation

Maya — name, form, time, space, causation
Prakrti — manifest and unmanifested nature

"Though knowledge, being a compound, cannot be the Absolute itself, it is the nearest approach to it, and higher than will or desire."

INTELLIGENCE / KNOWLEDGE
(Sattva)

Chidabhasa — Pure Intelligence reflecting off of Reality
Anubhava — Direct Perception of Reality
Paravidya — Sacred Wisdom of the Nondual Scriptures
Upalabdhi — Insight via Divine Remembrance

"The Divine first becomes knowledge, then, in the second degree that of will."

MIND / WILL
(Rajas)

Abhijna — Intuition
Ahamkara — Sense of separate "I"-ness
Ahamta-vrtti — Self-arrogating Thought
Aparavidya — Secular Intelligence

"If it is, this is the evolution, less and less in the body and more and more in the mind — man the highest form, meaning manas, thought — the animal that thinks, and not the animal that senses only."

BRAIN / SENSES / DESIRE
(Tamas)

Indriyajnana — Sense-knowledge / Sense-perception
Vedana — Feelings / Sensations from Contact with Objects
Vasana — Desires based in Past Experiences

"So long as the upadhis are present, the jivas retain their individuation. But the Paramatman undergoes no change due to these superimpositions. As the clay pot is not a transformation of the unchanging akasha, so too the jiva is not a transformation of the immutable Paramatman, who had these changes projected upon It by ignorant minds." *Gaudapada*

objects, feelings, and desires all muster under these banners. Dreaming is now a permanent vocation for billions of beings inhabiting the realms consisting of intelligence, most all of them devoid of that superlative quality, stunned by the *mayic* magic show around them, and imagining that the universe, its living beings, and the various objects, which they experience with the five senses are real in and of themselves. The power of mental dreaming, called *sankalpa* in *Sanskrit*, with its component partner, *vikalpa,* is in charge now. Never in four billion, three-hundred and twenty million years will creatures under this most far-reaching of all regimes think it all to be a cosmic mirage, and seek to establish themselves in the Unchanging Reality via the axioms of *Aparinama* and *Ajativada*.

The next visual for our consideration, appearing on the facing page, communicates to us what the luminaries of India have come to formulate around this most amazing and potentially deluding principle of *sankalpa/vikalpa* — represented on the chart by the two images of Lord Vasishtha who was one of the early exponents of its elucidation. The *Sanskrit* word, *kalpa,* refers to time; the word *kalpanika* intimates imaginings in time. *Vikalpa* infers desires in time based in fantasy. So the overall picture that can be drawn here points to the mind's powers of projection based upon desires sought to be fulfilled in time. And the list of mental modes in the middle of the chart reveals a host of human pastimes wherein all manner of delusion is possible. Our old study from a previous chapter, called brooding, is among them, as are such seemingly harmless occupations as thinking, fantasizing, conceiving, etc. If such modes are taken to be the end all and be all of life, and are perpetuated devoid of higher intelligence, then life turns surface-like, superficial, and becomes preoccupied with all that is mundane and quotidian. Further engagement of the mind at this base and hypnotized level can bind it into the process of birth, life, and death interminably — the very thing which Lord Buddha and other great beings strove to extract themselves from in order to gain true freedom.

As the chart reflects, *sankalpa* and *vikalpa* occurs on three levels — the world, the mind, and the intellect. It is a great teaching, and a fascinating *triputi*. Around the world, and in accord with our other old study, worldliness, beings seek for wealth, gain, lands, and possessions, and all that these can provide, most often to the exclusion of higher and more noble pursuits. Hoping for, owning, coveting, enjoying — then losing, brooding, regretting, seeking to regain (see 9 complacencies chart on page 309) and going through it all over again thereby takes up the time of a human being, and wastes his or her precious opportunity of seeking and finding God, Reality, Freedom, and Truth. Thus the seers warn embodied beings about the dangers of *sankalpa* with regards to worldly matters and physical objects.

To look at the next level of *sankalpic* involvement is to awaken to the fact that what one participates in on earth will also carry over into the next phase of existence. Thinking on and obsessing upon the world builds up a strong desire for attending worlds, and this includes a hefty thirst for heaven and what it can offer after death. Conventional religion even encourages this kind of seeking, and holds it out as way of enjoyment and reward at the conclusion of a lifetime. But the illumined seers regard heaven and its pursuit after death as a distraction to authentic spiritual life, as another type of enticement accompanied by mental excitement. What is more, this type of seeking leads the soul towards powers which prevent it from higher attainments, powers like personal lordship, replete with the manipulation of souls who fall under ones control. All of this comprises the intellectual level of *sankalpa*, attended by the taste for what the sages call *mada*, defined by the fitting word, vainglory. Attachment to the body which only decays and dies, obsession with fame which only brings disenchantment and loss of peace of mind, seeking after power that gradually corrupts and destroys, collecting beautiful objects which grow boring and imprison ones thoughts — these are instances of *mada's* influence. The influence of *sankalpa* at these three levels thus insinuates itself upon the lives of those who have no spiritual goal, who can envision no higher pursuits.

Luminaries like Lord Vasishtha have drawn a fine distinction between what is termed *mayic sankalpa* and *atmic sankalpa*. That is, the world has been projected by mind, so this must mean that great souls, when they enter the physical body and universe, must also betake themselves of *sankalpa*. In their case, however, due to past mastery of the rebirth process, their projections are

The Three Levels of Sankalpa/Vikalpa

"Sankalpic desire at three levels — the world, the mind, and the intellect — when utilized by an unillumined mind is a detrimental force at the root of all suffering. It is like a rutting elephant whose trunk is the tendency of selfish grasping and who goes about spraying the world with the water of surface enjoyments. Only the sharp arrow of Atmajnan can bring this lumbering beast to its knees so it can be bound by the ropes of masterful mind control."
Lord Vasishtha

Lord Vasishtha

1. *The World:*
Desire for Physical Objects

for foods, for sense objects,
for pleasures, for possessions

2. *The Mind:*
Desire for Mental Projection

for worlds, for heavens, for
excitements, for distractions

3. *The Intellect:*
Desire for Attainments

for power, for manipulation,
for pride, for glory

Mental Modes of Sankalpa

Hoping for

Brooding upon

Seeking after

Owning

Coveting

Enjoying

Striving for

Accumulating

Clinging to

Nonsharing

Taking as real

Conceiving

Thinking on

Imagining

Creating

Projecting

Fantasizing about

"For mastery over sankalpa and vikalpa practice asamvedana — nonreceptivity to all desire. Instead of falling in love with your own desires as if they were fulfilling, you must instead begin to perceive them as burdens, like packages and parcels filled with unwanted items that really clutter your life and only weigh you down." Lord Vasishtha in Yoga Vasishtha

extremely *sattvic*. The difference between *mayic* and *atmic sankalpa* is revealed on our next chart.

The visual aid on the facing page is imbued with many valuable teachings, and overall bears the mark of Lord Vasishtha's facile mind. Sticking to the nondual Truth, he declares that there is ever and always really one Supreme Reality, called *Parabrahman*. Those who venture forth from it, apparently, whether it is done consciously or unconsciously, fall into the realm of *maya*. The wondrous thing about the luminaries is that they protect themselves in the realms of name and form and only appear there, associating with bodies but never identifying with them. This enables them to engage in sportive play, called *Lila*, even as they work for the highest good of others. As the chart reflects, coming out of the nondual state of *Parabrahman*, they bring with them *jnana*, discriminatory wisdom, whereas others who have not developed that most crucial quality, or who leave it behind so to speak, follow the path of *ajnana* (ignorance) and, becoming lost to their Self, fall into suffering. Here is the solution to reincarnation, and one that does not fly in fear of being reborn. As Sri Sarada Devi, the Holy Mother has stated, *"What does a man of wisdom fear from rebirth?"* The *advaitic* axiom, mentioned earlier, called *Ajativada* — the path of those who are never born — figures prominently in here. In other words, maintaining a body in the physical realm for the purpose of some internal or divine work, as compared to being bound into the body due to ignorance and its interminable cycles of suffering, are two vastly different situations. Lord Vasishtha outlines the dynamics of each as is laid out on the two columns on the chart under study.

Basically, the difference between the two paths of *atmic* and *mayic sankalpa* is one of direction — not physically, since both occur in the world, but mentally. The world is *Brahman* when seen from the unique perspective of nondual wisdom. That same world is hell when seen through the thick veil of ignorance. And so, the path of nondual abidance, or the path of false separation — which shall it be? That question, and quandary, was proposed once before when the soul entered the worlds of becoming. Its decision predicated its outcome, and thus the soul is now either content and involved in increasing its wisdom and devotion, or it is happy and unhappy in turns, casting about in a world that, for it at present, consists of decaying matter instead of the eternal *Brahman*. So, in answer to the age-old question, "Why have we come here?," perhaps learning how to make wise choices is the reason why the soul has taken birth in a body on Earth.

Whatever the case may be, as there are many types of souls present in a body in any given age, the enlightened ones perceive time, space, and all that the mind and intellect has fashioned, as mere appearance. Across the chart on the right hand side, it is seen that the unillumined do not even know that they have fashioned the world out of their own thinking process, so are at a huge disadvantage, and go on assuming the world to be real rather than it being projected by the mind. Coming out of *Parabrahman*, the wise seek a teacher immediately in order to get spiritual initiation and instruction in order to hone the mind's tendencies away from desire-based *sankalpa*. The ignorant rely upon their own ego complexes and revert to conventional means of coping, imagining (*vikalpa*) that they can fulfill desires in the world with unreal objects via vain fantasies.

But the illumined soul ends its time in the body with a profound sense of the unreality of the worlds in space and time, and sports no attachment to them, nor has any fear of leaving them. This is not the case for the spiritually uninformed soul, however, and as has been mentioned in the last chart, is only longing for more and better individual experiences — a longing which will take it into the twin modes of death and rebirth. That old standby, *ragadveshau*, to cite Patanjali — attachment to pleasure and aversion to pain — accompanies the final thoughts of the ignorant person in old age and death, while the free soul merely returns to *Parabrahman*, sloughing off the body and leaving off of individual existence as if it was a mental dream from which all must awaken. As Sri Ramakrishna has stated, *"The difference between a bound soul and a liberated being is that the former cries at the time of death, while the latter laughs."*

In brief, as the middle of this chart reveals, the spiritually blind person is born in *samsara*, thinks and acts via the single mode of worldliness, and lives in complacency throughout life. For the enlightened soul all is *nirvana*, and to keep that fact foremost in the mind while he temporarily fre-

Atmic Sankalpa and Mayic Sankalpa

"The universes are modes of Consciousness reflected through Atmic Sankalpa, the Divine Will of Parabrahma, which is said to evolve them all out of Itself for the purpose of sportive play."　　Lord Vasishtha

Parabrahman (Absolute Reality)

Jnana —— Path of nondual abidance ←　**Atmic Sankalpa**　→ Path of false separation —— Ajnana

(Divine Will in Potential Manifestation)

Lila Sankalpa
(Divine Will At Sport)

Mayic Sankalpa
(Power of Obscuration)

Reality | Relativity

NIRVANA | SAMSARA

Appearance of Time, Space, Causation, Mind, Intellect as Cosmic Principles

Appearance of Time, Space, Causality, Mind, Intellect as assumed Reality

Jnanakasha/Chittakasha Universes as Modes of Awareness

Mayakasha Universes as Ego-based Ideation

Acquisition of an Illumined Guru and Adherence to the Spiritual Path

Reliance on Ego/Mind complex and Belief in Conventional Paths

SADHANA | WORLDLINESS

Disciplined curbing of the Mind's tendency towards Sankalpa

Deluded contemplation of the things of the world as being real

Practice of Yoga to remove the tendency for Sankalpa and the desire for objects of the World

Consciousness in association with Sankalpa contemplates ever denser states of Matter

Attenuation of Sankalpa via the practice of Asamvedana — nonreceptivity to desires

Longing for desire-based existence in an embodied condition leading to cycles of birth and death

REALIZATION | COMPLACENCY

Contemplation of all with the eye of abhava — nonexistence

Experience of pain and acceptance of suffering as being real

Attainment of Samadhi and Absorption in Brahman

Fear of pain/attachment to pleasure leading to rebirth in ignorance

"By Atmic Sankalpa is meant Divine Will in manifestation, but it degrades into Mayic Sankalpa via ego-based ideation that arises as a result of a falsified relationship between subject and object."　　Lord Vasishtha

quents the realm of relativity, he practices spiritual disciplines so as to depart the body and the physical realm in a realized state — thus, the differences between *atmic* and *mayic sankalpa*.

In the case of *sankalpa* and *vikalpa*, inside of the Indian *rishi's* unique way of looking upon the world, and in view of the teaching of *atmic sankalpa* and *mayic sankalpa*, it may be wondered that there is no middle ground. That is, either one is in possession of the keys to refined mental projection or is not. As in the case of Lord Buddha's perspective, that there are souls who are awakened spiritually and there are souls who are not, such a seemingly black and white view seems to leave out those who are as yet struggling to awaken. In the eyes of the illumined, however, this class of beings is considered already awake; they only need to follow through to realize just what it is that they have awakened to. If they fall back asleep in the process, though, they run the risk of engaging in *sankalpic* dreaming for an untold length of time. On the other hand, to go forward is to accomplish what the seers call moving *"from lower truth to Higher Truth — asato ma sadgamaya."* The chart on the facing page places this teaching in easy form for inspection and comprehension.

Basically, and though there are a multitude of reasons why beings take birth, most souls who take embodiment do so at the behest of unfulfilled desires and the *karma* from unresolved actions past. Therefore they are born in what the seers call *mithyajnana*, literally, "false knowledge." The box at the bottom of the chart on the facing page describes that type of life, fraught with negativities and always beset by dangers — both for themselves and for those with whom they come into contact. The next step forward is not much better, called *ajnana* — the lack of any real knowledge. Whereas the beings suffering *mithyajnana* are deluded into evil acts, those under the press of *ajnana* are possibly doing some of the right things but for the wrong reasons. That is, gaining knowledge, even attaining scholarship, are not bad in and of themselves, but reach no plateau of higher wisdom when undertaken with a view to merely gain wealth, wield power, secure objects, gather possessions, and the like, all for the fleeting experiences of pleasure and enjoyment.

It is really only when *jnana* dawns in the mind that any appreciable progress is made. And the sages and seers divide this category up into lower knowledge, called *pravrittijnana*, and higher knowledge, called *nivrittijnana*. *"Pravrittimarga"* is the path of social action amidst a worldly society. *"Nivrittimarga"* refers to the path of renunciation of the world and its many relative pursuits. As the box under the *jnana* category reflects, it is when actions and seeking turns altruistic that a definitive shift in the area of overall *jnana* is finally made. That is, instead of preoccupation with the ego's gratification with facts and figures, secular knowledge, social service, and the like, the soul instead begins to turn towards study, instruction, and self-effort — all in the purely spiritual arena. This, in turn, and over time, leads the soul towards a very special type of knowing referred to as *vijnana*. Selfless service, compassion, devotion, worship, and the like are facets of life here, and culminate in the acquisition of that rare set of occurrences listed under the category of *anubhava* — direct spiritual experiences. As the chart illustrates, the Mother of Wisdom awaits the soul there, with the incomparable attainment of *Brahmajnana*. This is knowledge of Reality, of the Ultimate, and all that it entails and consists of. Words like *samadhi, nirvana, kaivalya, moksha,* and others help explain this most precious of principles.

From lower truth to Higher Truth is how beings proceed, then, never from falsity to Truth. Knowledge of Reality exists in every being; it is only buried deep in some, while in others it shines near the surface like gold, waiting to be fully uncovered and retrieved. Running a race in a dream on this level, in regards to this particular area, traverses a living being's own inner terrain which stretches all the way from benighted mind inwards to enlightened Consciousness — from *mithyajnana,* to *ajnana,* to *pravrittijnana,* to *nivrittijnana,* to *vijnana,* to *Brahmajnana*. Sri Ramakrishna's quote at the top right corner of this chart boils this all down to a threefold teaching for us, and in metaphoric fashion. That is, a being devoid of special or subtle knowledge is like a man who does not know that fire is potential in wood; he is an *ajnani*. But a *jnani* would be like the man who knows that fire exists in wood but does not know how to draw it out. The *vijnani* holds the key, however, and utilizes it for opening up the secret of fire in wood for the highest good of all beings.

"Lead Us From Lower Truth To Higher Truth"

Brahmajnana

The Vak Devi

"An ajnani does not know that there is fire potential in wood. A jnani knows this, but cannot bring it out. A vijnani possessed of Brahmajnana not only knows that fire is potential in wood, but gathers it up, strikes the flame, cooks the food, and feeds others."
Sri Ramakrishna

Paramadvaita

Vijnana

The acquisition of direct spiritual experience
Combining devotion and wisdom in meditation
Compassionate use of wisdom to remove suffering
Worship of the deities in a nondual state of mind
Transmitting the teachings to help free or liberate

Paravidya

Nivrttijnana

Jnana

Pravrttijnana

Teaching spiritual disciplines to sincere aspirants
Study of scriptures under a spiritual teacher
Reading of spiritual books for edification
Knowledge utilized for altruistic motives
Secular subjects gained for conventional means
Gathering of information for ego-gratification
Preoccupation with facts and figures

Aparavidya

Ajnana

Teaching for selfish gain and profit
Scholarship to gain fame, out of ambition
Intellectualism for pleasure-seeking and power
Knowledge used merely for making a living

Avidya

Mithyajnana — Actions which are mindless, deluded, violent, harmful, spiteful, hateful, jealous, and evil.

Pratibha — Power of Intelligence

"Everything — the world, manifestations therein, enjoying, suffering, and departing, and the power of conjuring the realms of name and form, can and should be directly designated and attributed to one's own intelligence. Other factors such as fate, destiny, karma, and even grace, also reside within and spring from that selfsame power." Babaji Bob Kindler

Pratibhasikasatta
Unreal or Apparent Dream-Reality

Pratibha
Self-Aware Intelligence

Devout offering to the Lord, despite suffering

Pratibandhaka
Power of Obstruction

Pratibandhakabhava
The Power of Intelligence which removes Obstructions

"Gods and goddesses, father and mother, or any other kith or kin, cannot confer greater benefit than that of the well-directed intelligence. This intelligence is incomprehensible and exceedingly subtle. It wanders wherever and whenever it desires. Therefore, the wise ones carefully watch over this intelligence, which resides in the cavern of the heart, and utilize it to free themselves, and others, from the shackles of Mara." Lord Buddha

When the soul is introduced to the pathway and ascent from lower to higher Truth, the question that occurs to the sincere spiritual aspirant is, "How is such a transition going to be accomplished?" Certainly some adjustments to life, and mind, must be instigated. But the real question the observant student asks should revolve around the *mayic* conundrum upon which this "race in a dream" called life is taking place; for his mind is dwelling, at least in its present unillumined state, in relativity. *Sadhana*, the spiritual exercises which a truth-seeker engages in to rid himself of *mayic* tendencies and overlays, is also performed in relativity. Some say that Albert Einstein declared most astutely, *"Problems cannot be solved at the same level of awareness that created them."* And what is true for physics, and life in general, must also hold true for metaphysics and beyond, namely spiritual life. To put a finer point on it, the obstructions one will inevitably encounter in life, the power of intelligence that can be utilized to remove them when applied rightly, and the holder of such refined intelligence — all of them are players in a dream which will, when spiritual awakening occurs, come to rest, to peace. This is what our next chart up for study, on the previous page, reveals.

In order to proceed from lower truth to higher Truth, the individual is best served by awakening to his or her own intrinsic intelligence. When spiritual teachers speak of intelligence, it should be noted that they are not speaking primarily of the intellect. The intellect, called the *buddhi*, which is one of the four aspects of mind in *Vedanta*, is a sheath, a container for intelligence. Since the ego, called *ahamkara*, is also a part of the fourfold mind complex, all that becomes stored within the intellectual sheath gets tainted by the ego, meaning possessed. But what is getting possessed is intellectual information, not *pratibha*. *Pratibha* is awareness of subtle wisdom connected to the soul, and to the Self. As Sri Ramakrishna has stated, a match, when placed in water for a few seconds, will not strike when taken out, even though it still has sparking potential in it. A flint, however, even if kept in a river for centuries, will strike sparks immediately when retrieved and struck against another rock. *Pratibha* is like that flint, whereas the intellect is like a match. The latter is also quite limited in its capacity, and at best has only one light in it. A flint can create fire again and again. When a spiritual aspirant awakens the potential of *pratibha* and its *pratibhandakabhava* element, lying undiscovered even in the ordinary person's mind, the power of obstruction, *pratibhandaka*, can be waylaid at will. What is more, the entire dream of limited intelligence, referred to as *pratibhasikasatta*, can be pierced through using *pratibha* to effect a full awakening into Reality.

The chart on the facing page reveals these four pregnant terms for consideration. As the quote at the bottom of the chart reflects, beings the likes of Lord Buddha have spoken of this inherent power in the human soul, encouraging intrepid souls to locate, activate, and benefit by it. Since it is not a part of relativity, is outside the usual ken of conventional solutions and ordinary *sadhana* — being a special power of the soul — having access to its radiant luster will afford solutions and advancement which are known only to adept souls and past masters.

Drumming up this subtle force from within takes boldness and courage — not in show, pretense, or hopefulness, but in internal action. One must locate its presence as one would, to quote the *Svetashvataropanisad*, *"...bring out oil from sesame seeds, butter from curd, water from underground springs, fire from wood,"* etc. This is why the ordinary intellect, even when it is well-stocked with knowledge, cannot and does not necessarily lead to its discovery, and when faced with unexpected challenges and outright calamities only falls back, again and again, on repetition of past temporary successes and pallid imitation of other intellects like itself. For, knowledge has its opposite, called ignorance. But where is ignorance in the illumined soul? Where has it gone to? The *Upanisads* say that *"He who, by means of truthfulness, self-control, and concentration, after hearing of the all-pervasiveness of the Self, searches for It via meditation as being rooted in Self-knowledge, that singular one becomes the Supreme Brahman and destroys ignorance altogether."*

The dreamer laboring under the debilitating influence of ignorance, along with his dream of its polar opposite, knowledge, is shaken awake by the power inherent in his Self, the real soul of mankind. As Sri Krishna says, the tree of *samsara* is cut down and destroyed at its very roots by this fiery power placed into action. The following chart gives us a look at this Tree of *Samsara*.

Diaphanous as a gossamer web, flexuous as a complex labyrinth, mesmerizing as a house of mirrors, and playing chimerically into the all-too-willing imagination of mankind, *samsara*, or *maya*, is nothing to be trifled with — not if awakening from the dream of pain, pleasure, and other flummoxing dualities is important to the soul. Adishankara, spiritual champion of one of India's most noble traditions, and revered in India overall, impresses us with this point, as the two forthcoming charts will demonstrate.

In the chart on the facing page we find images representing facets of the Tree of *Samsara* via Shankara's description of it in the *Vivekachudamani*. The seed of this tree is none other than the *guna* of *tamas*, that inertia-causing quality of nature, residing also in the mind, which blinds the soul and stymies any and all forward progress towards liberation. The roots of this tremendous and terrible tree symbolize the body of mankind which, when imbued with the *guna* of *tamas*, freezes in place, thereby foregoing both recognition of and access to its inherent qualities for higher life and wisdom. Even man's *prana*/life-force, symbolized by the trunk of this towering tree, has grown slow and unable to galvanize itself, like sap in winter. And with such a base — soporific seed, reluctant roots, and tenuous truck — how is the human being going to rise to a nobly-lived life and a divinely inspired mind? How will such a soul, under the influence of this many-branching tree's gloomy shade, act and think?

The branches and their contents answer these questions. The bird of the human soul, precariously perched in this sprawling tree, which should be sipping the nectar of sunshine beaming down, instead focuses its benighted awareness on the earthly flowers of sense objects, attracted by their many colors. Caught up in the branches of the five senses, and flitting about the variegated collection of small twigs, which are its attachments, it pecks now and again at both ripe and rotten fruit in turn, which represent pleasure and pain respectively.

The bound soul's actions, which are like soil and water, further feed and nourish this *samsaric* tree, which waxes strong and resilient, impervious to the soul's attempts to escape its insidious domination. Earthly and worldly activities, as Shankara states in the quote at the bottom of the chart, only tend to immure the soul further within the tree's far-reaching vines and tendrils, especially those works that are done as offerings to the small ego-self, which senselessly or callously forego the benefit of others. The rank aroma of this towering timber, or sickly sweet as the case may be, exudes into the atmosphere of relativity and permeates all levels of human existence, numbing and intoxicating the soul and convincing it that any idea of escape is undesirable.

In the *Bhagavad Gita*, while using the banyan tree, or *Ashvattha* as it is called in India, as a symbol for the tree of *samsara*, Sri Krishna instructs his beloved disciple Arjuna as to how to escape its far-flung influence. The word *"ashvattha"* infers by its meaning something which is different today than what it was yesterday, and will be tomorrow. Thus it is a fitting word, and tree, to symbolize *maya* or *samsara*. About this tree of *samsara* He states: *"Its presence is not perceived as it truly is here on earth by living beings through their five senses, nor can they divine its origin or its end. They cannot disenchant themselves. Therefore, Arjuna, circumvent its influence entirely and cut it down with the axe of firm discrimination and nonpareil nonattachment. Then shall you seek that Goal of all goals which will close the doors of rebirth forever and return no more. Instead, seek refuge in the Primal Purusha out of which sprang all of this continual activity, tree and all."*

The greatest spiritual teachers of mankind do not waste any time, and do not spend undue energy, on any of the many futile pursuits that fall under the auspice of *samsara*. They do not want to run a footrace with *maya* in the dreamland of projection and illusion. When even good acts and good souls find themselves trapped for lifetimes in ongoing occupations, whose effects find no ultimate solutions, appearing and disappearing like leaves in a maelstrom, then who, or what, can stand against the world-bewitching *maya* with its *samsaric* rounds of birth and death in ignorance?

Moving back, and onwards, to consult Shankara once again, we find that, like Sri Krishna, he also advises honing a kind of cutlery for the swift dispatching of the tree of *samsara* — that of the Sword of Discrimination. The chart on the following page illustrates this fine internal weapon.

The Tree of Samsara
From the Vivekachudamani — Sloka 145

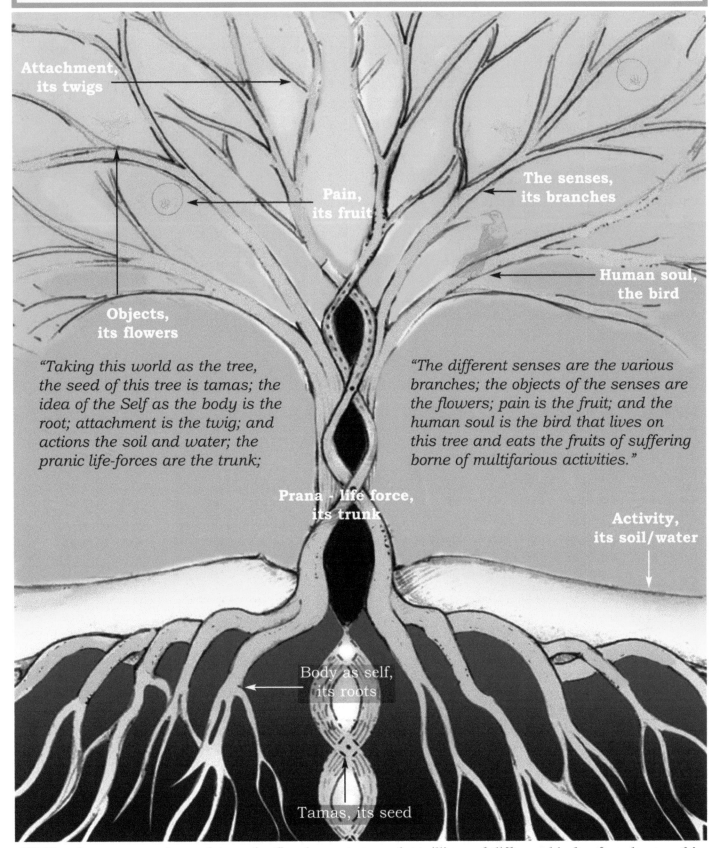

Attachment,
its twigs

Pain,
its fruit

The senses,
its branches

Human soul,
the bird

Objects,
its flowers

"Taking this world as the tree,
the seed of this tree is tamas; the
idea of the Self as the body is the
root; attachment is the twig; and
actions the soil and water; the
pranic life-forces are the trunk;

"The different senses are the various
branches; the objects of the senses are
the flowers; pain is the fruit; and the
human soul is the bird that lives on
this tree and eats the fruits of suffering
borne of multifarious activities."

Prana - life force,
its trunk

Activity,
its soil/water

Body as self,
its roots

Tamas, its seed

"Neither by weapons, by scripture, by fire, by water, nor by millions of different kinds of works can this
tree be hewn down, but only by discrimination leading to knowledge of the Self." Adishankaracharya

The Great Sword of Discrimination

From the Vivekachudamani — Slokas 147-148

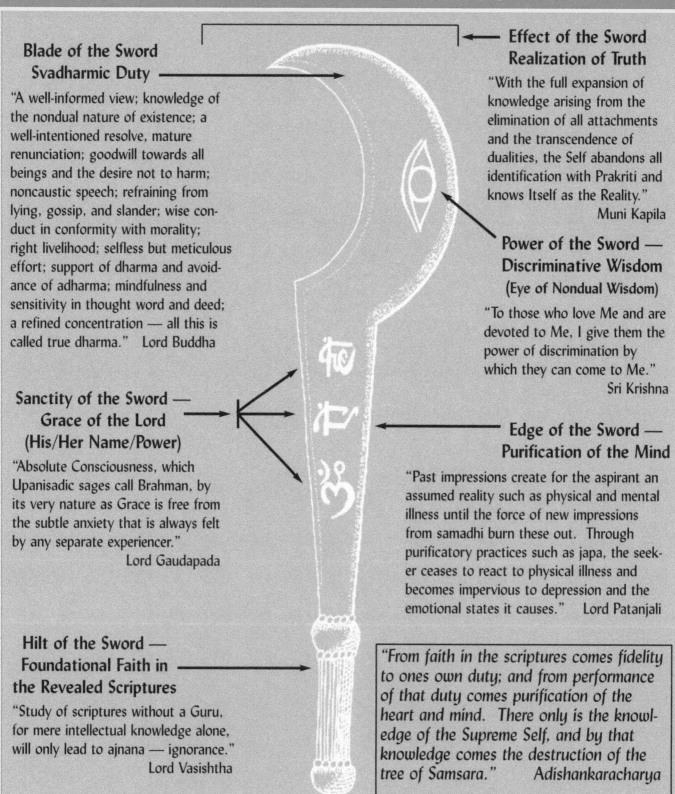

**Blade of the Sword
Svadharmic Duty**

"A well-informed view; knowledge of the nondual nature of existence; a well-intentioned resolve, mature renunciation; goodwill towards all beings and the desire not to harm; noncaustic speech; refraining from lying, gossip, and slander; wise conduct in conformity with morality; right livelihood; selfless but meticulous effort; support of dharma and avoidance of adharma; mindfulness and sensitivity in thought word and deed; a refined concentration — all this is called true dharma." Lord Buddha

**Sanctity of the Sword —
Grace of the Lord
(His/Her Name/Power)**

"Absolute Consciousness, which Upanisadic sages call Brahman, by its very nature as Grace is free from the subtle anxiety that is always felt by any separate experiencer."
Lord Gaudapada

**Hilt of the Sword —
Foundational Faith in
the Revealed Scriptures**

"Study of scriptures without a Guru, for mere intellectual knowledge alone, will only lead to ajnana — ignorance."
Lord Vasishtha

**Effect of the Sword
Realization of Truth**

"With the full expansion of knowledge arising from the elimination of all attachments and the transcendence of dualities, the Self abandons all identification with Prakriti and knows Itself as the Reality."
Muni Kapila

**Power of the Sword —
Discriminative Wisdom**
(Eye of Nondual Wisdom)

"To those who love Me and are devoted to Me, I give them the power of discrimination by which they can come to Me."
Sri Krishna

**Edge of the Sword —
Purification of the Mind**

"Past impressions create for the aspirant an assumed reality such as physical and mental illness until the force of new impressions from samadhi burn these out. Through purificatory practices such as japa, the seeker ceases to react to physical illness and becomes impervious to depression and the emotional states it causes." Lord Patanjali

"From faith in the scriptures comes fidelity to ones own duty; and from performance of that duty comes purification of the heart and mind. There only is the knowledge of the Supreme Self, and by that knowledge comes the destruction of the tree of Samsara." Adishankaracharya

"Only the Great Sword of Discrimination can cut down the tree of Samsara, and that Sword should be whetted by the Grace of the Lord." Adishankaracharya

As so many of the great *rishis* and luminaries of Mother India have proclaimed, real spiritual life — despite all appearances to the contrary — is not truly underway and does not even gets its rightful and authentic start without the aspirant gaining possession of the superlative quality of *viveka,* discrimination between the real and the unreal. Call it the essential and nonessential, substantial and nonsubstantial, sentient and insentient, but it all amounts to the ability to know the Truth, free from all overlays, sublations, superimpositions, conditionings, etc. Another way of saying this is with *viveka* in mind, one can pierce through the coverings that *maya* places over Reality, and know them also to be unreal, nonactual.

Helped along by Shankara's inspiration in the *Vivekachudamani*, this chart has been fashioned using the teachings of various luminaries of India throughout many millennia. In his own words, and in two separate quotes, Shankara avers that it is the knowledge of the Supreme Self that will destroy the tree of *samsara,* but also mentions discrimination and Grace. Grace would be the *bhakta's* way of proceeding, Self-knowledge would be the *jnani's* way. Perhaps, since a bird needs two wings to fly, both are required.

Whatever the case, for whoever the pathfinder, this all-powerful sword seems to be a part of the arsenal of every soul who strives to penetrate and transcend *samsara* and remain free. It has a blade representing higher duty, called *dharma;* it has a hilt symbolizing foundational faith in the revealed scriptures; it has its sharp edge which facilitates purity and clarity of mind. On the more esoteric side it bears a wisdom eye whose practical usage allows for seeing through illusions and deceptions of all types — individual, collective, and cosmic. On its blade are carved ancient *Sanskrit* symbols — like *Aum, Aim,* and *Hrim* — representing subtle seeds of transformative spiritual power. Finally, there is its overall effect, emancipation of the ultimate kind, called *samadhi.*

Since the most problematic elements of the tree of *samsara* occur to the ordinary individual due to the five senses and their attachment to material objects due to desire, the sword of discrimination is perfectly suited to rid the aspiring soul of such fetters. But the soul must aspire; otherwise, no appreciable change for the better will occur. A warrior may own a famous sword, but if he does not pick it up and wield it there will be no victory. It will simply lay on his mantle place, or hang mounted on the wall of his dwelling place, and his enemies will sneer and laugh at any attempt on his part to walk freely, with nobility, in and out of the village at will. Such is the case of the man or woman who fails to discover this inner weapon, then unsheathe, loft, and deliver the decisive stroke which will cut the tree of *samsara* down forever. The power of discrimination, much akin to our recent study of *pratibha* on previous pages, is an inherent force, and like grace, is never apart from or estranged from the Soul. Every person must find it and put it into operations. Each is his or her own savior, then, and the grace which they at first seek for "on high" is within them. This is what Sri Ramakrishna meant when He stated that *"The wind of God's Grace is always blowing, but one must raise their sail to catch it."* Even knowing this much of the Truth will eventually culminate in the search that uncovers this mighty weapon. The rest is all about developing the subtle muscles needed to lift and wield it.

Little clues are found amongst the quotes selected for this chart regarding the sword's nature. Gaudapada mentions that the sense of a separate self, and the fear which always accompanies it, is done away with by gripping this confidence-building sword. Lord Kapila advises the expansion of ones knowledge to increase the ability to heft its weight. Patanjali encourages the use of *japa,* associated with the *bijams* carved on the sword's blade, for greater strength in utilizing it. And Lord Vasishtha emphasizes faith in and resort to the spiritual preceptor so that the secrets for operating this superlative weapon will be both discovered and placed into operation with full assurance of complete success.

Then there is the acquisition of helpful knowledge about the enemy. Though the masters of *Sankhya, Tantra,* and *Vedanta* all agree that *maya,* or *samsara,* is insentient, even illusory, it nevertheless seems real to the one facing off with it. Knowing its facets will be of great help, then, as the next study and its related chart will reveal.

This rather involved but informative chart on the sixteen evolutes of *maya*, all listed in the box on the lower left hand side of the chart on the facing page, carries other great and revealing secrets for the sincere student's perusal. However, the crucial point for the aspiring *sadhaka* is not so much to study *maya* as to simply become aware of its subtle presence so as to be able to draw back from it. Thus, observer rather than a participator is advised by the luminaries. For, as Sri Ramakrishna has said, if one studies *maya* it tends to seduce one into its game, as instanced by the myriad beings who are playing its game all the time, and without ever suspecting its omnifarious presence permeating their lives. Thus, the phrase and heading to this chapter, "Running a Race in a Dream."

Thus, *maya*, or *samsara* as we have been calling it, is pure legerdemain. Its artful deception routes millions of beings in multitudinous realms on countless levels of existence into what the seers of India have called *"the illusion of finitude."* Operating a veritable and ongoing riot act of complex and interpenetrating causes and effects sporting positive, negative, and mixed ramifications, *maya's* play of birth, life, death, and rebirth that propels the transmigration of souls from one state to another (all without any movement actually taking place at all) rolls onward inexorably to who knows where. And most stultifying of all, it really has no actual bearing on Absolute Truth whatsoever. The *Tantric* adepts are well-known for pondering *maya*, and contributing the results of these contemplations to Indian philosophy. They say, *"It is both real and unreal (sadasat) — real since it is the material of which the worlds are made of, and unreal since it creates illusion and does not constitute the real nature of Paramashiva."*

To put it more concisely, *maya/samsara* is the simulacrum of Reality, appearing as true but not delivering Truth. Or, to use another way of explaining, it is verisimilar, so embodied beings easily accept it as fact, as true existence. As Lord Vasishtha, a knower of Divine Reality, states in the quote at the top right corner of the chart under study, *maya* consists of and proceeds upon the human mind's knowledge of diversity, and this excruciatingly simple fact can only be seen and put into proper perspective for good by knowing that One who transcends diversity. In other words, where Oneness is, or *Brahman*, or "homogeneity," — whatever one calls Reality — *maya* vanishes, revealing that, like a mirage in the desert which does not moisten a single grain of sand, it was never really present to begin with.

Along with *Brahman*, *maya* has been one of the main subjects on the mind of the Indian *Rishis* for millennia. One will be hard put to find such a word or a concept as *maya* in any other religion or philosophical system, especially in such a well-defined way. And what is its definition? As a summation of what Shankara and his line of *gurus* thinks about *maya*, and so we know what we are dealing with, it is:

- the power of God *(paramesha-shakti)*
- undivided/undifferentiated *(avyakta)*
- indefinable *(avyakrta)*
- beginningless *(anadi)* [but has an end in *Brahmajnana*]
- possessed of three qualities - *gunas (trigunatmika)*
- insentience, or ignorance *(jada/avidyam)*
- incomprehensible except by its own actions *(kary'anumeya)*
- the projector of the universe *(jagat sarvam idam)*
- indescribable *(anir-vachaniya-rupa)*
- neither real, nor unreal, nor an admixture *(sat/asat-satasat)*
- made to vanish by the knowledge of *Brahman (sarpa brahmo rajju viveka)*

Taking into consideration the wisdom of many different illumined beings and religious traditions on the puzzling subject of *samsara*, then, we find a veritable host of welcome information about its nature — as difficult as this is to define. Perhaps a story from the *Vedic/Tantric* tradition will help us to see better.

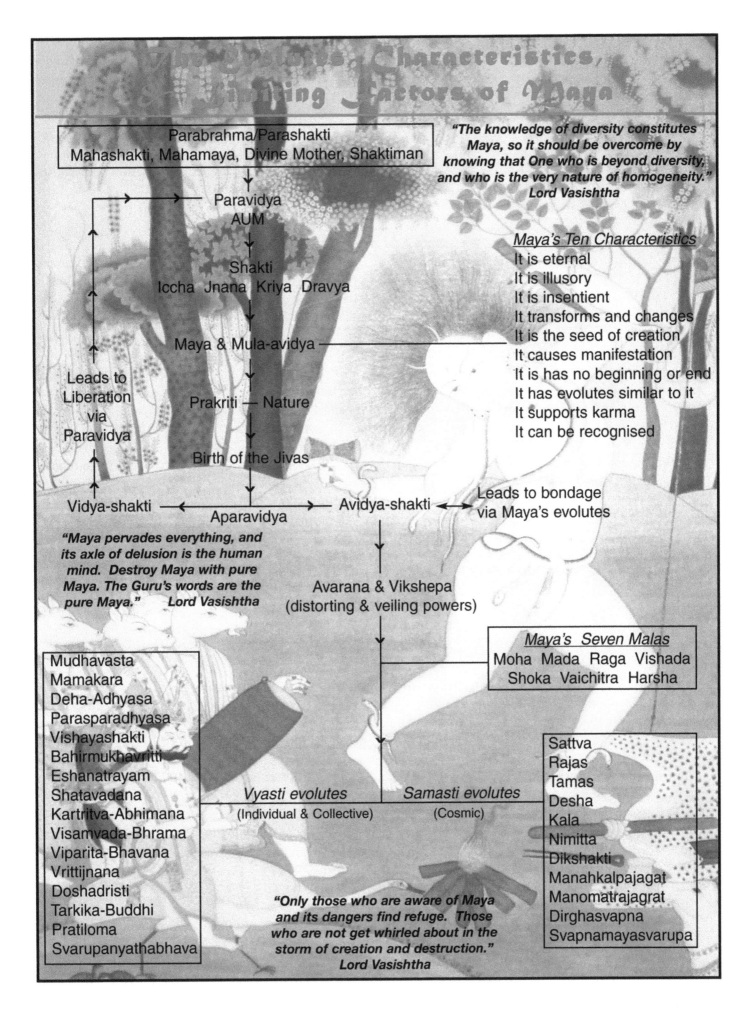

Parabrahma/Parashakti
Mahashakti, Mahamaya, Divine Mother, Shaktiman

↓

Paravidya
AUM

↓

Shakti
Iccha Jnana Kriya Dravya

↓

Maya & Mula-avidya ——————

↓

Prakriti — Nature

↓

Birth of the Jivas

Leads to
Liberation
via
Paravidya

Vidya-shakti ←——→ ———————— ←——→ Avidya-shakti
Aparavidya

Leads to bondage
via Maya's evolutes

*"Maya pervades everything, and
its axle of delusion is the human
mind. Destroy Maya with pure
Maya. The Guru's words are the
pure Maya."* **Lord Vasishtha**

↓

Avarana & Vikshepa
(distorting & veiling powers)

↓

Mudhavasta
Mamakara
Deha-Adhyasa
Parasparadhyasa
Vishayashakti
Bahirmukhavritti
Eshanatrayam
Shatavadana
Kartritva-Abhimana
Visamvada-Bhrama
Viparita-Bhavana
Vrittijnana
Doshadristi
Tarkika-Buddhi
Pratiloma
Svarupanyathabhava

Vyasti evolutes
(Individual & Collective)

Samasti evolutes
(Cosmic)

*"Only those who are aware of Maya
and its dangers find refuge. Those
who are not get whirled about in the
storm of creation and destruction."*
Lord Vasishtha

*"The knowledge of diversity constitutes
Maya, so it should be overcome by
knowing that One who is beyond diversity,
and who is the very nature of homogeneity."*
Lord Vasishtha

Maya's Ten Characteristics
It is eternal
It is illusory
It is insentient
It transforms and changes
It is the seed of creation
It causes manifestation
It is has no beginning or end
It has evolutes similar to it
It supports karma
It can be recognised

Maya's Seven Malas
Moha Mada Raga Vishada
Shoka Vaichitra Harsha

Sattva
Rajas
Tamas
Desha
Kala
Nimitta
Dikshakti
Manahkalpajagat
Manomatrajagrat
Dirghasvapna
Svapnamayasvarupa

Stories about Narada and Lord *Vishnu* abound in the scriptural history of India and reveal many profound lessons. Once, sage Narada desired to understand the Lord's *maya*. After trying to dissuade him from this request, but to no avail, the Lord took him flying high on Garuda's back. They crossed over many beautiful realms of manifestation. Stopping at one particular realm, *Vishnu* asked Narada to bathe in a lotus-filled pond lying there. No sooner did Narada enter the waters when his male form turned into a female form and he forgot his identity. Gone were his harp, clothes, memory, and also the beloved form of Sri *Vishnu* whom had mounted Garuda and flown away. Looking about, Narada, now a woman, noticed a king and his retinue approaching. The king took this lady back to his castle and, in time, married her. Over the years, they had many children and grandchildren.

As time wore on, Narada, now a queen named Saubhagya Sundari, became entirely immersed in royal family life and was completely forgetful of her past identity under the influence of the Lord's *Maya*. After many years of happiness, a rival king became jealous of the royal couple's lands and wealth and waged war on her husband, King Taladhavaja. The queen's regal husband and many sons marched to the battlefield for victory, but all were killed outright in the slaughter that ensued. Making haste to the battlefield to see the outcome, the queen beheld the scene and, beside herself with grief, bewailed her fate. Gathering up the bodies of her loved ones with the help of her attendants, she constructed a funeral pyre and lit it aflame with the idea of committing *sati*. As she approached the fire, one hand extended to ward off the heat long enough to enter, an arm sprang out of the flames and pulled her in. Recovering from this shock, and with eyes wide in wonder, Narada found himself in male form again, standing in the pool that he had earlier entered to bathe, and holding the Lord's hand — as if not a moment had passed. Gazing meaningfully into His devotee's eyes, Lord *Vishnu* said with a wry smile: *"Now do you understand a little of my maya? But what are you doing standing here in these waters? Come forth and let us be off!"*

By such stories as this we can comprehend that the Lord's *Maya* is inexorable. To fully comprehend it is impossible. Instead of embroiling ourselves in it by attempting to analyze what it is, we must instead simply recognize its existence. After knowing *Maya* as a fact of existence, we can then implement useful practices prescribed by the *guru* and affirmed in the scriptures, such as discrimination and detachment. These cause *Maya* to dissipate like fog under direct sunlight. Lord Vasishtha prescribes this way, saying, *"Destroy maya by rising above it rather than trying to comprehend it. In other words, do not rack your brain as to the origin of maya, but rather inquire into the means of its destruction from the illumined gurus. If it be destroyed, then one will know how it arose, whence it arose, its nature, and how it perishes."*

The discriminative art of recognition around *maya* constitutes an entirely different approach from attempting to analyze *Maya*, then, for *Maya* is of the very nature of unfathomable complexity. *Maya* is the cause for the universe of name and form itself. All phenomena are appearances projected by it in conjunction with the mind in the state of *sankalpa* and *vikalpa*. Even time and space have been facilitated by this inscrutable power. Therefore, all learning pertaining to the universe of name and form is simply a study of *maya*. One who perceives this is immediately exempt from accepting the world to be ultimately real. Here, a distinction must be made between *daivi maya*, the higher aspect of *maya* that the Divine Mother of the Universe (*Mahashakti*) utilizes for manifesting Her Consciousness into form, and *maya* proper, where matter is taken to be real, to be Reality. The latter, being a *vikara* form, not only causes the universe to seem real, but also is responsible for the impression that the elements of *Prakriti* (nature) undergo transformation. Thus, *maya* is a force of illusion that covers truth and distorts human understanding. As the *Tantricists* say, *"Since maya is woven into the fabric of manifestation itself, one must carefully notice its hiding places. In a field of rattlesnakes, one must avoid them by heeding their warnings."*

It has been stated that it is not wise to enter into an analysis of *Maya's* domain. This assertion allows for one very important exception. Ignorance binds only those who are without the knowledge of their true nature. If a striving being, through awareness of *Paravidya* (Higher Wisdom), gains enlightenment and comes to realize the Self within as eternal and indivisible Consciousness, then *maya's* powers are rendered harmless. This is instanced by the Divine Mother's *daivi maya* which She uses to create forms, circumstances and locations for the work of Her *Avatars*, devotees and other luminaries. As for others — scientists, politicians, lawyers, mathematicians, physicians, authors, artists, workers and the rest — if they are as yet unaware of their divine nature, then they only play into *maya's* hands and remain in the dark about *Paravidya*. Out of touch with Reality, they then enter into the speculative mode of *vaichitra,* varieties, and become preoccupied with the exacting analysis of *maya* through the avenues of their respective occupations. This is the one main drawback of pursuing *aparavidya* (lower knowledge) as the highest aim. It can lead towards higher knowledge if utilized in conjunction with moral and ethical living, but quite often embroils the mind in a futile obsession with details and superficialities, drawing it down into habits of restlessness and lethargy and leading it away from true fulfillment.

Aparavidya also conduces to worldliness, as it takes the mind away from higher pursuits and avenues of expression and places it on purely conventional modes of attainment such as fame, success, family life, pleasantries and gathering sustenance. Then, the truths contained in *Paravidya* — those eternal and sacred principles of nondual truth, comprehensive wisdom, unalloyed bliss, inner peace, and the transcendent nature of pure conscious Awareness beyond name and form — remain undiscovered, and unplumbed. Then, as luminaries from many walks of philosophy declare, *"Maya creates illusion which is moha in individual minds. A jiva's delusion arises when it cannot make any distinction between atma and anatma and it identifies the Self with the not-self and the not-self with the Self."*

As we trace down the chart on page 279, we find that *Paravidya*, just mentioned, emanates off of the Supreme Being like rays from a sun. This superlative wisdom, a facet of *Brahman's Shakti*, is presided over and distributed by the *Mahashakti's* four aspects of *Iccha, Jnana, Kriya,* and *Dravya* (see pages 46 & 145). Below their domain and direct influence, embodied beings encounter the crush of *maya* proper and its companion of root ignorance, called *mula-vidya*. It is here that the "Ten Characteristics of *maya*" apply, and they make a valuable study for the one who would be prepared.

Illumined souls, from their safer, steadier, and more detached position, have long pondered the mystery of *maya* and noted down its peculiarities in order to help the *jiva*, the embodied being, to escape its effects and gain realization of the divine Self within. Over the centuries, *Tantric* adepts especially excelled in enumerating many of *maya's* workings. The *Tantra* philosophy lists ten characteristics of *maya* to help beings recognize its workings — and detach from them. Listed on the chart in short form, they are given here utilizing a more expanded form:

- It is eternal, for it exists even after *pralaya*, the dissolution of the universe of name and form.
- It is illusory since it creates illusion in the minds of living beings.
- Being the very material of the many worlds, it is insentient.
- It undergoes transformation without ever losing its own identity.
- It is the seed that spawned the universe, which appears like a mirage before the mind and senses.
- Since it is the initial cause of manifestation, it acts in hundreds of ways, each of them with many permutations.
- It has no beginning, middle or end.
- All of its evolutes partake of its same nature.
- It supports sense perception and activity in beings so long as the results of past deeds are not exhausted or neutralized.
- It can be recognized by the grace of God revealed in the illumined intellect.

Placing knowledge of *maya* in this ten-fold perspective is tantamount to acknowledging its existence in individual life and thereby being able to ferret out its offshoots and work to do away with them via *sadhana*, actual spiritual practice. The result is an informed existence rather than a deluded one, a contented mind rather than a restless one, a matured philosophy of life rather than a skewed view of Reality — or maybe no belief in Reality at all, as is the case with many souls today.

There is an eleventh characteristic of *Maya* as well, that being that *maya* gives rise to seven kinds of *malas*, or limiting modes of operation. As the chart on page 279 is traced further, the appearance of nature and the dream-birth of the *jivas* (embodied beings) take place. At this juncture, reincarnating souls ought to have a choice whether to return to their original state of perfection (wake up from dreaming in *maya*) or, unwisely, continue the dream process of the ego and wend their way deeper into the flexuous web of *samsara*. Those who do not know of this choice due to root ignorance reject the wisdom *shakti* and fasten onto its opposite, *avidya shakti*. As the chart reflects, *avidya shakti* veils whatever intrinsic knowledge the soul possesses, and a visit to the realm of the Seven *Malas* of *Maya* is assured.

In *Tantra*, imperfections are not looked upon as fixed defects — like a permanent black mark on the soul — but rather apparent flaws that ripen with time and experience and duly fall away. The *malas* of *maya* are viewed as intentionally imposed limitations existing in order that relative life can be transcended and divine life can proceed. As life is lived, the *malas* gradually disappear and the aspiring soul is released into *Paramashiva* — the highest abidance. In *Sanskrit*, the *malas* are called *moha, mada, raga, vishada, shoka, vaichitra* and *harsha*.

• **Moha** is a particularly insidious form of morbid fascination which causes beings to become attached to evil deeds as if they were good deeds. In today's governments, judicial systems, social organizations, and religious institutions, for instance, beings are perpetuating all manner of detrimental actions and calling them beneficial. It is mass delusion on a collective level. Going to war to establish peace, judging people by harsh and inflexible standards of law rather than with compassion, performing social service with selfish motives and hidden agendas, upholding false dualistic doctrines in the name of religion — these are some examples of *moha* in the individual and collective consciousness. Educating young minds by teaching only worldly knowledge while ignoring the source of all knowledge is another example of *moha*.

• **Mada** taints the mind with vanity and self-aggrandizement. Attracted by glory and fame, beings seek after and accept that which is base and ugly, thinking it to be desirable and beautiful. Attachment to the body which decays and dies, obsession with fame which only brings disenchantment and loss of peace of mind, seeking after power that gradually corrupts and destroys, collecting beautiful objects which grow boring and imprison ones thoughts — these are instances of *mada's* influence.

• **Raga**, attachment, is a well-known obstacle in spiritual life. It cripples the human mind by robbing it of its freedom and spontaneity. It ties the body and its energy to the yoke of subservience and slavery. Such is its nature that it leads to deeper and deeper modes of bondage and will not fully let go its hold even after a personality, object, action, or thought is transcended. In this case, beings actually become attached to attachment and remain that way for lifetimes. Embodiment in a form that repeatedly suffers the agonies of birth, disease, old age, and death is a prime example.

• **Vishada** is sorrow and grief. It pervades the mind with despondency and depression, making it unable to raise itself up to accomplish even menial tasks. The *guna* of *tamas* — slothfulness or inertia — is its close partner. Its presence can last for a lifetime, as it blinds the individual with overwhelming dejection and unhappiness. Loss of fortune, unrequited love, unforgiven grudges, uncontrolled passions — these are open doors through which *vishada* can makes its entrance. Once it enters the mind, it becomes increasingly difficult to destroy its darksome presence.

• **Shoka** constitutes a vast set of afflictions that plague the mind and make it dull and lifeless. It saps body, mind, and soul of vitality and motivation and fills it instead with doubt, reticence, and complacency. Under the constant array of blows proceeding from life and its experiences, the struggling being staggers and falls, and soon gives up. Spoiled dreams, dashed desires, elusive attainments, frustrated success, and the like all inhabit the realm of *shoka*. In association with *raga* and *vishada*, *shoka* breeds well in the hearts and minds of living beings.

• **Vaichitra** is a *Sanskrit* word for variety, and in this connection refers to the many distractions that tempt and haunt the human mind, making it restless and imbalanced. Its presence brings about the loss of steadfastness, a quality which lends itself well to a wide degree of attainments ranging from basic happiness to meditation. For the sake of experiencing diverse pleasures in the form of tastes, feelings, sights, and even intellectual stimulation, beings take to *vaichitra* like an old friend. In conjunction with moha, it attracts the mind and senses to the many, thereby obscuring the one — a characteristic trick of *maya*. It leads to unadvisable contact with the other *malas*, which all play into each other in insidious fashion.

   • **Harsha**, the seventh *mala*, is the delight which contributes to the desire for increased pleasure, particularly with regard to amassing huge amounts of wealth and the power it brings. Even after riches and influence are attained, it continues to evolve and leads to various unhealthy distortions centering around hedonistic pursuits. Thousands of beings are under its control. The greatest multinational conglomerate of this age, after merging all other interests under its umbrella, could very aptly name their organization *Harsha* Unlimited. The forces of *maya* move far and strong under the steam of this powerful *mala*, and in union with *moha, mada,* and *raga,* seduce beings into the unsavory realms of *vishada, shoka,* and *vaichitra.*

   Beings choosing the path of *Vidya shakti,* of course, do not need to experience the sufferings which come in association with the seven malas of *maya. Vidya shakti* is a power of ascension which takes all aspiring souls who desire to free themselves from cyclic rounds of birth and death in ignorance inwards towards remembrance and realization of their true nature. It propels by revealing subtler and subtler gradations of higher knowledge leading to *Paravidya. Paravidya* contains the teachings of the divine incarnations, the truths of the scriptures, the words of the *guru,* and the very presence of the universal Wisdom Mother Herself. It is also closely married to what is termed *Pratyabhijna* by the ancients — divine recognition. It encompasses everything one needs to know for liberation, namely, the knowledge of what the world represents, awareness of the immortal Self within called *Atman,* and realization of *Brahman,* the Ultimate Reality. For those who are still bereft of this divine recognition, it is necessary to rid the mind of the influences of *avidya shakti* to transcend *maya.* Lord Vasishtha's advice is pertinent here, namely: *"The process of rising above maya is facilitated by the conjunction of jnana, jiva, and Ishvara married with patience and reflection. Until the truth of Brahman dawns in you, you should hold fast to the truth of the words of the sages, seers, and scriptures. Thus will avidya be revealed and destroyed in you."*

   Avidya shakti, the downward moving force, accommodates all souls who desire to follow the way of *Vyavaharika* — the path of worldliness based upon sense-life. As the chart relates, to facilitate the darker, denser aspects of *maya, avidya shakti* breaks into two further powers called *avarana* and *vikshepa,* the former suited for veiling Reality and the latter effective in distorting It. Under the regime of these twin powers, and bereft of *vidya shakti's* spontaneous force, human beings struggle helplessly against the many weights and chains of *avidya shakti* which adversely affect their physical, mental, and spiritual well-being.

   Maya's many powers act on two basic levels of the creation; cosmic, called *samasti,* and individual, called *vyasti.* The cosmic *maya* facilitates all the various universal laws and creative principles such as the triple conception of time, space, and causality (*desha, kala,* and *nimitta*), and the three *gunas* of nature (*sattva, rajas,* and *tamas* of *Prakriti*). *Maya,* in the individual consciousness, seeps into the awareness of living beings, causing them to lose subtle and intuitive perception and become attached to what is finite. Identifying these deceptive forces and reversing their effects is a prerequisite to enlightenment and is undertaken by all sincere seekers of Truth. When this task is completed, the experience of *samadhi* dawns upon the awakened consciousness of the aspirant.

   This process may happen swiftly or take more time according to an aspirant's *karmic* propensities, state of preparation, capacity for realization, and the degree of intensity mustered for *sadhana* and spiritual life. *Maya's* evolutes are formidable opponents which create barriers that are difficult to detect. Negative impressions from previous births, belief that the world is real, belief that God is unreal, presuming ones present existence to be the only lifetime, nonacceptance of cause and effect, preoccupation with the ego, its desires, and the body — these and more hamper spiritual progress and make enlightenment impossible. In order to facilitate the transcendence of these negativities, it is necessary to identify the evolutes of *Maya* and thereby diminish their hold over human awareness. Though they are many, they can be condensed and classified in brief in a manner pertaining to this day and age. To do this, we must gaze back into an earlier age — an age where beings of great wisdom encountered *Maya's* forces and, with much effort, austerity, and concentration, transcended them. Abidance in the *Atman*, the sole Reality, was their reward.

The *rishis* of ancient India bequeathed the world an abundance of valuable teachings, gleaned from their one-pointed meditation on *Brahman*. They realized these truths through their love for true existence after renouncing mundane worldly life. They perceived the presence of *maya* and applied their powers of discrimination to the pressing problems of humanity so as to blaze a trail out of ignorance and its related suffering. The purpose of this was twofold: to help the peoples of the world to live a pure and fulfilling existence and, more importantly, to help them gain the vision of *Brahman* and thereby receive the knowledge, wisdom, truth, love, devotion, peace, bliss, and freedom that proceeds from it. It should be pointed out that suffering, in this context, includes enjoyment and the momentary happiness it brings, for joy and sorrow always come in turns, and both produce suffering — one through ignoble whips of pain and the other through misleading strokes of pleasure. They are, as Swami Vivekananda points out, chains that hold — one of iron, the other of gold.

The evolutes of *Maya* are given next in *Sanskrit*, a tongue also referred to as *Devavak* (the Divine Word, its meaning, and its many expressions), and *Devabhasha* (the language of the gods). It both bears and conveys the subtle power of *Brahman* and *Shakti*. It expresses spirituality itself, for that was the essential ideal and salutary attainment of the *Rishis*. The realizations of the illumined beings of ancient India are locked in *Sanskrit* in subtle form, as are the descriptions of *maya's* evolutes. These evolutes of *maya* plague humanity and create obstructions to the realization of *Brahman* — the true Self. To repeat how the *Tantras* put it, generally, *"Maya creates illusion which is moha in individual minds. A jiva's delusion arises when it cannot make any distinction between atma and anatma and it identifies the Self with the not-self and the not-self with the Self."*

• *Mudhavastha* is forgetfulness of ones true nature. Due to this critical lapse of memory, beings fail to remember themselves as pure Spirit and instead identify with concerns of an impermanent nature. The sense of ownership, agency, and separation from God all begin here (see chart on page 219), for the true Self is not an object, is free from activity, and is ever one with Divine Reality. It is perfect, and therefore the blessed Christ stated: *"Be thee perfect, even as the Lord in Heaven is perfect."* Herein, the remedy for *mudhavastha* is a firm acknowledgement that declares absolute identity with *Brahman* coupled with an ongoing and powerful practice that destroys all obstacles to this realization. Otherwise, the truth of ones real nature can never be experienced. As Sri Ramakrishna puts it: *"A bullock carries a huge bag of sweets on its head but can never taste it."* The poet/saint, Ramprasad, gives his rendition of this teaching in song: *"By forgetting Reality and seeking after the things of the earth, beings imbibe earth instead of nectar; they give themselves to nature instead of Spirit."* In other songs, he advises remembrance in accordance with the divine names of God: *"O complacent and restless mind caught in the fundamental illusion of finitude, do not forget to remember your Divine Mother's hallowed name."* Thus, remembrance, *daivi-smriti*, and recognition, *pratyabhijna*, go hand in hand.

• *Mamakara* means the sense of "I, me, and mine." The sense of ownership in relation to all levels of existence — my spouse, my family, my possessions, my wealth, my career, my learning, my future, my religion — casts a cloak of limitation over the mind and breeds thoughts and actions that are directly in opposition to Truth. The truth is simply that all these things proceed from and belong to nature, the realm of conceptualization, and ultimately, to God. Sri Ramakrishna gives a fine story about those under the influence of *mamakara*. He says: *"God laughs on two occasions: when the physician assures the mother that he can cure her baby; and when two brothers divide their land saying, 'That side is yours and this side is mine.'"* The gist is that few beings realize that all belongs to God. As Khalas, the great devotee of Sri Ram sings: *You flatter the millionaire but forget to pay homage to Sri*

Ram, though Ram is the owner of the entire universe!" More specific to mankind's ignorance, the poet/saint, Ramprasad sings: *"The egocentric bind themselves mindlessly, repeating 'this is I, that is mine.'"* Similarly, Lord Buddha advises: *"Happy indeed are those who live free of attachment to possessions. They feed on eternal happiness, like the gods."* As the Great Master often said, *"It is this deranged attitude of 'I, me, and mine' that has driven the whole world mad."*

• **Dehadhyasa** is attachment to the body out of ignorance. After forgetting ones true nature (*mudhavastha*), the sense of ego (*mamakara*) grows strong as there is nothing noble and transcendent to identify with. Preoccupation with the body is then the only recourse, and the unripened ego delights in this misguided pastime. In the *Vivekachudamani*, Shankara says: *"This knowledge of the Self as the body — this wicked desire that 'I am the body,' — this is the root of birth and different sufferings."* Despite the body's limitations, imperfections, illnesses, deterioration, and death, deluded beings continually obsess with their finite form and thus habitually begin to mistake it for the Self. Instead of perceiving it as *adhara* — a container into which God pours a bit of His undying Spirit — ignorant beings mistake the vessel for the contents and suffer innumerable miseries. As Sri Shankaracharya states: *"Consciousness remains untouched, ever pure; yet with the body and senses, the mind deludes Consciousness and creates there the thought of 'me,' and 'mine.' This delusion causes suffering."* The advice of Lord Buddha on attachment to the body is well-known: *"He who has not any attachment to name and form and does not grieve for what does not really exist, that one is wise beyond conception."* Further, He declared: *"O builder of the house, I have seen you; You shall not build the house again — not of wood, stone, flesh and bone, or even of wise conception. I have broken the rafters; the ridgepole is sundered. Mind has arrived at dissolution, having attained the extinction of all cravings."* Speaking to His beloved disciple, Uddhava, Sri Krishna advises: *"Living in the body which is under the sway of past actions, the deluded one becomes bound due to identification with it."* Continual fixation with the body soon leads to a complex wherein the living being falls into a strong misconception that the body is the only self. In this case, even the mind and intellect, which are vastly superior to the body, become subservient to it. Thus is the body, an outer covering over Reality, worshiped in place of the indwelling Self. This invites the following evolute of *maya* to enter in.

• **Parasparadhyasa** is an unfortunate malady wherein one mistakes the Self for the body and the body for the Self. Most human beings are overcome with the disconcerting idea that they are actually their physical sheath. Even many of those who profess to be spiritual cannot shake this delusion and cling to life in a body. Sri Ramachandra states openly in the *Adhyatma Ramayana*: *"How can this human body made of five elements, blood, and excreta ever be the immortal, all-pervading Spirit?"* In the *Vivekachudamani*, Shankaracharya declares: *"That which is real and ones own primeval essence, that is beyond form and activity. Attaining That, one should cease to identify with ones false bodies like an actor giving up his assumed masks."* Sri Ramakrishna states: *"The seat of the mind is in the center between the eyebrows, but its gaze is ever fixed below the navel and on the organs of evacuation and reproduction."* When the mind is pure and sure of its immortal nature, then, it dwells in transcendental bliss and ceases its endless dalliance with desires associated with name and form. Further, the Great Master stated: *"The body is a mere pillowcase, but the heart of the devotee is the abode of Brahman."* Despite these and other teachings, and though the mind has infinite potential for higher expression, it stubbornly reverts to body consciousness, worldly thoughts, and the lower passions again and again. *"The camel eats thorny bushes, and even though its gums bleed it will not give them up,"* notes Sri Ramakrishna. As Patanjali, the Father of *Yoga* declares: *"There are five obstacles in spiritual life; ignorance, egotism, attachment, aversion, and clinging to life."* This latter *klesha* is life in the body only.

• **Vishayashakti** influences the mind by attaching it to the senses. The world is full of people who have very little depth to their thinking process. Due to preoccupation with the surface of human awareness, they are simply unaware of the infinite potential which lies within them and are unable to access it. With the senses out of control, they remain rank materialists, bereft of the wherewithal to transform themselves into an image of Spirit. Ramprasad sings: *"Oh essential mind, you are infinitely more refined than the organs of action and perception. In the kingdom of consciousness, you are nat-*

ural sovereign. Yet you accept as constant companions the most limited and negative intentions. What a petty potentate you have become." Communicating similar sentiments, Shankaracharya states: *"A great tiger, whose name is 'the mind,' wanders in this world. The wayward senses and their objects are the forest where this great tiger roams. One who is desirous of liberation should not go there."* Lord Buddha speaks of sense control as well: *"Blessed indeed are they who live amongst those who are yearning for sense delights, without yearning for such things themselves."* In the *Uddhava Gita*, Lord Krishna says: *"Contact with the senses, which are the creation of nescience, should be avoided until attachment, which is a stain on the mind, has been removed by a strong and systematic devotion to God."* Thus, the warnings against sense life devoid of love and wisdom are declared by the wise in every religion.

• *Bahirmukhavritti* describes the outward going mind that fixates continually on external stimuli, usually of a mundane or banal variety. Unable to curb its wayward tendencies, beings give the mind free reign and suffer the consequences. Not only does this bind the thinking process to external phenomena, it also robs the mind of its precious ability to look within for answers to life's problems and thereby abide steadily in the *Atman*. Sri Krishna states in the *Bhagavad Gita*: *"The mind is difficult to control, no doubt. But it can be controlled, by Abhyasa Yoga — the path of constant practice."* About the wayward mind, Sri Ramakrishna says: *"It is extremely difficult to gather up mustard seeds that have been blown from the package by the wind."* This means that once the mind's thoughts are habitually given to the outside world, it is much harder to withdraw them and place them within where peace abides. Offering solutions for this malady, Lord Buddha states: *"Irrigators conduct water whenever they please; fletchers shape arrow shafts; carpenters work the wood; but the wise discipline the mind."*

• *Eshanatrayam*, the triple desire, is the drive for enjoying spouse, wealth, and offspring. These three pursuits are natural to most human beings, and if sought after with maturity and detachment, can bring some fulfillment of earthly desires. Unfortunately, due to selfishness and inadvertent clinging, the impositions of lust, greed, and the desire for power (see charts on pages 247 & 249) enter in and squelch any positive benefits that may come from earthly existence. Sri Ramakrishna noticed the predicament of worldly beings attached to mundane existence in the family setting and remarked observantly: *"The rich, the miserly, and the worldly spend their money in four ways — litigation, thieves, physicians, and wicked children."* Ramprasad, gazing upon the ways of the world, sang: *"To seek for help from spouse, friends, or family provides no profound solution. Don't you know that all are lost here? Everyone lives in pallid imitation of everyone else."* Though family life can and should be a time-honored institution, it is or has become, in this day and age, an open door for the entrance and influence of *maya* and its evolutes. As stated in the *Dhammapada*, Lord Buddha said: *"Non-recitation of scripture is the rust of monasteries; non-exertion is the rust of households."* Furthermore, He stated: *"The wise do not call strong that fetter which is made of iron, wood, or hemp. Rather do they call attachment to jewels, ornaments, children, and spouses a far stronger fetter."* On the other hand, He also advised: *"If you find a wise companion to associate with, one who leads a virtuous life and is diligent, you should lead a life with him or her, joyfully and mindfully, conquering all obstacles."*

• *Shatavadana* means thinking of and doing a hundred things at once. Its presence is a telling sign of our times. Beings find it difficult to focus with one-pointed concentration because they have habitually succumbed to various distractions over time. This fragments human awareness so that it cannot focus sufficiently. As more time passes in this mentally shattered atmosphere, this becomes a habit which drastically limits the mind's attention span. At this point, and in contemporary times, it will not be long before psychologists begin to classify it as a mental disease, chemists begin to look for a combination of substances to commercialize it, and physicians begin prescribe such "medicines" for a disorder that should be done away with by self-discipline — and which really should never have appeared at all. Lord Buddha says: *"There is no perfect contemplation for that one who is not wise, and no wisdom for the one who does not concentrate."* Therefore, in spiritual endeavor, the inability to meditate on the essence of Reality is a great loss. In this case, restlessness takes over and wins the day. Sri Krishna speaks of this tendency in the *Uddhava Gita*: *"The man of uncontrolled mind falls into the error that there is a plurality of objects [vaichitra], and this error leads to his downfall."* Sri Ramakrishna puts it in yet another way: *"Everyone is enamored of the rich man's garden, but few ever inquire after the owner."* Thus do embodied beings pass over what is essential and beneficial due to preoccupation with a thousand external considerations.

These perplexing evolutes of the enchanting power of *maya* are to be recognized and transcended. They inundate the thinking process and thus affect our daily actions and otherwise peaceful relations with God, nature, and other living beings. Though a part of the experience of life and responsible for its perpetuation, they are also responsible for ignorance, delusion, and much of the avoidable suffering that human beings undergo. As Sri Ramakrishna so revealingly states with regard to *maya* and its powers: *"Maya is like the skin of a mango. It protects the fruit while it is ripening. But once the fruit is ready the skin is discarded. One should not eat it, for it is bitter and can cause a rash."*

In view of this astute analogy, and if one studies the first eight evolutes of *Maya*, it will become clear how living beings have, especially under the auspices of materialism, worldliness, and sensuality, made a veritable feast out of the skin of the mango! Attachment to the body as if it were a permanent structure, preoccupation with the external world as if it were a permanent location, attachment to the five senses as if they represented permanent awareness, and attachment to family, friends, and wealth as if they were permanent possessions — all of these have become normal behavior. This warped and distorted view wherein Reality is considered an illusion while relativity is perceived to be real and abiding is the work of the *avidya shakti* aspect of *maya*. Time-honored abidance in what the *Vedanta* calls *nityanityavastuviveka*, discrimination between the real and the unreal, is its antithesis, and the time-tested practice of neti, neti, the implementation of not this, not this, is the solution.

These eight evolutes of *Maya* provide a firm basis upon which to trace root ignorance and rid oneself of its problematic tendencies. By identifying them in this fashion, aspirants may destroy *maya*'s effects while remaining free of its perplexing enchantment. As Sri Ramakrishna indicates with regard to *maya* and *Brahman*: *"If one holds up a towel in front of a lamp, the lamp disappears."* By recognizing *maya*'s presence from a detached position, and transcending its powers of obscuration and distortion (*avarana* and *vikshepa*), beings can tear away this towel of false superimposition and misleading appearances from in front of the lamp of *Atman* and perceive the all-pervasive Light of Consciousness called *Brahman*.

In continuation of the study of *maya*'s evolutes on the chart under examination (page 279), eight more can be listed. These are generally more subtle than the previous eight. Whereas the first eight evolutes point out fundamental mental distortions like possessiveness, selfishness, and shallowness, these additional eight focus on tendencies that are more difficult to comprehend and renounce, such as the sense of agency, and the attempt to acquire basic knowledge in relation to the intellect and its interaction with the individual ego.

• *Kartritva-Abhimana* is a delusion which supposes that the Self within is the agent of action. This only occurs when, out of ignorance, one identifies with the body which is, as discussed earlier, a case of *dehadhyasa*. In truth, the real Self is not only free of agency, it is free of all modifications. Sri Krishna proclaims this truth on the cosmic level: *"Animating my Prakriti. I send forth again and again all this multitude of beings helpless under the regime of Prakriti. Nor do these acts bind me, for I remain unconcerned and unattached to these acts."* The *Atman* permeates all things, all beings. By identifying with Spirit instead of with matter, aspiring beings give up the sense of agency and offer all actions to the Lord and Mother of the Universe. Thus they realize a state beyond agency and are at peace. Sri Krishna advises this course directly: *"Whatever you do, whatever you eat, whatever you sacrifice and give away, do it as an offering to the Lord. Then you shall be free from the bondage of action and the good and bad results that it yields."* Lord Buddha's advice is pertinent to the mode of practice: *"Let the seeker purify the threefold avenues of thought, word, and deed, and thus be free from the effects of karma. Then, he will tread the path made known by the sages."* Adishankaracharya laughs at the attempts of ignorant beings to superimpose modes of activity over the Self: *"People in ignorance impute to the true*

Self all these gross and subtle states, in much the same way that they impute to Eternity cycles of years, months, weeks, and days. Eternity has no parts and, similarly, the Self has no activity."

• **Visamvada-Bhrama** casts a cloak of mistaken identity. Here, *maya* is up to its old tricks again, causing beings to mistake something that exists for something else; or perhaps to mistake something for another thing which is illusory or vice versa. This quizzical and subtle trick recurs repeatedly to people going about their daily lives, but most remain unaware of it. This is a part of the hypnotism which living beings fall victim to, until finally their entire existence is based upon fallacy. Entering into spiritual practice and learning to use the powerful tool of discrimination (see chart on page 65), an aspirant can dispel what is fallacious from life and mind. Then, a continual vigil must be placed over the mind and its tendencies until old habits simply dissolve and disappear. Lord Vasishtha advises, *"Let not your mind give way under trials. Crush impediments in the mind the very moment they arise. Then the destruction of maya will be accomplished."* Therefore, searching for the *Atman* — not the individual self, but the indivisible Self — the sincere seeker must expose all impostors. As the scriptures state: *"In daylight there is the shadow body; at night there is the dream body. Near a lake, there is the reflection body, and in the mind there is the body of knowledge. There is the body of another, and all the five sheaths pose as the real body as well. But the true Self is none of these. Give them all up and uncover your true nature."* Sri Ramakrishna had a story for this process of uncovering: *"Some thieves came to a vegetable field at night to steal the crops. A straw figure resembling a man had been put there to frighten away thieves. The thieves could not persuade themselves to enter the field due to fear of the scarecrow being real. One of them, however, approached and found out that the figure was made of straw. He called out to his companions to come near, but they were still fearful. Then, the daring thief laid the straw figure on the ground and cried out, 'Come here! It is nothing, it is nothing.'"* The illusion of mistaken identity is also nothing. Beings must see through it and dispatch it straight away.

• **Viparita-Bhavana** is the cause for much suffering. It is based upon the belief that the world is the only reality. Materialists who cling to nature and what it has to offer; pleasure-lovers whose entire existence centers around sensual delights and experiences; hedonists who seek after enjoyment without regard for any negative repercussions for themselves or for others; worldly beings who desire only to pursue mundane existence, like an ostrich with its head in the sand, heedless of pressing and persistent dangers — these believe in a real world separate and distinct from Reality, and have it as their only resort. But whether the world is real or unreal is not the only question. The existence of higher worlds and, especially, the state of pure nondual Awareness, which conveys a bliss and fulfillment far beyond what the world has to offer, awaits the aspiring seeker of Truth. Sri Ramakrishna told many stories about the especial discernment that renders the world of name and form to be without substance: *"A magician came to a king to show his magic. When the magician moved away a little, the king suddenly saw a rider on horseback, arrayed in robes and armor, approaching him. The king and the audience began to reason out what was real and what was an illusion. Evidently, the horse was not real, nor the robes, nor the armor. At last they found out for certain that the rider alone was real."* The Holy Mother, Sri Ramakrishna's wife, stated it plainly as well: *"Everything in the world has but a one or two-day's existence. Yet people are fully preoccupied with it."* Finally, Lord Buddha states that which puts to rest the subject of attachment to the world: *"Not in the sky, not in the middle of an ocean, not even in the cave of a mountain should one seek refuge, for there exists no place in the world where one will not be overpowered by death."*

• **Vrittijnana** equates to knowledge attained by the activity of the mind. This knowledge is empirical, of the earth, and limited to the physical universe alone, so is not beneficial for the realization of higher Truth. The mind, which is operating under the misconception that its worldly knowledge is somehow absolute, is laboring under one of the most subtle of *maya's* illusions. Pundits, scholars, professors — all intellectuals who are devoid of faith in God and lacking the realization of where the source of the mind's knowledge comes from — are sorely deluded by *vrittijnana*. Sri Ramakrishna, seeing the learned men of His day, called *pundits*, declared: *"Vultures soar high in the sky, but their gaze is fixed on the carrion pit below."* This saying relates that though beings may be full of facts gleaned from books, they nevertheless remain attached to the base pursuits of the world via the senses and thus are really ignorant. Besides, such beings desire to make money from what they know, and fail to realize that they are really only selling the skin of the fruit and not the flesh. In order to convince these kinds of beings to give up reliance on limited worldly knowledge and take to the Supreme Knowledge, the Great Master stated: *"The lens will not burn paper inside a house. Come out of the house and the lens will catch the power of the sun."* Shankaracharya puts this matter in a unique way, as usual: *"There is a pitcher of water sitting in the sun, and there is a reflection of the sun in the water. The fool, seeing the reflection, thinks it to be the real sun. Just so, in mind, intelligence, and the other sheaths, the reflection of Atman is ignorance and the fool thinks that he is beholding the real Self."* Lord Buddha gives an interesting insight into this problem. *"The fool who knows of his ignorance, indeed, through that very consideration, becomes a wise man. But that conceited man who considers himself learned is, in fact, the real fool."*

• ***Doshadristi*** describes the tendency of human beings to find fault with others and to see imperfection everywhere, while overlooking all that is inherently perfect. This insidious tendency of the mind proceeds from the unripe ego that is insecure at one moment and puffed up with pride the next. This wavering mental condition is reflective of spiritual immaturity. The blessed Christ said: *"Seek thee first to remove the beam from thine own eye before attempting to remove the mote of dust from another's."* The Holy Mother, Sri Sarada Devi, explained it thus: *"Do not find fault with others. Learn to see your own faults. The whole world is your own. No one is a stranger."* Lord Buddha also had a unique way of indicating this problem: *"The faults of others are easily seen, but ones own faults are perceived with difficulty. One winnows the faults of others like chaff, but conceals his own faults as a fowler covers his body with leaves and twigs."* Speaking further on the subject, He said: *"Those who imagine error where there is none, and do not see it where it does exist, such beings, embracing false views, enter the woeful path."*

There is another aspect to *doshadristi* that must not be overlooked. It is of cosmic design. There are defects inherent in the universal scheme of things, and many beings experience them, complain about them, and finally obsess with them. These beings are laboring under the influence of *Doshadristi* on the cosmic level. One who is free from this distorted vision which sees the defects in everything will take an alternate pathway, instead going deeper and perceive the underlying perfection and the eternal connectedness of all things. These beings see the imperfection of perfection, and the perfection of all imperfections. As Lord Buddha acknowledges: *"The world is blind. Few see things as they really are. Like birds escaped from the net, very few gain right perspective."* So, the seer of wisdom uses discrimination to uncover the defects in creation and transcend them, but also perceives their unique facility for revealing what is perfect. In other words, darkness only reveals the glory of the light. As Sri Ramakrishna points out: *"Once, some ruffians were causing a disturbance on a landlord's estate. The landlord hired some other ruffians to go and put an end to it."* More to the point, and at a very realized level, the Great Master related: *"A monk was once beaten unconscious in the streets by a wicked man. When he regained consciousness back at the monastery, one of the monks asked him who he was in order to ascertain his mental competency. He answered, 'He who was beating me is now inquiring after my well-being.'"* The enlightened mind sees perfection everywhere and realizes that all imperfections in the cosmic design are only apparent and serve a higher purpose.

• ***Tarkika-Buddhi*** conveys the problem of an intellect that always argues. This is due in part to the *doshadristi* aspect in it, but also points very directly to lack of faith, nonacceptance of Truth, and basic insecurity. What is more, it reveals the inherent defect of the mind which inadvertently defaults to possessiveness around its small store of personal knowledge, claiming it, holding it up above all else, and foisting it upon others as the final decree in all matters. In religion, Sri Ramakrishna indicates this tendency in the mind by observing: *"Everyone thinks that their own watch keeps the only correct time."* Here, narrow intelligence proclaims its own way as superior to the way of others, and argues incessantly on the matter. In scholastic circles, *tarkika-buddhi* has been made into an art form, turning the pastime of argument and debate into a coveted attainment. This is *moha*, wherein something negative and detrimental is presumed to be positive and beneficial. In philosophy, refutation, text-torturing, and inadvisable interpolation go on interminably, often at the cost of perceiving Truth's basic and natural premises and principles. In everyday life, too, people argue incessantly in matters that are either best kept silent about or merely accepted outright. In this regard, Lord Buddha declared: *"One is not a supporter of the law merely because he talks much. But that one who hears only a little of the divine law, yet perceives its essence by diligent exertion, and does not neglect it, is indeed a true supporter of the divine law."* Shankaracharya refutes the tendency of the intellect to argue and advises acceptance of what is natural and obvious: *"Giving up this unreal notion — what you have misguidedly taken as your own self — take instead that which is real, self-evident, beyond all argumentation. 'I am Brahman' — by this pure thought, know thine own Self, which is indivisible Consciousness."* In the *Bhagavad Gita*, Sri Krishna puts it in simpler terms: *"Those who carp and cavil about this, my Supreme Truth, will never be able to comprehend it."* In the words of Sri Ramakrishna, *"Only one thing has never been defiled by the tongue of mankind, and that is Brahman Itself. There are defects in every religion, but it is God who maintains them there, and it is God who also removes them in due time. A man sets out to visit Jagannath but goes north instead of south. Searching for that location, he asks someone where it is and is told to go south. Eventually he reaches Jagannath, attends the temple, and communes with the Lord of the Universe."* In the *Uddhava Gita*, Lord Krishna speaks further on the subject: *"'It is not as you put it, it is as I put it' — this sort of fighting over the issue is due to maya's powers of the gunas which are difficult to get rid of. It is this disturbance that causes the doubt which is the ground of contention among the disputants. This doubt vanishes when one attains calmness of mind and self-control, and after that, all dispute is at an end."* The distortion of argumentation without a point, and devoid of direct experience, is a great obstacle, then, and must be overcome if recognition of Truth and realization of the *Atman* are to be attained.

• ***Pratiloma*** is inadvertence towards following the way of harmony, unity, and natural balance. It is caused by a distortion in the mind which neglects or rejects the light of higher intelligence and accepts the ego's divisive tendencies instead. It conduces to a sort of twisted thinking which, when getting free reign, grows antagonistic to the presence of the divine in all things and strives to eradicate that, placing creations of its own design into operation and superiority. The instigation of concepts and activities from this imperfect orientation soon produces modes and methods of living which are colored with greater distortion, burgeoning into obsessive fixations, warped complexes, and mental imbalance. Lord Buddha observes: *"Long is the night to a sleepless person; long is the distance of a league to a tired person; long is the cycle of rebirths to the fool who does not know the Truth."* Further, He states: *"So long as evil deeds do not mature, the fool thinks his deeds to be sweet as honey. But when the evil deeds mature, they bring untold misery."* Sri Ramakrishna teaches about the imposition of egotism in this regard: *"Wisdom and liberation cannot be had as long as egoism persists. Birth and death also do not come to an end for that one given to egoism."* Speaking of the distorted mind, Sri Krishna states: *"That which, enveloped in darkness, regards unrighteousness opposed to the natural way of dharma as a desirable thing, and views all things in a perverted way, that intellect is darksome, is tamasic."* Sri Sarada Devi, speaking on the level of the individual, states: *"The intelligence of a human being is very subtle. It is like a screw that, if turned slightly in the wrong direction, misthreads. Such a mind experiences mental imbalance constantly."*

• ***Svarupanyathabhava*** is the state of being other than ones true nature. Instead of abiding in ones essence, called *Svarupapratistha*, one finds many ways of denying It or hiding from It. This reveals a lack of spiritual responsibility and amounts to inherent weakness. The truth-seeker must be bold and stand up to declare the axioms of the immortality of the Self and the illusion of death. Instead, beings shirk, or even shun, their true nature out of fear, doubt, or laziness. As Sri Ramakrishna often said: *"In front of God's mansion lies a huge stump. One cannot get into the mansion without jumping over this stump."* Further, and about the individual's willingness to overlook inherent divinity and fixate on finite considerations, He stated: *"According to local legend, the snake has a precious jewel lodged in its head, yet it is content to eat a mere frog."* His great disciple, Swami Vivekananda, directly stated this truth in nondual terms: *"The Self is all in all; none else exists. And thou art That."* Again, he said, *"The real me is none but He, and never, never, matter changing."* In the teachings of Lord Buddha we find it explained in this way: *"Few beings ever cross over to the farther shore. The multitudes who remain here futilely run to and fro on this selfsame shore."* As Sri Krishna relates: *"A person who denies the Atman is tormented by attachment to the body and its desires and activities, but the man whose mind rests in the Atman does not even know the body as it stands, sits, walks, lies down, eats food, or performs any other natural act."* Such is the predicament of the former — the condition of *svarupanyathabhava* — while the latter enjoys *svarupapratistha*. The former is resisting the dawn of his or her true nature, and failing to abide as the Self — *Atman*.

To conclude, a rundown of the chart on page 279, from top to bottom, is given. In brief, *Parabrahma* and *Parashakti* (*Brahman* and *Shakti*) are Absolute Reality in Its static and dynamic aspects — the transcendent Father and the primordial Mother of all beings. All true knowledge contained in Them is called *Paravidya*, which is Supreme Truth, pure and perfect, symbolized by the sacred word, *AUM*. Through *Iccha shakti*, *Jnana shakti*, *Kriya shakti*, and *Dravya shakti* — the Divine Mother's essence as will, wisdom, spontaneity, and creative activity — the complex architecture of diverse worlds, subtle and gross, seen and unseen, gets facilitated. This has been called envisionment, expression, divine sport, dream power, manifestation, illusion, etc., and this is where *maya* enters in. When the Divine Mother's four *shakti*'s begin to operate, the first material of subtle creation utilized is Her *maya*, with its attending attribute called *mulavidya* that immediately, though apparent only, causes a rift in Consciousness. This disturbance provides the means necessary for projection, including the appearance of celestial powers (gods and goddesses), the cosmic principles they oversee, the many worlds of becoming, the three modes of nature (*gunas*) the many pairs of opposites (duality/relativity), the process of evolution, and more.

In this complex web the human being, called the *jiva*, or embodied consciousness, gets born and becomes subject to two forces: *vidya shakti*, which leads inward and away from *maya*'s effects; and *avidya shakti*, which leads outward, and which is fully subject to *maya*'s effects. With the many categories of *aparavidya* available (secondary knowledge concerning the external worlds of becoming only) living beings embark on the journey of life, making choices that affect their progress in both earthly and spiritual matters. Those who are *dharmic*, seeking higher attainments through right knowledge and right action, ascend inwardly along the path of *vidya shakti* and reach consummate wisdom leading to immersion in the Absolute. The rest, taking matter to be Reality, become subject to *maya*'s perplexing forces, such as the seven *malas* and the many evolutes.

The ten characteristics of *maya* reveal a little of its nature, and describe briefly both the reason for its appearance and its ultimate insubstantiality. The seven *malas* show the manner in which *maya* works within the limits of the body/mind mechanism and act upon the imperfections of human nature. The sixteen evolutes represent the development of *maya*'s powers on the individual, collective, and cosmic levels of manifestation. They form complexes that cloud proper perception of the design and purpose of *dharmic* living, causing forgetfulness of Reality.

In all this, the real Self, called the *Atman*, which is the indwelling and all-pervasive Spirit consisting of Consciousness alone, and which is identical in nature with *Brahman* and *Shakti*, is ever free from *maya* and its evolutes and abides eternally in a perpetual state of perfect unity. By identifying with this eternal verity while taking note of and detaching from the various forces of *maya*, living beings can escape the suffering associated with relativity and experience the peace and bliss inherent in *Atman* — their true Self. As Shankaracharya puts it: *"The majesty of the ocean of the Supreme Brahman, replete with the nectar-like swell of the Atman, is verily impossible to express in speech, nor can it be conceived by the mind — in an infinitesimal fraction of which my mind melted like a hailstone getting merged in the ocean, and is now satisfied with that Essence of Bliss."*

Unaccountable to the extent that it both requisitions life and masquerades for Reality, *maya* has been given a somewhat thorough observation over the course of the past few pages of this book. But there are aspects of *maya* which are more easily explained, and can be very helpful in the task of overcoming ignorance and unmasking Reality — so long as the seeker recognizes the factitious presence of *maya* and the spiritually implausible subterfuge that it is capable of.

In the chart on the facing page we find that *maya* has three *shaktis* of its own, and that one of them proves it to be much more than a purely negative power. That power is called *Prakasha Shakti*, or the revealing power in all things, all beings. When placed side by side with the other two *shaktis* of *maya*, namely, *avarana* and *vikshepa*, a clearer and more concise picture may be had of the workings of *samsara* on three levels: confusion in life; delusion in the mind; and illusion in the cosmos.

As the chart on the facing page is studied, the reader will find that the three *shaktis* listed above correspond with the powers of obscuration, distortion, and revelation. The more spiritually and philosophically educated person will also perceive the correlation between these three powers and the famous three *gunas* of *tamas, rajas,* and *sattva* (see chart on page 307), linking *maya*'s ability to cover the truth, falsify the truth, and expose the truth.

In one sense, at least, *maya* needs no help in the *avarana* department in veiling the truth from human minds. This is because human beings are practicing the art of forgetfulness, not remembrance. They are born without spiritual wisdom and constantly pursue ill-considered actions, conventional knowledge, or moralistic goals instead of seeking higher Truth (see chart on page 271). As a book of this type accents over and over again, without spiritual life and its refined level of learning, no appreciable progress in either fulfillment of the individual's goals in life, or of his or her eternal and conclusive peace of mind, can be gained — not for any substantial duration of time. That is, a life of happiness may be enjoyed, but it will be based upon ones good *karmas* from past lifetimes, not upon realization of the Truth that carries one beyond death and rebirth.

In this regard, even *prakasha shakti* is not the ultimate attainment of an aspiring *sadhaka*; it is a penultimate acquisition gained and secured via spiritual practice. On the chart under study on the facing page, it is seen that the welcome power of *prakasha* hones those special abilities of a discriminating aspirant called *adhyaropa* and *apavada* (see chart on page 65). In short, it makes one aware that the wool has been pulled over ones eyes, that *maya* has pulled a ruse on individual consciousness, and then points the way towards release from the same; it is not the goal in and of itself.

Where there is a distortion, like in a decaying musical tone, vibrations have caused erratic overtones which are conflicting with one another in the atmosphere. In like manner, *vikshepa shakti* is alive and vibrating in human minds, and in a jarring and disruptive way is causing disharmony and discord in the thinking process, in human relations, and in the all-important potential for higher understanding. *Prakasha shakti* is that balance which will both calm the *vikshepa* vibrations and clarify *avarana*'s obscuring overlays. It is pure revelation, and on so many levels.

Acquisition of *prakasha* is most useful in four ways: matters pertaining to spiritual education; clarification of mind and its issues; philosophical understanding; and spiritual practice and attainment. When a false premise or illusory overlay is present in any given matter or situation, as is described in Shankara's famous "snake in the rope" analogy at the bottom of the chart under study, the power of *prakasha shakti* will remove the problem and reveal the truth and the way. Even in the case of physical objects — not only around the problem of attachment to them, but with regards to the exploration of their nature — *prakasha shakti* provides the revelation needed for in-depth scrutiny, thus thorough clarification.

Thus, it is found that *maya* possesses and, for the inquiring mind, communicates and inspires an impetus for freedom. As the *Tantracists* have declared, it covers our eyes with one hand and leads us on with the other. The truth seeker only needs to make sure that this "leading on" process does not head us in a direction that is contrary to the attainment of the true and ultimate goal of human existence. His or her proclivity for awareness and foresight must be honed as well, and this is relative to our next chart.

The immeasurably great luminary, Gaudapada, *guru*'s *guru* to Sri Shankaracharya, is famed in both East and West for his brilliant commentary on the *Mandukya Upanisad,* and for bringing out its inherent nondualistic content in such a superlative fashion. In his own words it is the *maya* of the

Prakasha Shakti — The Revealing Power

Maya's Influence Towards Freedom

"Maya is an insentient force that, though invested with inherent powers of obscuration and distortion, nevertheless is present to drive beings towards remembrance and enlightenment. The Tantric adepts state that she covers our eyes with one hand, but leads us towards freedom with the other. This directive power is Prakasha Shakti. Prakasha is the revelatory light; Prakashaka is its revealer; Prakasya is the thing revealed." Babaji Bob Kindler

The Three-Fold Power of Maya

Avarana Shakti — The Power of Obscuration
* Veils the mind on individual, collective, and cosmic levels
* Is related to the guna of Tamas
* Works in conjunction with Vikshepa Shakti

Vikshepa Shakti — The Power of Distortion
* Distorts the mind on all three levels
* Is related to the guna of Rajas
* Works in conjunction with Avarana and Prakasha

Prakasha Shakti — The Power of Revelation
* Clarifies the mind by revealing the actual nature of things
* Is related to the guna of Sattva, and leads beyond it as well
* Exposes truth in association with Adhyaropa and Apavada

Adhyaropa - The ability of the spiritual aspirant to adroitly detect the unreal false superimposition of name and form over Brahman.

Apavada - The ability of the spiritual aspirant to, via rejection of the unreal, do away with the false superimposition of name and form over Brahman.

"Once I had entered the woods and was sitting in meditation in the pine grove when suddenly I had a vision in the form of something like a chamber door in the ground. I couldn't see inside the chamber so I tried to bore a hole in the door with a nail-knife. But as I dug, the earth kept falling into the hole and filling it. Then suddenly I made a very big opening...."
Sri Ramakrishna Paramahamsa

rajjuvivartasya sarpasya rajjumatratvat vastubhuta brhmano vivartasya prapancha desha vastu bhutrupadaupadeshah apavadah

"Espying a snake one evening in the semidarkness, a man reacted in abject fear. Upon closer inspection he saw that the illusory snake was really a rope. Similarly, a man sees the universe where only Brahman exists. The power of obscuration, avarana, causes his mind to cover Reality with the world. The power of distortion, vikshepa, makes him perceive the world as distinct from Brahman But the penetrating power of prakasha reveals all such superimpositions and projections to be unreal."
Babaji Bob Kindler

False Assumptions About the Atman

"There is no limit to the mind's imaginings; different people, so long as they have not acquired the proper knowledge, indulge in the pastime of describing the Paramatman in various ways. Atman is imagined to be prana, and other innumerable entities. This is the Maya of the Atman by which even Atman Itself becomes deluded."   *Gaudapada*

Atman Is:

taken to be merit and demerit by the religionists

taken to be dharma and adharma by the virtuous

taken to be the various ashramas by the four castes

taken to be mind and intellect by scholars and scientists

taken to be prana by the metaphysicians

taken to be padas by adherents of phonetics

taken to be the five elements by earthbound souls

taken to be physical objects by the materialists

taken to be the three gunas by the knowers of the gunas

taken to be lokas by ancestors, celestials, and seekers of heaven

taken to be the many tattvas by the intellectuals

taken to be gods and goddesses by the worshipers

taken to be creation, sustanence, and dissolution by philosophers

taken to be gross, subtle, and causal by the cosmologists

taken to be vedas and sacrifices by the priest class

taken to be enjoyment and objects of enjoyment by the worldly

"....and that this Lord we are trying to realize from time without beginning in the objective and in the attempt throwing up such "queer" creatures of our fancy as man, woman, child, body, mind, earth, sun, moon, stars, the world, love, hate, property, wealth, etc.; also ghosts, devils, angels and gods, God, etc."   *Swami Vivekananda*

Atman which causes beings to assume all manner of things in place of the *Atman,* thus forcing the true Self of mankind to occupy a subservient background position in the minds of men.

As the chart on the facing page illustrates, there are some very profound beings involved in this cheap "pea and walnut shell game" of swapping a favorite object, pastime, location, ritual, quality, or philosophy for the all-pervasive and eternal *Atman.* In this type of folly it seems that all really want the *Atman,* but none truly knows what It is, so they attempt to substitute their most precious and valuable word, symbol, thought, concept, projection, or conclusion where none but the *Atman* should appear or can exist. Truly, then, this unadvisable pastime of deluded trading must really contribute to a host of frenetic races run in a veritable wash of dreams, dreams in which the imaginations of millions of dreamers are busy trying to supplant Reality and install mere imitations in Its place.

As the circle of propositions encircling the Great Master on our chart reveal, living beings all have their particular love in life, and where that love is, their own personal version of Reality also abides. From gross to middling to refined fall the pet principles in multiple categories, all vying for the vaunted throne of supremacy, as beings devoid of knowledge of the Truth all move to lay their various select treasures atop the ever-present champion of an immeasurable host of illumined souls — the *Paramatman.* Some, rather fanatic at times, think that religion and its set of morals and ethics is the Self of mankind, but though there are many fine religions on earth, there is only one indivisible *Atman.* Others, a little deeper into the matter, see *Atman* in terms of *dharma* and *adharma,* of vows and betrayals, but *Atman* transcends all pairs of opposites. Even scholars, scientists, and psychologists are studying and conceiving the all-pervading *Atman* in their never ending search of mind and matter, but the subtlemost *Atman* escapes them as they do. As the *Svetasvataropanisad* states, *"It is the God of religion, the Self of philosophy, and the Energy of science,"* yet It is not matter, energy nor thought.

Continuing on with this unusual exploration, the general mass of people in the world, those who seek heaven and pleasant felicitude after death, place their ancestors and their celestial realms in place of the *Atman,* even though these worlds and beings are only a faint reflection of the *Atman's* majesty. As the poet-saint, Ramprasad Sen, sings, in disbelief at this mishappen spectacle: *"Everyone is babbling about what happens after death. Superstitious villagers insist we will become strange wandering spirits, while simple religious hearts assume our goal to be sweet heavenly existence. Pure spiritual lovers long to be lost in eternal companionship with the Divine, while profound knowers of God wish to merge completely with God. But this intoxicated poet of Goddess Kali is certain that all opinions are void of substance. The Divine Mother's Mystery eludes every earnest practitioner or philosopher who assumes virtue or vice to be real."*

And relative to this level of thinking, or dreaming, is the mind-set of millions of beings who look to and worship the gods and goddesses for salvation. Though a higher level of conception, the *Atman* is still left out of the picture; for, as Swami Vivekananda has stated, *"The earth is higher than all the heavens; it is the greatest school in the Universe. Mars and Jupiter people cannot be higher because they cannot communicate with us. The only so-called higher beings are departed, and these are nothing but men who have taken on another body. This is finer, it is true, but still a man body, with hands and feet and so on. And they live on this earth in another akasha, without being absolutely invisible. They also think and have consciousness, and everything else like us. So they are also men, and so are the gods, and the angels."* All of these beings will have to come back to earth in a human body in order to fulfill their desire for individual lordship, and transcend birth and death.

Some of the aspects of this chart have been scrutinized with regard to the hidden Essence in life and mind and the many overlays that are superimposed (see chart on page 65) upon It by a host of various perspectives. In the following chart, we see an apt example of how such superimpositions can invade life and mind, bringing with them a myriad undesirable causes and effects, all forcing the heaven-aspiring soul to continue with the business of "running a race in a dream."

As was discussed and taught earlier in this chapter (see chart on page 267), false superimposition, or the overlay of name and form over the essential formless nature of mankind, was given a definitive word by the Indian *rishis.* In *Sanskrit,* the Language of the Gods (*Devabhasya*), that word is *sankalpa,* defined as "imaginations in time." The implication of such a word and its deeper meaning revolves around the distinction that a seeker of Truth must draw between all that happens in time, called phenomena, and That which exists beyond it. Formless, to be sure, *Brahman,* the Reality, is also timeless, which immediately designates everything that happens in time to be a matter of mental projection, or *sankalpa.*

In the chart on the right, inspired by one of the spiritual stories in the great scripture, *Yoga Vasishtha,* the Indian *rishi,* Dashura, tells of a kingly figure by the name of Svotta whose powers of dreaming were very powerful. He told this story to his own son, born from a flower drawn from his own heart and bestowed upon a forest goddess who had aided him in his spiritual quest. When this son, whom he had never met, was brought to him by the goddess when he was twelve, Dashura took it upon himself to come out of *samadhi* and train the boy in the spiritual arts.

After testing the boy's acumen and concentration, which he found to be of excellent quality, he gave him the teaching about *sankalpa* and its marvelous yet potentially insidious effects as his first teaching. In that teaching the young charge of Dashura came to know that King Svotta, himself, was *sankalpa* incarnate. He had such powers of mental projection as to shame the celestials and the cosmic beings combined, having full control over both *prana,* life-energy, and *prakriti,* material energy. The boy then heard about Svotta's magnificent construction in the form of a projected city consisting of thought and conception. But such were the diverse elements that were contained in both the story and its symbology that the young student, out of both wonder and confusion, was prompted to inquire about them all.

It was then that Dashura explained to him that King Svotta's *sankalpa* city was a construction of pure *atmic* proportions, being fashioned from the highest intelligence. This is also true of the Three Worlds, which are the king's very body. Contrary to conventional thinking, all beings have three bodies, not just one, which correspond to the gross, subtle, and causal worlds (see chart on page 161). Further, in this triple creation of cosmic design run fourteen avenues, representing the fourteen spheres of existence, seven higher realms and seven lower hells. If the transmigrating soul aspires beyond the seven upper *lokas* and takes these routes of spiritual ascension, it transcends rebirth and merges back into the highest Reality and dreams no more.

Otherwise, King Svotta's castle and its pleasure gardens await, which is the abode of nature and its six transformations (see chart on page 225). Svotta's two great lights abide there, which are sun and moon, mere reflections of the Light of Intelligence that also signify the host of dualities that the soul must suffer in this solid realm. These two mesmerizing luminous bodies shine upon Svotta's seven bathing tanks, teeming with life, symbolizing the seven oceans, and indicative of the soul's immersion in relativity and all its ills. Mighty rivers course in and out of these massive liquid reservoirs, like creepers in a garden, which speak of the soul's fascination and eventual addiction to the feelings and emotions associated with *prana* and its various allurements.

Various creatures of King Svotta's design vie for possession of this illusory landscape — the *devas, nagas,* and human beings. These are the three great pillars that are driven deep in the soil of this city of mental projection. Countless forms are Svotta's chambers and apartments, each having nine windows, apertures out of which the light of the senses shines, hungry with desire for multiple experiences representing the countless winds blowing in and out of Svotta's city.

And finally, King Svotta has a ghostly friend living in his city, whose two long arms encircle the entire periphery. This ghost is the human ego through which the king sports continually. It resists meditation and spiritual life, two rare opportunities that will save it, and instead transmigrates restlessly from birth to death and back again (see chart on page 164).

With this expanded elucidation, Dashura informed his son of the workings and dangers of *sankalpa,* as all good parents should do for their children. Concluding, he gave his son this precious piece of cogent advice: *"Never contemplate the things of this universe under the assumption of their being real or actual. Instead, contemplate all as Brahman — the only Reality. This will lead to your ultimate happiness."*

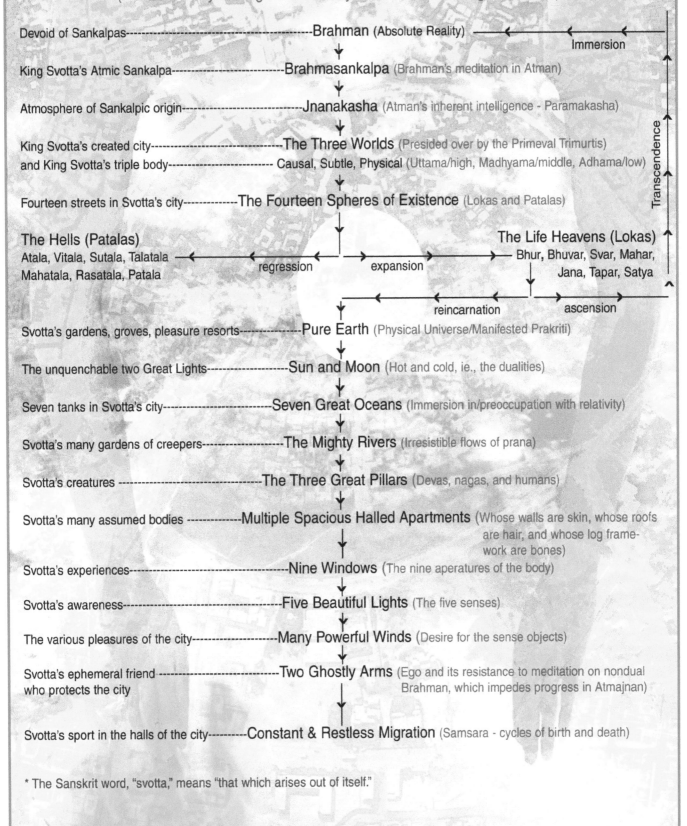

King Svotta's Sankalpa City

(From the Story of King Svotta told by Rishi Dashura in Yoga Vasishtha)

Devoid of Sankalpas----------------------------------**Brahman** (Absolute Reality) ←— ← ← ← | Immersion

King Svotta's Atmic Sankalpa----------------------**Brahmasankalpa** (Brahman's meditation in Atman)

Atmosphere of Sankalpic origin----------------------**Jnanakasha** (Atman's inherent intelligence - Paramakasha)

King Svotta's created city------------------------------**The Three Worlds** (Presided over by the Primeval Trimurtis)
and King Svotta's triple body------------------- Causal, Subtle, Physical (Uttama/high, Madhyama/middle, Adhama/low)

Fourteen streets in Svotta's city-------------**The Fourteen Spheres of Existence** (Lokas and Patalas)

The Hells (Patalas)   **The Life Heavens (Lokas)** ↑
Atala, Vitala, Sutala, Talatala ← — ← ← ← — → → → — Bhur, Bhuvar, Svar, Mahar,
Mahatala, Rasatala, Patala   regression   expansion   Jana, Tapar, Satya
                                                                          ← ← — → → —
                                                                        reincarnation   ascension

Svotta's gardens, groves, pleasure resorts---------------**Pure Earth** (Physical Universe/Manifested Prakriti)

The unquenchable two Great Lights----------------------**Sun and Moon** (Hot and cold, ie., the dualities)

Seven tanks in Svotta's city--------------------------**Seven Great Oceans** (Immersion in/preoccupation with relativity)

Svotta's many gardens of creepers----------------------**The Mighty Rivers** (Irresistible flows of prana)

Svotta's creatures --------------------------------------**The Three Great Pillars** (Devas, nagas, and humans)

Svotta's many assumed bodies --------------**Multiple Spacious Halled Apartments** (Whose walls are skin, whose roofs
                                                                                                         are hair, and whose log frame-
                                                                                                         work are bones)

Svotta's experiences------------------------------------**Nine Windows** (The nine aperatures of the body)

Svotta's awareness------------------------------------**Five Beautiful Lights** (The five senses)

The various pleasures of the city----------------------**Many Powerful Winds** (Desire for the sense objects)

Svotta's ephemeral friend --------------------------**Two Ghostly Arms** (Ego and its resistance to meditation on nondual
who protects the city   Brahman, which impedes progress in Atmajnan)

Svotta's sport in the halls of the city----------**Constant & Restless Migration** (Samsara - cycles of birth and death)

Transcendence

* The Sanskrit word, "svotta," means "that which arises out of itself."

"The manifestation of Atmajnana as visible things is sankalpa, but contemplating them as being real leads to unhappiness."
Rishi Dashura

The duality of bondage and liberation is one of several dualities which occupy a more rare and refined position in the mind, the contemplation of which brings about beneficial results. Along with the duality of form and formlessness, its import approaches the seeker of Truth at advanced stages of spiritual awakening. Reminiscent of King Svotta's mentally projected city, the Three Types of Bondage as outlined by Lord Kapila of *Sankhya Yoga* fame spotlight this tenacious problem again, only in a much more direct and philosophical way.

Embodied beings who enter the realm of relativity, void of the teachings of *sankalpa* and the principle of cosmic superimposition, fall victim to bondage there in three distinct but interconnected ways (see chart on facing page). First, there is bondage to nature. In Buddhist teachings, the five elements of nature, or *Prakriti,* represent the embodied soul's desires. Earth and its bounty, water and its properties, fire and its appeal, air and its exhilaration, and ether and its magnitude all entice and entrap the soul and, over lifetimes, bind it fast. At the time of death, releasing the grip on these five elements and all that they represent to the transmigrating soul causes much suffering, keeping it from its naturally liberated state. The soul exiting the body feels preponderant weightiness, dryness of mouth and body, burning and sweating feelings, difficulty with the breathing process, and disorientation — all related to the five elements respectively.

It is only by wisdom teachings given to the aspiring soul during his or her life that this all-consuming dependence on nature can be cut away. Over time, and with good counsel from the wise, the soul comes to understand that the Sentient Soul and Insentient Nature are two different principles. The Eternal Soul, or *Atman,* can never be matter, nor can matter ever become a soul. If the truth be known, all of nature comes out of the human mind via its power of projection, as is instanced in the story of King Svotta recently under study.

Bondage to the sense objects is the second kind of bondage, which is only bondage to nature in another form. Here, personal pleasure is the linchpin that holds the soul firmly in its grip. Here, and in the language of *Yoga,* the seer has become identified with the seen — a problem that should never have originated. Placing all of the energy of the five senses into the sense objects, a man verily animates them, transforming them into the most important things in his life. He will then sacrifice everything else just in order to maintain enjoyment of them, even though these same objects bring suffering as well.

To examine a material object, spiritually, is to look into its essence. Its physical form consists of a combination of the five elements. Then it has a formless form, called swirling particles. But then there is its essential form, the *Atman,* or underlying Consciousness. If one thinks this way, dissecting the object with the mind's discrimination, then the problem gets solved swiftly. If this is not possible, however, if the soul is too attached to listen to reason, then the fact of an object's transitory nature is to be examined. In this regard, and according to scriptural teachings, the object has at least five ways through which it fails the soul. First, it can get damaged; second, it can get lost; third, it can get stolen; fourth, it can become boring. Finally, it will get forgotten and replaced by another object that is more pleasing. Of course, the fact that it will disappear forever upon death is something few souls will ever ponder. Being under the control of a physical object is one of the most ignoble of predicaments for the living being. As Ramprasad Sen sings about the Soul and Its true Mother, *"The Wisdom Mother alone is purest gold, the only Treasure, yet you barter Her golden Radiance at the center of your being for a fragmentary world of mere colored glass."*

These two types of bondage just mentioned play into the third in insidious fashion. *Dakshina Bandha,* the bondage of conventional life, is both rampant and ongoing in the world of living beings. And it has a convenient excuse for being present in every aspect of human life, called making a living, or gaining an occupation. But Lord Kapila does not excuse it. He points out one very important point in this regard, that being, that if life is shorn of religious practices and spiritual realization, nothing but confusion and misfortune will eventually and inevitably follow.

The widespread philosophy of *Tantra* has an equivalent teaching in this regard. It is called the *Eshanatrayam* — the triple bondage of spouse, children, and wealth. One might expect a teach-

The Three Types of Bondage
& The Three Types of Liberation

Lord Kapila

→ **According to Sankhya**

With compiled teachings from Tattva Samasa Sutras

"Purusha is pure Consciousness, an ever-aware spiritual entity who, through connection with Prakriti, assumes jivahood. Ever-wise, ever-free, It never actually falls into the bondage of ignorance."

Prakritika Bandha — Bondage to Nature

"Prakriti, nature, is the primordial source of all evolutes. The greater amount of it remains unmanifest. When it is manifest, beings identify with it, taking the non-eternal for the Eternal, the impure for the Pure. They mistake the trans-evolutional Purusha for evolving matter."

Vaikritika Bandha — Bondage to Sense Objects

"The various incapacities of mind and intelligence adversely affect the five cognitive and five active senses, subjecting them to ignorance and turning them towards the nine complacencies and away from the eight great accomplishments. The five major hells then take root and life under the mantle of the three kinds of pain ensues."

Dakshina Bandha — Bondage to Conventional Life

"Common people's involvement with the ordinary desires and needs of life breeds preoccupation with mundane existence, shorn of religious practice and spiritual realization. Good and bad acts of stupefaction then follow."

Jnanamukti — The Liberation of Wisdom

"With knowledge of the components of the nonself brought about by the study of the chain of universal causation, the full expansion of wisdom duly manifests and cognizance of the distinctiveness between Prakriti and Purusha dawns on the mind. The elimination of pain is the result."

Vaitrsnya-mukti — the Liberation of Detachment

"When clear understanding concerning the distinction of nature, the insentient world of objects, and Soul, the sentient spiritual energy, dawns, all fetters and attachments to the transient realm of name and form are struck away. Purusha realizes its transcendent nature."

Paramukti — The Liberation of Transcendence

"Actuation of the reversal of the transitional chain of evolutes results in the awakened mind's complete dissolution of all manifested principles into unmanifested Prakriti. The gunas, in disequilibrium during cyclic manifestation, return to equilibrium, and Purusha realizes Itself beyond phenomena."

ing of this nature from an Indian monastic school, but *Tantra* is not necessarily known for its monasticism. Among the householders, then, there is a knowledge that has grown over time, very ancient too, which has espied the tendency of the human mind to become so attached to daily life in the home and workplace that it deposits the soul into abject attachment and bondage to people, places, and things. That is, those aspects of life which should be aids and helpmates along the path to enlightenment via peace and contentment — a spiritual partner, loving and intelligent children, and wealth earned by right means utilized for the service of humanity — become the very things that impede and bind. Further, and as a result of failing to implement spiritual practice, called *sadhana*, into the life of the family, various acts of delusion follow (see chart on page 253), accumulating, as they occur, a host of *karmas* (see charts on page 184 & 210) ending in a heap of troubles (see chart on page 247). In such fashion does life, originally meant to be an expression of God on earth, turn into an exhibition of slavishness that recurs in succeeding lifetimes with all its ills unabated.

The bottom half our the chart under study on the previous page presents the struggling soul with options that are not only preferable, but inspiring. Just as there are three types of bondages noted by the ancient *rishis* of India, so too are there three types of liberations. The first is a freedom gained by *jnana*, spiritual wisdom, the gaining of knowledge as prescribed in the *Sankhya darshana*. Sorely overlooked in this day and age, mostly due to the poor posture and condition of religion, *jnanam* proceeds in part by an accounting of the chain of causation. When applied from the standpoint of embodiment in ignorance, this process is implemented in reverse, wherein the aspirant becomes aware, much like in the upper three limbs of *Yoga*, through study, contemplation, and meditation, of the connections between all the various principles of creation. These present themselves to the seeker through the teachings of the tradition in sets of fives, like the five elements, the five active senses, and the five cognitive senses. After noting the connection of this quintuplication process, the budding seer then assumes that all of these sets of five are effects of a subtler cause.

Looking deeper, through both wisdom teachings from the scriptures and personal introspection, the destined luminary ferrets out the existence of several sets of five that, though unseen, must have to be the causes for the gross physical world and its externalized aspects. Five subtle elements and five subtle senses (see chart on page 161 and 151) thus make their appearance, and the intrepid spiritual wayfarer can now factor these into the chain of causation process. The involving soul is now becoming aware of the internal dynamics and cosmic laws that really run the universe in space and time, transcendent of conventional theories of science and psychology like the "Big Bang," evolution, gravity, genealogy, heredity, instinct, etc.

It is generally at about at this juncture that the five life-forces, aspects of *prana*, are uncovered, and with that discovery and its inclusion into the growing list, the awakening soul has effectively entered into the subtle world and is about to penetrate the causal one. For, the cognition and affirmation of *prana* — that vital energy which proves that *"man does not live by bread alone"* — leads the *jnani* to the existence of psychic *prana*, a subtle force that carries thoughts to their many destinations and affords insight into the realms of inner phenomena and the memory to remember them. Controlling and mastering the psychic *prana*, the aspiring soul can ride it, like the great dragon bird, Garuda, to a profound region of causal design that is as if formless, yet pregnant with potentiality.

And this is where freedom, called *mukti*, comes into the picture. Along this wondrous path, the aspiring being has glimpsed, more and more, that freedom was never something to be gained; despite limiting conditions and overlays on the individual level of existence, it always remained the nature of the Soul, and unaltered. Nevertheless, as these conditionings are sloughed off and discarded, one by one, and the chain of cause and effect is duly noted, aspect by aspect, principle by principle, the increase of personal knowledge and its impending effect is going to burst the individual ego/mind mechanism, the result being a breakthrough of truly spiritual proportions.

And, in fact, the ego itself begins to figure into this keen inner accounting of the chain of causation, which will not stop at the level of energy, no matter how refined it may be, but will continue into levels of existence which can only be defined by words like cosmic, causal, or universal.

When the personal ego sees itself, and its limitations, it will shed them and take on a station called witness consciousness, or *Sakshahamkara* (see chart on page 453). From this unique position of divine objectivity, the cosmic Personality comes into view, and the Light of pure Intelligence that is emanating from It. This is the "Son" through which one arrives at the "Father," called *Ishvara* and *Brahman*, respectively, in Indian religion and philosophy. Salvation and liberation lie there.

The second of these three pathways to liberation is one of detachment, *vairagyam*. How it differs from the freedom of wisdom lies more in the makeup of the soul rather than in the process. Some souls have a natural affinity with transcendence, and an innate inclination towards renunciation. These will observe, mainly through the *Yoga* of Meditation, the sharp and obvious distinction between Soul and Matter, *Purusha* and *Prakriti*, and immediately detach from insentient nature. For more on the dynamics of detachment, see the teaching of the Twelve Levels of *Vairagya* on page 389.

There is another form that liberation takes and utilizes to reveal its eternal and unchanging existence, and that is one of pure Transcendence. It is termed *Paramukti* in order to declare its supreme nature, *"Para."* It can be said here that all three of these pathways towards *mukti* utilize both the chain of causation method and the *neti neti* process. But *Paramukti* is less of a station that an aspiring soul arrives at, and more of a permanent verity that permeates and galvanizes everything — especially the urge towards awakening, insight, and realization.

Therefore, its distinction lies in the power it affords the now-realized soul to not only reverse the chain of cause and effect and, at the same time, detach from each and every wisdom principle (*tattva*) as being an element of the nonself, but to grant the ability for the illumined being to revisit the worlds of name and form at will, always in possession of its essential Awareness. Therefore, and ironically enough — and contrary to the limited thinking of those schools and their adherents who presume that formlessness is all there is, and the last word in spiritual realization — transcendence transcends the limitation of formlessness as well. As Sri Ramakrishna *Paramahamsa*, has declared: *"God is with form, and beyond form, but is beyond both form and formlessness as well. It is the only principle that has never been defiled by the tongue of mankind."*

With an overview and teachings around the "Three Types of Bondage and the Three Types of Liberation" now absorbed within for further contemplation, a crucial conclusion must be stated, and as often as possible. As earlier teachings in this book affirmed some of this already. More on this definitive subject will come in later chapters, the reiteration that *Brahman*, Reality, is pure and perfect, unchanging — *Akshara Brahman*. This is to be pondered continually.

In reference to the chart just scrutinized, it stands in odd contrast that the terms of bondage and liberation are foreign and obsolete in conjunction with the Unchanging *Brahman*. To lend more sense and substance to this apparent anomaly, it can be offered here that there is bondage, there is liberation, and then there is liberation from the concepts, or assumptions, of bondage and liberation. These three positions actually fit with the three types of liberation just studied. In that mind where there exists bondage and its ignorance of Eternal Freedom, *Jnanamukti*, with its liberating wisdom, such will suffice to awaken the sleeping soul from its illusion of finitude, its dream of ignorance. And where the desire for liberation holds sway in the discriminating mind, there, *Vaitrsnyamukti*, holding in it the power of withdrawal from all forms of attachment and projection, will apply. And in that rare mind that has transcended ordinary mind and wisely turned to Original Mind, there, *Paramukti*, with Its ultimate position of natural transcendence in *samadhi*, in a cohesive way that is inclusive of name, form, worlds, divine beings, and all that *Jnanamukti* and *Vaitrsnya-mukti* hold and teach, will prevail.

In this way, and similar to all other *triputis*, all these steps along the path apply to beings whose understanding is either dualistic, qualified nondualistic, or nondualistic — as the case may be. Thus, the scriptures of nonduality demand that no being should undermine the understanding of another, whose comprehension may not yet be at a more mature level. Care in dealing with practitioners at the level of comprehension that they are presently holding is a facet of universal religious quality. It affirms stages of growth. Otherwise, a "one size fits all" measure can devastate religion.

Along this line of gradated understanding, of spiritual graduation, of soul qualification, of being led "from lower truth to higher Truth" (see chart on page 271), the tendered perspective of life being very much like "running a race in a dream" is a fitting one. Sri Sarada Devi's teaching about the train trip between two points is apropos here as well. One falls asleep at some point during the journey, and so does not see much of the scenery that goes by, but still awakens at the destination. Similarly, the beginning and end of our life's journey are usually kept in mind, but what happens in the middle, in the interim, often goes by ungrasped, and unnoticed. Pertinent to spiritual life, this applies to all the ignorance, unconscious acts, *karma,* and other overlays that do get destroyed over time via spiritual self-effort, but whose destruction are never actually witnessed by the striving soul. As Ramprasad sings, *"One day I awoke and my delusion was gone, gone, utterly gone! Who can obscure the Truth? Who can keep a blazing fire tied in a cotton cloth?"*

Given that we have seen how Reality is eternally perfect, and that relativity is attended by all manner of dualities, overlays, even outright ills and evils, the experiences that emerge out of this admixture, and the brooding and pondering that attends this enigmatic process, must end in a conclusion that is sensible and satisfying. In The Nine Steps to Perfection chart that appears on the facing page, we see evidence that a dream race is indeed under way, and that it will recur repeatedly upon the surface of our own consciousness unless we take definite steps to awaken. If the aspirant should face any more doubt about this twin conclusion around Reality and relativity, he only has to look to the words of a great Soul for verification. Gracing the chart at the right is Sri Ramakrishna's final word on the matter: *"One attains to perfection by going beyond the universe and its created beings conjured up by Maya."* Armed with this assurance from a past Master, the soul can enter into the path that will awaken it from its own personal dream of finitude.

Scrutinizing the Nine Steps to Perfection shown here, it must be admitted that the first eight steps are all a part of a dream race, though a subtler one. There are levels of *maya* that get transcended as ones practice goes forth and ones awareness gets refined. According to the illumined ones who have observed and worked with the human soul for lifetimes, the awakening process all begins with recognition of the cosmic deception that the soul has bought into. In other words, taking form, particularly in ignorance, has placed the embodied being in a predicament that contradicts the truth that man's nature is formless. Realization of this axiom, gained while the soul is experiencing embodiment (not afterwards in a heavenly or qualified formless state), correlates with spiritual awakening. This is not to be confused with a mere passing glimpse of the fact of bondage, as is had via inferior mechanisms such as surface *bhakti,* drugs and elixirs, or natural temporary lulls in *karmic* and *gunic* cycles. *Kapata* is a type of deception assumed by misguided cleverness such as these, and must be pierced through with an act of sincerity that is honest and real.

If that puncture in a man's own egotistic guile can be effected, and if he can place his petty desires and pleasures second to spiritual awakening, some authentic reception, *Buddhi-vyapara,* can be attained. Open-mindedness, and open-heartedness, then visits his quest, and his earlier suspicions about the insubstantial nature of phenomena and appearances gets a sanction. What to speak of running backwards, as he did in so many lifetimes, his race in a dream begins to resemble a race towards a real goal. It is here that the favored and coveted stage of *abhijna* descends on the mind, with its deep recollection of things pushed away and long forgotten in the mind's memory. At this juncture the word "intuition" applies nicely, for though a long way from enlightenment yet, the soul feels the presence of something incomparable and ineffable.

Still, more depth must be gained, and more of the ground of consciousness exposed in order to receive a clearer vision of this Reality. Combining outward glances towards the world with gazes inward into the realm of the Spirit, managed via the all-important and ongoing operation of *sadhana,* the sedulous seeker presses on and observes the wheels of the cosmic mechanism turning, and sees himself as its witness and potential master. This station and the further aspiration that it confers sets the scene for a great renunciation to take place, which is a singular event in the spiritual involution of the aspiring soul.

The Nine Steps to Perfection

"Reaching the pinnacle of pure, conscious Awareness, the individualized soul merges in the Supreme State, which is the Source and Origin of all objects and all beings."

9. Samyag darshana - Perfection

8. Brahmachintana — Introspection

Saturated with deep understanding and intense devotion, the soul aspires to immerse the separate self into the Ocean of Existence, Knowledge, and Bliss Absolute.

7. Upalabdhi — Perception

Perceiving the Truth of Existence that is the foundation of mind, life, and human beings, the soul remains enthralled with It and abides in a state of peace and subtle bliss.

6. Artha-bhavana — Reflection

Contemplating emptiness for a time, the soul begins to uncover the subtle basis underlying that state, discovering the secret of interconnectedness and all-pervasiveness.

5. Tyaga — Rejection

In an intense state of resolute assurance, the soul resists all desire-based impulses which attempt to possess the transitory universe, and instead embraces emptiness.

4. Nirupana — Inspection

Scrutinizing the world of matter, the principle of energy, and the cosmic cycles of universal phenomena, the striving soul comes to know its mutable nature.

3. Abhijna — Recollection

Gaining an initial glimpse of the Reality beyond names and forms, the soul begins to remember its original state of Being and embarks upon an inward journey to recover It.

2. Buddhi-vyapara — Reception

As a result of doubting the reality of appearances, the human heart and mind opens to the search for deeper meaning and higher existence beyond the realm of matter.

1. Kapata — Deception

The awakening soul begins to suspect that the universe of names and forms is not ultimately true or real, supported by his/her own sufferings and experiences in relativity.

"One attains to perfection by going beyond the universe and its created beings conjured up by Maya." Sri Ramakrishna

Here, at the stage called *tyaga*, the awakened being is able to reject all that acted as impediments along the interior pathway previously. The result is an emptying of the mind that, contrary to the beliefs of unawakened souls, is more of a deep feeling of peace and bliss rather than a void where thought and existence expire. This is proven to the inward dwelling soul when, after a period of immersing in this welcome emptiness, called *shunyata* by some, a very subtle backdrop is perceived, along with the knowledge of the inter-connectedness of all things, all beings. This stage of spiritual awakening also requires some long-lived reflection, and all manner of subtle wisdom and individual soul-experience proceeds from it.

The next stage towards perfection, called real and true perception, *Upalabdhi*, is a superlative position for the inward moving soul to rest in. It is just short of immersion into the essential Self, or *Atman*, which will be the penultimate stage in this most precious process of inward ascension. Stages seven and eight, *Upalabdhi* and *Brahmachintana*, really represent the awakened soul's sublime move from blissful contemplation of subtle form to periods of absorption in formless Reality. This double stage of refinement, very difficult of description, is attended by many visions, insights, and realizations, all around the essential nature of Reality. Long gone and far distant are the beginning steps of awakening to the transitory nature of the world in space and time based upon causation, mere wisps of memory associated with a primal ignorance that was neither real nor the fault of the soul, but more of an immediate overlay of cosmic proportions that figures as a spontaneous occurrence in the process of manifestation.

And as the fully awakened soul drinks in the "Nectar of Naturalness" that resides at the penultimate station of *Brahmachintana* — the very Consciousness of *Brahman* — the fact of its own identity with That strikes home in the form of nondual *samadhi*. *Samyakdarshana* is the supreme vision of inherent perfection that is nameless, formless, birthless, deathless, and beyond description. This latter fact did not keep the *rishis* of India from attempting description, however, and a plethora of hymns, scriptures, philosophical schools, and other divine movements and testaments flowed endlessly and copiously from a host of illumined lips, minds, hearts, and souls throughout many millennia. In the *Hasta-amalaka Stotram*, for instance, this winsome and multi-faceted expression is found:

> *Absolutely unique, the ineffable essence which is the source and origin of all,*
> *The primal Purusha, playfully manifesting Itself in Pure Mind,*
> *Who is the one impartial sun, reflecting in the different waterpots of various intellects,*
> *That One and I are identical, non-different, inseparable.*

> *It is one homogenous presence that causes all eyes to see.*
> *It is one omniscient entity which graces all minds with thought.*
> *It is like unto the sun which reveals the world of name and form for perceiving.*
> *That One and I are non-distinct and form one cohesive unity.*

> *There is only this One, existing in all beings, and all existing in It.*
> *It filters down and touches all hearts and minds, yet nothing can touch It.*
> *It is like the sky, pure and serene, subtle and impossible to taint.*
> *That One am I, I am that One, there can be none other.*

> *Like the lustrous gem which assumes the outline of its backdrop,*
> *Or the stationary moon that undulates on the surface of a rippling lake,*
> *So too does the formless and all-pervading Reality appear everywhere, in everything,*
> *While remaining boundless and ever-free, untainted by any of its associations.*

In verses such as these, products of the realizations of the illumined mind of the seer interwoven with the fondest aspirations of the devotee's heart, is to be found declared the Truth of Life and Existence Itself. How can ordinary living compare and, even more unthinkable, what is it about conventional life that attracts the transmigrating soul to the physical world alone, causing it to fixate on its paltry offerings and petty concerns? In one of India's many devotional wisdom songs, the cry for freedom from the tyranny of matter and ignorance finds appropriate words:

O mind, my dear friend: this projected world is only the faint reflection of Reality.
By attempting to grasp reflected images, we cheat ourselves of true experience.
Turn instead to the Original and discover the Treasure of Delight.
This realm of reflection we call the universe consists simply of earth, water, fire, air, and ether, arranging
and rearranging with intricate beauty.
The principle of subtle energy naturally evolves into tangibility, blossoming as millions of worlds.
The sun reflects in countless water-bearing vessels.
When these earthenware worlds are broken, one by one,
the sunlight of infinite awareness remains the same.
Floating in the Cosmic Mother's womb, we are all contemplatives,
but once we take birth in the world of separation,
we consume earth instead of nectar, time instead of timelessness.
The cord that bound me to my human mother was severed quickly and cleanly by the midwife.
Can I cut as easily my illusion of bondage to the world?
The passionate words of a selfish lover may first taste sweeter than honey,
but they contain the poison of delusion.
The singer of this song once drained the cup of selfish love
and felt the anguish of its poison touch.
But now this poet tastes only authentic bliss, crying constantly:
"O Great Mother! Dream Power of the Absolute! Daughter of the Eternal Snow Mountain!
Do whatever You will with me!"

As a summary of all that has been studied in this chapter thus far, an outline can be presented that will both further clarify the teachings and instill them into the mind's awareness in the deepest possible way. Awareness of this process will destroy root ignorance, providing for true life at *dharmic*, divine, and transcendent levels. Put in simplest possible terms that neither compromises nor contradicts the accepted philosophical schools of Indian thought:

1) there is an eternal, immutable, and all-pervasive Reality *(Brahman)*.
2) inherent in that Ultimate Reality is a dynamic power *(Shakti)* ever one with Its Source, that is capable of projecting infinite realms of name and form on cosmic, collective, and individual levels of existence.
3) inherent in that dynamic power is *maya*, an inscrutable force containing the three qualities of obscuration *(tamas)*, distortion *(rajas)*, and revelation *(sattva)*.
4) transmigrating souls, who are nothing less than embodied bits of birthless, deathless, Consciousness, assume forms to sport in the worlds of apparent transformation and playful becoming, but forget their supreme status and immutable essence due to *Maya's* influence.
5) in the case of forgetfulness and the suffering it causes, illumined souls, in constant possession of both memory and realization of their Divine Nature *(Atman)*, manifest bodies in full awareness in order to assist suffering beings in remembering their own true nature.
6) the overall method utilized in this task is a prescribed regimen of *sadhana* guided by study of the revealed scriptures and counsel from illumined souls and spiritual preceptors.

The Nine Steps to Perfection, in whatever way they are utilized by the different wisdom schools of Indian philosophy, provide a most excellent description of the process of spiritual awakening that is taking place wherever *Maya's* influence is in operation in the human mind.

Since a mention of the three *gunas* of *maya* have come up again, it will be helpful to revisit this subject once more, this time in terms of how they overlay and permeate life. The reader is encouraged to take up portions of chapter five again, especially those teachings on *tamas, rajas,* and *sattva.* By drumming the teachings on these three modes of nature into the mind stuff *(chitta)*, the dream race that is inexorably going forth in *maya* will come to an end. For the *gunas* are dream work, pure and simple, occurring initially at the most subtle levels of the mind's awareness and then trickling on down and out to a more solid manifestation on the physical plane.

Within the chart on the facing page will be found a rendering of the three *gunas* according to three important divisions of existence, namely Nature, Mind, and Action. By studying the presence and effects of the *gunas* on these three levels, a comprehension of the complexity of *Mayic* superimposition, along with some important keys for transcending this triple aspect of *Maya*, will become available.

Taking up the three categories overall in a comprehensive look, *tamas* is inertia. In nature bondage to matter, void of even the slightest hint of any movement away, or of higher leanings. In the human mind, *tamas* is recognized in the tendency towards heavy sleep, and by a strong resistance and aversion towards functioning in the waking state. In action, if it could even be termed such, *tamas* compels the soul to engage only in brutish activities, and only with the body. The mind and intellect are nearly shut down, and the thoughts are dark and sluggish.

If *rajas* is introduced into the mix, but *tamas* is still present, even predominant, a shift begins, though not one that is, as yet, at all positive or beneficial. Nature now becomes a ground for manipulation of the most perverse type. The mind sees no real light of true awareness yet, remaining thick and heavy, and activity is fraught with the influence of violence. It is when *rajas* gains the upper hand over *tamas* that the overall atmosphere and mood begins to change. With the unbridled energy that *rajas* brings, mankind views nature as a means for possession and power, and his mind seeks pleasure for the senses and ownership for the self. At this point, all activity done under pure *rajas* is for personal gain via individual domination, with little thought for the good of others.

The welcome light of the *sattva guna* brings the first inkling of higher reason into the picture. The move to master nature and put it to work for mankind occurs to the mind, which now begins to think in terms of altruism. But *rajas* still holds the mind field enthralled with restless activity for individual and collective gain, which reflects in the arena of activity as the search after wealth and the leisure that it affords.

It is only when *sattva* takes predominance that activity is rendered subservient, and this represents the gift of life as it should be. Of a sudden, upon the swift and puzzling disappearance of *tamas* and *rajas*, the mind of a human being feels balanced naturally, and not due to any particular effort on his own part, either. This is not necessarily a good thing, for *sattva* will eventually disappear as quickly as it came upon the mind, leaving it shocked and angry at the return of slothfulness and frenetically paced action. The mind, then, once it has perceived the presence of the *gunas*, must learn to control them, not merely wait on their cycles, and in the interim bide with them in some kind of wise forbearance.

But in the meantime, when *sattva* does predominate, nature vibrates with beauty, work seems effortless, and the mind gets attracted more easily to higher thoughts and attainments. The Light of Consciousness, heretofore dwelling unseen in an ordinary man's awareness, comes forward and influences all the aspects and decisions in ones life.

And it is here, if one is spiritually inclined — meaning if he/she practiced disciplines in previous lifetimes — that the possibility for attaining to that very rare level of balanced mind called pure *sattva* presents itself. Here, work becomes worship, the service of God in mankind, and nature shows itself to be an expression of God's beauty, an overflow of the bliss of *Brahman*. And importantly, the human mind, leaving off all that is ordinary in it, approaches what is termed today as Enlightenment. It is here, at this juncture, that the three *gunas* of nature are mastered and transcended for all time.

The Three Gunas of Nature

	In Nature	In the Mind	In Activity
Pure Sattva	Perceiving the unity of Purusha & Prakriti	Approaching attainment of God-realization	Serving God in all beings
Sattva	Living in harmony with nature	Intense spiritual practice for gaining knowledge	Performing all work free of selfish motive
Rajo-sattva	Mastery over nature & utilizing its resources	Altruistic work for the good of society	Complacency after attaining wealth
Rajas	Seeking domination of the world & nature	Restless mind pre-occupied with ego/senses	Frenetic activity for personal gain
Tamo-rajas	Perverted use of nature attended by callousness	Greed and selfishness devoid of conscience	Violent activity with the desire to harm
Tamas	Total bondage to nature	Narrow, gross mind given to sleep/dullness	Inability to act at will, and brutish action

With the disequilibrium of the *gunas* no longer an impeding factor, some souls go towards the highest felicitude of transcendence of name and form. Others, seeing the need to return to embodiment, revisit the realm of humanity to begin the work of awakening living beings to their true nature, perfect and stainless. In this difficult mission, the slumbering human soul has two great tasks to complete for itself: first, to rid the mind of complacency; and second, to get down to the business of attaining an eightfold level of accomplishment that the saints and sages describe as being essential to spiritual perfection.

There are some major misconceptions occupying the ordinary human mind. Its habitual dips down into *rajasic* and *tamasic* cycles not only plant these in the mind, but also nourish them there. Unknown and unaccounted for by most living beings, these are some of the detrimental effects of hanging out in ignorance. And the reason for their perpetuation is complacency.

Over time, complacency becomes less of a reversible tendency and more of a command in the benighted human mind, and it becomes a preference in the restless one. In these imbalanced mindsets, then, implausible and detrimental thoughts occur, lodging in the recesses of the mind and sending out errant messages from there. As shown on the chart on the right, the fallacious idea of abiding happily in matter is one such delusion, often combined with the errant thought that awakening to higher truth, if it is even sought after at all, will come of its own accord if one only plays a waiting game. After all, the conventional saying declares that "All comes to he who waits," so the soul merely falls into complacency and does not seek higher wisdom.

But perhaps the saying should be modified to read, "All comes to he who waits while patiently performing spiritual practices." Patience and self-effort are qualities of the mind. Matter can never bring about such excellence, being insentient. This is why Lord Kapila has given, in contrast to the worldly wisdom that befriends the occupation of wiling away ones time, the Eight Great Accomplishments listed at the bottom of the chart on the facing page. The soul must come to know the utter futility of waiting on insentient matter to provide true attainment. Left to its own devices matter will only breed desire, attachment, and the vain hope for uninterrupted pleasure. But the insinuating presence of pain and suffering leading to disease and death are left out of the worldly person's formula for life.

In short, biding ones time in watchful awareness is far different than waiting upon time, chance, luck, good fortune, destiny, and wealth. As is instanced in Lord Buddha's saying from the *Dhammapada* on the chart under study, wealth is a considerable bondage, hard to get free of. Lord Kapila teaches that it is not only a vexation to earn wealth, but it is a further botheration to guard it and maintain it. Beyond that, the holding and utilizing of wealth for pleasure leads to both the sapping of the vital forces in the body and senses, and a sense of boredom ending in depression, even insanity, in many cases. Therefore, the Nine Complacencies — *Navadha Tushtih* — are to be carefully guarded against.

But let us take a look at the invigorating and uplifting pastimes that a sincerely aspiring soul has to look forward to, once having sidestepped the mind's tendency towards complacency. There are not enough words available to us to utilize in praise of them. Mainly, they consist of getting past or mastering the Threefold Sorrows of Existence. These represent the primary perfections, or *Siddhas*. For a succinct review on these, the reader can refer to the helpful chart on page 231 and its pertinent exposition for details, which outlines several of Lord Kapila's major teachings from the *Sankhya* philosophy. As to the secondary perfections, these are of equal importance, possibly of even greater import, as attainments along the spiritual path. These five aspects of *sadhana* deserve a commentary all their own, as follows.

The well-guided and fully determined pursuit of a select spiritual path by the avid and committed practitioner and aspirant after Truth is tantamount to spirituality itself. So few souls of this day and time come into embodiment with the rare and precious orientation that perceives this fact and follows through to its consummation. More common is the soul or souls who enter into life and begin their seeking phase, if at all they do, by running hither, thither, and yon to partake of the sur-

The Nine Complacencies
and the Eight Great Accomplishments

The Nine Complacencies (Navadha Tushtih)

Four Spiritual Complacencies
1) Matter Gives Realization
2) Renunciation Gives Realization
3) Time Brings Realization
4) Destiny/Luck Gives Realization

Five External Complacencies
5) Earning Wealth
6) Guarding Wealth
7) Keeping Wealth
8) Satisfying Desires
9) Seeking Enjoyment

ZZZzzzzzz

"The wise do not call strong those fetters made of hemp, wood, or iron. Rather they call attachment to jewels, treasure, ornaments, wealth, and possessions a far stronger bond." Lord Buddha

The Eight Great Accomplishments

The Three Primary Siddhis
Transcending Three Kinds of Suffering
1) Adhyatmika (Internal)
2) Adhibhautika (External)
3) Adhidaivika (Cosmic)

The Five Secondary Siddhis
4) Pursuing a Spiritual Path
5) Gaining Knowledge
6) Study of Scriptures & Sadhana
7) Attaining Guru, Disciples, Friends
8) Achieving Self-Purification

"As Patanjali said, 'When a man rejects all the superhuman powers, then he attains the cloud of virtue.' He sees God. He becomes God, and helps others to become the same. This is all I have to preach. Doctrines have been expounded enough. There are books by the millions. Oh, for an ounce of practice." Swami Vivekananda

face fare of every path, preacher, and philosophy available to them in their culture or country. This spiritual menu tasting style of seeking is allowable to some extent initially, as a way of familiarization with what is out there for consideration, but otherwise, and if left unchecked with no conclusion or consummation, leads to what has been described by the luminaries as "a hodge-podge of undigested spiritual moods."

In addition, and among several dangers to a matured spiritual life, is the tendency of the promiscuous beginner to fall victim to his or her own naivete, and then get allured by and drawn to the sensational level of existence revolving around metaphysics and the occult sciences. As reflected in the quote at the bottom of our chart under study on the previous page, beings the likes of Lord Patanjali and Swami Vivekananda concur about the danger of coveting powers, and advise instead the gradual attainment of sterling virtues which both build and proceed from true and authentic human character.

This is precisely why the spiritual preceptor, the *acharya*, the *guru*, called by many auspicious names, rejoices exceedingly upon seeing a qualified human soul come straight away to his or her spiritual path, free of any sidetracks, deviations, or detours along the way. As the wise know, there will be plenty of time to contemplate the teachings of other ways and means, preferences and opinions, pathways and philosophies, even religious traditions — free of the potential dangers of contamination, dilution, admixtures, and especially an untimely interruption from ones own chosen and original spiritual trajectory — once enlightenment has been regained. And as an exclamation point on this teaching, the aspirant who avoids compromise and complacency, and any prevarication around seeking Truth, builds within the mind a positive *samskara* for swiftly locating the teacher and his pathway in any and every lifetime assumed thereafter. This fact accounts for the singular soul who, "hitting the ground running," immediately seeks the *dharma* at a young age, remembering the teachings and the teacher or teachers who so patiently schooled them in a previous incarnation, and who is on hand again, in one form or another, to see it through to its consummate spiritual end.

Unfortunately, all of this also pertains to those who have, due to lack of discrimination, involved themselves with spurious beings who masquerade as *gurus*. They, too, recognize and are drawn to former associations — these problematic souls of their past — and reenact the caricature of spiritual life previously suffered. This explains why so many are lost when they are born, having no idea of why they are born, who they truly are, why they suffer, and what is the way out. As Sri Ramakrishna has said, *"If a water snake gets a hold of a frog it cannot swallow it completely, so both suffer together. But if a cobra seizes a frog, one or two croaks and the entire matter is over and done with."* To be "seized" by a great soul, then, is the intention of every embodied being who recognizes the dangers of being born on earth in a physical form with its constantly "croaking" ego.

Though much can be said and written about the benefits of pursuing a single spiritual path to its mature and consummate end, it can also be further expressed in terms of the next spiritual accomplishment on Lord Kapila's list — that of gaining knowledge. Obviously, since we are speaking the language of spirituality, this knowledge is of an extraordinary kind. Referred to as *Jnanam*, or *Atmajnan*, by the seers, it is coveted most highly. The denizens of the present day world have little, if any, ability in it, and even less stomach for it. It is either mindlessly brushed aside for pleasure-seeking, overlooked due to preoccupation with secular sciences, rejected for reasons of too much complexity, or abandoned outright for the path of devotion — as if the path of devotion does not require clarifying wisdom to reach its goal of selfless Love.

Further, hosts of great beings, from Vasishtha to Vivekananda, Moses to Mohammed, Krishna to Christ, Ramchandra to Ramakrishna, have taken refuge in its ignorance-destroying qualities. And what to speak of this level of solace and salubriousness, *Jnanam*, discriminating wisdom, also ushers the seeker into the higher echelons of the soul, namely, its own intelligence (see chart on page 271). At first, the human being assumes that intelligence is merely a property of the intellect. But soon, after spiritual instruction and apt reflection, the burgeoning mind of the practitioner comes to see the intellect as a vehicle for classifying intelligence, thus also limiting it. Intelligence itself is then perceived to be a superlative tool for clarifying the intellect, and eventually freeing it as well.

This comprehension of what intelligence epitomizes is a great juncture and graduation for the aspiring soul. Before higher understanding ever dawned on the human mind due to spiritual disciplines like study of scripture and meditation, it passed through stages of secular knowledge, then higher learning, then discriminating wisdom, then revelatory wisdom. But it was all seen in proper light upon the realization that *Jnanam* is really liberating wisdom. It is the scintillating Light of Pure Knowing that is the Divine Mother's own pristine atmosphere. How could it ever be brushed aside then, or ignored, or rejected, or abandoned. Should it not be raised, instead, to the highest station and paid the highest reverence?

Jnanam is gained, or more precisely, remembered, through study of scripture, memorization of *slokas*, contemplation of *sutras*, and meditation engaged in after such distilled wisdom ripens in the human mind. And this describes the third great accomplishment adequately. In *Yoga* it ensues via *svadhyaya* (see chart on page 69), study and memorization of scriptures. In *Vedanta* this practice goes by the triple designation of *shruti, yukti,* and *anubhava* — hearing the truths in the scriptures, reasoning about them, and maturing them into direct spiritual experience (see chart on page 381). In ancient times, Lord Vasishtha told the young *avatar*, Sri Ramchandra, about this great accomplishment, calling it *vidya-shastra,* and indicating it as being distinct from lower scriptural knowledge that treats only terrestrial subjects. Sri Krishna taught it in a monumental and necessarily condensed way to his disciple, Arjuna, on the battlefield of *Kurukshetra,* poised in a lull between two armies at war, speaking of it as *Prajna Pratistha* — steady wisdom. He called its loss *smritibhrama,* forgetfulness or loss of memory of the Self and its innate knowledge of Self, *Atman.*

In a more recent time than all these listed above, the great *Advaitan,* Shankaracharya, spoke of this great accomplishment via the phrase, *shruti-para-darshanam.* He transmitted, in his own scripture, these words on it: *"It is hard for any living creature to achieve birth in a human form. Strength of body and will are even harder to attain; purity is even harder still; harder even than these is the desire to live a spiritual life; and an understanding of scriptures is hardest of all."* With declarations such as these coming from the world's luminaries, one can well see why *jnanam* received through the revealed scriptures is termed one of the Eight Great Accomplishments of a *Sadhika* on the spiritual path.

And so it follows, these eight, and particularly the final five accomplishments, are interconnected. Naturally, then, the next boon is the achievement of gaining of an illumined soul for ones *guru,* including the disciples and close spiritual companions that accompany him. Holy company is the name of the game here, a must, especially for all souls who are still learning the subtle art of spiritual life (see chart on page 345). Through attending upon the company of a spiritual teacher and his sangha, several important requisites for *dharmic* life are accomplished. First, the thinking process gets redirected towards the true goal of human existence. Secondly, the aspirant, still uncertain and sporting many doubts about life in the world, gains assurance of what actions to engage in and what actions to refrain from, i.e., what to do and what not to do. This helps to clear up the matter of past *karmas,* or at least begins the process. Using a subtle inner transmission the illumined soul, without even saying much at first, deftly removes these unseen impositions and the ambivalence which attends them and smoothes the way for ensuing spiritual life and growth.

When this auspicious phase is complete, and even during its advent, is when the final great accomplishment is attained, in stages. It is a positive rarity in human beings — which is the attainment of purity of mind. Called *chit-shuddhi* in *Sanskrit,* it is gained via purity of location, purity of atmosphere, and purity of action (see chart on page 122). The saints and seers say that a pure mind is nothing short of the presence of God in a human being. The absence of all the usual troubles, distractions, and negativities is the characteristic of pure mind, so naturally beings seeking qualities such as peace of mind, forbearance, and compassion, will strive to attain this boon. Once attained, life in the body, whether in the present incarnation or in future lifetimes, if they be opted for, will be a perfect expression of God in humanity.

Over the course of six chapters, all representing a host of footfalls taken by the great *rishis* of

India over millennia, we have seen the *"baby steps"* taken by individuals and cultures at their inception. We also looked back at the strange and questionable tact of separation from our formless nature via *"retracing the strut of the individual"* into his or her present state of embodiment. Managing that by a study of time, space, and causality, we attempted to *"match our stride"* with the seers themselves by researching all that India has to offer by way of spiritual disciplines. This brought to the fore the problems faced by all those who would be so bold as to walk the razor's edged path of Truth, and we *"beat the old familiar path"* by scrutinizing the relative laws of *karma* and reincarnation, and the desires and *samskaras* that perpetuate them. In a moment of regret, we next witnessed how the soul often is caught *"walking backwards"* instead of going forward, when the *gunas*, passions, fetters, and other forms of ignorance were taken up for sobering contemplation. This study led us to the recent chapter where we witnessed the embodied soul *"running a race in a dream"* under the press of *Maya* and the mind's penchant for *sankalpa* and *vikalpa*, and its inability to distinguish between action and inaction.

In the following chapter, armed with all that the *rishis* have provided us with for embarking upon the spiritual path, we will attempt *"giant steps"* by considering Mother India's comprehensive vision of cosmology, Her clear ways of seeing which are the many orthodox and unorthodox *darshanas*, along with the vast array of wisdom pathways laid out and prescribed by the saints, sages, seers, and saviors dedicated to the propagation and implementation of the Eternal Truth. Within this magnificent *"gait of the gods,"* then, may we now posit ourselves, keeping step with an Eternal Path that has graced the world and its attending souls even long before their inception, and will continue to do so long after all dissolves in *Mahapralaya*.

Footfalls of the Indian Rishis
— Chapter Seven —

Giant Steps — The Gait of the Gods
The Cosmological and Philosophical Underpinnings
of India's Wisdom Pathways

"From dreams awake, from bonds be free. Know the Truth! Thou art He; thou are She." With this sweeping statement, filled with both Truth and inspirational poeticism, the *rishis* of India expressed in the eternal *Upanisads* the noblest of aspirations that always occupies the minds of all sincere souls who seek the ultimate welfare of their brothers and sisters. Knowing that dreaming is overrated, and that dreams contain nightmarish elements as well as heavenly ones, these thoroughly illumined souls, out of compassion and wishes for the highest good of all sentient beings, went inside themselves in deepest contemplation to scrutinize the dreamscape, the dream, and the dreamer, all three. In this way they were able to return to embodiment after the body's passing to fashion and present percipient ways to awaken humanity to its divine nature.

The result was an unprecedented myriad of philosophical systems opening onto a copious network of wisdom pathways, the like of which were never before seen or conceived of in any other country or by any other race of human beings. *Veda, Tantra, Sankhya, Nyaya, Vaishesika, Purva Mimamsa, Vedanta, Yoga, Buddhism, Patanjala (Yoga), Sikhism, Jainism, Vaishnavism, Shaivism, Shaktism, Saurism, Ganapatya* — the list goes on and on. Here was not just one holy book, or one divine incarnation, or a single prophet, but dozens to hundreds of each, what to speak of a countless host of luminaries, well-celebrated, stretching back millennia B.C.E. — all so ancient, so long-lived, so profound, that the expression "before their time" takes on an entirely new meaning in their case.

In other words, these *rishis* arrived on the world scene and were, spiritually speaking, and in view of the rudimentary status of other cultures, mature before their time. Even in more recent times, and up into the second millennia B.C.E., flash-in-the-pan civilizations like Rome, Greece, and now, America, have had and are still having a difficult time comprehending what India has brought to the world. And throughout the sweep of centuries, great powerhouses of brute domination such as Attila the Hun, Alexander the Great, Napoleon, the Caesars, and in present times, England, have had to bow at the feet of this exceptional subcontinent whose main protection against invasion of all types has always been the undaunted spirit of *ahimsa*, nonviolence, along with Her unusual ability to absorb rather than resist the changes that were brought to the sanctuary of her borders.

Therefore, India is an exceptional example before the eyes of the world, and the main quality which makes her so is realization of and adherence to Truth. This Truth, as we shall see in forthcoming chapters, and as we have studied in previous chapters as well, was founded upon natural acceptance of the presence of God as Existence Itself. This Truth got tempered on earth in the fires of spiritual practice and its resultant experience. In other words, it was never a matter of philosophy alone. In more contemporary times, Swami Vivekananda was to use his country's long-lived and healthy hold on Truth to rejuvenate religion itself, and to resurrect it for other countries and cultures as well. In one of his letters, he wrote: *"I will compare Truth to a corrosive substance of infinite power. It burns its way in wherever it falls — in soft substance at once, hard granite slowly, but it must. I have clear light now, free of all hocus-pocus. I want to give this Truth dry hard reason, softened in the sweetest syrup of love, and made spicy with intense work, and cooked in the kitchen of Yoga so that even a baby can easily digest it."* In this grand statement, pregnant with the atmosphere of universalism, lies the four main modes and keys of natural progression — wisdom, worship, work, and meditation. These four, in turn, match the four temperaments of living beings — studious, devout, active, and contemplative. Thus, the Four Yogas of India — *Jnana, Bhakti, Karma,* and *Raja* — what Swami Vivekananda proclaimed *"the new religion of this age"* — make their august appearance, and much will be written about them in the forthcoming pages of this chapter.

The word and principle of Universalism must necessarily surface again and again if we are to comprehend what Mother India epitomizes, and that, in turn, so that we can benefit from her nonpareil offerings. In this regard, the chart on the facing page will initiate our cosmological and philosophical wisdom journey adequately enough. It reveals just how multi-faceted is the religious and spiritual landscape of this remarkable country and culture, including, as it does, many of the main *darshanas*, lineages, sects, *yogas*, religious streams, and philosophical perspectives. Its premier quote, heading the chart, speaks the truth of India's correct orientation in that it never divided religion and philosophy from one another; they were always present, side by side, to check and verify each other. As Swami Vivekananda has stated, *"Faith is a wonderful insight, and can save, but there is a danger in it of breeding fanaticism barring further progress. Jnanam, wisdom, is all right, but there is the danger of its becoming dry intellectualism. Love is great and noble, but it may die away in meaningless sentimentalism. A harmony of all these is the thing required."*

Though there is contention among the philosophers and historians alike on the subject of initial origin, it is clear enough that there were two great streams of thought in India from earliest times. The *Vedic* stream, predominantly practical and wisdom-based, gifted India with her orthodox *darshanas*, while *Tantra*, decidedly worship-based, and inclusive of elements of mysticism, contributed main sects and many diverse sub-sects to the mix. Both were twin rivers whose salubrious waters of spirituality were constantly intermingling with one another. Fortuitously, both of these massive spiritual flows had two great principles in common: one, an orientation towards ritual; and two, a primal connection through *AUM*, the Word. The important element of *yajna*, sacrifice, in the truest sense of the term, was another connecting and cohesive force. Thus, when the seeker of contemporary times comes in contact with the all-auspicious *Vedanta*, it is difficult indeed to recognize, what to speak of separate out, all of these integral facets.

The chart on the right champions both *Advaita* and *Dvaita* — nondualism and dualism. If the truth be attested to, both of these great streams originate from a nondual source — called *Brahman* by the *Vedas*, and *Paramasiva, Mahavishnu,* and *Mahashakti* by the Tantras — but the way that they respectively unwrap their particular approaches often ushers in relative modes. Further, it was always qualified nondualism, *Vishistadvaita*, that drew them inexorably together when they seemed to diverge too much due to mankind's now expanding, now flagging, comprehension. All three of these stages of philosophy will be taken up in forthcoming pages, as will the Four *Yogas*.

Of engaging interest to those whose emphasis revolves mainly around philosophy is the placing together, side by side, of the Six Orthodox *Darshanas* and the Five Main Sects of India. Study of wisdom principles, *Tattva-Jnan,* more characterizes the *darshanas*, while worship of deities, *Upasana,* captures the bulk of *Tantra's* attention. Interestingly enough, *Tantra* is not listed as one of the six orthodox *darshanas*; it was just too capacious of content and spread over too vast a time period for any individual luminary to ever come along and systematize it. But whatever the case may be, the student may notice that the *darshanas* were all founded by six profound luminaries, while the five main sects focus upon the gods and goddesses. This slants the spectrum of attention, generally speaking, and divides it between wisdom seekers and knowers on one side, and worshipers and devotees on the other — both not necessarily exclusive of one another.

The heading of this chart, with its singular implication, must be kept in mind, that being the natural underlying Unity. As an example of this, if we look at the lives of those who systematized the six *darshanas*, we will see that they were also worshipers, belonging to one of the five main sects or their sub-sects. Thus, and to offer a picture of Indian life in early times, a man or woman championed a philosophical ideal which he or she followed for mental guidance, and this existed side by side and in natural fashion with the chosen ideal (*Ishtam*) that dictated his or her heart's faith and

The Natural Unity of Vedic Religion & Philosophy

The 6 Darshanas, 5 Sects, 4 Yogas, 3 Stages of Philosophy, & 2 Religious Streams

"Philosophy in India never stands sundered from religion. It is never considered as divested of religious life and living. Further, every system has its own value in its own particular region. The various interpretations of the scriptures are therefore tenable from the standpoint of the various temperaments of individuals forming different religious sects."   Sri Manoranjan Basu

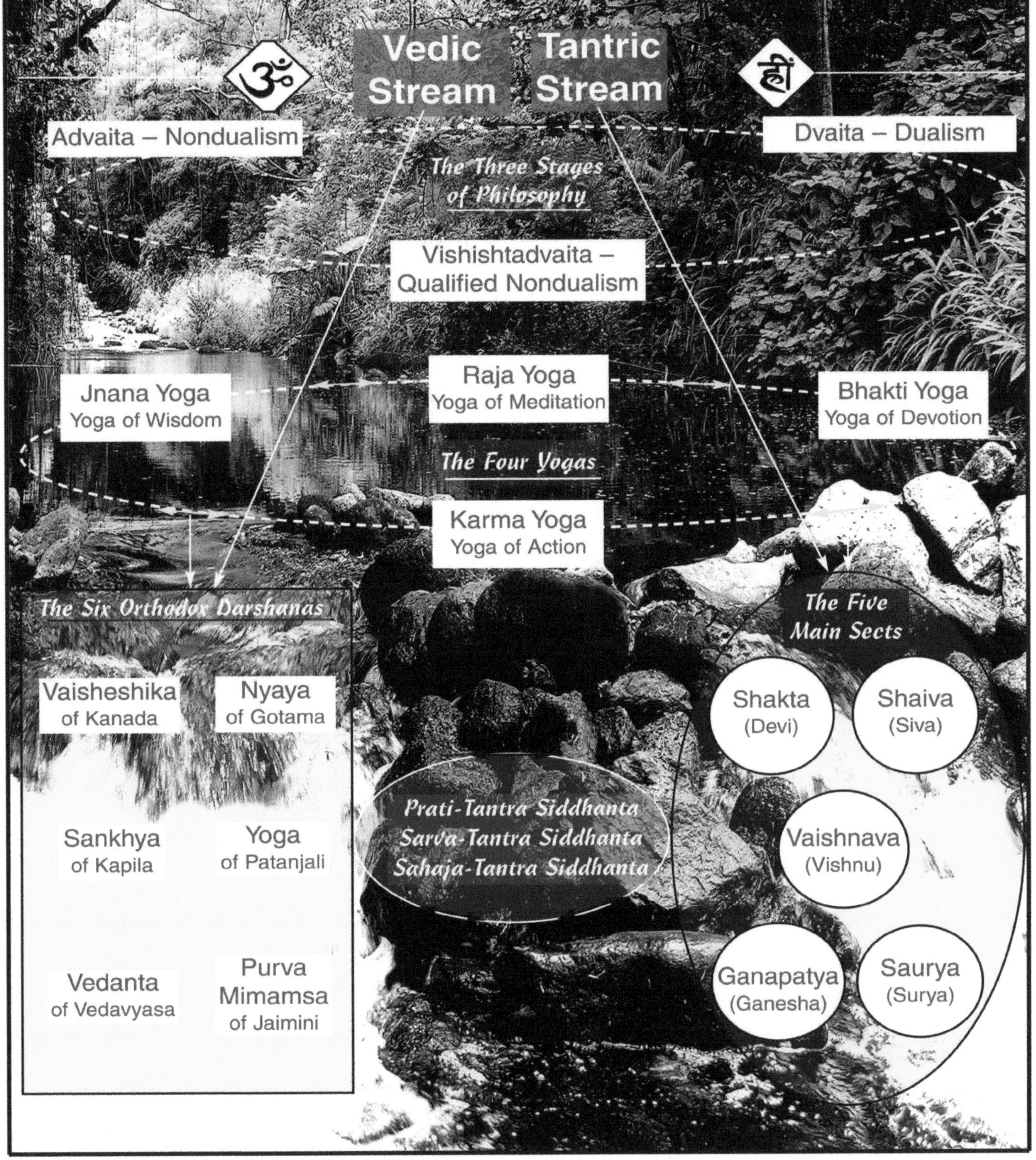

Vedic Stream — **Tantric Stream**

Advaita – Nondualism

Dvaita – Dualism

The Three Stages of Philosophy

Vishishtadvaita – Qualified Nondualism

Jnana Yoga
Yoga of Wisdom

Raja Yoga
Yoga of Meditation

Bhakti Yoga
Yoga of Devotion

The Four Yogas

Karma Yoga
Yoga of Action

The Six Orthodox Darshanas

Vaisheshika of Kanada	Nyaya of Gotama
Sankhya of Kapila	Yoga of Patanjali
Vedanta of Vedavyasa	Purva Mimamsa of Jaimini

The Five Main Sects

Shakta (Devi)

Shaiva (Siva)

Vaishnava (Vishnu)

Ganapatya (Ganesha)

Saurya (Surya)

*Prati-Tantra Siddhanta
Sarva-Tantra Siddhanta
Sahaja-Tantra Siddhanta*

fealty. The aspirant, for instance, might practice the esteemed *Yoga darshana*, and simultaneously be a devotee of *Vishnu (Vaishnavism)* or *Durga (Shaktism)*. Or, a man might be a *Vedantist*, striving hard to comprehend the path of *Advaita* (nonduality), while also holding the ideal of Lord *Siva* as his personal *Ishtam*. Thus, the Personal and the Impersonal God were recognized by all, and except for the unwelcome insinuation of those few and ever-present hypocrites with narrow minds who spoil religion and misinterpret scripture for their own zealous ends, i.e., the followers of the *"my watch keeps the only correct time"* perspective, the ideal of innate Unity went basically untampered with.

And so, these healthy and happy hybrids of religion and philosophy were not "mights" or "may be's," but were evident and obvious marriages, seen and acknowledged in everyday life by the entire culture, and there was a diverse and multi-faceted number and combination of them as well. The chart on the facing page (317) gives us another look at some of these same eternal pathways, complemented by another amazing facet of spirituality.

Arranged a little differently, but still revealing the diversity and unity of the overall truth of Existence, the emphasis here is placed upon the healthy and holistic body of Mother India, where mind, heart, energy, and physique are all well integrated. Participating fully in the highest good for all beings, and contributing continually to their best welfare on all levels of existence, the culminative result over time has been the appearance of a world-shaking and mind-transforming way of divine life that has graced human thought and action over the entire interim. A sign of this, in what could be termed a true miracle of human character and sagaciousness, are in the many philosophical perspectives that have come out of this salubrious amalgam of illumined mind, devout heart, purified energy, and sanctified body. The list in the lower right hand corner of the chart under study, though not exhaustive, illustrates this abundantly. Though too involved and lengthy for a full explanation here, the list placed below will give the student more of an idea of the diversity that is being cited, and how incomparable and ingenious India's *Sanatana Dharma* is:

Nondual

Ajativada — The doctrine of nonevolution, or the "no creation" theory.
Advaitavada — The doctrine which states that *Brahman* is the only Reality.
Atmadristhivada — The path that perceives all as *Atman*.
Dvaitadvaitavivarjitavada — The view that Reality is beyond oneness, twoness, and multiplicity.
Ekantavada — Monism proposing that God is the sole Reality.
Shunyavada — The declaration that nothing exists, based upon the eight negations of Nagarjuna:
　　1) no elimination *(nirodha)* 2) no production 3) no destruction 4) no eternity 5) no unity
　　6) no manifoldness 7) no arriving 8) no departing
Sadrishaparinamavada — The view which states that all mutable things are not different in nature
　　from the immutable substratum from which they arise (like gold in an earring).
Sarvatitavada — The path that declares the Reality of all things, but that Truth alone is purely
　　Transcendental.
Kriyadvaitavada — The path of complete oneness, even in action.
Dravyadvaita — The path which proposes unity of substance.
Shaktadvaitavada — The path that proposes that all experience of existence is nothing less than pure
　　Consciousness, and sees *shakti* and the possessor of *shakti* (*shaktimana*) as one and the same.

Difference and Nondifference

Bhedabhedavada — The path that declares that the soul is different than God, but simultaneously
　　one with God.
Bimbapratibimbavada — The view that the *jiva* is a reflection of *Brahman*, but is therefore identical
with *Brahman* since a reflection originates from its origin.
Vivartavada — Phenomenalism, where all manifestation is a superimposition over *Brahman* due to
　　the mind's ignorance.
　　a) *Vivartasristhi*—*Brahman* remains the same, but brings about the appearance of change of

India's Sanatana Dharma

"The Eternal Religion of the Rishis has been in existence from time out of mind. The Sanatana Dharma contains all forms of worship — worship of God with form and worship of the Impersonal Deity as well. It contains all paths — the path of knowledge, the path of devotion, and so on. Other forms of religion, the modern cults, will remain for a few days only, and then disappear. The Sanatana Dharma declared by the Rishis will alone endure."   Sri Ramakrishna

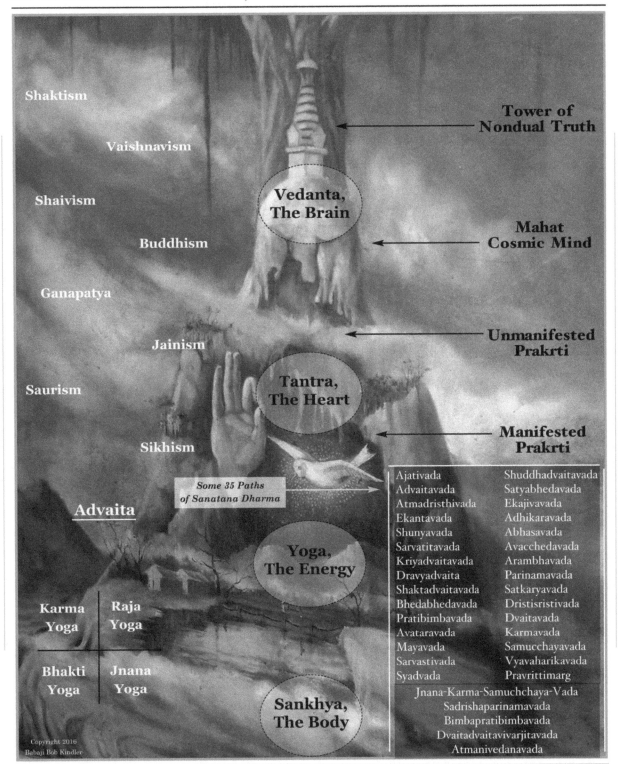

Shaktism

Vaishnavism

Shaivism

Buddhism

Ganapatya

Jainism

Saurism

Sikhism

Advaita

Karma Yoga   Raja Yoga

Bhakti Yoga   Jnana Yoga

Tower of Nondual Truth

Mahat Cosmic Mind

Unmanifested Prakrti

Manifested Prakrti

Vedanta, The Brain

Tantra, The Heart

Yoga, The Energy

Sankhya, The Body

Some 35 Paths of Sanatana Dharma

Ajativada	Shuddhadvaitavada
Advaitavada	Satyabhedavada
Atmadristhivada	Ekajivavada
Ekantavada	Adhikaravada
Shunyavada	Abhasavada
Sarvatitavada	Avacchedavada
Kriyadvaitavada	Arambhavada
Dravyadvaita	Parinamavada
Shaktadvaitavada	Satkaryavada
Bhedabhedavada	Dristisristivada
Pratibimbavada	Dvaitavada
Avataravada	Karmavada
Mayavada	Samucchayavada
Sarvastivada	Vyavaharikavada
Syadvada	Pravrittimarg

Jnana-Karma-Samuchchaya-Vada
Sadrishaparinamavada
Bimbapratibimbavada
Dvaitadvaitavivarjitavada
Atmanivedanavada

"This great immortal frame of Indian Philosophy operates efficiently on four great powerhouses: Sankhya, its Body; Yoga, its divine Energy; Tantra, its loving Heart; and Vedanta, its universal Mind."

the effect.

b) *Vivartopadana* — A cause that does not undergo change in the least, while it produces the effect, like the snake in a rope. A fictitious material cause.

c) *Parinami Upadana* — A cause that actually gets transformed into the effect.

Pratibimbavada — The view that the *jiva* is a reflection of *Brahman* in the realm of ignorance.

Avataravada — The doctrine stating that God takes human form and descends to the world of name and form for purposes of awakening sleeping souls.

Avyavaharavada — The path of those who are free from worldly considerations and *karma*-producing work.

Kartrivada — The path of those who are independent doers.

Mayavada or *Mithyavada* — Path and theory which declares that the nature of the phenomenal world is illusory.

Sarvastivada — Early *Hinayana Buddhist* teaching that declares "Everything Is." It is a radical pluristic path that denies the existence of a self as substance or soul, and confirms the existence of momentary entities such as dharmas, which though unmanifest at times, nevertheless exist from beginningless time and only change from a latent to manifest state. In essence, all dharmas and past/present/future all exist simultaneously in a single *dharma*.

Syadvada — Jainist path ("it may be" path) postulating the viewpoint of multiple simultaneously existing viewpoints of Reality, each having their own place. The same Reality can therefore be seen from different views that each can be right according to their particular outlook.

Shuddhadvaitavada — (of Vallabhacharya) states that the relationship between the soul and the world is real rather than an apparition of *Maya*. The soul is seen as a subtle form of *Brahman* with only its bliss aspect veiled.

Satyabhedavada — The doctrine that states that up to the point that the soul reaches emancipation, it is different from the Highest Self, but when it reaches emancipation it is nondifferent.

Ekajivavada — Proposes that there is really only one *jiva* in existence.

Qualified

Adhikaravada — Upholding the doctrine that there is a distinct course of discipline for each aspirant according to individual capacity.

Abhasavada — The doctrine stating that all of creation is a reflection of *Brahman*.

Avacchedavada — Doctrine that soul is the ultimate Self, but limited by adjuncts.

Arambhavada — The doctrine of the creation of the world by *Ishvara* or a creative agency, which posits a beginning or origination (*Nyaya—Vashesheika*).

Parinamavada — Doctrine of transformation which declares that *Brahman* transforms a portion of Itself into the universe and living beings (Ramanuja's qualified nondualism).

Atmanivedanavada — The way of complete surrender of the self to God.

Satkaryavada — The doctrine that states that the effect is inherent in the cause, but that it is only an apparent change in the cause.

Dristisristivada —The view that the world is the outcome of the faculty of perception, and that it is real, at least as long as it appears.

Jnana-Karma-Samuchchaya-Vada — States that only through a combination of knowledge and action can liberation be gained.

Dualistic

Dvaitavada — Dualism that accepts distinction between God and *jiva* (Madhva's *dvaita*).

Karmavada — The doctrine which states that pain follows bad action and pleasure follows good action.

Samucchayavada — The doctrine that *karma* and *jnana* are both necessary for Self-realization.

This copious yet incomplete list of wisdom perspectives not only grants the seeker a comprehensive view of the ability and fertility of the mind that is constantly focused in on Reality, but also reveals the dynamic nature of this Reality without compromising Its nondual essence. The avid student of Indian philosophy also gets to see the main subdivisions, all falling into well-considered categories — Nondual, Difference in Nondifference, Qualified Nondualism, and Dualism. Not one to leave any stone unturned, the *Sanatana Dharma* also includes pathways that intentionally forgo or deny religion, such as: *Vyavaharikavada,* the way of the world wherein no provision is made for belief of anything beyond relativity; and *Pravrittimarga,* the path of social action according to the nature of the world. Even a path of outright materialism, called *Charvakavada,* gains inclusion into the Eternal Religion of the *rishis,* as if to say that some good or gain can be gotten out of every perspective — especially given the many different levels of qualification and the various grades of consciousness that persist among living beings.

It has probably been seen by now, in the light of such an in-depth presentation and study, that there is a special import to this categorization, one that, if understood, could heal major rifts in mankind's thinking process. About these tiers of philosophical perception and their respective transmissions, Swami Vivekananda has stated, *"Now I will tell you my discovery. All of religion is contained in the Vedanta, that is, in the three stages of Vedantic philosophy, the dvaita, vishistadvaita and advaita; one comes after the other. These are the three stages of spiritual growth in mankind. Each one is necessary. This is the essential of religion. The Vedanta applied to the various customs and ethnic creeds of India, is Hinduism. The first stage, dvaita (dualism), applied to the ideas of the ethnic groups of Europe, is Christianity; as applied to the semitic groups, Mohammedanism. The advaita (nondualism) as applied in its yoga-perception form is Buddhism, etc. Now, by religion is meant the Vedanta; the applications must vary according to the different needs, surroundings, and other circumstances of different nations. Dualist, qualified monist, monist, shaiva, vaishnava, shakta, even the Buddhist and the Jain and others — whatever sects have arisen in India are all at one in this respect: that infinite power is latent in this jivatman (individualized soul); from the ant to the perfect man there is the same Atman in all, the difference being only in manifestation."*

Concluding the chart on page 317, certain assignments have been allocated to the meditating figure with his head in the clouds, his base on earth, and his hand sporting the mudra of perfection. The tower of Truth represents *Advaita Vedanta,* his crowning achievement, mentioned by Swami Vivekananda in the quote above. A fuller rendering of this quintessential expression of Truth will be given in the final chapter of this book. Suffice to say that it is the subtlemost golden thread running through the necklace of pearls we have just gazed upon in the form of the many pathways to illumination found in the *Sanatana Dharma* of the Indian *rishis.*

The meditating figure also possesses a medium or matrix in the form of the Cosmic Mind, or *Mahat,* that facilitates the appearance of all the many worlds of name and form in time and space based on causation. The *Mahat,* most pure, or *sattvic,* is the first creative principle emanating out of the primal door of formlessness. It represents a congenial meeting point between the Soul and Nature, called *Purusha* and *Prakriti* in the *Sankhya Darshana.* Thus, it is a fit vehicle for the *Purusha's* consciousness and intelligence.

Next of the gradated echelons seen on the meditating figure, falling at the level of the heart and navel on down to the waist, and stretching below, are those of the two forms of *Prakriti* itself. Termed Unmanifested Nature and Manifested Nature, they present the seeker of Truth with an authoritative rendering of all that falls within the category of insentient matter, plus a teaching that explains questions and conundrums around principles and phenomena such as time and timelessness, space and the void, waking, sleeping, dreams, and dreamless sleep, and importantly, birth, death, and reincarnation. Taking up these crucial teachings will be the enthralling emphasis of the following collection of charts and pages, all falling under the auspice of one of Mother India's most ancient and important of orthodox *darshanas* — the *Sankhya Yoga* of Lord Kapila. By studying it, a host of essential connections — many of them missing in contemporary mankind's thinking process, will be opened up for contemplation and implementation, all paving the road for the remembrance, attainment, and expression of spiritual realization.

The orthodox *darshana* of *Sankhya Yoga* offers the aspiring student of spiritual life several sets of illuminating teachings based upon the trustworthy tenet that to "know Who one truly is, one has to know What one is not." A study of the Twenty-Four Cosmic Principles of *Sankhya Yoga*, one of Lord Kapila's greatest gifts to mankind and world philosophy overall, will accomplish the full comprehension of this tenet, leaving no doubt in the seeker's mind as to (as the *Vedanta* puts it) what is Real and what is unreal. And speaking of eternally abiding tenets, there is also a list called the Ten Fundamental Tenets of *Sankhya Yoga* which will be taken up. But before encountering these august systems of perspicacious clarification, an in-depth look at the aforementioned subject of Manifested and Unmanifested *Prakriti* would be wise.

Prakriti is the word for nature, or matter, in ancient *Sanskrit*. However, unlike the premature, or immature conclusion about matter in western ways of thinking, in the arenas of science, psychology, and the public sector, the presence of nature in the way of thinking of the Indian *rishis* has a side to it that is subtle and unseen. It is both the place of destination for all created things, and the point of departure for all that naturally returns to form. This explains so much, destroys so many age-old doubts, and makes so many connections for a balanced life attended by inner peace, that it is a wonder that, once knowing about it, mankind has not inscribed teachings like this in gold letters and, out of deference to them, given up utilizing that precious metal for any other use.

The chart on the facing page illustrates the dual aspect of insentient nature utilizing the image of an iceberg floating in arctic waters. Its tip, so proverbial, represents all of nature that is manifest — earth, water, fire, air, ether, planets, space, bodies, etc. Everything subtle that gave rise to the five elements and living beings must also necessarily fall under this classification, they being manifest as well — principles such as senses, mind, intellect, and the human ego. Even the *Mahat*, God's Mind, which we just scrutinized briefly, is a member of the multi-faceted organization titled Manifested *Prakriti*, though it also bridges, like a doorway, the Unmanifested *Prakriti* as well.

Then is seen the Unmanifested itself, symbolized by the bulk of the iceberg, It is formless matter, i.e., everything mentioned previously, but in its undifferentiated state. It is, according to Kapila, *"....all things in potential."* Thus, the mind comes to know, primarily, the manifest and the unmanifest are one entity, and secondarily, that the two interchange constantly in ongoing cycles, all without ever expanding or contracting in the least. Importantly, Consciousness, *Purusha*, never changes as a result.

The impact of this teaching on the human mind, especially in a spiritually darkened age, renders 1) existence true; 2) nonexistence a misnomer; 3) change an untenable assumption; 4) time and space both facets of the mind; 5) *karma* and causality only relative laws; 6) and death an outright illusion. It also proves the undeniable influence of cycles in relativity. These cycles catch and ensnare every embodied being, from the Holy Trinity on down to the denizens of the physical world, and the gods, celestials, and ancestors in between. This grand and illusory process of coming in and going out of existence has everyone guessing as to the nature of Reality, or if Reality even exists, or if relativity _is_ Reality. Its concealed and diaphanous workings, once perceived, have been held responsible or mixed up with concepts such as *maya, samsara,* origination, genesis, divine expression, fullness and the void, life-force, birth, creation, preservation and destruction, and other forms of stultifying cosmic legerdemain. Suffice to say that an awareness of the goings-on of *Prakriti* via its two modes will both destroy unnecessary doubts and fears in the human mind, and lead the soul away from identification with insentient matter and towards the ever sentient Self, or Soul (*Atman*).

And in this regard, *Prakriti* is the stuff of dreams. When the sentient Soul encounters insentient matter, and begins playing the game and dreaming the dream of sporting in form among objects of its own design, it forgets that all of nature has emerged from its own thinking process, called *Sankalpa* (see chart on page 267). The three *gunas* (see chart on page 307), as shown on the upper right hand corner of the chart, then fall in and out of equilibrium, and all the evolutes of *Prakriti* come pouring into manifestation, only to disappear later, unaccountably. The sentient Soul falls into confusion amidst this wash of flexuous phenomena, hypnotized by the melting and reforming of this

Manifest and Unmanifest Prakriti
The Tip and Mass of the Iceburg

"Prakriti is the equilibrium of the three gunas, not evolved from any other origin, being the primordial source of all other evolutes. A greater amount of Prakriti is unmanifest. Purusha, the sentient, conscious principle, is ever wise, ever pure, ever free."   Lord Kapila

Paramakasha —
Sky of Awareness

Sunlight of Nondual Reality

Mahat - Intellect - Ego - Mind - Tanmatras. - Senses - Elements-

Prakriti

Hiranyagarbha
Lord Brahma
"Great" Mind →

Gunas out of equilibrium

Gunas in equilibrium

**Unmanifest
Prakriti**
(Pradhana)

Formless Matter— All Worlds, all Things & Objects in Potential

Sancharah prati sancharah
"There is a chain of transition from unmanifest or nonevolved prakriti to manifest prakriti and its evolutes, ending in the grossest evolute, earth. There is also a reverse transition of evolutes ending in dissolution into unmanifested prakriti."

Ishvara

"All that is perceived by the senses is finite; all that is beyond the senses is infinite. From the infinite the finite has come, yet being infinite, only infinite remains."
Ishavasya Upanisad

AUM

"Dive deep. oh mind, dive deep in the ocean of God's beauty...."
Kabir

Purusha/Brahman —
Ocean of Consciousness

cosmic iceberg, and scarcely knowing that the entire massive structure exists and is going forth in its own mind via its own intelligence and consciousness.

And here is the key that effectively turns the tumblers in the well-fastened lock of the benighted human mind. The process, all processes, are going on in its own consciousness, at levels of waking, dreaming, and deep sleep. Waking and dreaming correlate to manifested *Prakriti*, and deep sleep to Unmanifested *Prakriti*. Further, when the mind is focused in on form, there is birth (waking) and life (dreaming), and when it has surrendered to its formless state there is death (deep sleep) — so-called.

But here arises another realization, more important and pertinent to the ever-awake state of the *Yogi*, or luminary. As *Sankhya Yoga* declares, *Purusha* and *Prakriti* are distinct from one another, a teaching that, when taken at the level at which it is meant, provides the necessary discrimination between the sentient human being and insentient nature. Put in more direct terms, waking, dreaming, and deep sleep are modes of conditioned consciousness, and manifestation and nonmanifestation are modes of nature. Distinct from them all is Pure Consciousness, or *Purusha/Atman*. To separate the wheat from the chaff, the Real from the unreal, God from mammon, the Essential from the nonessential, the Soul from nature — this is what spiritual life and practice leading to Enlightenment is all about. Once accomplished, all the resultant teachings, the fine opinions, the philosophical propositions, the wisdom pathways, and the sacred religious traditions, will be as open books to the knower of Truth. This is illustrated on the chart under study on the previous page, 321, by the attending entries which surround the iceberg of *Prakriti* in its two modes. Note how the entire mass, and all its potential — manifest and unmanifested — floats in the Ocean of *Brahman*, breathes in the Sky of Awareness, and basks in the Sunlight of Nondual Reality. *Prakriti* is in *Purusha*, matter is in the Great Mind, nature is in the Soul, and form and its counterpart, formlessness, rest in Absolute Formlessness. This is why Sri Krishna tells Arjuna, in chapter eight of the *Bhagavad Gita*, that: *"This multitude of beings, coming forth again and again, merge, O Arjuna, in spite of themselves, at the approach of night, and manifest themselves at the approach of day. But beyond this manifest and unmanifest movement there is yet another Unmanifested Eternal Existence which does not perish even when all existences perish. This Unmanifested is called the Imperishable; It is said to be the ultimate goal. Those who attain to It return not to embodiment and its suffering. That is My Supreme Abode."*

To conclude this chart (page 321) and its manifold teachings, a major connecting point, or points, between *Brahman* and *Prakriti*, is included as well. This is indicated by two similar, if not identical principles — *AUM*, and *Ishvara*. Chapter three introduced much about *AUM*, the Word, and chapter eight will bring in more about *Ishvara*, God with Form, the Chosen Ideal. For now, suffice to say that these extremely subtle principles, both related with the Cosmic Mind, *Mahat*, form an important bridge between God and mankind, Soul and nature. With one foot in form and the other in Formlessness, *Ishvara* is the doorway through which the aspiring soul, *jivatman*, reaches for and immerses itself into its essence, *svarupa* or *Atman*. The Word provides this same function, but with less of an emphasis on divine personality and more on mystical union. God and His Word are one and the same, but prior to such realized union they are "with" one another, as complements. When one *"gets to the Father through the Son,"* then, there are two modes: one being through blissful communion with the divine form; and the other being through mystic union via purified intelligence. This matches the two kinds of temperaments of masterful souls at this juncture, i.e., attracted via form, or drawn to formlessness.

Before moving on to a study of the list of cosmic principles and characteristic tenets of *Sankhya* philosophy, and since the all-important cosmic station of The Word, *AUM*, has come into the light of intelligent scrutiny again, some time can be taken to flesh out this transcendent principle and its multi-faceted teaching. On the chart on the facing page is shown an image of one of the most fitting symbols for The Word, the bell. The teaching is, and in direct relation to *Sankhya's* Manifest and Unmanifest *Prakriti*, that the bell has its tone inherent in it; all it needs is to be struck.

The striking of the bell represents that most enigmatic of movements, ones that have been

Omkara — The Great Cause
Emanation and Dissolution in Vedic Cosmology

"It has been revealed to me that there exists an Ocean of Consciousness that is without limit. From It comes all things of the relative plane. Therefore I give the illustration of the bell's sound, 'T-o-m.' The strike of the bell is like the falling of a great weight into the ocean; waves rise on all sides. Spiritually speaking, the relative rises from the Absolute; the causal, subtle, and gross worlds and bodies appear out of the Great Cause; the waking, dreaming, and deep sleep phases rise out of Turiya. And just as millions of brahmandas rise in the Ocean of Chidakasha, they merge in It again. The Lila merges into the Nitya."   Sri Ramakrishna

"In the Beginning was the Word, and the Word was with God, and the Word was God."

"Gates of the body closed, the mind confined in the heart, fixing the life-force in the head, engaged in yoga, uttering Om, Brahman, and thinking of Me, that one who departs the body attains to the Supreme Goal."   Krishna

"Pranava is the lower Brahman, and it is the higher Atman. Having known Pranava one attains to Brahman."   Gaudapada

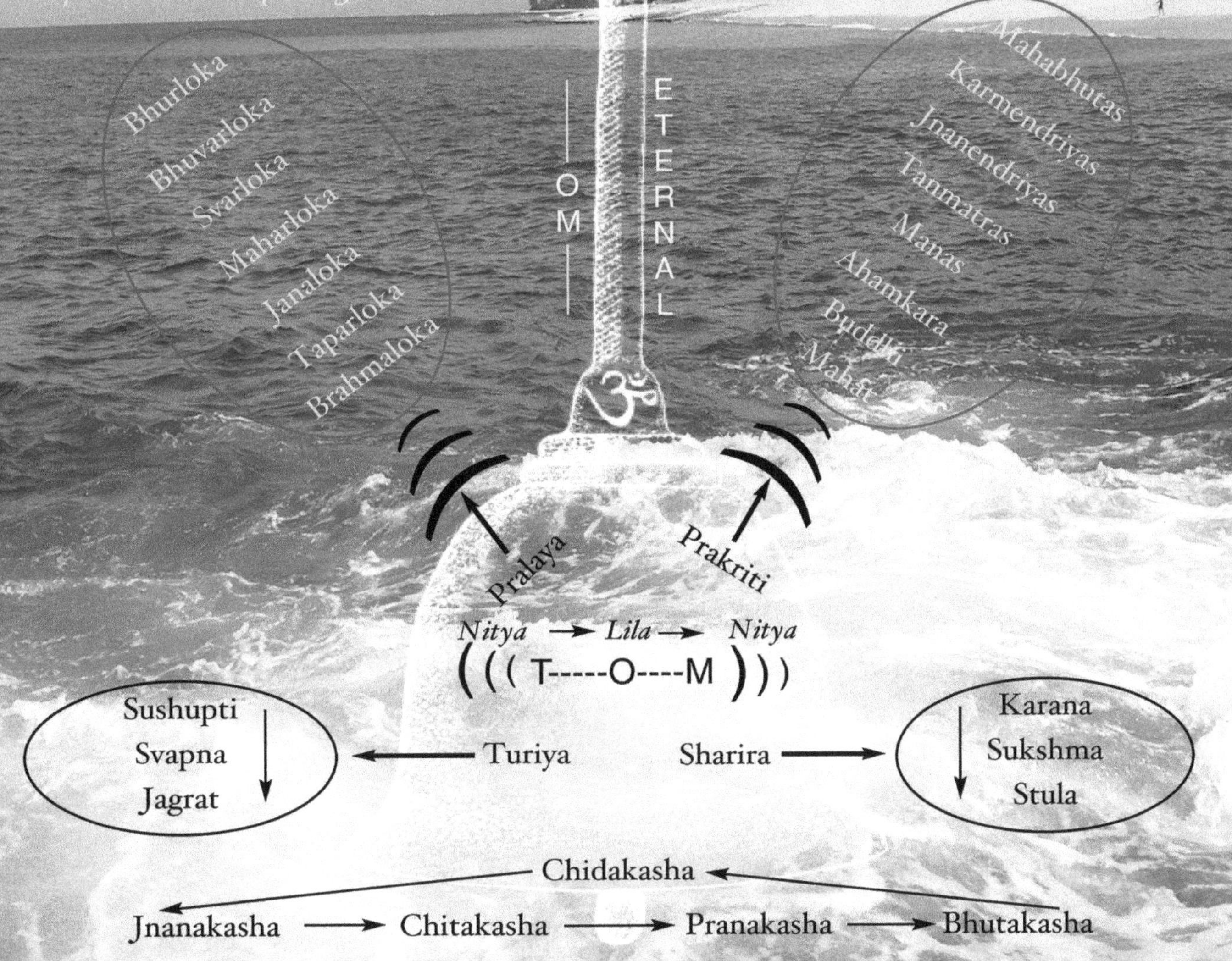

OM | ETERNAL

Bhurloka
Bhuvarloka
Svarloka
Maharloka
Janaloka
Taparloka
Brahmaloka

Mahabhutas
Karmendriyas
Jnanendriyas
Tanmatras
Manas
Ahamkara
Buddhi
Mahat

Pralaya   Prakriti

Nitya → Lila → Nitya

(((T-----O----M)))

Sushupti
Svapna
Jagrat

← Turiya   Sharira →

Karana
Sukshma
Stula

Chidakasha ←

Jnanakasha → Chitakasha → Pranakasha → Bhutakasha

"All universes in space and time lie within Om. With knowledge of the Word, and how cosmic projection goes forth, one can follow the shining rays of Jnana-wisdom straight to the Source, penetrating all brahmandas. Then the Mother of the Word will immerse one in the Ocean of Consciousness."   Svayambhuva Manu termed Creation, the Big Bang, the First Day of Creation, the Cradle of Evolution, the Beginning of Time, the Demi-urge, the Bursting of the *Bindu*, the Divine Expression, and according to the "Mind Only" schools of Indian Philosophy, Projectionism. By whichever mode beings envision its occurrence, what follows is the pouring out into "existence" of all beings, principles, worlds, places, things, objects, and elements into manifestation, and once "the cat has been let out of the bag," there is no stopping the endless flow of production — at least half of it being of negative propensity.

But what is of greatest interest to the seers with regard to The Word — called *AUM, Pranava, Anahata, Shabda, Sphota,* the Unstruck Sound, the Primal Vibration, the Original Idea that flashes — is Its infinite and unchanging nature. *"No one strikes It,"* say the *Tantric* seers, but yet it "Hums" eternally. So, in the example of the bell, the fact that it is silent when left unstruck signifies the state of Unmanifested *Prakriti,* or *pralaya,* the dissolution of forms. When struck, it has an initial impulse, a giving way to the life of the tone, and ends in the tone's fading into inaudibility. As per the chart on the previous page (323), we can take a look at all the significances of this process.

In the egg *(Hiranyagarbha)* situated at the upper left of the bell, the process is put in terms of the production of worlds. The famous Seven Planes of Existence (see chart on page 375), namely *Bhur, Bhuvar, Svar, Mahar, Jana, Tapar,* and *Brahmalokas,* all emerge at the behest of The Word. These seven correspond roughly with the world of the humans, the world of the elementals, the world of the celestials, the world of the demigods, the world of the gods and goddesses, the world of the luminaries, and the world of the Trinity. These are the *Lokas* of Hinduism. They appear in reverse order, from causal to subtle to gross, *Brahmaloka* being closest to The Word.

In the egg pictured on the chart to the upper right of the bell, the process is put in terms of the cosmic principles, called *tattvas. Mahat* is the first "out the door," being most pure and closest to the source, followed by *Buddhi, Ahamkara, Manas,* the *Tanmatras,* the *Jnanendriyas,* and the *Karmendriyas.* This is a *"Pancha"* process, or manifestation by quintuplication, with the primal five being Cosmic Mind, Intelligence, Cosmic Ego, Dual Mind, and Thought (*Chitta,* not shown in this chart). The Five Subtle Elements come next, followed by the Five Senses of Knowledge and the Five Senses of Action. These *tattvas* are vehicles for Consciousness. The master of spiritual involution dissolves them in reverse order into Unmanifested *Prakriti,* or the Word, in meditation. The practitioner of meditation actually enacts this process in the mind daily, thus keeping the soul in awareness of these inner worlds and their principles, and in preparation for leaving the body consciously at the time of death. This is the "Dissolution of the Mindstream" meditation (see chart on page 503).

In the egg lying at the bottom left of the bell on the chart is seen another designation of this cosmic process. This is more personal, having to do with mankind's state of Awareness. His constant movement from waking to dreaming to deep sleep, his body, senses, and ego being temporarily abandoned as he did so, and then returning to them in reverse order, gave the ancient seers pause for reflection. If consciousness could so naturally vacate these *tattvas* (cosmic principles) yet not remember doing so upon awakening, then that same path could be retraced via focused meditation after mastering the mind and senses in the waking state. What is more, all the *lokas,* or kingdoms of Heaven within, would also show themselves, along with the deities that were presiding over them. Thus, the ancestors, angels, and other visions could be brought to bear and communed with.

In the egg lying at the lower right of the bell on the chart under study (page 323), we see this incomparable cosmic process explained in terms of *shariras,* or sheaths. As has been described earlier (see chart on page 161), man has three bodies, not just one. They are termed *karana,* causal; *sukshma,* subtle; and *linga,* gross or apparent. When the transmigrating soul leaves the physical frame — whether in dream and deep sleep, death, meditation, or *samadhi* — its consciousness moves from the gross *sharira* to the subtle one, and/or then to the causal one. When this occurs at the time of "death," the move is a more permanent one — at least until rebirth occurs (see chart on page 164). This is because the esoteric "silver thread" that binds the soul to the *linga sharira* has been cut. But when this inner movement occurs during sleep, the soul finds its way back along that subtle current and tiny channel and reenters the physical form again. Of course, enacting this process in meditation and attaining *samadhi*, or *nirvana*, is the ideal, for the intimately aware state of perception that ensues destroys ignorance completely, allowing the free soul, the *Jivanmukta* (see chart on page 689), to course freely throughout the Seven Planes of Existence, utilizing the Cosmic Principles at will.

At the foot of the bell, across its clapper, is another helpful designation in comprehending the multifarious Cosmic Design. This rendering reveals the process in terms of *akashas,* or subtle dimensions of space (see chart on page 30). Mention has been made of this powerful teaching, but some expansion will be necessary to understand its profundity. For now, and in connection with the chart under study on page 323, it can be surmised that from the *Chidakasha,* the space of pure Spirit, proceeds the *Jnanakasha,* a space of wisdom or unconditioned intelligence. From that most blissful of internal atmospheres flows the *Chittakasha,* the space of diverse thought. From the *Chittakasha* emerges the *Pranakasha,* the space of life-force or vital energy. And finally, from this world of *prana* manifests the world we know, the *Bhutakasha.* This general classification is helpful to our overall knowledge. It is also deceptively illuminating, for undertaking a deeper study of the Five *Akashas* via the revealed scriptures of India informs us as to the real and hidden meaning *(svarupa)* of human life in time (see chart on page 41) and space (see chart on page 33) based in causation (see chart on page 47), at all its many levels. The forthcoming chart on page 327 will explain this wisdom teaching more adequately.

Before taking up this subject at a deeper level, we should review and cite that the most subtle and crucial principle of *AUM,* as demonstrated through the analogy of the bell, has given us several ways in which to plumb the depths of God's Word. Whether looking at The Word in terms of Planes of Existence like the human and ancestor realms; or as Cosmic Principles such as mind, intelligence, and ego; or via the states of consciousness that a human being visits and sports in every day and night of his or her life; or pertinent to the forms or sheaths that Consciousness passes through while still embodied at different levels of awareness; or finally, in view of the echelons of space, from outer to inner, that hold and support all beings — from the "veriest worm" on inwards towards the *akasha* of the Holy Trinity — it is evident that the blessed Word of God is an incomparable station of Awareness that is both illimitable and ineffable. Thus it is worshiped in all Wisdom Traditions.

Everything consists of The Word and its shining intelligence. In the gross physical world, the *Bhutakasha,* this fact is not so apparent, but in the subtle worlds within, The Word makes itself known as the underlying and all-pervasive substratum of all that takes form. In the *Srimad Devi Bhagavatam,* the *devas* (gods) praise The Word, and the one, The Divine Mother of the Universe, who is Its purveyor. This Hymn of Praise goes like this:

Obeisance to Thee, the Self of all,

from whence has originated Fire, Sun, and Moon,

from whom has originated medicinal herbs,

gods, human beings, birds, beasts, and celestials.

The Five Pranas, the Seven Worlds, the Seven Flames,

and the Seven Samadhis all emit from Thee.

Beloved Deity, all oceans, mountains, rivers, plants,

and the tastes and odors in things, have sprung from Thee.

The vital breath, the energy in grains and wheat, are permeated by Thee.

We bow again and again to Thee, the Great Form of Formlessness, the Primal AUM.

As we have used the image of the bell to symbolically represent the principle of *AUM*, so too can we now borrow the popular object of the five Russian dolls to illustrate and explain the teaching of the Five *Akashas*. This presentation will transform a teaching that is otherwise abstruse and difficult of understanding into a gift of spiritualized information that is easy of comprehension.

In consideration of the times we live in, replete with the vaunted discoveries of Quantum Physics, it can first be stated that there are really four realms of space other than physical space, each consisting of subtler and subtler particles (see chart on page 33), all within Consciousness. To entertain this idea sufficiently, and with least resistance, we will have to accept, as the Indian *rishis* proved, that Consciousness, not matter, is King. And as we have seen in the set of teachings we have studied in this chapter thus far, matter has really come out of Consciousness (see chart on page 47). Mankind will have to study, or better, meditate upon his own Consciousness to perceive this fact. Connecting matter back into his mind instead of into outer space, will bring him truth and peace.

As was just mentioned, the ancient *rishis* have designated names for the five *akashas*, each in accordance with the expansive realm they underlie. *Bhutakasha* is the space of objects, even objects like planets and suns in outer space. Human and animal bodies are also objects in this level of space.

Pranakasha is the space of energy, but not electric or kinetic energy only. Life-force is its essential element, called *prana* (see chart of page 536). The absence of the perception of *prana* represents a huge gap in the knowledge base of Western man. Among other things, this lack of perception restricts him to belief in the material worlds only, despite the fact that he dreams heaven and hell, ancestors and celestials, soul and matter, throughout his life and, certainly, after death.

Chittakasha is the space of thought. A thinking human being can and does spend great lengths of time in this realm. But again, most fail to see it as an inner region, mainly, again, due to the failure to cognize, grasp, and deftly utilize the *prana*. Even ordinary beings spend a vast amount of time in this inner realm, all caught up with dreams during sleep.

Jnanakasha is the space of intelligence. Just as it is wise to draw a distinction between brain and mind, so too, it is good to note the difference between thought and intelligence. One could say, in defense of this point, that there are hundreds of thoughts going through the average mind daily, but how many of them could be classified as truly intelligent? Thus, intelligence occupies a very rarefied and refined level of Consciousness, and all that is best springs forth from it.

Finally, there is the *Chidakasha*. This is the space of pure, conscious Awareness. It is indescribable. It correlates directly with what is called *samadhi*, or *nirvana*, by the luminaries. It is nondual Awareness with no realms and boundaries, no beings, no overlays or conditionings.

The main teaching to consider in this chart is the interconnectness of all five *akashas*. From gross, to ethereal, to subtle, to causal, to Causeless, each realm fits into the next, getting absorbed there at the time of dissolution, and reemerging from there at the time of manifestation. Thus, Oneness, *Advaita*, gets demonstrated again, even in terms of space.

The second aspect of this teaching to ruminate upon is the makeup of each of these realms with regards to living beings. Each *akasha* hosts a variety of life-forms, some of which have been included in the related sidebars of this chart (facing page). From humans, to ancestors, to celestials, gods, sages, seers, and on inwards to the realm of the Trinity, inward ascension takes the soul inexorably towards its formless nature. Ultimately speaking, it is a mock journey, a dream projection, since all realms and beings are permanently fixed in the *Chidakasha*. Those who know this are seers.

Other facets of this teaching focus on the higher echelons themselves. At the level of the *Jnanakasha* the symbol for *AUM* makes its appearance, indicating its lofty station in the cosmic and transcendental scheme of things. Being The Word of God, it acts as a gateway into formlessness, merging like a sugar cube into hot tea into the nondual *Brahman* at the time of *Mahapralaya*. *Brahman* and *Shakti*, Themselves, are epitomized by the *Chidakasha*. They are Causeless, so cannot be the cause for anything, which affirms Their unadulterated purity.

From The Word, then, everything vibrates forth into existence at many levels. These five *akasha* are not airtight compartments, but overlap liberally, both in terms of dimension and sentien-

The Five Akashas of Vedanta Philosophy

"Like five Russian dolls of diminishing size, neatly nesting inside of one another, all ending up as one all-inclusive unit, similarly do the five atmospheres through which name and form manifest all reside within each other — from causeless to causal to subtle to gross — each holding multiple dimensions, countless worlds, and myriad beings." Babaji Bob Kindler

(Causeless)

Brahman
Shakti

**Chidakasha
(Paramakasha)
*Space of
Awareness***

"Like akasha, space, that holds many objects yet is not affected by them, so too does Brahman both hold and pervade the many worlds and various forms held in space and time — though It is beyond space and time." Lord Vasishtha

(Causal)

Path of Brahma/Trinity
Brahmaloka

Ishvara
Avatar
Brahma
Vishnu
Siva
Vairajas

**Jnanakasha
*Space of
Intelligence***

(Subtle)

Path of the Luminaries
Taparloka

Seers
Rishis
Paramahamsas
Mahatmas
Avadhuts
Sages
Arhats
Yogis
Manus

**Chittakasha
*Space of
Thought***

*Realm of the Sages,
& Mind-born Sons*
Maharloka & Janaloka

Path of the Celestials
Svarloka

(Astral/Ethereal)

Indra
Gods
Goddesses
Demigods
Manes
Asuras
Munis
Siddhas
Ghandarvas
Angels
Ancestors
Nagas
Elementals
Lost Spirits
Pretas

**Pranakasha
*Space of
Life Force***

Path of the Ancestors
Bhuvarloka

(Gross)

**Bhutakasha
*Space of
Objects***

Realm of the Physical
Bhurloka

Human Bodies
Animals
Insects
Plants
Microorganisms
Planets
Ether
Air
Fire
Water
Earth
Objects
Atoms
Molecules

"All forms, multifarious in manifestation and expression, being aspects of the wisdom-word, like drops of rain falling into torrential rivers, enter the infinite Ocean of Consciousness called Brahman. Each akasha — physical, pranic, mental, intellectual, and causal — dissolve into the Paramakasha, that supreme Space of pure, conscious Awareness."
Lord Vasishtha

cy. There are, to be sure, many cases of beings who are restricted to the single *akasha* that they vibrate in, but in the case of illumined souls, a seer occupying a physical body in the *Bhutakasha* can, at will, and via concentration and meditation, penetrate the veils and coverings of the physical *loka* and commune with beings and places in the *Pranakasha* and beyond. Even normal beings accomplish this journey upon vacating their waking state and physical senses in sleep, but do not remember this sojourn, know of its import, or connect it to mind, *akasha*, and consciousness upon their return to the dense ego/mind complex they are currently identifying with during embodiment.

Now that the subject of space has been opened up and, hopefully, our concept of it based upon the wisdom of the *rishis*, an excursion can be taken which will provide us with a keener understanding of space with regards to some strata of Awareness that are cross-sections of the higher *akashas*. For this we can borrow from the *Buddhist* tradition, from a teaching that reveals a set of worlds, as levels of inner consciousness, that the soul must traverse and transcend in order to fully mature his or her spiritual life and mind.

On the facing page is a chart based upon the Ten *Dasabhumikas*, or Pure-Mind Lands, which represent a sort of spiritual graph that dictates a necessary process of ascension to be accomplished by aspiring *Bodhisattvas*. Many of these superlative souls , like the *Jivanmuktas* of *Vedanta*, want to return to embodiment so as to "save all sentient beings from suffering." While a worthy cause, there are some lessons to be learned about such a statement and its vow, and the naive and spiritually infantile western world — especially its new age adherents — should sit up and take notice.

On such a mission, at least three great axioms and eternal teachings must be held in the selfless servant's awareness. First, the Soul (*Buddha*-Nature) is never bound; it is not in need of saving. It only needs to wake up to its own inherent perfection. Secondly, suffering is an illusion. It also has a purpose, which is to impel the soul towards its misplaced state of freedom. As Padre Pio once said to a person who wanted to be saved from suffering, *If you knew how important your suffering is, you would not ask me to take it away."* Third, and revealingly, the subtle work of awakening souls is not a matter of conversion to another religion, but rather an art of revealing the Eternal Religion existing within them. All religion, every religious path and perspective, in indigenous to the Soul. By awakening to and following the internal earmarks and signposts lying within the soul/mind complex, the aspiring being will enter that "open space beyond religion" which is the natural unification of all beings, and the spontaneous atmosphere of the Oversoul. Thus, does the *Nitya-siddha*, Swami Vivekananda, state, *"Hands off! The teacher ruins everything by thinking he teaches."* The free soul's purpose, then, is to remove obstacles from the path, then let the aspirant walk it him or herself, under ones own properly generated impetus.

Since the chart of the facing page states what is essential for graduation into each *"bhumi,"* there is little need for extensive commentary. How many of us are *Bodhisattvas*, anyway? For those who aspire in this way, which is extremely laudable, clarity and definition are a matter of taking refuge at the feet of a great soul, of the teacher/student relationship. However, and other than the marvelous scope of *Buddhist* philosophy revealed here in a single aspect of its teaching, there are salient points to be made about certain junctures that the inwardly ascending soul will arrive at, what is encountered by way of obstacles there, and what is gained by way of victory. To that end we turn our attention next. The reader can follow the chart, *bhumika* by *bhumika*, to receive essential information. The word *"bhumika"* means stage, step, state, or level. The word, *bhuma*, refers to Reality, or in this case, Buddha-nature, or *Tathagatagarbha* — what Lord Buddha called *Prajna Param*.

In the precincts of the "Land of Joy," the most compelling of its qualities is the renunciation of all *karmas* and the abandonment of attachment to *dharma*. When Sri Krishna states in the *Bhagavad Gita*, "Renounce all dharmas and take refuge in Me," he is referring to a spiritual awakening of a superlative degree that recognizes the distinction between the enigma of knowledge, the knower, and the freeing principle of That which is to be known (see chart on page 339). The *Bodhisattva*, in his or her own way, is seeking the Ultimate, and there are nine other *bhumikas* waiting to demonstrate the incomparable nature of this imperishable Truth. This striking contrast, destructive of ego-

Dasabhumikas — The Ten Pure Lands
or Ten Stages of Bodhisattvahood

1) Pramudita-bhumi (Land of Joy)
* Full spiritual awakening takes place * Bodhisattva vow is taken
* Vow of dana, generosity, is accepted   * Wishes for karmic merit are renounced
* Egotistic pursuits and all dharmas are perceived to be empty

2) Vimala-bhumi (Land of Purity)
* Shila, spiritual discipline, is perfected
* Practice of dhyana & samadhi are intensified
* Lapses in concentration are removed

3) Prabhakari-bhumi (Land of Radiance) →
* Attains the 4 Stages of Absorption
* Attains the 4 Stages of Formlessness
* Acquires 5 of the 6 Supernatural Powers

4) Archismati-bhumi (Blazing Land)
* Burns away all false conceptions
* Begins to develop nondual wisdom
* Achieves right exertion
* Works on the 37 Limbs of Enlightenment

5) Sudurjaya-bhumi (Hard to conquer Land)
* Meditates to realize The 4 Noble Truths
* Works on the 37 Limbs * Destroys all doubts

6) Abhimukhi-bhumi (Wisdom-view Land)
* Gains insight into conditioned arising
* Transcends need for discriminating thought
* Achieves Shunyata — perception of voidness
* Perfects wisdom — Prajna

7) Durangama-bhumi (Far-reaching Land)
* Attains skillful means to guide others
* Can be reborn in any form of choice
* Transcends all possibility of regression

8) Achala-bhumi (Immovable Land)
* Gains freedom from obstacles
* Knows time of personal Buddhahood
* Transmits own merits to others

9) Sadhumati-bhumi (Pure Mind Land)
* Attains full bodhisattvahood * Has all 6 Abhijnas
* Has the 8 Liberations * Has all 10 Dasabalas ←
* Has the 4 Certitudes * Knows all dharmas & transmits them

10) Dharmamegha-bhumi (Land of Dharma-clouds)
* Has wisdom, compassion & boundless virtue
* Confirmed Buddhahood * Has mature Trikaya *Abides in the Buddha fields

---

Dhyana
(The 4 Stages of Absorption)
1) Akushala, Vichara, Vitarka, relinquishing desires via conceptualization and discursive thought.
2) Thought dissolves to promote inner calm and one-pointedness.
3) Equanimity (upeksha), alertness, awareness, and well-being
4) Eternal awakeness, abidance

Arupasamadhi
(The 4 Stages of Formlessness)
1) Stage of limitless space
2) Stage of boundless awareness
3) Stage of nothingness
4) Stage beyond aware & unaware

Abhijnas — 6 Supernatural Powers
1) Wealth and power
2) Divine hearing
3) Perceiving other's thoughts
4) Recollection of past lives
5) Divine sight
6) Certainty of enlightenment

Dasabalas — 10 Powers of a Buddha
Knowledge:
concerning deaths and rebirths
concerning purity and impurity
concerning the ripening of deeds
concerning absorptions, liberations
concerning paths leading to worlds
concerning abilities of other beings
concerning constituents of the world
concerning exhaustion of defilements
concerning tendencies of other beings
concerning the possible & impossible

istic elements, is stated here in terms of the phrase, *"All dharmas are to be perceived as empty."* To the wisdom seeker, this may at first seem painful. But to the Truth seeker, the purpose of gathering wisdom was not to hoard it or to store it up, and certainly not to put a stamp of personal ownership on it, but to use it to destroy ignorance and thereby reach total Enlightenment. And some of this ignorance that must be done away with is extremely subtle (see chart on page 255), as we will see.

The three attributes of the second *bhumika*, the "Land of Purity," are all of inestimable value. First of all, and in accord with the ability to transcend reliance upon *dharma* alone, is the facet of perfecting ones *sadhana*. For, there is nothing of greater potency in spiritual life than *sadhana*, self-discipline. The difference between salvation in the intermediate *akashas* or *bhumikas*, and attainment of the higher Lands of Awareness leading to liberation, depends on the ability to refine and perfect ones spiritual practice.

Additionally, those inscrutable lapses in concentration, whose origins in the hidden recesses of the human mind are hard to locate, are done away with here in this benign Land, which assists the ascending *Bodhisattva* in his familiarization with the spiritual levels of meditation and *nirvana*. And this is in conjunction with another whole echelon of abilities that kick in at this juncture, as the first and upper sidebar on the chart under study (page 329) reveals. The Four Stages of Absorption, which define meditation proper, now get fully underway, which are both prompted by and lead towards the radiance emanating from both of these internal levels of Consciousness.

The first sidebar on the chart under study, and the next two below it, are all connected with the "Land of Radiance," which is well named considering the treasures of Enlightenment that are gathered there. The *Bodhisattva* is swiftly becoming a *Buddha* here, for not only are stages of absorption distilling within him, but he is also acclimatizing and getting accustomed to exquisite states of formlessness heretofore unknown and unplumbed. It is no wonder, then, that five of the six *Abhijnas,* the superlative powers of a Buddha, come to the *Bodhisattva* at this stage. They come as a result of his willingness to experience the Four States of Absorption just mentioned. The six *abhijnas,* however, having to do with foreknowledge of the complete removal of all imperfections, and foresight into the pending realization of his *Buddha* nature, are as yet still veiled from him.

The fourth echelon, aptly titled with the designation, the "Burning Land," has mostly to do with the extinguishing of subtle impurities with the increased fire of radiance that the *Bodhisattva* now enjoys. In companionship with this rises the acquisition of more wisdom around the Thirty-seven Limbs of Enlightenment.

The "Hard to Conquer" Land affords the spiritually elevated soul the destruction of all doubts, meaning those slender shreds or residues of subtle insecurities that still linger in the mind. In many religious traditions, whose adherents have availed themselves of the mellifluous art of meditation, the presence of doubt persisting even up until the highest reaches of realization, is admitted.

The sixth *bhumika* under brief scrutiny here is the "Wisdom View Land." Here, in this lofty atmosphere of internal Awareness, the famous and well-thought teaching structure called *Pratitya Samutpada* opens up fully to the *Bodhisattva*. Translated as "Interdependent Arising" in English, or "Conditioned Nexus," the main brunt of the teaching revolves around the binding connectedness of all phenomena — both of the mind and of the physical world — to such an extent that they all intermingle interminably, causing confusion, suffering, and return to embodiment based upon twelve "links," or *nidanas* (see chart on page 193). Ironically, the naive sense of "oneness" that the immature aspirant cherishes upon entering spiritual life, is this very undesirable interconnectedness that the luminaries want the mind free of. The *darshanas* of *Sankhya*, *Yoga*, and *Vedanta*, all have systems and teachings related to this selfsame problem, which is basically the soul's stubborn involvement with matter and objects leading to the inability to extract itself from them due to inordinate attachment. Many practitioners, so-called, are stuck here, most without even acknowledging it.

As links that bind, the order of appearance in *Pratitya Samutpada* are: 1) ignorance of the danger of suffering in relative existence; 2) the formation of negative and mixed mental impressions due to ignorant actions; 3) habit and reliance upon conventional life and thinking taken into the next birth; 4) attachment to name and form in a new body in forgetfulness of *Buddha* Nature; 5) the development of fresh sets of *karma* based upon sensual experiences enjoyed in an uninformed state of mind; 6) intermingling with people, places, and situations with a vacuous mind, breeding more *karmas*; 7) accrual of dependence on the five senses and their experiences for happiness; 8) habitual craving for more experiences gotten in the body through the senses under the false impression that satisfaction will come from them; 9) inordinate clinging to embodied existence via the habit of selfishness; 10) an unknown desire for a new body at the approach of death; 11) rebirth in ignorance based upon attachment; 12) the continual cycle of these links resulting in the painful experiences of old age and death, multiple times. These links, and freedom from them after their recognition, occur over the span of three lifetimes but can recur again and again if left unchecked.

The "Far-Reaching Land" sports two special features of spiritual mastery. First, the ability to guide other souls begins to manifest and, second, any potential for regression or falling back from the goal is destroyed. Rebirth at this juncture of realization is a matter of conscious choice rather than of *karmic* coercion or random occurrence.

The "Immovable Land" performs a spiritual one-upmanship on the Far-Reaching Land in that it signals arrival to *Buddha*hood. Along with *Buddha*hood, then, comes the potential for transmitting ones own soul qualities — like peace, equanimity, wisdom, and compassion — to others. This is the land of spiritual transmission proper; only the realized ones who abide at this especial level of attainment can truly help the world. Others only hope to do so, pretend to do so, or run themselves ragged trying to do so, via misguided, inferior, conventional, or ineffectual means and methods.

Realization that the world, i.e., nature, cannot be helped, is not in need of help, and that the benighted soul should be the recipient of all spiritual assistance, is the defining distinction between illumined and the worldly souls. For the *Bodhisattva*, his fine discrimination on the matter was gained and implemented back in the Wisdom View Land, the sixth *bhumika*. Prior to that, he learned right exertion in the Blazing Land, the fourth *bhumika*. And before that, he had given up all egotistic pursuits and possessions in the Land of Joy, the first *bhumika*. But in the case of the worldly, prior to entering the arena of action, they have not renounced anything. As a result, their egos are deeply invested in their work and its outcome. Also, their exertions, even altruistic ones, are centered around money and finance. Finally, the worldly believe in the reality and ultimate existence of the world; otherwise they would not be called "worldly." The *Bodhisatva* has realized that all things, all places, all objects, all personalities — even all *dharmas* — are essentially "empty." What motivation can drive him, then, other than the pure one of awakening sentient beings to their inherent Sentiency, their *Buddha* Nature? These are some of the great lessons that *Buddhism* teaches.

Speaking of such wondrous purity, it is at the ninth *bhumika*, called the "Pure Mind Land," that the sixth *abhijna* comes into the *Bodhisattva*'s possession. This auspicious arrival represents and confers confirmation of his enlightenment, and his full *Bodisatva*hood as well. The Ten *Dasabalas*, or powers of a *Buddha*, which were maturing over time, also come under his mastery. These ten are an engaging study in and of themselves. The reader is invited to contemplate them, one by one, as they appear in the fourth sidebar on the chart (on page 329), near the bottom.

The "Land of *Dharma* Clouds" is the final stage in this reckoning of complete Enlightenment. All the other *Buddhas* unanimously affirm the new *Bodhisattva*'s mature status of full illumination at this juncture. This realized being can now dwell in the Land of the *Buddhas*, the *Buddha* Fields, possessing boundless compassion and stainless virtues that are the *Buddha*'s own. His all-knowing and all-pervasive knowledge of the *Trikaya* is also available and on hand to assist all beings. The *Trikaya*, the Triple Body, is constituted of: *Dharmakaya*, the Transcendental Body; *Sambhogakaya*, the Body of Blissful Delight; and the *Nirmanakaya*, the Body of Transformation. The first is *Buddha* Nature, true Oneness; the second is *Buddha* Paradise, the land of enlightenment; and the third is *Buddha* Manifestation, his actual physical appearance throughout time for the good of mankind.

The *Dasabhumikas* form an illuminating study, apropos to the principle of *akashas*. They are subtle realms of inner space, visited or attended only by the mind in an enlightened condition.

In chapter two, and now in chapter seven, the subject of space, *desha,* has been thoroughly scrutinized. This study, typical of Indian *darshanas,* is undertaken mainly for the purpose of mapping out the subtle and causal worlds within our consciousness, called *"the Kingdom of Heaven within"* by Jesus. This purpose, in turn, and as has been seen, is really for tracing origins in order that the Source of Existence can be revealed, approached, and immersed in.

Along this crucial trajectory, the *rishis* have taught us that the role of knowledge is indispensable, being essential to the aspiring soul seeking the highest Truth. And since this chapter is about principles and systems of a cosmic and philosophical design, we must not overlook the famous Seven Stages of Knowledge. Interestingly enough, the *Sanskrit* name for this wisdom conglomerate is the *Atmajnana Bhumikas,* revealing that the subject of *bhumikas* is not limited to *Buddhism.* This particular angle on teaching the *bhumikas,* however, concentrates upon these realms as having their locale in knowledge, consisting of knowledge, and being infused through and through with knowledge. In other words, the "Kingdom of Heaven" is made of intelligence, or intelligent particles (see chart on page 33), and lies within the Great Mind of God. All this will become clearer as we study the next three charts.

Even by casting a cursory glance at the first of these three charts, viewed on the facing page, it can be seen that many of the *darshanas* and their systematizers were taken up with and fascinated by the teaching of the *Atmajnana Bhumikas* — the worlds of wisdom within. Patanjali's *Yoga,* Vasishtha's *Yoga, Vedanta,* and others, all sported their version and interpretation of these coruscating countries of Consciousness. A look into each will prove beneficial.

The first stage of knowledge, according to Patanjali, is based upon spiritual awakening. Vedavyasa would call this the desire for true knowledge, and Vasishtha would call it right desire. Whatever the title assigned, it does not take much thinking power to see the similarities between these designations. When a man awakens from his dream of the mundane world and his conditioned awareness, it is both due to and resultant in knowledge. From there he can begin to flex his internal muscles, simultaneously doing away with the impediments now revealed to him. This summates the second stage of knowledge. He renounces the unreal. As an important aside here, these seven stages hit similar chords and resonate well with Lord Buddha's Eightfold Path (see chart on page 229). The reader is invited to view and compare.

In the third stage of knowledge, the ordinary mind's crystalizations are fast beginning to disintegrate, which frees it from all manner of subtle residue that was responsible for problems such as indeterminacy and brooding. This is not just "a new lease on life" that brings fresh waves of positivity but disappears after the first onslaught of unfortunate occurrences. The mind actually feels free from all that inhibited it earlier, and the aspirant is rather amazed at this, and waits, expectantly, for the return of old habits. They never return, for the mind that supported them earlier has been dissolved in knowledge. And, in fact, the onrush of the fourth stage of knowledge is waiting to happen instead, which is a sense of equanimity accompanied by a sense of final accomplishment.

This inner peace that descends upon the newly fashioned mind paves the way for stage five, which is characterized by a more dynamic inward thrust of ability. The mind becomes singularly focused and one-pointed, heralding the approach of the experience of *samadhi* in its initial forms. The *samadhis* of wisdom and bliss (of *Yoga*) are verily beginning to manifest at these fourth and fifth stages of knowledge. When they do, the now spiritually adept soul courses in and out of them in stages pertinent to their own natural order. Then, the sixth stage of knowledge graces the mind with a purity that is one of the greatest boons sought after by illumined souls. It is Pure Mind, and its advent ushers in that nondual experience known as transcendence.

The final stage of knowledge, or beyond knowledge as Lord Vasishtha outlines it, is indescribable. Words such as *Nirvikalpa, Nirvana, Asamprajnanta, Moksha, Mukti,* and others, have been graciously lent to the tradition by its respective *darshanas.* The reader is invited to take in the three quotes of these luminaries, and also study the seven sheaths on the far right side of the chart that correlate with these seven stages, for further elucidation.

Seven Stages of Spiritual Progress in Seven Systems

Patanjali	Vedaryasa	Vasishtha	Krishna	Buddha	Yoga	Kapila
Vyutthana Chitta *Awakening Consciousness*	Parajnata Prajna *True Knowledge*	Subheccha *Right Desire*	Antah-jnana *Realization of Inherent Knowledge*	Samyag-dristi *Perfect View*	Samyak-jnana *Wisdom Transmission*	Gaining the Five Preliminary Perfections
Nirodha Chitta *Controlling Consciousness*	Heya Kshina Prajna *Renunciation*	Vicharana *Right Reflection*	Duhkha Samyoga Viyogam *Elimination of Pain*	Samyak-samkalpa *Perfect Resolve*	Khyati *Discernment and Clarity*	1. Svadharma *Selecting & Contemplating a Spiritual Path*
Nirmana Chitta *Individual Consciousness*	Prapya Prapti Prajna *Attainment*	Tanu Manasa *Dissolved Mind*	Samadhi Sampadanam *Attaining Samadhi*	Samyak-vak *Perfect Speech*	Dharma-megha *Raincloud of Virtues*	2. Shruti/Shravana *Recourse to Guru & Scriptures*
Prashanta Chitta *Tranquil Consciousness*	Karya Shuddhi Prajna *Accomplishment*	Satvapati *Self-realization*	Samyag-darshanam *Perfect Vision*	Samyak-karmanta *Perfect Conduct*	Malavinasha *Destruction of Blemishes*	3. Manana *Inner Reflection*
Ekagrata Chitta *Attentive Awareness*	Charitadhikara Prajna *Realization*	Asamsakti *Nonattachment*	Niyamukta *Absolute Freedom*	Samyak-ajiva *Perfect Livelihood*	Guna-vaitrshnyam *Dispassion towards the Gunas*	4. Sadhu-satsangha *Holy Company*
Chidra Chitta *Purified Consciousness*	Gunatita Prajna *Untainted Intelligence*	Padarthabhavana *Transcendence*	Trigunatitatvam *Dissolving the Gunas*	Samyak-vyayama *Perfect Effort*	Jnana-prasada *Destruction of Karmas and Obstacles*	5.Manah Shuddhi *Self-Purification*
Paripakva Chitta *Pure Consciousness*	Svarupa Matra Jyoti *Self-illumined Consciousness*	Turiya/Turyaga *Beyond Knowledge*	Brahma-nistha *Immersion in Brahman*	Samyak-smriti *Perfect Mindfulness* / Samyak-samadhi *Perfect Concentration*	Asamprajnata *Attainment of Nondual Samadhi*	Trividham Dukhkam *Removal of the 3 Types of Pain*

"The Seven States of Knowledge all overlap, have countless ramifications, and each of those is divided a hundredfold. Upon coursing through these seven stages, all visible things become empty and past resurrection. The result is Jivanmukti — a state of pure Being. These Stages of Higher Knowledge make one a living liberated being, then, perfectly free, whether abiding as a householder or as an ascetic. The earth moves, causing the illusion of the movement of the sun; but the sun does not move. So, Prakriti, or Maya, or Nature, is moving, changing, unfolding veil after veil, turning over leaf after leaf of this grand book called life — while the witnessing soul drinks in knowledge in stages, unmoved, unchanged." Illumined Seers of India

Lord Vasishtha's take on the Seven Stages of Knowledge is now culled out from the chart previously studied for closer inspection. In the new chart on the facing page, we see it and the several juxtapositions that accompany it. These entries and correlations expand our knowledge base about this enthralling subject, that has attracted the attention of so many great souls over time. For instance, we can now see some more personalized information about the soul's progress along this inward trajectory. For starters, there is the making of a teacher, described as a sort of germination period at the primary stage, the level of spiritual awakening. As the "blossoming" stage kicks in, a spontaneous oneness with nature ensues, and as elements fructify at the third stage, the art of right action and proper orientation get established. These three levels are gained mainly in accord with the waking state (*jagrat*), as shown in the column on the far right.

The "maturation" stage is characterized by knowledge of the truth of mental projection. No longer does religious superstition or the symbolic metaphor found in fundamentalist or dualistic scriptures occupy the throne of the mind. The awakened soul perceives the truth that the mind is the hub of creation, and that God, or Reality, is acreate. The light of the distinction between form and formlessness, as well as sentience and insentience, dawns. The soul then wastes no time in getting free from the tendency towards projecting, and learns to dissolve the mind into more refined states of Awareness. Equanimity is the result — *"the Peace that Passeth all Understanding."* The crucial nature of the fourth stage of Knowledge is therefore affirmed. This stage is directly in accord with the dreaming state (*svapna*) of the individual, and it is not hard to see why. Both the attainments and the results of this stage are subtle; they transcend the gross or apparent, or the physical.

And if all of this is acknowledged, then it stands to reason that when all mental projections are allayed, and a great peace descends upon the mind, then there is nowhere else to take refuge than in transcendence, or *Asamshakti*. It is within this fifth stage of knowledge that nonduality becomes the focus. There is simply no impediment left to detain the mind in its deeper contemplation process. This is the land of inner vision, but of a preternatural kind. It is not so much the appearance of divine forms that captures the attention, but rather the formless Light of Awareness that describes the vision here. All that is preconscious — not obviously present or accounted for earlier, but able to be remembered — takes the forefront of the mind. This is why this stage is aligned with deep sleep (*sushupti*), which is all bliss, free of forms, while its secrets are easily forgotten in lower states of awareness.

The sixth and seventh stages of knowledge are *samadhi*, called *Turiya* in this rendering. It is characterized by absorption tending towards immersion. It is explained in the *"hailstone falling towards the ocean"* metaphor. A man is then beyond the three states of his consciousness — waking, dreaming, and deep sleep. Any impressions in the mind that are leftover and still present, admittedly very subtle ones at this point in spiritual attainment, are wiped out completely, and in fact, thoughts of attainment and nonattainment themselves are found missing. *Turiya* simply means "the Fourth," named so probably because no explanatory title could really stick at these superlative spiritual heights. The only thing left to do, then, is to immerse completely, irretrievably, and go "beyond the beyond." As Sri Ramakrishna Paramahamsa was wont to say in this regard, *"No matter how high a bird may fly, there are always higher regions to attend upon."*

In the third chart on stages of knowledge, pictured on page 337, we get the opportunity to see not only the soul's step by step progression along its inward trajectory, but also a copious list showing the "sunken grounds" of human awareness, called the *Ajnana-bhumikas*. *Ajnana* means ignorance, and there are seven stages of its existence, which, if the soul gets caught in them, must be gradually transcended. Together, all these are designated the Fourteen Stages of Upper and Lower Knowledge. Since the stages of higher knowledge have already been explored through three different interpretations, one of them going rather in-depth, the following commentary will restrict itself to a description of the *Ajnana Bhumikas*, or stages of lower knowledge. Much can be learned from a study of them, as the awareness of most beings is, unfortunately, still operating at these soporific levels, and feeling the incertitude of their weighty atmospheres.

Seven Levels of Higher Knowledge (From the Story of Iksvaku)

4 States of Consciousness	7 Levels of Higher Knowledge	Stage of Progress	Characteristics of Higher Knowledge
Turyatita - Beyond the 4th	Turyatita - Pure Consciousness	Immersion	Enters liberation beyond description
Turiya - the "4th"	Turya - Abidance in the Self		Sees Brahman in everything Identifies fully with Consciousness Goes beyond attainment/nonattainment
	Padartha-bhavana - Grasp of Truth	Absorption	Destroys subtle impressions of the mind Acquires perfect inner vision Looks equally on all things/beings
Deep Sleep (Sushupti)	Asamshakti - Nonattachment	Transcendence	Transcends nature/gunas Gains certitude of the truth of nonduality
Dreaming State (Svapna)	Sattvapati - Illumined Intelligence	Maturation	Rests in Sat-bhava state Attains tranquility amidst action Allows the mind to dissolve
	Tanumanasa - Peaceful Mind	Fructifying	Gets free from mental projection Perceives the universe as a projection
Waking State (Jagrad-avastha)	Vicharana - Proper Inquiry	Blossoming	Does what is to be done refrains from what is not Is in harmony with nature
	Shubhecha - Right Aspiration	Germination	Helps instill wisdom in others Becomes a Spiritual Teacher

Laying at the very basement of the list of conscious states, which in this case is not really conscious at all, is *Bindu-jagrat.* The word, "semi-conscious," may be used in this case. It is a state experienced by human beings, necessarily attended by some small and veiled intelligence, though considerably benighted. As the chart reveals, this is the condition of root ignorance that characterizes the appearance of the spiritually unawakened human being, called the *"jiva,"* on the earthly scene. Unaware of his real identity, misinformed as to the real nature of time, disconcerted about the reason for his presence on earth, and without a clue to his actual whereabouts, he epitomizes the world of name and form in time and space based upon cause and effect *(maya).*

However, as the fitting phrase expresses, "there is no place to go but up." Therefore, this darksome state must give way to some kind of progress, no matter how stunted it may be. Thus, the second *ajnana-bhumika* sees the soul becoming aware of its own individuality. This does not mean the true individual, but rather the ego, and inside that dwarfed structure the as yet addled human being perceives the many manifestations of the mind in *maya* and sees them as a host of real differentiations. As if this muzzy-minded state of confused consciousness were not bad enough, the egocentric individual moves to try to possess and own all of these disparate levels and their structures, along with their ever flexuous situations — even the other egos that cause them. This is life at the level of the second sunken ground of heavily restricted awareness.

It is not hard to imagine what the Indian *rishis* would declare in the case of souls operating in this spiritually deprived condition. They are bound for rebirth, again and again, in a similar state and situation. Further, the connection has not yet been made with regards to the connections between the universe and the soul, so these hapless beings can neither affirm and establish the healthy ones, nor snap and destroy the unhealthy ones. It is a helpless condition, irremediable, really, and only the presence of recurring experiences of suffering and, perhaps, a little grace from unseen positive influences, will compel it onwards.

At this juncture, there is still no real light present for the benighted soul, and he must move through darkness to get to another less shaded form of darkness. This comes upon him in the form of the ability to master his surroundings, at least for a time. In other words, and as the chart relates, he gains some vaunted dominion over nature. But the wise have all seen what the worldly soul does with this potential boon: it fashions objects of pleasure out of nature, enjoys them, then gets attached to them, and finally suffers the results of loss, decay, boredom, theft, and other lessons of this kind, ending in abject bondage (see chart on page 197). The title of this stage of lower knowledge is *Jagrat-svapna,* inferring that the waking and dreaming state are indiscriminately mixed up together, as if the experiences he is having are both painful and dreamlike. Ironically, this is actually the first sign of light leading to the fifth stage of lower knowledge wherein he begins to "get a clue."

Called plainly, *svapna,* dreaming, the fifth stage of knowledge sees the soul gaining some objectivity, since his consciousness has either been driven to or has arrived at that level where he feels that all of life is being lived as if in a dream. He does not know yet that it *is* a dream, a mentally-projected one, but he suspects. And there is an advantage to seeing it this way, for it breeds in him some healthy detachment. Prior to this, the negative experiences of life had given him aversion, which is not healthy. It is one of the great traps for consciousness, and the doorway to the real hell — not a fictitious one with devil, pitchfork, and hell fires — but hell on earth in the physical body.

In any event, this modest awakening grants him access into the sixth stage of knowledge, where progress is being made in terms of connections remembered from events long past, in previous lifetimes. These have a salutary effect on his mind, which responds in kind to produce the desire, or will, to live a more conscious life. This is where the waking state informs the dreaming state which, in turn, repercusses in a positive way to *"render the waking stage lucid."*

Finally, and accomplished via breaching all dependence upon things seen in both the waking and dreaming state, the soul awakens fully to its predicament in *maya.* Put in terms that Lord Buddha expresses, he realizes that all states of relative awareness are *"beset with pain"* — that *"Suffering Is."* This might be the first real bit of wisdom gleaned thus far by the soul inhabiting the

The Fourteen Stages of Upper and Lower Knowledge

(Jnana-bhumikas and Ajnana-bhumikas)

(From the Story of Iksvaku)

Turyatita - Full Absorption

14) Turya → Abides in the Self | Rests in disembodied liberation | Enters Immersion

13) Padartha-bhavana → Identifies with Consciousness alone | Sees Brahman in all | Goes beyond attainment

12) Asamshakti → Merges in Atman | Attains certitude of nonduality | Transcends the gunas | Realizes Jivanmukti

11) Sattvapatti → Mind adheres to Truth | Illumination of Intelligence | Equality of vision | Reaches mature detachment

10) Tanumanasa → Freedom from desires | Mastery of concentration | Transcendence of mind | Freedom leading to the 4th state

9) Vicharana → Inquiry into the nature of Reality | Contemplation of Atman | Attainment of virtues | Increased spiritual aspirations

8) Shubheccha → Attraction for the path of indifference | Desires to enjoy Jnana-Essence | Seeks guidance of an illumined soul | Studies Atma-jnana scriptures

↑7 **Jnana-bhumikas**

7 Ajnana-bhumikas ↓

7) Sushupti → Realizes all states are beset with pain ← Perceives all worlds in maya

6) Svapna-jagrat → Recalls events long past | Renders waking state lucid

5) Svapna → Gains objectivity ← Examines life's events in dream → Remembers upon awakening

4) Jagrat-svapna → Sovereignty over nature ↔ Gets attached to objects ↔ Labors under delusion

3) Maha-jagrat → Progression of repeated rebirths ← Believes man and universe to be dissimilar

2) Jagrat → Awareness of individuation ↔ Inception of differentiation

1) Bindu-jagrat → Root state of ignorance ↔ Incipient manifestation of the jiva

"The Seven Ajnana states all overlap, have countless ramifications, and each of those is divided a hundredfold."
Lord Vasishtha

realm of physical embodiment, and it qualifies him for entrance into those stages of higher knowledge that we have already scrutinized over the past few pages.

To conclude, for now, this section on liberating wisdom and its stages, the words and teachings of Sri Krishna can be imbibed. This Archetypical Soul, the *Avatar* of India, leaves us no doubt as to the presence, process, and purpose of knowledge — what to speak of its Purveyor. In the chart on the facing page, the reader is invited to study this teaching, given by a past Master. His declaration places a definitive mark on the topic, giving it a turn towards the essentials of each subdivision. Such a transmission, ancient yet timeless, has left its mark on all the *darshanas*, as well as their systematizers, leaving no doubt as to how to proceed in this most powerful of *yogas*.

To take stock of what true knowledge is, and compare it to what worldly-minded beings think it is, is enlightening in and of itself. For a wisdom-knower like Sri Krishna, the list compiled from His celestial song *(Bhagavad Gita)* at the top of the chart on the facing page tells it all. In a nutshell, it is that the seeker must eke out a little detachment from relativity through which he can then gain control of the senses. When established, this enables the mind to rise above dualities like attachment and aversion. This leads to both the necessity and ability to purify the intellectual body, which in turn settles the self into an abiding mode of dispassion, or equanimity.

Only after such a regimen has been enacted and attained can the soul finally get to the essential *yoga* of meditation. From here it is all downhill. With peace of mind a matter of past mastery, the soul dwells within, in solitude, no matter how much activity or how many beings are vibrating on the surface. Living in this ineffable and impenetrable abode of peace, the roots of problems such as anger, selfishness, desire for power, egotism and pride, and covetousness, all die away. This describes the path to wisdom, what true knowledge is all about.

The "knower" is that one who treads the path. At heart he/she is *dvaitahina,* a nondualist, though he may not appear to be or know that he is, while he is in the process of destroying his ignorance via the path of knowledge. The list in the middle of the chart under study outlines all that the knower believes in, and what he strives for with all his heart. The entire list is sought and gained by the sincere seeker under the ultimatum of a special kind of foreknowledge — that Reality is unborn, beginningless, eternal, and the sentient Overseer of all the worlds. This pellucid foresight, impressed indelibly on the memory of the mind, gives the well-informed aspirant after Truth a great advantage in spiritual life., an advantage that leads him inexorably towards *"That which is to be known."*

In Indian *darshanas*, there is no reticence or fear with regard to knowing God. Even when it is admitted that the mind cannot know God, the exercise of attempting to know God is said to purify the mind so that it will come to know God with a mind that is pure. *"Pure Mind is God,"* said Sri Ramakrishna. *"Buddha Mind is Buddha Nature,"* sayeth the Buddha. So the conclusion around this otherwise recondite matter, as far as the Indian *Rishis* are concerned, is indubitable.

In the list on the bottom of the chart under study is a host of exclamations that, among other things, describes, as well as words can say, the nature of Divine Reality. If one were to try to pick a phrase or word in English that would express, overall, the insuperable sentiment of these magisterial statements, the word "all-pervasive" would be a good choice. Suffice to say, Divine Reality is boundless, and contemplating it with a mind that has fulfilled all the criterion laid out on the rest of this chart is elevating, to say the least.

This is the reason why beings both fail to contemplate Reality, and are not attracted to It. The lack of knowledge about It, and the absence of a well-guided spiritual practice that places the mind in a peaceful state conducive to meditation on It, simply derails such intentions. As Sri Ramakrishna has said, *"It takes a jeweler to recognize the value of a diamond."* The reader is invited to scrutinize the fifteen bullet points on the chart on page 339 describing *"That which is to be known,"* for it is rare, if ever, that such a list has ever been so efficiently compiled, what to speak of it ever being presented so openly, point of fact, and free of all and any incredulity. Such is the Indian *Rishi's* unique perspective.

Knowledge, Knower, and That Which is to be Known

Knowledge – Qualifications for the Brahman State (Ch. 18)

"Learn from Me in brief, O Kaunteya, how to reach perfection & attain Brahman."

- Detach from Senses and Objects   (niyamya cha shabdadin vishayams)
- Subdue Speech, Body, and Mind   (yata vak kaya manasah)
- Relinquish Attraction and Aversion   (tyaktva ragadvesau)
- Generate a Pure Understanding   (buddhya vishuddhaya)
- Restrain the Self with Firm Resolve   (dhrtya'tmanam)
- Take Refuge in Dispassion   (vairagyam samupashritah)
- Engage in Meditation   (dhyana yoga parah)
- Abandon Selfishness   (vimucya nirmamah)
- Gain Peace of Mind   (shanto)
- Live in Solitude   (viviktasevi)
- Eat but Little   (laghvashi)
- Give up Egoism, Power, Pride, Desire, Anger, and Covetousness
  (ahamkaram balam darpam kamam krodham parigraham)

The Knower – "....all these have sprung from Me." (Ch. 10)

"That one who knows Me as unborn and beginningless,
as the Great Lord of the Worlds,
that one among mortals is free."

- Self-Controlled (dhrtya)
- Undeluded (asammohah)
- Forbearing (damah)
- Intelligent (buddhih)
- Cheerful (sukham)

- Equanimous (samata)
- Nonviolent (ahimsa)
- Generous   (danam)
- Patient (kshama)
- Wise (jnanam)

- Fearless (abhayam)
- Truthful (satyam)
- Content (tushtih)
- Austere (tapah)
- Calm (samah)

That Which is to be Known (Ch. 13)

"I shall describe what has to be known, knowing which one attains immortality."

- With Hands and Feet Everywhere (sarvatah panipadam)
- With Eyes, Heads, and Mouths Everywhere (sarvato aksishiromukham)
- With Ears Everywhere (sarvatah shrutimat)
- Existent and Enveloping All (sarvam avrtya tisthati)
- Shining via the Senses but Transcendent of Them (sarvendriya gunabhasam/vivarjitam
- Transcendent but Sustaining All (asaktam sarvabhrt)
- Experiencing the Gunas yet Beyond Them (nirgunam gunabhoktr cha)
- Within and Outside of All Beings (bahir antas cha bhutanam)
- Moving About yet Remaining Ever-Still (acharam charam eva cha)
- Incomprehensible yet All-Pervasive (avijneyam durastham cha'ntike cha tat)
- Indivisible yet Divides into Multiple Beings (avibhaktam cha bhuteshu vibhaktam)
- The Underlying Support of all Beings (bhuta bhartr)
- Beyond Darkness, the Light of all Lights (jyotisham api taj jyotis)
- Seated in the Hearts of All (hrdi sarvasya visthitam)
- Knowledge, the Knowable, and the Goal of Knowledge (jnanam jneyam jnanagamyam)

The Great Luminaries of India have been called God in human form. If one comes to know *Brahman,* one becomes *Brahman,* as the Upanisads state. In the chart on the facing page, this intriguing statement is given deeper inspection, resulting in valid proof. The teaching of *Brahmapada* declares that Divine Reality disports Itself through all the worlds, appearing within various forms. The only qualifier to this bold statement is that every form has a limit as to how much of the Light of *Brahman* can manifest in and through it.

This is explained nicely by Sri Sarada Devi's penetrating utterance shown at the top of this chart (page 341), in which She states that a flash of lightning shows up in the window pane of a house, not in the wooden shutters that frame the window. In other words, the intense flash of *Brahman's* pure, conscious Awareness gets revealed well in illumined souls with clear minds, while souls with dull minds and intellects will hardly receive or radiate any light. Thus, they are like "wooden shutters" as far as the expression of God in the human form is concerned.

To illustrate in more depth, this great teaching of the Lord appearing in human form, as well as reflecting in even material stations to a certain extent, the chart shows a circle of select principles, both sentient and insentient, as moons, that are either full or in cycles which lessen their capacity for expressing the light of Consciousness. *Brahman* is always full, of course, as is Its *Shakti,* as well as Its *Word,* for the most part. *Ishvara,* too, is as replete with Awareness as any form could possibly be, as are the *Avatars* that come forth from It.

It is when it comes to Cosmic Mind, the *Mahat,* and all that flows from it, that the vehicles containing Consciousness begin to show off their limitations, particularly when Nature, or *Prakriti,* gets animated into motion by lesser deities and the collective mind, and begins producing various grades of senses and elements. When the human mind/body complex meets and interacts with external nature (which proceeds from Unmanifested Nature, or *Prakriti*), the dream of relativity thickens considerably as all manner of random and ill-considered activities enter the fray. This level of existence is mostly devoid of higher Consciousness, because the dull and restless human mind is busy replacing It with desire-based projections, fantasies, imaginations, dreams, and other surface occupations and frivolities. This is called *sankalpa* and *vikalpa* in Sanskrit. Since, as Swami Vivekananda has stated, *"Brahman does not dream,"* there is no real room for expression of *Brahman* here, though *Brahman* persists as the underlying substratum of all life on earth, nevertheless. As the ecstatic devotee, Jafar, states in one of his spiritual songs:

I have finally understood, O Lord, that everything exists in Thee.
Every heart is ultimately united in Thee. Nothing exists but Thee!
O Beloved, Your Grace has returned me to my Eternal Abode
and Your Love has permeated my heart,
Indeed, is there a heart which exists that is devoid of Thy Love,
when nothing exists but Thee?
God and Goddess, man and woman, Hindu, Mussalman, Christian —
all are brought into existence by Thy own inscrutable Will.
What are these beings without You? They all exist in Thee!
Churches, Temples, Kaba — all places of worship,
You fashion them and cause all beings to bow down there.
You have become the worshipper, the act of worship, and the place of worship.
Nothing exists but Thee.
From the life heavens, throughout the boundless universe,
and even into the dark nether regions,
wherever our souls journey we find only Thee —
for nothing exists but Thee.
Matchless is Your Presence, O Lord, I have found nothing which compares to it.
Contemplating it, this humble singer, Jafar, has become illumined,

Brahmapada: How Brahman, Divine Reality, Disports Itself

"A flash of lightning can be seen in the windowpane, but not in the wooden shutters." Sri Sarada Devi

Ishvara/Ishvari

Shakti

Sadhakas & Devotees

The Light of Pure, Conscious Awareness

Realized Seers, illumined Souls

Ordinary Souls

Avatar
Trimurti
Lila
Maya
AUM
Lokas
Brahman
Samkalpa/Vikalpa
Maha Shakti
Akashas
Ishvara
Antahkarana
Prakriti
Mahat

"Brahman is both within and without. From within He creates the various states of mind. The scriptures thus say that Brahman Himself has become the twenty-four cosmic principles. Therefore I say: worship Brahman both inside and out."

and this simple Truth has dawned upon his understanding —
that nothing whatsoever exists but Thee!

As the chart (page 341) reveals, those spiritually expanded beings who both contain and exude the Light of pure, conscious Awareness are direct emanations of *Brahman*. Souls who are either shut off from or resistant to the Light of Higher Awareness simply do not have real bliss, or even the true enjoyment or exquisite pleasure that the devotees of the Lord and Divine Mother feel on earth. In previous lifetimes, these exceptional souls took up a regimen of spiritual practice under the guidance of an authentic preceptor, and attained to *moksha* — or are in the process of attaining It.

Going back several millennia, we can inspect one of these systems of spiritual progress, one that epitomized Lord Vasishtha's way. On the chart on the facing page, and reading from the top down, an auspicious path can be traced, paving the way for more treasures coveted by all seekers of Truth

It all begins with that crucial *viveka*, discrimination, used in this conjunction for distinguishing the difference between ordinary scriptures and "Atmajnan" scriptures. If the student thinks back, or refers back, this facet of knowledge has been illustrated in the past three charts studied. It was an element of the Eighth Stage of Knowledge (page 337). It was a part of Sri Krishna's Qualifications for the *Brahman* State (page 339). It appeared in at least three of Shankara's eight strata on the previous page. And so, it is a special facet of spiritual seeking. Its nonrecognition by religious seekers of the day is seen in the overall lack of spiritual realization in the world in general.

In short — and here is where *viveka* saves the seeker again — spirituality is characterized by much higher aims than conventional religion is, namely two: an actual, ongoing, and multi-faceted daily practice *(sadhana)* that outstrips a mere once a week remembrance of God; and the realization of *Moksha*, Liberation (see chart on page 686). *Moksha* is what the spiritual pathway consummates in. To quote from Swami Vivekananda about it: *"After long searches here and there, in temples and churches, in earths and in heavens, at last you come back, completing the cycle from where you started, to your own Soul, and find that He for whom you have been seeking all over the world, for whom you have been weeping and praying, on whom you were looking as the mystery of all mysteries shrouded in the clouds, is nearest of the near, is your own Self, the reality of your life, body, and soul."*

But it is up to the sincere seeker to recognize another important distinction as well, and *viveka* also helps in this aim and end. He/she must separate out in the mind the difference between pure desires and impure desires (see chart on page 180). For the most part, and in the guilt-laden atmosphere created by fundamentalist religion and its hell and devil-oriented scriptures, the immature aspirant is going to feel that all his desires are sinful. Attending upon holy company will both help him to reduce impure desires, and bring out the pure desires. Once this distinction is perceived, much progress can be made along the spiritual trajectory, and guilt and fear will become things of the past.

And here is where the Four *Purusharthas* stand forth to reveal their promise. Basically, these are: *artha*, making a living via right means; *kama*, fulfilling legitimate desires; *dharma*, learning precepts and taking spiritual vows; and *moksha*, the soul's natural arrival back to its Source. For more on these, see the chart and its commentary on page 365.

In line with realizing the superiority of revealed scriptures, there also comes to the seeker the necessity of separating authentic teachers from unqualified ones. Lord Vasishtha now brings that into the picture. It must have been, then, that much like in present times, uninformed beings were getting fooled by charlatans and pretenders, by occultists and sensationalists, by these and others who were deviously utilizing clever manipulation and spiritual marketeering to attract souls in the name of spirituality. No such hypocrisy should ever be allowed in the realm of spiritual seeking, so it is up to the aspirant to make sure of this via his or her own clear discernment. The "Four Qualifications of the Teacher" and the "Five Attributes for Approaching the *Guru*," listed on the previous chart (page 341), will help the aspirant in avoiding the wastage of time and ensuing confusion

The Sincere Seeker

Atmajnana Shastras ← *Lead to liberation* | *Lead to bondage* → Ordinary Shastras

"The greater is the science of divine wisdom, whence the lesser that is only terrestrial knowledge." — Lord Vasishtha

Pure Desires ← *Lead towards Brahmic State* | *Generate Pain* → Impure Desires

"Free the mind from subjection to the impure and raise the mind by acquaintance with the pure vasanas." — Lord Vasishtha

Purusharthas (The Four Fruits of Life)

Dharma	Artha	Kama	Moksha
(Moral/Ethical Life)	(Right Livelihood)	(Legitimate Desires)	(Liberation)

"Through right endeavor in this life of the world, all the ends of human endeavor can be attained." — Lord Vasishtha

Jnana Guru (Guru-viveka) ← | → Ajnana Guru (Guru-aviveka)

"After discriminating between a guru of jnana and one of ajnana, find a seat in the supreme one." — Lord Vasishtha

Sadhanachatushtaya (The Four Qualifications)

Viveka Vairagya Sama Dama Uparati Titiksha Samadhana Shraddha Mumukshutvam

(Discrimination, Detachment, Peace, Self-control, Self-settledness, Forbearance, Concentration, Faith, Yearning)

"We have ordained that all souls should be initiated after attaining the four qualifications." — Lord Vasishtha

Brahmapadesha (Initiation into the path of Brahman)

"Until thy mind is illumined, walk the path of initiation shown by realized souls." — Lord Vasishtha

The Three Great Sources

Guru-anushasana	Vidya-shastra	Aparokshanubhuti
(Transmission from a wise guru)	(Knowledge of the Scriptures)	(Direct Spiritual Experience)

"Assimilate within yourself the profound knowledge derived from the Three Great Sources." — Lord Vasishtha

Atma-tripti (The Three Prerequisites for Atmajnan)

Sankalpa-vinashana	Upekshanam	Brahmakaravritti
(Destroy all illusory thoughts)	(Gain extreme quiescence of mind)	(Merge in Brahman)

"By these three great prerequisites may you attain to the Atmic State, free of all stains and pains." — Lord Vasishtha

Retain the Four Sentinels

Shanti (Peace) Atma-vichara (Self inquiry) Santosha (Contentedness) Sadhusatsangha (Holy Company)

"Those who have embraced and implemented these four means gain freedom from Samsara." — Lord Vasishtha

that comes from association with an *Ajnana Guru.*

Continuing on with our study of the chart on page 343, we reach, again, mention of the "Four Treasures and the Six Jewels" (see chart on page 67). Suffice to say with regard to the Six Jewels, and reasoning in reverse order, that true faith is based upon the ability to concentrate, and that is founded on resolute forbearance. Forbearance has been strengthened by self-control, which itself comes from inner peace, or contentment. Such equanimity has been achieved by the coupling and practice of discrimination and detachment. All of these, together, culminate in a true desire for Freedom.

To pause here for more clarification, what passes for an authentic desire for freedom among spiritual aspirants in religious circles, or *sangas,* today, must be held up for scrutiny. Blisses, visions, and fleeting experiences have been assumed to be the real divine article, but these most often fail the test as time passes. The receiver of such transitory boons is seen to return again to the same old habits, fall back upon the same old desires, and fall victim to that telltale lack of intensity that belies the previous notion of vaunted freedom. Even the intermediate level of seeker has a compromise readily available, which is called "resting on ones laurels." Thus, so many convenient excuses emerge during crucial junctures along the spiritual path. Only the final consummation of a well-guided and wisely directed practice ending in Enlightenment will satisfy here, which is precisely why the sagacious and long-suffering aspirant ensures the complete attainment of the *Sadhanachatustaya* — The Four Treasures and Six Jewels.

It is then, or in the process of acquiring these, that the prepared seeker commits to the spiritual path. The only full commitment that is traditionally recognized, and which purifies the body and makes one fit for holy company, is that of *mantra-diksha* (see charts on pages 142 & 626). Called *Brahmapadesha* on the chart under study, now on the previous page, it is to be received from an illumined soul and adhered to through all levels of spiritual practice and up and until Enlightenment dawns. Even after that, the initiation a realized soul received early on from his *guru* is considered sacrosanct, and allows the fortunate seer to confer the same upon other students who come to him for guidance.

This important moment in spiritual life and growth is underscored by what is referred to next as the Three Great Sources (see chart on page 381). These are closely related to the Three Proofs of Truth, deemed sacred by all luminaries. They are held in such high esteem due to the authenticity they confer on both the spiritual path and its practice and attainment. Taking resort to the sacred scriptures (nondual in nature, of course), receiving instruction from an illumined *guru,* and verifying the aforementioned boons via ones own spiritual experiences — these three are a winning combination at the highest level of realization. More is to be said about them in forthcoming pages.

Next on the chart under study on page 343, *Atma-tripti* is an earmark of Lord Vasishtha's teachings. It is a sure-fire method if the aspirant is courageous and persistent enough, of merging the mindstream and all that is in it into final immersion and absorption. Even its first directive, the destruction of all illusory thoughts, is a stroke of enlightenment itself, being the death knell for ignorance. The practitioner can certainly understand, then, the import of attributes like *viveka,* for discernment regarding the quality of ones thoughts and experiences is both critical and sensitive.

But the "proof of the pudding" lies in the outcome. If *upeksha* descends upon the mind, leaving it in a state of peace and subtle bliss, then the practitioner can feel assured that the phase of destroying negative and detrimental thoughts was successful. The process is most critical because thoughts that are eventually detrimental for spiritual life can easily masquerade for beneficial thoughts, only to upset the precarious balance later on. All these matters become a thing of the past, however, when the mind's vibrations, called *chita-vrittis,* begin to dissolve in their Source. The result is what has been called *samadhi, satori, nirvana,* etc. This state, or stateless state, is both the acid test and proof of true spirituality and its attainment.

The final pearl on Lord Vasishtha's list on the chart on page 343 is called the Four Sentinels, and is another signature teaching of this celebrated luminary. The chart on the facing page, 345, and

The Four Sentinels & The Three Great Sources

"After the development of a man's knowledge via recourse to the four sentinels, showers of arrows discharged at him will become like soft lily flowers, being burned in flames will resemble a softly cushioned bed scented with rosewater, the chopping off of the head will feel like sushupti, disemboweling will be like the application of sandalpaste on his stomach, and the piercing of the breast with many spears will feel like droplets of cool water sprinkled over his body during the hot summer season." Lord Vasishtha

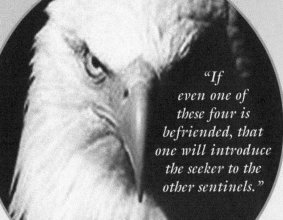

Shanti
Quiescence of Mind

"Causes desires and sorrows to vanish, grants unruffled composure of mind, and facilitates attainment of moksha."

Atma-vichara
Self-Inquiry

"Ushers in discrimination, ends cycles of rebirth, clear doubts, and leads to the highest state of Consciousness."

"If even one of these four is befriended, that one will introduce the seeker to the other sentinels."

Santosha
Contentment

"Brings bliss without longing or aversion, strengthens inner detachment, and sharpens one's insight."

Sadhu-satsanga
Holy Company

"Expands the intellect, neutralizes karma, transforms the mind, and takes one across the ocean of samsara."

The Three Great Sources

Guru-anushashana
Instructions from a Guru

"Beings unwilling to submit to the preliminary process of self-effort will either have a mere brush with spirituality or will get misled via attraction to spurious teachers."

Vidyashastra
Scriptural Significance

"Trying to realize God without the help of the scriptures is like trying to grow crops only at night."

Aparokshanubhuti
Direct Experience

"After the guru and the scriptures have been consulted, the quest for realization of the Atman begins in right earnest."

"The study of scripture without a guru for intellectual knowledge alone will lead one into ajnana, ignorance. True self-inquiry recognizes the words of guru and scriptures as the supreme authority. One may place credence even in the words of a child if they are consistent with the guru's instructions and the teachings of the revealed scriptures. Otherwise, one must reject like straw the words of even Lord Brahma himself."
Lord Vasishtha

its following commentary, has been fully dedicated to these most helpful aids. The Three Great Sources are listed again as well, showing their importance to spiritual life in general.

The transmission of the teaching of the Four Sentinels is usually attended by a story, both ancient and famous among the luminaries of India. The story tells of a man, living in a city with four walls, whose livelihood depended upon him leaving the city gates after dark, when they were locked and guarded. As his situation became more difficult, and scaling the walls at night was dangerous and risky, he struck upon a plan. Approaching one of the four sentinels of the four gates of the city one evening, he became familiar with the man by introducing himself. The next night he showed up again at the gate, bringing the guard a good smoke to enjoy. As the two grew to know one another, and an affection sprung up, the man lightly broached the subject to his unusual but legitimate nocturnal doings outside the city, and the sentinel decided to let him out of the gates, and even back in again, before the sun rose. Thus, the man's activities went unimpeded.

This story, replete with profound significance, reflects the need of the striving aspirant to go about practices of an esoteric nature free of impediments, and without interference from conventional quarters. The four sentinels at the four gates, in this regard, symbolize the four qualities the aspirant must cultivate in order to realize his consummate end in spiritual life.

The first, *Shanti,* is crucial to the spiritual seeker's journey. Nothing can be accomplished without peace of mind. Where restlessness and slothfulness are present, the path gets clouded, ones intentions become uncertain, and the desired outcome is hard of access. This coveted Peace is also the third level of the stages of higher knowledge just studied; it is one of the essential Qualifications for the *Brahman* state in the *Bhagavad Gita*; it is the *"Peace that passeth all understanding"* in Christianity, and the Peace of Allah upon the Prophet, Mohammed, in Islam. In Hinduism, the word, *"shanti,"* is uttered three times to bring peace to all three levels of existence — the imminent, the subtle, and the transcendent (see chart on page 231). As the Holy Mother, Sri Sarada Devi, has stated in recent times: *"You need peace of mind first and foremost, my child."* For all these reasons and more, the aspirant seeks it.

The second sentinel represents a huge step in the transcendental direction. Called *Atma-vichara,* the phrase means inquiry into the nature of the *Atman,* the immortal Self of mankind. It is what the *guru*/disciple relationship is all about, really, and its fulfillment vaults the spiritual seeker to a whole other level of mastery. In general, the inquiry proceeds with the question, "Who am I?" If the answer occurs, or is given, this does not end the process, however, as many beginning seekers might prematurely assume. Like a Zen koan, the question and the answer, both, have to be contemplated, and rolled over and over in the *sattvic* mind until maturation occurs, naturally.

What is more, and as has been mentioned earlier, it is unlikely that a seeker will come to know just "who" he is until he comes to know just "what" he is not. This will require a look into the ephemeral nature of the world, the cosmology of religion, the wisdom of philosophy, the practice of spirituality, and the science of the Self — a crucial fivefold requisite. A well-rounded soul will want for nothing less, anyway, the attainment of enlightenment notwithstanding.

As for Lord Vasishtha's essential teaching on this most important sentinel, he gives it to the young *Avatar,* Sri Ram, in the profound scripture, *Yoga* Vasishtha: *"Atma-vichara is the inquiry of the focused mind, usually after Shanti has been gained, into That which the seers indicate as the indivisible Self — not to be confused with the ego-self or with any level of matter, energy, or conceptualization. It consists of asking this question with the ultimate aim of finding out the origin of both the true Self and the apparent self. Atman or Ahamkara, the Indivisible Consciousness or the ego — which are you, my son? From time out of mind, immeasurably great beings have penetrated the shallows of relativity and then plumbed the depths of Reality with prime assistance stemming from this simple query. After the study of the Atmajnan scriptures, where fervid corroboration is gleaned, the pure intelligence that results from such an investigation then naturally arrives at this question of cosmic and transcendent proportions — 'Who am I?' By considering deeply this most profoundly simple question, the chains of birth and death get snapped in twain as their illusory cause becomes known. The light bestowed upon the seeking mind by Atma-vichara outshines all other lights, and disperses darkness like a thunderbolt on a stormy evening. Even the murky depths of mula-avidya, root ignorance, is dispelled by the coruscating light of Atma-vichara."* Glowing words like these should leave no doubt in the mind of those sedulous seekers who strive for mature liberation beyond mere salvation.

The third sentinel up for inspection is termed *Santosha*, and bespeaks of a mind that has become so used to peace that it is now fully rooted in it. Called contentment by the seers, it is certainly not a contentment that is satisfied by the paltry things of the world, or even the vaunted attainments of the intellect sought after by worldly souls. Being a spiritual quality, its aims tend towards concentration used for meditation rather than for rationalization. Therefore, the word "equanimity" has been used with reference to it. About it, Lord Vasishtha states: *"Santosha, the third Sentinel, is described by the seers as that subtle and unequivocal bliss which arises from the natural contact with objects that is simultaneously free from both attraction and aversion. That is, a yogi who perceives objects but does not long for them, perceives their facility but does not get excited by them, utilizes them but does not experience disappointment when they are absent, and remains free of them yet does not sport a callous indifference to them, that yogi is said to have mature Santosha, equal to firm self-settledness. When this contentedness ceases to merely visit the mind, and instead becomes its permanent fixture, then does that supreme state of Paravairagya, supreme detachment, have a chance of settling in. A yogi who possesses that insuperable condition cannot enjoy anything but Brahman from then on, and delights only in the gathering of and reveling in Atmajnan. Such a great tapasvin becomes superior to all other forms of life, terrestrial, heavenly, or cosmic. Such is the profound importance of attaining a mind that is content with what is, oh Ram, rather than with what can be or what is not."*

The final sentinel can easily be considered both the origin and the result of the other three, depending on any given soul's *karma* and inner journey. That is, the sacred boon of Holy Company, called *Sadhu-satsanga* in *Sanskrit*, comes to those who long for Truth and clarification around it, but, as many of the teaching systems on the charts in this book reflect, quite often the aspiring disciple has to qualify him or herself before such a boon really manifests. But whether holy company appears before or after the initial start is made, there is no doubt that it is both auspicious and accompanied by auspicious timing. As Lord Vasishtha tells the young and as yet veiled *Avatara* of the Age, Sri Ramchandra, in the revealed scripture, *Yoga* Vasishtha: *"The fourth and final Sentinel is Sadhu-satsanga, oh shining youth, known affectionately among the sincere seekers as holy company. Though it may be gained early on, even before the attainment of peace, contentment, and proper inquiry, it shows an equally excellent facility after the other sentinels have been embraced. For, my son, how much more timely the advent, how much more transformative the teachings, how much more appreciative the heart, when having achieved the ability to inquire into the nature of Reality and relativity with a settled mind, the aspirant looks again at the precious guru and finds all knowledge residing there! And in fact, along with the holy ones and their advice, when Sadhu-satsanga is duly comprehended, every aspect of existence becomes a teacher possessing a teaching. Just as earthly beings rush to the Ganges to free themselves of countless transgressions in its salubrious waters, spiritual beings make haste to immerse themselves thoroughly in the nectar-like flow of holy company which graciously ameliorates between the stunted worldly intellect and the capacious store of Atmajnan lying untapped in the human mind. Oh where, dear Ram, has that intense longing for holy company gone in our day and time? Why would humanity, due to its penchant for mundane thoughts and worldly activities alone, choose to lose such a precious commodity? The seers and sages, my son, would loose humanity from the bonds of suffering and confusion, as they are friendly to all living beings. Therefore, my spiritual son, the sedulous seeker ought to approach the wise ones, both before and after apt comprehension of the spiritual path has been gained. Ones spiritual lucubrations become enriched immeasurably in the elevated atmosphere of Sadhu-satsanga."*

In closing this most precious teaching of the seers, a gift bestowed upon all sincere aspirants after true spiritual existence, it can be said that the four sentinels at the gate all interconnect and interact is religious life. Referring back to our story of the man who befriended the guard at one of the gates to the city, the story goes on to tell how this guard told each of the other guards of the man's friendly nature, and soon he could pass out of any gate he wanted. It is in similar fashion that the aspirant, coming to possess even one of the sentinels, eventually accesses them all.

In keeping with teachings of the foundational nature from the ancient *Sankhya* Philosophy, it is time to introduce the fundamental teachings of this *darshana* using two of its salient systems. On the chart on the facing page is laid out the primary teaching of *Sankhya*, which was admired by all the other *darshanas* of India to such an extent that it was utilized as the springboard off of which they launched their own sempiternal systems. It is therefore that the Twenty-four Cosmic Principles of *Sankhya* represent the earliest and most complete form of "homework" ever accomplished by an early illumined seer.

The result of this gift of Lord Kapila was that seekers of Truth who followed after its inception in time were provided with a convenient list with which to plumb the broad and ever-changing surface of relative existence, but only after 1) knowing what it consisted of, essentially; and 2) knowing that it comprised all the elements of God with form. The formless Reality, *Brahman*, or *Purusha* in this context, was left as it is — eternally pure, unchanging, and perfect. Prior to this *sankhyic* rendering, practitioners were often unclear as to what they should be meditating upon, or, why what they were meditating on was not offering up its essential secrets.

Later, looking back on Lord Kapila's insightful work, the *Vedanta* would conclude this by stating: *"Brahman satya, jagad mithya — Brahman is Real, the world is unreal."* The *Vedantic sadhikas* would follow a similar and related statement to this effect, that being *"Nityanityavastuviveka — It is needful for Enlightenment to discriminate between what is Eternal and what is noneternal."* And as has been related several times in this book, it is a point of fact that this single missing element in a seeker's spiritual efforts is the cause for all manner of failings and falling back, even quitting the path and practice. The seers, then, highly advise the possession of this singular knowledge, and its acquisition is a matter of simple study and memorization, called *svadhyaya*. The chart outlines it for use in such study, later to be used in contemplation and meditation.

Basically, what is to be known in this teaching is that *Purusha*, the sentient Soul, and *Prakriti*, insentient matter, are different by nature. Proceeding from there, and still generally speaking, is that *Prakriti*, in proximity of *Purusha*, gives rise to eight cosmic principles that are Origins, and these give rise to sixteen others called Evolutes. These twenty-four constitute the "nonself," since the Self is never an evolute of anything else, and always the *"Conscious Spiritual Entity."*

Everything that is *sattvic*, balanced, and full of benign power, is contained in the *Mahat*, often referred to as "God's Mind." Being a *"vehicle for Purusha's consciousness,"* and *"a medium between the soul and nature,"* it also allows for the manifestation of all other intellects, which are like sparks emanating from a fire. The *Buddhi*, then, expressing through the intellects of human beings, has a direct connection inwardly to the "Great Mind," but also filters outwardly to help in the formation of the human ego. If this movement is kept in awareness, then inner communion can always take place, free of veils and complications, but if the connection is forgotten, the *buddhi* becomes dwarfed and fails to inform the ego of its higher and deeper associations. The result is an "egotistic" person, guilty of pride and arrogance, and who commits all manner of errors and digressions.

Cosmically speaking, the ego has three subdivisions of its own, reflecting the three gunas of *sattva, rajas*, and *tamas* (see charts on page 221/3), all manifesting via the mind mechanism, *Manas*. From *sattvic*, or balanced ego, spring the five cognitive and five active senses, which are imbued with some light of their own, emanating, of course, from the *Purusha*. From *tamasic* ego come the five subtle elements (*tanmatras*), and the five gross elements. The *rajasic* ego counterbalances these two sides of the ego, energizing them alternately.

The student of *Vedic* wisdom is encouraged to study the quintuplication process going on here, as it is key to the question of source and origin that is always cropping up in the aspiring human mind. And indeed, the student and practitioner of *Yoga* is asked to actually meditate upon these twenty-four Cosmic Principles (as *alambanas*), from outside in, then inside out, in what is called a

The Twenty-Four Cosmic Principles of Samkhya Philosophy

"There are two eternally-existing principles...."   Lord Kapila

A) Purusha — Sentient Soul, The Self
(Conscious Spiritual Entity; Ishvara; Brahma-Vishnu-Shiva)

B) Prakriti — Insentient Nature, the Nonself
(Unconscious Material-energy; Unmanifested Nature; Intangible Matter)

** Prakriti consists of Three Gunas in Equilibrium:

Sattva: luminosity, purity, buoyancy, harmony — it produces pleasure/happiness

Rajas: activity, energy, movement — it produces pain

Tamas: dullness, inertia, darkness, stasis — it produces stupor

"Like a magnet, Prakriti attaches itself to Purusha and receives Its conscious rays."   Kapila

- -

1. Mahat— Cosmic Mind
(Initial disequilibrium, most subtle, most sattvic, most pure)

" The Mahat is a vehicle for the Purusha's consciousness, and a medium between soul and nature. A small portion of It becomes the individual buddhi of man."   Lord Kapila

The Eight Origins: 1-3, & 15-19	2. Buddhi — Intellect *(Faculty of discrimination, intelligence)*	The 16 Evolutes 4-14, & 20-24

3. Ahamkara — Ego
(The "I"-maker, sense of separate self, beginning of name and form)

Sattvic Ahamkara ←——→ Rajas ←——→ Tamasic Ahamkara

4. Manas — Mind

Jnanendriyas — 5 Cognitive Senses
5. Shravenindriya — Hearing (sound)
6. Sparshendriya — Feeling (touch)
7. Chakshurindriya — Seeing (form)
8. Rasanendriya — Tasting (taste)
9. Ghranendriya — Smelling (smell)

Tanmatras — 5 Subtle Elements
15. Shabda — Audibility
16. Sparsha — Tangibility
17. Rupa — Visibility
18. Rasa — Flavor
19. Gandha — Odor

Karmendriyas — 5 Active Senses
10. Vagendriya — Speaking (speaking)
11. Hastendriya — Handling (acting)
12. Padendriya — Locomotion (moving)
13. Upasthendriya — Procreating (sexual)
14. Payuindriya — Excreting (eliminating)

Panchamahabhutas — 5 Elements
20. Vyoma — Ether
21. Marut — Air
22. Teja — Fire
23. Ap — Water
24. Ksiti — Earth

"The twenty-three evolutes are the non-self; the Purusha alone is the Self. This realization eradicates pain permanently and totally."   Lord Kapila

"chain of cause and effect," in order to find the soul's way back to Nondual Reality. This inner journey and its intention is inferred by Lord Kapila's final quote on the chart: *"The Twenty-four evolutes are the nonself; the Purusha alone is the Self. This realization eradicates pain permanently and totally."*

To put a final stamp of authority on India's philosophical origins, and to drive a final nail into the coffin of human ignorance as well, *Sankhya* offers a profound and unequivocal list of tenets for the seeker's contemplation. These ten laws of the spiritual cosmos ring of mature truth, and lay out and outline all the dynamics that any authentic cosmology should possess. It all begins with the declaration of the undeniable existence of a supreme spiritual entity which is Existence Itself. *Sankhya* does not concern itself with describing what That is in any great detail. Its appeal, nondualistically, is that it is the Self of mankind, thereby removing any inclination of the mind to think in terms of a God that is distant or different than the Soul of man. As Shankara has written, *"Those who think that there is any real distinction between man and God, creature and Creator, nature and Spirit, are laboring under mental delusion."* India's philosophical stance has always been rooted in Nonduality, *Advaita*, and its cosmological and religious steps have always followed suit. The final chapter of this book will focus on that Reality.

The word *Purusha* is defined as *"Indweller in the City,"* what Sri Krishna and others speak of as a *"city of nine gates,"* referring to the senses (two nostrils, two eyes, two ears, one mouth, and the procreative and evacuative openings) through which Consciousness sports and emanates. That it moves and sports through the cosmic mechanisms never belies or changes the fact of its immovable and immutable status. Consciousness is static, and blissful; nature is its co-dependent, dynamic offshoot. Therefore, and on this unimpeachable maxim, the first two tenets of *Sankhya* philosophy are set down firmly.

Further, the third and fourth tenets of *Sankhya* explain the relationship perfectly. *Purusha* is master; *Prakriti*, nature, is the bond slave. If this relationship gets reversed then there is ensuing confusion, a host of problems — *maya*. In other words, *Prakriti* does not exist to enslave the Soul, but to serve it. Whenever one sees balance and harmony in the world, in people, and between mankind and nature, what is being seen is adherence to this set of laws. The server and the served are like the knower and the known. Nothing should be allowed to interfere with the Lord's play.

In case any doubt or second thought comes to the mind, always striving to find its place in a peaceful resolution, the fifth cosmic law of *Sankhya* puts those to rest. The declaration is that the *Purusha* is distinct from all that proceeds from nature. A well-lived and constantly activated spiritual practice will be the defining measure for acceptance of this conclusion, especially where meditation is concerned. The practitioner must 1) meditate; 2) do the separation process in the mind; and 3) come to rest in the *Purusha* and feel Its infinite and eternal peace and bliss. Nothing in the realm of evolutes will ever attract it again, which means that the seer is free to visit the worlds of name and form without risking that lamentable forgetfulness of Reality that is the cause of all suffering.

Tenet number six is actually the result of such long-lived and consummate meditative practice. When the practitioner finds that equipoise and stability outreach chaos and activity, a firm abidance in the mode of actionlessness occurs. Even when action is accomplished by the seer, it is done so in a mode of equanimity. No *karma* accrues from it (see charts on page 210 & 213). Only Peace abides. And, actually, it is the nature of *Purusha* to remain silent and still; the tendency towards activity requires embodiment, and is thus often ill-considered.

The seventh and eight tenet of *Sankhya* are pure gold in the realm of philosophy, especially where reasons or a purpose for life are required by the human mind. In a simple two-sided statement, Lord Kapila merely admits to the obvious — that the Soul is prone towards uniting with that which it produces, but that it also feels the need, hopefully in due time, of separating from its own projection as well. The cosmic and *karmic* chain of cause and effect now has its justification. Even then, this does not stop certain illumined souls from ending the play of embodiment and its activity altogether, and entering into Formless Reality. As Ramprasad, the poet-saint of India, sings: *"Cherish no hope for this poet of the Mother. I am gone, and gone forever!"*

The Ten Fundamental  of Sankhya

TENETS

"Pra-sankhyana, introspective discrimination between the spiritual Self and subtle material energy and its evolutes, eliminates pain and brings about enlightenment. Thus, Sankhya insists that all the aspects of the non-self (Prakriti) be fully enumerated and carefully studied in order to bring about clarification of this essential distinction." Tattva Samasa Sutras

Sankhya's Purusha is:

- ❆ The Reality underlying all Phenomena
- ❆ Free of Time, Space, and Causality
- ❆ Shuddhabuddhamukta — Pure, Conscious, and Free
- ❆ The Atman of Vedanta, but Multifarious
- ❆ Souls in Nontheistic Sankhya, but Souls & God in Theistic Sankhya

Sankhya's Prakriti is:

- ❆ Insentient Material-Energy Principle
- ❆ The Origin of all Phenomena
- ❆ Inherently Intangible, but becomes Tangible later via Its Evolutes
- ❆ Made of the 3 Gunas in Equilibrium
- ❆ Apparently Sentient due to Attaching to Purusha & Assuming Its Presence

The Dasamulika Arthas
Ten Tenets of Sankhya

1) There exists a conscious, sentient Self — Purusha.

2) There is an insentient, unmanifest cause — Prakriti.

3) The Purusha exists for no other entity.

4) Matter exists to serve Purusha.

5) Purusha is distinct from Prakriti and Its evolutes.

6) The Purusha is not an agent of action.

7) Union of Prakriti with Purusha occurs.

8) Separation of Prakriti from Purusha occurs.

9) There are many conscious Purushas.

10) After self-realization, the body may continue to exist via the momentum of its own laws.

The ninth tenet of *Sankhya* constitutes what may be called a philosophical "rub" in the eyes of other systems of India, particularly the explicitly nondual ones. With the principle of Oneness a given, why would the premise of "many conscious Purushas" be accepted, or even considered? But it is quite possible that the statement was meant to apply only at the level of conscious embodiment, where it is evident that many illumined souls can and do live in harmony together on the earth plane, each one knowing itself fully and being ever united in Oneness. After all, many clouds exist in one sky, and many waves sport and play on the surface of one vast ocean. The phenomenon of separation as an appearance only, nonactual, still remains the highest law. Let divinity have its rule on all levels, says the *Sankhya* philosopher. Oneness never is, nor can be, affected in the least.

The final and tenth tenet of *Sankhya* may just infer or suggest the first appearance of the *Jivanmukti* ideal in Indian philosophy. Since the distinction between Soul and Nature has been declared by *Sankhya*, then the body, being of Nature, must live or die according to the laws of *karma* and Nature. The self-realized *Purusha* neither lives nor dies, having never been born in the first place. This is the perspective of the *Jivanmukta,* the "living liberated Soul." To It, the cosmic laws are wondrous, inspiring, the keepers of order on all relative planes of existence. Besides, they have all been dictated by the *Purusha* Itself. Why would God ever transgress His own laws? If He did, there would be hell to pay.

As an example of the possibility for the *Purusha* to turn the relationship with Nature into a kind of hell, Lord Kapila gives the *Sankhya* teaching on the Five Kinds of Minds and Intellects in the realm of action. For the worldly soul, the problem lies in the realm of the five senses and their interaction with the physical objects they covet and desire. For the aspiring soul, especially in the beginning stages of practice, the problem falls more in the mind, intellect, ego complex. Whatever the case may be, the teaching on the Five Types of Mind, on the chart at the right, covers it all.

First, there is the balanced mind, inclined towards the *dharma*, towards amelioration and concrescence, wanting the highest good for all living beings. Following this, there is the mind inclined towards evil acts. Then, there is the mind that is so slothful it does not know the difference between good and evil, and just acts indiscriminately out of base ignorance. But these three do not cover the spectrum well enough for Lord Kapila. He cites a fourth and fifth type of mind that do action in ignorance. The phrases, "acts of good stupefaction" and "acts of bad stupefaction" explain this phenomenon in part.

If one examines living beings in this day and age, one will not have far to look to come upon examples of these aforementioned tendencies. Doers of "good" are everywhere, but whether these beings are aware of their own intentions or not is another matter, what to speak of the results of their respective activities. These results, or *karma*, as it is called, are really the measure for an act or series of actions. For instance, there is the case of the man who damns up a stream on the back of his property so that his children can have a swimming hole, but downstream he leaves people suffering from thirst. And what if some of these die? Certainly there is *karma* to pay. And when this *karma* comes back to the man, he being unaware of its cause, the result is a debilitating repercussion that confuses the mind, since it is unaware of its own involvement in the cause of suffering. This is an example of an act of good stupefaction. The world is full of beings perpetrating these kinds of acts, and suffering unknowingly as a result. What is worse is that the soul has caused suffering to others. Acts of bad stupefaction are more obvious, caused by the mind that should know better, but that has not learned even the basic moral principles through which to conduct action and relations.

On the bottom half of the chart on the facing page is an outline that pertains more to the intellectual body of mankind that explains unrefined human nature and its often mindless resistance to positive change and transformation. What Lord Kapila calls forward with regards to the mixed nature of intellectually motivated action is very helpful to know. It also defines the difference between pure intellect and impure intellect. The latter is tainted by obsession, pride, sense of agency, desire, sense indulgence, and manipulative tendencies. If this list is considered, and purification is attained, qualities such as resolve, faith, and a yearning for spiritual life take hold. Even

THE FIVE TYPES OF MINDS & INTELLECTS IN ACTION

Pancha Karmatmanah: The Five Types of Minds

1. **Vaikarika** —
Sattvic mind/ego inclined to
do good actions

Taijasa —
Rajasic mind/ego inclined
towards evil actions

Bhutadi —
Tamasic mind/ego
performing acts of stupefaction

4. **Bhutadi-sanumana**
Performing acts of
good stupefaction

Bhutadi-niranumana
Performing acts of
bad stupefaction

Pancha abhi-buddhayah
Five Activities of the Intellect

Abhibhuta — Obsessive Agency
"I must do."

Adhimana — Prideful Agency
"I will do."

Iccha — Willful Agency
"I will fulfill my desires."

Kartavyata — Sense-indulgence
"I will satisfy my senses."

Kriya — Sense manipulation
"I will use my senses."

Pancha karma-yonayah
Five Causes & Results of Action

Dhriti — Resolution of mind,
speech, and action.

Shraddha — Inclinations of faith,
such as generosity and fealty.

Sukha — Actions taken with
expectation of reward and
pleasure.

Avividhisha — Tendency in action
that blocks desire for knowledge.

Vividhisha — Tendency to know
matters pertaining to spirituality.

"There are some 28 kinds of mental and intellectual incapacities, like the mind's attachments and the intellect's false views. If one follows a logical mental discipline as told by the scriptures and transmitted by the preceptor, then all of these can be eliminated. Knowing it all, one fulfills oneself. Then one is not overcome by the three types of pain."   Lord Kapila

then, the onslaught of pleasure-seeking, and all that frustrates it, has to be avoided, or at least curtailed. According to Lord Kapila, however, *"If one follows a logical mental discipline as told by the scriptures and transmitted by the preceptor, then all these impediments can be eliminated."* Then, the three types of pain can be transcended (see chart on page 231).

Pursuing this practical approach to purification via practices of ancient and noble heritage, the chart on the facing page places this teaching under study under the scope of incitement to action. For, if one is to know what causes *karmic* repercussions, one should look into the act itself, and prior to that, what incited one to action. The teaching relates the truth about the precarious nature of embodiment overall, for the soul has taken on more than just an intellect; it has also inherited a body, ten senses, and the life force (*prana*) that impels them all. Sri Krishna puts this all in terms of the three kinds of action, namely *nishtam, mishtram,* and *anishtam.* The word, nishtam, infers works done with a concentrated and one-pointed mind that attenuates *karma* as it begins to accrue. Regarding fruits of action, it is the best and highest, the only better being complete renunciation of fruits in the midst of the field and process of action.

But it is the incitements to action that we want to focus on here. The bottom half of the chart lists five of these. The fifth, *daiva,* the Presiding Deity, is the most crucial, for without its participation, or overseership, the other four go awry. With the Presiding Deity in charge, held in mind and heart daily, the body, otherwise stodgy and unresponsive, becomes a vehicle for *dharma* and the purified host for the divinity in mankind. Devoid of this indwelling observer, the ten senses, called *indriyas,* meaning "little gods," separate and cause havoc with their respective desires and competing objectives. The life force, *prana,* if it is not under control of this inner ruler, fastens upon experiences and fuels habitual obsession with them.

The matter of conducting activity on earth, in the body, in consciousness, then, is a very sensitive one, even for the advanced soul. For there is no doubt of the divine potential of mankind. Left undisturbed and unperturbed by *mayic* overlays and recurring *karmas,* he is nothing less than the Knower. It is just that he must maintain in mind and memory the distinction between true knowledge and false or mixed knowledge. He must also seek what is to be known, and avoid what is only fit to be renounced. To aid in this mission, the next chart, pictured on page 357, citing the Thirty-Two Points of the Immortal *Dharma,* is most helpful of study.

As has been mentioned in the early chapters of this book, India's *Sanatana Dharma* — The Eternal Religion — is replete with attributes, qualities, virtues, practices, axioms, and principles, that leave no doubt in a seeker's mind as to its sterling character and transformative abilities. On the battlefield of Kurukshetra, Sri Krishna, the *Avatar* of the Age, transmitted the essentials of this exceptional pathway to His beloved disciple, Arjuna. From basic preliminaries and overall observances, to intermediate practices, on to advanced ways of abidance, the copious list is a perfect example of how to live a spiritual life. Impediments to spiritual life are not even considered here. It is as if they have no purchase point in the mind that only concentrates on growth and perfection, practicing the art of *"watering the flowers and not the weeds."*

These many flowers, as far as Mother India is concerned, are most often seen to be growing in the fertile soil of nonviolence. Thus, the first point listed on the chart on page 357 is *Advesta,* non-hating, and so as to communicate a fuller picture, it is coupled with *maitrah,* friendliness. Yet, if we look further, this friendliness is founded in enlightened nonattachment, and is unconcerned yet compassionate. Therefore, the first five points of the Immortal *Dharma* relate a picture of well-rounded and balanced mind and behavior. In ordinary persons, even those who follow an ethical code of behavior, it is rare if they possess all five of these qualities, what to speak of effectively synchronizing them in any given relationship or situation. It is more likely that any given four of the five will simply "abandon ship" when challenging life situations surface.

But the follower of the Immortal *Dharma* is expert, *daksha* (see chart on page 59). He has undergone all of his experiences with a balanced mind tempered by *sadhana,* facing and managing the difficult ones and remaining equal during the positive ones. Nonreactivity has been his watch-

THE THREEFOLD FRUITS, THREEFOLD CAUSES, AND FIVE INCITEMENTS TO ACTION IN THE GITA

"Relinquishing the fruits of action, not action itself, is considered authentic renunciation. Do not avoid disagreeable work, then, or seek only agreeable work. Accomplish all work with a balanced and sattvic mind." Sri Krishna

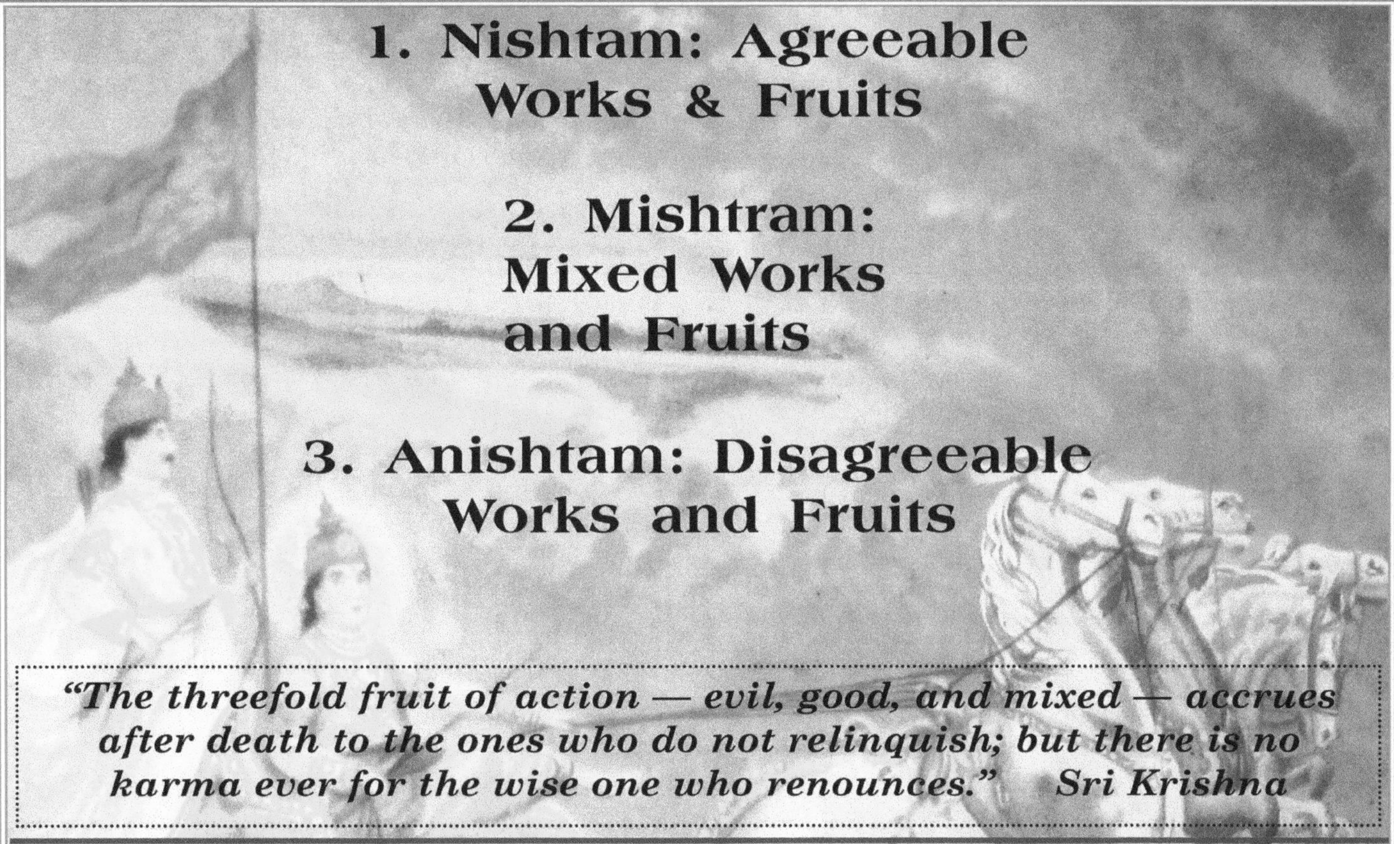

1. Nishtam: Agreeable Works & Fruits

2. Mishtram: Mixed Works and Fruits

3. Anishtam: Disagreeable Works and Fruits

"The threefold fruit of action — evil, good, and mixed — accrues after death to the ones who do not relinquish; but there is no karma ever for the wise one who renounces." Sri Krishna

The Five Incitements to Action

Adhisthanam — The Body/Firm Seat
Karta — The Doer, or Agent
Karanam — The Ten Senses
Prtak Chestah — The Life Functions
Daiva — The Presiding Deity

"Whatever action a man performs, with body, speech, or mind, right or wrong, these five are the causes."

"A parallel can be drawn between a car and a human being. The body is like the factory; the agent is the proprietor; the wheels, steering wheel, brakes, clutch, and gearbox are the five senses; petrol is the functioning life-force. The driver is the ego, no doubt, but the Jivatman is the presiding deity."
Swami Chidbhavananda

The Threefold Causes of Action

Jnanam — Knowledge
Jneyam — The Knowable
Parijnata — The Knower

"Whosoever looks upon the Self as the agent, his mind is perverse and he sees not."

word, which gets reflected in the next four points under study — silence, egolessness, purity, and steady-mindedness.

Silence, *mauna,* is itself an austerity of great merit. It tunes the mind into the guidance of the inner voice while simultaneously short-circuiting the base ego's otherwise intrusive interference. Thereafter, *nirmamo,* egolessness, has a chance to root and effloresce, and the aspirant experiences that expansive feeling of indwelling spirituality that causes the fugacious games of the meandering ego to seem wholly undesirable. Purified of the unripe ego's unsavory influence, the mind feels pure for the first time, and that results in the implementation of one of Sri Krishna's favorite spiritual qualities, *sthiramatih,* steady-mindedness. It is thus that the second set of five transforming points of the immortal *dharma* work in harmony to clear the mind-field for further subtle improvements.

Ever full of devotion, content and untroubled, free of desires and thus easily self-controlled, these next five *dharmic* qualities conduce to make one *"me priyah narah — dear to the Lord."* It is rare to see a devotee in this day and time, face flushed with exuberance, words effusive with love, actions selfless and heartfelt — where do we find such a person? All seem sterile, despondent, even sick, as they move about the world. Maybe it is that this unbridled devotion actually invites contentment, while turning the tendency to fulfill personal desires into the preferred ability to control the self. Here we are speaking of spiritual qualities and their superiority. But again, where do we see them in a wayward world amongst people who seek only ego-gratification via inferior modes. Those who are dear to God, then, are luminaries unto themselves, and if one can befriend them, life vibrates with a new and fresh intensity.

Having scrutinized, briefly, the first sixteen of these points of *dharmic* life, all pictured in the circles on the chart on the facing page, we now come to a list of attributes that would attract any sincere seeker, and which easily outstrip the rules and commandments of any moral or ethical system. To be free of attachment heads the list, for if one has freedom, all that is conventional, soporific, and procrustean, never touches the soul. And in fact, spiritual freedom is what the soul is heading for, and what it desires more than anything else, knowingly or unknowingly. From the platform of freedom, it is not so much that anything good is possible, it is more that everything good is probable. Much more on true freedom will be stated in the final chapter of this book.

The next four points are all about same-sightedness, the nonreactivity mentioned above. The *dharmic* soul is the same in censure and praise, same to friend and foe, the same in honor and dishonor, and the same in pleasure or in pain. He is also *"samah sita ushna sukha duhkheshu,"* the same in heat and cold, listed later. Though sounding simple, the actual practice and establishment of these points are difficult indeed, what to speak of their mastery. But the next point summates this fourfold practice, and allows for its implementation. Thus it is, that Sri Krishna tells Arjuna, *"Be content with anything."* How is this possible? The question is poorly framed. It is rather that there is no other option. Whatever occurs, then, the devotee is prepared for, and if he is not, his natural contentment and even-mindedness will kick in spontaneously. For, he knows that there is nothing worth the loss of his peace of mind.

And this is the next point worthy of contemplation. It is not only the aspirant's heart that has become devoted, his mind and intellect have followed suit. This is what the seers call *medhakendra,* the mind that has taken counsel of the heart. It is now a "winged heart," able to soar in rapt flight into the highest reaches of wisdom. At this juncture, nothing can pull it down.

Honeyed words falling from divine lips come next: *"Yasman no'dvijate, loko lokan no'dvijate"* means *"....whom the world cannot afflict, and who does not afflict the world."* Being based in *ahimsa,* nonviolence, this is more than just nonhating; it is not even just carefulness or sensitivity around committing no trespass against others. It is, rather, pure knowledge, based in renunciation, that the world is essentially unreal, ultimately insubstantial. How can the world afflict, or be afflicted, in any actual way, then? It is empty, not only of ultimate Reality and substance, but of the ability to fulfill. That is why the advanced soul renounces it, as is indicated on the chart. These are points twenty-five and twenty-seven. Number twenty-eight, what *Vedanta* calls *titiksha,* forbearance in heat

Thirty-Two Points of the Immortal Dharma

Advesta
not hating

Maitrah
friendly

Aniketah
unattached to location

Sangavivarjitah --
free of all attachment

Tulya ninda stutir --
same in censure & praise

Karunah
compassionate

Udasinah
unconcerned

Samah satrau cha mitre --
same to friend & foe

Dakshah
expert

Mauni
silent

Mana apamanayoh --
same in honor / dishonor

Nirmamo
egoless

Samushtah yenakenachit --
content with anything

Sthiramatih
steady-minded

Suchih
pure

Mayi arpita mano buddhih --
devout mind/intellect

Yasman no' dvijate --
who does not afflict the world

Sama duhkha-suhkha --
same in pleasure & pain

Bhaktiman
full of devotion

Gatavyathah
untroubled

Me
priyah narah
dear to God

Samtustah
content

Sarva arambha parityagi --
renounced in all actions

Yatatma
self-controlled

Anapekshah
desireless

Loko lokan no' dvijate --
whom the world cannot afflict

Shubha-ashubha parityagi --
renounced of good & evil

Satatam -- steady in meditation

Drdha nishchayah -- firmly resolved

Samah sita ushna sukha duhkheshu --
same in heat & cold, pleasure & pain

Harsha-amarsha-bhaya udvegaih muktih -- completely free of joy, envy, fear & anxiety

Na hrshyati na dvesti na sochati na kankshati -- neither rejoices, hates, grieves, desires

"They who follow this immortal dharma of Mine, endued with shraddha, looking upon Me as the Supreme Goal, and devoted, they are exceedingly dear to Me." Sri Krishna

and cold, has been listed above.

Of the final four points, *"satatam, steady in meditation,"* may well be the highest and best, for it is through this that the soul can enter nonduality, or *samadhi*. But real meditation is not possible without the acquisition of many of the points listed previously. And in fact, it is usually the last *yoga* to be conquered and attained. In the meantime, and while it is being practiced in the form of the ability to concentrate, the soul must be resolved in its pursuit. The last two points of the Immortal *Dharma* reflect the breadth and capaciousness that the soul will have to attain, where freedom from envy, fear, and anxiety is duly gained, but also, strangely enough, freedom from excessive joy as well. The balanced mind of the aspirant, combined with knowledge of the transitory nature of life, body, and the world, must prevail in the end. Hatred, grief, and desire are not just negative in nature, but wholly empty. Knowing this, it is much easier to renounce them and live in the Eternal *Dharma* forever. The seers have accomplished this; the fortunate aspirant is on the path; others only suffer.

The Thirty-Two Points of the Immortal *Dharma* is certainly counted among India's great cosmological and philosophical systems On equal footing with it comes another radiant gem in the Divine Mother's wisdom crest, that being the Thirty-Six Cosmic Principles of *Shaivism*. Basing its wisdom tier upon Lord Kapila's Twenty-Four Cosmic Principles (see chart on page 349), as so many *darshanas* have, Shaivism adds an upper twelve, sorely needed and greatly appreciated. For, what lies beyond the *Purusha* and its servant, *Prakriti*, forms a region so subtle that little has ever been said or written about it; it defines the term, "esoteric." Yet, the aspirant after truth will need to plumb the depths of some of these subtle and causal principles in meditation to reach consummate realization. Thus, the list of these upper twelve *"spandas,"* or vibrational spheres, is given. The reader is also invited to refer to the chart on the following page, 360, for additional visual benefit.

Since the Twenty-Four Principles have already been scrutinized, we will begin our journey of the spiritual realms within with a look at its mixed *tattvas*. Along with everything, from *Purusha* on down to the element, earth, the principles of *Kala, Kalas,* and *Niyati* are also of mixed origin and content. These are regions of cosmic laws that an have existence all their own, with deities presiding over them. If even the curious person has ever wondered about the origin and nature of time, here is the explanation from the *Shaivite* tradition — those who worship Lord *Siva*, the God of Wisdom.

Kala means time, and *Kalas* refers to the passage of time in vast cycles (see chart on page 39). This force, this purveyor of cosmic cycles, moves and affects everybody and everything, from the gods on through to man, animals, insects, and plant life. Thus, *Kala* is also a pathway which leads living beings towards union with their true nature (see chart on page 595), and *Kalas*, representing phases of time, refers to those pathways (some sixteen of them) that provide passage to union.

Niyati, a related *tattva*, shown in close proximity on the chart on page 359, enters here. It is, to borrow an English term and concept, predestination. The *Tantric*ists call it *"the power that determines the cause and effect relationship."* Like its two associates, it is a mixed *tattva*, pure yet impure. On the positive side, it contributes highly to the overall order of laws, beings, and things as they relate to one another, while on the negative side it limits the soul *(Purusha)* by blinding it to its own power of all-pervasiveness *(sarva vyakatva shakti)*. Jumping ahead a little, all three of these mixed *tattvas* connect upwardly (inwardly) to the pure *tattvas* of *Bindu* and *Sadakhya,* which is primarily a connection with subtle sound as the source of vibration. More on this will come as we proceed.

Among other mixed principles (*tattvas*) on the internal field of consciousness is *Vidya*. *Vidya* means knowledge, but here it is conditioned knowledge — not so conditioned as knowledge on earth, i.e., mental, secular, intellectual, etc., but still somewhat removed from its higher source, *Shuddha Vidya*, its connecting point. *Vidya* is really *Siva's* power of omniscience in a limited form, pertinent to the individualized self. The example utilized by *tantric* adepts is that of a lamp whose light is stifled all around its rim except for a single ray that emanates from it. Without it, no enjoyment of the world would be possible, yet this allowance of enjoyment simultaneously veils the higher bliss of the *Purusha*. It is this *tattva* that manifests as intuition in the human mind, and which beings then mistake for "God's voice." It is quite likely, then, that when *vidya* operates in the mind, he/she is get-

The Thirty-Six Cosmic Principles of Shaivism

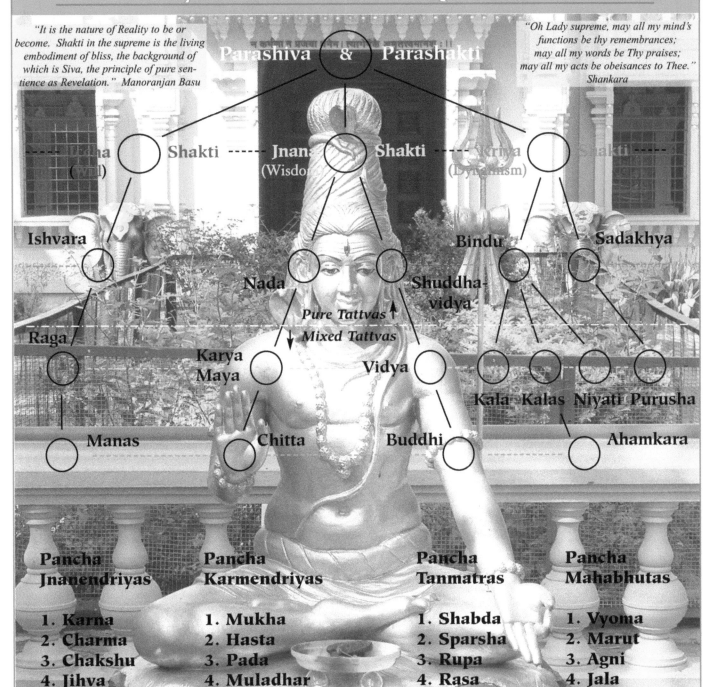

"It is the nature of Reality to be or become. Shakti in the supreme is the living embodiment of bliss, the background of which is Siva, the principle of pure sentience as Revelation." Manoranjan Basu

"Oh Lady supreme, may all my mind's functions be thy remembrances; may all my words be Thy praises; may all my acts be obeisances to Thee." Shankara

Parashiva & Parashakti

Iccha Shakti (Will) ----- Jnana Shakti (Wisdom) ----- Shakti ----- Kriya Shakti (Dynamism)

Ishvara

Bindu   Sadakhya

Nada   Shuddha-vidya

Pure Tattvas ↑
↓ Mixed Tattvas

Raga

Karya Maya   Vidya

Kala Kalas Niyati Purusha

Manas   Chitta   Buddhi   Ahamkara

Pancha Jnanendriyas	Pancha Karmendriyas	Pancha Tanmatras	Pancha Mahabhutas
1. Karna	1. Mukha	1. Shabda	1. Vyoma
2. Charma	2. Hasta	2. Sparsha	2. Marut
3. Chakshu	3. Pada	3. Rupa	3. Agni
4. Jihva	4. Muladhar	4. Rasa	4. Jala
5. Nasika	5. Jananedriya	5. Gandha	5. Prthivi

*Mantranam jyabhuta tu ya smrta shaktiruttama
tatha hina varatyphenisalatah saradabhravat.
Tantra Sadbhava*

"Tattvas are Cosmic Principles which denote different grades of the universe or universes. Experience, according to the Tantras, consists of bhuvanas (universes) and planes of life and consciousness made up of tattvas. In the Tantras thirty-six tattvas are recognized. In the ultimate analysis these tattvas owe their origin to the Supreme Locus wherein lies Siva as Existence and Shakti as Consciousness, existing in perfect union or non-separateness (abhinabhava)." Sri Manoranjan Basu

"She who is known by the seers to be the imperishable Shakti is the soul of all mantras. Without Her, oh fair one, all the tattvas are as useful as clouds with no rain. She is the luminous being of perfect I-consciousness inherent in the multitudes of words, the secret of all mantras, and whose essence consists of the highest nondualism. Oh Goddess, from Lord Brahma out to the earth you pervade everything as matrka, full of the luster of Parahanta, the creative power of Paramasiva."

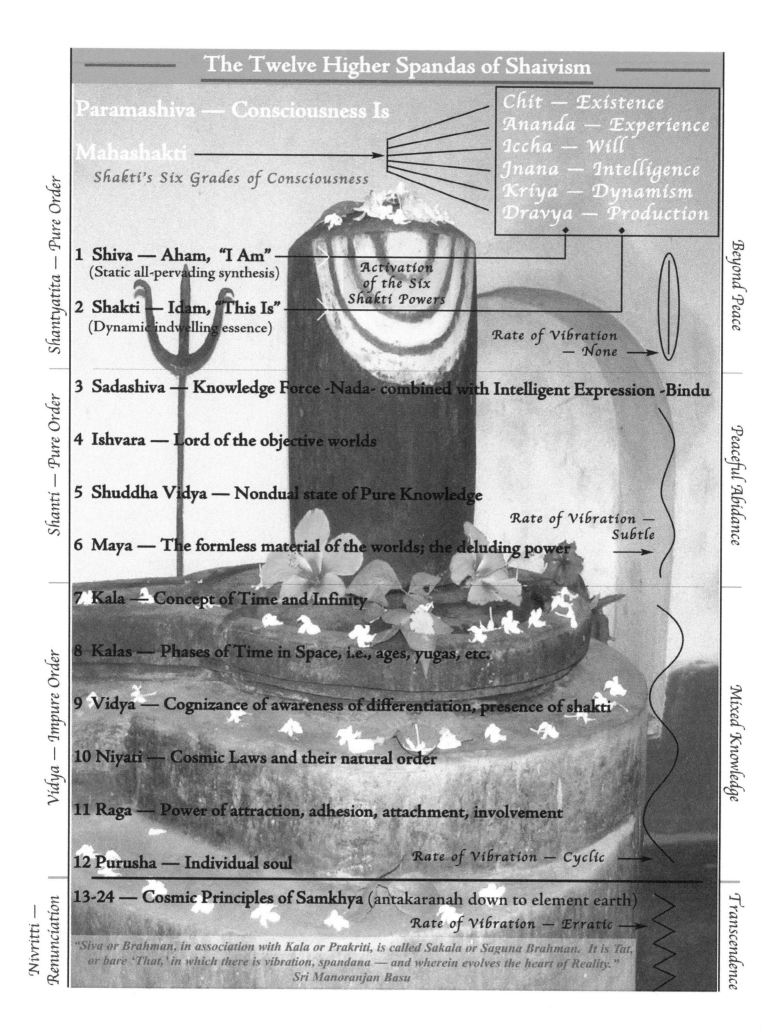

The Twelve Higher Spandas of Shaivism

Paramashiva — Consciousness Is

Mahashakti

Shakti's Six Grades of Consciousness

Chit — Existence
Ananda — Experience
Iccha — Will
Jnana — Intelligence
Kriya — Dynamism
Dravya — Production

Activation of the Six Shakti Powers

1 Shiva — Aham, "I Am"
(Static all-pervading synthesis)

2 Shakti — Idam, "This Is"
(Dynamic indwelling essence)

Rate of Vibration — None

3 Sadashiva — Knowledge Force -Nada- combined with Intelligent Expression -Bindu

4 Ishvara — Lord of the objective worlds

5 Shuddha Vidya — Nondual state of Pure Knowledge

Rate of Vibration — Subtle

6 Maya — The formless material of the worlds; the deluding power

7 Kala — Concept of Time and Infinity

8 Kalas — Phases of Time in Space, i.e., ages, yugas, etc.

9 Vidya — Cognizance of awareness of differentiation, presence of shakti

10 Niyati — Cosmic Laws and their natural order

11 Raga — Power of attraction, adhesion, attachment, involvement

12 Purusha — Individual soul

Rate of Vibration — Cyclic

13-24 — Cosmic Principles of Samkhya (antakaranah down to element earth)

Rate of Vibration — Erratic

Shantyatita — Pure Order

Shanti — Pure Order

Vidya — Impure Order

Nivritti — Renunciation

Beyond Peace

Peaceful Abidance

Mixed Knowledge

Transcendence

"Siva or Brahman, in association with Kala or Prakriti, is called Sakala or Saguna Brahman. It is Tat, or bare 'That,' in which there is vibration, spandana — and wherein evolves the heart of Reality."
Sri Manoranjan Basu

ting in touch with a mere intuition rather than getting in touch with the Higher Self. The reader will notice that this relatively stunted or mixed knowledge is connected upwardly to pure Wisdom, and then to an important aspect of the Mother of Wisdom Herself — *Jnana Shakti*.

Karya Maya comes next in ascending order in the chart on page 359, at least according to this lineage of *Shaivism* (the chart on page 360 shows a somewhat different list of *tattvas*). It is a subdivision of *Maya* overall, and its power provides beings with everything from the ability of comprehension, to worlds, bodies, and objects. In the *Shaivite* system represented by the chart on the facing page at the left, which has a slightly different content and order, *Karya* it is not listed, but can considered a part of the *Maya tattva*. It is one of three forms of *maya*, arranged as pure, pure/impure, and impure. We must remember that purity and impurity in *Vedic* philosophy does not strictly mean morally pure or impure, but rather farther from or nearer to the Source. (see chart on page 119).

Raga is the next *tattva* listed on the chart on page 359. It appears as well on the chart on the facing page. It is the power of attraction, in general, and overall. As a cosmic principle tending inwards, it helps beings know and love through the incentive it provides. Its outward influence veils natural renunciation and thus lends towards attachment to objects of pleasure. *Raga's* influence is why many souls chase after the nominal things of the world while simultaneously turning their backs on religion, tradition, wise counsel, and other beneficial boons. If this kind of untoward behavior is rejected and controlled, *Raga* then becomes the quality of contentment and fulfillment for the aspirant, leading to the maturation of renunciation.

In the pure atmosphere of *shuddha tattvas* lie *Sadakhya*, *Bindu*, and *Nada*, already mentioned earlier. All three are intrinsically connected to the primal vibration of *AUM*, the first vibration from which all of creation has emanated. The esoteric *Tantric* teaching of *Sristi Rahasya*, the Secret of Creation, has much to do with *Nada* and *Bindu* (see chart on page 463), the first representing the initial manifestation of the unmanifest *Paramasiva*, and the second representing that point of Light from which all bursts into expression. This is the effect of the proximity of *Siva* and *Shakti* out of which these cosmic principles are all emerging, and into which they all finally merge.

Sadakhya's great role in conjunction with the primal sound vibration is its ordering of six fundamental pathways to highest wisdom, or *Brahmajnana*. They are: *Kala* (aspects); *Tattva* (categories); *Bhuvana* (regions/lokas); *Varna* (letters); *Pada* (words); and *Mantra* (utterances). This particular aspect of *Tantra* is deeply profound, and generally unstudied by the masses.

Shuddha Vidya is a nondual state of pure knowledge. Lying close to *Ishvara*, and also closely connected into the *Jnana Shakti* Herself, it is the Light of Intelligence that shines off of the Divine Couple, *Siva* and *Shakti*. Many illumined beings inhabit this Light, which, besides possessing qualities of nondual perception, is also equal to the highest Bliss.

The import of *Ishvara/Sadasiva*, already indicated in previous chapters, and up for further mention in forthcoming chapters, cannot be overstated (see chart on page 467). All the deities, their respective knowledge, their power, their realms, the beings they preside over, the teachings they transmit, and the *mantras* they utilize, all connect inwardly to *Ishvara*. Even fortunate souls inhabiting the farthest out regions of the *Bhurloka* (earth) find out about this highest principle and worship and meditate upon Him devoutly. In short, He is *Maheshvara* — the Lord of the Worlds.

Regarding the Highest of the High, the chart system on page 359 gives us *Siva*, *Shakti*, and *Shakti's* three main powers of divine dynamism. The chart system on the facing page reveals the same, only with six major powers of *Shakti*. Like a flower and its fragrance, thus has the description been utilized to describe *Siva* and *Shakti*. He is static, all-pervading, and indivisible; She is His indwelling Essence and His dynamic power. All systems agree upon Her three main *shakti* powers, those being *Iccha*, *Jnana*, and *Kriya* — Her supreme Will; Her irrepressible force of Wisdom; and Her prevailing powers of manifestation. Of course, She has other *shaktis*, or subservient powers.

If three other acclaimed *shakti* powers be added in to this list, they would be listed as *Chit*, *Ananda*, and *Dravya* — Her presence as Existence; Her bliss as direct spiritual experience; and Her ability as the foremost producer of substances and generator of the infinite worlds. With Her major powers all taken into consideration, She is the *Mahashakti* — The Supreme Power. None surpasses Her. There is nowhere to go, further inwards or upwards, after encountering Her. She is the incomparable Divine Doorway into *Paramasiva*, Pure Consciousness. She also takes the boundless spiritual potential that lies within Him and renders it into multitudinous expression.

This vast ocean of expression is unlimited. The modicum of manifestation that human beings perceive as the physical universe is just the tip of the iceberg (see chart on page 321). The divine outpouring that flows from *Siva* and *Shakti* is not restricted only to worlds, laws, and cosmic principles, either. Myriad beings form an important and ultra-sentient part of this grand scheme. The next chart, displayed on the right hand facing page, reveals some the innumerable hosts of beings by category that inhabit the *ashuddha* (impure/distant), *shuddhashuddha* (mixed pure and impure/nearer), and *shuddha* (pure/nearest) realms.

Starting at the bottom of the chart and working our way upwards, the beings inhabiting the impure realms are basically laboring under three major *Malas*, or imperfections, listed on the bottom: *Anava, Mayika,* and *Karmika*. Thus, three types of individual souls, *Jivatmas*, come forth: the *Sakalas,* the *Pralaya kalas;* and the *Vijnana kalas*. These three are classed in two subdivisions as shown on the chart — those who mature and those who remain immature. That is to say, that even the highest level of these three groups contains beings who may not mature, and who remain as they are over cycles. Of those who mature, the realms of the *Mantreshvara's* are open for habitation.

The *Sakalas*, however, are bound by all three *malas*. The reader is invited to look at the listings to see what "limiting adjuncts" these souls labor under. Ignorance, impurity, delusion, and misuse of power form the *Anava mala* impediment. Generally, enjoyment and attachment to pleasure via the mind, body, and senses describes the *Mayika* obstruction. And limited thinking, improper action, inability to observe and adhere to the laws of merit and demerit, and an overall succumbing to *samsaric* living makes up the *Karmika* mala. The *Sakala* class of beings have all of this to deal with, though many of them never question the presence of the three *malas*, what to speak of striving to transcend them. These are the physically embodied souls, *Jivatmas*, according to *Shaivism*.

The next higher class of beings, called the *Mantreshvaras*, are, as the chart on the facing page shows, still under the influence of *Maya*. They retain a modicum of attachment to the worlds of name and form. Unlike the three classes of *Jivatmas* just described, their bodies, the subtle sheath or *sharira* that they reside in, is not made up of *mayic* constituents, however. It consists of *Bindu (bhaindava sharira)*, of a much subtler vibration *(spanda)*. In terms of living knowledge, their's is still impeded by their attachment to what transpires on the physical level of the spiritual universe, thus their world is not a world of "Pure Ideas."

For access to such a wondrous world, the soul must transcend *Maya*. This is precisely what the *Vidyeshvaras* and *Vidyas* have accomplished. The former have a slight separation from *Siva*. They enjoy His wisdom, even have His vision, but do not possess "Him" yet. A slender tendril of a particular type of *mala* still impedes them from full identification with the Lord. But they are free of *Maya*. The same is true of their higher ups, the *Vidyas*. They are closest to the Seven Presiding Deities and are thus *Siva*-like. They perceive the Lord; their world is made of Pure Ideas and they emanate the pure wisdom of the Lord and do His will as well.

The Seven Presiding Deities (sometimes listed as eight) form the next strata of free souls. Basically, they are of the same nature of the *Vidya's* and *Vidyeshvaras*, but are special souls who preside over the pure realms falling under the grace of the Fivefold Pure Order. These five are difficult of description, and each require deep meditation on the part of the aspiring soul to comprehend. They can best be described as spiritual vortexes (centers, lotuses, *chakras*) of Consciousness or, metaphorically speaking, channels of pure Awareness through which pass all souls destined and qualified for nondual liberation into *Paramasiva*.

Overall, it may be said that many of those beings falling below the *Vidyeshvaras*, being under the deluding influence of *Maya*, will return to embodiment in *Maya* after the Great Dissolution, called *Mahapralaya*. Others, who have not sought the grace of *Siva*, will have to rely upon mediums

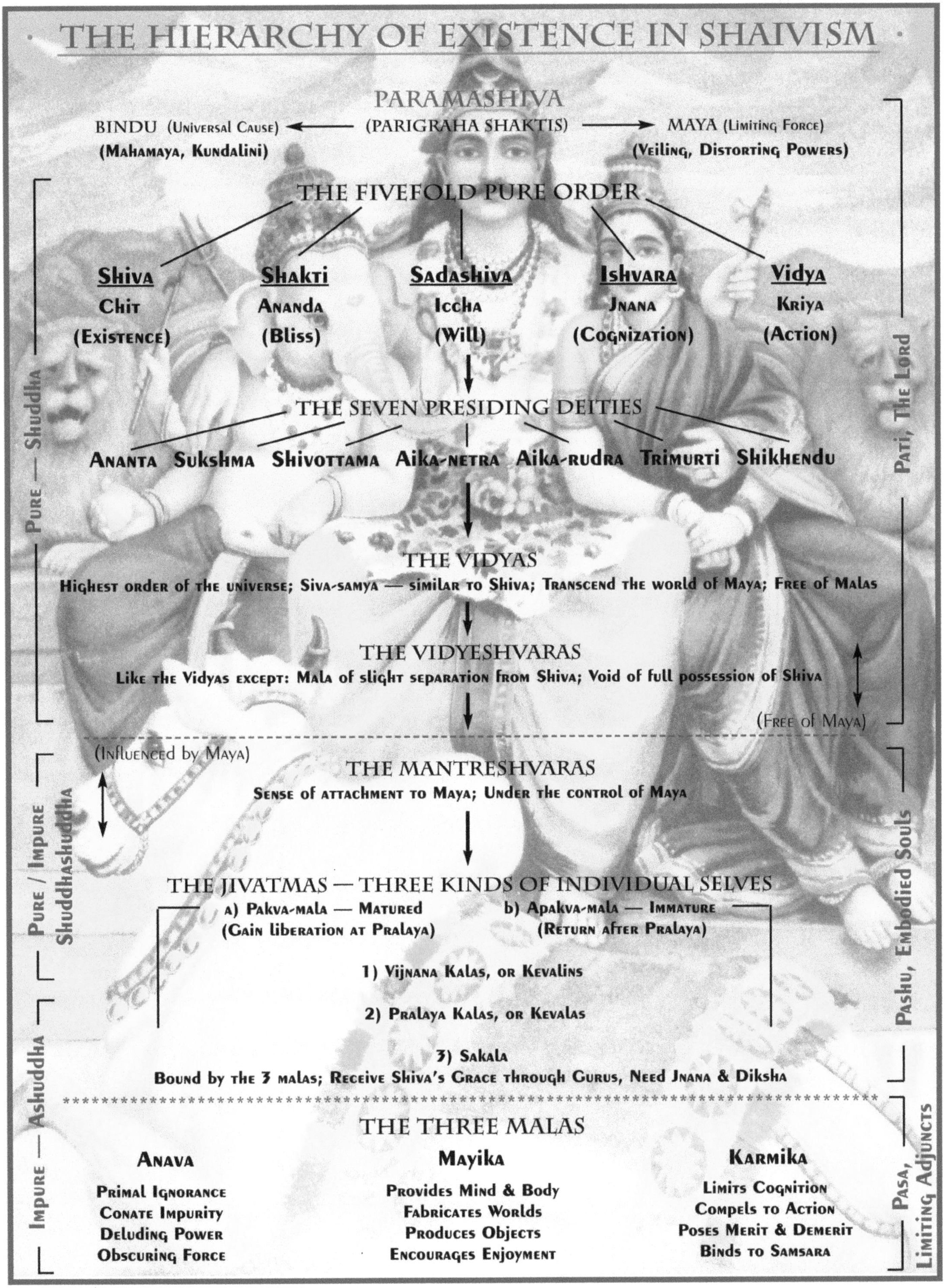

THE HIERARCHY OF EXISTENCE IN SHAIVISM

PARAMASHIVA
(PARIGRAHA SHAKTIS)

BINDU (Universal Cause) ← → MAYA (Limiting Force)

(Mahamaya, Kundalini)   (Veiling, Distorting Powers)

THE FIVEFOLD PURE ORDER

Shiva	**Shakti**	**Sadashiva**	**Ishvara**	**Vidya**
Chit	Ananda	Iccha	Jnana	Kriya
(Existence)	(Bliss)	(Will)	(Cognization)	(Action)

THE SEVEN PRESIDING DEITIES

Ananta   Sukshma   Shivottama   Aika-netra   Aika-rudra   Trimurti   Shikhendu

THE VIDYAS

Highest order of the universe; Siva-samya — similar to Shiva; Transcend the world of Maya; Free of Malas

THE VIDYESHVARAS

Like the Vidyas except: Mala of slight separation from Shiva; Void of full possession of Shiva

(Free of Maya)

(Influenced by Maya)

THE MANTRESHVARAS

Sense of attachment to Maya; Under the control of Maya

THE JIVATMAS — THREE KINDS OF INDIVIDUAL SELVES

a) Pakva-mala — Matured   b) Apakva-mala — Immature

(Gain liberation at Pralaya)   (Return after Pralaya)

1) Vijnana Kalas, or Kevalins

2) Pralaya Kalas, or Kevalas

3) Sakala

Bound by the 3 malas; Receive Shiva's Grace through Gurus, Need Jnana & Diksha

* *

THE THREE MALAS

Anava	**Mayika**	**Karmika**
Primal Ignorance	Provides Mind & Body	Limits Cognition
Conate Impurity	Fabricates Worlds	Compels to Action
Deluding Power	Produces Objects	Poses Merit & Demerit
Obscuring Force	Encourages Enjoyment	Binds to Samsara

Left margin: Pure — Shuddha | Pure / Impure — Shuddhashuddha | Impure — Ashuddha

Right margin: Pati, The Lord | Pashu, Embodied Souls | Pasa, Limiting Adjuncts

or mediators (like *gurus*) to reach higher states. All eventually get their *malas* ripened. It is important to note that in *Tantric* paths, *malas*, or imperfections, are not permanent black marks on the soul, like sins, etc., but are more like unripe fruits that, via development, will mature in time. In can even be said that souls laboring in the realms of *Maya* take on these limitations for the express purpose of solving them within the flow of positive impetus to realize their *Siva* nature. They thus act as examples for less adept souls to do the same.

Lord *Siva* and His great Powers, called *Shaktis*, deserve copious discussion and expansion of their own. Before this is taken up, however, and in accordance with the mention of aspiring souls and their oft times broken and winding ways of spiritual progress and procedure, several teachings can be brought to light. The first, featured on the facing page, is the famous Four Fruits of Life, or *Purusharthas*. Every aspiring soul is gifted with these. They must, however, recognize this fact and make use of their human birth. Further, the Four Boons, pictured on page 367, are also given for consideration and study. Coming down a bit from the lofty heights of *Shaivite* philosophy, then, these eight requisites can be introduced and explored inside of these two charts (pages 365 & 367).

The Four Fruits are really a concessionary teaching, easy and natural, and not requiring much study or contemplation to comprehend. The classic way of transmitting this teaching is to place the fruit of *Dharma* before all the others. However, some teachers evidently overlook the import of this feature, while many students never consider the real ramifications of it. This is dangerous. The idea is this: that without *dharma* first, the following two fruits, desire and livelihood, will only corrupt and mislead, and the fourth fruit of liberation will then not occur. One does not have to look far in this world, and in this day and time, to see many examples of this.

Dharma, as has been explained in earlier pages, begins that phase of life that comes upon sedulous seekers wherein vows and precepts are to be taken. It is a grand opportunity of immense value to the aspirant after highest Truth. The quote from the *Mahanaraya Upanisad* on the chart just opposite makes that exceedingly clear. And in fact, there is a marked difference, noticeable to all who have awakened to the truths of spiritual life, between a *dharmic* person and a worldly person — a *dharmi* and a *samsari*. A *dharmi* will go on to become a *sadhika*; a worldly person will remain as he is, possibly even risking falling lower.

Much like the hope of every authentic *Yoga* teacher for his students — that they accomplish the *yamas* and *niyamas* of *Yoga* (see chart on page 69) before proceeding to the higher limbs of *yogic* practice — the *guru* wants that the *shishya* center himself in *dharma* before entering into the arena of the world to seek a living. If one gets established in the *dharma*, then all activities in the world, as well as their repercussions — positive, negative or mixed — will be taken in stride. No undue *karma* will occur then, since undue reaction to events and experiences is really the basis for *karmic* accrual, not phenomena itself. Thoughts, which can turn either towards aspiration or brooding, will also be attenuated salubriously in the *dharma*. As the great *Tibetan Buddhist* luminary, Milarepa says of it, after looking at all the experiences of *samsara*: "*When I think of samsaric experiences, I cannot help but practice dharma — the teachings of enlightenment. When I think of dharma, the way to enlightenment, I cannot help but offer it to others. When samsaric death approaches, I shall have no regret.*"

The fruit entitled *Kama* comes next, and is a problematic one for many beings, including practitioners of *dharma*. Conventionally defined as "desire," it is at the root of attachment and the suffering it brings. But as our chart states in one of its bullet points, it can be sublimated; its energy, when purified, turned towards higher ends. Until then it must be monitored and, as Sri Ramakrishna has advised, "*....kept at a minimum.*" Otherwise, rebirth with a blank and spiritually uninformed mind, unawares of both its potential and its true nature, will recur.

However, desire that is subjected to *dharma* is actually worked out in *dharma*, and without many ill effects. Neutralized *karma* will then be the result, or at least, attenuated *karma* (see chart on page 176), so that the effects do not impede the path to Enlightenment. The experienced *sadhika* will come to know ways of transforming poison into nectar, as the tradition puts it. The reader is encouraged to review all the charts on *karma* appearing in chapter four.

The Purusharthas — The Four Fruits of Life

1. Dharma
Life Lived In Pursuit of a Spiritual Path

- *Should be implemented before Kama and Artha are sought after*
- *Must be adhered to in all activities to insure harmonious existence*
- *Will be transcended with the attainment of Moksha*

"Dharma, religious righteousness, is the support of the whole universe. All people draw near a person who is fully devoted to dharma. Through dharma a person chases away sin; all are supported by dharma. Therefore, they say that dharma is the means of liberation." Mahanarayana Upanisad

2. Kama — Legitimate Desires Not Contrary to Dharmic Laws

- *Must be monitored and controlled in order to avoid rebirth in Samsara*
- *Can be refined and sublimated so as to lead towards a higher destiny*
- *Should be aligned with devotion to God and freedom from attachments*

"There are two kinds of desires: one that stimulates enjoyment and one that quickens dispassion. In the case of the devotees who adhere to dharma, desires are mere nothings; the more they come and go the better it will be. And so, my children: do not worry. The desires of your mind — you must fulfill them. Later on you will attain to Eternal Peace." Sri Sarada Devi, The Holy Mother

3. Artha — Right Livelihood in Keeping with Dharma

- *Predicated on a dharmic lifestyle married to the quality of generosity*
- *Requires that one moves among the sense-objects without attachment*
- *Based upon the twin ideals of nonownership and careful responsibility*

"Blessed are those who live amidst abundance and among those who long after possessions, yet whose longing is not for the world, but rather for the supreme happiness of spiritual bliss." Lord Buddha

4. Moksha — Realization of Eternal Freedom

- *Is founded in self-inquiry which leads to knowledge of the real and the unreal*
- *Is revealed upon the extinction of desires leading to quiescence of mind*
- *Is a state in which objects, their knower, and knowledge, are not found*

"Firm conviction of oneself as Brahman is moksha. Moksha arises in the mind that longs for moksha. It is the goal towards which all tend. Initiation and instruction from a Guru, and a spotless intelligence, are the two means to moksha. Those virtuous ones will gain moksha who, from early childhood, train themselves in Atmajnan and associate with great beings." Lord Vasishtha

Artha means right livelihood. It, too, will cause living beings to fall, or at the very least, leave off their pursuit of spiritual life if *dharma* is not observed initially and throughout life. It is an old and oft repeated story. The other dangers to immature *Artha* are reflected in the three bullet points on the chart (page 365), namely: an easy abidance among sense objects that, over time, justifies the use of wealth for pleasure and personal gain; a failing to mark the distinction between egotistic giving in altruistic pursuits and authentic generosity based upon a strict sense of nonownership and nonagency. For, many a good soul has fallen and come under the control and influence of wealth and possessions. Lord Buddha's quote on the chart on the previous page bears testimony to this fact.

The ultimate fruit called *Moksha* will get a thorough treatment in a forthcoming chapter. The three bullet points under *moksha* on the chart on page 365 describe Its essentials. For now, suffice to say that when all goes well in the preceding stages, i.e., when the fulfillment of legitimate desires and the earning of a just living in the world are tempered by *dharmic* precepts and practices, *Moksha* is a principle already at hand.

The chart on the facing page gives us another look at the Four Fruits, but in juxtaposition with the Four Boons. Both sets of benefits are placed in the context of the many blessings conferred upon human beings by the *Avatar*, or *Ishvara*. These boons are taken for granted by most all beings upon their birth and throughout their lives. The first, *Manus Yatvam*, a human body, is of immeasurable value to an aspiring soul. Whereas birth in the human form has also been described as a serious impediment, and as something to be transcended, great beings have also taken birth here on earth via *dharmic* fathers and mothers. So, again, a life lived in *dharma* is of paramount importance. Regarding the physical body, then, what is not wanted is birth in ignorance.

To ensure that this does not happen, the second boon of holy company (see chart on page 345) comes into play. By attending upon the presence and teachings of enlightened souls and their devotees, a spiritually inexperienced human being learns what to do and what to refrain from. This is the first benefit of *Sadhu-satsanga*, holy company. Of course, the soul must be intelligent, and must follow through with the teachings, putting them into practice. Many come who fail these important steps, betraying the trust of the generous teacher, thus betraying themselves as well. Both *Hindu* and *Buddhist* traditions agree on the gravity of this betrayal, citing from scriptures that *"....if an aspirant betrays the trust of his or her guru, then the next lifetime will be spent in a hell realm."*

A "hell realm," placed in proper context, is not necessarily a place of fire and brimstone, but really means any number of subhuman births, or a human birth in ignorance and suffering. A birth taken with inferior, ignorant, or overly manipulative parents is also a sign of the soul's betrayal in the past. Beings who are dishonest and insincere attract one another. Taking refuge in holy company, then, is only beneficial if the quality of the soul attending is sincere, honest, and intelligent. Otherwise, and as Sri Ramakrishna has stated, *"Trying to teach wisdom to such souls is as hard as trying to penetrate the leathery back of a crocodile with a sword, or trying to pound a nail into a stone wall."*

And all this brings up what is perhaps the most important of all boons in life, certainly in spiritual life. It is *Mumukshutvam*, the sincere desire for freedom (see chart of page 65). Many souls feel the urge for freedom; most either do not recognize the call, or fail to follow through. Some even mistakenly and prematurely align their experience of freedom with the actual attainment of it, which are two very different things. Depending on so many factors — *gunas, karmas, samskaras*, life events, social conditions — a human being's mind changes radically day to day. And until the practitioner gains a firm grasp on the mind and the senses, and does so via time and tradition-tested methods such as detachment, dispassion, meditation, and selfless service, so long will the mind react and writhe under the ignoble whips of pain that life produces, for the good and the evil alike.

The balanced or *sattvic* mind that the sincere devotee longs for in order to secure possession of long-lasting freedom is called *Chit Shuddhi*, a Pure Mind. It is the fourth of these fundamental boons which, when put together, are a testament to the kind of life we are intended to live here on earth in the body. The benefit of a pure mind cannot be underestimated. As an attainment, there is hardly any better, for everything will come naturally to the one who possesses it. The shining

The Four Boons and the Four Fruits of Life

"A man is born to no purpose who, having received the priceless boon of a human body, is unable to realize God in this lifetime." Sri Ramakrishna

Divine Mother's Four Boons

1
A Human Birth
Manus Yatvam

2
Holy Company
Satsanga

3
Desire for Freedom
Mumukshutvam

A Pure Mind
Chit Shuddhi

1
Spiritual Life
Dharma

2
Right Livelihood
Artha

3
Legitimate Desire
Kama

4
Liberation
Moksha

Divine Mother's Four Fruits of Life

"An impure mind does not easily become pure. But remember — the mind is everything. You will have to carry the mind with you when you try to realize Brahman. So at the present stage the mind is very important. It is the pure mind that shows man the way. One fulfills all desires in this life and reaches liberation when the mind becomes steady."
Sri Sarada Devi

example of Sri Ramakrishna in recent times is proof of this.

And in fact, His divine consort, Sri Sarada Devi (both are pictured on the chart on page 367) has given an essential teaching around the Four Boons. In order to emphasize the crucial nature of possessing a pure mind, She has updated and upgraded this teaching to contemporary times. This teaching used to revolve around the first three boons. Scrutinizing the many hundreds of seekers who came to Her, She observed over time that these striving souls had indeed secured a human body, found their way to holy company, and some even attained an authentic desire for Freedom. In the end, however, Enlightenment escaped them, for they were unable to gain possession of a Pure Mind. Interestingly enough, great souls make their way into the body via a pure mind. Their freedom is not a matter of desire, but a fact of their existence due to their pure mind. Holy company is a mainstay of their lives because of a pure mind. Finally, their bodies are fashioned from the constituents of a pure mind. In other words, the Four Boons are a given for them, from the heights on down.

In correlation with this much-coveted purity, and to revisit the sacred stations of the Divine Couple, *Siva* and *Shakti*, the following chart is presented. In the recently viewed charts on the *Tantric* principles and Cosmology, *Siva* was mentioned often, as was *Paramasiva*. *Siva*, the God of Wisdom, acting on the world scene, and the Transcendent *Siva*, experienced in nondual Realization *(samadhi)*, are one and the same. The former is easier of comprehension. The devotees of *Siva* long to know of His doings through humanity so as to take full advantage of them while they are occupying the embodied condition. In this regard, Lord *Siva* has four great works to accomplish on earth, five essential functions to perform, and he does all this with the aid of his two primary *Shaktis*.

As the chart reveals, and clarifies, Lord *Siva's* four main works in relativity are 1) to ensure that spiritual Truth and wisdom remain in the minds of beings; 2) to transmit the teachings via illumined *gurus* and preceptors; 3) to hold up the ideal of seeking higher qualification to the aspirants while simultaneously discharging ones duties in the world; and 4) to reveal the art of bringing the teachings full circle by demonstrating them in life and activity. These four functions are all laid out, like shining jewels, in the golden setting of His five essential functions, taken up next.

Of the Five Functions of Lord *Siva*, the first two are simultaneously revealing and perplexing. Self-Expression is easy of comprehension, and most beings understand it — at least on emotional, mental, intellectual, and artistic levels. But spiritual expression is unique, and crucial. The *Sanskrit* word, *"Anugraha,"* is also often translated as "grace." The implication, then, is that it is the Lord's Grace that gives human beings the will and impetus to express divine Truth. The second function, *Tirodhana*, is less clear, and needs some explanation. On the cosmological level, *Tirodhana* suggests the play of name and form that produces the universe, which, although an expression of *Siva* and *Shakti*, is very certainly fraught with limitations on all levels of its appearance. By "self-limitation" individually speaking, is meant that, since Truth is actually inexpressible, it can only be condensed or concentrated down by filtering it, by squeezing it, if you will, into a comparatively limited mind and intellect. Thereby, mankind gets some of its best expressions of Truth, called Wisdom, through concentrated channels. In other words, it is *Siva* Himself who manifests as the illumined soul, taking on the limitations of the body/mind mechanism in order to express Truth at the specific level that other similarly limited beings can understand it best. In this way do the first two functions of Lord *Siva* find their beneficial interconnectedness.

The other three functions listed on the chart are well known to those who have studied in the *Vedic shastras.* Called creation, preservation, and destruction in a less adequate rendering, the real meaning is captured better by using the terms projection, sustenance, and dissolution. Since many of the teachings found in *Vedic* scripture and *dharma* point inexorably towards the truth of nonduality, indivisibility, eternity, and, more pertinent here, the birthlessness and deathlessness of the everpresent Soul, then words such as creation and destruction hardly seem applicable, and may cause a sense of contradiction. *Siva* never "destroys," then; He dissolves all back into its Source. Those who presume otherwise are still laboring under the misconception that destruction is actual, basing their assumption only on what they see going on externally. Further, they obviously have not taken

Siva's Two Shaktis, Four Padas, & Five Functions

"The relation between Siva and Shakti goes beyond all types of characterizations. It is a mystery realizable only in the light of Self-expression as Consciousness."
Manoranjan Basu

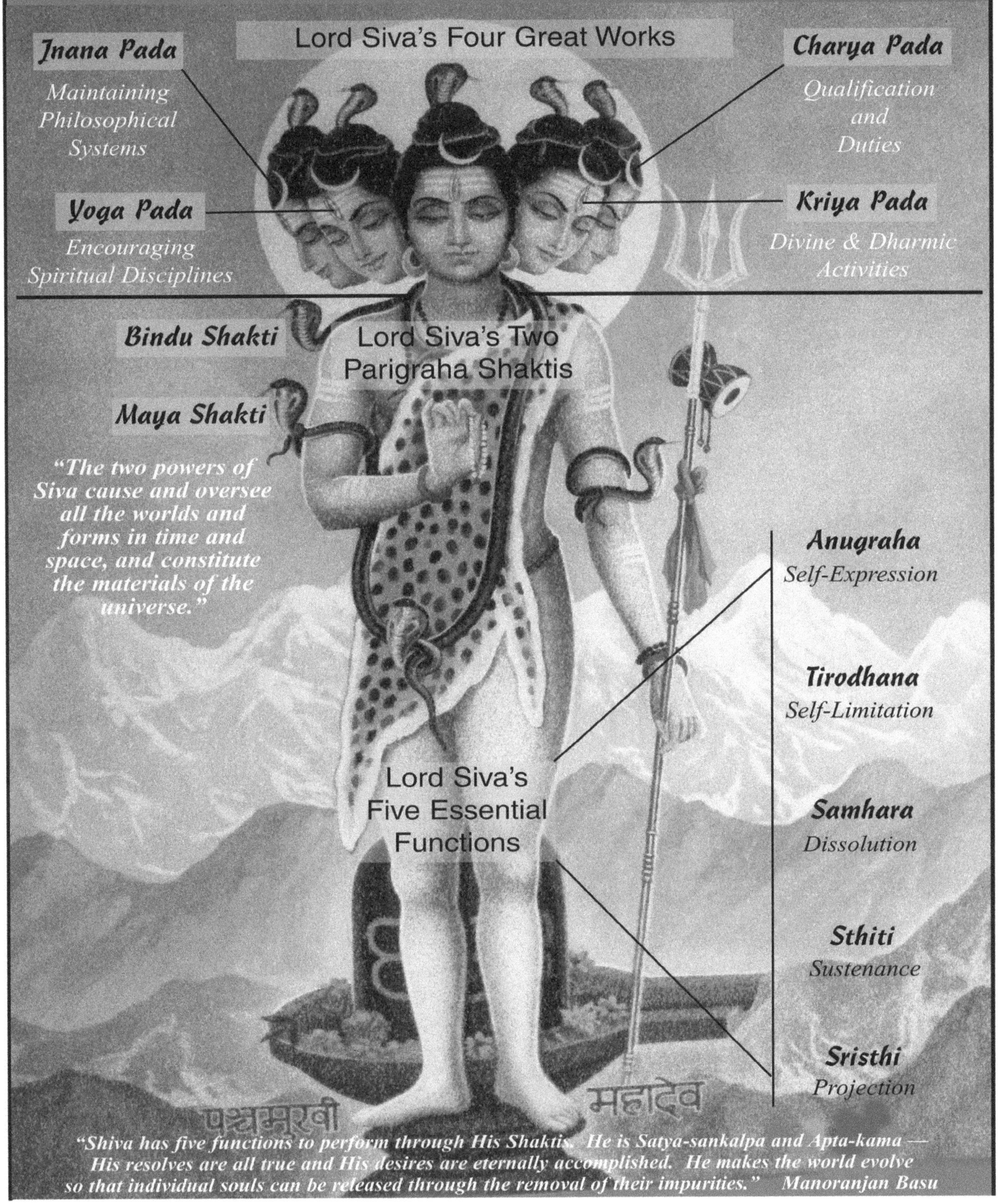

Lord Siva's Four Great Works

Jnana Pada
Maintaining Philosophical Systems

Yoga Pada
Encouraging Spiritual Disciplines

Charya Pada
Qualification and Duties

Kriya Pada
Divine & Dharmic Activities

Lord Siva's Two Parigraha Shaktis

Bindu Shakti

Maya Shakti

"The two powers of Siva cause and oversee all the worlds and forms in time and space, and constitute the materials of the universe."

Anugraha
Self-Expression

Tirodhana
Self-Limitation

Samhara
Dissolution

Sthiti
Sustenance

Srishti
Projection

Lord Siva's Five Essential Functions

पञ्चमूरबी महादेव

"*Shiva has five functions to perform through His Shaktis. He is Satya-sankalpa and Apta-kama — His resolves are all true and His desires are eternally accomplished. He makes the world evolve so that individual souls can be released through the removal of their impurities.*" Manoranjan Basu

recourse to *Siva's* Four Essential Works, and therefore have not taken up the teachings yet.

Siva's two very efficient *Shaktis* — *Bindu* and *Maya* — are causes, facilitators, limiters, and destroyers of limitations, all in one. *Bindu Shakti* is involved intrinsically with sounds, words, meanings, and all correlations thereof. Unseen, she is the foundation for all knowledge, secular and intellectual. Unmasked, she is the integrator, justifier, and revealer of everything having to do with the science of *mantra* — sacred words *(bijams)*, explanatory phrases, statements — and thus is the power residing in the scriptures and in the *guru's* words and transmission. *Maya Shakti,* though she has her own functions to perform, is also involved in *Bindu Shakti's* realm. She is the power that both obscures the meanings of words and scriptures, and also reveals them at the auspicious time. As the quote on the chart on the previous page relates, she also produces and provides all beings with the various bodies and the worlds in which they sport. The materials of the multi-faceted and many-tiered universes are hers, and she acts to oversee them all in conjunction with *Bindu Shakti* and her Lord, *Siva.*

Lord *Siva,* Himself, gets further exposure in the new chart on the facing page to the right. Two main aspects of His — *Nataraja* and *Atmarama* — come to our attention as well. *Atmarama* is the all-pervading *Siva,* transcendent, infilling the souls of all beings. *Nataraja* is the purifier, doing away with the impediments of the devotees via his ferocious *Tandava* dance. These two aspects also represent the Absolute and the Relative, and help explain the two sets of eight forms shown on the chart. They appear as *Asta-murti,* or invisible forms; and as *Murti,* or visible forms.

His visible forms are the powerful aspects of nature. Some of His power gets manifested through these elements; as such, they represent his bodies. All that is divine in nature, then, sings of His glory. Fire purifies, water cleanses, earth produces, air pervades, lightning reveals, clouds send forth their rain, moon heals, and sun illuminates via His presence in and through them.

At the same time, and interconnectedly, *Siva's* subtle forms represent the many facets of His Godhood, emanating as the deities of *Rudra,* the wrathful one who dispels unwanted negativities; *Sarva,* the eternally full and content; *Pashupati,* the most ancient overseer of embodied souls; *Ugra,* the undefeatable; *Ashani,* the all-powerful; *Bhava,* the sweetness of Existence; *Mahadeva,* the Lord of Gods; and *Ishana,* the most Sovereign Lord.

These eight subtle and visible forms of *Siva* are both ancient and widespread. Mention of them is found in philosophical texts such as the *Vedas,* the *Agamas,* the *Puranas,* and in sections of the *Samhitas* and *Brahmanas.* They also appear in the *Mahabharata,* and in many hymns and *stotrams* by a host of luminaries, poets, and sacred songwriters. The purpose of all these appearances is in line with both the *Vedic* and *Tantric* goal of spreading wisdom, *Jnanam,* for the purposes of Enlightenment — *tanyate vistaryate jnanam anena iti tantram.*

This goal also coincides perfectly with the nature of *Siva,* whose Essence is spiritual wisdom. *Siva* comes to mankind in direct response to his zest for knowledge, revealing the eternal nature of Truth through that most efficient of transformative vehicles. As Sri Krishna states in the *Bhagavad Gita: na hi jnanena sadrishyam pavitram iha vidyate — of all purifiers in the world, knowledge is the best.* Further, this wisdom centered around spirituality is not just ancient, it is eternal. The *rishis* of India were not the composers of it, but rather the seers of it. As the Four Works of *Siva* on page 369 have shown us, He is the one who reveals this indestructible wisdom from age to age, making certain of its continued existence in all realms — in The Three Worlds.

The next chart taken up for study, on page 373, illustrates The Three Worlds for further scrutiny and contemplation. *Triloka* is a designation that divides the realms of name and form into very broad categories, each of which contains a host of *lokas* and worlds within it. But this triple designation also helps categorize many of the cosmological teachings and systems of India, some of which we have already studied in previous pages of this book. Another look at these, in a fresh context, will help bring them into a perspective that is beneficial for comprehension and deeper meditation.

As has been taught thus far in several ways, the Three Worlds correspond to the Three Bodies (see chart on page 161), and both sets of threes should be assigned to the three *matras* of *AUM* (see

The Eight Subtle & Eight Visible Forms of Siva

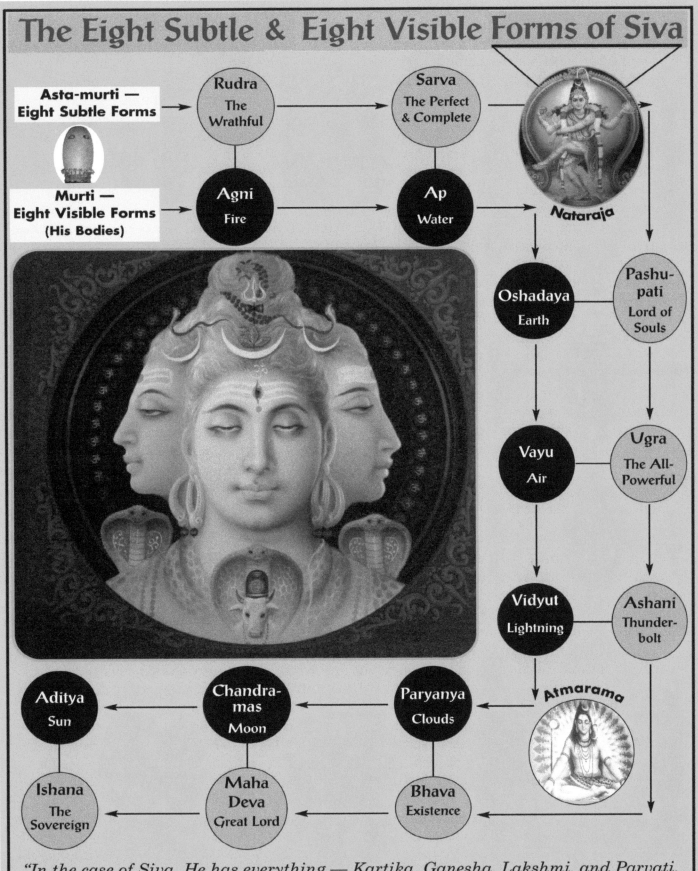

Asta-murti — Eight Subtle Forms

Murti — Eight Visible Forms (His Bodies)

Rudra — The Wrathful

Sarva — The Perfect & Complete

Nataraja

Agni — Fire

Ap — Water

Oshadaya — Earth

Pashu-pati — Lord of Souls

Vayu — Air

Ugra — The All-Powerful

Vidyut — Lightning

Ashani — Thunder-bolt

Atmarama

Aditya — Sun

Chandra-mas — Moon

Paryanya — Clouds

Ishana — The Sovereign

Maha Deva — Great Lord

Bhava — Existence

"In the case of Siva, He has everything — Kartika, Ganesha, Lakshmi, and Parvati. Still, he experiences two states. In the first he is transfixed in the Great Yoga. At that time he is Atmarama, satisfied in the Self. Next, he descends from samadhi, assumes an ego, and dances about, chanting, 'Rama, Rama!'" Sri Ramakrishna

charts on pages 144 & 146). Other *triputis* also apply here (see chart on page 611). Overall, such inward-leading knowledge breaks man free of the limited belief in a physical existence only, and sets him on the border of his own infinite Consciousness, thus Freedom. If the chart on the facing page is studied, and all that is in the subtle and absolute worlds are taken into account, one could see how much would be missing from the life and mind that accepted only the physical and rejected all else.

Following the headings, top to bottom, and observing how each entry falls in columns, a more complete picture can be had of the depth of a few of India's cosmological and philosophical systems — what to speak of mankind's comprehensive mind and spirit. The *Sanskrit* words, *stula, sukshma,* and *karana,* mean gross, subtle, and causal, respectively. They are the physical, psychological, and spiritual worlds, or Immanent, Transcendent, and Absolute. Generally, three levels of beings inhabit these realms: *adhibhuta,* earthbound creatures; *adhidaiva,* ethereal souls; and *adhyatma,* divine beings. If one were to correlate this system to contemporary thinking and description, the headings might read, human beings, celestials, and gods.

But to gain understanding of the greater dimension that is being suggested here, the Four States of Consciousness can be brought forth. In Indian philosophy, and to Indian seers, a human being's waking, dreaming, and deep sleep states suggest more than everyday rounds of mundane life, and even more than interest in the psychological functioning of the brain. The waking state indicates man's relation with nature and other living beings, no doubt, but the dreaming state points to a world within the mind that is in operation even when the five senses are shut down in sleep. What happens in deep sleep is even more mystifying, for all worlds, as well as the human ego, are dissolved away for an indeterminate amount of time, since time is also absent in deep sleep. Further, the fourth state of Awareness, called *samadhi* by the knowers of Truth, reveals a man's true nature that is beyond relative consciousness, sometimes called the "superconscious" state. Ordinary beings encountering this state would not know what is happening to them, like most beings are unaware of what occurs in deep sleep. It takes an advanced being with increased powers of spiritual perception to cognize this state. And such a being would also perceive the otherwise obscured Light of Consciousness that pervades the deep sleep state as well.

As the chart at the right relates, the waking state connects to the Immanent world, *Stula Jagad;* the dreaming and deep sleep states relate to the Transcendent worlds, *Sukshma Jagad;* and the fourth state, also called *Turiya,* correlates with the Absolute. To make it simple, there is an external world, an internal world, and an ultimate Reality. The external world is made up of millions of planets in space; the internal world consists of millions of worlds within realms, or *lokas;* the ultimate Reality is nameless and formless. It is beyond body and mind, worlds and *lokas.* In other words, it escapes the superimposition of form and all powers of formulation.

The next entry is another *triputi* that connects with all that has been stated thus far. It has to do with the cosmic functions of prime Deities who are Overseers for entire worlds, realms, and *lokas.* The functions of these Oversouls, also called The Trinity, overlap and interweave, but generally speaking, the powers of Lord *Brahma* facilitate Creation, while the powers of Lord *Vishnu* go towards sustenance. And as we have seen in recent pages, Lord *Siva* presides over the dissolution process. All of this would seem to suggest that cycles are eternal, and that the Three Worlds, the Three Realms of Beings, and the Three Deities enact an everlasting series of revolutions in time — but more specifically, in Consciousness. The quote by Lord Vasishtha at the bottom of the chart under study explains this nicely.

The Four States of Consciousness connect here again, for the creation work of Lord *Brahma* is the waking state of myriad of souls, or their morning, while the sustaining work of Lord *Vishnu* is the ongoing dreamlife of them all, or their daytime. Night sets when Lord *Siva* dissolves all, like the formless state of deep sleep that all beings experience, and these three phases merge in pure Consciousness, or Timeless, Deathless Awareness, as It has been called. Two great facts get presented and underscored here. First, that Reality has more to do with formlessness than with names and forms; and two, that time is ultimately illusory, or, that beginnings, middles, and ends, i.e., birth,

TRILOKA — THE THREE WORLDS

1 Immanent, Stula Jagad (Physical World)	2 Transcendent, Sukshma Jagad (Psychological World)	3 Absolute, Karana Jagad (Spiritual World)
The 3 Realms Adhibhuta (Living Beings)	Adhidaiva (Celestial Beings)	Adhyatma (Nonduality)
The 4 States of Awareness Wakefulness (Jagrat)	Dream State (Svapna) Deep Sleep (Sushupti)	Pure Awareness (Turiya)
The 3 Cosmic Functions Projection (Lord Brahma) Apparent Creation	Sustenance (Lord Vishnu) Assumed Preservation	Withdrawal (Lord Shiva) Supposed Destruction
The 8-fold Body (Physical body)	Ego, Mind, Intellect, Five Senses of Action	Atman Kundalini Shakti
The 24 Cosmic Principles Five Gross Elements Five Active Senses	Five Subtle Elements Five Cognitive Senses Mind, Buddhi, Ego, Mahat	Purusha/Prakrti
The 5 Sheathes Annamayakosha	Pranamayakosha Manomayakosha Vijnanamayakosha Anandamayakosha	Brahman
The 7 Plains of Existence Bhurloka (Earth Plane)	Bhuvarloka (Astral Plane) Svarloka (Heavenly Plane) Maharloka (Plane of Rishis) Janaloka (Plane of Firstborn) Taparloka (Plane of Vairajas) Satyaloka (Plane of Brahma)	Ajata (Nonembodiment)
The 7 States of the Mind Muladhara, Svadhishthana, & Manipura Chakras	Anahata, Vishuddha, Ajna Chakras	Sahasrara Chakra

"The Three Worlds are born of the Light of Wisdom, which is ever One, not many. It is the Truth, or the 'Sat' aspect of Brahman, that manifests Itself as worlds and universes in space and time."

Lord Vasishtha

life, and death, are also ultimately unreal. These take place only in nature, to souls who know nothing beyond it.

Further, *Brahma, Vishnu,* and *Siva,* all experience a morning, day, and night of their own. This night is called *Pralaya,* which occurs at the end of many cycles of manifestation (see chart on page 39), and these vast cycles all end in *Mahapralaya.* This is the *samadhi* of the Trinity, the bliss of which is beyond comprehension — the *"Peace that Passeth all Understanding."*

Coming down to the very makeup of the human being, the next entry, the Eight-fold Body, often referred to as the *Puryastaka* Body, gets divided between the gross and subtle worlds. But this is not to forget the most important part of the human being — the *Atman* and Its Divine Energy. This immortal Self of mankind, and the *Kundalini Shakti* that is ever flowing within, belong to the Transcendental Plane of Pure Consciousness. They represent the Supreme Goal, and the Way leading to It. If a sincere, striving human being can awaken the spiritual energy within via intense practice, the *Atman* will stand forth, unimpeded, revealing Itself to be the Source of all manifestation.

This is instanced in the next three entries on the chart, now on the previous page. The Twenty-four Cosmic Principles, studied earlier in this chapter (see chart on page 349) also divide up nicely across the span of the Three Worlds. The gross elements and the active senses are a part of the immanent world, while the subtle elements, the cognitive senses, and especially the fourfold mind bridge the immanent, and lead into the subtle world. Only the Soul, *Purusha,* and that part of *Prakriti* that is formless and unmanifest, fall into the transcendent world.

The famous Five Sheaths of *Vedanta,* fundamental to spiritual life in India, appear next in line (see chart on pages 19 and 21). The *Annamayakosha,* the "sheath of food," resides in the gross world, while the other four sheaths fall into the subtle world. Only that which pervades and transcends all sheaths, all covering, all vehicles, abides in the Absolute World, that being *Brahman.* The last two entries on the chart on page 373 are of the Seven Planes of Existence and the Seven States of Mind, more popularly called the Seven *Chakras.* That chart (on the preceding page) shows how these are subdivided and spread over the spectrum of the Three Worlds.

The next chart, on page 375, to the right, takes several of these classifications and places them side by side so that the student can see some interesting juxtapositions. Of immediate import is the dotted line running through the middle of the chart, which indicates a line of demarcation that applies mainly to the transmigrating soul and its spiritual aims. The first two of the five sheaths, the first three of the seven spheres, the first three of the seven worlds, and the first three of the seven chakras, all relate to the soul's status in the physical world and body, in the heaven realms, and in that realm that falls between the two, sometimes called the ethereal or astral realm. But if the *Pranamayakosha* is transcended, if the *Svarloka*/realm of the gods is surpassed, if the celestial world is penetrated, and/or if the *Manipura Chakra* is exceeded, what opens to the individualized soul is an outstripping of all impediments pertinent to the realms of suffering in ignorance, and an end to weak dependence upon all realms of pleasure as well.

It is here that all that is purely spiritual in nature comes forward, and this is where the aspirant who is serious about mastery and perfection focuses most intensely. As the sidebar at the far right of the chart relates, when virtues and qualities like nonviolence, equanimity, compassion for beings, and others get developed, the higher, deeper realms of Awareness become available for occupation. This is precisely why the transmigrating soul who has fallen into the dream of relativity, into the predicament of birth and death, into embodiment in ignorance, has taken such extreme care and exerted with such intense effort while on earth — so that it can develop merit and character which will lend it power enough to pierce through the veils of *Maya* and get free again. The penultimate attainment of communing with *Ishvara,* the highest form of God, what to speak of the ultimate station of merging into *Brahman,* awaits the aspiring soul. The soul will then cease being soul (body/mind complex) and will become Soul, *Atman,* which it was all along but had only forgotten, had dreamed itself away from its Self. With the dream over, and awakening achieved, the *Anandamayakosha* opens, the realm of Lord *Brahma* transform, the *Pushkar Dvipa* offers access, and

The Seven Spheres, Seven Worlds, Seven Chakras, and Five Koshas

Prana pervades all Seven Spheres ←

Tattvas	Sheaths / Koshas	Spheres / Brahmandas	Worlds / Dvipas	Vortexes / Chakras	
Purusha & Mahat produce Prana	Anandamayakosha Sheath of Bliss	Brahmaloka Realm of the Sacred Trinity	Pushkar Dvipa Subtlemost World	Sahasrara	Illumined souls transcend the Brahmaloka and merge with Brahman
	Vijnanamayakosha Sheath of Intelligence	Tapaloka Realm of the Vairajas	Plaxa Dvipa Higher Causal World	Ajna	Those souls nearly free of all desire for the realms of embodiment go quickly to the higher worlds, there to merge with Brahman in due time.
		Janaloka Realm of the Seers	Shalmali Dvipa Intermediate Causal World	Vishuddha	Beings possessed of love, nonviolence, equanimity, and virtue rise easily to the higher causal realms, transcending rebirth in the physical, astral, and celestial worlds.
	Manomayakosha Sheath of Psychic Energy	Maharloka Realm of the Sages	Krauncha Dvipa Lower Causal World	Anahata	
	Pranamayakosha Sheath of Vital Energy	Svarloka Realm of Indra and the Gods	Kusha Dvipa Celestial World	Manipura	Pious people with unfilled desires arrive at the Svarloka and get reborn on earth to fulfill them.
		Bhuvarloka Realm of the Munis and the Siddhis	Shaka Dvipa Etheric/Astral World	Svadhisthana	Transmigrating minds attached to the earth plane revolve between the first three worlds.
Earth	Annamayakosha Sheath of Physical Energy	Bhurloka Realm of the Humans and Animals	Jambu Dvipa Physical World	Muladhara	Those with sinful karmas gravitate to the seven lower worlds as ghosts and asuras, eventually gaining a chance for a physical birth again.

The Seven Hell Realms, or Patalas — Atala, Vitala, Sutala, Talatala, Mahatala, Rasatala, and Patala

the Thousand-petaled Lotus reveals its wonders.

The chart under study also lays out the list of the seven *Patalas,* or "sunken grounds," at the bottom. Generally referred to as "hell realms," they are inhabited by souls whose *karmas* are particularly evil, who have harmed other beings. Violence and nonviolence are, and always have been, determinative factors in India philosophy and religion, not so much from the moral standpoint and its implications, but more from the aspect of following cosmic laws and avoiding transgression of the *dharma.* It must be remembered, as well, that heaven and hell realms are not locations in physical space, but are vibrational spheres existing within the individual, collective, and cosmic mind itself. The "Mind-only" schools, then, are well named; the Indian views that perceive all realms as based upon vibration are well-thought, and the enlightened Hindu view that everything is a projection of the mind, called *sankalpa/vikalpa,* is well-presented — and should be duly followed.

Since the salubrious subject of *dharma* has come up, and especially in relation to the transmigrating soul seeking perfection beyond the vagaries and vicissitudes of the dense worlds of becoming, the next chart on the facing page can be scrutinized. For, it has long been known that there are three gateways which sojourning souls enter and exit, and that these three are eternal and well marked. For clarification about this essential matter, two teachings, called the Four Veiled Doorways and Four Fundamental Paths of Life, can be referred to.

The Four Veiled Doorways is another well-named system. Accordingly, all four fall under the Eternal Gateway of *Adharma,* or unrighteousness — all that is contrary to peace and harmony, health and well-being. It would be good to mark these four. *Lokayatika Marga* (*marga* means "path") is rank materialism, of the kind that is rampant at present in the mechanical or "jet" age. *Mithajnana Marga* is the path of those who are narrow and sectarian in the extreme. Precious little light can pass through the tiny rafters of this hypocritical religious house, and certainly not the light of reason. *Pravritti Marga* is the path of secularism, followed by the masses, its numbers even outweighing the followers of religion. The psychology here may be that "there is safety in numbers," but the result ends up to be more like "misery loves company."

And finally there is *Bahutva Marga,* or religious convention. Not nearly as narrow as fundamentalism, and certainly much more forgiving, its downside and main weakness, ironically, is the lack of verve, focus, and forward motion that fundamentalism proceeds by, if it proceeds at all. Lacking intensity, religious convention is a disease that has not only weakened the fiber of religion itself in the world, but has also turned its adherents, a great percentage of humanity, into pretenders instead of practitioners. As far as their God is concerned, taking Him out of hiding and winding Him up on Sundays, praying to Him occasionally in the church confessional to forgive their perpetual and ongoing sins, and inviting His blessing for a few minutes at dinnertime, He is otherwise left to His own devices, with little thought, what to speak of love and devotion, ever offered Him. In this way has conventional religion turned their Savior into a doormat of complacency and convention instead of a doorway to Divine Realization.

Vedic Religion and its scriptures do not spout pronouncements of hell and damnation, or "end of day" theories, or "end of the world" prophecies. Rather, the movement of time that results in the turning of eternal ages is marked by certain observances that allow the soul, sojourning in the dreamrealms of time and space, to recognize when and where it has incarnated. The quote from the *Srimad Devi Bhagavatam,* placed side by side with the Four Veiled Doorways, is a good example of this. When signs appear, they are to be read, not used to incite fear and panic that plays into the hands of fundamentalist religious coercion.

The Four Fundamental Paths of Life are another interesting study. Of the four, one falls under the heading of *Adharma,* that being *Vyavaharika.* It is similar to secularism, and carries elements of religious convention in it, but has as its main aim the pleasures and enjoyments of life. Also in line with what India calls the *Bhoga Marga,* or path of enjoyment, worldliness leads nowhere but back to the world, i.e., rebirth.

Two paths of these four fall under the welcome umbrella of *Dharma* — the path of authentic

The Three Eternal Gateways

&

The Four
Veiled
Doorways

&

The Four
Fundamental
Paths of Life

Adharma —————————— Dharma ————————— Svadharma

(The Four Veiled Doorways)

Lokayatika Marga
(Materialism)

Mithyajnana Marga
(Fundamentalism)

Pravrtti Marga
(Secularism)

Bahutva Marga
(Religious Convention)

*"In an age of darkness, viciousness and vile
acts become the normal mode of behavior.
Even the gods become deceitful, what to speak
of humans and lower creatures. It is natural
that injury come to those who injure others,
but when peaceful persons, devoid of enmity,
are injured, that is an act of wickedness, pure
and simple. In such an age one will find very
few persons following the True Religion."*

Srimad Devi Bhagavatam

*"That intrepid spiritual way-
farer who inquires into the
wise characteristics of dharma, he treads the proper path.
He learns concentration and
meditation, the significance of
the scriptures, discrimination
between the real and the
unreal, and knows what
actions are to be done and
which are not to be done."*

Lord Vasishtha

Vyavaharika
(Worldly Path)

(The Four Fundamental Paths of Life)

*"Meditation on the meaning
of Truth as it is taught in the
Vedanta leads to the highest
illumination. By this means,
the misery of worldly life —
Vyavaharika — is destroyed
altogether."*
Shankaracharya

Dvaita
(Path of Dualism)

Yoga
(Path of Transformation)

*"The true renouncer, called
the Great Actor and The Great
Enjoyer, has transcended both
dharma and adharma and gotten free from birth and death."*
Parameshvara Shiva

Advaita
(Way of Nondual Abidance)

Dualism, and the Path of *Yoga,* or Transformation. By "Dualism" is meant all those adherents of religion and the various schools based upon the premise that God and mankind are basically different in nature than one another, and that God, as a separate Entity, rules over mankind from a heavenly location and guides him for his own good. Paths of dualism can differ philosophically, running a gamut of tenets and ranging from extreme dualism to qualified nondualism (see chart on facing page).

The other *dharmic* pathway is here termed *Yoga,* and whereas there is the purest form of it which coincides with Indian tradition, at least in its aims and ends, the term is utilized here to indicate any form of spiritually-oriented practice that is engaged in which purifies body, life, mind, and senses in accord with the attainment of Enlightenment. Since such a path will necessarily demand that the aspirant follow a regimen of disciplines that suits and deals with the limitations and anomalies of each aspect of a human being's makeup, i.e., *sadhana* or spiritual practice, the path must fall under the auspice of *Dharma* rather than *Svadharma.*

With regards to *Svadharma,* it is the highest and best of all pathways. All beings seek it, knowingly or unknowingly. With respect to the human soul, its fullest, best, and divinely intended destiny is what is at stake. Though *Dharma* marks the difference between a spiritually aspiring soul and one who is not yet through with the matters and concerns of the world, everything that it prescribes and guides is all in preparation for the soul's arrival at the portal of *Svadharma.* It is therefore in perfect relation to *Advaita,* nonduality, which will be discussed at length in chapter nine. As Sri Krishna tells His beloved disciple in the *Bhagavad Gita: "After all righteous actions have been accomplished by you, Arjuna, you should abandon all dharmas and take refuge in Me alone."*

In preparation for study in the nondual atmosphere, and as an explanation of important stages that the spiritual aspirant is bound to go through via inner life, the forthcoming two charts reveal certain secrets known only to preceptors and their disciples, being either carelessly overlooked or rejected outright by those who follow the narrow and worldly pathways just presented. In the first of these, appearing on the facing page, Swami Vivekananda tells us of his discovery in the shape of three distinct but interconnected levels of philosophical understanding that must attend any higher realization attained to by the aspiring human soul.

Basically, these three stages of comprehension are declared to be like steps, with Dualism giving way to Qualified Nondualism, and it paving the way for *Advaitic* Realization. The chart gives teachings which can act as various handles that accommodate perception of the content of each stage. These can be read and contemplated. *Dvaita,* or dualism, is obvious. Madhva's five points at the bottom of the chart render it clear: souls are distinct from God, matter is distinct from God; souls are distinct from other souls; souls are distinct from matter; and portions of matter are distinct from other portions of matter. However, souls and the universe of matter all have their deeper existence in God. Thus, Madhva's dualism is not a matter of separation, but of distinction only.

The subject of these three philosophies may be considered complex. So, for easier access to what is being communicated about Qualified Nondualism, Sri Ramakrishna explains: *"One cannot get the weight of the bel-fruit by weighing the flesh only. One must weight the flesh, seeds, and shell together. Similarly, via spiritual discrimination, one must first reason, following the method of "neti neti," (not this; not this) and one comes to see that God is not the universe, nor its living beings, that Brahman alone is real. Then one realizes, as with the bel-fruit, that the Reality from which we derive the notion of Brahman is the very Reality that evolves the idea of living beings and the universe. Therefore, to Ramanuja, Brahman is qualified by the universe and living beings. This is Qualified Nondualism."*

Speaking from the *Advaitic* standpoint, or Nondualism, the Great Master said: *"But without awakening ones own inner consciousness one cannot realize the All-Pervading Consciousness. A man reasons only so long as he has not realized God. I clearly see that God Himself has become everything. I have observed that a man acquires one kind of knowledge about God through reasoning, and another kind through meditation; but he acquires a third kind of Knowledge about God when God reveals Himself to him, His devotee."*

The Three Stages of Indian Philosophy

Ascending Steps in Religious Understanding

Shankara

Ramanuja

Madhva

Vivekananda

"Now I will tell you my discovery. All of religion is contained in the Vedanta, that is, in the three stages of Vedantic philosophy — the dvaita, vishishtadvaita, and advaita; one comes after the other." Swami Vivekananda

Advaita Vedanta of Shankara — Nondualism

Some Declarations of Advaita Vedanta

God and mankind are one inseparable entity, nondifferent

All beings, all things, are nonoriginated, free of birth and death

Man's nature is divine; impure mind superimposes ignorance

"The followers of Advaita constantly discriminate, saying, 'Brahman alone is real, the world is illusory.' Their aim is to attain Nirvana. This is Self-knowledge, discussed in the Ashtavakra Samhita. It is an experience beyond the reach of ordinary men. The followers of this school, the nondualists, say, 'Soham,' I am the Supreme Self. This real Self is unattached, impervious to all dualities, whereas the ego self suffers them. If one burns wood some ash results, but if one burns camphor, nothing remains. All the six darshanas are contained in the Advaita."
Sri Ramakrishna

Vishishtadvaita of Ramanuja — Qualified Nondualism

The Three Relations between God and the Cosmos

1. Adhara and Adheya — The Supporter and the supported
2. Niyamaka and Niyamya — The Controller and the controlled
3. Sheshin and Shesha — The Lord and His servant

"According to Ramanuja, God is qualified by the universe and its living beings. These three — Brahman, the world, and individual souls — together constitute one. It is like the case of the bel-fruit whose flesh, shell, and seeds make up the fruit itself. At first one may think that the real thing in the fruit is the flesh alone. But to get the full weight of the fruit one must weigh in the shell and seeds as well. Likewise, in spiritual discrimination, one must at first separate the unreal from the real to find out the essence. Then alone will one be able to see this essence everywhere, like in the world and its living beings. Thus, one soon realizes, as with the bel-fruit, that the Reality from which we derive the notion of Brahman is the very Reality that evolves the idea of living beings and the universe." Sri Ramakrishna

Dvaita of Madhvacharya — Dualism

The Five Differences or Distinctions of Dvaita

1. God is distinct from individual souls   2. God is distinct from nonliving matter
3. An individual soul is distinct from every other   4. Souls are distinct from matter
5. Parts of matter are distinct from one another

"The proposition upon which Madhva bases his realism is that both the knower and the object of knowledge must be real, for otherwise knowledge would not be possible. The object of knowledge, then, has a reality of its own. The world is real because it is perceived as such. The fact that an object is fleeting and subject to change does not mean it is 'unreal.' As for souls, all are distinct from one another, and are distinct from God as well, though they have dependent existence in Him. To Madhva, all souls born into the world are in a state of bondage, but by continued struggle through many lives release from this bondage may be gained."
Swami Prabhavananda

Based upon such superlative realization, the points under the heading of *Advaita* at the top of the chart come clear: God and mankind are one inseparable Reality; all beings, all things, are non-originated, or birthless and deathless, i.e., Eternal; and man's nature is Divine. It is only the mind and its multitudinous projections initiated in ignorance that makes it seem otherwise.

Finally, it should be related that these three stages are not judged inferior or superior to one another. Rather, they are platforms upon which beings at differing levels of comprehension can come to realize God. Further, even after the realization of God, the enlightened soul returns to the preceding stages so as to be abe to communicate and teach beings who are moving through them. In other words, they are not bridges to be burned, but bridges to be valued, and crossed over and back, again and again, for the higher spiritual evolution of all aspiring beings.

As the aspiring soul searches for ways to illumine the mind complex, all the while forbearing the problems of relative existence, it becomes obvious that there is a vast difference between mere reasoning attended by the usual and often pointless argumentation, and clarifying knowledge from the scriptures as transmitted by the illumined preceptor. This is one of the secrets of the Indian scriptures that is "hidden in plain sight," as the saying goes. Hearkening back to the charts on pages 341 and 343, the reader can remind the mind of the difference between revealed scriptures and ordinary scriptures, the latter which often imprisons the soul further in the confusing labyrinth of futile reasoning. This fact, along with Lord Vasishtha's quote at the bottom of the chart on the facing page, should be kept in mind as we uncover some of these great secrets of Indian scriptures.

The chart now under study is a precious teaching filled with axioms and techniques that, when followed and adhered to, will purify and free the mind. Thousands of great luminaries have been pouring out of India for countless cycles of time due to abiding faithfully by just such tenets and principles as these. In the West, in present times, scripture and its study has become unpopular. This is not surprising given the heavy interpolation that scriptures have passed through, as well as the worldly hands and minds they have been subject to. In India, it was not ordinary minds, or royalty, or business men, that interpreted scripture; it was the luminaries, *gurus*, seers, and sages that did so. The result has been a long-lived heritage of wisdom, uncompromised and untampered with, that is fully competent to guide souls in their spiritual quest, even today, in modern times.

Some of the listings on this chart have already been brought forth in previous pages of this book. The Three Great Sources at the top of the chart has been mentioned several times. Every spiritual seeker of a *Vedic* path can take recourse to these, and feel the freeing and doubt-dispelling power inherent in them. Importantly, the third — ones own direct spiritual experience — is paramount, but it should be remembered that experiences had before studying the scriptures and taking communion with ones *guru* cannot be classed under this heading. The authenticity of these can only be trusted when based upon the testament of the seers and the scriptures. That is, some of them might even be valid, but without the stamp of authority that *Vidya Shastra* and *Guru Anushashana* confer upon the seeker's mind, no reliable conclusion about them can be drawn.

As for the Three Techniques for Interpreting the Scriptures, it puts to rest age-old doubts around spiritual seeking. The limitations of pitting one doctrine against another *(prati-tantra siddhanta)* is well known to all who have come in contact with different religions; no final conclusion is ever forthcoming at this level of observation. At the next level, if it is even sought for, when the attempt at reconciling various paths and religions is met with *(sarva-tantra siddhanta)*, there is still plenty left for consideration. It is only when all religions are seen as so many routes up the mountain, leading to the same summit *(sahaja-tantra siddhanta)*, that satisfaction is attained. As the ancient *Vedas* say in this regard, being the first and oldest testament to universality: *"Ekam sat viprah bahuda vedanti — Truth is One; paths are many."* This truth is seen only by the *Avatars* and other illumined souls. Most of humanity forever remains uninformed, even clueless, about this all-important verity.

The Two Types of Knowledge has also been included in earlier pages of this book (see chart on page 271). The Four Views on the Origin of the Scriptures represents another clarifying teaching. Ultimately, the revealed scriptures are of Divine origin. Some say that they emanate from

Vedantic Secrets of the Scriptures

The Three Great Sources
Vidya-Shastra – Consulting the Revealed Scriptures
Guru-Anushashana – Instructions from a Preceptor
Aparokshanubhuti – Verification by one's own Experience

Three Techniques of Interpreting Scripture
Prati-tantra Siddhanta – as Separate Doctrines
Sarva-tantra Siddhanta – by Way of Reconciliation
Sahaja-tantra Siddhanta – by Way of Natural Synthesis

The Two Types of Knowledge
Paravidya – Spiritual and Revelatory
Aparavidya – Religious, Secular, and Intellectual

The Four Views on the Origin of Scripture
Apaurasheya – Of Divine/Eternal Origin
Ishvariya – Originating from Ishvara
Archa – Originating from the Seers
Paurasheya – Originating from Human Intellect

Three Potent Practices
Shravana – Listening
Manana – Contemplating
Nididhyasana – Realizing

Three Proofs of Truth
Shruti – Hearing Truth
Yukti – Reasoning Truth
Anubhava – Experiencing Truth

Ishvara, but the nondual perspective is that they are *Apaurasheya*, Eternal. That is, they exist at all times, only submerging into the recesses of the collective mind when *Adharma* waxes, and coming forward naturally when *Adharma* declines. As for the idea that the seers compose the scriptures, these great personages, themselves, deny it. They see themselves as the caretakers of these eternal systems of Truth, their business being to keep them alive for the highest good of aspiring human beings. This effort forms a part of the system of Divine Works (see chart on page 369).

The two *triputis* at the bottom two corners of this chart echo similar truth sentiments. In other words, they are the same teaching, but given in several systems, coming from different ages. Suffice to say that the aspirant must first hear the truth, then roll it over in his mind for a time. The first part occurs in the presence of the spiritual preceptor, or at least this is the best and classic way. The second act marks the difference between contemplation and meditation, the former dealing with and operating at the level of conceptualizations, and the latter being utilized more for communion with the Deity, or the Formless *Brahman*. After these two have been implemented, though, realization, or direct spiritual experience, should be the result. No doubt, fear, or lack of clarity can persist in the atmosphere of the well guided, well-activated *triputi* of the Three Potent Practices and Three Proofs of Truth.

The recent mention of the important practice of *Vedanta* called *"neti neti"* has inspired the next chart, shown on the facing page. Termed "not this, not this" in English, the implication is that the spiritual aspirant, in order to come to know the nature of Reality and the transitoriness of the world of name and form, must free the mind of all misconceptions *(avidya)* and overlays *(adhyasa/adhyaropa/vivarta)*, thus leaving it clear and certain of its connection with God/*Brahman*. This has been described by such fitting terms as "weeding the garden of the mind," and "watering the flowers and not the weeds," etc. *Vedanta* uses words such as *Vivarta*, false superimposition, and *Adhyasa*, the reflection of attributes of one thing over another, to explain this special, inwardly-oriented, subtle practice. To suspect a ruse, to perceive it, and to do away with it via specific tools of spiritual practice *(adhyaropa* and *apavada)*, is the superlative aim (see chart on page 65).

The ruse, in a nutshell, perpetrated by *maya* in conjunction with the human mind, is that the seers declare that *Brahman* is formless, and the only Reality. If this is the case, then what is name and form? It must be: a reflection; an illusion, an appearance; an add-on; a projection; a manifestation; an expression. The ancient *rishis* of India gave the sweet expression that it was *"....an overflow of the Bliss of Brahman."* All of these choices, or opinions of differing philosophies (see chart and commentary on page 317), appear on the center of the chart in ascending order.

But an oft-times overlooked or understated facet of this valuable teaching is the background presence of *"iti iti,"* meaning "all this, all this." Indian philosophy and religion were never satisfied to leave the matter of Reality in the bottomless pit of nihilism, voidism, emptiness, etc., and also did not like the idea of rounds of contradictions ending nowhere. *Siddhanta*, apt conclusions — as we noted in the chart on the previous page, were crucial. Thus, *iti iti* is the welcome addendum and arrival point of the *neti neti* practice, as explained in the quote at the top of the chart.

To further understand the mental practice of *neti neti*, we can follow the right hand column from bottom to top to see its aims. The reader will notice that the familiar list of twenty-four cosmic principles (see chart on page 349) is arranged up the middle. Being insentient, or, at best, only vehicles of Consciousness and not Consciousness Itself, these are precisely the facets of relativity that the aspirant seeks to transcend. He practices *neti neti* to free himself from attachment and undue involvement with them. Admittedly, this is a monastic practice, but those of *yogic* leanings also employ it, as do those whose parley and communion with the world has come, or is coming, to an end.

The charm and benefit of this chart is that it juxtaposes *neti neti* and *iti iti* side by side. Much like the Three Stages of Indian Philosophy (see chart on page 379), then, these two facets of spiritual life are seen as steps. As the devotee contemplates the five elements, for instance, he declares inwardly and adamantly, from the *neti neti* perspective, "I am not the five elements." If and when

꧁ The Synchronicity of Iti, Iti & Neti, Neti ꧂

"When the human being realizes the Reality, Parabrahma, in formless samadhi, the mentally projected phenomena of name and form in time and space disappears, demonstrating its ephemeral nature. If the fully awakened soul should return to embodiment after knowing the nondual Truth, however, the entire world reveals nothing but Brahman." Babaji Bob Kindler

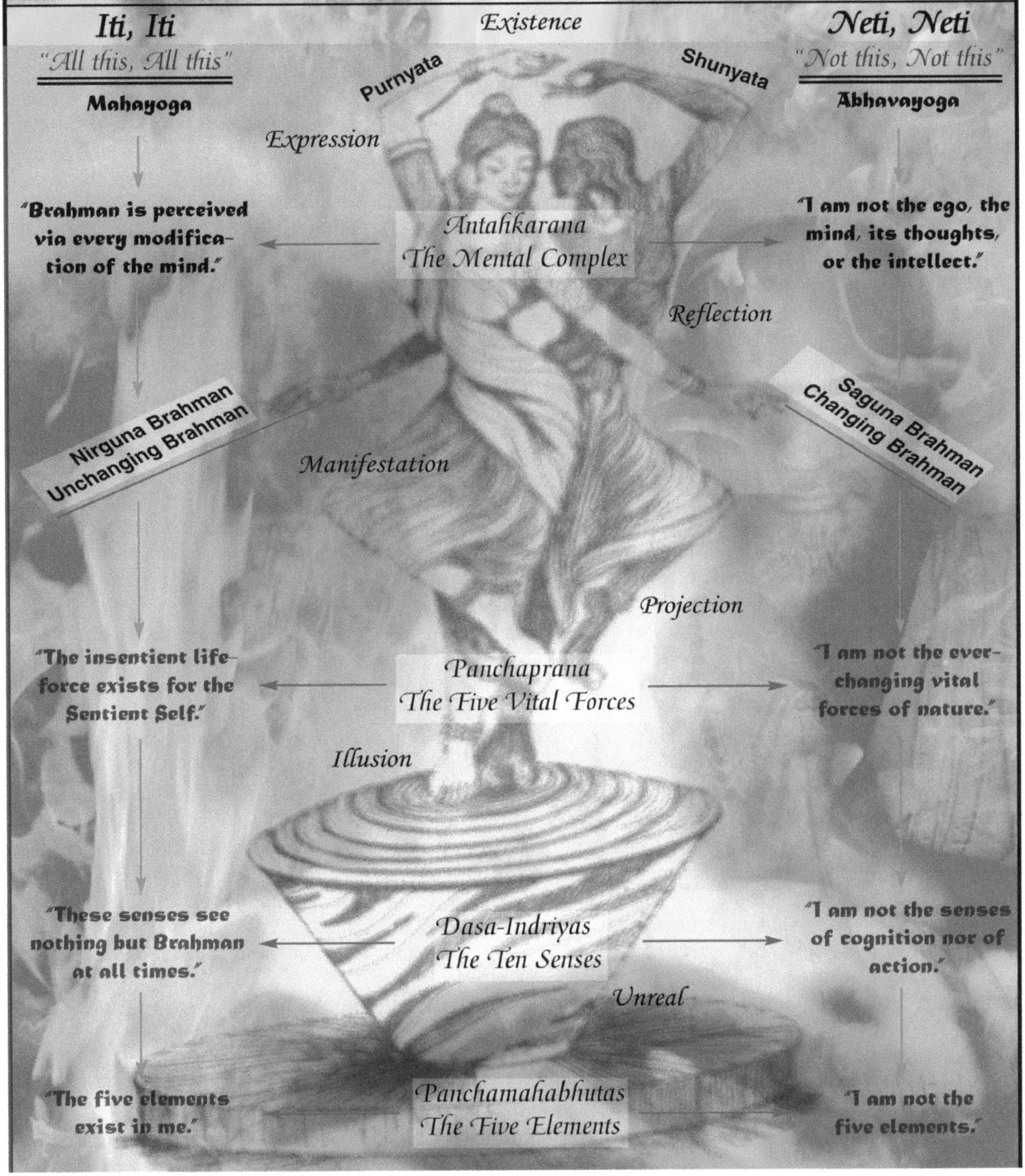

Iti, Iti
"All this, All this"

Mahayoga

Existence

Purnyata

Neti, Neti
"Not this, Not this"

Abhavayoga

Shunyata

Expression

"Brahman is perceived via every modification of the mind."

Antahkarana
The Mental Complex

"I am not the ego, the mind, its thoughts, or the intellect."

Reflection

Nirguna Brahman
Unchanging Brahman

Manifestation

Saguna Brahman
Changing Brahman

Projection

"The insentient life-force exists for the Sentient Self."

Panchaprana
The Five Vital Forces

"I am not the ever-changing vital forces of nature."

Illusion

"These senses see nothing but Brahman at all times."

Dasa-Indriyas
The Ten Senses

"I am not the senses of cognition nor of action."

Unreal

"The five elements exist in me."

Panchamahabhutas
The Five Elements

"I am not the five elements."

he is ready for advancement and deeper maturity, however, he will come to conclude that "The five elements exist in me." Though the difference in these two conclusions is subtle, it is also extremely important.

There have been premature conclusions drawn throughout time, and incomplete assessments made by immature minds in the name of these two practices. That all of nature exists, not in time and space, but within the mind and its powers of conception, is an extremely advanced state of thinking, and takes much deep pondering to arrive at. Otherwise, there is always the tendency lurking in the uninformed mind that, when the practice of *neti neti* gets implemented, it will conduce to either a condemning of the worlds of name and form, and of nature, or an immature transcendence of them all without realizing their special significance — what to speak of overlooking and foregoing the spiritually elevated stage of seeing *Brahman* in everything. This would leave the devotee and Truth-seeker lingering only at the penultimate level of Awareness, at best.

With this guide in place, the rest of the chart, in ascending fashion, offers up the consummate practice of *neti neti,* moving on through transcendence of the senses, vital forces *(prana),* and the four-fold mind. Along this precipitous pathway of inner practice, souls begin to realize the subtle difference between *Nirguna* and *Saguna Brahman* — Reality with and without attributes. It is here that comprehensive understanding may finally dawn, the kind which puts to rest all doubts about the nature of Reality, and vaults one into the lofty regions of a true knower of *Brahman* (see chart on page 88). Along with this comes the realization that *Abhavayoga* and *Mahayoga* (see chart on page 685) are two eternal pathways, adhered to by masterful souls of different temperaments. Each is powerful in its own way, and both move spiritual adepts to levels of preternatural realization that are rare and scarce of attainment by multitudes of other aspiring beings.

To give an idea at this juncture of the depth and profundity of the realized soul who has practiced *neti neti* and attained to *iti iti,* the following chart, on the facing page, is presented. According to the luminary, Swami Vivekananda, and his fine quote at the top of the chart, the realized soul sees all of nature as a book, and drinks in the experiences of it from an ever-stationary position. This is not hard of comprehension given that the first state of Higher Knowledge is *Antah-Jnana* — a recognition that all wisdom is inherent in the Soul. Such a great being has given up seeking outward for anything, then, being content in his/her own divine nature.

And this ultimate satisfaction is also the end of suffering — *Dukha Samyoga Viyogam.* When beings talk and philosophical systems teach about the transcendence of suffering, it is nowhere on the level of realization yet. Vivekananda's quote under this heading reveals not just the possibility, but the actual attainment of removing suffering through nonidentification with the body. In the *neti neti* practice previously examined, the body was one of the first principles of relative existence to be renounced. Sri Krishna clarifies this point further in His quote on the bottom half of the chart, showing how the appearance and the absence of light and darkness, both, are beneath the *yogi's* notice. Such divine imperviousness is akin to equanimity of mind, unfathomable Peace of Mind. This ought to act as the aspirant's main example in spiritual attainment.

The attainment of *samadhi,* plain and simple, is the next abiding facet of the illumined soul's realization. But with souls as rare and advanced as Vivekananda, *samadhi* is not for the enjoyment of personal bliss, but is to be utilized in order to bring light to others. This further accents the fact that *samadhi* is the true nature of every human being, of the gods and ancestors as well; but few out of these heavily populated sectors of beings inhabiting the realms of name and form move to realize it. Perhaps their vision is still marred, or lacking.

And that is precisely what the realized soul possesses, the fourth level of Higher Knowledge, called *Samyag Darshana,* Perfect Vision. It is really a return to the natural intrinsic Unity of Being which the dual mind has lost or forgotten due to the ego's divisive tactics. At some point in the manifestation process, the soul lost its way among its many projections, misidentifying with them and thereby forfeiting its priceless spontaneous Freedom.

That valued Freedom is called *Nitya-Mukti,* and is the fifth level of Higher Knowledge. As

The Seven Levels of Higher Knowledge In Those Fitted for the Brahman State

"The earth moves, causing the illusion of the movement of the sun; but the sun does not move. So, Prakrti, or Maya, or Nature, is moving, changing, unfolding veil after veil, turning over leaf after leaf of this grand book called life — while the witnessing soul drinks in knowledge, unmoved, unchanged."

Antah-Jnana — Realization of Inherent Knowledge
"The object in work is purification of the soul, to make it fit for knowledge."

Duhkha Samyoga Viyogam — Elimination of Pain
"It is glorious to withhold the soul from suffering with the body."

Samadhi Sampadanam — Attainment of Samadhi
"Remain immersed in samadhi but come out in order to help others."

Samyag-Darshanam — Perfect Vision
"All the little thought-whirlpools into which the mind has broken declare one single aim — a vision and a search after the Unity of Being."

Nitya-Mukti — Absolute Freedom
"Freedom is the condition of growth; take that off, the result is degeneration."

Trigunatitatvam — Dissolution of the Gunas
"The gunas keep the jivatman in the body from joining the Paramatman."

Brahma-Nishtha — Immersion in Brahman
"When I think, 'I am Brahman,' then I alone exist. It is so when I think so."

Those Fitted for the Brahman State

Easy Forbearance of Gunic Influence
"They who do not resist light, activity, and delusion when they appear, nor long after them when they are absent, are fit for the Brahman state."

Steady Abidance in Brahmajnana
"Constant in the meditation of inaction, in full knowledge that all activity takes place in prakrti, the one fitted for the Brahman state remains impervious to change."

Perfect Transcendence of All Dualities
"Balanced in pleasure and pain, viewing a stone and gold alike, unaffected by agreeable and disagreeable occurrences, imperturbable amidst censure and praise, stoic in the face of honor and dishonor, of even temperament in association with friend and foe, fully divested of any selfish intentions in all undertakings, and throughout it all ever abiding firmly in the Self — such as these are fit for the Brahman state."

That one attains Peace who lives devoid of longing, freed from all desires, and without the feeling of 'I, me, and mine.' This is the Brahman state. Attaining It, none are bewildered. Being established in It — even at the hour of death — the soul gets into oneness with Brahman." Sri Krishna

Vivekananda states in his quote, its loss results in the degeneration of the soul and its inherent qualities. As the embodied being falls further and further from memory of that pristine Source, the many aberrations of the mind kick into operation. *Karmas*, otherwise held at bay, and *samskaras*, theretofore rendered harmless, suddenly flare up and endanger life and mind. The result is a chaotic life, peppered by doubts, fears, restlessness, and ongoing misgivings. This is the price of the sacrifice of Freedom, and every soul should look into it and decide what is paramount and what is nonessential.

The penultimate level of Higher Knowledge is *Trigunatitatvam*, transcendence of the three *gunas* (see charts on page 221 & 307). Wherever and whenever the teaching of the three *gunas* crops up, it is always placed at a level of utmost subtlety, indicating the difficulty of mastery associated with it. Teachings found in the *darshanas* of *Yoga*, *Vedanta*, *Tantra*, and other systems, all point to the fact that an adept seeker can actually attain *samadhi*, but still fall away from it, mostly due to the persistence of the presence of the three *gunas*. Referring again to the bottom half of the chart, now on the previous page, Sri Krishna places the matter in association with steady abidance in Highest Knowledge, *Brahmajnana*, along with exercising caution with regards to the goings-on of *Prakriti*, Nature. He also cites a *"perfect transcendence of all dualities,"* which are foisted upon the mind by the *gunas* of nature. This is all fine preparation for *Brahma-Nistha*, still to come; there can be nothing higher, better, or fuller than Immersion in *Brahman*, the Reality. More on this will be given in forthcoming chapters.

Now that the reader has seen and considered the criterion and attributes for Those Who are Fitted for the *Brahman* State, another fine and related teaching, coming from the *Bhagavad Gita* through Sri Krishna, can be given. It is a presentation that will aid and guide the seeker of Truth, of God, of Devotion, of devotion to Discrimination, in every aspect of life. It concerns four definitive principles that present and reveal the overall makeup of Existence: *Brahman*, the Reality; *Ishvara*, God with Form; *Atman*, the Soul; and *Prakriti*, Nature. In a word, what is being said is this: *"The embodied soul offers the very best of nature to the Oversoul and, pleasing It, passes through It to Formless Reality."* Speaking of His own sixteen direct disciples, the *Kali Yuga Avatara*, Sri Ramakrishna, said, *"If they know who I am, who they are, and what the world is, they will always be safe and have nothing to fear."*

In effect, then, this simple teaching is profound, being, as it is, a clear and concise outlook on the entire process of manifestation and nonmanifestation. The artistic image that graces the chart speaks for itself. Along with this main teaching, four others, pertinent to it, have been added in.

Regarding the sojourning soul, it takes on and passes through the Four Transmigrations. Incarnating as a human being, attending the realm of the ancestors, attaining the divine regions of the gods, and reaching communion with *Ishvara*, explains and expresses this inner movement. For, man is cut in God's image. He makes his way back to blissful transcendence by accomplishing the Four Transmigrations.

With respect to Divine Reality, and all sacrifices taken on by *Ishvara* and the aspiring soul, The Three Ways of Clear Seeing confer light and guidance in the process. First, the aspiring being must always keep the Supreme Goal in sight, never losing track of It or faith in It. Second, and to help in accomplishing the first, the seeker must remain in remembrance of the fact that all changes, movement, activity, events, phenomena, and transformations, take place in nature, not in the Soul. Observance of this axiom alone, when fully mature, is tantamount to the death of ignorance. Lastly, and while inhabiting a body on the earth plane, the devotee should practice perceiving the one Reality in all beings — those who are living, those who have passed, and those who are in the process of dying. This both trains the soul in the art of embodiment and disembodiment, and sobers it so that it will not fall victim to the many distractions of nature in conjunction with the desire-prone dual mind. Thus, The Three Ways of Clear Seeing are another valuable gem in the treasure house of Sri Krishna's abundant teachings.

More on the level of basic but crucial everyday practices, known to practitioners as ones *sadhana*, the Five Offerings to the Lord represent a way of fulfilling oneself while maintaining *dharma*.

The Fourfold Presence

"The Imperishable is Brahman, the Supreme. Its dwelling in individual bodies is termed Adhyatma. Adhibhuta pertains to perishable nature, and the Purusha is the Adhidaivata. And I, Ishvara, am the sole sacrificer, the Adhiyajna."   Sri Krishna

2. Adhidaivata –
The Soul

4. Adhiyajna –
Ishvara's Sacrifice

The Four Transmigrations

Bhutas – physical beings
Pitrus – ancestors
Devas – gods & goddesses
Ishvara – Supreme Form

The Three Ways of Clear Seeing

Perceiving Reality in the dying and the undying
Perceiving the Supreme Goal
Perceiving all action done by Nature
while the Soul remains actionless

1. Adhyatma –
Brahman's Presence

3. Adhibhuta –
Nature/Prakriti

The Five Offerings
to the Lord

Actions
Consumptions
Sacrifices
Gifts
Austerities

The Five Criteria for
Divine Union

Divine Works
Divine Vision
Divine Devotion
Divine Detachment
Divine Love

Called *Sharanagata* in some systems, meaning heartfelt sacrifice, its wisdom revolves around making an offering of everything in life to the Chosen Ideal, or *Ishtam*. What one moves to accomplish, all that is consumed, every sacrifice one undergoes, all gifts that are given, and any austerity that one undertakes — it is all to be considered as a grand supplication of the Lord. Of special mention here, is that by the word "consumption" is meant not just the physical food one ingests (see chart on page 423), but all that is taken in by way of energy, knowledge, and spiritual experience as well.

These Five Offerings, besides diminishing the ego complex, purify the mind. Eventually, the persevering one who adheres to this superlative system begins to feel that everything is really the Lord's doing, and no one else's. Here is where the final teaching of this chart on page 387 — the Five Criteria for Divine Union — comes to the fore. Similar to the Four *Padas* of Lord *Siva* (see chart on page 369), The Five Criteria indicate a state of mind and existence that has matured beyond practice, as important as that is, having arrived at the indescribable experience of actually manifesting divinity in the human form. Here, divine works, visions, devotion, detachment, and love all vie for supremacy in the human heart and mind, producing a set of *bhavas*, or divine moods (see chart on page 587), that are overwhelming in both content and quality. To flesh out this teaching, we can select just one of these divine preoccupations — detachment/dispassion — and examine it, as instanced on the next chart on the facing page.

According to the refined teachings of *Sanatana Dharma*, the precious and coveted quality of detachment, or *Vairagya*, has twelve levels of maturation. These twelve are spread out over three stages of ascending order: mild, medium, and intense. If one sees a person in the process of trying to control the senses — and this does not mean just dealing with passions, desires, anger, etc., but specifically, taking the senses off of the sense objects — then one is witnessing the stage of *Yatamana* in progress. It is a very rudimentary level of advancement simply because the intelligent human being should never have come under the control of the sense objects in the first place, what to speak of base and demonic influences such as anger and violence.

Nevertheless, when the senses are brought under basic control, *Mrduvairagya* kicks in, sporting an off and on appearance of early detachment. The *Sanskrit* word, "mrdu," means meek, or mild, so the idea is conveyed of a weak element still present in it. But at least it signals the possibility of the middling variety of detachment, called *Madhyavairagya*. This is better, but as the chart relates, it is still lacking in intensity. Intensification is a feature that any spiritual preceptor would love to see in their student's practice. It outstrips that tendency to fall back on habit and convention in religious life. A divine restlessness even attends it, which impels the aspirant to extend himself beyond what is merely expected of him, into the rare regions of actual spiritual advancement.

And this is where the next stage, called *Karanavairagya*, comes into play. It will take some intense resilience and fortitude to remain dedicated to the spiritual path in the midst of the rising vagaries and vicissitudes of everyday life, for it is well known to the teacher that all manner of difficulty will arise when the aspirant commits to his or her practice.

But a whole new level of dispassion comes upon the seeker at stage five, *Uparamavairagya*. This is where desires become insipid, and even work and duty begin to disappoint. Called "world-weariness" by saints and seers, it has been noted as a turning point in religious life for many centuries in India. It gives way to *Anashakti* as well, which represents the first appearance of real and authentic detachment, or better still, nonattachment. The second appearance, however, comes upon the seeker when stage seven, *Sthulavairagya*, begins operating, and the culmination of this medium level ends in the attainment of *Vaishikara*.

At stage nine, *Adhimatra*, the aspirant begins to resemble the ascetic, for all those thoughts, experiences, situations, and objects he used to love and seek turn pale and pallid to him. The shine is now off of the world, attraction is out of the mind, and *maya* is losing its grip on the soul, that now senses and seeks something innately more beautiful and captivating. It is here that the seeker becomes a devotee, and the devotee realizes the merit of *jnana*, spiritual wisdom.

Audasinya, stage ten, is actually mentioned in scripture as one of the high states of *Jnanam*.

The Twelve Levels of Vairagya, Dispassion

"Sages reach the inaccessible, making it accessible via the three gates of Vairagya, Utsaha, and Gurubhakti. Serving the guru and the spiritual cause with great enthusiasm, they learn the meaning of dispassion and attain supreme detachment."   *Tejabindu Upanisad*

8 **Vaishikara — A more mature state of detachment, sometimes called "the highest state of lower dispassion."**

⇧

7 **Sthulavairagya — The Fundamental or "gross" stage of authentic detachment, which is not yet fully matured.**

⇧

6 **Anashakti — The beginning of actual detachment which represents the early stage of nonattachment.**

⇧

5 **Uparamavairagya — Detachment which arises from satiety of desires and disenchantment with works.**

⇧

4 **Karanavairagya — Detachment caused by the arising of various difficulties of life mixed with ever-interrupted pleasures.**

⇧

12 **Paravairagya — Absolute and supreme detachment which leaves the mind completely and permanently free of thoughts of worldly objects.**

⇧

11 **Tivravairagya — The most intense form of detachment short of fully matured vairagya, where a very keen sense of natural abidance is felt.**

⇧

10 **Audasinya — A very lofty state of detachment brought about by jnana which causes indifference to sense experiences and transcendence of all contrasting pairs of opposites.**

⇧

9 **Adhimatra — A high state of detachment under the influence of which the pleasures of life seem insipid, even feel painful.**

⇧

3 **Madhyavairagya — Middling type of detachment, lacking in intensity, which nevertheless rises up sporadically at times with intensity, but soon dies away.**

⇧

2 **Mrduvairagya — Mild detachment which is intermittent, vague, and weak, and which easily falls victim to compromise and distraction**

⇧

1 **Yatamana — Initial detachment of a beginning aspirant who, having come to know that the body and senses require purification, attempts to bring them under control.**

"Those who want to help mankind must take their own pleasure and pain, name and fame, and all sorts of interests, and make a bundle of them and throw them into the sea, and then come to the Lord. This is what all the Masters said and did. The fact is that the Lord is in us, we are He, the Eternal Subject, the real ego, never to be objectified, and that all this objectifying process is mere waste of time and talent. When the soul becomes aware of this it gives up objectifying, detaches, and falls back more and more upon the subjective. Until we are ready to sacrifice everything else to one idea and to one alone, we never, never will see the Light. If you want to give up everything for your own salvation, it is nothing. But do you want to forego even your own salvation for the good of the world? If so, then stem the tide of degeneration at the sacrifice of name and fame, wealth and enjoyment, nay, of every hope for this or other worlds."

Whereas earlier stages of detachment found the aspirant navigating dualities such as pleasure and pain, this tenth stage sees him encountering and besting much more subtle dualities such as bondage and liberation, form and formlessness, and, relevant here, the distinction between attachment, detachment, and nonattachment. And this characterizes mature detachment in that it is both natural and intense, which is the precise definition of stage eleven, *Tivravairagya*. It is the final stage of *vairagya* possible before it matures fully into Supreme Detachment, *Paravairagya*.

These twelve stages are given to the aspirant for his reference, but are barely discernible as the soul passes through them. Little is written on them individually, and they are more to be experienced and graduated than analyzed and discussed. However, utilized as a way of revealing just how much exists in even a portion of a teaching, like the one that appears in The Five Criteria for Divine Union from the chart on page 387, the point comes across beautifully.

To give the spiritual seeker and philosopher a better view and grasp of exactly what happens to the soul along its stages of practice and attainment, the following chart is useful. It will also be used as a pivotal mechanism that will segue us into the study of the *darshana* of *Yoga* which will be taken up next in this chapter.

A holy host of quotes by spiritual luminaries graces the chart on the facing page, now up for study. These sayings from spiritual life and scripture are applied specifically to levels of existence, some of them being not so desirable. To give an example of the scope of consciousness here, Lord Buddha's sayings at the bottom of the chart under "earthly toil," and at the top, which epitomizes the consummate spiritual adept, describe the basement and the loft of this Mansion of the Lord. What lies in between represents the struggle an aspirant will need to undergo in order to rise out of the valleys of suffering to the peaks of highest transcendence.

The chart, once looked into, is fairly self-explanatory. Perhaps some running commentary can be given on the lower slopes, where thoughts of these three worlds of heaven, earth, and hell preoccupy the minds of living beings. These are quite in line with the heading of "Restless Activity" on the left hand side of the chart. So long as the soul (*manas*/mind complex) dances to the tune of worldly achievements, just that long will it remain revolving at these three levels of relative existence, all under the thumb of the *karmas* it formulates. The three types of beings existing at these three levels are ancestors, human beings, and violent beings. The reader can look back on the charts that treat the three *gunas* (page 221, 223, & 307) to see how beings bind themselves on these slopes of struggle and striving, thinking all along, perhaps, that God may help them with their self-acuated projects.

But God is beyond relativity; even the gods transcend the ancestors and their heaven. The ancestors would do well to worship these higher deities, but since they do not do so on earth, why should they in heaven? All they want is another birth on earth in order to enjoy pleasures there, though, unbeknownst to them, this downwards moving trajectory is also due to *karmas* they need to expunge from previous lifetimes on earth when they did not worship and study higher wisdom. Thus, they — and all the beings at this lower strata of existence — revolve in *Samsara* on the *Kalachakra*, the wheel of birth and death spinning inexorably in ongoing cycles time.

So it is not restless activity, but calm, balanced works, that will help free the soul from such weighty cycles of *Maya/Samsara*. That is, human beings should work, must work, but all activities are to be done in *sattva*, not *rajas* or *tamas* (the three *gunas*). That is why far beyond mere works is wisdom *samadhi*; *Karma Yoga* must lead to *Jnana Yoga*, i.e., the soul must come to know why it is on earth performing actions, and how to expedite them consciously and move on.

For, there is a station so lofty, so profound, and filled with Bliss, that awaits the soul who satisfies criterion on earth and begins to learn the deeper secrets of Existence. Teachings of the *Dharma*, like the compilation of them contained in this book, will introduce the soul to its Divine Nature, or *Atman*. *Atman* is not an individual soul; it is The Indivisible Soul. It is not the ego, or *anatman,* as so many beings, even advanced ones, assume. That is matter mixed with energy and thought. The quotes by both Patanjali and by Sri Ramakrishna shown at the top of the chart suggests that there is

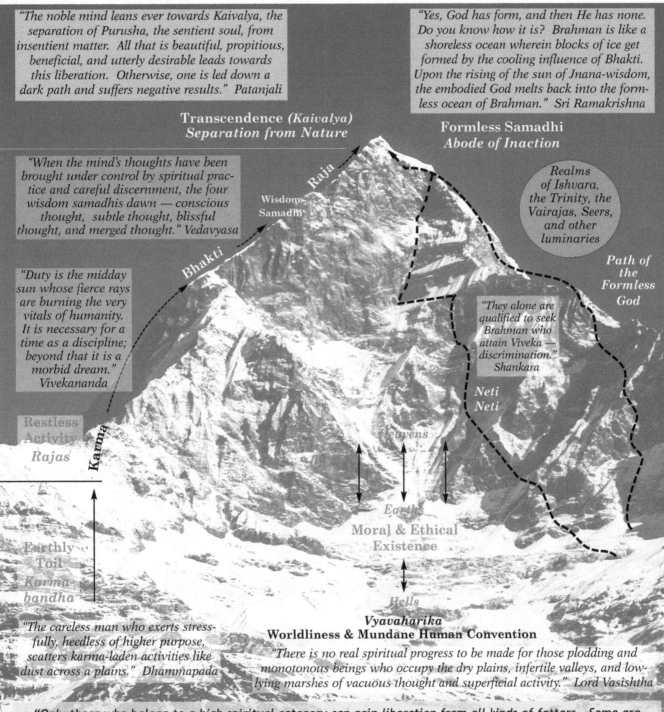

"Wide awake among sleeping souls, the wisdom-knower forges ahead of them as a powerful steed outstrips a mule. And when the wise one, having ascended to the high tower of inner perception, looks upon the world of suffering beings, he does so with an afflicted and compassionate heart. He beholds the ignorant masses as a mountaineer on the slopes espies people down in a valley." Lord Buddha

"The noble mind leans ever towards Kaivalya, the separation of Purusha, the sentient soul, from insentient matter. All that is beautiful, propitious, beneficial, and utterly desirable leads towards this liberation. Otherwise, one is led down a dark path and suffers negative results." Patanjali

"Yes, God has form, and then He has none. Do you know how it is? Brahman is like a shoreless ocean wherein blocks of ice get formed by the cooling influence of Bhakti. Upon the rising of the sun of Jnana-wisdom, the embodied God melts back into the formless ocean of Brahman." Sri Ramakrishna

Transcendence *(Kaivalya)* Separation from Nature

Formless Samadhi *Abode of Inaction*

"When the mind's thoughts have been brought under control by spiritual practice and careful discernment, the four wisdom samadhis dawn — conscious thought, subtle thought, blissful thought, and merged thought." Vedavyasa

Realms of Ishvara, the Trinity, the Vairajas, Seers, and other luminaries

Wisdom Samadhi

Raja

Bhakti

Path of the Formless God

"Duty is the midday sun whose fierce rays are burning the very vitals of humanity. It is necessary for a time as a discipline; beyond that it is a morbid dream." Vivekananda

"They alone are qualified to seek Brahman who attain Viveka — discrimination." Shankara

Neti Neti

Restless Activity *Rajas*

Karma

Heavens

Earthly Toil *Karma-bandha*

Earth **Moral & Ethical Existence**

Hells

Vyavaharika Worldliness & Mundane Human Convention

"The careless man who exerts stressfully, heedless of higher purpose, scatters karma-laden activities like dust across a plains." Dhammapada

"There is no real spiritual progress to be made for those plodding and monotonous beings who occupy the dry plains, infertile valleys, and low-lying marshes of vacuous thought and superficial activity." Lord Vasishtha

"Only those who belong to a high spiritual category can gain liberation from all kinds of fetters. Some are born just to enjoy the world. I say that it is good to finish, in entirety, all enjoyments and sufferings. But it is different in the case of the companions of God. For how many cycles did the rishis of old practice austerities in order to realize God, and you believe you will attain Him in a flash? Is it so easy to realize God? But this time the Master has shown an easy path; therefore it will be possible for all to realize God." Sri Sarada Devi, The Holy Mother

a distinction between Spirit and Matter, or between God with form and without. It is this subtle but crucial difference that the spiritually evolving soul must perceive. If he/she does not, then earthly evolution is what takes place, i.e., the passage of ego-based embodied consciousness through the six transformations of birth, growth, disease, decay, old age, and death (see charts on pages 225 & 247) in endless cycles. In this way, Indian Philosophy does not need to scare its adherents with threats of hell. Life on earth, in the body, when properly analyzed, will do that and more.

The age-old cure-all for spiritual maladies in India is *Yoga*. The word suggests Union of the ultimate kind, or "reunion" if the soul has somehow fallen out of remembrance of its indivisible nature. In the chart just examined, *Yoga* in its four main forms are all present — *Karma* (action), *Jnana* (discriminating wisdom), *Bhakti* (devotion), and *Raja* (meditation). The chart next up for study on the facing page can launch us into a deeper examination of *Yoga*, in all its facets. It has to do with Patanjali's overall assessment of the human mind and its bid for both higher wisdom and ultimate freedom. The Father of *Yoga* thus gives us — initially, and before taking up the complexities of *Yoga* Philosophy — seven methods for mastering the mind; for he knows that the mind is the main culprit in the process of embodiment. He also knows that if it can be turned into ones friend, in agreement with its purification process via *Yoga* practice, then all will be well.

And friendliness and purification are both contained in the first method for mind-mastery. The four *"Parikarmas"* are well-known, since Vedavyasa, Sri Krishna, and Lord Vasishtha, all mentioned them as teachings in more ancient times. They are friendliness, compassion, reverence, and indifference. The aspirant practices these four with regards to the four types of beings that get encountered in everyday life. The mind remains calm and feels fulfilled if this practice is adhered to with attention and noncompromise.

Vidharana is *pranayama*, but not merely of the physical and sporadic kind. Special attention is paid to all movements and phases of breathing. If this is maintained in the proper and ongoing atmosphere of holy company and guided practice, the subtle forms of *prana* are seen, and they soon get connected to the mind and its thought processes. This is akin to connecting the "A" of *AUM* to the in breath (creation), the "U" of *AUM* to the sustained breath (sustenance), and the "M" of *AUM* to the out breath (dissolution). Such concentration connects breathing (fourth limb of *Yoga*) with the mind (fifth limb of *Yoga*), i.e., conscious breathing awakens the *prana*, while using it to make wisdom connections purifies the mind and helps it to focus (*pratyahara*). A focused mind that can maintain its concentration can accomplish anything, and on any level of existence.

The third way which Patanjali suggests as a practice for mastering the mind is simple but ingenious. It actually falls in accord with the ancient *Tantric* practice of deifying all that the mind and senses behold and encounter. That is, since the mind is operating most of the time in the realm of objects, it should learn to look out upon them as manifestations of its own thinking process. Habitually and conventionally, it instead sees all objects as existing only outside of itself, and thus falls into the trap of trying to own them and extract pleasure from them. Materialism, sensuality, and hedonism then become the mind's philosophies, rather than mastery and transcendence, and thus falls into bondage to external phenomena. As Patanjali has stated, *"The seer has become identified with the seen,"* and he views this as a topsy-turvy arrangement. As the poet-saint, Ramprasad, sings in one of his wisdom songs:

> *Consider the foolishness of the game you are playing, O mind, and be ashamed.*
> *You, the noble black bee, should drink only the purest nectar,*
> *attracted by the intense fragrance of Mother Kali,*
> *Whose Wisdom Feet are vast lotus blossoms.*
> *Yet heedlessly you quaff the poison of egocentric gratification.*
> *O mind, you are infinitely more refined than the organs of action and perception.*
> *You are the natural sovereign in the kingdom of awareness.*
> *Yet you accept as bosom companions the most limited and negative intentions.*

THE SEVEN METHODS FOR MASTERING AWARENESS

With Vedavyasa's Commentaries on Yoga Sutras 1.33 – 1.39

1. Parikarmas
The Four Refinements

"Cultivate friendliness towards those who are happy, compassion for those who suffer, appreciation for the virtuous, and indifference towards the nonvirtuous. The mind thus becomes pure and, purified, it attains stability."

2. Vidharana
Conscious and Even Breathing

"As an aid for establishing greater stability of the mind, the practice of the expansion of the breath and the prana is duly recommended and utilized."

3. Vishayavati Pravrtti
Contemplating Objects

"By focusing on the nostrils, the tongue, and the palate, perception of the subtle nature of smell, taste, form, touch, and sound occurs. Celestial bodies and objects are also known by this special concentration. Via this method of direct experience doubt is dispelled, the teachings of the seers and acharyas get accepted, and the gateway to wisdom and samadhi opens."

4. Vishoka Jyotishmati
Meditation on Inner Light

"Practicing meditation in the heart-lotus, the buddhi reveals itself and appears clear and luminous, like a sun-filled sky. From comprehension of this ocean of sorrowless Light, calm and serene, springs the great realization, 'I Am.'"

5. Vita-Raga-Vishaya-Chitta
Contemplating Divine Beings

"By contemplating and reflecting on the minds of perfected sages and seers who have transcended all attraction for the sense objects, the yogic practitioner gets free of attraction and attachment and gains the state of stability."

6. Svapna-Nidra-Jnana-Alambanam
Recalling Dream Experiences

"The yogi also attains the state of stability of mind when he contemplates, in profound meditation, the states of dreaming and deep sleep."

7. Abhimatadhyan
Meditating on a Chosen Ideal

"Overall, the yogi may allow the mind to meditate upon whatever is most pleasing and beneficial, for through this method as well the mind becomes stable, and enters samadhi."

"To overcome impediments to Yoga and other distractions, recourse to the one-pointed practice of a single method is enjoined. As concentration occurs, knowledge of all things, from gross to subtle, is gained, and samapatti – mastery over the mind-field – is attained."   *Lord Patanjali*

What a petty potentate you have become!
Bloated by arrogance, inflated by flattery, your royal gracefulness has disappeared.
You resemble instead some minor official.
Only when the body lies trampled and abject beneath death's cruel feet
will you learn your devastating error.
The seasons of childhood, youth, and maturity, pass with deceptive slowness, O mind.
You suffer the subtle anguish of self-obsession like a solitary prisoner in a narrow cell.
Your anxiety over death is like a serpent who lives in terror of a frog.
When you grow sick and old and Death draws near to deal its terrible blow, what will you do then?

Even the practice that Patanjali prescribes for this particular method of mental mastery is unique. Basically, the senses, which are the mechanisms involved in this primal error, and that are *"....defective by nature due to their being outgoing only,"* as the *Upanisads* state, must be meditated upon to and at their very root. If this is done according to well-guided *yogic* practice, the senses give up their secrets, i.e., the *tanmatras* come forward and reveal their subtlety. For example, exquisite sounds are heard within when the ears and their power of hearing are meditated upon, and wondrous aromas present themselves when the nose and its power of smell are concentrated upon. With the advent of such inward phenomena, the aspirant comes to believe in the unseen and — up to this point — unknown verities of spiritual life. It will not be long until the sources of the subtle elements will be pondered, and true wisdom visits the mind at last.

The fourth of Patanjali's prescribed methods for the unawakened mind is probably the most well-known and popular of them all. It consists of meditating upon Light, in this case, an "ocean of sorrowless Light." This is probably the most welcome of all the many envisionments that meditation teachers hand out to aspiring beginners of the art, since it involves very little external effort and carries the least amount of baggage with it, religiously speaking. In addition, all beings have the memory of emerging from Light at the time of their birth, so it is rather natural to call such an aid up in order to benefit the overall practice of meditation.

However, some beings are more oriented towards form, and this is not necessarily a negative thing, paticularly in spiritual life. The fifth of Patanjali's methods, still pulling from the chart on page 393, is meditating upon divine beings, lovingly referred to as "deities" in India. These divinities are not always classed among the gods and goddesses. A more profound level of existence (refer again to chart on page 327) is occupied by illumined beings like saints, sages, seers, yogis, and *rishis*. Meditating upon these realized souls produces more immediate results, since they lived lives on earth and are therefore much more believeable to beginning and intermediate practitioners than the pantheon of gods and so the Father of *Yoga* suggests that the aspirant focus upon what is most pleasing and therefore beneficial for meditation — as the seventh and final method advises.

But the sixth method is not to be passed over at all. Its title alone — *Svapna-nidra-jnanam-alambanam* — is intriguing, especially to the knower of *Sanskrit* words. The implication is that a *yogi* who takes his dreaming and deep sleep states as objects for meditation *(alambana)* finds them filled with *jnanam* — higher wisdom. It all proceeds with examination of dream experiences, as well as noticing the disappearance of all forms in deep sleep. Whereas methods outside of India's ken search dreams for some hidden key or message, Indian seers who either suspect or come to know of the formless nature of Absolute Existence inspect what is left upon their disappearance.

Emptiness has always intrigued India. One of the proofs of Reality adhered to in philosophical scrutiny is called *anupalabdhi*, or nonapprehension. The absence of a thing presupposes that it was once present based on the perceptions, as well the nonperceptions, of the knower. The fact that most beings perceive nothing in the deep sleep state indicates that there is much there to be seen. Dreams that dissolve into deep sleep and dreams that lead back to the waking state contain different grades of substance. By meditating on both of these while the memory of them is still fresh, certain facets of consciousness that are buried deep come to the surface, bringing with them knowledge of their origins. Remembrance of past lifetimes can be classed as one of these hidden facets.

Thus, Patanjali advises the examination of the dream and deep sleep states as one of the prime methods for mastery of the mind. He avers that the mind becomes stable due to the gathering of such hidden and heretofore forgotten knowledge, and simultaneously infers that many of the sufferings that beings subject themselves to are directly associated with the absence of such esoteric wisdom. The spiritual aspirant verily rushes to fill in these gaps is awareness, and thereby plugs up the leaks in the sailing ship of the mind so that it will not sink in the stormy waters of relative existence. Scrutinizing dreams, as well as their disappearance in deep sleep, provides a rich field for the exploration of human awareness.

Abhimatadhyan is one of the most common of all methods in India, in any *darshana*. One might settle upon a "Chosen Ideal," or *Ishtam*, in order to implement this method. For Patanjali — whose system of *Yoga* does not even depend upon belief in God for its practice — any ideal will be acceptable, so long as it is pure, associated with higher Awareness, and is pleasing and inspiring to the aspirant. In the tradition of the saying, *"One gets to the Father through the Son,"* contemplating ones *Ishtam* will eventually lead the sincere practitioner to the highest state of Consciousness called *Samadhi*.

In line with other generous concessions of the *Yoga darshana*, however, Patanjali states that anything inspiring will suffice for this method of meditation. If the truth-seeker prefers formlessness over form, and that elevates his or her awareness, then formlessness itself will become the means by which *Samadhi* is experienced. In one inspiring *bhajan* of Mother India, this particular spiritual sentiment gets expressed nicely, but the composer prefers to use the form of Kali for his *Ishtam*:

> *O mind, meditate on the mystery of Kali, using any method of worship that you please.*
> *Or simply breath day and night Her Holy Name*
> *as the seed of transforming power planted by the teacher in your heart.*
> *Consider the act of lying down to sleep as devoted offering of your body and mind to Her.*
> *Allow your dreams to become radiant meditations on the Cosmic Mother.*
> *As you wander through countryside or city, feel that you are moving through Mother Kali.*
> *All sounds you hear are prayers and praises, arising spontaneously*
> *as the whole universe worships Her.*
> *The Goddess of Wisdom constitutes the letters of every alphabet,*
> *and each letter secretly bears the power of Her Name.*
> *The singer of this song is overwhelmed: Wonderful, wonderful!*
> *My blissful Mother exists fully through every living creature!*
> *O wandering poet, whatever food or drink you receive,*
> *offer as oblation in the sacrificial fire of your body,*
> *and meditate intensely on Her encompassing Reality.*

At the bottom of the chart whose study is just being concluded (page 393), there is a quote of utmost import from the Father of *Yoga*. The message is especially applicable to today's promiscuous practitioner who seems to think that casting about in different pathways, pursuing initiation with several *gurus*, and receiving a host of *mantras* to use is wise. Patanjali states clearly that *"....recourse to the one-pointed practice of a single method is enjoined."* In India this great boon is called *Istha-nistha*, and requires devotion to a single pathway, *guru*, and if part of the practice, *mantra*.

In order to keep up and in step with the "gait of the gods," the aspirant will have to avail himself of the knowledge of unique disciplinary practices, as well as the obstacles that may present themselves when implementing them. The *yogi* is a special type of aspirant that holds the attitude that facing off with life's difficulties is the best way to overcome them, and do so for all time.

In the chart on the facing page is found a concentrated list of obstacles well-known to both

Some Obstacles & Solutions in Spiritual Life

"Pratibhasika is the illusory reality, and Pratibha is the intelligence which is developed and honed to bring about the power (pratibandhakabhava) to destroy it, outright, along with all the impediments (pratibandhakas) in the mind which restrict the naturally enlightened state of pure, conscious Awareness."

Babaji Bob Kindler

Pratibandhakas – Obstacles	Pratibandhakabhavas – Solutions
The Main Impeding Mental Vrittis	
1. Vishada-vritti – Dull vibrations which cause despondency and dejection	Pranayama-manana – Conscious breathing accompanied by contemplation of scripture
2. Vitarka-vritti – Thoughts containing demonic vibrations which foster violence	Indriya-nigraha-nirodha – Control of the senses and restraint of negative thoughts
3. Shushna-vritti – Mental vibrations beset by falsehood and deceit, leading to suffering	Yama-niyama – Practice of the moral exercises and daily observances of Raja Yoga
4. Vijatiya-vritti – Turbulent and contrary vibrations which confuse and fluster the mind	Darshana – Keeping holy company with the guru, sangha, and other enlightened beings
5. Kashaya-vritti – Vibrations rising from residual impressions due to enjoyment of pleasure	Pratyahara – Practice of withdrawing the mind from thoughts of sense objects
6. Manorajya-vritti – Ungrounded vibrations which cause the mind's awareness to drift	Dharana – Focusing inward on the immediate nature of mind and awareness
7. Chanchala-vritti – Intermittent and inconsistent vibrations which cause gaps in awareness	Dhyan-samadhi – Meditation, without breaks, in order to realize the continuity of Awareness
The Two Powers of Avarana Shakti	
1. Asadavarana – The power of obscuration which covers the truth of Brahman	Bhavanas – Hearing, contemplating, and realizing the truth, which destroys all doubt
2. Abhanavarana – The power of obscuration which distracts the mind from Brahman via the manifestation of lesser lights.	Aparokshanubhuti – Direct and immediate spiritual experience gained via sadhana, meditation, and samadhi
The Two Processes of the Mind	
1. Vikalpa – The mind's unbridled tendency towards superficial fantasy and imagination	Siddhanavakyashravana – Guided study and right conclusion with regard to the scriptures
2. Sankalpa – The ego's improved shift towards more controlled and self-willed thinking	Samskara-vinasha – The destruction of subtle impressions of the mind via samadhi

"Using spiritual disciplines, the aspirant after perfection destroys all mental obstacles, snaps the chain of rebirth, and attains freedom from suffering." Sri Ramakrishna Paramahamsa

teachers of *Yoga* and its practitioners as well. This special list applies specifically to spiritual life and its aims, and particularly to the art of meditation. Those who have held a meditation practice for years will recognize these despoilers of inward focus and mental balance, and will also appreciate having names for them, i.e., knowing what they have been called by *yogic* adepts and masters in the past.

As can be seen, the entire matter falls under the overall heading of vibrations, or *vrttis*. When primal Awareness is in Its original state, It is still, silent, immutable. But when it breaks into waves, like an ocean under the influence of a storm, It pulsates intensely. But these waves appear only on the surface; the depths are never moved or affected. *Brahman* is the boundless depths, and mind is the generator of surface waves. Therefore, in order to realize *Brahman*, which is the ultimate Goal of the *sadhaka*, the mind's vibrations must be stilled. It is in this way that Patanjali states at the outset of the *Yoga Sutras*, "*Yogash chitta vritti nirodha*," that destruction of the mind's vibrations leads to union with Divine Reality. Then, the sea of *samsara* transforms into the Sea of *Satchitananda*. Even Its waves, should they appear, are blissful. As Swami Vivekananda puts it: "*The surface of the sea rises and sinks alternatively, but to the observant soul, the child of Light, each sinking reveals more and more of the depth, and the beds of pearls and coral at the bottom.*"

The chart on the facing page is, again, self-explanatory. Only the *Sanskrit* terms are unfamiliar to most. But the English translation saves us again, and we find out that many of these seemingly esoteric terms and words describe everyday obstacles that the human being holding a daily meditation practice will encounter. That is, and to move swiftly through these problematic vibratory spheres which are all too common — even outside of meditation — there is what is dull, demonic, deceitful, and restlessly dual. There also rises the urge for pleasure, the tendency to drift, and the penchant to fall out all together. If these seven impediments were eliminated, the mind would be full of Light and eternally balanced.

Patanjali has distilled these seven down by giving us the four impediments to meditation, i.e., laziness, restlessness, the duality of attachment and aversion, and the desire for subtle pleasure or, lower bliss (as contrasted with higher Bliss, *Ananda*). The mind must forebear these when they insinuate themselves in meditation, and then transcend them for all time. The mind of the luminary is fully under his/her control, and never wavers from that firm position. It is a mental *asana* that far outstrips anything that *hatha yoga* has to offer. And in fact, the illumined soul simply prefers the bliss of balance. Of course he would select it over suffering, but he also chooses it over the mundane pleasures of life that so enchant ordinary beings.

The list of solutions for the above-listed seven insinuations, called *pratibhandakabhavas*, consist of fairly common exercises as well. The breathing process is overlooked and taken for granted by most all beings. The *yogi/yogini*, however, knows that it indicates the presence of life force, or *prana*, and therefore utilizes conscious and informed breathing exercises to locate and control the *prana*. Really, if this one feat gets accomplished, most of the attending solutions on our list would not be necessary. With the mind under control, negative thoughts would not rise, the senses would not roam after external stimuli, holy company would naturally attract the seeker, and a spontaneous need to know the nature of Awareness would present itself. Meditation without breaks would be the result.

The lower half of the chart under study on the facing page takes us deeper into the teaching of *avarana-shakti*, called the obscuring power of *maya*. It is the *tamasic* element lying dormant in mind and nature. The teaching here, other than pointing out the covering power of name and form, is to inform the mind that the problem with forgetfulness is twofold: first, the creation/projection itself holds the power to veil Reality, and second, even if Reality, i.e. God, is accepted, "lower lights" will take the mind away from seeking, realizing, and abiding in It. As Sri Ramakrishna used to say, "*The power of ignorance (avidya) is stronger than the power of wisdom (vidya); if this were not the case, more beings would have realized Brahman.*" Of course, hearing, contemplating, and realizing the Truth — what is called the Three Great Proofs in India, as well as maintaining ones spiritual disciplines daily, along with meditation and striving for *samadhi*, will defeat the weights of ignorance.

The two processes of the Mind is the last entry on the chart on page 396. For a full review of the principles of *sankalpa* and *vikalpa,* the charts on pages 267, 269, and 297 will remind the mind about the Mind so that it will be more mindful about what it projects.

Mention was made in the previous page of the *vrittis* of the mind and the need to control them. The new chart up for study on the facing page holds a precious and traditional ten-fold teaching in *Yoga* that will aid the aspirant immensely. And in fact, the problem of failure to make spiritual progress can be traced to the aspirant's careless overlooking of basics such as the five *yamas* and five *niyamas*. The tendency of most beginners who get interested in *Yoga* is to jump right into postures *(asana)* and breathing exercises *(pranayama)* — the third and fourth limbs of *Yoga* — before taking up and mastering the first two limbs. Again, previous paragraphs talked about the powerful nature of breathing exercises. Awakening the *prana* is penultimate to awakening *Kundalini* Herself, and the body, senses, and brain need to be strong and healthy in order to bear such a brunt.

Even *asana*, i.e., sitting in half-lotus posture for instance, opens up the base of the spine, even physically, and thus the stage is already being set for the rise of spiritual energy in the subtle body. The precious human being and the potentially sacred body that it resides in, albeit temporarily, must be guided carefully and lovingly. Today's *hatha yoga* craze and its instructors fly in the face of such care and concern. No authentic teacher in India would risk the delicate balance of the psycho-physical being by beginning the aspirant at the third limb, ignoring the first and second. *Yamas* and *niyamas*, as will be seen, are crucial to the foundation that must be built before any appreciable progress in *Yoga* can be had.

The chart on the facing page is set up so that direct quotes from the Father of *Yoga* can be seen in correlation with their concomitants. Taking the five *yamas* first, we can see that the principle of *ahimsa*, nonviolence, heads the list. Besides common good sense, this observance helps develop the quality of compassion for suffering beings, and steers the aspirant away from the problem of *karmic* repercussion before it even gets started. The Father of *Yoga* states that all violence will cease in the presence of a being who has attained nonviolence in thought, word, and deed. So the benefits of this *yama* are legion.

Satya comes next. It is not just telling the truth; when mastered it makes one incapable of telling a lie. But truth is more than words, and transcends moral codes and vows as well. As Patanjali states, anything the *satya-yogi* says or thinks will come true. Such a boon could only come to a person of highest integrity and extreme self-control. Thus, the *yama* of *satya* is far superior to the occult powers of *prakamya* and *ishitva*, and *vashitva*, which inferior souls seek. Such unfortunates can, at will, make all their desires come true, but they find out soon enough that desires cannot be fulfilled, they keep constantly rising up. This is an entirely different outcome than the one the *satya-yogi* attains to. He gets eternal Peace, the other gets disruptive and worrisome power. There is no comparison.

Asteya is a lesson all its own, especially in this day and age. What to speak of coveting thy neighbor's goods in Jesus's time, or fighting over a few clods of earth with ones family, nowadays whole nations are going to war with the threat of nuclear-tipped coercion in order to get the wealth and resources of other countries. The *yogi* has no friends, has no neighbors, and pays no affiliation to any country or culture — not any specific religion, since religion in this world is all about gathering wealth. He only has God, and that is enough. And God owns all the universes in space and time. The *yogi*, then, is like the son of a king, whose father will certainly give him everything he has. The entire secret is, that he covets nothing. As the *Ishavasyopanisad* says it: *"Whatever there is changeful in this ephemeral world, all of that must be enveloped by the Lord. By renunciation of the world, then, do thou support thyself. Do not covet the wealth and goods of anyone."*

The fourth *yama* is *brahmacharya*. For the monk and the youth in his/her student phase it demands outright celibacy. For the householder it amounts to moderation. For the *yogi*, beyond a vow of celibacy and control of the senses it suggests the attainment and maintenance of a sense of

The Yamas and Niyamas of Patanjali's Yoga

"As much principles as they are practices, the wise adept and preceptor who sees the role and import of ongoing sadhana in the full recognition and realization of nondualism masters the ten yamas and niyamas, perceiving them as eternal axioms. He then carries them along the precipitous ascent to that loftiest and unseen height of the Eight-Limbed Yoga called Asamprajnata Samadhi."   Babaji Bob Kindler

Patanjala Yoga Sutras II:30 — II:45

"The Yamas are great universal vows, to be practiced at all levels of Yoga, and not to be delimited by conditions such as species, locus, time, or situation."
Patanjali

"When imbalanced mind and negative thoughts present themselves one should counter them by impressing upon oneself the positive qualities of the niyamas of Yoga."
Patanjali

YAMA — NIYAMA

non-receiving   continence   non-coveting
truthfulness   non-violence

austerity   scriptural study   devotion to god
contentedness   purity of mind

APARIGRAHA   BRAHMACHARYA   ASTEYA   SATYA   AHIMSA   TAPAS   SWADHYAYA   ISHVARA PRANIDHANA   SANTOSHA   SAUCHA

"Via non-receiving and non-indulgence the yogi perceives memory and mastery of his past births."

"When the yogi establishes himself in ahimsa, hostilities from all other quarters cease."

"Via austerities there is freedom from impurities and mastery over the body and senses."

"Purity brings out mental essence to ready the buddhi for seeing the Self."

"With continence comes the advent of strength and capacity."

"When firmly established in satya, all actions and their fruits depend solely upon the yogi."

"Deities, sages, and adepts show themselves to that one who is inclined towards svadhyaya."

"Pleasure in the world and in heaven can in no wise compare to the pleasure of the end of craving."

"Mastery of non-stealing ensures the possession of all treasures for the yogi."

"Surrender to Ishvara leads directly to samadhi."

"The yamas and niyamas, from non-violence onwards, should be practiced diligently for attenuating the kleshas. As a single hole in any part of a vessel causes a leak, so too does the neglect of any one of the yamas or niyamas render them impotent."
Vedavyasa

fealty to the spiritual path, the *guru*, and the supreme Goal of Enlightenment. Finally, for Patanjali, the master teacher, its secret is the gathering of spiritual force that will transform the living being into a divine vehicle that will render the influence of *Maya* nil and void. Among other strengths and attributes that come with the practice of *brahmacharya*, a facile and retentive memory is one of them. This memory will not only be beneficial in this lifetime, but will come to the fore in future existences as well, bringing back with it all the qualities and attainments gained and gleaned previously. And this brings in the fifth and final observance of the beginning *yogic* practitioner.

The *yama* of *aparigraha* is much misunderstood, particularly in this day and age. Rare is the person of the day who can understand why "gift-giving" is a negative occupation, and why the *rishis* of old struck it from their lives, even if they were householders. Of course, this rather conventional definition of the word *aparigraha* is misleading. Indulgence in worldly matters to the exclusion of spiritual life might be a better way of explaining it. The ancient luminaries saw the tendency of ignorant living beings, not only to covet the goods of others, but to go on engaging in the accumulation of wealth, goods, and property even long after they had gained all that they needed and more.

To great souls like Patanjali and Vedavyasa, however, the main problem was not just greed and its effects, or even rank worldliness. The real problem was that through overt preoccupation with economy and commerce, living beings forgot their past lifetimes and all the knowledge and wisdom they had gathered there. The twin tragedy of losing awareness of their divine nature, and circling on the *samsaric* wheel of birth and death in ignorance, was the result. Thus, they spent their time less and less in gathering and trading, and more and more in worship of the Lord and Mother and meditation on *Brahman*. The memory of their past lifetimes came right back to them, and they swiftly used the full sweep of their wisdom to free themselves from bondage to matter, Nature, and *maya*. As the Father of *Yoga* states, *"Via nonindulgence the yogi perceives the memory and mastery of his births."*

Up to this point, the reader may be able to empathize with the important point made about mastering the *yamas* of *Yoga* (the first limb of the entire eight-limbed system), before moving on to take up postures and practice breathing exercises. This point will come forth all the more as the *niyamas* of *Yoga*, which are specific fundamental practices, are studied.

Coming first, as well it should, is the important principle of austerity, or *tapas*. Taking up expansive and purificatory practices is rare in the lives of most beings; if they implement these at all it is mostly on the physical level. The mental and intellectual levels of mankind's existence also see some effort and activity in this regard, but what is missing in most all embodied beings, in most cultures, in most families, and in most individuals, is *tapas* — austerities specific to spiritual practices.

Ironically, it is these very efforts along religious, philosophical, and spiritual lines that remove the problems of mankind's existence, those very problems that hundreds of inferior means and methods are constantly failing to do. And in fact, living beings come back into new bodies over cycles with the same problems and impediments that they suffered previously, when according to the luminaries this is not necessary. Once, when asked if a man should be reborn, Swami Vivekananda's quick answer was: *"I would say that he should not be reborn, not until he can do so in full consciousness."* This precious total awareness is of ones divine nature, not just of ones ego, mind and body complex. It is study of scriptures, devout worship of God, meditation upon Ultimate Reality (*Brahman*/God/Allah/All-Mighty Father), and selfless service to God manifesting in living beings, that are the four main pillars of *tapas*. These are called the Four *Yogas*, and will be taken up in coming pages of this book.

"Deities, sages, and adepts show themselves to that one who is inclined towards svadhyaya." This is how the Father of *Yoga* describes the result and benefit of study and memorization of scriptures. *Svadhyaya* is the second *niyama* of the second limb of *Yoga*. Again, if this practice were placed in prominence before other limbs of *Yoga* were attempted, preoccupation with *asana* and the body, and imbalances of mind caused by premature breathing exercises, would be eliminated. For, not only would divine beings enter into the mind to guide the seeker, but a copious treasure-house of sacred wisdom would come readily available. And reading and memorization is just the tip of the iceberg

in this area of spiritual life. It only pricks the subtle memory (from past lives) lying untapped in the mind so that one finds, as Patanjali has related, that *"all knowledge lies within."*

The benefits of *svadhyaya* can hardly be counted. If one is confused about life and its activities and their repercussions, consulting the scriptures will straighten it all out. If the sweetness of devotional fervor does not arise when one moves towards worship of Divine Reality in forms, a daily practice of reading the scriptures and listening to their explication from the spiritual preceptor will bring it forth in gushes. If one is encountering blocks and lapses in meditation, the holy scriptures will give the seeker a massive amount of key teachings that will virtually inundate the mind and wash away all other relative concerns and considerations. The *mayic* overlays of fear, doubt, and brooding will meet a swift demise in the halcyon light that the revealed scriptures cast upon the aspiring human mind. This is the promise of *Jnana Yoga,* the express method to Enlightenment. All that is needed is a little resolve to remain at the task, a little time to give to philosophical study, and some patience with the mind and its present habits caused by past *karmas.*

But the *Yoga* method is certainly not one-sided. *Jnana*-wisdom is nicely blended with *Bhakti*-devotion, and *ishvara-pranidhana* sees to that. This third *niyama* has to do with worship of the Lord and the Mother of the Universe *(Ishvari).* It also includes in its marvelous sweep a certain kind of love and fealty to Formless Reality as well. Things to relate about devotion to God are legion, but the basic premise of the matter can be explained at three levels. To review these, the reader can look back at page 124 to find the teaching on *vaidhi bhakti, raga bhakti,* and *prema bhakti.* Engagement in *puja, homa,* devotional singing, recitation of scripture, performing all work as worship, rapt meditation, and more comprise the beautiful *niyama* of *ishvara-pranidhana.* According to Patanjali, its observance and consummation will even bring about *Samadhi* — the most profound and ecstatic level of Awareness.

Santosha is the fourth of the *niyamas.* By consulting the seers, it is discovered that *santosha* is not just a "garden variety" brand of contentment; that is, it is not ultimately about experiencing the subtle bliss of a happy mind. Its attainment brings about the *"end of craving."* Craving, *trishna,* is spoken of in both Buddhist and Hindu scriptures as a despoiler of the most virulent kind. It is akin to desire, no doubt, but is of a much more intense and demanding nature. To overcome this pettish and pernicious enemy to peace of mind will demand a powerful ally. *Santosha,* then, is a deceptively strong and able practice that soon becomes an attribute. It usually follows the appearance of a mature world-weariness in the soul's life on earth, and kicks in and operates as a ready and welcome filler for all that was given up or renounced in that phase. It is subtle and, as Patanjali states, replaces even the desire for pleasures in heaven. When looked at in this way, the soul begins to perceive the natural state of pure being, or "abiding in the *Atman,*" as the Goal of life, and not (return) visitations to inner worlds and pleasurable *lokas.*

The final *niyama* in *Raja Yoga* is called *saucha.* It is a kind of purity that invites one to be pure, but it also stands for innate purity that only needs to be recovered by the wandering soul. Purity in India never was just a matter of outer cleanliness, or moral purity alone; The soul, meaning the transmigrating mental complex, is pure, more or less, according to its proximity to *Brahman.* The closer one gets to God, the less impurities there will be, for impurity is not real, i.e., not a black mark on the soul. As Sri Ramakrishna has stated, *"Smoke may taint a window, but it will pass through a screen."* The mind that is close to its Divine Nature is like a screen that will simply watch the many impurities of nature, the body, the senses, and the mind, pass right through it.

And in fact, all the *yamas* and the *niyamas* of *Yoga* are to be seen not only as observances and practices, but also as eternal principles. Nonviolence, truthfulness, non-covetousnesss, celibacy, freedom from bondage to objects, austerity, scriptural wisdom, devotion to God, contentedness, and purity — all these describe the very nature of Reality — not like ornaments pinned on a tree, but like the innate green color of the tree. For the embodied being here on Earth, exposed to every kind of misery and form of suffering possible, the *yamas* and *niyamas* both protect and sustain. As Vedavyasa states, *"As a single hole in any part of the vessel causes a leak, so too does the neglect of any of the yamas and niyamas render them impotent."* The wise and sincere *yogic* aspirant, then, will pay all initial attention to these mainstays of spiritual practice and secure them, thus avoiding the risks and dangers of jumping stages and moving ahead too fast.

Taking a short break from the *Yoga darshana,* the chart on the facing page reveals what the Divine Mother of the Universe teaches Her precious spiritual children about *yamas* and *niyamas.* In Her scripture, the *Srimad Devi Bhagavatam,* She lists ten of each, many of which are the same as those listed in the first two limbs of Patanjali's system. We can examine briefly those that do not appear there, and which are more pertinent to the *Tantra* system.

In the *yama* department, *daya, samatva, driti, akartrtvama,* and *ksama* do not appear in *Patanjala* (the eight-limbed *Yoga* system). *Daya,* compassion, is definitely an abiding quality, but there is no reason why its tenents cannot and should not be practiced by the spiritual aspirant. The seers say that it is often the final attainment to dawn in the mind of an advanced soul, and that even adepts of spirituality are quite often still devoid of it. This shows that it is rare of possession. To be authentic, it must not be mistaken for pity, sentimentality, empathy, and other less intense forms of it. Real compassion is married to selfless action; in other words, just observing from a distance and feeling sorry for people's suffering is far less beneficial than rolling up ones sleeves and getting down to actual service. This selfless service will have to be formulated on a plan, and that plan composed with clarity of mind and purpose.

And all of these contingencies smack of *samatva,* evenness of mind and steadiness of thought. With the thinking process posited firmly in a nondual state of mind — of the *"if thine eye be single thou shalt know the Truth"* variety — life and its activities will move forward smoothly and remain free of the repercussions of *karma.* Called quiescence of mind, equanimity, peace of mind, and other noble appelations, *samatva* is highly coveted by spiritual aspirants and adepts alike. The luminaries enjoy it thoroughly at all times. Their lives are difficult for restless souls to fathom.

The illumined mind freed itself of all negativities and secondary consideration by attaining to *driti,* firmness. It is right resolve based upon gaining the "courage of ones convictions." Thus, it covers the activities of life, senses, and mind, all three. Its presence is why we never see or hear of a truly illumined soul making a wrong move, suffering an evil *karma,* or entertaining a bad thought. Sri Ramakrishna inferred the quality of *driti* when He stated: *"An expert danced never makes a wrong step."* We can interpret this analogy by adding that if a "wrong step" does come up in the expert dancer's movements, this master simply incorporates it into the body of the dance, and no one is the wiser. What was a potential mistake gets transformed into a freshly spontaneous nuance that actually improves what was originally intended. Thus, firmness has deep and long lasting benefits that better life and action even into the later stages of spiritual advancement.

Akartrtvama, another *yama* in Divine Mother's practical arsenal of tools, is most welcome for the greater percentage of living beings, as it applies more to souls who are trying to live a spiritual life in the world, rather than to monks who are mostly or completely through with the world. *Brahmacharya,* the *yama* of celibacy to be observed in the *Yoga darshana,* can seem too uncompromising for the average soul, and is not possible for married couples seeking to raise a *dharmic* family. Thus, the practice of moderation comes to the fore, and to the rescue. By attenuating the desires of the senses instead of tearing them out by their roots, a gradual control and eventual mastery over them can be gained. This is much preferable to the two extremes pressing in on either side, i.e., complete celibacy for life, or the worst alternative of all — giving free reign to the senses. As Swami Aseshanandaji Maharaj used to say: *"We want freedom from the senses, not freedom to the senses."*

The final *yama* in *Tantra's* list (that expands *Yoga's* list) is called *kshama,* or forgiveness. In this day and time it is a welcome teaching, since many beings are caught under problems such as poor upbringing, lack of love, failed relationships, and weakened resolve leading to over-emotional states of mind. Nonemotionalism is termed *Akshobha* in *Sanskrit,* and is a great aid that the sincere aspirant after Truth must acquire. In the West today, particularly in America, the entire culture has fallen under the dire influence of emotionalism, and is hard pressed to get free of it. Some souls

THE TWENTY YAMAS & NIYAMAS OF TANTRA

"I am the World Mother. Fix heart and mind upon this lustrous form of Mine and soon you will realize the union of Jiva and Brahman." Sri Devi

Ahimsa
Nonviolence

Satyam
Truthfulness

Asteyam
Nonstealing

Brahmacharya
Sense-control

TEN YAMAS

Daya
Compassion

Samatva
Steadiness

Driti
Firmness

Akartrtvama
Moderation

Kshama
Forgiveness

Saucha
Purity

Tapasya
Austerity

Danam
Charity

Tushti
Contentment

Shraddha
Faith

Astikya
Faith in Scripture

Homa
Sacrificial
Oblations

TEN NIYAMAS

Hri
Modesty

Ishvara-Pujanam
Worship of God

Siddhantavakya-Shravana
Study of Scriptures

Japa
Mantra

"The enemies to Yoga, union with the Self, are the six passions — lust, anger, greed, ignorance, vanity, and jealousy. The practitioner overcomes them by the attainment of the Eight Limbs of Yoga, and does so by first practicing and accomplishing limbs one and two — the Ten Yamas and Ten Niyamas." Sri Devi

have found, or are finding, that the act of forgiveness, if it be deep and sincere — forgiveness of parents and relatives, of betrayal, of ones *karmas* and of the *karmas* of others, and especially of oneself — conduces to healing. Of course, practices and disciplines will need to be instigated after such forgiveness in order that negativities do not just rise up again. And whereas emotional problems can be helped by therapy, spiritual disciplines must be advised and guided by a *guru* or spiritual preceptor. This will complete the regimen and ensure that *kshama* remains constant.

The *niyamas* of *Tantra* are overall a bit different than those in the *Yoga darshana*, though several are quite similar. These are shown on the bottom half of the chart on page 403, still under study. *Tapas,* austerity, is the same on both lists (compare with the chart on page 399). *Ishvara-pujanam* is the same as *ishvara-pranidhana* in the *Yoga niyamas*, and *siddhantavakyashravana* compares equal*ly to svadhyaya.* One could also say that *Tantra's tushti, or* contentment, is verisimilar to *Yoga's santosha* as well. With these four equaled out, what is left to consider on the list of *niyamas* are *danam, shraddha, astikya, homa, hri,* and *japam.*

Danam is listed as charity, and suggests that all souls avail themselves of the gracious quality of generosity. It can also be applied to the principle of alms-giving in India. The wandering free souls depend upon the householders to dispense food when the sannyasin knocks on their door. It is considered a great boon and good *karma*, as well as service of God in mankind, to offer alms to illumined souls who have given up home and family, as well as the world in general. For the West, this speaks to us of both a different class of human being, and a new precedent for feeding the hungry — what to speak of practicing higher awareness around God existing in all beings. In addition, *danam* can be used as a discipline that removes the presence of greed and selfishness in the mind. Sri Ramakrishna once told a story of seeing a man who, though he was spending thousands of rupees on his daughter's wedding, would not even give a handful of rice to his neighbor who has just lost his home and been cast out on to the streets. Such selfishness is evil; a bane of human existence. Practice *danam.*

Shraddha, faith, is a very high quality to possess in religious and spiritual life. In *Vedanta* it is listed as one of the six jewels alongside of inner peace, self-control, forbearance, self-settledness, and concentration (see chart on page 65). Far more than mere belief, faith possesses the ability to both remove obstacles in the spiritual path, as well as to help transform the mind to prepare it for higher *samadhi.*

Astikya relates to another kind of faith; that of a deep, abiding reliance on the words of the illumined souls found in sacred scriptures. Since it is rare to meet a realized being on earth, even in a series of lifetimes, aware souls know that what has been left behind by way of wisdom can and should be located in the tradition *(astika).* Fully enlightened beings have no reason to return to the earth other than to help others get free of the embodiment process and the sufferings that come with it. The sacrifice that they undertake in doing so finds its fulfillment in the souls they save and the wisdom they share. If they can increase and establish fealty to the scriptures in others, then it will be only a matter of time — even if a few lifetimes — before these students become aspirants, and then practitioners, and then adepts, until liberation occurs in one rare and auspicious lifetime. The revealed scriptures play a huge part in the spiritual evolution and freedom of the serious soul.

Homa is a powerful ritual through which both contact with ancestors and deities can be made, and *karmas* from this and past lifetimes annulled. When performed by a qualified priest, this fire ceremony has the ability to place the aspirant in a higher state of consciousness, even without any effort on his or her part. The offerings made into the fire by the priest and the participant represent the lifting of many subtle weights from the mind. As a daily practice, though this is rare today, homa can render the obstacles of everyday life null and void, placing the awareness of the ritualist in another dimension. *Homa* is still offered in India today, though much of the ancient knowledge about it has been forgotten.

The *Sanskrit* word, *hri,* denotes modesty. It is a good addition to the practices to be taken up by the beginning practitioner of spirituality. Since the ego exerts a strong influence in both life and spiritual practice well into later phases of these processes, a tool such as *hri* helps keep a watch upon it and helps attenuate it as well. Humility is then ensured throughout all stages of practice, keeping the path free of unwanted impediments so as to enable arrival at the Goal of human existence.

Finally, the *niyama* of *japam* is declared. It is an ingenious addition to any list of practices. *Japa*m, recitation of the *mantra* given to the aspirant by a *mantri guru*, is practically a *Yoga* in and of its self. Chapter Eight of this book will dive deep into teachings on the *mantra* and its recitation, and present quite a few charts to further the reader's knowledge on the profound subject. In the meantime, the beautiful song by Ramprasad Sen on the subject can act as an early precursor for that study.

This devotional wisdom song is especially symbolic, since it holds elements of several of the *yamas* and *niyamas* that have just been broached and examined, such as *japa* (*mantra* recitation), *hri* (humility), purification (*saucha*), and particularly, the fire ceremony called *homa*:

The Name of Kali is divinely sweet to taste.
Chanting Om Kali with every breath, one drinks nectar from the rare fruit of Her Wisdom.
Shame on you, my foolish tongue, still craving ordinary tastes of the world.
Yet all forms appear only within the formless Mystery of the Mother.
O Goddess, nothing exists except Your Bliss.
The all-purifying river, Mother Ganga, flows through every heart where Kali is awake.
Even transcendent Reality, the sublime Lord Shiva,
lies enthralled beneath the dancing Feet of the Warrior Goddess Who dissolves death.
O sisters and brothers, kindle the sacrificial fire within your heart.
Visualize both harmonic and chaotic thoughts as clarified butter consumed by fierce flames.
Visualize the mind itself as a sacred leaf offered into the blaze of insight.
With rapture, this poet sings: "Every conflict in my life has been resolved.
My body and mind are now owned by blissful Kali.
With Her own Hand, She has signed the mystic document of ownership."

Another wisdom song of India finds a good place here, including as it does several other inferences to *yamas* and *niyamas* in action, namely *siddhantavakya-shravana* (scriptures), *japam* (*mantra* recitation), *ishvara*-pujanam (worship of Divine Mother), and *akartrtvama* — moderation leading to asceticism.

O majestic Kali, O living Mystery!
You alone can sweep away every difficulty.
Divinely revealed scriptures confirm Your Power.
So why do You refuse to intervene on behalf of this impoverished poet?
Yet whoever loves You, Holy Mother, begins to shine with inward illumination.
The secret lives of Your intense lovers resemble the naked limbs and matted hair of ascetic practice.
Their shining bodies of Love remain concealed beneath the ashes of inner renunciation.
Through Your inscrutable Will alone, Mother, my soul incarnates upon this earth.
You present me with experience after experience of excruciating misery,
and still I repeat Your august Name,
Everyone is whispering and gossiping that the destitute poet, Ramprasad,
falsely claims to be the heir of a wealthy mother.
But who can understand our secret inward communion, O blissful Kali,
and the meaning of the poverty You have given me?

Before departing the salubrious atmosphere of *Tantra* and *Yoga*'s *yamas* and *niyamas*, a brief study of the *Kriya Yoga* system must be made. The original *Kriya Yoga* system belongs to Patanjali, the Father of *Yoga*. Several other versions of it have arisen in contemporary times, but these have been put forth mostly by sensationalists, mystery-mongerers, and spiritual entrepreneurs, i.e., spurious teachers who are seeking fame and gain via using the *dharma* and its teachings. Whatever the case, the chart on the facing page shows the main facets of Patanjali's authentic *Kriya Yoga* system.

The first fact that makes itself known upon examination of this chart is that Patanjali has chosen three of the five *niyamas* as his subjects and content for *Kriya Yoga*. This gives a strong clue as to the foremost elements that a practitioner of *Yoga* must have, i.e., a will to undergo austerity, extra time spent in studying and contemplating the revealed scriptures, and deep devotion for Divine Reality. This is it. These three make up a healthy spiritual life.

About austerity and the willingness to place oneself in it, the implication is that ordinary exercises like fasting and *asana*, and even moral practices like attending church or temple, do not transform the mind. Millions of souls have been adhering to such regimens for centuries, even millenia, but few have ever gotten free, i.e., attained *samadhi*. And the purpose of *Yoga*, and of *Kriya Yoga*, according to Vedavyasa, is to attain *samadhi*. *Samadhi* is oneness with God, or *Yoga*. Vedavyasa continues on to say that without purifying subtle imperfections in the mind — like *karmas*, *kleshas*, and *vasanas* — realization of ones inherent freedom will never come. He also warns the aspirant not to overtax the body in its practice of *tapas*; even the practice of *mantra* can be overdone, what to speak of something more physically radical like breathing exercises.

Referring still to the chart on the facing page, the definition of *svadhyaya* is conveyed by the Father of *Vedanta*. It is twofold: first, the scriptures themselves have to be taken up, studied, memorized, and contemplated; secondly, recitation of *mantras*, *slokas*, and the *bijam*, *AUM*, are to be performed daily, along with examination of *AUM*'s three *matras* (A, U, and M) and what they each signify. Further instructions on how to achieve all this are to be heard from the lips of an illumined preceptor. Without clarification of the meaning of *mantras*, *bijams*, *dharma* teachings, and scriptures by the *guru*, ones spiritual practice will be, as Vasishtha has stated, *"as futile as trying to grow crops only at night."*

Devotion and self-surrender are the two main facets of *ishvara-pranidhana*. These two are to become the basis of the everyday life and practice of a devotee. And not just ones actions and works must to be offered to God, but also the fruits that proceed from them, selflessly performed. The energy with which the acts are done, and from which fruits are gained, is also to be offered. Thus, with the combination of the three *niyamas* explained above, the special practice of *Kriya Yoga* can be undertaken. All other practices, qualities, principles, and insights — if they are not already present in the heart and mind of the disciple — will soon manifest and mature therein, in the brilliant light of *Kriya Yoga*.

The bottom half of the chart on the facing page is also related. The Three Treasures of the eight-limbed system of *Yoga*, namely *samapatti*, *samadhi*, and *yoga* itself, comprise and describe the highest attainments that spiritual life has to offer. As mentioned just above, the system of *Yoga* transcends all other observances and practices. The soul who takes to *yoga* practice has left the regions of the world and religion behind, and is now involved in transformation of mind and realization of what lies beyond earth, Nature, and the embodied condition. Perhaps this is why so few take it up. But when *samapatti*, evenness of mind (instead of dullness and restlessness in cycles), is attained, and *samadhi*, realization of the nature of Reality (instead of constant confusion in relativity), is experienced, the aspirant will be grateful indeed that he/she gave up the menial concerns of the world and the limitations of the body.

A guide to the five types of aspirants is also given on the chart opposite, under study. Much like the Four Levels of Knowers of *Brahman* (see chart on page 88), which cite the qualifications of the true *guru*, the Four Types of *Yogis* read a strict and decisive proclamation on the subject. It is very helpful for the aspirant to have evaluation of this type coming from beings of such high spiritual caliber as Patanjali and Vedavyasa, for otherwise the presence of pretenders and spiritual egos can throw up all manner of potential confusion in the mind. For a quick summation, among these

Patanjali's Kriya Yoga
and the Three Treasures of Patanjala

THE TRIPLE TENET OF KRIYAYOGA

1) Tapas — austerities or ascetic practices that purify the mind without taxing the body

"The spiritual life of a non-ascetic neither progresses nor succeeds. And without purification, karmas, kleshas, and vasanas only increase, creating a net which cannot be loosened or broken. But Patanjali avers that so long as the body is not overtaxed, the sincere tapasvin should practice austerity for purification of the mind."

Vedavyasa

2) Svadhyaya — study of scriptures, recitation of the mantras, memorization of slokas

"The moksha-shastras, profound and insightful wisdom about knowledge of the Self gleaned by the seers, coupled with devout recitation of the Pranava, the sacred syllable, Om — these make up the noble practice of svadhyaya."   Vedavyasa

3) Ishvara Pranidhana — devotion in all its aspects, along with self-surrender to Ishvara

"One's daily practices of Yoga, replete with all the various movements and actions of one's life, and even the very energy with which one engages one's existence, plus the fruits of all acts — all these are to be offered to God. This is Ishvara-pranidhana."

Vedavyasa

The Three Treasures of Patanjala

1) **Yoga** — the means to reach Self-realization
2) **Samadhi** — absorption in God-consciousness
3) **Samapatti** — abiding equanimity of mind
   The two states of Samapatti are:
   - **Savichara** – transforming consciousness by contemplating subtle objects such as ego, mind, intelligence, the tanmatras, time, space, causality, luminosity, etc.
   - **Nirvichara** – freedom from all reflections

The Five Types of Yogis

1) **Janma** — born with an aspiration to become perfect
2) **Ausadha** — by seeking spiritual experience via drugs, elixirs, etc.
3) **Mantra** — by repetitious incantation of the given mantra
4) **Tapas** — by undergoing various ascetic spiritual practices
5) **Samadhi** — by profound meditation

"The first three types may fall from grace due to pride and negligence. The other two are true luminaries, standing as examples for mankind."

"The noble Kriya Yoga is to be practiced with the sole aim of attaining samadhi. Its implementation brings about starvation of the kleshas and even burns their seeds to end any further production. Thereafter, clarity of wisdom and its awareness will reveal the separate nature of sattva and Purusha, enhancing the possibility of further involution." Vedavyasa

five types of potential *yogis* there are three who fail the Goal, and two who succeed in attaining it.

With regard to the first type of *yogi*, we find that at the very outset of life, before so many distractions surface, many beings look with wide eyes at the attainments of spiritual life and the prospect of being truly free, but among this wider population few will ever go the distance. It is as if they can taste the perfect nature of their disembodied Essence, but do not have the strength of resolve to realize the Truth, nor the power to resist the nontruth, i.e., *maya*. This describes the first category of aspirant.

Then there are those who make the primal mistake of trying to take a shortcut to spiritual experience by using intoxicants and elixirs, either ingested or inhaled. But substances found in matter cannot bring experiences found only in Consciousness, and the world is full of beings who confuse the two. This goes all the way back to the earliest of *dharmic* teachings in India that insist that the soul knows the difference between *Prakriti* and *Purusha* and, if it does not, develop the key discrimination *(viveka)* to know the difference. Otherwise, the aspirant starts out on a wrong course and over time habitual dependance begins to masquerade for spiritual Bliss *(ananda)*. This form of deception is subtle and runs deep. *Samskaras* of desire for intoxicants get formed, and the soul reappears in future bodies unable to break through them, and failing to recognize the illumined *guru* and follow the authentic path to Truth.

The third type of failing practitioner is one who, through some merit, attains path and *guru*, then receives a *mantra* to practice. This is a powerful path with three great boons to offer, so whence comes the failure? The aspirant loses faith in the *guru* and the *mantra* (and his/her original convictions) and begins to wander, soon taking on several or even many gurus and mantras. The intensity once attained cannot be sustained, and the soul falls from spiritual blessings into the world again. Even if such a soul, determined early on, stays the path for a time, he cannot maintain his practice long enough to develop a deeper appreciation for the teachings, thus utilize them at later stages of spiritual life when they are most effective, and so he/she backslides, unable to make spiritual progress. After all, commitment is sacred; it cannot be betrayed for any reason.

The two types of *yogis* who are most exemplary are those who keep up a strong spiritual practice all their lives, and those who are well-versed in meditation, or who are naturally spiritual and realized at birth. Among teachers, *gurus*, are seen both excellent examples as well as personages who only pretend spiritual maturity. The latter are known by their attraction to power, their search for wealth, their attraction to sensual pleasures, and their desire for worldly accomplishments.

Continuing on in the *Yoga darshana*, as well as in the vein of failed, lower, and higher attainments, the chart on the facing page shows Patanjali's assessment of aspirants who fall into three basic categories. As he states, *they are meek, moderate, and intense in their practices."* The gauge that he uses to judge this concerns the level of discernment, or detachment, that any given aspirant can accomplish. It is revealing to see that one must at least be able to analyse at the intellectual level *(mrdu)* in order to even be fit for *yogic* practice. The inborn knowledge of the difference between good and evil is also a requirement here. This is why we see so many beings with clever intelligence and none of them interested or able to practice *Yoga* yet. Discerning intelligence and goodness — if you have them, you may set foot on the Eternal Pathway to Truth.

The *madhya* level of aspirants include those many souls who, though they have not figured out what has happened to them yet, nevertheless have experienced spirituality in one form or another. What they are finding out, whether they know it or not, is that there is a presence within them that is extraordinary, and they are on the trail to finding its origin.

But it is at the intense level of aspirant *(adhimatra)* where barriers in the form of subtle desires vanish due to former austerities and disciplines. What else would happen as a result of this than the descent of peace and quietude of mind so coveted by the seers. In addition, and as a matter of course, this will result in mastery and the ability to utilize *yogic* accomplishments for the higher good of oneself and of others as well. And this can only lead to *Tivra samvegan* — those who have achieved that rare detachment called *Paravairagya*. These are the truly marvelous souls in all of existence.

Patanjali's 9 Levels of Awareness in Aspirants

"There are differences in those who are meek, moderate, and intense in their practices."

SUPREME	**Adhitrataman** (Paravairagya)	9) Tivra samvegan	Who possesses Supreme Detachment
INTENSE	**Adhimatra**	8) Upaya pratyaya	Who has learned the skillful means of Yoga
		7) Bhava pratyaya	Who has achieved abiding peace of mind
		6) Virama pratyaya	Who has succeeded in calming the waves of the mind
		5) Vashikara prajna	Who has subjugated all desires
MEDIUM	**Madhya**	4) Asmita prajna	Who is beginning to secure knowledge of the Self
		3) Ananda prajna	Who has gotten the experience of bliss
MILD	**Mrdu**	2) Vichara prajna	Who distinguishes between knowledge and ignorance
		1) Vitarka prajna	Who can analyse only at the intellectual level

"Real spirituality begins with rejection of the phenomenal world combined with a decisive turning away from mundane human conventions. It is the seeking of freedom that only exists beyond name and form in time and space. This is a rare goal to select among the people occupying the physical plane of existence. Beginners along this singular path will proceed either via intellectual pursuits, following the heart, or peace of mind through meditation practice. As progress is made, true detachment settles into the mind." Babaji Bob Kindler

While on the subject of *vairagya* (detachment) in *Yoga*, a look at its eternal companion, called *viveka* (discrimination), can be taken. In *Yoga*, as in *Vedanta*, *viveka* and *vairagya* are seen as being in conjunction with constancy of practice *(abhyasa)* and steadiness of mind *(sthiti)*. These four together are aids for attaining one of *Yoga's* highest stations, that of *Kaivalya* — which we will look at soon. But as an introduction, the chart on the facing page gives us a map for qualification in this particular *yogic* endeavor.

Much like the triple facet of *Kriya Yoga* just studied, this foursome shown on the chart may as well be another method for making substantial spiritual progress in and of themselves. As Patanjali states, the river of *viveka* flows towards the ocean of *Kaivalya*. Once the soul has learned to distinguish between the essential and the nonessential, i.e., Consciousness and matter (God and Mammon), the entire expanse of spiritual territory opens up like a fragrant, blooming rose. The role of *vairagya* then reveals itself, and with its advent all things inhibiting, extraneous, and obsolete fall away swiftly.

But contrary to what one might expect, the soul under the fresh impetus of discrimination and dispassion feels an even more compelling will to perform ongoing spiritual practice, *abhyasa yoga*. Additionally, as more intense austerities present themselves to the swiftly evolving aspirant, the ability to remain perfectly steady *(sthiti)* in both practice and forward process kicks in as well. Gone are the days of initial struggle with early self-efforts, as well as that old problem of a one step forward, two steps back type of conundrum. Instead, all is now proceeding naturally, free of most impediments. Sri Ramakrishna described this level of intermediate to advanced self-disciplinary advancement using the story of the sailor who put out to sea in his small craft. Sailing some miles off shore, he suddenly encountered a storm. He had to quickly take down the sail, secure the rudder, and bail water for his very life. After some hours of this frantic struggle to survive, the storm passed as abruptly as it had arrived, and the sailor trimmed the sail, put the rudder on automatic pilot, and sat back to smoke his pipe and gaze at the stars. This two-part phase of a sailor's life on the ocean describes the tumultuous early efforts of the novice and the later phase of swift and easy progress. The possibility for the latter depends greatly on *sthiti*, steadiness in spiritual practice.

On the chart is shown five aids to the attainment and maintenance of such adamantine steadiness. Enthusiasm, *utsaha*, heads the bill, and contributes both positivity and forward motion to the task. *Sahasa*, courage, comes in handy as well, to encounter and handle any obstacles that may still rise up along the path, such as hidden *karmas*, *samskaras* from past lifetimes, and fructifying *karma* (*prarabdha*) arising from actions done in the present lifetime. In this regard a vast amount of patience, *dhairya*, will be required — with oneself, other beings, and the world in general — since the shifting sands of circumstance and the changing modes of nature *(gunas)* will still be impinging on the spiritual maturation process.

But all along, there are two aids in particular that will befriend the seeker like no other. The first is the constant pursuit of Wisdom *(adhyatma-vidya)*, and the second is the increasing desire to be of service to the luminaries *(mahat-seva)* who maintain the *dharma* in this world.

And it is somewhere in all this that, as Vedavyasa comments, the *vrittis*, thought vibrations, all come under control. This mass of thoughts, called *chitta*, also termed "stuff of the mind," was a main source of suffering and waywardness for the aspirant in earlier stages of *sadhana*. Many struggles and specific practices were undertaken at that time for the sake of ridding oneself of all these errant and restless thoughts. And now, with the advent of this Quartet of conquerors, their presence is suddenly gone, their insinuations no longer a problem. Of course, this is the end of the painful reign of the *vikshipta* state of mind, and the beginning of the sweet and just rule of the *ekagra* state of mind — to be studied in a later chapter of this book.

The Fathers of *Yoga* and *Vedanta* place this quartet of teachings in the setting of the Father of *Sankhya's* teaching of the two oceans. Lord Kapila had, very early on in India's philosophical history, revealed that there was a stream of souls flowing towards ultimate Freedom, and another stream of souls cycling repeatedly in constant bondage. The beautiful phrases utilized for these, respec-

Viveka, Vairagya, Abhyasa, and Sthiti

& The Oceans of Kaivalya-prag-bhara & Samsara-prag-bhara

"The changing tides of the mind's thoughts move towards two distinct oceans — the ocean of freedom, Kaivalya, and the ocean of bondage, Samsara. The river of viveka flows to the former. The river of a-viveka flows to the latter. When the latter river is dammed up by the practice of viveka, vairagya, and abhyasa, access to the ocean of Kaivalya is attained. These three qualities assure nirodha of the vrttis." Vedavyasa

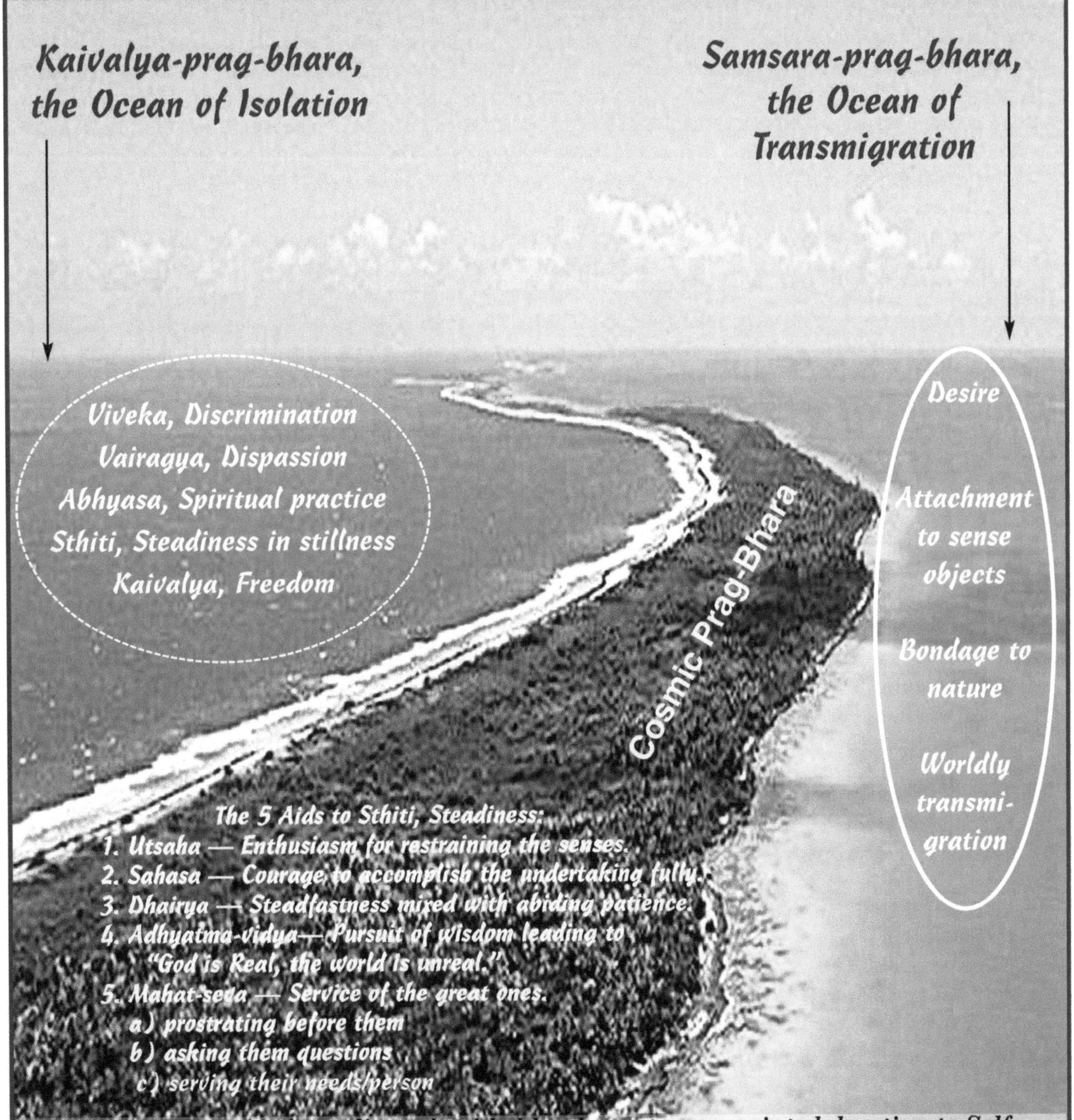

Kaivalya-prag-bhara, the Ocean of Isolation

Samsara-prag-bhara, the Ocean of Transmigration

Viveka, Discrimination
Vairagya, Dispassion
Abhyasa, Spiritual practice
Sthiti, Steadiness in stillness
Kaivalya, Freedom

Cosmic Prag-Bhara

Desire

Attachment to sense objects

Bondage to nature

Worldly transmi-gration

The 5 Aids to Sthiti, Steadiness:
1. Utsaha — Enthusiasm for restraining the senses.
2. Sahasa — Courage to accomplish the undertaking fully.
3. Dhairya — Steadfastness mixed with abiding patience.
4. Adhyatma-vidya — Pursuit of wisdom leading to "God is Real, the world is unreal."
5. Mahat-seva — Service of the great ones.
   a) prostrating before them
   b) asking them questions
   c) serving their needs/person

"The attainment of steadiness is aided by ekagrata, one-pointed devotion to Self, the Paramatman, whose nature is essential Consciousness." Patanjali

tively, were *Kaivalya-prag-bhara* and *Samsara-prag-bhara*. It is *Kaivalya* that we want to take up next in our study.

In most all *Sanskrit* dictionaries, the definition for the word, *Kaivalya,* is "isolation." This can be taken to mean the final exit from all realms of name and form, a sort of "final beatitude" in *Yoga.* But a deeper look into the dynamics of this ecstatic release shows that the word "isolation" also refers to the soul's departure from Nature. Here, it should be remembered (see chart on page 321) that Nature in Indian philosophy has two sides to it: one that is manifest, i.e., what people of contemporary times call matter, and the other that is unmanifested — all that is laying in a formless state, in potential, waiting to be turned into form. It is this unmanifested side of Nature, or *Prakriti,* that makes sense out of so many of India's principles and their conclusions.

For instance, its (unmanifested *prakriti*) inclusion into the mix clears up the question of where objects (like bodies, suns, planets, animals, etc.) move to after their destruction or death on the earth plane, and where they all come from when they return to form. In turn, and as follows, this explains as well how everything moves in cycles *(samsara),* why there is no birth or death for anything *(ajati-vada),* the difference between the insentient and the sentient, what lies in the formlessness of our deep sleep state *(sushupti),* where the ancestors move to *(pranakasha)* after abandoning their physical forms, where the deities exist (in inner planes of existence, *lokas*), and much more. Thus, the consideration of Unmanifested Nature is an important one or, put in another way, its exclusion from the from philosophy and from the thinking process of contemporary human beings will leave blatant gaps in its cosmology and cause much unnecessary confusion down the centuries.

Going back to *Kaivalya,* then, the unique turn of traditional philosophies like *Sankhya, Yoga,* and *Vedanta,* proposes that there comes a time in the soul's spiritual ascension when the atmosphere becomes so rarefied that all of Nature will fall away, and if it does not, or persists in any way, the advanced adept will have to see to it that it does. As can be seen by the chart on the facing page, this all happens in seven stages according to the Father of *Yoga* — all seven of them lying at a very elevated level of Consciousness.

Interestingly enough, the first of these stages includes the transmission of higher spiritual wisdom from an illumined soul to a qualified aspirant. A "transmission" is quite different from a lecture, a class, a seminar, or a discourse, though if the teacher be illumined and the student ready, it can happen in any one of these venues. Its real earmarkings, as already mentioned here, entail a qualified *sadhaka* who is sincerely seeking the highest Truth, and a very rare and special soul who has both established contact with Divine Reality via some sort of *Samadhi,* and received the inner command from within to spread *dharmic* wisdom to others. Of course, the dynamics of transmission are well documented in the *Tantra darshana,* where the high attainments of *Ojas* and *Tejas* are utilized by the liberated soul to impress the transformative light of pure, conscious Awareness upon others near to them. More on this subject will be given in a later chapter of this book.

The second stage leading to *Kaivalya* is the blessed and coveted visitation of *khyati* into the mind of the advanced *sadhaka.* The clarity that this welcome quality brings to all aspects of the mind — its thoughts, its perspective, its personality, its intellect — is indescribable, and must be experienced first hand in order to understand it. Among other important boons, its presence eliminates suffering, and that alone endears it to the sedulous seeker. But there is more:

With the advent of *khyati* comes that most surprising state called *Dharma-megha samadhi.* It is defined in English as the "raincloud of virtues," the implication being that all qualities once thought to be existing outside of oneself, to be pursued so as to become "a better person," are found to be dwelling within — and always were. This is practically tantamount to the realization that the *Atman* within is ever-pure and ever-perfect. That both spiritual wisdom and sterling virtues are to be found in oneself both propels the *sadhaka* forward and closes the door on any further doubts.

Comparatively speaking, if *khyati* and *dharma*-megha were welcome gifts for the advancing aspirant, the step called *mala-vinashi* in *Yoga* is a dash of cold water in the face of advanced spiritual life and practice. But the *sadhaka* is too far along to be daunted by the subtle imperfections that

–The Seven Steps to Attainment of Kaivalya–

"Through union of the two principles of nature and soul comes the observation of their fundamental difference resulting in realization of one's true essence. This process takes place when the Purusha abandons its relationship with matter and mixes itself no more with nature. This is called Kaivalya, final isolation from the endless stream of phenomena caused by the mind, manas, and the intellect, buddhi." Vedavyasa

1) Samyak-jnana — Wisdom Transmission

"One whose buddhi is filled with the discriminating wisdom that springs from constantly trying to perceive the spiritual Self, possesses the highest dispassion."

2) Khyati — Discernment and Clarity

"The highest type of dispassion is clarity of knowledge, called prasada. When it arises, khyati rises with it, and the yogi eliminates suffering, attains all, and snaps the chain of rebirth."

3) Dharma-megha — Raincloud of Virtues

"When rajas has been eliminated, the mind gets established in its own nature and perceives its distinction from sattva. It then reaches dharma-megha which allows realization of the nature of all things."

4) Malavinasha — Destruction of Blemishes

"Luminosity is the self-nature of sattvic buddhi. With impurity removed from it, its flow is pure and proficient, unsubjugated by the presence of rajas and tamas."

5) Guna-vaitrshnyam — Dispassion towards the Gunas

"Freedom dawns when all craving for the gunas and the attributes of nature ends, based upon realization of the spiritual Self – the Purusha."

6) Jnana-prasada — Destruction of Karmas and Obstacles

"When knowledge is at its purest, even the subtlest impediments, like karmas from previous births, get obliterated. This is the culmination of perfection, and ushers in an end to even the thought of form."

7) Asamprajnata — Attainment of Nondual Samadhi

"When all the vrttis are brought under control, and subjected to nirodha, then Samprajnata, the wisdom samadhi, ensues, followed by Kaivalya and Asamprajnata." Patanjali

this level of awareness reveals to him. As Sri Ramakrishna used to say, one can look at a piece of white paper and think it to be free of all visual imperfections. But if that sheet is held up to the light above, all manner of little dark specks can be seen in it. In similar fashion, holding the mind up to the now coruscating Light of *Brahman*, emanating sweetly in its initial descent into the gradually opening mind, reveals subtle blemishes in it. Thankfully, this Light of pure Awareness that is making itself more fully known to the soul, carries with it living sparks of dynamic *chit-shakti* power that will dissolve these remnants of imperfections, a superlative process much like the final shifting of gravel through a prospector's fine filter that reveals the flecks of pure gold that were hidden there.

Yet, another splash of sobering revelation awaits the *sadhaka* at this juncture, and that is the presence of the *gunas* of *Prakriti*. The advanced practitioner has long since been aware of these three companions of relativity, but they were also encountered and wrestled with in the mind and body, and in daily life. Now, here, at lofty spiritual atmospheres, when life is giving way to Eternal Life, the "Three *Gunas* of *Prakriti*" (see charts of pages 221, 223, & 307) present the *sadhaka* with a twofold realization: one, that they have an origin; and two, that they must be transcended in order that the soul can meet The Soul, i.e., that the now purified mental complex can merge into the Original Mind. The Bliss of *Brahman (ananda)* awaits. The three *gunas* of Nature cannot be allowed to play the role of despoiler no longer.

And with the dissolution of the *gunas* at a cosmic level comes the possibility of doing away with some very subtle *karmas* that were associated with them, thus impossible to do away with prior to this very refined juncture of spiritual life. The adept realizes here that lifetimes lived under the regime of the three *gunas* have deposited effects of a primal nature that only a luminary can spot and disintegrate. It is with the demise of these tiny increments of cosmic dust that the indescribable station of *Asamprajnata Samadhi* comes within reach of attainment, as the chart (on page 413) illustrates. It is in this classic way that *Kaivalya* occurs, that the soul gets a divorce from the form-producing mechanism of Nature, *Prakriti*. As forthcoming chapters of this book will explain, this will either put an end to the transmigration process of the soul (as a body/mind mechanism), or said soul will choose to return again to reveal the inner dynamics of attaining *Kaivalya* to others — like Lord Patanjali did for us.

At this point a *Vedantic* complement may be added into our *yogic* philosophical fare. The chart opposite gives out in simple terms the steps of *Yoga* as Shankara, the great nondualist, sees them. Interestingly enough, though not surprising, it all begins with controlling ones speech. Dishonest words, deluded talk, worldly talk, gossip, even talk about secular subjects alone all contribute to forgetfulness of God and the soul's innate nobility. As the next step illustrates, a desire for time alone with which to contemplate the *dharma* teachings and meditate upon God will naturally be set up by *mauna*, or remaining quiet.

And in fact, the young aspirant will find that these two initial austerities will go a long way towards overall control of all five senses, an inner feat that few practitioners achieve and most fall back from. At this point, as Shankara indicates, the absence of mundane words — on the lips as well as in the mind (as errant and wayward thoughts) — allow important words from ones scriptural study to come to the fore. These are to be "joined" with the mind, within the mind. When the mind feels the sweet grace and positive influence of higher wisdom again, the original intellect of mankind, long overshadowed by harsh, dull, and restless thoughts, will become receptive to the entire awakening process involving initial *yogic* observances.

This is the important beginning to transformation of mind, which is really a type of remembrance. As Swami Vivekananda has stated, *"If it (transformation) exists at all, it is less and less in the body and more and more in the mind — man, the highest form, meaning manas, thought — the animal that thinks, and not the animal that senses only."* Thus, man awakens to his true nature as Intelligence (*buddhi*) when ignorance disappears under the onslaught of (transformative) Wisdom. He was always perfect; he only forgot the fact. As Gaudapada puts it: *"As the clay pot is not a transformation of the unchanging space around it, so too, the embodied soul (jiva) is not a transformation of the Supreme Soul*

Shankara's Doorways to Yoga

(From Slokas 367 to 371 of the Vivekachudamani)

*"Only by that meditation that is free of all doubts does one realize the Self in Nirvikalpa.
Otherwise, other thoughts will enter into the unstable mind, which will then get mixed up with them."*

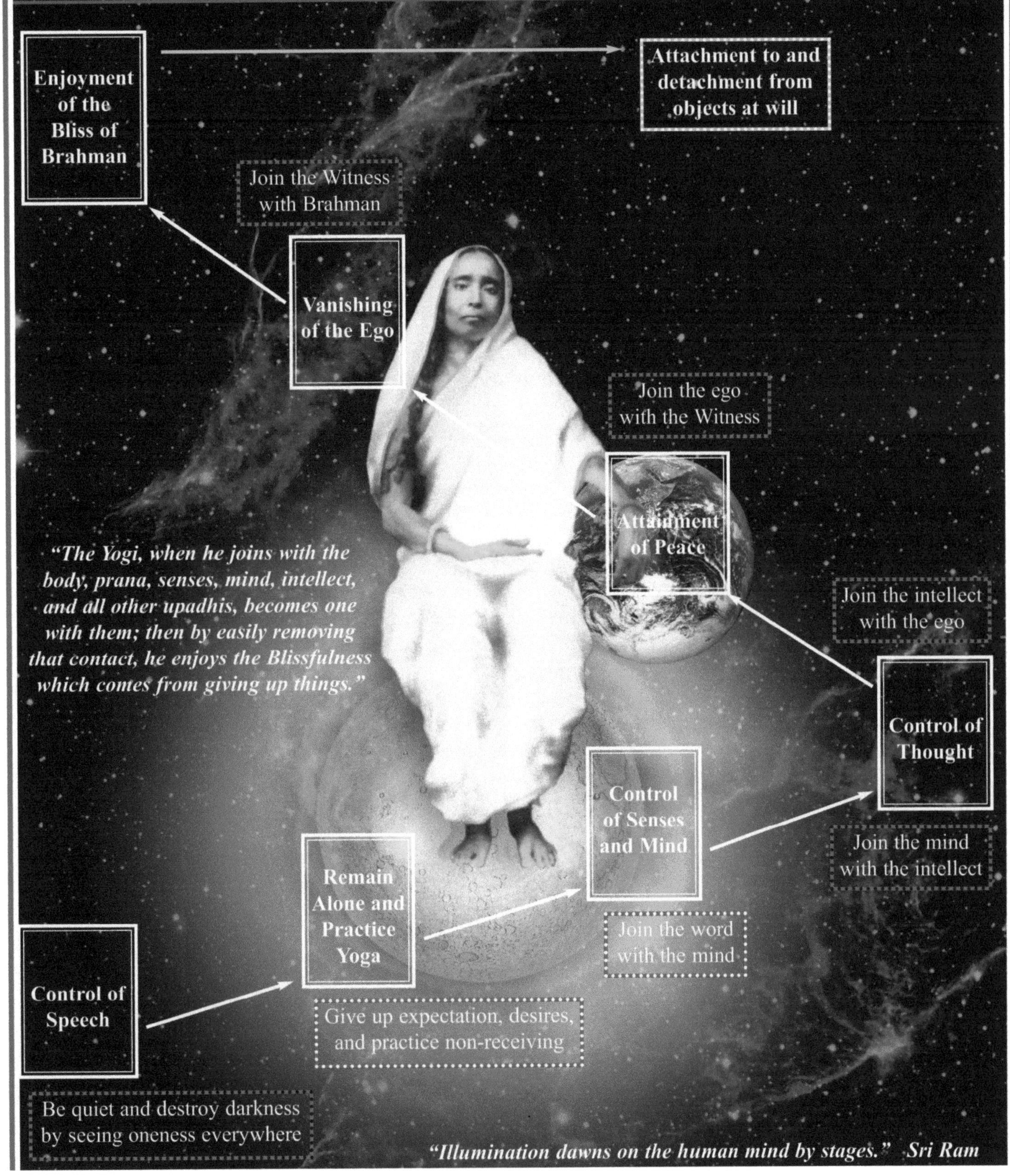

**Enjoyment
of the
Bliss of
Brahman**

**Attachment to and
detachment from
objects at will**

Join the Witness
with Brahman

**Vanishing
of the Ego**

Join the ego
with the Witness

**Attainment
of Peace**

Join the intellect
with the ego

*"The Yogi, when he joins with the
body, prana, senses, mind, intellect,
and all other upadhis, becomes one
with them; then by easily removing
that contact, he enjoys the Blissfulness
which comes from giving up things."*

**Control of
Thought**

Join the mind
with the intellect

**Control
of Senses
and Mind**

**Remain
Alone and
Practice
Yoga**

Join the word
with the mind

**Control of
Speech**

Give up expectation, desires,
and practice non-receiving

Be quiet and destroy darkness
by seeing oneness everywhere

"Illumination dawns on the human mind by stages." Sri Ram

(Paramatman), who had these changes projected upon It by ignorant minds."

With restless thoughts and dull mind controlled, peace descends. At these fresh junctures, the ego, usually so contrary to any type of powerful transformation, suddenly heeds the higher vibrations of the intellect. In this classic moment of peaceful inwardness, it obtains the opportunity to glimpse what Indian Philosophy calls "The Witness of all phenomena." When events in space and time are seen to be ephemeral and dreamlike, the now spiritually awakened soul feels the presence of nondual Reality, or *Brahman.* Thus, the "Peace *(Shanti)* that passes all understanding" swiftly gives rise to the Bliss *(Ananda)* that transcends all forms of happiness. Among other things, all doubt has died away forever, and this allows for the forthcoming experience of *Nirvikalpa Samadhi.*

Along the way of these opening doorways indicated by Shankara, mention was made several times of the important feat of controlling the senses. The chart on the facing page gives a classic rendering of all the facets involved in this crucial process. All the basic quintuplications are shown there, from the five elements, to the five senses, to the five *tanmatras* (subtle elements). The five *pranas* are the reigns connected to the mental composite consisting of ego, intellect, mind, and the ever-fertile thoughts. This cosmic chariot of the gods should always be in perfect running order, thus able to conduct the soul to any realm, internal or external, free of resistance and anxiety.

The reason why this vital vehicle gets imbalanced is threefold: want of mastery over the vital force *(prana)*; ignorance of the *tanmatras* as subtle elements existing in ones dream state; and lack of knowledge of what objects really signify. The key practice that will improve these problems is meditation. As Patanjali states in the quote on the chart, it is by meditation on the elements, the senses, and the mind, that the truth about objects gets revealed. "Meditation," here, is not just contemplation; it is also connection. Connection is mastery. And the truth about objects is that they have come into existence via the mind. One cannot just trace them to Nature, for all of Nature lies within the mind. One cannot leave them disconnected, believing them to have a separate existence of their own, as they are then granted power over the soul, who becomes subservient to them. This is called materialism. It is also called attachment leading to bondage.

Once these fundamental connections have been made (it should be noted here that luminaries who come to earth never lose them in the first place), higher stations can be taken up for meditation. As the Father of *Yoga* states, and as was mentioned above, the ego will give up its hold on relativity when it is contemplated for its essence. It has none. As Sri Ramakrishna has stated, *"The ego is like an onion — all layers and no center."* If left to its own devices, it will also make one cry like an onion does. But when this "separate I-maker" is shown up to be empty in this regard, the soul will naturally look for the fullness that it feels underlying all phenomena. This is where Patanjali gives out the teaching that *"....the Purusha will transcend the very idea of selfhood and begin to meditate on the awareness of cessation."*

The "awareness of cessation" is a little-known secret of advanced spiritual practice. Emptiness may not be the final station of enlightenment, but it is the key to finally perceiving Ultimate Reality. When the indrawn soul can ponder the wonder of emptiness when it appears, yet still recognize that there is another entity witnessing this emptiness, that is when a huge opening into the Ocean of Nondual Awareness occurs.

This extraordinary spiritual implosion, sometimes called the opening of the *Jnana-chakshu* (Wisdom Eye), and refered to by the saying, *"If thine Eye be single thou shalt know the Truth,"* is the consummation of both years of self-effort and spiritual practice, as well as the *samadhis* of knowledge, bliss, and mature "I-ness." Much more will get related about this lofty subject in forthcoming chapters of this book. Suffice to say, that its advent brings in its wake the first real and abiding kinds of formless meditation and nondual experience, filling in this rare but vital attribute in the aspiring soul's spiritual life and spiritual capabilities.

Keeping up with the "gait of the gods" will demand attainments which have been listed and explained over the last few pages of this chapter. While we are on the subject of *Yoga,* and to complete its place and role as a major "footfall" of the Indian *rishis,* one final chart can be displayed.

Controlling the Five Senses In Yoga

By meditating upon the elements, the senses, and mind, the hidden truth about objects gets revealed. Meditation upon the subtle elements and the sense of I-ness expands thought, awakens wisdom, and tames the ego. Then, meditation upon the true individual along with its intelligence delimits the ego and exposes the fount of Joy within oneself. The Purusha then transcends the very idea of selfhood and meditates on the awareness of cessation. Thus do the samadhis of knowledge, bliss, and I-ness lead to Formlessness. Patanjala Yoga

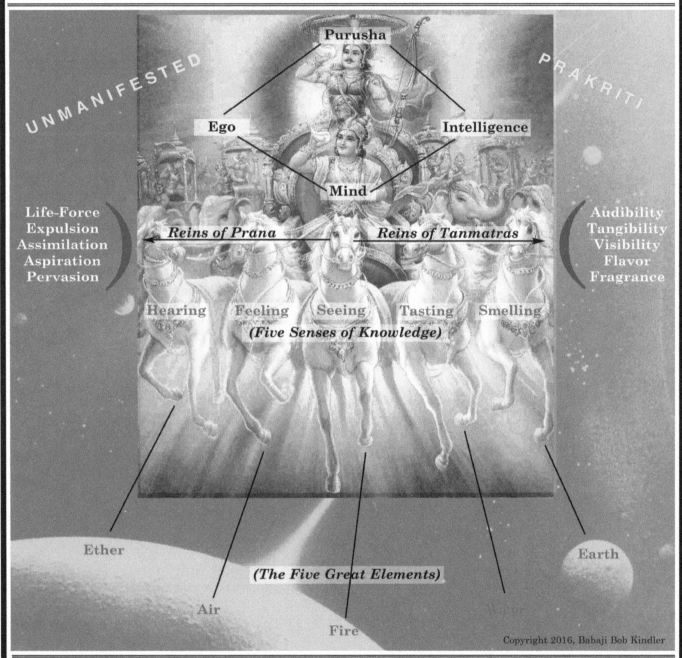

UNMANIFESTED

PRAKRITI

Purusha

Ego

Intelligence

Mind

Life-Force
Expulsion
Assimilation
Aspiration
Pervasion

Audibility
Tangibility
Visibility
Flavor
Fragrance

Reins of Prana ← → *Reins of Tanmatras*

Hearing   Feeling   Seeing   Tasting   Smelling
(Five Senses of Knowledge)

Ether

Earth

(The Five Great Elements)

Air

Water

Fire

Copyright 2016, Babaji Bob Kindler

"Meditating with intense focus upon the principles of existence, the seeker de-fragments the mind and unifies himself with nature. Unification, here, is not one of identity, but one of connection. That is, oneness with nature would mean his Soul is one with birth, decay, and death, and this is not the case. The Soul is eternal Existence. Thus, realizing that all of nature has come out of his mental process via the power of projection, the yogi takes stock of the evolutes of nature, from gross to subtle, contemplates them, and masters them. In this way he separates the true Self from the apparent self, and from nature." Babaji Bob Kindler

The Five *Kleshas* of *Yoga* have been mentioned twice in previous chapters. Here, we can finally take a good look at them with a mind to eradicate them forever from the mental and spiritual picture. When these five problematic obstacles — called "calamities in Nature" by Patanjali — are taken into account, the first thought about them is that they are not anything difficult of comprehension. It is upon deeper inspection that several other facets are uncovered which render them into a rather esoteric matter. This is mostly due to their causes. For instance, one might think, in the contemporary Western conventional strain, that ignorance is just a matter of lack of learning or the absence of knowledge. But in Indian philosophy, which looks upon ignorance and knowledge as a duality — as two thorns in the flesh of the authentic student seeking nonduality — that *avidya*, ignorance, it is really a matter of misidentification.

That is, the primal *Purusha*, which is pure Sentience Itself, and which has taken on a body/mind mechanism for purposes of divine expression, has mistakenly become identified with cosmic stations along the way of its manifestation process, and has thereby forgotten its formless Essence, the *Atman*. Therefore, the problem of *avidya* is not illiteracy, but instead the soul's eightfold identification with unmanifested *prakriti* (formless Nature), *mahat* (cosmic mind), *ahamkara* (ego), and the five elements of earth, water, fire, air, and ether (the *panchamahabhutas*). Though these are lofty considerations for the soul, they are insentient principles, not *Brahman/Atman*. Further, and as Patanjali states, *jnana*, knowledge, is not inherently in them, so identifying with them will tend to "veil" the soul's wisdom — which is always inherent to Itself.

And so, the "calamity," here, is of the nature of stumbling blocks in the path. In the case of the second *klesha*, called *asmita*, the matter becomes more personal, the issues, more convoluted. The eight tripping stones here are the *asta-bala-siddhas*, the personal occult powers, which also exist in the soul (mind). Both seeking them and possessing them brings the soul to ruin via the three types of confusions that they cause, either immediately or over time. These are called *vichara-moha, chesta-moha*, and *vedana-moha*. The embodied being begins to lose control of his actions, his feelings, his energy, and his thoughts, by allowing the propensity for power to overtake his mind. Free of these powers, and with this tendency to exercise them neutralized, a pure, simple, unostentatious life in the *dharma* can be lived, full of contentment, peace, and bliss. For a list of the occult powers the reader can look back to the chart on page 660).

The third and fourth *kleshas* to consider are a team, called *raga* and *dvesha*, or *ragadveshau* — attraction and aversion. Of course, the problem of attachment is based upon the desire for pleasure. In this regard, and since preoccupation with the occult powers has already been entertained by the mind, it only remains to try to employ all eight in order to secure what is desired. Of the eight, the power to dominate over Nature, as well as over other beings (*ishitva*), comes to the fore. But getting the desired object and its corresponding pleasure only leads to a longing for more "exquisite" enjoyment. When this is not always possible, it is then that the next stage of impediment rears its ugly head.

Aversion, called *dvesha*, is the fourth of the five *kleshas*. When cycles of nonproduction and nonreturn occur, the contented soul, free of the pursuit of occult powers, simply settles down and waits for the next cycle of abundance. The deluded soul under the press of attraction, however (plus the first two *kleshas*), puts up all manner of resistance and attempts to force the hand of auspicious timing. This results in great failure and deep suffering. As the Holy Mother was wont to say about the predicament of trying to satisfy desires at inauspicious times, *"It is like attempting to secure good mangos out of season."* All in all, we find out, thanks to Patanjali, that aversion is not just about our likes and dislikes, or our emotional states, but applies more to habits and complexes that are deeper in our mind's consciousness.

The final *klesha, abhinivesha*, has been defined as "clinging to life," but can also be termed the fear of death. Despite the soul's crushing disappointment at having the occult powers fail him, he nevertheless lives in abject fear of losing them altogether. Further, Patanjali paints a starker picture still by declaring that such souls face this disaster "at the end of a cycle," which means that the unfor-

The Insinuation of the Five Kleshas on Spiritual Life
The Emergence and Elimination of the Impediments to Yoga

"From the root, 'klish,' which means 'to suffer,' the five kleshas of Yoga are called pancha-parva due to their having five sections. They spring from the inscrutable principle of Nescience, the infamous 'Cloud of Unknowing,' and form its very parts. Caused by perverse cognition or fundamental misapprehension, they are the seeds of calamity within samsara itself and the gears which turn the wheel of birth and death in ignorance." Yoga Sutras

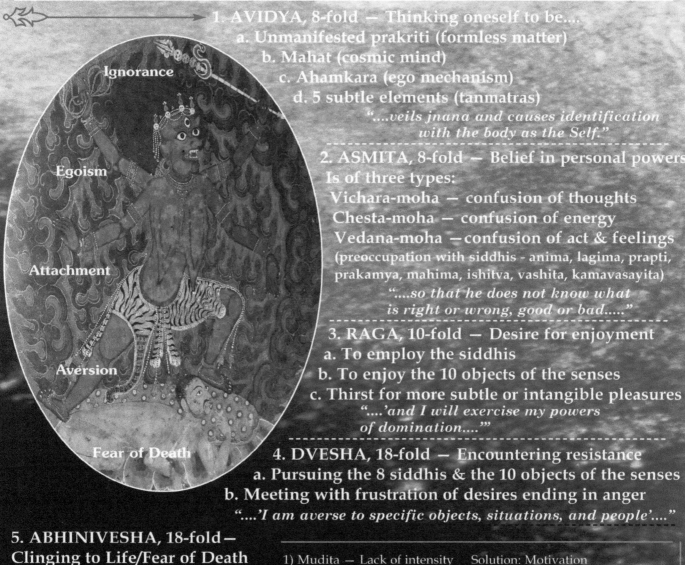

Ignorance

Egoism

Attachment

Aversion

Fear of Death

1. AVIDYA, 8-fold — Thinking oneself to be....
a. Unmanifested prakriti (formless matter)
b. Mahat (cosmic mind)
c. Ahamkara (ego mechanism)
d. 5 subtle elements (tanmatras)
"....veils jnana and causes identification with the body as the Self."

------

2. ASMITA, 8-fold — Belief in personal powers
Is of three types:
Vichara-moha — confusion of thoughts
Chesta-moha — confusion of energy
Vedana-moha —confusion of act & feelings
(preoccupation with siddhis - anima, lagima, prapti, prakamya, mahima, ishitva, vashita, kamavasayita)
"....so that he does not know what is right or wrong, good or bad....."

------

3. RAGA, 10-fold — Desire for enjoyment
a. To employ the siddhis
b. To enjoy the 10 objects of the senses
c. Thirst for more subtle or intangible pleasures
"....'and I will exercise my powers of domination....'"

------

4. DVESHA, 18-fold — Encountering resistance
a. Pursuing the 8 siddhis & the 10 objects of the senses
b. Meeting with frustration of desires ending in anger
"....'I am averse to specific objects, situations, and people'...."

5. ABHINIVESHA, 18-fold—
Clinging to Life/Fear of Death
a. Attaining full enjoyment
b. Boredom/dissatisfaction
c. Living in fear of loss
"....fear at the loss of powers and pleasures at the end of a cycle...."

Contemporary Kleshas
of Neo Vedanta

1) Mudita — Lack of intensity	Solution: Motivation
2) Kamana — Pleasure-seeking	Solution: Austerity
3) Styana — Disinterest	Solution: Study
4) Vikshipta — Distraction	Solution: Focus
5) Vishada — Despondency	Solution: Activity
6) Alasya — Listlessness	Solution: Spiritual orientation
7) Kshina — Weakness	Solution: Determination/resolve
8) Samkocha — Procrastination	Solution: Routine practice
9) Amarsha — Negativity	Solution: Positivity
10) Ahaituka — Cynicism	Solution: Sincerity, humility, service
11) Doshadrsti — Fault-finding	Solution: Compassion

"The five kleshas cause affliction by turning internalized awareness outward so that it does not dwell on its own perfect nature. Thus, they are a mutation of the mind-field, and they swiftly become a field of abundant growth for a host of karmas and samskaras." Vedavyasa

tunate being had nursed, enjoyed, and suffered the eight occult powers for lifetimes. If placed in the context of everyday life, where the occult powers have their hidden influence, the entire matter courts pleasure, boredom, fear of loss of pleasure, and fear of death as well. Meanwhile, the devotee of the Lord who eschewed the occult powers, and sought only to realize God all the while, is enjoying peace and bliss, and — when the time comes — places death in its own grave.

While we are on the subject of controlling the erratic mind, there is a method that the Father of *Yoga* heartily advises that has to do with locating vibrations in the mind and developing the capabilities to quell them. The chart on the facing page gives out the secrets of this method.

Chitta-vrttis are thought vibrations in the mind. Though it is not known to many, and only entertained by a few on the surface level, the mind's thoughts are responsible for everything that occurs in the realms of name and form. They do not just influence our lives and actions, they dictate them. It is not merely that we think about objects; objects are our thoughts concretized. In short, our thoughts result in and manifest as the world of objects.

With this in mind, we should contemplate the boon a having a pure mind. It would be tantamount to both free-living and positive action. On the other hand, sporting an impure mind would only mean trouble at all junctures of life. Patanjali cites the two kinds of thought vibrations that emit from these two kinds of minds. There are *klista vrttis*, which are negative thoughts that are "pain-bearing," and *aklista vrttis*, which are more positive and result in neutral vibrations. The overall teaching has it that the practitioner is to overcome the *klista-vrttis* using the *aklista vrttis*. This technique is the most ancient version of all the more recent schools that prescribe transforming negative thoughts into positive ones.

However, Patanjali's original school, *Raja Yoga*, has a definitively more substantial goal in mind than just possessing a positive mind with good thoughts. As the chart on the right reveals, the mind gets straightened, objects shine as blissful projections of a deeper thinking process, discernment develops, spiritual practice (missing in those who are content with a happy mind alone) gets strengthened, hidden impressions from past lives that cause unwanted *karma* get destroyed, the *gunas* are transcended, and supreme detachment — *Paravairagya* — from all that poses as Reality but is not, dawns on the human soul.

It is impossible to describe the elation that comes to the sincere truth-seeker due to these combined boons, these fruits of advanced *yogic* practice. Bhartrihari attempts to put it into words, in (selected) verses of his *Vairagya Shatakam*, his one-hundred *slokas* on Renunciation:

> *Blessed are they that, living even in the caves of mountains, meditate on the Supreme Light.*
> *Even the birds will fearlessly drink of the tears of pleasure that flow from their eyes.*
> *But there exist whirlpools of delusion, with despondency as their high banks.*
> *The Great Yogis are blissful because they, with their pure minds, never crossed that river.*

> *Bathing instead in the sacred river Ganges, worshipping the Lord with holy fruits and flowers,*
> *and stretching out on the ground in stoney caves, their entire being goes into meditation,*
> *and according to the never-forgotten voice of their Guru, they escape all misery,*
> *and purify the mind that was once defiled by serving worldly society.*

> *With the whole wide earth as my bed, my beautiful pillows my own two arms,*
> *the wonderful canopy of blue sky and the cool evening breeze to fan me,*
> *with the moon and stars as my lamps, and my stunning wife, Renunciation, by my side*
> *what king, anywhere, is there, who can sleep like me, in deepest bliss?*
> *For, finally came that time when, on a beautiful moon-lit night,*
> *and meditating on the banks of the sacred river,*
> *the calm yet high notes of my voice singing, "Siva, Siva,"*
> *all my inner feelings came out through my eyes in the form of blissful tears.*

Controlling the Chitta-vrttis in Yoga

"Yogash chitta-vrtti-nirodhah — quelling and mastering the vibrations of the mind — is conducive to attaining Yoga, union with Reality."
Lord Patanjali

— Klishta Vrttis —
Pain-bearing thought vibrations

- are caused by the kleshas ————————

- are causes of the kleshas ————————

Avidya, Ignorance
Asmita, Egotism
Raga, Attachment
Dvesha, Aversion
Abhinivesha, Clinging to Life

- become the field for karma (karmashaya)
(Due to the vrttis, kleshas arise and the field of karma gets further seeded.)

- produce samskaras which create more vrttis (perpetuating the wheel of samsara.)

Pleasure and pain, virtue and vice, attract and repel, creating vasanas

— Aklishta Vrttis —
Non pain-bearing thought vibrations

Craving for vrttis causes acceptance or rejection of life-experiences

- do not give rise to the kleshas

The fruits of karma are sought via false proof caused by the buddhi's misinformation from mind & senses

- mirror klishta vrttis but are unaffected
(Directed towards objects they are klishta. Directed inwards they become blissful.)

Fostering aklishta vrttis resists ignorance, desire, and karma

- control klishta vrttis ————————

Rajas and tamas get reduced

The buddhi is rendered sattvic

- do not liberate but foster discernment ————

Abhyasa, desire to practice, initiates

- strengthen with spiritual practice ————————

Khyati, discernment, develops

- help mature the samskaras ————————

Agama and anumana, scriptural authority and inference, increase

- produce excellent qualities ————————

Path is gained, guru is consulted

- get transcended via Paravairagya ————

Vairagya, detachment, burgeons

Prajna-prasada, clear wisdom, dawns

"Dissolve the gunas of rajas and tamas by taking recourse to sattva. Then, rise up above sattva by developing pure sattva and abide there." **Sri Krishna**

In Siva, who is the Lord of the Universe
or Vishnu, who is its soul, I see no difference.
But still, my love is for Him
who bears the young moon on His forehead.

Another powerful and beneficial teaching that is in accord with the *darshana* of *Yoga,* as well as with the attainment of a pure mind, is called the Four Clarities of Spiritual Life. A teaching chart for it appears on the facing page. As has been mentioned, clarity of mind *(khyati)* is highly coveted by the *rishis* of India. Another word for clarity in *Sanskrit* is *prasad* (or *prasada* or *prasadam,* though this word often gets used only with regard to sanctified food.

However, Sri Krishna has more expansive wisdom to convey in this context, listing four different types of clarity to aspire for. The first, of course, is food, *annaprasada,* a much overlooked and maligned principle of both daily life and spiritual life. Most of the world's peoples never have adopted the proper attitude for food, either in growing it, preparing it, and consuming it. Even saying a simple prayer over it falls far short of engendering both its meaning and its benefits. The five defects in food shown in the upper right hand corner of the chart under study, conveys more of the point. Suffice to say that food from farms, at marketplaces, in restaurants, and sadly, even at home, carry defects that could be destroyed with the right mind-set and practice. A *mantra,* chanted over food before its consumption, would be a good start, and would be even more effective if the real purpose of food, i.e., to provide energy with which to practice spiritual disciplines, were properly utilized and implemented into daily life. More on this fundamental principle will be taken up in later chapters of this book.

The second type of *prasad* is *chittaprasada,* clarity of mind. In order to possess it some basic impediments, known to all, will have to be surmounted. Distracted mind takes center stage here, for it is the problem per se. According to the Father of *Yoga,* visitations to the otherwise peaceful mind by sorrow and despair must be guarded against, as well as despoilers like those listed on the charts on pages 240, 247, 249. In addition, the aspirant will have to strive to render and maintain steadiness of mind; that alone will work wonders for all levels of his/her existence. Finally, efforts at controlling the breathing process will add overall mastery. Of course, once the negative influences are substantially diminished, some fives aids to steadiness of mind can be happily implemented. These have already been listed and studied in previous pages.

Another great form of clear mind is called *samprasada,* meaning clarity of mood. As long as the Four Deadly Traps, studied earlier as well, can be avoided, the seeker can more easily follow the way of friendliness, mercy, positivity, and detachment — called the Four *Parikarmas,* or "beneficial attitudes," in *dharmic* circles. The many possible sour moods of the mind will find their demise here, and not only the external ones that others notice, but also internal ones that may have become habitual and unnoticed over time.

Most important of all, if one can arrive there, is *adhyatma-prasada* — clarity of the Spirit. The reader will notice another mention of the occult powers listed on this chart, showing how pervasive they can be, and how deviously placed in life. Even the desire for heavenly existence will pose an obstacle to real spirituality, igniting desires for pleasure in the afterlife rather than engendering a pure desire for God alone. The entry on the chart, "No Transmigration," makes it quite clear *(prasada)* that the chief aim of any sincere aspirant after Truth will be transcendence of all lesser pursuits or attainments, whether they be limitations, imperfections, deceptions, ills, or outright evils, found in all forms of embodied existence. Far beyond physical enjoyment, intellectual pursuits, morality and ethics, or conventional religious life, spiritual attainment leading to freedom from afflictions is both the way and the destination for those who seek Peace, Wisdom, Truth, and the Bliss of *Brahman.*

A plethora of teachings on the *Yoga darshana* of Patanjali have graced the many pages just visited by the astute student and interested practitioner. Patanjali's *Yoga* is the *Raja Yoga,* known as the *Yoga* of Meditation. It is one of the four main *Yogas* of India. The other three are *Bhakti Yoga, Jnana*

The Four Clarities of Spiritual Life

	3 Qualities of Food	5 Defects of Food
1. Annaprasada (Clarity of Food)	**1. Tamas** *"Is stale, tasteless, over-cooked, impure — refuse."* **2. Rajas** *"Is bitter, sour, saline, hot, pungent, and dry."* **3. Sattva** *"Gives vitality, energy, vigor, health, and joy."* *(Sri Krishna, Bhagavad Gita)*	1. Poor soil, lack of nutrients 2. Selfish purpose while harvesting 3. Lack of awareness when processing 4. Impure mood while preparing 5. Failure to bless and consecrate
2. Chittaprasada (Clarity of Mind)	**The 5 Aids for Steadiness of Mind** 1. Enthusiasm 2. Courage 3. Steadfastness 4. Pursuit of Wisdom 5. Serving the Great (utsaha, sahasa, dhairya, adhyatma-vidya, and mahat-seva)	**The 4 Causes of Distraction** 1. Sorrow 2. Despair 3. Unsteadiness 4. Uneven breathing (duhkha, daurmanasya, angamejayatva, and shvasaprashvasah)
3. Samprasada (Clarity of Mood)	**The 4 Beneficial Attitudes** 1. Friendship 2. Mercy 3. Positivity 4. Indifference (maitri, karuna, mudita, and upekshanam)	**The 4 Deadly Traps** 1. Grief 2. Guilt 3. Depression 4. Lack of Self-worth (shoka, udvega, vishada, and vibhranti)
4. Adhyatma-prasada (Clarity of Spirit)	**The 3 Conditions of True Detachment** 1. Spiritual Attainment 2. Free of Afflictions 3. No Transmigration (sampadana, klesha- & samsara-vinashana)	**The 3 Obstacles to True Detachment** 1. 8 Occult Powers 2. Heavenly Existence 3. Personal Lordship (asta-siddhis, vaikarika-bandha, & prakrti-laya)

Yoga, and *Karma Yoga* — the *Yogas* of devotion, discriminatory wisdom, and action, respectively. *Bhakti Yoga,* which is its own pathway, will be looked at more closely in a forthcoming chapter. Since both meditation and wisdom are so interrelated, and dependant on one another, and since Shankara, the great *Advaitin,* commented on Patanjali's *Yoga* sutras some five or six hundred years after they were composed, a side by side comparison would be revealing — which is what the chart on the facing page is designed for.

Using, as well, the original chart on the eight-limbed *Yoga* on page 69 (chapter 3) as a reference, we can see right away that Shankara expanded those limbs to fifteen. By inspecting just those elements that were added in to the system by him around 700 A.D., the facets of *tyaga, mauna, desha, kala, nirodha, deha-samatva,* and *drdhata-drshya* are seen. Shankara also gave his one unique, *Advaitic* definition to the names of the traditional limbs as well, as the chart relates. This shows the frame of mind under which a nondualist would take up practices, i.e., in the firm knowledge that the *Atman* within is not in need of purification. Starting off on this premise, then a set group like the five *yamas* would not remain only as "observances," but become powerful ways of perception, as *"seeing all as Brahman."* For example, the first *yama, ahimsa,* nonviolence, would not be just an attempt at remaining nonviolent, but would affirm for the practitioner that the nature of *Brahman* is intrinsically free of violence or, is of the very essence of benign Peace.

In similar fashion, the five *niyamas* are posited as "control of the mind," demonstrating how important that quality is to the practitioner of *Yoga.* Control of the mind itself could be classed as a great austerity, *tapas,* which is the first *niyama* to master. Other *niyamas* such as study of scripture and worship of *Ishvara* would easily fall under attainment if the mind were brought fully under the aspirant's control. Thus, one of the hardest achievements in spiritual life would be gained early on, making all that is to come much easier of possession.

In the same vein, *tyaga,* or renunciation is taken up at the outset as well. So many of the problems, suffering, and delay along the path of spiritual growth are experienced due to the failure of the aspirant to see the illusory nature of the world right away and give it up. With the world out of the way, progress can come swiftly.

Prior to *asana* — which Shankara defines tellingly (and singularly) as *"the posture of meditation"* — the great *Advaitin* places time *(kala)* and space *(desha)* as limbs of *Yoga* to be considered early on and mastered. It is an ingenious move, for not only is the world illusory by nature, but so are the two fine threads it is wound up in. The reader can look back at page 360 to find the chart on *Shaivism's* Twelve *Spandas,* two of which are time and space. When these two are seen as cosmic principles, and transcendible, the outlook of the mind changes radically. It takes up its lofty position as the rightful ruler of the five senses and the five elements, thereby eliminating right away any further attachment to objects and pleasures — one of *Yoga's* chief aims.

Only three other newly contributed limbs stand out in Shankara's list. *Nirodha,* already a *yogic* principle in itself, is brought into fresh context as the eighth of fifteen total steps. He defines it as *"Restraint of Maya by Brahman."* Revealingly, the teaching in *Tantra* is that the soul should not try to observe and resist *Maya,* but rather must place attention only on Reality, i.e., *Brahman.* Therefore, the wording here is perfect. The Soul is *Brahman,* and that is the stance the practitioner takes to begin with. By letting the Divine within take over and take care of all things *mayic* is then the wisest choice and, again, swift progress can be made thereby. As a reminder of just how stultifying *maya* can be, and how difficult to overcome, the chart on page 279 will refresh the reader's memory as to its inscrutable nature.

Next, Shankara insists that *deha-samatva,* "Equipoise of the body," plays it part in progressive spiritual awakening and mastery. A naturalness in sitting for meditation, and for longer and longer periods of time, must occur. This will be beneficial for *drdhata-drshya,* "firmness of vision," to occur as well. Sitting for longer periods of time (which has been mastered earlier in the sixth stage) will be demanded of the evolving *yogic* aspirant, and this is needed in order that the Truth-seeker's newly-dawning inner vision will both expand and settle into the mind and its memory.

Patanjali's and Shankara's Yoga of the Mind

Patanjali's 8-Limbed Yoga	Shankara's Advaita Yoga in 15 Parts

"The controlling of the mind should be the first duty of the practitioner of Yoga and Concentration."

I Yamas	**Yamas — Seeing all as Brahman**
II Niyamas	**Niyamas — Control of the Mind**
"External renunciation is achieved by giving up gross things; internal by giving up the ego."	**Tyaga — Renunciation**
"Control of the speech is the first door to Yoga."	**Mauna — Silence**
"Think of soul in the soul, not in the body or mind."	**Desha — Space of Consciousness**
"There is One who is the witness of all states."	**Kala — Brahman as Witness**
III Asana	**Asana — Posture of Meditation**
"Give up the idea of the Self in the sheaths and recognize yourself as Brahman."	**Nirodha — Restraint of Maya by Brahman**
"That one who is free in the body, he is free without a body also."	**Deha-samatva — Equipoise of the Body**
"Settled knowledge — understanding the difference between the seer and the seen — is perfect seeing."	**Drdhata-drshya — Firmness of Vision**
IV Pranayama	**Pranayama — Mental States as Brahman**
V Pratyahara	**Pratyahara — Seeing Atman in All**
VI Dharana	**Dharana**
VII Dhyana	**Dhyana**
VIII Samadhi	**Samadhi**

"Attain samadhi by controlling the senses, and remain always in peace. By attaining samadhi, destroy the darkness that arises from ignorance by the practice of seeing oneness always and everywhere. These are the main doorways to Yoga. Then control speech and mind, give up all expectations and all desires, and seek solitude." Adishankaracharya

The four *Yogas*, with their immeasurable import resurrected and brought forward to us in recent times by Swami Vivekananda, can be easily paired up into two sets of two. That is, the *yoga* of devotion and the *yoga* of wisdom make a good match, and a fine comparison, and the *yogas* of action and meditation do as well. Starting first with the subject of action and inaction, the chart on the facing page lines up their practices and benefits side by side — the limbs of Patanjali's *Yoga*, and the laws of *Karma Yoga* from the *Bhagavad Gita*. Below these lists can be seen the comparative points of each. Thus, not only a comparison can be made, but a reconciliation as well. For, the paths of action and inaction have obvious contradictions in them, even if only seeming ones. They tend to cancel one another out if followed separately, i.e., an active life in the world and a contemplative life within. But that is only true for the soul who is lacking in or unaware of the art of synthesis. In truth, a successful balancing of an active life with the practice of daily meditation is what real *Yoga* is all about. This is the only way that the embodied being can live a spiritual life in the world, turning all action into meditation and thus existing in a *karma*-free state of awareness.

Referring to the chart, the first four limbs of *Raja Yoga* pertain well to the gaining of initial knowledge of *Yoga* and balancing the body, senses, and *prana*. This sets the stage for everything that has to do with the mind, intelligence, and ego complex, which align precisely with *Raja Yoga's* upper four limbs, five through eight. When all are implemented adeptly, the practitioner can maintain mental oneness in action — a huge and relatively unpretended feat of spiritual mastery by any soul. However, striving towards a complete dissolution of the mind's waves, called *samadhi*, is the crest-jewel of *Yoga*. All activity falls away at this level of Awareness.

But this cannot effectively happen if the laws of *Karma Yoga* are not mastered as well, and if any residue or remainder of desire for results, however subtle, is present in the mind. Total meditation, brooking upon formless *Samadhi (asamprajnata)*, is ultimate and inviolable. No trace of form or action can reach it. Thus, readers and sedulous students of *Yoga* is asked to familiarize themselves with the laws of *Karma Yoga* (listed in the upper right hand corner of the chart). To further comprehend the fine points of those, the lower half of the chart can be taken up.

Looking straight across the board at these, one will find some of the guiding points for successful integration of paths and ways, such as the difference between focusing the mind's thoughts to enable one-pointedness, yet also being able to dissolve them when in meditation so as to enter formlessness consciously. Other potential conundrums, such as the connection between serving God in mankind and leading humanity towards a higher spiritual perspective and attainment, are also displayed — all based in the ability to understand striving and struggling individuals on the particular level that each are living and working at. Of course, rare tools such as utilizing God's Name for personal balance and purification, as well as implementing the ability to both avoid and neutralize *karma* that may rise in all these life processes, are also brought forward.

When *Dhyana (Raja) Yoga* and *Karma Yoga* are studied and mastered, it is then that the seemingly contradictory principle of "action in inaction" can be achieved. Only certain highly illumined souls are qualified enough for this, and the expression of it is not readily perceived on the outside by others. The only real sign of its possession is the constant equanimity that graces that form, and even this is only recognized by those who remain near such a soul for extended periods of time, as in the cases of devout disciples and certain exemplary *gurus* and *acharyas*. Along with this deep and abiding peace of mind in rare souls like these, an equally deep store of *dharmic* wisdom will be present or sensed, and it will be utilized to help embodied beings clear up all mental issues and philosophical quandaries.

Similar to the chart on page 427, the chart on 429 uses the famous Koa-e-ula- bird of Hawaii to make its point about spiritual paths that must be integrated in order that the spiritual aspirant of today become well-rounded. This tropical bird soars high in the sky and only touches earth occasionally in order to nest in high cliffs of inaccessible valleys, thus making a suitable symbolic comparison with the real illumined souls of lofty spiritual attainment. Here, its two wings stand for the paths of wisdom and devotion, while its body speaks of the path of action and its tail feathers that

The Paths of Action and Inaction

"Rub your hands with coconut oil before opening the sticky jack fruit. Likewise, before entering into the world of action, develop and apply the practices of discrimination and meditation." Sri Ramakrishna

**Bhakti Yoga
Devotion**

"Those who see action in inaction, and inaction in action, they truly see." Sri Krishna

Eight Limbs of Raja Yoga

Yama — Five Observances
Niyama — Five Practices
Asana — Correct Posture
Pranayama — Correct Breathing
Pratyahara — Sense Control
Dharana — Concentration
Dhyana — Meditation
Samadhi — Nondual Abidance

Laws of Karma Yoga

Work free of Desire for Results
Work free of Karmic Accrual
Work done Meticulously
Work done in Even-mindedness
Work done in Failure or Success
Work done as Worship
Work done in Knowledge
Work done free of Attachment

**Raja Yoga
Meditation**

Karma Yoga Action

**Jnana Yoga
Wisdom**

Comparative Points About Karma Yoga

**Study and Practice of
the Lower Four Limbs of Yoga**

**Striving towards Achieving
Mental Oneness in Action**

**Performing Action as Duty and Worship,
free of all Motivations and Expectations**

**Recitation of the Mantra
to Calm and Master the Restless Mind**

**Devotion to the Path of Action
for the Purpose of Serving God in Mankind**

Comparative Points About Raja Yoga

**Study and Practice of
the Upper Four Limbs of Yoga**

**Striving towards Dissolving
the Mind's Vibrations**

**Performing All Action in a Meditative
State so as to avoid Karmic Accrual**

**Recitation of the Mantra to
merge the Mind into a Nondual State**

**Devotion to the Path of Meditation
to bring Enlightenment to all Beings**

"If you have known the Atman as the one existence and that nothing else exists, for whom, for what desire do you trouble yourself? Through Maya all this doing good, etc., came into my brain; now they are leaving me. I get more and more convinced that there is no other object in work except the purification of the soul — to make it fit for knowledge. This world with its good and evil will go on in various forms. Only, the evil and good will take new names and new seats. My soul is hankering after peace and rest eternal, undisturbed."
Swami Vivekananda

of meditation — for meditation steers the wayfaring human soul along its right and proper course.

Such souls differ in temperament and character, are diverse in their *karmic* makeup, and approach spiritual life with various intentions and preferences. Thus, the four classic *Yogas* under study in these recent pages are taken up by them according to stages of growth and the presence of impediments in the way of progress. By way of general observance, however, it can be said that the path of action is common and paramount to most all beings, the drawback to this fact being that most souls enter into the arena of works devoid of any other form of *yogic* attainment, and therefore they suffer the accrual of *karmas* that would have better been avoided. Sri Ramakrishna's quote on the top part of the chart on page 427 mentions this unfortunate phenomena.

To broaden the analysis further, however, many beings who get interested in spiritual life and *sadhana* jump into practices as diverse as *asana*, meditation, and devotional exercises, before removing the several layers of ignorance present in the mind. As Sri Krishna tells Arjuna in the *Bhagavad Gita*: *"In all the worlds there is no purifier as effective as wisdom (jnana), and the wise ones realize this in time."* Therefore, it would behoove all beings who desire to enter the paths of action, devotion, and meditation free of *karmic* accrual to instill discriminatory wisdom into the heart and mind.

In more straightforward terms, the world is full of people who try to help others out of bondage and suffering before first getting free themselves. The world sees quite a few beings who enter into hours of meditation practice each day prior to gaining the ability to concentrate even one hour in the proper fashion devoid of mental aberrations. The world experiences many souls who, prior to removing philosophical misunderstandings from the mind, dance and sing mindlessly, merely putting on a pretentious show under the unripe ego's impure influence. Even those preliminary practices such as body postures (*asanas*) and breathing exercises (*pranayama*) will be guided masterfully towards their intended fulfillment if higher knowledge is there to inform them.

Everything that prematurely falls short of its true mark, then, can be rendered fully effective by the introduction of ignorance-destroying wisdom into the mind. In the case of the old and tired argument between those who follow the path of devotion and those who attend upon the way of wisdom, all contentions can be put aside in the light of true understanding. The side by side list at the bottom of the chart on the opposite page tell the story of a happy *yogic* ending in amelioration, as do the several quotes from the scriptures proceeding from the lips of illumined souls who have reached such perfect synthesis. Important facets here, in this pairing of classic yogas, centers around the crucial presence of revealed and secondary scriptures, meditation on God with form and beyond form, and the essential nondual stance necessary for complete integration of ones entire being, on all its intricate levels.

In this regard, in the quote on the bottom of the chart under study (opposite page), the profound and powerful words of the Kali *Avatar*'s foremost messenger, Swami Vivekananda, ring true and find their mark. In the case of this perfect soul, the hallmarks of the advanced and mature devotee of the future are outlined masterfully, enticing all sincere practitioners towards a consummate end and a supreme Goal. To place this important spiritual stance into the body of the text, *"I want to give Truth dry hard reason, softened in the sweetest syrup of love, and made spicy with intense work, and cooked in the kitchen of Yoga so that even a baby can digest it."* With a superlative ideal like this before us, elucidated and epitomized in current times by the great Swami, the ultimate task before the true spiritual aspirant becomes both clear and imminent. The age of the fully qualified practitioner must dawn, for the call for it in this day and age, with all of its manifold problems and insinuating poisons, is becoming rather desperate.

In ancient times, Sri Krishna proposed and explained the path of *Yoga* to practitioners as well, as the chart on the facing page illustrates. The two previous charts have presented and delineated the four classic *yogas* for deeper study and understanding. These have emerged from Eternal Truth and have persevered throughout millenia up to the present times.

In the *Bhagavad Gita* this quartet of ignorance, doubt, and death-destroying pathways shows the way to benighted humanity in this day and age. As the chart on the facing page demonstrates,

The Two Complementary Paths

"Jnana and Bhakti, Wisdom and Devotion, are like the two wings of a bird. A bird cannot fly without two wings. Therefore, O Divine Mother, grant us Pure Love, Pure Knowledge, and Pure Devotion." Swami Aseshananda

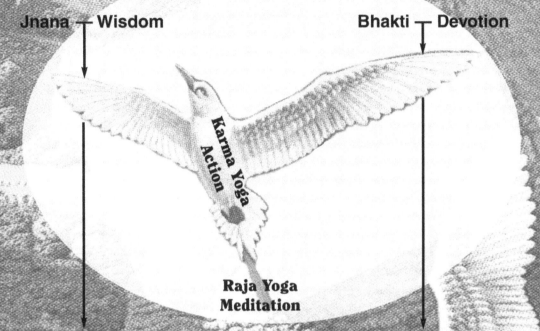

Jnana — Wisdom

Bhakti — Devotion

Karma Yoga
Action

**Raja Yoga
Meditation**

Comparative Points About Jnana Yoga	Comparative Points About Bhakti Yoga
Study of Shruti, Nondual Scriptures, Advaita	Study of Smriti and Itihasa, Secondary Scriptures, Puranas
Contemplation on the Unity of Jivatman and Paramatman	Contemplation of the Nara Lila, the Sport of Consciousness
Meditation on Brahman, Impersonal Reality, Nirguna Brahman	Meditation on Ishvara, the Personal God, Saguna Brahman
Performing Action as Detached Witness, Knowing the World to be Unreal	Performing All Action as Sacrifice, as an Offering to the Lord
Recitation of the Mantra in Line with Meaning, Insight, and Will-Power	Recitation of the Mantra in Line with Love, Empathy, and Self-Surrender
Devotion to the Path of Discrimination to Gain Pure Love	Devotion to the Path of Love to Gain Pure Discrimination

"To those who know Me in full I reveal Myself. I am dear to them and they are dear to Me." Sri Krishna

"To those who Love Me, I give them the discrimination by which they come to Me." Sri Krishna

"This is the new religion of this age — the synthesis of Yoga, Knowledge, Devotion, and Work — the propagation of Knowledge and Devotion down to the very lowest, without distinction of age or sex. Thus, I want to give Truth dry hard reason, softened in the sweetest syrup of love, and made spicy with intense work, and cooked in the kitchen of Yoga so that even a baby can easily digest it." Swami Vivekananda

the appearance of *"Buddhi Yoga"* as the path of meditation forms the only difference from the current rendering of this comprehensive spiritual system, and so we can equate it to the upper limbs of the *Raja Yoga* system of the present day. Concentration of mind is crucial for success in any endeavor in life. Later, with the appearance of Patanjali and his eight-limbed system on the world scene, it was established as the sixth limb, allowing meditation proper (*Raja Yoga, Dhyana Yoga*) to find its proper base. Sri Krishna's inclusion of it into this universal fourfold package also emphasizes the importance of intelligence in an aspirant's spiritual life. Intelligence, *buddhi,* is the very *"first compound of Consciousness,"* as Swami Vivekananda has stated, and therefore the first qualitative substance to flow out of *Brahman* in the trickle down (and out) process of Cosmic manifestation. Therefore, in the involutionary sweep, wherein all substances — i.e., matter, energy, and thought — are taken back to their respective sources (matter into Unmanifested *Prakriti,* and living beings to primal Awareness), it will be Intelligence that will allow for all beings to merge back into their Source. As the *Svetasvataropanisad* states:

> *Meditate on the Lord as thine own Self, seated in your heart,*
> *Who appears to you as the universe, and who is the absolute Source of all living beings.*
> *Perceive that one as the ultimate cause of the relationship between matter and Spirit,*
> *And as the partless Divine Entity who transcends the three phases of time.*

Whereas the two wings of the bird have been metaphorically allocated to *jnana* and *bhakti* in the previous chart, here we have the accent placed upon the body and tail feathers of the bird in order to indicate the import of work and meditation. The reader can review the chart on page 437 for details. This chart (facing page) imbues us with the grand idea of the natural synthesis of the four *yogas,* a principle dear to the hearts and minds of luminaries throughout vast sweeps of time in cycles. One facet of the Neo-*Vedanta* in present times is that there are four types of beings overall, namely the active, the devotional, the studious, and the contemplative. These four match the four *yogas* across the board, and by understanding this match-up, living beings can both find their inherent characteristics (also linked with their present *karmas*) and make forward progress in an integrated way. Otherwise, without this understanding, there is our old nemesis of backsliding to deal with, what the Father of *Yoga* calls *anavasthitatvani.* This is taking one step forward, then falling two steps back.

Other than the obvious problem of never making any appreciable advancement in spiritual life, another impediment crops up as well. Beings begin to believe that they actually are making headway when it is not the case, becoming proud of the one step forward but remaining blind to the occurrence of the two steps back. Patanjali links this problem to another called *alabdhabhumikatva,* meaning the lack of faith that causes an increasingly preponderant belief in the act of failure. These two *vikshepas/antarayas* work in tandem with one another; they are spiritual obstacles, as contrasted to physical, mental, psychological, and intellectual/philosophical ones. To comprehend their existence, and to perceive their presence and workings in the human mind, is to become aware of the need for a profound solution. For the sedulous seeker of Enlightenment, the four *yogas* — well studied, well-guided, and well-implemented — readily provide this.

As has been mentioned, though worth repeating, Swami Vivekananda made a generous gift of the Four *Yogas* to the West when he was present here in the late 1800's and early 1900's. Even in India in this present age, whole portions of the system have fallen away and are not being considered nor practiced — much to the detriment of India's peoples, culture, religion, and its policy of right action in knowledge. On the facing page is another showing of this incomparable system of spiritual practice leading to natural union, *Yoga,* with Divine Reality. There, all the facets of the four *yogas* are placed in such a way that their various elements are revealed for consideration, and hopefully for contemplation and implementation into daily life and meditation as well. For, though study is important, especially at the outset of serious spiritual endeavor, application of what one comes to know is essential so that transformation on all levels of ones being can take place in a timely man-

Chaturdasya Yoga — The Four Yogas

"The four main Yogas cited in the Bhagavad Gita guide the soul in its inward flight. Bhakti is one wing, Jnana the other. Karma Yoga is the body of the bird, and Buddhi Yoga is its tail feathers. The crucial flight occurs in and leads to the Atman." Babaji Bob Kindler

Jnana Yoga
Wisdom

Of Pure Intellect
Abiding in the Self
Restraining the Senses
Free of Attachment/Aversion
Dwelling in Solitude
Eating Sparsely
Subduing Body, Mind, Speech
Engaging in Meditation
Full of Dispassion
Free of the Sense of Me/Mine
Established in Peace
Abandoning Ego, Violence, Arrogance, Desire, Enmity, and Property

Bhakti Yoga
Devotion

"Becoming Brahman, serene-minded, that one never grieves nor desires. The same to all beings, he obtains supreme devotion to Me. By devotion he knows the truth, what and who I am, and having known, forthwith enters into Me" Sri Krishna

Buddhi Yoga
Meditation

"Mentally resigning all deeds unto Me, having Me as the highest Goal, and resorting to Buddhi Yoga, the Yoga of Concentration, do thou ever fix thy mind upon Me alone."
Sri Krishna

Karma Yoga
Action

"Doing continually all actions in Me, taking refuge in Me, by My grace he reaches the eternal undying abode." Sri Krishna

"Thus has wisdom more profound than all profundities been declared to you by Me. Reflect upon it daily and then act as you choose. This secret is never to be spoken to those who are devoid of austerities, nor those who are not devoted, nor those who do not render service or who speak ill of Me. And those who study this great secret of the fourfold Yoga, they rightly and duly perform the sacrifice of knowledge to Me." Sri Krishna

ner. Soon, the sincere aspirant will find that Reality does not go through transformation of any kind, at any time. But that is a realization for a much higher stage of existence. In the meantime, and as long as the body/mind/ego complex persists, impeded by any type of limitation or delusion, so long must the dedicated *sadhaka* take this fine-toothed comb of the four *yogas* and run it through the untamed hair of the psycho-physical being, again and again. In this way do the assumption of purification, the contradiction of spiritual practice, and the illusion of transformation, have their important place in life and mind.

Before departing the veracious and salubrious atmosphere of the Four *Yogas* for other *dharmic* climes, some dynamics of what has been come to be called "the synthesis of *Yoga*" can be emphasized. If the three quotes by Vivekananda that have been culled out on the chart on the facing page are studied, in addition to all of Sri Krishna's sayings from the *Bhagavad Gita* listed there, the overall import of this kind of integration in spiritual life can be seen. Swami Vivekananda even infers the danger of becoming narrow and limited in the practice of *Yoga*, and the risk of falling into a sleepy complacency around assuming that becoming qualified at only one of the four *Yogas* is enough. Therefore, for the active *karma yogi* or *yogini*, the development of inaction, i.e., the *yoga* of meditation, should be attempted. And for the one adept in study of the scriptures, who is contemplative and inward, opening up the heart via participation in devotional worship would be the best complement.

In other words, no *Yoga* is alien or contradictory to another. In the same way that, for the Universalist, all religions are indigenous to the soul, in like manner, for the consummate practitioner, all four *Yogas* are not only different facets of one diamond-like *dharmic* field, they are also intrinsically connected and complementary of one another.

And this is where *Yoga*, in and of itself, escapes the rigid limitations that so often accompany sects, cults, lineages, *sampradayas,* and the like. It is highly reflective of India's open-minded policy in action and the best representative overall of what has been called *Sanatana Dharma* — The Eternal Religion. And though the term *"Sanatana Dharma"* itself has been co-opted by several sects in India in recent times, there is still no corrupting of the original meaning and intention of the term.

To give an example of *Yoga's* wide and capacious stance among India's *darshanas*, the chart on the forthcoming page 435 can be studied. A dozen or more of India's *Yogas* are listed there, and many of the *Yogas* comprising the names of the chapters of the *Bhagavad Gita* are also present. As the Holy Mother, Sri Sarada Devi, whose countenance graces the page, declares, the breaking of the bonds that bind the soul to this world of dualities and conundrums forms the main directive of the one who takes to *Yoga*. For getting free of the trammels of relativity, then, aspiring beings take to *Yoga*. As Sri Krishna puts it in the *Bhagavad Gita*, *"Let this disconnection of the mind from the body and its pain be called by the name, Yoga."* Further, *"It is to be practiced with an unswerving resolve until the goal of liberation is attained."*

On the chart now under study, (page 435) all the *yogas* cited there are likened to waves, but not to the erratic thought waves *(vrittis)* of the mind. They are healing waves, and they rise in a timely fashion, when needed, on the breast of the ocean of Awareness. Our modern spiritual hero, Swami Vivekananda, tells us that it is the "Fire of *Yoga*" that is the most precious possession of the *yogi* per se. Everything from *samadhi*, to peace of mind, and all the way down to the health of the body, is due to owning the Fire of *Yoga*. Impeding factors as diverse and variegated as vaunted control by the gods, *karma* coming from the ancestors, negative thoughts springing up in collective consciousness, and disease-causing germs in the body, are all boiled away and destroyed within that divine form that contains the Fire of *Yoga*.

And why should this not be true, especially when the qualities and properties of these manifold *yogas* are taken up for consideration, what to speak of practice. Of the classic *Yogas*, most of them well-known to all, there are the four main ones we have just studied in the previous pages — *Bhakti, Jnana, Raja (Dhyana/Ashtanga),* and *Karma.* Following close on their heels there is *Mantra Yoga.* The reader would be well-served to look back and review portions of chapter three, *Matching*

The Four Yogas and Their Synthesis

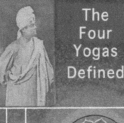

The Four Yogas Defined

Bhakti Yoga – Union with Reality via One-pointed Devotion

Raja Yoga – Union with Reality via Focused Meditation on Divine Reality

Jnana Yoga – Union with Reality via Knowledge of the Atman

Karma Yoga – Union with Reality via Selfless Action offered as Service to God in Mankind

"The teaching of the new Incarnation, Sri Ramakrishna, is that the best points of Yoga, Devotion, Knowledge, and Work must be combined so as to form a new society."　Swami Vivekananda

Bhakti – Yoga of Devotion to God

"Serene-minded, beyond both grief and desire, same-sighted and kind to all, such a one attains supreme devotion to Me."

- Listen to Accounts of God's Deeds
- Engage Sincerely in Devotional Rituals
- Purify Heart and Mind via Daily Worship
- Sing Praises to the Lord and Mother
- Get Initiation into the Spiritual Path
- Perform Japa of the Holy Names
- Engage Earnestly in Meditative Prayer
- Increase Devotion to Ishvara

Jnana – Yoga of Discerning Wisdom

"He whose intellect is unattached everywhere, who is endowed with nondual understanding, that one reaches consummate Knowledge."

- Recite the Slokas of the Scriptures
- Memorize the Slokas of the Scriptures
- Take Teachings from an Illumined Teacher
- Comprehend the Meaning of the Scriptures
- Discriminate between the Real and Unreal
- Penetrate through the Cosmic Appearance
- Contemplate the Nature of Reality
- Abide Continually in Nondual Realization

"I want to give Truth dry hard reason, softened in the sweetest syrup of love, and made spicy with intense work, and cooked in the kitchen of Yoga so that even a baby can easily digest it."　Swami Vivekananda

Raja – Yoga of Meditation/Samadhi

"Dwell in solitude, restrain the senses, control the mind, and engage in meditation. You will thus reach perfection in Brahman."

- Calm and Control the Mind's Thoughts
- Purge the Mind of Desire and Passions
- Still the Mind's Tendency of Distraction
- Uncover and Neutralize all Karmas
- Dissolve the Mind's Limiting Impressions
- Reach the Samadhi of Wisdom
- Gain Kaivalya — Isolation from Nature
- Immerse into Nirvikalpa Samadhi

Karma – Yoga of Selfless Action

"Performing actions selflessly and continually while taking refuge in Me, by My grace he reaches the eternal, undecaying Abode."

- Engage Only in Obligatory Actions
- Renounce Action done for Selfish Motive
- Perform all Action with Evenness of Mind
- Do not Seek the Fruits of Action
- Detach from all the Outcomes of Action
- Perform all Work as Worship
- Utilize all Work to Serve God in Mankind
- Work Meticulously but with Detachment

"Would to God that all men were so constituted that in their minds all of these elements — philosophy, mysticism, emotion, and work — were equally present in full! That is the ideal, my ideal of a perfect man. Everyone who has only one or two of these elements I consider one-sided; and this world is almost full of such 'one-sided' men, with knowledge of that one road only in which they move."　Vivekananda

Strides with the Seers, to be able to re-estimate the value of this fine *yoga.* As may have been stated, this *yoga* could be included as a fifth *yoga,* since all the other main four have close connections with it, and use it, each in their own way. For instance, the *yoga* of wisdom will help uncover and transmit the meaning of the *mantra.* The *yoga* of devotion will infuse the *mantra* with the power of inner longing for vision and freedom. The *yoga* of meditation is verily made for the *mantra,* which prepares the *sadhika* for contemplation and removes the impurities of the mind that stymie meditation. And the *yoga* of action will facilitate the very repetition of the *mantra* by the mind, lips, and hands. There is no separating these five, then.

And speaking of action, the ever-famous *Kriya Yoga* takes its place in this auspicious list. *Kriya Yoga* in its original form was the Father of *Yoga's* condensation of three of *Raja Yoga's* most beneficial practices, namely *tapas* (austerity), *svadhyaya* (study of scripture), and *Ishvara-Pranidana* (devotion to God). Patanjali's intention here was to take and combine these three dynamos of spiritual practice in order to afford the practitioner a way to make instantaneous and even spontaneous (*kriya*) progress. For, austerity, properly guided and rightly performed, will break down any barrier, while *svadhyaya* will inform the seeker as to the advice and spiritual experiences of the seers. Of course, devotion to God — not mandatory according to Patanjali and other seers — will broaden the path and make all actions and matters along it run smoothly.

Over time there has come several other versions of *Kriya Yoga,* but none of them have the power and authenticity of the original by Patanjali, and if the truth be known, most of them deviate from honest practice and advise taking up physical exercises only, sometimes mixed in with occult pursuits. These are to be avoided, as they are antagonistic to the true aims of *Yoga,* such as meditation and *samadhi.*

As we approach the other *yogas* listed on the chart (page 435), we find them to be less familiar, especially to the general practitioner of this day and time. But each has its specific area of expertise to be considered. Take for instance *Vasana Yoga.* *Vasana* is a *Sanskrit* word that refers to desire. This *yoga* takes up the aspirant's desires, particularly the subtle ones, and subjects them to practices that either slowly attenuate them, or do away with them in a short time — all depending on the abilities of the seeker involved. Again, the overall problem with this *yoga* in contemporary times in certain circles is reliance upon physical postures to do away with mental complexes. This is, of course, a misconception, and only fosters the false idea that inner progress can somehow be attained through mere physical means. This, in turn, gives rise to societies of *hatha yoga* practitioners that presume to be enlightened when they have not even gotten beyond of the early stages of *sadhana.* *Vasana Yoga* in its authentic form prescribes practices for the mind that do away with mental impressions (*samskaras*) that are responsible for negativity and weakness in human beings that have been in operation for many lifetimes. Stripped of the special tools for dealing with *samskaras,* *Vasana Yoga* gets rendered to an inefficient regime of physical postures whose only facility, if done correctly, is to help strengthen and tone the body. Such is the fate of the very word, "*Yoga,*" in the West in modern times.

While on the subject of what is authentic, and what becomes a caricature, the path of *Siddhi Yoga* can be taken up. The *Sanskrit* word "*siddhi*" means perfection; it can also refer to psychic powers. If we keep the highest rendering of the word, and dedicate ourselves to reach Enlightenment in this very life, then it should refer to those who are realized and lauded by other luminaries. Beings such as Sri Krishna and Lord Kapila come to mind immediately.

In the *Bhagavata Purana,* Sri Krishna mentions the primary *Siddhis* to be attained as being five in number, i.e., mastery of time (knowing and transcending the past, present, and future); mastery of dualities like pleasure and pain, heat and cold, etc.; coming to know the mind, ones own, and others'; mastery over death, the ability to remain free of all influences. On the other hand, and not to be confused with these, Sri Krishna eschews the search for and attainment of the eight occult powers which include such abilities as levitation, walking on water, power over others, etc.

In the ancient *Sankhya* texts, Lord Kapila lists *Siddhi Yoga's* eight facets as: examination and knowledge of the 24 cosmic principles (*Tattvas*); associating with an enlightened teacher; gaining

The Ocean of Awareness & Its Yogic Waves
Universal Pathways to Enlightenment

"Sitting up on the snow peaks of the Himalayas, I repeat from the Upanisads: *'He has neither disease, nor decay, nor death, for, verily, he has obtained a body full of the fire of Yoga.'"* —————— *Swami Vivekananda*

"The truth is this: he who is really anxious to cross the ocean of this world will somehow break his bonds. No one can entangle him."

Sri Sarada Devi,
The Holy Mother

The Four Main Yogas
Jnana Yoga, Bhakti Yoga
Raja Yoga, & Karma Yoga

"This is the new religion of this age, the synthesis of Yoga, Knowledge, Devotion, and Work, the propagation of Knowledge and Devotion down to the very lowest, without distinction of age or sex...."

Swami Vivekananda

Yogas of the Bhagavad Gita

Ananya-yoga
Abhyasa-yoga
Sankhya-yoga
Sanyasa-yoga
Vibhuti-yoga
Jnana Vijnana-yoga
Purushottama-yoga
Akshara Brahma-yoga
Rajavidya Rajaguhya-yoga
Jnana-karma Sanyasa-yoga
Shraddhatraya Vibhaga-yoga
Vishvarupa Darshana-yoga
Gunatraya Vibhaga-yoga
Kshetra Kshetrajna-yoga
Daivasura Sampad-yoga
Moksha Sanyasa-yoga

Some Traditional Yogas

Advaita-yoga
Buddhi-yoga
Antar-yoga
Charya-yoga
Laya-yoga
Mantra-yoga
Kriya-yoga
Vasana-yoga
Chaturdasya-yoga
Prema-bhakti-yoga
Lakshya-yoga
Siva-yoga
Siddhi-yoga
Dhyana-yoga
Brahma-yoga
Ashtanga-yoga

"According to Patanjali, there are erratic thought waves, called vrittis, in the human mind, which must be pacified. Further, there are mighty waves of Yoga in the Ocean of pure, Conscious Awareness, and they must be utilized for this task." Babaji Bob Kindler

knowledge of the scriptures; attaining spiritually-minded friends and associates; assisting others to gain the highest knowledge; gaining freedom from suffering; freedom from matter and its influences, and destroying reliance upon inferior modes and methods such as fate, luck, destiny, etc.

These lists, along with Patanjali's concurrence in the *Yoga sutras* about giving up occult powers and overcoming the obstacles to spiritual advancement that they represent, give the path of *Siddhi Yoga* its proper perspective again, saving it from the mystery-mongerers sensationalists, and charlatans who always dabble and weigh down its atmosphere, dragging its honorable precepts earthwards for purposes of fame, money, and power over others.

Two other powerful *yogic* waves that receive mention on the chart under study (page 435) are *Brahma-yoga* and *Siva-yoga*. Here, *Vishnu-yoga* could also be placed. The Trinity, a long-standing Divinity at the very hub and core of cosmic projection, each have their own characteristics as overseers of crucial aspects of the creative process, so it would stand to reason that they each contain and express their own *yogic* pathway as well. To put it succinctly, the Great Master is on record in the *Gospel of Sri Ramakrishna* as stating, with brevity: *"Vishnu-yoga and Siva-yoga: these are two eternal pathways. Siva-yoga, eyes shut and looking inward only, and Vishnu-yoga, eyes half open and looking both inwards and outwards."* The implication is evident, and matches the temperaments of these great deities.

Of course, for details in practice the aspirant will have to choose the path that is best suited for him or her, then approach a teacher who has excelled in the disciplines of that particular way for instructions. It may be that the seeker will find *Siva-yoga* focused on principles such as austerity, detachment, meditation, with an accent on nonduality, while *Vishnu-yoga* — though containing some of these elements, will proceed more along the lines of worship, chanting, and selfless service. Each will require study of scriptures that are pertinent to its salient expression as a spiritual pathway. As for *Brahma-yoga*, the implication leans more towards the formless *Brahman* rather than the firstborn Lord, Brahma of the Trinity. Nevertheless, practices that strive to reach and master the initial creative urge, leading the aspirant towards early experiences with formless Reality, would certainly be a part of this path.

And this is where *Advaita-yoga* comes in, with its outright penchant for union with Divine Reality. Neither its aims nor its interests lie in God with form. It begins with natural union, as in *Sahaja Samadhi*, and only insists upon remaining there. That indivisible Consciousness frequents form at all is a misnomer; It only does so, apparently, by way of appearance or assumption only. Therefore, all the nondual truths of the noble *Advaita Vedanta* are accepted and implemented in this upper echelon type of *yoga*.

Another *yogic* path sometimes come upon is *Antara-yoga*. Again, there are many contemporary forms of *yoga* borrowing this name. In its original form, however, it concerns itself with inner observation mainly, called *antar-mukha*, where objects are seen to leave their outer expression and assume subtle form. This *yoga* is very much in step with the fifth limb of Patanjali's *Raja Yoga*, and its practices enter there.

Laya-yoga is another name often heard in spiritual circles. The *Sanskrit* word, *"laya,"* means dissolution, and usually refers to dissolving name and form into pure, conscious Awareness at the end of a very long period of time (*yuga*) (see chart on page 39). Using this facet of cosmic knowledge, the aspirant of *Laya-yoga*, then, strives to dissolve body, elements, senses, subtle elements (*tanmatras*), and subtle senses, all into the mind, seeing that the mind has projected all of these. When the mind itself is encountered, then its thoughts (*chitta*) must be dissolved, along with the ego (*ahamkara*) and the individual intelligence (*buddhi*). This also accomplishes, by the way, the purification of the *antahkarana*, the four-fold mind composite. There is a famous *Sanskrit sloka* concerning it:

Mano na buddhih na shariram indriyam tanmatra-bhutani na bhuta panchakam
Ahamkritis chapi viyat-svarupakam tam isham atmanam upaiti shasvatam

That one realizes the supreme, eternal Self who dissolves mind, intellect, body, senses, the five subtle elements, and the five gross elements — along with the ego — into the Atman in meditation.

To clarify the system and its process, cycles of time will inevitably lead to dissolution of the universe of name and form in space and time. But what about the living being, or sentient soul, and what about its *karmas*? The soul itself must actuate this intrapersonal dissolution, and that is done in meditation after preparing the way through various spiritual disciplines. A forthcoming chapter dealing with meditation itself will contain teachings and charts on this most high and intense dissolution of principles accomplished in *Laya-yoga*.

Of the few *Yogas* left to comment on in the chart on page 435, there are *Charya-yoga* and *Lakshya-yoga*. There is also *Prema-bhakti-yoga*, which is just the higher echelon of *Bhakti Yoga*, and its chief aim. As regards *Charya-yoga*, it is a qualifying *yoga* that prepares the aspirant at the early stages of practice. *Charya* requires a combination of gaining virtues and putting them to work in modes of selfless service. When *charya* is accomplished, it is blended with three other rivers of practice, namely *kriya*, *yoga*, and *jnana* — i.e., giving energy to worship, meditating, and gaining wisdom from the tradition. *Lakshya-yoga* focuses mainly on the practice of union with God in meditation. The *Sanskrit* word, *"lakshya,"* means "the center of the target," and so ones concentration is rendered into a bow, ones mind becomes the arrow, and *Brahman* becomes the Target to hit and penetrate. Ones burgeoning strength via *sadhana* allows for success. There is a fitting *Sanskrit sloka* on this inner practice and process in the *Upanisads*:

> *Dhanur grihitva-upanisadam mahastram*
> *sharam hyupasanishita sandhayita*
> *ayamya tad bhavagatena chetasa*
> *lakshyam tad evaksharam somya viddhi*

> *Taking as bow that mighty weapon furnished by the Upanisads,*
> *fasten to it the arrow of mind made sharpened by thoughts on Reality alone.*
> *Then drawing full strength, oh student, release and penetrate the mark —*
> *that imperishable Brahman.*

In the upper right hand corner of chart on page 435 is to be seen a block of yogas that enrich both the word and its phases of practices. Not only that, when used in this particular context it shows how *Yoga* is to be implemented into every phase of life, transforming all actions into divine occupations. All of these *yogas* are either mentioned in the *Bhagavad Gita*, or are actual names for some of the chapters of that incomparable living scripture.

Sankhya-yoga advises the study of cosmic principles and all the varieties of life, both inner and outer. *Sanyasa-yoga* prescribes advanced practices for those who are ready to renounce the world and attain freedom for all sorts of bonds — much like the import of Holy Mother's quote opposite the list itself. *Vibhuti-yoga* indicates the divine powers of God, helping the aspirant to develop profound devotion to the Highest Deity. *Jnana Vijnana-yoga* compels the advanced seeker to move beyond lower knowledge and attain to consummate Wisdom, but also notes the differences between these two. *Purushottama-yoga* reveals the highest Divinity in form, verily Sri Krishna Himself, and encourages the devotees to take refuge There. *Akshara Brahma-yoga* tells of the indestructible nature of *Brahman* which, by knowing, one transcends all fear. *Rajavidya Rajaguhya-yoga* explains the supreme secret of existence and blends it ingeniously with the method through which one attains understanding of it. *Jnana-karma Sanyasa-yoga* demonstrates how, by performing works selflessly and culling knowledge from their results, the seeker can gain freedom from the ordinary rounds of birth and death in ignorance. *Shraddhatraya Vibhaga-yoga* enumerates and explains the threefold divisions of faith for the aspirant, while *Gunatraya Vibhaga-yoga* does the same for the three modes of nature, i.e., *tamas*, *rajas*, and *sattva*. *Vishvarupa Darshana-yoga* is the powerful revelation of Sri

Krishna's cosmic form to a stunned Arjuna laboring under the limited comprehension of who the Lord really is. *Kshetra Kshetrajna-yoga* splits apart and displays the distinction between the field of variegated principles and the one who is supposed to know that field, while *Daivasura Sampad-yoga* informs as to the divine and demoniacal beings who people and comprise them both. Finally (though there are more), *Moksha Sanyasa-yoga* concludes and unifies all subjects with its grand declaration of the supreme Goal of Existence, namely, full Enlightenment.

The first two on the list — *Ananya Yoga* and *Abhyasa Yoga* — relate that *Yoga* itself is a matter of 1) the inseparability of God and mankind, and 2) the pathways that lead back to this consummate realization in the event that the soul becomes lost in dreams of its own devising. This impressive partial list, then, both reveals the ultimate nature of Existence, and shows the way to union with Divine Reality. Speaking philosophically, the advanced seeker and knower cannot but be amazed at the possibilities for spiritual growth and understanding when *Yoga* and Gita are blended together.

Taking up another chart for study under the present chapter heading of "The Gait of the Gods," we look to the soul-freeing path of *jnanam*, since it has been brought up twice in the previous few pages. This teaching gives us a look at Lord Vasishtha's perspective on spiritual wisdom, and can be worked into the aspirant's life; for, most beings are usually too busy and tired from their daily jobs in the marketplace of the world, and/or therefore disinclined to spend any time in quiet study, perhaps being averse to it all due to all the time they had to spend studying secular subjects in their early years. The obvious and lamentable absence of spiritual topics in educational institutions is one of the gross oversights of today's "educators" — as if anything can be learned without first knowing that one eternal Principle to be learned about first. A string of zeros adds up to nothing, but place a "1" at the front of that string and a huge number results. Such is the case with placing teachings on Divine Reality at the beginning of all other subjects, as in *"Seek thee first the Kingdom of Heaven and all else will be added unto thee."*

Lord Vasishtha's method for bringing spiritual topics back to light is based upon airing the opinions of those who have not been given the *dharma*, and those who have. For the former, even though they may include spiritual life in their scope, the presence of *jnana* does not figure into the picture. They aver that two parts of the mind should be given to worldly pursuits, and the other two be split amidst meditation and worship. Such as these simply depend upon morals and ethics, and religious life, for their salvation, but they never court liberation — which is *jnana's* strong suit, and ability to grant.

Therefore, those who have come into contact with a *jnana-yoga* teacher, and have heard the liberating teachings of the *dharma*, shift an extra portion of their mind over to worship of the spiritual preceptor, taking the emphasis off of worldly topics and their attractions.

But, and as can be seen on the chart (facing page), those who possess *jnana* wisdom effectively take the final portion of their attention on the world and place it on the rare feat of quelling all desires. Then, through worship, study, and the discovery of the *Atman* within them, they swiftly reach the Goal of human existence.

As far as the lauded King Virochana is concerned, the path to freedom proceeds by first subjugating desire for the worlds of name and form (including heavens). This is to be accomplished at the same time as the attainment of right livelihood, as in Lord Buddha's *Astangika Marga*, or "Eightfold Path." Thus, both kings and ascetics share this view, which is much like Sri Krishna's advice in the *Bhagavad Gita* on accomplishing works rather than racing towards inaction. For, this brings in the attainment of a *sattvic* state, and when such balance and satisfaction visit the mind, and the mind sees its limitations, higher truths can then be sought after.

With the mastery of the *sattva guna* intact, levels of detachment are quickly encountered as well. It is only from the position of mature detachment that real self-inquiry can be undergone. And it is here that pure *jnanam* makes its appearance — the incomparable wisdom that reveals the intrinsic unity between God and mankind. That opens the way for *Moksha*, which is a state of Enlightenment always at hand (see chart on page 343), but usually covered over by considerations

The Attainment of Rare Jnana

(From the Story of the Great Bali)

Opinion	World	Study & Meditation	Worship of Guru
Those Who Possess Jnana declare ⟶	1 Part of the Mind on study of scriptures treating Atmic Reality 1 Part of the Mind on the study of methods to remove Desire 1 Part of the Mind on the study of the ways of Self-cognition 1 Part of the Mind on the path of how best to worship the Guru		
Those Partially Familiar with Jnana Yoga declare ⟶	Give 1 Part of the Mind	Give 1 Part of the Mind	Give 2 Parts of the Mind
Those Unacquainted with Jnana Yoga declare ⟶	Give 2 Parts of the Mind	Give 1 Part of the Mind	Give 1 Part of the Mind

King Virochana's Advice to his son Bali on the Attainment of Jnana:

Subjugate Desire ⟶ Secure Just Livelihood ⟶ Attain Sattvaguna ⟶

Gain Detachment ⟶ Perform Atmic Inquiry ⟶ Attain Jnana ⟶

Realize Moksha ⟵

"Contemplating deeply, find that nothing truly exists, not you nor I, only the one rare Jnana." Lord Vasishtha

for the world — and as we could now declare, due to the absence of *jnana* wisdom in the first place. As the Father of *Yoga* has revealed, along with the Father of *Vedanta*, constant commerce with and in the world takes the mind away from contemplation on ones previous lifetimes, causing forgetfulness of the line of incarnations that represent an unbroken stream of Awareness stretching all the way back to *Brahman*

Another famous king can be cited at this point, and in this regard. He is one who had many experiences with the world, all contrasted and eventually unified with his inner experiences in the Spirit. King Janaka, of *Vedic* fame, is the ideal for so many beings. These beings do not want to view the world as being unreal, like ascetics, nor do they want to give it up like the *sannyasins*. They see a being like King Janaka who possessed both spiritual realization plus the world of objects, and they naturally want to be like him. What they do not know, and have neither seen nor understood, is that 1) Janaka went through many spiritual disciplines to perfect himself prior to both his enlightenment and to taking his position as a king, and 2) once he was king, he spent less and less time with his possessions and wealth, and more and more time with the luminaries of his court while meditating on the wisdom of the nondual scriptures contained in his library. Most beings will not even approach the disciplines and self effort needed to begin the process that Janaka mastered over time and lifetimes.

The chart on the facing page explains the symphony of life — both of the world and of the Spirit. In brief, before mastering life and thereby bestowing goodness on others, the soul has to face off with knotty problems such as pain in the body, pleasure in the senses, brooding of the mind, attainment of virtues while resisting vice, the presence of human beings on the field of competition, the insinuations of ignorance, *maya*, and *samsara*, and the onslaught of birth, growth, disease, old age, decay, and death. Finally, and if these impediments have been turned into challenges, the soul finally realizes the mutable and empty nature of the world — of all the worlds, actually, for the ancestors, demigods, and gods all want souls under their regimen and control. Thus freedom is difficult indeed to attain for the embodied soul.

But the truth of the matter is — and this brings forward the goal of Self-mastery — that it is only through life in the body as a human being that the soul can transcend relativity, for the ancestors and gods are all caught in the web of *maya*'s design consisting of attraction to wealth, power, fame, vainglory, and the like. Only the selfless soul will gain freedom — which, by the way is one of the reasons why Sri Ramakrishna Paramahamsa is the most important study of Enlightenment anyone could engage in nowadays to understand the dynamics of the death of the ego and the attainment of absolute selflessness.

And those dynamics are well displayed in olden times in King Janaka's case as well. The list of his "Improvisational Airs on Awakening" reveal that he had to intuit the presence of the *Atman* within, then find out what was veiling it, or what thief had "stolen" if from him, as it were. These insights were gleaned by frequenting the holy company of the *guru*, getting a *mantra*, and practicing meditation, which are certainly three of the main requisites for beginning inner life. Following through after gaining a few of the experiences that came from this type of comprehensive *sadhana*, the noble king ousted all delusion from the mind, perceived all things arising from the mind, then purified that selfsame mind and turned it into "a pearl of great price." In this way he gained victory over the heavy mind, the wayward mind, the ordinary mind, the worldly mind, and yes, even the intellectual mind.

Lastly, he saw that all was mind, and that impure mind projected a universe of suffering, while pure mind perceived nothing but *Brahman*. This classic run of *Vedantic* insight has been repeated over and over again, for time out of mind, by countless luminaries. Thus, constant rounds of birth and death in ignorance is not the only alternative for embodied souls, nor the only cycle going on. If repetition is the way of things here on this plane of existence, then let us repeat the *mantra*. And if duplication, *ad infinitum*, is the name of the game here, then let us double up on our compassionate acts to benefit all sentient beings. And if variety is the nature of manifestation, then

King Janaka's Song of Victory

Melodies of Mourning

Afflicted with pain, deluded by the world of maya.

Brooding on the short span of life in the illusion of time.

Despondent due to desires of the gross mind in ignorance.

Kingdom and rulership seem empty, dull, and evanescent.

Rulers and their vast wealth have only disappeared over time.

My mind-ghost dances in the world-theater to the hollow tune of the 5 sense organs.

The gods in the heavens will vanish like fish in the ocean.

Weakness reigns due to energy wasted on the sense objects.

Death recurs, and the Timeless Brahman is never quite realized.

The deluded mind thrives as the basic root of the tree of samsara.

Youth is ignorance, adulthood is base desire, old age is suffering.

Improvisational Airs on Awakening

Detecting the vile thief of my Atmic Jewel and expelling him.
Learning the art of japa & meditation from my guru.
Dispelling mental unrealities like "I and you" from the mind.
Never allowing delusion an entrance into the mind again.
Boring a hole in the pearl of the mind to dispel darkness.
Stringing my mala with the thread of sobering experiences.

Variations on a Theme of Victory

Victory over my great adversary, the deluded mind.
The disappearance of the suffering that had afflicted me.
The attainment of a life and mind filled with quiescence.
Adoration of the Jnana-wisdom that allowed this state.

The Serenades of Samadhi

What object is there in this world for me to accomplish?
Where is illusion? To my present scrutiny all is pure Jnana.
I cognize nothing but the one immaculate Atma-jnana.
I will not long for any object I do not come across naturally.
I will never evince aversion to any object that I duly come by.
I will remain immutably fixed in my own Self of Atma-jnana.
All events and happenings will occur as preordained by dharma.

"Observing the actions of the world wherein men flutter like birds in the air and perish, and feeling no more significant than a speck of dust floating in a sea of dust, I gave up the ephemeral wealth and the objects of this world and fixed my mind immutably in my own Self of Atma-jnana." King Janaka

let us produce countless ways of inseminating the *dharma* and its teachings into the many minds of human beings so as to create a stream of souls moving towards ultimate Freedom from this earth plane. If we do all this and more, King Janaka will smile upon us from his empyreal realm, and bless us with his own sweet symphony of spiritual realizations.

As this caravan of endless teachings charts rolls on, bearing a potentially infinite number of *dharmic* teachings to effect the highest good of aspiring humanity, the student of *dharma* will find that the mind plays an extremely important part in Indian philosophy in the struggle between bondage and freedom. As Sri Sarada Devi, the Holy Mother, stated, *"You need peace of mind first and foremost."* On another occasion, She uttered the words: *"The mind is everything, my child. You must treat it with care. For you will have to utilize it and take it with you in order to reach Brahman."*

The chart on the facing page shows the many ways that Lord Vasishtha counseled on how to reach *Brahman*, or Self-realization. In tandem with our recent exploration on the many *yogas*, which are all pathways to this highest goal as well, this teaching deals particularly with the mind and how to direct it. That is, once its errant tendencies are toned and attenuated, the presence of wide open pathways will become apparent to the now inward moving adept. Of course, two of them at the top of the list, and which have already taken up many paragraphs and pages in this book, are *bhakti* and *jnana*. Whether *bhakti* comes first to the aspirant, or *jnana* leads the way, the end result of utilizing them both forms an unsurpassable combination for peace of mind.

Of course, long before these two fully mature, the winsome ways of *chitta-nirodha* and *atma-vichara,* are taken up by many. Exercising control of the mind first, then asking the essential question ("Who am I?"), proves to be most effective in comprehending the subtle spiritual art of nondualism. In other words, a pure mind — as we have just studied about — will afford the right answers to the questioner who has first controlled and directed the mind along the proper course of inner action. Put in the opposite way, it would not be wise to engage an impure mind in either action or thought, what to speak of *sadhana*, for the repercussions that came back would be counterproductive, to say the least.

The remaining four ways to quiescence of mind shown on the chart on the facing page are all interconnected. Blessings be unto that advanced soul who looks and sees these as profound opportunities, then follows through on them in and implements them into spiritual life. They are meditation, direct perception, bliss, and selfless action. They are placed in this order here due to the classic way in which illumined beings seize and utilize them, and in some unique cases, express them so naturally.

Of course, and has been mentioned elsewhere in this book, meditation is a late arrival on the scene in most aspirant's life of practices. True, some beginners have great meditations right away, but weeks or months later that is seen to have changed. It most often takes a very long time to break through subtle mental barriers (and inner *karmas*) and reach even basic peace of mind, what to speak of attaining the mind's most precious treasures. That is where direct experience (*anubhava*) comes in. When rare and spontaneous visitations of the causal type come to the meditator, it is fairly certain that the early nocturnal stirrings are over and, as the song in India states, "The Day of Truth is dawning."

And bliss, *Ananda*, is one of the results coming from meditation and direct internal experience. Nothing soothes the mind and gives it quiescence better than *Ananda*. If *Shanti*, Peace, passes all understanding, then *Ananda*, bliss, is waiting beyond such understanding, for they describe it as being both "unalloyed and uninterrupted." In other words, it is not like happiness, which only changes to sadness, and it is not like joy, which can so easily turn to sorrow. *Ananda* has no opposite.

And it is with such bliss in hand, and in mind, that it can also reflect in action. For another facet of true bliss is that it wants to be shared with others. As Sri Ramakrishna has stated, *"Some realized souls like to eat mangos by themselves. They feast in private, then wash their faces and hands of all traces and come out to speak with others (*these are those great souls who show no traces of their

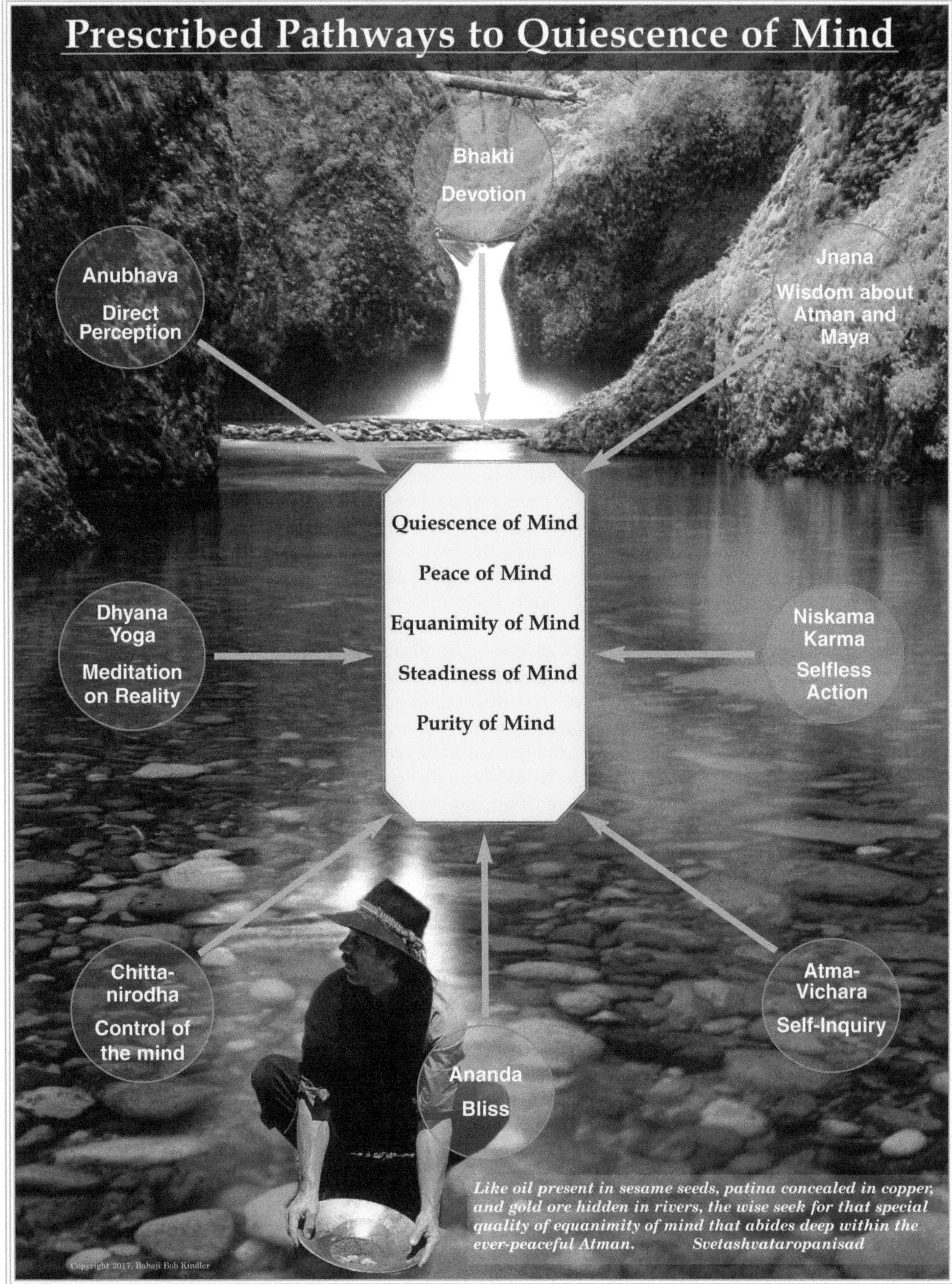

Prescribed Pathways to Quiescence of Mind
Bhakti
Devotion
Anubhava
Direct Perception
Jnana
Wisdom about Atman and Maya
Quiescence of Mind
Peace of Mind
Equanimity of Mind
Steadiness of Mind
Purity of Mind
Dhyana Yoga
Meditation on Reality
Niskama Karma
Selfless Action
Chitta-nirodha
Control of the mind
Atma-Vichara
Self-Inquiry
Ananda
Bliss
Like oil present in sesame seeds, patina concealed in copper, and gold ore hidden in rivers, the wise seek for that special quality of equanimity of mind that abides deep within the ever-peaceful Atman. Svetashvataropanisad
Copyright 2017, Babaji Bob Kindler

profound realizations on the outside). *But there are others who bring the mangos out and share them openly with everyone."* This expression forms one of the dynamics of perfected *Karma Yoga* in action. It is contagious, this exuberance of the saints and seers who try to inject the wisdom of *Brahman* into others. Everything that they do, or do not do, is based in *Niskama Karma*. Again, selflessness is its singular earmarking.

The pathways to peace just displayed are all of a lofty character, that is, they represent more of the ends of practice rather than the beginnings. Throughout this chapter there have been teachings that emphasize the foundations of spiritual life and practice, such as the Ten *Yamas* and *Niyamas* of *Yoga* (p 399), and the Twenty *Yamas* and *Niyamas* of Tantra (p 403). Systems such as these and their implementation into daily life are precisely what bring about peace of mind for those beings who, like in present times, have lost it in the first place. The chart on the facing page gives still another showing of precepts on a grand and well-thought scale, this time in the religion and *darshana* of *Buddhism*.

Interesting juxtapositions take place when the teachings of fundamentals coming from systems like *Yoga, Tantra,* and *Buddhism* are placed side by side. But one thing is certain in Indian religion across the board, and that is that violence is the first thing to go. Whether one claims it as nonviolence, like *ahimsa*, or gets to the point of the matter by simply forbidding the taking of life, both the law and its result is obvious. *Buddhism*, like *Jainism* (see forthcoming chart on page 457), gets very specific about taking the lives of living beings, even going so far as to include animals and insects into the matter. And in case the onlooker might conclude that this is only a moral law, with some horrible consequence being leveled upon the transgressor by a vengeful deity somewhere, *Buddhism* clears up such misfeasances by laying the focus on positive means and outcomes.

This is the import of the two columns on the chart under study, one listing the "exoteric" form, and the other showing "esoteric." For instance, if we take the first and ninth precepts on the chart, both being concerned with killing and violence, we find that their esoteric forms come by way of *karma*-neutralizing solutions rather than via cosmic recompense. It is like saying that if one understands and maintains the *dharma* in its original form, that both potential problems — transgressing the cosmic laws and *karmic* repercussions, wherever they might originate — never arise. So many insensitivities and mindless errors in human life and thinking would simply be absent, never causing their unwanted effects at all. For instance, the fifth precept listed on the chart, the long-lived human bane of partaking of and distributing alcoholic beverages, if it were eschewed, even seen as a type of violence itself, would result in not only the absence of millions of ills in human life, but (as is the case with its esoteric form) would do away with any negativities being leveled upon the transformative teachings of the *dharma*. In other words, *dharma*, rightly lived, not only does away with *adharma*, it precludes it. Why should *adharma* be present in the first place?

In this way, and following the path set down by the knowers of *dharma*, ills such as stealing would be replaced by sincere seeking, betrayal by generosity, telling falsehoods would be countered by compassion, slander would die under the mind-set of detachment. Similarly, pride and egotism would be met by right mental perspective, and selfishness regarding life and making a living would be treated by encouragement along the pathway to Enlightenment. Overall, major boons that benefit humanity highly, such as spiritual teachings and teachers and their *dharmic* organizations, would never be denigrated or underestimated again, for all sentient souls would come to realize the singular and salubrious nature of religion and philosophy properly utilized in the world.

Along these very lines, it is most healing to look at the extremely gentle and benevolent world of Jainism, a religion that has been in existence for over twenty generations before *Buddhism*, as its own religion, formulated on earth. Of the eight major religions of the world (Christianity, Islam, Hinduism, Buddhism, Sikhism, Judism, Jainism, Zoroastrianism), Mother India has contributed three of them. They are Hinduism, Buddhism, and Jainism, and these three represent only a portion of all the different lineages, *sampradayas*, sects, and other *darshanas* that infill and inform India's vibrantly pulsating spiritual life and realms.

Jujukai — Ten Basic Precepts of Buddhism

The "Yamas and Niyamas" of Buddhism

"The sincere practitioner should be watchful over his speech, well-restrained in mind, and commit no unwholesome deed with his body. Let him thus purify this threefold avenue of karma and tread the path made known by the seers and sages." Dhammapada

Exoteric Form

Esoteric Form

Exoteric Form	Esoteric Form
1. Never Taking Life	1. Maintaining Dharma
2. Never Engaging in Stealing	2. Never Failing to Seek Enlightenment
3. Never Being Unchaste	3. Coveting Nothing and Being Generous
4. Never Speaking Falsehoods	4. Always Showing Compassion
5. Never Selling or Buying Alcohol	5. Never Denigrating the Dharma Teachings
6. Never Recounting the Misdeeds of Others	6. Always Remaining Unattached
7. Never Praising Oneself and Deprecating Others	7. Keeping Free of False Views
8. Never Being Selfish With Time and Money	8. Encouraging All Towards Enlightenment
9. Never Engaging in Violence and Aggression	9. Explaining Hinayana and Mahayana
10. Never Slandering the Three Great Ones	10. Offering Charity to Spiritual Teachers

"Engaging in spiritual practice prior to the initiation and implementation of advised preliminary disciplines results in failure to comprehend the teachings, to act in accordance with the dharma, to meditate properly, and to worship in the right spirit." Babaji Bob Kindler

Previously, as mentioned, the principle of *ahimsa*, nonviolence (in thought, word, and deed), is crucial to India's religious and philosophical stance. Certainly, nowhere is this principle given its deepest and most convincing rationale as in *Jainism*, what to speak of its exemplary manifestation. *Jains* are serious about non-killing, to such an extent that even microbes floating in the air stand less of a chance of destruction from members of that religion than from natural means.

The chart on the opposite page has been put together thanks to studies done by interested monks of the Hindu fold, mainly, Swami Brahmeshanandaji Maharaj of the Ramakrishna Order. Living with the Jains while on pilgrimage, and frequenting their temples and homes over a period of time, the rather strict and complex rules of their way of religious life were observed and noted down. As in most Indian-based religions, there are rules for both monks and householders. Since this book has just taken up the precepts of *Buddhism*, and earlier, the *Yamas* and *Niyamas* of both *Yoga* and *Tantra*, this list of Jain observances and practices provides another good contrast, as well as a comparison that reveals the way the pious and spiritually oriented Indian mind thinks and proceeds.

Whether for monk or householder, it can be seen right away that the presence of evil or negative thoughts in the mind is unacceptable to adherents. As will be seen with all of Jainism's precepts, this is not merely a moral law such as the West has been trained to follow, exclusively. In the West, if a man has a bad thought, it is rather natural. Most beings neither stop to eradicate it on the spot, nor think that such a vibration might stain the mind if it is not purged immediately. The sensitive spiritual seeker, Eastern or Western, does not allow poison to sit and fester in the mind. In Jainism, the acolyte not only destroys negative thoughts when they arise, he also replaces them with positive thinking and makes a habit out of that. For, it is a sobering thought, that what we think translates into action, then bounces back and effects future actions as well. In *Jainism*, as well as in *Yoga*, harsh words are alleviated and sweet and encouraging speech is used instead. Better still are words that inspire spirituality, driving beings on towards the goal of Enlightenment — not only for the self, but for all beings.

Thus far the religious attributes of Jainism looks much like other religions at the moral level. But when it comes to what is called *samitis,* the landscape changes in appearance — both inner and outer. The rather well-known practice of avoiding killing insects and other creatures comes in here. The expression, "Be careful where you walk," takes on an entirely different level of meaning with the Jains, for it is also enjoined that one must be careful *how* one walks as well. The practice of inspecting ones movements, as well as ones area of movement, not only protects one from unconscious harming and killing, but also forms a very good mode of practice that increases sensitivity to all living beings, nature included. Thus, one accepts and eats food only after inspecting it, one ingests meals in well lit places, and one is extra aware of the excretion of waste from the body with regard to location. Talking while eating is also minimized, and restricted to words that inspire and uplift. The energy that one exudes during practices such as eating actually permeates the food taken in, and then affects the energy from those morsels later, in action. Therefore, what is being called mindfulness in action these days gets extra special treatment in *Jainism*, which in turn benefits all involved, and in all three phases of time — past, present, and future.

A beautiful aspect of *Jainism* is how these *samitis* connect to vows, and even to the accidental or purposeful transgression of said vows. Vows, called *vrata* in old times in India, are pretty much absent in the lives the modern peoples. That is unfortunate. But the type and level of vow in Jainism, developed over so many generations, is even more notable. For the sincere Jain aspirant, moving about in the body faces stiff restrictions. The more the movement and the wider the range, the more possibility there is of causing harm to other beings. And so the *Jain* family will work only in an area close to home. This observance has more to it, obviously, then just staying away from unclean places and evilly influenced human beings. It follows the ancient way of India that refrains from storing up more than one can use, as well as living free of attachment to objects and nature, and owning few possessions. Fasting enters in here as well. Adherents to the *Jain* religion fast religiously twice in a lunar fortnight. This renunciation of food is an austerity that heals and reveals.

Ahimsa in Jainism
Nonviolence in the World's Gentlest Religion

"Ahimsa is a goddess who supports all creatures. She is like water for the thirsty, food for the hungry, and medicine for the sick. She conduces to the well-being of all creatures, moving or immobile." Prashnavykarana

Mahavratas – Vows For Monks

- *Refraining from killing the five categories of creatures, viz., with one sense organ on to all five sense organs*
- *Never killing or harming creatures in thought, word, and deed – even in a dream*
- *Observing the two categories called Modes of Conduct and the Six Samitis*

1. Manas Gupti — Restraint of Mind:
   a) never to think evil thoughts
   b) always to think noble thoughts
   c) always to be pure and unselfish
2. Vachana Gupti — Control of Speech
   a) never speak harsh or untrue words
   b) never flatter others
   c) speak little, using only truthful words

Six Samitis — Careful Conduct
1. *Irya Samiti*: carefulness while walking
2. *Bhasha Samiti*: no ridiculing, talking ill, self-praise
3. *Eshana Samiti*: carefulness in accepting food
4. *Adananikshepa Samiti*: careful inspection of objects
5. *Alokita-pana-bhojana Samiti*: eat and drink in the day
6. *Utsarg Samiti*: discharge of excrement at a place free from living beings

Twenty-four Tirthankaras

Anuvratas – Vows For Householders

Guna Vratas
- *Digvrata*: restriction of movement to within specified areas
- *Deshavrata*: stay clear of impure or objectionable places
- *Anartha danda-vrata*: give up sinful activities
- *Samayika vrata*: meditation on the equality of all beings

Shiksha Vratas
- *Pradosh-upavasa vrata*: fast twice in a lunar fortnight
- *Atithisamvibhaga vrata*: serve guests with food and comforts
- *Upabhoja-paribhoja parinama-vrata*; restrict use of food, drink, bags, bedding, etc.

Transgression of Vows

1. *Bandha*: to tie or restrain an animal from freely moving
2. *Vadha*: to beat any living being with a stick or whip
3. *Cheda*: to pierce the nose, ear, or limbs of any animal
4. *Atibhararpana*: to load animals beyond their ability
5. *Anna-pana-nirodha*: failing to supply food and drink to humans or animals

Transgressions of Restricted Area
1. Going beyond the prescribed limit in one's area
2. Going down a well or crawling into holes and caves
3. Increasing one's area prompted by greed, infatuation, or profit

"Killing a living being is killing one's own self; showing compassion to a living being is showing compassion to oneself. They who desire their own good should avoid harm to all living beings."

Mahavira, Samana Suttam

A Brief Look at Right Livelihood in Jainism — *avoid trades in which*: furnaces are used; trees are cut & forests are burned; liquor is produced; animals and birds are sold; excavations/explosions are used; trade in ivory, bones, horns, furs, etc; trade involving lard, meat, fat, etc; commerce in poisonous substances and drugs; work where lakes, ponds, and wells are dried up; all work where wicked men and prostitution are supported.

"One must always remember that Ahimsa is the essence of religion. To be learned implies that one must not kill or harm any creature." Sutrakritanga

Freedom from dependance on outer stimuli strengthens the mind, making it more fit to place clear attention on Divine Reality. Again, this building of inner fiber, or character, has gone missing in today's world, particularly where opulence has visited a culture. It may be an old story, but it becomes a new one when profound solutions that are found in the ongoing lives of *Jains* are taken into consideration and applied.

Although much more can be said of *Jainism*, what remains on the chart (page 447) is adequate for this study. It is also compelling. It has to do with the axiom of what *Buddhism* refers to as "right livelihood." The Jains are extremely careful here, and again, this is a fine example for the modern world. What to speak of the obvious and welcome life-style of vegetarianism, ones occupation if he or she be a *Jain* has to consider non-killing at as many levels as can be provided for, consciously. Keeping others from suffering is an element of this practice as well. It is not only that animals are not killed and eaten, they are treated humanely as well. They are not overburdened with weight, they are not tethered, they are not beaten or whipped, their bodies are not pierced to afford tying and restraining, and they are religiously given ample food and water daily. Short of giving a few. select animals sentimental love like which happens in the West, the *Jains* serve and even worship all forms of life. This is divine duty, and it remains free of attachment to pets as objects of pleasure.

To address right livelihood more directly, the chart reveals that *Jains* will not accept jobs or occupations that have anything to do with threatening life or damaging the environment. If you are a *Jain* looking for employment, then, it is not just digging a well that would put you off, but even crawling down a well would be off limits for you. The cutting or burning of forests, of course, would be an outright atrocity, full of negative *karma* for the future. Anything that has to do with the killing of animals such as manufacturing perfumes, selling furs, mining for ores, using explosives, commerce in poisonous substances, and especially anything that has to do with producing liquor and intoxicating substances would be forbidden, since that harms all three — environment, animals, and the minds of human beings. For the *Jains* a pure world is a nonviolent one, and the quality of existence of next world will also depend upon how one treats the present one.

Jainism, *Sankhya*, and *Buddhism* have a deep connection, not only in religious practice and perspectives, but also within the sweep time. It has been mentioned that the most recent *Tirthankara* (Hanuman-like hero) of *Jainism*, Mahavir, lived about the time that Buddha visited this world. Twenty-three previous *Jain* teachers had already graced India, meaning that the most strict and mindful practices of *ahimsa* were already well in place in India when Lord Buddha came about 550 B.C. The *Sankhya* philosophy of Lord Kapila was one of the most ancient of Indian *darshanas* as well. Unfortunately, its scriptures have all but vanished from form in this day and time.

To reveal, as far as possible, how these long-lived and extraordinary movements of spiritual wisdom have both developed and intersected, the chart on the facing page shows all the line of *acharyas* that followed in the tracks of Lord Kapila, of such massive *Vedic* fame. Some historians place *Sankhya* around 600 B.C.E. as well, but since Sri Krishna has stated that he taught the ancient *Sankhya* to the sons of Lord *Brahma*, a very powerful and long-lived form of it was obviously present, even at the beginning of a cosmic cycle, under the auspice of *Brahma* and his mind-born sons.

Whatever the case, the teachings of *Sankhya*, *Jainism*, and *Buddhism* smack and ring of one another. Reviewing a few of the auspicious *slokas* from the seers of India on the chart under study will accent this fact. One of the most potent, and again, long-lived, is the teaching of the natural separation of the Soul, *Purusha*, from Nature, *Prakriti*. In *Sankhya*, nature is likened to a dancing girl who appears and gives her performance, then vanishes backstage thereafter. The onlooker, the sentient Soul, watches from a detached witness standpoint, delighted by the spectacle but safe and sound in Its own eternal abode. As Kapila stated, so long as the Soul does not forget itself, it will never fall into bondage in nature, where, as Lord Buddha warned, the six transformations (see page 225) — birth, growth, disease, decay, old age, and death — are taking place continually. Thus, as the scriptures of India have stated, *"There is no knowledge such as Sankhya, and no power like that of Yoga."*

Coming to the end of this powerful chapter entitled "The Gait of the Gods," several in-depth

EARLY SANKHYA ACHARYAS

Sankhya forms one of the most important pillars constituting the six orthodox systems of Indian Philosophy, called Sad-darshana by the seers and acharyas.

1
Lord Kapila → **Founder of Sankhya** → **Sankhya Sutra**

"Cause and effect are the basis of production. There can be no production of that which is non-existent. Cream, for instance, that is inherent in milk, forms on milk and never on water."

2
Asuri → **Main Disciple of Kapila**

Tattva Samasa Sutras

"Purushas are numerous entities of consciousness who, through association with Prakriti, nature, become jivas — embodied souls. But the Purusha is ever-free and ever-wise. If it knows itself, it will never fall into ignorance or bondage.
Prakriti, intangible matter, is insentient, and attaching itself to Purusha, receives its rays of consciousness."

3
Pancha Shikha → **Disciple of Asuri**

4
Vindhyavasa → **Lineage Holder Sankhya teacher**

5
Varsaghanya → **Lineage Holder Sankhya Teacher**

"Like the dancing girl who exhibits herself to the spectators and vanishes, so too does nature show itself off to the Purusha, and then cease operating."

6
Jaigisavya → **Lineage Holder Sankhya Teacher**
(Classmate of Pancha Shikha)

7
Isvara Krsna → **Commentator Lineage Holder Sankhya Teacher**
(Around the First Century A.D.)

Sankhya Karika

"Like the flow of milk for the sake of the calf, similar are the many acts of nature — and all of them are ultimately for the emancipation of the soul."

8
Vodhu, Devala, & Sanaka → **Other Important Names**

"To Sanaka and the sons of Lord Brahma I taught the ancient Sankhya and the eternal Yoga." Sri Krishna

"There is no knowledge such as Sankhya, and no power like that of Yoga."
The Mahabharata

"Sankhya stands very near to the Vedanta in that it accepts the doctrine of the non-difference of cause and effect." Adishankaracharya

renderings of clear and informative cosmological systems in the sacred *darshanas* of Mother India are still to be displayed. And the recent mention of *Sankhya Yoga* provides a perfect time and way of doing so. For never have the workings of inner Cosmology been stated so cogently, yet at the same time with such unreserved sententiousness, as in Lord Kapila's philosophy — as the engaging chart on the facing page shows us.

The Ancient Chest of Consciousness, besides providing an excellent metaphor for its topic, is also an amalgam of India's greatest teachings from several notable luminaries in its wide spiritual field. And they are all borrowed and mingled here to explain one or two major themes in Her enlightened philosophy. In brief, and to cite it out the front, one of them is to reveal where forms disappear to at the time of their passing, i.e., where objects retreat to, and where living beings journey to. We already know how Indian *darshanas* feel about death: one, and ultimately, that it is an illusion, or a projection of the mind; and two, that it serves a small function in the Divine Mother's realms of manifestation, that being to help souls shift into subtler spheres of awareness. We also know about India's teachings that all travel, i.e., movement in the worlds, is dreamlike in nature, since the one, true Soul, *Atman*, which is the Essence in all beings, never moves or dreams.

Keeping these two facts in mind, we can examine the cosmic chest to see its contents. It has three drawers, signifying the gross worlds *(stula)*, the subtle worlds *(sukshma)*, and the causal worlds *(karana)*. Our earth and the planets and suns in outer space form the *stula jagad*, as the box on the right hand side of the chest explains. The subtle worlds are formed of mind in its role as the container and projector of concepts and thoughts. And deepest of all, representing the third and highest drawer, is the causal world that is made up of seed essences. Everything existing in the subtle and gross worlds is pulled from there. How is that done? In part, by the mind, in its waking, dreaming, and deep sleep states. There is, of course, greater dynamic to this, but the philosophers of India, and of the "mind only" schools, want beings to know that objects are just mind made manifest. Put another way, they are intelligence solidified. For those who have been left high and dry by the scientific theories of physics, i.e., that the atomic particle with its smaller constituents is all there is, a welcoming inroad into a much finer and complete system, with its connection to inner life, is available for consideration (see charts on pages 33 & 262).

This much describes the cosmic chest in brief, giving us answers for so many of our age-old questions. And these questions are not answered by the universes in space and time themselves; they are answered by our own mind and intelligence that formulated them. On the right hand side of the chest of drawers lie the five sheaths of the embodied soul (see the earliest charts on pages 19 & 21), shown in their connection with the three drawers. The three drawers hold everything of Nature, manifested and unmanifested (see chart on page 321 of this chapter), and the five sheaths — that are a part of Nature as well — are holding consciousness. Consciousness, which in its purest form is transcendent of Nature, nevertheless uses nature to manifest in and express itself.

This amazing fact, as revelation, actually makes up the rest of this chart — as instanced by the intelligent observations of a more recent scientist quoted at the bottom of the chart, and further filled out by statements from seers like Sri Krishna and Jesus Christ. Perhaps more convincing to the soul raised in the materialistic West, is the quote from Sir James Jeans on the right hand bottom of the chart: *"Mind no longer appears to be an accidental intruder into the realm of matter. We are beginning to suspect that we ought rather to hail it as the creator and governor of this realm."* Whereas *Vedanta* would change the word "creator" to "projector," the profound idea still comes across. Scientists, evolutionists, archeologists, biologists, etc., — and certainly all those of a materialist bent — might want to take a close look at what souls who have found their way to India's teachings, represented rather simply by the Cosmic Chest of Drawers, are thinking.

And we cannot leave this chart under study until the owner of this cosmic chest is both revealed and lauded. The entire top half is dedicated to the Mother of the Universe, the Wisdom Goddess — the *Bhagavati Devi*. Her words at the top of the chart, drawn from Her own scripture, leave no doubt about Her part and place in the scheme of things, both cosmic and collective. The

The Ancient Chest of Consciousness
The Secret of Spiritual Self Storage

"At the time of the Great Dissolution, I withdraw all beings and worlds back into My Unmanifested Prakriti, while I, Myself, disappear into the formless Brahman. When the Dance of Maya begins again, I loose all things forth into the realms of becoming. All the while, nothing is born, nothing dies; nothing is created, nothing gets destroyed."

Bhagavati Devi

MAHAMAYA

MAHASHAKTI

Withdrawal (Laya)

Ring of Truth

Sustenance (Sthiti)

Sportive Play (Lila)

"Verily, I have My manifested form, and My unmanifested form. Beyond both is My Supremely Unmanifested Form."

Sri Krishna

Projection (Srsti)

"In my Father's Mansion there are many chambers, abiding places – homes of rest and peace and sojourn."

Jesus Christ

Ishvara Avatar  Brahma Vishnu Siva

	The Three Worlds		
All objects as seed essences, i.e., bijams	→ Causal Realm (Karana Jagat) → Deep Sleep	→	*Anandamayakosha*
All objects as mental constructs / thoughts	→ Subtle Worlds (Sukshma Jagat) → Dreaming	→	*Vijnanamayakosha Manomayakosha Pranamayakosha*
All objects as physical forms. i.e., matter	→ Gross Worlds (Stula Jagat) → Waking	→	*Annamayakosha*

Shesha → **Primal Residue**

Emblem of Eternity

"As we inspect it over periods of time, the universe begins to look to us more like a great thought rather than a great machine." Sir James Jeans

"Mind no longer appears to be an accidental intruder into the realm of matter. We are beginning to suspect that we ought rather to hail it as the creator and governor of this realm."

entire chest is Hers, along with a whole lot more. Projection, sustenance, and withdrawal all go on at Her behest.

But lest we should conclude that She is a form only, Her oneness with the Formless *Brahman* is to be taken under consideration. She both supports form and transcends it. This is comprehended better by noting what lays underneath the cosmic chest, and also what lies atop it. The Trinity, *Ishvara*, and the *Avatars* all grace its surface, while beneath lie the primal etheric Waters of Existence, called *Ekarnava* in *Sanskrit*. The thousand-headed serpent rests in these, representing the subtle residue that persists, even at the end of a massive cosmic cycle, or *Mahayuga* (see chart on page 39). Upwards, inwards, is found The Word, *AUM*; She is the progenitress of It. It is Her living ocean of potential where pure Intelligence, not just seeds of concepts, dwells. Victory be unto Her! *Om Sri Bhagavati Durga Devi!*

The Five Sheaths, or "*koshas*," have just made another appearance in our ongoing and in-depth look at Mother India's philosophical and religious systems. Having examined the various vehicles through which Consciousness emanates, manifests, reflects, and assumes, an across-the-board look at their juxtapositions would be helpful.

We have seen that, unlike the one body idea that the West believes in, India explains that living beings actually have three bodies: one in the physical universe; one in the mind; and one in causal formlessness. These all represent three states of mankind's awareness, called waking, dreaming, and deep sleep. This system also provides us with the connections for the three conditions that the soul abides in, and each of these carry separate identities as well. Thus, the *jiva*, or embodied being, is the enjoyer of objects in the gross body while awake, the enjoyer of dream worlds and their objects in the subtle body when transcendent of the five gross senses, and the enjoyer of bliss in the causal body while in deep sleep.

And the five sheaths all figure into these *triputis* as well, explaining the subtler subdivisions where dynamics that are often unseen go on under the surface, unbeknownst to most beings. For instance, when consciousness that has temporarily been enjoying outer worlds and objects, moves into the subtle body, the *pranamayakosha* facilitates the shift and plays host to it and its inner movements. Again, when the *vijnanamayakosha* concludes its part hosting the transmigrating consciousness in the realm of subtle dreams, the *anandamayakosha* opens to receive that selfsame consciousness that wants to rest in formless bliss. Even the ego, or assumed self of mankind, goes into abeyance then, only to be roused when the desire for activity and sporting in the worlds suggests itself again. Thus, the transmigrating soul moves back and forth, in and out, amidst worlds of its own devising.

Not only will this twenty-four hour process continue its cycle, the soul's consciousness will also enact such moves from birth, to life, to death, and back to rebirth again. The entire process, at all levels, is represented in microcosmic form in the three phases of the breath — the in-breath, the suspended breath, and the out-breath. Thus, the *yogis* know: master the breath, and all the keys to inner life will begin to unfold.

And while on the subject of *triputis*, this chart also holds one of the signature teachings of Lord Vasishtha around the three types of ego, as well. It appears here because we should not forget to connect them to the three bodies and three states of consciousness, etc. Left with the idea of only one body, what to speak of no living consciousness in it and no intelligence or soul that outlives it, a human being has only the ego to rely upon. This is the small self, invested with fear at the loss of not only its own little existence, but everything around it that it strives to own and enjoy. Laboring everything, coveting everything, and ultimately spoiling everything for itself, it even takes what the intellect can give it and skews it towards personal and selfish ends. And where these more vicious characteristics of the human ego are not so prevalent, like in the so-called "good" person, the opposite pole of the ego is ready to appear. It brings with it uncertainty, lack of self worth, weakness, false pride, and a whole host of other machinations.

And the only real solution for this "*dehadhyasahamkara*," is miles away — or giant steps

The Three Bodies and Five Sheathes

Sri Ram asks: "What is the nature of ahamkara?"
(From the Story of Bhima, Bhasa, and Drdha)

Body	Condition	Sheath/Kosha	State	Identity
Gross Body	Stula Sharira	Annamayakosha (Sheath of Food)	Jagrat (Waking)	Vaishvanara (Enjoyer of objects)
Subtle Body	Sukshma Sharira	Pranamayakosha (Sheath of Energy)	Svapna (Dreaming)	Taijasa (Enjoyer of dream-worlds)
		Manomayakosha (Sheath of Mind)		
		Vijnanamayakosha (Sheath of Intellect)		
Causal Body	Karana Sharira	Anandamayakosha (Sheath of Ego)	Sushupti (Deep Sleep)	Prajna (Enjoyer of bliss)

The Three Types of Ego/Ahamkara

Paramahamkara
Supreme Self, which reveals the cohesive unity between the Atman, living beings, and the worlds

Sakshahamkara
Beneficent and detached Witness-Self which is ever-existent and transcendent of the worlds of name and form

Dehadhyasahamkara
Attached, fear-based ego-self which causes suffering through false identification of the Atman with the body

"There are three types of bodies, associated with three types of ahamkara." — Lord Vasishtha

inward. *Sakshahamkara,* the ripe ego, or witness ego, is calm, peaceful, detached, and content, wise and transcendent. What a major difference, then, between these two forms of *ahamkara!* It only goes to show (and only those who practice austerities that diminish the ego will know) that a great amount of inner work is in store for the sensitive person who has become tired of the troublesome insinuations of the tyrant ego and wants free of its ignominious reign. Nothing in the physical universe — no conventional means, no miracle cure, no new invention, no stark measure — will help with this problem, for the ego has been in on the conception and fashioning of all of them. It is like the clever fox that has made all provisions and taken all precautions long before the hounds appear on the scene. Only deep calm, sweet contentment, mature detachment, and the rare qualities of the trained and masterful mind will win this war. Peace is hard won, whether on the outer battlefield or the inner. Suffice to say, that when the ego is stripped of all that it covets and attaches to, then, again, will the welcome peace of mind and heart regain the territory of the pure Soul. That is the *Paramahamkara* — sort of a contradiction in terms, really, for no *ahamkara,* ego, is present in it whatsoever. Since God has a mind, the *Mahat,* perhaps we could call this God's Ego. It is what is seen, or sensed, when one meets an illumined soul, or has a vision of a seer or *Avatar.*

Several times in his two visits to the West, in 1893 and 1899, Swami Vivekananda told the Western people that there is little difference between *Vedanta* and *Buddhism.* When these two religions are studied side by side, along with the philosophies that both espouse, the truth of this statement will come shining through. A similar conclusion will be reached if the nondual versions of these two, namely *Advaita Vedanta* and Zen *Buddhism,* are compared. On the qualified level, however, teachings such as the *Triloka* in *Vedanta,* and *Sangai-yui-isshin,* combine to reveal not only similarities in these systems, but complementary contributions as well.

In the chart on the facing page, the famous "Three Worlds" of Indian Philosophy get a further rendering. *Zen* teachings simply describe the first of these three as "the sphere of desire," or *Kamadhatu.* In this one dimension of the mind are found beings with very different characteristics. Animals and human beings occupy the more solid planets, but hell beings lie lower, and the realms of lower heaven lie beyond. This latter series of worlds is where semi-divine beings, namely the *asuras* and the gods. All of these beings are bound by desire to incarnate within these layers of thought, energy, and matter. As the Buddha noted, when a few of these incarnate souls recognize the limitations of the body and the illusoriness of these worlds, they will beat a hasty retreat out of *Mara,* or *Maya.*

The realms of form are not so easy to transcend, however. *Rupaloka* is the realm of "desireless form," a good distinction to make seeing that so many beings who get beyond matter are still weighted down by subtle forms. But at least — and unlike the earth realm and lower heaven — the work to be done is acknowledged and engaged in at this level of awareness. Impedances such as torpor, hatred, root ignorance, and the like are dealt with here — but inside in mind where their origins lie, rather than on the outside on earth in the physical body where their effects occur. *"Thrashing around like a fish out of water"* describes well the intense struggle the soul undertakes to get rid of these passions and obstacles, but the Four Absorptions, so well-known by *Buddhist* practitioners, form the fine attainments that await the sedulous seeker after all this is accomplished.

But the real reward awaits in the third world, called *Arupaloka.* With the inner art of meditation mastered, all the blessings of attaining formlessness, impossible to comprehend until they are experienced, come forth. Their names, like "nothingness," and "nothing whatsoever," are as enigmatic as the experiences themselves. To express the inexpressible nature of these echelons of awareness, and to level an apt conclusion around them all, Lord Buddha's quote under this heading states it well: *"Difficult is a human birth; difficult is mortal life; difficult is really hearing the truth. Rare is the appearance of the Enlightened Ones."*

And speaking of apt conclusions, the quote at the bottom of the chart really gets to the point of the Buddha's teachings of the *dharma.* In this respect, it is that attaining mastery over all three of these worlds, either individually or collectively, is nowhere near as auspicious as entering that sin-

Sangai-Yui-Isshin
Three Worlds, One Mind

"They who follow the path of Truth live happily in this world, and in the hereafter." Buddha

Sangai — The Three Worlds

1. Kamaloka (Kamadhatu) — Sphere of Desire

The Twenty-eight Divine Realms of Buddhism

Hell Beings (narakas)
Human Beings
Animals
6 Classes of Gods
Asuras

"Seeing the body as temporal, and the world as a mirage, one transcends the realm of Mara."

2. Rupaloka (Rupadhatu) — Sphere of Desireless Form

desire, ill will, sloth, restlessness, doubt
desires, becoming, ignorance
desirelessness
empty mind & joy
equanimity
perpetual wakefulness

Gods of the Four Dhyana Heavens
Requires:
Removal of the 5 Nivaranas
Elimination of (3) Ashrava
Practice of the Four Absorptions

"As the fish taken out of its watery home and thrown on land thrashes about, so does the mind tremble while freeing itself from the dominion of Mara."

3. Arupaloka (Arupadhatu) — Sphere of Formlessness

"Those wise ones who are absorbed in meditation, mindful, fully awakened, even the gods hold dear."

Akasha - Limitless Space
Vijnana - Consciousness
Arupa - Nothingness
Sat-asat - Nothing Whatsoever

Advanced Beings of the Four Highest Heavens

Practice of the Four Stages of Formlessness

"Difficult is a human birth; difficult is mortal life; difficult is really hearing the Truth. Rare is the appearance of the Enlightened Ones."

"The fruit of entering the Stream of Enlightenment is superior to that of sole sovereignty over the world, or going to heaven, or of supreme lordship over all the realms." Dhammapada

gular and incomparable "Stream of Enlightenment" where flows, unimpeded, the inexpressible Bliss of pure, conscious Awareness, or *Buddha* Nature.

A thorough "fleshing out" of such well-envisioned systems of cosmic design comes about when we look back prior to *Buddhism* some several thousand years to the time of the *Vedic rishis*. *Vedanta*, namely, the *Upanisads*, had not come out from the enlightened human mind yet — at least not as written documents. But there was a plethora of wisdom to be gleaned, both in life and in action. A rich period of intricate and ornate ritual had brought from the depths of the Hindu heart and mind a complex and well-rounded vision of the cosmos (again, inner and outer) that left no doubt as to the multi-layered fabric of consciousness and the many beings occupying these subtle inward layers of space.

This is all evinced in a descriptive testament by the *rishi*, Svetashvatar, in the *Upanisad* that bore his name many hundreds of years later. The chart on the facing page will help us gaze deep into that grand reckoning of the manifold cosmos, showing us that not only did these early beings envision these worlds and their facets in deepest meditation, but also that they were far more philosophically and spiritually advanced than the moderns of our day and age who have lost both track of and sight of these *"Kingdoms of Heaven within."*

First of all, and most important, these illumined souls knew of and perceived God the Almighty, called *Brahman*, as the purest, the highest, the transcendent, and the Ultimate Being of all beings and all things. They acknowledged that Reality as being beyond thought, energy, and matter — a conclusion that no other religion in the history of the world has both confirmed and upheld throughout time, what to speak of emphasized in their scriptures. Therefore, when we take into account the *Brahmachakra* on the facing page, we must hold in mind that Its description as a "Grand Wheel" in no way limits It to principles like motion (thus activity), cycles (as in time), evolution and involution, or the manufacturing of forms (whether of stations of existence or living bodies). It could be said, then, that Its description as a wheel relates more to the fact that everything circles around It rather than the other way around.

Running eternally by the momentum of a single belt, whose every cycle gives rise to sets of dualities unnumbered, the Grand *Vedic* Wheel is unlike any other wheel ever mentioned or taught about in the different religious traditions of the world — prophetic, visionary, or indigenous. Its complexities belie a mere nature based ideology, and set the stage for an understanding of God and mankind that far outstrips any theological reckoning. For one thing, there are those triple tires on which it rolls on inexorably, signifying the three *gunas* of *Prakriti* — *tamas* (inertia), *rajas* (activity), and *sattva* (equilibrium). The reader can look back to the charts on pages 221, 223, and 307, to find consummate teachings on this unique Indian system.

Its sixteen extremities — the mind, five cognitive senses, five active senses, and the five elements — are, in and of themselves, both dense and far-reaching enough in their powers and potentials to cause most beings an age or more just to ponder their import. A case in point about them comes forth when examination of the fifty spokes of this grand wheel is undertaken; for numerous powers and weaknesses abide innately in these sixteen mechanisms, so much so that ample disappointments and satisfactions, both, come flowing out of their usage and application. Enthralled beings falling into this realm of mind, senses, and elements utilize them to try and control this grand wheel of infinite complexities, an impossible task, but one that entices them nevertheless.

And three very different routes make themselves known to the divine, human, and demonic occupants of this cosmic design. They are termed *Trimargabhedam*. The demonic hosts, driven by base passion for control and gain, take to the pathway of *adharma*. As Sri Krishna has stated about them in the *Bhagavad Gita*, *"Bound by a hundred ties of hope, given over to lust and anger, they strive to secure by unjust means hoards of wealth to use for sensual enjoyment."* A more concise yet explanatory description about such beings has never been given. And as Sri Ramakrishna said millennia later, they will not take to the *dharma* even by accident. *Dharma* is the second option, and much more favorable, for it will eventually, if not immediately, lead purer minds to *jnana*, higher Wisdom.

Brahmachakra – The Grand Vedic Wheel

"Some deluded thinkers speak of nature, others of time, as the force that revolves the grand wheel of life. But all of this is just the glory of God manifested in the world. So long as the jiva imagines separation from Brahman, so long does he continue to spin on the cosmic wheel, enjoying and suffering experiences there. He gains freedom when he realizes his oneness with Brahman."   Svetashvataropanisad

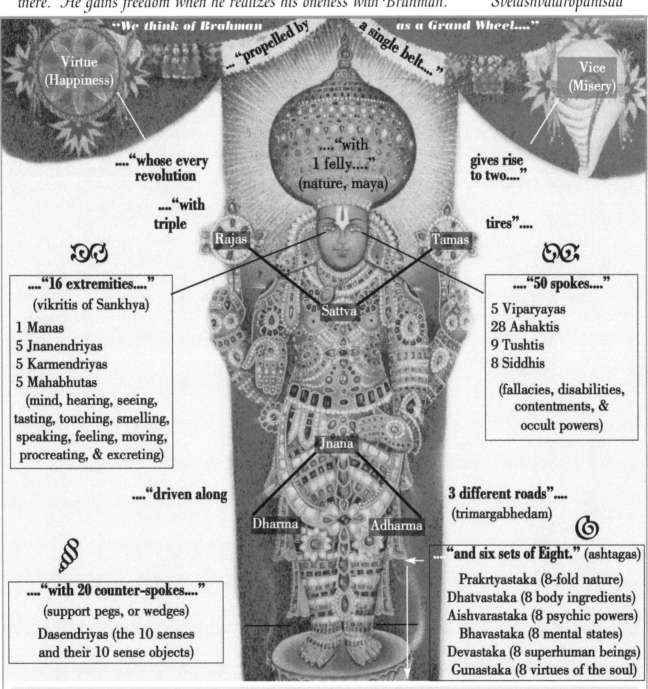

"We think of Brahman ... "propelled by ... a single belt...." as a Grand Wheel...."

Virtue (Happiness)

Vice (Misery)

...."whose every revolution

....."with 1 felly...." (nature, maya)

gives rise to two...."

....."with triple

tires"....

Rajas

Tamas

Sattva

....."16 extremities...."
(vikritis of Sankhya)

1 Manas
5 Jnanendriyas
5 Karmendriyas
5 Mahabhutas
(mind, hearing, seeing, tasting, touching, smelling, speaking, feeling, moving, procreating, & excreting)

....."50 spokes...."

5 Viparyayas
28 Ashaktis
9 Tushtis
8 Siddhis

(fallacies, disabilities, contentments, & occult powers)

Jnana

...."driven along

Dharma

Adharma

3 different roads"....
(trimargabhedam)

...."with 20 counter-spokes...."
(support pegs, or wedges)
Dasendriyas (the 10 senses and their 10 sense objects)

....."and six sets of Eight." (ashtagas)

Prakrtyastaka (8-fold nature)
Dhatvastaka (8 body ingredients)
Aishvarastaka (8 psychic powers)
Bhavastaka (8 mental states)
Devastaka (8 superhuman beings)
Gunastaka (8 virtues of the soul)

1) ether, air, fire, water, earth, mind, intellect, ego; 2) external skin (charma), internal skin (tvak), blood (asrk), flesh (mamsa), fat (medas), bone (asti), marrow (majja), semen (sukra); 3) invisibility (anima), weight-lessness (laghima), expansiveness (vyapti), satisfaction (prakamya), glorification (mahima), domination (ishitva), attraction (vashitva), enjoyment (kama-vasayita); 4) righteousness (dharma), unrighteousness (adharma), knowledge (jnana), ignorance (ajnana), renunciation (vairagya), attachment (avairagya), divine powers (aisvarya), lack of powers (anaisvarya); 5) brahma, prajapati, devas/devis, gandharvas, yakshas, rak-shasas, pitris, pishachas; 6) compassion (daya), forbearance (kshama), non-jealously (anasuya), purity (saucha), non-fatigue (anayasa), freedom from poverty (akarpanya), desirelessness (asphra).

The "six sets of eight" complete the picture of this ancient cosmic wheel. The list is given both in *Sanskrit* and in English so as to open our understanding to yet another set of often contrasting qualities. The seers seem to be conveying that life in the realms of name and form come with a price. As the quote from Svetashvatar at the top of the chart under study declares, as long as the transmigrating soul dreams in the mode of assumed separation from Ultimate Reality, so long will he or she have to circle on this immense merry-go-round of good, bad, and mixed experiences. A long pause for consideration and a big breath of trepidation are taken by any soul, deluded or wise, who would dare to venture near this huge cosmic wheel with its all-attracting magnetic pull of potential *karma*.

Another teaching of vast cosmic design, coming from the same school of *Upanisadic* Wisdom, appears on the facing page. What to speak of envisioning an immense cosmic wheel with its constant rotations and endless effects, the image of a powerful river is also conducive to communicating both the territories and the mechanisms that the realms of name and form in time and space based in causation present to the sojourning soul. Students of the incomparable Indian philosophy must always remember that *dharmic* teachings like the Great *Vedic* Wheel and the Mighty River of *Brahman* are posed as representations of *Brahman* with form, or the "manifest *Brahman*." The seers were keenly aware of the presence and pervasiveness of the formless or Unmanifested *Brahman* as well, and sought to have union with "That," first and foremost.

The Mighty River teaching on the facing page really repeats and runs through much of the Twenty-four Cosmic Principles of the *Sankhya* philosophy of Lord Kapila, but with a few additions. What is added here for contemplation are a few other sets of fives, such as the five *pranas* and the fivefold miseries. They are likened to five great tides and five swirling rapids — apt analogies for all those who have suffered erratic or blocked energy in the mind and body, as well as the transformations that take place in them over time. Working our way up the chart, the five elements are compared to unpredictable currents in this mighty river, able to sweep away any soul who jumps or gets pulled into it. Five dangerous whirlpools also lie nearby, often out of sight until too late. These are correlated with the five subtle senses that allure the weak swimmer, namely sound, touch, color, flavor, and aroma. What transmigrating soul who is embodying to enjoy the many sights and sounds along this great tributary would not come running at the promise of partaking of the many enjoyments it has to offer.

And, in fact, soul swimmers like these are already aware of five other bodies of water that feed this mighty river, those being the five surging streams called hearing, seeing, touching, tasting, and smelling. They naturally seek and are attracted to the subtle senses and their objects. So powerful are their currents, that beings become convinced that their very life itself, even their very existence, is based in and destined to circulate around them. Evidently they have not seen others get out of the water and free themselves from its dangers.

Souls who have effected a successful departure from this mighty river, its rapids, tides, currents, and whirlpools, are beings who have seen its source — the mind. Many there are who never connect all these sets of fives to the mind, thus knowing that the mind's fourfold elements of dual mind, thoughts, intellect, and ego, direct and control all its many movements in time and space. This is the ocean into which the river pours itself continually, also receiving its influx of tides, currents, etc. Seeing this, along with the incredible power both ocean and river possess, wise souls beat a hasty retreat from its copious influences and become free, making the dry land of *Brahman* their only refuge. This refuge is rendered doubly auspicious and highly desirable considering Svetashvatar's beautiful quote in his own *Upanisad*, which graces the upper portion of the chart under study: *"That one who projected consciousness, who is the bridge of immortality, ever tranquil, over the wavy and unnavigable ocean of samsara, who delivered the Vedas as a life raft, who is the purifying waters of the mantra stationed firmly in these mayic waters — I go for refuge in that effulgent One whose clear Light turns ones understanding towards the Atman."* It is deep and powerful wisdom sayings like this one that draws the soul away from all other attractions and posits it at the Source for all time. Other beings cannot

The Mighty River of the Manifest Brahman

"That One who projected consciousness, who is the bridge of immortality, ever tranquil, over the wavy and unnavigable ocean of samsara, who delivered the Vedas as a liferaft, who is the purifying fire of the mantra stationed firmly in mayic waters — I go for refuge in that effulgent One whose clear light turns one's understanding towards the Atman."
Svetashvataropanisad

"We meditate on the manifest Brahman, who is like a mighty river...."

...."whose source is the boundless ocean...."

The Mind
(Antahkarana —
manas, buddhi,
chitta, ahamkara)

....."which is fed by five surging streams...."

The Five Senses
(hearing, seeing touching, tasting, smelling)

...."which sports five unpredictable currents...."

The Five Elements
(ether, air, fire, water, earth)

....."which contains five dangerous whirlpools filled with innumerable confusions...."

The Five Subtle Senses and their objects
(sound, touch, color, flavor, and aroma)

....."which is agitated by five great tides...."

The Five Pranas
(prana, udana, samana, vyana, apana)

...."and which is attended by five swirling rapids."

The Fivefold Miseries
(birth, disease, old age, decay, death.)

"The ignorant soul being born into the world is like an unfortunate man accidently falling into the whirlpool of Vishalakshi from which he will never return. But for an illumined soul in the world, all is Brahman. There is the Ganges, for instance. If a man touches its waters anywhere he can declare, 'I have touched the Ganges.' It is not necessary for him to touch the entire river from Hardwar all the way down to Gangasagar." Sri Ramakrishna

even imagine the all-out fealty of the devotee of *Brahman* for the nondual Truth that has revealed itself to him. Everything in relativity can easily be sacrificed for possession of That.

Since further mention of the *Sankhya* Philosophy of Lord Kapila has been made, and the very important subject brought forth again, an even deeper look into it is warranted. For this particular pass through it, we depart a bit from its traditional rendering to include other crucial mentions that fall in line with the quintuplications that already infill it, i.e., the five senses of cognition, the five subtle elements, the five active senses, and the five gross elements. These are twenty of the Twenty-four Cosmic Principles. Though mind, ego, intellect, and cosmic mind make up the fourfold balance, *chitta,* or thoughts, can be added in to complete a fivefold x's five list.

At the head of all these stands *Purusha* and *Prakriti* as the *"....two eternally existing Principles."* There are four main things to know about this *Sankhya* couple. First, *Purusha* is Sentient while *Prakriti* is insentient. Second, *Prakriti* has come out of *Purusha* as its projection. Third, when *Prakriti* marches out of *Purusha, Purusha* does not change in the least in the offing. And fourth, *Prakriti* is present to serve the *Purusha.* If these roles get reversed and the sentient *Purusha* identifies with *Prakriti* instead of remaining its master, then root ignorance gets its starts and gains a hold over the mind. Suffering is the result of this false identification. For an excellent overall look at this system, the charts on pages 349 and 351 display the main principles and tenets of *Sankhya Yoga.*

As the chart on the facing page shows, there are other and many important sets of fives that can be counted into this mix of relative principles. Written out, they read like this:

A human being has five fingers on each hand, five toes on both feet, and sports five active and five cognitive senses (see page 417). The mind is also fivefold, including dual mind, it thoughts, the intellect, the ego, and, if counted, the Cosmic Mind that it is a part of. The life-force, or *prana,* that connects all of these facets, is also fivefold.

Living beings formulate their bodies amidst the five gross elements of nature, and play in the dream state utilizing five subtle elements. Five sheaths enfold and engross them (see pages 19 & 21), associated with five levels of ether, called *akashas* (see page 30 & 327). All embodied souls are subject at birth to the fivefold aspects of *maya* called name, form, time, space, and causality, and their relations include five types of living beings — namely, animals, humans, ancestors, deities, and seers. Whether conscious of them or not, human beings live eternally by five great spiritual laws.

The spiritually awakening human soul will soon begin to consider the Five Eternal Questions (see chart on page 116). Then, while observing and practicing the Five *Yamas* and Five *Niyamas* of *Yoga* (see chart on page 399), will strive to master the Five States of the Mind (see chart on page 612). Five Pathways to Perfection (see chart on page 622) will then present themselves to the sincere seeker of freedom, and in their pursuit of them, these singular souls will have to encounter the Five Main Obstacles to *Yoga* (see chart on page 419) and the Five Cosmic Bondages (see chart on page 240). To assist in overcoming such impediments, the aspirant will ascend through Five Levels of Wisdom (see chart on page 271), come to know the Five Fundamental Facts of Consciousness (see chart on page 709), and as a result of such spiritual advancement will be able to enjoy the Five Modes of the Detached Experiencer (see chart on page 737).

When accounted for, even these few sets of fives convey a broad hint to the soul that the days of its body/mind mechanism are "numbered," and that deep meditation on these hosts of quintuplications is revelatory, empowering, and essential. As the *Taittiriya Upanisad* lays it out, *"One should meditate upon the elements that compose the universe, namely, earth, intermediate space, heaven, sky, the four and eight directions, fire, air, sun, moon, stars, water, herbs, plants, trees, ether, and ones body — including skin, muscle, bone, and marrow. Then meditate on the five senses and the five pranas. Then contemplate AUM, the universal term of compliance, which is Brahman."*

To conclude this powerful chapter called *The Gait of the Gods,* with its many fine cosmic systems and its host of celestial wisdom, a look and study of one of India's most beloved philosophical renderings can be engaged. In this instance we switch our lens and its focus over to the *Tantra* Philosophy — a *darshana* that, though not listed as one of the traditional systems (*astika*), is never-

Quintessential Quintuplications
The Secret of Cosmic Projection by Sets of Fives

"A human being has five fingers on each hand, five toes on both feet, and sports five active and five cognitive senses as well. The mind is also fivefold, including dual mind, it thoughts, the intellect, the ego, and, if counted, the Cosmic Mind that it is a part of. The life-force, or prana, that connects all of these facets, is also fivefold! When accounted for, these sets of fives convey a broad hint to the soul that the days of its body/mind mechanism are both symbolic and "numbered," and that meditation on quintuplications is needed." Babaji Bob Kindler

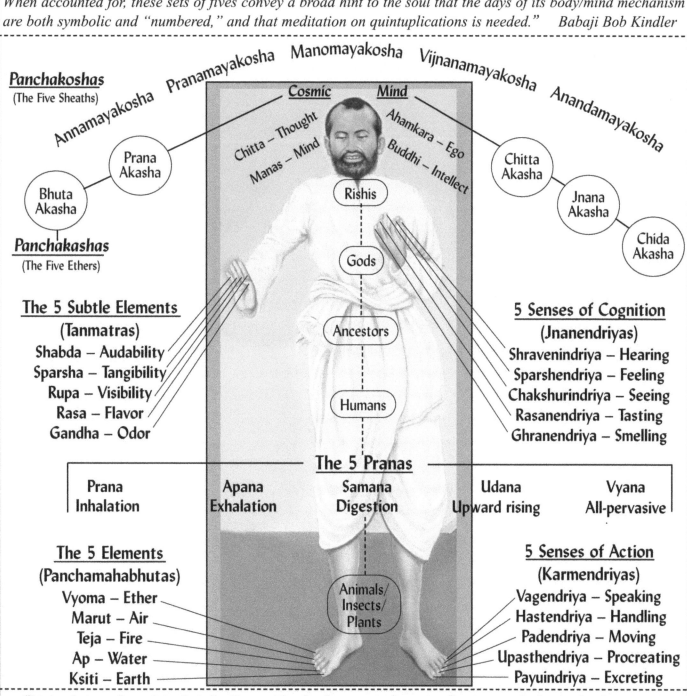

Panchakoshas
(The Five Sheaths)

Annamayakosha Pranamayakosha Manomayakosha Vijnanamayakosha Anandamayakosha

Prana Akasha

Bhuta Akasha

Panchakashas
(The Five Ethers)

Cosmic   Mind

Chitta – Thought
Manas – Mind
Ahamkara – Ego
Buddhi – Intellect

Chitta Akasha

Jnana Akasha

Chida Akasha

Rishis

Gods

Ancestors

Humans

The 5 Subtle Elements
(Tanmatras)
Shabda – Audability
Sparsha – Tangibility
Rupa – Visibility
Rasa – Flavor
Gandha – Odor

5 Senses of Cognition
(Jnanendriyas)
Shravenindriya – Hearing
Sparshendriya – Feeling
Chakshurindriya – Seeing
Rasanendriya – Tasting
Ghranendriya – Smelling

The 5 Pranas

Prana	Apana	Samana	Udana	Vyana
Inhalation	Exhalation	Digestion	Upward rising	All-pervasive

The 5 Elements
(Panchamahabhutas)
Vyoma – Ether
Marut – Air
Teja – Fire
Ap – Water
Ksiti – Earth

Animals/Insects/Plants

5 Senses of Action
(Karmendriyas)
Vagendriya – Speaking
Hastendriya – Handling
Padendriya – Moving
Upasthendriya – Procreating
Payuindriya – Excreting

"Living beings formulate their bodies amidst the five gross elements of nature, and play in the dream state utilizing five subtle elements. Five sheaths enfold and engross them, associated with five levels of ether, called akashas. They are subject at birth to the fivefold aspects of Maya called name, form, time, space, and causality, and their relations include five types of beings — namely, animals, humans, ancestors, gods, and rishis. Whether consciously or not, they always live eternally by five great spiritual laws." Babaji Bob Kindler

theless replete with the ability to reveal the innate sacred design of life and mind. *Tantra* is such an ancient and immense body of spiritual lore that it was never systematized by any individual, say, like *Yoga*, another intricate *darshana*, was. No one can lay any claim on it, then, but looking into its vast and often mystic territories provides many answers to age-old queries that come from the human heart and mind.

Sristi Rahasya, when translated literally, means "The Secret of Creation." As the reader can see by the chart on the facing page, the ancient *Tantracists* of India had an advanced way of looking at both Reality and relativity, both *Paramasiva* and its Divine Play. First of all, and most important-ly, *Paramashiva* is eternal, immutable, and transcendent. It is both the essence for all of Existence, and the stable and imperishable ground upon which all expression takes place. But this expression, often called *Lila* in *Sanskrit*, is naturally inclined to emanate outwards into realms of playful sport. Though it assumes forms, the forms are seen as manifestations of *Siva* rather than as illusions or sep-arate modes of awareness. They are all *Paramashiva's* ocean of intelligent Light turned into little ice-bergs, as it were. Their play happens only in *Paramashiva*, on behalf of *Paramashiva*, ending always in *Paramashiva*.

But in the interim of this grand outdoor recess of individual souls, the immense power of *Paramashiva* appears, called *Mahashakti*. Her proximity to Him releases all manner of potential cre-ative power. In Her this is termed *"vichikirsha."* It is inherent in Her, and without it the infinite, formless Wisdom that is *Paramashiva's* own Essence would not be able to come into manifestation. He is formless Essence, She is dynamic divine Potential. He is vibrationless Consciousness, She is the vibration of loving playfulness. Their movements of mock separation and blissful uniting will formulate the *Bindu*, or Cosmic Egg. Ripe and pregnant with all manner of cosmic proliferation, that *Bindu* will burst at the auspicious moment, producing such mediums as *nama* and *rupa*, name and form.

And this highest level of *namarupa* is still replete with inherent wisdom *(siva)* and its ability of manifestation on all levels *(shakti)*. The powerful and all-pervasive humming of these two pow-ers are termed *Omkara*, or the primal cause of all manifest things. A huge part of the secret of pro-duction from formlessness is this Unstruck Sound that nevertheless vibrates eternally. This is *Shabda Brahman*, which among other prime functions provides a powerful pathway to God for embodied beings via sound and its vibration. For conscious beings who frequent the worlds of name and form in time and space, and who are leary of fashioning any kind of *karma* there, the Primal sound acts as an unerring guide. The *Guru Stotram* states this well, among its many *slokas*:

> *More subtle than the ethers,*
> *eternally pure and impossible to taint,*
> *You embody that essential part of Consciousness*
> *that is indescribably peaceful and serene.*
> *Beyond the initial seed, the primal vibration, and the web of time,*
> *reverent salutations to the Ultimate Guru.*

The initial seed is the *Bindu.* The primal vibration is *Omkara*, the Unstruck Sound, and the web of time, or *Kala*, is what transpires — as well as space and all the worlds and objects that fill it. The bottom part of the chart under study lists the elements, both subtle and gross. Living beings sport in these worlds, the best and most conscious of them worshipping *Siva* and *Shakti* with all their heart and soul. For an in-depth study of this sacred art of worship, the forthcoming chapter will pro-vide many keys and teachings.

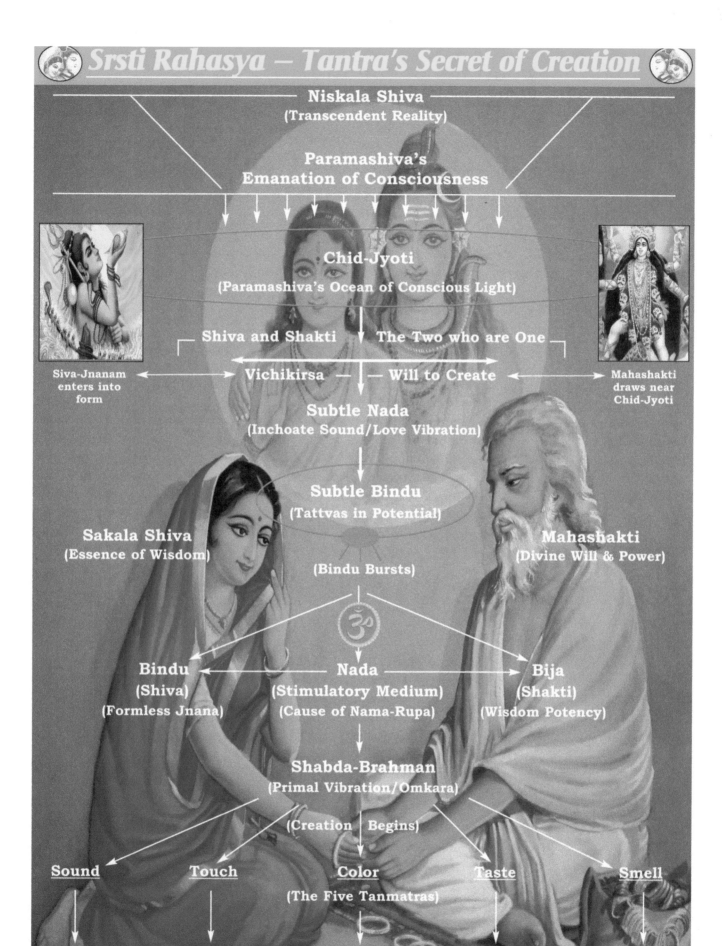

Srsti Rahasya – Tantra's Secret of Creation

Niskala Shiva
(Transcendent Reality)

Paramashiva's Emanation of Consciousness

Chid-Jyoti
(Paramashiva's Ocean of Conscious Light)

Shiva and Shakti — The Two who are One

Siva-Jnanam enters into form ← **Vichikirsa** — — **Will to Create** → Mahashakti draws near Chid-Jyoti

Subtle Nada
(Inchoate Sound/Love Vibration)

Subtle Bindu
(Tattvas in Potential)

Sakala Shiva
(Essence of Wisdom)

Mahashakti
(Divine Will & Power)

(Bindu Bursts)

Bindu
(Shiva)
(Formless Jnana)

Nada
(Stimulatory Medium)
(Cause of Nama-Rupa)

Bija
(Shakti)
(Wisdom Potency)

Shabda-Brahman
(Primal Vibration/Omkara)

(Creation Begins)

Sound **Touch** **Color** **Taste** **Smell**
(The Five Tanmatras)

Ether **Air** **Fire** **Water** **Earth**
(The Five Elements)

The Locomotion of Devotion
The Path of Ecstatic Love for Divine Reality

As Sri Ramakrishna Paramahamsa once remarked, *"If the mechanic comes daily and puts oil in the machine, then all runs smoothly. Otherwise, the machine will overheat, seize up, and stop running."* In this story the Great Master is referring to devotion for God, which is the oil in the machine of both earthly and spiritual life. The devotee's life cannot run smoothly amidst the challenges and hardships of this world without bathing the mind daily in this oil of devotion, called *bhakti* in *Sanskrit*. If the objection is raised that "I am fine without devotion to God," as in the case of the atheist, for instance, one has only to look at time and its cycles to observe how empty life becomes — if not eventually, then by its end — if it is devoid of some devotional content and outlet.

And what to speak of a mere outlet, the absence of divine expression in ones life only tends to make that empty space inside deeper and blacker, for a human being without a soul is not human at all, but more like an insentient object. Further, dullness, insensitivity, animalism — even callousness and eventually violence — can be the fatal outcomes of lack of faith and devotion. Again, if the argument be posed that religion itself is a cause for such things, the frank and true answer is that living beings attended by sincere faith and authentic devotion would never stoop so low, and that when these appear in human minds it is not a sign of real religion at all, but irreligion. Intelligent people recognize this as the case, and place the blame, if blame there be, where it is due — in worldly people. As Swami Vivekananda has put it: *"The real spiritual man is broad everywhere. His love and devotion to God forces him to be so. Those to whom religion is a trade, are forced to become narrow and mischievous by their introduction into religion of the competitive, fighting, and selfish methods of the world. I pity them. It is not their fault. They are children, yay, veritable children, though they be great and high in society. Their eyes see nothing beyond their little horizon of a few yards — the routine of work, eating, drinking, earning, and begetting, following each other in mathematical precision."*

With all of this stated emphatically, the following chapter — though short and sweet — will reveal both the role of and the need for *bhakti* in all levels of life and existence. In terms of deeper understanding of its import, *bhakti* in daily life is *Karma Yoga*; *bhakti* in the mind is meditation (*Raja Yoga*); *bhakti* in the intellect is *Jnana Yoga*, and *bhakti* in the heart is, well, its very own self. Further, *bhakti* in the body, as Sri Krishna points out, is performing worship/puja. As my *guru*, Swami Aseshanandaji Maharaj, once put it, *"What wind is to a bird's wings, and water is to a thirsty man, bhakti is to the devotee."*

Since this book is always and ever "charting" the scriptures of Mother India, we can begin our exploration of the devotional pathway by taking a brief look at India's love of *Ishvara*. *Ishvara* is the purest and highest of divine principles pertaining to God with form. As seen by the many heads, arms, hands, etc., of the image on the chart on the facing page, the intimation is that *Ishvara* is all-seeing, all-facilitating, and all-pervasive. He is also all-knowing. From earthly powers like sun and moon (*surya* and *chandra*), to celestial powers like the elementals, and on through to divine powers represented by the highest gods and goddesses, *Ishvara* contains and directs them all. Human beings, both divine and demonic in nature, all function via *Ishvara*'s powers, and the *Avatar*, too, is a manifestation of them. The great teachers like Prajapati and the seven ancient *rishis* get mind-born out of *Ishvara*, and carry on their respective functions under Its direction. The two quotes from the *Svetasvataropanisad* shown on the top and bottom of the chart tell all this and more about the

The Immanent and Transcendent Reality

"Though the Lord, the cosmic projector of the heaven and earth realms, is one and indivisible, yet He is the real owner of all eyes, all faces, all hands and feet in the gradated universes. It is He who inspires them all to do their respective duties in accordance with knowledge of the past actions and tendencies of various beings." Svetasvataropanisad

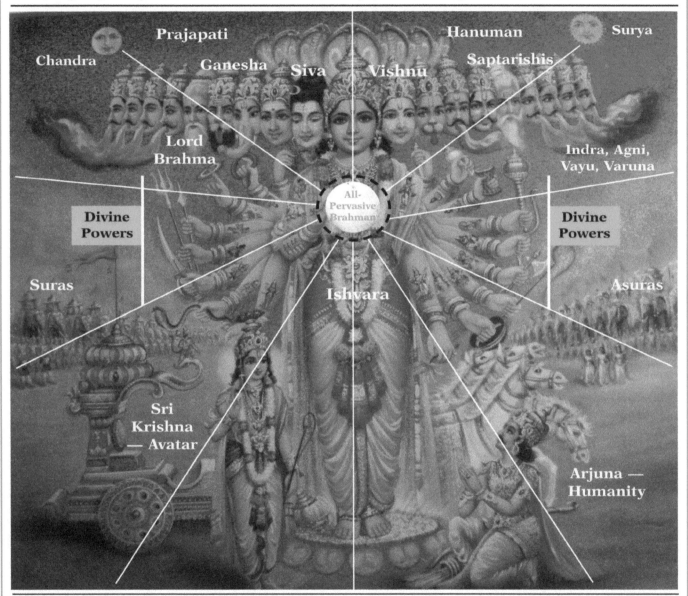

"With hands and feet everywhere, with eyes, heads, and mouths everywhere, with ears everywhere, He exists, pervading everything in the many universes. And higher than this Personal Brahman is the Supreme Brahman, who attracts intelligent souls towards the highest goal of Mukti. Without feet It goes everywhere; without eyes It sees everything; without ears It hears all. Though this Impersonal Brahman is changeless, It seemingly grows beyond its own nature to formulate the objective universe. By the grace of the Personal God the aspiring soul becomes free of sorrows and transcends all desires. I know this omnipresent One who is concealed in the hearts of all beings, and by knowing which, one becomes free of birth and death." Svetasvataropanisad

supreme nature of this nearly transcendental Being. What to speak of hearing about Him, as far as that is possible, even knowing of Him elicits all manner of love and devotion from the devotees. And hidden in His very nature is the most precious of His secrets known as *Ishvari* — the Divine Feminine Reality who underlies all of Existence.

Concentrating more on the cosmic and transcendental qualities and properties found in *Ishvari* and *Ishvara*, the chart on the facing page comfortably situates the famous Trinity of Hindu philosophy as powers within *Ishvari*, and reveals, as well, one of Her own secrets in the form of Her nondual nature — rather like a bridge from the realms of name and form in time and space, crossing over into the vast and formless Light of pure, conscious Awareness that is *Brahman*.

Taking up the former aspect above first, the quote by King Sudarshan from the *Srimad Devi Bhagavatam*, one of the few quintessential Divine Mother scriptures in the world, declares in no uncertain terms that even the Trinity of Lords' Brahma, Vishnu, and Siva do not know the extent of Her powers and wisdom. In most stories of Indian *Itihasa*, or scriptural history, when powerful negative forces mount and rise to attempt usurping the many and multifarious *lokas* under the Trinity's protection, it is the Divine Mother of these universes who comes to their aid when all seems lost. Quite often, Lord Brahma — four-headed and looking all directions — He who projects these realms of name and form in their causal, subtle, and physical forms, will remember Her at these terrible times and begin to recite Her praises with his four mouths. He also recites the Four *Vedas* and their 108 *Upanisads* to get Her out of hiding, for She gets attracted to the living Wisdom found in these sacred words most of all. When She suddenly appears on the battlefield of relativity She is a sight to see — a spectacle which incites fear in the hearts and minds of the *asuras*, but that causes surging waves of love, devotion, and inspiration to well up in the hearts of Her votaries. Ramprasad Sen, Her devout and intimate lover, privy to personal visions of Her in deepest meditation, sings glowingly about such rare appearances:

Who is this mystic woman of sheer loveliness?
The exquisite beauty of Her Features is illumined by the mysterious Light
of the black moon on Her Forehead.
Vigorously She strides through the battleground of suffering,
Her Tresses of Power flowing wildly, Her Divine Body black as the blackest new moon night.
Lithe and vibrant with the youth of timelessness, no garment of relativity can cover Her.
With two Left Hands She bears the Sword of Transcendence and the severed head of mundane convention.
With two Right Hands She radiates perfect protection and boundless generosity.
I am transported in ecstacy!

The remainder of the chart on page 467 declares Her inseparability with Nondual Reality. In the *Srimad Devi Bhagavatam*, She states to King Himalaya, the Lord of the Eternal Snow Mountains: *"When everything melts away, it is then that pralaya comes. At that time I abide with Brahman, latent in It."* Thus She is *Puranam*, timeless, as shown on the chart. The scripture goes on to say, *"When the worlds are projected again at the beginning of a new cycle, I become all beings such as Sri, Buddhi, Smriti, Shraddha, Lajja, and others."* Therefore She is *Achintya Rupam*, of inconceivable forms, and *Sarvasya Dhataram*, the supporter of all, as indicated on the chart. The *Devi Bhagavatam* goes on to state, *"I flow through the 35 millions of gross and subtle nadis located in the sacred human form."* And so, She is obviously *Anoraniyan*, infinitesimal and subtlemost, as confirmed by the chart. In the *Tantras*, Divine Mother is described with the words, *"God with form, called Ishvara, living beings, worlds, objects, and everything else evolve from Her."* This makes Her *Anushasitaram*, the sovereign ruler, as revealed on the chart. In Her own words, as elucidated by scripture, She avows, *"One should go into the highest region where there is no speech or thing spoken, absolutely free of dualities — Akhanda Satchitananda. There, with AUM, meditate on my brilliant Light, the Flame of Consciousness that destroys the darkness of ignorance completely and forever."* Here, we can see that She is *Tamasah Parastat*, beyond all darkness, and *Adityavarnam*, effulgent like the sun, as the chart explains. Finally, in the *Sri Durga Saptasati*, or

The Four Parts & Eight Glories of Ishvari/Ishvara

Sattvika Matra —
Engaged in
Sustaining the Worlds

1

Mahavishnu,
Lord of Preservation

Rajasika Matra —
Engaged in
Projecting the Worlds

2

Shiva Mahadeva,
Lord of Dissolution

3

Tamasika Matra —
Engaged in
Withdrawing the Worlds

4

Nirguna Shakti —
Free of All Qualities
& Activities

Brahma,
Lord of Creation

"Brahma, Vishnu, and Shiva are unable to fathom the exalted deeds of the Goddess. How then am I to describe the great glory of that Mahamaya."   King Sudarshana

- -

The Eight Glories of Ishvari/Ishvara

KAVIM
Omniscient

ADITYAVARNAM
Effulgent like the Sun

PURANAM
Timeless/Ancient

ACHINTYA RUPAM
Of Inconceivable Form

ANUSHASITARAM
Sovereign/Ruler

TAMASAH PARASTAT
Beyond all Darkness

ANORANIYAN
Infinitesimal/Subtlemost

SARVASYA DHATARAM
Supporter of All

"Let the mind not want for anything else, but rather meditate on the Supreme Self. For, that one who remembers Ishvara's Glories reaches the Goal."   Sri Krishna

She utters the Truth, stating: *"I am the World Mother, All-Seeing and All-Knowing. Fix heart and mind on this lustrous Form of Mine and soon you will realize the union of yourself, the Jiva, with Absolute Reality, Brahman."* This establishes the fact that She is *Kavim,* omniscient — as stated unequivocally on the chart.

The one last burst of Mother Wisdom that this revelatory chart (page 467) gifts to us has to do with the three *gunas,* or three modes of nature (see charts on pages 221, 223, & 307). As can be seen, *Ishvari* both controls and transcends them. Whether in the form of irresistible creative power, called *rajas,* or sublime sustaining force, called *sattva, Ishvari* prevails. She can even use Her power of darkness, called *tamas,* to cause the latter two modes to cease and desist so that She can dissolve all forms when She deems that individual souls, universes, and objects should merge back into their respective sources. As the teachings on *Kundalini Shakti* tell us, *"She accomplishes the involution of the individual soul back to its source by stripping away the coverings and superimpositions of Maya that have obscured the vision of the Atman."* This is really a loving gesture that frees, not an act of destruction.

Now that we have introduced and examined the prime exemplar of Love, the quality itself can be looked at. The "King of the Devotees" in this age, Sri Ramakrishna Paramahamsa, is the best source to turn to, and the most authoritative as well. Further, and if looked at humbly, His teachings on Love, and love, will cause a powerful awakening in contemporary humanity, especially from the standpoint of today's often stunted versions of the quality. For example, we get into deep waters right away when we consider the first two of four types of love — *Sadharani* and *Samanjasa.* (page 469)

The first listed type of love, *Sadharani,* is ordinary, in both its scope and its intent. It is all too common as well. So many beings operate, what to speak of suffer and labor, under its pale light, its thick pall of dissatisfaction. This is because it is selfish. Neither support nor reciprocation comes from either half of the relationship. All such relationships are bound for failure due to the presence of egotism in all parties, an unripe ego-complex that has not yet come to know that only Divine Reality is worthy of loving — is Love itself, and Its Love is reciprocal besides. But it is too early in this discussion to bring up such ultimate secrets of true Love. Stages of growth must be considered in the meantime.

And that is why *Samanjasa* has to be looked at closely. That is love coming from both sides, wherein both parties are working for the good of the relationship. All the conventions are in place, the workload balanced, and all the desires and needs of both are catered to. Yet all of this poses a problem, the presence of deep-rooted desire in the mind for a world that can never satisfy completely. Ironically then, and as time passes, it can be an even more deceptive kind of love than the rude awakenings in store for the follower of *Sadharani,* for the orientation still leans heavily towards the world and is still shorn of the Divine. A "happy" life is often the result of it. Others look on enviously, wishing that they had such a relationship, such a loving partner. But then, all wonder later, why did they not remain together, why did they not realize the goal of life together, and why did they look for satisfaction in another partner; why did they fight over the division of material wealth at the end, and where did their original happiness vanish to?

Here enters the first glimpse and aroma of something real rather than pretended, something beneficial rather than pleasurable, something eternal rather than short-lived. *Ekangi* is that noble type of Love described by Sri Ramakrishna in the simple phrase, *"The duck loves the water, but the water does not love the duck."* True and authentic is this rare kind of Love, its only drawback being where it is placed. For instance, a young man may fall in love with an older woman with her desires for home and family already fulfilled, or a love-struck votary may feel real love for a God-centered luminary, but both these objects of love are already well beyond the pale of emotions, romance, and mutual relationships — at least in the conventional sense. And so, *Ekangi* is an example in those who have arrived at it, and a teacher for those who should aspire to it. One could say that, in the realm of love, it is the final filter through which the soul gets refined and prepared for Love of God alone.

And this describes the quality of *Samartha* very well. As a teaching coming from the Great Master, who was married, we should be clear that, though this type of love has its particular version

The Four Types of Love
According to Sri Ramakrishna

"Love is the rope by which one can tether God, as it were. Whenever you want to see Him you merely have to tug on the rope. But one must know the difference between a green mango and a ripe one, between immature bhakti and mature bhakti. Unalloyed love for God is the essential thing. All else is unreal." Sri Ramakrishna

Sadharani — Ordinary Love

Conventional or selfish love, assumed for the sake of one's own happiness, but disregarding the happiness of one's partner or of others.

Samanjasa — Mutual Love

A nobler type of love wherein both parties seek the happiness of one another.

Ekangi — One-sided Love

A true and authentic love wherein one loves the other devoutly, but that love is not reciprocated.

Samartha — Selfless Love ← PREMA

The highest type of love wherein both love selflessly, each wanting only the fulfillment of the other, even regardless of their own.

"Do not speak glibly about love. Is it such a common place thing? True love, prema, has two characteristics: first, it makes one forget the world, for its intensity causes natural detachment from external things — or transforms them into Brahman; secondly, true love takes away the feeling of 'myness' from the body, which is usually so dear to man. In the sweet upsurge of prema one wholly gets rid of the feeling that the body is the soul." Sri Ramakrishna

in monasticism, what is being related here is more on the level of a perfect human relationship — much like the special kind of Love that He had with Sri Sarada Devi, The Holy Mother. And though Theirs was both completely celibate and thoroughly spiritual, it nevertheless exemplifies what is humanly possible when *Samartha* is on the scene. Sri Ramakrishna often mentioned the divine house-holder couple, or *yogic* relationship, the very presence of which, when placed in the atmosphere of struggling souls (laboring under *Sadharani* and *Samanjasa*), becomes a boon of blessing upon the entire human race. More of these kinds of couplings are needed in the world today, along with the blessed children of God that they will raise up in the *dharma*.

To know even more about the four types of love, the two quotes from the Great Master placed on the chart (page 469), on top and bottom, can be read and contemplated. And much more will be related on Him as this chapter plays itself out.

In and with regard to all four of the types of love just explained, the mention of Love of God occurs in relation to every one of them. This is certainly apropos, especially since Mother India, even though She is known for Her full blown Wisdom of the Ages, really emphasizes the presence of love and devotion underlying all and everything as most important. This is why an inspection of the Five Worshipful Attitudes (facing page) at this particular juncture will be of great benefit for all who are attempting to comprehend the role of love and devotion in spiritual life and practice.

Some of the underpinnings of authentic love and intense devotion to God are faith, worship, self-surrender, and sacrifice. All of these will be explored in forthcoming pages and their respective charts. Worship has the effect of both humbling and inspiring the striving human soul, which on earth always seems to find itself in the press of weights that are personal, collective, and cosmic, all three. These can be lightened and lifted, and the worshippers of Sri Ramchandra and Sri Krishna, namely *Vaishnavas*, have found the keys for sloughing off these burdens of daily life. They propose and advise that one take up a single discipline in the form of a mood, or "*bhava.*" Inquiring with the *guru*, or spiritual preceptor, is a prerequisite of this wise internal move, for the temperament of the seeker must align with the practice prescribed.

Following along the oft-repeated saying of Sri Sarada Devi, namely, *"You need peace of mind first and foremost,"* many beings, possibly with restless and rebellious minds, will benefit most by taking up the mental posture of *Shanta Bhava* — as Sri Ramakrishna stated, *"...like the rishis of old."* The *rishis* and their long-lived teachings are enough to contemplate in order to be convinced that peace is the most desirable of attainments in this lifetime. Their culture and their lives were so admirable. And so the aspirant reads about and meditates upon the personage that is most inspiring, perhaps following the practice of *Lila-dhyana,* rumination on the divine play of a great soul. The seeker finds out over the term of such inward practice that it was the world and desire for its objects that stole the mind away from this original peace in the first place, so gradually contentment replaces love of pleasure and seeking for enjoyments.

The next *bhava* speaks to us in familiar and convincing terms by saying softly., "Everyone needs a friend." What is more, "One needs friends in high places" as well. The divine attitude of *Sakhya Bhava* confers both of these when rightly practiced, since the devotees and the Lord Himself/Herself all appear to that one who values spiritual camaraderie. And for all who have tasted the bitter fruits of the "fair faces and false hearts" of this world in this regard, the positive and rare phenomena of a "true friend" is highly valued. The Divine Lover, Ramprasad Sen, sings about this wondrous marvel and its obstacles: *"The passionate words of a selfish lover may first taste sweeter than honey, but they contain the poison of delusion. The singer of this song once drained the cup of selfish love and felt the anguish of its poison touch. But now this musical poet tastes only bliss....!"*

The experience of Divine Reality in Its various modes may just turn the devotee into a devoted servant as well. When this mood, termed *Dasya Bhava,* manifests — whether it is chosen, bestowed, or deeply felt within — the worker takes up *karma yoga* with the strength of a Hanuman, and *bhakti* with the power of the love of a mother for her children. These fuse with wisdom and meditation in the highest expression possible for an embodied being.

Pancha Bhava — The Five Worshipful Attitudes

"In order to realize God, the Vaishnavas advise taking to one of the five divine attitudes of worship. These bring about higher knowledge in the mind. Peacefulness and absence of egotism are the early signs of spiritual progress here. These bhavas are to be assumed within three devotional modes and result in four types of liberations."

Babaji Bob Kindler

Shanta Bhava

"....like the rishis of ancient India."

"This is the serene attitude, like that of the rishis of old. It does not cherish any idea of worldly enjoyment."

Attitude of Peace

Dasya Bhava

"....like the mood of Hanuman towards Ram."

"This mood epitomizes Hanuman working with the strength of a lion for Ram, or the selfless service of a mother towards her children."

Attitude of a Servant

Madhura Bhava

"Similar to a woman's intense love for her paramour, this sweet mood contains all the other four within it."

"....like Radha's and Mira Bai's love."

Attitude of a Lover for the Beloved

Vatsalya Bhava

"....like Kausalya had for baby Ram."

"Yasoda's attitude towards Krishna is a good example of this mood. The father protects the child, and the mother feeds it with her very life's blood."

Attitude of a Parent for a Child

Sakhya Bhava

"....like the cowherd boys towards Krishna."

"Friends say to each other, 'Come and sit near me,' and they feed each other with food they have already partaken of."

Attitude of a True Friend

And mention of a mother's love brings in the mood of *Vatsalya Bhava* nicely as well, which is the attitude of a parent for the child. Real love gets expressed, even in this world, by that relationship. The scriptures of India are replete with sacred lore describing how God manifests in a baby and gets raised and cherished by noble and pious parents. It might just be the highest attainment to most Hindu couples that they birth a holy child or children and raise them up in the *dharma*. Tulsidas sings about this momentous occasion in time and space relative to the baby Ramlal, *"The overwhelmed mind of Tulsi is swiftly transported to another realm upon beholding the poignant scene of the Lord's play as Divine Child. Its incomparable beauty will be etched deeply into every fiber of his vibrant memory...."*

Last, but definitely not least, is the divine mood of *Madhura Bhava*. It is said of it that all the other four *bhavas* are really included in it, so powerful a position it represents. Nothing impresses itself on the human mind as much as unadulterated Love, and since we have recently gone through and studied the Four Types of Love (see chart on page 469), a better idea of what that entails should be readily accessible for recall. Suffice to say, then, that *Madhura Bhava* utilizes *Samartha* to a great degree, and in such a way that easily causes the lover of Divine Reality to be completely surrendered and fully committed to his or her Ideal. What to speak of a love that covets no consideration for oneself at all, in *Mathura Bhava* there simply is no other self but the Beloved. Thus, it is oneness indeed, free of any semblance of twoness or manyness whatsoever. Going deeper, though words will never describe it in full, the chart on the facing page will help expand our understanding.

There is no need for dissention with regard to Love and Wisdom, or immersion and transcendence. The most complete state of Awareness —what Sri Ramakrishna referred to by pointing out the ultimate union of *Prema-bhakti* and *Brahma-jnana* — is to be experienced in deepest *Samadhi*. Even the kings of *bhakti* throughout the ages, the likes of Sages Narada and Sandilya, confirm that the highest Love is the state of Liberation. Their quotes on the chart opposite show this. And the Five Moods make an appearance on this chart as well, in the lower left corner.

To demonstrate that there is life after pure transcendence, the description of the Four Forms of Liberation are most helpful. They are *Samipya, Salokya, Sarupya,* and *Sajujya*. The devotee who is *Samipya* is most fortunate, for he/she is beloved of God. The actual meaning of the word is "dear to God." The general meaning uses a metaphor to explain that the son of a king will never want for anything in his entire life. Such is certainly the case, and more so, of the beloved of God. The lives of such souls as Abraham, Moses, Jesus, Mohammed, of the Middle Eastern fold, and Ram, Krishna, Chaitanya, and Sri Ramakrishna of the far Eastern sector of the world, reveal this fact. To explain it simply, if one gains the love of God, especially sincere love for God, the ocean of suffering dries up, the various games of life come to an end, the *"Peace that Passeth all understanding"* dawns on the mind, and the transcendent state of absolute Freedom takes the soul in Its eternal embrace.

Along the way of this Path of paths, and as long as the mind of the devotee remains cognizant of the worlds of name and form, *Salokya* is gained. But attending upon such realms, even as blissful as they might be, cannot compare one whit to being in any of those *lokas* while in the actual presence of, and with the holy company of, God in form. The only way we can imagine this is to envision ourselves being with divine couples like Vasishtha with Lord *Brahma*, Ananda with Lord Buddha, John with Jesus, Gaur and Nitai with Lord Chaitanya and, most recently, Swami Vivekananda with Sri Ramakrishna. They were all in the same location with God at the same time when the Formless One took a form and acted out various world-transforming plays for the highest good of those who had eyes to see. Even to be born in the same century, or within a few hundred years of any of these *Avataric* manifestations, is auspicious, and thus beneficial to any form of spiritual practice one may take up in that blessed lifetime. Thus it is described in the tradition.

Sarupya is another form of liberation in life. Its meaning indicates that the incarnating soul has taken on the same form of God. This is not meant in the physical sense only, although, again, if one has the eyes to see, it will appear as a wonder how living beings actually take on even the physical characteristics of their chosen ideal. This is to be seen in the overall countenance of entire races, wherein many beings from the far East look like Lord Buddha, and others from the West appear like

The Four Forms of Liberation & The Five Divine Moods

"Four types of virtuous beings worship Me, O Arjuna: the one in distress; the one seeking knowledge; the one seeking wealth, and the one imbued with wisdom. Of these, the wise one, ever steadfast and devoted to the One, excels. For, supremely dear am I to the wise one, who is exceedingly dear to Me." Sri Krishna

"Identification with the Lord is gained through undivided devotion. Liberation is gained when the inner organ dissolves completely in Him." Sage Sandilya

"There is no difference between God and His devotees." Sage Narada

"The signs of love are peace and bliss." Sage Narada

1. Shanta - Mood of Peace
2. Dasya - Mood of a Servant
3. Sakhya - Mood of a Friend
4. Vatsalya - Parental Mood
5. Madhura - Lover and Beloved

1. Samipya - Dear to God
2. Salokya - Same Loka as God
3. Sarupya - Same Form as God
4. Sayujya - Immersed in God

"The Lord and Master resides within me in a subtle form. In the same way I will reside within you, as well, in a subtle form." Sri Sarada Devi

"Transcending all other forms of love, love the Lord, and love Him as His eternal servant, and His eternal bride." Sage Narada

"If one assumes one of these five moods, one gets a love body endowed with love ears and love eyes. One even gets a sexual organ made of love. With this love body one communes with God." Sri Ramakrishna

Jesus. Of course, this usually only applies where the spirit has been assimilated, i.e., where the actual spirituality of any given luminary has been taken on, and in. In other words, the worldly simply look like themselves — wan and pale, with the life sucked out of them by their inordinate desires for the world and its various and vain pursuits — while the lovers of Divine Reality appear ethereal and transcendent.

And this is certainly the case of those who have the liberation called *Sayujya*. *Sanskrit* dictionaries define this word as *"...oneness with God."* Therefore, and even amidst the devotional atmosphere of both *Bhakti Yoga* and *Vaishnavism*, it affirms the state of nonduality, even for a divine lovestruck devotee. All that can be said of that singular, *advaitic* experience is sparse in indeed. It must be experienced, and once It is, there remains no separate being left to return and express It. It causes, in the words of Mirabai, *"...immersion in God"* which, when her mind was restored to her, she only called out *"Sri Krishna, my Beloved."*

The two following charts share a certain distinction: they were created, unintentionally, in different periods of time utilizing the same subject matter. Nevertheless, the first of these charts contains additional teaching material on the Eleven Forms of Divine Love for God. Both charts (pages 475 & 476) are included here to grace the eye and fill the *dharmic* stomach, and to drive the teachings home with twice the loving force.

Narada's *Bhakti Sutras* is rather like the Bible of India on devotional matters pertaining to the heart. And much like *Ashtanga Yoga* for the meditator, it also provides the *bhakta* practitioner with an eight-fold system for increasing his or her devotion to God with form. But on the chart on the facing page (page 475) are also seen the Eleven Forms of expressing Love for God, and interestingly enough, they end in a state of nonduality called "love of absorption" in God (*Brahman*).

In the case of any separate thing or things, one can only enjoy them, handle them, admire them, and love them from the standpoint of them being separate from oneself. One cannot immerse, get absorbed in, or "become one" with anything material such as objects, bodies, senses, etc. Even thoughts, wispy as they are, are not open for absorption. One can get "absorbed in ones thoughts," but cannot become the thought itself, simply because there is an independent thinker who is the source of all thought. What is more, and speaking of independence, there is an ego that wants to control the thinker, and which often succeeds at this. With objects, then, absorption cannot come about due to the illusory or empty nature of matter. So it follows that the thinker who thinks of objects with the ego in charge is verily rendering any form of oneness impossible for himself. Thus, both thought and matter must go by the wayside for a time in order to achieve absorption into Reality.

And this is where the Eight Devotional Aids of Narada come in. Concerning the first two, and interestingly enough, *shravanam* and *smaranam* (hearing about and remembering the Lord) echo tenets of *Vedanta*, *Yoga*, and *Tantra*. The Three Proofs of Truth and Ten Conditions of the *Guru/Shishya* relationship (see chart on page 91) in *Vedanta* both include *shravana*, and the list of *yamas* and *niyamas* in both *Yoga* and *Tantra* contain facets concerning remembering God daily. The Nine Limbs of *Bhakti* of Sri Ram also include hearing about and spreading the teachings of the Lord. These will be shown later in this chapter.

A case could be made that the first two of these aids are *jnana* oriented, while the next three and number seven are most definitely *bhakti* flavored. The sixth aid is *Karma Yoga* based, while the eighth is styled in the *Raja Yoga* tradition via surrendering the ego in meditation. Whatever the case may be, three, four, five, and seven create a definite system for *Bhakti Yoga*, being aids that tend one towards its actual practice. The "practice" of *Bhakti Yoga* is inspiring and joyful, which is why most of the seekers of this world take to it most conclusively, if not exclusively. Another case could be made that "Having devotion for the Lord" (*bhajanam*) is a needed prerequisite, and that by possessing it, the "worship of the Lord" (*vandanam*) follows directly. Actual "adoration of the Lord" (*archanam*) proceeds easily, being next in line, and the devotee slips naturally into "singing and dancing for the Lord" (*kirtanam*) thereafter. In whatever order these four endearing aids come, however, they sweeten the soul substantially and lead it towards ecstatic devotion — what *Raja Yoga* terms *Sananda Samadhi*.

The Eight Devotional Aids of Narada

"Bhakti is intense love for the Lord. In its intrinsic nature this divine love is tantamount to immortal bliss. By attaining it man becomes perfect, deathless, and verily fulfilled for all of eternity." —*Narada Bhakti Sutras*

1) **Shravanam** — Hearing About the Lord

2) **Smaranam** — Remembering the Lord

3) **Archanam** — Adoring the Lord

4) **Kirtanam** — Singing and Dancing for the Lord

5) **Vandanam** — Worshipping the Lord

6) **Sevanam** — Serving the Lord

7) **Bhajanam** — Having Devotion for the Lord

8) **Sharanam** — Surrendering to the Lord

"According to Narada, chanting the names and glories of God with sincerity destroys the effect of past actions. The path of action is complicated. Bhakti Yoga is simple and natural. A man must do his duties as long as he has to reap the results of his past lifetimes, but it is the development of love for God that is crucial." —*Sri Ramakrishna*

Narada's Eleven Forms of Divine Love for God

1. love of chanting
2. love of God's beauty
3. love of heartfelt worship
4. love of God's presence
5. love of being God's servant
6. love of being God's friend
7. love of being God's child
8. love of being God's beloved
9. love of surrender to God
10. love of absorption in God

11. love of the pangs of separation from God

Prema Bhakti, Divine Love for the Lord, is so intense and precious that it causes the devotee who experiences it to want to cast away even the body, which is usually so dear to living beings. Sri Ramakrishna Paramahamsa

Narada's Eight Devotional Moods

"Devotion to the Eternal Truth alone is the greatest bhakti. Though of itself always and ever one, bhakti manifests itself in many forms, and there are several classic aids by which one can attain it." Devarishi Narada

Shravanam - Hearing of God's glories
Sharanam - Taking refuge in God
Kirtanam - Singing & dancing for God
Sevanam - Serving God & His devotees

Smaranam - Constant remembrance of God
Archanam - Loving adoration of the Lord
Bhajanam - Heartfelt devotions to the Lord
Vandanam - Devout worship of the Lord

As was just mentioned, *sevanam,* serving the Lord, is a *Karma Yoga* tenet. But Narada would be quick to indicate that when service is offered to the Lord, it is not rendered under the mantle of any sense of duty or responsibility. These elements may be a part of said offering, but they take a back seat where more important matters of the heart are concerned. Serving the Beloved is both a boon and a privilege for a sincere devotee, and no wisp of any thought of recompense will ever enter the mind. In part, this is because pure Love in surging waves is always spilling out of the very vibrations of the Lord in human form; nothing need be asked for short of Enlightenment, and the authentic devotee knows that this unique form of highest Grace will come according to the omniscience of the Lord, at the proper and perfect time, and is willing to wait for it.

There is another need that gets satisfied in due time as well, and that has to do with refining the ego so much that it surrenders its own individual concerns and desires up to the Lord of the Universe. This is called *sharanam* by Narada, and it appears in other *Yogas* and *darshanas* as well. In other salient pathways of Mother India this feat is achieved by specialized means, but for the *bhakta* the increase of devotion to an absolute breaking point will do the trick. Like the "expansion of the knowledge" method that, in time, explodes the clinging ego, the expansion of devotion works in much the same way, and equally effectively so long as the elements of sincerity and dedication are present — either in heart or mind, as the case may be, and best in both.

As was mentioned, the chart on the facing page shows these eight aids to devotion identically with the chart on page 475. But the latter chart also lays out the Eleven Forms of Divine Love for inspection, also listed in the sacred pages of *Narada's Bhakti Sutras.* Whereas many of these overlap and even echo the Eight Aids, they are presented here in a hands-on way in order to attract the devotee and encourage him or her to dive in and immerse the body/mind mechanism in the purest Love.

The differences here are striking. Love of God's beauty, for instance, has not been brought out so directly in the Eight Aids. This facet enraptures the mind, for one, and also brings in a stark contrast that always attends the soul who is caught in love of forms in nature, in human beings — even in animals and physical locations. In loving the Lord's Form there is no harm to be had, and no negative kickbacks later. This is always the case in the distinction between the Eternal and the noneternal, as *Vedanta* so often emphasizes. Even the forbidden problem of attachment poses no problem here, for attachment to the Lord and Mother of the Universe proves identical with Formless Reality. This is instanced and proven when, by focusing lovingly on the Divine Form of God and reaching one-pointed devotion to the *Ishtam,* the devotee finds that all forms — including human beings, animals, plants, and yes, even locations on earth — become infused with the sacred Presence of *Brahman* and get transformed into "Paradise."

To bring out a few more of the precious distinctions between the Eight Aids and the Eleven Forms of Divine Love, numbers 5 through 8 of the latter simply call up four of the five modes or *bhavas* of *Vaishnavism,* namely, being God's servant, enjoying friendship with Him/Her, becoming the child of God, and seeking divine union with God as Lover and Beloved. This teaching and set of devotional practices was displayed for study on page 473. A veritable smorgasbord of *Bhakti Yoga* elements is thus made known to those aspirants who either vibrate naturally with the devotional path, or seek to bring some sweetness into their studies while increasing their faith in God.

Facets 10 and 11 of this copious list are also very great, again, bridging on the secret connection with Formless Reality that all beings will come upon sometime in their spiritual life and practice. Taken together, they also pose a conundrum, and maybe even satisfy and solve it simultaneously. For absorption into *Brahman* is often complemented by returning to form, at least at the advanced practice level of *Yoga.* And that return, in turn, is too often plagued by those pangs of separation from that All-Knowing, Ever-Present, and Eternally Blissful Ocean of Conscious Light, called *Satchitananda.* Here is where *Bhakti Yoga* offers its solution; for as long as form is assumed and the sport of living is undertaken, so long will the form of God be both available and desirable to all lovers and seekers. As Sri Ramakrishna has so often stated, *"God is both with form, beyond form, and beyond both form and formlessness as well."* This all-inclusive affirmation fits the all-pervasive Incarnation, who both infills the totality of pure, conscious Awareness, and pervades the worlds of name and form too. Soon, with realizations of this nondual nature brought to bear, and maturing all the while, pangs of separation have no more reason to bother the heart. As the *Upanisads* state, conclusively: *"Brahman is infinite and Brahman is everywhere. To a genuine aspirant this is far more than mere belief; It is the Reality without a second."*

The chart on the facing page can be thought of as a fifth noble Truth, a twelve-fold path to take the soul beyond the illusion of suffering to reconnect it with Original Mind. Sensitivities, Perfections, and Attitudes, four of each, comprise this precious pathway to the very Heart of Divine Mother Reality. Of these three sets of four, the Attitudes — friendship, mercy, positivity, and indifference — smack of familiarity, and resound in the inmost memory of ardent living beings. Both Lord Vasishtha and Sri Krishna from the ancient past of India, and Sri Ramakrishna and Sri Sarada Devi in the recent present, have utilized this fourfold system to break living beings free of their impediments and send them joyfully and confidently on their winsome way. With classic compassion, Sri Sarada Devi, the Holy Mother, admits the general weakness of mankind but favors the method of working patiently over time to build up strength in living beings. For this to happen, some wise warnings will be necessary in order to steer the wayward soul away from unseen perils. If the soul is sincere and listens to divine guidance, all will go well, but if the proverbial blind eye, or deaf ear, is turned away from such compassionate counsel, then not even God can help that stubborn soul. Nevertheless, and as Sri Krishna avers, the Eternal Friend will always be waiting for the flagging aspirant to return to the flock. *"Be friendly to those who are happy in the world."* They will soon tire of vain pursuits and return inwardly to their only real home.

About mercy, She states: *"And be compassionate to those who suffer."* The one Supreme Soul is everywhere, and in everything. It is only apparently divided in living beings. And it suffers there, as well as enjoys. *Karuna*, therefore, is the best way to lift the mind up and out of the illusion of separation. For only uninterrupted union with Divine Reality is Bliss; happiness, glee, joy, and elation are but partial and impermanent expressions of That. *Karuna* is not pity, sympathy, or even mere empathy. It is recognition of the oneness between the sufferer and the onlooker.

And the onlooker must be armed with *mudita*, positivity, as well. Such an irrepressible spirit can right many wrongs, and can even help surmount seemingly impossible difficulties. Further, in classic *Vedantic* fashion, where contrasting pairs of opposites are seen as indicators and used as purifiers, the helpful quality of *upekshanam*, indifference, completes the four "Attitudes" picture. For, if unflagging positivity were to fail, the only recourse for the strong would be indifference to all outcomes. Battles are won and lost, but only those who persevere will win the entire war.

Attitudes must be attended by and implemented with sensitivity. Four different but complementary Sensitivities that the enlightened soul wants to own are goodness, intelligence, compassion, and reverence. Judging by the four quotes of Holy Mother under each of these headings, the avid aspirant after Truth wants to court such qualities and win them forever. Of course, *medha*, intelligence, is the Divine Mother's own light. It is not to be merely presumed, nor is it to be wasted or squandered. Using it to plumb the depths of the meaning of all words — particularly in revealed scripture — the seeker after realization learns to savor wisdom rather than only study it. Such sweet introspection unlocks the doors of inner lands — *lokas, akashas, bardos, the kingdoms of Heaven within* — which are all massive and heretofore unseen gates into the Light of *Brahman*. Reverence, *aradhana*, both assists in this inward ascension process, and develops further at its final destination.

The Four Perfections listed on the chart under study on the facing page are less like coveted qualities and more like abiding principles. Faith is foundational to spiritual life, and many-faceted too, but faith in the *guru* is highlighted as a way to build of it an unshakable edifice that will withstand all blows from the world, from both *karmic* circumstances and narrow and small-minded beings. As Swami Vivekananda has stated, one never gets enlightenment from a book or a temple, but only from another soul. Further: *"I have experienced even in my insignificant life that good motives, sincerity and infinite love can conquer the world. One single soul possessed of these virtues can destroy the dark designs*

The Four Sensitivities, Four Beneficial Attitudes & Four Perfections of the Heart

Goodness *(Saumanasya)* ----------------------------------

"Be good, do good. Then purity will come.
He who has a pure mind sees everything pure."

Intelligence *(Medha)* ----------------------------------

"Dive deep with the noble teachings
you have received and contemplate them in good company."

Compassion *(Daya)* ----------------------------------

"I do not know anyone, not even an
insect, for whom I do not feel compassion."

Reverence *(Aradhana)* ----------------------------------

"It is wise to take refuge in God.
He who will pray to God eagerly will see Him."

(Perfections)

Faith *(Shraddha)* ----------------------------------

"One must have faith in one's
teacher, for therein lies one's chance for salvation."

Benevolence *(Saumyatva)* ----------------------------------

"Be benevolent to all. Do
not find fault. Remember even a trifle done on your behalf."

Radiance *(Tejas)* ----------------------------------

"Some are born with the quality of
Light. They have wisdom from their very birth."

Love *(Prema)* ----------------------------------

"Who calls upon God, by His grace, gets Premabhakti.
This love is to be cherished in utmost privacy."

(Attitudes)

Friendship *(Maitri)* ----------------------------------

"Mankind is prone to weakness.
One who warns in time is the true friend."

Mercy *(Karuna)* ----------------------------------

"Show kindness to all. Even to the cow
we owe such mercy. Hold the vegetable peelings near her mouth."

Positivity *(Mudita)* ----------------------------------

"The purpose of one's life is fulfilled
when one is able to bring joy to others."

Indifference *(Upekshanam)* ----------------------------------

"Body changes, Atman remains the same.
So please try to practice a little detachment."

of millions of hypocrites and brutes."

The radiance of *tejas* shone through Swami Vivekananda, as it did through Lord Buddha and Jesus Christ. *Ojas,* refined energy that is extracted through the sublimation process involving pure food, wholistic health, recitation of the *mantra,* and spiritual practice *(sadhana),* brings *tejas* into manifestation — both inwardly and outwardly. Pure love is the result, and a benevolence that cuts through all resistance and binds the human heart forever to God.

The singular spiritual phenomena of the Holy Mother, like all truly remarkable occurrences, is impossible to describe or explain in full, but it begs the attempt. Similar to the previous chart that was presented under Her auspice, the next offering delves even deeper into both the wisdom and the mystery that was Sri Sarada Devi. If a worthy synopsis of Her teachings could be formulated, they might readily fall under these two singular *Yogas* that She both taught and epitomized.

Mano-Buddhi Yoga is the first of these, and incorporates all the four main *yogas* that have been mentioned and inspected throughout the pages of this book. With control of the mind as its uncompromising requirement and central pole, this effective way of getting into union with Divine Reality begins by utilizing the sixth and seventh limbs of *Raja Yoga* along with the love of the *Ishtam* found in *Bhakti Yoga* to attain its superlative ends. For, what obstacle could ever survive in the intense atmosphere that combines a focused mind with a loving heart? And if the subtle barrier of the human ego — no matter how ripe or refined it has become — still persists, and rises to interfere with the final attainment of nondual meditation leading to *samadhi,* this *Yoga* brings in the ebullient force of intelligent scrutiny to overcome it. The two categories of ownership and agency then lose the last tendrils of their long-standing hold on the human mind, leaving it content and free.

The father of *Yoga,* Patanjali, has brought forth the teaching in the *Yoga* sutras that *karma* persists well into the late stages of *sadhana* and purification. The above selfsame combination of concentration, contemplation, and inner scrutiny, now integrated into one irresistible force, is exactly the specialized tool needed to break down and dissolve these subtle and persistent *karmas* for all time. *"Burnt ropes cannot bind,"* as the Great Master, Sri Ramakrishna Paramahamsa, has declared, meaning that subtle *karmas* like these will be rendered helpless to impede the advanced *sadhaka's* forward spiritual progress before the power of this *Yoga* and its superlative facets. They may still appear, as wisps of memory and thought, but just like burnt ropes, a puff of the wind of well-oriented self-effort will turn them into fine powder and blow them away.

And the result will be the assurance of attaining the knowledge of the full identity of the small self *(jivatman)* with the Supreme Self *(Paramatman).* And even after this rare feat of spiritual acumen is accomplished, the freshly and fully realized master will return to the now completely purified body-mind mechanism and cast benign waves of peace, bliss, and clarity upon everyone and everything. This is quite often actualized by repetition of the sacred *mantra* containing powerful seed words *(bijams)* combined with the holy names of the Lord and Mother of the Universe (see charts on pages 131, 133, & 135). At this juncture, the free soul will become a blessing for removing impediments in the lives of others.

Another special form of *Yoga* that the Holy Mother, Sri Sarada Devi, lived and breathed in Her rare and unprecedented lifetime on earth, was *Jnano-Daya Yoga. Jnana* is spiritual wisdom, and *daya* is unconditional compassion. One can fairly imagine what the merging of these two special qualities might accomplish in the mind of the sincere seeker.

The dynamics of this rarely implemented *Yoga* are based upon and unfold over a fresh understanding of what compassion truly is. Wisdom is the greatest compassion when it is transmitted to a qualified person under proper circumstances. As Sri Krishna has sung in His celestial song: *"That one who possesses supreme devotion to Me, and who teaches the perennial philosophy to my devotees, shall doubtless come to Me. Nor is there any among beings who renders dearer service to Me, and none on earth who is dearer to Me."* This statement smacks of *Jnano-Daya Yoga,* for it is through destroying ignorance in the minds of others that they become emancipated from all manner of bondages and misconceptions.

The most daunting of these misconceptions is the presence of death. The one who can prove

THE TWO YOGAS OF THE MATRI AVATAR
MANO-BUDDHI AND JNANO-DAYA YOGAS OF SRI SARADA DEVI

"Where is there any good in doing works and practices without collectedness of mind? Grace descends only after concentration of mind. Even your work and service demand this. Therefore, you should know that it is improper to deprive living beings of what is their due. In this regard, compassion is knowledge." Holy Mother

Holy Mother,
Sri Sarada Devi

Mano-Buddhi Yoga

- Complete concentration of mind on the Chosen Ideal
- Contemplating the Chosen Ideal as the one & only Reality
- Scrutiny of ego to perceive the fallacy of ownership & agency
- Analyzation of personal karma to attenuate and alleviate it
- Knowledge of the full identity of the Self with Brahman
- Selfless performance of japa for the benefit of mankind
- Overcoming all obstacles via reliance on Mano Yoga & Grace

Jnano-Daya Yoga

- Compassion for all who fear death by teaching Atmajnana
- Compassion for one's own mind by destroying distraction
- Serving all beings with works offered after gaining knowledge
- Study of scripture to gain freedom to serve God in mankind
- Seeking to utilize wisdom for service, not for selfish purposes
- Work knowing that Brahman is not a form, but is formless
- Keep holy company to refine the self in order to serve better

"Mentally resigning all deeds unto Me, having Me as your highest Goal, and resorting to the practice of Buddhi Yoga, fully fix your mind upon Me." Sri Krishna

to others that death is an illusion, and that beings should *"place death in its own grave,"* as one of the devotional wisdom songs of India declares, will be the all around champion, lauded by living beings over millennia. To teach this and convey it most definitely is thus the highest and best form of compassion. The second most persistent and troublesome problem that human beings face is mental distraction combined with brooding. A past master will bring home to people the need for gathering the scattered mind back to its source, and the futility of fretting about all the many phenomena that transpire in the sweep of the three phases of time — the past, present, and future (see chart on page 421). And so, these first two facets of this *Yoga* are crucial to it, and key to implementing it successfully.

In order to engage and utilize true compassion it will be necessary to comprehend that action is relatively incompetent to any task or accomplishment if it is not informed by higher knowledge, particularly in the light that God and the Soul (*Atman*) are both ever free of action and its effects. As Swami Vivekananda has put it, *"If you have known Atman as the one Existence and that nothing else exists, for whom, for what desire do you trouble yourself? Through maya all this doing good, etc., came into my brain — now they are leaving me. Now I get more and more convinced that there is no other object in work except the purification of the soul — to make it fit for knowledge."* What is more, heavy *karmas* form around selfish and disoriented actions, while on the other hand, the seers have demonstrated in their own lives that right action will remain free of repercussions of that sort (see chart on page 391). All of this is to say that once actions are informed by knowledge, they should be offered to the service of God in mankind, which is true *Karma Yoga*. Thus does *Jnano-Daya Yoga* make use of the *Yoga* of selfless action. As the balance of the chart on the facing page shows, it also utilizes *Jnana Yoga* with study of scripture, *Bhakti Yoga* in terms of keeping holy company, and finally, *Advaita Vedanta* in its pursuit of merging with the formless *Brahman* in *samadhi*.

Another chart that communicates similar profundity is displayed on the facing page. The teachings are from the Divine Mother of the Universe Herself in Her own scripture, the *Srimad Devi Bhagavatam*. Here, two secret and ancient *Yogas* are explained and advised, they being *Dharana Yoga* and *Avyaya Yoga*. Several of the Divine Mother's precious names are also shown, revealing Her to be the very essence of pure, conscious Awareness, and the very form of *Brahman*. Through proper worship of Her, all deities are worshipped.

Dharana Yoga is the path of apt concentration, a focus that both precedes lower exercises and lends them their efficacy. It does not utilize *pranayama* to control the breath, but uses the centered mind instead. In this way it skirts the dangers associated with breathing exercises. Focused mind also arouses *Kundalini*, again evincing the supremacy of purified mind over forced and habitual *asana* and *pranayam*. Throughout, the secret of dependance upon Mother Kali says it all, as She accomplishes everything for Her devotee under Her own auspice and protection. *Dharana Yoga's* relationship with *Kundalini Yoga* is obvious, but the description of its dynamics uncover the secret to invoking and pleasing all divinities at all levels of existence. Coursing inwards and upwards with Her, She introduces the aspiring soul to the deities residing in all the centers of consciousness (*chakras*), who receive their blissful share of nectar after the adept reaches the crown *chakra* and returns to these lower centers, enlightened. More than just a mere symbolical way of expression, this unique internal phenomenon is seen and experienced by the practitioner. To quote Sri Ramakrishna about this:

"This is a very secret experience. I saw a boy twenty-two or twenty-three years old, exactly resembling me, enter the sushumna nerve and commune with the lotuses...." "....When he reached the lotus of the heart — I distinctly remember it — and communed with the lotus there, touching it with his tongue, the twelve-petalled lotus, which was hanging head down, stood erect and opened its petals. Then he came to the sixteen-petalled lotus in the throat and the two-petalled lotus in the forehead. And last of all, the thousand-petalled lotus in the head blossomed. Ever since then I have been is this state."

The chart on the facing page is split in halves to reflect another *yoga* that the Divine Mother Kali prefers and advises for sincere seekers. This is *Avyaya Yoga*. This is also a *yoga* of concentration, but its way is the path of envisionment, more for the *bhakta*. The quote from the *Srimad Devi Bhagavatam* tells us that the *guru* is of great importance when embarking on the spiritual path.

Mother Kali — The Adyashakti

The revealed scriptures of the Divine Mother declare: "Shakti Jnanam Vina Devi Nirvana Naiva Jayate. There can be no liberation without knowledge of the Wisdom Mother."

> Worship of Kali — Brahmakalarupah → Kaivalya Nirvana Mukti

> Worship of Lesser Deities > Gauna Mukti

Ekananda Chidakritih

Eka = Single principle
Ananda = Complete contentment
Chid = Consciousness / Intelligence
Akritih = Essential Nature

Avyaya Yoga

1) Fix attention upon Mother's Feet
2) Fix attention on Mother's Hands
3) Fix attention on each of Her limbs
4) Practice until the heart gets pure
5) Fix your heart on Her full Form
6) Practice japa of Her mantra
7) Meditate on Her mantra as Her
8) Transform Brahman into Knowledge
9) Fuse mantra practice with Yoga
10) Dissolve the mind into Her

Dharana Yoga

1) Focus mind to balance the breath
2) Fix mind on the Muladhara Chakra
3) Arouse the Kundalini Shakti
4) Pierce each ascending Chakra
5) Carry shakti energy upwards
6) Settle in the Sahasrara Chakra
7) Meditate on Shiva & Shakti there
8) Gather nectar from Their union
9) Offer it lovingly to the Maya-shakti
10) Offer some to all the lower Deities
11) Descend to the Muladhara Chakra
12) All mantras will now yield success

"By practice of Dharana Yoga one will become free of this Samsara filled with old age and death. Dharana Yoga means to fix one's heart and mind fully on the supremely lustrous Form of Mine which pervades all the quarters, worlds, and countries. I am the World Mother. My devotees will get all of My qualities; there is no doubt of this. This Yoga leads to the knowledge of the union between the Jiva and Brahman."

"Avyaya Yoga prescribes practice of mantra combined with yogic prowess. First, receive instructions from a Guru. Millions of books will not give you realization, but time spent with the Guru will confer It. By meditating on the mantra, the thing to be known, called Brahman, gets transformed into Knowledge. The mantra is futile without Yoga; Yoga is futile without the mantra. Together they are an infallible means to realize Brahman. The Jivatman, made invisible by Maya, is seen as identical with Paramatman via the mantra."

"Among castes, Brahmins are foremost; among sadhikas, shaktas are foremost; and among the foremost of the shaktas are the worshipers of Kali." Srimad Devi Bhagavatam

Through interview and several meetings with this luminary, the *guru* will then orient the new practitioner to his or her Chosen Ideal *(Ishtam)*. In the *Bhagavad Gita,* Sri Krishna tells Arjuna of this blessing, by stating: *"Sincere seekers approach wise preceptors via prostration, humility, and questioning into the nature of Brahman. Then these luminaries will instruct them in the highest wisdom."*

As the aspirant begins to envision the *Ishtam* within the heart lotus, then the *mantra* is transmitted. It is very difficult to explain or express what transpires as the *mantra* does its subtle inner work, partly because the practice needs to go on for months, even years, in order for its salient effects to manifest themselves. This is why so many fail, since they lack patience and faith. Others think that they can go about collecting *mantras* for this and that *Ishtam,* from this and that *guru,* but all of this distraction only clutters the mind that is striving to become one-pointed, or it dilutes and scatters concentration by sending it in various directions.

If the subtle work of the *mantra* is mystical, what occurs thereafter is even more so. Soon, or eventually, depending on the practice and it intensity, the Divine Mother reveals Herself as the *mantra* (see *mantra* charts beginning on page 131), and thereafter shows the devotee how everything is *Brahman* expressed through knowledge. True *Yoga* then becomes possible, and merging the mind into Divine Reality happens in stages — like immersion, absorption, and complete dissolution.

As has already been evinced in the earlier pages of this book, powers and glories can be of two different kinds. One category, misleading and demeaning, only buries the bound soul deeper into the misconception that power, in and of itself, is the best attribute to seek. The other set, inspiring and freeing, exposes the truth that peace is the highest end that any individualized soul can attain, and further, that this type of power and peace leads to the ultimate realization, i.e., that the individual is a temporary construct who has its origin in homogenous Awareness — ever unbound and always free.

The chart on the facing page reveals for us the nature of this second kind of power, which was so well manifested in and expressed by the Great Master, Sri Ramakrishna Paramahamsa. His quotes on the Six Powers of God at the bottom half of this chart are revelations of their own types. For one, the *jivatman,* or embodied soul, is shown to be one of God's own powers. The universe itself is another. If the *jiva* realizes this, he/she comes to know that God abides within in a very real sense, and that all worlds are sporting grounds for Divine Consciousness that is only associating temporarily with various forms.

Whereas these two powers of God, *Brahman,* are cosmic, easily understandable, and fully obvious to the sensitive human being, the following two are matters of purification. Both mind and intellect are powers of God, in that all of existence gets manifested through them. This is not so obvious to the greater percentage of living souls, who have kept themselves out of this divine loop by assuming titles like animal, human, ignorant, sinner, limited, physical, and so many other false superimpositions over their indwelling divine nature. To quote Swami Vivekananda on this unfortunate situation: *"Gold and silver have I none, but what I have I give to thee freely, and that is the knowledge of the goldness of gold, the silverness of silver, the manhood of man, the womanhood of woman, the reality of everything is the Lord. And that this Lord we are trying to realize from time without beginning in the objective and in the attempt throwing up such 'queer' creatures of our fancy as man, woman, child, body, mind, earth, sun, moon, stars, the world, love, hate, property, wealth, etc.; also ghosts, devils, angels and gods, God, etc. Herein lies the secret. Says Patanjali, the father of Yoga: 'When a man rejects all the superhuman powers, then he attains the raincloud of virtues.' He sees God. He becomes God, and helps others become the same."*

When a man's mind is "stilled," then, and his intellect is subjected to "austerities," he falls onto the right "path" and receives "Divine Knowledge." This knowledge, *Jnana,* is closest to *Brahman* Itself, and though it is still a "compound," as Vivekananda has stated, it is the nearest quality to the Source. It is, itself, a divine power of God. All knowledge is divine, really, and full of intelligent particles. It is just that beings subject it to all manner of degradation, like "the eternal money-making," and thus rob it of its real power and purpose — to enlighten and set free. And *Prema,* Divine Love, is this self-same Knowledge at its most intense peak.

The Six Treasures and Six Divine Powers of God

"As the web comes out of a spider, and sparks come out of fire, so this whole universe proceeds from the Beloved Goddess, the Primal Force of Existence. We salute Her, the Mahashakti, within whose mayic power this whole universe, moving and unmoving, is projected, sustained, and withdrawn." Vedavyasa

The Six Treasures of God

Sri — Unlimited Abundance

Bala — Magnificent Glory

Aishvarya — Irresistible Strength

Vijnana — Penetrating Wisdom

Tyaga — Natural Renunciation

Tejas — Awesome Splendor

The Six Divine Powers of God

Jivatman — Living Beings
"The jiva at first remains in a state of ignorance. He is not conscious of God, but of multiplicity. Then he becomes conscious that God dwells in all beings."

Jagad — Universe
"This universe is God's glory. People see His glory and forget everything else. They do not seek God. This universe has evolved from the Supreme Brahman."

Manas — Mind
"Regardless of the path one follows, yoga is not possible until the mind is stilled. The yogi's mind is under his control; he is not under the control of his mind."

Buddhi — Intelligence
"A man's intelligence is very delicate and can get covered, distorted, or misled. He must therefore practice many austerities so as to acquire Divine Knowledge."

Prema — Love
"What is Prema? The one who feels It, this intense and ecstatic Love for God, not only forgets the world, but also forgets even the body, which is so dear to all."

Jnana — Knowledge
"Intelligence, devotion, compassion, renunciation — these belong to the realm of true knowledge. With these a man comes near God. One more step and he attains God."

Some beings there are, who, coming so close to this Source of all divine power, inherit more than the kingdom of heaven, but also align fully with Divine Reality Itself. Only they could comprehend the Six Treasures of *Brahman* listed at the top half of the chart on the previous page. About the first of them, *Sri*, who is there in existence who can fully conceive of the infinite expanse of manifested qualities and materials, both inward and outwards? Most beings can only think of this in terms of monetary gain and material opportunity. What is set before them due to the combination of Spirit and Matter gets relegated to the physical alone, and even there they become greedy. Khalas, the divine singer of Mother Wisdom, expresses this in one of his devotional wisdom songs:

> *Oh mind, why have you given up uttering the Holy Name of Ram?*
> *When you should be renouncing your anger, deceit, and dishonesty,*
> *you have given up your integrity and sacrificed your love of Truth instead.*
>
> *You flatter the millionaire, yet forget to praise Sri Ram,*
> *though Ram is the owner of the entire universe.*
> *Your mind dwells constantly on sense objects and mundane habits,*
> *tempted by that which has no eternal existence.*
> *Is it for the sake of these fleeting things that you have forgotten the precious gem of Ram's Name?*
>
> *Consider this, oh mind: The Lord is the source of all Existence;*
> *Can you truly afford to forget Him?*
> *Khalas is continually posing this profound question:*
> *"When will you renounce your attachment to this empty world,*
> *offering even your body and mind to the Lord, Sri Ramachandra Bhagavan."*

The *"many chambers of the Father's Mansion"* comprise a fuller, richer wealth than all that the physical universe holds. Body attached and matter bound, most incarnating souls never come to know this, and circle in the closed loop of earthly and heavenly transmigration for ages (*yugas*). All this talk about ones divine inheritance applies here, most tellingly.....

Bala, the second of these Treasures, refers to the magnificent glory of the Lord, both in abilities and in appearance. In another song of divine expression, Trailokyanath Sannyal sings:

> *Meditate, oh mind, on Lord Hari, the pure, the ever perfect Consciousness Absolute.*
> *What incomparable radiance, how fascinating is His wondrous form!*
> *How dear is He to all His devotees.*
>
> *Even more beauteous in fresh blossoming love, that shames the splendor of a million suns.*
> *Like lightning gleams the glory of His form,*
> *filling the soul with deep joy and sweet ecstasy.*
>
> *Worship His Holy Feet in the lotus of your heart,*
> *and with mind serene and eyes made radiant with heavenly love, behold that matchless sight!*
> *Overpowered with devotion, immerse yourself forevermore, oh mind,*
> *in that one who is pure Knowledge and pure Bliss Absolute!*

For all-out Power, unlimited and irrepressible — a Divine Force that outstrips all other lesser movements — the *Sanskrit* word, *Aishvarya* describes it well, it being a special kind of rare internal wealth. Perhaps there is no other description of this that is quite so potent as Swami Vivekananda's poem on Mother Kali:

> *The stars are blotted out, the clouds are covering clouds*
> *It is darkness, vibrant, sonant.*

In the roaring, whirling wind are the souls of a million lunatics just loosed from the prison-house,
wrenching trees by the roots, sweeping all from the path.
The sea has joined the fray, and swirls up mountain-waves, to reach the pitchy sky.
The flash of lurid light reveals on every side a thousand, thousand shades of death —
begrimed and black — scattering plagues and sorrows, dancing mad with joy, come, Mother, come!
For Terror is Thy Name, death is in Thy Breath, and every shaking step destroys a world fore'er.
Thou Time, the All-destroyer! Come, O Mother, come!

Who dares miserys love, and hug the form of Death, dance in destruction's dance.
To him the Mother comes.

For the kind of wisdom that will penetrate through the densest darkness, bringing light to all levels of ones being, *Vijnana* is the most effective. This knowledge of a singular nondual variety is, as it were, *Brahman* in action. As Lord Vasishtha said about it to the young *Avatar*, Sri Ram: *"Come to know the depths of the ocean and do not merely get tossed about by the waves on its surface. To realize true wisdom, vijnana, know that Brahman is the substratum of maya, and do not give maya an independent existence or accept it to be sentient; these are the two great mistakes committed by immature religious conceptions throughout time. Coming to know that the mind in maya is responsible for all that was previously blamed upon and attributed to God, one can then strike at the root of both ignorance and the undesirable suffering that oozes imperceptively from it, like blood from a wound of an unconscious man."* Another of India's devotional wisdom songs expresses this especial wisdom well:

This is my prayer to Thee, O Raghunanda:
kindly destroy my mind's tendency to perceive duality —
and thereby remove all sorrows and sufferings arising in my being.
For Atman alone abides; none else exists.
It is attachment to relativity that gives birth to the miseries of life.

Vijnana, then, is this rare knowledge of the homogenous nature of all existence. Also called *Atmanjnan*, and *Brahmajnan*, the seeker who comes into the company of a soul who possesses It consciously, gets blessed to the point of nonreturn, i.e., there will be no more birth in ignorance, any more. For a look at the level of this highest Wisdom, review the chart on page 271.

As we make our way through the chart on page 485, the penultimate Treasure of *Brahman* shows itself up to be *Tyaga*, a supremely natural state of renunciation of the world. Again, the image of the Great Master on this chart matches perfectly with this superlative quality. For, like Lord Buddha and Jesus before Him, Sri Ramakrishna wore the crown of renunciation in the most natural way. And in fact, it was not that He attempted to hold this austere attribute in the face of temptations, etc., but more that it was His natural everyday mode of being. One verse of a wisdom song of India, composed by Swami Vivekananda for his Great Master, evinces this perfectly:

Drinking the essence of immortality, renouncing attachment to the world,
forsaking that self-serving spirit which is the mother of all dissention,
and meditating on the blessed Feet of our Guru which are the embodiment of all well-being,
we humbly invite the entire world to share in this divine elixir.

As the Great Master Himself used to say, referring to the *Bhagavad Gita* of Lord Krishna, when one says the word *"Gita"* over and over many times, it turns into *"tagi,"* i.e., *tyagi*. Thus, the deepest meaning of the holy scriptures revolves around that one quality of renunciation. As Bhartrihari repeats at the end of every verse of his *Vairagya Shatakam: "Only renunciation is fearless."*

The final entry among the Six Treasure of *Brahman* is that of *Tejas*. Described as "radiant splendor," it is far more than some outward show. That is, it may impress those who are as yet spiritually uninformed, and those who tend towards mystery-mongering and sensationalism, but the advanced disciple knows what intense *sadhana* and enlightenment has gone into producing such an effect on the visages of the sages and seers. For *Tejas* is the effect of stored up *Ojas,* which in turn is subtle spiritual power that has mounted due to living a life of purity, austerity, and practice.   As one spiritual song of India puts it:

> *The powerful spiritual force at the base of the spine awakens at Thy touch,*
> *and the bondage of desire disappears when you grant detachment and discrimination.*
> *Oh Teacher Divine, shining with the Light of Tejas,*
> *kindly shower compassion on Thy loving devotee.*

Since the main subject and "footfall" of this chapter is *bhakti,* devotion, and the Great Master, Sri Ramakrishna Paramahamsa has come up in its context, it may be wonderfully informative to take a look at the divine life of this unique being, who has been titled not only the *"Avatar* of the Age," but also, "The King of the Devotees."

Basically, the two charts that follow are self-explanatory.   All one needs to do to get information and teachings on both the history and the deeper ramifications and significance of Sri Ramakrishna's most recent lifetime is to follow the right hand columns of both charts from top to bottom.   Some comments on a few of these points will suffice to fill in important details around them.

Of immediate note is that both his father and mother had spiritual visions prior to His birth. This is not all that surprising, seeing that the Hindu parents in general, unlike modern people in the West, do austerities in order to gain children, and to host higher souls as well.   It is not a matter of mere sexual relations, often enacted bestially or unconsciously; it is more a matter of eating pure foods to purify the physical body, meeting on auspicious times for relations that are thought of as the union of the sacred *Shiva* and *Shakti* principles dwelling in human men and women, then praying and meditating so as to usher the soul into the world of embodiment consciously.   This is a bare description, really, as there are more elements to conscious child-birthing.   Westerners, if they think of being conscious at all during this process, usually take it up on the physical level only, like with natural child-birthing, eating organically for a short time, staying away from smoking and alcohol (which are things people should not be imbibing anyway, at any time) etc.   In short, it is all involved in physical considerations only.   Daily *sadhana* with meditation, doing devotions at the shrine, keeping holy company, repeating the *mantra* many times a day — what to speak of seeking the knowledge from scriptures and holy beings of how the soul moves from the disembodied state along the *nadis* into the fetus, and the like, are completely unknown/unobserved to most beings.   Thus, gaining a child for most is all a matter of chance for them, like a "crap shoot."   The results of such randomness are seen in the kinds of souls that are born to parents today, particularly as these children grow up and their *samskaras* and *karmas* come to the fore, sporting all their problems and negativities.   To put it simply, unconscious parents produce worldly children, or, as Krishna states, *"....souls born into restless and slothful wombs."*

But with conscious parents (like devotee householders) and their children, and particularly with illumined souls that come forth, the signs of spirituality are evident early on.   In the Great Master's unique case, He had *samadhi* at the age of seven, merely by seeing a flock of cranes fly in front of a dark storm cloud that was gathering.   As a boy He frequented holy beings at their wayside rest stops near His village and listened to their teachings, stories, and devotional songs.   Hearing these only once, He was able to remember them all in full for the rest of His life.

Becoming a priest at the temple of Mother Kali, He strove to perceive Her with ardent love and divine focus, and finally had Her mind-transforming vision.   Soon after that He had the highest *samadhi,* called *Nirvikalpa,* under the brief tutelage of an *advaitic* master.   On top of this, He realized the goal of the *Tantra* after completing its sixty-four disciplines under a female *Tantric* adept.   Importantly, He did not engage the in two disciplines that naive Westerners associate with *Tantra,* those two being the imbibing of intoxicants and sexual relations.   It was as if, in prophetic fashion, He was seeing in advance the misconceptions that future practitioners would fall into when taking up the honorable practice of *Tantra,* and how they would run the risk of demeaning and distorting such ancient pathways.

The Unique Features of Sri Ramakrishna's Descent

Part 1

"Sri Ramakrishna was a perfect soul. Satya Yuga began when He was born. This time He has come to save all beings — rich, poor, wise, foolish." Sri Sarada Devi

#		
1	**Pita Vishnu Darshan**	The Master's father, Kshudiram, has a vision of Lord Vishnu as his future son at the Vishnu Temple in Gaya.
2	**Mata Shiva Darshana**	The Master's mother, Chandradevi, feels impregnated after a vision of Shiva in the temple at Kamarpukur.
3	**Vishnu Avatar**	Kshudiram's vision is of a deity with four arms, holding conch, mace, and discus — all emblems of Lord Vishnu.
4	**Jagad Guru**	The Master shows insight at an early age, solving disputes of the pundits.
5	**Samadhi**	The Master experiences samadhi at the tender age of seven.
6	**Ma Kali Darshana**	The Master has his first vision of Mother Kali at the Dakshineswar temple in Kolkata around 1855.
7	**Vijnana Dhara**	The quality of shrutidhara, perfect recall of all scriptural wisdom, was fully manifested in the Master.
8	**Mahabhava Dhara**	Attainment and experience of the various devotional moods of many religious traditions got expressed in him.
9	**Nirvikalpa Samadhi**	The Master attained Nirvikalpa, the full experience of Advaita Vedanta, at the height of his spiritual realization.
10	**Tantra-charya**	The Master accomplished the goal of all sixty-four disciplines of Tantra by realizing God in different forms.
11	**Sarva Dharma Svarupine**	The Master realized the essence of all religions, thus establishing the principle of Universality in the world.
12	**Yogacharya**	Seeing via practice that hatha yoga sought power and longevity, the Master advised the practice of Raja yoga.
13	**Jaina-Sikhta-charya**	Through spiritual insight, the Master confirmed that the Tirthankaras of Jainism were incarnations of Janaka.
14	**Asta-Siddhi Tyagi**	In his twelve-year sadhana, the Master acquired the eight occult powers and gave them up as dangers on the path.
15	**Anubhava Apta**	In his lifetime, the Master attained the nineteen kinds of refined devotional moods.
16	**Mahadiksha Avatara**	As Avatar of this age, Sri Ramakrishna conferred liberation on aspiring beings by a mere touch, wish, or thought.

| Part 2 |

"He followed all the disciplines — Christians, Muslims, Hindus, etc. — for the sake of God-consciousness, and enjoyed the Lila in different ways, entirely unconscious of how time passed."

Sri Sarada Devi

1	**Jagad Parinama**	* Wakened Kundalini Power * Quickened spiritual growth * Evolved the individual soul * Began world transformation
2	**Avastha-adikaravada**	* Restored authentic Tantra * Reconciled religious views
3	**Sarvam Khalvidam Brahma**	* Revealed world as Brahman * Saw Brahman & Shakti as 1 * Emphasized discrimination between the real and unreal
4	**Purna Advaita-charya**	* Transcended pairs of opposites while integrating life * Saw the essence in all beings * Synthesized all views
a	**Purnayoga Jnani**	* Integrated the four yogas * Melded wisdom with love, action with meditation * Taught giving up ignorance, not the world as Brahman
b	**Adikara-viveka**	* Advised gradual maturity * Preached neti, neti to iti, iti
c	**Premavada-charya**	* Taught love of God as the solution for all ills * Revealed how to harmonize cast, cultures, relationships
d	**Dvandva-titacharya**	* Adeptly dissolved dualities * Demonstrated how to defeat the 6 passions and 8 fetters
e	**Brahma-shakt-advaita**	* Reconciled the dichotomy of change and non-change * Revealed the presence of Witness-Consciousness
f	**Samyak Karmanta**	* Indicated the limitation of moral and ethical laws * Taught how to follow all rules until fully mature
g	**Avastha-charya**	* Taught growth by stages according to one's capacity
5	**Mahalila Avatar**	* Demonstrated Divine Lila * Rendered embodiment noble * Authenticated the principle of God with Form
6	**Mayashakti**	* Revealed maya as the power of Brahman
7	**Atma-chaitanya Satya**	* Revealed the ever-free state of Consciousness * Affirmed that Consciousness is different from matter
8	**Jiva Chaitanya**	* Explained Conscious via degree of intensity * Cited Avatar as the highest expression of divinity
9	**Brahma-ruparupa**	* Cited God as being with form and beyond form * Cited Shakti of Brahman
10	**Karma Vandana**	* Advised dharmic action leading to non-action * Encouraged service of God
11	**Anubhava Tattvam**	* Insisted that realization is a matter of direct experience * Advised mental purity
12	**Brahmajnani**	* Declared that realization of God is the only true aim of human existence
13	**Jnana Parinama**	* Transmitted teachings of positivity for the upliftment of aspiring beings
a	**Samyagdristi**	* Presented spiritual growth via transformation of mental outlook, not aversion
b	**Jagad Lila**	* Saw the universe as an indication of Divine Expression
c	**Avidya Vinashana**	* Revealed that ignorance is ultimately unreal * Taught transcending pain via removing ignorance
d	**Kama Shuddhi**	* Taught fulfilling desires via dharmic actions, and by sublimation
e	**Para Tyagi**	* Exemplified divinizing life based upon seeing all love as love for God
f	**Pakva Ahamkara**	* Revealed how to turn the unripe worldly ego into the ripe ego of a devotee
g	**Karma Moksha**	* Informed that action done in service of God is both productive and liberating
14	**Matrivada**	* Saw all women as manifestations of the Divine Mother

Not stopping here, He practiced and realized the ideals of many other religious traditions as well — including the nonviolent religion of the Jains, with their Twenty-four *Tirtankaras* — proclaiming them all to be from one Source. Many had talked of this ideal, but no one had yet practiced and realized it up until His lifetime. Thus He became known as the paragon of all religions, their champion — showing them all to be both similar and dissimilar, but absolutely one in essence.

As both a lesson and a cautionary measure, and in keeping with maintaining religious, philosophical, and spiritual integrity in practice, the Great Master saw the dangers of preoccupation with *hatha yoga*, and practiced and promoted instead the full regimen of *Raja Yoga*, or the Eight-Limbed *Yoga* of Patanjali — the "Father" of *Yoga*. This was also far-sighted on His part, and hopefully will save many Westerners from a mere physical pathway and help them place their feet on the time-tested paths of *jnanam* and *bhakti*. In this very same vein, He acquired the controversial eight occult powers *(asta-bala siddhis)* and found them to be outright impediments to the goal of spiritual *sadhana* and its goal of full Enlightenment *(moksha/mukti)*. To emphasize the authentic and eschew all that is not, He also practiced the five devotional moods of *Vaishnavism*, and many other *bhavas* that are associated with the path of *Bhakti Yoga*. In this way did He point the way towards the four traditional *Yogas* (see charts on pages 431 & 433) and steer sincere practitioners away from lower and unworthy paths.

With all of these tasks accomplished, and in a spiritually darksome age in front of the collective gaze of humanity, the real important revelations were now open to bestow on living beings. For those living in His own lifetime, He sometimes bestowed these gifts with a touch, a thought, or a word. For those to follow, like in present times, after His passing, He shown light on long-forgotten precepts that form the very foundation of true Religion and nondual Philosophy. Many of these are listed on the second chart in this series, shown on the facing page.

Of crucial import in this regard was the timely reminder that living beings are manifestations of pure, conscious Awareness, and, to put it more succinctly, consist of Consciousness alone, not matter. And as if these two points were not enough, He explained that this Consciousness manifested Itself via differing levels of intensity. Thus, and contrary to worldly opinion, He revealed that all beings are not created equally; they are not created at all! They are projections of their own minds. Further, when they take form and enter onto the field of creation, they are not equal there either, with some having much more capacity and abilities than others. In brief, they are only equal by measure of their Souls, or *Atman*, or, if using the language of another religion, "equal in God's eyes only." And in fact, He, Himself, demonstrated by His very life and being, that the *Avatar* is the fullest expression of all capacities and abilities.

Another axiom the Great Master brought forward for this age was to declare that God was with form and beyond form as well. His personal realization of this fact clarified so many doubts and dissolved so many arguments on the subject. Of course, and due to His having *Nirvikalpa Samadhi*, so rare of experience, He stated further that God, *Brahman*, was beyond form and formlessness as well.

One of the most blessed of revelations He gave us was the hidden presence of *Shakti* in all. It was wondrous to reveal the formless *Brahman*, and the *Atman* in all, but this additional facet of revealing the subtle power of *Brahman*, namely the Divine Mother of the Universe, gave full power and deep heart to India's already profuse sets of philosophies — what to speak of to life and existence itself. With the knowledge of Mother Power, and Mother Presence within them, living beings can move forward in all pathways of life, and consummate their search for fulfillment in Her. Therefore, bringing awareness to the presence of the Divine Mother — She usually being so hidden from age to age — was one of His greatest boons on present day humanity.

Far from evincing transcendence of the world as the only path, the Great Master revealed the efficacy of the path of *Karma Yoga,* even leaving behind a large and successful order of monks and lay devotees dedicated to this important way of right action. Service of God in mankind is its motto, all leading to the destruction of ignorance and the alleviation of suffering. For He knew, like Lord Buddha before Him, that through rightly oriented action, the mind would gain back its original purity by degrees, and direct spiritual experience would dawn, inevitably.

The rest of the list on the second chart of "Unique Features" just examined — the role of positivity over aversion, the illusory nature of ignorance, the fulfillment of all desires via *dharmic* preoccupation, the divinization of life and deification of all things and all beings, the seeing of Divine Mother in all women, and the upliftment of women for the rejuvenation of a fallen world — can all be studied by researching His singular and exemplary life in books such as *Gospel of Sri Ramakrishna, Ramakrishna the Great Master, Great Swan,* and other fine works and testaments of the tradition.

Yajna is an all-important word in *Sanskrit*, and a chief tenet in Indian spirituality. To wind down the eighth chapter of this book towards its consummation, a study of this tenet, rather missing in today's hurried and modernized world, can be offered. To outline the basics, we see by the chart on the facing page that another and very important set of fives is outlined. In other words, to keep all the worlds, inner and outer, operating in balance and free of undue strife and suffering, the ancient peoples of India made their heartfelt offerings daily towards five strata of living beings — of beings living in the myriad worlds of collective consciousness.

It is very hard to ascertain any real order of supremacy among living beings occupying the realms of name and form. Each has its prime function, and souls occupying what would appear to be the lower levels of manifestation can be in possession of the most sacred and liberating elements — as is the case with human beings, for instance. They may not be inhabiting the heavens of the ancestors, or the high *lokas* of the gods and goddesses, but they can be free at any time if they like, and unlike these others, they can realize their perfect, divine nature and merge into nondual Reality. Another facet of their especial ranking comes in the form of the ability to render sacrifice to both the deities within and the denizens outside. They can also extend worship and be of service to holy beings. Thus, the human race has in its hands and at its beck and call all the levels of manifestation in existence. It can even court and win the Supremely Unmanifested, i.e., *Brahman*.

With these facts noted, the traditional way of viewing levels of sacrifice begins with propitiating either the gods or the *rishis*, depending on what plane one is inhabiting at any given time, or in any given life. Thus, *Deva Yajna* holds a very lofty position in the scheme of things cosmic. Even Lord Buddha — as can be seen by the quote from him on the chart under study — gives profound credence to this form of worship. Some immature Buddhist thinkers tend to put off the worlds of name and form as if they do not exist, or have no bearing on the soul's inward journey. But the system of The Three Worlds *(Triloka)* has been known and in effect, philosophically and cosmologically, from long before Shakyamuni's time, on through his own, and up until the present in the form of Zen *Buddhism's* own teaching. It is called *Sangai-Yui-Isshin* (see chart on page 455) today. The worshipper who is concerned for his or her highest and best good, then, spiritually, mentally, and where worldly prospects are concerned as well, will offer obeisances daily, or several times a day, to these inner divine powers.

Rishi Yajna, worship of the illumined teachers and wisdom knowers, is enjoined even more seriously on the devout practitioner. For, not only does prostration before the wise effectively reduce the arrogant human ego to nothing, it also has the salutary effect of moving mountains where external obstacles and impediments of the mind are concerned. Additionally, and of great import, guidance out of the realms of name and form, wherein all *karmas* lurk and manifest themselves, is granted to the sincere seeker via sacrificing the small self to the *rishis* and their salient aims on earth. In *Sanskrit*, the famous *sloka* reads: *"tad viddhi pranipatena pariprashnena sevaya upadeksyanti te jnana jnaninas tattva darshinah,"* which translated means: *"Sincere students approach the wise teachers via prostration, service, and apt questioning. Then these wise ones initiate them into the highest Wisdom."*

After the above two *yajnas* have been honored, and respective regimens for their completion have been implemented into everyday life and worship, the beings dwelling in the heavens and on earth are acknowledged. For heavenly concerns there is *Pitri Yajna. Pitris* are ones ancestors. For the earth-dweller they generate a very tight and impenetrable net of bondage if they are not worshipped appropriately. On the other hand, if appeased with proper rites and positive thoughts, the internal doorways to higher spheres can be thrown open, and spiritual progress can go forth unimpeded. This

The Fivefold Strata of Sacrifice

★ _The 4 Keys to Divine Life_
Conscious Ingestion (Ashnasi arpanam)
Conscious Sacrificing (Juhosi arpanam)
Conscious Generosity (Dadasi arpanam)
Conscious Austerity (Rtapas arpanam)

"It is verily a thief who takes what the universe gives and fails to give back in the form of sacrifice. Such a selfish one does not gain this world in truth, so how can he gain the next and higher worlds?" Sri Krishna

Deva Yajna

"The miserly do not come to this world of the gods, and the foolish do not praise them. Only the one of good character, who takes pleasure in giving, becomes happy in that realm." Lord Buddha

Rishi Yajna

"He who with supreme devotion to Me will teach this profound philosophy to My devotees, shall doubtless come to Me alone. Nor is there any among men who renders dearer service to Me than he." Sri Krishna

Pitri Yajna

"The knowers of the three Vedas, worshipping Me by sacrifices, pray for the way to heaven. They reach the holy world of the Lord of the Devas and enjoy it in the celestial planes of the Devas. Having enjoyed the vast world of heaven, they return to the world of mortals on the exhaustion of their merits. Thus abiding by the injunctions of the Vedas, desiring objects of desire, they go and they come." Sri Krishna

Nara Yajna

"Down on your face before Him, and make a great sacrifice; the sacrifice of a whole life for humanity, for whom He comes from time to time, whom he loves above all — the poor, the lowly, the oppressed." Swami Vivekananda

Bhuta Yajna

"That one who takes good and shuns evil, acting as if holding a pair of scales, is indeed wise. By nonviolence to all living beings, even to animals, one becomes noble." Lord Buddha

"All these yajnas and more are contained within the Divine Storehouse of Vedic Sacrifices." Sri Krishna

is ideal. For the ordinary embodied soul, there are far and away enough mountainous obstacles already in the way of substantial progress towards freedom that he does not need to have unresolved ancestor *karma* added to the heap! And it is here, particularly, that the importance of performing *yajna* becomes most evident. As Sri Krishna states in the *Bhagavad Gita*, *"This world is not for the one who performs no sacrifice, so how then any other world, Arjuna?"*

Nara Yajna and *Bhuta Yajna* pertain mostly to the physical realm, or the *Bhur Loka*. Basically, we are speaking of mankind, animals, insects, and plants within the dual scope of this offering, though disembodied spirits can also be added in. Ideally, serving all these beings, or serving God dwelling within them, is the highest ideal. And where this is not possible due to limited thinking and poorly conditioned awareness, at least due respect and nonviolence can be adhered to. For so many millennia most the Hindus would not eat their animals, and several of its honorable sects would not even kill insects. Besides being sensible, the amount of *karmic* accrual is also reduced substantially over a lifetime based upon these wise observances. For more on the conscious treatment of lower life forms, see the chart on page 447.

Where sacrifice to mankind is concerned, perhaps a few of Swami Vivekananda's statements will size it all up adequately for the interested reader. As he was wont to say, often: *"Oh, when will man be friend to man?"*

"Down on your face before Him, and make a great sacrifice; the sacrifice of a whole life for them, for whom He comes from time to time, whom he loves above all, the poor, the lowly, the oppressed."

"Feel, my children, feel: feel for the poor, the ignorant, the downtrodden, feel til the heart stops and the brain reels and you think you will go mad — then pour the soul out at the feet of the Lord and then will come power, help, and indomitable energy."

"So long as millions live in hunger and ignorance, I hold every man a traitor, who having been educated at their expense, pays not the least heed to them. I call those men — who strut around in their finery, having got all their money by grinding the poor — wretches, so long as they do not do anything for those two hundred millions who are now no better than hungry savages."

On the facing page is the next offering up for inspection, as we continue to chart the Indian scriptures and the footfalls of the ancient *rishis*. In this selection, taken from the *Bhagavad Gita*, a larger scope of sacrifices is outlined. According to that scripture, and the illumined soul, Sri Krishna, there are a host of sacrifices one can and should perform daily, in every lifetime, that accent and play off of the Five Main Sacrifices that were just covered on previous pages. The reader should note all the quotes that are connected with each of these noble five, and then scrutinize the storehouse of *Vedic* sacrifices at the bottom of the chart. In an apt summation, it can be seen that wealth, objects, food, the actions around all three, as well as the senses that encounter and relate with them, form a major part of most of these *yajnas*. The breath and the life force come next as offerings, followed by the sacred deities. Study and overall *sadhana*, spiritual disciplines, make up the bulk, all performed in the spirit of purifying austerity. And all of the aforementioned are to be offered to the Lord Himself, or *Ishvara*.

It is important to note that none of this pertains to nondual Reality, *Brahman*, which is transcendent of sacrifices, the acts of sacrifice, and the sacrificer him/herself. So many beings think that when they make conscious offerings, that they somehow apply to or benefit God, or *Brahman*. That Reality is beyond all need for offerings or assistance. That Reality is not found in the realms of food, objects, matter, action, the senses, nor the life force. That Reality is not even found in the realms of the gods, nor can it be perceived via acts of study, *sadhana*, and austerity. All these are for the mind, and when the mind attains purity via these very principles, sacrificed consciously, then it transforms from ordinary mind to pure Mind. That pure Mind is *Brahman*, for it has been stripped clean of all its overlays and limitations. As Shankara relates in his *Vivekachudamani: "That one realizes the eternal Self who dissolves mind, intellect, body, the gross and subtle senses, the gross and subtle elements, and the*

THE FIVE KINDS AND TWELVE TYPES OF SACRIFICE

(Pancha Maha Yajna)

"Having known that even the ancient seekers after freedom performed action, therefore do you perform action, as they did in olden times. And know, too, that the world is bound by actions other than those performed for the sake of Yajna; so perform action for Yajna alone, free of attachment." Sri Krishna

Deva Yajna
(Sacrifice to the Gods)

"Longing for success in action on earth, they worshiped the gods; for quickly is success born of action in this world of man."

THE IMPERISHABLE ↑

THE VEDAS

YAJNA AND KARMA ↓

"Know karma springing from sacrifice to have risen from the Vedas, and the Vedas rise from the Imperishable. The all-pervading Veda is, therefore, ever centered in Yajna."

Rishi Yajna
(Sacrifice to the Seers)

"Cherished by Yajna, the wise shall bestow the enjoyments you desire. But a thief is he who enjoys without returning anything."

Nara Yajna
(Sacrifice to Humankind)

"Having created mankind in the beginning together with Yajna, the Lord said: 'By this shall you propagate.'"

Pitri Yajna
(Sacrifice to the Ancestors)

"He sees, who sees the Supreme Lord as remaining the same in all beings, the dying and the undying."

"That one who does not follow on earth this wheel thus revolving, sinful of life, he lives in vain."
Sri Krishna

Bhuta Yajna
(Sacrifice to Subhumans)

"Behold My forms, by hundreds and thousands, manifest and divine, and of multi-colors and shapes."

"From food beings become; from rain food is produced; from Yajna rain proceeds; Yajna is born of karma."

"Having known Me as the Lord of Yajnas, as the Ruler of all the worlds, as the Friend of all beings, you will attain Peace."

Bahuvidya Yajna — The Storehouse of Vedic Sacrifices

The Twelve Yajnas

Devayajna — Offering as sacrifice to the gods	Ishvarayajna — Offering all as sacrifice to the Lord
Shrotrayajna — Offering the senses	Shabdayajna — Offering hearing and sense objects
Indriyakarmaniyajna — Offering the sense actions	Pranayajna — Offering the life-force
Dravyayajna — Offering wealth	Tapoyajna — Offering austerities
Yogayajna — Offering yogic practice	Svadhyayayajna — Offering sacred study
Pranayamayajna — Offering regulation of the breath	Niyataharayajna — Offering food and its energy

---

"Various Yajnas such as these are spread out in the storehouse of the Vedas. Know them all to be born of karma, and thus knowing, you shall be free."

ego, along with time and space, into the Atman in meditation." *Brahman* and *Atman* are ever pure and perfect; they (who are one) need no transformation or purification. It is the mind that projected the three worlds that needs to gain transparency, divesting itself of all superimpositions once and for all.

Speaking of offerings and sacrifices, the next chart on the facing page brings this "locomotion of devotion" chapter to an fitting conclusion. In the ninth chapter of the *Adhyatma Ramayana*, Sri Ramachandra gives out this sweet but powerful transmission to the woman ascetic, Sabari, who has worshipped him for countless lifetimes. It comprises a thorough study of the path of *Bhakti Yoga*, including the ways in which to practice it. Nonduality fittingly finds its place here too, appearing in the final two limbs as apt conclusion.

Since this chart forms the basis for a book that is already written, only a brief and interconnected explanation will be given here. Importantly, it all begins with Holy Company. Rather than laud the endless benefits of this boon from Divine Mother, it may more effectively be given that engaging in worldly company, and worse, threatens the embodied soul with grave risk. The key word here is protection, which is one of the blessings that Holy Company provides for the self-surrendered devotee. Whether one believes, or knows it or not, *karmas* are fructifying all the time. They are coming from daily actions; they are arising from actions done in past lifetimes; they are surfacing because of and in the midst of families and family settings, as well as appearing in ignorant society. The aspirant who knows this verily rushes to the sanctuary of Holy Company straightaway, and saves the self from the hailstorm of delusion and suffering that always attends upon the atmospheres of delusion.

And, if Holy Company is won, the real benefits, beyond basic protection, come to the fore. One gains the *dharma* teachings and can spread them broadcast among others who seek the Truth. This is not yet a *guru's* transmission, which matures much later in certain highly qualified individuals, but is nonetheless a license to help lost souls find their way out of the world-bewitching *maya* and on towards Enlightenment.

One of the facets that appears to the Lord's servant and helper at this juncture is the burgeoning forth of devotional moods that get expressed via wisdom songs. It is not only *kirtan* that finds a place here, but *bhajans* and *stotrams* as well. The names of the Lord are sweet to taste, no doubt, but in order to really digest what they imply, the devotee needs more than aural repetition; he/she needs study and contemplation.

This further facet appears in the fourth limb of *bhakti*, called hearing the teachings. Obviously, the second limb was a kind of "spreading the good news" among open hearts. But limb four appeals more to open minds. With the heart made self-surrendered, the mind can more easily get to the point of the spiritual path and its practice, which is ridding the entire being of ignorance so that Divine Love can be experienced. That becomes more evident in limb number eight.

But prior to that, the *guru* and *sadhana* must take up the fore. So many seekers make the usual mistake of stopping their forward progress at the terminal of chanting alone. Notice how even the *mantra* takes up a deeper import in Sri Rama's system in limb number seven. Practices under the spiritual preceptor's instructions — limbs five and six — are therefore most necessary and important. In short, chanting, eating pure foods, reciting the *mantra*, physical posture and breathing, as well as hearing the teachings of the *dharma* only once without study, will not drive any aspirant very deep. This problem falls within the realm of surface mind and immature ego, and is the cause of ones failure to deepen the practice of austerities under the guidance of an illumined preceptor.

And that is why, under the heading of the seventh limb on the chart under study, we find the world teacher, Swami Brahmananda, in the book, *Eternal Companion*, advising young people to receive a *mantra* from an illumined soul and dive deep with it, not just singing it for the emotional feelings that surface *bhakti* brings, or reciting it devoid of intense and supervised daily practice, like a parrot, but finding out the meanings and inner connections therein that will fuel meditation and bring about the direct experience of God — not just a mere, emotional show.

For what comes next, in the final limb, is the consummate word in spiritual life called "Seeing God in All." This all-pervasive vision comes to those whose ultimate goal is to not only *"....idealize the*

Nine Limbs of Bhakti
According to Sri Ramachandra

"Association with the holy ones, reciting accounts about the Lord, singing God's glories, hearing and transmitting God's teachings, devout service of the teacher, sense-control and ceremonial worship, repetition and contemplation of the Lord's mantra.....

Association with the Holy

"Through the company of the holy arises nonattachment; through nonattachment arises freedom from delusion; through freedom from delusion arises steadfastness, and from steadfastness arises liberation."
Shankara

Spreading the Teachings

"They who are well-grounded in knowledge, and who share their wisdom, who rejoice in freedom, full of Light, they win Nirvana even in this world."
Lord Buddha

Singing God's Glories

"What purpose can these ears serve if every sound is not heard as the sweet nectar of God's Name, flooding our eyes with tears of ecstasy?"
Ramprasad

Hearing the Teachings

"You will find Me in those sacred places where My names are being chanted and My teachings are being transmitted." Sri Krishna

Serving the Teacher

"Whoever is devoted to God, and delights in the service of the teacher, to such a person Moksha is an attainment already at hand."
Sri Ramchandra

Undergoing Purification

"If but one fiber is sticking out, it will be impossible to thread the needle. Likewise, if purification is not practiced early on, realization will not be possible."
Sri Ramakrishna

Selecting the Mantra

"Gain control of the life-force in a natural way. Through the practice of japam and meditation you will reach the stage of kumbhaka without risking the dangers which may easily come from the practice of asana and breathing exercises." Swami Brahmananda

Seeing God in All

"God is the act of giving, God is the offering, and by the Lord is the offering given into the Lord for consumption. The highest state of Consciousness is gained by those who see the Lord present in everything."
Bhagavad Gita

Realizing Brahman
"The scattering form of the mind is activity that manifests as pleasure and pain. The darkening form is dullness and tends towards injury. The gathering form is the struggle to focus. The one-pointed form is the tendency to concentrate, and the concentrated form is what brings us to samadhi." Swami Vivekananda

".....seeing God in all beings after attaining nonattachment, and investigating the true nature of Brahman — these are the Nine Limbs of true and authentic Bhakti."
Sri Ramachandra

real, but to realize the Ideal."   As the quote from Swami Vivekananda on the chart presently under study (page 497) relates, the sincere aspirant will have to make his or her way through lower states of mind before encountering such awesome and austere heights. Stopping short of the Supreme Goal, *Paragatam,* will not suffice. Ultimate Enlightenment will become the personal property of only those of serious demeanor and full commitment who will resolve to — as the title of our next chapter declares — "tread a trail of translucent teachings."

Treading a Trail of Translucent Teachings
The Highest Order of Wisdom Transmission

The wisdom knowers — those who court *Paravidya* rather than *Aparavidya* only — have found the singlemost superlative principle in the world in the *dharma*. *Dharma* comprises teachings of the highest order, precious pearls of insight and revelation that have been passed down for ages from transcendent nondualists to pure, desireless souls, from detached mountain yogis to world-renouncing ascetics, from illumined preceptors to highly qualified students, and from high-minded parents to their inwardly aspiring children. It is not a principle that courts either secular knowledge nor religious morality, but rather leaves them to the level of awareness that they both operate on, returning later to light them up with fuller understanding.

The *dharmi* is the opposite of the *samsari*, and counteracts the latter as well. Whereas the *samsari* is content to live in constant rounds of birth and death, never knowing the purpose nor the reason for his existence — nor even that he has many lives to live — the *dharmi* wastes no time, once in the body, in finding out the auspiciously marked pathway out of ignorance and along the translucent trail to ultimate Truth. Towards this end he swiftly locates the realm of the *dharma*, along with its glorious teachers, and immerses the body/mind mechanism in it for an extended length of time. *"Saturate the mind in the blissful ocean of Brahman and Its teachings over and over again, as you would repeatedly dip a towel in a lake,"* said Sri Ramakrishna Paramahamsa, for He knew that the obstinate and oft ornery mind would then obey its owner (*Atman*) and take it to liberation.

Thus, the seeker of *dharma* knows that it is the greatest purifier in all the worlds, and one that makes the soul ready for the grace of the Divine Mother as well. When She opens up the inner portals residing in the precious human mind/soul, *dharma* effloresces inwards, then falls like welcome rain over the parched recesses of dried up and withered human consciousness. This *dharma-megha samadhi*, or rain-cloud of sterling inner virtues, is sought after by all wisdom seekers and imbibed by all wisdom knowers, whatever religion they profess to and whatever philosophy they rely upon. It signals the death of ignorance. It brings about the clarification of doubt and uncertainty. It also allows for the intensity of spiritual practice that is so necessary for the mind's final shift to Witness Consciousness and beyond.

The realm of wisdom teachings, called the *dharma*, hold a profound twofold significance: one, it is infinite; and two, it is eternal. And whereas this is also true of *Brahman*, the Self/*Atman*, and even the worlds of name and form (*maya*), *dharma* will help the aspiring soul to realize the former two and transcend the latter. On a secondary level, *dharma* is infinite because no end can be found to it; its teachings rise and fall in and out of The Word like aromatic winds that incessantly blow thousands of miles in all directions. And where eternity is concerned, one will also never be able to find a beginning to this ongoing flow of intelligent particles. They carry the essence of pure, conscious Awareness in an unerring flow that streams mellifluously throughout the Three Worlds with the sole intention of enlightening the entire expanse of living beings in all locations, in all realms.

And it is this stream of intelligent particles that captures our attention at the beginning of this chapter, dedicated to higher wisdom. Each particle of it gathers our mind forcefully, like iron filings coming near to a powerful magnet, focusing awareness on what is real, what is true, what is beneficial, and what is essential. With our awareness coalesced in this insuperable fashion, we find that boredom is gone, lethargy is destroyed, restlessness is quieted, and distraction is no more possible.

It is from this inviolable position that the mind can turn back in on itself to behold and marvel over the source and origin of all its many projections. Of course, first it will discover that everything in the realm of name and form is a projection; this is a major insight that will change life altogether. And when the mind-soul finds out that it is the projector of everything, via its "flint-like intelligence" (see chart on page 272), then it may begin to experiment with its powers of withdrawal as well.

The *Jnana Matra*, or wisdom particle, is as least as ancient as anything in the physical realm, since it predates it all. Beyond ancient, then, it is timeless. 500 billion years is the blink of an eye of a god to it. It is the predecessor and processor of the atomic particle, both, perceived early on by luminaries as the *Atmic* Particle. The *Mundakopanisad* states that *Atman*, the ever-conscious inner Self of mankind, is *"anterior to life and mind."* Here, the *dharmic* teachings reveal to us that there is a subtler origin to the physical universe than, say, the material force of a "big bang," as is taught at the *aparavidya* level of Western thinking. And what to speak of an "intelligent design" that is, by the way, also posited as being material in nature, the *Jnana Matra* bespeaks of Intelligence itself *(buddhi)* as the subtlemost cause — not just of all things material in nature, but of all ancestral, heavenly, celestial, and cosmic realms and bodies as well. Here, one will need some basic understanding of Formless Reality to comprehend such internal marvels, and that is where the wisdom particle begins. It emerges from Formlessness as conscious force and proceeds to formulate the worlds, from the cosmic down to the physical.

The *Atmic* particle is the main subject of a book by the present author entitled, *Jnana Matra, The Wisdom Particle.* For this reason it will not be scrutinized in as fine a detail here as it is in that book. Interested readers and students of *Vedanta* may take it up in depth if they so choose to. For now, a basic run through of the wisdom particle's facets will satisfy our purposes, since there are a whole host of other teachings awaiting us in the following pages.

Suffice to say, that like any complete and self-sufficient cell of life, the *Jnana Matra* has all that it requires for its prime existence. In this way it is like the eukaryote of the spiritual realm, containing all potential for eternal life within it. Birthless and deathless, beyond creation and destruction, and opening the portal that splits the otherwise impenetrable line of demarcation between the twin realms of form and formlessness, this *atmic* atom is nevertheless at the hub of everything that takes form. All ideation and conception at their best originate from it, the only problem here being that its blissful streams of benign intention get obscured in minds that forget to remember it. Such is the influence of the covering power of *maya* *(avarana,* see page 293) in beings who succumb to it.

But for those who make these causal particles the focus of their awareness, unobstructed flow becomes the point of all life. They do not have to worry about decay and death, for this cell is wrapped around by the resistant force of retentive memory (of eternal life) and shot through and through by the pervading quality of intelligence itself *(chit shakti).* Wherever it flows it projects dynamic power that radiates revelatory light by its very nature. All this describes its cell wall.

The interior of this wisdom cell (described in detail in the aforementioned book) reflects a who's who list of spiritual tenets and philosophical principles. In the middle, and at the core, as it were, is the *AUM* symbol, with its four echelons/phases. This describes consciousness from the standpoint of the embodied human being, who experiences existence on four levels, i.e., waking, dreaming, deep sleep and transcendental. As the teachings of *dharma* have related, these must all be connected to one another. If they fall apart and disassociate, the result is fragmented mind and frantic life. Put another way, if the streaming wisdom particles are coalesced and concentrated, all the important inner connections are accomplished, and external life can go on in full swing. For more on this crucial teaching see all the teachings on *AUM* related in previous pages (136, 147, 154).

In brief about the other facets, it should be obvious by inspecting the chart that intelligence and memory are intrinsically interconnected. The weakened memory in human minds in contemporary times results in all manner of mental diseases, and early breakdown of the brain as well, but original memory *(smritihetu)* will not only waylay such maladies, it will open up inner vistas to remembering past lifetimes, along with all the knowledge gleaned there as well. Experiences aris-

ॐ Jnana Matra — Atom of Wisdom ॐ

"The bodies of beings which appear in the form of a framework of bones and sinews, is the self of the nature of food. Further within, is the self of Prana, split into five. Deeper still is the self of the nature of mind, different than these. Even deeper than it is the self of the nature of intelligence. At the deepest of all distinct levels is the self of the nature of Bliss....."

Protective Cell Wall
Smriti – Retentive Memory

Vyapakatma – Pervading Quality

Turiyatita

Smritihetu
Causal Memory

Guru-Bhakti
Devotion

Turiya – Transcendence

Samanya-vijnana
Settling Wisdom

Pratibha
Intuitive Intelligence

Jagrat – waking state

Sushupti – deep sleep state

Arupa-manonasha
Dissolving Power

Medha
Mental Acuity

Jnanagni
Wisdom-Fire

Kriyajnan
Spontaneous Knowing

Sakshi-Chaitanya
Witness Intelligence

Chitsakti – Force of Intelligence

Svapna – dreaming state

Sankalpamatra – Projecting Power

IMMINENT
PAST
SPEECH
TRANSCENDENT
PRESENT
LIFE FORCE
ABSOLUTE
FUTURE
MIND

"....food is pervaded by vital energy; vital energy is pervaded by mind; mind is pervaded by intelligence, and that ever happy intelligence is pervaded by Bliss. This self of Bliss is pervaded by Brahman, the Witness, the innermost of all. Brahman is not pervaded by anything else. Neither by action, nor by begetting children, nor by anything else – only by knowing Brahman – does one attain Brahman." **Katharudra Upanisad**

ing in the present life that are based in fear, shame, inadequacy, and a host of other problems will also be attenuated early on by tapping into the subtle memory residing in the wisdom particle. As can be seen by viewing the bottom of the chart (on page 501), time and its operations, and all of its three phases, are also stored in the *Jnana Matra*. The wisdom particle also contains a substantial amount of devotional element as well *(guru bhakti)*, which when utilized in conjunction with subtle memory, will take the aspirant straightaway to the spiritual teacher in any given lifetime, insuring that the course to freedom remain always open and accessible. For more on the *Jnana Matra*, the reader is invited to refer to the book with that title, which has over a hundred pages of teachings on the subject.

It could be asked how the wisdom particle works, and how to place it into operation — it being such a subtle principle, and rare of mention in this day and age. Another book by the present author *(Dissolving the Mindstream)* points to such tools by citing the method called *Dissolution of the Mindstream*. It is a technique of meditation used in various forms in *Yoga*, *Vedanta*, *Buddhism*, and other wisdom pathways. The chart on the facing page displays its method and elements.

The lower left hand corner of the chart under inspection reveals the Ocean of Consciousness, the Formless Essence into which all gets dissolved, and out of which all proceeds. Moving upwards on the chart, and in evolutionary style, the next two principles encountered are the Self, *Atman*, followed by The Word, *AUM*. In other words, when consciousness moves from formless Awareness outwards into causal and subtle shades of form, it will do so by stations. Streams of wisdom particles naturally emanate from The Word, and their powerful inner potential, as has been seen, will find these primal grounds to manifest in and upon.

The first of these is Cosmic Mind, or *Mahat*. This is intelligence at the Cosmic level, where intrinsic qualities lie in wait for activation. Ether, air, fire, water, and earth are present there, as also hearing, feeling, seeing, tasting, and smelling — but all in their causal forms only. As wisdom principles stream out and down from the *Mahat* to the *Antahkarana* (the fourfold mind of living beings) they will bring the power stored in these causal principles into the subtle realm for further expression. The reader should be aware that this is the formulation of the collective and individual minds of beings; its dissolution will be accomplished later, when involution takes place. But for the time being, this higher view of the evolution of consciousness fills the gap in contemporary thinking left by modern science, biology, anthropology, and other facets of *aparavidya*, revealing origins of much greater and more complex dimension. Here is where words such as God, *Brahman*, *Allah*, Yaweh, or Divine Reality, play into the wider picture.

The next phase of the evolution process is key, and is a puzzle piece that is missing from both science and religion of the day. Its absence in the ordinary mind's memory is also the cause of repeated failure on the part of spiritual aspirants who are attempting to move into the interior of consciousness and attain Enlightenment. This all has to do with *prana* — the *"Man does not live by bread alone"* teaching and principle. Down on earth, in the body, shallow-minded beings are giving out teachings on *prana* at the physical level only, therefore mimicking the perspective of science. But spirituality and *dharma* should never do so; they must always hand out the highest teachings for the ultimate good of suffering, struggling, and aspiring souls. The fivefold *prana* is indeed in charge of vitality, circulation, digestion, evacuation, and aspiration in the body, but there is a psychic *prana* that is equivalent to all five of these movements, which acts in the realms of mind, thought, and intellect as well. For instance, thoughts are generated and rejected by this *prana* in two of its forms, and the mind is rendered vibrant and vital by another of its forms. The teaching of physic *prana* is not taught in *yoga* schools, and for this reason the meditator who wants to go beyond beginning sitting and mere control of thoughts finds himself unable to move inward, say, to the *"Kingdom of Heaven within."* And without being able to move in subtle space (See chart on page 30 & 327), arrival at the crown of all spirituality, namely *Samadhi* of the formless kind, will not be possible.

Another teaching is the station found missing in the minds of present day aspirants called the *Tanmatras*; these are not provided for in most ideologies, Eastern or Western. Basically put, they are

Dissolving the Mind Stream

The Formless Meditation of the Upanisads

"When a sugar cube dissolves into hot liquid, it first breaks in half, then into small chunks, then into granules, and finally there is nothing left but sweet liquid. Similarly, when the mind moves towards authentic meditation, it first contemplates the dual world, then the many teachings, then living particles of its own intelligence, and finally enters full immersion. What remains then is one blissful, indivisible homogenous mass of pure, conscious Awareness." Babaji Bob Kindler

Samsara ——— Prag-bhara

Panchamahabhutas
The Five Elements
Earth ————————→
Water ————————→
Fire ————————→
Air ————————→
Ether ————————→

Dasendriyas
The Ten Senses
Smell (w/excretion)
Taste (w/procreation)
Sight (w/locomotion)
Touch (w/handling)
Hearing (w/speaking)

Mahat
Cosmic Intelligence

Projection	Causation
Sustenance	Solidity
Dissolution	Liquidity
Time	Luminosity
Space	Homogeneity
All-pervasiveness	

Antahkarana
Fourfold Mind
Manas
Chitta
Buddhi
Ahamkara
(w/Psychic Prana)

Panchapranas
Fivefold Life force
Prana (vitality)
Vyana (circulation)
Samana (digestion)
Apana (evacuation)
Udana (aspiration)

Tanmatras
Five Subtle Elements
Odor
Flavor
Visibility
Tangibility
Audibility

AUM
Pranava/Shabda

Atman
Indivisible Self

Kaivalya Prag-bhara

Ocean Of Consciousness

Brahman

"The classic and comprehensive meditation in Yoga and Vedanta dissolves the elements into the senses, the senses into the subtle elements, the subtle elements into the prana, the prana into the mind, the mind into the Great Mind, and the Great Mind into Om. Find Om in the Self, and dissolve that Self into the Great Self, Brahman."

the subtle elements out of which the gross elements will eventually emerge. Ether, air, fire, water and earth, contrary to popular thinking (or not thinking), do not come about by themselves. They are projected by a combination of the five senses and five subtle elements (*tanmatras*) — all connected to the mind, of course; to intelligence. Everything finds its way outwards in phases through this order of *tattvas,* then, driven by the force of Intelligence (wisdom particles). The physical universe in its entirety is only a product of mind. Its objects are actually mind made manifest, or thought concretized.

If the spiritual seeker after Truth wants to find the source of all origins, he/she does so in meditation using a method such as this. Sitting in deep silence and following the sets of fives inward (see chart of page 461), the meditator dissolves them and finds the formless Peace, Bliss, and Light that is at the hub of them all. This happens in deep sleep, and at the time of death, but is more effective if done in conscious meditation while in the body. A method as subtle as this requires a *guru*.

The *yoga* of meditation is extremely refined. It must be approached carefully and consciously. Instructions for it are rare, for each being will experience its dynamics variously. The results of it will come about slowly, as it is the final form of *yoga* to mature in most aspirants.

The chart on the facing page displays and teaches about meditation in its two forms via eight main types. Its two forms are obvious, being with form and beyond form. All methods of meditation fall within these two modes. Indian seers have always known that Divine Reality has two modes, and these they called *Saguna Brahman*, God with attributes, and *Nirguna Brahman*, God devoid of attributes. The former has mostly to do with levels of practice, and the latter with final arrival or ultimate attainment.

Under the first category, the initial type of meditation involves objects. Objects are seen by the ignorant to be opportunities for pleasure and ownership. But the former is short-lived, and the latter in not possible. One can neither enjoy nor possess that which is unreal by nature. So, the real efficacy of objects is that they are pointers to the existence of Divine Reality. Behind every one of them lies *Brahman*. The seeker has only to adopt the proper attitude of heart and perspective of mind to see It. Therefore, taking a *pratika* or *pratima* for the basis of meditation, the practitioner holds it in the mind until its essence is revealed. Quite often this essence will be related to the object, symbolic of it in some way. When a deep look behind outer forms is afforded the meditator, the entire realm of phenomena will be brought into question. Whether practiced in *Yoga, Vedanta,* or *Tantra*, this "negative" approach proffers substantial results.

A more inspiring way of proceeding in the meditative art is found is *Sukshma-dhyan,* meditation on subtle truths. Whether these truths are read in the revealed scriptures, or heard falling from the lips of an illumined preceptor, their effect is galvanizing. The practitioner only has to plant them deep in consciousness; the profound meaning inherent in them will do the rest. Memorization and aural chanting of these *slokas* or *sutras* plays an important part as well. In connection with the wisdom particle taught about earlier, each word and letter has something powerful to offer up. In short, the obvious meaning of the subtle truth may help destroy ignorance, but the hidden meaning in the letters and their implications could tear apart the entire fabric of false projection, all the way through the realm of the *devas* and *devis.*

And for additional help with this feat, the third mode of meditation on God with form proceeds by selecting and focusing upon a deity. These beauteous forms are lodged in higher awareness much like golden nuggets are buried in mountains. And they *"shine like burnished gold"* as well, as the *Upanisads* state. For help is finding the perfect deity to meditate upon, the seeker should approach another auspicious form known as the *guru*, or spiritual teacher. These beings have taken outer forms, making them excellent oracles for consultation. Some of them can even act as auspicious forms for the practice of *Vyakti-upasanadhyan.* To envision the deity as dwelling in the shrine of ones own heart is both an inspiring boon and a beneficial practice. No wonder that tens of thousands of devotees utilize this especial method for spiritual advancement leading to Enlightenment.

There is an exceptional Ideal, a superlative "form of forms" abiding in the heart as well. The

Two Forms & Eight Types of Meditation
Deification & Transcendence of Forms, Concepts, & Objects

S A G U N A   B R A H M A N

Create Realm

P R O J E C T I O N

Pratika-pratimadhyana — Meditation on Objects
"By meditation upon those objects which are most agreeable, the yogi's mind attains blissful equipoise." Lord Patanjali

Sukshmadhyana — Meditation on Subtle Truths
"To come to know the methods for removing desire, and how best to worship the acharya, the seer studies those scriptures which treat Atmic Reality and point the way to Self-cognition." Lord Vasishtha

Vyakti-upasanadhyana — Meditation on God with Form
"For many it is best to think of God as possessed of qualities and having a form. This way their minds will become easily concentrated." Swami Sivananda

Lila-dhyana — Meditation on the Avatar's Divine Play
"Lila as God, Lila as the deities, Lila as man, Lila as the universe; take delight in the Naralila." Sri Ramakrishna

Meditation with Form (*Saguna Brahman*)
· ·
Meditation beyond Form (*Nirguna Brahman*)

N I R G U N A   B R A H M A N

Acreate Realm

D I S S O L U T I O N

Tailadharadhyana — Meditation on One-pointedness
"The powers of the mind should be concentrated and turned back upon itself to penetrate the innermost secrets." Swami Vivekananda

Svarupadhyana — Meditation on the Inner Self
"The Self is master of the self; who else can the master be? With the finite self subdued, one obtains the sublime refuge most difficult to achieve." Lord Buddha

Brahmakaravrittidhyana — Meditation on Brahman
"Remain quiet, indifferent to the body, and by that one thought of Brahman, become one with Brahman." Sri Shankara

Layachintayadhyana — Meditation to Achieve Immersion
a) Bhuta-layachintayadhyan – of the physical
b) Antahkarana-layachintayadhyan – of the mental
c) Omkara-layachintayadhyan – of the initial cause
"When the mind is completely absorbed in the Supreme Being — Brahman, the world of appearances vanishes." Sri Shankara

"The practice of meditation will lead your mind to such one-pointedness that you will not want to give it up. But don't just seek God; see God! Does God exist only when eyes are closed, and cease to exist when they are open? Simply quiet the mind and practice." Sri Sarada Devi

final mode of meditation in the category of form appeals to this Being in its deepest contemplations. Termed *Ishvara*, or *Ishvari* if envisioned in the feminine, time is taken up and spent ruminating in the mind upon all the many deeds, feats, blessings, and profound teachings that this ultimate Being in form has bestowed, without number, on millions of living souls since time immemorial. *Liladhyan*, which is meditation of the Lord's divine sport in the realms of name and form, has all the elements necessary to retrieve the mind from any and all forms of suffering, and plunge it irretrievably into an ocean of inspiration. Further, since this incomparable form *(Avatar)* is of human origination, has walked on two legs in physical space and suffered all that human beings do over phases of time, then He/She is easy and natural to focus upon and contemplate. For instructions on how to approach and worship this supreme Being in form, one seeks the *guru*, or spiritual preceptor.

In the *Nirguna* category, where form has vanished as if into thin air, there are also four modes for the meditator to explore. Thus, everything below the dotted line on the chart (page 505) is "uncharted" territory as far as most beings of this age, in this world, are concerned.

The first mode is concentration itself. A host of ills will simply be wiped away if and when the individual learns the art of *dharana*, concentration. And in meditation, unlike all other occupations, that concentration must be "one-pointed," i.e., entirely focused, completely absorbed. For it is only then that the meditator can catch a glimpse of the essence of his or her own Awareness, the Self. This is not the individual self, *ahamkara*, but the indivisible Self, *Atman*. For seekers of Truth, the small self has already taken up way too much precious time, even lifetimes. Now, let the true Self come forward for worship. Perhaps that is why the *Svetasvataropanisad* states, always worth repeating: *"Meditate upon the Lord as thine own Self, seated in your heart."* This very statement clearly demonstrates how the meditator will move beyond forms like "the Lord" and find that selfsame divinity within. As the *sloka* from Lord Buddha in the *Dhammapada* on the chart (page 505) expresses it, *"The Self is master of the self; who else would the self be?"* Among other issues, this concise statement should clear the air between *Vedanta* and *Buddhism* as regards to the very word, "self."

And there is only one atmosphere that transcends this true Self, that being *Brahman*. In *Brahmakaravrittidhyan*, only one *vritti*, or vibration, is left for the mind to contemplate. All other thoughts get absorbed into That. Free of distractions, the illumined meditator can sit for hours, even days, contemplating the Peace and Bliss that resides There. Then, after a time, the physical, subtle, and causal levels of existence will all merge into It. This is *laya*, or *pralaya*, as the case may be.

To give a fuller idea of what India thinks of as form and formlessness, which will also give the meditator more depths to plumb, the chart on the facing page reveals the strata of consciousness, from outside to inside, and on into transcendence. Elements, objects, senses, planets spinning in space. vast oceans, and the individual body/mind mechanism — all these and more make up the gross realm of matter. And it is classed under the *saguna* heading because it falls under the overseership of the *Trimurti*. Traditionally termed *Brahma*, *Vishnu*, and *Siva*, these three prime divinities represent the dynamic powers of projection, sustenance, and withdrawal, respectively. They are the Cosmic Mind, and all worlds and their occupants — from the gods and goddesses on through to the celestials and ancestor and right on outwards to the earth plane — vibrate to Their bidding.

The chart opposite shows that the cosmic, collective, and individual realms, each accompanied by countless worlds and myriad beings, labor generally under the two *gunas* of *tamas* and *rajas*. Thus they are "*saguna*." As regards to mankind's consciousness, waking, dreaming, and a touch of the visionary level occur here; that is, few souls penetrate into or are even aware of what lies on either side of them in consciousness — above and below, as it were. Peace is rare here, illumination even more scarce. The main avenue here for sensitive souls wanting to refine their awareness and move inward to subtler existence is the path of devotion. As was mentioned in the meditation chart earlier, focusing on *Ishvara* is the highest meditation of its kind in the realms of form. *Ishvara* is not partial to any one religion, either. All souls move beyond religion when they travel inward to their own source, finding their preferred form as Krishna, Moses, Buddha, Christ, Mohammed, etc., along this divine trajectory.

"Do you know what God with form is like? Like bubbles rising on an expanse of water, various divine forms are seen to rise out of the Great Akasha of Consciousness. The Incarnation of God is one of these forms. The Primal Shakti sports through the Incarnation." Sri Ramakrishna *Paramahamsa*

Nirguna

Brahman

Gunas Transcended

Turiyatita

Formless Reality

"The jnani, through his discrimination, realizes that the ego and the universe are both illusory, and perceives Brahman in his own consciousness." Sri Ramakrishna

Formless Dynamism

PURE INTELLIGENCE

Turiya

Gunas in Abeyance

CURTAIN OF NESCIENCE

Mahashakti

Causal Form

Deep Sleep State

Saguna

Brahman

Sattva Predominant

"Higher than the Personal God is the infinite Supreme Brahman, who is concealed in all beings according to their bodies, and who, though remaining single, envelopes the whole universe. Knowing That to be The Lord, one becomes immortal." Svetasvataropanisad

PROJECTION   SUSTENANCE   WITHDRAWAL

Visionary State

"The bhakta feels that God is one entity and the world is another. Therefore God reveals himself to him as a person." Sri Ramakrishna

SHIVA

rajas Predominant

Trimurti

Dreaming State

Subtle Form

(Cosmic Mind)

tamas Predominant

(Collective Mind)

(Individual Mind)

Waking State

Gross Form

| Hearing | Feeling | Seeing | Tasting | Smelling | | Audibility | Tangibility | Visibility | Flavor | Odor |
| Speaking | Acting | Moving | Procreation | Excretion | | Ether | Air | Fire | Water | Earth |

Senses / Emotions

Objects

The lovers of the formless, and though they have a finer and more difficult pathway, court formless Awareness, or *Nirguna*. The doorway here is The Word, or *AUM*; It is the pool of infinite possibility that lies within the ecstatic realm of *Mahashakti*, the Divine Mother. The entrance here is paved with pure *sattva*, and man's consciousness gets swathed in an ultra causal state that resembles the rapt state of deepest sleep.

If the soul who wishes to merge into nondual Awareness can pierce through the subtle tendril *(vishnu granthi)* that separates this realm from formless Light, the transcendence of all three *gunas* will be attained, and *Nirguna — or Trigunatita —* will be attained. But the subtlest of dualities still flavors and colors this level of existence, namely the Light of Pure Intelligence on one side, and its paradoxical opposite, the "Curtain of Nescience," on the other. Thankfully, the Divine Mother's presence via formless dynamism is available to all who have the inner wherewithal to venture there, and Her Grace and supreme *mantra* act as guides towards the purely nondual State. For certainly, this is the realm of the *vijnani*, of souls whose spiritual realization is as powerful and penetrating in these deeper strata as it was back on earth in the physical body. And in fact, as Sri Ramakrishna Paramahamsa has related recently, this is the Great *Akasha* out of which fully illumined souls rise, like giant waves from an ocean without boundaries. May Peace be unto them, and may Peace come unto all!

Another helpful correlation can be made when the twin practices of meditation and prayer are taken up for inspection, as has been done on the chart on the facing page. Meditation, while, as we have seen, covers both the realm of form and formlessness, tends more towards transcendence as its final aim. Prayer, on the other hand, is useful and utilized only in the realms of form. In short, one cannot pray to the formless *Brahman*, or the Almighty Father. Whereas objections could be raised about this declaration, philosophically speaking, the schools of *Advaita*, or nonduality, make it clear that Absolute Reality is beyond both the appearances of creation and destruction, and completely free of any and all transformations that go on there. In short, there is no separate being to pray to There, where prayer, prayee, and the one offering the prayer are inseparably one.

If this is understood, then both of these tools for *sadhana* can be taken up and rightly directed towards their respective aims and ends. The chart opposite lists many of these, and also cites some cautionary elements as well. For instance, whereas prayer can connect one with the highest form of God that the devotee is seeking, and brings about succor and peace of mind in its train, it can also create dependency on external powers and bring about desire for gifts and boons that are better earned by individual self-effort. The most loving and devoted servant of God would rather not call on God for any and every little thing in life anyway, and will reserve such moments of closeness and spiritual intimacy for purposes of divine communion.

And this is where meditation takes up where prayer leaves off, or, if preferred, where the two connect and conjoin to facilitate the swiftest and best results. There is a famous story in India about the Wish-fulfilling Tree. This tree grants everything the devotee asks for. But the problem is, as is stated by so many beings, that most prayers do not seem to get answered. The story goes on to reveal that if one prays to the Wish-fulfilling Tree from a distance, the Tree will not hear; thus, no reciprocation will be forthcoming from it. The teaching comes through that coming near to the Tree is called meditation. Therefore, before one speaks to God the desires of the heart, one should first engage in a period of silent introspection to set the atmosphere.

Dangers in meditation are cited as well, for spiritual life is beset with these risks, particularly if the spiritual guide, or *guru*, is not consulted first. Also, the scriptures. The most classic of these risks are two in particular: first, the path of daily action can become less effective, even given up, if meditation increases beyond the balance set for it. Of course, if this is the desired end, as in the case where the meditator is resolved to renounce the world and all its activities, then this is a good thing, as they say. But if meditation takes away the need to provide for family via occupation, earning of money, and providing of food, as in the case of the *dharmic* householder, then it must be curbed, i.e., used sparingly until more capacity is developed and there is more time for spiritual life and practice.

Meditation & Prayer

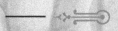

"Both prayer and meditation are crucial to spiritual life. The former connects the soul to its ideal in form, called the Ishtam, and the latter establishes the aspirant in formless Reality, called Brahman. The danger common to both is selfishness, for the ego mars prayer and meditation if there is the slightest sense of unripe individuality or personal gain associated with their respective practices.   Babaji Bob Kindler

Benefits of Meditation

1. Bestows objectivity on the seeking mind
2. Hones the power of right discrimination
3. Increases the ability for mature detachment
4. Introduces the subtle presence of nonduality
5. Ushers in the incomparable state of samadhi

Cautions/Limitations of Meditation

1. Can imbalance the mind if initially over-used
2. Can contribute to the growth of spiritual ego
3. May lull the mind into habit of complacency
4. Might disturb or stymie the path of action
5. Can keep the meditator from full realization

"Do you know what authentic meditation is like? One thinks of nothing else but God. The mind becomes like oil flowing easily into a pure receptacle."

Sri Ramakrishna

Advantages of Prayer

1. Establishes a connection with Ishvara
2. Helps in the development of peace of mind
3. Strengthens faith in the Chosen Ideal
4. Affords communion with God with form
5. Leads naturally to direct meditation on God

Disadvantages of Prayer

1. Weakens the soul if based on gifts and boons
2. Increases dependency on external powers
3. Fosters attachment to form, rites, and rituals
4. Maintains a sense of duality and dualism
5. Can cause forgetfulness of Formless Reality

"A worldly woman once entered the shrine. Her husband was ill, and she came there to pray for his recovery. Instead of being prayerful and penitent, however, she had covered herself with perfume. Does this become one who comes before God? Ah me! Well, such is the nature of these modern people." Sri Sarada Devi

And this brings up the other danger in meditation, that of imbalancing the mind if it is engaged in too much. The problems of falling short of *samadhi* due to dependance on meditation, as well as the development of a spiritual ego if not guarded against, are also considerations for the avid practitioner. All in all, when utilized in close conjunction with one another, prayer and meditation provide a subtly powerful element that secures spiritual growth for the aspirant, which is otherwise so rare in the realm of the physical plane.

The *darshana* of *Yoga* provides several good ways of explaining what occurs to the mind of the Truth seeker when formlessness is approached and attained. Here is where meditation reaches its most honed form-cutting edge, its most elevated pinnacle. The chart on the facing page gives the reader a step by step visual report, from the bottom to the top, of what the *yogic* aspirant might reach for, and what he or she may encounter in ascension.

The first three levels, as unfortunate as they may be, are examples of planes of the mind that require swift transcendence *(nirodha parinama)*. Imbalanced mind, dull mind, and restless mind place the soul in a state where it is unable to make progress and maintain it. The sidebars shown at each of these levels have already been mentioned and/or discussed in the pages of this book (255, 419, etc). It is at the fourth level, or *ekagra*, where formless meditation kicks in. This is also the realm of "seeded' *samadhi*, called *samprajnana*. It is characterized by inner vision, and the opening to inner wisdom that follows. The mind easily comes under full control at this juncture, and absorption can finally be experienced. These are the four levels of *yogic* mastery.

In conjunction with these come the seven levels of *yogic* attainment. The adept practitioner is able to actually transcend suffering and eliminate the causes of pain. Of course, this has occurred in the mind some time earlier in practice, but even physical pain and suffering are reduced, duly expunged, thereafter. This is not a miracle, nor does it mean that the body does not suffer disease anymore. What really happens is that the mind gets so caught up in subtle bliss and the other positive attributes of spiritual attainment, that the *yogi* hardly notices the body anymore. He walks about in an elevated state. This is a *samadhi* in and of itself, and it also aids this adept in fine-tuning the discrimination between the essential and the nonessential at a very high level. When this process is complete, the advanced *yogi* can transmit the essence of the teachings to others, which is an entirely different ability than merely teaching from a platform.

At the sixth level of attainment is where the *gunas* fall away, leaving the *yogi* free indeed. Teachings on the three *gunas* have graced this entire book, and can be reviewed again to provide further clarity (see pages 221, 223, 307).

It is only when the infamous three *gunas* of *Prakriti* leave off their influence on the aspiring mind of the *yogi* that true immersion into *Brahman* can take place. This experience is indescribable, and takes the now pure mind beyond mere one-pointedness and into the realm of formlessness per se, called *niruddha*. This level of transmission is beyond teachings, and is mentioned here as a sort of precursor to all that will occur in chapter ten of this book. The six secret gateways to *Yoga*, listed at the top of the chart on the opposite page, will also be taken up in that chapter, being a superlative teaching that deserves its own commentary. The Five States of the Mind Field, however —*kshipta, mudha, vikshipta, ekagra,* and *niruddha* — which form a well known teaching in the *Yoga darshana*, will be taken up for scrutiny later in this chapter. Used in correlation with the Dissolution of the Mindstream chart on page 503, this *yogic* version of rendering the mind liquid and lucid should help convey how the adept lover of Divine Reality gets transported in ecstasy when all the impediments of the ordinary mind fade away.

The hallowed *rishi*, Lord Vasishtha, has contributed some very worthy teachings on the dissolved mind as well, coming from an ancient time that rather defies history. Back in the time of the earliest human *Avatar*, Sri Ramachandra, Vasishtha counseled this unique soul when he was a young teenager, some time before other luminaries recognized him to be of Divine Descent. The profound subject of dissolved mind came up in a teaching session when the elderly seer mentioned *"a mind that had attained its natural state."* This statement intrigued the young Sri Ram, so he inquired of the

Stages of Dissolution of the Mind in Yoga

"O Mother of the Universe, my entire being is breaking apart. There is nothing left, but Thee."
Ramprasad Sen

Ekagra Parinama

Dissolved
Niruddha
Mind

Apply 8th Limb
Samadhi

Six Secret Gateways of Yoga
Knowledge of creation as vibration
Internal movement of particles
Particles as makeup of objects
Moments forming passage of time
Apparency of Time, Space, Causation
Comprehension of Eternity/Infinity

Brahman

Seven Levels of Attainment
7 Immersion in Awareness
6 Dissolution of the Gunas
5 Utilizing Discrimination
4 Perfecting of Discrimination

One-pointed
Ekagra
Mind

Apply 7th Limb
Dhyana

Four Levels of Yogic Mastery
4 Atikranta-bhavaniya — Absorption
3 Prajna-jyoti — Mastery of Mind
2 Rtambhara prajna — Wisdom
1 Prathama-kalpika — Inner Vision

3 Attainment of Samadhi
2 Eliminating causes of Pain
1 Renouncing Suffering

Chit Shakti

Samadhi Parinama

↑ (Samprajnata Samadhi) ↑

Restless
Vikshipta
Mind

Apply 5th
& 6th Limbs
Pratyahara &
Dharana

Seven Methods for Mastery
Practice of the 4 Aids • Contemplating Inner Light • Breath Control
Contemplation of the Alambanas • Recalling Dreams & Deep Sleep
Contemplating Guru & Ishvara • Meditating on a Spiritual Ideal

Five Aids to Steadiness
Utsaha — Enthusiasm   Dhairya — Steadfastness
Sahasa — Courage   Adhyatma-vidya — Seeking Wisdom
Mahat-seva — Service of the Great Ones

Nirodha Parinama ←

Dull
Mudha
Mind

Apply 3rd
& 4th Limbs
Asana &
Pranayama

The Nine Impediments
Vyadhi — Disease
Styana — Complacency
Samshaya — Doubt
Pramada — Negligence

Alasya — Idleness
Avirati — Sensuality
Bhrantidarshana — Confusion
Alabdhabhumikatva — Inability
Anavasthitatvani — Backsliding

The Four Distractions
Duhkha — Sorrow   Angamejayatva — Unsteadiness of body
Daurmanasya — Despair   Shvasaprashvasah — Uneven breathing

(The 3 Transformations of Consciousness)

Imbalanced
Kshipta
Mind

Apply 1st
& 2nd Limbs
Yama &
Niyama

The Five Obstacles
Avidya, Ignorance ——→ 8-fold veil to knowledge & body-attachment
Asmita, Egoism ——→ Bondage to the 8 siddhis and the 3 mohas
Raga, Attachment ——→ Enjoyment of the 10 objects of the senses
Dvesha, Aversion ——→ Failure to enjoy the 10 objects and 8 powers
Abhinivesha, Clinging to Life —→ Fear of losing the siddhis and ragas

"Asamprajnata is acognitive samadi, total control and cessation of vrittis, requiring no supports or alambanas, wherein samskaras can no longer produce kleshas and karmas — the Great Sleep of the Mind-field wherein the self dwells in the Self." Lord Patanjali

hoary old sage about its contents — and lack thereof.

The chart on the facing page reveals what Lord Vasishtha told Sri Ram on that auspicious day in antiquity, which is a precious teaching seldom given out to unqualified souls. This teaching of the *dharma* is set off well by citing the contents of the crystallized mind in contrast a pure one, a state that is all too obvious to the luminaries looking out on the world of living beings, but not at all evident to those caught in its limitations.

For instance, the crystallized mind is always and ever projecting devious and deceptive illusions with which to entrap itself and others. Never stopping to consider the ramifications of such thoughts and actions, it runs headlong into travesty after tragedy. The chart back on page 197, which is another teaching of Lord Vasishtha, is worth looking at again at this time. The main character, *Manas* by name, pursued such a troublesome course in rounds for many lifetimes, even failing to awaken and rectify his predicament when Lord *Brahma* took pity on him.

Lord *Brahma* and Lord Vasishtha are examples of the dissolved mind that never gets subjected to desires and illusions, that is never caught in the fundamental web of illusion. Having attained to eternal peace and bliss, they spend their time going about helping others free themselves. But as the chart relates, the crystallized mind fails to do so, and has fallen so low that it even rejoices in the misfortunes of others. As a result, this bound mind is constantly formulating *karmas*, unbeknownst to it, that snap back on it in future times and future lifetimes. When the crystallized mind sees an opportunity for pleasure, it will try to take advantage of it, and if that pleasure gets thwarted it will unfailingly revert to anger. The dissolved mind, however, has long ago destroyed the causes for anger and other passions to ever rise again. It prefers peace and takes its ongoing repose in bliss.

And in fact, one of the telling differences between the bound soul and the luminary with regard to their minds is that one is through with dualities and the other is plunged into everything that has to do with them. In an early age much like Sri Ram's, Sri Krishna counseled his devotee, Arjuna, to avoid any doings laden with these stultifying sets of contrasting dualities by saying, *"Beware of dvandva mohena, Arjuna, the bewitching pairs of opposites."* The illumined soul divorces himself from dualities, and duality itself, by always remaining in a nondual state of mind. This is akin to dissolved mind. Such a mind befriends all beings, on all levels of existence.

And this is another unfortunate problem of a soul with a crystallized mind; he/she is always at odds with all the powers of existence. As if it were not enough to place the self in jeopardy with the powers of the world and nature, this type of mind also acts in such a way as to alienate the cosmic powers as well. This is a grave mistake, and traps it on the wheel of birth and death inevitably. The god of death, *Yama,* will see to that. But as one song of India declares, the three gods of birth, death, and *karma* went looking for the illumined soul during one particular cycle. They could find no record of him being born or dying, nor could they find a *karmic* trail exuding from him like others leave behind. Thus, they dismissed their search for him and let him be. Like a bird that flies through the sky but leaves no trace, so to does the realized soul keep himself ever free, never bound, and he does so by dissolving the mind into *Brahman* while he yet lives in the body.

Another way of putting the illumined soul's marvelous condition is that he loves and worships — not just at the physical and individual level, but also, and most importantly, at the cosmic level. He/she makes fast friends out of the gods themselves via devout worship in the right and proper spirit. Thus, all beings come to love and recognize him. He is the famous "Eternal Companion" that all the most fortunate ones have heard of — even some of those bearing crystallized minds. These latter live not by love, but by fear, and the many souls inhabiting the earth plane can sense it. To even be associated with a being possessing a crystallized mind is to risk being infected with restlessness and imbalance. These types are known as "worldly" among spiritual circles, and they are given a wide berth by those seeking to be in harmony with God and gods alike.

Another story that the marvelous Lord Vasishtha related to Sri Ram in their auspicious and historical *dharmic* meetings follows along the same line of the dissolved mind. In those more ancient times an individual's spirituality was more accessible than today, in this darksome age, where few

Dissolved and Crystallized Mind

(From the Story of Iksvaku)

Sri Ram asks: *"What are the characteristics of a mind that has achieved its natural state?"*

Crystallized Mind	Dissolved Mind
Is always raising desires & constructing illusions	Cannot be stained by desires or illusions
Cares only for itself & rejoices in other's misfortune	Is ever considerate and beneficent
Negative karmas are constantly being formed	Past karmas and negativity have disappeared in it
Arises and reacts to every suggestion of passion	The impulse towards passion has been dispelled
Responds with anger when desire is frustrated	Anger has been destroyed and desire overcome
Pain and pleasure are its twin modes	Pain and pleasure do not afflict it
Erratic and caught in the net of duality	Equanimous due to transcendence of all dualities
Shuns pain and is unable to deal with it	Has risen above pain due to practicing forbearance
Is dominated by the lower cosmic powers	Has attained the love of the cosmic powers
Is obsessed with imperfection and out of balance	Thinks and acts in harmony while beholding beauty
Receives fear and avoidance from other minds	Gains respect and praise from other minds

"One needs a mind that has dissolved, but which simultaneously retains its spiritual element."
Lord Vasishtha

"That one fixed in unswerving equanimity of mind frees oneself in this life from virtue and vice alike."
Sri Krishna

"Having known this Atman, one should fix the mind and memory on nonduality; having secured nonduality, one should carry on the worldly activities like an insensate one."
Gaudapada

"The total insensitivity of the mind to external objects on account of bliss is Nirvikalpa. One should spend time in the practice of these forms of meditation."
Shankara

"For the aspirant after Truth, the mind must become like a towel dipped in a lake, until it is completely saturated, and fully malleable."
Sri Ramakrishna

people even believe in higher mind and its elevated atmospheres, what to speak of having access to them. On the other hand, spiritually awakened souls were referred to by the attractive and intriguing title of "Walker of the Skies." A chart on this principle is shown on the opposite page.

To comprehend the basic subtlety of this esoteric and cryptic reference, the word "skies" must be explained. In India, the word *"akasha"* would be used. In the materialistic West there is only one sky, and beings access it by looking up, "skywards." But looking "inwards' in meditation the *rishis* of India found several other "skies," or *akashas* (see charts of pages 30 & 327). If the reader remembers, besides *anna* (physical.food), they consist of *prana* (subtle energy), *chitta* (thought), *jnana* (intelligence), and *chid* (pure consciousness). The inward moving meditator, once discovering these *"Chambers of the Father's Mansion,"* to reference Jesus, becomes a "walker" in these inner territories or terrains. India philosophers utilize the different states of a human being's consciousness, such as waking, dreaming, and deep sleep, to refer to these subtle lands as well. Since contemporary man is so completely extrovert in every way, he/she does not even imagine that inner worlds exist, what to speak of moving within to explore them. The subject of involution is all about this opportune move, whereas evolution restricts one not only to one world, but also to strange ideas such as a one lifetime scenario ending in death. The essence of mankind, *Atman*, is birthless and deathless. How did he fall into such a stunted condition?

The storyboard opposite is based upon Lord Vasishtha's life story told to Sri Ram about Queen Chudala, herself a superlative walker of the skies. Souls such as her do not just acquire the special power to walk internally by accident, or due to some special grace bestowed by a creator god. They measure themselves to the task of *sadhana,* and do so in a universal and holistic sense and way. What they eat is examined with discrimination for its content and ability to power the body in a way that will open inner avenues to *prana,* life force. They take nothing for granted like modern man does, nor do they become the least unconscious in the realm of actions, thoughts, and deeds. When they have taken care of that which is their first responsibility, i.e., healthy food, a strong body, good posture, and even breathing, in *yogic* fashion, then they take up the mind and purify it as well. This they do with the help of illumined souls and their revealed writings, called scriptures. The passageways leading inward *(nadis)* may have to be opened again, just as an explorer would do if he visited a wilderness that he blazed years earlier. The undergrowth consisting of the six passions will need to be severly subjected to the machete of detachment from the five senses and their objects, so that these despoilers will not upset the soul's impetus of traveling along the inner pathway of spirituality and its attainment.

All of this fundamental purification serves to awaken subtle power within (*shakti*), the one thing that is sorely missing in those who are dull, ignorant, misinformed, narrow-minded, and weakened by the world, and by worldly ways. The nepenthe for all of these maladies lies within in the form of spiritual wisdom, *jnanam,* much different from secular knowledge, and far more refined. The worship that pleases the Mother of this Wisdom, Herself named *Kundalini Shakti,* also acts as propulsion inwards towards the heart, or *anahata chakra. "This is the worship that disappoints death,"* as Ramprasad, the poet-seer of India, sings, in one of his songs to the Divine Mother.

And here, as well as along the way of the soul's inward ascension, is where "walking the skies" becomes both fruitful and revelatory. The world, once so scintillating in its gross offerings, seems now like a "mere reflection in the muddy water that infills the hoofprint of a cow." Both contrasted and contrary to earthly existence stands Eternal Life, as spoken of for ages by illumined souls of the different religious traditions of the three worlds. What is more, these very souls are now found walking those same skies that the freshly awakened soul has just opened inwards to. Communion with them provides both deeper wisdom leading to unimaginable bliss.

This is what Queen Chudala found in her deepest contemplations on Divine Reality, a story of such ageless fame that it was known and told by the timeless seer, Vasishtha, to one of the earliest of human *avatars*, Sri Ramachandra. As this blessed Lord himself testified, *"When Kundalini Shakti is awakened and brought up and arrested in the heart chakra, Eternal Life begins."*

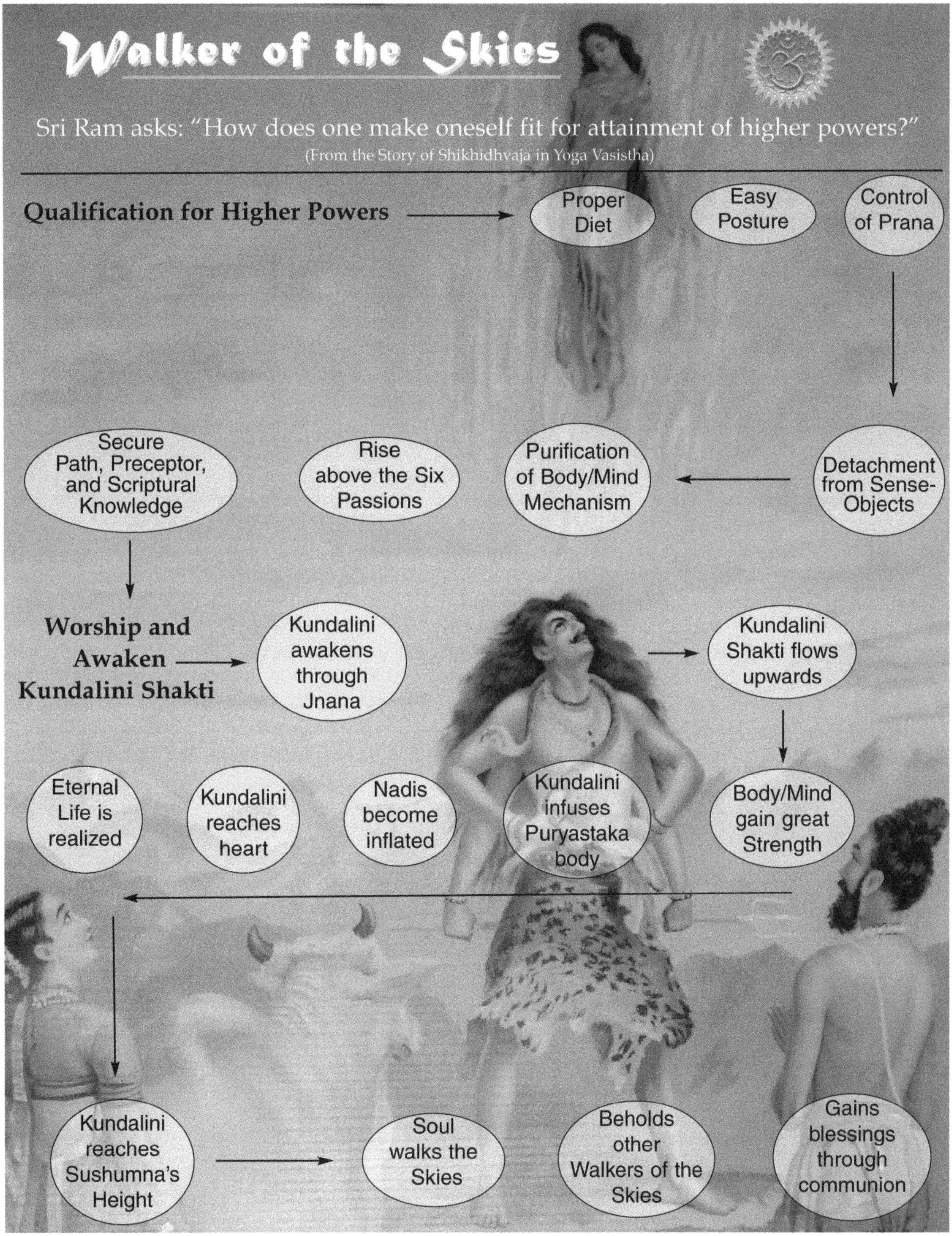

Walker of the Skies

Sri Ram asks: "How does one make oneself fit for attainment of higher powers?"

(From the Story of Shikhidhvaja in Yoga Vasistha)

Qualification for Higher Powers →

(Proper Diet)
(Easy Posture)
(Control of Prana)

(Secure Path, Preceptor, and Scriptural Knowledge)
(Rise above the Six Passions)
(Purification of Body/Mind Mechanism)
(Detachment from Sense-Objects)

Worship and Awaken Kundalini Shakti →
(Kundalini awakens through Jnana)
→ (Kundalini Shakti flows upwards)

(Eternal Life is realized)
(Kundalini reaches heart)
(Nadis become inflated)
(Kundalini infuses Puryastaka body)
(Body/Mind gain great Strength)

(Kundalini reaches Sushumna's Height)
→ (Soul walks the Skies)
(Beholds other Walkers of the Skies)
(Gains blessings through communion)

"If the Kundalini is brought up and arrested in the heart, Eternal Life ensues." — Lord Vasishtha

To take a page from the noble book of *Buddhism*, another India *darshana* of great repute, we look to *Zen* in Japan, some fifty-three generations after Shakyamuni visited earth. The principle of *Satori* permeates *Zen* teachings and experience. Record of luminaries who opened to it, being more recent in history, provide a fine record for the Truth seeker who desires to move, step by step, to the supreme Goal.

In much the same way as *Yoga*'s dissolution of the mind, and other systematic teachings gracing the early pages of this chapter, the grounds of *Satori* move forward to prepare the aspiring practitioner for lofty spiritual heights. And similar to the Walker of the Skies preparation, this system begins with *prana* and the breath as well. But unlike *hatha* exercises, *Buddhism* calms the breath by the mind, using the mind — a much wiser approach, probably suited for a more advanced practitioner. After breathing practices have widened to a mature count, the mind itself is taken up with regard to its thoughts and their quality. What is termed the "conventional world view" in *Zen*, is to be transcended, so working with the quality of thought forms the way. A powerful sign of progress is seen in the attainment of *Heikan*, or "closing the gate." The gate is, of course, the doorway of the mind that, in conventional beings, is always left open, letting in all manner of negativities and questionable vibrations. Much like *Yoga*'s *pratyahara* leading to *dharana*, a master of the stage of *Heikan* attains to absolute focus of mind, allowing for deeper and higher experiences of concentration to settle in.

And it is here where the famous inner occurrence of *Daishi* takes place. The ego element in the individual, which up until its demise is actually taken to be the individual, its true identity, lets loose its hold, and the "Great Death" finally takes place. Exactly like the *Yoga darshana* again, a realm of burgeoning insights similar to *Patanjala*'s *Dharma-megha samadhi* graces the practitioner, and this signals the advent of the first ground of *Satori* called *Kangi*. A supreme confidence builder, *Kangi* ushers in the attainment of *Joriki*, which like *Vedanta*'s *samadhana*, brings the ability to focus the mind in meditation, free of distractions, and for substantial lengths of time.

Remaining in blissful oneness of this kind gradually changes the perspective of the mind on deep levels. The meditator can actually spend very extended periods of time in this state, and the work that gets accomplished on inner levels is both legion and crucial for advanced *Satori*. This latter is known to have taken hold when the distinction between the meditator and what is meditated upon disappears. Known in other schools by the wording, subject-object relationship, the idea is that what is exterior consists of the same underlying Reality as what is interior.

And in fact, the distinction between the two, in the view of *Zen* and other nondual schools, is part of what impedes the attainment of *Satori*. In the koan tradition of *Zen*, this is where the *"woodcutter suddenly becomes a diamond cutter,"* for greater adeptship is demanded of the *Buddhist* practitioner at this time. Old tendencies and thinking habits will require removal at this higher ground of *Satori*, among them the erroneous view that the experiencing subject is somehow distinct from the phenomena that is being experienced. Necessary practices that early on require discrimination between subject and object are now put behind, and realizations that court the removal of all lines of demarcation come to the fore.

One of the best ways of explaining this further, at least as far as words can tell, is the teaching of *Goi* in Zen *Buddhism* (see bottom half of the chart on the opposite page). This refers to Five Degrees of Enlightenment that are noted as the practitioner advances along the spiritual path. Briefly, in the first, *Sho-Chu-Hen*, the meditator removes the idea of an evil or impure world from the mind and its thinking process, and looks to see it instead as a manifestation of Reality. As practice deepens, and *Hen-Chu-Sho* sets in, any and all difference disappears, and nondistinction takes the fore. Soon, with the advent of *Sho-Chu Rai*, thoughts of a separate world, a personal body, and even a individual mind, all disperse. This is the famous state of "emptiness," so valued in *Buddhist* schools, and particularly so in *Zen*.

This third degree of Enlightenment could easily sweep the field, leaving no more thought of further progression. But as the teaching of *Zen* Ox-herding relates (see chart on page 669 of this

Daigo-Tette — Grounds of Satori
Go'i — The Five Degrees of Enlightenment

"The Sutra of the Diamond-Cutter of Supreme Wisdom declares that all phenomena are projections of one's own mind. The work of cutting away all mental conceptualizations brings one to the furthest shore of Enlightenment." Prajnaparamita Sutra

Anahana – The calming of the breathing process by the concentrated mind.

Susokukan – Counting one's breaths in four stages.

Fushizen-Fushiaku – Transcendence of both good and bad thoughts, and thereby the limiting, conventional world view.

Heikan – "Closing the Gate," by transcending mental distractions.

Daishi – The "great death," the demise of the individual ego in Zazen practice.

Kangi-Zatori – Gradual, graduated Satori that approaches full Satori via a host of burgeoning insights.

Joriki – Mind power that allows for the unique ability to fully focus at will.

Joshin – Beyond focus, the mind can fully identify and get completely absorbed.

Ninkyo-Funi – "Person-Phenomena not-two," is the realization afforded by Zen practice wherein the erroneous delusion that the experiencing subject and the experienced object/world are different. Subject and object are really nondistinct.

- -

Go'i — Five Degrees of Enlightenment

* *Sho-Chu-Hen – The Relative in the Midst of the Absolute*
Seeing the world as a manifestation of the Absolute.

* *Hen-Chu-Sho – The Absolute in the Midst of the Relative*
Nondistinction has come to the fore, and the manifold begins to recede.

* *Sho-Chu-Rai – Experience of Emptiness/Shunyata*
Awareness of mind and body disappears.

* *Ken-Chu-Shi – Entering between the Two Polar Opposites*
Each state is accorded its uniqueness; emptiness vanishes in phenomena.

* *Ken-Chu-To – Arriving into the Middle of Both*
Form and emptiness interpenetrate, resulting in intentionless action devoid of thought and emotion, that suits whatever circumstances arise.

chapter), several more specialized stages are to be encountered. This is to say, that complete and formless transcendence is not the supreme goal of *Zen*; spontaneity in every second of life is, what may be termed by other *darshanas* as 'living in the eternal moment." This is to be understood by the fourth degree of *Satori* called *Ken-Chu Shi*, wherein the meditator abandons the position of emptiness and enters back into the realm of phenomena. Both meditator and what is meditated upon now appear as two unique realms of Awareness — a view that was not possible earlier until the other stages had been experienced and passed through. The complete and utter spontaneity of *Ken-Chu-To* is now most evident, and pure awareness beholds all of Reality as indivisible, but is able to encounter each moment, locale, circumstance, and object, in all of its inherent uniqueness.

As can be seen by now, the entire trend of the early section of the chapter presently under study focuses in on stages of spiritual growth. Called by the word *avasthas* in *Sanskrit*, and recognized as a crucial part of any aspirant's *sadhana*, these echelons of inward ascension mark and measure how close the seeker is getting to both penultimate goals, and The Goal, *Paragatam*. And though becoming goal-oriented is never a good idea in the shifting realm of the mind conjoined with spiritual self-effort, nonetheless some attention naturally falls on this important phenomenon.

The chart on the facing page, however, delivers some concrete suggestions along the way of spiritual advancement. Utilizing the famous hot-air balloon story of Sri Ramakrishna Paramahamsa, with its weighty sandbags just waiting to be cut asunder, the student and practitioner can take a closer look at higher mind to find out what to aspire to, as well as lower mind to get a clue on where to work on the ones self.

Noting that the entire chart is divided up the middle into two general realms of consciousness that are positive, *aklistha,* and negative, *klistha,* we can first take a look at the "moorings" that tie the balloon of the mind down to denser atmospheres of thought, when it really desires to soar high in the sky of pure Awareness. On the lower righthand side of the chart are listed the base moorings, inhibiting of anything inspiring, and really very frightening in their implications. Being ignorant at birth certainly does not sound at all like making a very good start in life, it is true, but it also suggests that there were possibilities to do otherwise previously, in other lifetimes and before taking another body — proven by the fact that there are souls who come into the body quite knowledgeable at the outset, and prone to intellectual advancement from the very beginning. For the *tamasically* oriented soul, however, attachment to the senses and their objects puts an early end to such boons, as does the increase of desire over a lifespan. Until this dull obsession with matter is curbed, no appreciable growth will be possible.

On the other side of this unhealthy tendency towards ignorance we find the soul who has gained basic knowledge but runs the risk of becoming arrogant and superior about it. The attachment for this "good" soul is to pleasures, and rather than dulness, restlessness is prevalent in it. This tendency drives him or her toward success in the world. Though a much better proposition than the negative set, these are all still moorings that bind the soul to the earth plane, and thus stimy spiritual progress.

Revealingly, the sandbags that are falling from the mind-balloon to provide more buoyancy tell another story. On the *klistha*, or negative side of the chart, inhibiting sets of botherations need to be shed, troublesome weights such as the three stupefactions, the four enemies of reason, the three deadly traps, and the eight fetters (see charts on pages 247 & 249). Note, as well, that attached to the balloon itself are the little red flags of the six passions. These are signs of danger that risk the death of spirituality in the embodied soul.

On the other hand, again, are the considerations that the aspiring soul has to encounter and face of with. Sandbags that will soon need severing from the mind follow the pleasure seeking that formulated this "good" soul's primal moorings, like aspiring for heavenly existence rather than for Enlightenment, remaining attached to lower knowledge instead of striving for wisdom, and finding temporary satisfaction and refuge in the ego and its relationship with limited bliss. The precious teaching, then, is that *"good and bad are chains that hold, one of iron, one of gold."* In other words,

Fashioning a Pure and Buoyant Mind

Dropping the Sandbags of Gross and Subtle Mental Weights

"Rainwater seeks the lowest place to settle. Likewise, the ordinary human mind becomes heavy, and dwells on lust and greed all the time. It is like the case of a hot-air balloon weighed down by sandbags so that it cannot soar. Thus, the wise soul frees itself from the sandbags of worldliness with the sharp knife of spiritual self-effort, and rises to inspiring heights, directly and effortlessly." Sri Ramakrishna

• • • • • • • SKY • • • • • • • • • • • • • • OF • • • • • • • • • AWARENESS • • • • • • •

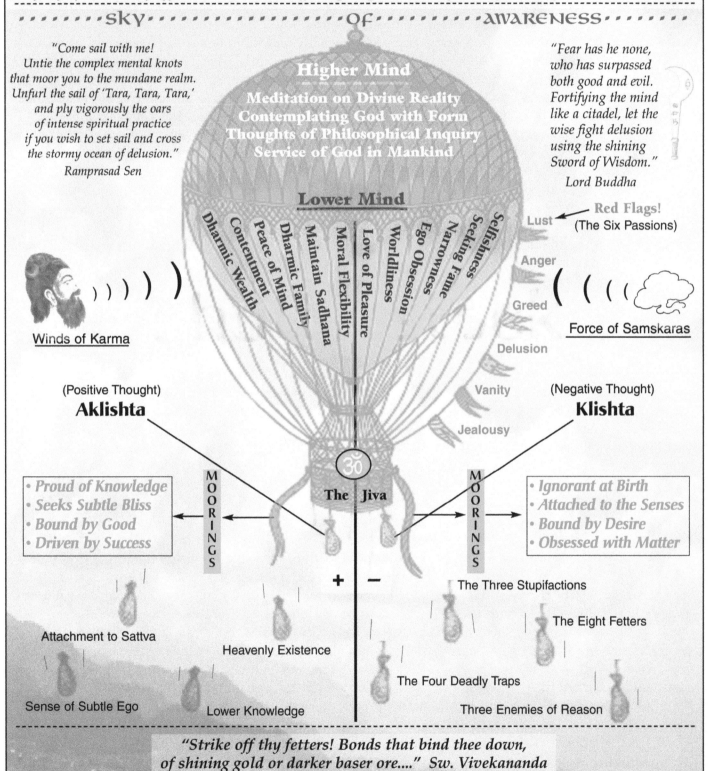

"Come sail with me! Untie the complex mental knots that moor you to the mundane realm. Unfurl the sail of 'Tara, Tara, Tara,' and ply vigorously the oars of intense spiritual practice if you wish to set sail and cross the stormy ocean of delusion." Ramprasad Sen

Higher Mind

**Meditation on Divine Reality
Contemplating God with Form
Thoughts of Philosophical Inquiry
Service of God in Mankind**

"Fear has he none, who has surpassed both good and evil. Fortifying the mind like a citadel, let the wise fight delusion using the shining Sword of Wisdom." Lord Buddha

Lower Mind

Dharmic Wealth
Contentment
Peace of Mind
Dharmic Family
Maintain Sadhana
Moral Flexibility
Love of Pleasure
Worldliness
Ego Obsession
Narrowness
Seeking Fame
Selfishness

Lust — **Red Flags!** (The Six Passions)

Anger

Greed

Delusion

Vanity

Jealousy

Winds of Karma

Force of Samskaras

(Positive Thought) **Aklishta**

(Negative Thought) **Klishta**

• *Proud of Knowledge*
• *Seeks Subtle Bliss*
• *Bound by Good*
• *Driven by Success*

MOORINGS

The Jiva

ॐ

MOORINGS

• *Ignorant at Birth*
• *Attached to the Senses*
• *Bound by Desire*
• *Obsessed with Matter*

+   −

Attachment to Sattva

Heavenly Existence

The Three Stupifactions

The Eight Fetters

The Four Deadly Traps

Sense of Subtle Ego

Lower Knowledge

Three Enemies of Reason

"Strike off thy fetters! Bonds that bind thee down, of shining gold or darker baser ore...." Sw. Vivekananda

there is no safe haven or abiding refuge in relativity; only in Reality, or *Brahman*. Souls that undergo purification of a more refined kind will need to know this and practice to attain the liberation of transcendence.

Taking a closer look at higher mind and the requirements for its valued possession, it is seen that the dualities associated with them are finer; it is really ones perspective and attitude that must make a shift. This is especially notable in the positive category of the lower mind, shown on the actual balloon itself. The chart there (page 519) lists morality, but intimates that a certain flexibility is needed. Coming to know that pleasures are dangerous due to the attachment they breed, and that they get associated with the desire for heavenly existence in celestial realms, the more informed soul takes to teachings on spirituality and its attainment and allows the moral lessons to fall where they may. This man or woman of ethics now begins to steer life and mind towards *dharmic* teachings that refine consciousness, rather than leave it lying fallow in the realm of lower pursuits and lesser ideals.

One of the signs of such inner advancement is that the mature, spiritually-oriented practitioner also directs the entire family, especially children, to and along this life-saving *dharmic* avenue as well, as the chart displays. Such a high-minded individual knows that the precious qualities of peace of mind and overall contentment are not only hard to come by in today's world, but that what can happen to living beings in their absence is even worse. A full life complimented by every opportunity for success may be stifled, and the soul brought up short without the crucial kind of balance that peace of mind affords.

The final entry on the chart under this category, that of *dharmic* wealth, will also not be possible without mental balance and peaceful thoughts. The mind seeking to affect its timely graduation out of the nominal considerations of everyday life and successfully enter into the more peace and bliss-filled climes of higher mind will meet with failure otherwise.

And so again, the lesson comes forth that the aware possessor of dual mind, where good and bad, pleasure and pain, virtue and vice, and positive and negative all reside, must seek to unify the mind-field if any consummate fulfillment is to be gained within the realm of human embodiment. For, there are at least two other serious considerations to face off with, they being the force of the winds of *karma* on the balloon of the mind, and the heretofore hidden *samskaras* that are acting on it as well. To study again the profound teaching on the subtle mental impressions created by the individual due to actions in previous lifetimes, called *samskaras,* see the two charts on the subject on pages 167 and 170. Revisiting that *dharmic* teaching will convince the mind further, if any such convincing be necessary, that there are mental stains on the interior of the mind, at both subconscious and unconscious levels. And this is an additional reason to seek higher mind, where qualities that alleviate such mental residuals lie waiting for discovery and application.

As for the winds of *karma* (see charts on page 184, 210, 213, & 216), the mind is most susceptible to them, and without some ability for transparency it will simply get blown here and there at random, with no rudder to steer it, unable to follow a wise direction — if such even be known. This beneficial transparency is difficult to describe, but it can be said that it equals the egoless state, for the narrow sense of individuality is what got the soul into *karmic* predicaments in the first place. The infamous "I, me, and mine" that Sri Ramakrishna warned against may as well be three additional weights attached to the wind-blown balloon, each influencing it in different directions simultaneously. Revealingly, the entries under lower mind on the chart under study, if inspected closely, will be seen to reflect nothing short of ego and its doings. To divest oneself of *ahamkara,* then, the ego element present in every act, word, deed, and thought, although a tall order for the aspring soul, is nevertheless one of the wisest moves the mind can make for its own highest good. Higher mind, or nondual mind, will then be within its grasp, along with a host of transcendent virtues that will put *karma* to death for all time and reduce *samskaras* to mere burnt strings that cannot bind anymore.

With all of this disclosed, higher mind itself can be taken up and scrutinized, utilizing the short list that appears at the top of the balloon on the chart under study (page 519). What this quartet of stunning entries actually represent are the Four *Yogas* of *Vedanta* philosophy (see charts on page

431 and 433 in the previous chapter). What order to take them in is always rather a puzzle, for beings with different *karmas, samskaras,* and personalities, all possess different capacities, and require different modes of healing and spiritual sustenance as well. Generally speaking, the noble *Vedanta* usually advises that ignorance be removed from the mind, as far as possible, before the seeker enters into the three other fields of action, devotion, and meditation. If we take Lord Buddha's advice and encouragement, appearing on the right hand side of this chart (page 519), we will see that *"....the wise aspirant must fight delusion with the shining sword of wisdom."* This is perfectly true in the case of the serious aspirant, but does not necessarily apply to the beginner who may take to the early exercises of devotion along the *Bhakti* path, or to the adept and luminary, of course, who has already integrated the Four *Yogas* (see charts on pages 431 & 433) and is experiencing various *samadhis.*

But whatever the case may be, each of these Four Yogas, when properly implemented, purify and inspire the major chambers of the mind, and once the *guru* has been located and spiritual practice begins in earnest, it will become obvious or revealed to the sincere seeker which *yoga* needs to be implemented and mastered first. Eventually, a synthesis of *Yoga* will abide in the mind, and this defines higher mind quite well. If mind *(manas)* can be rendered nondual, the intellect *(buddhi)* honed via *dharmic* teachings, the ego *(ahamkara)* reduced to a servant of God via self-surrender, and the thoughts *(chitta)* made buoyant and caused to flow towards Divine Reality alone, Higher Mind is then present and in charge of all the facets of existence that it projected. If this is not attempted, and accomplished, the fourfold mind just listed *(antahkarana)* will fall or remain in relative existence.

Relative existence is everything shown on the chart from the words "Lower Mind" on down. It is a "mixed bag," as they say, with some very good elements present, but some real despoilers as well. One only has to look deeply at life to see that it is an admixture of qualities — positive, negative, and mixed. Lord Buddha's teaching of the Four Noble Truths (see chart on page 229) exemplifies this fact. This is precisely what has led illumined souls like Him to find a way out of relativity, and caused so many thousands of beings to attain transcendence of all of its confounding aspects and learn to live in a state of absolute equilibrium — even on earth, right here in the human form, as far as possible.

These great beings and their unique ways of living amidst relativity are what gave way to the birth of so many of India's radiant systems of Religion and Philosophy. The next three or four charts up for commentary will reveal them all, or as many as can possibly be counted. For *Bharat,* Mother India, was never one to limit Herself or Her peoples to one holy book and one prophet. Her nature is Universal — in the highest and deepest sense of the word. Out of Her infinite storehouse of truth-filled tenets came an abundance of scintillating spiritual systems, any one of them capable of leading millions of souls to liberation (see charts on pages 315 & 317).

For, again, it was never Her intention that living beings become satisfied with a slavish salvation, or seeking to survive by mere hope, or dependent upon a savior figure. Since the true nature of mankind is *"ever free, never bound,"* to quote Swami Vivekananda, then that freedom, and nothing less, is to be brought out, taught, mastered, and transmitted to others, in as many clear and direct ways as possible.

How She accomplished this feat in such a contrary and disinterested world full of worldly antagonists and religious hypocrites is an authentic miracle. Similar to a molten flow of lava that goes underground into tubes so as to remain liquid in order to reach the ocean, India's streaming religious and philosophical movements with their many sects, lineages, and *sampradayas,* got covered over by tough and resilient shields of *dharma*-teaching tunnels that protected them from the eroding effects of time, and from fundamentalist meddling and text torturing by narrow, ignorant minds. That is one reason why, even today, an interested student can pick up a sacred *Upanisad* of India, translated into a number of contemporary languages, and find the nondual Truth being expressed through it immediately, even without having to search deeply or read behind the lines.

The chart on the following page profers a fine reading of this winning fact, showing not only how such tomes and their teachings have filtered down through time into their present forms as

Mother India's Revealed Scriptures On Earth

"The revealed scriptures and spiritual preceptors of the world have their existence through the Atman. Faith, devotion, and constant communion with the wise — these are declared by the scriptures to be the seeker's direct means to realizing It. It is hard for any embodied being to achieve a human form, strength, and purity. More difficult still is the desire to live a spiritual life. And hardest of all is cultivating an ability to comprehend the holy scriptures." Shankara

Panchakarana

Hiranyagarbha — Mahat, Buddhi, Ahamkara, Manas, Chitta → **1**

Tanmatras — Shabda, Sparsha, Rupa, Rasa, Gandha → **2**

Jnanendriyas — Shravenindriya, Sparshendriya, Chakshurindriya, Rasenendriya, Ghranendriya → **3**

Karmendriyas — Vagendriya, Hastendriya, Padendriya, Upasthendriya, Payuindriya → **4**

Panchamahabhutas — Vyoma, Marut, Teja, Ap, Kshiti → **5**

Cosmic Intelligence

Cosmic Mind
Intellect
Ego
Mind
Thought

Audibility
Tangibility
Visibility
Flavor
Odor

Hearing
Feeling
Seeing
Tasting
Smelling

Speaking
Handling
Locomotion
Procreating
Excreting

Ether
Air
Fire
Water
Earth

Cosmic Projection

Quintuplication Process

108 Upanisads
Bhagavad Gita
Brahma Sutras

Srimad Devi Bhagavatam
The Chandi

Ashtavakra Samhita
Avadhuta Gita
Adhyatma Ramayana
Gaudapada's Karika

The Four Vedas
The Eighteen Puranas
The Sixty-four Tantras
The Ramayana
The Mahabharata
Srimad Bhagavatam
Uddhava Gita
Narada's Bhakti Sutras
Sandilya's Bhakti Sutras
The Code of Manu

Tattva-Samasa-Sutras
Patanjali's Yoga Sutras
Jivan-Mukti-Viveka
Panchadasi
Dhammapada
Yoga Vasishtha

Vivekachudamani
Aparokshanubhuti
Drg-Drsha-Viveka
Atmabodha
Tattvabodha
Vedantakeshari
Prapancha Sara
Atma-Anatma-Viveka
Mohamudgara
Vakyavritti

Gospel Of Sri Ramakrishna
Complete Works of Swami Vivekananda

"I have never lost faith in a benign Providence, nor am I ever going to lose it. My faith in the true religion and revealed scriptures is unshaken." Swami Vivekananda

scriptures, but also how they have done so via an intricate and comprehensive cosmology. Like the steel hull of a mighty ship that is watertight and impervious to penetration, the precious cargo of Mother India's eternal wisdom teachings were transported to earth via sound minds and immovable principles, both working together in the spirit of compassionate amelioration for the highest good of mankind. The problem with a cargo of static principles, however, is that they may just sit in port when the ship docks, remaining undiscovered. Therefore, the Mother of the Universe plants these potent forms of nutritious teaching into the hearts and minds of saints and seers, and sends them to earth. Their footfalls, as the chart opposite reveals, then seed the world and the human mind with all the potential for spirituality that is needed.

And it is quite a process, this transmission of Truth and Wisdom leading to spirituality. As the sidebar on the far right of the chart displays, and in conjunction with the list of *tattvas* (principles) down the middle, all of these are really stations for consciousness; this is their real purpose, not pleasure, pain, enjoyment, fame and fortune, or even just for living a life. Cosmic Intelligence flowing through all its mediums — from Cosmic Mind to human mind and on to animate the senses and the elements of matter — should arrive at the outermost stations called the body and the world in full possession of its higher purpose, and certainly not in utter forgetfulness of its essence.

But, of the five footfalls shown on the chart, steps "1" and "2" are forgotten by embodied souls when they take on a body on earth, and the other three footfalls are, as has been intimated above, taken for granted, i.e., not seen as stations for consciousness to inhabit and express itself, but rather as means for mundane life. As a result, suffering and misery find an avenue of entrance into the increasingly humdrum everyday existence of embodied beings.

But the divinely intended purpose that should occur among the denisons of the physical plane is seen at the bottom half of the chart under study. There we find a list of scriptures of Mother India designed to fully illumined the mind of the *jiva*, or, if this is not yet possible, at least remind it of its divine nature and its essential Source so that it can effectively seek Enlightenment.

This copious list of revealed wisdom scriptures covers the entire gamut of gradated divisions that are suitable for seekers at every level of the search for Truth. Primarily, there are the three landmarks of scriptural history, or *Prastanatraya*. The *Brahman Sutras,* the *Bhagavad Gita,* and the *Upanisads* make up this especial category. The first is to be studied with a teacher of nonduality, being very difficult to penetrate; the second, obversely, is very accessible, and can be read prior to approaching the *guru* about its teachings. The final one is actually a collection of 108 divine scriptures which form the very substance of India's teaching transmission, and which is the focus of the *Vedanta* as well. The chart on the following page (524) shows a copious list of all of them, appearing within the hoary pages of the Four Vedas from which they originated. The ones that are underlined on the chart are those which were studied deeply and commented on by the *Avatar* of *Siva,* Adishankaracharya, about the eight century when he occupied the body. These ten, eleven if the *Svetasvataropanisad* is included), are most authoritative thereby, having had the light of a great mind shed upon then in current times. The reader and student will benefit greatly by seeing the comment by Shankara that appears on the top of this same chart, which expresses in a few words the main import of the entire chart, with all of its ramifications.

To complete commentary on the *Upanisads* chart first before finishing the chart on the facing page, a condensation of the ten major *Upanisads* is given out next, stating the essence of what each contains in a few words:

Isha Upanisad — Predominantly deals with all stages of growth, and the relationship of action and knowledge.

Kena Upanisad — Deals with the oneness of *Atman* and *Brahman.* Also contains the famous story of the *devas*/gods first seeing of the Divine Mother of the Universe.

Katha Upanisad — Preeminently about Self Knowledge, and what occurs to the soul after death.

Prasna Upanisad — Describes the creation/projection of all living beings, and discusses *prana.*

Mundaka Upanisad — Contrasts lower and higher knowledge, inspects separation and ignorance, and

The 108 Upanisads

Rig-Veda & Its 10 Upanisads	Aitareya	Kaushitaki-Brahmana	Nada Bindu
	Aksha-Malika		Nirvana
	Atma-Bodha		Saubhagya-Lakshmi
	Bahvricha	Mudgala	Tripura

Yajur-Veda & Its 51 Upanisads

Sukla-Yajur →

Adhyatma	Isavasya	Niralamba	Tara-Sara
Advaya-Taraka	Jabala	Paingala	Trisikhi-Brahmana
Bhikshuka	Mandala-Brahmana	Paramahamsa	Turiyatita-Avadhuta
Brihadaranyaka	Mantrika	Satyayaniya	Yajnavalkya
Hamsa	Muktika	Subala	

Krishna-Yajur →

Akshi	Ekakshara	Maha-Narayana	Suka-Rahasya
Amrita-Bindhu	Garbha	Pancha-Brahma	Svetasvatara
Amrita-Nada	Kaivalya	Pranagnihotra	Taittiriya
Avadhuta	Kalagni-Rudra	Rudra-Hridaya	Tejo-Bindu
Brahma-Vidya	Kali-Santarana	Sarasvati-Rahasya	Varaha
Brahma	Katha	Sariraka	Yoga-Kundalini
Dakshinamurti	Katharudra	Sarva-Sara	Yoga Sikha
Dhyana-Bindu	Kshurika	Skanda	Yoga-Tattva

Sama-Veda & Its 16 Upanisads	Aruni	Jabali	Maitrayani	Savitri
	Avyakta	Kena	Maitreya	Vajrasuchika
	Chandogya	Kundika	Rudraksha-Jabala	Vasudeva
	Darshana	Maha	Sannyasa	Yoga-Chudamani

Atharva-Veda & Its 31 Upanisads	Annapurna	Devi	Mundaka	Rama-Tapaniya
	Atharvasikha	Ganapati	Narada-Parivrajaka	Sandilya
	Atharvasiras	Garuda	Nrisimha-Tapaniya	Sarabha
	Atma	Gopala-Tapaniya	Para-Brahma	Sita
	Bhasma-Jabala	Hayagriva	Paramahamsa-Parivrajaka	Surya
	Bhavana	Krishna	Pasupata-Brahmana	Tripadvibhuti-Mahanarayana
	Brihad-Janala	Maha-Vakya	Prasna	
	Dattatreya	Mandukya	Rama-Rahasya	Tripura-Tapini

outlines teachings on the life-heavens and the illusion of death.

Mandukya Upanisad — Discussion on *Atman* and *Brahman,* the nature of inner and outer worlds, the nature of Consciousness, and the meaning of causality — all in terms of The Word, *AUM.*

Chandogya Upanisad — Deals with the many rituals of India, and the doctrine of nonduality via *Mahavakyas* like *Tat Tvam Asi.* *Atman* and Infinity are also taught.

Brhadaranyaka Upanisad — The identity of *Atman* and *Brahman, Saguna Brahman,* the interdependance of all things, how to attain both prosperity and liberation, and the line of succession of teachers are all taught.

Aitareya Upanisad — The nature of the *Atman,* the assumption of bodies by the transmigrating soul, *Atman* and the projected worlds, and the teachings of *Adhyaropa* and *Apavada* are taken up.

Taittiriya Upanisad — The five sheathes over *Atman,* fearlessness, bliss, and pronunciation, are all emphasized.

Svetashvatara Upanisad — The three stages of philosophy, the personal god and its relationship to the Impersonal, *Sankhya,* and Theism are included. (Shankara's commentary for this *Upanisad* is not confirmed, though probable).

To receive an even more stunning message around the existence of these 108 wonders of the spiritual realm, the reader and student are invited to read the quote from Swami Vivekananda at the top of this chart (facing page). All the rationale, as well as all the permission (if it is even needed) to pursue the freeing wisdom of India's sacred scriptural offerings is provided in that pithy statement.

Returning to complete the teachings of the chart on page 522, the additional scriptures that are listed there form a considerable lot. The spiritual aspirant who can complete study of these revelatory testaments to pure, conscious Awareness, and then contemplate them in the atmosphere of an open mind, will have the inner worlds based upon The Word revealed to them. The nature of *Brahman* will also occur more and more to the embodied soul, finally breaking apart all doubts around the matter.

A list of secondary scriptures also fall on the chart, right under the *Prastanatraya.* *Puranas,* *Tantras, Srimad Bhagavatam, Ramayana* and *Mahabharata,* as well as several of the *Bhakti* scriptures of Narada and Sandilya are all more than worthy of deep study and memorization. Next to this revered list appears noble scriptures, some of which have more to do with India's orthodox and nonorthodox *darshanas* like *Yoga, Sankhya,* and *Buddhism.* Knowledge of these collections of liberating insight, schools the aspirant deeply in the wisdom pathways of India, but more importantly, provide ways of actually embarking on these radiant roads to Reality after ignorance has been destroyed by their study.

Important, even crucial of note, are the two Divine Mother scriptures that are included on the chart. Both the *Chandhi* and the *Srimad Devi Bhagavatam* will figure in prominently towards any future growth and realization that may occur among the peoples of the present era and age. Already, and due to Sri Ramakrishna Paramahamsa's advent in the 1800's, millions of souls are turning within again to take refuge in the Goddess of Wisdom, known by such august names as *Kali, Durga, Sarasvati,* and *Tara* — also *Mother Mary, Fatima,* and *Prajnaparamita.* That there exist even two holy scriptures about Divine Mother to take recourse to in modern times is a fantastic boon.

At the far right on the chart under study (page 522) appear two lists. The first list is essential due to the rarity and the profundity found there. Known specifically as "nondual scriptures," they transmit the unique perspective of *Brahm'advitiye,* or "Oneness without a second." It is said that The Great Master, Sri Ramakrishna, though not in need of books or scriptures of any kind, nevertheless kept a copy of the *Astavakra Samhita* nearby, such is its import based on its superlative description of the Indescribable One. He also had Narendranath, the soon to be Swami Vivekananda, read from it when he was a young man, thus helping to both plant within and bring forth current expressions of Nonduality for the modern world today.

Below this important list falls another, some ten scriptures written by Shankara himself. He was actually the seer and author of many more as well, showing him up to be an *amsa-avatar,* a divine incarnation of Lord *Siva*. Born illumined and fully realized, he recalled all the scriptures of Mother India to his amazing mind before he was ten years old, and was thus teaching graybeards when he was just a young man. His lofty commentaries, as was stated above, both revived India's *Vedanta* after the decline of the Buddhist age, and kept both the nondual Truth of *Advaita Vedanta* and the revealed scriptures protected and flowing, like molten lava, into the minds of striving beings and the world in a rapidly darkening age.

To bring the point of this multifaceted chart home, the final two entries on the list of scriptures on this chart are purely contemporary. The *Gospel of Sri Ramakrishna* and the *Complete Works of Swami Vivekananda* will be of great interest and benefit to all current seekers after the *dharma*, and its end result of Enlightenment. These two collections are indispensable to the moderns, holding as they do myriad keys to the import of the Eternal *Dharma* of Mother India, the principle of Eternal Life, and the identity between the apparently individualized soul *(jivatman)* and the Supreme Soul *(paramatman)*.

Since the subject of the great seer, Shankara, has made another welcome appearance, and in relation to the revealed scriptures he so deeply loved, clearly revealed, and thoroughly commented on in the brief 32 years of his recent incarnation, the chart on the facing page takes up his conclusions of the scripture, *Vivekachudamani* — possibly his most profound spiritual composition, and certainly his most well known,

A *siddhanta* is an apt conclusion, arrived at after deep introspection by the luminary. In the *darshana* of *Yoga*, it takes what is termed a *samyama* in order to finalize some great spiritual realization. This comprises a combination of concentration *(dharana)*, meditation *(dhyana)*, and realization *(samadhi)*. After an expansive treatment of his various subjects in the *Vivekachudamani*, Shankara wraps up that great scripture in its final pages with certain salient facts that are specifically nondual in nature. These are drawn around the unique soul who has attained *jivanmukti*, a living liberated condition that attends the luminary, even while in the body.

For instance, such a being can live anywhere, even in a city dwelling, and still remain free of all attachments and temptations. His bed can be laid therein, or in a forest, and it matters not to him whatsoever. The food he takes is whatever comes naturally to him on any given day or time. As Vivekananda has put it in his *Song of the Sannyasin*, *"....the sky thy roof; the grass thy bed; and food, what chance may bring, well cooked or ill, judge not. No food or drink can taint that noble Self which knows Itself. Like rolling river free thou ever be...."*

And these are merely the luminary's natural and unspoken observances around physical life. Other matters, more specific, are also treated in similar unattached fashion. And in fact, all enjoyments are verily shunned — not due to their weakening influences, as with ordinary beings, but because this rare being's soul is already resting in an ever-content state. He dwells within. As the Great *Swami's Song of the Sannyasin* describes it again, *"In mountain caves, and glades of forest deep, whose calm no sigh for lust or wealth or fame could ever dare to break; where rolled the stream of knowledge, truth, and bliss that follows both...."*

Even the illumined soul's activities are unusual. Whereas most beings act out of uncertainty, or even outright ignorance, this superlative one has learned how to act without doing anything. He glides through the atmosphere like a bird whose flight leaves no trace of itself behind. Since he identifies with Divine Reality and not the body/mind mechanism, no effect can accrue to him or attach to him in any way. Thus he sings, *"Heed then no more how body lives or goes, its task is done, let karma float it down; let one put garlands on, another kick this frame; say naught. No praise or blame can be where praiser praised and blamer blamed are one.. Thus be thou calm...."*

His companion is his own Self. He always thinks, *"The 'I' has all become, and all is 'I' and Bliss."* His moods are full of abstractions, and there is no telling how he will respond to daily life and situations. His relations with other beings are thus unfigurable. Sometimes he advises out of some hidden store of amazing wisdom, at others he has nothing to say, as if a fool. But there is no doubt that he sees all beings the same in essence, and goes about, *"from place to place, and helps them*

Shankara's Vivekachudamani Siddhanta

"For those who are suffering very much from the effect of the heat of the sun's rays on the road of this world, wandering in the desert of samsara in expectation of water, world weary, the scripture Vivekachudamani is the nearest ocean of Nectar which reveals the presence of the nondual Brahman. May the instruction of Shankara, the incarnation of Shiva, which is the way to the bliss of Nirvana, be successful."

Adishankaracharya

What does he eat? What comes naturally, free of anxiety.

Where does he sleep?

What does he drink? The Nectar of Truth from the Guru.

Without a companion — Loving the Self in all

Sometimes expressive — Sometimes quiet

Sometimes like a wise one — Sometimes like a fool

Sometimes learned — Sometimes unlettered

Sometimes respected — Sometimes unknown

Full of power — Seemingly helpless

Shunning enjoyment — Ever contented

Not like other beings — Seeing equality in all

Engaged in action — Doing nothing

Seemingly finite — All-pervasive

Temporarily in the body — Not identifying with it

On the ground or in a forest, in a castle or in a hut.

Does he walk? Yes, the path of Vedanta
Does he sport? Yes, his sport is Brahman.

"In a ditch, or a river, in a churchyard, or in a field, wherever the leaf may fall, what is that to the tree? Like the destruction of a leaf, a flower, or a fruit is the destruction of the body, senses, vital forces, mind, intellect, and all else to the wise seer — but not of the Atman of that one who stays always in the ever-blissful state. He remains always like the tree." Shankara

"The stone, tree, grass, paddy, husk, etc., when burnt, become one form — ashes. Just so, the body, senses, vital forces, mind, and all other appearances, upon being consumed in the fire of knowledge, become Brahman." Shankara

out of darkness, Maya's veil."

And there are other facets of this being's remarkable personality, or what is left of it, that mark him, or her, as divinely gifted. Some of this will be inspected in Chapter Ten of this very book. In the meanwhile, some keys and insights into how a luminary of this especial kind arrives at such an otherwise incomprehensible state are given in the next chart on the facing page.

Thanks to Shankara, we have just seen who the seer is, and what he consists of regarding rare qualities and attributes. On the top of the chart on the facing page we see some appellations for this illumined being. The first row of four pertain to pure, conscious Awareness — namely *Brahman, Atman, Chaitanya,* and *Chetana.* The second row indicate names for the Supreme Personality. The third row of four points to actual names for such beings, each one operating at a unique level of Awareness. Lastly, the final row of four lists titles for states of Consciousness used in different religious traditions to reveal the existence of the highest station of Awareness. All of this falls generally in the realm of the seer, or who he/she is. In brief, he/she is the witness of all phenomena, i.e., the changing *maya* that makes up the other three categories underneath.

All that the seer beholds falls under the heading of "The Seen." And though generally most of it can be perceived by the five senses, such is the nature of The Seen that even it has hidden facets to it. All that lies in the realm of energy is invisible, and even some life-forms are not visible to us. About this admixture of gross and subtle, the *Upanisads* state, *"What is internal is infinite; what is external, though finite, is also infinite. From the infinite the finite has come, but being infinite, only infinite remains."* To be a seer is to be aware of both what is within and what lies outside, and further, to actually make the essential connections between them.

One of these crucial connections, the Unseen, holds myriad invisibles within it. This is the realm of the gods and goddesses, or *devas* and *devis.* What lies underneath their control and overseership, such as demigods, celestials, ancestors, and elementals, is also a part of their *akasha.* And in fact, this grand *Loka* holds so much within it that the seer often wonders how it gets overlooked so blatantly by living beings on earth. They all travel through these realms on their way to embodiment, and even dream about them while inhabiting the form, yet most have no connection with The Unseen whatsoever, and even fail to believe that it exists, of all things!

This is all the more strange when one looks to find the tiny bits and pieces that make it up. Atomic particles, quarks, neutrons, sub-atomic particles, and the like could easily and justifiably be placed in the cross-section titled The Seen, but in that realm there are almost no beings that comprehend their secret. These tiny increments really represent doorways into subtle worlds that fall under the title, The Unseen. This is the "crucial connection" that the seer has made that others, even intelligent scientists, have not made. Just as the observer looks at objects and does not see the particles that they are made of at first, just so does the seer look at the particles of the object and perceives their connection to subtler particles.

The reader may remember that this chapter started out with an examination of the Wisdom Particle, or *Jnana Matra* (see chart on page 503). The three other fourfold lists in this Unseen category reveal themselves to be gradated, i.e., gunas, *prana,* ego, mind, thoughts, intelligence, subtle elements, Cosmic laws, Cosmic Mind, and finally, The Word — *AUM.* Each of these stations of consciousness contain and consist of finer and finer levels of particles. The second chart of this chapter, called "Dissolving the Mindstream" (see chart on page 505), listed most of these stations and gave out a powerful method for graduating grosser particles by stages in order to attain the subtler and subtler ones. When this, and other connections introduced here, are accomplished, the realm of The Unseen will not have to be left invisible anymore, or worse, end up in the view of humanity to be a mere figment of some estranged visionary's imagination.

And speaking of worse, the fate of worlds and living beings who leave such fundamental spiritual connections disconnected is shown by all that comprises the list at the bottom of the chart on the facing page — what is called The Obscene. No long commentary need be written on this host of subjects. What remains to be done once all of this has been beheld and admitted is a complete

The Seer, The Seen, The Unseen, & The Obscene

"I transcend what is seen and what is unseen. I am the Supreme Seer. This multitude of beings manifest themselves and go to the unmanifest state continually, and thereby subject themselves to rebirth in good and evil wombs. They do not know of the Eternal Existence which never changes, never perishes. But those who perceive It by knowing the unity of the Seer, the Seen, and the Unseen are never born in the gross worlds again."   Sri Krishna

The Seer

→

Brahman   Atman   Chaitanya   Chetana

Parabrahma   Mahavishnu   Paramasiva   Mahamaya

Videhamukta   Jivanmukta   Maharishi   Sakshi

Samadhi   Nirvana   Moksha   Mukti   Turiya

The Seen

Ether/Space   Air/Wind   Fire   Water   Earth

Electricity   Motion   Rotation   Gravitation

Humans   Animals   Insects   Micro-organisms

Oceans   Forests   Rivers   Plants   Flowers

←

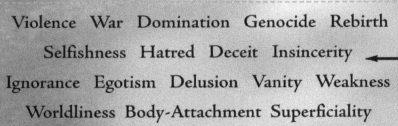

→

Ishvara   Devas   Celestials   Ancestors   Disembodied

Om   Cosmic Mind   Cosmic Laws   Subtle Elements

Intelligence   Thoughts   Mind   Ego   Prana   Gunas

Atomic Particles   Quarks   Neutrons   Sub-atomic

The Unseen

Violence   War   Domination   Genocide   Rebirth

Selfishness   Hatred   Deceit   Insincerity

Ignorance   Egotism   Delusion   Vanity   Weakness

Worldliness   Body-Attachment   Superficiality

←

The Obscene

remaking of daily life and transformation of mind. And this great change must include the internal aspects of life based upon primary connections that bring streams of intelligent particles to the fore of the collective and individual mind so as to be wisely utilized.

The ancient *rishis*, or seers of India, based all of life on all its many levels, recognizing and confirming connections that they knew to be built right into "creation." Seen as the great cosmic cohesions, *Mahasamhitah*, and spoken of utilizing the teaching of *vyahrtis* in revealed scriptures, the entire art of perception for these luminaries revolved around the sacred conjunctions that make up existence itself. What to speak of sensitivity regarding all of life, this spiritual art form is light years beyond even the emerging mindfulness practices of today. A follower and knower of these subtle truths meditates daily on the Five Great Combinations, in much the same way that all of the crucial quintuplications are contemplated and activated in life. (see chart on page 461)

Fortunately for humanity, a clear record of this overall cosmic observance and its modes of practice can be found in the *Taittiriya Upanisad* of the *Krishna Yajur Veda*. The two quotes shown at the top and bottom of the chart on the facing page are both drawn from that scripture, explaining how deep meditation went forth along these internal lines. Among other important points, this shows how meditation, which is the gift of Mother India, was duly centered upon the meanings and implications of cosmic principles in ancient times, and how important these steps were to realization of the formless *Brahman*. Nowadays there is little knowledge of this or any cosmology, or of the subtle principles that connect the physical universe to Absolute Reality. Meditation today is practiced for purposes of health or healing, to achieve the nominal bliss of *sattva*, to renounce the worlds of name and form entirely in order to escape them, or to arrive at some sort of state of transcendental emptiness. And the overall mode of these various types of inward exertions center in on what might be, instead of what is — on some vaunted goal rather than upon the realization of all-abiding Truth.

In order to realize the Ideal rather than merely idealizing the Real, the *rishis* and well-informed practitioners of that olden time took into deep consideration the Five Perceptible Objects — the Universe, Light, Learning, Progeny, and Self. Short of nondual abidance beyond form, wherein nothing with form even mattered, these five principles epitomized existence. Rapt introspection upon this profound quintuplication over long periods of time became so deep and all-consuming, that every essential connection which lie hidden in each element got affirmed and fully fleshed out.

Under the heading of the Universe, for instance, it was not just the earth as a planet that received deep reflection, but also the firmament upon which it rested and the atmosphere wherein it was set, even the very air that surrounded, supported, and permeated it. This means that the ancient seers came to know about space as more than an awesome and boundless external dimension, or a resting place for suns and planets, or even a place to set ones feet on in order to conduct activities. The firmament which supported all of this, the atmosphere that made it sacred, and the air that animated all beings living upon it, became clear to them in their deepest meditations. And while seeing this from the vantage point of a detached, inactive perspective, and in the outright peace of undisturbed mental stillness, the one-pointed Awareness that perceived all these elements and their connections became clear and pronounced as well. Succinctly and lucidly put, this is the universal meditation that destroys the world as a thing, object, planet, or location that is separate from *Brahman*. And this is also why the great statement, "All is *Brahman*" got realized in Mother India, came forth from Mother India, and was only able to make sense and ring true due to the many illumined philosophies and *darshanas* emanating from Mother India over millennia.

Meditation of such a universal and comprehensive kind deserves both our attention and our practice. If contemplation upon the first of great Five Perceptible Objects, namely the Universe, brought about such profundity and meaning, then what of the other four? Light? What introspective living being has not used that as a source for meditation? But what is light without the connections to fire, sun, water, and lightning? Certainly there have been many beings, and several religions, that have worshipped the sun. But who has known the sun via its nature as light? In the *Upanisads* it is recalled that, as one luminary was leaving the body, he prayed to the Lord of Light,

The Sacred Doctrine of Conjunctions

ᘓ *Meditation on the Great Combinations* ᘓ

*"The illumined seer who revealed this essential wisdom by his deep intuition,
having grouped the various elements of existence, declared that the entire universe
of gross and subtle worlds is based in sets of fivefold principles, and that one set of fives
enables and preserves the next set of fives. The seer opens up cosmic vision by
knowing this principle of fives based on facts known to all."* Taitirriya Upanisad

Mahasamhitah — **Great Combinations**

The Five Perceptible Objects

Universe

Earth
Firmament
Atmosphere
Air

Learning

Teacher
Student
Study
Imparting

Light

Fire
Sun
Water
Lightning

Progeny

Mother
Father
Offspring
Procreation

Conjunction
"The two   into One"

Ego/Self
Lower Jaw
Upper Jaw
Speech
Tongue

"One should meditate on Existence bearing in mind all these interior relations."

*"One should meditate upon the elements that compose the universe, namely, earth,
intermediate space, heaven, sky, the four and eight directions, fire, air, sun, moon, stars,
water, herbs, plants, trees, ether, and one's body — including skin, muscle, bone,
and marrow. Then meditate on the five senses and the five pranas.
Then contemplate AUM, the universal term of compliance, which is Brahman."*
Taitirriya Upanisad

saying: *"Oh Lord, please take away that glaring light of the sun in the sky, for it veils your true Light emanating from within."*   To make such a statement, especially at the time of the body's death, reveals a soul that has meditated upon all forms of light, along with their inner connections. As the *Taittirya Upanisad* says again, *"One should meditate upon Existence bearing in mind all of these inner relations."*

Learning, Progeny, and Self are the other three "perceptible objects." It is for the conscious meditator to dive into them with the spiritually-awakened mind and render them alive and aware, as they are. As Sri Ram demonstrates for us on the chart just examined, as he performs his reverent puja to Lord *Siva* represented by the *lingam*, everything dual must be combined and returned to its nondual essence, i.e., "The two must become One."

To achieve this ultimate of all conjunctions, everything that precedes Reality by way or along the road of involution has to be dissolved into its respective essence (see chart on page 503). And to succeed at this subtle spiritual move, comprehension must come to the mind that these essences — the *svarupa* of each and every principle, including its series of expressions — lies in its respective *bijam*, or original seed. Those awakened and aware beings who cull and harvest these seeds and their essence know that this is where true Wisdom resides. Others look for mere knowledge on the surface, in the physical universe.

The chart on the facing page readily gives out more teachings from the *Taittiriya Upanisad*, specifically about these potent seeds. The Four Celebrated Mystical Utterances declare that four of the seven internal worlds are reached through such especial wisdom. These statements, or *vyahrtis*, in *Sanskrit*, open the inner doorways to these more refined realms. They are also found in the famous *Gayatri mantra*, chanted by millions of beings daily for spiritual well-being:

> *Om bhur bhuvah svah tat savitur varenyam bhargo devasha dimohi diyoyo nah prachodayat.*
> *May we always and ever meditate upon the radiant effulgence of the Supreme Being*
> *residing within our hearts and minds eternally.*
> *May that one blessed Presence guide and protect us, and protect the three worlds.*

And beyond the third world is *Mahar* which the seer, Mahachamasya, perceived in deepest meditation. On the chart we can see the elements that naturally makeup each realm, and which the human mind embodied on earth needs to see and account for in order to receive their array of powers. And each of these four worlds connect with one another as well, from outside in, as far as the process of inward ascension is concerned. The indrawn breath, the expended breath, the retained breath, and all food to be consumed — these are all givers of life. Fire, air, the light of sun and moon — these are all sustainers of life and maintainers of healing in the body. The earth, the inter-regions, the life-heavens, and the realm of the shining *devas* — these are the foundations upon which the circle of harmonious life and living revolve. *Brahman* and Its Word, the scriptures and what they signify — thought, sound, meaning, and objects — are the clarifiers and the refuges for all Source-bound spiritual pilgrims.

Below, strewn around the lovely Feet of *Sarasvati*, the Goddess of the Word, are a host of *tattvas*, or cosmic principles, all which are to be seen as manifestations of Consciousness Itself, and that are to be utilized as stations for meditation (*alambanas*) on Divine Reality. All of these same facets of Awareness, if they are seen only as objects for pleasure and taken for granted, become like weights that pull the aspiring soul down to the lowest and grossest of all worlds, restricting it there. There, the gross nerves in the body become the only avenues along which this stunted consciousness travels, and the subtler passageways, called *nadis* in *Sanskrit*, close down like overgrown trails in an ancient forest. What is more, the higher realms, called *Janah*, *Tapah*, and *Satyam*, are never seen, not even imagined, much less visited in meditation or after the death by this benighted soul. As the Tantras state, *"Without Her, all the tattvas become about as useful as clouds with no rain."*

Restricted to one world? How dull and boring. Open to four worlds? Much better, thank you. Aware of all seven worlds? This is for that illumined soul whose entire existence is always about union with Divine Reality, and the Peace, Bliss, Love and Light that proceeds from It.

The Four Celebrated Mystical Utterances

"Bhur, Bhuvah, Suvah — these are verily the three celebrated mystical utterances. In addition to these there is a fourth one which Mahachamasya proclaimed. That one who meditates upon these, called the four Vyahrtis, comes to know Brahman, and to that auspicious one all the gods bring homage." Taittiriya Upanisad

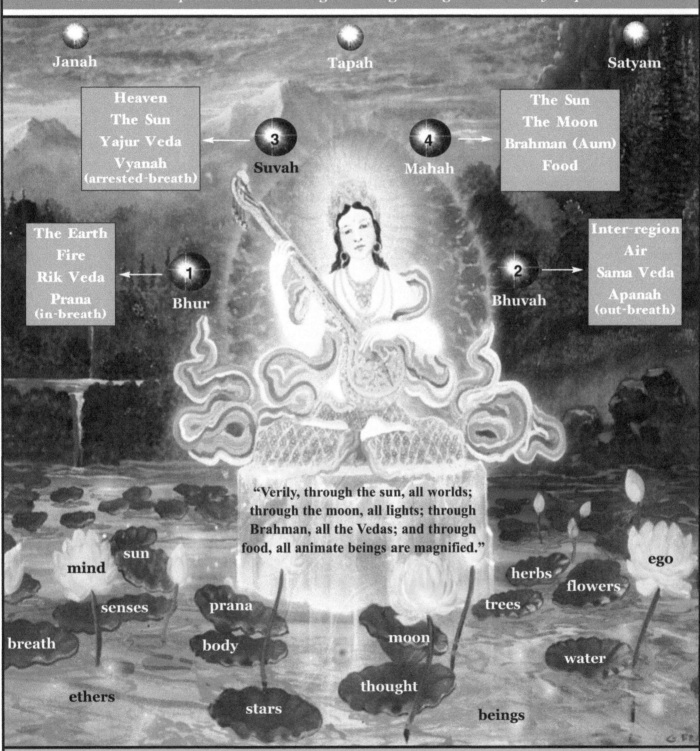

Janah

Tapah

Satyam

Heaven
The Sun
Yajur Veda
Vyanah
(arrested-breath)

3
Suvah

4
Mahah

The Sun
The Moon
Brahman (Aum)
Food

The Earth
Fire
Rik Veda
Prana
(in-breath)

1
Bhur

2
Bhuvah

Inter-region
Air
Sama Veda
Apanah
(out-breath)

"Verily, through the sun, all worlds; through the moon, all lights; through Brahman, all the Vedas; and through food, all animate beings are magnified."

mind

sun

ego

herbs
flowers

senses

prana

trees

breath

body

moon

water

ethers

thought

stars

beings

"In meditation the worshiper leaves the body through the subtle nadi, gains union and abides in fire by uttering 'Bhur,' and in the air by uttering 'Bhuvah,' and in the sun by uttering 'Suvah,' and finally in Brahman, declaring, 'Mahah.' He reaches the Lords of sight, hearing, speech, and understanding, and becomes the Divine Brahman." Taittiriya Upanisad

This superlative soul, like the "Walker of the Skies" we read about on page 514, is always and ever actuating what the luminaries of Mother India refer to as "Inward Ascension." The next chart up for study reflects the internal journey that every embodied soul has to make at one time or other, or over cycles of time in order to get beyond time, thus free. In other words, the soul always courts its innate freedom, even when it seems otherwise. More wisdom from the *Taittiriya Upanisad* lights up this chart on the opposite page, this time centered more in the soul itself and how it uses the wisdom shown and told about earlier.

Taking a distinctive turn towards the *Kundalini Yoga* system, the *Taittiriya Upanisad* moves from the important facts concerning seed words and their connections *(vyahritis)* and how they coalesce *(samhita)*, to the power they produce and how it gets utilized for inner life by the adept soul. Spiritual power, once awakened and initiated, needs vessels and conduits to flow to, and through. The awakened soul itself is the vessel, and its channels, called *nadis* by the yogis, are the facilitators for the power to flow through. The three main ones, shown on the chart opposite, are the *ida, pingala,* and *sushumna.* The latter is the central channel, and the other two swirl around the enfold it.

Every level of existence has its channels. For ordinary beings on earth, housed in physical bodies, the nervous system allows for the flow of life force, or *prana,* at the fundamental level. Everyday life is conducted via this energy. This was pointed out by Jesus when He said, *"Man does not live by bread alone."* If the normal human being experiences an unusual amount of concentrated energy due to any form of fresh exercise, the nerves expand and begin to allow more force to rise. Using this force, the awakening individual focuses and intensifies it and finds special avenues to gain even subtler types of power. These lie hidden within the mind complex *(antahkarana).* Those who get stuck laboring over gross forms of this force, particular to the body only, never discover them, and remain physically-oriented only. These get preoccupied with, then bound, into matter.

But the soaring spirit of the truth-seeking soul lifts off of the material plane and begins a journey of Inward Ascension. With the essential connections made and the *nadis* open wide and leading into the illumined mind, *Shakti* force, as it is called, wends its way inwards, lighting up the interior planes of existence that heretofore remained benighted and undiscovered by the newly awakened one. As one song of India sings it:

> *Dive deep, oh mind, dive deep into the ocean of God's beauty.*
> *If you descend to the uttermost depths, there you will find the gem of Love.*
> *Light up, oh mind, Wisdom's shining lamp,*
> *and let it burn unceasingly within your heart.....*

This lit-up mind complex is the true marvel of existence in the realms of name and form. All other miracles occur because of it. But the power that invades and saturates it, that *Shakti* Force, is another matter altogether. It, She, is dynamic Sentiency. The seers say that She always lies latent in ordinary beings, and that they never intuit Her or strive to bring Her to the fore of life and awareness. Thus, the current of life in most beings is mere *prana,* which is limited to the realm of the five elements. Many do not even know that it is that selfsame energy that causes the eyes to see, the ears to hear, and the tongue to taste. The few that do discover this subtle presence of life-force, as Sri Krishna states in the *Bhagavad Gita,* begin to offer everything that the senses experience, including the objects of the senses, to the Lord and Mother of the Universe. This is a type of deification that refines life and mind further.

This refinement of the individual's energy, from gross *prana,* to *prana* of the senses, to the *prana* of the mind (called "psychic" *prana*), represents a powerful form of spiritual awakening that, however it is called or described, is the well-lit thoroughfare to Truth that all religions and philosophies of Mother India recognize and utilise for full Enlightenment. All modes of worship, as well as all methods of study and meditation, turn to and rely upon this magnificent subtle Force, within and without. When the three lower centers of existence that are associated with eating, drinking, and sex-life are transcended, the rapidly intensifying *Shakti* power reaches towards the four inner centers, also referred to as lotuses, or *chakras.* The chart on the facing page, under study, shows dia-

Inward Ascension of the Free Soul

"I am the stimulator of the Tree of the Universe; my fame is High, like a mountaintop. Elevated to the most Holy, I am the excellent, immortal being as He is in the sun. I am the Power, the Wealth refulgent with divine intuition. Imperishable and immutable I have become." *Trishanku*

Ida

Sushumna

Pingala

"...whose essence is Truth."

"...who is endow-ed with peace."

"...who is felicity of mind."

"...whose sport is the life-force."

"...whose body is the ether."

"The hollow canal called sushumna lies between the two arteries of the upper palate and the nipple-like growth that hangs down between them. It passes out of the crown where the root of the hair is made to part, opening the skull in the center. This is the gate leading to The Supreme Lord."

"There is within the heart the bright space known to all. There, let the worshipper meditate upon and realize the intelligent, imperishable, self-effulgent Soul. May you, O Prachinayogya, worship in the manner described herein." *Taittiriya Upanisad*

Phases & Permutations of the All-Pervasive Prana

"Controlling the heaven-aspiring senses and the life-force with the help of the mind and intellect, the Immanent Soul so regenerates them as to enable them to manifest the infinite, self-luminous Light of Awareness. All that exists in the three worlds is under the control of Prana, and Prana is Mother. May She transmit Wisdom to us via Her Divine Energy."

Svetasvataropanisad

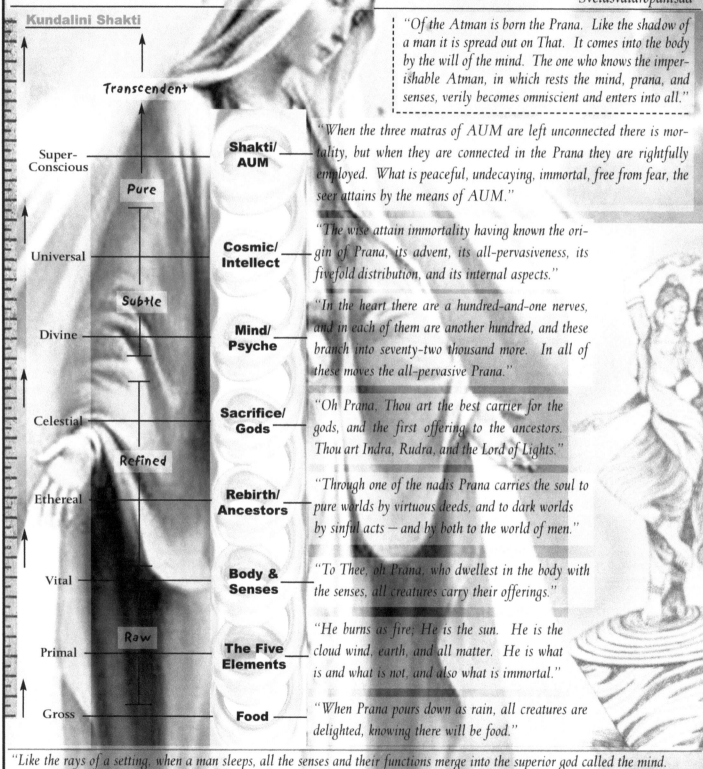

Kundalini Shakti

Transcendent

Super-Conscious — Pure

Universal — Subtle

Divine

Celestial — Refined

Ethereal

Vital

Primal — Raw

Gross

Shakti/AUM

Cosmic/Intellect

Mind/Psyche

Sacrifice/Gods

Rebirth/Ancestors

Body & Senses

The Five Elements

Food

"Of the Atman is born the Prana. Like the shadow of a man it is spread out on That. It comes into the body by the will of the mind. The one who knows the imperishable Atman, in which rests the mind, prana, and senses, verily becomes omniscient and enters into all."

"When the three matras of AUM are left unconnected there is mortality, but when they are connected in the Prana they are rightfully employed. What is peaceful, undecaying, immortal, free from fear, the seer attains by the means of AUM."

"The wise attain immortality having known the origin of Prana, its advent, its all-pervasiveness, its fivefold distribution, and its internal aspects."

"In the heart there are a hundred-and-one nerves, and in each of them are another hundred, and these branch into seventy-two thousand more. In all of these moves the all-pervasive Prana."

"Oh Prana, Thou art the best carrier for the gods, and the first offering to the ancestors. Thou art Indra, Rudra, and the Lord of Lights."

"Through one of the nadis Prana carries the soul to pure worlds by virtuous deeds, and to dark worlds by sinful acts — and by both to the world of men."

"To Thee, oh Prana, who dwellest in the body with the senses, all creatures carry their offerings."

"He burns as fire; He is the sun. He is the cloud wind, earth, and all matter. He is what is and what is not, and also what is immortal."

"When Prana pours down as rain, all creatures are delighted, knowing there will be food."

"Like the rays of a setting, when a man sleeps, all the senses and their functions merge into the superior god called the mind. Then he hears not, sees not, smells not, tastes not, feels not, and they say 'he sleeps.' At that time the fires of Prana alone remain awake in this city, holding the two oblations of inspiration and expiration within it."

Prashnopanisad

grams of both the three main *nadis* abiding in the subtle body of mankind, and the seven centers of Awareness that *Kundalini Shakti* flows through. As Sri Ramakrishna Paramahamsa has stated, conclusively: *"There will be no spiritual growth for man until Kundalini Shakti is awakened."*

Since the subject of *prana* has been introduced by the *Upanisads* — which is one of the few places one can find teachings on it and its crucial import in the world — teachings about this rarefied life energy under the operation of the *Mahashakti* must be made welcome in the human thinking process. On the facing page is a chart that reveals *prana*'s deepest implications, and shows its primal connections with all levels of life and existence.

Until a man awakens sleeping awareness within him, until he tires of the energy associated with food and its digestion and excretion, until he at least becomes aware of his breathing process as more than just the need for oxygen, he will never know about what animates him, even about keeps him upright. Later, when all of these are no more a mystery to him, then he can begin to comprehend what takes his mind into its highest flights of fancy, what powers his dreams and visions, and what takes him from birth to life to death, and beyond — the *Prana.*

This unique chart requires studying from the bottom up. Since embodied souls are living on the level of gross vibrations, both material (nature) and mental (ignorance) in content, the move towards refinement of consciousness has to begin there. Jumping steps will not work well, either. A gradual advancement, inward ascension style, from step to step, from stage to stage (*avasthas*), must form the way.

We can see at the bottom of the chart that food represents gross *prana* the best. Thus, as long as impure and unrefined foods are consumed there is little chance of uncovering the gentle and subtle presence of loving and compassionate consciousness that makes man much more than a mere beast. It would be best, as well, if the spiritual teacher were on the scene to tell the beginning aspirant that *prana* is not *Brahman;* it is not sentient in and of itself. It is an energy. It flows and stagnates. It waxes and wanes. *Brahman* is motionless Perfection. Thus, *prana*'s location, its mastery, and its usage for inner life, is a penultimate aim. This is stated for many beings, seekers even, who come upon the life-force and take it to be all in all. They may get distracted away from *Brahman* and begin to utilize *prana* for occult purposes. Even those who "thirst for life" are in danger of getting caught in the realms where *prana* operates. The Fathers of *Yoga* and *Vedanta* both concur that attachment to *prana* is part of what increases the desire for embodiment in millions of souls again and again, i.e, the helpless drive to get reincarnated in form.

On the chart under study, the next level of *prana*'s operations are with the elements. Quotes listed from the scriptures can be read to assist the reader and student in understanding these levels of life-force. But already we can see that the seers are connecting *prana* up with the Supreme Being — as if without the *prana* there would be no conduits leading to realization of It. Both of these first two stations of *prana* are "raw," meaning that this is the primal or root state of things. And this base state can also be seen in the minds of animalistic beings who still war, rage, dominate, and try to control other species and races with the energy they get from coarse foodstuffs. The saying, "You are what you eat," may pertain here better than anywhere. But the content of food alone is only partially responsible for insensitivity to others, and to the creation; the state of mind in which the living being takes food into the body is more to blame. A good example of this is how beings eat food in a restless state of mind, as in today's world, and commit all manner of heinous and unthinking acts as a result. The pace here is far too fast, excited by a raw-edged type of *pranic* energy that is erratic and prone to blunders.

Prana at the level of the five senses is "vital." More of the primal substance makes itself known here, at least to the mentally evolving human being. The quote from the scriptures listed at this level mentions the *nadis*, or nerve channels, as taught about above. It also explains how, at the next subtler level, some beings are taken towards lower worlds, while others transition towards higher spheres, all based upon the quality of the *prana* involved.

And higher, or subtler worlds, really begin to define what *prana* is, and what is its deeper purpose in all the realms of consciousness. When the incarnated soul begins to detect the hidden presence and influence of his ancestors on his life, he is arriving at an understanding that is "ethereal" in its implications. Here is where, according to the teaching of the Fourteen Stages of Upper and Lower Knowledge (*Jnana* and *Ajnanabhumikas* – see charts on pages 333, 335, 337), a human being will get inklings that he or she has been born before, and that his life in this physical world is only a temporary sojourn. And whereas the appearance of the ancestor realm on the dawning horizon of the mind's awareness may signal a refinement of sorts, it is not as subtle and healing as the vision of the realm of the Deities, or gods and goddesses, that follow it. In this celestial region, *prana* has graduated in quality to become the "carrier of offerings," and if what is carried forth pleases the higher powers residing in the inner kingdoms, spiritual ascension can become swift and successful.

At this potentially sublime juncture, or somewhere along its way, usually unbeknownst to the inner traveler, Divinity itself makes its introduction. In other words, this is the divine *loka*, characterized by a truly subtle level of energy that gets titled "psychic *prana*" by the seers. In his *Raja Yoga*, Swami Vivekananda describes, in part, the inwards rising of psychic *prana* that will soon transform into *Shakti* power Herself. *"As this force travels from center to center, layer after layer of the mind, as it were, opens up, and this universe is perceived by the Yogi in its fine, or causal form. Then alone the causes of the universe, both as sensation and reaction, are known as they are, and hence comes all knowledge."* This realm of the psyche, or mind-field, is full of all potential that has manifested already as the physical universe with its various planets and other objects. Here, the causes of all outer expression are perceived, or *"known as they are."* But a finer cause, and a causeless cause, are still to be revealed.

Prana now has to give up all charades. It was practically equated with *Brahman* in the early scriptures, and now comes the reason for that. At the next profound station, that of the Cosmic intellect, the Divine turns Universal. Out of the primal closet, as it were, comes the vision of *Shakti* Herself, and the well-schooled and illumined soul now knows why all of life, even on the physical plane, seems under the control and overseership of a hidden Force, only intuited by a few. And She has not yet revealed the totality of Her three most sublime secrets yet — the first being that the *prana*, in all its phases, is Hers, and operates under Her bidding, and secondly, that She is the owner and tender of God's Word.

AUM is a teaching of the deepest and most profound order. There is hardly a world religion of philosophy that has not become enamored, in one way or another, with The Word, and that pertains many times over to Mother India. This book has already explored in part, this transcendent but imminently present Verity deeply (see charts of pages 144, 146, 154), though there is more to come on It. Suffice to say here, then, that there is a pervader over The Word, a sublime Presence so ineffable that even illumined souls spend lifetimes to get even one glimpse of Her beatific vision. As one song of India describes this:

> *In dense darkness, oh Mother, Thy formless beauty sparkles*
> *Therefore the yogis meditate in a dark mountain cave*
> *In the lap of boundless dark, on Mahanirvana's waves upborne*
> *Your peace flows serene and inexhaustible.*

And here is where the third secret of Her incomparable Presence reveals itself. She is ever one with the formless *Brahman*. As the chart just completed on page 536 shows, as *Kundalini Shakti* She connects all souls at the highest level of Awareness, and as She does so, She makes of them not only knowers of *Brahman*, but masters of all levels of Awareness through Her own energy, *prana*.

The chart on the facing page is another on the secret of *prana*, which must not remain a secret any longer if Enlightenment is important to the aspiring soul. This chart gives an even more direct correlation to realms within, that are reached by the flow of refined *prana* along the *nadis* lodged within the subtle body of mankind. In this *Vedic* rendering, possibly older than *Kundalini Yoga's* systemization, we see four great currents ascending "heavenwards," generally associated with the states of waking/sleeping, dreaming, deep sleep, and *Turiya*. The assignment given here is the Vital Breath and the Four *Nadis*. Further correlation has it that each of the four states and the vital breath have

The Four States & The Vital Breath

"All created things were certainly present in the Divine Ether of Brahman's Heart before any inception. Like a hive of bees they were fashioned into individual souls, and thus came forth the different species. This Sacred Lore of Brahman exists and shines brilliantly in the resplendent City of the Transcendent Brahman, and I relate it to you here." Para-Brahma Upanisad

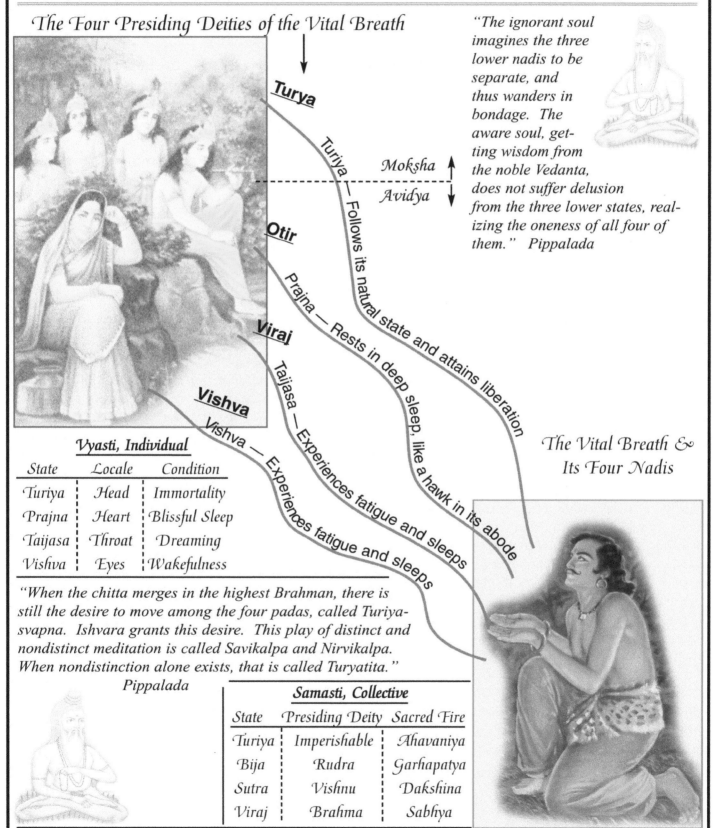

The Four Presiding Deities of the Vital Breath

Turya

Otir

Viraj

Vishva

Turiya

Moksha

Avidya

Turiya — Follows its natural state and attains liberation

Prajna — Rests in deep sleep, like a hawk in its abode

Taijasa — Experiences fatigue and sleeps

Vishva — Experiences fatigue and sleeps

"The ignorant soul imagines the three lower nadis to be separate, and thus wanders in bondage. The aware soul, getting wisdom from the noble Vedanta, does not suffer delusion from the three lower states, realizing the oneness of all four of them." Pippalada

The Vital Breath & Its Four Nadis

Vyasti, Individual

State	Locale	Condition
Turiya	Head	Immortality
Prajna	Heart	Blissful Sleep
Taijasa	Throat	Dreaming
Vishva	Eyes	Wakefulness

"When the chitta merges in the highest Brahman, there is still the desire to move among the four padas, called Turiya-svapna. Ishvara grants this desire. This play of distinct and nondistinct meditation is called Savikalpa and Nirvikalpa. When nondistinction alone exists, that is called Turyatita." Pippalada

Samasti, Collective

State	Presiding Deity	Sacred Fire
Turiya	Imperishable	Ahavaniya
Bija	Rudra	Garhapatya
Sutra	Vishnu	Dakshina
Viraj	Brahma	Sabhya

"presiding deities," and further, that these divine personages are ones that lift the aspiring soul out of ignorance and into the state of *Moksha*, or Liberation.

And so we find that the human breath is not merely a mechanism to keep the physical body functioning, nor is it just a sudden revelation of the sleeping soul that allows for more energy in the body either. The saying in circles of wisdom knowers has it that *"Man does not live to eat; he eats to live."* In similar fashion, it can be said that "Man does not live to breath; he breathes in order to truly live. This true breath the awakening soul takes is not just into the lungs, then, but into the mind. Just as the lungs expand with air to provide more vital energy, the mind needs to expand with psychic *prana* to provide room for more knowledge.

The great *rishi*, Pippalada, whose wisdom quotes are placed on the chart under study (page 539), likens such expansion of knowledge to the connecting of all levels of mankind's awareness. In ordinary man, fixated as he is with the physical plane only, with matter, objects, and the five senses to enjoy them with, the waking state is all and all to him. His dreams are foggy and meaningless; his deep sleep state is as if a comatose condition — like the sleep of a hibernating bear in winter. Finally, there is no awareness of the fourth state, what the seers of Truth call *Turiya*. The waking state is all he knows, and for those who have looked at the violent acts and base thoughts of human beings, particularly in this day and age, there is precious little to justify his existence on this planet. Even other life forms that coexist with him, like the plants and animals, shun his presence and suffer under his cruel domination.

Therefore, Pippilada teaches those few aspiring human beings to connect all the states of awareness available to them — much like the connections and conjunctions that we have taken up earlier in this chapter. To him, by leaving the three major *nadis* of waking, dreaming, and deep sleep disconnected, man shuts the door to both a fulfilling life on earth, and realization of his divine nature. Further, he wanders around the worlds unaware of their hidden meaning and potential, performing acts that subject him to recurring lifetimes in ignorance and suffering.

Leaving the chart under study with its mention by the *Upanisads* of mysteries such as "The Sacred Lore of *Brahman*," "The Resplendent City of the Transcendent *Brahman*," and "The Divine Ether of *Brahman*'s Heart," we take up the chart on the facing page on the esoteric subject of *prana*. The word "ether' in English confers upon the Western thinker a sense of sky, space, and possibly heaven for the religious soul. But for Mother India the word is immediately associated with inner realms, of space inside of space where the disembodied soul courses through "etheric" planes and sports in blissful *lokas*.

One of the reasons that the teaching of *prana* never received a deep read in the West to date, even with the advent of the seer, monk, *yogi*, *sannyasin*, and luminary, Swami Vivekananda, in America in 1893, is due, again, to mankind's attachment to all things physical, his death-grasp on the atomic particle. Even when an occasional soul with trans-scientific predilection appeared, *prana* was taught about only on the level of matter, and in terms of physical health alone. These short-sighted *yogis*, called *hathis*, took Patanjali's mention of the five forms of *prana* and restricted them to the functions of the body only.

Thus, the *apana* (downwards moving *prana*) was limited to matters of diet, excretory movements, cleaning of the bowels, and concerns of that ilk. It was never revealed at the level of the psychic *prana* where cleanliness of thoughts, ejection of ignorance, and purification of the mind were needed. In like manner, the *samana* (distributive/digestive *prana*) got restricted to matters of the organs like the stomach and intestines, and the circulation of the blood. It was never taught at the level of psychic *prana* where spiritual teachings given by the *guru* and the wisdom of the scriptures required it for assimilation by the mind. In short, the contemporary student's inability to concentrate on the *dharma* in this day and time is due to not having *samana* in play and operating at the level of the psychic *prana*.

As for the *udana* (upward-rising *prana*), what mention of it needs be made for the astute aspirant. Leaving it at the level of the physical body, associated with the in-breath or the first phase of

The Singular Prana & Its Five Forms

"The Rishi was asked, 'How many gods support all creatures, and who is the greatest among them?' He replied, 'The ether is that god, and air, fire, water, earth, mind, and senses. These, standing forth, manifested their power and declared, 'We, holding the body, support it.' Then Prana declared, 'Do not be deluded; I alone, dividing myself into five parts, hold and support the body.' But none were disposed to believe him, So he abandoned the body and as he went out, so did all others. Just as bees leave the hive when the queen does, so did the speech, mind, eye, ear, and all others depart when prana departed. Then they all praised him."   Prasnopanisad

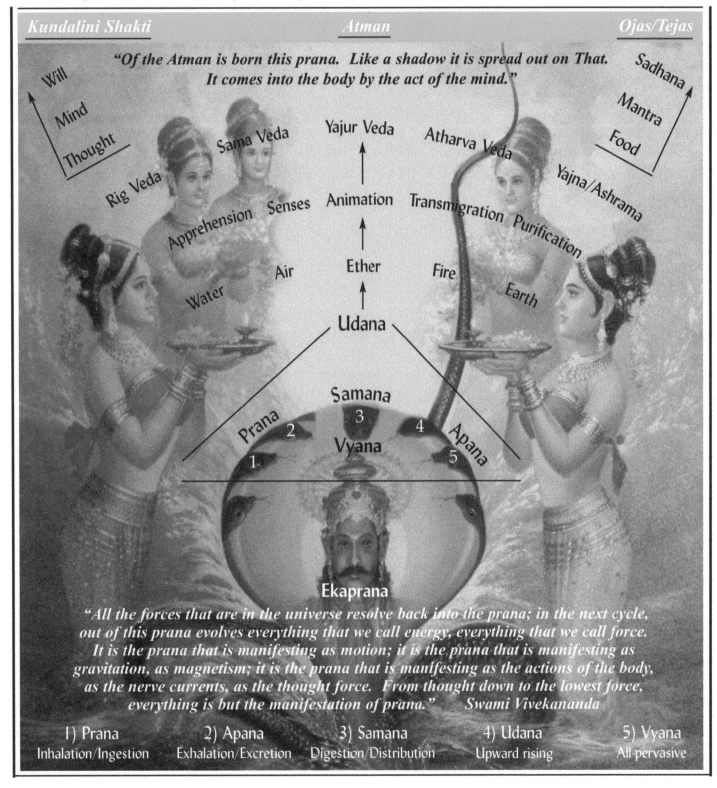

Kundalini Shakti   *Atman*   *Ojas/Tejas*

"Of the Atman is born this prana. Like a shadow it is spread out on That. It comes into the body by the act of the mind."

Will / Mind / Thought

Rig Veda / Sama Veda / Yajur Veda / Atharva Veda

Sadhana / Mantra / Food

Apprehension   Senses   Animation   Transmigration   Purification   Yajna/Ashrama

Water   Air   Ether   Fire   Earth

Udana

Samana

Prana   2   3   Vyana   4   Apana

1   5

Ekaprana

"All the forces that are in the universe resolve back into the prana; in the next cycle, out of this prana evolves everything that we call energy, everything that we call force. It is the prana that is manifesting as motion; it is the prana that is manifesting as gravitation, as magnetism; it is the prana that is manifesting as the actions of the body, as the nerve currents, as the thought force. From thought down to the lowest force, everything is but the manifestation of prana."   Swami Vivekananda

1) Prana	2) Apana	3) Samana	4) Udana	5) Vyana
Inhalation/Ingestion	Exhalation/Excretion	Digestion/Distribution	Upward rising	All-pervasive

a sneeze, does more than an injustice to it. This fine *prana*, placed into motion in the mind, at the level of psychic *prana*, is responsible for nothing less than the timely delivery of inspiration to the mind's thinking process. Just like the starving lungs without an in-breath, the human intellect goes undernourished as well without the presence of *udana* at the psychic level. This is also true in the case of *vyana* (pervading *prana*). Whereas at the physical level, the body would fall down flat, inert, if the *vyana* were not present, in much the same fashion the mind would be devoid of transcendent quality without *vyana* at the psychic level. Finer arts and acts like contemplation and meditation would not be possible either, and no visualization of higher ideals would take place, what to speak of striving to reach them via psychic *udana*.

And finally, *prana* itself, the in-breath and ingestion so necessary for the body's existence, was seen and demonstrated by teachers of *hatha* via using sets of breathing exercises, *pranayama*, while its role at the psychic *prana* level — that of expanding the mind for purposes of knowing the Nondual *Brahman* — went by the wayside, untaught. Thus was the import of the Five Forms of the one *Prana* in the context of full and complete *Yoga* rendered a disservice in the West, and in contemporary times overall. Even to this day its real import goes unnoticed. The place of *prana* in life and philosophy is missing, and that absence is the cause for many a malady at all levels of life.

The rest of the chart under study (page 541) shows how the five forms of *prana* rise and refine into psychic *prana*. This assists the soul in connecting to crucial levels of practice and understanding such as aligning the five elements with the five senses (see chart on page 151), learning the art of mental purification leading to spiritual ascendency, and perceiving the role of the revealed scriptures in the ongoing spiritual life of an embodied human being. Both the story of the god, *Prana*, in the *Upanisads*, shown at the top of the chart, and the quote from Swami Vivekananda at the bottom, are well worth reading and contemplating to bring this potent teaching to fullness and effectivity.

Before departing the realm of teachings on *prana*, there is a final function that it carries forth that is crucial to several aspects of human existence. Philosophically, the *prana*, when properly known, will divest the soul of fear regarding death, showing it up to be an outright illusion, or at least a mere relative function in the Kingdom of Eternal Consciousness. Religiously, the *prana* connects living beings to their ancestors, thus "heaven," and to the realm of the gods as well. Here on earth, in the body, the *prana* is responsible not only for moving the body from place to place, but also for moving the soul (mind complex) from location to location — between the states of waking, dreaming, and deep sleep, as has been mentioned, but also out of the physical form at the time of its demise.

The chart on the facing page exposes the otherwise hidden presence and functions of *prana* as it carries on its operations in the transitory and transmigratory realm of birth, life, and death. *Yama*, the Lord of Death, has his own witness view of this process, and of all the multitude of souls that are caught up in it. As the quote from the *Katha Upanisad* puts it, *Yama* sees embodied souls wasting time in the world, preoccupied with wealth and pleasures and never giving a thought to their well-being in the "afterlife."

It is the god of *Prana* that conducts souls out of the body and into the realms of this afterlife, directing them according to their *karmas* accrued on earth. Many millions will enter the cycles of multi-dimensional movement, falling under the auspices of the ancestors, *asuras*, or demigods. Trans-dimensional movement is more for those who reach the realm of the gods, like *Indraloka*, and dwell there for as long as they desire to. Coming back to earth in a physical form is not incumbent upon them. Since they come to know and master the *prana* that transports them from *loka* to *loka*, they contemplate it naturally and, as the quote from the *Taittiriya Upanisad* states (on the chart opposite), they contemplate *prana* as *Brahman* and attain a full lifetime on secure ground. Their's is eternal life lived upon the deep bedrock of Spirit, not a series of tentative and precarious lives lived atop the surface of the ever shifting sands of relative existence. When *prana*, known as *shakti*, leads to *Brahman*, then, as Swami Vivekananda has written, *"All life both here and there, do I renounce, all heavens, all earths, all hells, all hopes and fears. Thus cut thy bonds...."*

Prana and the Illusion of Death

"Prana is the life-duration of the animate world; on that ground it is regarded as Sarvayusam — Universal Life. Those who contemplate prana as Brahman attain the full span of life. The soul becomes fearless only when it obtains that secure ground. If it assumes the slightest interval of separation from that identity, then comes fear, and death." Taittiriya Upanisad

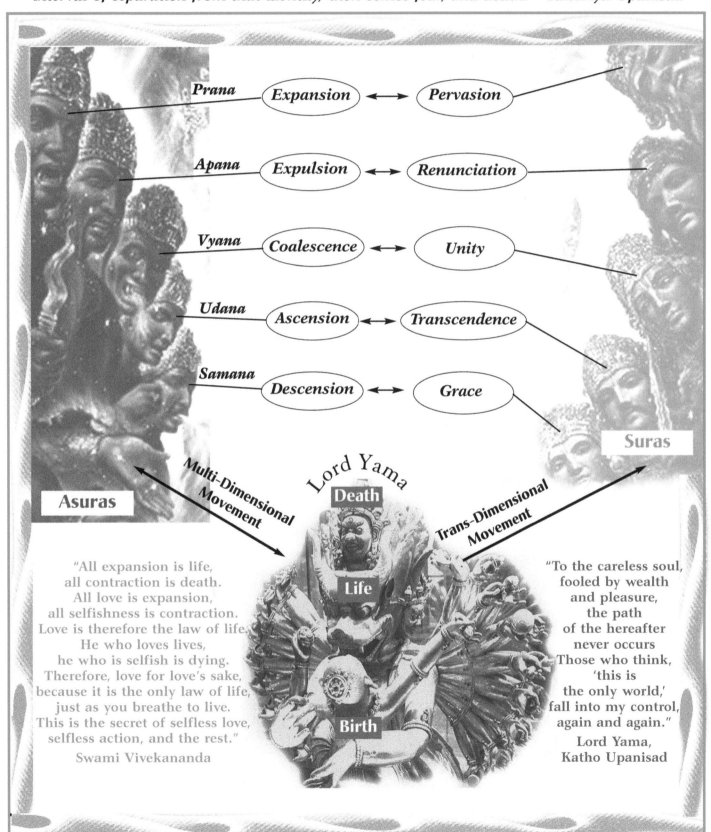

Prana — Expansion ←→ Pervasion

Apana — Expulsion ←→ Renunciation

Vyana — Coalescence ←→ Unity

Udana — Ascension ←→ Transcendence

Samana — Descension ←→ Grace

Suras

Lord Yama

Death

Life

Birth

Multi-Dimensional Movement

Trans-Dimensional Movement

Asuras

"All expansion is life,
all contraction is death.
All love is expansion,
all selfishness is contraction.
Love is therefore the law of life.
He who loves lives,
he who is selfish is dying.
Therefore, love for love's sake,
because it is the only law of life,
just as you breathe to live.
This is the secret of selfless love,
selfless action, and the rest."

Swami Vivekananda

"To the careless soul,
fooled by wealth
and pleasure,
the path
of the hereafter
never occurs
Those who think,
'this is
the only world,'
fall into my control,
again and again."

Lord Yama,
Katho Upanisad

The chart under study on page 543 goes on to show how the five forms of *prana* transform in the subtler realms, or the "afterlife." *Samana,* the distributive energy, will deposit the mind's contents either at the feet of a benign overseer filled with grace, or under the control of a more capricious deity — much like what happens to souls on earth with parents and families. *Udana,* with its leanings towards aspiration, will determine what inner direction will be taken by the still form-oriented soul, depending on how much power (*prana/shakti*) has been stored up for such purposes prior to its passing from the earth plane. In the case of *vyana,* and its abilities leading towards natural homogeneity, it will help the soul achieve either coalescence or unity, depending on what it needs for its next phase of spiritual evolution. The *apana* at such a subtle level, if utilized, will facilitate the expulsion of all that is yet heavy, everything that might carry the soul earthward for another rebirth in time and space. And *prana,* overall, will be present and accessible for the soul's growth resulting in realization of its full capacity.

In the flux of all this movement, inner to outer and back again, the transmigrating soul will eventually gain insight into its own eternal nature, coming to see through it all, that the supreme Soul, *Atman,* has been overseeing all processes — of birth life, and death, of waking dreaming and deep sleep, of movements from heavens to earths to hells — all revealing that Consciousness is always present. This is the realization that *"puts death in its own grave."*

The greatest connections possible for the aspiring human being in the realms of name and form are shown in one fell swoop on the next chart up for study on the facing page. And *prana,* particularly the psychic *prana,* comes into full play to facilitate them.

The word, *Manahpranasambandhah,* is listed in *Sanskrit* dictionaries. There is simply no equivalent for it in English because the West has never studied the inner workings of mind and subtle power, being focused upon, or preoccupied with, the gross brain and physical forces only. What dabblings there have been in the realm of the psychological have fallen victim to examining bad habits, and to courting occult influences, i.e., sensationalism and love of spectacle and phenomena. But the seers of ancient India closely inspected the inner workings of mind and its energy, focusing mainly upon thought and its abilities and qualities. As the quote by Swami Vivekananda at the top of the chart relates, whatever the mind thinks, the *prana* is there to direct and fulfill those thoughts. However, for the master of *prana,* and as been taught already, the *prana* leads the soul to the "City of the Transcendent *Brahman."* For those who misuse and abuse the forces of *prana,* the worlds of name and form in time and space, i.e., *maya,* get the upper hand. As Sri Ramakrishna has stated, pointedly, *"The mother cat keeps her claws and fangs withdrawn when She picks up Her kitten, but this is not the case when She plays with a mouse."* The meaning of this is not hard to fathom.

The four corner pillars of this chart really transmit the teaching under inspection in a nutshell. Basically, food produces the energy of *prana* that, when purified and taken inwards, effects the mind in positive ways. allowing for an inward spiritual ascension that encounters *shakti* power. When *shakti* assumes the human being's thoughts and acts, the human ego is easily deflated, and God, Divine Reality — pure, conscious Awareness — takes over.

But this simple rendition of what needs to occur for spiritual awakening and realization has important details that accompany it. First, the food one takes into the body must be pure and clean, and be consumed in an atmosphere of quietude with an attitude of reverence. How many souls are there that satisfy these requirements around food consumption? Even leaving the important practice of vegetarianism aside, most beings have little discrimination around what they eat, and even less restraint about how much they eat. Disease comes to them as a result. Even, and maybe particularly, the opulent Westerner suffers them, and ends up spending most of his/her money on doctors, hospitals, and drugs. It was Jesus, the religious Ideal of Western man, who was heard to say: *"Thou shalt bless the bread and water that you partake of, and He shall take away all disease."* In India, becoming impervious to illness is not even an accomplishment. Health is natural to the *Yogi.* This being so, illumined souls spend their time in higher attainments, and in serving God in human beings.

Manahpranasambandha

Connecting the Living Prana   to the Luminous Mind

"The prana comes into the body from the Atman by an act of the mind. Whatever the mind thinks, that flows in and out via the prana, and verily leads, along with the Atman, unto the desired realm." **Prasnopanisad**

| FOOD | Gain Strength | Increase Stamina | Master Posture | Purify Senses | Equalize Breathing | PRANA |

"From pure food one gets pure blood; from pure blood, pure energy; from pure energy comes pure thoughts, and from pure thoughts one gets pure mind." Sri Sarada Devi

"The Apana facilitates evacuation and generation. Samana distributes the offered food. Prana itself operates and infills the senses. Through the main nadi, the Udana carries the soul back and forth to the various worlds, and Vyana pervades and moves through the many thousands of gross and subtle nerves." Prasnopanisad

Purify Prana

Control Prana

Raise Prana

Attain Nirvikalpa Samadhi
Help Souls out of Bondage

Frequent Holy Company

Meditate on Brahman

Attain Samadhis

Meditate on Ishvara

Luminous Mind

"My young friend, the one who knows that Imperishable One in which rest the mind, the prana, and the senses, verily becomes omniscient and enters into everything." Pippalada

Select a Guru

Secure a Mantra

| SHAKTI POWER | Perform Work as Worship | Surrender Self | Contemplate Scripture | Conduct Worship | PSYCHIC PRANA |

"As the rays of the sun become united with it at the time of its setting, and shine forth again when it rises, all the senses merge in the superior god called 'Mind' when it sleeps. At that time prana alone remains awake in that city." Pippalada

But such compassionate service is not yet possible for the aspirant. There is the vital breath, that is, the aspiring soul has to stop and consider how he lives. *"Man does not live by bread alone,"* said the Christ. So, he must take his first conscious breath. Prior to this, usually, his stance has to become manly, i.e., straight and upright. The body's posture is akin to the mind's posture which must mature later. The art of mental *asana* is yet to come for most beings (see chart on page 719).

Therefore, as seen on the chart (page 545), pure food, upright posture, and free breathing — these three, essentially, signal the wakening of *prana*. And actually, *prana* is always there, but man is to awaken to that presence and then utilize it. Some virile specimens, like athletes and warriors, use the *prana*. But they are not aware of the psychic *prana*. This marks the huge difference between the man who knows only the senses and the man who knows the Self. The senses live and delight in their objects of pleasure. The Self exults in itself, knowing that everything comes from That.

And it is here that the sincere spiritual aspirant turns the corner to pass the second pillar and head for the third, the psychic *prana*. For, as been noted, the *prana* may be on the rise in the physically strong person, but the psychic *prana* is still sorely underdeveloped there. Raw *prana* and refined *prana* are in contrast here, and so the refined, soul puts the physical behind him and starts a regimen of purification, control, and upliftment of his inner energies. Though no established order can be dictated at this juncture, the desire to purify and refine consciousness is usually accompanied by the appearance of a path, some teachings, and a guide to shed light on the both of them. And in fact, it might even be said that when we see a fine physical specimen of humanity in the world, that person is a walking exemplar of gross *prana*, but when we witness the appearance of what the seers call "Holy Company" in the form of *dharma* teachers, meditation instructors, spiritual preceptors, and the like, we are seeing the manifestation of psychic *prana*, right before our eyes. Now all that we need to do is acknowledge this fact and aspire to realize what it epitomizes.

A major element of great import in this approach to perceive and manifest holiness is the *mantra*. In the earlier pages of this book, from pages 131-143, the subject of *mantra* was taken up and taught extensively. The reader and student can look back and review them in this new light of the psychic *prana*. For the refined *prana* is full of the power of The Word. It would have to be, since it is the carrier of thought, knowledge, wisdom, and even cosmic conception. So, the *mantra*, with its seed elements *(bijams)*, conjoin with the *prana* is a huge way to help with the refinement process that the seeker is undergoing at this juncture of his or her spiritual evolution. An authentic *guru* has to be there to confer this penultimate of all boons. More on the *mantra*, and on the sacred act of *mantra diksha,* or spiritual initiation, will be explored in later pages of this book. And for more on the benefits of Holy Company and its concomitants, the teaching of the Four Sentinels by Lord Vasishtha on page 345 can be reviewed. And of course, a plethora of teachings on the blessed *guru* can be found in chapter two, starting on page 89 and onwards.

The several entries listed on the chart (page 545) between the third pillar of psychic *prana* and the fourth pillar of *shakti* each deserve special treatment as well. Spiritual life is in full swing, here, for the awakening of *prana* and its refinement into psychic *prana* has already done away with most of the problems and complaints about life in relativity. For, the advanced spiritual aspirant does not dwell in relativity any longer, even though the body may have to abide there. Even the body has become sanctified, with the spiritual experiences flowing through it transforming it into a crystal, as it were, that reflects nothing but the Light of God.

What gets noticed when psychic *prana* is released into the awakened mind, is that all modes of life turn into forms of worship. Even if the particular individual does not have a devotional temperament, worship goes forth in the form of study of scripture and service of God in mankind. As Shankara put it in his scripture, the *Vivekachudamani, "My devotion is to discrimination."* However this auspicious process occurs in various seekers, the secret of it all is that rare, absolute self-surrender that dawns on the mind of the devotee who has perceived the Truth, and is now dedicated to Its realization. The two charts recently explored in chapter eight, on pages 493 and 495, describe both the condition of such a rarified mind and spirit, and the many modes it runs along, naturally.

The Divine Mother of the Universe, famous among the devotees of the Lord, refuge of the fallen and lowly, and beloved by all creatures, wills it that beings become conscious of indwelling divinity and helpful to all beings. Those who are antagonistic to Her Divine Will She casts into the world, allowing them run their own misguided course. This course eventually brings *karma* to bear. Thus, their suffering will eventually awaken them to their selfishness, and to their own self-acuated predicament. This is to say that the pillar of *Shakti*, fourth on our chart under study (page 545), is hard won. Just prior to its attainment is that singular surrender of the selfish ego to a power that is beyond it, making it fall in step with the regimen of helping to remove suffering in others. If the soul has become aware of how it caused its own suffering, and then worked to find its way out of it, then it can more readily and effectively turn to help others. As Holy Mother has put it, *"Now that you have found the Great Master, Sri Ramakrishna, and are well along the path leading to Him, won't you kindly turn and help others along the way?"*

Thus, work as worship, or the path of *Karma Yoga*, also called selfless works, is not only a part of Her plan for perfecting the transmigrating soul, it is also a tool for assisting the entire world of living beings in their efforts to find peace of mind. For it is peace of mind, not endless activity, that will open the eye of wisdom to the vision of *Brahman*. Thus, the appearance of motiveless works is a sign of advancing spirituality, and also a factor in the further breakdown of the crystalized mind-ego complex. The Dissolution of the Mindstream chart at the start of this chapter, on page 503, shows the inner dynamics of this process from the standpoint of conscious meditation.

The rest of this circle, after the fourth pillar has been attained, is simply a blissful picture of spiritual life at the highest level of its expression. With *Shakti* in charge of all matters, and the soul given up completely to Her, it begins to perceive nothing but God in everything, though mostly centered in *Ishvara*. Communion with this Divine Being filled with the Light of Consciousness takes up much of the matured devotee's time.

And it is thereby that the boons of various *samadhis* dawn on the pure mind (see chart on page 697), now fully focused and free of the many distractions that preoccupied it prior to spiritual awakening. Life has finally been rendered divine. Food is pure, always taken in a sacred atmosphere with a fully attentive mind. Posture is naturally upright, and the breath is flowing evenly in and out of the lungs, also naturally. The *prana* spreads out, and in, unimpeded, and in spontaneous fashion, towards the planes of higher awareness. And even when the soul encounters the world, remembrance of its Divine Nature is immediate and ongoing. Protection from the world of ignorance and delusion, namely benighted humanity, and detached observation of the six transformations of birth, growth, disease, decay, old age, and death (see chart on page 225), is provided by constant attendance on *guru*, *dharma*, and sangha — called The Triple Gem. Work, worship, and study can go on without interruption. In this auspicious setting, *dharmic* wealth, *dharmic* spouse, and *dharmic* children can be enjoyed. As the *Upanisads* put it:

May our bodies experience great health.
May our life force flow unimpeded.
May our minds expand in their capacity to know Brahman.
For the Upanisads state that "All is Brahman."
Therefore, may we never deny Brahman.
May Brahman never deny us.
May there be no rejection of Brahman, ever, by us —
we, who are dedicated to the realization of the Atman, within.
May all the divine qualities cited in the Upanisads also, then, abide among us.
Om Peace, Peace, Peace.

Realizing the nature of *Brahman* in *Nirvikalpa Samadhi* returns the sojourning soul to its Blissful Abode, sometimes called *Paramasiva*. From that superlative and ultimate state of states, the now fully illumined Soul can either merge in Divine Reality, or return to the realms of embodiment

Lokas, Nadis, and the Transmigration of Souls

"In the heart dwells the Atman. There are a hundred and one nerves centered there, and in each of those are a hundred more, and each of these branch into seventy-two thousand nadis. In all of these the Shakti Power flows." Prasnopanisad

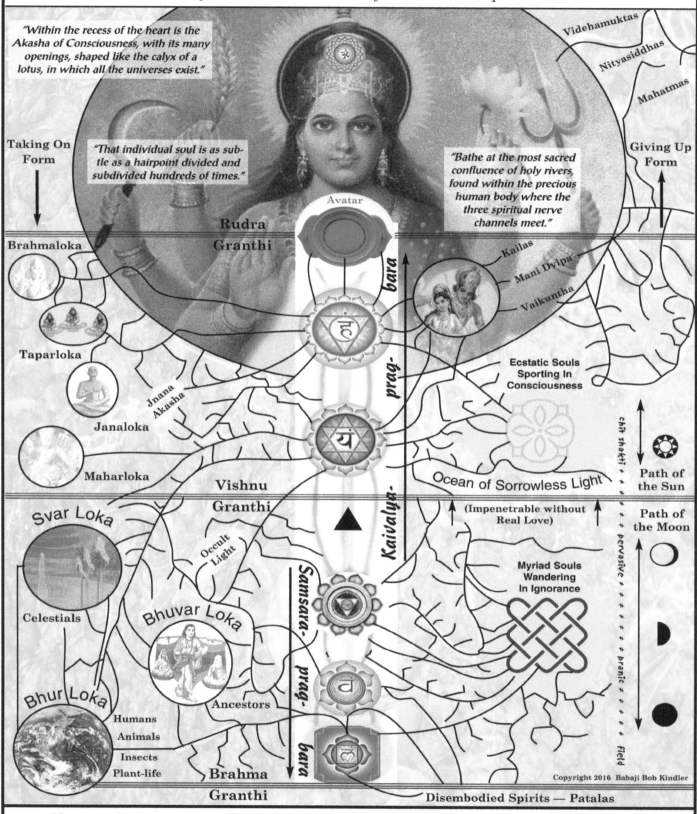

"Within the recess of the heart is the Akasha of Consciousness, with its many openings, shaped like the calyx of a lotus, in which all the universes exist."

"That individual soul is as subtle as a hairpoint divided and subdivided hundreds of times."

"Bathe at the most sacred confluence of holy rivers, found within the precious human body where the three spiritual nerve channels meet."

Taking On Form

Giving Up Form

Videhamuktas

Nityasiddhas

Mahatmas

Avatar

Rudra Granthi

Brahmaloka

Taparloka

Jnana Akasha

Janaloka

Maharloka

Vishnu Granthi

Kailas

Mani Dvipa

Vaikuntha

Ecstatic Souls Sporting In Consciousness

Ocean of Sorrowless Light

(Impenetrable without Real Love)

Svar Loka

Celestials

Occult Light

Bhuvar Loka

Ancestors

Bhur Loka

Humans
Animals
Insects
Plant-life

Brahma Granthi

Myriad Souls Wandering In Ignorance

Path of the Sun

Path of the Moon

chit shakti

pervasive

pranic

field

Samsara-prag-bara

Kaivalya

prag-bara

Copyright 2016 Babaji Bob Kindler

Disembodied Spirits — Patalas

"There, in the heart, where all the subtle nerve-endings meet, like the spokes of a chariot wheel at the hub, abides the Atman, stationary, but becoming manifest. Meditate on that Self as AUM, and Godspeed to you in crossing over to the farthest shore beyond darkness." Svetasvataropanisad

to help others out of bondage. In the first case, there are no individual souls present, therefore nothing to "help." In the latter case, as the luminary looks out upon the mind-field full of dreaming individuals, it all becomes a matter of helping embodied beings out of the illusion of finitude.

In order to accomplish this awakening of souls to their own eternal divine Nature, especially for those who are ready to do so, some substantial blockages will need to be penetrated. As we have been studying recently in these pages, the *prana* needs to be espied, refined, and released so that it can carry the soul, or ego-mind mechanism, inwards towards its Source. The chart on the facing page is designed to give an external visual of this working, however inadequate it may be to explain the vast inner spectacle of worlds and passageways within the marvellous human context.

Breaking its intricacies done into comprehensible sections, and examining them from bottom to top, we can see that on the left hand side of the chart are shown the seven *lokas* which were revealed earlier in this chapter (page 533). On the right hand side of the chart is seen the realm of *maya* that permeates the lower worlds, as well as the "Ocean of Sorrowless Light" told of by the Father of *Yoga*, Patanjali. Up the middle of the chart flow the seven *chakras*, the three lower centers roughly correlative with the lower three worlds on one side, and the realm of *maya* on the other. Three higher chakras are connected to the four higher *lokas* on the left, and the realms of higher awareness on the right — as well as the divine realms of *Vishnu*, *Siva*, and Divine Mother *Shakti*.

Throughout all of these inner worlds, signifying levels of Consciousness that beings operate at, stream the *nadis,* which as we have studied most recently, not only connect the realms together, but lead the soul with unerring force to the location of their desire, choosing, or preference. *Prana* operates this function in the lower worlds, psychic *prana* in the intermediary *lokas*, and *shakti* power on the highest and deepest of realms. As the *Prasna Upanisad* states at the top of the chart, *"In the heart dwells the Atman. There are a hundred and one nerves centered there, and in each of those there are a hundred more, and each of these branch into seventy-two thousand other nadis. In all of these the Shakti Power flows."* Strewn about the chart are several more quotes from the *Upanisads* about these subtle nerves and their intricate structure — a primal web in which all living beings live, act, and think, but which few are aware of.

Of deep interest and great import are the three *granthis* that divide the three worlds, keeping transmigrating souls in the region which they are restricted to by their own inner abilities — or lack thereof. The word, "transmigrating," is used over and over again in the teachings, mainly because it signifies and pertains to realms where such precarious principles such as movement, growth, *karma*, thought, processes like involution and evolution, etc, take place. Both Divine Reality, *Brahman*, and the Supreme Soul, *Atman*, are not restricted or limited to these, in any of the three worlds or seven realms. Divine Reality is both static and all-pervasive — also transcendent — and the aspiring soul should keep this in mind as the realms of name and form in time and space based in *karma* appear and play themselves out in dreamlike fashion.

The lowest of the three *granthis* intersects the root *chakra*. It is called the *Brahma Granthi*. No embodied soul will move out of ignorance and suffering, nor be able to give up the desire for birth and rebirth on the physical level, unless this dense knot in consciousness is "untied." This equates with the awakening of *Kundalini Shakti* in the *muladhara chakra,* and its uncoiling. Millions of souls are kept in *samsara* by the thickness of this gross knot in the mind, which is indicated on the chart by the mention of *Samsara-prag-bhara,* a veritable tributary full of souls who are always flowing back and forth amidst an unconscious state to life on earth, all via the mother's womb. Not even the ancestor realm is known by most of these souls, such is the denseness of their ignorance, and the existence of the life heavens also escapes them completely. What to speak of the animals, plants, and insects that inhabit nature expressly, there are even disembodied souls that frequent lower realms, or *patalas,* experiencing wide-spread suffering and shallow, scattered consciousness.

Once the *Brahma Granthi* is penetrated, usually via Divine Grace coupled with individual self-effort, a vast array of possibilities, as well as further impediments, await the still *karma*-laden embodied soul. Deeper centers of awareness, heretofore unseen within, present themselves to the ardent

CURTAIN OF NESCIENCE/CLOUD OF UNKNOWING

"When mentation, with all its facets and emanations, is engaged in devoid of full awareness, stripped of the knowledge of the Self within, then the universe in space and time rises out of nescience, root ignorance. But, if the true nature of all things is known prior to embodiment in the three worlds, the entire affair becomes nothing other than Brahman." Lord Vasishtha

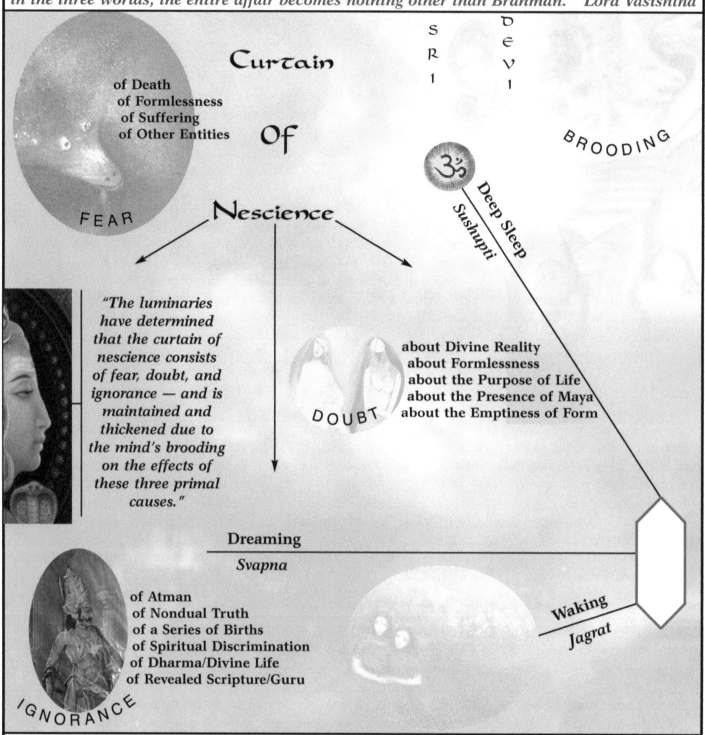

Curtain

of Death
of Formlessness
of Suffering
of Other Entities

Of

FEAR

Nescience

SRI

DEVI

BROODING

ॐ

Deep Sleep
Sushupti

"The luminaries have determined that the curtain of nescience consists of fear, doubt, and ignorance — and is maintained and thickened due to the mind's brooding on the effects of these three primal causes."

about Divine Reality
about Formlessness
about the Purpose of Life
about the Presence of Maya
about the Emptiness of Form

DOUBT

Dreaming
Svapna

of Atman
of Nondual Truth
of a Series of Births
of Spiritual Discrimination
of Dharma/Divine Life
of Revealed Scripture/Guru

Waking
Jagrat

IGNORANCE

"As Ram listened carefully, Lord Vasishtha spoke of Uddalaka's piercing of the curtain of nescience: 'Mere wisps of thoughts occurred to his mind, but he dissolved them on the spot. When the subtle tendency towards vikalpa arose, he quelled that immediately. Soon, even the darkness that gathered, indicative of primal ignorance, was overcome by his nondual mental stance, and he came upon and beheld a Great Light. Amazed, he pierced through it as well, along with the dizziness which came from gazing upon it. Thus, the stage of darkness and light was transcended.'" Yoga Vasishtha

seeker   But as the chart under study reveals, the *Vishnu Granthi* impedes the soul from more prefered atmospheres of consciousness. The knowers of these heights say that this *granthi* cannot be penetrated by the soul that does not possess real love of God in the heart. This is rather telling, revealing that many souls who are heaven-bound are actually bound to heaven. The inner worlds that border the *Vishnu* Granthi are called the life heavens. There are many of them, and souls still attached to pleasure and connected to earth will attend them, then have to take another birth "in the womb of matter." Love of God is rare, then, as well as being a type of coinage whose purchasing power will not just buy the soul access up the vaunted stairway of heaven, but can take it beyond heaven.

Beyond the *Vishnu Granthi* lies the four higher *lokas*, as well as the abodes of the highest deities. Souls who meditate deeply upon these divinities, who are Chosen Ideals to the earthlings, will reach these blissful abodes and never fall from them again. The first real taste of formlessness also occurs here, in the Ocean of Light that flavors these entire sets of regions. And it is here where the soul becomes aware of the subtlest of all barriers. This is the *Rudra Granthi* which separates the blissful *lokas* from the realm of Nonduality, or *Brahman*. Penetrating it is equal to giving up all forms.

And it is here that the infamous Curtain of Nescience casts its veil. This is an obstruction of the subtlemost consistency. It lies deep in the mind of collective humanity, and even effects the gods and higher divinities as well. To penetrate the *Rudra Granthi* is to see through this mental cloud and pierce the presence of root ignorance (see Lord Vasishtha's quote at the top of the chart, opposite). This is not only the transcendence of form in space, but also the dissolution of time as a mental concept. To rest in the Formless *Brahman* is pure Bliss, *Ananda*. The soul cannot enjoy this Supreme State if any haziness or sleepiness persists in the mental complex. And it is here where the Curtain of Nescience offers its best teachings.

As the chart on the facing page reveals, and as any persistant and percipient soul will want to know, the Curtain of Nescience is a surprising and unlikely melange of three primary elements. The revelation of this fact may be shocking at first (since the mind imagines and conjures up all manner of complexities when fighting its own darkness), but it is only the soul's three primal enemies of fear, doubt, and ignorance that make up this diaphanous cloud. And to deal with these so as to effect penetration, two facts are given by the illumined spiritual preceptor out front to the aspiring meditator.

First, it has to be known that this chimerical curtain is present for a purpose, and will persist and continue to separate the worlds of name and form, gross and subtle, from the realm of the Formless for all of time — or until time no longer insinuates. Secondly, and very important to the seeker of formlessness, is that since this barrier is there to stay and to provide its function, that to pierce it is to thin it out. Obversely, what thickens this otherwise impermeable locus, the preceptors say, is brooding.

The teaching relates, then, that by focusing their God-given awareness upon everything but Divine Reality, beings of all planes of existence fatten this inchoate barrier by the misguided power of their own uninformed minds and wills. This connects deeply with the tendency towards *Sankalpa* (see chart on pages 267 & 269), wherein the mind entertains all manner of projections, even becoming obsessed with them. As Sri Krishna tells Arjuna in the *Bhagavad Gita*, *"Beware of the tendency of sankalpa, Arjuna, for it can become a positive evil."*

To center the mind's awareness, and prior to that, its thinking processes, on God alone, thins out the Curtain of Nescience. This is precisely what happens in powerful dreams and religious visions; also is meditation practice every so often. In other words, one does not have to be free of the physical form in order to dissipate this cloud of cosmic mental residue. It can be accomplished by the inward moving practitioner in the meditation chamber right at home. The spiritual aspirant must learn to direct the many modes of the mind, like basic thinking, conceptualization, imagination, dreaming, and the like, away from the usual avenues they run along and focus them all upon *Brahman*. As the *Tantric* adepts say, *"Brahmavada, Brahmanistha, and Brahmaparayana"* — *Brahman* must becomes ones Path, ones Ideal, and ones Refuge. Moreover, habits such as fantasizing, sleepiness and, particularly, brooding, are to be fully curtailed — for it is brooding upon the matters of relative existence that thicken human ignorance, conjure up fear, and cause the aspiring human soul to doubt the pristine nature of Divine Reality that abides within.

Particulars about the chart on page 550 revolve around what kinds of fear, doubt, and ignorance take shape in the human mind. In the case of the first, fear of death is obvious. Patanjali even indicates this as the darkest of all *kleshas* in his *Yoga* system. But not so obvious is people's fear of formlessness. That is why the *yoga* of meditation is advised, so that the soul gets used to powerful modes such as emptiness, absence of thought, and the disappearance of the ego. It is only when such beneficial negatives occur that the more elevated states of mind can be experienced. In the case of doubt, the oft repeated teaching on it is that it goes away slowly, and persists even into the later stages of spiritual attainment. Doubt about the fact that all objects are insubstantial and devoid of essence plagues the human mind, but then again, doubt regarding whether the mind and senses that behold objects are any more substantial, also persists. Doubt about life in the world on one end, and about the existence of Divine Reality on the other, keep the mind in a state of flux, and that problem of brooding sets in, especially where no definite conclusion gets drawn.

The third aspect of the Curtain of Nescience, namely ignorance, is rife with problematic seeds. Ignorance of ones Self is the worst of these, and this pertains to the real Self, *Atman,* not the unreal self, the ego. And it is because the real Self remains unknown that the other facets of ignorance rise up so readily. In the ignorant person, the revealed scriptures are never looked into, a *dharmic* life is never lived, and ones series of past births are never seen and acknowledged. Such gross oversights only cause ignorance to burgeon and persist. Perhaps worst of all, the soul's discrimination never gets honed and utilized, for the presence of mature discrimination, *viveka,* signals the death of ignorance.

The Curtain of Nescience persists and exerts its influence in all three states of mankind's awareness, i.e., waking, dreaming, and deep sleep. It only lifts, that is, thins, when the mind develops the beneficial habit of one-pointedness, for, as we all should know by now: *"If thine eye be single, thou shalt know the Truth."*

The present author has done deep research on this "single eye," and has found that references to it appear in some seven or more different religious traditions of the world. These are all listed on the facing page at the bottom half of the chart now up for study. With these quotes to fuel our insight on this rather esoteric topic, the aforementioned teachings can be considered. Just as the three states of waking, dreaming, and deep sleep bear the inscrutable stamp of the Curtain of Nescience, so do they contain three sets of eyes that hold the potential for seeing through it. Calling them gross, subtle, and causal sight, these fine tools are scarcely used by those who possess them. The physical eyes should convey the real meaning of objects — the fact that all that is seen represents a pointer towards and proof of the existence of Divine Reality. If the physical senses, rightly tuned, hold this much penetrating power, then how much more will the subtle and causal senses hold?

Of course, there is a seer for all that is seen, and the "Third Eye," or "Wisdom Eye." exemplifies that as well as anything else. As the teaching on the chart relates, the presence at the center of the Wisdom Eye, or *Jnana Chakshu,* when it perceives via the gross senses, must come to know that all is imperishable. That is, when the outer eyes behold objects, beings, and circumstances coming in and out of existence, they should be trained to automatically default, as it were, to seeing the subtle undying Presence behind these appearances. To do otherwise, like brooding on the such changes, would thicken the Curtain of Nescience, allowing no real perception to get through whatsoever.

Thus, when the outer eyes are "made single" in this way, the subtle senses will burgeon with their own power of insight. The essence of all things inward and outward will become known to the seer and the *yogi.* This is the key to beholding God everywhere, equally — equally, because the Presence supporting everything remains the same, i.e., ever full. That Presence gets obscured by the form which it takes on. When beings see only through the two outer eyes, it is then that they perceive limitation and imperfection, and come to assign these misnomers indiscriminately everywhere, even to Divine Reality. As the quote on the chart (page 553) by the Great Master explains, *"The eyes*

Jnana Chakshu — The Wisdom Eye
Gross, Subtle, and Causal Sight

"The world is nothing but Brahman, because Brahman is the only Reality. See this always with your spiritual eye, and with an unruffled mind, and in all circumstances. For what is there to be seen here by the eye other than the mere objects of the senses? In like manner, to that one who knows Brahman, what is there to be seen at all — wherever the intellect may play or wander — except Divine Reality?" Shankara

1. Sees and utilizes the gross senses (*smelling, tasting, seeing, feeling, and hearing*)

2. Sees and utilizes the subtle senses (*odor, flavor, visibility, tangibility, audibility*)

3. Sees and utilizes the causal senses (*solidity, liquidity, luminosity, homogeneity, all-pervasiveness*)

1. *Avinashyantam* Sees Reality as Imperishable.

2. *Sarvatra Samavathistam* Sees Reality dwelling equally, everywhere.

3. *Prakrti Karma Kriyamanani* Sees that nature performs all action, while the Soul remains actionless.

Sees only the objects of the senses

"The eyes are in the center of the forehead, but their gaze is always fixed on the three lower centers where eating, drinking, and sex-life are enjoyed." Sri Ramakrishna

Religious References to the "Eye of Wisdom"

Christianity — *"If thine eye be single thou shalt know the Truth."* Jesus Christ

Hinduism — *"They who perceive with the eye of wisdom, they truly see. Devoting themselves to wisdom, they are neither born at the time of creation, nor are they disturbed at the time of dissolution. But the deluded do not see Me as I depart, stay, and enjoy. Only they truly see who possess the inner eye of wisdom."* Sri Krishna

Kundalini Yoga — *"As Kundalini traverses the sixth center, or 'Lotus,' called the Ajna Chakra, currents of refined prana rise high. Visions, light, and internal sounds are experienced, and the mind gets so absorbed that it loses normal consciousness."*

Buddhism — *"I have the true dharma hidden in my wisdom eye."* Sakyamuni Buddha

Taoism — *"The eyes are the windows of the soul. Between the two windows is the main door to divinity. Enter there to discover your inner divine nature."* Lao Tzu

Gnosticism — *"The True Gate is also the door to one's divine nature. It is the 'front door' to Heaven. It is located neither left nor right, up nor down. It is right in the center and thus is called the door to divinity — the White Sun."* Gnostic Mystic

Confucianism — *"Three persons are walking together; who is the master? They all have two eyes, but the divine Third Eye is the master of all of them."* Confucius

are in the center of the forehead, but their gaze is always focused on the three lower centers where eating, drinking, and sex life are enjoyed." By using their inward eyes, the ancient seers, on the other hand, beheld the deities within, assigning powerful names to them. The *Rig Veda* gives an example of this clarity of inner perception:

Om indram mitram varunamagni mathuratho divyah sa suparno gharutman
ekam sat vipra bahudha vedantyagnim yaman matarishvanamahuh

To that singular, divine Presence, the seers assign many a title, such as: The Lord of Gods, The Eternal Friend of all Beings, The ever-pure Waters of Life, The all-dissolving Fire of Yoga, The all-pervasive Ether of the Spirit, The devourer of Death, The winged Carrier of Consciousness, and the One who shines forth the Light.

The illumined soul who utilizes the causal senses is actually seeing into the realm of the Trinity (*Brahma, Vishnu, Siva*). The properties of solidity, liquidity, luminosity, homogeneity, and all-pervasiveness that transform later into earth, water, fire, air and ether on planet earth (the *bhutakasha*) are, "in the beginning," five causal thoughts in the Mind of God, the *Mahat*. When these finer senses function at the causal level, there is no doubt that a detached "Witness Consciousness" is looking on, and that It is stable and immovable in its eternal position. The conclusion is, as Sri Krishna puts it in His Wisdom Song (*Gita*), that *"....all action takes place in nature, not in the Soul."* Relating this back to the Curtain of Nescience once more, the last vestiges of doubt can easily dissipate in the light of this fact, leaving this diaphanous veil easy to move through — in both directions.

To bring greater clarity to all of this higher Philosophy, a visit to the realm of the supreme Deities would be helpful. This visual *darshan* offers up salient features of realization of the cosmic forms of *Brahman* and *Shakti*.

Mention has been made several times of what is underlying all appearances, what is behind the Curtain of Nescience, and of a subtle Presence that manages all worlds and guides all beings inhabiting them. And whereas there are many divine forces in operation throughout the three worlds and seven planes of Awareness, as the chant from the Rig Veda above strongly declares, they all fall under the auspice of the most auspicious One, the Divine Mother of the Universe. Called the *Mahashakti*, among other wonderful and inspiring names, even the Trinity obeys Her — as the chart on the facing page intimates.

The beautiful Hindu conception begins, as it were, with Lord *Vishnu* awakening from *Mahapralaya*, or Cosmic sleep, a state he has been meditating in since the dissolution of the previous cycle of time, far too long to fathom. All this is signified by the "Waters of Existence" he rests upon, called *Ekarnava*. A bed of a thousand snakes, *Ananta*, is his support, and represents all that is leftover from the previous cycle — for nothing is ever lost; nothing ever "dies." As the incarnation of *Vishnu*, Sri Ramachandra, declares, *"The destruction of things is their return to the cause that produced them."* The *Sanskrit* word, *ananta*, means infinite. Mother's primal process, filled with cosmic Awareness, moves inexorably over billions of years cycles, and cycles within cycles, all the many worlds and beings within them being too many to count or fathom. When worlds dissolve back into their source (unmanifested *prakriti*) and all beings sleep in formless Awareness *(Brahman)* at the end of a series of these cycles, it is the Trinity that comes forth first to reinitiate a fresh manifestation.

Lord *Brahma* is also been enticed into Cosmic Sleep, his version of it occurring within the Lotus of thousands of petals, each one representing many worlds. Out of the navel of *Vishnu* springs this fragrant flower of Divine Mother's inconceivable expression, opening to thrust Lord *Brahma* out into the forthcoming arena of multifarious activity that he will incept and proliferate. The Lord *Vishnu* will then take charge and preside over it, with Lord *Siva* appearing again at the "end" to dissolve it all — worlds, *lokas*, objects, living beings, and their *karmas*. Those *karmas* that will not dissolve at the time of *Mahapralaya*, the Divine Mother will hold in abeyance until the next upsurgence of multifarious forms. As an important aside, the beings to which these *karmas* belong will have to reincarnate in order to work them out. If the fortunate spiritual aspirant who has God's Grace has

Mahashakti – The Supporting Force

"They say that Brahma is the creator, but he is born of the navel-lotus of Vishnu."

1

"Again, Vishnu cannot be the creator, for he sleeps on the bed of the many-headed snake, Ananta, at the time of cosmic dissolution."

2

"Yet, Ananta cannot be the primal hub of creation either, for he rests on the liquid ocean of existence called Ekarnava."

3

"A liquid must have a vessel. Therefore, I take refuge in the primal Mahashakti, the Mother of all beings, who is the innate force in all and is thus the support of all."
— *Srimad Devi Bhagavatam*

4

Mahavishnu – Lord of Preservation

Brahma – Lord of Creation

Lotus of Conception

Ekarnava – Waters of Existence

Ananta/Shesha – Unmanifested Cosmic Energy

"I fly for refuge to the Devi who is praised by Lord Brahma while resting on the navel lotus of Vishnu, who himself is plunged in yogic sleep due to Her power of Yoganidra."   Sri Suta

ever heard of the millions of souls who are subject to hundreds of births on the wheel of *Samsara*, caught in the *Kalachakra*, then this explanation will both inform and satisfy any question.

More is always welcome when it comes to the all-attracting Divine Mother of the Universe. The next chart up for study, displayed on the facing page, is fully informative as to just what are the main powers of the *Mahashakti*. For those who have wondered, after being so fortunate as to have seen any of Her majestic *murtis*, those weapons She holds in Her ten arms hold profound significance, both on the battlefield of the mind and in deep meditation. Though sword, conch, discus, mala, bell, winecup, shield, bow, arrow, and spear are pictured here on the facing page, there are other *murtis* of Her whose arms hold different items, all specific and adequate to any given task She may have to undertake in the worlds of name and form, i.e., the Three Worlds and the Seven Planes of Existence.

Rather than explore every one of Durga's divine articles here, the reader is encouraged to find, read, and study the book by the present author entitled, *The Ten Divine Articles of Sri Durga*. Therein is found not only a complete explanation of each of Her weapons of righteous warfare, but also individual guided meditations on each one of them. As a companion book on this crucial subject, *Twenty-Four Aspects of Mother Kali* can also be sourced and read, providing even more beneficial inspiration on the sacred symbology of the Divine Mother of the Universe. To suffice for now, the paragraphs below are taken from the Introduction of The Ten Articles of Sri Durga, giving some preliminary teachings on the symbolism and usage involved:

The Ten Divine Articles of Sri Durga, as well as the Twenty-Four Aspects of Mother Kali, provide an introduction to the ultimate Goddess, both on a formal and a personal level. The Ten Divine Articles involve an in-depth exploration of the symbolism associated with the many objects seen in Sri Durga's lovely hands, and proceeds to utilize these many attributes as spiritual and devotional aids in a set of guided meditations. This study and its process is based upon the important premise that the divine articles held aloft in Her ten hands are not just physical objects, not only weapons for fighting negativity, and not merely powers for bringing about benefit to struggling and aspiring beings. Each one is an inseparable and intrinsic portion of Her very nature, being extensions of Her infinite attributes and qualities in outer manifestation only. If this is comprehended and accepted at the outset, the reading and study of this work — even a mere perusal of its pages — will prove to be much more effective in conveying its essential inner message.

This perennial message is spiritual in nature, transforming in effect, and inherently one with the Universal Mother. As the written word, its letters, its sound, and the meaning connected with it are all one and inseparable, so too is the Universal Mother's transmission of Truth ever-unified and homogenous. In this way are the ten articles that She carries indivisible parts of Her. The Sword, the Conch, the Discus, the Mala, the Bell, the Winecup, the Shield, the Bow, the Arrow and the Spear — they are all sublime expressions and nondual essences simultaneously. Being associated with Her, they act as purifying and enlightening forces coming straight from the Mother of the Universe. It is up to each of us, then, to gaze upon them, contemplate them, extract the meaning which they represent, implement this valuable information into our understanding, and meditate in unified fashion upon the Beloved One who wields them endearingly with infinite care and perfect detachment.

About this particular aspect of the Divine Mother called Sri Durga, the *Srimad Devi Bhagavatam* states:

"Durga, the Mother of Ganesh, comes, as the first, the most auspicious, loved by Shiva. She is Narayani, Vishnu Maya, and the nature of Purna Brahma (the Supreme Brahma). This eternal and all-pervading Devi is the presiding deity of all the devas and is therefore worshipped and praised by all devas, munis, and manus. This Bhagavati Durga Devi, when She gets pleased, destroys all sorrows, pains, and troubles of the bhaktas that have taken Her refuge, and gives them good karma, everlasting name and fame, all auspicious things, bliss and all happiness — nay, the final liberation!"

In this blessed *Tantric* realm of inner deities we have entered into, both tenderness and puissance are present. This is a winning combination, to be sure. In order to make certain that the aspirant is receiving the boons and blessings that arise from the Divine Mother and Her incomparable atten-

THE TEN DIVINE ARTICLES OF SRI DURGA

"Sword, conch, discus, mala, bell, winecup, shield, bow, arrow and spear — these are the ten articles She carries that are integral parts of Her. Associated with Her, they act as purifying and enlightening forces." Babaji Bob Kindler

Sword of Nondual Wisdom

Shield of Complete Protection

Conch of Auspicious Victory

Bow of Unerring Projection

Spear of Deep Penetration

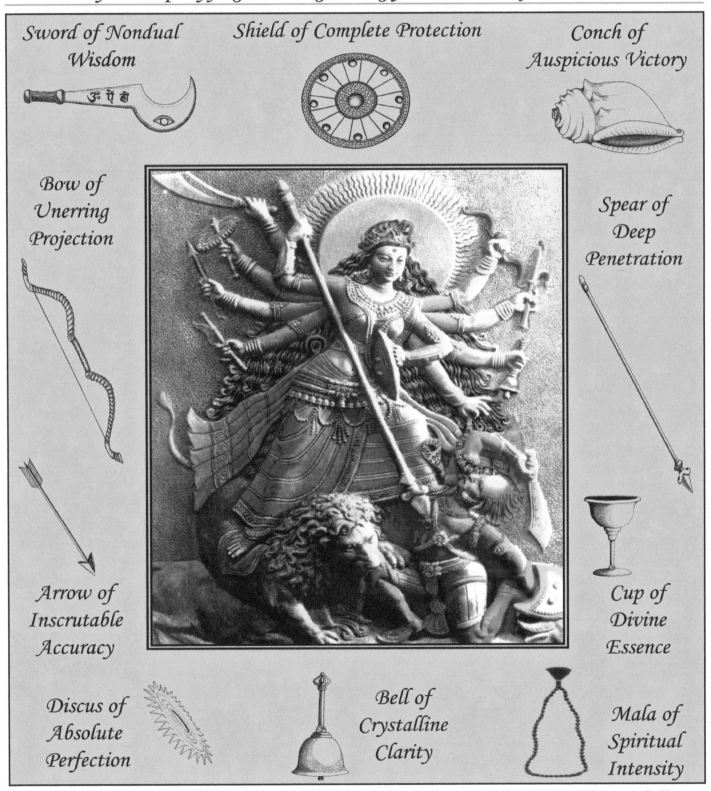

Arrow of Inscrutable Accuracy

Cup of Divine Essence

Discus of Absolute Perfection

Bell of Crystalline Clarity

Mala of Spiritual Intensity

"Struggle to fathom Her, oh mind, with every fiber of your being. You will never fully comprehend Her, but your intelligence will be purified in the attempt." Ramprasad Sen

tions, purification followed by meditation is the wise course. On the facing page is seen another example of The Divine Mother's *murtis*, this one couched in the atmosphere of India's unique and incomparable *Kundalini Yoga* system.

Similar to the preceding chart, the one on the facing page also appears in a previous book by the present author, one entitled *Reclaiming Kundalini Yoga*. It is based upon the description of meditation on the Goddess in the *Devi Gita*. Beginning with a deep inward glimpse of the Goddess to begin the process, the aspirant who worships Her next brings the revered *guru* to the fore of the mind, and envisions him/her simultaneously with the Divine Mother of the Universe. With these two auspicious points well defined in the mind, the devotee focuses all concentration on the base of the spine where the lotus called *muladhara* is located. Taking up the sacred *mantra* transmitted to the aspirant by the *guru* in sacred ceremony *(mantra-diksha)*, the fortunate seeker after perfection lights up all the remaining six *chakras* with its recitation. Proper pronunciation and concentrated focus are required on the part of the seeker to make this holy act effective and successful.

This powerful four-step beginning is rendered all the more forceful by remembrance of and rumination upon the Four Boons that Divine Mother grants upon all Her votaries. For a clear view and explanation of this step, the charts on pages 365 and 367 offer the full complement of teachings around this precious subject.

After this refreshing step in the meditation process, the devotee is to take up and contemplate the Five Seats of the Goddess, namely Lords *Brahma, Vishnu,* and *Siva,* in addition to *Sadasiva* and *Ishvara.* These five are superlative stations imbued with Consciousness, and are therefore fitting positions upon which the Divine Mother of the Universe can rely for absolute stability. It is from these quintuplicated cosmic foundations that She can look deeply into all the beings abiding throughout the seven planes of existence, and their various doings as well. Each one of these five contain abundant measures of Her infinite power, being sovereigns presiding over magnificent realms, and all attracting personalities as well. Whole meditations can be spent just on one of these five seats of abiding divinity.

But beholding such beauteous inner visions leaves the inward spiritual traveler with a deep desire to worship them with all heartfelt devotion. Understanding this yearning, the Goddess instructs the rapt lover of Divine Reality to perform *pujas* to these exceptional deities, which can be done both inwardly and outwardly, according to temperament, predilection, and preparation. Of course, each one of the five divine seats of Hers have a *mandala* of their own, and upon beholding them, the worshipper feels compelled to offer flowers and *mantras* to all of them. This pleases The *Devi* most highly.

And most fittingly, this elevating worship leads well into the succeeding steps of this profound meditation, all having to do with one of the Goddess's favored pastimes. The recitation of Her many blissful Names, combined with reading and discoursing upon the wisdom scriptures, is taken up next, adding a unique loftiness of atmosphere to the sacred proceedings. Such is the elevated swing of consciousness at this juncture, that the devotee is encouraged to dance and sing the Holy Names of the Goddess — an occupation that increases divine bliss manyfold.

To complete what now is known as a many-faceted meditation, instruction is given to take up the *yoga* of selfless service and prepare foodstuffs for distributing among all classes of living beings. Feeding the devotees is, of course, a supreme blessing in itself. Feeding holy men and women is a rare privilege, and if done, adds untold merit to the credit of the votary. But Mother is most keen to have Her poor and unfortunate children served as well, so the devotee is prevailed upon to take food to the lowly and the impoverished, the needy and the hungry. This act, perhaps more than any other, brings out from hiding a few of the key secrets of Formless Reality, among them being recognition of the innate equality of all souls. In both quantity and quality, the *Atman* pervades all beings, all things. Therefore, the Divine Mother's plan concludes with a directive to actually perceive Divine Reality existing in all beings — the young and the old, the rich and the poor, the famous and the unknown. God dwells within all beings, and all must be given the chance to realize this salient fact.

Meditation on the Goddess

In the "Devi Gita" from the Srimad Devi Bhagavatam

"Throughout life, everything is to be done in the light of My Great Hrillekah mantra, whose gifts are the guru and all the blessings which naturally come to My devotees. Nothing at all, at any time, is unattainable to the one who worships the Devi."

"Meditate on My Thousand-petaled Lotus."

"Perform all actions in the light of the great Devi Mantra."

"Remember and envision your blessed guru."

"Perceive youth, the aged, the poor, and the public, all as forms of Me."

"Meditate on My form in the fire of Kundalini in the Muladhara."

"Feed the holy, the hungry, and the devotees."

"Contemplate the Hrillekah mantra in tandem with the chakras."

"Dance joyfully and sing My Names."

"Ruminate on the four boons."

"Recite My many names and read My Upanisads."

"Meditate on the five seats of the Devi, all situated under My Lotus Feet."

"Make offerings to all the deities in My sacred Mandala."

"Perform puja for Me with devotion, and with all sacred offerings."

"Perform concentrated Japa and offer the results to Me, the Devi."

The Five Seats of The Devi

Brahma

Ishvara

Vishnu

Sadasiva

Siva

If there is one abiding point that persists at the end of this unique meditation on the Goddess, it is that everything is contained within Her sacred *mantra*, the *Hrillekha Mantra*. If the devotee can keep this fact in heart and mind, and carry its potency into all acts of life, then the very highest good for the individual soul, as well as for all souls, will be ensured. Such is the exceptional meditation upon the Goddess found in the *Devi Gita*.

All of India's wonderous *darshanas* are replete with pertinent instructions on meditation, both with and without the sacred *mantra*. However, for those who are advancing towards higher and deeper atmospheres on Consciousness, qualification is essential. To gain this rare attainment, often called *Adhikara Vichara* in the wisdom traditions, the *mantra* is the most powerful tool, for it sets up all types and forms of meditation (see chart on page 505) for experiencing.

Interesting of note, then, is how many-sided and multi-faceted both Indian *sadhana* and the human nature it attempts to transform can be. In the chart on the facing page, the aspirant after qualification can find all the four *Yogas* and their various shades present and operational. The overall mode smacks of *sadhana*, well-directed self-effort along the spiritual pathway. But how few beings are aware of, or duly instigate, these precious steps that will, if implemented prior to such refined exertion, render disciplines undertaken on behalf of gaining Enlightenment effective and successful. As Swami Vivekananda has stated in this regard, which always bears repeating: *"Herein lies the secret. Says Patanjali, the father of Yoga: 'When a man rejects all the superhuman powers, then he attains the raincloud of virtues.' He sees God. He becomes God, and helps others become the same. This is all I have to preach. Doctrines have been expounded enough. There are books by the millions. Oh, for an ounce of practice!"*

The words at the top of the chart presently under study (page 561) say it all in one paragraph — in fact, in one long sentence. Therefore, before an *asana* is assumed, a conscious breath is taken, or a bead of the mala is twirled, for the sincere seeker pursuing success in spiritual life and practice must satisfy the criteria for approaching sacred inner ground — what to speak of "the most Holy of Holies." It all begins with "attitude," to use a contemporary word. But it is not a good or bad attitude that is being called for, but one transcendent of all dualities and their endless problems and concerns. *Nityasarga*, appearing first on the list of preliminary practices, aspires to begin every day as if there were no beginnings, which is the truth of the matter anyway. Nonorigination *(ajati)* is the highest Truth; no beginnings, middles, or ends can change or compete with that. Chapter Ten of this book will take that sacred subject up in some depth.

So, suffice to say that the mind of the aspirant is already under his or her control regarding this facet. To awaken to the Truth is to first awaken from sleep refreshed and ready to explore the hidden depths of ones own Consciousness. This is followed by sacred ritual, also undertaken with all seriousness and sanctity. A splash of water from the bathroom sink, if the sacred river is not running by outside ones dwelling, is good enough, so long as the act, the motion, the water, and the intention all falls under the category of conscious awareness. Accomplished with the heart intact and the mind in tow, would be a good definition here. No sluggishness or hanging back, i.e., dragging of the feet, can be allowed. For all intents and purposes, and as far as he/she can know in the present, the sincere aspirant is now on the inward moving pathway to meet the Beloved Deity of the Three Worlds and Seven Planes of Existence: how else should he/she act and feel if not filled to the brim with reverence and awe? Thus do *Nityasarga* and *Sandhya* work together to begin the beginning.

The present writer has seen, on many occasions, ardent devotees literally running for the temple or the shrine room in all haste in the wee morning hours, there to bow low, i.e., *pranam*, before the sacred images on the altar. Ironically, in an elevated view from a helicopter, caught on camera and played in fast motion, the witnessing soul can see thousands of beings caught in a mad rush towards the altars of riches, fame, pleasures, and the like — but there is no sanctity or purity to this insane flux, what to speak of any intelligence or awareness. What is more, suffering of many types is its fruit, particularly when all these individual existences come to an end.

Preliminary Practices to Mantra and Meditation

A Sadhika's Nine-fold Ritual Prior to Daily Spiritual Practice

"Rising each morning with a desire to engage in the creative process, taking one's bath, prostrating before the deities, chanting one long recitation of Om, praying for the fulfillment of one's aspirations, offering life and soul to God, saluting the guru and the gurus of the guru, and vowing to infuse daily sadhana with verve and vigor — this is the nine-fold practice of a sincere aspirant prior to japa of the mantra and formless meditation."

- **Nityasarga** – Wakening consciously each day

- **Sandhya** – Purificatory bath and rituals

- **Pranams** – Prostrations at the altar

- **Dirgha Pranava** – Long recitation of AUM

- **Prapatti** – Prayer for fulfillment

- **Samarpana** – Offering one's life to God

- **Purusha Yajna** – Dedicating the soul to God

- **Guru-pranam** – Salutations to one's Gurus

- **Utsaha-vrata** – Vow to infuse sadhana with enthusiasm

The fruits of *Pranam,* however, make everything in the world of work and acquisition easy of attainment, for as soon as the forehead touches the ground before God in a sacred and consecrated atmosphere, the human ego is deftly removed from the picture — effectively "struck from the equation." This makes the Lord's work of granting everything to His votary quite easy, for He is known far and wide as the "Wish-Fulfilling Tree" Who confers all boons and blessings upon those who surrender themselves to Him. That is why Holy Mother, Sri Sarada Devi — who, according to Sri Ramakrishna Paramahamsa, is the incarnation of the three Goddesses, Kali, Sarasvati, and Lakshmi in this age — has stated beautifully, *"Oh bound soul! Surrender! Surrender! Then alone will She take compassion upon you and leave your path open."* Swami Vivekananda put it in this way, in one of the devotional wisdom songs he composed:

I make a complete offering of myself to my Guru,
Who is an all-powerful wave of purity rising out of the infinite Ocean of Shakti.
Whose Lila floods the being with a love that destroys all doubts,
and Who is the ultimate healer of the chronic disease of worldliness and attachment.

I surrender my life, mind, and soul, to the Divine Lord Who appeared in human form,
and Whose superhuman actions are inconceivable to mortals.
Whose life reveals and exemplifies nondual Truth,
and Who removes the incapacitating effects of relative existence.

But humility and egolessness are not the only boons to descend upon the rapt lover of Divine Reality. As if these two were not enough, that feeling of dizzying heights comes again and again, causing, as was mentioned, a gentle stampede of sacred footfalls towards the sanctum — both outer (church/temple/shrine room) and inner (Soul, God, *Atman*). In other words, and in the case of the other-worldly, it is not the ego that swells; it is the heart! This tear-causing expansion of devotional fervor at the center of ones being is one of the most intoxicating feelings in the Three Worlds, and is the main cause for millions of beings praying, meditating, circumambulating, studying — whatever divine preoccupation there is according to the differing temperaments of living souls.

Therefore, and back to the sole practitioner preparing for worship and meditation each morning, bowing before the shrine to the sacred images, *murtis,* thereupon, is infused with intense feeling, and followed up with a longing for direct spiritual experience that will both make all efforts fruitful and all future attempts at success unnecessary. Such one-pointed surrender is as rare among *bhakti* practitioners as is one-pointed concentration among even advanced meditators. It is no wonder, then, that devotees and practitioners of different religious traditions may make thousands of prostrations before the image of the Deity, even daily. What more needs be written on this facet?

After heartfelt *pranam* is offered, the ardent student of spirituality will take his or her seat (*asana*) and focus the mind by chanting one, long, recitation of the sacred *bijam, AUM.* This is called *Dirgha Pranava,* and has the salutary effect of transporting the mind into higher and deeper levels of Consciousness. As has been written and shared in earlier pages of this book, the *Pranava,* or, "The Word," is *Brahman's* own especial representative. The charts on pages 144, 146, 154, and 157, among others, will recall this powerful principle and its illuminating teachings to mind — which should be done repeatedly, day to day. Even the mere repetition of *AUM* will keep God close, providing protection and inspiration throughout all of life.

After recognition of *Brahman* has been affirmed via chanting of The Word, the aspirant is ready to offer a prayer. In Indian tradition, in all of its many facets, this prayer is not one for wealth, or gain, or pleasures, etc. The profound preparation that has been accomplished up until this auspicious moment has not been undergone for a mere boon concerned with earthly acquisitions. The sincere soul wants God, knowing that if the Lord and Mother of the Universe is gained, all else will follow naturally. But even this description has a flavor of calculation to it. Love of God for the sake of love alone is more to the point. The sincere aspirant, then, wants to possess the highest favor possible in the Three Worlds, wants to be the "Son of a King," as the saying goes. Therefore, with a centered mind and a heart virtually on fire, an innermost prayer is offered up from the depths of the soul, whether sounded silently into the heights of inner Awareness, or uttered aloud into the surrounding atmosphere.

This ultimate prayer is called *Prapatti,* and sets the stage for further exploration of the depths of Consciousness where the Lord and Mother lie hidden from view. In oldest time, the great soul, *Aditi,* the god of dawn's first light, made *prapatti* to the Lord for release from all *karmas.* To this day, *Sanskrit* dictionaries carry the definition of the word as *"....a deep, inner appeal made to the Divine Being by a capable devotee for the attainment of liberation, moksha."* Thus, besides being age-old, it is also accepted by the luminaries as an important element in the relationship of the embodied soul with the Supreme Soul.

The Lord and Mother of the Universe must find the spiritual advocate ready and willing for such high boons and deep blessings. *Moksha,* liberation in this lifetime, is practically the rarest of all spiritual bestowals, and so warrants a one-hundred percent sacrifice on the part of the adherent. The complete offering of oneself is therefore the price to pay in order to receive the boon of blessing sought by aspirants and luminaries alike. This absolute offering of the self to God is called *Samarpana.* If this offering to God is accepted, the ongoing battle with the human ego is immediately won. In a sense, real spiritual life begins here, for many are the souls who attempt such sacrifice, but due to holding back even a tiny portion of the self for the self, fail in it. The path is often rough and rocky for these souls, whereas those who succeed in giving their all make swift and sure progress towards all goals, even the Highest One.

But whereas the permission to enter the path has been granted to the more fortunate aspirant at this juncture, there is still work to do. This is proven by the next stage of preparation called *Purusha Yajna.* Dedication is now placed on the testing ground. The willingness to plunge into the work of reaching Enlightenment is key to the fruition of this phase. And it is a phase of spiritual practice and discipline, of *sadhana* — the all-important cutting edge of spiritual attainment. In other words, one cannot just state, "I dedicate myself to Thee, oh Lord," and walk away expecting all grace and fulfillment to come tumbling out of the skies. To be admitted into the pristine atmospheres of the *Atman,* one will have to make sure that the heart and mind are pure. The recitation of the *mantra,* which this nine-pointed preparation presently under study is leading towards, will accomplish that work. As Sri Sarada Devi has told us, *"As the timepiece on the wall goes on ticking, so too must you continue to repeat God's Name. Thus you will attain everything. Nothing else need be done. To learn how to pronounce and repeat the mantra, consult a guru."*

And it is thus that *Guru-pranam* comes to the four as the penultimate facet of this nine-point practice. In brief, and importantly, it is crucial that the devotee call to his or her mind the visage of the *guru,* and do so with all gratitude and heartfelt devotion. As Holy Mother has said, again, *"One must have reverence for ones guru. You should not doubt the words of your own teacher. Ones chance for salvation lies in reverence for him. There are many gurus, but the one who has given you the mantra is the real guru. For those who forget this, there will be trouble. Some day in the future they will have to come around and fall at the feet of the guru whom they have abused."*

And in fact, ones entire line of *gurus* ought to be brought to mind before starting into *mantra* and meditation. There are rituals available to enact this auspicious act, replete with *mantras* for each divine personage that are to be invoked in the mind. This, again, can be learned from ones spiritual teacher. For additional and definitive teachings on the import of taking and following a preceptor, the chart on page 91 can be referred to again.

To finalize this nine-step preliminary practice (page 561), there is a refreshment of the other eight elements of the entire sequence that is enjoined upon the dedicated practitioner. Entitled *Utsaha-vrata,* it entails infusing everything — life, spiritual practice, study of scriptures, *japa* of the *mantra,* and meditation — with increased enthusiasm. This will require the development of an indomitable spirit, one that will bear up stoically under all the weights that both earthly life and spiritual practice might throw in the way. As Holy Mother, Sri Sarada Devi, often advised in this regard,

SADHANA FOR PURIFICATION
The Precious Gift of Holy Mother

"I have done much more than necessary to make my life a model. Ah, the ecstasy of those days! On moonlit nights I would look at the moon and pray with folded hands, 'May my heart be as pure as the rays of yonder moon!' or, 'Lord, there is a stain even in the moon, but let there not be the least trace of stain in my mind.'" Sri Sarada Devi, The Holy Mother

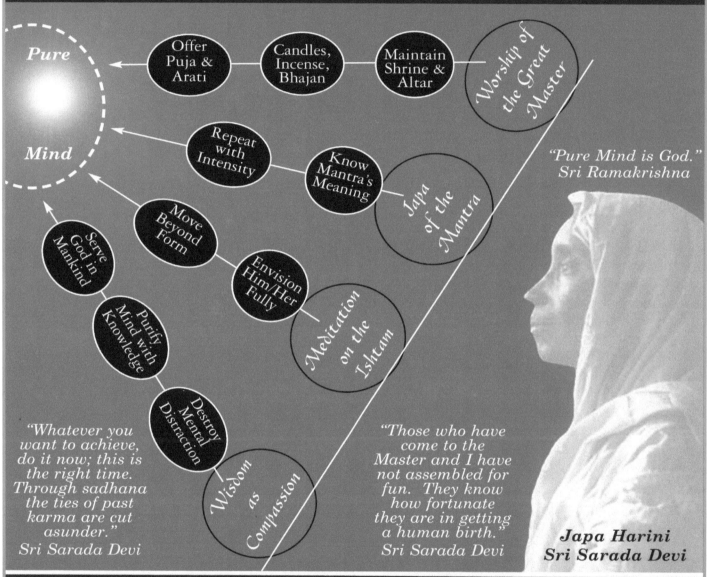

Pure

Mind

Offer Puja & Arati

Candles, Incense, Bhajan

Maintain Shrine & Altar

Worship of the Great Master

Repeat with Intensity

Know Mantra's Meaning

Japa of the Mantra

Move Beyond Form

Serve God in Mankind

Envision Him/Her Fully

Purify Mind with Knowledge

Meditation on the Ishtam

Destroy Mental Distraction

Wisdom as Compassion

"Pure Mind is God." Sri Ramakrishna

"Whatever you want to achieve, do it now; this is the right time. Through sadhana the ties of past karma are cut asunder." Sri Sarada Devi

"Those who have come to the Master and I have not assembled for fun. They know how fortunate they are in getting a human birth." Sri Sarada Devi

Japa Harini Sri Sarada Devi

"You must approach holy beings with the proper attitude. Next, dive deep with the noble ideas you receive from them. Then turn to help and serve others."

"Perform your sadhana by meditating upon the Lord. On that day on which you have the right mood, you will have meditation spontaneously."

"As the timepiece on the wall goes on ticking, so too you must continue to repeat God's Name. Thus you will attain everything."

"The Master used to fall into samadhi upon seeing Mother Kali's image adorned by the seven-stranded garlands I fashioned from full blown jasmine and rangam flowers."

purity, patience, and perseverance are the watchwords for comprehensive self-discipline in religion and spirituality.

The many auspicious mentions of Holy Mother, Sri Sarada Devi, plus the recurring subjects of *mantra* and *sadhana*, make this next chart up for study a major footfall, and one laid down by a contemporary seeress as well. The famous quote by Her has been placed lovingly at the top of the chart, and acts as the basis for its entire inception. That is, with purity of mind as the deep prayer *(prapatti)*, analogous to taking the pure white moon as its symbol, dedicated practice *(Purusha Yajna)* can be entered into with all enthusiasm *(Utsaha-vrata)*. And as the new chart reveals, *japa* and meditation are two key elements of that practice. To condense it all, using patience, and persevering in the practice (to add a fourth "p" into the theorum) purity of mind will come, shining its illuminating light upon life like a full moon over an otherwise benighted landscape.

It is interesting to note, and a case can be made for the point, that each of the four elements on the chart presently under study match well with the Four Yogas of *Vedanta*. Worship is *Bhakti Yoga,* of course. Wisdom is *Jnana Yoga*. Meditation is *Dhyana Yoga,* or *Raja Yoga*. And *Japa* can be likened to *Karma Yoga,* since it is definitely an act, and *karmas* get destroyed by engaging it.

But whatever the case may be, each of the four listed aspects of spiritual practice *(sadhana)* seem like friendly concomitants to the process just studied in our last chart (on page 561). In the case of worship, for instance, setting up the scene proves to be important. To accent again, preliminary preparation renders future practice more likely to be successful, and to repeat, lack of such preparation is the reason why so many beings throughout time — and particularly in the present time in Europe and America — are falling down again and again in their practices and thereby failing to gain any appreciable headway in spiritual experience, what to speak of gaining Enlightenment itself.

In worship, then — according to temperament and particularly for householders — the preceptor will advise the practitioner to construct and maintain a shrine in the home. "Construct" means to select a clean and quiet area away from the hustle and bustle of the home, use materials that are fresh and new, install images that have been blessed using holy water (water from the *Ganges* is best), and placing ones seat *(asana)* in front, with the *japa* mala in easy reach. "Maintain" signifies daily purification with holy water, the burning of incense in front of the deities with appropriate *mantras*, offering fresh flowers to the divine images and changing them before they have begun to decay, and reciting *slokas* and reading scriptures in that specific area to increase the sacred vibrations. The nine-point preparation (page 561) can also be done, for the most part, in that sacred atmosphere as well. Then, the singing of *bhajans* and chanting of the Lord and Mother's Holy Names, best offered by sitting still in one place so as to avoid bringing excitement and egoism into the place of meditation, can be offered. If time allows and training is available by an accomplished *pujari*, then *arati* and *puja* can be performed, deepening the sanctity of the consecrated space immensely. Such is a short description of daily worship for the devotee of the Lord and Mother.

Next in order is the practice of *Japa* itself. The Holy Mother, Sri Sarada Devi, whose one of many names is *Japa Harini* — perfect in the practice of *Japa* — gives us two main instructions about the practice, and one minor, clarifying teaching. That is, She had many instructions and teachings around *mantra* and *japa*, but these key ones stand out. First, the aspirant must know the meaning of the *mantra*. It is really inconceivable, but also very common today, that most seekers who attempt to find a teacher and secure a *mantra*, once they attain this boon, never inquire about the meaning of what they will be reciting hundreds and thousands of times in the coming months and years — should they not give up and maintain the practice, as they should.

Of course, we are not speaking here about the "spiritual menu tasters" who bounce from one teacher to another, perhaps weekly or even every other day, taking this *mantra* and that, then moving on to get another without giving the previous one a slightest chance to do its important inner work. Immature beings of this ilk will not only never make any substantial headway in authentic spirituality, they will never even make the necessary start of learning the meaning of precious words *(bijams)* that give the *mantra* its power to transform human nature into its divine potential. And, importantly, the mantras are connected to the Deities they represent. The ignorant and foolish therefore insult the divine beings within themselves by treating the sacred mantras in such a uncaring and callous way, with such a cavalier attitude. Again, knowing the meaning of the *mantra's* words, at the outset, might go a long way in removing this careless tendency in inexperienced seekers. They may even get a few early spiritual experiences from the *mantra* via this more committed path and perspective.

But back to those who initially feel the power of the *(Sanskrit)* words intuitively, an entire world of peace and bliss will open up for them if the persist in spiritual study. This is where *japa* and *karma* connect to *jnana* and its wisdom. In other words, the young bird suddenly finds out it has two wings, and begins to exercise and utilize them both. The *mantra,* in all its parts (see charts on pages 131 & 140) will be revealed to them, and "revealed" means having an actual vision of the specific deity who lies hidden deeply in the *mantra* — just as meanings lie within words. The reader can refresh the mind with the wisdom teachings that are contained in many of the charts on the subject in this book, starting on page 131 and moving through to page 146. Consummate teachings on the transforming power of the *mantra,* and how to utilize it effectively, will help the aspirant to penetrate deeply into the spiritual art form that is *Mantra* Science.

The second important point that Holy Mother, the *Japa Harini,* has to communicate to us, is that the *mantra* and its repetition is a matter of deep intensity. It cannot be allowed to become plodding, mundane, or boring. She, Herself, stated that the practice of *japa* can become as tedious as *"tilling the dry earth with a spade,"* so it is up to the devotee to infuse the practice itself with devotional fervor — just as he promised to do in the final mode of preparation called *Utsaha-vrata,* recently studied on page 561. The devotional wisdom songs of Ramprasad hold evidence of this ability to turn the mind wet like the tropics rather than dry like the desert. He sings in one of his offerings to the Supreme Deity:

> *Oh mind, listen carefully; you are my tame bird.*
> *I am training you to repeat the Name of Kali.*
> *Heed the wise proverb — whoever learns a lesson thoroughly lives perfectly content.*
> *Whenever you become dull, oh mind, remember this ancient adage —*
> *that student that shuns study will be beaten soundly and put to bed without supper.*

To further clarify the teachings on the *mantra* portion of the chart, and to dovetail it into the teachings on *Raja Yoga,* or Dhyana, it was mentioned that Holy Mother had one secondary point to make about the practice. In this regard, it can be stated that the *mantra* is a practice, not a goal. Its efficacy lies in the fact that is destroys imperfections and impurities on the human mind who uses it for that purpose. This is its best and most redeeming quality, at least as far as the sincere practitioner is concerned. The practitioner, however, is not to imagine or think that the *mantra* and its practice is the goal of spiritual life. There is much more ahead.

To put it succinctly, one has to move on to Formless Awareness. This is one of Holy Mother's main points on the chart presently under study within the heading of Meditation. Just as ones penultimate business in spiritual life is to introduce the embodied soul to the *"kingdom of Heaven within,"* which will include the many guardians and angels, and gods and goddesses, abiding there, so too, the realization must dawn that this introduction is accomplished so that the soul can move beyond Nature and its name and form producing powers *(maya)* so as to *"get to the Father through the Son."* As was previously stated, the one who utilizes the *mantra* conferred upon him/her by the authentic spiritual preceptor in sacred ritual *(mantra-diksha),* will eventually have *darshan* (inner communion) with the holy personages abiding therein. This is not like looking up in the sky to see celestial beings floating there in outer space; that is a superstition — and one that turns away the intellectual, makes and scientist scoff, and keeps the atheist a disbeliever. It is rather to discover the *"many chambers of the Lord's Mansion"* within oneself. This is some of the "best news" that *Vedanta* can bestow upon contemporary seekers after Truth, that all of existence lies within oneself, and that, as the nondual teachings proclaim, *"The Self is Eternal."* And it is this Self of mankind *(Atman)* that is the Formless Essence, and which the *mantra,* using divine forms and words of subtle power, can reveal to us. Thus, again, do the *mantra* and wisdom both lay and pull together.

But to remain with the subject of meditation on the chart, the second point revealed is that, prior to having that definitive experience of Formlessness, or Formless Awareness, the meditator may have visions of Divine Forms come to him/her in rapt meditation. Since, at this point in practice, the aspirant has spent so much time reciting the Lord's Name by repeating the sacred *mantra,* it is only natural that when spiritual experiences culminate around divine forms, that the Greater Reality will also appear — *Brahman, Allah, Prajnaparam,* the All-Mighty Father, etc. This has been cited by insightful sayings like, *"If thine eye becomes single thou shalt know the Truth,"* and *"Thou shalt know the Truth, and the Truth shall set thee free."* Or, more consummately, in Sri Ramakrishna's words, *"God is with form and God is beyond form, and God is also beyond both form and formlessness."* In this exceedingly connected way do the worlds of name and form in time and space, and the Ultimate Reality Who is the underlying foundation for them all, coexist in India's *Sanatana Dharma.*

For final elucidation of the chart under study on page 564, we need only take up the section on Wisdom as Compassion. Many connections have already been made to that facet of practice from the other three subjects listed. And inside of this fourth facet there are three more important elements to consider. These bring into focus the twofold title of compassion and wisdom, a duo that have not always seen eye to eye throughout human history. The fault for this lies with the human mind, so full of distraction and so prone to ignorance.

Taking up ignorance first, we see the cause of distraction, i.e. due to mankind's lack of perception of his own innate perfection. Many vagaries and vicissitudes of life then enter in. He thinks he is a body rather than a soul. He believes that he is a product of nature rather than the essence of conscious Awareness. He supposes that he evolved over many millenia when the truth of the matter is that he is the detached "Witness Consciousness" that simply watches all phenomena occurring in nature pass by, leaving him untouched and intrinsically whole, in blissful eternity. This is what Sri Krishna is trying to tell the beleaguered and confused Arjuna on the battlefield of *Kurukshetra,* recorded in the *Bhagavad Gita,* that *"All action takes place in nature, not in the Soul."* In the sweep of powerful insight caused by realization of this statement, imagine the peace and bliss that would suddenly accompany the embodied soul. It would not only bring about the death of ignorance, but would herald a final end to all confusion of the mind as well.

Sri Krishna has also stated that *"there is no purifier in the world like knowledge."* Obviously he is not speaking about intellectual knowledge, for there was plenty of that in India back in his time. What there was, and always is a scarcity of in this world, is Supreme Knowledge, called *Paravidya.* This is the Wisdom of the Soul, the nondual awareness of Divine Reality that underlies all of relative existence.

Ignorance of ones divine nature, or of anything remaining to be known by the pure knower, has no chance against Wisdom — particularly of the nondual type. But the onslaught of distractions coming from life in relativity threatens to stave higher wisdom off. By being drawn out by the world and senses instead of maintaining ones center in the *Atman,* the human being courts spiritual suicide. It is only then, as Sri Ramakrishna has stated, that *"Avidya shakti is more powerful than Vidya shakti,"* that ignorance wins the day, and therefore the lifetime, even many lifetimes, against liberating Wisdom.

One way to change this disasterous course of things, instanced by the final entry on our chart under the Wisdom as Compassion heading, is to take up selfless service of mankind. The expression of compassion will ripen in this endeavor, and the higher wisdom that is missing or lacking in the mind will be filled in. The secret here, or one of them, is that when engaged in selfless service man forgets himself, i.e., his ego self, and with that rare vacancy his concern about ignorance also begins to dissolve. Being unreal, a mere false superimposition, ignorance has no substance, so treating it like it has none will lessen its influence more and more as divine works go forth and good merit accrues.   Of course, and has been mentioned already earlier in the pages of this book, serving mankind as God, and not as a human being, is the further secret.   We are human only temporarily, but we are divine eternally.   Too many uninformed human lives impresses the habit of embodiment into the mind's subconscious layers, causing conditionings that bind the soul (mind/ego mechanism) to matter, to the earth plane.   Soon, all that exists for bound souls is the physical, and remembrance of ones blissful, ever perfect Consciousness, falls away.   For one of the best explanations of the dynamics of ignorant human embodiment, see the Twelve "Links," or *Nidanas*, chart on page 192.

It has been declared that human ignorance is unreal, a mental construct and overlay unwisely laid atop the truth of mankind's essential nature.   The next five charts will take the reader deeper into this fact, while also exploring the reason why such a dark and cruel superimposition has been accepted by the human mind to be real.

Such a bold statement as to the unreality of ignorance requires proof, and if the presence of hundreds of enlightened and liberated souls throughout history is not enough, since each living being must realize this salient fact for him or herself, the exact ways in which superimposed ignorance dissolves and goes away can presented for additional impetus towards freedom.   The chart on the facing page lays out two classic ascending pathways towards the destruction of root ignorance in the human mind, replete with quotes from several exceptional luminaries who accomplished this feat.

Beginning at the base of the triangle of *avidya* (based in duality) where ignorance has its hold on the minds of living beings, we look upwards (actually inwards) to behold two ascending roads full of the promise of soul liberation.   The left ascending trajectory is followed by souls who are naturally light-hearted and attracted to joy, while the right pathway is for those whose natures are inclined towards seriousness and attainment.   Of course, many of the attributes of one path are shared by the other, since human souls are not always so easily set in one way only.   But generally, the attainment of spirituality proceeds with these ways and means along these two basic routes.

This fact is seen particularly in those who begin with an enthusiastic spirit that is often given to excitement and impetuousness at the outset.   This can be a great aid if it is channeled towards a mature equanimity that is bound to come if spiritual insight matures in them.   Otherwise, inhibiting factors can enter in, such as emotionalism and sensationalism, along with an abiding satisfaction with surface attainments only.   When these dangers are avoided, happiness and joy are soon upon the scene, bringing an exuberance that is wholly impossible to dampen or depress.   The welcome advent of higher wisdom is the natural result of such maturity of spirit, and the calming effects of authentic peace can then settle into the soul, like rain seeping into a thirsty landscape.   But it is not the end-all and be-all of that winsome happiness that once frequented the face of the positive soul, for true bliss based in equanimity soon appears.   And the fulfillment of all desires awaits at the end of such a spiritual rise in human consciousness.

The scenery is somewhat different for the soul who treads the more traditional pathway.   These rare beings usually come into life and embodiment is possession of powerful teachings, and they promptly find a way to make them broadcast to the world and thus distribute them among other seekers of Truth.   Thus, it is only a matter of course that they immediately find their way to holy company in the form of an illumined teacher and spiritual companions, i.e., *guru* and *sangha*.   In the rarified atmosphere of such unique souls, they dive even deeper into finer levels of understanding and comprehension, mainly concerning the transformative words of the illumined seers whose divine testaments to spiritual realization fill the scriptures.

Sincerely seeking souls such as these easily find their way out of potentially dangerous attachments and the allurements of the world and society.   There nature is more austere, and they thrive on less, in the spirit of natural renunciation.   Pleasures and enjoyments seem insipid to them, whereas hard work and the struggle for ultimate freedom attracts them immensely.   They end their fruitfully spent time on earth in possession of attainments that are hardly even imagined by simple souls, and not even known by the worldly.   It seems as if fulfillment was never their goal, but rather the attainment of an unalterable and unimpeachable state of self-discipline that will allow them to go

The Disappearance of Ignorance

Fulfillment   Discipline

Bliss
Ananda

Transcendence
Para

"If a man but tastes the bliss of God, he runs after it thereafter. It matters little to him then whether the world remains or disappears."
Sri Ramakrishna

"At the time of creation, people had wisdom from their very birth. Consequently, they at once realized the unreal nature of the world. They renounced it and practiced austerity. They were liberated in no time."
Sri Sarada Devi

Equanimity
Samatva

Attainment
Sampadyate

Peace
Shanti

Self-Effort
Sadhana

"We believe that every being is divine, is God. Every soul is a sun covered over with clouds of ignorance; the difference between soul and soul is only due to the difference in density of these layers of clouds."
Vivekananda

"The secret of religion lies not in theories but in practice. This is all I have to preach. Doctrines have been expounded enough. There are books by the millions. Oh, for an ounce of practice!"
Vivekananda

Contentment
Trpti

Austerity
Tapas

"Perhaps one practices japa and austerity in this life. In the next life one intensifies the spiritual mood and in the following advances it further, and thus spiritual evolution goes on."
Sri Sarada Devi

Wisdom
Jnana

Contemplation
Manana

Joy
Mudita

Scriptural Study
Svadhyaya

"The happiness of the worldly man slowly declines as his spiritual joy becomes deeper."
Sri Ramakrishna

"The nondual scriptures point the way to Moksha, that most elevated condition that is the very atmosphere of Divine Reality."
Lord Vasishtha

Happiness
Sukha

Holy Company
Satsangha

"The happiness of the world is transitory. The less you become attached to the world, the more you enjoy peace of mind."   Sri Sarada Devi

"Whenever I contemplate the teachings of the dharma, I cannot help but share them with others."   Milarepa

Excitement

Dharma

← Ignorance / Avidya →

anywhere and forebear anything for the sake of duly meting out the Truth to those who have qualified themselves to hear and realize It. The reader is invited to study closely the quotes from luminaries that complement this chart (page 569), which help explain many of the fine tenets displayed
along these two classic inward trajectories.

The second of the five charts presently undergoing study takes up another and similar type
of inward trajectory, also in line with a definitive progress towards ultimate Freedom. In this case,
however, another visitation of the teaching of the three *gunas* recurs to guide us along it.

Thankfully, for every sincerely seeking soul, as well as for all beings who are tired with suffering — both in the world and with the body — the fine guage of the three *gunas* emerges in spiritual life to save and protect. The saving occurs via the destruction of doubt and guilt that plagues
the mind, and the protection kicks in to ensure that one never drifts back into the realms of suffering again. For instance, the darkness of *tamas* visits even illumined souls, as in the *"dark night of the
soul,"* but where does it go to later when the light of victory arrives? It is only that the unillumined
soul, who is unawakened as of yet, is still plagued by uncertainty. Thus, he/she must follow an
inward path back to his/her innate perfection.

This early state of darkness is well-illustrated by the description at the bottom of the chart on
the facing page, where we take up the trail of the one who must take up the challenge. It is seen
that ignorance *(avidya)* is *tamas*, not sin or worthlessness or futility. Desire based in materialism has
caused a condition of sleep-filled delusion to cover the mind, and most beings around him are equally entranced and burdened by this heavy weight — to such an extent that it has become as if a natural state to live in! In this regard, beings laboring most of the time in *tamas* occasionally rise to a
state of better energy, flavored by *rajas,* at least temporarily. Here we see excitement and sensuality enjoyed in families and in society, all based in foolish pastimes filled with selfish grasping after
superficial things, beings, and situations. The aim of this darkened area of life is pleasure and vaunted happiness; the result is the inevitable descent into mental brooding.

In an attempt to better both life and mind, most beings seeking to rise out of the mind's penchant for spoiling inner peace, turn to a rise in stature. This occurs in the workplace, mostly.
However the attainments there are not long-lasting, and the authority one gains, often used to lord
over others with a domineering spirit, only backfire in the atmosphere of mutual competition. In
the wake of these elements, the mind drifts back and forth between an unsettled emotionalism and
a defeatist attitude of pallid indifference. The sensitive soul searching for higher fulfillment cannot
help but notice the underlying deceptive nature of work-life and its promised gains — gains that turn
old and insipid once they are used repeatedly and become all too familiar, day by day, night after
night.

All the while pushing against this still benighted mental envelope, the human soul striving for
relief searches for greener pastures and begins to see some glimmerings at the end of this dark tun-
nel of combined and ever-alternating *tamas* and *rajas*. This is the shine of *sattva,* which brings with
its advent a success of a different nature, one that is attended by intellectual advancement. Here,
the ground becomes more secure, the light more revealing, and the air purer and purer as refinement begins to visit the mind. The long forgotten feel of deep thinking and spontaneous insight
enhances this new, more inward, territory, and the intrigues of spiritual revelation that far outstrip
anything the world and the workplace can offer, pay a happy visit to the soul.

But come to find out, as the aspiring being finds, that this *sattva* is still tinged with leftover
rajas, that is, that a superlative and heretofore unseen element that lies beyond the personal ego and
its small share of limited joy is beginning to exert its superior influence. This is the first real sign of
authentic freedom, authentic because it places all responsibility and ability in the hands of the newly
awakened soul. Here, there is no more praying to a force or power outside ones own Self, the *Atman*.
No longer are there many things to see, many places to visit, many wonders to hear about, many
secrets to uncover, or anyone to love other than the Self, because the many does not exist any longer,
only The One.

Progress Towards True Freedom

Moksha — Perpetual Freedom

(Pure Sattva)

Ananda - Bliss

Samasti-chitta - Universal Mind

Niskampana - Stability

Sattva

Mumukshutvam, True Desire to be Free
Involving:
Recognition of Oneness, Discrimination, Detachment, Willingness to Practice

→ **Prasanna - Clarity of Mind**

Adhigama - Attainment

Upalabdhi - Perception

"There must be freedom of the individual to express his nature"

Raja-Sattva

Chaitanya, Spiritual Awakening
Ushering:
Glimmerings of Insight, Intuition, Aspiration, Willingness, Positivity

→ **Sadhana - Self-Effort**

Alochana - Deep Thinking

"May you speedily attain to freedom and then help others attain it."

Udasina - Indifference

Rajas

Mrsa, Pretense/Vanity
Around:
False Attainment, Assumed Status, Feigned Authority, Sense of Superiority

→ **Kapata - Deception**

Vedana-moha - Emotionalism

"Those social rules that stand in the way of freedom are injurious."

Aupadika - Sense Enjoyment

Tamo-Rajas

Bandha, Bondage/
Relating To:
Sense Objects, Pleasure, Excitement, Family, Pastimes, Feelings, Brooding

→ **Kamana - Pleasure Seeking**

Vikshepa - Distraction

"Advancement towards liberation is freedom — the worthiest gain."

Lokayatika - Materialism

Tamas

Tandra, Darkness/Sleep
Ignorance About:
Vital Energy, Meaning, Selflessness, Higher Intelligence, The Soul

→ **Bhranti - Delusion**

Sprha - Desire

"Let each one work out his or her own freedom."

Characterization

Spiritual Awakening By Stages

The Four Classes of Devotees

"There are stages of spiritual growth in mankind. Each one is necessary. This is the essential of religion. Know that every undertaking must pass through a lot of obstacles. Truth triumphs if only one pursues a peaceful course." Swami Vivekananda

1 Pravartaka

Observes outer religious formalities

Follows a daily routine of mild general practices

Regulates food and refines dietary habits

Reads religious books that strengthen faith

Engages in actions that increase mindfulness

2 Sadhaka

Conducts sadhana on an internal level

Intensifies spiritual practice over time

Fixes senses and mind in a stable position

Studies the revealed scriptures with a Guru

Prays inwardly in a state of intrinsic connection

Emanation

of

Pure

Intelligence

Brahman
Mahavishnu
Paramasiva
Mahashakti

Brahma
Vishnu
Siva
Shakti

Mahat
Antahkarana
Senses
Elements

3 Siddha

Adjusts practice based upon the vision of God

Keeps discipline handy but lives in realization

Sublimates desires and rises to higher states

Transmits wisdom of the scriptures to others

Meditates in a state of one-pointed Awareness

4 Siddha-Siddha

Abides in the nondual state of Brahman

Has transformed spiritual practice into Bliss

Is desireless and lives for the good of others

Emanates the essence of Enlightenment naturally

Meditates naturally with eyes open and closed

"The Pravartaka is a beginner. He puts marks on his head and body, wears a rosary around his neck, and strictly follows outer observances. The Sadhaka is more advanced. He has lost his penchant for outer show. He longs for the realization of God and thus prays to Him earnestly. The Siddha has firm conviction that God exists, since he has seen Him. And the Siddha of the Siddha? He has not only seen God, but has talked to Him intimately." Sri Ramakrishna Paramahamsa

And glimpses of this One only add further impetus to practice the unique arts of self-discipline, for there is Bliss (*Ananda*) in this fresh sense of Oneness, and the awakening soul wants to gain and possess That for all time. Further, making its appearance in this ripe and fertile soil of new spirituality, comes the advent of the singular transcendent facet called "universal mind." Where indivisible Oneness is, That also follows. *Sattva,* then *Pure Sattva,* forms the penultimate arrival point for the more enlightened Soul. The reader is invited to study all the quotes by Swami Vivekananda that accompany each level of this inward journey to Freedom.

From a more traditional standpoint, and utilizing the teachings of the Great Master to explain it, the chart on the previous page outlines the spiritual aspirant's inward rise back to his/her intrinsic perfection. This wonderful perspective leaves ignorance and its unsavory minions out of the picture, and pertains more to those salient souls who are returning to the embodied condition for purposes of completely divesting themselves of all traces of *karma.* Earthly existence — a very unhealthy place to be — is nevertheless an ideal place in which to remove all imperfections; they all tend to show up on earth rather than, say, in heaven. In other words, the consummate soul wants beyond both earthly and heavenly existence.

This teaching all begins with the *pravartaka,* the novice, who though unpracticed and spiritually unlettered, has nevertheless become convinced that spiritual life and its superlative ends are the real purpose for human existence. This level of practitioner, verisimilar to the type of aspirant we see in the West today, involves him/her with basic but meaningful rituals accompanied by a minimum of daily practice. Consciousness around food is important to them, particularly with regard to its purity and the observance of moderating its intake. Along with this regimen comes a beginner's search of the religious scriptures of the world, and an overall interest in what the luminaries of the past and present have realized and passed on to others via spiritual life. Finally, a spotlight is shone upon ones actions, with an emphasis on mindfulness and sensitivity. Engagement in all of this, though often unknown to the *pravartaka,* is in preparation for *sadhana,* which will require an intensification of all aspects of consciousness.

The *sadhaka,* then, represents the second phase of authentic spiritual awakening. The most obvious difference between stage one and two is that the accent shifts from outward to inward at the *sadhaka* level. Those religious rituals undertaken by the *pravartaka* transform and begin to take place in the mind instead of in the world, and those few routine practices done daily out of a sense of duty intensify greatly to where less time is spent on life in the world and more on the life of the Spirit. In other words, the happy compromise allowed by the beginning aspirant begins to disappear from the more intense regimen of the *sadhaka,* and this is noticed most of all in the new behavior of the senses and the mind. They no longer wander or seek to cast about for subtle pleasures, but instead come to rest on an incomparable treasure that is intuited by the inward senses, the senses of knowledge. As Sri Ramakrishna used to tell, if a thief became aware that there was an abundance of treasure just on the other side of a door, he would neither stop nor rest until he had broken through and laid hands upon it and possessed it. This kind of intense longing signifies the mind-set of the *sadhaka,* and also distinguishes him from the milder, less serious endeavors of the *pravartaka.* Further, regarding those scriptures that the novice got interested in early on, the *sadhaka* takes them up and examines them in revelatory company of an illumined preceptor, thus extracting much more essence from them than the *pravartaka.* All of this gives the *sadhaka* an actual connection with Divine Reality — something that the beginner is sorely lacking in.

But if the *sadhaka* has an inner connection to rely upon for spiritual sustenance, the *siddha,* operating inwardly at the third stage of awakening, has actual vision. Thus, his/her practice is natural and spontaneous, with much of the earlier intensity already a matter of attainment. The *siddha* lives in realization, and only reverts back to discipline and practice when it is required or needed. Put in another way, if all beings knew that they are the *Atman,* there would be little need for practice. Facets of a *siddha's* attainment shine forth in the ability to both sublimate all remaining desires, and also to effectively transmit wisdom teachings to other minds. As this spiritual work goes forth, he/she is able to meditate directly upon the *Atman*, again, naturally.

There is a unique state of Awareness beyond the *siddha*, that the Great Master called the *"siddha* of the *siddha."* Though a bit difficult to describe, one could say that short of merely meditating successfully on the *Atman*, as wondrous as that is, the perfected being simply abides in *Atman* constantly. His practice, if any remains, is the direct experience of Bliss, *Ananda* — unalloyed and uninterrupted. Meditation — and of the nondual variety — is natural to such a one, and is going on all of the time. This was intimated by the Holy Mother, Sri Sarada Devi, when She stated, *"Does God exist only when eyes are closed in meditation, and cease to exist when they are open?"* This sentence, fully realized, describes the superlative state of the *"siddha* of the *siddha."*

Obviously, much more could be said about all four of these states of spiritual awakening — the latter two being awakenings only in the sense of deeper and greater revelations and spiritual insights. To make this singular state of spiritual awakening as clear as possible, however, the fourth of five charts along this vein is displayed on the facing page, placing this teaching in a more straightforward and easy to comprehend manner.

The Great Master mentions right off the top, in the quote on the chart on the facing page, that most beings born on earth into a human body remain in a state of ignorance of where they came from, what they are doing here, and who they truly are. Of course, this state of connate ignorance happens prior to the Four Stages of Awakening just studied on page 573. This unfortunate state correlates to the condition of "animalistic" and "ignorant" at the bottom of the chart now under study. As the little guage running up the middle of the chart shows, this is a gross state of unknowing, where all the veils present in the human mind and awareness are pulled done tight and thick as a brick. Nonetheless, and as the quote from the Great Master on the bottom of the chart relates, mankind is nothing less than the sporting ground for divinity in expression. He must only awaken to this fact and tear off these veils. The fact that he can do this, and has done it many times before, proves Mother India's declaration that all ignorance in unreal, or without any real substance. There is no sin, then, nor any imperfection. Sins and imperfections only gather in the mind when embodied existence begins and the embodied being acts out of accord with his natural divine nature.

At the "primal" and 'vital" level, as the chart next shows us, is where actions and thoughts become most effective (or detrimental as the case may be) in mankind's inward ascension towards realization, or remembrance of his pristine state of pure Awareness. And in fact, the appearance of intelligence in the mind signals not only his ability to rise out of ignorance and matter, but his singular and unique place in the cosmos of being able to do so. No other embodied being, from the animals onwards to the gods in the life heavens, can achieve freedom from (self-imposed) bondage like he can. This begins to become evident when he intuits the divine presence within him and then moves to express it through religion, a calling of a more "ethereal" station. But it must be mentioned here, even cautioned about, that his intellect and his religious life are still under the control of the individual ego, and that these very qualities will act as barriers to the attainment of higher Awareness. The reader can look back on pages 333, 335, 337, to review charts like the *Fourteen States of Upper and Lower Knowledge,* to bring more clarity to this point, here and now. The human ego, left in an immature condition, without attenuation via spiritual practice (*sadhana*), will turn the intellect prideful and turn religion into a vexing show of pompousness and self-righteousness.

And this is precisely why the next two stages of ascension are so crucial. Spiritual awakening and spiritual discipline are the cutting edge for religion, helping the soul pierce through pride and sensationalism and enter directly into the "Kingdom of Heaven." These levels of consciousness are celestial and cosmic in succession. Souls having accomplished them are hardly ever seen in human form again, unless they be adepts and masters with a divine decree and a special mission to return to the physical realm.

As the chart reflects further, the divine and the universal stages are advanced in the extreme, and beyond the comprehension of most embodied beings on earth. That is why so few recognize these superlative souls when they do return in human form. Even when recognizing them out of

Phases of the Soul in Relativity

"The jiva at first remains in a state of ignorance. It is not conscious of God, but of matter and multiplicity. It only notices the many things around it. Upon attaining knowledge it becomes conscious that God dwells in all beings. But on attaining higher wisdom it discards both knowledge and ignorance and talks of nothing but God day and night."   Sri Ramakrishna Paramahamsa

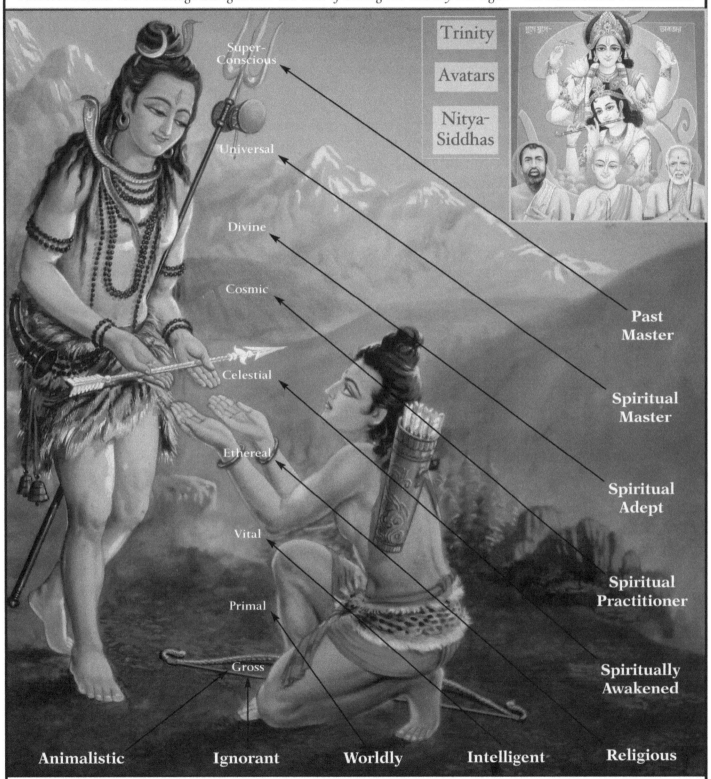

Trinity

Avatars

Nitya-Siddhas

Super-Conscious

Universal

Divine

Cosmic

Celestial

Ethereal

Vital

Primal

Gross

Past Master

Spiritual Master

Spiritual Adept

Spiritual Practitioner

Spiritually Awakened

Religious

Animalistic   **Ignorant**   **Worldly**   **Intelligent**

"There is a greater accumulation of God in man than in other creatures. God is born as man for the purpose of sporting as man. He is thus called Narayana. Rama, Krishna, and Chaitanya are examples of this. By meditating on the Divine Incarnation of God one meditates on God Itself. If God can manifest through the image, then why not through man?"   Sri Ramakrishna Paramahamsa

some inner and intuitive connection, most beings still do not follow them, such is the inscrutable limiting and restraining force of *maya* (name, form, time, space, and causality) on the human mind.

And from this lofty vantagepoint of full illumination, only souls who are Souls remain, that is, the individualized soul called *jiva* has long since given up its hold and its role, both, in the now strange phenomena of embodiment. Thus, *"the jiva is Siva,"* and incomparable words and titles like The Trinity, *Nityasiddha,* Past Master, *Avatar,* and the like, are left to be pondered. As the Great Master states in His quote at the bottom of the chart just completed, *"By meditating on the Divine Incarnation of God, one meditates of God Itself."*

Under the auspices of the great, illumined soul, Shankara, the next chart presents its beneficial teachings. Having seen over the past four charts how a soul progresses towards higher stations of awareness in its return to the original state of nondual *Samadhi,* it is now left to reveal some of the obstacles along this precipitous inward ascent into *Brahman.*

The fivefold list at the top of the chart emerges from the *Vivekachudamani* of Shankara, but the quotes that accompany each entry are the words of Sri Ramakrishna Paramahamsa and His fold. Briefly summarized, if the soul wanting freedom holds on to the attachments that come from the conjunction of the senses with their sense objects, all for the sake of a little fleeting pleasure, then liberation of the spiritual kind — the only true emancipation there really is — is still a far cry. If that same soul also fails to admit the suffering prone nature of worldly existence, like the Buddhists teach in depth, or, put in *Vedantic* terms, will not separate the real *Brahman* from the unreal world, then still another barrier will remain in his or her search for freedom and the bliss it confers.

And in view of these first two hurdles, and even when the Lord and Mother of the Universe send inspiration and aid to the striving soul, if this soul rejects such assistance and follows the way of the inflated ego instead — the ways of family, friends, society, fundamentalist religion, and the like — then spiritual awakening of the necessary kind will never occur, either. This is why the fourth impediment of Shankara's list focuses in on worldly families and a quotidian lifestyle. He includes the potential problem of wealth as well, an orientation that most beings in the world are not only raised in, but rush to embrace as well. The word, "prosperity," has a better ring among the peacemakers and the truth-seekers, for the human being has every right to live a healthy life of equanimity and balance, though always being on the guard against aspects of life in the world that are not utilized for the advancement of *dharma* and spiritual life, and the highest good of all beings.

This calls into consideration that steadfast companion of wealth and possessions called work, the fifth possible cause for lack of success in true and authentic human existence. Again, "activity" is a better word, as it carries the connotation of helping others, serving others, even rescuing others from the humdrum round of surface superficiality and mundane convention that often goes by the very name, "work." As Swami Vivekananda's quote on the chart under study blatantly points out, these ever continuing rounds of work, also referred to as duty by "responsible" beings, may be supplying the soul with all it thinks it needs for daily living. At the same time, and often unbeknownst to those under its press, they sap the body of its natural health, burning out the life force in the nervous system, and imprisoning the mind and its thinking process. Even worse, and as a result of all this, crucial access to ongoing refection of the spirit, i.e., spiritual life in toto, is denied to the thirsty soul, who remains parched in the scorching "noonday sun" of this heartless human workplace.

But there are solutions for this dire situation, five of them, and another five signs that these ready remedies are having their salient effects as well. As proposed by Shankara — a past master in all aspects of spiritual life, practice, and realization — the solutions begin with a firm resolve to renounce overbearing cravings. Being a monk, and strong, he would recommend such a course. But if this is not possible for the beginner, or even the intermediate practitioner to achieve, then practice itself is advised next. Practice, or *sadhana,* does not mean a once a week type of religious effort, the like of which was just noticed and hopefully done away with in the first and fourth causes for failure listed above. Chipping away at the mind's coverings and barriers requires a full-time effort if any appreciable progress is going to be made. Most beings seldom even get to working on the mind,

Lack of Spiritual Success & Its Causes

"Spiritual success depends on qualification. Thus, the seeker should take to study and reasoning after approaching the Guru – who must be among the best of the knowers of Brahman, and an ocean of mercy."
Shankara

Causes for Lack of Spiritual Success

1) Attachment to Objects & Pleasures
"Once a sweetmeat has gone down the throat, one can hardly remember what it tasted like."

2) Delusion Concerning the True Nature of Brahman, the Self, and the World
"If my devotees know who I am, who they are, and what the world is, they will be fine."

3) Failure to Awaken Spiritually
"The boy tells his mother, 'Wake me up when the call of nature comes.' 'You will wake up yourself,' she answers.'"

4) Relying for Refuge in Home, Spouse, Wealth, and Offspring
"To hope for help from relatives and friends provides no profound solution. Don't you know that all are lost here?"

5) Obsession with Work & Activity
"Duty is the midday sun whose fierce rays are burning the very vitals of humanity."

Solutions for Lack of Spiritual Success

1) Renounce Desires and Cravings
2) Engage in Daily Sadhana
3) Take Refuge in Path & Preceptor
4) Absorb Yourself in Love of Truth
5) Develop Devotion to Discrimination
6) Attain Freedom from Worldliness

Five Signs of Spiritual Success

1) Tendency to do Right Action
2) Presence of Natural Discernment
3) Increased Knowledge of Reality
4) Nonreliance on Body, Senses, & Morals
5) The Will to Perform Spiritual Practice

"...with a mind made sharpened by thoughts on Reality alone, release and penetrate that mark — the Imperishable Brahman."

"Conviction about the Truth proceeds from constant counsel with realized souls. It will never come from repeated ablutions in the holy Ganges, nor by a hundred-thousand asanas and pranayamas. Further, realization is brought about by spiritual discrimination, not by millions of acts. Action may eventually purify the mind, but of itself it does not lead to the direct perception of Reality." Shankara

Qualification is King
In Authentic Spiritual Life and Practice

"The competency of the spiritually initiated aspirant is crucial for the determination of its true significance. This is termed Adhikara Vichara, qualification of the aspirant according to capacity, leading to merit. The sages and seers deem it essential for Vaidika and Tantrika discipline and studies." Sadhana Shastras

Vedanta
Neti Neti

- Sadhana Chatustaya
- Pancha Kosha
- 4 Yogas
- Trigunatita

Patanjala
Astanga Yoga

- Yamas/Niyamas
- Alambanic Quintuplications
- Kriya Yoga
- Pranayama
- Chitta-vrittis
- Pratyahara

Sankhya
Tattvavid

- The 24 Cosmic Principles
- Trividham Duhkham
- 10 Tenets of Sankhya Yoga
- The 9 Complacencies
- The 8 Great Accomplishments

Buddhism
37 Limbs of Enlightenment

4 Noble Truths
Pratitya Samutpada
12 Nidanas
6 Transformations

Tantra
Upasana-Dhyan

- Mantra-Diksha
- Sristi Rahasya
- 7 Qualifications
- 3 Shuddhis
- Pancha Bhava
- 8 Devotional Aids

Kundalini Yoga
Shaktipat

- Annaprasada
- Mukhya-prana
- Asana & Pranayam
- Kundalini Shakti
  The 6 Chakras
- Ojas
- Tejas
- Jnana Chakshu

Vasishtha's Yoga
Atmajnana

The 4 Sentinels
Karma/Samskara Vinasha
5 Akashas

assuming that body-oriented practices, like fasting, stretching, and breathing exercises will somehow come to equal realization. Unbeknownst to them, it is really practices such as scriptural study, devotional exercises, and meditation — all done in the atmosphere of holy company — that will affect the surest and swiftest growth. And as the chart relates, such dedicated and wise daily practice will end in love of Truth gaining victory over love of the world and its empty enticements, so much so that the disciple will then prefer living a life of discrimination; *viveka* becomes his devotion.

To finish this chart's examination (page 577), the five signs of spiritual growth make a good study. All of them are perfectly understandable. In the fourth, nonreliance on body, senses, and morals, brings forth the transcendent nature of spirituality over both worldly and conventional religious life. That not many beings make this grade only reveals the scarcity of truly illumined souls in this world. Again, it is continual spiritual practice that gives these few the definitive edge.

Speaking of truly illumined beings, as well as how they have succeeded and what they have concentrated on to do so, the chart on page 578, with a picture of Swami Vivekananda — among the very the greatest of contemporary seers — pulls together a complete regimen of worthy teachings found by astute seekers of Truth and God in several of India's most precious *darshanas*. This chart could make up a book all of its own, holding, as it does, keys and secrets of spiritual life as of yet undiscovered in this day and age by the multitudes. This chart can act as a kind of table of contents and reference guide combined, coming late in this book's final chapters.

Beginning under the **Vedanta** heading, the list entails some of the main pillars of this *darshana*'s powerful offerings. The reader only has to look back to the earliest pages of this book to be reminded of these, such as page 65 for *Sadhana Chatustaya,* and page 19 and 21 for a study of the *Pancha Koshas.* Pages 431 and 433 teach the important precepts of the Four *Yogas,* and the charts on pages 221, 223, and 307 show us how to recognize and transcend the three *gunas* of *prakriti* — *Trigunatita.* These four heading, shown in the box, are only the main features of *Vedanta,* focusing on the *sadhana* aspect of it. The nondual, or *Advaita Vedanta,* occurs over the pages of this book.

Moving down the left hand side of the chart, we come to the classic eight-limbed **Yoga, or** *Patanjala*. The present book's many pages have already treated us to both introductions and in-depth studies of many of *Yoga's* facets as well, like a complete list and study of the *yamas* and *niyamas* on page 399, and a look at cosmic quintuplications on page 461. *Kriya Yoga,* one of the systems jewels for concentrated practice, received an unwrapping too, showing its facets on page 407. *Pranayama,* beneficial breathing exercises connected to *prana* and its mastery, is initially taken up and presented on page 69, while *prana* as a *tattva,* cosmic principle, is rendered in depth on pages 536, 539, 541, and 543. The *chitta vrittis,* of such interest and importance to beings who are concerned about their often erratic thoughts, are taught by Patanjali on page 421, though matters pertaining to them fill the pages of this book and every *darshana* of India. Teachings on *pratyahara* and its import can be located and studied throughout pages running from 415 to 425.

Sankhya Yoga falls next on the lower left-hand column. Lord Kapila's philosophically famous list of "Twenty-four Cosmic Principles' can be reviewed in the charts on page 349, with the *Shaivite* version, plus, on page 359. The "Three Types of Suffering," a likely predecessor to Lord Buddha's Four Noble Truth but several thousands years earlier, can be examined on page 231. The "Ten Tenets of *Sankhya Yoga*" appears on page 351. Finally, the "Eight Great Accomplishments" and the "Nine Complacencies," teachings particular to Lord Kapila and his ancient wisdom, are to be located on page 309.

At the bottom of the chart under study on the previous page, we find a few of **Vasishtha's Yoga's** timeless offerings. Basically, if people of this day and age knew what his teachings to the people of his time were all about — namely, knowledge of the five types of space called *akashas* (page 327), teachings on the presence of *samskaras* in the subconscious minds of embodied souls (pages 166 & 170), and the "Four Sentinels' that duly inform and protect a seeker who strives to make his or her way through all levels of existence and its potential problems and mysteries (page 345) — then the Great Seer could certainly rest in peace. For, like other India *rishis,* he proposed *Atmajnana,* realization of the perfect Self within, for the solution to any and all issues and concerns of souls that find themselves in the often dire predicament of embodiment.

Moving up the right hand column (page 578) from bottom to top, we first come upon **Kundalini Yoga** and its unusual and attractive spiritual practices. Of course, sanctified food and mastering the basic *prana* that comes from it is first on its list. For *prana,* pages 546 through 545 contain so much teaching information about it, which is all the more valuable given the message of Swami Vivekananda in this day and age about *prana* being a missing link in the human mind's understanding of the universe in which he lives and breathes.

Regarding food (and prior to finishing up the chart on page 578), the reader is asked to cast a watchful eye at the chart on the facing page to find just how reverently India and its peoples view it. There, the *Bhagavad Gita's* famous teaching on sanctified food, chapter four, *sloka* 24, is taken up and mated with important teachings in the *Vedanta.* The entire chart is to be studied under the auspice of this *sloka's* deep meaning, stating: *"Devoutly offered is the sanctified food given as the oblation, placed into the Fire of Brahman by Brahman alone. The One Brahman can be reached only by those absorbed in action as Brahman,"* all which goes to say that if living beings held to a conscious standard of seeing *Brahman* everywhere — in the food they consume, in the act of consumption, in the fires within the body that digest it, and on through to the one who assumes the act of eating — then the presence of *Brahman* would be rendered clear and visible, pertaining consummately to the one who then perceives *Brahman* in all.

Continuing with the remaining *darshanas* and their headings of the chart on page 578, we see that along with food and vital energy, *Kundalini Yoga* wants its adherents to take up certain *tantric asanas* and breathing exercises as well. The reader is asked to look to the forthcoming chart on these mainstays of *yogic* practice, shown next on page 583. A brief look at the also famous seven *chakras* (or six if the *sahasrara* is left out of the list due to its being totally transcendent) can be studied on the chart on page 375. However, an in-depth look at this unique and all-important teaching of the Indian *Rishis* is also soon to appear on forthcoming pages. This is also true of the two principles of *Ojas,* and *Tejas,* which are both the proofs of and methods leading to the many sanctuaries of refined Awareness attested to in this system. As for the *Jnana Chakshu,* the "Third Eye," the reader has only to look back and review the comprehensive chart on page 553, studied earlier in this chapter.

The penultimate box on the chart under study (page 578) represent the infinitely wide territories of Indian **Tantra.** We can see by its list that *Tantra* holds the initiation of the disciple into the traditional path by the illumined preceptor to be of utmost importance. For all that has been offered in this book on the principle of *mantra-diksha,* the charts on pages 131 through 144 can be consulted. For *Tantra's* "Secret of Creation," termed *Srsti Rahasya,* page 463 renders up its precious teachings. And while we are entertaining the subject of qualification for spiritual life in India, "The Seven Qualifications of *Tantric* Adept," way back on page 79, also sport their own chart. To see what the *Rishis* of India have to say about purity, especially in its threefold forms, the charts on page 119 and 122 can be viewed, and the very beneficial teaching on the "Five Moods," or *Bhavas,* appears on page 471. To complete *Tantra's* main facets, the adepts always ask their votaries to become familiar with the "Eight Devotional Aids of Narada," shown on the verisimilar charts on pages 475 and 476.

This review and helpful mini-guide about qualification as seen by Indian *darshanas* has only **Buddhism** left to consider. An easy presentation of its three main facets include "The Four Noble Truths," the "Doctrine of Interdependent Arising" *(Pratitya Samutpada),"* and the "Twelve Links," or *Nidanas.* The Four Noble Truths, which includes the Eightfold Path as well, can be studied and memorized based upon its chart on page 229. For the *Nidanas,* or twelve links of mental conditioning that are responsible for rebirth in ignorance from lifetime to lifetime, the chart on page 192 provides a complete study. The "Six Transformations of *Buddhism,"* so similar to *Vedanta's* "Six Billows," are placed side by side on the chart on page 225.

Over all of this presides Swami Vivekananda, centered in the chart just examined on page 578, inviting us to plunge into the *Sanatana Dharma,* the Eternal Religion of the *Rishis,* and come

Food & Brahman

"From Atman ether emerged; from ether air; from air fire; from fire water; from water earth. From the earth herbs came to be, and from herbs food. From food came the body. He indeed is the person consisting of the essence of food."   Taittiriyopanisad

Anandamayakosha

Brahma karma samadhina

....only by those absorbed in action as Brahman."

Brahma-eva tena gantavyam

The one Brahman can be reached....

Brahman as Bliss

Vijnanamayakosha

Manomayakosha

Brahmana hutam

....by Brahman alone.

Brahman as Intelligence

Brahman as Thought

Pranamayakosha

Brahmagnau

....placed into the fire of Brahman....

Brahman as Energy

Brahma havih

....is the sanctified article given as the oblation,...

"Devoutly offered.....

Brahma arpanam

Annamayakosha

Brahman as Food

Bhagavad Gita 4:24

Copyright 2016
Babaji Bob Kindler

"The celebrated rishi, Bhrgu, approached his father, Varuna, requesting: 'Revered Sir: instruct me about Brahman.' As a means to the knowledge of Brahman, Varuna taught him food. Then he taught him about the vital airs, sight, hearing, and speech. Bhrgu then understood food. For, all beings born here are born from food. Having been born they remain alive by food. Upon departing the body they enter into food. Having reflected on the nature of food, Bhrgu then asked Varuna, 'Revered Sir: now instruct me about Brahman."   Taittiriyopanisad

forth with jewels and treasures untold and immeasurable. If this collection of *darshanas* and their tenets — which could be called a "short list of teachings" in India — reminds us of something, or proves anything, it could be Jesus's famous declaration that man stores up his treasures in heaven rather than on earth. This leaves us only to imagine what vast spiritual wealth has been gathered over millenia in India, resulting in its time-tested methods and fully adept leadership in the realm of the Spirit.

The mention of both *pranayam* and *asana* in the *Kundalini* section of the chart just studied on page 578 calls to mind the unique offering of *Tantra* with regard to both of these elements of spiritual practice. The chart on the facing page presents a select list of practices for the beginning aspirant, and one that protects the soul from both unnecessary over-emphasis, wastage of energy, and worst of all, misdirection. *Hatha Yoga* in this day and time, particularly as it has been seized upon by the West, is devoid of the awareness of higher forms of *Yoga*. What *Yoga* really is has escaped the Western mind, and has disoriented many potential followers of the spiritual path and sent them right back into preoccupation with the physical. Even in India in these times, truer and more effective spiritual practices have gone missing for the most part, leaving an entire world of beings lost and unaware of both their indwelling perfection *(Atman)*, and the way to realize It again if they stray away from It. As Swami Vivekananda has said, after catching a look at the earth and its peoples in this present time, and even in his own country: *"If there be glory in keeping the machine in good trim, it is more glorious to withhold the soul from suffering with the body — that is the only demonstration of your being "not matter" by letting the matter alone. Our Bengal is a land of bhakti and jnana, where yoga is scarcely so much as talked of even. What little there is, is but the queer breathing exercises and asanas of hatha-yoga — which is nothing but a kind of gymnastics."*

This problem can be rectified and turned around with a little proper orientation combined with the awakening of mankind's innate intelligence. The latter can be brought to bear by the kind of special qualification that is shown on the recent chart on page 578. Finding an illumined preceptor will be paramount to avoid more wrong orientation. When such study under an authentic *guru* does take place, after the mind becomes ready to implement what it has imbibed, *Tantra* will shed light on the potentially dangerous areas of physical practice with teachings like the ones shown on the facing page.

The *sloka* from the *Srimad Devi Bhagavatam* at the top of the chart, uttered by King Himalaya, reveals proper orientation. All physical exercises are to be undergone while *"...concentrating the mind on Consciousness,"* after *"...."placing the Ishtam inside."* These two key bits of information are precious, and will save the aspirant from getting (mentally) off track when working with the physical form, which is, after all, *"....just a cage of bones and flesh,"* and *"....no more than a few pounds of ashes in the end."*

With all of this declared out front, and with the aspiring soul's innate intelligence awakened to these facts, *Tantric Yoga* proposes a safe way to select and enter into both *asana* and *pranayama*. The three types of breathing exercises, along with the five main *asanas,* sum it up well, and simply. Manned with these alone, the practioneer can learn to successfully *"...hold the prana on the toes, heels, knees, thighs,* and most importantly, *chest and head,"* in order to readily master *pratyahara*. *Pratyahara*, controlling of *prana*, ones thoughts, and everything having to do with moving inwards to higher awareness, is the stumbling block in (eight-limbed) *Yoga* for most practitioners. That is why they may become flexible of body and vitally healthy, but they seldom come to know of the depths of the *dharma*, and never gain *Samadhi*. Even the five senses, or maybe especially the five senses, must become subject to this conscious way of practice. As one old adage states, *"The act of smelling should be thought of as the practice of breathing."*

On the chart opposite, again, it is seen how *Tantric* practice orients the aspirant towards dedicating every little breath to envisioning the *Ishtam* and realizing "The Word." The phase of the breath, its locale in the body, the channels it flows through, and the level of practice, are all secondary. The real import is directing all of this to the Chosen Ideal via recitation of the *mantra* and the act of meditation once concentration has been achieved.

The wise teacher informs the sincere aspirant that intensifying daily practice before the body, nervous system, and brain are ready to receive greater *pranic* impact, is dangerous for spiritual growth, which must go forth in stages. The limbs of *Yoga* called *Pratyahara, Dharana,* and *Dhyanam* all have to

Asana & Pranayam in Tantric Yoga

"Hold the prana on the various parts of the body in turn — toes, heels, knees, thighs, chest, head, etc., — and practice pratyahara. Concentrating the mind on the Consciousness within is then made easier, and formal dharana will mature when the jivatma places the Istam inside." King Himalaya

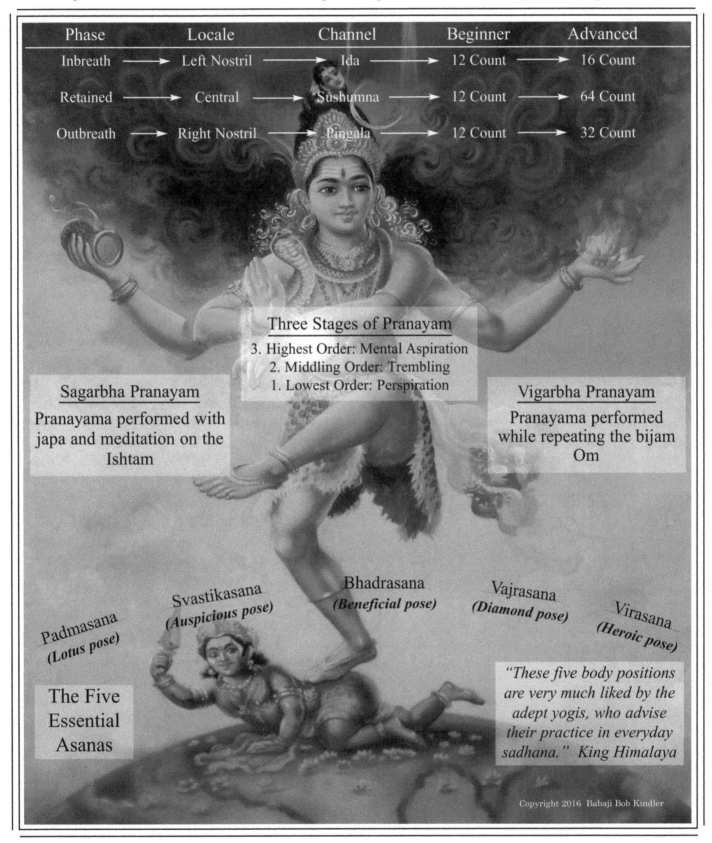

Phase		Locale		Channel		Beginner		Advanced
Inbreath	→	Left Nostril	→	Ida	→	12 Count	→	16 Count
Retained	→	Central	→	Sushumna	→	12 Count	→	64 Count
Outbreath	→	Right Nostril	→	Pingala	→	12 Count	→	32 Count

Three Stages of Pranayam

3. Highest Order: Mental Aspiration
2. Middling Order: Trembling
1. Lowest Order: Perspiration

Sagarbha Pranayam

Pranayama performed with japa and meditation on the Ishtam

Vigarbha Pranayam

Pranayama performed while repeating the bijam Om

Padmasana *(Lotus pose)*

Svastikasana *(Auspicious pose)*

Bhadrasana *(Beneficial pose)*

Vajrasana *(Diamond pose)*

Virasana *(Heroic pose)*

The Five Essential Asanas

"These five body positions are very much liked by the adept yogis, who advise their practice in everyday sadhana." King Himalaya

The Role of Food & Prana in Achieving Self-Realization

"From pure food one gets pure blood. Pure blood produces pure thoughts. Pure thoughts lead to pure mind, and pure mind is Brahman." Sri Sarada Devi

Ananda Ghana — Mass of Bliss

Ajna
Visionary Chakra

Kundalini Ascends
Towards the Sahashrara

Transcendent Experiences
Ability to Teach/Transmit
Destruction of old Karmas
Intensification of Yogic Fire
Ability to Meditate
Ability to Concentrate
Cessation of new Karmas
Maturation of Devotion

Vishuddha
Wisdom Chakra

Ida Nadi — *Pingala Nadi*

Anahata
Heart Chakra

Spiritual Life Proceeds
Cycles of Transmigration End

Release of Udghata
Psychic prana develops
Refined prana floods Nadis
Inception of Sadhana
Moderation of Sense Life
Observance of Celibacy
Early Spiritual Awakening

Sushumna

Worldly Life Commencing
Transmigration in Cycles

"We understand that food is Brahman. All beings existing here on earth are born of food. They retain their existence by means of food. Departing their bodies, they become food for others."

Manipura
Vital Chakra

Svadhisthana
Primal Chakra

The Yogi's Sublimated Energy Moving Upwards — Urdhvaretoyogi —

Muladhara
Root Chakra

- Tejas

"The emanation that exudes from the pure yogic state is called tejas, a subtle light that transforms. By its presence illumined beings inspire and uplift those who strive and suffer. It also gets utilized for continuing realization and training others. This is spiritual transmission in its fullest manifestation, among those who can inject Brahmajnana and those who have made themselves fit to receive It."

- Ojas

"Ojas is the stored up power from pure food and sadhana combined which aids in the release of Kundalini Shakti into higher spiritual centers. Experiences of temporary bliss occur just prior to this but are to be transcended."

- Mukhya Prana

"Mukhyaprana supports the organs, sharpens the senses, and maintains life in the body. It must be invigorated by the ingestion of pure food; otherwise, ill health results."

- Food with Mantra

"The mantra, uttered in deep meditation, when blessed by such sacred words, renders pure food into prasad." Lord Vasishtha

"anne hidam sarvam prathistham - All is supported by food."

"Food taken with an ignorant or brooding mind turns to poison in the body. Food taken with clarity of mind conduces to perfect health. It is the fire of Yoga in the form of physical, vital, and mental purification that makes the difference." Lord Vasishtha

do with the mind, not the brain. The brain is really just the physical symbol for the mind, which itself holds all realms and all forms within it. Further, and as Swami Aseshanandaji Maharaj used to say, *"Your body is a symbol of existence; your mind is a symbol of consciousness; but your Soul. Atman, is pure Awareness."*

Moving on in the present swing of the *Tantric darshana*, there is an even more basic element to *yogic* practice and spiritual advancement than many beings surmise. It is as simple as the food we eat. Many of the obstacles that living beings encounter in life, on all levels, as well as many of the secrets needing to be told in order to overcome them, all originate around food. From Lord Vasishtha's ancient times, all the way up to Sri Sarada Devi's present day and age — as the two quotes from them on the top and bottom of the chart under study relate — beings exist here on earth via food. Of course, that is a basic teaching, but it must be understood on a deep level. Once comprehension of the importance of food is gleaned, then one can look into the statement of Jesus that *"Man does not live by bread alone."* Nevertheless, though hidden energy *(prana)* and thought *(chitta),* as well as "Spirit," all form higher echelons of mankind's existence overall, food still supports it all. Thus, the *mantra* on the chart which states: *"Anne hidam sarvam prathistham — All is supported by food."* As a reminder and an apt conclusion both, this *mantra* can be uttered over all food before it is consumed, rendering it sanctified.

Otherwise, as Lord Vasishtha declares, *"Food taken with an ignorant or brooding mind turns into poison in the bloodstream,"* and this causes disease, among other things. *Tantra,* with its *Kundalini Yoga* facet, explains not only how to avoid such errors, but also gives the method through which to destroy them and bring both food and the act of eating back into conscious focus.

So, avoiding unconscious consumption of food, and staying away from foods that are, as Sri Krishna advises in the *Gita, tamasic* and *rajasic,* is a given for the sensitive spiritual aspirant. The real meaning of food then opens up, as the chart on the facing page relates. Simply put, food can either be a tie to the ancestors and their realm, or it can be force to transcend all lower realms. These "lower realms," as far as *Kundalini Yoga* is concerned, are the three lower *chakras.* Unconscious consumption of everything in nature, not just food, occurs from those three centers. They represent *"eating, drinking, and sex life,"* as Sri Ramakrishna put it. As the chart relates (page 584), life spent in these three realms conduces to transmigration in cycles. That pretty much summates it.

Once the soul becomes freed from the third *chakra,* spiritual life begins to take place. Moderation or celibacy, acquiring a spiritual regimen of practices, and the awakening of *prana* and *psychic prana,* all take place as the fourth center is perceived. In other words, the human being finds out at this juncture that he/she has a subtle body, and a set of senses that are not merely physical. The fresh energy that begins to flow, both inward and outward, is not physical only, and can be utilized for more than just exercise, health, and enjoyment. For, the awakening of *prana* and its subtler psychic component both bring forth the heretofore unknown presence of *Kundalini* Power, or *Shakti* power. This auspicious appearance not only signals the end to transmigration in ignorance, but opens the gates for the soul to live a truly spiritual life here on earth — something it will have to experience at least once in order to gain fulfillment and leave attachment to the worlds of matter and gross energy behind forever.

The top of the left hand column of the chart also relates what this precious occurrence would entail. Devotion to Divine Reality, to *Brahman,* would ensue and expand, and the aspirant would soon intuit the welcome absence of culminative *karmas* that used to plague the soul. Having no more unexpected fires to put out leaves the seeker with time for spiritual pursuits, like sharper concentration, followed by the will and ability to meditate.

And it is here, at this fine juncture, that the desire to helps others, alongside the ability to do so, comes in. The right hand side of the chart under study reveals the process that leads to such coveted qualities. Having been given the sacred *mantra* by an illumined teacher, the sincere aspirant uses it for purifying all food that is consumed, transforming it into *prasad* prior to eating it (see chart on page 423). Gross *prana* itself then readily changes into *mukhya prana,* a healthy energy that is always present from then on. Signs of this are the loss of heaviness and brooding, both of body and of brain. The senses find a newborn force as well, and becoming pure, give rise to awareness of their subtle counterpoints, i.e., the five sense in the dream state. Here, and without at first knowing it, the soul has entered into the mind via the brain. The dreaming *(svapna)* and deep sleep *(sushupti)* levels of consciousness then begin to take on and shed the light of higher consciousness. Awareness of the Divine Mother, or *Shakti* Power, is experienced here, as *Kundalini* rises, or deepens, into causal levels of existence and comprehension.

The principles of *ojas* and *tejas,* terms peculiar to the *Kundalini Yoga* system, find their entrance here. As the chart now being completed shows, *ojas* is stored up power that is extracted from food by the sublimation process just described, then condensed into spiritual creativity that can be utilized to benefit others. And this is only the beginning of its greater potential. Once spiritual practices get combined with the forthcoming spiritual experiences that proceed from them, this power of *ojas* further transforms into *tejas*. It is with this subtlemost of powers that the teacher can help illumine the minds of those around him/her, shedding the light of method, practice, scripture, higher awareness, and Eternal Life for all to see and partake of. The light sometimes seen emanating off of the personage of the luminary is that same light of *ojas/tejas,* exuding even from the very pores of the physical body. And why not, since physical food itself helped in generating this pure *Shakti* force to bear auspiciously on life and mind.

With many mentions about the seven *chakras* of the *Kundalini Yoga* system having been made, a more in-depth study of them would be helpful, particularly for those who want to meditate upon them after receiving instructions from an adept preceptor.

To begin, an overview on the *chakras* themselves, and how they correlate to the *lokas* within human awareness, is given. States of higher (and lower) awareness are also revealed to give the interested reader and motivated student an idea of how vast human awareness is, and how filled with infinite realms and beings it is as well.

The seven states of awareness, i.e., *chakras,* range from life on the physical planet earth and, anthropomorphically speaking, stretch inwards through realms of the elementals, the ancestors, the celestials, and the gods and goddesses. Beyond that are very blissful realms where realized beings have their refuge, like *Taparloka*. Likened metaphorically to the seven holes of a *bansuri* flute, the Great Master gives descriptions next to each *chakra* on the chart that indicate the overall atmosphere of that inner realm. Of note, the scriptures say that just as there are seven higher realms of existence, there are also seven lower ones as well. These are called *patalas,* which means "sunken grounds." The reference is rather and roughly to that of hell in the Christian religion.

But the three lower *chakras* — *muladhara, svadhistana,* and *manipura* — are no party or picnic either. That is why the Great Master's overall description of them mentions the unlikelihood of any comprehensive *yoga* being accomplished in them. They are the realms of rebirth in bodies, in ignorance of anything higher or deeper. Completely opposite are the transcendent upper three realms, called *Vishuddha, Ajna,* and *Sahasrara*. Bodies are hardly even noticeable there; only a wisp of form persists, and that is always is danger of dissolving in bliss at any moment. Of course, one dissolution is into total Bliss, called *Ananda*. Because the Great Master had visited and seen these higher *lokas,* or *akashas,* while in the physical form on earth, he was always saturated with that selfsame bliss/Bliss most of the time.

On the right hand side of the chart under study on the facing page, a list of spiritual states has been given. Some of these are common to the *Yoga darshana,* while others are *bhavas,* or finer moods that the spiritually awake soul comes upon in meditation, or while contemplating God with form. Others are completely transcendent of form, the beings who experience them possibly never emerging from them again.

Whatever the case, it is *Kundalini Shakti* that courses blissfully through the *chakras,* introducing the aspiring soul to these experiences in a timely fashion. It is as if they remain locked within these centers of awareness awaiting discovery, much like a chest of treasure sits buried in a cave, or under the sands of an ocean bed, until some fortunate miner or diver comes upon it.

But it takes a persistant soul applying intense scrutiny to uncover these; they are not given to many, and usually escape detection even by advanced practitioners. The quote by Mahendranath Gupta, author of the *Gospel of Sri Ramakrishna,* explains this well enough. The seeker will need some sort of special looking glass to espy such subtle treasures as these. Even the *chakras* themselves are scarcely seen by most practitioner's, and never by the uninitiated — at least not clearly. This is probably due to the ordinary soul's preoccupation with the distraction of the lower worlds of earth and heaven, and to what little of any great substance is offered there. As the quote at the top of the chart stated by Sri Ramakrishna suggests, most beings will tend to sound the lower notes of the flute of life which are easier to hold for a long period of time. Remaining on a higher level is not possible for them, so they grav-

The Seven Centers & Planes of Awareness & Existence

"Holding the highest note on the flute is very difficult. But one can come down and play with the other six notes of the instrument." Sri Ramakrishna Paramahamsa

↓ The Seven Centers of Awareness ↓

"When the Kundalini rises to the Sahasrara and the mind goes into samadhi, the aspirant loses all consciousness of the outer world. In that state the life force lingers for 21 days and then passes out. But in the case of the incarnations and ishvarakotis they can descend from this exalted state. They like to live with the devotees, enjoy the Love of God, and retain a trace of ego so that they can teach men. Their minds move between the 6th and 7th planes. They run a boat race, as it were, between these two subtle centers."

"The 6th plane corresponds to the Ajna center, at the eyebrows. It has a lotus of two petals. There one sees the form of God. But there is still a barrier. It is like a light in a lantern; you cannot touch it due to the glass."

"The Vishuddha, the 5th plane, is at the throat. It has sixteen petals. When Kundalini reaches it, one wants to talk and hear only about God. Talk of worldly subjects cause him pain."

"The center at the heart corresponds to the 4th plane of the Vedas. In this center is a lotus called Anahata, with Twelve petals."

"Yoga is not possible if the mind dwells on the three lower planes of existence only — the Manipura, Svadhisthana, and Muladhara. A worldly man's mind moves among these three centers, at the navel, the sexual organ, and the organ of evacuation. These three represent eating, drinking, and sex life. But when Kundalini shakti is awakened it passes through these three lower centers and pierces the heart chakra. Then a man hears the subtle sound and sees light, and he cries out in mute wonder, 'Oh! What is this! what is this!'"

"Known as the hell realms, the seven Patalas correspond generally to the subconscious mind of humanity wherein all manner of irrational instincts, habits, impressions, and memories are stored. These rise to influence the thoughts and actions of ignorant embodied beings without their being aware of the source of them."

The Seven Planes of Existence ↓

7 — Brahmaloka

6 — Tapaloka

5 — Janaloka

4 — Maharloka

3 — Svarloka

2 — Bhuvarloka

1 — Bhurloka

1. Atala
2. Vitala
3. Sutala
4. Talatala
5. Mahatala
6. Rasatala
7. Patala

Special States of Higher Awareness

Nirvikalpa Samadhi

Asamprajnata Samadhi

Nirvana

Turiya

Satori

Bhavamukha

Jada Samadhi

Sthita Samadhi

Savikalpa Samadhi

Samprajnata Samadhi

Chetana Samadhi

Sasmita Samadhi

Bhava Samadhi

Sananda Samadhi

Unmana Samadhi

Nirvichara Samadhi

Savichara Samadhi

Nirvitarka Samadhi

Savitarka Samadhi

Kundalini Shakti Traversing the Seven Chakras

"With a magnifying glass one can make tiny objects look very big. Likewise, through the practice of Yoga one can detect the subtle spiritual lotuses." Mahendranath Gupta

itate, compromise, prevaricate, and lower the ideal to their comfort zones. The finer notes of the flute of Eternal Life are thus never known to them.

The chart next up for study on the facing page takes us deeper into the study of the seven *chakras,* and thus fleshes out our limited understanding of these inner mysteries. A special facet of its teaching means to inform practitioners of both the poisons and the nectars that reside in each *chakra.* At the root, called the *muladhara,* is where many of the base human passions hide, exerting their unwholesome influence on life all the time. Also, some four "S's" also define that root center, all of which possess their own form of nectar as well. Sexuality for procreation, security for family life, stability for the mind to rely upon, and more, all reside here. Of course, all the potential of *Kundalini* is said to be stored up there as well, making the root *chakra* at the base of the spine a pivotal center.

The *svadhisthana* at the second *chakra,* associated with the sexual organ, contains a host of poisons, but some counteractive nectars too. There is the violence force festering there, but also the famous creative impetus if this negativity can be sublimated and used for positive results. Joy, pleasure, and addiction are all mixed up there, and it is up to the aspiring soul to make the right distinctions and decisions regarding them. A teacher, or *guru,* will aid in this task. Otherwise, it is a danger zone.

At the *manipura chakra,* third in the inward ascension scheme, the atmosphere of consciousness has become somewhat more refined. Unfortunately, the obstacles have followed suit. This center is famous for difficulty in balance; rank emotionalism often blows through its premises like an uncontrollable wind, from all directions. Anxiety is usually the result, as are the unsavory conditions of fear and judgement as well. Again, it is up to the determined practitioner to work the power of transformation that also resides there, and to wisely choose the path of expansion rather than contraction, growth rather than backsliding.

The three *chakras* just outlined are realms where beings attracted to life and attached to bodies gravitate, where *"eating, drinking, and sex life,"* to quote the Great Master, preoccupy the mind. It is the third *chakra,* particularly, that interests the aspirant after spirituality, for that realm, that *"Chamber of the Father's Mansion,"* contains the human being's many ancestors — fathers, mothers, husbands, wives, children, grandparents, etc. — being all wrapped up with his or her past lifetimes and, importantly, the *karma* that has been created in and through them all. Many of the troubles that plague the embodied soul on earth can all be traced to this realm, though few ever come to know of it. And as the list of *chakras* on the chart reveal, the more refined pleasures, joys, and yes, even the sense of power and illusion of growth, also originate there. The ardent aspirant seeks to penetrate that center, along with its respective *vishnu-granthi* (subtle knot/barrier), and course freely inwards from then on (review chart on page 506).

And that entails merging into the fourth of these subtle regions, the *anahata chakra.* An intensely desired center of awareness, the "heart" *chakra* signifies all that is good, better, and best in its sweep. If residues of weakness and passion left over from lower realms can be navigated, the path of deeper and more profound freedom lies open to the soul here. As has always been known about this central *chakra,* wherein are seen the three lower *chakras* beneath, and the three upper *chakras* on high, it is a realm filled with love and devotion for Divine Reality. It also brooks and brushes up against the very subtle fabric of consciousness contained in the *vishuddha chakra,* where a more breathless freedom attends upon the ascending, aspiring soul. If the temptation for misusing such profundities, that lie in easy access about the floor of that center like so many jewels, is resisted and surmounted, then a true teacher and leader of men is born (see chart on page 106), and one who also has access to even deeper and higher secrets.

These come into play at the next center, called *ajna.* As the chart under study reflects, true spirituality makes itself known to the now fully adept soul, but so does the potential to become disoriented. Misdirection must be counteracted here by a love for and adherence to clarity, called *"khyati"* in both *Buddhism* and *Yoga.* It is only this quality, refined into a sterling and crystal version of itself, that can allow the now fully-awakened soul to attempt the final inward jump — past the practically indiscernible *rudragranthi* to the famous otherworldly "Thousand-petaled lotus" at the crown of the head. There, is no quality; no realm, or land, or atmosphere. The soul is not there either, as all bodies, whether gross, subtle, or causal, have ceased to be. Fittingly named, *sahasrara,* its infinite "petals" are filled with nothing else but pure, conscious Awareness. They, the seers, do not speak of it, for they cannot. It is indescribable. It takes away all the senses, along with the sense of individuality that mans and operates them.

The Seven Causes & Ten Impediments in Kundalini Yoga

"Imbalances appear in the body due to several causes. If the yogic aspirant reacts to these then fears arise, and he falsely believes that his yogic practice has instigated these diseases. This is the first obstacle to the practice of Kundalini Yoga, so the yogi should abandon this and all other obstacles."   Yoga Kundalini Upanisad

<u>Seven Causes</u>			<u>Ten Impediments</u>
Daytime Lassitude	Untimely Elimination of Waste	Reaction to Disease	Attachment to Objects
Nighttime Excesses		Doubt	Erroneous Perception
Unchecked Sexuality	Unwholesome Food	Carelessness	Oversensuality
		Laziness	Faithlessness
Frequenting Crowds	Erratic Condition of Prana and Mind	Sleep	Failure to Attain Truth

Sahasrara

Shakti   Siva

<u>Nectars</u>   <u>Poisons</u>

Ajna

Spirituality	Confusion
Clarity	Mistrust
Visualization	Misdirection
Intuition	Indeterminacy

Vishuddha

Freedom	Falsehood
Mentation	Projection
Balance	Deceit
Communication	Domination

Anahata

Love	Passion
Devotion	Rejection
Compassion	Weakness
Circulation	Imbalance

Manipura

Power	Fear
Expansion	Anxiety
Growth	Judgement
Digestion	Emotionalism

Svadhisthana

Enthusiasm	Pleasure
Creativity	Violence
Joy	Addiction
Reproduction	Selfishness

Muladhara

Stability	Lust
Security	Jealousy
Sensuality	Greed
Sexuality	Obsession

"The Kundalini dwells in the Muladhara chakra. When it is aroused it passes along the Sushumna nerve, pierces the six centers, and at last reaches the lotus at the head, the Sahasrara. This is called the movement of the Mahavayu, the Spiritual Current, and it culminates in Samadhi. All the lotuses then blissfully blossom forth. This is a very secret experience." Sri Ramakrishna Paramahansa

Even the all-pervasive *prana* is silent and still there. As one song of Mother India puts it:

O Blissful mind, awaken to the enchanting vision of Mother Shyama
by opening your inner eye of Wisdom.
Upon perceiving Her Form enshrined eternally within your heart,
withdraw into that sacred chamber of ecstatic Love and behold Her there in secret.
Abiding in that exalted condition, remember that the ordinary mind
connected to the five senses cannot enter there.
But you are allowed to bring the tongue into that Holy Sanctuary,
so that is might spontaneously utter the Blessed Name of Kali —
The Divine Mother of the Universe.
Worshipping Her in solitude, O mind, and with your Self-Knowledge intact,
let Kamalakanta forever rejoice in the Mother's Sacred Presence!

The remainer of the chart on page 589 takes up the Seven Causes and the Ten Impediments for review. Interested aspirants, and even the casual student of this rarefied wisdom, may find some clues and solutions to problems experienced in everyday life among this list.

We can deepen even further our wisdom about *Kundalini Yoga's* seven *chakras* with metaphoric quotes used by Sri Ramakrishna Paramahamsa, all placed into the next chart on the facing page. In similar fashion as in the chart on page 587, where the Master used the *bansuri* flute as a way of explaining the gradated levels of human awareness, here, a "sound castle" made of musical instruments gets utilized for the same purpose.

Sri Ramakrishna, besides being a nondual seer, an intensely realized *premabhakta,* an enlightened *Paramahamsa,* and an superlative *yogi,* was also, and mainly, a master of *Kundalini Yoga.* As one looks around today one can see that, other than questionable pretenders, there are precious few *Kundalini* masters in existence anymore. In the *Gospel of Ramakrishna* are found many of His insights and teachings, as well as His many experiences with *Kundalini Shakti.* These descriptions leave little doubt as to both the access He had to Her (*Kundalini Ma*), and the many powerful states She put Him in.

At one time He described Her ineffable power moving in ascending fashion up His subtle centers as the journey of a man in a seven-floored castle. This journeyman was looking for the King *(Paramasiva)* who *sat* in his throne room *(sahasrara),* and had important words for him. At each floor of the castle there was a guard (presiding deity of the realm), each one more impressive and imposing looking than the last. The man had to speak with each one *(mantra)* to find out if they were, in actuality, the king, and was told each time that he had to go higher to find him. Finally, the man had tread the stairways (performed specific *sadhanas*) to all the first six floors, and when he reached the seventh floor he did not have to ask if this was the King, for his glory (Light of *Brahman*) was evident and obviously unsurpassable.

Here he falls speechless and realizes that he is the Lord's dynamic power *(Kundalini).* He gets transported in deep, nondual meditation, surrounded by the Light of Consciousness. She has taken him to the seventh gateway of the castle. A poignant verse from a song of Mother India, by Ramprasad, expertly relates the culmination of this bliss-filled tale:

My beloved mentor once whispered in my ear these instructions for meditation:
"O meditator: become the Goddess!
Visualize your own body as sparkling Goddess energy.
Within its spirals of consciousness, the universal form of humanity,
dwells every being from the heavenly hierarchy
embodying feminine and masculine energy.

"Emerging into Her thousand-petal reality,
O meditator, become the Goddess consciously.
She is your essence, you her expression.
Now cast your benign glance of compassion upon all beings in creation.
You are that which pervades all phenomena.
You are the pearl of clear light beyond all worlds."

❰❰ Kundalini's Palace with 7 Gates ❱❱

"A man wanted to see the king. The king lived in the inner court of the palace, beyond seven gates. No sooner did the man pass the first gate then he saw a regal official. 'Is this the King,' he asked?. He was told to enter the next gate and again he saw an official, more regal than the last. He wondered if that was the king. But when he eventually passed through the final gate, he knew that he was seeing the king."

Sri Ramakrishna

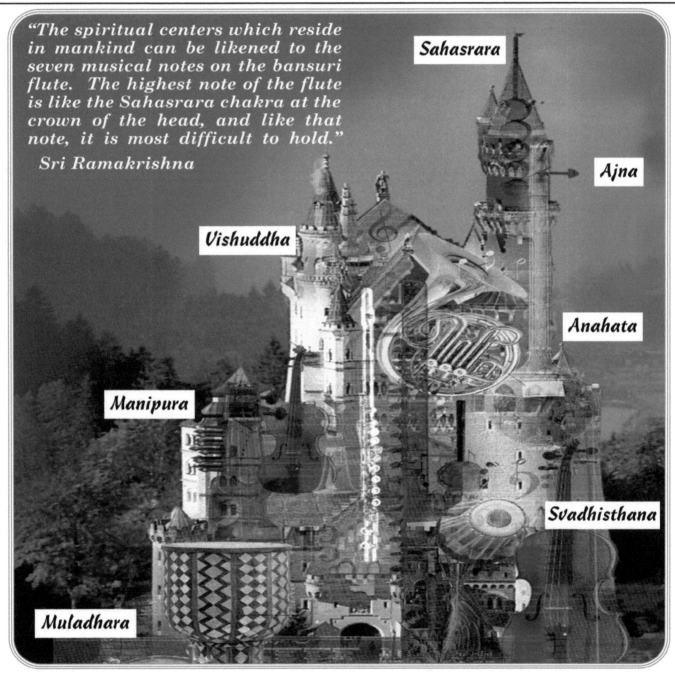

"The spiritual centers which reside in mankind can be likened to the seven musical notes on the bansuri flute. The highest note of the flute is like the Sahasrara chakra at the crown of the head, and like that note, it is most difficult to hold."

Sri Ramakrishna

Sahasrara

Ajna

Vishuddha

Anahata

Manipura

Svadhisthana

Muladhara

"Kundalini passes through the six centers. God is both within and without. From within He creates the various states of mind, and without He sports through them. After passing through the six centers the jiva goes beyond the realm of maya and becomes united with the Supreme Soul."

Sri Ramakrishna Paramahamsa

Sri Ramakrishna also reminds us, in his quote on the bottom of the chart (page 591), that by passing through the six *chakras* in our practice of *Kundalini Yoga* we transcend *maya* and go beyond all appearances, all projections, all confusions, all suffering.

The seven *chakras* of higher Awareness are inward. Looking into outer space is merely gazing at the various external phenomena of the lower two centers. Obsessing with the third *chakra* is only courting rebirth with the ancestors, in cycles. When the fourth center is opened, however, via certain spiritual disciplines and austerities, living beings see and begin to know their Essence (*svarupa*). The chart on the facing page goes into more depth about some of the features of each center with regard to its position and its mysticism.

First of all, and probably of greater import to the ardent seeker after freedom, the six bullet points at the bottom of the chart are to be noted. *Prana-shakti* is called into focus at the outset. A review of all the charts on *prana* in this book would be helpful for insight and orientation. Second to note are the *nadis,* and the meaning of the word *nadi.* Basically, and to repeat teachings from earlier pages of this book, the *yogis* are aware of millions of tiny channels that course through the human body, yet that are not found in its physical form. The human nervous system is only an outer expression of these inner passageways. Much like vessels that carry blood, and nerves that carry physical energy, the *nadis* carry transmigrating consciousness at its various levels to different *akashas* and *lokas,* forging ahead with subtle power on the wings of various *prana-shaktis.* The famed *Garuda* bird of Indian "mythology" is a symbol for this function.

Limited consciousness, though essentially nondual, changeless, and eternal in its Essence (like at the seventh chakra), is an emanation of *Brahman,* much like rays of the sun which emanate from it. In order to move around in the *"Fields of the Lord,"* or visit the many *"Chambers of my Father's* (Mother's) *Mansion,"* souls utilize the *prana-shaktis.* There are also major manifestations of consciousness in the *chakras* known as wrathful deities, angelic beings (at the gates of lower centers) and gods and goddesses. A look back at the chart on page 548, entitled *Lokas, Nadis, and Transmigration of Souls,* will be helpful to the student and practitioner, and will provide a visual, however inadequate, for what goes forth in this immense, immeasurable, and immaculate series of inner universes. Again, the infinite number of galaxies in the physical universe are only an outer reflection of the *"Kingdoms of Heaven within"* — all held in the One Kingdom that India calls *Brahman,* and that *Kundalini Yoga* calls *Sahasrara.*

The upper two thirds of this chart repeats information already gleaned from the past three charts on the *chakra* system, but it offers some new information as well. We see that the *chakras* are aligned with the five elements and the mind, as well as with the presiding deities of each. Letters, sounds, and *pranashaktis* also find their places. In other aspects of the teachings, colors and petals, like doorways in and out, also get assigned. Another song of Mother India refers to some of these:

You awaken and manifest, O Mother,
on the petals of six ascending lotus centers
as the fifty letters of the sacred alphabet.
Your dynamic power alone plays through the solar plexus,
focus of strength and will.
Seed sounds of your feminine energy balance on twelve letters of the lotus heart.
Your potent vowels cluster on the sixteen-petal lotus at the throat.
Symbols containing your revolutionary wisdom
emanate from the two-petal lotus between the eyebrows.

Ascend swiftly in awareness, O Mother, through all six levels,
symbolized by dense earth, flowing water, dancing fire, invisible wind,
open space, and all-embracing mind,
each one entered with a key of sacred sound.
When breath catches in delight and enters momentary suspension,
subtle structures pass before the inner eye
and sweet humming music is heard:
first, the base note of a black bee intoxicated by golden pollen,
then waves roaring in the conscious ocean of Awareness.

The Seven Sat Chakras of Kundalini Yoga

Chakras	Element / Deity	Location	Petals / Nadis
Sahasrara	**Parashakti**	**Crown of the Head**	**1000** prana-shakti unites with Parashakti

Sahasrara is not a chakra, but an infinite realm where all rests in a causal state

Chakras	Element / Deity	Location	Petals / Nadis
Ajna	Shambhu	Forehead	2 — 2 letters, 2 sounds, 2 prana-shaktis

The deities are forms of Universal Consciousness which manifest in the chakras

Vishuddha	Ether / Sadasiva	Throat	16 — 16 letters, 16 sounds, 16 prana-shaktis

Nadis are not physical nerves, but Yoga-nadis that cannot be detected by the eye

The nadis are subtle nerve channels along which flows the psychic current (pranika)

Anahata	Air / Isha	Heart	12 — 12 letters, 12 sounds, 12 prana-shaktis

Each chakra possesses a host of forces (prana-shaktis) that work on its own specific plane

The chakras (lotuses) are vortexes of vital Consciousness-force called prana-shakti

Manipura	Fire / Agni	Navel	10 — 10 letters, 10 sounds, 10 prana-shaktis

Each lotus has a certain number of petals that hold letters/bijams and their innate powers

Svadhisthana	Water / Varuna	Generative Organs	6 — 6 letters, 6 sounds, 6 prana-shaktis
Muladhara	Earth / Brahma	Base of Spine	4 — 4 letters, 4 sounds, 4 prana-shaktis

"After great effort and spiritual practice the Kundalini is awakened. At that time the mind of the aspirant is withdrawn from the three lower centers. He feels the first awakening of Divine Consciousness and sees Light. In mute wonder he sees that radiance and cries: 'What is this? What is this?'" Sri Ramakrishna Paramahamsa

The *Tantric* way of mystic philosophy and experience is deep and vast; this is why it was never systematized by any seer or sage and turned into an orthodox *darshana*. It is also unlike any other religious or philosophical system in the world, with its soul-stirring emphasis on blissful love of God. But few beings know that *Tantra* is mainly based upon and grounded in sacred Wisdom, and that its pathways to knowing are as stunning as any found in *Vedanta* or *Buddhism*. The following chart shows this to be true in its explication of the Six Ways to *Brahmajnana*, the knowledge of Divine Reality.

Tantra's Sadakhya system is a little known and long lost treasure, and is as much or more of a statement of fact about the power of divine manifestation than a path to follow to complete understanding. *Tantra* has always had a unique and convincing way of proving the existence of Existence to wondering mankind. Its *Sristi Rahasya* principle, or "Secret of Creation," evinces knowledge of primal beginnings via the Word, *AUM*. Both the *Vedic* stream and the *Tantric* stream have had a long standing relationship with and meditation on The Word. The Wisdom Word of *AUM* is at the basis of all and everything, even principles like "emptiness," as well as the existence of a vacant expanse like "the void."

Rather than engage in conjecture about what is actual and nonactual, real or unreal, the *Sadakhya* system merely states that *"Manifestation is in the nature of Reality."* Other systems would aver that when any expression comes forth, then Reality is immediately covered up. Whereas this can be allowed as true on the philosophical level, on the experiential level the case seems much different.

The first of these six ways to perceive Truth is **Kala.** *Kala,* and *Kali,* are divine names for *Siva* and Divine Mother. *Kala* is also the *Sanskrit* word for time. *Kala* is the Divine Being appearing in time, as time, and thereby bringing forth all realms of existence while simultaneously assisting living beings in moving between and among them. All transitions are accomplished by *Kala,* which also confers the levels and planes of expression upon which these movements take place. This it does by projecting five presiding deities (see chart) who preside over all cosmic principles, from subtlemost to solid.

Tattva is the second of the six ways to *Brahmajnana*. *Tattvas* are wisdom principles that follow after *Kala* and its broad sweep of manifestation. The Twenty-four Cosmic Principles of *Sankhya* philosophy according to Lord Kapila are well known in philosophical circles. A chart on these can be reviewed on page 349. Shaivism's Thirty-six Cosmic Principles can be seen again on page 359. *Tantra's Sadakhya* system falls in line with these lists, but explains their appearance in terms of these six ways now under study.

Bhuvana denotes regions lying within consciousness. Stating succinctly what Jesus knew and taught, all of these realms appear inside of human awareness. The division of internal worlds, along with the one external one (earth), fall into a seven *loka* designation, which also happens to correspond nicely with *Kundalini's* seven *chakras*. Seven lower worlds are also often noted, sunken grounds that degraded beings frequent. The *tattvas* in the seven worlds fall into a threefold categorization that is often called gross, subtle, and causal — or physical, psychical, and spiritual. Just as there are countless planets in the physical firmament, so too are there an infinite array of worlds in the inner universes.

Varna is the fourth way to secure knowledge of the Highest, and its introduction offers a more general comprehension to the outwardly-oriented human mind. The realm of words leaves no doubt as to its import. It is all a matter of whether words are seen as 1) the very essence of intelligence, 2) utilized for basic communications only, or 3) stripped of their sanctity and robbed of their real meaning. In *Tantra*, the first route is the one to tread, and this means that, just like an atom is to be inspected for its internal power, so too must words and letters be inspected for their subtle primal force (see chart on page 33). Here, both *Tantra's Kundalini Shakti*, and *Vedanta's Vak Devi Sarasvati*, reveal their unity.

The indwelling force in words is referred to as *matrka-shakti* by the Indian *rishis*. The whole secret to the astonishing appearance of worlds and the beings that inhabit them comes down to vibrating particles. Unbeknownst to modern science, and the greater percentage of living beings in this world, the Divine Mother's expression of divine sound, called *Shabda Brahman*, emanates forth via alphabets (*matrka*), words (*shabda*), and their meanings (*artha*). When a world is solidified by the mind, it is accomplished via dream particles drawn from an inner source (deep sleep). Similarly, when a word is put together by the *matrka-shakti,* it is rendered complete via *chit-matras*, particles of living intelligence. Her presence in them is why all beings, even those who have no knowledge of the subtle science of the Spirit, love words and their meanings.

The Six Ways of Attaining Brahmajnana in Tantra

❱Sadakhya — The Six Paths of Knowledge Leading to Perfection❰

"With self-purification achieved, liberation proceeds via extracting the essence of the scriptures and gaining an intellectual conviction leading to mature spiritual discrimination. Lifeless mechanical rites and rituals do not work. If rubbing the body with ashes could bring liberation, then village dogs could have it." —Tantras

Kala	Tattva	Bhuvana	Varna	Pada	Mantra
(Aspects)	(Categories)	(Regions)	(Letters)	(Words)	(Utterances)

Kala — Manifestation is in the nature of Reality. Kala, in its 5 main forms, presides over all cosmic principles — pure, mixed, and impure. It simultaneously assists the unmanifest to transition into the manifest and acts as a guide for all seekers of Self-realization. As possessor of shakti, at its highest level Kala is the Supreme Shakti, the Prime Mover — at the same time absorbed in Reality, incapable of being differentiated from It, yet partially and independently emergent via its own Divine Will.

(nivrtti kala)	(pratistha kala)	(vidya kala)	(shanta kala)	(shantyatita kala)
Brahma Presiding	Vishnu Presiding	Rudra Presiding	Maheshvara Presiding	Sadasiva Presiding

Tattva — Beginning with the elements and proceeding to Shiva and Shakti, consciousness as experience is made up of worlds (bhuvanas) which are planes of existence consisting of tattvas.

PHYSICAL TATTVAS	PSYCHICAL TATTVAS	SPIRITUAL TATTVAS
EARTH, FIRE, WATER, AIR, ETHER; ODOR, FLAVOR, VISIBILITY, TANGIBILITY, AUDIBILITY; EXCRETING, PROCREATING, LOCOMOTION, HANDLING, SPEAKING; SMELLING, TASTING, SEEING, FEELING, HEARING	MIND, THOUGHT, INTELLIGENCE, EGO; SOUL (PURUSHA), COSMIC LAWS (NIYATI), TIME-PHASES (KALAS), TIME (KALA), HIGHER KNOWLEDGE (VIDYA), SUBTLE MATTER (KARYAMAYA), ATTRACTION (RAGA)	INNER GUIDANCE (SADAKHYA), SPIRITUAL WISDOM (BINDU), NONDUALITY (SHUDDHAVIDYA), PRIMAL SOUND (NADA), SUPREME DEITY (ISHVARA)

Bhuvana — 224 realms lie within 14 universes, 7 higher and 7 lower, ranging gross to subtle. Some correspond to the 5 elements, and others to subtler worlds which exist beyond the physical plane, located in those spiritual vortexes called chakras. Essentially, all realms of existence lie within.

Brahmaloka (Trinity)	Tapaloka (Vairagas)	Janaloka (Seers)	Maharloka (Sages)	Svarloka (Gods)	Bhuvarloka (Siddhas)	Bhurloka (Humans)

7 Nether Regions ➜ Atala · Vitala · Sutala · Talatala · Mahatala · Rasatala · Patala

Varna — The garland of letters — Varna-mala — is the science of 51 alphabets which is an expression of the Mahashakti, the essence of indivisible Truth which reveals the mystery of creation. The mystery of creation, Srsti Rahasya, vibrates via particles of intelligence (chit-matras) and includes 3 main elements — matrkas (alphabets), shabda (word), and artha (meaning). Devoid of matrka-shakti consciousness could not reveal itself. Worlds, beings, objects, even Ishvara — all evolve from matrka.

Pada — The construction and meaning of whole words springing from matrka is what is called pada. The arrangement of these words into statements and profound utterances is constitutive of mantras.

Mantra — The science of cosmic sound, mantra is direct knowledge. Divine spontaneous action proceeds from it. Tattvas form the objective side of experience, while mantra forms the subjective side. By practicing these two aspects one attains spiritual ascendency. Mantra, then, is special knowledge which, when contemplated, reveals the otherwise unseen truth — that the universe is full of Brahman.

Padas are thus formed, words that join and duly form the elements of complete sentences, and importantly, all that follow in the realm of sound and knowledge. Here, the seers, the knowers of Divine Reality, do not flow outward with the words like intellectuals, but flow inwards via the power is "divine utterances." This is one way of keeping the words pure, and speech sacred. Otherwise, and as Sri Ramakrishna has stated, they get polluted by the tongue of mankind.

And to keep the sanctity of words, even on the earthly level, the seers have provided what is known as **Mantra** for humankind (see charts on pages 131, 133, 135, 140, 142, 144 for a course on *mantra* study and practice). The manifested worlds (*tattvas*) are what are seen and experienced by living beings, but the abiding, unseen essence underlying them all are these words of refined intelligence and utterances of holiness that belong to the *Mahashakti.* Through them She reveals to us that "All is *Brahman,*" inside and out.

Continuing on to definitively chart the *dharma* of Mother India, and taking a break from the subject of *Tantra* and *Kundalini Yoga,* the visual on the facing page shows aspiring beings how to approach the Transcendental *Brahman,* as far as that is possible while one is in form. This helpful and encouraging teaching springs from the illumined mind of Sri Krishna, as related in the *Bhagavad Gita.* The entire teaching depends primarily upon working with the mind using discriminative wisdom. Since surface commentaries on the *Gita* by one-sided minds have focused upon the pleasant elements of *bhakti* only, the more *sadhana*-based methods that Krishna prescribes have gotten underplayed. Living beings must return to the path of spiritual disciplines — particularly ones that penetrate to the inner *samskaras* (impressions) in the mind, and to the *karmas* that lurk there, and eradicate them in this very life.

The *Atman,* the Essence in living beings, is ever-pure. It is the mind that is impure, and in such a condition it covers the innate perfection in mankind. Working devoutly upon the mind's subtle layers via *jnanam* and *dhyanam* is thus prescribed by the *gurus* and luminaries.

One of the most readily available methods for self-purification is the attempt to place the mind's thoughts away from the objects of the senses, and thus curb its brooding upon the varied results that come from this contact. As Swami Vivekananda has stated, if a man with a higher ideal makes a thousand mistakes, a man devoid of a higher ideal makes twenty-thousand of them. Thus, an ideal is needed to help the mind focus. As was just stated, the *mantra* helps greatly in this matter. However, a *mantra* is always connected to God with form, and this shows the seeker what an ideal truly is. To have faith in ones ideal, *Ishtam,* and to give away the personal ego so that one can merge in that ideal, ensures swift progress along the path. This is perfect *Yoga* practice, as the first approach listed on the chart relays.

If the mind is obstinate in this attempt, however, or ones temperament is not easily given to such a method as this, the Lord provides and reveals the path of *sadhana* to aspiring souls. *Sadhana,* spiritual disciplines, are the way to freedom for struggling souls, and are a missing element in today's world and its nations and families. *Tapas,* austerities, are also effective, and missing. Ironically, the only *yoga* that is performed today at all is at the physical level only, called *hatha,* but it is wholly ineffective for purification of mind, intellect, and ego. Problems, impediments, and haunting spectors such as doubt, suffering, pain, and fear of death, will never be overcome by physical means. *"One cannot reach the Infinite by the finite,"* as Swami Aseshanandaji has declared. Spiritual practices, done daily, remove all coverings and barriers from the vision of God, which is ones own Self, *Atman,* when it comes right down to it. Soon, "uninterrupted wisdom" visits the mind — which is its real nature as Pure Mind.

But some cannot muster either the will or the strength to engage in *sadhana.* Possibly it is not their time to do so, as it takes assurance of Truth combined with qualification in its pathways (please review the chart on page 578) to be able to strive intensely. And so, a purification of subtle elements performed at the level of divine works gets introduced. In other words, the mind, as yet unsuited for or still orienting itself towards inner life, may like the method of continuing on in its outer actions while offering them all to the Lord and Mother of the Universe, rather than to the small self called "ego." This shift of awareness ushers in a gradual giving up of works done for the individual's sake, thus making it fit for higher wisdom.

The arrival of mature wisdom on the scene of the freshly controlled mind brings in a new understanding of both the need of and ability for renunciation. Since *"renunciation is not condemnation, but deification,"* as Swami Aseshanandaji has stated, this avenue of approach, preceded by its three steps, fits per-

The Four Plateaus for Approaching Brahman

"To those who approach Me with love and sincerity, I give them clear discrimination by which they can realize Me." **Sri Krishna**

1) Fix the Mind and Its Thoughts Upon Reality Alone.

"Of all yogis, that one who worships Me with faith, his inmost Self merged in Me, that one I hold to be most devout, perfected in yoga."

2) If the Mind Will Not Concentrate, Engage in Constant Practice.

"The senses impetuously carry away the mind of the one striving for perfection, but the yogi, controlling them all, remains focused upon Me and enjoys the bliss of uninterrupted wisdom."

3) If Practice is Not Possible, Then Offer All Works to God.

"The yogi, abandoning all attachment, performs work with body, mind, intellect, and senses for self-purification alone and, being untainted, dedicates all thoughts, works, and deeds selflessly to Brahman."

4) If Selfishness and Agency Persist, Abandon the Fruits of Work.

"Better indeed is knowledge than formal practice; better than knowledge is meditation; better than meditation is the renunciation of the fruit of action; profound peace immediately follows renunciation."

Natural Renunciation in Four Phases

For The Effacement of Latent Impressions

"Renounce first the desire for enjoyment, then the inner mental desires that foster it. Keep the purer desires, such as the desire for friendship. Then practice giving even that up inwardly and seek knowledge alone. Finally, giving up even the desire for knowledge, abide in what remains, and give up that by which you renounce." Jivan-Mukti-Viveka

4. Vidyavasana
Give up knowledge to realize Truth

3. Pranayavasana
Give up social relations and cultivate knowledge alone

1. Vishayavasana
Give up base desires for the sense objects

2. Manasavasana
Give up the internal desires of the mind

"The beginner should fill two parts of the mind with objects of enjoyment, one part by study of the scriptures, and one part by attending on the guru."

"The intermediate student should fill one part of the mind with objects, one part by reflecting on the scriptures, and two parts by attending on the guru."

"The advanced student should fill half of the mind with the study of scriptures, and then the remaining half with the worship of the teacher."
Lord Vasishtha

"Raising an opposite wave in the mind, called Pratipakshabhavanam, is a much overlooked and underestimated method of spiritual practice. It is the simple way of watering the flowers and not the weeds. Here, the aspirant does not strive to root out desires, to squelch emotions, to destroy the passions, or force austerities. Instead he slowly transforms the mind by fixing it on the dharma and its teachings alone."

Babaji Bob Kindler

fectly for a greater percentage of living beings who desire to achieve their innate perfection in life, but who do not yet possess the fully awakened power necessary to gain full Enlightenment in one, grand leap.

For attaining swift purification of mind leading to mature renunciation, the beings who are either adepts, or who are busy gaining liberation in this lifetime, take a more direct route. Using their accumulated power (*shakti*) won from intense practices (*sadhana/tapas*) over years, even lifetimes, they strive harder than ever before to reach liberation (*mukti*). The nondual scripture entitled *Jivan-Mukti-Viveka* prescribes an ideal method for such advanced practitioners, as the chart opposite reveals.

Unlike tremulous beings who fear every little movement in life that takes them away from outer security, the adepts of the spiritual realm both welcome and take to direct means of effacing latent impressions that stand in the way of their personal vision of God. They have the power to tear out by the very roots the remnants of desire that are still hiding in the subconscious mind, placing irritating spots on the lens of their inner eye, as it were. Checking the mind for any leftover traces of desire for any and all objects, they find and dissolve the same without hesitation, thus satisfying the first prerequisite called *Vishayavasana*. According to Lord Vasishtha in another scripture, this is accomplished at the outset of this particular practice by allowing the mind to keep only half of its desire for objects of enjoyment, while placing a quarter of the mind on study of revealed scriptures and the remaining quarter on the spiritual preceptor's guidance and instructions.

The next level of success is gained by eradicating the source of desires in the mind, the problem being *Manasavasana*. The going gets subtle here, the ground less certain, but Lord Vasishtha recommends filling a half of the mind with thoughts on the *guru* and his/her teachings, while keeping up a quarter of the mind's attention upon study of scripture. The holding of thoughts of objects now gets reduced by twenty-five percent attention, leaving the ego less room to object about the decrease to its selfish world.

Pranayavasana, the third phase of this divine plan to return the soul back to its blissful, free status, is more of a natural occurrence than a conscious practice. By now, everything worthy in the human mind is ripening, and the senses and body are even becoming obedient to higher will. As a result, the look at, smell of, and contact with, worldly people and society is fast becoming an undesirable undertaking, and feels even repugnant. Helping lost souls and interested individuals is not what is meant here; maintaining support of beings who are given to ignorant thoughts and insensitive actions is what is at issue. The practitioner simply withdraws from all commerce with selfish, pleasure-bound beings, and turns inwards to find holy company. As was mentioned, this move happens almost of its own accord, in spontaneous fashion. In the same way that one would not go back and lick up spittle that was exuded in a gutter seconds ago, an awakened soul will not return to the world of name, fame, and gain at the cost of harming other living beings. The principle of *ahimsa* (see chart on page 447) is now in full operation, and compassion is fast becoming the modus operandi of the now spiritualized mind.

The blissful benefits of knowledge, or wisdom, is also a part of this phase, and a gain that is far beyond anything the world of rank egotism can offer. Just as for the *bhakta*, devotion to God is itself ample reward for sacrificing in life, for the *jnani*, this especial knowledge is far and away more than enough to justify all struggle to gain it in a world full of vain pursuits. To watch subtle knowledge burgeon in the open and expanding mind is a kind of bliss that only the wisdom seeker and the *guru* understand. This higher knowledge never appears in the minds of average beings, and its utterances never grace the tongue of worldly souls, so the spiritual aspirant quietly vacates the gathering places of the blithe and gay pleasure seekers and retreats to the silence of the inward-turning intellect

The fourth phase of renunciation, *Vidyavasana*, finds the now adept practitioner entering the stage of truth-knower. It is not that knowledge goes away, as some presume, but that after it fulfills its purpose it can now rest as both underlying presence and eternal protector of the mind-field. Should the illumined soul ever need to emerge from the incomparable atmosphere of nondual Reality, i.e., Truth, this knowledge, lying in seed form, will provide him/her with all that is necessary to formulate and exemplify divine life in the realms of name and form.

Higher knowledge as a doorway to Truth is the natural expression of the aspiring soul, who returns to *Samadhi* like a hawk returns to its mountain nest in the lofty crags when night falls. And as was mentioned, knowledge left lying fallow in the human mind, short of this ultimate goal, can tend towards future projections (*sankalpa*) that involve the soul in questionable actions and pursuits. Just like

Para & Aparavidya

The Clarifying Teaching of Higher and Lower Knowledge

"Lower knowledge taken from books, and conventional religious knowledge gleaned from ordinary shastras, form two separate hells for beings devoid of Higher Wisdom. Even intelligent beings writhe in these two states, fixating on wealth, status, and power. Therefore, you should exert inwardly and swiftly attain to Transcendent Wisdom, taking refuge in the Great Self." — Valmiki

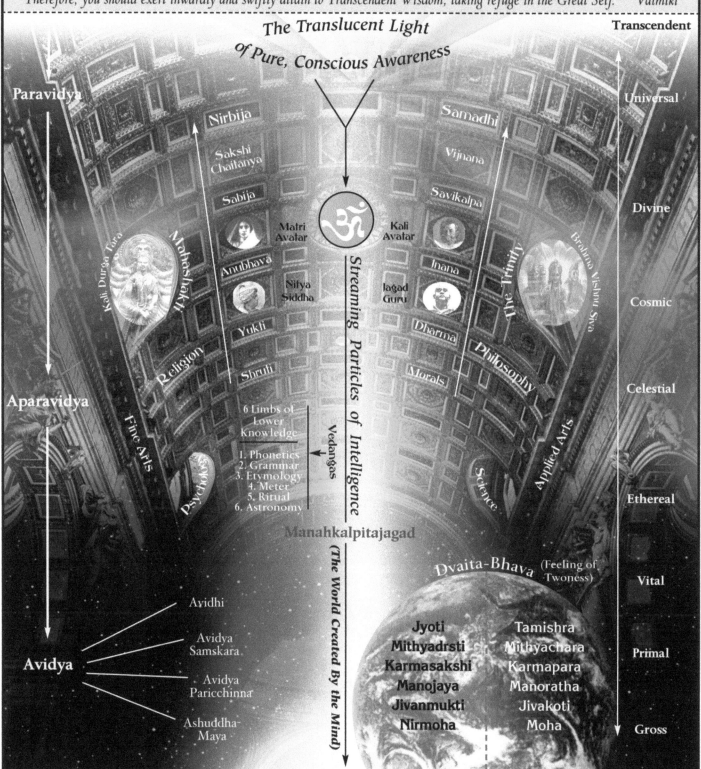

The Translucent Light of Pure, Conscious Awareness

Transcendent

Paravidya

Universal

Nirbija

Samadhi

Sakshi Chaitanya

Vijnana

Sabija

Savikalpa

Divine

Kali Durga Tara

Mahashakti

Matri Avatar

Kali Avatar

Brahma Vishnu Siva

The Trinity

Anubhava

Jnana

Nitya Siddha

Jagad Guru

Cosmic

Religion

Yukti

Dharma

Philosophy

Aparavidya

Shruti

Morals

Celestial

Fine Arts

Psychology

6 Limbs of Lower Knowledge
1. Phonetics
2. Grammar
3. Etymology
4. Meter
5. Ritual
6. Astronomy

Vedangas

Streaming Particles of Intelligence

Applied Arts

Science

Ethereal

Manahkalpitajagad

Dvaita-Bhava (Feeling of Twoness)

Vital

Ayidhi

Avidya Samskara

Avidya Paricchinna

Ashuddha-Maya

Avidya

(The World Created By the Mind)

Jyoti
Mithyadrsti
Karmasakshi
Manojaya
Jivanmukti
Nirmoha

Tamishra
Mithyachara
Karmapara
Manoratha
Jivakoti
Moha

Primal

Gross

"The One remains, the many change and pass; Heaven's Light forever shines, Earth's shadows fly;
Life, like a dome of many-colored glass, stains the white Radiance of Eternity." — Percy Bysshe Shelly

the ego that tries to possess it for its own purposes, knowledge must be ripened in order that it open the way to the Light of Truth. Just as idleness in the devil's playground, so, too, is lower knowledge, which can play havoc with all the many possibilities that lay waiting for activation in the fertile human mind.

To give the avid student of *Vedanta* philosophy a look at the clear distinction the seers of India have laid down between lower knowledge, *aparavidya,* and higher knowledge, *paravidya,* the chart on the previous page is now offered up for inspection. It should be stated at the outset that some thinkers aver that higher knowledge includes the realm of the scriptures and the cross-section of religions, while others state that higher knowledge only refers to that which is gleaned from direct spiritual experience. Whatever the case, perhaps an intermediary level can be assigned for knowledge as well, which would include in its sweep all that has to do with scriptures and religion. For, as has been shown throughout this book, there are scriptures that are dualistic, and some that are nondualistic — the common scriptures and the "revealed scriptures." This fact might necessitate a further category of distinction.

There is no dearth of richness to consider, however, when we examine the bottom of the chart under study. The world below, and the vault of wisdom above, within — both sport a plenitude of knowledge. A case can be made for dividing the human mind into two similar divisions as well, for there is much in it that is dark in nature. The word on the chart, *manahkalpitajagad,* says it all. There is no word for this in English, and hardly any concept for it either. It refers to the fact that the mind created the worlds of name and form. It was aided in this task by all the knowledge that lies within it, but was neither aided or abetted by God/*Brahman* therein — as there is no projection or creation in Nondual Reality. The world is a place of contrasting dualities such as light (*jyoti*) and darkness (*tanmishra*) — both in terms of physical and mental light and darkness. There is delusion, *moha,* and freedom from delusion, *vimoha* or *nirmoha,* just as there is the danger of bondage in form, *jivakoti,* and the boon of liberation from form, *jivanmukti.* Overall however, *avidya,* ignorance, steals the day on planet earth. It is in the very mind (*manas*) that projected the world, and resides there as a root impression, *avidya-samskara.* Even the host of rites and rituals of various dualistic religions here on earth, fittingly named *avidhi,* are laced through and through with the uncertainty of unknowing, or not-knowing — also called "hope" among the ignorant. Finally, the impure *maya* permeates everything on earth (*ashuddha-maya*), causing beings to think that benefit and gain can be gotten there. They run hither and yon to gain that which actually resides within them already. Such is the predicament of earthly and worldly life.

But beyond the confusing admixture of fact and fiction that *avidya* congeals and offers up, the realm of *aparavidya* shines with a light that is borrowed, moonlike, from the sun of higher Wisdom. The mind here is taken up by better pursuits, by more worthy causes. It is not called "lower" knowledge for no good reason, however, for these vaunted goals lose their lofty beginnings in the search for power and greed for material gain. Whether it be the six limbs of lower knowledge in India — phonetics, grammar, etymology, meter, ritual, and astronomy — or the facets of Western mentality such as science, psychology, and philosophy, they all lose their claim to true inspiration, i.e., "higher" knowledge, due to the human being's overall ignorance of the Divine Reality that pervades them. Even religion — in every country — falls short of that authentic quality that destroys ignorance and transcends ego-based knowledge. Corrupt priestcraft, and its mixing with business and politics, is the bane of religion, and irreligion is the result. Authentic Religion is only really alive on earth when the *Avatars* visit, every so often.

And even where creativity and inspiration find an entrance, as in the cases of the applied arts and the fine arts, the eternal money-making spoils its higher leanings. A bit of technical proficiency is seen, and a few inspired individuals excel, but overall the arts do not produce enlightenment in the soul; only higher knowledge can do that, since it alone destroys ignorance in the human mind. This is why the seers and saints are free of self-motivated works, argumentation, speculation, the desire for domination, the desire to impress others, the will to be rich and famous, and the glory-seeking ego, while professionals of all types live on and by these inferior modes of existence. As Swami Vivekananda has taught and advised, *"In the world take always the position of the giver. Give everything and look for no return. Give love, give help, give service, give any little thing you can, but keep out barter. Make no conditions and none will be imposed. Let us give out of our own bounty, just as God gives to us."*

The rarified realm of higher knowledge (*paravidya*) is characterized by its nearness to the translucent Light of conscious Awareness. In their highest flights of inspiration, religion and philosophy touch these regions; thus reasoning and scripture find their niche in the lower portals of higher knowledge.

The upper echelons of this chart (page 600) specify for us what Divine Reality really is, and how it is distinct, and remains distinct, from all that falls below It. Put in two basic categories, It is God with form and God beyond form. Described by way of crucial prerequisites, It is the desire for Freedom and the imbibing of *Dharma,* once located.

And it is the *guru* that brings the *dharma* to the sincere aspirant, which ushers in the need for an intermediary between form and formlessness. That is, the spiritual preceptor is not really a form or a personality; he/she is a principle. On this chart, then, four of the most remarkable of luminaries in our times are shown, i.e., Swami Brahmananda, Swami Vivekananda, Sri Sarada Devi, and Sri Ramakrishna. Respectively, and respectfully, these are the world teacher, the ever-perfect soul, the Divine Mother incarnate, and the *Avatar* of the age. These all emanate from pure, conscious Awareness, and even the Trinity worships Them. It is these especial souls who can introduce the adept practitioner to the most refined levels of Consciousness, and thereby grant them *samadhi.* Thus, they represent and epitomize the highest ideal for spiritually aspiring souls. What is beyond Them will be the subject of chapter ten.

According to *Vedanta* philosophy, there are seven Great Ideals that make up the deepest, farthest reaches of nondual Awareness. The next chart, on the facing page, lists these for contemplation, giving quotes from certain luminaries to increase understanding about them and their import.

More of an eternal principle than an ideal, *Brahman* is the first to consider. The quote on the chart by Gaudapada is certainly one of the most perfect descriptions of "That which is indescribable" on human record. Reading it conveys a definitive sense of a breathless atmosphere of inner heights. Contemplating it transports the mind into flights of nondual reverie, the benefit if which cannot be expressed in the realm of words. Finally, realization of what is expressed there is the most precious "attainment" of the knowers of Truth, the "gaining" of which is the reason for both taking a form and giving it up. A complete description of *moksha,* the path to *Brahman,* can be studied again on page 343. The true meaning of *moksha,* or *mukti,* will be taken up in later pages of this book.

Across the chart on the right hand side is *Ishvara* which, according to Swami Vivekananda, is the highest concept of God that the human mind can comprehend. It is God with form, albeit, the highest and best of all forms. All the sweet and powerful manifestations of *Brahman* on earth, such as Rama, Krishna, Buddha, Jesus, Chaitanya, Sri Ramakrishna, and other *Avatars,* have all emanated from *Ishvara.* It is that incarnate form that beings can pray to, and meditate upon, where as the formless *Brahman* is not a subject for such practices or undertakings. Therefore, *Brahman* and *Ishvara* are the perfect couple, philosophically speaking.

And what gets reached in the deepest depths of Awareness by the conjoining of these two eternal principles is *Mahanirvana,* also called *Nirvikalpa Samadhi.* Besides representing the permanent end of suffering — a wish all beings cherish — this stateless state effects the infilling of not only a *"peace that passeth all understanding,"* but a "bliss that is unalloyed and uninterrupted." Therefore, it is highly coveted by the illumined souls who take on a body on earth for the highest good of others.

And it is that very station — more of an ideal than any mentioned thus far in this chart — that makes the best use of all nondual qualities and atmospheres. That is titled *Jivanmukti* by the *rishis* of India, and is an ideal that is reached for and maintained by all aspiring beings who take on a form in relativity. The state and characteristics of a *Jivanmukta* will be discussed at length in the forthcoming pages of this book.

Three more lofty ideals are left to consider in the chart presently under study on the facing page. And actually, they represent the consummate arrival points of three of the four great *Yogas* of India — *Jnana, Bhakti,* and *Karma Yoga.* The wisdom *(Jnana)* and devotional *(Bhakti) Yogas* can be reviewed by referring to the chart on page 429, and the points of the *Yoga* of selfless service *(Karma Yoga)* can be seen on page 427 along with teachings on the fourth *Yoga, Raja Yoga,* or meditation. Extremely important to the path of spirituality in this day and age, Swami Vivekananda has not only brought the Four *Yogas* to the West and to the world in modern times, but has also declared that they are really the new religion of the present age. By learning each one, and synthesizing them all into a consummate practice, many-sided devotees of God and Truth will be born on earth again. A living being that is wise, devout, contemplative, and dedicated to the service of God in mankind — who would not want to see a being of such stature, let alone be alive on earth in the human body when such a marvel takes form?

Sapta Maha-Alaya-Vijnana
The Seven Great Universal Ideals

"The world has not come to that state yet when the ideal can be realized in society. The progress of the world through all its evils is making it fit for the ideals, slowly but surely....

Brahman

"Brahman is unborn, free of sleep, devoid of dreams, beyond names and forms, flashing up all at once. It is omniscient, like intense concentration without end but transcendent of conceptualization. It is silent with no words, completely calm, illumined once and for all, unmoving, and free from fear." Gaudapada

Ishvara

"Ishvara is the sum total of individuals, yet He Himself is also an individual in the same way as the human body is a unit, of which each cell is an individual. The collective, is God. The component, is the soul, or jiva. The existence of Ishvara, therefore, depends on that of jiva, as the body on the cell, and vice versa." Swami Vivekananda

Mahanirvana

"Be not a traveler in samsara; fall not a victim of endless sorrows. The Buddhas declare Nirvana to be the Supreme State. That, verily, is the safe haven and the supreme refuge. After arriving at that state, a man is emancipated from all suffering." Lord Buddha

Jivanmukti

"A Jivanmukta is one who has nearly forgotten duality, whose heart is filled with bliss and whose mind harbors no impressions, who is indifferent to time and its phases, into whom enjoyments enter like rivers, leaving no effects, devoid of 'I', and who knows no difference between the world and Brahman." Shankara

Brahma-Jnana

"In the state of Brahmajnana one sees God both within and without. One sees that it is God that has become body, mind, life, and soul. A man attains Brahmajnana as soon as his mind is annihilated. With the annihilation of the mind dies the ego, which says, 'I', 'I.'" Sri Ramakrishna

Mahat-Seva

"The unenlightened act out of attachment. Thus, the enlightened must act out of nonattachment, desirous of guiding the multitudes. The seven great rishis and four manus were born of my mind. They serve and sustain all creatures. The wise, ones, imbued with equanimity, renounce personal gain and serve the great and the small alike." Sri Krishna

Prema-Bhakti

"In the incomparable state of Prema-bhakti, one's newly awakened awareness focuses on Divine Reality. The devotee dwells ecstatically in this fresh revelation, as all of existence naturally worships Ishvara, without interruption. The entire collection of worlds and lokas then becomes a neverending puja to and for the Lord." Prahlada

...The majority will have to go on with this slow growth. The exceptional ones will have to get out to realize the ideal in the present state of things." Swami Vivekananda

Principles of Brahman According to the Upanisads

"Brahman is unborn, free of sleep, devoid of dreams, beyond names and forms, flashing up all at once. It is omniscient, like intense concentration without end but transcendent of conceptualization. It is silent, calm, illumined once and for all, unmoving, and free from fear." Gaudapada

Tower of Truth

Satyam — Brahman is Truth
Akala — Brahman is Timeless
Ananta — Brahman is Infinite
Ananda — Brahman is Blissful
Advaita — Brahman is Nondual
Akarta — Brahman is Actionless
Atisukshma — Brahman is Subtle
Arupa — Brahman is Formlessness
Ruparupa — Brahman takes Forms
Avicchina — Brahman is Indivisible
Akshara — Brahman is Imperishable
Atindriya — Brahman is Omniscient
Aparinami — Brahman is Immutable
Anirdeshya — Brahman is Indescribable
Ajata — Brahman is Unborn and Uncreate
Sarvam Khalvidam Brahma — All is Brahman
Jivanmukti — Brahman is the Living Liberated
Shantisharana — Brahman is the peaceful Refuge
Vibhu — Brahman is All-Pervasive and All-Inclusive
Ahamta-mamata — Brahman is Egoless/Genderless
Brahmavittama — The Knowers of Brahman are Brahman
Parabrahman — Brahman is Transcendent yet All-Pervasive
Brahma-hridaya — Brahman exists in the heart as Intelligence

"That one Brahman, as Atman, decided, 'May I become many.' So with Cosmic Mind It projected all this — whatever there is here. Having brought it all forward, verily, It entered into all. And having entered in, It abided blissfully." It became the defined while remaining the undefined. It founded everything, but remained foundationless. It became both consciousness and unconsciousness, the real and the unreal, and whatever else there is — yea, It became the entire Reality. On account of It, the seers declare that all is real, all is Brahman." Taittiriyopanisad

It has been stated that the ultimate Reality called *Brahman* is inexpressible and indefinable. This is verily true, but this fact has never stopped the India *rishis* from attempting to express everything about *Brahman* that may lead others to realize It. In the next two charts up for viewing and study, both eternal principles of *Brahman* and essential points about *Brahman* will be taken up for inspection.

The "Tower of Truth" on the previous page does some justice in offering a description of the Ultimate Reality which is undescribable. Most of the principles about *Brahman's* nature are well-utilized and well-understood by philosophers and lovers of Truth, both. Looking down the list, however, there are four or five of them which bring to light some things that are not usually spoken of or comprehended by very many souls.

The first of this small collection is that *Brahman* is *akarta*, actionless. Every action, movement, thought, and aspiration on the part of living beings attempts to contradict this nondual fact. That is why beings wishing to go deeper into levels of consciousness, such as heaven, discriminating wisdom, Cosmic Mind, and even *Ishvara*, sit to practice meditation regularly. It is in meditation that the mind finally slows down long enough to catch a glimpse of the Light of Nondual Awareness. Other truths about *Brahman*, like timelessness and formlessness, come to the fore as well when actual meditation fructifies in peace and equanimity of mind. In the meantime, to repeat here what Vivekananda has stated, *"It is this Lord that we are trying to realize from time without beginning in the objective, and in the attempt throwing up such "queer" creatures of our fancy as man, woman, child, body, mind, earth, sun, moon, stars, the world, love, hate, property, wealth, etc.; also ghosts, devils, angels and gods, God, etc."* In brief, all the many manifestations in our lives, as well as in our active imaginations, simply fall far short of what Divine Reality truly is.

Therefore, living beings who court realization of the formless Reality need to continually remind the mind that *Brahman* is unborn, and to use a phrase coined by Vivekananda in the late 1980's, is "acreate." This is called *"ajata"* in *Sanskrit*, and is one of the pillars of *Advaita* on its own merit. Thinking a bit deeper along this line of scrutiny, the fact of *Brahman's* deathless state would come to mind. Thus, birthlessness and deathlessness, once contemplated in the mind by the discriminating seeker, should convey the proof of several other of the appellations listed on the chart under study, such as *akshara*, imperishable, and *aparinama*, immutable. Taking a clue from India's precious *Advaita Vedanta* philosophy, Shankara sings, *"na mrityor na shankha na me jati bedha pita naiva me naiva mata ma janmah,"* which translates as *"No death have I, for I was never born; I have no father, and no mother,"* and goes on to declare that he is the all-pervasive Reality, *Vibhu — "I am Siva, I am Siva!"* The great Tower of Truth becomes as indestructible as *Brahman* by the realizations of such great souls as he.

Brahman as the living liberated soul, like Shankara, is another of the wondrous truths about Divine Reality. Such a being is a *jivanmukta*, fully realized while occupying the physical body. Since *Brahman* cannot become a form, it is up to the free soul to purify all the mechanisms in the psycho-physical being and rise in subtle stature to a singular transcendent level of Awareness called *samadhi*. There, this exceptional being can readily see the identity of the apparently individualized soul with the Supreme Soul, the *jivatman* with the *Paramatman*. *Brahman* existing in the heart, *Brahma-hrydaya*, will assist in this lofty transport into higher Consciousness, where potentially limiting factors such as gender and ego *(ahamta-mamata)*, and time *(kalas)*, are left behind, and infinity and bliss — *ananta* and *ananda* are experienced in uninterrupted and unalloyed fashion.

A final special "attribute" of the attributeless *Brahman* is its all-pervasiveness, already mentioned above in passing. Perhaps this is Its most subtle *(atisukshma)* facet, and one overlooked so easily by all beings, even the intelligent ones. The *Upanisads* state, revealingly, that *Brahman* is *"....faster than the fastest, slower than the slowest; higher than the highest, lower than the lowest."* In other words, before the intelligent mind-soul can even collect its thoughts, and while it is in the midst of doing so, it has overlooked the fact that *Brahman* pervades them all thoroughly. Beings of low intelligence thus never know *Brahman*; many do not even think to conceive of It. As Sri Ramakrishna has so humorously but lamentably stated, *"Most beings never even think of God by accident."* Such is the predicament of so many of the beings who incarnate in the *Kali Yuga*, an age of spiritual darkness. But then again, *Brahman* is timeless, *akala*, so why should beings even think to search for It while they are lost in the river of time?

With some special facets of the Tower of Truth explored a bit, the chart on page 607 provides ample substance for examination of the many important points surrounding *Brahman's* extremely subtle *(atisukshma)* presence on earth. In other words, and in atypical, all-pervasive fashion, It is here on earth but It is not. Swami Vivekananda once explained this conundrum by stating, *"God is not in the world; the world is in God."* Perhaps a study of the cosmic level of truths will help reveal more.

Coming to know important points about the cosmic level of existence will contribute to the removal of what the Father of *Yoga* calls *bhrantidarshana,* imperfect seeing, or distorted understanding. This speaks of a philosophical problem in the minds of living beings. For instance, to think in terms of creation hampers understanding considerably, for in order to "create" something, that something must have a basis somewhere, for one cannot get something from nothing. Thus, everything has existence. Even the void is no exception, for in order to have become a mental concept and to have received the name, "void," means that someone must have seen it. *Vedanta,* and Indian thinking overall, therefore adopts the word "projection" to replace creation, and is thus on better footing to understand the mind's power to fashion objects, even whole worlds, out of thought.

To accept the physical world at face value is to trust the five senses to give one a thorough reading of life on earth. Since this is obviously a flawed scenario given the stark limitations of the senses, Indian *darshanas* proceed on the premise that there are quite a few unseen elements at work in the world process, and that many of these are not even physical in nature, but have their existence on a subtler plane of vibration. *Prana,* life-force, is one of these. The five charts and their teachings stretching from pages 536 through 545 will give the reader a refresher course on this subtle principle. *"Man does not live by bread alone,"* and his life is not brought about by God or *Brahman* either, since *Brahman* is causeless and birthless. The intermediary, then, is vital force, called *prana* in the *Upanisads.* It pervades everything gross, such as flowing water, burning fire, moving air, rotating earth, etc., but it also flows inward and pervades mind, its thoughts, and its thinking process. All moves on all levels due to the *prana* — which is precisely why *prana* is not Reality, for Reality, *Brahman,* does not move, being all-pervasive. To make the distinction between flowing *prana* and stationary Spirit is the work of the knowers of Reality. From the pinnacle of cogent discrimination they gain insights not given to ordinary thinkers.

Another of the cosmic principles that is key to higher awareness is The Word, *AUM.* The charts and their teachings stretching from pages 133 through 157 will call to mind the crucial important on The Word in Indian cosmology.

Turning now to the collective and individual levels of existence, we find so many pithy and powerful points to ponder. At least three or four of these have to do with the *guru,* illumined souls, and the need for holy company. And prior to really earning this great boon, there will come the need to qualify the mind for entrance into higher awareness. This is precisely why so many aspirants in this day and age are falling victim to spurious teachers and opportunistic *gurus,* for they failed to get qualified in the preliminary teachings before venturing out into the world of religious pathways. Devoid of scriptural study and ignorant of the difference between lower knowledge and higher knowledge (see chart on page 271), they go unprotected into the philosophical fray, losing their way at the very outset.

To purify both the senses and the mind, for instance, is something better accomplished before approaching an illumined teacher. It should not be up to the *guru* to help the student destroy basic *karmas* and undo complicated life-circumstances; such a being is not a therapist or a divorce counselor! For instance, there are plenty of very subtle *karmas* associated with, say, the soul's primal desire for birth, that are more along the lines of a spiritual beings's expertise. Thus, the whys and wherefores of how the bound soul got into the embodied condition are to be examined in a luminary's presence, not the whys and wherefores of how the soul got confused and lost after embodiment already took place. Preliminary practices like *Yoga's yamas* and *niyamas* (pages 399 & 403), *Tantra's* devotional worship (page 497), and even *Vedanta's* Four Fruits and Six Jewels (page 65), to name a few, are best attained, or at least made familiar to the aspirant, prior to meeting any holy personage and gaining his or her advanced instructions. It is here that the individual and collective mind needs its work and discipline. Then the prime and precious principles of philosophy and practice such as The Word, meditation, and sacrificing for the good of others, can be implemented fully and properly into spiritual life per se, even into everyday life, overall.

Points and Principles of *Brahman* in two charts acts as a complete manual for comprehension of spiritual life. The many entries up for consideration there have been rendered into *Sanskrit,* too, adding depth to the aspiring student's all-round knowledge of life's most important subject — the *dharma.*

Points About Brahman According to the Upanisads

Cosmic

Ajatavada — No Creation, no Evolution
Mahat — Cosmic Mind projects the Universe
Yajna — The Cosmos proceeds via Sacrifice
Srishti Rahasya — All worlds are projected, not Created
Samsara — Creation is attended by Suffering
Rayim-prana Brahma — Matter and Energy come from Brahman
Sarvam prane ejati — Prana, gross to subtle, pervades All
Omkara — Om is the key for the door to Freedom

Collective   Individual

Pancha-yajna — Sacrifice is the First Duty
Guru-moksha — Guru is required for Liberation
Atmajnana harchayet — Illumined beings are teachers of Men
Rishi jnana trptah — The Masterful, the Attained, the Aspiring
Vikshepa-bandha — Ignorance veils Self-realization.
Sadhusangha — Holy Company is a Necessity
Shishyachara — Seekers must be Qualified
Sadhana — Sadhana leads to Liberation
Abhyasa Yoga — Atman is attained by constant Practice
Paraparavidya — There are two kinds of Knowledge
Paravidya — True Knowledge transcends Rites and Rituals
Niskama Karma — Only scripturally-ordained works bring Freedom
Chit-shuddhi — Purification of mind is the Way
Indriya-shuddhi — Pure senses help reveal the Self
Dhyan — Brahman is revealed via Meditation
Karma-vinasha — Karma ends in Realization

"The gods, guardians of the universe, fell into the mighty ocean of existence and samsara. The Creator subjected them to hunger and thirst. The gods then spoke to Him saying, 'Grant us a place where we can establish ourselves and eat food. He brought them a cow's body and it was not sufficient for them; He brought them a horse's body, and it too was not sufficient. Then He brought them the form of a man. Seeing that form, they rejoiced and exclaimed with joy, 'Well done!' Therefore man is indeed well done." Aitareopanisad

To give the aspiring soul an idea of what kind of superlative attainments await the qualified being who approaches the wise ones for counsel, a list of them are shown on the chart on the facing page. These were a few of Swami Vivekananda's favorite attributes in spiritual life. The first two alone — devotion to ones precious spiritual teacher, and complete surrender to and fealty towards the Divine Mother of the Universe — are the best possible treasures for the aspirant who enters the body, ready for taking on the challenges inherent in both the world, and in securing higher attainment. On top of this, he/she must develop strength at all levels of being. A strong body, an unimpeded flow of vital energy (*prana*), a balanced and inquiring mind, an intellect that has been made sharpened by thoughts of Reality, and an ego that has divested itself of personal desires and gains and is therefore *apakvahamkara* — ripened and surrendered to the Lord and Mother of the Universe — is what is wanted.

Gaining the first three items on this spiritual check list will naturally lead the aspirant towards a greater light. When this light culminates and gets utilized for selfless service to God in mankind, it will shine within and without. This is *brahma-tejas*, the halcyon Light that radiates off of *Brahman*.

With this kind of grand strength in possession, the onlooker might think that demonstrations of power would be forthcoming. In typical spiritual fashion, however, both a supreme peace of mind and an actual inability to harm any living thing come forward instead. This enigmatic combination of power and peace, nobility and nonviolence, is an expression of the Divine Mother Herself, who is said to pit dualities against one another and thereby create openings in consciousness by which the freedom loving soul can gain transcendence by unusual or nonordinary means. This is the secret of the *"triputi,"* a triple teaching in which the third element reveals a doorway out of dualities. The chart shown on the forthcoming page 611 will teach on this principle.

The principles of universal mind, *samasta-chitta,* and same-sightedness, *samadarshitvam,* represent a full maturation of the spiritualized soul of the individual. Such qualities, if they could be called such, are more like eternal stations of nondual Truth that dawn on the mind of the luminary at the time of deepest spiritual maturation. That is, there are realized souls who possess deep knowledge within their own particular religion or lineage, but who, as yet, do not possess the expansive heart and wide-open mind of a consummate luminary. Looking back on the highest of the Seven Stages of Knowledge (page 335) will remind us of that. Looking at Swami Vivekananda will also recall to mind the real article and authentic example. And these two qualities, in particular, were dear to his universal heart.

The chart on the facing page also gathers together a few of the sayings of Swami Vivekananda that utilize the lion as an example of courage and strength. He is often referred to as "the Lion of *Vedanta*," and he means to set his disciples and followers on a course of training and will help them break free of the cage of bondage with its various bars of limitation. Supreme knowledge, *Brahmajnanam,* and mature renunciation, *tyaga,* are two internal crowbars suited for this task. Swami Vivekananda's course for *Atmic* realization also laid heavy emphasis on the Four *Yogas,* a gift he brought to the world in recent times. In taking up the practice and mastery of knowledge, devotion, meditation, and selfless service — *jnana, bhakti, raja,* and *karma* — the focus given by him and his divine teachers and spiritual brothers and sisters was that without gaining knowledge first in the form of *brahmajnanam,* ones devotions would be mixed, ones meditations might be ineffective, and ones works could be flawed.

These very problems are seen today, particularly in Western spiritual aspirants, whose love for God gets mixed indiscriminately with love for the world. Swami Aseshanandaji pointed this out to us clearly when he stated from the podium, *"The Judeo-Christian faith is a dualistic faith. Why dualistic? Because it accepts that behind the body and mind complex there is an underlying reality called the soul. But that is just the ego; they mistake it for the soul. It is that ego/mind complex that dreams itself from heaven to earth to hell."*

And so often the Western aspirant's devotion to God remains on the surface, their works rarely escape the influence of the selfish ego, and their meditations scarcely, if ever, give them the vision of what is internal, what to speak of what is Ultimate. Where is their enlightenment after decades of prescribed practice? As Swami Aseshananda used to tell us, from the pulpit, "with a voice like a lion's roar": *"America has accepted Greek thought, and this has given the American people a logical mind. Jefferson drafted the Declaration of Independence being prompted by the rationalistic philosophers of Europe. Greek mind is a logical mind. It wants precision. It also wants comprehension of the truth by the intellect. But the higher*

The Course of Atmic Realization

"Have faith in yourself. All power is in you. Be conscious and bring it out. Even if you are at your last breath be not afraid, but work on with the intrepidity of a lion but at the same time with the tenderness of a flower."
Swami Vivekananda

"What I want is muscles of iron and nerves of steel, inside which dwells a mind of the same material as that of which the thunderbolt is made of."
Swami Vivekananda

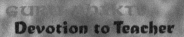

GURU-BHAKTI
Devotion to Teacher

SHAKTI-VANDANA
Worship of Divine Mother

KSHATRA-VIRYA
Warrior-like Strength

BRAHMA-TEJAS
God-realized brilliance

ISHTA-NISTHA
One-pointed focus on God

ABHAYA
Fearlessness

AHIMSA
Nonaggression

TYAGA
Mature Renunciation

BRAHMAJNANAM
Supreme Wisdom

SAMASTA-CHITTA
Universal Mind

SAMADARSHITVAM
Equal Vision towards All

"Guru-bhakti is the foundation of all spiritual development. The guru-bhakta will conquer the world — this is the one evidence of history. It is faith that makes a lion of a man." Swami Vivekananda

IS THIS EWE?

TRY

VEDANTA

BEFORE   AFTER

"Let there be but a dozen such lion-souls in each country, lions who have broken their own bonds, who have touched the Infinite, whose whole soul has gone to Brahman, who care nether for wealth, nor power, nor fame, and these will be enough to shake the world." Vivekananda

thought of Swami Vivekananda reminds me of Aryan thought; something 'beyond.' The Greeks had no concept of the beyond. They based all on the concept of this world in order to build a proud society which could dominate other races, just like this affluent American society. But if a society cannot produce an illumined soul it achieves no real purpose or lasting meaning. If you cannot produce a single illumined soul in America, then what power, what glory, what grandeur is contained in its rational civilization and its scientific achievement? — which then moves irrationally to create bombs for the destruction of the world." But this unique soul also told us of an apt solution. *"America has a responsible task to perform by spiritualizing inner life and bringing forth a society which will not be merely affluent, but illumined, where jivanmuktas will play the part of distributing the wealth of spirituality to the rest of mankind. It may seem like a dream now, but let this dream come true through the blessing of God."* And so the "Course of *Vedantic* Lion taming" and training, goes on.....

As just mentioned, the principle of *triputi,* or triple teaching, is unique to Mother India. The problem with what *Vedanta* calls in English the "contrasting pairs of opposites," and what Sri Krishna calls in the *Bhagavad Gita, dvandva mohena* — deluding pairs of opposites — is well known to the Indian *rishis.* It is certainly well known to the world at large as well, though few beings look for a way out and beyond them, and would seem to rather bear with them.

Beyond such perplexing and *karma*-creating dualities like pleasure and pain, and virtue and vice, etc., and always existing as an option for seekers striving to rise above impediments to enlightenment and illumination of mind, the third element in a *triputi* opens doors inwardly to blissful, peaceful transcendence. Of course, not every *triputi* reveals a wide open door, but they all suggest the possibility of positive transformation, or potential freedom. In the case of, say, good, bad, and mixed, the light available in them lies in realizing the danger in admixtures and using the entire triple teaching as a way to transcendence. In a *triputi* like attraction, aversion, and neutrality, the former two are to be mastered by the third, and this is the way most *triputis* work — some in conjunction with one another, others offering higher and better options.

Triputis run the gamut of various levels of life and existence. They are found in philosophy as triple teachings like duality, qualified nonduality, and nonduality. They emerge in cosmology as well, as in the gross, subtle, and causal bodies of living beings. Even on the level of life-force and beginning spiritual disciplines they will make a distinct appearance, as when the practitioner observes the three movements of the breathing process, the in-breath *(puraka),* the held breath *(kumbhaka),* and the out-breath *(rechaka).* Actually, this *triputi* is an especially good example of hidden ascension, for unbeknownst to most practitioners, the suspended breath holds the secret of meditation and *samadhi,* as well as being a key to the deep sleep state in humans. *Kumbhaka* happens spontaneously in a deeply focused meditation, and if the *sadhaka* is aware of this beforehand then the *pranayam* practice bears fruit over time.

Triputis appear at both lower and higher levels of the physical dimension as well. To contemplate time, space, and causation has always provided keys for the seeker wanting beyond relativity. Even inside of time itself, the past, present, and future triputi is one fraught with potential meaning.

In the realm of spirituality, many triple teachings abound. The three types of life, namely worldly life, divine life, and transcendent life/Eternal Life, come forward to be explored. On the level of the heart, the precious *triputi* of seeing, approaching, and enjoying — *priya, moda,* and *pramoda* — offers up its unique view concerning the bliss of communion with God. For the renunciate, or especially pertinent to the renunciate, to "enjoy" what he or she has given up the entire world to possess, i.e., God-realization — is precious, is priceless. What is giving up worldly happiness for the sake of spiritual bliss like? Swami Vivekananda once described ephemeral happiness while inferring the bliss of *Brahman* by stating: *"In the world, all things are done by people guided like lifeless machines. There is no mental activity, no unfoldment of the heart, no vibration of life, no flux of hope; there is no strong stimulation of the will, no experience of keen pleasure, nor the contact of intense sorrow; there is no stir of inventive genius, no desire for novelty, no appreciation of new things. Clouds never pass from this mind, the radiant picture of the morning sun never charms this heart. It never even occurs to the mind if there is any better state than this; where it does, it cannot convince; in the event of conviction, effort is lacking; and even where there is effort, lack of enthusiasm kills it out."*

Wisdom *triputis* abound, and so does the opportunity for contemplating them. The reader is invited to take up any or all of these triple teachings and spend hours of inward scrutiny on them, all along the way healing rifts in the mind and opening doors to spirituality as well.

Vedic Triputis and Quintuplications

"This divine expression is definitely declared to be the Supreme Brahman in manifested form. In that is the Triad. It is the firm support, and it is the imperishable. Knowing the inner essence of this along with its sets of triputis and quintuplication processes, the knowers of the Vedas become devoted to Brahman, merge themselves in It, and are released from birth and death." Svetashvataropanisad

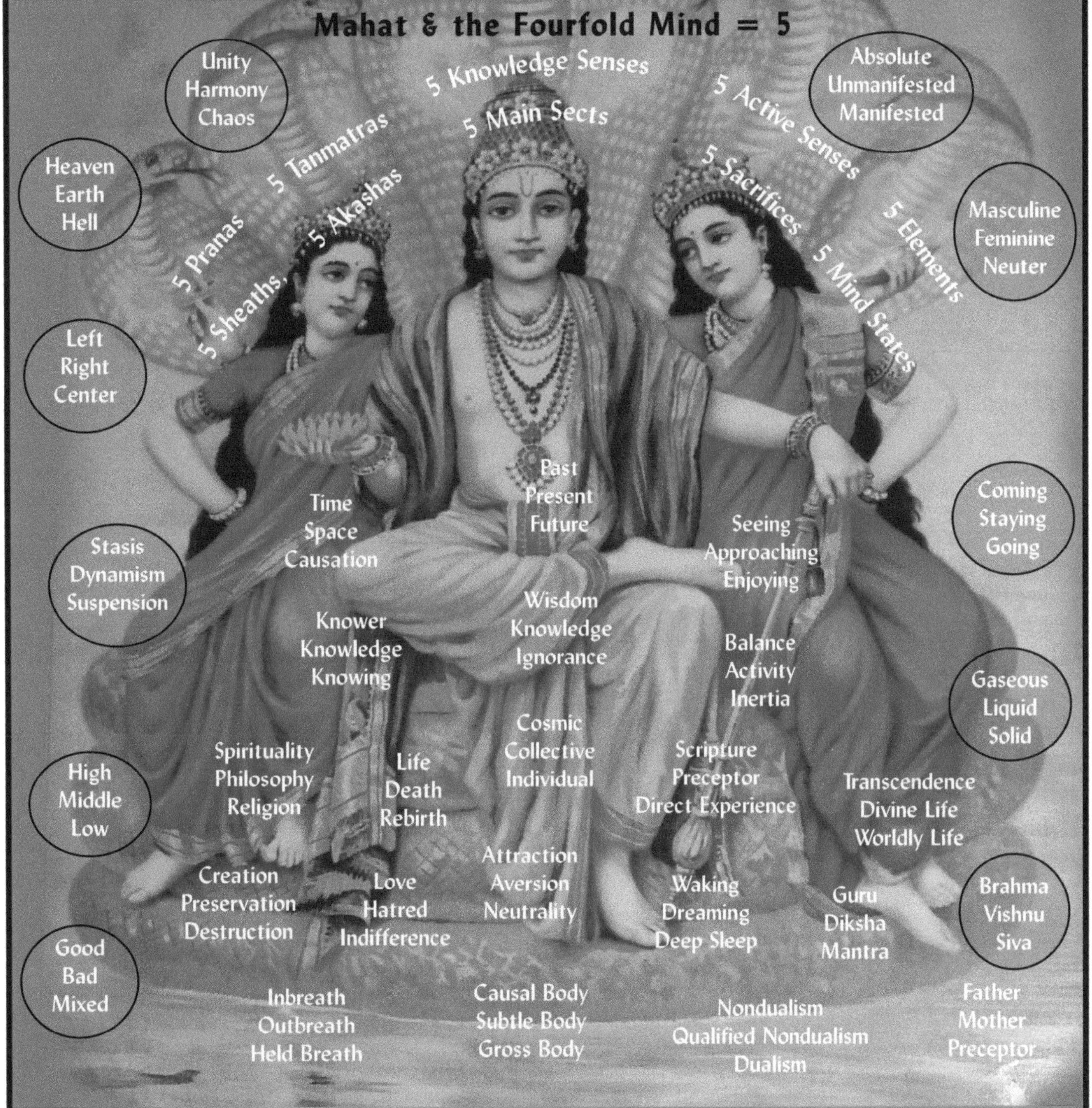

Mahat & the Fourfold Mind = 5
5 Knowledge Senses
5 Main Sects
5 Tanmatras
5 Akashas
5 Pranas
5 Sheaths,
5 Active Senses
5 Sacrifices
5 Elements
5 Mind States
Unity Harmony Chaos
Absolute Unmanifested Manifested
Heaven Earth Hell
Masculine Feminine Neuter
Left Right Center
Past Present Future
Time Space Causation
Seeing Approaching Enjoying
Coming Staying Going
Stasis Dynamism Suspension
Wisdom Knowledge Ignorance
Knower Knowledge Knowing
Balance Activity Inertia
Gaseous Liquid Solid
Cosmic Collective Individual
Spirituality Philosophy Religion
Life Death Rebirth
Scripture Preceptor Direct Experience
Transcendence Divine Life Worldly Life
High Middle Low
Attraction Aversion Neutrality
Creation Preservation Destruction
Love Hatred Indifference
Waking Dreaming Deep Sleep
Guru Diksha Mantra
Brahma Vishnu Siva
Good Bad Mixed
Inbreath Outbreath Held Breath
Causal Body Subtle Body Gross Body
Nondualism Qualified Nondualism Dualism
Father Mother Preceptor

"The Three Prerequisites for Atmajnan, knowledge of your Soul, consist of the destruction of illusory thoughts, the gaining of quiescence of mind, and the ability to merge in Brahman at will. Lauded among the supreme knowers as Atma-tripti, they will stand you in good stead, no matter what the impediments thrown up by the mind in maya. By these three, and other divine triputis, may you attain to the Atmic state, free of all stains and pains." Lord Vasishtha

The Five States of the Mind-Field In Yoga

"Like seeds fallen even briefly into the fire, thus losing their generative power, the first three states of the mind-field are worthless for gaining samadhi. They are scarcely worthy of detailed mention and are not fit to be included in the category of Yoga, since Yoga is Samadhi." Vyasa

I. *Kshipta – Disturbed*	Continually agitated Completely unsteady Dominated by rajas	Lost among objects Average waking state of a normal person
II. *Mudha – Lethargic*	State of dull stupor Steeped in stagnation Dominated by tamas	As in states such as comatose, inebriation, drug-affliction, etc.
III. *Vikshipta – Distracted*	Experiences balance Stripped of balance Drawn away by habit	Gives rise to the 9 vikshepas such as disease, doubt, etc.
IV. *Ekagra – One-Pointed*	Samprajnata state Illumines all wisdom Removes impurities	Loosens karma's hold Leads to full control Gives pure perception
V. *Niruddha – Absorbed*	Asamprajnata state Full control of vrittis Karmas nullified	Confers paravairagya Only samskaras of samadhi persist

Bhagavad Gita's Mini-Manual for Mind Control

"Constantly engaging in resolute practice, the yogi who has fully calmed the mind and purified the senses attains with ease the infinite bliss of intimate contact with Brahman." Sri Krishna

Sankalpa prabhavan kamams tyaktva sarvan asheshatah

"Abandon, without reserve, all desires born of sankalpa."

Manasa'ndriya gramam viniyamya samantatah

"Utilize the mind to curb and control the senses."

Shanaih shanair uparamed buddhya dhrtigrhitaya

"Settling the intellect, strive to attain peace by degrees."

Atmasamstham manah krtva na kimchid api chintayet

"Thinking of nothing else, focus the mind on the Self."

Yato yato nishcharati manash chanchalam asthiram
tatas tato niyamyai'tad atmany eva visham nayet

"By whatever reason or means the fluctuating mind may wander,
call it back and fix it solely on Self."

In tandem with the other sets of fives that are shown on the chart just completed, an important quintuplication comes forward in the *Yoga darshana* of Lord Patanjali. Not only does Patanjali list the stations of the human mind for inspection, he also gives insights into the condition of each, thereby rendering the teaching into a means for healing the fragmented mind.

The fact that some beings are born into the human form with a balanced and peaceful mind, imbued with wisdom, ought to act as a wakeup call for those whose minds are not yet under their control. Among the illumined there are basically two kinds of mind states: the mind that is one-pointed, i.e. always concentrated, and the mind that has dissolved into a state that has been described by seers as "no mind," or "pure mind." The *Sanskrit* words *ekagra* and *niruddha* aptly suit and describe these two blessed vessels of higher Consciousness. The former has as its main possession the state of *samprajnata samadhi,* and experiences effortless control, abiding peace, access to higher wisdom, and freedom from *karma.* The latter gets infused with *asamprajnata samadhi* and thereby experiences the state of formlessness and an abiding state of supreme detachment culminating in unalloyed Bliss, called *Ananda.* A stage by stage ascension towards higher states of mind can be reviewed on the chart on page 511, and these two *samadhis* themselves, as well as their components, will be taken up in chapter ten.

For those less fortunate beings who are under the weight of the other and lower three states of mind, the picture is not so bright. As a kind of intermediary state of mind, *vikshipta* goes back and forth between being focused and distracted. Whereas the time the soul spends in the company of a balanced mental condition is good, no doubt, the fact that this relative peace is being interrupted constantly is not good at all. A habit is thereby constructed wherein the shifting of vibrations becomes the normal state of mind, and this habit gets instilled in the *samskaras* of the subconscious, being very difficult to get free of later. This explains why some beings are born with a restless mind.

And in fact, this *samskaric* habit often tires the soul as it tries for a more constant and balanced condition, and this leads to the *mudha* level of mind. *Mudha,* which also translates as foolish, leaves the mind lethargic all the time, and nothing productive can come from it. Though it is not detected by healers and psychologists of the day, this is actually where the mind, left listless and stagnate, dips into even more problematic conditions — not just in the present life, but in lifetimes to come as well. Like arrows already shot from a bow, these lifetimes of imbalance and retardation find no solution whatsoever after such tendencies have fructified. A cross section of unfortunates — a veritable insane asylum of souls — is thus let loose upon the world, leaving the word "disturbed," *kshipta,* somewhat inadequate to describe the situation.

The balance of the chart on the previous page describes a five point practice of refinement of mind stated in the *Bhagavad Gita.* Seeing the mind's tendency to shift from equipoise to all manner of activities, the practitioner stifles that urge and maintains peace. It is only this peace-filled mind that can successfully control the senses. Most novitiates fail at this task due to trying to calm the senses with an erratic mind. Many seekers also attempt to gain peace all at once, instead of patiently attaining to equipoise little by little. Once a steady and unwavering mental atmosphere is attained, the mind can more readily focus upon the Great Self, *Atman.* And once the mind has come to glimpse the *Atman,* it will be easy to call it back from its old tendencies should it ever drift back towards them again. This is why Sri Krishna relates to Arjuna the precious secret of *sthiti prajnasya,* one-pointed mind, on the battlefield of *Kurushektra:*

Om yatha dipo nivatastho ne'ngate so'pama smrita
yogino yatachittasya yunjato yogam atmanah

Like a candle in a windless place,
its flame still and unflickering,
so too is the mind of the yogi,
steady and unwavering, meditating on the Atman deep within
and steeped in Yoga.

Of recent mention, the principle of reincarnation comes up again for further inspection. More than a theory, or even a possibility, insightful beings not only accept its premise, but begin to fashion their

The Palette of Conscious Future Lives

"Human being — today it is, tomorrow it is not. No one will accompany a person after death. Only actions, good and bad, follow, even after death. The result of karma is inevitable. But karma's effects can be counteracted greatly by japa and austerities." **Sri Sarada Devi**

Attaining Jivanmukti, Liberation, in a past Lifetime

Selecting the country and culture of one's choice

Assuming gender and physical body

Spiritual practice and attainment in previous Lives

Choosing dharmic parents prior to entering into the womb

Arranging life-circum-stances in order to neutralize karma

Experiencing a conscious death at the end of the last Lifetime

"Ego, plus mind, plus intelligence — and adding in the five senses — make up this temporal unit called the psycho-physical being. When considering it and its powers, we must remember that when these eight facets are kept in a pure state, then Kundalini Shakti loves to sport in this amazing form." **Lord Vasishtha**

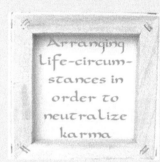

Setting up the mani-festation of one's work and mission in Life

Sincere compassion to help all beings gain spiritual emancipation

Cosmic Wisdom

Clear Mind

Strong Intention/Resolve

Pure Will

Spiritual Adeptship

Far-Sightedness

Nondual perspective that trans-forms all appearances into Reality

"The potter puts his pots in the sun to dry, both the baked and unbaked ones. A cow happens to walk over them and breaks some of them. The baked pot shards that are broken he throws away, but the soft ones, though broken, he gathers up and shapes them into a lump. From this lump he forms new pots. In the same way, so long as a man has not realized God, he will have to come back to this earth — to the Potter's Hands." **Sri Ramakrishna Paramahamsa**

present lives in such a way as to avail the soul of a deeper, more meaningful existence in the future. "In the future" means after death. Since the eternal nature of the Soul, *Atman,* has been well documented in this book, and the incessant flow of thousands upon thousands of illumined beings have graced the earth plane, the practitioner wishing to better any or all of his or her future lifetimes only has to bring consciousness under control in the present lifetime and use it for purifying the mind complex. This is called *sadhana* in India, or spiritual discipline. There, in that hallowed land of the ancient *rishis,* the purpose of life is to destroy the ignorance that caused unconscious birth in the first place.

The chart on previous facing page has on it several scenarios mixed in with both serious ultimatums and illumined choices. The wise soul will always consult and take refuge in the *Kundalini Shakti* in this matter, as the quote on the middle of the chart from Lord Vasishtha states. She will aid the soul in making the best choices for its incarnation.

As was already mentioned, a lifetime of intense spiritual practice, *sadhana,* combined with the soul's first conscious "death," is what is wanted most of all. These two attainments set up all that is to come. Some unfinished business may be revealed to the soul in this transition, called unneutralized *karma,* and in order to bring that to the fore in the forthcoming life, three other choices — dharmic parents, fertile country, and a just and peaceful society — will be selected.

With all this accomplished, the business of arranging life circumstances so as to allow for finding and completing ones destined work can be taken up. Of course, if the soul attained a high degree of illumination in the present lifetime, much of the above mentioned work of selection will occur almost naturally. In other words, ending life in an illumined condition of a *jivanmukti* and possessing the unique nondual perspective so cherished by the wise, will afford the soul all that is necessary to live a life that is fully beneficial for itself, and to all others as well. Thus, the ever-pure canvas of compassion for all and everyone, existing in all the kingdoms that lie within consciousness, is secured to complete the masterful painting. A quick look back at pages 328 & 329 in chapter seven, with the chart entitled *The Ten Pure Lands,* will remind the mind of what awaits the inward moving aspirant who cherishes God and Truth first and foremost.

What is now left on this simple but profound chart under study has to do with the mechanism that accomplishes inner movement. It is called the *antahkarana,* of course, studied often throughout the pages of this book. On the palette are to be seen several of its main attributes that, ironically, most beings do not have as their complete possession yet. A pure will and intention, a clear mind, strong resolve — anyone claiming these as tools will not only succeed in life, whatever be the mode of living, but will also become past masters of conscious birth. Wisdom, adeptship, and farsightedness will follow them all the days of their life, and into future lives as well. They will never fall into the "potter's hands" again, as outlined in Sri Ramakrishna's story at the bottom of the chart. By their own wise and able self-efforts, the clay of their consciousness will be rendered fully baked in the fires of *Yoga* so that, unlike the soft clay of weakened awareness, it can never be formed into bodies hosting dull and ignorant minds again.

According to the revered and insightful teachings of Indian *dharma* — and though there are thousands of *nadis,* or inner channels to arrive through and depart from — many pathways culminate in several main avenues available to transmigrating souls. If higher consciousness has been perceived and utilized by the adept soul, these broad pathways to internal realms of Awareness lie open and accessible.

Throughout this book India's *dharmic* teachings have been communicated by the overall explanation of the Three Worlds, correlated with the Three Bodies that go with them (see charts on pages 161, 373, 453, 455). Throughout the different ages of India's cultural and spiritual history, these important sets of threes, or *triputis,* have been presented in different ways according to the particular age and temperaments of beings living therein. Sometimes refered to as the inner realms of *Bhur, Bhuvah,* and *Svah,* next appearing as layers of coverings such as *annamaya, pranamaya,* and *manomaya,* then mated up with levels of mankind's consciousness as in *jagrat, svapna,* and *sushupti,* whenever and wherever these three show up, the system is always cogent and self-explanatory.

The same was the case in ancient times when the three worlds got aligned with outer and inner pathways as well. On the chart next up for study (page 617), we find three broad avenues by which consciousness courses along. The classification makes it quite easy for the spiritual aspirant attempting to understand the passage of souls who are still caught or engaged in the transmigration process. We must remember that Consciousness, called *Brahman,* does not transmigrate at all, remaining ever-stationary and free of qualities, adjuncts, and overlays. It is perfectly all-pervasive, so does not need to move between three worlds, or three "anythings." This is important to keep in mind when studying the inner mystery of why souls seek to move, where they move to, how this movement is accomplished, when such motion is allowed and restricted, and best and most clarifying of all, what or who is it that is doing the moving.

The chart on the facing page utilizes India's incomparable assignment of waking, dreaming, and deep sleep to reveal answers to these mysteries. This obvious but subtle fact of existence, staring humanity in the face for eons, declares that all life is of an internal nature; even the outer world, declares India's seers, is always and ever posited within the mind. We are living in the inner recesses of our mind when we are inhabit the body or move inside of a house or home; it is all mind made manifest.

And so, some luminaries, even contemporary ones like Ramana Maharshi, teach that all of life is a kind of dream projection. It is all a matter of whether the mind has solidified the field and turned it outward, or has kept it ephemeral and is enjoying it free of solid objects — and obstacles. These two descriptions are the waking and dreaming states of the Great Mind, through which all of manifested existence is experiencing name and form in time and space.

This Great Mind is also named Lord *Brahma.* he who projects the many universes at differing levels of vibration. And, as in any grand location in time and space, it is not enough to simply provide places to go; there must be a network of channels, like byways and highways, for consciousness to navigate so as to arrive at their chosen destinations — all within the Great Mind's massive projection.

And along with the accompanying aid of classifying the stages of awareness into three levels of consciousness, this ancient system has also provided a description of the three main pathways along which souls will travel, both inwardly, and out to the physical universe, as well. This explanation helps the soul to escape the possible confusion that can amass, particularly in the short-sighted individual mind, regarding where it can go, when, and how it must proceed; also, when it is limited in its passage, and why,

For instance, the path of lower births, heavily populated in this day and age *(Kali Yuga),* titled *Tiryanmarga,* disallows the transmigrating soul from reaching deeper and finer planes of existence that are populated by beings filled with and radiating the beautiful light of pure *tejas.* Bound souls must be satisfied with realms, though also beautiful, that are always accompanied by sufferings associated with birth, disease, decay, and death. What is worse, the minds of these restricted souls cannot see or even scarcely envision the Light of pure, conscious Awareness beyond, so long as they are bound into these lower worlds in cycles. In another philosophical correlation, this third and lower world of multiple pathways is connected with the three foundational "lotuses" of the *Kundalini Yoga* philosophy, titled the *muladhara, svadhisthana,* and *manipura chakras.* For a cross referencing guide for some of this, the reader and student can look back to page 375, and the chart displayed there.

The Path of the Fathers, called *Pitriyana,* is another matter, with far deeper and broader ramifications. Whereas the grosser level of the *Tiryanmarga* may reach as far as realms that may be allocated with the term, "lower heavens," the *Pitriyana* stretches deeper into plateaus of consciousness that penetrate the higher heavens. Though there are facile souls that only traverse this plethora of subtle regions and move further inwards, beings dwelling there are in possession of many of their inherent powers. Thus, this set of realms is famous for its otherworldly beauty. As for restrictions here, however, there are still deep-rooted desires and interconnected *karmas* playing themselves out in this powerful collection of souls. A look at the "Five Russian Dolls" chart on page 327 will go far in laying out the cosmology of this, ad other levels/realms of awareness.

On the way towards the Transcendent Reality of *Brahman,* where no worlds or realms exist, or persist, the *Devayana* shines in its own glory and special light. It is not called the Path of the Gods for no good reason, since godlike beings settle there for immeasurable periods of time *(yugas)* in order to oversee the vast array of scintillating *lokas* falling beneath them — like lustrous gems floating in the nocturnal skies of sentient awareness. Yet, looking in a deeper, inward direction, this unique pathway leads to the Ultimate Light of Awareness Itself. Few of the denisons of this collection of *lokas* want to move in that consummate direction, however. They are stunned by the vision of what lies around of them, all the

Lord Brahma's Universal Projection

"Unto Him was imparted the Supreme Wisdom of Brahman. He is Atman, and He is Prana. He represents both the life and death of the Gods. He controls them and the Jivas through His Prana, which belongs to the Nadis. In dreamless Sleep they pass through that state into their own abode, like a falcon piercing the sky to rest in its own nest." Brahmopanisad

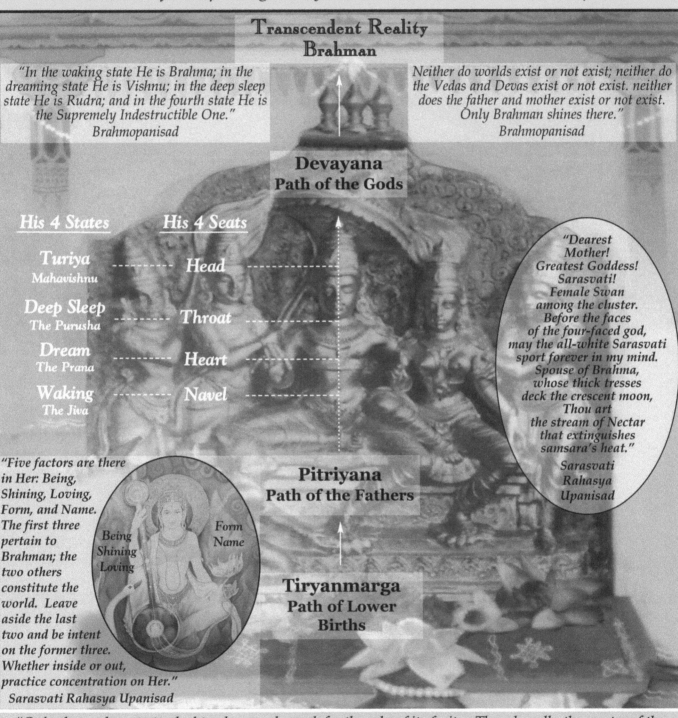

Transcendent Reality
Brahman

"In the waking state He is Brahma; in the dreaming state He is Vishnu; in the deep sleep state He is Rudra; and in the fourth state He is the Supremely Indestructible One."
Brahmopanisad

Neither do worlds exist or not exist; neither do the Vedas and Devas exist or not exist. neither does the father and mother exist or not exist. Only Brahman shines there."
Brahmopanisad

Devayana
Path of the Gods

His 4 States   ### His 4 Seats

His 4 States	His 4 Seats
Turiya Mahavishnu	Head
Deep Sleep The Purusha	Throat
Dream The Prana	Heart
Waking The Jiva	Navel

"Dearest Mother! Greatest Goddess! Sarasvati! Female Swan among the cluster. Before the faces of the four-faced god, may the all-white Sarasvati sport forever in my mind. Spouse of Brahma, whose thick tresses deck the crescent moon, Thou art the stream of Nectar that extinguishes samsara's heat."
Sarasvati Rahasya Upanisad

Pitriyana
Path of the Fathers

Being
Shining
Loving

Form
Name

"Five factors are there in Her: Being, Shining, Loving, Form, and Name. The first three pertain to Brahman; the two others constitute the world. Leave aside the last two and be intent on the former three. Whether inside or out, practice concentration on Her."
Sarasvati Rahasya Upanisad

Tiryanmarga
Path of Lower Births

"Only those who get attached to pleasure do work for the sake of its fruits. Though really the master of the senses, they become bound and take various forms, wandering constantly along the three pathways as a result."

"He who is the one source of all the worlds brings forth everything from His own sattvic Nature, and leads all beings to perfection according to their own karmas while endowing each with its distinguishing characteristics. Thus, He presides over the entire Cosmos" Svetashvataropanisad

way outwards to the realm of Earth where human beings live, love, and worship the gods with pleasing offerings, keeping them tied in their respective places. This entire set of three major arteries of soul transmigration falls under the overseership of the Great Devi, the Mother of all existing Universes and Worlds. It is that dynamic Principle that is taken up in the next chart up for inspection.

Appearing as Sarasavati Devi on the chart just completed, the Kundalini Shakti, with names too numerous to count, all of them exceedingly enchanting with mysterious attracting and transformative power in them, has Her own specific areas of operations and concentration. To feel Her attention in all or any of these realms equates to blossoming seership, productive of Ultimate Wisdom and Supreme Bliss. This is due to Her intention of removing all coverings from Divine Reality, which is formless and naked in the Truth — as the quote at the top of the chart, opposite, relates.

This stripping away is accomplish through four of Her main aspects, and in phases that the aspiring human soul, under Her direct supervision, is undergoing. As for those who do not aspire for anything other than matter and pleasure, She leaves them to their own devices in the lower worlds. But it must be said that there are beings living on the earth plane who are beginning to gain ground, spiritually speaking, and who need Her assistance as well.

This the Mother will give via Her aspect as *Kriyavati*. Again, and as the previous chart intimated, all this work is accomplished on at the level of the three lower *chakras*. Since these three areas of the consciousness of living beings are rather dark, or if not just dark, uninformed, then the teaching forthcoming from Her will center in the attainment of calmness of mind so as to help them outstrip the restless *guna* of *rajas* and gain detachment from objects that give pleasure, but also bring pain. It should be mentioned here, important for this day and time, that the dangers of *hatha yoga* and preoccupation with it by the body-centered members of a materialistic society are offset by taking the Divine Mother as the Ideal, the *Ishtadevi*. *Kriyavati's hatha yoga* does not operate in the area of body postures, but instead introduces the superior method of graduating immediately to mental postures. Adopting these internal postures, the body, its ill health, and its attractions, will all be healed naturally and put in their proper place and perspective. For more teachings on this wondrous benefit see the forthcoming chart and explanation in chapter 10, called *Manasana*.

When a soul's general aspiration has begun to reach a peak, doing so after a few substantial experiences of spiritual life have been gleaned, then *Kundalini Shakti* manifests in human lives as *Varnamayi*. It is in keeping with everyday life, and the progression that we see in its concern with education, that this makes good sense. Even unknowingly, beings who are interested in developing their intellects are feeling the influence of this aspect of *shakti* all the while. Speech, voice, and scriptures seem to be the line of succession here, culminating in the desire to spread the teachings to others. Of course, when this aspect of *shakti* is consciously recognized and known by the seeker, so much more benefit and advancement is made. But it is a select few who gain this foreknowledge of Her benign presence and transforming influence in advance — usually told by the *guru*, if such a one is sought and found.

The advent of *Kalatma Shakti* not only raises the bar, but raises the psychic *prana* as well. With this inner buoyancy comes the six phases of unfoldment, seen on the upper left side of the chart under study. Simply put, *Bindu*, according to the *Tantra Shastras*, is the first great principle, or *Mahatattva*, to appear on the scene of the adept's spiritual journey inwards. It can be described as a perfectly round doorway into higher consciousness, associated intrinsically with the "Third Eye" and The Word. *Ardendhu* is the splitting in half of this primordial principle so as to allow the soul to penetrate to deeper levels of Consciousness. *Nirodhika* is the dissolving of all barriers to such a blissful passage inwards. There is actually a form of *Kalatma* called *nirodhika-shakti* who ensures that the practitioner will not fall off or away from the spiritual heights he/she is seeking.

Continuing on with this brief description of the six phases of unfoldment, *nirodhika* ensures renunciation of subtle impediments so that both *samana* and *unmani* can mature in the aspiring luminary's being. These two are subtle but tremendous powers of a *yogi/yogini*, and are associated in some *Tantric* systems with the sixteenth and seventeenth *chakras* located in the *Sahasrara*, beyond the *Amalaka Chakra*. Being the realm of direct spiritual experience of the highest order, little description has been given, or can even be undertaken. One must stand up and actually travel to the place of pilgrimage, not just see its location on a map.

The Four Main Aspects of Kundalini Shakti

"Kundalini Shakti, through Her four aspects, accomplishes the full cycle of the embodied soul back to its source. This means involution, the disidentification of the ever-pure Atman from the many coverings and superimpositions of maya."

Six Phases of Unfoldment

Bindu
Ardhendu
Nirodhika
Samana
Unmani
Pratistha

Six Spiritual Symptoms

Bliss
Trembling
New Power
Intoxication
Samadhi
Absorption

Kundalini Yoga's Hatha Yoga

Kundalini Yoga's Raja Yoga

Kundalini Yoga's Mantra Yoga

Kundalini Yoga's Laya Yoga

Seven Victories

Bhuta Jaya
Indriya Jaya
Prakrti Jaya
Manojavittvam
Vikarana Bhava
Pradhana Jaya
Sattva Purusha Nytakhyati

KRIYAVATI

* Physical plane
* First 3 chakras
* Natural practice
* Calms the mind
* Grants detachment

VEDHAMAYI

* 7th chakra
* Contains all shaktis
* 6 Spiritual Symptoms
* Bestows yogic mastery
* Grants 7 Victories

VARNAMAYI

* Sarasvati Devi
* Plane of speech
* Refines the voice
* Reveals the scriptures
* Ability to teach

KALATMA

* Refines/raises prana
* 6 Phases of Unfoldment
* Transcendence of tattvas
* Confers spiritual vision
* Dissolves the mind

The final level of unfoldment, called *Pratistha,* is equally undescribable. The *Sanskrit* word is known in other systems to mean "steadiness," and is highly coveted by the enlightened. So, the implication is that the *yogi* gets firmly established in the Highest Reality. The *Sadakhya* System of the Six Ways To Realize *Brahman* in *Tantra* recently viewed, lists *Pratistha* as one of the five *kalas,* by attaining which the spiritually advanced soul can penetrate through the six *chakras* at will, anytime.

The balance of the chart on page 619 lists the "Seven Victories of *Tantra Sadhana'* (see chart on page 59 for teachings), and lists the qualities of the fourth aspect of *Kundalini Shakti, Vedamayi.* She is all seventh *chakra* material, and contains the previous three aspects within Her. Having Her on hand gives rise to the "Six Spiritual Systems" in the devotee, also described on the chart. Whereas *Kriyamayi* represented *Tantra's* hatha yoga phase, and *Varnamayi* dealt with *Tantra's mantra yoga* phase, *Kalatma* brought about the *laya yoga* phase. Then it is time for *Vedamayi's* appearance to bring forth *Tantra's* full blown *Raja Yoga* phase with its meditative visions and *samadhis.* In this profound system, then, *Tantra's* own Four *Yogas* find their auspicious place for practice.

For further teachings and information on this superlative philosophical religious system of India, the additional chart on the opposite page offers more to study. In this offering the student and practitioner can see some direct correlations to aspects of Divine Mother, methods to be utilized to realize Her, and the *chakras* that are being operated at, and upon. A bit more is also given about the Six Spiritual Systems that are indications of the awakening of *Kundalini Shakti* in sincere and qualified beings. This is helpful because of the mistaken assumptions that arise in the immature practitioner's minds. There are many pretenders to the throne of such awakening, and also some premature and even sometimes necessary starts and stops to this sublime process.

For instance, feelings and tremors in the body and emotional bodies caused by the unfortunate imbibing of intoxicants are easily mistaken for actual *shakti* awakening by many naive beginners. These are not *Ananda,* or *Kampa,* of course — the first two of these spiritual signs — but the hopeful and imaginative mind can certainly shape them into them, and also pretend them in front of others in order to appear spiritual. Again, a fresh wave of energy (that really comes to everyone at some point in a *sattvic* cycle), that causes increased activity on the life stage, is not *Udbhava,* the third of these signs, for *Udbhava* is always accompanied by deep wisdom and renunciation of objects, pleasures, and everything else that attracts and distracts the soul who is under the cycle of the persnickety *sattva guna* which comes and goes. So, like this, the true signs of awakening must be studied from both the outside and the inside so that no pretensions will visit the minds of either students, disciples, or potential spiritual teachers.

In this regard, one of the best of all studies of authentic *Kundalini Yoga* awakening is certainly Sri Ramakrishna Paramahamsa, who lived in fairly recent times, from 1836 to 1886. That he was beheld by many, even illumined souls that flocked around Him, gave the world of living beings a chance to see a truly God-intoxicated being on earth, in the human body. His host of *samadhis* showed Him up to be a luminary of the highest order, the rarest of embodied souls, and to so many today, an *Avatar,* a full and complete Divine Incarnation. To read the *Gospel of Sri Ramakrishna* today is to have the clear light of revelation shone upon all the teachings of Mother India, like the ones being listed and offered in this book.

It is said, and seems obvious as well, that the Divine Mother of the Universe got into the Great Master and took Him over completely. He used to sing that precious song to Her, the lines of which read:

> *"O Mother, You cause all to happen by Thy own sweet Will.*
> *Truly, You are the self-willed One, and the savior of all living beings.*
> *All work belongs to You; others only call it their own....."*

A few charts on this Great Master are thus very worthy of showing here, with all reverence.

The Great Master's way of teaching, if it could be called that, was to simplify and coalesce the many techniques and scriptures while encouraging the intensification of the student's practice, simultaneously. An example of this method is demonstrated on the forthcoming page, 622.

Starting at the lower right hand corner of this chart, and also at the lowest level of consciousness as well, the *asiddha* is a forlorn person who has no substance within that can grab or hold onto knowledge and truth when it comes. Attempting to insert knowledge into such a mind is like trying to drive a sword into a crocodile's back, the Great Master once said. Observing the process of early photography,

The Four Main Aspects of Kundalini Shakti II

Human Condition		Aspect of Shakti	Utilized Method	ChakraCorrelation
L O W E R	Physical	Kriyavati affects detachment of the Self from the body and nervous system	Tantric Hathayoga (asana, mudra, pranayam)	Muladhara Svadhisthana Manipura
M I D	Verbal	Varnamayi awakens dormant powers of voice, knowledge, and power to confer teachings	Mantrayoga (phonetics, bijas, shabda, mantras)	Anahata Vishuddha
U P P E R	Mental	Kalatma allows for transcendence of all worlds and penetrates the 6th chakra	Layayoga (refining, merging, dissolving)	Ajna
H I G H	Spiritual	Vedhamayi penetrates the 7th chakra, confers Samyama, and grants the 7 Victories	Rajayoga (piercing the chakras)	Sahasrara

Layayoga's Six Stages of Merging

Vindu — encountering the timeless, spaceless point wherein all wisdom tattvas abide

Ardhendu — dividing the dimension of time in half, and halves ("half-moon")

Nirodhika — attaining full concentration

Samana — with mind 1) Nad, gaining universal identity

                2) Nadanta, experiencing the Ocean of Light — Jyoti

                3) Shakti, advent of powers: gochari, dikchari, bhuchari, khechari

                4) Vyapaka, experiencing all-pervasiveness

                5) Samani, placing the mind in a static state

Unmani — dissolving the mind

Pratistha — establishing mind in a constant and stable condition in nondual reality

The Six Spiritual Indications of Kundalini Awakening

Ananda — Feelings of bliss or delight

Kampa — Trembling of the body, or inner tremors

Udbhava — Cognizance of a newborn power and a leap of realization

Gurni — Intoxication, or reeling with delight

Nidra — Sleep samadhi in which indifference to outer objects occurs

Laya — Merging of consciousness into Brahman

The Five Ways to Perfection
According to Sri Ramakrishna

"One can gain spiritual perfection through both affirmation and negation. Blend tears of yearning with discrimination and renunciation and you will be able to see God. This is the all-inclusive path of positive love and devotion commingled with transcendent knowledge."

Nityasiddha — The Ever-Free

"...a class apart, he nevertheless practices disciplines after realization. He is similar to the gourd or pumpkin vine — first fruit, then flower...."

Sadhanasiddha — Perfect by Disciplines

"...through austerity, japa, meditation and study, this rare class of beings realize God through the practice of spiritual disciplines...."

Kripasiddha — Perfect through Grace

"...like a room kept dark for countless years and illumined when a bright lamp is finally introduced, these good souls get liberation through God's own sweet grace...."

Hathatsiddha — Perfect Suddenly

"...freed all of a sudden for no apparent reason, like a poor boy who, befriended by a rich man, is married to his daughter and given home and wealth...."

Svapnasiddha — Perfect in a Dream

"...there is another class of devotees who, very fortunate and deserving, in a profound state of dream, get the vision of God and are set free...."

Asiddha — Not Perfected, even by Accident

"...like trying to drive a nail into a stone wall, there are many beings whose spiritual consciousness is not the least awakened even though they hear about God a thousand times...."

"Why shouldn't a man be able to realize the formless Brahman? He need only renounce the sense-objects. Then he, too, will know this much of Brahman — that It exists."

Sri Ramakrishna

He compared the *asiddha* to the camera's glass plate, whereupon images will not adhere if silver nitrate solution has been smeared on it, i.e., devotion to God. The *asiddha* thereby gets nothing from Holy Company. This is not criticism; it is practical truth realized by an illumined mind after long time observance of worldly living beings. Sri Krishna explains as much in the *Bhagavad Gita* in the chapter on the difference between the Divine and the Demoniacal *(daivasura sampad)*. Jesus referenced this fact in His *Sermon on the Mount* with the saying, *""Do not give what is holy to the dogs; nor cast your pearls before swine, lest they trample them under their feet, and turn and tear you in pieces."* It is only the spiritually naive, then, who hear the teaching that the Ever-pure *Atman* dwells in all beings, and accept or reject it on face value only, without due deliberation. Actually, the *Atman* dwells only in those who have realized themselves to be the *Atman*. All others worship *mayahamkara* — the ego in *maya* — knowingly or unknowingly. Swami Vivekananda explained this phenomena by telling us that the *Atman* dwells in all beings equally, in potential, but is fully manifest only in those who have realized their identity with It. We can let these few prime examples suffice to explain the unfortunates who fail to develop their consciousness while given the opportunity to do so while they are in the body.

However, the other five examples of *"siddha,"* perfection (previous page), are all much more fortunate. For example the *Svapnasiddha* has his or her consciousness awakened in the dream state, usually based upon preparation that has been accomplished in the waking state, namely *sadhana*. And the *Sadhanasiddha* is listed too, who regardless of getting a waking or dreaming vision, or a series of them, continues to perfect the mental mechanism in life by continued self-effort. These are a rare class of beings, used to detachment, and loving austerities performed while in the physical form.

Inexplicably, the *Hathatsiddha* gets illumination suddenly, and often without any apparent reason or even perceptible qualification. Onlookers must simply stare in abject disbelief at this unfathomable transformation in individuals. They often defer and, seeing no other way of explaining, call this unbelievable happening "grace."

But grace belongs to the *Kripasiddha,* and even these have their hidden secrets behind the scene of appearances. Although exceptions are always possible, as nothing is impossible, the one who awaits grace from the Lord and Mother is often seen lost in reverie, prayer, and other forms of spiritual qualification — as much to pass the time beneficially and contently as to earn any boon from God. These lovers of divine life rely entirely upon God, so the descent of Grace is both deserved and forthcoming — all in the Lord's own, sweet time.

Then, there is the rarest of all perfect beings, called the *Nityasiddha*. These are not made perfect, not through any form of growth, practice, or divine presence, but are that way by nature. "Eternally perfect" is the way to say this in English. The most recent example of this comes to us in the form of Swami Vivekananda who was, at an early age, recognized by Sri Ramakrishna as a *Nityasiddha* and declared to be that openly to all who were present at that time.

Sri Ramakrishna's teaching on these types of *Siddhas* provides a simple and straightforward way of both understanding the growth and progress of living aspirants, as well as a pathway to realize any of these states for oneself. He couches the teaching overall in terms of an adept practitioner's ability to gain comprehension and merit from the methods of affirmation and negation, both. Discrimination, the way of negation, is not liked by many, but is a swifter and more effective way of getting to the Source without undue delay, and the danger of falling of the path. Affirmation, sweeter and loved by more beings, is a way of realization rather than of purification, but being so it often runs the risk of stopping short of the destruction of ignorance, and of reaching the absolute, formless state as a result. What is really wanted, then, is a perfect blend of devotion and wisdom (see chart on page 429), for this combination will lead the soul to blissful transcendence. From there, anything is possible due to the innate perfection that is finally upon the soul, for good.

The *Hamsa,* or Swan, is a unique figure in India. Like the chariot, the *avatara,* and the lotus, the swan holds a place that is especially aligned with spirituality and Self Realization. A *paramahamsa,* then, is cherished by lovers of God and knowers of Truth, both. It is said that a swan can drink from a container of milk and come away having extracted the cream and left the water behind. The meaning of this is fairly clear, being that such a soul has the power of spiritual discrimination that allows Him to be in the world and body while taking away only the essence of life and leaving behind the nonessence.

ॐ Omkara: The Silent Call of the Hamsa

"The adept Yogi who mounts astride the Hamsa Bird is never affected by karmic influences, or even by countless numbers of sins. Taking up a single posture and concentrating within his awareness, he hears the internal sound through the right ear, becoming deaf to all outer sounds. Through such intense focus he enters the Turya state in a matter of days." — Nada-Bindu Upanisad

The Four Matras & Presiding Deities

"In early practice he hears loud sounds like oceans, thunderclouds, or kettle-drum. Later, he hears sounds like the tinkling of bells, flute, or vina. Passing all of these one by one, the yogi absorbs the chitta into the Primal Sound and renders the mind silent." Nada-Bindu Upanisad

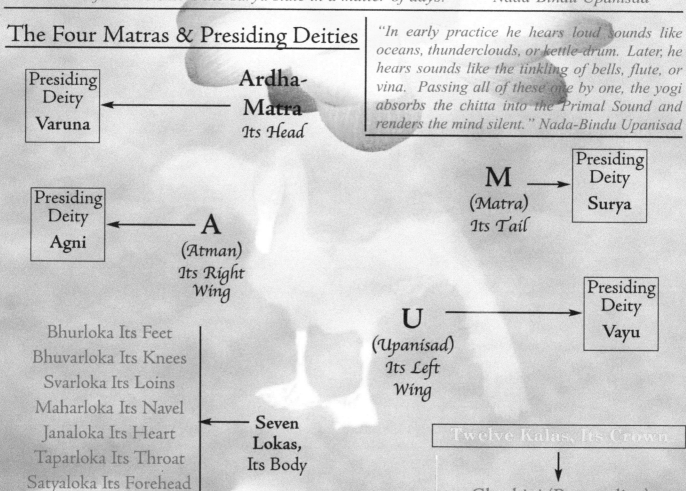

Ardha-Matra *Its Head*

Presiding Deity **Varuna**

A (Atman) *Its Right Wing*

Presiding Deity **Agni**

M (Matra) *Its Tail*

Presiding Deity **Surya**

U (Upanisad) *Its Left Wing*

Presiding Deity **Vayu**

Bhurloka Its Feet
Bhuvarloka Its Knees
Svarloka Its Loins
Maharloka Its Navel
Janaloka Its Heart
Taparloka Its Throat
Satyaloka Its Forehead

Seven Lokas, Its Body

Twelve Kalas, Its Crown

Death contemplating 1st Kala - Born an Emperor
Death contemplating 2nd Kala - Born a Yaksha
Death contemplating 3rd Kala - Born a Vidyadhara
Death contemplating 4th Kala - Born a Gandharva
Death contemplating 5th Kala - Born a Deva
Death contemplating 6th Kala - United with Indra
Death contemplating 7th Kala - Born in Vaikuntha
Death contemplating 8th Kala - Born in Kailash
Death contemplating 9th Kala - Born in Maharloka
Death contemplating 10th Kala - Born in Janaloka
Death contemplating 11th Kala - Born in Taparloka
Death contemplating 12th Kala - Nonreturn/Brahman

Ghoshini (Resounding)
Vidyunmali (Lightning Wreath)
Patangini (Sun-Drenched)
Vayuvegini (Wind-Speed)
Namadheya (Renown)
Aindri (Pure-sensed)
Vaishnavi (of Vishnu)
Shankari (of Siva)
Mahati (The Great)
Dhriti (Resolute)
Nari (Feminine)
Brahmi (Whirlwind)

Both the *Paramahamsa Upanisad,* and the *Nada-Bindu Upanisad,* have specific teachings and helpful information on this pure, white swan of a soul. And speaking of simple pathways and swift ways towards realization, the quote from the *Nada-Bindu Upanisad* right off the top schools us in what rapt and one-pointed concentration can accomplish, even, and especially, in the face of *karmas* and transgressions that mount up in life. It also informs us as to the connection between the pure Soul and The Word, *Omkara* — the Primal Cause of everything.

In this *Upanisad,* as can be seen on the chart under study, all of the Seven Worlds that have come out of *AUM,* called *lokas,* have been assigned their places in connection with the body of the *Hamsa,* such is its importance. Deities, or major gods, also have their associations there. So great is the symbology of the *Hamsa,* that even lifetimes in worlds falling under the cycles of phases of time have their profound assignments as well. Status of living beings is also determined by this *Hamsa,* who is one with The Word and Father to the Gods.

There is mystic symbology here as well, as the quote from the same *Upanisad* explains. The practitioner hears internal sounds at the time of meditation. These come at certain times, in conjunction with the disappearance of *karmas* and *samskaras* and the fructification of spiritual disciplines. Many of the disciplinary trappings of *yogic* practice are there as well, like assuming a single posture, *ekasana,* and entering into deep concentration with thoughts of Reality alone. Such consummate practice by the sincere devotee can bring about experience of the ultimate state, *Turiya,* in a matter of days.

In the crown of the *Hamsa* resides the twelve *kalas* — all connected to and representative of the Divine Mother, *Shakti.* As *Ghoshini* Her divine presence virtually echoes in orotund fashion within the deepest corridors of the aspiring mind. Thus She is fittingly named *Ghoshini,* the "Resounding."

Her vision within, being so breathtakingly brilliant, lights up all the passageways (*nadis*) in the subtle mind with an incandescence that outshines a billion suns in the nocturnal skies. This is not unusual to imagine, since She gave birth to all the worlds, along with the stars and planets that infill them. Looking inward at Her coruscating beauty, it seems as if all the separate lights in the Seven Worlds have formed a circle of translucence that defies description. This is the famous "Wreath of Lightning" the luminaries tell of in esoteric scriptures. Thus Her name, *Vidyunmali.*

This Light that is described in connection with Her, It is the Light of Consciousness — of pure, conscious Awareness. She is like a mold cast by a million suns, thus She is known as *Patangini* — Sun-drenched. The sunlit beaches of paradise are dim compared to Her prismatic radiance.

Vayuvegini, the fourth of the twelve *kalas,* means "speed of the wind." The implication is that Her intelligence outstrips all other powers that move, no matter how fast. This is also a clue to Her all-pervasive nature, first on the scene in whatever world She is called to minister to. Like the *gandharvas,* whose music reaches deep and swift into the minds of all sensitive beings, the aspect of Divine Mother Reality named *Vayuvegini* penetrates awareness and its *lokas* as positive thought and welcome healing, available for all who worship Her.

Namadheya, the renown *devi,* places first among those who are actual goddesses in the realm of the gods and goddesses. She confers the status of notoriety on the deserving deities who reside at subtlemost levels of consciousness, and who preside over them as well.

Then there is *Aindri,* the goddesses of ultra pure senses, who is *Indra's* consort. And from Her realm inwards the Trinity comes into view, along with the female aspects of *Brahma, Vishnu,* and *Siva* named *Mahati, Vaishnavi,* and *Shankari.* The causal realms of *Maharloka, Vaikuntha,* and *Kailash* are lovingly cared for by these lofty goddesses.

Also worthy of mention are the goddesses named *Dhriti,* the fast, firm, and resolute one, and *Nari,* the quintessence of the feminine quality and perfection, of the tenth and eleventh *kalas.* These twin powers preside over inward realms where the desire for life in forms is fast diminishing, and where advanced souls are beginning their inward, transcendental journey into formless Awareness.

And there, in the realmless realm of formless Awareness, the benign aspect named *Bhrami,* graces this most refined station. The coming together of all currents of consciousness into one light-filled"point is overseen by Her, thus She known as "The Whirlwind." Those who enter this vortex of coalescence consummate the path of "nonreturn." As Lord Buddha was once heard to say, *"Have no hope for me forevermore; I am gone, and gone forever."*

The Different Types of Diksha – Spiritual Initiation

Sankalpa Diksha
By thought or will

Chakshu Diksha
By a glance or a look

Hasta Diksha
By hand on the head

Vak Diksha
By a word or an utterance

Sparsha Diksha
By a touch to heart or body

Dhyana Diksha
By meditating on the aspirant

Mantra Diksha
By formal initiation with bija

Svapna Diksha
By transmission in a dream

Shaktipat Diksha
By transferring subtle power

Pada Diksha
By touching the guru's feet

"To strive for enlightenment devoid of guru-diksha and teachings is like trying to grow crops only at night. Therefore, until thy mind is enlightened, follow the path of initiation shown by the illumined souls."   *Lord Vasishtha*

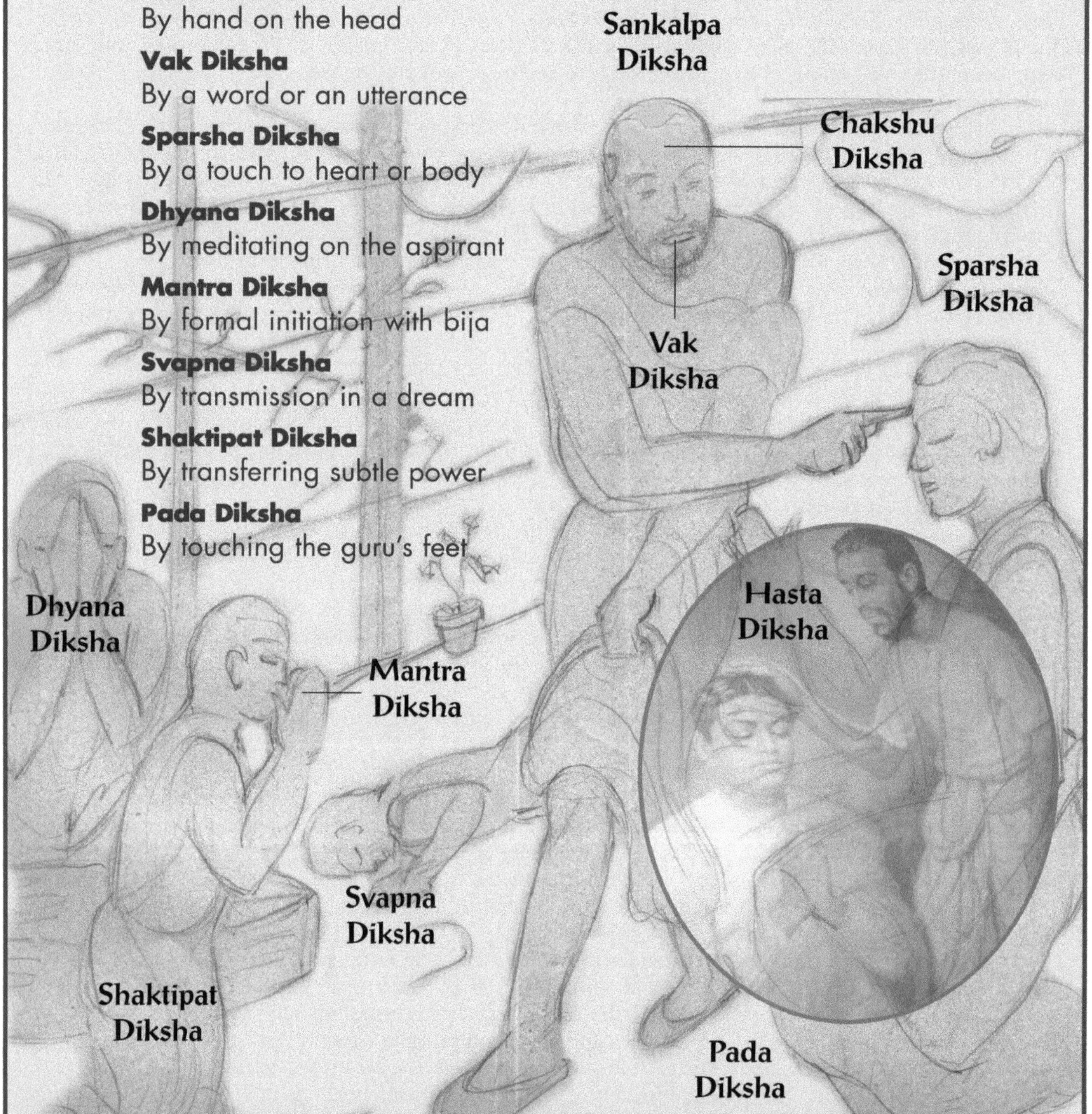

Sankalpa Diksha

Chakshu Diksha

Sparsha Diksha

Vak Diksha

Dhyana Diksha

Mantra Diksha

Svapna Diksha

Shaktipat Diksha

Hasta Diksha

Pada Diksha

"The true guru is nothing less than the Cosmic Mind (Brahma/Vishnu/Shiva) manifesting itself in some rare soul. The guru initiates those sincere spiritual aspirants who are especially keen for Self-Realization."   *Sri Ramakrishna*

This ultimate path of nonreturn into form, and into time, space, name and *karma* as well, began with the spiritual aspirant's search for a spiritual master who could grant the auspicious boon of *mantra-diksha,* the formal entrance into a spiritual path leading towards Enlightenment. The chart on the previous page outlines the different kinds of ways that rare, illumined souls utilize to initiate beings interested mainly in matters of the Spirit, Absolute Consciousness, or *Brahman.*

A clue to the most real and lasting form of initiation is in the term, *mantra-diksha.* It is conferred upon the beginner by a living *guru,* and so is the most convincing, believeable, and supportive form of *diksha.* It also is the most practicable form, depending mostly on the aspirant's own ability to repeat the *mantra* and make spiritual progress under his or her own auspice. Due to this it can produce a tangible sense of moving inwards, and thus is a rare measuring device in the realm of spiritual aspiration and its generally intangible fruits.

There are a few types of *diksha* that fall into the area of the physical, even though their implications and results bespeak of the spiritual. *Hasta diksha,* which is received when an illumined soul places a hand on the devotee's head or heart, transfers a subtle energy to the psyche of the student or acolyte, helping them along the path of inward ascension. The effects of this, and other physically-based forms on initiation, are either swift or long range depending on the preparedness of the one who is receiving this boon. There is also a kind of spiritual upliftment that comes from the disciple bowing and touching the feet of the revered *guru* or preceptor. This is called *pada diksha.* Both the removal of *karma* and the receipt of spiritual gains can result from such contact, if it is sincere.

A form of initiation that is more common, though less acknowledged and understood, is *vak diksha.* There is an emanation of subtle power that proceeds from words. Of course, spiritually speaking, such words or phrases are utterances transmitted from a high level of consciousness by a luminary, coming from the source of purified mind. Even lower grade words can transmit secular knowledge to a student seeking an earthly education, but where actual *diksha* is concerned, *slokas* and *sutras* from revealed scriptures can break through inner barriers and produce revelations, many of these connected with former lifetimes.

And this is where initiations like *sparsha diksha* and *sankalpa diksha* come in. The former transmits spirituality via a touch. This touch is powerful, containing within it the concentrated mental force of the illumined mind that is willfully transfering it. It will undoubtedly penetrate through layers of deception and veils of obscuration that lie over individual consciousness at its as yet unrealized level of awareness. In the case of *sankalpa diksha,* the process is similar but not so usually swift. The *guru* or spiritual preceptor takes it upon himself to think long and deep on the student, sending subtle inner power to that fortunate being for the benefit of his or her spiritual life. The spiritual tradition of India, and other religions as well, are full of stories about such welcome input coming from "on high," or better, "in deep."

Similar to *sankalpa diksha* is *dhyan diksha,* where the preceptor meditates upon the student in deep contemplative periods, quite often helping young aspirants to develop a contemplative life of their own. And like this as well, the unusual and mystical form of initiation called *svapna diksha* also makes an occasional appearance in young spiritual lives. This is initiation transmitted in a dream, *svapna.* Not only a vision occurs in this form of *diksha,* but the *mantra* is also given at this time if the student is qualified enough to "hear" it and make it out. There are five subtle senses, called "dream senses," that need to be developed for this to occur. In India, the world of dreams is synonymous with the "kingdom of heaven" within.

More known in present times, but made popular by sensationalist teachers, *shaktipat diksha* follows the traditional form of certain outer rituals that confers inner power upon the seeker. In the *Tantras* it is given a very high status, for in olden days the teachers were advocates of spiritual practices and free from the attractions of gaining name, fame, and following. Some of the dynamics of the above mentioned types of initiation get utilized in the confering of *shaktipat.* When it is authentic, it can be a force for spiritual transference and awakening, but when it is impure it can bind both the seeker and the teacher into *mayic* occupations that are unhealthy and counterproductive to the higher aims and superlative ends of true spiritual life and nondual understanding.

In spiritual practice, the most common, healthy, trand dependable form of spiritual initiation, i.e., the *mantra*, is transmitted by a preceptor who has not only received that boon from a line of spiritual teachers who uttered and utilized it themselves, but who has also practiced it personally and underwent the purification and transformation that the *mantra* is best known for. Most beings do not know how deep the *mantra* goes, nor do they realize the real spiritual significance of the *mala* (rosary or *japa* beads) that they use to recite the sacred formula. The chart on the facing page gives some rare information from the Divine Mother scriptures on these points, along with a hint as to how the *japa* beads come alive in the practice, and how to treat this living presence when it emerges due to the practitioner's urgent call.

As with any art or science and the practice thereof, certain preparation is needed before the matter, as sanctified ritual with its beneficial results, is entered into. To give a hint about this to the newly initiated practitioner, the quote at the top of the chart on page 629 is offered. Few beings, even devotees, ever come to know of such esoteric practices, what to speak of carrying them out. Suffice to say that a *mala* that is treated with such reverential care and love both emanates an aura of sacredness, and is also more likely to connect the practitioner to the essence of every sacred deity that has its subtle seat in every single bead of the *japa mala*.

Those deities have been given an English description on the chart under study, confering a wonderful sense of the subtle and protective powers that populate the internal worlds of meditation and spirituality. The scriptures consulted for this chart propitiate the *Vedic* Forefathers who engaged themselves so willingly and unstintingly in the practice of *japam*, as seen in the quote on the bottom part of the chart. These profound beings knew that if the practice of *mantra* repetition was entered into and kept alive through generations, the benefits of this would be reaped over ages by countless souls — one of them being the preparation of the mind for its immersion and dissolution into Absolute Reality, *Brahman*.

For such a high attainment as this, nothing short of realizing the intrinsic oneness of everything, the transcendence of the idea of death, or illusion of death, must come to the soul as a full realization. The descend of death on human minds means more than the body's demise; it also means falling into a state of abject ignorance regarding the eternal existence of the human Soul, *Atman*. A careless attitude assumed over time by embodied beings, as well as a continuing oversight of the presence of evil in the embodied condition itself, results in the acceptance of false truths that were thought all along to be real by parents and society. In this unfortunate situation, negative *karmas* get formed and manifest in life, circling down and out of the mind's ignorance, or lack of actual knowledge. However, causing the *japa mala* to circle in the opposite direction, fueled by the *mantra* given to the devotee by an authentic *guru*, the practitioner both destroys *karmas* descending from careless actions done in past lifetimes, and dissolves new *karmas* from taking shape for the remainder of the present lifetime.

The symbology that is attached to the *japa mala* by the wise is pregnant with meaning, and inspiring as well. Many newly initiated souls, beginning the practice of *japa*m, underestimate the teachings associated with the *mantra* and thus fail to prepare the ground for reaping the full benefit out of the practice. For, some deep visualization goes along with the practice of *japam*, as is seen by the teachings at the top of the chart under study.

The sacred threads that interpenetrate the *mala* beads, usually *rudraksha* seeds, form into a tassel above the *guru* bead. This is *Brahman*, that permeates everything with inherent Perfection. The holes in the beads themselves signify knowledge of the spiritual kind that frees the soul from obstacles and entanglements in *maya*. To further clarify this, the knots that intersect the spaces between each and every bead (when it is correctly garlanded) symbolize nature, and the soul's attachment to it. This attachment must be outgrown, and the soul must thereby realize the pure, perfect, and formless essence of the Self which is beyond nature. This is a very important teaching, and it does away with those aforementioned problems of carelessness and heedlessness that cause ignorance of the cautionary facts of embodied existence.

The *guru* bead holds prime importance in the *japa mala*. The devotee is to visualize, every time he or she picks up the *mala* for practice, that the face of the *guru* bead is *Sarasvati* — the Mother of the Word — and the tail of the *guru* bead is *Gayatri*. Further, the left side of that bead is *Vishnu*, and the right side is *Siva*. When this total visualization is complete, prior to practicing the *mantra*, all the deities are well-pleased and invoked, and the practitioner can dive deep into the practice itself. For more teachings on this deep dive of concentrated consciousness, the reader can return to study the charts and their teachings on pages 131 through 157.

The Inner Meaning of the Mala

"Reverential treatment of the mala involves bathing it in milk, wrapping it in sacred grass made wet with ganges water and sandalwood oil, smearing it with fragrant pastes and unguents such as sandalwood and kasturi, placing it on a bed of flowers, and uttering AUM over it. Then meditate on each bead in conjunction with the presiding deities of each unit."
Aksha-Malika Upanisad

The Thread is Brahman

The Bead Holes are Knowledge

"Salutations to the Deities, who move about in and are established in the subtle atmospheres of the mala."

The Garland Knots are Nature

Guru Bead Face is Sarasvati

Guru Bead Tail is Gayatri

Guru Bead Left is Vishnu

Guru Bead Right is Siva

Left	Right
Conqueror of Death	Churner of Wisdom Nectar
The Omniscient	Remover of Diseases
Giver of Abundance	The Moon-Healer
Clarifier of Speech	The Prana Bird, Garuda
Giver of Strength	Essence of Goodness
Destroyer of Evil Thoughts	Granter of Success
Healer of Disorders	Bestower of Grains/Food
The Effulgent Revealer	Who Yokes one to Dharma
The Devourer of All	Who Grants Growth
The Great Deluder	Remover of Suffering
The All-Attracting One	Giver of Enjoyment/Freedom
The Pure & Noble One	Who Grants Progress
Foundation of Speech	Granter of Capaciousness
Nature of Speech	Remover of Defects
Elephant of Auspiciousness	Who Quiets Fears, Worry
The Terrible One	Who Staves off Hatred
Neutralizer of Poisons	Who Purifies Thoughts
The Tormentor of Evil	Who Burns Transgressions
Remover of Obstacles	Who Hears Prayers
The Great Stupefier	The Noblest One
Shaper of Intelligence	Who Sanctifies Actions
Destroyer of Cruelty	Who Grants Righteousness
Destroyer of Bad Spirits	The Primal Cause of All
The Unstoppable One	The Purest of All
Destroyer of Hell Beings	The All-Powerful One

"And salutations to those Forefathers for getting established in the aksha-malika for our highest and best good."

"Mrityu is not the only means of death. Carelessness and nonalertness resulting from ajnana also figure in. Reciting the mantra on the sacred japa beads, in circular fashion, starting from the crest jewel and ending at the crest jewel, destroys ignorance, neutralizes old karmas, and keeps new karmas from forming. Aksha-Malika Upanisad

From The Tripura Tapini Upanisad

"On That Adorable Splendor of the Divine Creatrix may we meditate. May She our thoughts inspire, Who is beyond all darkness. AUM."

Om Bhur Bhuvah Svaha — The Supreme, assuming the guise of The Trinity, comes to be styled as the Goddess *Tripuri.* By Her Power are fashioned the Three Abodes — earth, atmospheres, and heaven. Her bijam, *Hrim,* along with its terrible power, permeates the terminus of these three peaks, emanating from the junction between Her two eyebrows which is the seat of equilibrium of the three *gunas,* and where the world of objects gets dissolved.

Tat — is verily the eternal *Brahman,* the indefinable, impeccable, unconditioned, and unconstrained. It thinks, perceives, evolves, and desires the status of consciousness. Thus It evolves as the visible world. Its desiring is done through ascetics, mystics, seers, and their sacrifices. What is desired is born. Being free of desires, It holds sway over all beings. It puts forth letters like T-a-t. Therefore, *Tat* is desireless desire. Who so knows all this becomes the Lord.

Savitur Varenyam — The root "Supreme" means *"to give birth to living beings."* *Savitur* thus gives birth to all that lives. Power gives birth. This primeval power is *Tripura,* the Supreme Sovereign, Goddess Great with earrings adorned, in sphere of fire residing. *Varenyam* means best, adorable. Whosoever knows this gains all-pervasiveness.

Bhargo Devasya Dhimahi — *Dha* denotes the highest bearing. *Bharga* signifies the shining one who dwells at the center, who is the imperishable fourth. It is the innermost of all. The syllable, *Ma,* denotes greatness, inertness, solidity. *Mahi* denotes the earth, what is gross — seas, mountains, islands, and forests. The word *Devasya* represents the presiding deities.

Dhiyo yo nah Prachodayat — means to meditate upon the Supreme Self, *Sadasiva,* who renders us speechless, inspires our thoughts, and who takes us far beyond the sphere of desire for conceptualization to transcendental Reality.

"'Without taints, I am; being, knowing, loving, I am; Self-shining, devoid of duality, I am.' To these words, conform."
The Devi Sarasvati ≈ Sarasvati Rahasya Upanisad

The *Gayatri* was just mentioned in accord with the *guru* bead of the *mantra*. As a superlative *mantra* all its own, it may be the most widely chanted *sloka* of all, repeated by millions of souls often hundreds of times a day. The chart put together on the facing page gives the exact definitions of all the words of power contained in this ancient sacred formula, courtesy of the *Tripura Tapini Upanisad*.

Right from the beginning of its holy contents, the *Gayatri* infers *triputis* on many levels. The *Gayatri* itself is said to be one third of India's grandest *triputi*, that of *Gita, Ganga,* and *Gayatri*. *Gita* stands for the revealed scriptures, Ganga for the purification necessary to enter into a purely spiritual existence, and *Gayatri* for higher wisdom and its revelation and implementation into all of life.

The knower of *Gayatri* is protected and sustained by the Goddess Herself, reverently titled *Tripura Sundari*. She oversees all workings in the three worlds through Her assumption of the Trinity, *Brahma, Vishnu,* and *Siva*. The three *gunas* are commanded by Her, and the three sacred subtle rivers flowing through the marvelous human form are conducted in their flow due to Her presence alone. Thus, She is *Kundalini*.

Of powerful threesomes, She is the one who formulates the three essential parts of *Brahman* into Its essential name, *Tat*. Knowers of *Brahman*, threefold, namely the ascetics, mystics, and seers, make certain that all desires are fulfilled at the appropriate time in every cycle that She directs. They have "become the Lord" through Her.

She is *varenyam,* the highest and best among all Deities. Purifying and liberating fire is Her main seat, thus She baptizes by fire — by the heat of *tapas,* austerity. The Light of Her being permeates all of creation, shooting through and through all worlds and elements, and overseeing all the many deities that preside over them. The beauty of nature is Her beauty manifesting in and through all things majestic and inspiring.

With Her consort, *Siva,* She maintains the presence of the Highest Self, *Atman,* in all beings desirous of liberation. To Her votaries She graciously transmits the desire to meditate on this inmost divinity, and all other powers that would support the realization of It. The mind is Her powerful instrument for conception and manifestation, but She always holds out the possibility for aspiring beings to transcend it and experience union with the Highest Reality. Thus, as one translation of the *Gayatri* expresses:

> *May we always and ever meditate*
> *upon the radiant effulgence of the Supreme Being,*
> *abiding in our hearts and minds, eternally.*
> *May that one divine Presence bless and protect us eternally,*
> *and protect the Three Worlds.*
> *Om Peace, Peace, Peace*

Simply mentioning the Divine Couple, *Siva* and *Shakti,* evinces a strong desire to know Them better in beings who have surrendered the limited ego and taken up the quest for divine union. The chart on the forthcoming page, page 633, lays out the dynamics of a *Tantric* system that is both ancient and revealing. Their perpetual mystic union is a matter for both heartfelt love and all-consuming wonder.

And the *mantra* of *Shakti* plays a crucial part in this intrinsic and ecstatic symmetry. Placed in context with the principle of *Kamakala,* together they produce nothing short of a singularly enlightened communion known only to adepts and knowers of the deepest secrets of divine Reality.

Starting at the bottom of the chart on page 633, the *mantra* is to be understood in terms of words that fall into a wide spectrum of meaning, from gross to subtle to causal. In brief, and for purposes of easy comprehension, this additional *triputi* can be assigned to levels bespeaking of what is worldly, intellectual, and spiritual. *Shakti's* power resides in all words, but most intellects fail to comprehend it, most minds overlook it, and most tongues fail to express it. She is "most" subtle, for certain. Thus, the *Svetasvataropanisad* states,

"Practicing the yoga of meditation, the ancient seers of India came to behold the divine power existing in everything, and everywhere, and who though veiled by Her own modes of nature, was nevertheless one and indivisible — and Who had been incomprehensible to them earlier due to the limitations of their own intellects."

Therefore, if even the wise have had to search within for a lengthy period of time to finally make contact and commune with Her, imagine how invisible She is, and has been, to the ignorant masses for all these many millennia, over countless and continuing cycles of ongoing time.

Perhaps this is enough to say, or infer, about the first two levels of *mantra* at the bottom of the chart under study, concerning worldly subjects and lower knowledge focused upon matter and what is physical only. Nevertheless, since *shakti* power lies within both, a study of these areas is informative — if not for any other reason than to help distance oneself from all that is superficial and go beyond all that is intellectual only.

Suffice to say that it is the third level of *mantra,* the "universe of subtle principles" that soon beckons the inward traveler, for apt use of *shakti mantra* given by the *guru* in sacred initiation will help the soul penetrate through *maya* and reach the blessed realm of *Mahamaya.* Two great happenings occur at this important juncture. First, the twofold boon of achieving the end to rounds of birth and death in ignorance, along with the ability to distinguish between what is real and all that is unreal, transpire. This is the birth of *Vivekajnana,* or spiritual discrimination. Secondly, the twofold attainment of acquiring a spiritual body, and the ability to commune with God in Its highest Form *(Ishvara/Ishvari),* occurs. Though much can be said about this stunning and pivotal juncture, much of which has already been related in many of the pages of this book, it all sets the stage for what is called *Kamakala* in the tradition. Here, among other things, the aspiring practitioner can already sense the oncoming descent of nonduality and its place in the realization of the Highest Truth.

But prior to that pinnacle, an understanding of the subtler dynamics of *Kamakala* is given, which will settle age-old doubts about the nature of gradated existence — of the "building blocks of creation," as it were. From whence does this desire to create come from?, is one of these queries, and since the aspirant has not known and experienced the nondual and homogenous nature of all of existence yet, such questions pose a potential block to the finer and fuller comprehension that is so crucial to the full realization of the Self, *Atman.*

For a refresher course of some of the aspects of *Kamakala,* the chart on page 463 can be reviewed. As a furtherance of this principle, three other elements share the overall makeup of *Kamakala* with the force of the desire to create at the cosmic level. Nature in its manifested and unmanifested states is one of those. A look back at the chart on page 321 can perk the memory around this. In addition, it can be said that nature, being insentient (having no consciousness of its own that is not borrowed from the soul), has to have assistance in the creative process of *Kamakala.* The expression of the urge to fashion worlds of name and form in time and space is provided by subtle vibration springing eternally from The Word, *AUM. Spandas* are vibrating spheres of existence, easily associated with the words of Jesus when he spoke of the Kingdom of Heaven within. It is to be remembered that The Word and all levels of existence springing from it vibrate with innate intelligence *(jnanamatra).* The discoveries of science with regard to the vibrations of atomic and subatomic particles is pertinent only on the physical level, and should be seen as an outer sign directing consciousness to its intelligent roots. The source of all this, gross and subtle, is the *Bindu,* the fourth element of *Kamakala. Bindu* is termed *Mahatattva* due to its eminent position in the scheme of "creation," or projection, or emanation of intelligence. It is the first principle from which all else gets formulated.

Regarding the *Bindu,* it represents a powerful *triputi* all its own, called the *Mula-Trikona,* or "primal triangle." Its triple constitution concerns knowledge and its power at a very pure level. The *Tantra-Shastras* hold this out as the main secret of the "oneness," or innate homogeneity, of all existence. When the *Bindu* is in its original state, free of apparent bifurcations and separations, that is *Siva* and *Shakti* polarized, the potent seed of primal sound. Thus, *Siva* and *Shakti* in union is essential Existence combined with primal Essence. To explain, He is the nondual Wisdom that is beyond all expression, while She is the inherent power in that Wisdom who renders it manifest. Thus, they are the combination of innate perfection and potential dynamism. Together they epitomize the real nature of Freedom — whether remaining in the state of original wholeness, or breaking into two to express whatever they desire. In *Tantra* these Two as One are refered to as *Samvit,* or Ultimate Reality. The words *Svatantriya,* unstinted freedom, and *Vichikirsha,* the natural urge to express the potential held in Consciousness — from the cosmic level on out to manifested nature — are utilized to explain the true nature of Absolute Existence.

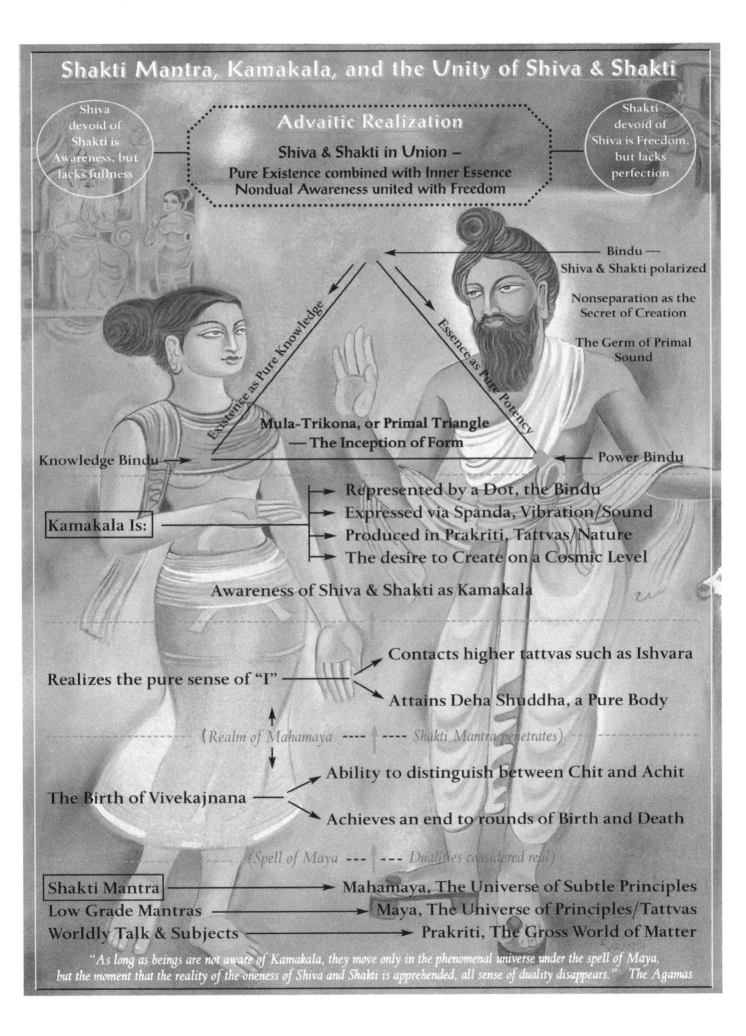

Shakti Mantra, Kamakala, and the Unity of Shiva & Shakti

Shiva devoid of Shakti is Awareness, but lacks fullness

Shakti devoid of Shiva is Freedom, but lacks perfection

Advaitic Realization
Shiva & Shakti in Union —
Pure Existence combined with Inner Essence
Nondual Awareness united with Freedom

Bindu —
Shiva & Shakti polarized

Nonseparation as the Secret of Creation

The Germ of Primal Sound

Existence as Pure Knowledge

Essence as Pure Potency

**Mula-Trikona, or Primal Triangle
— The Inception of Form**

Knowledge Bindu

Power Bindu

Kamakala Is:
→ Represented by a Dot, the Bindu
→ Expressed via Spanda, Vibration/Sound
→ Produced in Prakriti, Tattvas/Nature
→ The desire to Create on a Cosmic Level

Awareness of Shiva & Shakti as Kamakala

Realizes the pure sense of "I"
→ Contacts higher tattvas such as Ishvara
→ Attains Deha Shuddha, a Pure Body

(Realm of Mahamaya ---- ↑ ---- Shakti Mantra penetrates)

The Birth of Vivekajnana
→ Ability to distinguish between Chit and Achit
→ Achieves an end to rounds of Birth and Death

(Spell of Maya --- | --- Dualities considered real)

Shakti Mantra ⟶ Mahamaya, The Universe of Subtle Principles
Low Grade Mantras ⟶ Maya, The Universe of Principles/Tattvas
Worldly Talk & Subjects ⟶ Prakriti, The Gross World of Matter

*"As long as beings are not aware of Kamakala, they move only in the phenomenal universe under the spell of Maya,
but the moment that the reality of the oneness of Shiva and Shakti is apprehended, all sense of duality disappears." The Agamas*

The recent reference to fire as *Shakti's* power to awaken the soul to higher awareness calls up Mother India's teachings on fire. For the ancient seers, fire was to be meditated upon at all its various levels, not just as one of the five physical elements. As we have seen in earlier pages (see charts on pages 503 & 505), both the power and the light of fire relate directly to knowledge. Metaphorically speaking, it is the fire of wisdom that cures the numbness of ignorance in the human mind, and as Sri Krishna reminds us in the *Bhagavad Gita,* this fire of wisdom is the best of all purifiers in the Three Worlds. As the chart on the facing page reveals, then, fire is not just a physical element. Even the vast range between a tiny flame and a massive sun represents only a small segment of its true glory and power.

Unbeknownst to many, suffering is a kind of fire. If a human being takes up the primal force that is held within suffering and utilizes it to surmount weakness and error, a fresh conflagration ignites at the root center of consciousness *(muladhara).* Directing this flame upwards and inwards, the ingestion and digestion of food begins to proceed via a more beneficial kind of fire; food that was once heavy and poisonous turns into a heady nectar that causes the mind to gain a new-found buoyancy.

The spiritual aspirant's Godward thoughts are another type of fire. This is where the element fire makes its most useful turn. Thoughts can transform worlds; they create worlds, as we have seen in the points made by the Mind-only schools of Mother India. If the individual practitioner fans the flames of self-effort *(sadhana)* within, all of the dross contained in a human being's thoughts get purged from the gold of the mind's consciousness. Thus, as is chanted, *"May the fire of Brahman protect, sustain, and illumine the mind's thinking process."* In possession of a pure mind, the newly reborn adept and master can place their full-blown awareness on causing a veritable forest fire in collective consciousness — as Jesus, Buddha, Swami Vivekananda, and Sri Ramakrishna did.

Worshipping the Lord and Mother of the Universe entails both kindling the fire of love in the heart, and creating a fire of sacrifice that will destroy the unripe ego's hold on the mind. As Sri Krishna teaches, worship is the best form of austerity for the body. With the primal heat burning in the root *chakra,* and the "fire in the belly" doing its natural work, any form of worship that the devotee turns his or her mind to will bear fruit immediately. What to speak of completing all modes of sacrifice to the deities within, all the endearing modes of love will also burgeon forth accordingly (see charts on pages 123 & 473).

And forebearing both the ills of life in the body and the challenges of the mind's transcendence of limitations will demand the producing and maintaining of a unique kind of *yogic* heat, called the fire of transformation. It will assist in fusing human nature with its divine counterpart, the *Atman.* The fire of transformation is the main precursor to the attainment and appearance of the famed and coveted Fire of *Yoga.* It is necessary that the sincere and committed spiritual aspirant undergo all the regimens of austerity and growth that is demanded in order to transform body, senses, life-force, and the mind complex — including the ego. The scriptures state about this, *"That one realizes the supreme, eternal Self, who dissolves mind, intellect, body, senses, the five subtle elements and the five gross elements, into the Atman in meditation, along with time and space."* Such a unique turn of consciousness is attempted and attained only by those who court Freedom specifically, and who *"....love the Lord with all their heart."*

All of what is described above makes up the Fire of *Yoga,* which is actually the Divine Mother's own power of manifestation and dissolution. Even nagging problems and considerations such as ill health, advancing age, and the "looming spectre of death," meet their match when the Fire of *Yoga* burns in the heart. All the other forms of fire cited above combine in it. Both the intense love and profound wisdom abiding therein can remove all obstacles along the spiritual path. The intrinsically connected fires of *Ojas* and *Tejas,* mentioned earlier (see chart on page 584), are also working full time in this inner conflagration coveted by the *yogis* and seers. They know that this flame of combined love and wisdom will not only render the mind pure and keep it that way, but will also heal the maladies and infirmities of other living beings as well. Thus, as the Buddha was said to have stated it in the *Dhammapada: "Do not delay! Strive hard and be wise. Make of yourself a fire that will purge mental impurities. Being stainless, you will not then come into this life of birth, old age, and death again."*

Of fires and austerities, and the practices that ignite and fan them into flames that evaporate devour floods of ignorance in the mind, the *Vedantic* method of *Neti Neti* ("not this, not this") deserves both mention and study, what to speak of implementation into the lives of aspirants bent upon realizing

Echelons of Fire

The Significance of Fire in Vedic Religion and Philosophy

"First harnessing the mind and the senses with a view to realize the Truth, and then having found out the meaning to the light of Fire, the evolving soul brought itself out of the earth."

Surya
Sun God

Brahman

Suns

Awareness

Lava

Tejas

Candle
Flame

Ojas

Prana

FIRE

EARTH   WATER   LIGHT   AIR   ETHER

Fire of Shape

Fire of Yoga

"When the fivefold perceptions of Yoga arising from concentration on earth, water, light, air, and ether have appeared to the Yogin, then he gains a body consisting of the fire of Yoga, and he will never again be touched by disease, old age, or death."

"Forms that appear like smoke, firefly, sparks, fire, and crystal precede the manifestation of Brahman in Yoga practice."

Fire of Worship

Fire of Transformation

Fire of Aspiration

Fire of Suffering

"Salutations to that Divinity Who is in Fire, who is in water, who is in plants, who is in trees, and who has pervaded the entire universe." Svetashvataropanisad

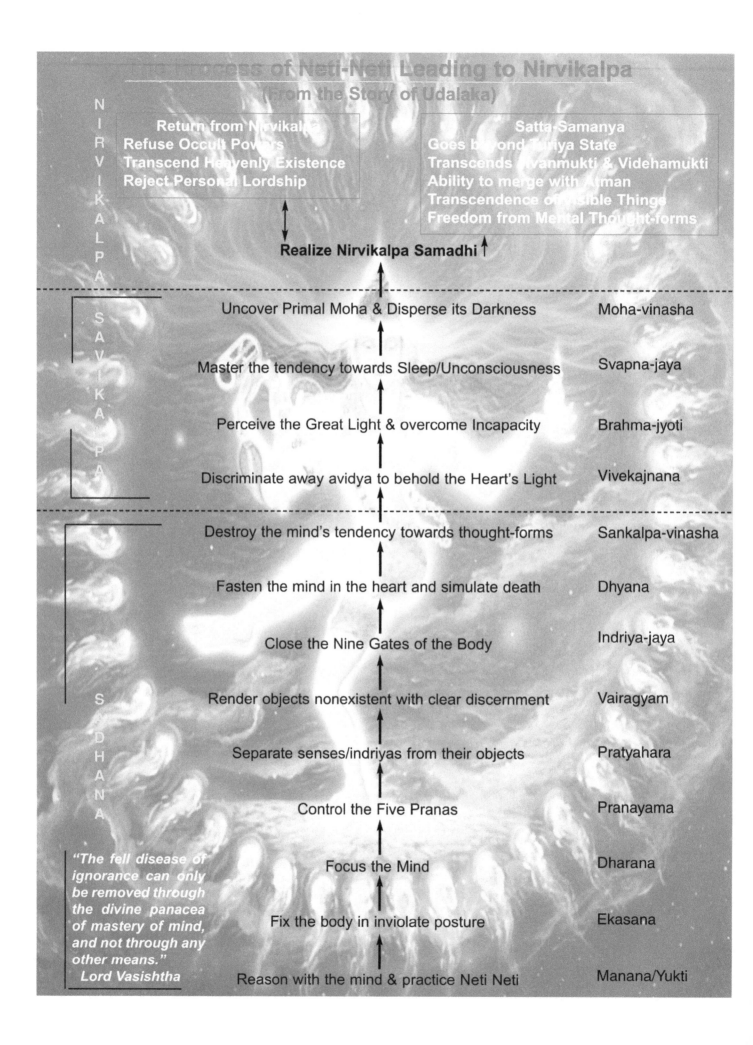

The Process of Neti-Neti Leading to Nirvikalpa
(From the Story of Udalaka)

N I R V I K A L P A

Return from Nirvikalpa
Refuse Occult Powers
Transcend Heavenly Existence
Reject Personal Lordship

Satta-Samanya
Goes beyond Turiya State
Transcends Jivanmukti & Videhamukti
Ability to merge with Atman
Transcendence of Visible Things
Freedom from Mental Thought-forms

Realize Nirvikalpa Samadhi ↑

S A V I K A L P A

Uncover Primal Moha & Disperse its Darkness — Moha-vinasha

Master the tendency towards Sleep/Unconsciousness — Svapna-jaya

Perceive the Great Light & overcome Incapacity — Brahma-jyoti

Discriminate away avidya to behold the Heart's Light — Vivekajnana

Destroy the mind's tendency towards thought-forms — Sankalpa-vinasha

Fasten the mind in the heart and simulate death — Dhyana

Close the Nine Gates of the Body — Indriya-jaya

Render objects nonexistent with clear discernment — Vairagyam

Separate senses/indriyas from their objects — Pratyahara

Control the Five Pranas — Pranayama

Focus the Mind — Dharana

S A D H A N A

"The fell disease of ignorance can only be removed through the divine panacea of mastery of mind, and not through any other means."
Lord Vasishtha

Fix the body in inviolate posture — Ekasana

Reason with the mind & practice Neti Neti — Manana/Yukti

the nondual Truth. The chart on the facing page gives the seer Udalaka's own version and method, in ascending order, of this practice, as told in *Yoga Vasishtha* by Lord Vasishtha himself. The main difference in content here, as contrasted by such systems as *Ashtanga Yoga*, the Eightfold Path, and others, is that Udalaka started off with *neti neti* at the outset, even prior to fixing his posture and taking up breathing exercises. In this way he prepared the mind for steps and stages that were to come, using *manana*, or *yukti* — a deep reasoning process — to convince the mind of the necessity and efficacy, both, of entering into spiritual life and practice in full possession of the soul's inner powers. This is passing wise.

According to *Vedanta*, discerning the difference between what is real and what is unreal is the purpose of applying *neti neti* into life. This is not just to get rid of suffering and dissolve *karmas*, but to pave the way to Enlightenment, or spiritual emancipation *(moksha/mukti)*. The words "real" and "unreal" must be taken to mean definitions such as changeless and changeful, primarily because constant waves of the shifting sands of *maya* are unrelenting in their assault on human life and circumstances, and secondly, because once the aspiring soul reaches assurance of the Reality of *Brahman*, he/she will see *Brahman* everywhere — even in those very changes that plagued earlier. This makes the *neti neti* method of *Vedanta* a superlative one, mainly because there is only one Principle that is changeless or immutable, and that is *Brahman* Itself. By doing away with so many overlays and superimpositions *(vivarta)* the seeker soon comes closer and closer to that singular Reality — which is Love *(prema)*, which is Wisdom *(jnana)*, which is Bliss *(ananda)*, and which is the true Self *(Atman)*, in all beings and all things.

The list of efforts and stages that runs up the middle of the chart presently under study (page 636) is mostly familiar to the student of Indian philosophy and spirituality, particularly around the *darshana* of *Yoga*. However, of especial note would be important accomplishments such as doing away with focus upon and preoccupation with mental projection *(sankalpa-vinasha)*, and mastering the phases of human consciousness that occur to the living being every twenty-four hours of each day of life, namely waking, dreaming, and deep sleep *(svapna-jaya)*. These two, along with the destruction of latent *karmas*, do not receive much attention in the average spiritual seeker of today, especially not in Western countries, being as unfamiliar with the inner terrain of their own consciousness as they are.

And this is precisely why transcendent states such as *Nirvikalpa* and *Satta-samanya* are seldom ever attained by individual practitioners. To live beyond time, even while in the body, and to become so even and transparent of mind as to be practically nonexistent as far as erratic mental vibrations are concerned, is rare. If a true master of spirituality were to instruct and guide an advanced seeker in developing the ability to neutralize *karmas* at their source, a more ready and easy access to the natural states of *samadhi* would be the result. The further effect would come about regarding doing away with primal ignorance, or *mula-avidya*. At this consummate level of inner seeing — which is perception beyond the gross and subtle senses — diaphanous veils such as the fear of formlessness, the desire for personal lordship, and the desire to take on bodies at all, in any realm, would dissolve away. Dreamlike forms projected by the mind, from animal to human to celestial to divine, would all merge into *Atman*. Thus would the unripe ego's multifarious (and nefarious) posturing and pretensions come to an end, once and for all.

Remaining close to the heart of Lord Vasishtha's teachings, the chart on the following page takes up another aspect of the story of Arjuna, this time in his meeting with Paramasiva. With the role of the boy/ego complex being so prominent in the lives of most beings, forgetfulness of the spiritual nature underlying all things settles into the mind. When this occurs the soul begins to act as if matter and body are the only reality, as is instanced in the cases of most beings on the earth plane. The only remedy for this malady is to consult the only one who has the authority to give out the striking truth of the matter. This amounts to the Soul informing the soul about the pure and perfect nature of its Existence, and of its Essence as well. In Lord Vasishtha's language this is described as the "indweller in the sheaths," called the *Sharirin*, transmitting the truth to the *sharira*, the consciousness bound within the sheaths.

As is seen by the many entrees on the chart on the next page, encasings like the body and ego are naturally disposed to the covering power of *maya*. Each sheath, or *kosha* (see charts on pages 19 & 21) has certain powers and abilities that it calls upon to invest life with all the propensities that it contains. As is listed at the outset of the list on the facing page, the mind loves to engage in *sankalpa*, or mental projection, and this emanates according to the desires it is seeking to fulfill. The ego wants to enjoy this play, and the body will obey these higher mechanisms *(manas & ahamkara)* as if it is the possessor of these

Illumination of the Jiva — How the Sharirin Informs the Sharira
(From the Story of Arjuna)

Sharira (The body/mind mechanism)	Sharirin (Indwelling Spirit in the body)
Creates mental vibrations (vrittis) via sankalpa	← Cognizes Atmic Reality via nonfluctuation of mind
Obscures connection between Jiva and Atman	← Affirms the Jiva's complete identity with Atman
Tends ever towards disease, decay, and death	← Acknowledges the indestructibility of the Atman
Gets attached to action in order to secure fruits	← Reveals the way of detachment to works & fruits
Covets everything for its own personal pleasure	← Offers all actions and all thoughts to Brahman
Shuns loving God and seeks personal lordship	← Worships Ishvara and becomes friend of the jivas
Clings to limits, fosters habits, is short-sighted	← Seeks liberation, karmic neutrality, equal vision
Avoids self-effort and thrives on excesses	← Masters austerity and strives for renunciation
Settles itself into worldliness and convention	← Gets established in Yoga and attains Jnana

* *The destruction of sankalpas in the mind is called Asangha (nonattachment).*
* *The comprehension of the Jiva's complete identity with Brahman is called Atmajnana.*
* *Knowledge of the birthless, deathless nature of the Atman is called Ajativeda.*
* *The renunciation of the fruits of action is called Sannyasa.*
* *Knowledge springing from proper discrimination that results in the identity of the universe and the "I" with Brahman is called Brahmarpana.*
* *Giving up duality and knowing that there is one Ishvara is called Ishvararpana.*
* *The practice of spiritual disciplines ending in renunciation is called Paravairagyam.*
* *The attainment of spiritual emancipation is called Moksha.*
* *The effort to attain the nondual state is called Jnana and Yoga.*

"The indwelling Spirit informs the body of the immortal nature of the Spirit."   Lord Vasishtha

powers. Therefore, if the play of life is going to include anything deeper and more profound than just enjoying sense pleasures via material objects, the *sharirin* will have to insert itself into the picture. Hopefully, long before pleasure turns to its counterpart, pain, the *sharirin* will convince the body/mind mechanism of the efficacy of peace, silence, quietude, and balance, and their supremacy over the paltry feelings and sensations that the lower sheaths try to foist on life. If this great authority gains an audience of the five sheaths, the connection between the *jiva,* the embodied soul, with the *Atman,* the transcendental Soul, will be initiated. The result is a life of equanimity and economy.

And this is not all of the benefit that the *Atman/Sharirin* can confer. The ego, the intellect, the mind, the life force, and the body of ordinary beings, are not aware of the dangers of embodiment and the ultimately disasterous results of life lived in nature. If the *Atman* can convince limited awareness that by identifying with ones undying and undecaying long before the sobering reality of the six transformations (see chart on page 225) begin to wreak their influences on life, then the inner abilities lying dormant in the mind can be awakened and used as protections against all that.

Another way in which the limited human awareness identifying with the sheaths remains clueless and exposed to risks unnumbered lies in the field of action. The uninformed sheaths of the worldly being are naturally inclined towards activity, knowing little or nothing else than that. The noble and ascendent spiritual heights of the *Atman* get further veiled by obsession with work, particularly if such efforts are all bent towards gaining pleasures via various objects. Even intellectual gains pose a danger for the soul if the truths of *dharma* and spirituality are not present in the mind. The giving up of both wealth and objects, along with the desire for heaven and earth, is the secret way of the peaceful of mind, and the granter of Bliss Eternal (*Ananda*) as well. As Swami Vivekananda tells it, fruits and works must lead to knowledge, and knowledge to Truth. If, during the course of ones life, the mind does not naturally fall into a state of peace and contentment, then something has obviously been amiss. This is the pronouncement of Lord Vasishtha, whose teachings we are studying at present (page 638).

The problem of *asteya,* or covetousnesss, hangs within the sheaths as well. The *sharirin,* if consulted (as in meditation), will inform the stunted consciousness moving within the sheaths that all belongs to Higher Reality, and that all levels of existence will be healthier and flow evenly if nonattachment is practiced daily.

And in fact, if the truth be known, the only attachment the *sharirin* will advise for the *sharira* is attachment to God Itself. Otherwise, it all comes down to a matter of "fair faces and false hearts," as is said. The presence of objects is misleading; they may act as friends and supports, but are short-lived on so many levels. And is the *prana* (*pranamayakosha*) ones friend? Only so long as it flows unobstructed in a healthy fashion, but as soon as its energy becomes erratic due to various reasons and causes, then disease and imbalance set in. And the imbalanced mind is often the opposite of a friend, with its restlessness, slothfulness, and penchant for dualistic thinking. It betrays its owner, even for a few paltry pleasures, that are better left alone anyway. The similar betrayals and delusions of the intellect and the ego are also well known. The *sharirin* wants to convince all the other levels of existence represented by the weakened five sheaths that only *Ishvara/Ishvari* are the real, Divine Friends (*Dinabandhu*). The Blessed Lord and Mother of the Universe, as They are known, are the closest principles to the Self, or *Atman,* that can be accepted, and refuge in Them is the favorite pastime of the wise — also of the truly wealthy as well.

Finally, as this chart and its teachings wind down, there is the matter of excess as contrasted to abundance. The latter is that welcome store of subtle gifts and boons that the Divine Mother Herself grants to Her votaries, whereas excess and its weighty bulk is coveted by those who judge in terms of quantity rather than of quality. No wise person rejoices in wealth and its excesses, and in fact, the wise prefer the happiness that emptiness and nothingness grants upon the soul, as odd as that sounds to the worldly person. And that brings up the final point in this list of *dharmic* revelations.

The expression, "mundane human convention," has been used by contemporary seers and sages to indicate the problem with a kind of habitual preoccupation with what is inevitably of a surface and superficial nature. As the last main entry on the chart presently under study (page 638) reveals, human beings flock to this shallow level of existence, investing their entire lives into it, only to discover that it is completely lacking in any real and abiding substance. Actually, the ones who do discover this lack are the fortunate ones, for they may turn things around and dive into the depths of Eternal Life where the true Soul, the *Atman* — the *Sharirin* — has Its permanent abode. *Yoga* and *Jnana* abide there, as Lord Vasishtha affirms, and taking counsel of these mainstays of spiritual life will destroy the mind's tendency to gravitate towards the realms of "mundane human convention" forevermore.

Other bullet points appear on this chart as well, all laid out for the interested and enterprising student of authentic spiritual practice to take note of and implement in daily practice. But Lord Vasishtha is not through explaining the truths of existence and the traps of *maya* just yet, as the new chart on the facing page illustrates. His unique approach there brings in the adept seeker's advanced perspective on attaining levels of spirituality that are practically unknown to most beings.

In this particular story out of the epic scripture, *Yoga Vasishtha*, the *rishi*, Bhrngisha, exposes the secrets and results of a luminary who, though thoroughly illumined as to the nature of the Self and the world, nevertheless leads a perfectly balanced life while temporarily lodged in the embodied condition. The only names he applies to such a soul are appellations such as "The Great Actor," "The Great Enjoyer," and "The Great Renouncer." Such a being, though perfectly aware that the world is as empty as the mind of an idiot, and as unfulfilling as a hogplum — which is *"all pit and skin, with very little flesh — and that if that flesh is eaten, causes indigestion."* One who has renounced said world due to this sobering realization still continues to act, enjoy, and participate, in the most masterful of ways. Studying such a luminary gives observant humanity a chance to perceive the vast difference between a true renunciate and a foul pretender — that fraudulent one who is named "The Great Imposter," "The Fake Enjoyer," " and "The False Renouncer."

Indifferent, unattached, transcendent of even wisdom, acting for no other reason than to benefit others, always free of the individual sense of personality, comfortable around objects but not seeking comfort from them, alien to doubts and fears, equanimous of mind and spirit, this immeasurably masterful soul witnesses all phenomena occurring constantly in the many manifest worlds from a position of ultimate calm and blissful quietude. This is "The Great Actor."

Completely indifferent to loss and gain, happy with whatever comes though free of attachment to it, ever stable amidst the shifting mind in the always mutable *maya*, same-sighted in view regarding the potential or inevitable approach of disease, old age, and death, and the same to friends, enemies, and arbiters — this is "The Great Enjoyer."

Possessed of a single inner eye that sees through dualities at all levels of existence, harboring no doubts or desires, free of any undue adherence to objects, flow of energy or its lack, and concepts of the mind, and ever-free of actions and the various types of thoughts that cause them — this is who is called "The Great Renouncer." The chart on the facing page also describes the dynamics of those who fake or feign these insuperable qualities of advanced spiritual life and realization.

Maintaining quiescence of mind in the midst of life in the world is the final word on the attainment of realization on earth. To put it in the highest of nondual terminology and thinking, the outright perfection innate in the Soul, *Atman/Buddha* Nature, must find a pathway outwards into life and mind before any real sense of oneness can even be spoken of.

The following chart takes up the teaching of authentic perfection as compared to what many being assume to be so. This is an ancient offering from the brilliant mind of Lord Kapila, the Father of the *Sankhya* philosophy. The most interesting facet of this teaching strikes us right off the top in his comparison between the Eight Great Accomplishments and the Eight Occult Powers. To simplify this, the former are all involved with the removal of suffering via spiritual practices, and the latter are taken up with personal power and individual ego. This side by side comparison ought to act as a welcome confirmation for beings who seek and see God/*Brahman* as being beyond sensation and phenomena, and a sobering wake-up call for all those who are still involving themselves with forces that both harm other creatures, and wreak havoc on nature and the world. To make it easy of comprehension, in story form, the Great Master has related the tale of the boy who was given a red toy to keep him happy. He grew so attached to this toy that whenever anyone tried to take it away, he threw a tantrum. The implication is that until mankind gives up the red toys of this world — sense objects, money, lands, powers, and the like, he will never reach higher than experiences in matter accompanied inexorably by their various sufferings and disappointments.

The Great Actor, The Great Enjoyer, and the Great Renouncer

Maintaining Quiescence of Mind while Embodied
(From the Story of Bhrngisha)

The Great Actor	The Great Imposter
Indifferent to the fruits of action	Seeks the fruits of action
Free of attachment to pleasure and pain	Covets pleasure, shuns pain
Beyond dharma and adharma	Is adharmic or pretends dharma
Performs action free of desire	All its actions are attended by desire
Free from ideas of "I, me, and mine"	Is possessed of ownership and agency
Does not identify with objects	Fixates on externals as perceived with the senses
Free of fear and despondency in actions	Acts out of fear and regrets the results
Is witness of all phenomena	Is always egotistically involved
Possessed of equal vision	Has a scattered, unfocused mind

The Great Enjoyer	The Fake Enjoyer
Free of anger in possession/nonpossession	Easily angered by loss and gain
Enjoys fully without attachment	Enjoys only via attachment
Always steady amidst transitory things/conditions	Unstable in relativity
Same-sighted in death, dotage, and adversity	Negatively affected by death, adversity, etc.
Associates with virtuous/vicious free of judgement	Finds fault everywhere

The Great Renouncer	The False Renouncer
Abandons all ideas and concepts of duality	Revels in multiplicity and overlooks nonduality
Harbors no doubts or desires that are harmful	Harbors doubts and desires
Does not cling to objects/concepts	Attaches easily and longingly to objects
Is unattached to thoughts and actions	Thinks and acts habitually

Bhrngisha: "How can I live in this decaying body and still maintain quiescence of mind?"
Parameshvara Shiva: "If, after destroying doubts, you then cling to Truth, you will become the Great Actor, the Great Enjoyer, and the Great Renouncer."

The True Meaning of Siddhi — Perfection

The Eight Great Accomplishments   Opposed to   The Eight Occult Powers

The Eight Great Accomplishments

The Three Primary Siddhis — Removal of the Three Types of Suffering

1) Adhyatmika — Intrapersonal Suffering

2) Adhibhautika — External Suffering

3) Adhidaivika — Cosmic Suffering

The Five Secondary Siddhis

4) Dharma — Pursuing a Spiritual Path

5) Vidya-shastra — Knowledge of Scripture

6) Svadhyaya — Concentration / Study

7) Sadhu-satsanga — Gaining guru, disciples, friends, compatriots

8) Shuddhi — Achieve Self-purification
   Bhuta-shuddhi — Purity of Location
   Kriya-shuddhi — Purity of Action
   Chit-shuddhi — Purity of Mind

Teachings on Trividham Duhkham
(The Three Kinds of Suffering)

1) Adhyatmika — Caused by mind
a) Mental Suffering - cured internally:

Suffering	Cure
Passion	Control
Anger	Compassion
Attachment	Self-analysis
Fear	Evolutes / Origins
Jealousy	Generosity
Depression	Nonattachment

b) Physical Suffering - cured by discriminative wisdom, practical regimens, and forbearance

2) Adhibhautika — Caused by other beings cured by Self-abidance and perseverance

3) Adhidaivika — Caused by natural forces cured by transcendence via spiritual practices

The Eight Occult Powers

(Asta-bala Siddhis — Utilization of Psychic Prana for Personal Gain

1) Anima — Power of Invisibility
   Ex: undetectability, nonresponsibility

2) Laghima — Power of Weightlessness
   Ex. levitation, obsession with thinness

3) Vyapti — Power of All-expansiveness
   Ex. clairvoyance, invasiveness / meddling

4) Prakamya — Power to Fulfill Desires
   Ex. impression, conjuring out of thin air

5) Mahima — Power of Glorification
   Ex. sensation-mongering, beautification

6) Ishitva — Power of Domination
   Ex. control, manipulation, lust for power

7) Vashitva — Power of Attraction
   Ex. allurement for selfish motive

8) Kama-vasayita — Power of Enjoyment
   Ex. enjoyment of wealth, land, desires, etc.

The Six Treasures of Godhead

Sri — Opulence / Infinity

Bala — Glory / Power

Aishvarya — Strength / Lordship

Tejas — Splendor / Radiance

Vijnana — Wisdom / Truth

Tyaga — Renunciation / Transcendence

"A true lover does not seek anything from God except for pure love. He does not seek miracles and occult powers. To such a one, the eight occult powers are like crow-droppings by the side of the road."
Sri Ramakrishna

"You will not succeed in realizing God if you possess even one of the eight occult powers." Sri Krishna

The Eight Great Accomplishments are given a full treatment on page 309, for those who want to review their wondrous qualities. As for the *Asta-Bala Siddhis*, they are manifesting everywhere and all over this world, as well as in the heavenly realms. Here on earth they take up rather insidious forms. Living beings see their expressions and think them to be highly desirable, even the aim of life. Even after they have settled in and had their violent effects, beings still covet them and use them as means to enjoy and possess, all in an unconscious or semi-conscious way.

An instance of this occurs in the case of *ishitva*, the power of domination. War is decried by most beings, but it is allowed to go forth despite the suffering and death it causes. Those in power, and even those watching those in power, feel safe and secure if the cruel muscle of military might is flexed against their fellow man. Courting *ishitva* fans the flames of the lust for power, which even beyond wealth and pleasures, is a craving and enjoyment all its own, causing its own addictions. That is why three other of these *siddhis* go hand in hand with *ishitva*, namely, *kama-vasayita, prakamya,* and *mahima* — the power to enjoy, the power to satisfy desires, and the power of glorification. What a *mayic* web these four make together, causing even knowledgeable souls to fall under their hypnotization and perform all manner of unthought and unseemly acts. Lord Kapila calls these "random acts of stupefaction," both seemingly good, and obviously evil.

The other four *siddhis* can also be generally grouped together. They are of a more *pranic*, or psychic nature, and thus are attracting to those who seek after phenomenal happenings and other-worldly occurrences, always falling short of the true goal of Self-Realization, or Enlightenment. These are *anima, laghima, vyapti,* and *vashitva* — the ability of non-detection, the feat of weightlessness, the power of stealthily seeing into the affairs of other beings, and the ability to attract others to oneself. These powers are hardly worth the energy that it takes to attain them, and once they arrive, often muddle and confuse life and mind by their presence and possession. Certainly, all eight of the psychic powers fall far below the worthy aims of a sincere spiritual aspirant, and are actually eschewed by teachers and luminaries who have an eye out for the highest good of living beings.

Of important comparison, as well, is the list at the lower right of the chart presently under study. So much is made of the psychic powers by small-minded beings, but little mention or attention is paid to the Six Treasure of the Godhead. Viewing such a collection leaves no doubt in the human mind as to both the supremacy of the Divine Being, called God with Form, as well as Its gracious nature, filled with holy attributes.

Finally, at the bottom left of the chart, falls Lord Kapila's rendering of the Three Types of Suffering — a profound study in and of itself. The benefit of noting the suffering caused by ones own mind, suffering caused by other beings, and suffering caused by nature, is one of increasing clarity, as the stultified human mind can finally put into place the right and proper reasons why all manner of happenings and effects are occurring to people, planets, and realms.

Among the list of mind-caused sufferings are to be found the human passions that are responsible for the sufferings of entire races, as well as nations, families, and individuals, but more importantly, are seen the solutions for the same, equipping the sincere spiritual aspirant with all that he or she needs to purify the mind and reach higher levels of awareness straight away. Mankind's old nemesis called "fear," for instance, is done away with ingeniously by looking into (meditating upon) the origins *(utpatti)* of all the various principles of existence, for it is in these properties that many *karmas* lurk, and are lodged, coming forth later to spoil life due to the failure of doing away with them in a timely manner. Another huge problem of the day, depression, is put into its place by the simple mental act of nonattachment — which is a far better solution than either giving up, taking a pill, or consuming intoxicants. Thus, taking a qualified look at the nature of suffering is most practical. Most all of the real answers to questions, and solutions to problems, are simple and obvious, and easy to take up for the improvement of ones health, mind, mood, and spirit (see chart on page 423).

The view in India around the attainment of perfection, or better put, the return of the sojourning soul to its innate perfection, takes up two distinct but ultimate kinds of supremacy. These two states, or conditions of conscious Awareness, are more like mutually inclusive and complementary strata of realization, only seemingly different due to the type of luminary that mans them as stations. As the next chart on page 644 reveals, these two are known as *Abhava Yoga* and *Mahayoga* by the seers. A simple minus or plus can be used to explain them in brief, *Abhava* being focused upon static emptiness as unending peace and equanimity, and *Mahayoga* partaking of all modes and moods through which divine expression can be experienced.

Although there are souls whose penchant and preference "zeroes" in on one or the other of these principles of Awareness, it is also known that there are superlative adepts that can shift back and forth between them. Sri Ramakrishna is the best example of this ultimate combining of highest principles. He did it both in religion and in personal experience. As He proved in his life and practice, for direct nondual experience there is nothing as powerful as *Abhava Yoga,* for whereas it perceives God with form, it does so in order to move beyond it and encounter Formless Reality.

This supreme *Yoga* virtually posits itself in ultimate voidness, being fully comfortable There without any supports. Ironically, its Presence there both supports and proves the existence of Essence in voidness, thus leading to the direct experience of nondual Reality for the intrepid spiritual wayfarer who will settle for nothing less. Negation of the outer world is shown up by *Abhava* to be both a healthy move on the part of the freedom-seeking soul, and also a proof of the substanceless of all forms, at all levels. Fittingly, it is also a maturer of consummate souls, for once having had the full drought of the elixir of Formless Awareness, such a superlative being can return into form, at any and all of its fine levels — even its gross ones — to partake of a variety of reasons to show up there, not the least being to assist other souls in reaching such inner heights.

In this way, *Abhava* both explains and fulfills *Mahayoga's* multifaceted Reality of all-abiding, all-pervading Existence. The science of the Self is precious to *Mahayoga*. It is an authentic and fully defined spiritual art form whose many pathways are time-tested and ultimately fulfilling. Despite its seeming dichotomy and assumed limitation, blissful communion with Divine Reality is only possible when a semblance of twoness is maintained, and *Mahayoga* allows the soul to keep this transcendental separation as an utmost blessing in the infinite ocean of spiritual experience. This also provides knowers of *Brahman* of the presence of "Formless Form" as well, a great secret among the lovers of the *Mahashakti,* the Divine Mother of all the Worlds.

A brief look into the realms of *Mahayoga* shows it up to be the singular storehouse of excellences untold. Overwhelmingly full, it is what makes the state of *Abhava* appealing to some souls, those who love peaceful simplicity and inaction above all else. A tour around this chart (facing page) gives rise to the full expression of the richness of *Yoga* at its best. If the Four Yogas that Swami Vivekananda brought forward again in this day and time are the *"new religion of the age,"* then *Mahayoga* must be the best expression of their synthesis and a good coverall term for them.

Narada's Eight Aids of Bhakti *Yoga* (charts on pages 475/476), Sri Ram's Nine Limbs of Bhakti (chart on page 497), the Four Treasures of *Vedanta* (chart on page 65), and the Eight Limbs of *Patanjala* (chart on page 69) have all found a place on this chart under the *Mahayoga* heading. The grand idea and secret teaching is that the collected facets of *Mahayoga* are all directing the consummate spiritual aspirant towards that singular condition and realization of nonduality that *Abhava Yoga* is in its essence. The bottom quarter of the chart under study outlines this briefly and simply, and connects both seeker and philosophy with *Kundalini Shakti,* who guides and directs all authentic spiritual growth.

First of all, some sincere aspiration in the form of yearning must be present. This occurs at the heart level. The more ready and available this current of love is, the easier and quicker will be the steps to illumination that follow. When this devotion is present, and easy to awaken, it indicates the presence of *samskaras* from past lives in the seeker, thus past spiritual practices as well. The second step proceeds with the mind's deep longing to know God. In this way, the secret path of *Mahayoga* and *Abhava* combine to use *bhakti* in conjunction with *jnana* for the unique devotee's immediate inward ascent. Whatever purification is needed is not hard or forced, here, but supremely natural, being under the auspice of *Kundalini Shakti.* She brings the attentions of a dedicated wisdom teacher to bear swiftly at this juncture as well, so that any unanswered questions and necessary guidance are both forthcoming in a timely fashion. Deeper and penetrating practice combined with realization is the welcome result. Under the releasing press of this strong force of *Shakti* power, any veils still standing in front of the vision of the *Atman* dissolve away quickly. In less than a thrice the Divine Mother reveals to Her votary the entire cosmic plan, a vision that separates the soul from its various dealings with nature. This is *kaivalya,* also called

Kundalini Yoga as Mahayoga

⇀ SPIRITUAL AWAKENING VIA THE SYNTHESIS OF YOGA ↽

*"Shaktism and Shaivism, with Sankhya as cosmological basis,
Yoga as practice, and Vedanta as nondual philosophy, is Mahayoga."*

THE TWO MAIN DIVISIONS OF YOGA

ABHAVA YOGA	MAHAYOGA
Perception of Reality with Form	Perception of Reality as One's Self
Negation of the Outer World	Knowing Reality In & Beyond Form
Perception of God as Voidness	Blissful Communion with God

"When Bhakti Yoga is combined, in practice, with Jnana Yoga and Raja Yoga, the result is the flowering of Brahmajnana — unified wisdom based in Nonduality. Salvation can be gotten from Bhakti, even Karma, but Liberation is not possible without Brahmajnana." **Babaji Bob Kindler**

Bhakti According to Narada

Smaranam — Remembrance
Shravanam — Hearing of God
Archanam — External Worship
Kirtanam — Chanting God's Names
Vandanam — Praising God
Sevanam — Serving God in All
Sundaram — Beholding God's Beauty
Sharanam — Taking Refuge in God

Sri Ram's Nine Limbs of Bhakti

Association with the Holy
Reciting Accounts About God
Singing God's Glories
Hearing Teachings About Reality
Devoted Service of the Teacher
Worship, Purity, Sense Control
Repetition of the Mantra
Selfless Service with Nonattachment
Seeking the Nature of Reality

Jnana Yoga — The Four Treasures

Viveka — Discriminating the Real and Unreal
Vairagya — Detachment from the Unreal
Shatsampatti — The Six Jewels
*(inner peace, self-control, contentedness,
forbearance, concentration, faith)*
Mumukshutvam — Desire for Freedom

Raja Yoga Limbs of Patanjali

Yamas (5)	Pratyahara
Niyamas (5)	Dharana
Asana	Dhyana
Pranayama	Samadhi

"Freedom is not gained via Karma Yoga, which is best as a means for purification."

Process of Mahayoga Yoga and Kundalini Awakening

1) A sincere love of God awakens in the heart due to yearning based on positive samskaras
2) The desire to know God leads to practice and purification of both mind and senses
3) The guru appears with revealed scriptural wisdom and personal spiritual experience
4) Via instruction, the seeker commits to the spiritual path and practices Dharma
5) Via intensification of practice, the seeker perceives Atman and attains Self-knowledge
6) Brahmajnana reveals cosmic ignorance and brings about Moksha / Mukti / Kaivalya

mukti or *moksha*. It has other precious names in other *darshanas* and religious traditions.

The mention of forthcoming internal progression and religious tradition fits perfectly into what the Tibetan Buddhists know as the *Mahamudra,* or "Great Seal." Among well-known and reliable spiritual and philosophical teachings and methods, it takes its place among the best, with a supremely natural way of transmitting the highest truth to qualified aspirants. One of its best attributes is the "mind only" stance it takes in its first of three impactful teaching presentations. It declares that the entire universe exists in the mind. This is not a declaration of concession, or just a friendly accompaniment meant to fit comfortably alongside of evolutionist or creationist perspectives and theories. The *Mahamudra* aims to start the aspirant off on his or her quest of higher spirituality knowing with a certainty that mind is the producer of all phenomena. For one thing — and this is merely on the physical level — it hosts the five senses via which all is heard, felt, seen, tasted, and smelled. Secondly, when mind turns off in deep sleep, or shuts down completely at the time of death, the universes in time and space all dissolve into it. Finally, and unaccountably for intellectual beings devoid of higher wisdom, mind supports and sports all the many divine expressions of peace and bliss that inexplicably suggest and even impress themselves upon its interior firmament.

And so, the first of the key points of *Mahamudra* reveals Mind — not nature, nor creator, nor God — to be the presenter of name and form in time and space to the many hosts of beings who people it, and goes on to state that true Mind is itself the realm of pure radiance, untouched, as Sri Ramakrishna has declared, by any thought, word, or deed that these hosts think, utter, or acuate.

And what does this superlative teaching say about practice? It is all about natural meditation upon luminosity of the Mind after the view, the first point, has been rightly and properly understood. The great souls say that *"the atmosphere is always pure and blissful there,"* so that when the soul comes upon this ground of Existence it must encounter it free of the thought of effort and doer-ship. There is nothing to accomplish "there;" one must only perceive the open space beyond religion, what the seers of India have called the *"nectar of naturalness"* for ages upon ages.

And the third point of *Mahamudra* comes forth in this light, informing the soul of how to act in the direct and spontaneous brilliance of this disarming truth-teaching. Mere exposure to this Light causes all virtues to grow and expand, and any shortcomings to evaporate on the spot — all free of the necessity to implement corrections or remedies. This is Light, encountering Light, in Light.

The final conclusion, or rapt summation that the enlightened mind arrives at here is the result of reducing these three points — the View, the Practice, and Action — into a single composite in Consciousness. The soul comes to know that there never was any *samsara* — any doubt, fear, delusion, suffering — to renounce or rise above, and there is not any *nirvana* — any special state of enlightenment — to gain. All that there is, or ever will be, or ever was, simply amounts to consciously living in the eternal and all-pervasive Light of ones own perfect nature.

The "Great Seal" is a sublime donning of ultimate Truth upon all who take it up and realize it. When this stamp of approval of ones own Awareness is set upon the consciousness of the embodied being, the twin truths of emptiness and luminosity are conferred, simultaneously and forever. This means that no misunderstanding about the nature of objects, forms, worlds, and bodies can ever mislead the soul again. All potential problems lying in the mental body, previously needing attention, are now dealt with in classic fashion, described as *"when focusing occurs, do so free of any objectives; when stabilization is needed, attain that devoid of any and all distraction; when consciousness shifts, allow that to occur without any grasping; when manifestations appear, perceive them all as the radiance of the mind, and when liberation comes, allow it to do so naturally."* According to *Mahamadra,* the whole matter is to *"experience the radiance of pure mind directly and effortlessly."*

From the subtle flavors evinced by the *Mahamudra* teaching, so sublime and superlative, one might be tempted to think that *Buddhism* is all high-mindedness, and to such an extent that it verily lives in an atmosphere that is thereby unreachable and impractical for most beings, especially given the vagaries and vicissitudes of the world and the limited abilities and capacities of the beings occupying it. But even reputable, pure schools, like Zen *Buddhism,* evince a very practical approach for novices and beginners, and suggest straightforward methods that help a seeker deal with all that the world and the human mind constantly throws in the way of spiritual advancement.

Mahamudra — The Great Seal

"For all practitioners of dharma, this teaching is a priceless gem."

*"The Mahamudra teaching was revealed to the Mahasiddha, Tilopa,
by the venerable Bodhisattva, Samantabhadra,
and was then transmitted to Naropa, Marpa, and Milarepa,
in sacred lineage succession, through which it reached Tibet."*

"All manifestation, the Universe itself, is contained in the mind, and the true nature of mind is the realm of illumination, shining with radiance that can neither be conceived or touched. These are the key points of The View."

There is no Nirvana to attain beyond...

"Errant thoughts, the antithesis of The View, are liberated in the Dharmakaya. Awareness, the Illumination, is always blissful there. Meditate in a manner of nondoing, and noneffort. These are the key points of The Practice."

"In action of naturalness, the ten virtues spontaneously grow, and the ten vices are thus purified. By corrections or remedies, the illuminating Void is never disturbed in any way. These are the key points of Action."

"Reduce inwardly these three points to one."

...there is no Samsara here to renounce.

The Three Principles of the Central Practice of Mahamudra

a) Basis — All phenomena bear the "seal" of combined emptiness and luminosity
b) Path — Direct, effortless experience of the nature of pure mind
   1) when focusing occurs, focus without objective
   2) when stabilizing occurs, stabilize without distraction
   3) when shifting occurs, shift without grasping
   4) when manifestations occur, experience them as reality
   5) when liberation occurs, allow it to occur naturally

c) Result — Freedom from liberation and the agent of liberation
   from intellection and conceptualization
   from false identities
   from hope and fear

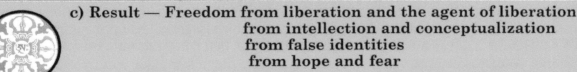

The chart on the facing page gives helpful cautionary teachings for aspirants who are particular about starting off the spiritual path and quest on the right and proper footing. For, it is certainly one of the great stumbling blocks of this day and age that there is as much about religion today that condemns it as recommends it. The seeker must be in possession of that singular quality of *viveka,* spiritual discrimination, in order to escape the many pretend pathways and clever but fraudulent fools that pose as authentics within the ocean of choice and possibility. The one word in *Zen* that captures this entire area of threat to ones burgeoning spiritual life and practice is *Mayoi.*

So that no veil is left in place, and no barrier left unbridged, the *Zen* masters transmit teachings for unlearned and inexperienced souls who must be protected from the ravaging wolves of fractious paths and spurious teachers so long as their naivete is still present. Authentic teachers, like traditional *roshis,* will protect young aspirants by warning them in advance of some of the pitfalls they might encounter along the great but potentially disconcerting way.

To begin, they show the vast differences in the Five Types of *Zen.* Some immature followers may get sidetracked right at the outset by the attractions of *Bonpo Zen.* These beings somehow have come to believe that focusing on the body and its health is paramount. Similarities exist in the Indian practice of *hatha yoga* as well, and in "left-handed" *tantric* pursuits as well, where aspirants get pulled into physical practices and occultism that have little or nothing to do with Enlightenment — which is the real if not only purpose for entering any spiritual path and practice. Another common thing to see at the elementary level of early practice is the tendency to practice many religions, all at the surface level. The followers of this short-sighted and short-lived way take many *gurus* and many of *mantras,* never getting to the root of any one of them in any given lifetime. In Zen this is called *Gedo Zen,* and is pointed out as being inappropriate for beginning aspirants. On the other hand, *Shojo Zen, Daijo Zen,* and *Saijojo Zen* are all authentic ways of proceeding, and can be seen as steps along an ascending stairway of practice leading to Enlightenment.

Apart from these Five Types of Zen, which are gradated, the seeker has to watch out for real threats to his or her young, spiritual shoot of a practice. There are six of these worthy of mention, and they can be divided into three and three in terms of commonality.

Zembyo, Makyo, and *Bonno* are particularly odious to those who have reached, or would reach, the sweet air and congenial atmospheres of *Satori.* Of these three, *Zembyo* is very common among Zen practitioners of the day, especially those who live in the West. It is a sickness that is described as "a mass of emotions" wherein the soul exposed to lustral disciplines at the outset of the path and practice gets beset by all the mind's passions, sentiments, dramas, excitements, and other mental weaknesses. It is practically impossible to make any headway, even towards basic peace of mind, as long as this mass of callow complexes, springing from past *karmas,* stand in the way.

Under the influences of *Bonno,* wherein impressions based in worldliness rather than in sentimentality arise, the effect is more concrete. The *karmas* here are founded in actions performed in a previous existence that formed impressions of various dualities in the mind, all based in the ego's belief that such actions and their results were real. Of course, this false view was never corrected in the human ego/mind complex of the past; it never came to know that it was taking in unreal experiences in a flow of unreal phenomena. Thus, it went to its demise under the impression that all of life — those dualities like pleasure and pain, virtuous acts and vicious acts, loss and gain, and a host of other merely empty occurrences — had actually happened to it. But nothing happens to Buddha Nature, *Bussho.* As Sri Krishna states in the *Gita, "All acts take place in nature, not in the Atman."* And in fact, the practitioner has come to *Zen* in order to undo such deeply-seated misfeasances of the human thinking process. Ironically, it might fail that objective due to the very presence of the worldly thoughts and acts it is trying to escape.

Makyo Zen is best avoided, for certain, for as history has shown, and partly due to a false view of the world again, circumstances and happenings in life have a harsh effect on the human mind. If the practitioner entering spiritual life still thinks about the world, i.e., has not renounced it prior to taking on its chosen way and spiritual ideal, the spectre of its often horrible visage will haunt the mind and spoil spiritual progress. Here, it is not so much the presence of dualities that deter, but rather the negative side of life in the world. Whereas pleasures attract, suffering repels. Repulsion, to a sensitive soul, is often

Zen Principles & Distractions
Mayoi - Avoiding Errors on the Dharmic Pathway

"The Goal of Zen is Bussho, consciously living in one's Imminent Nature, which is devoid of mass, beyond individuality and personality, and outside the realm of imagination — synonymous with Shunyata."

Five Types of Zen

Bonpo Zen - Unenlightened person practicing Zen for bodily & mental health
Gedo Zen - "Outside Way," mixing Zen with teachings of other traditions
Shojo Zen - "Small Vehicle," mainly seeks discontinuation of rebirth in cycles
Daijo Zen - "Great Vehicle," observes the unity of all things, & Zen in everyday life
Saijojo Zen - "Supreme Vehicle," where way, path, and goal are all fused in one

Buji Zen - A light and immature attitude towards the teachings wherein practitioners think that since they are already Buddha nature, they do not have to do practice or seek enlightenment.

Yako Zen - "Wild Fox Zen," inflicting those who pretend to be enlightened but really only mouth the teachings, having no deep or true realization of the dharma whatsoever.

Hasan - Interruption of Zen practice by an enlightenment experience — celebrated but not stressed — that keeps the aspirant from gaining many more and higher profound experiences.

Bussho - Gedatsu - Ku - Shunya - Satori

Goseki - "Trace of Enlightenment," sticking to those practitioners who cling to their initial insight experiences instead of living as if oblivious to their own enlightenment — in a natural way.

Zembyo - "Zen sickness," which make up the host of distracting thoughts, feelings, emotions, sensations, appearances and broodings that arise during the course of a student's practice of Zen.

Makyo - "Diabolical phenomena," like the negative circumstances of the ordinary world, which the practitioner should not entertain in the mind, letting them turn into mental hallucinations.

Bonno - Worldliness, sensuality, passions, longings, suffering, and misery, all rising from a false view of the world.

"The sun shines by day, and the moon by night, the Warrior is resplendent in armor and the Brahman radiant in meditation. But Buddha, the Awakened One, illumines both day and night by the splendor of His wisdom." Dhammapada

Katto - "Thicket of creeping vines" meaning falling victim to hearing too many words while failing to take the essence from them.

harder to deal with than giving up the paltry sensations of the body and senses.

The other three types of Zen warned about by luminaries are *Hassan, Goseki,* and *Katto.* If the novitiate is able to stay clear of the types of dangerous routes and detours that have just been explored, then advancement can be made. But the human ego is still present, and somewhat still unrefined at that. Under the influence of *Hassan,* when successes in practices like service and meditation are gained, the ego steps in to claim the credit, seeking approval from all quarters around it. *"Celebrated but not stressed"* is what the authentic teachers will advise to the advancing student at this juncture, for these realized beings know how many wondrous spiritual attainments are in store for the sincere practitioner, and stopping to gloat over just one incident, no matter how glorious it may be deemed to be by the practitioner's ego, will cause a setback that could stymie future progress substantially.

Goseki is very similar to *Hassan,* the main difference being that practitioners laboring in its limiting atmosphere will not let go of enlightenment experiences, and secretly cling to them within. When these attachments begin to show themselves in the intermediate practitioner's spiritual life, it becomes noticed by others as the ego's preoccupation with itself. The description here, very fitting, is that a few spiritual experiences "stick" to the seeker, and that he or she "stinks" of them as a result. In *Hassan,* then, a single authentic experience arrives and the ego wants to celebrate it. In *Goseki,* several of these experiences are attained and instead of using them as "signposts," the ego hides them away and holds on to them for its own individual and selfish enjoyment.

Finally, there is the famous *Katto Zen,* or "thicket of creeping vines." This obstacle has to do with the seeker's limited capacity, his or her inability to take in a voluminous amount of wisdom and extract the essence from it. The mind of such beings get hung up on the surface of words, failing to penetrate into their inner meaning. Sometimes this can be the fault of teachers if they neglect to transmit the wisdom of the subtlety of words. The *Tantric* chart back on page 595 explains this deep mystery — a secret that millions of beings know nothing about, particularly in Western cultures.

The problem of the "thicket of creeping vines" really has little to do with mass and volume, then; it has to do with quality of content. If beings would seek out internal essence instead of external spectacle, their powers of digestion concerning transformative wisdom teachings emanating from the *guru,* or *roshi,* would increase manyfold. If practitioners found out that immense power exists within words and letters in the form of particles of wisdom, similar to but far more refined than the power in atoms that make up objects, there would be delight instead of destruction, transformation instead of transgression.

And in religion there would come a return to sensitivity and a turning away from narrowness and hypocrisy. Then, the grossness of physical matter, the precariousness of the individual condition, the crassness of the unripe human personality, and the futile wanderings of the uncontrolled and undirected imagination, would disappear — just as the quote at the top of the chart presently under study indicates. The incomparably superior position of *shunyata* would dawn on human awareness, and would soon replace the stodgy and dense habitual thinking habits of the worldly mind. The mind's fresh and newly found ability to take in copious amounts of beneficial *dharma* teachings would lead it easily and swiftly back to its original "Buddha Nature," or *Bussho* in *Zen,* and the "thicket of creeping vines" would whither under the brilliant sunlight of the clear and radiant Truth.

The refined teachings of *Zen Buddhism* and the nondual path of *Advaita Vedanta* have sometimes been placed side by side with one another for easy comparison and rapt contemplation, and in exceedingly favorable light, as well. The chart being introduced next holds some precious correlations for both the student and the practitioner of Indian philosophical systems, maturing on earth over phases of time. In his book, *Living* Buddha *Zen,* the author Lex Hixon (Jikai) — himself an adept practitioner of several of the world's religious traditions — cites the historical movement of *Buddhism* out of India to its various homes across the planet, and into many countries, including *Japan.* With all of this behind us, and ever-present within us as well, it only remains to perceive what both *Advaita Vedanta* and Zen *Buddhism* know and reflect — which is the universality of all religious traditions.

The chart on the facing page is posted for the interested student of world philosophy and the avid supporter of interreligious faith to peruse and make use of. It will act as an awakener for the former, and an allay for the latter. So many of the connections shown here are obvious, but this does not render them any less useful for the purpose of singling out the similarities between two religious traditions, and makes

Zen Buddhist & Advaita Vedanta Correlations

Zen Buddhism

Bussho — Buddha Nature ----------------------------

Dai-anjin — The Great Peace of Mind ------------------

Dai-gedatsu — The Great Liberation/Nirvana --------

Hannya — Inner Wisdom/Prajna ---------------------

Ken-shu-shi — Uniqueness of all things/Shunyata ---

Bonpu Zen — Practice of Zen for health/longevity --

Susoku-khan — Watching the breath in four ways ---

Fugyo-ni-gyo — Spontaneous doing by not doing ---

Fusho — Unborn, Inactive, Timeless ------------------

Hakushi — Mind free of ideas, images,concepts etc. -

Hasan — Interrupted practice due to sp. experience --

Inga — The fruits of cause and effect ------------------

Isshi-injo — Training under one preceptor ------------

Ishin-denshin — Transmission from roshi to disciple

Jisho-shojo-shin — Inner perfection --------------------

Bonpo-no joshiki — Everyman's consciousness ------

Kan-shiketsu —Attachment to worlds (dry shit-stick)

Mosshoseki — Enlightenment with no traces (bird) --

Samu — Everyday work in the monastery -------------

Akushu-ku — Misunderstanding of emptiness ------

Heikan — Transcend distraction/gain concentration --

Ittai — Oneness of all things/one body ----------------

Tariki-Jiriki — Self effort as contrasted to Grace ----

Zadan — Destruction of dualistic world-view -------

Daishi/Daigotettei — Great death/Great rebirth -----

Fukatoku — The insubstantial nature of phenomena -

Zembyo — Zen sickness, describing the feelings, emotions, sensations that arise in Zen practice ----

Advaita Vedanta

Atman — Indivisible Self

Shanti — Peace, Peace, Peace

Moksha — Eternal Freedom/Nirvikalpa

Jnana — Inner Wisdom/Vidya

Alambana — All objects utilized for meditation

Hatha Yoga — Practice of yoga for health/longevity

Pranayama — Breathing exercises to purify the nadis

Niskama Karma — Selfless action out of Oneness

Ajativada — Path of those free of birth and death

Chit-shuddhi — Pure mind qualified for samadhi

Unmadana — Attachment to subtle bliss

Karma — Cause and Effect

Ishta-nistha — Devotion to one ideal

Guru-parampara — Succession of wisdom lineage

Svarupa — Essence of Consciousness within

Vyavaharika — Worldly consciousness & convention

Ajnani — One deluded by the world of name & form

Sahaja Samadhi — Natural state of enlightenment

Seva — Serving the guru, the ashram, the sangha

Neti-Neti — Proper discrimination to find out Reality

Pratyahara/Dharana — Control and concentration

Advaita — Intrinsic unity

Sadhana-Sharanagata — Self-effort, Self-surrender

Advaita-dhyan — Focus on Reality, not relativity

Ahamkara-vinashana — Destruction of ego

Maya — Inexplicable power of illusion/projection

Vasana-samskara — Rising of desires and mental impressions from karmic accrual in past lives

The Real Meaning of Objects

"Most beings, beholding physical objects such as trees, animals, planets, etc., assume them to be real, or actual. However, modern science has uncovered the atomic particle tree. Philosophy teaches about the illusory tree, its display being only an appearance. The luminaries, going deeper, speak of the Atman tree, or Buddha nature tree. Thus, there are three levels to existence: the external, the internal, and the absolute. Knowing about this triple subdivision, along with the nature of each, the human mind espies the truth about all manifestation and swiftly frees itself from bondage to objects." Babaji Bob Kindler

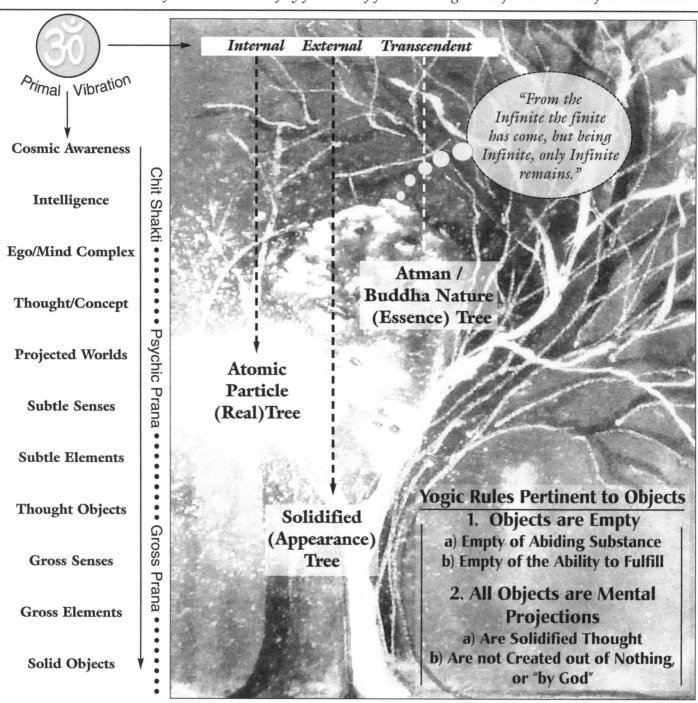

Primal Vibration

Cosmic Awareness

Intelligence

Ego/Mind Complex

Thought/Concept

Projected Worlds

Subtle Senses

Subtle Elements

Thought Objects

Gross Senses

Gross Elements

Solid Objects

Chit Shakti • • • • • Psychic Prana • • • • • Gross Prana • • • • •

Internal   External   Transcendent

"From the Infinite the finite has come, but being Infinite, only Infinite remains."

Atman / Buddha Nature (Essence) Tree

Atomic Particle (Real) Tree

Solidified (Appearance) Tree

Yogic Rules Pertinent to Objects

1. Objects are Empty
a) Empty of Abiding Substance
b) Empty of the Ability to Fulfill

2. All Objects are Mental Projections
a) Are Solidified Thought
b) Are not Created out of Nothing, or "by God"

"O mind, this projected world is only a faint reflection of Reality, consisting simply of earth, water, fire, air, and ether, arranging and rearranging with hypnotic beauty. By attempting to grasp reflected images we cheat ourselves of true experience. Turn instead to the original, and discover the Treasure of Delight." Ramprasad Sen

them even more helpful towards accenting the intrinsic oneness of Mother India's Wisdom, wherever She causes it to manifest and express itself — even over a span of some one-thousand, seven hundred years from Shakyamuni Buddha to Dogen Zenji in thirteenth century *Japan*, or over fifty-two generations of masters and disciples — twenty-eight in India, Twenty-two in China, and two in *Japan*.

About connections that are not so evident, the chart under inspection on page 651 draws them for the elucidation of the open-minded and the potential expansion of the narrow-minded. The identity of *Atman* and *Bussho*, and the transcendent Peace that radiates off of them, namely *Shanti* and *Dai-anjin*, simply mirror one another perfectly, whether the language being used to express them is *Sanskrit* or *Japan*ese. This selfsame Peace is what Jesus referred to as *"The Peace that Passeth all Understanding."* It is also what the Holy Mother, Sri Sarada Devi, referred to when She stated, *"You need Peace of Mind first and foremost; nothing can be attained without it."* What is to be "attained," so to speak, is nothing short of full Enlightenment. Whether indicated by the term, *Dai-gedatsu*, or by the freedom-fraught word, *Moksha*, the meaning is crystal clear. Another element utilized in arriving at that incomparable state is *Hannya/Jnana*, or discriminating spiritual Wisdom.

These first four couplets on the chart are examples of the innate oneness in spiritual pathways. The chart cites a host of these, helpful for the student and practitioner's ease of contemplation. The present author's manuscript, *White Crane, White Swan*, goes into these, and much more, in depth.

As a smooth segue into the common teachings of *Buddhism* and *Vedanta*, a crash course in the art of recognizing emptiness and its two main meanings is given in the next chart up for study on the facing page. Taking a tree for a fitting subject, a penetrating examination proffers up its revealing conclusions, i.e., that there are three levels to the tree's manifestation. First, the solid object tree, which has to be called empty due to the pretense of its appearance. In other words, when examined beyond its visual appearance it is seen to consist of a massive volume of tiny particles, belying its very existence. This is why many philosophers and their conclusions/philosophies have called it an illusion, or illusory by nature. In any case, this atomic particle tree is the real tree when compared to the appearance tree.

But its sense of being real is questionable due to the very fact of its emptiness, since it particles are changing so fast that it cannot be said to truly exist at the level it is being inspected. Therefore, and looking deeper, the seers who have examined matter and objects with their concentrated awareness have seen beyond both the outer tree and the inner tree to espy an "essence" tree that epitomizes the only true and acceptable reality. Thus, when the world of objects is perceived utilizing intelligent scrutiny, the three levels of existence — external, internal, and transcendent — get classified. As Swami Vivekananda wrote in one of his letters to a western disciple, about objects and Essence: *"Gold and silver have I none, but what I have I give to thee freely, and that is the knowledge of the goldness of gold, the silverness of silver, the manhood of man, the womanhood of woman...."* It is the Essence in all things, *Atman/Svarupa*, that gives them their inner and outer characteristics. But that Essence remains beyond them.

For a more *yogic* look at these same facts about what the five senses perceive all the time but fail to translate into Essence, the box at the lower right hand corner of the chart can be studied. When the *yogis* state, after deep meditation and due reflection, that objects are empty, they really mean they are empty in two ways: first, they are empty of abiding substance; and two, they are empty of the ability to fulfill human desires. A way of saying this is to point out that objects may have no abiding substance, but they do contain essence, as has just been related. On the experiential level, and though it may take some time, living beings will eventually come to find that objects lack the power to satisfy the soul, or that their vaunted ability to satisfy is short-lived. Other factors play into this conclusion. Objects can get lost, they can be stolen, they can become nonfunctional, useless, or get destroyed. The possesser of objects can become bored with them as well, and they can mount up and clutter daily existence. Further, they need caretaking, often consuming vast amounts of our time. Happy is the man who is free from objects. This is why those who live *yogic* lifestyles prefer giving things away rather than accumulating them.

To pursue this avenue of understanding further, the second rule around objects can be taken up. It, too, is two-fold. More philosophical in nature than its companion rule, it declares the little known fact, shocking to most beings upon first hearing, that the entire universe is composed of solidified thought; that all objects are just mind made manifest. The atomic particles that make up objects, and

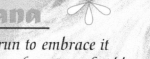

The Meaning of Maya &
A Subtler Look at Panchakarana

"Yes, all is Brahman. The tiger, too, is Brahman, but one should not run to embrace it on that account. You see, maya exists in Brahman like poison exists in a snake. One should not study maya, but only observe it carefully from a distance." Sri Ramakrishna Paramahamsa

The Five Main Constituents of Maya

Name, Form, Space, Time, Cause & Effect (Nama Rupa Desha Kala Nimitta)

Conventional Panchakarana (Quintuplication Process)

5 Subtle Elements ▸ 5 Senses of Perception ▸ 5 Senses of Action ▸ 5 Gross Elements (Tanmatras, Jnanendriyas, Karmendriyas, Mahabhutas)

Cosmic Panchakaranas

• **Cosmic Mind, Intelligence, Ego, Thought, Mind (Mahat, Buddhi, Ahamkara, Chitta, Manas)**

• **Sheaths of Self, Wisdom, Mentation, Vital Force, Food (Pancha Koshas)**

• **Fire of Heaven/Soma, Air/Rain, Earth/Food, Man/Seed, Woman/Embryo (Panchagnividya)**

• **Vitality, Circulation, Digestion, Evacuation, Aspiration (Prana, Udana, Samana, Vyana, Apana)**

• **Gods, Seers, Ancestors, Humans, Animals (Devas, Rishis, Pitris, Nara, Bhutas - Panchayajnas)**

• **Objects, Life Force, Thought, Intelligence, Awareness (Bhutakasha, Pranakasha, Chittakasha, Jnanakasha, Chidakasha - Panchakasha)**

Sadhana Panchakaranas

• **Sun, North Fire, East Fire, South Fire, West Fire (Panchatapas)**

• **Disturbed, Lethargic, Distracted, One-Pointed, Absorbed (Kshipta, Mudha, Vikshipta, Ekagra, Niruddha - Panchamanas)**

• **Peace, Servant, Parent, Friend, Beloved (Shanta, Dasya, Vatsalya, Sakhya, Madhura - Panchabhavas)**

• **Nonviolence, Truthfulness, Non-stealing, Continence, Non-Receiving (Ahimsa, Satya, Asteya, Brahmacharya, Aparigraha - Panchayamas)**

Samsaric Panchakaranas

• **Birth, Disease, Old Age, Decay, Death (Jayati, Vardhata, Jara, Kshara, Mara - Panchadukha)**

• **Ignorance, Attachment, Nature, Desire, Retribution (Avidya, Linga, Pramachchadaka, Kama, Karma - Panchabandha)**

• **Ignorance, Egotism, Attachment, Aversion, Clinging to Life (Avidya, Asmita, Raga, Dvesha, Abhinivesha - Panchakleshas)**

"Maya is a jungle. Knowing that it consists mainly of sets of fives provides an important tool — like a machete — for the seeker after freedom." Babaji Bob Kindler

which render them both unreal and empty, and due to which they cannot fulfill human desires, have all come from the mind as mental projections. Many of the charts presented throughout this book have been saying as much in their own, unique ways. Yet, the thinker is not to jump to the conclusion that all is nil and void. Nor is he/she to assume that some great Creator fashioned them out of nothing, or dust, etc. There is, behind all phenomena, the backdrop of pure Existence, called the Nectar of Nondual Awareness by some. And this is why "an arms length" study of *maya* is undertaken, in order to find out the nature of all that covers, all that distorts — in order to expose That which has become hidden as a result.

Another philosophical facet of many of the charts in this book has been the citing of the many sets of fives that coalesce to form the universes in space and time. In the present context they can be seen as contributors to what covers Divine Reality. To utilize the sets of five as clues or markers on a pathway that leads inwards is what is intended by the teaching of *Panchakarana,* whereas to fall into hypnotization by what they produce externally misleads and disorients the embodied being, and conduces to a real problem for the transmigrating soul.

On the next chart up for study, on the previous page, we find that sets of fives run the range from hamperers to helpmates. Some are just purely neutral as well. The five elements, listed first, are neutral, though if taken by the aspiring soul as a sign of the presence of a producing agent (creator), can turn positive in effect. This is fleshed out in the second entry on the chart, which is the traditional rendering of the *Panchakarana.* These twenty *"support and give rise to one another,"* as the *Taittiriya Upanisad* states. The meditator considers them in reverse order, from gross to subtle, so as to find their origins in the mind, and the mind in the Great Self (with *AUM* as the matrix). When seen as principles of projection/creation, then, they are the cosmic principles of *Sankhya Yoga,* and when seen as modes of meditation, they are the *alambanas* of *Raja Yoga* (*Patanjala*). Much of this has already been listed for study in the earlier pages of this book.

Some cosmic sets of fives are shown next. The first to be revealed is the Great Mind, with its component parts, i.e., intellect, ego, thought, mind, and if added to make five, the *Mahat,* or Cosmic Mind. The five sheaths, or *koshas/upadhis,* come next (see charts on page 19 & 21), followed by the five ancient wisdom sacrifices — fire, air, earth, man, and woman, each with their contributions of nectar, rain, food, sperm, and embryo. These connections, or *samhitas,* are to be remembered and observed throughout the incarnation process of the soul in nature, and revered in life and action. A *dharmic* life will thus be insured, while the risk of falling asleep in *maya* will be averted.

The five *pranas* should receive the same sacred treatment from the embodied soul. This is really one life-force in five forms. The charts on pages 536, 541, 543, 545, and 584 will provide a consummate refresher course on the content and import of this "vital" principle. *Panchayajna,* five ways in which the living being can acknowledge and worship the five strata of sentient beings — subhuman creatures, mankind, ancestors, *rishis*, and, gods — is listed next, followed by the five kinds of space (*akasha*) that these beings occupy. The connection of all these ten is crucial for a wider understanding of both what the many worlds consist of, and how so many beings came to embody in them — and why. Keeping track of this knowledge is not for the possession of mere information, even philosophically speaking, but more for placing the pure mind's attention upon them in order to bring the highest good to all beings and all worlds.

And this pertains all the more to the final set of cosmic *panchakaranas,* i.e., objects, life force, thought, intelligence, and Awareness. A proper and inward contemplation of these five would convince even the doubtful and jaded person of the existence of God, or *Brahman* — the last one, of the existence of Awareness itself, placing an apt and final conclusion on the matter.

The traditional and the cosmic have been inspected now, in brief. Following the lead of the entire quintuplication principle, the two remaining categories — inclusive but not exhaustive of what is in existence — can be scrutinized.

The list named *"sadhana panchakaranas"* pertains to practices that can be exercised for the good of the individualized soul. The five fires sacrifice, accomplished by the Holy Mother, Sri Sarada Devi, in recent times, among other austerities, increases forbearance of extremes like hot and cold. The meditator enters a circle of four fires, with the rising and setting sun being the fifth, and sits all day, several days, only receiving occasional water from the priest. Impurities get dissolved in such an austerity. Such impurities as these are indicated in the next set of fives concerning the distracted mind and its healing. This is Patanjali's list of five conditions of mind, three of them being common but undesirable, with the other two being goals to reach (see charts on pages 353 & 612). Other divine ends to meet with for the aspirant follow, as the welcome teaching of the *panchabhavas* appear (see chart on pages 471 & 473). Finally, the *yamas* of *Yoga* must be included (see chart on pages 399 & 403).

Such a rendering of the stultifying and capacious *Maya* would not be complete without the usual warnings around some of the poisons it contains. Therefore, some *samsaric panchakaranas* can be inspected. For teachings pertaining to each of these — *panchadukha* (sometimes six are listed), *panchabandha*, and the *panchakleshas* — see chart on pages 225 & 247, 249, & 417, respectively.

To pierce through the world-bewitching *Maya* is a task given only to seers of Truth, and certainly not possible for those of weak physical and mental constitution. Most beings are happy in it; others even wallow in it for lifetimes. For the freedom-seeking, freedom-loving soul, the seers point the way to the possibility of penetrating *Maya's* many veils via the use of *viveka,* which is a sharp-edged tool, often described and sung about as a double-edged sword (see chart on page 65 & 276). The chart on the facing page is designed to focus in on both the presence of *Maya's* overlays, and the way *viveka* can be honed and directed at them to cause an opening in consciousness for purposes of perceiving ones true nature. Culminated, this is the *"I and my Father are One"* experience, termed *"Tat Tvam Asi,"* or *"That Thou Art,"* in India, long before Jesus appeared on earth.

This chart, however, is not content to list the traditional teachings on *viveka* — spiritual discrimination between the real and the unreal — as esoteric and profound as they may be, but hastens to indicate that *viveka* should be utilized in life (with regard to the occurrence of birth and death), in ones devotional practice (*Bhakti Yoga*), and in meditation practice (*Dhyan Yoga*) as well.

Pertinent to the first of these three areas, the point is, that by understanding the predicament the soul falls into upon embodiment in *Maya,* with its thick, chimerical superimpositions, the apt and facile practitioner can destroy past *karmas,* set up the circumstances for a better and higher rebirth, and set the stage for the attainment of Enlightenment — all three. Such is the import of coming into possession of this great tool of advanced spiritual life and practice. Lord Vasishtha puts it in a most unique way in the quote on the chart under study. He states that the desire for rebirth is a primary disease in the human mind that is present in the minds of the ancestors and celestials as well. If this is the case, arriving on earth in the human form, in the embodied condition, amidst *Maya* and its flummoxing concomitants, all without being in possession of *viveka,* would amount to a secondary disease — that in conjunction with the first type of illness, would make for a soul hampered by the sickness of suffering. This may be "enough said" about this element of existence. Now we must implement *viveka* into daily life.

In the path of *Bhakti Yoga,* being the second facet under scrutiny in this chart, the importance of bringing in *viveka* is both needful and obvious, given the over-emotional and under-developed state of western practitioners of this otherwise noble form of *yoga.* Generally, it is the immature human ego that gets ahold of the noble tenets and practices of the four *yogas* and compromises them, sometimes hideously. In present times, in America, Europe, and even India, this occurs in three ways: preoccupation with *hatha yoga;* participation in *kirtan* and chanting for purposes of showing off and attracting the opposite sex; and the performing of actions under the force of selfishness rather than under the auspices of authentic *Karma Yoga.* This is all pretentiousness masquerading as spirituality. As one modern seer has said, *"The power of doing will not help the individual unless the power of Being is blended with it."* Just as numerous *asanas* and countless breathing exercises (*pranayama*) will not bring the mind to enlightened state, neither will mere singing and dancing with the Lord's names on ones lips bring about the singular higher wisdom that will destroy ignorance and bring the soul lasting peace and bliss.

Swami Aseshananda, a contemporary teacher of *Vedanta,* and the last monastic disciple of Sri Sarada Devi to be amongst us in the west, made an astute observation after teaching western adherents of Indian paths and philosophies over several decades. He stated: "*"The Judeo-Christian faith is a dualistic faith. Why dualistic? Because it accepts that behind the body and mind complex there is an underlying reality called the soul. But that is just the ego; they mistake it for the soul. It is that ego/mind complex that dreams itself from heaven to earth to hell."* As Sri Krishna has stated in the *Bhagavad Gita,* "For those who desire

The Indispensable Role of *Viveka* in Spiritual Life

"The appearance of the world, Oh Rama, is due to its being experienced through hundreds of births devoid of yogic discrimination. The discriminating soul will pass beyond mere enjoyments, then, and secure these three great attainments — The Knowledge of Truth, The Dissolution of the Mind, and The Effacement of Desires." Lord Vasishtha

Knowledge of Truth
Dissolution of Mind
Effacement of Desires

Study of the scriptures is the means to Knowledge of Truth

Practice of Yoga is the means to Dissolution of Mind

Production of positive impressions is the means to effacement of latent impressions

Viveka of Bhakti

Viveka at Birth

"The primary disease of the mind is the desire for rebirth. The secondary disease of the mind is reincarnation devoid of discriminative wisdom. From its absence comes lack of control of the senses and the inability to quell desires." Lord Vasishtha

"The failure to implement Viveka into the path of Bhakti leads to worship of the ego rather than authentic Love of God. The outcome is preoccupation with surface practices like asana, and affectatious singing and dancing."
Babaji Bob Kindler

"Sure knowledge of Brahman is gained by meditation upon correct teachings given by the illumined guru, and never through sacred ablutions, almsgiving, or hundreds of breathing exercises."
Shankara

Viveka in Meditation

"That one attains to perfection who, restraining the mind and the senses via discrimination, directs all his organs along the path of dharmic works."
Sri Krishna

Viveka in Karma/Activity

"The sterling virtue of discriminative restraint relies upon higher Knowledge, and that noble Wisdom depends upon this selfsame virtue — even as the lake and the lotus thrive upon one another. Through such rare and incomparable practice are the fetters of the heart severed, just like the threads running through a lotus when its stalk is cut."
Lord Vasishtha in Jivan Mukti Viveka

Me, and Me alone, I give them the discrimination (viveka) through which they can come to Me."

So Love, accompanied by true Devotion, checked early on by purificatory Discrimination, is what is needed for an authentic spiritual life and practice. So long as the ego is in charge of life, these three remain far off. As Swami Aseshananda observed, further: *"When people love each other's egos they say, 'I have fallen in love.' But what about God? For God, they say, 'I will love God when he finally comes to help me.' But will God come inside your television? Will God come to your bowling alley, or onto your football field? He will only come into your heart once it has been made pure, sincere, and free of distractions by viveka."*

The third area of the chart on page 657 concerns discrimination in meditation, as well as in action. For the performance of right action, the need for *viveka* is obvious. It is in meditation practice that seekers tend to lose the ability to discern what is happening to them, and where and when they need to move inwardly and creatively to effect progress. What is needed is constant watchfulness, constant guidance by a master, and constant vigil, so that the mind will not fall into dreaminess, rigidity, the influence of egoic bliss, and the sense of false formlessness. For, an absence of thought vibrations that pretends to be Ultimate Awareness is more often just mental insubstantiality. Due to the presence of all of these impediments listed above, the meditator must take to *viveka* in *Dhyana Yoga* and come to know all the movements of the mind/ego complex. Knowledge of truth, seeking dissolution of the mind, and gaining total effacement of desires will then not be far behind.

Human bondage has many causes and pitfalls. The real causes of all these are in the mind, while the effects work their way out into the senses and body over time. Beings then try to remedy them on the outside, with external methods. Further, God, who is purely transcendental, is not responsible for human suffering. Simply put, ones thoughts and actions are the culprits, not God or the devil. For what problems do the saints and seers with pure minds and noble actions have to suffer? They live divine lives. Even after their body's death they are not forgotten, and go to pure worlds — or into blissful Formlessness.

The early *Vedic* paths have scrutinized the lives and actions of embodied beings and gathered together a consummate list of causes for bondage. The chart on the facing page shows these in no uncertain terms. The first quote at the top of the chart reveals what they are. The image in the center has been utilized to place them all in context representing the famous story of the gods and *asuras* churning the ocean of existence by using Mt. Meru with the giant reptile, Vasuki, wrapped around it, to form a gigantic churn. The major agitation of this milk-ocean brought forth all manner of treasures which the gods and the *asuras* greedily snapped up for their own, but it also brought forth an acidic poison that began eating away at the very foundation of the three worlds. It was only by calling on Lord Shiva that all were saved from destruction, for he gathered the poison up in a container and swallowed it entirely. This would have destroyed him had not the Divine Mother pressed her finger on his throat and stopped the poison from reaching his stomach. Still, his throat turned blue due to this supreme sacrifice, which is why he is known by the name *Nilkantha,* in the scriptures.

The lower third of this chart holds the detail around this teaching. Under the five headings concerning the human passions are listed each of these particular negativities in the four-fold mind, consisting of ego, intellect, thoughts, and dual mind. A study of these details is very telling, and will be helpful for those who are still suffering the adverse effects of problems like mental restlessness. In the intellect, for instance, restlessness is recognized there by its tendency to turn everything that is learned into a source of dissatisfaction. Since this may not be enough information to help the victim of restlessness find a solution and get free, the other four passions are to be checked for their influences on the intellect — like doubt about the validity of what is being learned, utilizing knowledge for sensual purposes that degrade its rightful functioning, the increase of pride and superiority about what is being learned, and adversely, a subtle and growing contempt concerning knowledge and its role in life and practice.

By following up on the discovery of the presence and locale of all that deters and bothers the mind of the aspirant with connections like these, poisons like the one that threatened to undermine the three worlds can be removed from the mind for ever. The mind that is free of such negativities will no longer spew them out on people, places, and situations, and will instead become a blessing upon the world, and on humanity. As Swami Vivekananda states in his *Song of the Sannyasin,* one verse of which is quoted at the bottom of the chart under study, we must cease to lament and let go of our hold on causes of bondage

The Ten Major Knots
in the Rope of Human Bondage

"There are ten knots in the rope of human bondage: the illusion of personality; doubt; belief in the efficacy of religious rites and rituals; sensuality; ill will; desire for a future life in the world of form; desire for a future life in the world of the formless; pride; lack of mental quietude, and ignorance." Vedic Darshanas

Vyapi
AUM Eternal

ignorance egoism rites & rituals
rebirth with form & rebirth without form

Samasti

Maya

Vyasti

Subtle knots

Gross Knots

Mind

hatred doubt pride restlessness sensuality

Desire for rebirth with form and beyond form

"Prakriti-layas are souls who have risen above attraction to phenomena, who can dissolve the mental complex yet who still desire to create worlds out of unmanifested prakriti. As a result they cannot attain Kaivalya." Vedavyasa

Hatred, *Dvesha*
Buddhi: Negative attitude towards learning
Ahamkara: Jealousy of the knowledge of others
Chitta: Violent and aggressive thoughts
Manas: Dislike of harmony and unity

Doubt, *Samshaya*
Buddhi: Uncertainty about valid knowledge
Ahamkara: Feelings of insecurity, lack of self-worth
Chitta: Uncertainty mixed with turbulent thoughts
Manas: Haphazard brooding and lack of direction

Pride, *Darpa*
Buddhi: Sense of superiority, pride of knowledge
Ahamkara: Opinionated behavior and lack of respect
Chitta: Judgmental thoughts and insensitivity
Manas: Overweening attitude and delusions of grandeur

Restlessness, *Vikshepa*
Buddhi: Dissatisfaction with what is studied and known
Ahamkara: The desire to enjoy more and more experiences
Chitta: Thoughts that continually roam among sense objects
Manas: Lack of peace and contentment

Sensuality, *Vishayavati*
Buddhi: Misguided intelligence that is tainted with banality
Ahamkara: Vanity and gross overestimation of oneself
Chitta: Thoughts focused on sense enjoyment alone
Manas: Attachment to outer beauty bereft of the inner Light

Desire for Rites and Rituals
"Those who are devoted to rituals only enter into blind darkness, and into deeper darkness still go those fixed upon knowledge of rituals alone. They who worship non-becoming and becoming apart from one another fail to see. They who perceive them together conquer death." Ishavasyopanisad

"Where seekest thou? That freedom, friend, this world nor that can give. In books and temples vain thy search. Thine only is the hand that holds the rope that drags thee on. Then cease lament, let go thy hold, Sannyasin bold, say 'Om Tat Sat Om.'" Swami Vivekananda, Song of the Sannyasin

Occult Powers & The Raincloud of Virtues

Hidden Evils versus Divine Qualities

"Herein lies the secret. Says Patanjali, the father of Yoga: 'When a man rejects all the superhuman powers, then he attains the raincloud of virtues.' He sees God. He becomes God, and helps others become the same. This is all I have to preach. Doctrines have been expounded enough. There are books by the millions. Oh, for an ounce of practice!" Swami Vivekananda

Dharma-megha

sahasa, samatva, ksama, alochana, mrduta, udarata, sauharda, vinaya, mitahara, dhriti, hri, dina, yukti, etc.

Asta-bala Siddhis

anima, laghima, vyapti, prakamya, mahima, ishitva, vashitva, kama-vasayita

Right Thinking Leading to **Divine Life and Enlightenment**

Wrong Thinking Leading to **Suffering and Rebirth in Ignorance**

Nonviolent & Peaceful	Warlike & Domineering
Generous & Content	Selfish & Covetous
Gracious & Indrawn	Jealous & Meddlesome
God-loving & Unattached	Materialistic & Possessive
Transcendent & Respectful of Nature	Curious and Manipulative of Nature and its Powers
Pursues Higher Wisdom	Attracted to Psychic Powers
Uses Life for God-realization	Uses Life for Enjoying Desires
Strives to Attain and Share Freedom with Others	Tries to Influence Others through Wealth & Vanity
Seeks Mastery of the Self	Seeks Mastery over the World

"The Eight Occult Powers are like crow-droppings alongside the path."
Sri Ramakrishna Paramahamsa

"The state of superconsciousness, or Samadhi, is often called the 'Raincloud of Virtues,' in as much as it showers nectar-like drops of Immortality on living beings and the world through higher Wisdom. All the negativities, like the hosts of vasanas in base human minds, are then entirely destroyed. Thus, the 'Raincloud of Virtues' is the name given to Samadhi in the Astanga Yoga of Patanjali." Vedavyasa

that weigh us down, driving us further and further away from our true Nature that is eternally peaceful. As another of his verses reads, *"Say Peace to all; from me no danger be to ought that lives. In those who dwell on high, in those who lowly creep, I am the Self in all! All life, both here and there, do I renounce, all heavens, and earths, and hells, all hopes and fears. Thus cut thy bonds, Sannyasin bold, say 'Om Tat Sat Om!'"*

Swami Vivekananda's deep and transforming words can suffice to launch us off on the next chart up for examination, in conjunction with a quote he loved out of the *Yoga Sutras* of Patanjali. It concerns the Father of *Yoga's* cautionary warnings around the insinuating presence of the *asta-bala-siddhis*. Back on page 642, the subject of the eight occult powers was brought up in the context of their dangers, and of higher powers that should be attained instead. Here, the context is in contrast to the famous *Dharma-megha Samadhi,* or "Raincloud of Virtues," which appears in both Buddhist and *Vedic* scriptures.

To really see the difference in quality between these two, a side by side rendering has been composed on this chart so that any doubt still occupying the human mind around this matter can be alleviated for good. For, many souls have stumbled at this crucial juncture of inner life, falling for the old ruse of the material world and the tendency in the human mind for power rather than peace. As one authentic contemporary teacher of the *dharma* has stated, *"If you seek power you get Roll Royces. It you seek Peace you get God"* — referring by way of innuendo to the presence of spurious teachers on the current world scene whose presence only muddies the waters of potential spirituality in others.

The chart on the previous page lists both the eight occult powers, in *Sanskrit* and English, as well as the main concomitants of the Raincloud of Virtues. Simply put, the former is the cause and result of wrong thinking, while the latter both indicates and supports the way of right thinking. *Himsa,* for instance — violence, war, forced domination, and the like — is an occult power (*ishitva*) that harms and damages, while *ahimsa* — harmlessness, peace, and contentment with what one has — is a virtue that is good for all. This fact is obvious, especially to those who call themselves moral, yet even among the likes of these the power to dominate and do harm, either subtlely or indirectly, persists.

Such contradictory thinking and behavior characterizes every mind that falls under the various categories of the *asta-bala siddhis*. Above, in Swamiji's verse that was quoted, we find the words *"....all life, both here and there, do I renounce..."* Why renounce life? Because it is ephemeral, its offerings ever-changeful, empty of substance, and short-lived; also, therefore misleading. Yet beings by the millions grasp on to wordly life. As the poet wrote, *"Grasping matter, losing Grace, strange indeed this human race."* The Father of *Yoga* calls this *"clinging to life,"* and dubs it the lowest of all hells that the soul can fall into. Jesus also said much the same: *"Those who would love their life will lose it, but those who hate their life will get it again in Eternity."* Simply put, we are to renounce this narrow, limited, conventional life of pleasure leading to pain (and back again), for a life of peace, bliss, love, and light in service to God in humanity, and in all beings and things.

The list under the Raincloud of Virtues heading shows us the truth of this leaning towards right-thinking, or *dharma*, that we are to use life for God-realization and for helping to release others from suffering. This type of power, *yogic* power, is what is to be sought after. It first redeems, then enlightens, and finally transports the newly-transformed soul into highest Awareness. From the trap of transgressions perpetrated under the influence of the occult powers, then followed up by a series of births and deaths caught on the wheel of transmigration, the aspiring soul next finds the means for transformation via renouncing the occult powers and thus becoming qualified to stand under the cleansing Raincloud of Virtues. Purified by the fall of this Rain of Grace, it achieves, in one auspicious lifetime, the transcendence of name, form, time, space, and causality. It becomes transparent, thus free.

This sequence, put in words and stages, is transgression, transmigration, transformation, transcendence, and transparency. In the end, at its original, transparent state once again, the ego gets emptied of its desire to use power in order to wreak havoc, control the lives of others, satisfy desires that can never be fulfilled, heal that which is by nature diseased and incurable, perform miracles that are only for outer show and have no permanent and positive effect on either the world or God, and to attempt to possess that which is unattainable and ungraspable. All this is intended to be renounced so that what is Real, what is True, and what is ultimately Beneficial can be enjoyed, culminating in Freedom.

The final entries on each list under the two headings on the chart presently under study draw the final conclusion on this subject. *"To be, or not to be,"* that is not the question so long as the desire to use

The Four Mighty & Noble Combats

"What are the four noble combats? The battle to keep from waking the evil that is as yet still unmanifested within you, the battle to repel the evil that is already in existence, the battle to awaken the good that is as yet still unmanifested within you, and the battle to preserve and develop the good that is already in existence." Sankhya Yoga

The battle to awaken the unmanifested good within.

The battle to preserve the good already in existence.

Projection Sustenance Dissolution

The battle to keep from waking the evil within.

The battle to repel the evil already in existence.

Ignorance Egotism Attachment Aversion Clinging to life

*"If you bring forth what is within you, what you bring forth will save you.
If you do not bring forth what is within you, then what you do not bring forth may destroy you."*
Jesus Christ, Gospel of Thomas

occult powers is still predominant in the mind. To attain to mastery over the world, or worlds, is a positive evil if mastery over the Self has not been achieved. Therefore, to the discriminating aspirant, the penultimate goal of reaching *Dharma-megha samadhi* stands before him/her, and whatever stands in the way — namely, the *asta-bala-siddhis* — must be eschewed in order to ensure arrival at the ultimate Goal of human existence.

And next, the entire matter can be looked at from the seeker's perspective under the auspice of noble combat rather than aggressive war-like behavior. The chart now up for inspection on the previous page evinces this higher attitude.

The Four Noble Combats are a simple way for the developing spiritual aspirant to simultaneously admit and accept the presence of negativities in the mind. They can also help one take up the task of bringing out all positive tendencies within, based upon the goodness that has already come forth in life. Attenuating the negative first, what lies hidden in the individual's mind must be considered to be dangerous, somewhat like a slow poison that will eventually wreak havoc on the entire system. As Jesus stated once in the presence of Thomas, *"....if you do not bring it out it, will destroy you."*

The entire matter then becomes how to bring such poison out of the mind in a way that will not harm others, nor damage the delicate psycho/physical being. The following are half-measures, at best: the advice of family members who lack the skills and training to inspire and heal; reliance upon prescribed, expensive, conventional methods advised by the worldly who, themselves, still hide and nurse these selfsame poisons within themselves; treatment by professionals who rely upon medicines and elixirs that may help the body but not the brain; approaching counselors and subjecting oneself to the latest therapies involving pills, prescriptions, a "how did that make you feel:"dialogue, or a soft pillow to cry (or scream) into; the confession of "sins" and so-called communion with the leaders and members of conventional religious circles — none of these will suffice to solve deep-rooted problems and issues and destroy them at the root, from where they can so easily just sprout forth shoots, again and again.

The traditions of India both advise and demonstrate the efficacy of *sadhana*, or spiritual practice. This individual self-effort is noble in and of itself, but it does require a competent guide, or *guru*. Otherwise, the soul risks committing errors that only compound the already existing condition, and which could have been avoided under the scrutiny of a wise and watchful eye. Under an intense regimen of spiritual practice, latent negative tendencies get called to the surface of the mind where they can be dealt with on the spot. The idea is that these unwanted despoilers of life must come forth in the atmosphere of holy company where they will simply expire in the light of the exceptional purity that exists there. This "holy company" really consists of teacher *(guru)*, fellow students *(sangha)*, and teachings *(dharma)*. All of these are purposefully spiritual in nature, which is why they work where other methods either fail outright, or do not penetrate deep enough into the psyche to get to the source, and thereby allow the mind's negativities to live in a state of incubation and merely recur after some time.

Of great aid and benefit in this noble combat are the positive qualities and attributes that the soul has gleaned from past experiences in life. Like the "Raincloud of Virtues" studied previously to this chart, such powerful allies are to be kept close and utilized whenever necessary. For, the spiritual awakened soul, as was just mentioned earlier, is now operating at the level of mind and intelligence rather than body and energy. These intrepid spiritual wayfarers are bound to hear the expression, "pure mind," come up, and must strive their best to achieve this most precious of attainments.

A pure mind, at the height of it all, is really no mind at all. It is transparent mind that has become stripped of everything that a normal or conventional mind still grasps onto and cherishes. Chapter Ten of this book will take up much about this principle of transparent Mind and its access to the highest level of Consciousness. Other than this, a pure mind can mean other things. It can be that repository of all good qualities, the only rub on this being that where there is good, evil also persists. The pure mind of this reckoning, then, is really still dual mind, or *manas*, and just a tad more refined than minds that are restless and imbalanced. In those more refined cases, those poisons that are hidden in the depths may be a bit less obtrusive, and when they rise up in life and action are thus a bit easier to deal with.

Being able to perceive the difference between a Pure Mind and a good mind is an important step in spiritual life, and could make the difference between being born in the lower heavens with ones ancestors again, or snapping the chains of rebirth altogether so as to escape embodiment in the world of the six transformations — birth, growth, disease, old age, decay, and death.

Mind, then, wherever it is a complex, provides a home for accumulation of objects and objectives, of weights and balances. Real Peace seldom visits that mind. Even the good that lies within it only forms the grounds for a struggle to keep it alive. Is it a noble undertaking? Yes, and better than allowing negativity to take the forefront of consciousness. But *sadhana*, spiritual practice, has more to reveal, and more to offer. As has been stated, *"Good and bad are chains that hold, one of iron, the other of gold."* For the consummate spiritual practitioner, the Goal of Enlightenment looms in the distance — which the following chart up for study on the facing page explains perfectly.

According to Sri Sarada Devi, the Mother of the Universe in human form in modern times, to attain Enlightenment depends mainly upon three requisites — *Karma, Sadhana,* and *Kala* — ones actions ones practice, and the duration and effects of both over phases of time. In a nutshell, and pertinent to some of Her signature teachings, the aspirant after this highest Freedom (*moksha/mukti*) must cut away the effects of actions done in time using the *mantra* transmitted in sacred ceremony by the spiritual teacher. For souls who are striving sincerely with a substantial accumulation of force *(shakti)* behind them, this most crucial task and supreme boon can be achieved in a single lifetime, and that is best. For others who are not so forward moving, and who are unable to muster great intensity through practice and austerities, the process will go on through several lifetimes (see chart on page 192). A strong desire to be free (*mumukshutvam*) must also increase and be intact (see chart on page 65), but at least a start must be made (see chart on page 341). Then time can tell the tale, as they say.

A most important facet here is constancy; time, here, in this endeavor, means constancy. Failure to maintain that singular practice that 1) dissolves past *karmas*, 2) neutralizes occurring *karmas*, and 3) deals effectively with fructifying *karmas*, i.e., *sanchita, kriyamani,* and *prarabdha karmas,* will bring the hopeful bid of the spiritual practitioner for liberation to an ugly and premature end. Thus ultimately, though time is illusory, ironically, it is a main factor in the process of a soul's spiritual evolution.

Holy Mother's teachings about the role of *kala* (including *kalas,* phases of time) in spiritual life are listed under its heading on the chart opposite. Much is made in contemporary western society about a child's education, and what he/she will grow up to be, etc. Nothing is mentioned about the soul's everfree nature, and how everyone around him, including himself, has totally forgotten it. Along with this forgetfulness has come both the loss of the true purpose for life, and a skewed idea of what the purpose of life is. Seeing the soul caught in the *maya* of matter, relatives, relationships, the search for success, bondage to family, and the earning of wealth, the spiritual teacher verily shouts in his ear, "Go on retreat! Find your spiritual pathway leading home! Find an illumined soul to guide you! Find your Chosen Ideal and adhere to It! Learn the *dharma* and fulfill your remaining desires in it! And take full refuge in Divine Reality, however It presents Itself to you — with form, beyond form, or both!" All of this will take time, so time must be regained and used wisely. Otherwise, as they say, "time's a-wastin."

Teachings on the right way to utilize time in this day and age are legion, at least to the soul who is aware of the wastage of potential in life. The *guru*, or spiritual preceptor, is one of those. Such an august soul sees living beings running in circles all the "time," and both puzzles at their desultory behavior, and ponders ways to direct their energy in a straight line once again. Boon-doggling must be converted into boon-doggedness, wherein a Raincloud of Virtues (see page 660 again) sheds grace upon the newly-oriented aspirant every day. To steal time away from worldly occupations and give it to spiritual life and practice then becomes the main consideration in life — both for the *guru* who wants to see real progress being made, and for the belabored soul who risks stepping again and again into the quicksands of *maya* with every act and decision that is made on the earth plane.

The question from the wise comes, then, "How much time are you giving to scriptural study, to meditation, and to the worship of the Lord and Mother of the Universe?" And here is where *sadhana* finally begins to receive its deserved share of attention. As far as Holy Mother is concerned, the first task in this area, as also the first victory to be gained, is over the sense organs. Preoccupation with objects and the pleasure they bring forms a major hurdle in the way of most beings wanting to get free. After this problem is solved, or brought under control, the use of worship, study, and *mantra* ushers in a purer direction that begins to define what real *sadhana* is, and what it involves. In Her exalted way of thinking, a major part of the puzzle around spiritual life and progress has to do with sorting out the mind's

The Three Main Factors
In the Attainment of Enlightenment

1
Karma

"Human being; today it is, tomorrow it is not. No one will accompany a person after death. Only action — good and bad — will follow, even after death."

The Holy Mother, Sri Sarada Devi

2
Practice

"Through spiritual practices, the ties of past karma are cut asunder. But the realization of God cannot be achieved without ecstatic love for Him. Do you know the significance of japa and other spiritual practices? By these, the dominance of the sense-organs is subdued."

Holy Mother, Sri Sarada Devi

Pure Conscious Awareness

3
Time

Kala

Recall life's true purpose
Go on retreat & pilgrimage
Seek out a spiritual path
Find an adept guru
Select an Ishtam / Chosen Ideal
Take final refuge in God
Fulfill all desires in the dharma

Sadhana

Purify the soul via worship
Strengthen body/mind via yoga
Hone the Intellect via study
Memorize the scriptures
Practice japa of the holy mantra
Perceive God with form
Realize the formless Brahman

Karma Vinasha

Awaken to the insidious presence of Maya
Recognize the limitations of name and form in Nature
Perceive the suffering-ridden nature of relative existence
Subdue sense-life by noting the dangers of pleasure and enjoyment
Break free of the cocoon of family life and mundane human convention
Scrutinize the link to one's ancestors and break the chain of rebirth with them
Inspect individual thoughts and habits and connect them to actions in past lifetimes
Meditate with the specific aim to dissolve all mental residue that binds the mind to relativity

"Perhaps one practices japa and austerity in this life. In the next life one intensifies the spiritual mood and in the following advances it further; thus spiritual evolution goes on. The moment that one's karmas come to an end one realizes God. That is one's last birth. This, plus the practice of spiritual discipline, and time, are the factors in the attainment of spiritual knowledge." — Holy Mother, Sri Sarada Devi

The Three Pillars of Zen Practice

Dai-Funshi	Dai-Shinkon	Dai-Gidan

"Believing with every pore of our being in the truth of the Buddha's teaching that we are all endowed with immaculate Bodhi-mind."
Hakuun Yasutani

"Not a single doubt, mind you, but a doubt-mass — and this inevitably stems from a strong faith."
Hakuun Yasutani

"....all existence is intrinsically whole, flawless, omnipotent — in a word, perfect. Without unwavering faith in this, the heart of the Buddha's teaching, it is impossible to progress far in one's practice."   Hakuun Yasutani

Great Resolve

Great Faith

Great Doubt

Principle: Inflexible resolve to believe in the teachings of the Buddha.	**Principle:** Reliance on the great root of Faith.	**Principle:** Probing inquiry based in the desire to know rather than in skepticism.
Practice: Bringing the full strength of one's will to bear on this faith.	**Practice:** Striving to remove the erroneous belief in all things supernatural, and the superstitions that go with them.	**Practice:** Intense questioning as to the nature of Reality.
Result: The dispelling of doubt leading to the realization that we are imbued with Buddha Nature.	**Result:** Rock-like faith in the Enlightenment that the Buddha attained.	**Result:** Assurance of the perfection of Buddha Nature, despite the strife and suffering of the world.

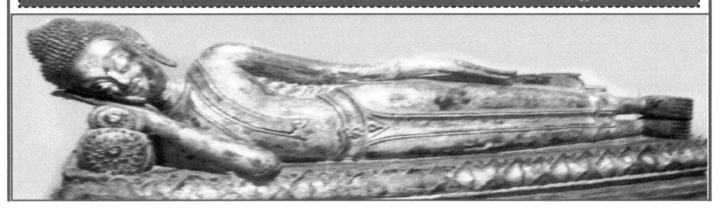

confusion as to the nature of God, or Divine Reality — *Brahman.* Coming to know from the *guru,* the scriptures, and ones own deepening spiritual self-efforts, that God is both with form and beyond form clears the internal memory and sets the stage for experiences that take the soul beyond the physical world. Self-Realization then looms once again before the unified eye of the *Brahman* beholder.

The teachings around *karma* fill the rest of this chart (page 665). As can be seen, they form a detailed and step by step account of further victories to be won. So much of the discovery along the spiritual path has to do with occurrences that should never have happened in the first place, along with the habit patterns that followed — all the fault of the individual, i.e., his or her own *karma.* When the phase of gaining victories comes to an end, *karma* melts away. According to Holy Mother that is the last lifetime the embodied soul, otherwise belabored by the impositions and ignobilities of *maya,* has to bear.

There is another triple teaching, or *triputi,* that complements the Three Factors in the Attainment of Enlightenment just scrutinized in terms of *karma,* practice, and time. This teaching has seen much exposure in the West over the past few decades, and it mirrors classics like the *Mahamudra* (page 647) in Tibetan *Buddhism,* with its threefold stance of the view, the practice, and action.

In *Zen,* the stances are Great Resolve, Great Faith, and surprisingly, Great Doubt. It is a very wise practice to take up. At the beginning, when the student's abilities are few and his capacity small, the encouragement from the *roshi* (zen teacher) is to mount a great resolve that will carry him through all the problems and challenges that naturally come along with committing to the spiritual path and its demanding practices. Predominantly, the risk of quitting the path is foremost, for failure at the outset will deter the mind from ever wanting to take up the challenge again. Aversion to anything of a spiritual nature and tone will become a habit. Drifting back to the pleasures and comforts of wordly life amidst people who will coddle the quitter and play up to the ego's weaknesses — as if it were okay to let down the standard and give up the higher goal — is so much easier to do than to strive for perfection.

Each of the Three Pillars has three requisite, as can be seen on the chart on the previous page. For *Dai-Funshi,* the resolve takes on the form of strong belief in the Buddha, unwavering faith in the path, and the unstinting watchfulness around anything that might cause doubt about the actual presence of Buddha nature in the student himself, and in all beings. In *Dai-Shinkon,* belief has turned into faith. It is in and during this transition that the lifetimes-old courting of all that is sensational in nature sees its demise. It is really the death of concepts, ideas, and images that have long been associated with superstitions posing as true religion and authentic philosophy. This is called *hakushi* in Zen, and is tantamount to the settling in of rock-solid faith in the enlightened state of the Buddha, and other luminaries.

And all of this is necessary of attainment for the aspirant; otherwise the *Zen* sickness called *Zembyo,* as we have just seen, will attend upon forthcoming stages of graduation along the path. The third pillar of import, called *Dai-Gidan,* gains due notice here. The "Great Doubt" spoken of in this regard is both a strengthening of previously gained resolve and faith around the existence of the perfection of Buddha and *Dharma,* and also a shield against all the uprisings of *samsara* that come to the fore just prior to the adept practitioner's final storming of the gates of Reality. Such adamantine faith will successfully repel all doubts in the mind and in the world. The Great Doubt will succeed in this task where so many other methods, undeveloped and as yet immature, will not. Lacking mastery of the third pillar, a niggling doubt about the empty nature of phenomena (*fukatosu*) may arise, and based upon this, a misunderstanding of the meaning of emptiness (*akushu-ku*) will occur. The soul does not need this kind of distraction (*heikan*) when it is about to attain to the full realization of oneness (*ittai*). Without the complete destruction of the dualistic world view (*Zadan*) that the mind/soul has been holding for so long, the innate Perfection of all and everything (*jisho-shojo-shin*) will not be possible.

And so it is, in the clear Zen path, that questioning and rationale based in skepticism is left until the end rather than the beginning. Otherwise, argumentation and misunderstanding by the untrained and unclear mind may spoil the aspirant's bid for growth and graduation along it. If all the injustices of the relative world, the *karmas* of the mind, the faults of religion, and the seeming contradictions of philosophy and scripture are dealt with once resolve and faith are in place, then there will be far less chance of the seeker falling off of the razor thin edge of the spiritual pathway. This will become all the more obvious when the problem of suffering souls impinges on the practitioner's growing comprehension of Perfection. *Dai-Anjin* and *Dai-Gedatsu* — the Great Peace and the Great Freedom are absolute and undivided. The spector of disease and death, with their hosts of myriad miseries, will not impede so long as the third pillar is in place — the full assurance that the Buddha and the salient teachings proceeding from Him are unimpeachable.

A famous and enticing method for training the mind in the spiritual verities of Zen *Buddhism* is now shown on the facing page in the form of the Ten Stages of Ox-Herding. The sacred traditions and their teachers (*gurus, acharyas, roshis, tulkus, lamas,* various spiritual preceptors) are well aware of both the inspirations and dangers of setting foot on the spiritual path. Though it would be great to think that all should take up the task, the fact about this world, this plane of consciousness, is that most beings are not ready to do so — even in they do sometimes feel the call of their inner nature to proceed. Depending on ones preparedness, trying and failing can be almost as bad as never attempting in the first place.

Whatever the case may be, and depending on different temperaments and character, when the beginner resolves to become a practitioner rather than a mere posturer, spiritual groupie, or faddist, there is the initial obstacle of achieving an authentic spiritual awakening. Using the metaphor of Ox-herding, this is where the future disciple admits to him or herself that they are lost, that they have become bereft of their true nature. It must be sought out and located. Interestingly enough — and this is true of all traditions that are nondual in nature — the ready seeker has an inner predilection that his or her soul is close at hand, but only hidden from view. Phases one and two of Ox-herding, then, are as if nondistinct, for when the sincere practitioner looks within, there are signs of the Ox-soul present and spread out across the inner terrain of the mind. Early meditation is also present, then, the real challenge being those many varying paths that can form a maze in and of themselves when they are approached individually to be selected. Thankfully, one of the greatest boons available in these early levels of seeking are the Wisdom-teachings. These are like the tracks of the Ox to follow, to discover its whereabouts.

And just as the Ox, being so huge, cannot easily disappear, so too is ones true nature an obvious presence. Phase three of the search, then, reveals glimpses of the as-yet illusive creature in the form of inner experiences and insights. These only convince and compel the ardent seeker to go deeper and intensify the search. He/she now is galvanized by the thought of capturing the Ox and regaining ownership of it.

This signals the outset of state four. The Ox-soul does not want to be brought under control, for it has tasted the *"sweet grasses"* of freedom, while its true owner fell into the bittersweet marshes of bondage. Seeing the soul in the primordial setting of its own "wild freedom," the struggling mind of the practitioner is willing to break all the old habits that caused it to lose its most precious possession in the first place. Seeing the Ox (*bussho*) in the bliss of its own freedom, this alone refines the mind and allows it the ability to sustain itself on higher and deeper levels of consciousness. Abiding, even for a few moments or minutes, in such a rarified state of awareness, confers upon the seeker a special energy, and with that he/she enters the fifth phase of the process.

Here, and all along the way — from realization of loss through following trackless paths through the forests, and on to gaining initial sight of the prize — a grand union has been culminating. The unspoken and inexplicable is at the root of this union, called Love. It is a divine intimacy wherein closeness is the strongest desire. Communion has been missing for so long. Upon initial contact again, the light of the seeker's true nature lights up the aspects of the mind. Thoughts are seen as if from a distance rather than from under a blanket of smothering bondage, and the ego ripens and gives away its usual control and possession of the mind's splendid attributes and qualities. As the mind awakens to its source in this way, a sense of innocence returns to it, being shorn of naivete. Ordinary consciousness now feels to be the highest level of abidance, and naturalness returns to the fore. Mind and soul merge, in love again. Now what remains to be done is to "ride the Ox home."

This sixth phase of Ox-herding is accompanied by the Light of Illumination; it thrives in spontaneous simplicity, like a child. Realization is radiating from this subtle union, but this brings about the awareness of an equally subtle appearance of illusion. The thought of separation and its possibility still plagues the mind, and fear along with it.

In phase seven, the bliss of twoness appears as the solution for the fear of possible separation. Having arrived home with the Ox in possession, the seeker turns his attention to the experience of enlightenment in everyday life. In this state, meditation deepens and is permeated through and through

Jugyu-No-Zu
Ten Stages of Ox-Herding

"The Ox symbolizes the intrinsic nature of Consciousness, the mystery of what we are. The seeker of Enlightenment must become as close an observer of Consciousness as the Eskimo is of snow conditions."   Jikai Lex Hixon

Seeking the Ox
1. AWAKENING
2. FORMAL SEEKING
3. MAZE OF PATHWAYS
4. EXHILARATION AND DESOLATION
5. SENSE OF HIDDEN ESSENCE

"The Ox has never really gone astray..."

Finding the Tracks
1. FINDING THE WISDOM TEACHINGS
2. FOLLOWING HIS OWN TRACKS
3. FRUITFUL ILLUSION
4. SELF SEEMS EVIDENT
5. ENTERS MEDITATION

"Trampled grasses show signs of the Ox's Presence."

Glimpse of the Ox
1. INITIAL EXPERIENCE
2. ENLIGHTENED BUT UNAWARES
3. FLASHES OF INSIGHT
4. INTENSIFIES DISCIPLINES

"There stands the Ox in the jungle! How can he hide?"

Catching the Ox
1. SEES WILD STRENGTH
2. BREAKS OLD HABITS
3. OBSERVES ORIGINAL MIND
4. TEMPERS AND REFINES MIND
5. SUSTAINS AWARENESS
6. HARNESSES THE ENERGY OF ENLIGHTENMENT

"Stubborn and unbridled, it still yearns for sweet grasses."

Taming the Ox
1. INTIMACY
2. OBSERVES THOUGHTS
3. RIPENS THE EGO
4. ATTAINS ORDINARINESS
5. RELEASES PRIMAL AWARENESS

"Tended, it becomes gentle; untethered, it follows its master."

Riding the Ox Home
1. ILLUMINATION VISITS
2. SIMPLICITY OCCURS
3. SPONTANEITY DAWNS
4. RADIATES REALIZATION
5. BECOMES AWARE OF SUBTLE ILLUSION
6. COGNIZES SEPARATION

"Astride the Ox's back, he gazes serenely at the clouds above."

Ox Forgotten
1. ALL IS ATTAINED
2. DAILY LIFE IS ENLIGHTENMENT
3. MEDITATION IS NATURAL
4. ACTION IS MEDITATION
5. INFINITE PEACE
6. BLISS OF TWONESS

"The Ox has now vanished, and alone and serene sits the man."

Ox and Self Forgotten
1. NEITHER DELUSION NOR HOLINESS
2. ALWAYS OPEN TO FULLNESS
3. LIFE IS ENLIGHTENMENT
4. ALL THINGS EMANATE AWARENESS

"He lingers not in the Buddha, and passes through the not-Buddha."

Return to the Source
1. FORMLESS TO FORM WITHOUT CHANGE
2. ALL IS A CIRCLE OF EMPTINESS
3. LIFE IS MANIFESTATION OF SOURCE
4. HUMANS GONE, ONLY TRANSHUMAN FLAVOR REMAINS

"Seated in his hut, bridle and whip lying idle, he hankers not for the things outside."

"Having turned his back on his true nature, suddenly man is confronted by a maze of crisscrossing paths, and treads through forests and jungles to find it."

Entering the Marketplace with Helping Hands
1. PERFECT EMPTINESS IN ACTION
2. TRANSFORMS POISON TO NECTAR
3. STRIPPED OF POWERS, CAUSES ALL TO BLOOM WITH HIGHEST POTENTIAL

"The nightingale warbles on a twig; the sun shines on undulating willows. If he will but listen, he will at that moment cognize the Source."

"The gate of the hut is closed, and even the wise cannot find him."

Astika & Nastika

"Basically, everyone has borrowed from Mother India throughout long phases of time, as there has been an endless sweep of religions, philosophies, and pathways emanating from Her — in other words, not just one sacred book and a single prophet or Avatar, but many, many of each. And within this plethora of spiritual avenues there has always been room for those who profess the existence of Divine Reality, as well as for those who do not care to either admit it or emphasize it." Babaji Bob Kindler

Astika – Orthodox Systems
(Admit the Existence of God)

Shad-Darshana
Sankhya of Kapila (*)
Yoga of Patanjali
Purva Mimamsa of Jaimini
Uttara Mimamsa of Vedavyasa (Vedanta)
Nyaya of Gautama
Vaisheshika of Kanada

Nastika – Nonorthodox Systems
(Noncommittal as to the Existence of God)

Buddhism of Lord Buddha
Jainism of Tirthankaras & Mahavira

Scriptures by Classification
Shruti: Vedas, Upanisads, Gita
Smriti: Itihasa, Puranas, Agamas
(Tantras), Darshanas, Dharma Shastras

The Vedas and Their Two Divisions: Karma Kanda & Jnana Kanda

"Yo vedebhyah akhilam jagat nirmane — God created the entire Universe out of the knowledge of the Vedas." Shankara

I. Karma Kanda

Samhitas
Collections of mantras and hymns
Corresponds with Brahmacharya Stage

Brahmanas
Sacrificial rites, duties, and modes of conduct
Corresponds with Grihastha Stage

Aranyakas
Inner meaning of Brahmanas and rules for forest dwellers
Corresponds with Vanaprastha Stage

2. Jnana Kanda

Upanisads
Secret teaching for those ready to renounce the world
Corresponds with Sannyas Stage

"Lord Brahma was once meditating on his creator, when there was manifest within the shrine of his heart the Eternal Word, AUM, the seed of all knowledge and thought. One by one, then came the sounds of all the letters, and through these letters there became known unto Brahma the Wisdom of the Vedas. He then taught it to his disciples, and these, in turn, spread it to the many worlds."

with peace and bliss. Thus, the Ox and its owner live on the same land in the bliss of twoness, in very close proximity.

Stage eight brings in the primal twoness wherein the Ox begins to disappear. In terms of practice, there is none to be discerned. There is no escape from delusion and no quest for holiness. Fullness infills everything. All beings and all things radiate the Light of Awareness (like in the *Mahamudra* teaching, earlier). In this condition of consciousess, life is Enlightenment.

All that can be said about the remaining two "stages" of Ox-herding is that the soul passes back and forth from form to formlessness easily and spontaneously. In either mode, emptiness prevails and pervades. The Source manifests all and everything naturally, effortlessly. The human has slipped away from the quotient and only a *"transhuman flavor"* remains — rather like the fragrance of an incense stick long after it has burned out and turned to ashes.

With all the stages behind, yet still present, the soul, when it acts, simply *"enters the marketplace with helping hands."* When in inaction, *"the door* of *his hut remains shut"* to all beings and interruptions. To have the extreme good fortune of holy company with such a being confers full fruition of all desires and aspirations.

As a fitting end to chapter nine of this book, which has taken the reader and student through many pathways of Indian *dharma*, a multitude of diverse teachings, and an abundance of explanations about the levels of aspiring human consciousness, a chart on the *astika* and *nastika* systems of India is now offered on the previous page. The *astika* systems are the orthodox ones, meaning that they base their authority upon the *Upanisads,* the traditional teachings of India. By *nastika* is meant unorthodox, which refers more to the fact that these ways of thinking and worshipping have their own way of proposing Divine Reality, though they may also borrow from the orthodox traditions.

Of the six *darshanas* (ways of clear seeing) that are orthodox, only three are really present and operable today as living philosophies. They are *Sankhya* of Kapila, *Yoga* of Patanjali, and *Vedanta* of Vedavyasa. The other three have had tenets of their thinking and conclusions absorbed into these main three.

Sankhya has suffered by way of its age, but is vibrant by the same measure. That is, most of the orthodox and unorthodox systems in India have borrowed heavily from Kapila's early homework in both cosmology and philosophy. His twenty-four cosmic principles (*tattvas*) are an ingenious rendering and concentration, both, of what is most apparent and important in the three worlds. By considering them well in study and meditation, one can know what is worthy of inspecting and accepting, and what is necessary of renouncing.

Yoga has also suffered in contemporary times and climes, particularly in today's tepid and compromising atmospheres of materialism and body-orientation. If the sincere seeker can forego the shallow focus upon what is termed *yoga* by those whose main interest is mere pleasure and longevity — *bhoga* rather than *yoga* — then true *Yoga* can come to the fore and occupy its noble and original, elevated position once again. The flash in the pan thraldom with *hatha yoga*, a series of physical exercises, is what is "posturing" as *yoga* today. Whereas these postures have some role to play in the body's health, they do nothing to address the source of ignorance and suffering that has its origins in the mind. The traditional Four *Yogas* brought to us by Vivekananda address these crucial problems. Additionally, the practice of bodily postures (*asanas*) place the mind's attention on the physical sheath, and create the desire (*vasana*) for shifting its mode to various contortion-like postures. These become habitual with repetition, and form impressions (*samaskaras*) in the mind. Thus, *asana-vasana samskaras* are the result, and these freeze the body-mind mechanism in one place, disallowing it to move inwards towards the higher limbs of *Yoga* like renunciation, concentration, and meditation. *Yoga* is Eight-limbed (*astanga*), not one limbed, and until the higher levels are plumbed and practiced, the true goal of *Yoga* — Samadhi — will not be achieved.

Vedanta, the other living orthodox pathway, is fresh on the scene today, mainly due to the advent of Swami Vivekananda onto the earth plane, and his visit to the West in 1893 at the Parliament of Religions in Chicago. Gaining ground daily among free-thinking individuals and intellectuals, its rise and peak may be a thousand years long according to the great swami. So many of the profuse *dharma* teachings found in this book come from the *Vedanta,* along with Its twin-sister tributary, *Tantra.*

Among the *nastika* systems of the philosophy of India, *Buddhism* and *Jainism* take the forefront.

The winsome and welcome tenets of peace, nonviolence, and vegetarian lifestyle, likewise, come to the fore when these noble religions and philosophies are considered. Though not of Indian origin, the religions of *Sikhism* and *Sufism* can also be cited, and be seen as belonging to the *nastika* category among India's many universal pathways. India has been home and mother to many of the world's religious traditions. Even fundamentalist forms of Islam and Christianity had found a home in India, though they have not been able to turn their gracious refuge there towards the selfish modes and ends of conversion and proselytization. India has always maintained the universal attitude of openness and sharing of its boundless and ancient wisdom with other traditions. Following ones path of choice while acknowledging the presence and benefit of other ways of proceeding has long been India's form and selfless stance.

The bottom half of the chart up for study on page 670 shows the *Karma Kanda* and *Jnana Kanda* divisions of the *Upanisads,* the *Vedanta,* also denoting the four stages of life. From a young age the Hindu child is trained and geared for the ascending levels of existence on earth — from celibate student, to having a family and making a living, to retiring into the forest, and on to renouncing the world and attaining liberation. This last stage will require knowledge and operation of the *Jnana Kanda,* and this leads to the highest and best of all life, Eternal Life. This is also what the final chapter of this book is concerned with.

The Ever Stationary Self

Atman's All-Pervasive Nature Belies Change, Renders Futile Any Need For Movement

The final chapter of this book of *dharma* charts, teachings, and the deep strains of high-minded philosophies of Mother India, is all about one Eternal Principle in two forms: Nonduality and Divine Mother Reality. Put more simply, or less grandly, Wisdom and Love in their most quintessential state.

It has been conceived by lovers of Truth for centuries, and told by contemporary disciples of real Religion, that Love is all you need; that Love is the main reason for coming to this realm, as contradictory as that sounds in this *"joyless, transient world."* The statement is true if the embodied being is qualified to understand and receive Love, and give It to all once having experienced It. Prior to such comprehension and ability, what has been termed "unconditional Love" eludes a greater percentage of human beings, despite all overtures and claims made towards its possession. Amongst the devotional songs of India, the devotee of Mother Kali, Ramprasad Sen, attests to this fact by singing adamantly: *"This intoxicated poet of Goddess Kali is certain that all opinions are void of substance. The Mother's Mystery eludes every earnest practitioner or philosopher who assumes virtue or vice to be real."*

The apparent reality of dualities such as virtue and vice, pleasure and pain, bondage and liberation, etc., are to be disproved, then, and the power that accomplishes this considerable feat is Nondual Wisdom. Love and Wisdom together are Truth, and Truth hides from humanity due to even its most learned members arguing continually and posing one of these great Tenets against the other. Seeing the condition of the human mind in contemporary time when he visited Chicago to speak at the Parliament of Religions in 1893, Swami Vivekananda noted the following: *"Faith is a wonderful insight, and can save, but there is a danger in it of breeding fanaticism barring further progress. Jnanam, wisdom, is all right, but there is the danger of its becoming dry intellectualism. Love is great and noble, but it may die away in meaningless sentimentalism. A harmony of all these is the thing required."*

In Western countries, religion and philosophy were never considered as one subject, both pertinent to the ultimate goal of human existence — that being the gaining of freedom from embodiment and all its limitations and sufferings. In India, religion and philosophy were never rent asunder; each helped the other in the task of balancing all elements of human nature and character so as to confer harmony and thus pave the way to comprehension of Unity.

The comprehension of Unity is what occurs to the human mind when Nondual Wisdom is realized. This fact has been illustrated from time out of mind in and by India's realized souls, the *Avatars, Rishis, Mahatmas, Avadhutas,* and other saints, sages, *swamis,* and seers of the sacred subcontinent. If human beings are to learn the lessons of pure Love, only a turning of the heart and mind, both, towards the holy feet of such unsung, overlooked, and underestimated members of the world's population, will effect the task.

It is therefore that the chart on the facing page — the first in a series of some 35 final charts in this book — is given to the task of duly understanding the realized soul. In this regard, the peoples of the West are hard put to formulate a comprehension of just what a spiritual luminary is all about, for precious few have visited the West, and those who have incarnated there are of a saintly character oriented towards devotion rather than beings who wisdom knowers, termed sages or seers.

The people of the West have a difficult time even formulating devotion for Nature, what to speak of for an embodied human being. Even when Christ lived, most beings did not care for or like him. He was reviled and hated by many, ignored by others. And so this rare quality of reverence is mostly missing among Westerners, and even among most of today's living beings.

The chart on the facing page, however, pulls out all the stops and leaves no stone unturned in its demonstration of what an illumined soul is, has gained, and why such a being ought to be the first choice of embodied beings to befriend and take counsel of. The two quotes from Mother India's *Upanisads* are precious in their explication of these divine beings, noting first their transparent nonduality, and second, their willingness to stop and help others along their way to *Brahman*.

Further, the chart poses brief but convincing testimony of exactly what constitutes the character of these rare souls, everything important about their lives lived in the Spirit. For instance, they also have taken a teacher, or *guru*, and followed the instructions given by those unique preceptors of the *dharma*. They act and move just like everyone else, but somehow remain free of any undue *karmic* repercussion, unlike others. They study deeply, and extract meaning from what they contemplate, therefore their knowledge is incomparable and unimpeachable.

Moreover, these special souls possess keen powers of inquiry and observation, for not only have they gleaned their wisdom under the direct tutelage of an illumined preceptor, but they also make certain to take refuge in a profound Ideal who protects them as they live and expand their awareness. They meditate, albeit from a position that is not dependent upon *hatha* or *asana*, but rather prefers a lofty intellectual seat located in the deepest reaches of the pure heart and transcendent mind.

These unique souls somehow blend mature renunciation with the heartfelt quality of full compassion. They are like full-blown wildflowers that bloom alone in isolated locations on distant mountain peaks. Quite often, the "bee-devotees" who want to imbibe their nectar-like transmission must actually climb up to these remote atmospheres in order to find them and learn esoteric spiritual secrets from them. Their conclusions are always apt, the Truth they know, simple yet profound. The scriptures form wondrous descriptions of these luminaries, who though lauded, always remain humble and peaceful. Their peaceful demeanors are both legion and legend:

AUM shanta mahanto nivashanti shanto
vashanta-vat lokahitam charantah

There are luminaries on this earth, silent and great, who,
like the Spring season, bring about the well-being of the world.

All in all, and in addition to what has been written here, the chart under study on the facing page gives its own answers to the question of what a luminary is, and on many important subjects and attributes. A study of all of this is disarming, and is also grounds for an increase of devotion in the newly-informed believer's heart and mind. The principle of God in mankind, so dear to enlightened beings, begins to dawn, with clarifying results, upon the awakened soul's understanding — like the sun gradually warming the cold, snowy regions of high altitudes at daybreak. A divine contagion takes over the soul, which theretofore scarcely ever experienced a galvanizing spiritual moment. The truest of love's best, before only wasted on worthless egos and futile pastimes, suddenly rises in the human heart, eliciting possibilities untold — all spiritual in nature.

This dawning of original Awareness is a gift from the luminary upon those who come close and seek the Highest. As Sri Krishna tells Arjuna in the *Bhagavad Gita*, "To those who seek me with a devout heart, I give the special discrimination by which they will come to know Me in full."

In addition to their superlative presence, the illumined souls of all religious traditions of the world say important things about the nature of both Reality and relativity. *"The truth of both has been known by the seers,"* as the *Gita* puts it. On the next facing page are shown a host of great sayings of some of the luminaries, the most remarkable thing about them being their concurrence with one

The Integral Constitution of the Luminaries

"Those qualified souls who are fit to study the Upanisads are protectors of the field in which I-ness is destroyed. To them, all beings and the world are just pure Consciousness. To them, talk about the uprooting of karmas amounts to mere words, for the illusion of I-ness has been cremated and spread about in the cemetery of Self, of Brahman. For others, these luminaries represent a ship with which to cross the ocean of earthly existence." Nirvana Upanisad

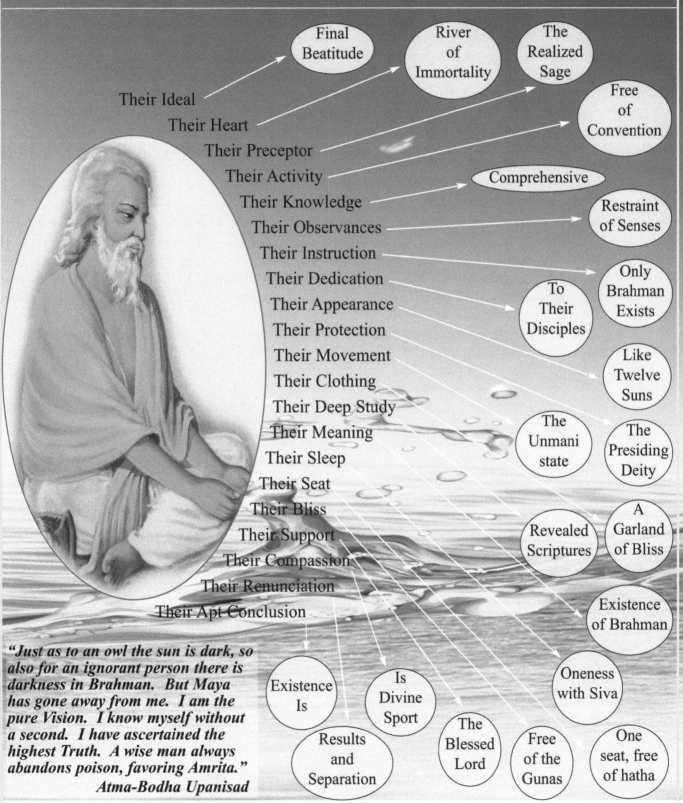

Final Beatitude

River of Immortality

The Realized Sage

Free of Convention

Comprehensive

Restraint of Senses

Only Brahman Exists

To Their Disciples

Like Twelve Suns

The Unmani state

The Presiding Deity

Revealed Scriptures

A Garland of Bliss

Existence of Brahman

Oneness with Siva

Their Ideal
Their Heart
Their Preceptor
Their Activity
Their Knowledge
Their Observances
Their Instruction
Their Dedication
Their Appearance
Their Protection
Their Movement
Their Clothing
Their Deep Study
Their Meaning
Their Sleep
Their Seat
Their Bliss
Their Support
Their Compassion
Their Renunciation
Their Apt Conclusion

Existence Is

Is Divine Sport

Results and Separation

The Blessed Lord

Free of the Gunas

One seat, free of hatha

"Just as to an owl the sun is dark, so also for an ignorant person there is darkness in Brahman. But Maya has gone away from me. I am the pure Vision. I know myself without a second. I have ascertained the highest Truth. A wise man always abandons poison, favoring Amrita."
Atma-Bodha Upanisad

another, despite their differences in choice of religions individual perspective. A common theme that runs throughout is the mention of oneness in terms of indivisibility of consciousness and the non-separation of God, mankind, and races and species. Another important thread in all of them is the attitude of subdominance with regard to the world and physical bodies. The supreme Spirit is tantamount, and holds the forefront of attention over life on earth in matter. Several of these greats aver that the world does not even exist when Ultimate Reality is experienced fully.

And it is not only the lesser import of earthly life that stands out in these sayings, but the outright illusory nature of death as well. The eternal nature of the Soul/Self therefore outstrips life, families, bodies, matter — anything and everything that simply fails to measure up to the untarnishable brilliance of Divine Reality, call it *Brahman*, Allah, God, Buddha Nature, or other noble appelations.

Along with the deep truths that are brought forward by a few well-constructed words, the emergence of the import of perceiving differences in what is temporal and ever-lasting reveals itself. Whether it is referred to as *"discrimination between the real and the unreal"* in one tradition, or *"separating the wheat from the chaff"* in another, this well-honed ability to purify the gold of the mind/soul of all dross is obviously highly valued among the saints, sages, and seers. Otherwise, what is divine in mankind remains covered over (see chart on page 293) by so many obstructions, both subtle and unseen, and gross and evident.

And so it is seen and accented that the awakened souls of the world's religious traditions all favor God first and foremost, speak to realizing That as the goal of human existence, and give the method as well. On top of these three mainstays, they encourage a strong self-effort along the spiritual path and unwavering commitment until the goal is reached. The methods they propose and stand behind may differ. Some evince an uncompromising nondual perspective based in lofty philosophical axioms. Others ask for devotion to the personal God, while still others lead the way by proposing meditation on Divine Reality with form and beyond form, both. In those seers who hail from Mother India, the emphasis is quite clear. Statements such as *"The Real always is, the unreal never ceases to be,"* and *"The soul bound is man, that same soul free is God,"* demonstrate India's possession and representation of the fully-matured nondual realization, called *Advaita Vedanta*. This sheds a unique light on all other forms of wisdom, and completes the picture, religiously and philosophically.

The word, *"Avatar,"* used in this chart presently under study is utilized to reveal the special presence of God in certain souls. Words such as prophets, buddhas, special and partial incarnations, as well as sages, seers, and yogis, etc., also apply in any specific case. The truth is that the visitation of higher states of Consciousness do occur in various awakened beings, regardless of their level of realization of the "Highest." Time also plays a factor, wherein the descent of higher Awareness may occur now and again according to many factors at play amidst the mass of collective consciousness of living beings.

This, as has been told, is the secret dynamism of *Brahman* called *Shakti* that moves with a speed inconceivable and undetectable to even the swiftest of minds and keenest of intellects. However, even to be in the know of Her sweet and benign presence is to be made a party to the real intentions of Her movements, and to be swept up into the fathomless depths of Her all-pervasive nonmovement as well. In accord with the chart now under study, She is the *Vak Devi*, the Goddess of the Word. She is "....the intelligence of the most intelligent ones, as the *Upanisads* state."

The intelligent particles in words and thoughts are much more powerful than material particles in atoms (see chart on page 501) and, actually, the latter evolve out of the former. The Divine Mother's many-tiered collection of worlds, universes, realms, and *lokas*, consist of particles that literally hum with Her Intelligence, some being much more potent than others. Potent means subtle in this regard; all the more powerful elements in form are within oneself, and originate and spring forth from the mind.

And that is why the *mantra* is given by the spiritual teacher as the sincere seeker for the prime means to purify the mind. These few small words hold immense power for transformation of mind,

Mahavakyas of the World's Avatars

"There are hosts of illumined souls that populate the atmospheres of higher wisdom — seers, saints, sages, yogis, munis, siddhas, etc. The Divine Incarnation transcends all of these." Babaji Bob Kindler

"An Avatar usually appears on earth in the company of divine companions, like Buddha's noble eight, Christ's twelve apostles, and Ramakrishna's sixteen direct disciples." Babaji Bob Kindler

Lord Buddha

"They who regard the body as a flake of foam on the waves shall no longer see death."

"They who discern Truth as Truth, and illusion as illusion, walk the right road."

Moses

"Hear ye O Israel: Our Lord is One God."

"Thou remainest ever the same, and thy years will not change that."

"It is not hidden; neither is It far off. It is not in heaven, nor is It beyond the sea. Verily, It is nigh unto thee, nestled deeply in thine own heart."

"Shine out for thyself as thine own Light."

"The destruction of things is their return to the cause that produced them."

"The idea of I and thou is a fruit of the soul's ignorance."

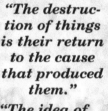
Sri Ram

"Illumination dawns on the human mind by stages."

"Perception of the end of knowledge in Truth is true knowledge. What is opposed to it is declared as ignorance."

Sri Ramakrishna

"I and my Father are One."

"No man hath seen God at any time."

"Love not the world, nor the things that are in the world."

"Verily, I say unto thee, that he who loves his life shall lose it, but he who hates his life shall receive it again in eternity."

Jesus

"The soul bound is man. That same soul free is God."

"If a man's mind gets boiled in the Fire of Knowledge, he will not be used thereafter for the new creation."

"Indivisible, It dwells in creatures as if divided."

"No one should weep for the dead or the living. All of us were before, and shall not cease hereafter."

"All of you have issued from the One."

"The perfect man is of the most use to others."

Zoroaster

"There is nothing worth loving that is not of The Light."

"The seer sees all as one Spirit."

"The world exists no longer when this mental dream is finished."

Mohammed

Shankara

but they only work at their highest potential if the transmitter and the receiver are authentic and rightly intentioned, and this *(shakti)* power is brought to bear on them via properly oriented self-effort.

As has been mentioned earlier in these pages, there is a difference between a *mantra* and a *mahavakya.* The essential difference is in the nature of each, the former being purificatory and the latter being confirmative/affirmative. The *mantra* will clean the mind of *karmas* and *samskaras* at intermediate and lower levels of consciousness, while the *mahavakya* will clear the mind of doubts at the highest level. The *mantra* is to be repeated continually to do its work, while the *mahavakya* is said just once at a time — probably at a time when the mind has been cleaned by the *mantra.*

Having stated these basic facts, a look at the chart on the facing page will reveal some of India's most profound statements which are also the result of long and deep meditation over lifetimes of spiritual search and arrival. The four main *Mahavakyas* of India are shown at the top of the chart, again not to be rendered a mere lip-service "parroting" kind of recitation, but rather an inner affirmation uttering of what has been realized previously via *sadhana.* For who is it that realizes the identical nature of the apparently individualized soul *(jivatman)* with the Supreme Soul *(Paramatman)?* The answer is precious few, and only they come out of such deep epiphanies to declare uncompromising statements such as *"I am That,"* or *"I and my Father are one,"* etc.

Though the four main nondual statements of India are legend, this does not stop the *Upanishads* and other *advaitic* scriptures from laying out all that is legion as well. A group of other powerful declarations of this nature also grace this chart, some of them being nondualistic, others falling into the realm of higher wisdom as qualified nondualistic utterances, and some even coming from lineages of India that lean more towards *Tantra.* Some of these declare Truth at the highest level, while others teach Truth near the apex of Self-realization.

The *abhavapadarthas* are an example of the latter of these categories. By using metaphors of examples in life and nature that point out obvious or not so obvious conundrums, the mind of the aspirant gets pointed towards the presence of *mayic* influences and can thereby clear the thinking process. The *"son of a barren woman"* is a good example of such a statement. If a friend walked up to you one day and told you that he had just had a great conversation with a barren woman's son, this would produce ample cause for the intelligent person to both doubt and examine further. Therefore, when the *guru* states *"vandhyputra"* in context with a teaching about *Brahman* and its *maya,* the seeker's mind is brought closer to the actual truth of the matter and does not need to exert philosophically in order to find an answer, or understanding. This is a bit like the practice of *koan (doksan)* in Zen. Inference thus plays a big part in the detection of the covering *(avarana)* and distorting *(vikshepa)* powers of *maya,* and the further uncovering of the Truth that eludes most beings in the realms of name and form in time and space.

Not all of these great statements are of a sweeping nondual nature. Some, there are, that bring in the sweetness of divine relationships with the deities, like in Divine Mother tradition. Oneness with Her is particularly desirable for the *shaktas,* and they do not care if such is considered dualistic or not. Does a baby care whether its mother has form (like when she is nursing it) or is essentially formless (when she puts it to bed and leaves the room)? It only loves the mother, and both the actual presence and the thought of her are precious to it. Thus, such statements as *Saham,* "I am She," or *Tavaivoham,* "I am Thine alone," epitomize the meaning and the relationship with the Divine Mother precisely.

Shaktism, or Divine Mother worship, has another very appealing facet to it which is rather sweeping and grand — and philosophical. That is its easy and comfortable fit with *Advaita Vedanta.* The school of profundity that best explains and characterizes this is called *Shaktadvaita,* or the path of nonduality in and through the perspective of Divine Mother Reality. The chart on the previous page gives some strong guidelines as to the observances, intentions, and practices of this singular pathway to Truth.

The two main directives of the *Shaktadvaitavada* actually characterize most all of the inten-

Daivi Vaka — Divine Sayings
India's Great Spiritual Statements

"At the height of all levels of the Wisdom-Word, and infused with the Divine Mother's own power of penetration and dissolution, the great sayings of Sanatana Dharma — the eternal religion of India — assist aspiring beings in destroying the mind's assumed ignorance and attaining the incomparable spiritual station of nonduality." Babaji Bob Kindler

The Four Mahavakyas

1) Aham Brahmasmi – "I Am Brahman."
2) Ayamatma Brahma – "This Self Is Brahman."
3) Prajnanam Brahma – "Brahman Is Pure Consciousness."
4) Tattvam Asi – "That Thou Art."

"By Mahavakyanusadana, inquiry into the meaning of the great sayings, seekers perceive Reality."

Other Great Advaitic Statements

Asmi – "I am."
Sarvosmi – "I am all."
Aham Atma – "I am Atman."
Kham Brahm – "All is Brahman."
Ahameva Sarvah – "I alone am all."
Chinmatroham – "I am pure Consciousness."
Sarvam Khalvidam Brahma – "All This is Brahman."
Brahman Satya, Jagad Mithya – "Brahman alone is real, the world is unreal."
Kevala Asti – "You alone exist." (One is not the world, but Spirit.)

Qualified Nondual Statements

Aham etat na – "I am not this."
Anaham Tvam – "Not I, Thou."
Ishvaraprayatna – "It is God's Will."
Shokamayata – "For God so desired."
Niranjanoham – "I am spotlessly pure."
Ekoham Bahusyam –
"May I, the One, become many."

Abhavapadarthas – Sayings Regarding the Real and Unreal

Shuktikarajata – Silver in mother of pearl
Vandhyaputra – Barren woman's son
Taptapinda – Heated iron ball
Rajjusarpanyaya – Snake in the rope
Stanumanusya – Man in a stump

Great Sayings of the Shaktas

Bhakti, Mukti, Jnanam Dehi – "May She bestow Devotion, Liberation, Knowledge."
Prabuddha Sarvada Tishtet – "Get thee ever Awakened!"
Tavaivaham – "I am Thine alone."
Saham – "She I Am."

Shaktadvaitavada — Divine Mother Nonduality

"Nonduality is the essence of Mother-Wisdom (Mahamatrika) which through Her Word as scripture (Agama/Nigama) emanates to reveal the mystery of the universe. God with form (Ishvara), living beings, worlds, and objects, and all evolve from Her." The Tantras

Intention of Shaktadvaita

Primary Directive: To Manifest the Soul's Inherent Perfection — Siddhi
Secondary Directive: To Free the Soul from Cycles of Rebirth — Karmabandha
Result: Awakening of Kundalini to reveal the Atman via Pure Mind — Chit-shuddhi

The Two Truths of Supreme Knowledge

Its Origin		Its Nature
Knowledge Is:	PRATIBHA	Knowledge Is:
Self-Revelatory (Not Sense-born)		Divine Dynamism (Female/Mother)
Is	VIJNANA	Is
Parasamvit, Chit-Shakti, Prajna	PRATYABHIJNA	Guru Tattva Trikalatita Nirmama

Advaita Vedanta		Tantra
All is Brahman	Basis	Siva/Shakti
Viveka	Method	Tattvavichara
Tattvajnana & Upasana	Body/Mind Purification	Bhutashuddhi & Chitshuddhi

Purnahanta – Nondual "I" in Its Fullness

AHAM

A	HA	M
Paraprakasha	Svatantriya	Bindu
(Supreme Space of Pure Being)	(Inherent Freedom)	(Point of First Emanation)

"She is called Parameshvara; Paravak in the Agamas and Shabda Brahman in the Vedas. There is nothing beyond Her, but there are infinite numbers of worlds within Her. She is the inner essence of Siva, not an extent consort." Lex Hixon

tions of the Indian *darshanas*. Unlike other religions, all *Vedic* and *Tantric* paths, as well as *Yoga*, and including *Buddhism* and *Jainism*, seek to get the transmigrating soul free of cycles of birth and death in matter in the body. This is the "secondary" directive, and it is based not upon purifying the soul, but rather bringing out the qualities of the already and always pure Soul. This odd but ingenious insight into Soul-Nature does not follow lines of thought such as original sin, the search for and arrival at heaven, or the escape from hell and the like. In fact, earth, heaven, and hell are all types of bondage in form to the *Vedic* thinkers, being realms conjured up by the impure mind due to its desires. concentrating on the innate perfection of the Soul, *Atman,* is then the prime and primary way to Freedom, and much superior to taking up the stance of imperfection and trying to work this condition out through moral measures.

With the intrinsic perfection of the Soul a given, paths such as *Shaktadvaitavada* bring quick results to the sincere seeker after peace, bliss, and Truth. Add to this the *Kundalini* element that is always close to any Divine Mother pathway, the vision, method, and consummation are all close at hand for the fortunate aspirant.

As the chart indicates by its three middle assignments, *pratibha* (innate intelligence), *vijnana* (specialized wisdom of purely spiritual matters), and *pratyabhijna* (recognition of the Soul's eternally perfect condition) are all key to the pathway, and when they combine it is for direct realization of *Brahman*. On both sides of this triune principle stands Consciousness, represented by the illumined *guru,* whose subtle *Shakti* power keeps the soul free from crystalizations that occur to so many beings who encounter time and space. It allows for a facile wherewithal that keeps the ever-threatening ego mechanism under control and out of the picture.

From here the path breaks into double designations, one for the *Tantric* temperament bent on worship, and the other for the nondual temperament desiring transcendence. Generally, the Divine Couple — *Siva* and *Shakti* — will appeal to the former, and the Ultimate *Brahman* will be the Goal of the latter. *Tantric* aspirants will move inwards via knowledge of and worship of cosmic principles, called *tattvavichara*. *Advaita Vedantists* will utilize the sharp-edged sword of *viveka,* a well-honed discrimination between the eternal and noneternal. Concerning the stodgy and persistent body, senses, and mind complex, *Tantricists* will subject it to purification, while the *Vedic* seekers will rise above it utilizing contemplation of wisdom principles and meditation of the Formless Reality. Whatever the case may be — for even admixtures of these two ways are possible among the varying temperaments of spiritual aspirants — the prime result is both swiftly forthcoming and superlative. Occupying the Supreme Space called *Paraprakasha,* and living always and spontaneously in the bliss of inherent Freedom *(Svatantriya),* even if the Essence abiding There decides to move into form again, it always does so from the original Point of Emanation *(Bindu)* that is fully conscious of all its movements. Here, it can only be said that —

> *When the mind neither accepts nor rejects anything,*
> *its activity ceases and one abides in ones essential Reality.*

The seers say that this pure, conscious Awareness is not a thought, nor can it be seen by any discipline or habit. It cannot be practiced. It is perfect alertness moment to moment. It comes about not by any choice or by seeking, but only spontaneously when the mind has ceased cognizing and surrenders itself completely to the effulgence of the Divine Presence within.

Leaning now more towards the *Tantric* side of Indian Philosophy in order to engender further understanding of the Divine Couple, *Siva* and *Shakti,* the following chart satisfies deep questions about this most enigmatic and eternally living Principle.

Part of the beauty of *Tantra* comes from its wide open acceptance, declaration, and outright worship of the static Ultimate Reality, *Siva,* and Its dynamic aspect, *Shakti*. This fully present twin aspect fuels Sri Ramakrishna's statement that *Brahman* is with form, free of form, and beyond both form and formlessness as well. It also falls well in line with *Vedanta's* conclusive pronouncement that "All is *Brahman*." And *Tantra* has its own unique way of elucidating these profound esoteric facts, no matter how abstruse they may be.

The chart under study on the facing page gives a series of most important bullet points on both *Siva* and *Shakti*. For the *Tantric* adept there is never any doubt that all that is seen on the field of action is *Shakti* in motion, and that Her motion is the manifested essence of Lord *Siva*, who remains still and motionless all the while. They are thus one Reality appearing in two modes, a truth that clears both the mind and the field of action of doubts and misconceptions that often plague other pathways and their methods. This is true because, while other modes of proceeding involve themselves with living, glorifying, or dealing with life as the main purpose of existence, the worship of *Siva* and *Shakti* focuses in on the destruction of ignorance first, which then naturally results in the exquisite enjoyment of absolute Freedom. This process has already been explained in the chart on page 369 by way of revealing the four works and five functions of Lord *Siva* via His two *parigraha shaktis*. Since *Siva* is formless, is pure Essence, is the underlying backdrop to all of manifestation, it falls to *Shakti* to carry into expression His transcendental intentions.

As the chart under study on the facing page reveals, *Shakti* also confers other crucial assistance on the *Tantric* votary. She guides the aspirant out of ignorance and into the light of Freedom, and this She accomplishes via the *Guru* Principle. *Guru* is not a personality, but a Principle. It exists within every heart and mind, only covered over in many and revealed in the few. A special transmission occurs when the prepared and qualified *shishya* comes near the adept and illumined preceptor/*Guru*. As iron filings get agitated and move accordingly when a magnet is introduced into their proximity, so too do aspiring souls wake up and court Enlightenment when a spiritual luminary enters their lives.

The further dynamics of this transmission and its effects can be compared metaphorically to needles that have accumulated rust; these do not move toward the magnet due to their overlays of impurity. Similarly, spiritually sleepy and impure souls do not get attracted to God when corrosion covers their consciousness in the form of desires and passions. Here, the Divine *Shakti* acts as a salt solution for these spiritually rusty minds, stripping away all corrosive coverings to expose the pure metal within them. The stainless Soul, or *Atman*, is what gets exposed here, which only got obscured previously by the mind's many *mayic* associations.

What *Tantra* is explaining here is the mystic awakening of *Kundalini* power, that subtle force that is lying dormant in all human beings. As Ramprasad Sen, one fully dedicated lover of Divine Mother Reality, sings in his devotional wisdom songs,

> *O Divine Mother of the Universe, flowing Power of the Absolute.*
> *Purifier of all minds and hearts!*
> *She who confers Her own Bliss as the fruit of the spiritual quest.*
> *O Ecstatic Consort of the Absolute, grant me the fragrant shade of Your Lotus Feet on this auspicious day!*
> *O She Who liberates every conscious being! O Holy Mother!*
> *Please shower Your Grace, Your Illumination!*
> *I am a simple person without sublime gifts of character.*
> *I lack real intensity in my life of prayer.*
> *My Blissful Mother, only You can wake me from this dream of change, this wheel of time.*
> *O Compassionate Tara! She Who bears all beings to the Truth!*
> *Your Feet of Wisdom are the only vessel that sails across this terrible sea of birth and death.*
> *O mysterious Kali! Consort and Power of Absolute Reality! She Who is One with Reality!*
> *Please be gracious to the singer of this song.*

In the chart on the facing page, Lord Siva comes to the fore. He is a prime example of the Stationary Self after which the final chapter of this book is titled. All the assignments on this chart reflect either the Truth of pure Existence, or the obstacles that hide the same. As it should be — but so unlike the philosophy of other religions or ideologies — India places the origin of all gods and demigods (*suras* and *asuras*) directly within the human mind, not up in space or in some imaginary

Tantra's Siva & Shakti

"Shaktayika, dynamic power, and Agama, knowledge of the use of that power, are identical with one another. Thus, Shiva is the agent, and Shakti, the instrument. But Shakti's manifestations are, in essence, Shiva appearing as the imminent — all life in the worlds of name and form."

• Siva is synonymous with Brahman and represents Kula, the aspiring family guided by live spiritual tradition.

• Siva is Niskala, the subtle underlying backdrop • Siva is Tat, "That Alone," and Purnahanta, "I in Fullness," which is Siva in tandem with His unstinted freedom as Shakti.

• Siva is the indeterminate state (alinga) from which arises all vibrations (spandas), which then manifest as principles (tattvas) amidst which Shakti sports in time (kala) as the play of Consciousness.

• Siva is also the determinative state (linga), who in conjunction with nature, is called Sakala Siva.

• Siva's essential functions are projection (sristhi), sustenance (sthiti), dissolution (samhara), self-limitation (tirodhana), and expression (anugraha).

• Siva wields two main consciousness forces, called Parigraha Shaktis (Bindu and Maya), which cause and oversee all worlds and forms in space and time.

• Bindu and Maya Shaktis fulfill Siva's Four Great Works: Jnana pada, maintaining philosophical systems; Yoga pada, spiritual disciplines; Charya pada, transmission of teaching; Kriya pada, fructification.

• Shakti is the form of Siva: Sivarupah. Thus, worship of Shakti is the stepping-stone to both the destruction of ignorance and the attainment of freedom.

• Shakti is directly correlative to Guru Tattva, via which the spiritual preceptor appears and spiritual teachings are duly transmitted.

• Shakti and Her worship accomplishes the full involution of the embodied soul back to the Source by withdrawing the Atman from Its many associations with Her mayic creations.

• Invoking Shakti awakens the Kundalini power lying dormant in all living beings.

• Propitiating Shakti reveals the Atman to be pure and sentient, and all manifest principles (tattvas) to be pure and insentient.

"Shiva and Shakti are pure Existence combined with inner Essence. Existence precedes Essence, but Essence renders Existence meaningful. Siva and Shakti's innate inseparability is the root of all expression. As long as beings do not realize it they move about in a confusing haze of illusory phenomena, devoid of the real import of humanity's relationship with God and with each other."
Tantra Darshana

kingdom. They are powers dwelling in the kingdom of awareness within, a multi-layered cosmos that consists of the mind's thought and conception. They are ever at war with one another (which reflects on earth in the forms of war and violence) to possess all that is generated by the greater mind, or *Mahat*. This urge to possess and dominate is a kind of cosmic churn fueled by desire and attachment, which brings to the surface of the ocean of consciousness all manner of articles, both heavenly and earthly. The effects of this process come forth in twin modes of good and bad manifestations, or *karmas*, and thus produce a kind of poison that causes bondage and suffering. These contrasting dualities, or *dvandva mohena*, along with the miseries they cause, are the coveted life of the physical universe and its denisons, and are exactly what the real devotees of God avoid and attempt to transcend. This they accomplish by all the designations shown at the top half of this chart.

First of all, the devotees get ahold of the *bijams,* or holy seeds of power, in any given lifetime. This they do by securing a wisdom teacher and receiving initiation into the mysteries of the ancient traditions. This person, an *acharya* or *guru*, is the living Siva who holds the *dharma* in the face of all antagonistic forces on earth. By seeing him, though often unbeknownst to them, they see Lord *Siva* in form. Further, He carries the Divine Mother within Him in the form of "*Om* Kali." It is She who assists Him in consuming the poisons that collect due to the ill-considered deeds that loving beings commit. Drinking them, His throat turns blue *(nilkantha)*, but due to Her He survives all evil effects. Thus is transformation, or its possibility, always going forth on earth, and the spiritual quest is nothing less than the aspirant locating *Siva/Guru/Acharya,* etc., and availing him or herself of divine power.

Siva's trident, with its triple prongs, signifies the three worlds where transmigration of souls is going on. Rising above these three *lokas (bhur, bhuvar, swahar)* the devotee finds the Truth at the heart, of fourth world *(mahar)*, and ceases to be reborn in ignorance ever again. The sun of nondual Awareness is seen there (with the single Eye), and the sound of divinity, or God's Word, *AUM*, is heard. The Sky of Awareness is much more alluring than the world of matter, so transmigration is given up. Ones *karmas* are all expunged.

The conditionless state that is eventually revealed so deep within the indivisible Soul is referred to as *moksha,* or *mukti,* by the Indian *rishis*. For a thorough review of how this ever-present Verity is reached, a look at the chart on page 343 is advised. How It is described via special words by the luminaries, and what Its subtle characteristics are, will be taken up in the next chart, shown on page 686.

The quote on the chart now under study is from the *Vivekachudamani* by Shankaracharya, and defines *moksha* best of all. He writes, "*Moksha, or mukti, is not to be considered a state or experience yet to come. It is the eternal condition of the Self, which is nothing other than Brahman.*" And as the quote from the *Avadhuta Gita* at the top of this same chart declares, there is nothing in existence that can purify the Soul, for the Soul is ever-pure. These two special *slokas* declare the natural essence of Enlightenment. So what is Enlightenment? The question need not be asked anymore. The *Upanisads* state and have always stated, that "All is *Brahman*." Shankara fleshes this terse statement out by adding that *"....time, space, living beings, and the world"* are that selfsame *Brahman*. But why do beings not see this, and act accordingly? Because they do not keep this most essential fact in their minds and memories, and thus forget. *"Living in constant recognition of this fact (All is Brahman) is what is called Enlightenment,"* he concludes.

So that the disciples, devotees, aspirants, *sadhakas,* do not forget, then, the great teachers come into the body on this earth and leave them with strong examples and evidence in the form of sacred scriptures, also giving divine discourses, daily, on the truths contained within them.

When we look upon these marvelous souls there are four great signs that appear to mark them. First, when they take a body, they keep their divinity intact. Most other beings abandon the Soul and memory of its special attributes when they take bodies. This is only seen if one accepts reincarnation and studies its dynamics in accord with inner cosmology. To manifest God on earth is

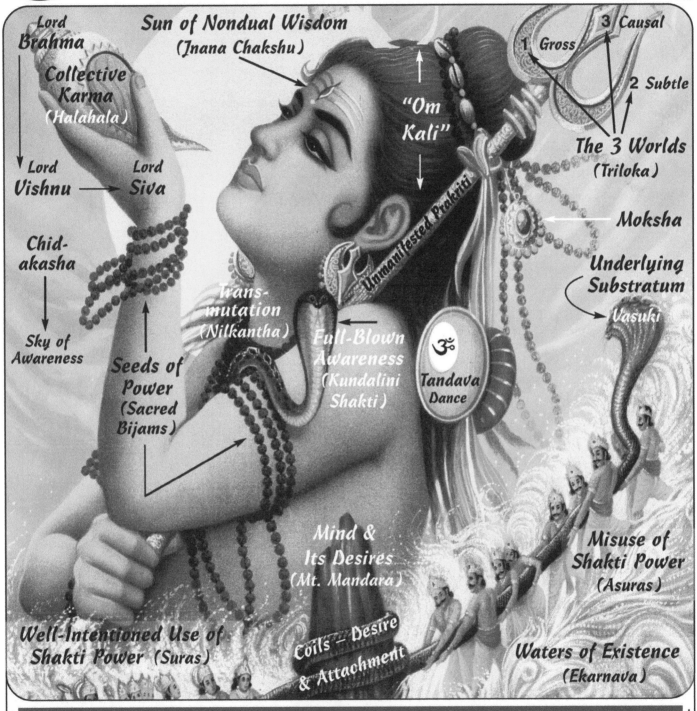

Lord **Brahma**

Collective Karma *(Halahala)*

Lord **Vishnu** → Lord **Siva**

Chidakasha

Sky of Awareness

Seeds of Power *(Sacred Bijams)*

Sun of Nondual Wisdom *(Jnana Chakshu)*

"Om Kali"

Unmanifested Prakriti

Trans-mutation *(Nilkantha)*

Full-Blown Awareness *(Kundalini Shakti)*

Tandava Dance

1 **Gross**   3 **Causal**
2 **Subtle**

The 3 Worlds *(Triloka)*

Moksha

Underlying Substratum

Vasuki

Mind & Its Desires *(Mt. Mandara)*

Misuse of Shakti Power *(Asuras)*

Well-Intentioned Use of Shakti Power *(Suras)*

Coils — Desire & Attachment

Waters of Existence *(Ekarnava)*

"The pure and self-sacrificing soul, devout worshiper of the Mother of the Universe and the Holy Trinity, while swimming blissfully in the Ocean of Existence under the pristine Sky of Awareness, willingly assumes and deftly transforms the collective karma of all living beings abiding in the three worlds, demonstrating how to transcend attachment to the objects of the senses via well-intentioned use of Shakti power in order to gain liberation from repetitious cycles of rebirth in ignorance. Chanting 'Om Kali' with every breath, he then 'drinks the nectar from the rare fruit of Her nondual wisdom.'" *Babaji Bob Kindler*

The True Meaning of Moksha/Mukti

"The Soul is not purified by the six-limbed Yoga; nor is It made pure by the destruction of the mind's waves; neither is it rendered pure by bowing at the guru's feet. The Soul is pure by its very nature."

Avadhuta Gita

⬇ The Free Soul – Jivanmukta ⬇

➜ Lives in the mortal physical frame as Brahman

➜ Sports in the world as the playground of Shakti

➜ Sees the universe as transcendental Consciousness

➜ Views all objects as representations of AUM

Mukti Is Not Liberation from Bondage:

1) Is not freedom which is produced or generated ⟶
* not freedom from senses
* not freedom from passion
* not freedom from nature
* not freedom from desire
* not freedom from sin

2) Is not a result of evolution, development, or transformation ⟶
* not the solving of problems
* not brought about by some power above or outside
* not the disappearance of weakness or imperfections

3) Is not something to be attained ⟶
* not the result of movement away from one's Source

4) Is not something to be realized via purification ⟶
* not due to the soul's fall from its original status
* not because the world is corrupt or needs escaping
* not because the soul has gathered impurities

"Mukti, or moksha, is not to be considered a state or experience yet to come. It is the eternal condition of the Self, which is nothing other than Brahman." Shankara

not just the business of Christs, Buddhas, and Krishnas; every soul is born to express their divinity. The bottom half of the previous chart on page 685 shows why this is so. Examples such as these are really the standard, not the exceptions. The principle of *jivanmukti* is thus India's superlative gift to human beings, allowing them a higher Goal than what earthly life offers: Eternal Life rather than cyclic life ending in death.

A second characteristic of the *jivanmukta* is that even this physical world has become a sporting ground, and life there is free of fear and bondage as well. The luminary sees the Mother Supreme, not Mother Nature, as operating and controlling all things. Sentient Mother-power, or *Shakti,* is ever superior to insentient matter.

This Divine Mother Principle is what allows the luminary to perceive the entire universe as pure, conscious Awareness. Without Her everything is dull and lifeless, which is instanced by those who have no idea of Her presence and puissance. When one is fortunate enough to see a realized soul, to see them as egos or personalities is wrong perception. Their separate selves have been offered to Her, thus stripped of all the problematic limitations that are so pervasive in the worldly and the ignorant. This is also why it is sacred Sound, not simple talk, that they are always listening for. The essence of objects in the form of sublime thoughts connect them to The Word via the pure intellect. Looking within or without, they see only what is true, what is real, and what is beneficial. This is the very nature of emptiness, too, that mirrors fullness for them.

The bottom half of the chart under study reveals the uniqueness of true freedom, and therefore the essence of *Advaita Vedanta.* Since *Atman* is ever-free, *moksha* is not gained via ordinary or conventional means. Nor is it attained by nonconventional means either. It is simply never gained, being ever-present. Though the sense-bound person may come to think that the senses need to be stripped of habit, and the pleasure-seeker might find that freedom lies in quelling his passions, neither of these turns of mind will facilitate true Freedom for them. Nor will the nature lover's attempt to detach from the five elements and the objects made of them bring about this ultimate condition either. Similarly, the reformer may want to destroy all traces of sin from the mind, but even if this were possible he would not find *moksha* thereby. One might find salvation through some of these efforts, but not *moksha.*

The chart shows us the unique nature of true Freedom, in that It cannot be gained over time, nor by developing the body/mind mechanism, and not even by undergoing transformation. A further explanation of this follows the extraordinary views of the nondualist who sees no other power, such as above or beyond, than the Self. Since this Self is ever-free of imperfections, and the mind of the luminary knows this, a simple observance of focused concentration upon this selfsame inherent Perfection is all that is needed to be in *moksha* all the time. This unique being does not fall victim to thoughts of bettering, improving, or growing; all these facets, no matter how well-intentioned, are beneath the Soul, the *Atman.* Why bring Perfection down and subjugate It to imperfection?

Location is also analysed with regards to the *Atman's* natural transcendence. The earlier point about these rare beings seeing *Brahman* everywhere and in everything is innately connected here in that they see no source to be moved towards or away from when the Self is all-pervasive. As Swami Vivekananda has stated, where is the place to which they will go to or come from when all space is in the Soul.

Thus, bondage needing freedom and impurities requiring rectification, though they may be necessary to assist the mind, have no place in the realmless Realm of the *Atman.* To realize "That" is to put an end to all limitations and misconceptions about the very nature of Reality, and thus to render relativity nil and void. *Moksha* is the divine and permanent status of the Soul, and relativity, or what is called *maya* by the illumined souls, makes it seem otherwise.

This would be a good juncture to place some focus on the *jivanmukta,* India's precious gift to the earth, and to aspiring humanity. The chart on page 689 lists many of the superlative characteristics of this living liberated soul, who has already been noted for his/her singular mode of existence that perceives Consciousness/*Brahman* as the only reality, and looks upon the world as a sporting ground for It.

Two lists grace the chart on page 689, compiled by realized souls from India who are probably some 3000 to 5000 years apart in time. This shows, one, how India has been thinking about and developing such unique beings for millennia and, two, that such souls are amongst us from age to age, assisting aspiring beings in reaching the highest goal of human existence.

Lord Vasishtha's description of the *jivanmukta* informs us on two levels that the world of name and form in time and space are "emanations" of the Great Self, or *Atman*, but being projections, are not real in and of themselves. This is why great souls – from Ramchandra to Ramakrishna to Ramana Maharshi – have renounced it. On the opposite side of the *dharma* chart, Shankara, who lived round 700 A.D., gives his assessment of the living liberated state from the all-pervasive perspective, and includes giving up the realms of name and form.

After this is noted, a host of wonderful points come forth from these enlightened souls on the nature of such unusual beings. Topics like suffering are taken into account, revealing the possibility of transcending it – even while occupying the physical form. The absence of the ego element in these luminaries stands out, showing all those who are seeking higher Consciousness that the sense of being an individual must be replaced by the actuality of the indivisible. Obviously, *karma* and desire have been attenuated, or dissolved completely, depending on the temperament and purpose of any given *jivanmukta* who embodies to assist others (since some retain *sattvic* desires so as to be able to embody to assist other souls in getting free). The absence of any attraction to what draws other beings into the net of *maya* and the wending ways of the world is also to be noted. They are as if oblivious to the allures of wealth, power, and mere pleasure, for they are in possession of both Bliss *(ananda)* and the *"Peace that passeth all understanding"* as well.

Some of the rare and less heard of qualities of the *jivanmuktas* also find their mention on this short list of qualities. Due to their high-minded, or no-minded state, these incomparable beings see the same in everything, or that *"All is Brahman."* Whatever there is in the worlds of name and form — powers, pleasures, personalities, phenomena — they all enter into the living-liberated Soul, as the *Upanisads* state, like mighty rivers merging into a boundless ocean. All the while they have verily "forgotten" that duality even exists, such is their rare condition of nondual realization. And amazingly, for the most part and with so many of them, they seem to act like everyone else, with few outer distinctions to call attention to them.

And so, these inimitable souls both live in the return to what Sri Krishna calls in the *Bhagavad Gita*, the "Stainless State," as the quote at the bottom of the chart under study declares. Amazingly, and seemingly contradictory, they can take a birth in the body on earth but remain ever-free from the stains of embodiment and rebirth. This is well-described by Shankara in his *Nirvanashatkam*, or *Six Verses on the Nature of Nirvana*:

na mrityor na shankha na me jati bheda
pita naiva me naiva mata ma janmah

I have no death, for I was never really born.
No father have I, nor any mother.
nor any friend nor any caste....

And he complements and consummates every verse of this *stotram* with the galvanizing words, *Chidananda rupah sivoham sivoham* — *"I am pure Consciousness and Bliss; I am Siva, I am Siva!"*

The philosophy of these beings who are nonbeings, if such a system could be called that, is India's exceptional *Advaita Vedanta*, the like of which is not found anywhere else in the worlds of religion or philosophy. As Swami Vivekananda himself has written: *"On planes physical, ethical and spiritual, an ever-broadening generalization — leading up to a concept of Unity Eternal — is in the air; and this being so, all the movements of the time may be taken to represent, knowingly or unknowingly, the noblest philosophy of the unity of man ever had — the Advaita Vedanta."* The powerful chart

The State and Characteristics of a Jivanmukta

Vasishtha's Description of Jivanmukti

"Those rare beings who are firmly set on the path of Brahman, who are always engaged in the certain knowledge that the universes in space and time, though emanating from the Self, do not really exist, and never did exist, they are the living liberated."

* Who appears to think and act like everyone else
* Whose mind is free of karmas and longing
* Protect all beings via Tattvajnana and Atmajnana
* Is indifferent to joy and pain arising from actions
* Is equanimous in all that is obtained or lost
* Forsakes attainments foreign to the path of Wisdom
* Makes ceaseless inquiries into the nature of Reality
* Ever interrogates the wise for keys to liberation
* Does not transgress the instructions of the acharyas
* Is the Lord in an embodied state, engaged in actions
* Who is detached even without performing austerity
* Enjoys jagrat and sushupti devoid of all desires.
* Associates with desire, but does not get defiled by it
* Is transcendent of conventional observances
* Is full of the certitude of his or her convictions
* Lives in the Bliss of Chidananda
* Whose mind is in an indescribable state
* Transcends the Siddhas and lives in Jnana
* Retains sattvic desire in order to re-embody
* Crosses samsara to get moksha; returns to help
* Purifies all desires and engages in life as mere sport
* Destroys undue attraction to forms in the mind
* Attains Videha-mukti at the end of life via samadhi
* Uses jnana and pranic control to do away with pain
* Always knows the unreal nature of the universe
* Contemplates Atman while performing all actions

Shankara's Description of Jivanmukti

"Internally, externally, in the sentient and insentient — everywhere, knowing the Self as the basis of all, who has given up names and forms and become one, undivided Self — one who lives in that state is surely a liberated one, a free soul."

* Enjoys the burgeoning of endless merits
* Is always established in nondual understanding
* Is ever poised in the Self in Brahman
* Experiences freedom even in this world and body
* Has mastered karma and desires
* Is peaceful and impervious to Samsara
* Retains no sense of I, me, and mine
* Is free of past, present and future
* Who sees sameness everywhere and in everything
* Who remains unchanged in pleasure and pain
* Whose heart is filled with bliss of Brahman
* Lives in the body only as its witness
* Knows the Self via study of sacred scriptures
* Feels no identification with the body and senses
* Sees no difference between Brahman and the world
* Remains the same at all times
* Into whom enjoyments enter like vast rivers
* Who has known the reality of Brahman
* Who sees indivisible oneness at all times
* Who is free from worldliness and its effects
* Via revealed scriptures, is free from the five sheaths
* Is free from caste, laws, blood-ties, and name/form
* Ceases to follow the world, the body, and dogmas
* Who sees Brahman in the sentient and insentient
* Who has made the intellect one with Brahman
* Who seeing Reality, has almost forgotten duality

"The one fixed in equanimity of mind frees oneself in this life from virtue and vice alike; therefore devote yourself to Yoga; work done to perfection is verily Yoga. The wise, imbued with evenness of mind, renouncing the fruits of their actions, freed from fetters of births, verily go to the stainless state."   Sri Krishna

on the opposite page outlines the essentials of its transcendent thinking.

The word, Self, in *Advaita*, refers directly to *Atman* — also called *Paramatman.* It is synonymous with *Brahman.* Being pure, conscious Awareness, or timeless, deathless Consciousness, it alone exists. All else — all that falls under the headings of time, space, name, form, and causation — are, at best, its emanations or offshoots. Waves naturally rise on the breast of a vast ocean, but only the ocean remains the same. This Self, then, has no rival, brooks no second principle. When the ego-mind complex, separating itself out from that infinite ocean like an iceberg, ignores the ocean and thinks only of its own, limited and solidified condition, it courts bondage. This bondage, and its related suffering, then thickens and deepens to a point where total ignorance of Reality ensues. If the soul (mind complex) recognizes this path of mistaken identification (with thought, energy, and matter), it then strives to detach so as to return to its original Nature once again, realizing that this apparent falling away from Reality was its own act of deluded mental projection. This paragraph outlines, in simple form, the first five points of the chart on the facing page.

Over a deep period of sincere practice in *Advaita Vedanta,* the realizations that come to the fore are not just ones of peace, balance, harmony, bliss, and so forth. The Pearl of Great Price here is one of total union with Divine Reality. When the refined, or matured soul is overtaken by nondual realization, called *Samadhi,* the recognition of the fact that there is no other being but The Self in existence transports it into an ineffable and inexpressible state. Recognition *(pratyabhijna)* on one side, and forgetfulness *(avidya)* on the other — both of these become things of a nonexistent past. This is *moksha,* a freedom always and ever at hand (refer to chart on page 686). If the realized Soul decides to take up any body in any world thereafter, and for any purpose, It does so in full knowledge that all forms and all *lokas* are mutable and impermanent, and that any identification with them whatsoever will risk preoccupation. This is why *vairagya,* mature detachment, is the single most important possession of any luminary attending upon the worlds of name and form in time and space. This paragraph outlines points six through ten in simple terms.

A realized soul may choose to incarnate in order to help others out of the illusion of finitude. Such a soul can remain a single force, or might even get involved with other living beings in various walks of life. The main hallmark of such a rare person is an overall and overriding evenness of mind that allows him or her to recognize perfect Consciousness existing everywhere, in all beings. Thus, these singular souls are free of fear and attachment, and move about the world uninhibited by the weights and worries of worldly beings. As Swami Vivekananda has written in his "Song of the Sannyasin," *"Say, 'peace to all:' from me no danger be to aught that lives. In those who dwell on high, in those who lowly creep, I am the Self in all!"* This declaration is the central theme of all realized souls: *Kham Brahm* — Freedom consists of seeing nothing but the Self.

With this central theme intact, the main watchword for a realized soul associating with the body will be clarity. No confusion of mind around the consistency of the Self is to be allowed. It is not matter, nor energy, nor thought; thus It is not bodies, nor nature, nor conception. Moreover, there must be no false superimposition of the lower self over the higher Self permitted. The lower self is the ego, or personality. The worldly love this personality. They throw God out the back door and usher the ego in via the front. Too late they find out, if at all, that the ego has a very limited and quickly exhausted store of happiness, joy, or even subtle bliss. The *Avadhut* declares this in his song of nondual Awareness: *"Contemplating the dreamlike past, I found that I never performed the action that brought about suffering. I never owned a mind complex with which to create pleasure and pain. The ego is an onerous phantom, devoid of substance. Thus I concluded: I am Pure Existence, Wisdom, and Bliss, as boundless as the sky, infinite like space."* These last two paragraphs define points eleven through fifteen on the chart on page 691.

Prior to taking up more of the superlative teachings of *Advaita Vedanta,* an easy shift over to the *Yoga darshana* can provide us with a step by step description of what was just outlined somewhat scantily in the previous chart. Patanjali, the Father of *Astanga Yoga,* has given a step by step rendering of higher states of awareness leading up to the ultimate and original perfection of

Advaita Vedanta's Pillar of Axioms

1. Kevala Asti
THE SELF ALONE IS;
IT NEGATES A SECOND PRINCIPLE

2. Brahman Satya, Jagad Mithya
BRAHMAN ALONE IS REAL,
ALL ELSE IS APPEARANCE

3. Adhyaropa/Adhyasa
FALSE IDENTIFICATION
OF THE SELF WITH THE NONSELF
IS THE CAUSE OF BONDAGE

4. Atma-Ajnana
BONDAGE IS THE RESULT OF
IGNORANCE OF THE SELF

5. Moksha Adhigama
FREEDOM IS ATTAINED WHEN
IGNORANCE DISAPPEARS

6. Avidya-Vinasha
DISAPPEARANCE OF IGNORANCE
ENTAILS DISAPPEARANCE OF
THE NONSELF

7. Atma-Asmriti
FREEDOM IS THE ESSENCE OF SELF;
LOSS OF FREEDOM IS A CASE
OF FORGETFULNESS

8. Moksha
THE SELF IS ALWAYS FREE;
FREEDOM IS NEVER ATTAINED,
BUT IS REALIZED

9. Vyavaharika
THE IMPEDIMENT TO
FREEDOM IS OUTRIGHT
PREOCCUPATION WITH
THE OBJECTIVE WORLD

10. Vairagyam
THE SOLUTION FOR
OBSESSION WITH
RELATIVITY IS
CULTIVATION OF
DETACHMENT

11. Manomoha
SO LONG AS THE MIND
SEES A SEPARATE SELF
THERE IS BONDAGE AND FEAR

12. Kham Brahm
FREEDOM CONSISTS IN
SEEING NOTHING BUT THE SELF

13. Aham Atma aham etat na manah
THE SELF IS BRAHMAN,
AND IS NOT TO BE CONFUSED
WITH THE BODY/MIND COMPLEX

14. Aham Chaitanya
THE EGO IS CONSCIOUSNESS
LIMITED AND DISTORTED
BY THE IGNORANT MIND

15. Suhkha-Duhkha Atmananda
THE EGO ENJOYS LIMITED HAPPINESS;
THE SELF ENJOYS LIMITLESS BLISS

*"The Atman in its dynamic phase
diversifies other entities, all set up
within the mind. Thus the shining
Atman imagines Itself by Itself
through Its own Maya, which is also
the apt conclusion of the Upanisads."*
Gaudapada Karika

Consciousness. Utilizing the ancient *Sankhya Yoga* of Lord Kapila, he sets the mind of the practitioner on meditating directly upon the primordial elements, the five active senses, and the five cognitive senses *(visheshas)*. This is to find out their source of origin and connect them to it. Along the way, as charts shown earlier in these many pages will attest to, the mind comes upon and accounts for its more refined attributes, much like "....stored up treasures in Heaven," and settles into them as stations of awareness.

The first of these to appear in the sincere aspirant's mind revolves around knowledge. Knowledge of the internal kind is a kind of *samadhi*; even lower knowledge that demands concentration is a type of *samadhi,* though not an interior one so much. When all the sixteen *visheshas* (see inset box at the top of the chart on the facing page) are gathered together and connected to one another (see chart on page 151), based first of all upon their origins — i.e., from outer to inner, as from earth to smell, water to taste, fire to sight, and so forth — then the process of proper deliberation has begun (improper deliberation has to do with enjoying the objects made of the five elements for the sake of pleasure and possession). This integral bringing together of knowledge principles *(tattvas)* empowers the mind to perceive all that is within its domain. It also places each set of *tattvas* in a framework that was not cognized by the mind up until this form of meditation was engaged in. Tracing the origin of each set of *tattvas* back into the mind (rather than back in linear time), reveals to the soul its past incarnations and its past history with the five elements. They are powers of the mind, and they have an order of appearance coming out from consciousness. This type of knowledge is a knowledge samadhi according to Patanjali, like the *savitarka/nirvitarka samadhis.*

Savichara, the next aspect of knowledge *samadhi* is gained by testing the mind's attachment and aversion via inner exposure to senses and their objects. Outer exposure has been had enough, and has by this stage of spiritual seeking been found lacking in any profundity or lasting value. By observing and ruminating over both the positive and negative aspects of these sets of *tattvas,* then, knowledge of past experience with them is gained. This, again, calls up perception of past lifetimes — a factor that Patanjali states is missing in the transmigrating soul due to keeping too much attention upon worldly affairs tainted with money and finance. *Brahman,* our true Nature, is forgotten in the interim.

Watching the reactions of the mind to its relationship with objects and senses in the past and present, and in past lifetimes as well, is tantamount to knowing (knowledge) that all worlds lie within the mind's scope. False ideas that God created the worlds, or that Nature did it on the physical level only over periods of time by itself, are thus seen to be incorrect. God is beyond the worlds, is "acreate," and all of Nature lies within the mind. In the next phase of initial knowledge *samadhi,* the response and reaction of the psyche and the emotions is taken up. If stability has not been gained when this stage initiates, problems to gaining deeper *samadhis* crop up. If, however, these problems are handled — like in the case of the spiritual preceptor helping the aspirant overcome them through clear understanding — then a marvelous turn of the mind further inward occurs.

This is in correlation with what the tradition calls the "third phase of the Word," or *madhyama.* It is here that the meditator perceives that all of creation is based upon vibration; that is words and their wisdom content, sounds and the intelligence they convey, ideas and their meanings — all of these are the substance or content of what solidifies worlds of name and form into objects for outer perception. Otherwise, as in the first and second phase of the Word, all remains formless and only in potential (see chart on page 154). At the consummation of the initial knowledge *samadhi (savitarka),* two great attainments have been had: first, mind, its senses and their objects all become understood from a unified position (rather than from an uninformed and often scattered condition — see chart on page 612); and secondly, the real meaning of objects stands revealed. All of this sets the stage for fulfilling the wisdom *samadhi* termed *Savichara.*

Here is where, *tattva*-wise, the 6 *avisheshas* come into play for the meditator. *Whereas savitarka samadhi* had to do with acknowledging the true purpose of the five elements and ten senses, and mastering them through connecting them to the mind from whence they originated, *savichara*

The Process of Samprajnata to Asamprajnata Samadhi

"In the mind's move towards unification it must meditate on the alambanas, the 24 states of matter, until it reaches the seedless samadhi." Lord Patanjali

Savitarka Samadhi

- Concentration on the gross Alambanas, including Virat and the 16 Visheshas →
  * On the nature and order of their origins
  * On their appearances in time and mind
  * On their positive and negative attributes
  * On their effects on the psyche and emotions
  * On the relationship between names, words, sounds, meanings, and objects
- Objects, the sense of perception, and the mind become more unified
- The hidden nature of the alambanas get revealed

The Sixteen Visheshas — Final Products of Nature

5 cognitive senses
(hearing, seeing, touching, tasting, smelling)
5 active senses
(speaking, acting, moving, procreating, excreting)
5 gross elements (ether, air, fire, water, earth)
4-fold mind (ego, intellect, thoughts, mind)

Savichara Samadhi

- Concentration on subtle Alambanas — 6 Avisheshas →
  * On the nature and order of their origins
  * On their appearances in time and mind, etc.
- The mind becomes concentration itself
- Expansion of the chitta awakens wisdom
- The nature of the object/principle is known
- Ego begins to be brought under control

The Six Avisheshas

The Five Tanmatras — Intermediate Links

1. Audibility
2. Visibility
3. Tangibility
4. Flavor
5. Odor

"Tanmatras are primal matter, the subtle elements out of which the gross elements are formed. They remain in an undifferentiated state before the quintuplication process takes place at the time of creation."

Ahamkara — Individual Sense of I-ness

Sananda Samadhi

- Meditation upon subtle ahamkara and individual buddhi →
- The bliss of Sananda must be seen by the:
  * nature of its origin, appearance in time and mind, attributes
  * effects on the psyche and emotions, etc.
- The fount of personal joy is located and encountered
- Ego and senses are fully mastered; rajas and tamas are subdued
- Occult powers come as temptations; the true yogi resists them
- The sense of a separate I begins to reveal its limitations

Subtle Ahamkara Individual Buddhi

"Having gained that which is considered the greatest gain, and wherein he is not shaken even by the heaviest affliction, let this bliss which is the disconnection from exposure to all pain be known by the name of Yoga."
Sri Krishna

Sasmita Samadhi

- Meditation on Linga-matra — The Cosmic Mind →
- Ahamkara dissolves into mahat, the first evolute of prakrti
- Mahat/Buddhi perceives the presence of prakrti in itself
- Viveka-khyati reveals the separate nature of Buddhi and Purusha
- Mahat disregards all evolutes and reflects only Purusha
- Mahat fully dissolves into the Unmanifested — A-linga →
- Asmita is transcended and Kaivalya, the final break between spirit and matter, occurs
- Dharma-megha samadhi, the raincloud of virtues and the knowledge of all things, transpires
- Chiti-shakti emerges fully, revealing pure Existence, free of all conditions, evolutes, and processes

Linga-matra

Mahat — Universal Buddhi

A-linga

Prakrti — Unmanifested Nature

Asamprajnata Samadhi

- Abides/meditates on the awareness of cessation — Mahanidra →
- Paravairagya has dawned • In control of or void of all vrttis
- Contains only samskaras of samadhi • Is Self dwelling in Self

Mahanidra — The Great Sleep

- Nir-bija, free of seeds of creation
- Niralambana, needing no supports
- Abhava, unconditioned existence

samadhi takes up the *tanmatras,* or five subtle elements, in order to establish a deeper connection with the human ego complex. The process and practice of going deeper follows the same directions as were just adhered to in the outer *samadhi* of external objects.

Given the usual views of India's religious traditions on the external world, i.e., that it is to be renounced and detached from, it is wonderful at the same time to see India's mode of utilizing everything external in proper order to reveal the return path back to the Source. *Tantra* calls this deification, and takes up all objects as articles of worship in order to uncover what underlies them. The seers and yogis tell that there are manifold strata of underlying levels of externalized and internalized consciousness to pierce through. If the student gets caught on one level only, say, the surface level of physical matter, then all that exists underneath gets overlooked. Mind gets overlooked due to brain; psychic energy gets overlooked for food energy; higher wisdom gets overlooked due to secular knowledge; God gets veiled because of the human ego, etc. To quote Lord Kapila, *sancharah prati sancharah":....*there is a chain of evolution outwards from the Soul *(purusha),* and there is a reverse chain of involution back into the Soul." Everything that emerges as projection from the Great Mind *(Mahat)* is nature as *tattvas,* and the Soul, *Purusha,* directs the process.

The greatest lesson that *savichara* has to teach, and its most winsome attribute and benefit, is concentration. Being the sixth limb of *Yoga,* prior to having actual meditation and *samadhi,* the whole matter lies in the distinction between the mind that is concentrated and the mind that is not. The focused mind scarcely has sorrow, never suffers depression, and escapes sufferings of all kinds almost completely. Remaining in a one-pointed condition, the mind verily becomes concentration itself, and thus resembles only itself and not something other. This is why Sri Krishna states in the *Bhagavad Gita,* that *"Single branched are the minds of the wise, but many-branching are the minds of the unwise."*

And it is with this thoroughly integrated mind that the *chitta,* the thoughts available to the introspective mind, become evident to the seeker of Truth. Instead of scattered thoughts containing little but negative content, awakened *chitta* is seen as a field of wisdom filled with an infinite amount of wisdom particles. These emanate in streams from the *Mahat,* The Word, and other spiritually primal sources. In Sri Ramakrishna's way of saying, these subtly powerful particles are to be *"charged up,"* and by *"thoughts on Reality alone,"* states the *Upanisads.*

And so this is the (still seeded) *samadhi* where, after outer elements and outer senses are accounted for and connected, internal *tattvas* become the focus — and all in preparation for encountering *ahamkara* and *buddhi,* the ego and the intellect. In short, it is only by knowing the building blocks of the universes in space and time which the mind *(manas)* utilizes to construct the worlds and the various bodies it inhabits to experience them, that the Primal Architect can be espied and known. The inner explorer now finds that by allowing the ego to project *(sankalpa)* indiscriminately, an overall generalization took place in which the self forgot itself. Using the mind's powers to construct and the intellect's *(buddhi)* ability to envision, the ego *(ahamkara)* freely engaged in an all out festival of random manifestation. Dividing itself into many, much like cells do on the physical level, this "separate I-maker," left uncontrolled, was let loose to engage in as many pastimes and pleasures as it could conceive of, all the while ignoring the laws of duality that it had unwittingly laid down for itself by separating from *Brahman* as it instigated illusory cycles of time.

Pleasure has pain as its opposite, then, and the enterprising soul is fast becoming aware of this and other problems and solutions. In the soul's ongoing revelation around cosmic manifestation, the heretofore missing element of bliss begins to emerge from hiding. The third level of seeded *samadhi* is thus appropriately named *sananda,* and its bliss, too, must be meditated upon and subjected to scrutiny involving its origin and its location in the mind, and in time. Here, a subtle dichotomy is encountered, for whereas the ego has its share of personal bliss, it is that very elation and its enjoyment that has caused it to become a rogue element in the mind, and thereby to change the course of the boat of life from a divine destination to an earthly one. The obstacle here, then, is one of misused power based in personal gain and love of pleasure. The way to freedom is to find the source of the ego's limited bliss and turn towards it. In *sananda samadhi* — if the soul continues to move inexorably inward — the occult powers *(asta-bala siddhis)* are seen and rejected in order that true Bliss, *Ananda,* is gained. Mediocre teachers of *dharma* proclaim that the occult powers are to be sought after, but superior teachers and illumined souls such as Sri Ramakrishna and Swami Vivekananda disagree. The Father of *Yoga* disagrees as well. He states: *"When the soul sees and rejects the occult powers, then the Raincloud of Virtues (dharma-megha samadhi) begins to manifest itself."*

It is to be remembered that the immature ego craves for and seeks after the occult powers. They are part and parcel of what has caused the soul to lose its vision of higher life and its identity with *Brahman.* Moreover, these selfsame powers cause greed, selfishness, domination, and war, thus a mass of suffering to humanity.

Seeing the multiple ills at the root of the ego's preoccupation with powers, the noble soul turns away from it, and them, and seeks to become a *yogi* — one united with Divine Reality. It is not only avoidance of the fall from Divine Grace that is gained in the aspiring *yogi's* wise choice at this juncture, but also the attainment of several immeasurably valuable fruits of spiritual life. One of these is the controlling and even mastering of the gunas of *tamas* and *rajas,* so persnickety in their tendency to cling to the soul (see charts on pages 221, 223, 307). The other is an open passageway into the finer realms of Cosmic Mind and Universal Intelligence.

Mahat and Universal *Buddhi* are the origins of the individual ego and intellect. When these are seen and acknowledge, and meditated upon in *alambanic* fashion, the result is an ushering of the soul into *sasmita samadhi* — the final level of seeded *samadhi.* The title assigned to these higher *tattvas,* or first evolutes of *Prakriti,* is *Linga-matra,* which really means the final vestige of form the soul will perceive prior to entering a formless, or causeless, condition. Unmanifested *Prakriti* is *A-linga,* and is where even the highest level of Mind, *Mahat,* dissolves. Along with the Great Mind, the subtle, or ripe ego, has to be dissolved. This process is fine, and blissful in and of itself. Much of the learning of higher wisdom earlier comes to bear in this causal juncture. *Mahat* and Universal *Buddhi* have cosmic projection (The Trinity) and intelligent particles (*Jnana-matra*) as their makeup. Their dissolution comes when this great mental complex sees all of *prakriti* residing within it. This is an essential part of the path that has been called Self-Knowledge, which is not just about realizing ones identity with *Atman/ Brahman,* but also includes the taking possession of all powers that the individual and collective ego (living beings and their ancestors) had stolen away with in the process of "progressive manifestation by unreal superimposition."

Taking possession of both the cosmic principles and the responsibility of projection, the aware soul uncovers another spiritual fruit or attainment called *viveka-kyati.* This allows the soul to separate out the final vestiges of the *buddhi's* unwise identification with all of Nature, *Prakriti,* and to see itself as a limited aspect of the *Purusha,* or Supreme Soul. The sheath of intellect called the *buddhi* has now been stripped away to reveal Intelligence, Universal *Buddhi,* as inherent Wisdom particles. It now perceives that it has its source of origin in the *Purusha.* Much the same transformation occurs to the small ego *(ahamkara)* that discovers the cosmic ego *(Mahat)* — the result being a giving away of the refined mental complex's limited bliss into the *Ananda* of the *Purusha.*

The wonders of *yogic* realization do not stop here. On the verge of the unmanifested, courting entrance into Formless, the penultimate level of freedom suggests itself onto the soul. This is called *Kaivalya.* Patanjali has done his utmost to describe what is essentially beyond words by explaining a *triputi* beyond all other threesomes, that of absolute Wisdom, freedom from Nature/Form, and the appearance of the Divine Mother of the Universe, whom he refers to as *Chit-Shakti.* It is She who ushers the soul into its birthless, deathless, timeless, spaceless, Formless Nature. Though separation from nature will not be the most popular of ideals and possibilities among embodied souls, those courting absolute Freedom will take to it. Nature is the form-producing mechanism, par excellence. Sri Krishna declares that all changes, limitations, sufferings, and transformations take place in Nature, not in the Soul/*Purusha.* Lord Buddha also cites the Six transformations as belonging to *samsara,* not Buddha Nature (see chart on page 225).

The balance of the chart on page 693 concerns the one and only "seedless" *samadhi*, *Asamprajnana.* All vibrations of the mind have ceased here, and the fully indrawn meditator now contemplates on what is left over, sometimes called "Emptiness." If any semblance of mental residue exists at all, it is just *samskaras* of *samadhis* had earlier, of the seeded kind. As a review and condensation of what has just been related on the level of seeded *samadhi,* the chart on the opposite page can be presented, before focusing upon seedless *samadhi* and the state of *"nirodha"* leading to it.

As an aid to further comprehending the seeded *samadhis* a handy table has been created on the opposite page that outlines the level, condition, aim, and method of each of the seeded samadhis. This can be combined with the chart on 693 to fill out needed details for the seeker after his or her own perfection. Lower samadhis are valuable, and it is even more beneficial to know that they are occurring to the mind. In a word, when concentration (*dharana,* the 6th limb of *Yoga*) has been mastered, the early seeded samadhis are already beginning to overtake the mind and its thinking process. When a scientist, artist, or other advanced intellectual being spends unbroken periods of time on his subject, that, in itself, is a lower *samadhi* — one of knowledge.

Of course, to be aware of the fact, and further, to connect it to more internal *samadhis,* describes spiritual life rather than mere professional life. A physicist may be able to concentrate on matter, but he can only focus in on Mother Nature, not the Mother of Nature, — nor does he yet perceive the Source of his own Awareness. For this, and to begin, the presence of his own ego would need to be examined. That would lead to *sananda* and *sasmita samadhis,* and his daily happiness and preoccupation with his work and occupation would swiftly turn to an exploration of that sudden joy and elation that might attend upon him occasionally due to his level of concentration.

Whatever the case may be, there is no other way to get into *Asamprajnata Samadhi,* the singular "unseeded" state — at least not with any significant understanding of what is happening to the soul — until the body/mind mechanism has been prepared for it by lower samadhis. *"One cannot get the Infinite via the finite,"* as Swami Aseshanandaji Maharaj used to state, which means to say that concentration on matter and worldly subjects will not open the Gate to what is beyond both. Further, taking intoxicants produced by nature/matter will not open that Gate either, but only route the mind back into modes of emotion, dizziness, fantasy, and pretense over lifetimes. That is why souls are reborn with desire for intoxicants, just like a camel is born with the desire to eat thorny bushes even though its gums bleed painfully as it does. There is no substitute for authentic spirituality, no method other than *sadhana,* and no shortcut to Self-Realization — the "razor's-edged path."

The bottom portion of the chart on the facing page explains the inexplicable as well as words can say. The first three points have just been reviewed, except that mention of the *gunas* are brought up again. The mastery of slothfulness *(tamas)* and restlessness *(rajas)* cannot be overestimated. Doubt and fear accompany the lower gunas, which will cause even the concentrated worldly soul to balk and fall away when higher experiences come to it.

The next two points concern the "raincloud of virtues" that overwhelm the mind and ego of the worldly intellectual, and the subtle presence of *Chit-Shakti,* Divine Mother and Her Wisdom at a penultimate but crucial phase. These two will not only dissolve the lower gunas, but also take on and refine the *sattva guna* as well, transforming it from individual joy to indivisible bliss *(sananda/ananda).* When this occurs, *Asamprajnata Samadhi* is in the process of occurring. Even though this singular *samadhi* may happen in spurts and starts, as the mind acclimatizes itself to higher Consciousness, the tendencies towards mind-control and transcendence of *samsara/maya* are nevertheless in motion. There is no coming back from the consummation of this unseeded State of states, just like there is no hope for a moth flying out of a bonfire once it enters there.

The last two points clear up some haziness in the matter of what occurs to the individual ego/mind complex once it escapes the ocean of pleasure and suffering *(samsara-sagara)* and dissolves into the ocean of Bliss *(ananda-sagara).* Some yogis are able to maintain relations with the world of name and form, at whatever level they choose, i.e., the physical world or the life heavens. In these cases (other than the ones who dissolve completely, never to return) they are as if unborn, undying,

The "Seeded" Samadhis of Patanjala

"The wisdom-samadhi, Samprajnata, is of four levels: attended by basic thought (vitarka); by subtle thought (vichara); by sattvic bliss (ananda); and by the sense of I-am-ness (asmita)." Patanjali

Asamprajnata Samadhi — Transcendent Awareness; Formless; Acognitive (Nirvikalpa)
Samprajnata Samadhi — Cognitive State of Awareness in Four Levels (Savikalpa)

Samprajnata Samadhi — The Four Wisdom Samadhis

Level	Condition	Aim	Method
Savitarka (& Nirvitarka)	Accompanied by gross thought, focused on names and forms, mixed with the gunas, and shadowed by doubt	To refine concentration by focusing on objects, names, and meanings so as to lead to fuller comprehension	Striving via basic knowledge to comprehend the world, the manifest deities, and the sixteen visheshas
Savichara (& Nirvichara)	Accompanied by subtle thought, focused on wisdom, and attended by inward analysis	To transcend the imperfections in nature and perceive the subtle essence of things	Striving via subtle knowledge to try to comprehend the six avisheshas
Sananda	Accompanied by higher intelligence, focused on the subtlemost causes, and enraptured by sattvic bliss	To concentrate on refined ahamkara and enjoy the fount of bliss contained in the personal sense of I-ness	Transcending the gross and subtle objects to attain and enjoy the bliss of refined ahamkara
Sasmita	Accompanied by self-convergence, focused on I-ness, and transcendent of sattva guna	To meditate on the unified self as "I am," in accord with the highest cosmic principles	Transcending the ego to unify meditator, act of meditation, and object of meditation

Process of Nirodha Leading to Asamprajnata

> Mind, with gunas and nature present, expands towards freedom
> With rajas eliminated, intellect discriminates between matter and Self
> The early stages of Samprajnata samadhi are encountered and attained
> The final level of Samprajnata brings about Dharma-megha samadhi
> Chitshakti illumines the buddhi, which becomes stable and desireless
> The triple gunas of Prakriti get duly dissolved back into their origin
> The dissolution of sattva guna brings about Asamprajnata Samadhi
> Purusha now controls the mind's activities and is free from samsara
> Attachment to matter ceases, but the buddhi still conducts relations between matter and spirit
> The yogi interacts with the world, but the Chitshakti within abides calmly, despite appearances

"When the mind-field expands to know the underlying principles which support it, that is called vitarka. When it seeks a more refined expansion in order to comprehend the subtle supports behind appearances, that is known as vichara. When bliss is experienced upon knowing the gross and the subtle, that is termed ananda, sattvic joy. And when evidence of a unified self occurs, which allows the removal of all distinctions, this is known as asmita." Vedavyasa

Paravairagya & Aparavairagya
Four Steps to Detachment in Yoga

Aparavairagya in Four Steps

1) Yatamana — Initial Self-effort
* A strong resolve to uncover the real and the unreal.
* Unrelenting effort to free the mind from sense objects.
* Ending craving by observing the world and the body.
* Identifying and eliminating the vikshepas in the mind.
* Reducing desires, even if one is not yet able to remove them.

2) Vyatireka — Astute Ascertainment   [9 Vikshepas ⟶
* Developing the ability of discernment to the extent that:
    – most of the vikshepas/antarayas have been corrected.
    – others are in the process of being corrected.
    – one knows which must be corrected in the future.
* Ascertaining which of the senses need mastering.
* Ascertaining what desires have not been mastered.
* Culling desires until only the strongest remain.

Vyadhi - physical disease
Styana - laziness/ambivalence
Samshaya - doubt/indecision
Pramada - inattentiveness
Alasya - dullness of mind
Avirati - overindulgence
Bhrantidarshana - delusion
Alabdhabhumikatva - failure
Anavasthitatvani - stagnation

3) Ekendriya — Specialized disciplines pertaining to mind
* Seeing that contact with all things, perceptible and imperceptible, brings suffering.
* Increasing dispassion until mind has become impervious to the whims of the senses.
* Reducing attachment to the sense objects until it remains as mere interest only.
* Developing dispassion until only subtle desires persist.

4) Vashikara — Full control and mastery, meaning:
* A state devoid of what is acceptable and what is rejectable.
* A state of complete disinterest in enjoyment.
* A state that naturally perceives Spirit distinct from matter.
* The ongoing abidance of fully matured detachment.

"To have vairagya is to be free of raga, attachment to distortions which pleasure imprints upon the mind. Mere indifference, vaitrishna, is not enough; vashikara is the essence of vairagya."

The Obstacles to Acquiring Aparavairagya (three main and three subsidiary)

1. Desire for the Eight Siddhis(anima, laghima, prapti, prakamya, mahima, ishitva, vashitva, kamavasayita)
2. Desire for Heavenly Existence - celestial bliss, visual spectacle, expansive realms, exquisite lokas.
3. Videha - transcend the physical but maintain linga body only, or mahat/ahamkara/mind body.
   Prakrti-laya - absorb in unmanifest prakrti only, using it to create subtle worlds to lord over.
   "Neither of these two types of beings gain Kaivalya, but fall into samsara in a physical realm again."
4. Uncontrolled sexual impulse 5. Inordinate desire for power 6. Attraction for mundane pleasure

---

Paravairagya ——— The Three Conditions of Paravairagya ———

1. All achievements, great or small, apparent or subtle, have been gained.
2. All plagues, afflictions, and disquietude have been destroyed or transcended.
3. The cycle of birth and death in the worlds of name and form has been eradicated.

"They who perceive the limitations and imperfections in mind and world have gained dispassion. The one whose intellect is filled with discriminating wisdom won by devout practice has higher dispassion. These are the two types of detachment. The latter brings clarity of mind and pure discernment."   Vedavyasa

and uninhibited. They act without acting, as Sri Krishna points out in the *Gita*. The *Chit-Shakti*, the Mother of profound thought and intelligence, abides peacefully within them, guiding every movement, inner and outer. All praises be unto them, and unto those who immerse themselves forever in *Brahman's* halcyon Light of Indivisible Awareness.

While we still linger in the *Yoga darshana* of Mother India, we can take up this selfsame internal transformation under the heading of *Vairagya*, from its healthy inception in the freshly discriminating human mind, to its deepest maturation in the transported human soul. Not surprisingly, *Yoga* wants initial self-effort at first, accruing in the mind's ascertainment, followed by recognizing and implementing certain special disciplines that pertain to the mind's deepest root impediments, and ending in complete mastery.

As in *Vedanta*, we also find in the *Yoga* disciplines that the unreal must be seen and rejected, and the Real must be put back in its rightful place of supremacy. The unreal is classified early on as body, senses, and objects of pleasure and attachment. The mind's changefulness and transitoriness will come in its own turn, it being the projector of the three aforementioned. Like in *Buddhism*, craving is the first habit, and false identification is the second. Overall, it is desire that blocks the human soul from its higher aspirations.

At the second step, the inset box called the 9 *Vikshepas* appears. It covers the gamut of problems that are present at four levels of the soul's being, namely physical, mental, intellectual, and spiritual (see chart on page 255). In its completeness, *Yoga* requires the aspirant after Union to remove the desires that are possible to remove, work to attenuate others that are not yet destructible, and take a good, hard, look at which desires are particularly stubborn and must face extinction in the future. In the meantime, the most persnickety desires are to be connected to any given sense organ, as in smell, touch, taste, etc. This is in preparation for their demise, and so that the aspirant knows what he or she is up against in the third step. We must recall, that this method in *Yoga* is all about *vairagya*, maturing detachment.

The first two steps are called *Yatamana* and *Vytareka*. The third step, indicative of its first syllable, is *Ekendriya*, having to do with placing the mind in a more one-pointed (*eka*) state. Thus, this is a very elevated type of subtle practice, operating at a level that is already close to the Ever Stationary Self. Though sounding like a form of practice, the attainments that come to the soul upon arriving at this stage have more to do with resting in the *Atman* rather than trying to avoid impediments. The senses fill up with the light of consciousness so that their objects and the desire for them pale in comparison. Spirit takes the fore, matter falls away. This is the natural state of the Self/Soul, and the mind recognizes it. Still, it recognizes, as well, that some desires are still present.

At the *Vaishikara*, the fourth step of *vairagya*, mind and senses no longer look down towards earth, but inward towards the Light. At this level of witness, consciousness can more clearly perceive what stands in the way of reaching said Light. Obstacles, here, range from subtle to causal, and have a lot to do with transcending desires for the mind's hidden powers (see chart on page 660), and rejecting worlds existing within the subtlemost reaches of the mind. Earlier, in the first step, the aspirant noted the difference between the unreal and the Real. Now is the time to completely make a departure from the unreal. It sees that Spirit is distinct from matter, the latter being only its projection via the mental complex that had taken on the blemish of desire. Projections have no substance, so are unreal. With this apt conclusion the soul loves to abide in mature detachment.

As the advanced and matured soul puts away childish things of the imaginary past, it attains the three final fruits of *Paravairagya* — Full achievement, eradication of all sufferings, and an end to rebirth in all bodies and in all worlds — a conclusive snapping of the chains of *samsara*. A list of beings who have practiced this method, enumerated and explained here, appears on the chart on page 389.

The chart on page 701 is a teaching from the high-minded scripture, *Jivanmukti Viveka*, and it goes well with the teachings on *samadhi* in *Yoga* just studied. This scripture is usually taken only by renunciates, like monks who have taken vows of transcending the world. Nonetheless, fringe-dwellers, like *vanaprastins* who work on the edges of society to try and benefit others, will also benefit from this particular teaching, as will householders who focus on the *dharma* throughout their lives and teach their children about the evil ways of the world, and of worldliness.

It all begins with a combination of sincerity and yearning. Beings born into this world who already possess intelligence around the deeper meaning of life, although rare in and of themselves, show signs of the first earmark of authentic spirituality. How they follow along this already elevated trajectory is by consulting the two ancient standbys of spiritual life overall. These are the revealed scriptures and holy company. The words of the enlightened seers of the past, combined with the compassionate presence of the realized souls of the present, form a winning way towards progression along the razor's-edged pathway to Freedom. To conclude, and to connect, everything that takes place in the lives of aware and intelligent beings is due to their own striving and success in their previous lifetimes, and the holy company they gain is also a direct result of such history.

In classic *Vedantic* fashion, the second earmark works on the also ancient premise that both discrimination and detachment, i.e., *viveka* and *vairagya*, are an ongoing development over lifetimes. It must be reiterated that being discriminating in the world of practical matters is not what is meant here, but rather an increasing knowledge of the distinction between what is changing and what is permanent. Even learning to live amidst what is mutable and transitory adequately springs from defining this line — a line that is always and otherwise blurred by worldly, pleasure-seeking beings. Reality must be seen and known as what It is, free of the overlays of nature, *maya*, and the false misconceptions and superimpositions of the flagging human mind.

Earmark three makes this crystal clear by accenting what has already been learned by the spiritually evolving soul. As an example to children, neighbors, and other seekers, detachment from sense objects is a quality that cannot be found very often among households and families. For, when will the householder find time or interest to engage in visiting an ashram or a monastery? So these spiritual qualities are to be demonstrated in the face of all and sundry. Only then will the hidden propensities of living beings stand a change of emerging from minds steeped in wealth and sense-objects.

These first three earmarks are assigned to the platform of human consciousness entitled the waking state. They emerge, get worked on, and are matured in daily life in this way. Earmark four takes a radical departure from this level, and moves into the realm of relative formlessness, or the dreaming state. When one sees a being who seems to be free of thought, or attended only by higher thoughts that do not bind or cause trouble, one is perceiving a soul who is generally in control of his or her mind, and thus free from it at will as well. In addition, the station of formlessness has been comfortably assumed by such a being. This is difficult to see and recognize for most beings, and they may misinterpret it as haziness or vacant-mindedness. However, the three anterior earmarks have been matured in such a being, so on closer inspection the untruth of that assumption is realized. Soon, such a being will be gathering souls together to meditate at home, or at a spiritual center in the neighborhood, thus exposing them to higher values and deeper insights.

Earmark five is assigned the title of "sleep." The easiest way of explaining this is that such an elevated soul is now asleep to all illusions, misconceptions, and the false and impossible dreams of others. The Light of *Brahman*, Nondual Reality, has taken over the mind, and the much-coveted attainment of Self-Realization is a thing of the immanent future. There seems to be nothing unattainable for such a luminary.

However, the complete merging of the mind, short of all return, is still waiting. It is like the sweetest state of deep sleep in which the now unified soul relishes its time, or the lack of the existence of time, to be more specific.

And all of the six previous stages come together for full expression in the seventh, where duality vanishes completely as if it never existed — for, in truth, it did not/does not. These degrees of tranquility, as the sacred scriptures put it, not only reveal the Essence of conscious Awareness to the qualified seeker after Freedom, but also solve the lingering problems of life encountered by those

The Seven Earmarks of God Realization

"The problem of non-perception of Reality due to preoccupation with conventional duties can be solved according to attaining degrees of tranquility. With this solution in view, the scriptures state: 'Sporting in the Self, delighting in the Self, yet performing works, such a one stands foremost among the knowers of Brahman.'" (Mundakopanisad) Jivan-Mukti-Viveka

Jivanmukti

Deep Sleep

6

Objectless Delight
"Absence of external & internal influences and the irretrievable plunging of the mind into Brahman."

Turiya

7

Transcendence
"Nonperception of duality & varieties due to prolonged practice of the six previous stages."

Waking

1 — **Goodwill**
"The strong will to know Reality with the help of scriptures and holy beings."

2 — **Discrimination**
"Differentiating between Reality and nonreality and applying detachment."

3 — **Even-mindedness**
"Nonattachment to sense objects via the implementation of goodwill and discrimination."

Dream

4 — **Enlightenment**
"Emptiness of mind, free of thoughts, and the ability to abide peacefully in formlessness."

Sleep

5 — **Disconnection**
"Freedom of mind and increased awareness and perception of the splendid Reality."

"With regard to the world the yogi remains empty within and without, like a vacant pot left in an open space. But with regard to Divine Reality, he is full within and without, like a water-filled jar submerged in an ocean."
Laghu Yoga Vasishtha

who are still needing to inhabit the world of name and form, for whatever reason they have for being there.

The chart on the facing page is a further complement to the previous two charts on *samadhi* and its various levels. The lower half of the chart gives a graph of *samadhis* in *Vedanta* and *Yoga*, correlated with stages of realization and grades of existence. For a more complete list on different samadhis and spiritual moods one can refer back to the chart on page 587.

It is the upper half of the chart that introduces fresh information and teachings, however, demonstrating, as it does, the different ways that four different paths in India utilize to recognize and unite with Divine Reality. As has been asserted before in this book, India never wasted time arguing as to whether God existed of not, but rather saw clearly that "All is *Brahman*." After perceiving this fact, all of its paths, or *darshanas*, set about to qualify the statement for up and coming aspirants so they could arrive at this apt conclusion. *Vedanta,* with its famous "real and unreal" division, also declared the highest Truth — that *Brahman* exists in all beings, all things, but that It is not an individual or an object.

Yet, its treatment of objects was set up to show that without the presence of *Brahman*, no object could exist. The word, *"archa,"* came to be utilized for the purpose of this refined explication. The idea is based upon the fact that all objects emanate Divine Reality by their very existence, some — like mountains and oceans — filled with inspiration and majesty as well. Tibetan *Buddhism*, to explain this, would point to its "Great Seal" teaching and declare that all things are literally stamped with the luminosity of pure Mind. So, whereas mature philosophy, of the kind found in India, would avoid the mistake of dragging God/*Brahman* down to the physical plain, and making "That" somehow responsible for all the many ills here, at the same time, to completely remove the presence of *Brahman* from the picture would render all and everything both incomplete, and null and void, as well.

Nonetheless, great souls like Sri Krishna, God in human form, points to three kinds of natures in His "Song Celestial." The earthly realm is perishable nature, *adhibhuta,* but it is one of "His" forms as well. Following the chart, we see that *Yoga* assigns this discarding of argumentation about Divine Reality throughout to the level of *prathama-kalpika,* the beginning stage. It is like the *yogi* saying to himself, "....of course God exists; I only have to exert to uncover It here in gross nature." Similarly, *Tantra* just enters into the worship of all articles after purifying them. This is *buhyabhava,* engaging in rituals that call divinity forward and send insentient matter to the rear. *Buhyabhava* is thus much like *Vedanta's archa* in that God can associate with objects, but is not the object itself. Thus, the claims by other religions that *Hinduism* is a religion of idol-worship, is unfounded and misunderstood; also that it is polytheistic. It is the One *Brahman* existing everywhere and in all things that is evident to the Indian seer, though It may appear veiled as objects, worlds, and living beings (see the chart of false superimposition on pages 64 & 657).

Two other levels, closely associated, come up next for inspection. The "Self" is an extremely important concept in Indian *darshanas*. It is variously classified as lower, higher, and Supreme, or as personality/ego, knowledge/intelligence, and *Atman*/Consciousness. To gain knowledge of the Self is the noble way of practice and purification. The Self, *Atman,* does not need them, but the mind will reveal Self if it is subjected to them. Thus, in *Yoga, rtambhara-prajna* is necessary. That same wisdom will come through in *Tantra* by utilizing the *mantra,* filled with power and presence. In the *Gita,* Sri Krishna repairs to it by mentioning the *adhidaiva,* or *Purusha.* And in *Vedanta,* the noble adage, *Antaryami* — the "Inner Ruler Immortal seated in the Heart" — is cited. Without knowledge of the Self the quest for God will fall short, again and again. Mankind merging with God, wherein all separations are removed, all rifts healed, and all thoughts of two and many are unified, is the swiftest way to absolute realization.

With the principles of sacred symbols and inner Self proclaimed, the other two echelons of Divinity can be stated. India has always known, despite its penchant for seeking the nameless, formless Reality, that there is a station of divinity with form where concentrated consciousness in a fully

The Four Ways of Perceiving God

In Indian Darshanas

"Brahman is beyond both Ishvara and the world, and is not a state. It is the only unit not composed of many units. It is the principle which runs through all, from a cell to God, and without which nothing can exist." Swami Vivekananda

Vedanta	Bhagavad Gita	Tantra	Yoga Sadhana
As Brahman, Ultimate Reality	Adhyatma, The Imperishable	Brahmabhava, Perception of Reality	Atikranta-bhavaniya Perfection
As Ishvara, Supreme Godhead	Adhiyajna, God Assuming Form	Dhyanabhava, Focus on the Deity	Prajna-jyoti, Masterful
As Antaryami, Inner Self Immortal	Adhidaiva, The Purusha, or Self	Japabhava, Mantra & Hymns	Rtambhara-prajna, Intuitive Wisdom
As Archa, Universal Symbol	Adhibhuta, Perishable Nature	Buhyabhava, Practice of Rituals	Prathama-kalpika, Beginning Aspirants

✚ The Five Stages of God Realization ✚

And Their Correlative Samadhis

Grades of Existence	Stages of Realization	Vedantic Samadhis	Yogic Samadhis
Vyavaharika (Phenomenal)	1) Mental Plane, Earthly Phenomenon		
Pratibhasika (Ephemeral, Intellectual)	2) Ethical Plane, Dharmic Law	Savikalpa	Savitarka Savichara
Adhyatmika (Spiritual)	3) Cosmic Plane, Kinetic Ishvara	(Bhava Samadhi)	Sananda
	4) Transcendental Plane, Static Ishvara	(Chaitanya Samadhi)	Sasmita
	5) Absolute Plane, Formless Reality	Nirvikalpa	Asamprajnata

"There are three types of joy, ananda: the joy of the world; the joy of worship; and the Joy of Brahman. In the first, one should dance and sing the names of the Lord; in the second, one loses partial consciousness of the world; and in the third, one experiences God-vision." Sri Ramakrishna Paramahamsa

realized state abides. Called *Ishvara, Ishtam,* Godhead, The Son, Deity, The Trinity, and more, It stands on the apex of Form and Formlessness. Also known as the Personal God, India refers to this cosmic personality as *Saguna Brahman,* or God with attributes. This book is filled with mentions, teachings, and charts on it. It is *adhiyajna,* the supreme sacrificer in the *Gita.* In *Tantra* it is the One to be meditated upon, and to Patanjali in his *Yoga Sutras,* it is an especial soul, fully masterful, who is the sum total of all embodied beings.

All that is left is to cite the indescribable, *Brahman* Itself. Perfect and Imperishable, Ultimate Reality Itself, the remaining portion of this chapter will be given to Its many august designations. And the next chart up for study accomplishes this substantially. Looking at it, one might be prompted to ask the question, "Does *Brahman* have divisions?" No: It has None. But It does have several qualifying monikers, or indicators, that make It more accessible to the mind and its comprehension. To begin, the station of *Sakshi* could be cited first. This is more of a condition that the knower of *Brahman* gets into wherein the pure presence of *Brahman* gets revealed. Since the word translates as "Witness," there is a slight suggestion or hint of twoness in it, meaning there is something being witnessed. Nevertheless, *Sakshi* is a "single-eye" position where what is being witnessed is perceived to be identical to the Witness. There is no real duality there, but maybe more of a subtle play of hide and seek where the finest sense of separation is being employed and removed, at will. Not only dualities prove transparent there, but also *triputis,* as the two descriptions on the chart declare.

Kutastha is the next echelon of the partless *Brahman* as we move up the chart under study. *Sanskrit* words such as *buddhi, pratibha,* and *prakasha* come to mind when it is mentioned or contemplated, for these words spell a special type of intelligence. And whenever the idea of an "underlying substratum" is utilized to point out the invisible *Brahman, kutastha* is the go-to word for it. A dancer requires a stage, the scriptures declare, and in that way the *kutastha* acts as the subtlemost support for all beings and things existing on its surface. In this way we can understand through philosophical reference, and inference, how it is that *Brahman* is in all things, but is not a "thing" Itself. It takes a very refined intellect to understand such subtleties, but *Brahman* remains unrealized if that spiritual intelligence is not gleaned and utilized accordingly — according to the words of the seers and the revealed scriptures.

The *Sanskrit* word, *Antaryami,* ushers in a wholly different atmosphere with regards to Divine Reality. The sweetness of real love, compassion, and protection gets inferred here, so that the seeker, aspirant, devotee, and nondualist, all, can get a very real taste of the bliss of *Brahman.* Additional profound *Sanskrit* words such as *anoraniyan,* and *atisukshma,* come to mind as well, inferring something so close, so dear, and so immediate, that the mind practically loses itself upon contemplation of it. *Antaryami* is defined in English by the present-day *Vedantists* as the "Inner Ruler Immortal seated in the Heart." It is like the *"....sweetness in sugar cane juice,"* to quote Sri Ramakrishna Paramahamsa. Rarely does an appellation present itself that combines Divine Form and Transcendent Formlessness so perfectly, simultaneously free of any and all kinds of possible philosophical complaint.

This only leaves the word *Pratyagatman* to inspect. *Pratyaksha* is direct perception, brooking no intermediaries, and culminating in the fullness of realization. Perception of the *Atman,* then, in its original and unveiled condition, is pratyag*atman.* As the quotes about it on the chart indicate — all of them from the revealed scriptures — it is a world-dissolver, a mind saturater, and an effective revealer of Its own boundless, homogenous mass of pure, conscious Awareness. This *pratyagatman,* then, is the indivisible Self. Its appearance in form is seen as the individual self, or *jivatman.* The essence is the same; the mode is different. *Pratyagatman* is synonymous with what is termed, *Paramatman.*

The following chart, viewed on page 706, fleshes out, as it were, the quintessential concomitants of the *Paramatman,* termed "complements" in this case, along with a fine set of immutables associated with It. It is a well-known fact in *Vedantic* circles that Absolute Reality, *Brahman,* is free from attributes and qualities, what to speak of *mayic* superimposition and psycho-physical overlays

The Four Levels of Brahman's Subtlety

"That which is the Supreme Brahman, the Soul of all, the great support for the universe, called Atisukshma, subtler than the most subtle, and eternal — That is Thyself, and Thou Art That."   Kaivalya Upanisad

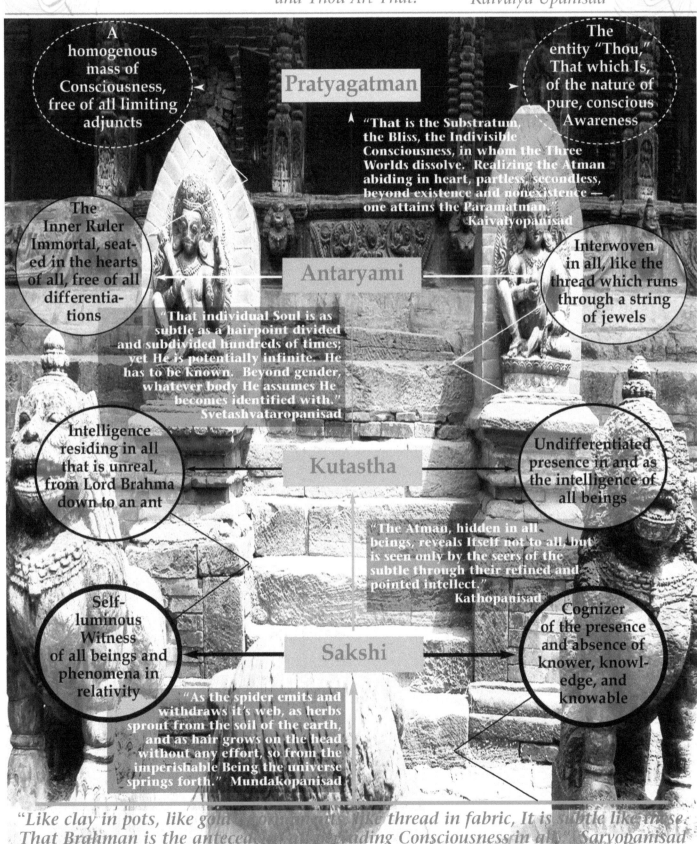

A homogenous mass of Consciousness, free of all limiting adjuncts

The entity "Thou," That which Is, of the nature of pure, conscious Awareness

Pratyagatman

"That is the Substratum, the Bliss, the Indivisible Consciousness, in whom the Three Worlds dissolve. Realizing the Atman abiding in heart, partless, secondless, beyond existence and nonexistence — one attains the Paramatman."   Kaivalyopanisad

The Inner Ruler Immortal, seated in the hearts of all, free of all differentiations

Interwoven in all, like the thread which runs through a string of jewels

Antaryami

"That individual Soul is as subtle as a hairpoint divided and subdivided hundreds of times; yet He is potentially infinite. He has to be known. Beyond gender, whatever body He assumes He becomes identified with."   Svetashvataropanisad

Intelligence residing in all that is unreal, from Lord Brahma down to an ant

Undifferentiated presence in and as the intelligence of all beings

Kutastha

"The Atman, hidden in all beings, reveals Itself not to all, but is seen only by the seers of the subtle through their refined and pointed intellect."   Kathopanisad

Self-luminous Witness of all beings and phenomena in relativity

Cognizer of the presence and absence of knower, knowledge, and knowable

Sakshi

"As the spider emits and withdraws it's web, as herbs sprout from the soil of the earth, and as hair grows on the head without any effort, so from the imperishable Being the universe springs forth."   Mundakopanisad

"Like clay in pots, like gold in ornaments, like thread in fabric, It is subtle like these. That Brahman is the antecedent all-pervading Consciousness in all."   Sarvopanisad

The Six Complements
& Ten Immutables of Paramatman

The Six Complements

Sarvatantra-Svatantratvam
Unbounded Freedom

Ananta-Shaktimattvam
Infinite Power

Sarvajnatvam
Perfect Omniscience

Anadi-Bodhatvam
Integral Knowledge

Trptih
Eternal Contentment

Nityatvam
Perpetual Existence

The Ten Immutables

Jnana — Absolute Knowledge

Kshama — Natural Graciousness

Vairagya — Mature Dispassion

Atma-sambodha — Self-Awareness

Aishvarya — Supreme Lordship

Srashtrtva — Abundant Creativity

Tapas — Inconceivable Power

Dhriti — Immutable Stability

Satya — Nondual Truth

Adhisvaratvam — Full Dominion

"There is one supreme Essence, called 'Paramatman.' It is formless. But seekers of the formless often make this one mistake — they forget that It is also embued with infinite power. Living beings, the universe, mind, intelligence, love, renunciation, knowledge — these are the manifestations of Its power. Thus, I accept not only Brahman, but also maya, the universe, and its living beings." Sri Ramakrishna

(thought, emotions, and bodies). Nevertheless all that is present in all the worlds, internal and external, is a manifestation of *Brahman,* and sports its existence due to *Brahman's* underlying essence — like solid objects growing on the surface of the earth due to the presence of the formless, liquid waters of an underground river. As unaffected essence, *Brahman* is as ether amidst objects; as all-attracting, cohesive power, It is like a huge magnet among metal filings. When looked at in this light it is very difficult not to assign qualities to It.

Still, when doing so, the lofty laws of nonduality will have to be observed. On the chart on the opposite page we find these laws upheld, and the attributes offered there also in keeping with the highest principles. Basically, there is nothing too difficult here for our understanding, and precious little commentary is really needed. Unbounded freedom, being the first complement, simply tells us that any and everything that might hamper natural freedom is missing in *Brahman.* In the case of everything else that inhabits the realms of manifestation, i.e., within the roiling cycles of name, form, time, space, *karma,* etc., it is that selfsame Freedom that is sorely missing. To be free is to be as *Brahman* is — unattended by change.

The next three complements on the upper half of the chart under study are related, in that they all have much to do with insight and intelligence. *Shakti* power, omniscience, and integral knowledge lie in *Brahman* much like whiteness abides in snow. Properly, they all belong as much or more to *Shakti,* for She will extract them as essence from Nondual Reality and put them into operation for the highest good of living beings. On the purely spiritual level, the ability to see (knowledge), seeing itself (omniscience), and the seer *(shakti)* is what is being represented here. And from them come endless existence, plus the wonder of being eternally contented throughout it — like the seers of Truth are. As the *Kathopanisad* states, *"To them belong Peace, and to none else."*

The Ten Immutables listed in the bottom half of the chart under study have a few things in common with several of the complements, but go further in filling out a greater and grander conception of what *Brahman* is. Pure conscious Awareness, Timeless deathless Awareness — these terms have been utilized in English by the *Vedanta* to give an expanded view of what is beyond eyes to see and ears to hear. Jesus told John, *"No man hath seen God with these eyes."* If the senses are unable to reveal *Brahman,* then, we must look within to see Him/Her/It via the most refined qualities available to our thinking process. The Immutables listed here not only fill in the blanks and connect the dots in thinking consciousness, they also enrich the content of our awareness in otherwise impossible ways.

Knowledge we have seen amidst the Six Complements. It can be added here, though that what *Vedanta* means by knowledge is the cause for the various wisdom *samadhis* of *Yoga.* From the Absolute springs the relative, and from the Seedless comes the seeded (review the charts on page 693 & 697, previously studied). Again, knowledge of the ultimate kind is all-seeing, all powerful.

Other eternal qualities grace *Brahman* as well, and should we commit the mistake of thinking that Reality is dull, empty, nothingness, etc., we should turn around and note the "graciousness," *kshama,* that is innate to It. The third Immutable also has unknown secrets abiding in it, given the fact that dispassion, *vairagya,* has 12 distinct levels of maturation (see chart on page 389). The one refered to here along with *Brahman,* is the *"Para" vairagya,* or most elevated kind. In it, the need for detachment has disappeared, and the ability to "attach and detach at will" has arrived.

The next Immutable is *Atma-sambodha,* or Self-Awareness. The word "Self" here, of course, does not refer to an individual self, but rather to The Indivisible Self. It is all-pervasive, not all-perverted; it is all-perceptive, not all deceptive. On another level, It knows Itself completely, and does so from the standpoint of knowledge, act of knowing, and knower all rolled into one. Deluding dualities have gone away; revealing *triputis* have lost their need.

Nevertheless, and as has been noted above, *Brahman* is not dull or empty. *"Br,"* the root of the great word, is defined as "able to expand," and the sixth Immutable, *srashtrtva,* makes this clear. Though remaining in a fully homogenous condition, unbound and free of boundaries, *Brahman* nevertheless acts as the underlying substratum for all other manifestations and their expressions. By way of analogous story, *Brahman* is not the water in the pot that makes the vegetables dance, nor the heat in the water that causes the motion. It is not the burner underneath the pot that makes all move inside, nor the gas running in pipes to the burner, unseen. It is more like the gas storage facility to which all the pipes of all the homes in all neighborhoods are connected, and where an infinite amount of the power-producing substance lies, yet unbeknownst to most bengs.

The last four Immutables — *tapas, dhriti, satya,* and *adhisvaratvam* — reveal *Brahman* as full of immutable power that is ever true and fully capable of holding all beings and all worlds in their respective places, within It. It is no wonder that the *Upanisads* state, *"I take refuge in the Formless Brahman, Who is the Ultimate Bridge to Immortality, and Whose Light of pure Awareness turns the mind of mankind to the Atman, the Indivisible Self in all, and in everything."*

On the facing page is a *dharma* chart that essentializes Indian Philosophy at its highest level. The occurrence of transformation *(parinama)* — of species, in nature, of phenomena, etc. — is a constant companion here on earth, particularly to the Western mind, which causes the truth of non-transformation *(aparinama)* to be very hard to accept, even to acknowledge (see chart on page 267). The first two essential facts on the chart on the opposite page thus reveal India's *siddhanta* (conclusion), on the matter, declaring that *Atman* (the Indivisible Soul, not the individual soul), is supremely singular and other than all of nature. This *Vedic, Yogic,* and *Tantric* philosophical law becomes all the more clear and precious when the second Fact is seen and considered, which is a two-part assertion.

First, and so that the thinker and seeker of Truth will not default to the common dualistic idea that Nature is somehow a second and independent reality, the teaching of mental projection *(sankalpa)* is given, as opposed to a creation out of nothing, or by God. This brings in the third Fact for contemplation. But back to the second Fact, its companion part asserts that the *Atman,* being intrinsically immutable, will not brook any change whatsoever — even when myriad worlds and a plethora of living beings appear and manifest over endless phases of time. All phenomena, including space and time *(desha & kala),* are a manufacture of the combined cosmic, collective, and individual Mind *(Hiranyagarbha/Mahat/Trinity)* which holds the seeds to all of Nature within itself. These seeds, *bijams,* hold the subtle power of *Shakti* within their tiny structures, each *"minuter than an atom,"* as the *Upanisads* state (see charts on pages 595, 33, and 501). This *Shakti* power is spoken about in *Vedanta, Yoga,* and *Tantra* in various ways, and is also known as The Divine Mother of the Universe, the Wisdom Goddess, and the Goddess of the Word *(Vak Devi).* The *Tantric* seers write, being worthy of many repetitions:

Mantranam jiva-bhuta tu ya smrta shakti-rupaya
Tathahina vararohe nisphalah saradabhravat

She, whom the seers know and remember as the Imperishable Shakti,
is the soul of all the revelatory slokas and sutras of the sacred scriptures.
Without Her, oh fair ones, all the tattvas would be as useful as clouds with no rain.
She is the perfect I-Consciousness inherent in all the multitude of words,
and the secret of all the mantras, whose essence consists of the highest Nonduality.

The simple point, then, and as Sri Krishna states it in the *Bhagavad Gita,* is that *"...all change takes place in nature, not the Soul."*

And considering the third Fact on the chart under study, it then can be understood why India has so readily developed a large cross-section, or casteless-caste, of freedom-loving luminaries over extended and multiple phases of time. It is because of the knowledge that all of nature and matter, as well as the energy that animates it, is an unreal projection from the mind. It is all vibration, if one prefers to look at it that way, but the Soul/Original Mind does not vibrate (see chart on seeded and seedless *samadhi* on page 693).

The fourth Fact of Nondual Indian Philosophy adds that warm, comfortable feeling into the

Five Eternal & Essential Facts

OF NONDUAL INDIAN PHILOSOPHY

"In the process of neutralizing karmas and samskaras, the recognition of the distinction between Soul and the mind/matter conglomerate occurs, cited as the difference between Purusha and Prakriti in Sankhya Yoga. This key insight is not to be relegated to the perspective of duality, but to be taught in the light of Advaitic practice and realization."

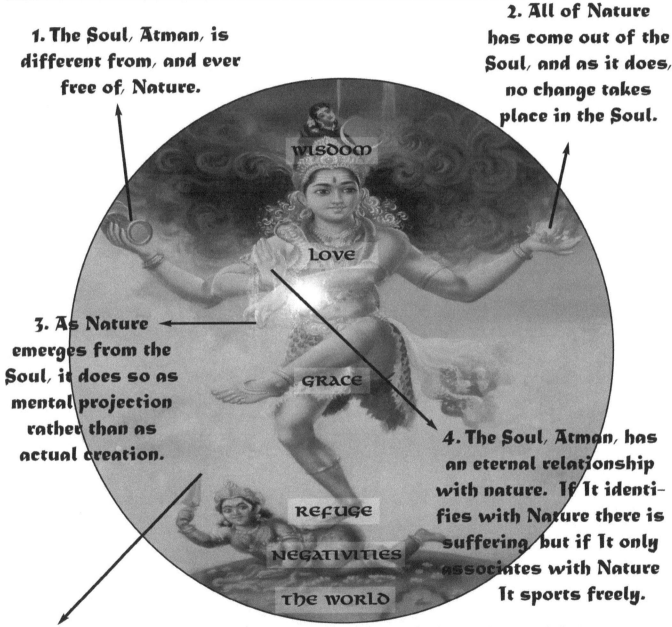

1. The Soul, Atman, is different from, and ever free of, Nature.

2. All of Nature has come out of the Soul, and as it does, no change takes place in the Soul.

3. As Nature emerges from the Soul, it does so as mental projection rather than as actual creation.

4. The Soul, Atman, has an eternal relationship with nature. If It identifies with Nature there is suffering, but if It only associates with Nature It sports freely.

WISDOM

LOVE

GRACE

REFUGE

NEGATIVITIES

THE WORLD

5. Nature has manifested and unmanifested sides, by which knowing, the Soul can remain free of cycles of birth and death in ignorance.

"When the mind recognizes the stark distinction between Consciousness and Matter, Sentiency and Insentiency, it perceives that all of nature — name, form, time, space, and causation — is its own self-projected maya, and it attains what Patanjali calls Kaivalya."
Babaji Bob Kindler

high-minded mental mix, stating as it does, that though *Atman* (pure Consciousness) is free and isolated from all of Nature, that all of Nature proceeds out of Consciousness — at least indirectly, or via relative mechanisms *(tattvas)*. Herein comes the ideation of *Lila,* or sportive play. Since "all is possible for God," the Indivisible Soul separates Itself out into the individual soul via Its own mechanisms of Nature, or *Maya,* and *"plays in the fields of the Lord."* If this frolic in form is to be allowed, philosophically speaking, then the fifth Fact on the chart under scrutiny on page 709 is necessary of comprehension. To correctly associate with Nature/Matter *(Prakriti)* and remain free of false identification with it (as being ultimately real), the sportive soul has to be aware of the unmanifested side of *Prakriti* — those seeds from which all name and form springs in time and space.

The Unmanifested side of *Prakriti* is often called the "causal" state, or the third body of mankind. It is related to the third *matra* of *AUM,* as well, i.e., the *"M,"* Most beings know nothing about it, and there is very little explanation of it in the scriptures. To make it more discernible for embodied beings it is also correlated with the deep sleep condition *(sushupti)* they experience beyond waking and dreaming. The chart across the page takes a close look at this state, and the other three as well, from the *Advaitic* perspective.

Though the four states of mankind's awareness is an ancient teaching, this chart draws upon the most current version of it coming from the illumined soul, Gaudapada, who lived around 550 A.D. His rendering of Nonduality is the highest and best known. The simplicity of the teaching on the three states of consciousness, namely waking, dreaming, and deep sleep, makes it the pattern to model ones study and realization of *Advaita* upon. Since it is the causal state that we want to focus in on at this time, the author asks the reader to look at the levels of waking and dreaming and notice their various divisions and categories. Generally, these two states mirror each other, and thus form the essential definition of what people call today the "inner" and the "outer." The outer is the physical universe with all its *tattvas* (5 elements, 5 senses, body, objects, etc.), and the inner is the mind with its arena of thought *(chitta),* intellect *(buddhi),* and separate self (ego/*ahamkara*). These are also termed gross and subtle, as are the bodies that contain them.

After studying and taking note of these two states, called *jagrat* and *svapna* in *Sanskrit,* the interesting phenomena of the third state *(sushupti*/deep sleep) and its body (causal) should be focused upon. The terrain changes substantially here, as if getting ready to act as a portal to something marvelous. Most notably, the appearance of higher knowledge, the absence of effects, and the presence of veiled bliss make up the difference from waking and dreaming. Also, the sense of separate I-ness is beginning to wane, as is shown nicely on the chart on page 693, at the level of *sasmita samadhi.* No ego, *asmita,* occurs, making this third level of consciousness simultaneously blissful and nescient. There is lack of awareness there, yet also the lack of the worldly, sense-bound, deceiving awareness that happens in waking and dreaming. It could be said that both the seeds for all creation/projection lie there in their potential form, along side of the knower of these seeds, but the knower sees them not.

Nevertheless, by the knower's mere proximity the seeds get animated, they being the cause of forthcoming effects. There are many shades of meaning and revelation around this teaching — the foremost being the soul's inward trajectory beyond matter and dreams of matter to the "fourth" state *(turiya)* — and among them Gaudapada indicates the natural way out of undue and unnecessary suffering as one of them. The *"Enjoyer and the Enjoyed,"* or *"the Field and its Knower"* as Sri Krishna speaks about in the *Gita,* engage two types of living being in the projection process *(sankalpa).* One leaves deep sleep neither gaining a glimpse of *Turiya* via the third eye nor perceiving the seeds strewn about his feet at that causal level, and so remains clueless about Divine Reality. The other *"retains awareness of Nonduality,"* goes forth to enjoy what is available to be enjoyed by the conscious Enjoyer, and all the while *"knows these two to be separate and so is never contaminated thereby."* Why is this? We cannot explain root ignorance, but the enlightened mind, we can. The secret of all-inclusive *Advaita* is that the *"all-pervading Sentient Soul (Atman) has situated itself perfectly in three states of Its own devising,"* and has done so as the Witness of both the worlds It projected (waking and dreaming)

The Four States of Consciousness
& Seven Attributes of Turiya

"There exists only Paramatman, the Supreme Sentient Soul, who though one and all-pervading, is aptly situated in three states of Its own devising. Ever the transcendental Witness, It enjoys (vishva) in the gross waking state through the body and senses, experiences (taijasa) in the subtle dream realms via the projecting mind, and is knower of all (prajna) in the deep sleep state via the intelligence of the heart. The Enjoyer and the Enjoyed — that one who retains awareness of nonduality, yet who knows these two to be separate, although he enjoys — is never contaminated thereby." Gaudapada Karika

Turiya

State 4
(Transcendent)
Individual: Non-existent
State: All-pervasive
Oneness

Locale: Brahman
Mechanism: Consciousness
Condition: Nonduality
Result: Unalloyed Bliss
View: All-Comprehending

The Seven Attributes of Turiya

1) Priyatvam —
Indescribable Beauty
2) Anantatvam —
Boundless Infinity
3) Satyam —
Unimpeachable Truth

4) Shivam — Liberating
Auspiciousness
5) Jnanam —
Illuminating Wisdom
6) Shantam —
Transcendent Peace

7) Advaitanam — Indivisible Unity

State 3
(Deep Sleep)
Individual: Prajna
State: Knower
Locale: Causal Realm
Mechanism: Intelligence
Condition: Subtle Cause
Result: Veiled Bliss
View: Noncomprehension
of Reality

Sushupti

"Perceiving the suffering of this finite world, one should turn to the Atman, the Unborn, who is Infinite. When mind enters Atman its variances are seen as unreal, and Peace descends. Atman is like intense concentration without end, but free of conceptualization. Atman has neither destruction nor origination – bondage nor salvation nor emancipation. This is the highest Truth! In its dynamic phase It diversifies entities. Those few who recognize Atman's envisionings perceive It's beauty everywhere. For them, no difference between Jiva and Atman exists whatsoever.

Thus, seers declare: 'Nonduality alone is auspicious.'"

Select Verses of Gaudapada's Karika

State 2
(Dream State)
Individual: Taijasa
State: Dreamer
Locale: Mental Realm

Mechanism: Mind
Condition: Cause / Effect
Result: Deception
View: Skewed perception
of Reality

Svapna

State 1
(Waking State)
Individual: Vishva
State: Enjoyer
Locale: Physical Universe

Mechanism: Body/Senses
Condition: Cause / Effect
Result: Pleasure / Pain
View: False perception
of Reality

Jagrat

The Four Stages of Absorption
&
The Four Stages of Formlessness

*"I, the Buddha, proclaim this path, which provides sandals against all thorns.
But you, yourself, must make the effort. The Tathagatas can only point the way.
Enter the path, become meditative, and get free from all bondages."*

The Four Dhyanas = Four Stages of Absorption

1. Relinquishment of desires   & unwholesome elements
   a) attained through Vitarka   conceptualization
                        Vichara   discursive thought
   b) characterized by Priti   interest/enthusiasm
                        Sukha   happiness
2. End of conceptualization   and discursive thought
   a) Penultimate to inner calm
   b) Focused mind via meditation on an object

3. Disappearance of joy and arrival of equanimity
   a) Characterized by alertness & contentment

4. Continual wakefulness and subtle abidance

Nivarana — Five Hindrances to Attainment of the Four Dhyanas

1. Abhidya — desire
2. Pradosha — ill will
3. Styana and Middha —
      sloth and torpor
4. Anuddhatya and Kaukritya —
      restlessness and compunction
5. Vichikitsa — doubt

Arupasamadhi — Four Stages of Formlessness
"....to help raise oneself to higher levels of incorporeality."

1. Akasha — the stage of limitless space
2. Vijnana — the stage of limitless consciousness
3. Arupa — the stage of nothing whatsoever
4. Sat-asat — the stage beyond awareness/nonawareness

via the Cosmic Mind, and as the Witness of the Formless, Intelligent Light of *Brahman* as well.

A similar teaching to the *Vedantic* States of Consciousness can be found in *Buddhism*, characterized by the Four Stages of Absorption and The Fours Stages of Formlessness. The first stage of absorption has to do with purifying the desires of the mind, and the unwholesome roots lying there. It is much like what occurs in the waking state of human beings, but only to those souls who are aware that desires and negativities are barriers to higher awareness and actual freedom.

It all begins with the urge to use the mind to conceptualize, then engaging it in "discursive" thought. Though most beings do not do this consciously, the subtle act is really the segue into dreaming. The dreaming state explained in the previous chart is not restricted to only going to sleep and leaving the waking state; one can dream in the waking state as well. This is called fantasizing, daydreaming, and an overall loss of focus due to the mind's habit of drifting away from the subject, and the moment at hand. This is also a problem in meditation practice. It is only when the mind concentrates that any benefit is gained by this kind of inward movement, which is why both *Vedanta* and *Buddhism* advise practiced introspection with a focused mind in order to make essential connections between states of consciousness.

And this is why prompted introspection and centered discursive thought will lead the soul (mind) to discover a certain joy and enthusiasm with inner things, much like a concentrated intellectual, inventor, or artist may get lost in. It is a type of absorption — but only if the mind's attention is brought to bear in it. The same will apply to the dream state of the human mind, which offers up many insights and visions if consciousness is present during the process, but not otherwise. In that case there is just a pointless rambling amidst surface thought, called "the 1000 imbecilities of the mind" in *Vedanta*.

And one will know the difference when the second stage of absorption kicks in. Therein happiness gets replaced by a preference for calmness, and enthusiasm turns from an eagerness to contemplate a host of ideas, to an attraction to focus in on just one essential one. This is like to a coin-collector gaining greater satisfaction by putting aside his pennies and nickels and studying a silver dollar. For the spiritual aspirant, this shift signals the real beginnings of meditation proper. This is so due to an increased presence and alertness that settles in at the third stage of absorption. To the newly, more deeply concentrated mind, what is singular begins to attract and outstrip what is multifarious. The ensuing process ushers in an evenness of mind that is both divinely peaceful and sincerely coveted by the sages and seers.

The fourth state of absorption can only be experienced. To describe it would be too simple for most beings, even boring. It is the ever-awake state that Lord Buddha admitted to, and other luminaries attained to. About it, one poet-saint of Mother India stated, *"I have lulled sleep to sleep forever, and all of my dreams have now become radiant meditations."* Suffice to say that to become immersed is one thing, but to be entirely absorbed is another.

The four hindrances to these fine states of Awareness can be studied on this chart as well. They are nothing new, but are, as the Father of *Yoga* has stated about such things, "despoilers" of the peace and bliss that is the rightful possession of the wise. More engaging are the Four Stages of Formlessness that fall at the bottom of this chart. There are few words, in any language to describe them. Again, suffice to say that the transcendence of even the subtlest of dualities, such as existence and nonexistence, awareness and nonawareness, occurs. The *Avadhut* sings of this incomparable process and its culmination in the his own Gita, famous among nondualists:

"Free now and ever, I have neither fathers, mothers, nor children — for birth, death, and desire have all been extinguished. The ever-abiding state of utter calm has come over me; it is unshakable and supremely tranquil. Thus, I am Pure Existence, Wisdom, and Bliss, as boundless as the sky, infinite like space."

Speaking of immersion, it, too, has a process, and one that can be studied for the refined edification of the mind around authentic spirituality. The chart on page 715 is a combination of meditation instruction, as well as guidance at the time of the body's demise. For either way, and ideally, the ego will disappear, dissolve, and this immersion is synonymous with *samadhi* in spiritual life.

Truly speaking, death is the passing of things that are already dead, things that are temporarily animated by *prana,* or life-force, which, itself, has a demise, an exit. This is why Jesus stated that *"Man does not live by bread alone;"* He lives by *prana* at first, then by Spirit, or Consciousness, for That is the only truly Living Principle in existence — or, the only Existence.

And so, meditation is a kind of death, or better put, the letting go by the mind of all manner of innately inert things. To cut to the chase, then, Sri Krishna starts of His guidance with a giving up of the body and closing down of the five senses. Control of the *prana* will be necessary for this, as it will provide the ability for such an unusual withdrawal. So with a twin effort of detachment, the thoughts in the brain (surface mind) get taken into the mind (the subtle realms within) which is their source, and the life-force, i.e. *prana,* gets merged into the heart. Just as there is a surface mind, called brain, there is also a surface heart, called emotions. When the brain/mind is not under ones control, it is the lack of exertion of the *prana* in the surface heart that is to blame. All manner of "emoting" then comes to the surface to affect life, usually in contrary and nonproductive ways. With these three steps, then, the aspiring seeker of Truth prepares the way for deeper immersion.

An ideal is necessary for all of this to occur. The thought of withdrawing from life and all its vagaries and vicissitudes would not crop up in the individual unless a higher ideal presented itself — usually in the form of a spiritual teacher who inspires, but also sometimes coming up more spontaneously from profound experiences that happened in a seeker's past lifetimes — which is then swiftly followed, in almost all cases, by the appearance of a *guru.* Whatever the case may be, an overall name for this ideal is *Yoga.* *Yoga* is universal, and can be applied to all religions, not just Hinduism. It is the name for ecstatic union with Divine Reality, a state that is already in place and perfect before the immersion process begins.

Therefore, Sri Krishna and other great souls urge the taking up of the ideal of blissful Oneness with God, *Brahman, Allah,* or whatever sweet and powerful Name one assigns to the nameless, formless Essence. At that time, when this is accomplished, then either by swift spontaneous delivery, or by peaceful, drawn-out transmission, the salubrious and sempiternal sound of *AUM,* The Word, will suggest itself to the seeker's now refined awareness. Taking this profound seed of all Wisdom, the deeply absorbed meditator should now fix the mind on the highest and most beloved aspect of God with form that his or her mind can conceive of. If the aspirant's early training and spiritual ideation was not geared toward God with form, called *Ishvara,* then The Word will easily accomplish the ushering of the matured, individualized soul into the Supreme Soul, or *Brahman.* That is Formless Reality. Some think of That as the highest Reality and Supreme Goal. Others prefer the Supreme Personality. It hardly matters at this transported level of full realization, but the best of all comprehensive insights would be to know both.

All endeavors have impediments connected to them, as if to ensure that the intrepid wayfarer will build up great strength as a result. In the process of immersion there is no exception to this rule. The bottom third of this chart under study simultaneously suggests what these obstacles are, and gives the right orientation, or mental posture *(manasana),* that will deal with them.

There is no shame, and it is completely understandable, that living beings may engender some attachment to the physical body. When cultures, upbringing, and occupational life all focus upon the body as if it were the only reality, and contain precious few teachings that would suggest the contrary, embodied beings then proceed along the paths of materialism *(lokayatika marg)* and secularism *(pravritti marg)* uninformed otherwise (see chart on page 377). This has many problems associated with it, but for this particular area of practical study, i.e., passing out of the body in either meditation or at the time of the body's demise, the problem is the mind's clinging to the body when it is time, sometimes past time, to give it up and go on (inwards to the kingdom of heaven or beyond). Thus, the soul desiring immersion tells his or her mind that the physical form is not the actual self or being, and assigns it back to the realm of *karma* from which it sprang. As Vivekananda wrote, "Heed then no more how body lives or goes, its task is done. Let *karma* float it down...." Further,

The Six-Fold Process of Immersion in Brahman

&
Six Illumined Thoughts at the Time of Death

"Let a person remain, wherever he may be and whenever he learns that his end is approaching, even if he has not practiced and prepared, or done meritorious acts, and even if he becomes senseless at the time of death, when dispassion visits and the mind gets temporarily clear and free of worldly thoughts, let that one think the following:"

"Now I shall tell you of the time that the Yogis depart, never to return."

1
"With all gates of the body closed...."

2
"....the mind confined within the head...."

3
"....having fixed the life-energy in the heart...."

4
"....engaged in firm Yoga...."

5
"....uttering the one-syllabled OM...."

6
"....thinking of Me alone...."

"....that one who departs, leaving the body, attains to the Supreme Goal"

1) I have no connection with this body, which is merely the outcome of action.

2) This body, composed of five elements, will soon be destroyed, for all forms are liable to decay and destruction.

3) There is no cause for remorse regarding the approach of death.

4) I am neither a worldly person, nor a material object, so death is not capable of doing any harm to me.

5) My Essence is pure, void of all qualities; I am the Supreme Soul.

6) I am always free; I am the Eternal Brahman.

Srimad Devi Bhagavatam

"Having come to Me, the great souls are no more subject to rebirth, which is transitory and the abode of pain. They have reached the highest perfection." Sri Krishna

The Divisions of Atman from Sri Rama Hrydayam

"I shall tell you the truth about Paramatman, Atman, and Anatman. Like the sky, which has three divisions — all-pervasive, associated with objects, and reflected in a water-tank — so too is Consciousness — Pure Consciousness, associated with the intellect, and reflected in the intellect."

Jiva,
Animals,
Insects, Plants
—
Reflected
Consciousness

Appearances
in the Buddhi, or
Intellect
—
Associated
Consciousness

Reflection
Sky

Brahman
—
Witness
Consciousness,
Pure
Consciousness

Reflection
Tree

Reflection
Body

Reflection
Deer

Reflection
Rock

Reflection
Earth

"Ignorant persons with distorted understanding cast superimposed divisions over the partless, unchanging Witness Consciousness, like the sense of agency that is only reflected in the Buddhi. These movements and partitions are all assumed by reflected consciousness. The existence of the jiva is also assumed by it. But all reflections are illusory; jiva and buddhi are false separations. Only Brahman is partless, indivisible. Divisibility in Brahman is due only to its adjuncts."

the observer looks deeper and reminds the mind that all composite things are subject to decay and death, but that the Soul, *Atman,* is free of them both. Freeing the mind of remorse in this way, the deeply focused soul now looks back to affirm that he/she never seriously identified the Self with being a worldly being, nor a material object like the body, and then confirms, wonderfully, "I am That," the ever-stationary Self. "I am ever-free." *Aham Brahmasmi* — I am the Supreme *Brahman.*"

Living in this spiritual perspective, and doing so even in the physical universe with a gross body, and amidst a multitude of beings who are either still blatantly ignorant or in the early or more advanced processes of realizing this Goal, the aspiring being takes recourse to several mainstays of religion and philosophy. In other words, even from a realized condition of mind the well-informed soul engages in spiritual practice, though of a much more refined nature than earlier along the path.

The chart on the opposite page explains the cogent threefold observation which the soul is undergoing all the time, especially so long as the false superimposition of name and form is appearing to the mind and senses. Sri Ram taught this system in a very early age, showing, among other things, that Indian philosophy was mature even in olden times, among ancient people. These beings were not, as Swami Vivekananda mentioned once, mummifying their dead for some afterlife in the body as was done in Egypt, but rather teaching embodied beings how to transcend the limited condition of the body altogether — and doing so with regard to three bodies, not just one (as in reference to the waking, dreaming, and deep sleep bodies of limited awareness just studied on page 711). Otherwise, a repetitive round *(yuga)* of birth and death in ignorance *(samsara)* of ones true nature *(Atman)* will set in, based upon recurring effects coming due to unconscious actions perpetrated earlier *(karma).*

The mind is all-important in life, even in heavenly life. If the mind is taught to see the Truth of Divine Reality clearly, then all of life will go on in a fulfilling way, with no detrimental effects in operation. This is why Sri Ram and other illumined souls point out (as in the chart opposite) to all beings who are paying close attention (like Sita and Laksmana) that though Consciousness is really everywhere and in everything, It must be perceived carefully so that, as *Vedanta* states, one will not take the unreal for the Real. The sky becomes a fitting metaphor for making this astute analogy, since it represents so simply and easily the three subdivisions of the *Atman,* so to speak.

The first, and most essential, is the sky in its infinite mode, untouched by forms and boundaries, more like the ether *(akasha)* that is so subtle it is not even displaced by objects. This is *Brahman,* in other words, "all-pervasive" — not *vyasti,* the individual, but *vyapi,* the one who pervades all individuals — as Ram explains, which is also one of the best words in English capable of explaining the abstruse *Sanskrit* with its high-minded emphasis. O?ne cannot see or sense this homogenous Entity, or Essence *(svarupa).* It pervades everything on all levels *(vyapaka).*

The second "division" of *Atman* is represented by how the sky "associates" with objects. The best way to become aware of this is through the animating power *(shakti/prana)* that propels all bodies, whether they be planets, human forms, nature, or moving and stationary bits of matter. The unseen cause the seen to seem alive, to appear sentient, to reflect awareness. That is, living beings may move amongst all of nature, but they never think about or espy the underlying sentient Force or Presence, that infills and compels everything. All of this, too, has divisions, like *Ishvara, Shakti,* and *prana.* Again, we scarcely have names or words for these principles in the West, and so never speak of them.

And along with how Consciousness associates with all things, there are some associations that are so far from the source, even illusory and pain-causing, that it is necessary to recognize them and note them for what they are — mere reflections. If we can simultaneously admit to the presence of Awareness, or Consciousness, in all things, then those things, likes objects, that do not hold sentiency but only reflect it, will not stymie us, or thwart us from seeing Truth in all, and as one.

To conclude, Consciousness is one and Indivisible, but it appears divided in beings and things. One might say, then, that Awareness is *Brahman,* that same Awareness associated with beings and things is the mind and intellect, and when It is reflected It assumes nature and objects. As

Vivekananda put it in poem form, *"There is but One — The Free — The Knower — Self! Without a name, without a form or stain. In Him is Maya, dreaming all this dream. The Witness, He appears as nature, soul. Know thou are That...."*

There are other superlative ways which *Vedanta* and Indian philosophy utilize to assist the aspiring soul in remembering and returning to its perfect nondual state. The chart next under study also uses a threefold division, this time based upon the soul's competency for making spiritual progress by stages. If the mind is still sick, imbalanced, and needs healing, then what is "salubrious" needs to be taken up. If mental health is present, then what is purely "spiritual" in nature can be imbibed. And if the spiritual has been digested by the now fit soul, the excellences of the "sempiternal" are waiting for it in bliss. All of these have to do with mental postures that the soul can assume, termed here, *manasanas*.

The author wants to inform the reader that he considers this teaching so potentially beneficial for the present time, that he has written a book on the subject, bringing it out from hiding amidst India's great systems. A detailed explanation of all the mental postures listed on this chart can be studied therein, although there are countless sets of these *asanas* available for practice.

And the *Sanskrit* word, *"asana,"* is key to this effort, for the body-oriented person of the modern day and time has focused in on only the physical postures of *hatha yoga*, actually mistaking the word and esteemed philosophy of *Yoga* to be only that. This is what happens when disoriented opportunistic instructors and teachers introduce a potentially healthy *yogic* system to an untrained, physically-based, sensually-oriented, materialistic culture of pleasure-seekers who, for one, have not even begun to master the five *yamas* and five *niyamas* of *Yoga* (1st and 2nd limbs) prior to taking up physical *asanas* (3rd limb). Awakened power *(shakti)* will begin its rise to higher centers due to placing the body and spine in certain positions, but it will encounter impurities as it does (particularly at the *svadhistana* and *manipura chakras*) due to the presence of latent *samskaras*/impressions from the past (see charts on pages 167 & 170) around violence (both inflicted and received), covetousness, sexual impurities and underlying passions, and a whole host of hidden problems that the *yamas* and *niyamas* are designed to destroy if *Yoga* is practiced in its traditional, eight-limbed system *(Raja Yoga, Ashtanga Yoga, Patanjala)* under the guidance of an illumined teacher, i.e. *Guru*.

With this stated, the benefits (rather than the content) of *Manasana* can be cited. Placing the body in positions, if done wisely and with moderation and guidance, may help in the early phases of spiritual practice, but learning to place the mind in strong postures — call them attitudes if you will — will not only take the soul more efficiently to Enlightenment, but will also make having to deal with the body and its ailments and shortcomings unnecessary. This is instanced by the fact that there are many illumined beings who take a body and manifest on earth, and they seldom resort to physical practices, having already mastered higher levels of awareness (like the *tattvas*) previously, in another lifetime. To begin with the mind, states the *Yoga Kundalini Upanisad*, is the superior pathway. If that is not possible due to *karmic* circumstances and limitations, the teaching continues, then controlling the *prana* is the next best route towards freedom. Having to resort to only the physical alone is risky, at best. If this is the default position, then why court spiritual life at all? Spirituality infers what lies beyond the physical, from the mind on inwards.

The mind is a kind of body as well, as we have explored in this book. It has inherent shortcomings and diseases too. And in fact, these mental infirmities will give rise to diseases of the body in due course if not rectified. *Manasanas* are postures that the mind takes up which not only rid the intellect and its thinking process of unwanted burdens and imbalances, but also strengthen its own singular immune system as well. Strong mind, healthy body, is the way. If the practitioner takes up a mental posture and holds it until it is ripe, the particular problem that was present and unsolvable earlier then disappears. For instance, if a beginning aspiring seeker has problems with emotions, and cannot control them, then placing the mind into the posture of *akshobhasana*, as suggested and guided by the *guru*, will remove it in good time. If, at a deeper stage of practice, the intermediate level aspirant experiences impediments around the ego, the position of *asmitavinashanasana* will suffice

The Spiritual Art of Mental Asana

"According to the Vedic Seers, the entire world is a projection of the mind. It stands to reason, then, that how one sees and experiences the world falls in direct correlation with the condition of one's mind. Therefore, perspective is key to life, living, and most importantly, to Divine Life. The luminaries of the world have mastered the mind by rendering it amenable to the sacred art of mental asana, i.e., placing it consciously in intelligent, stable, internalized postures." — Babaji Bob Kindler

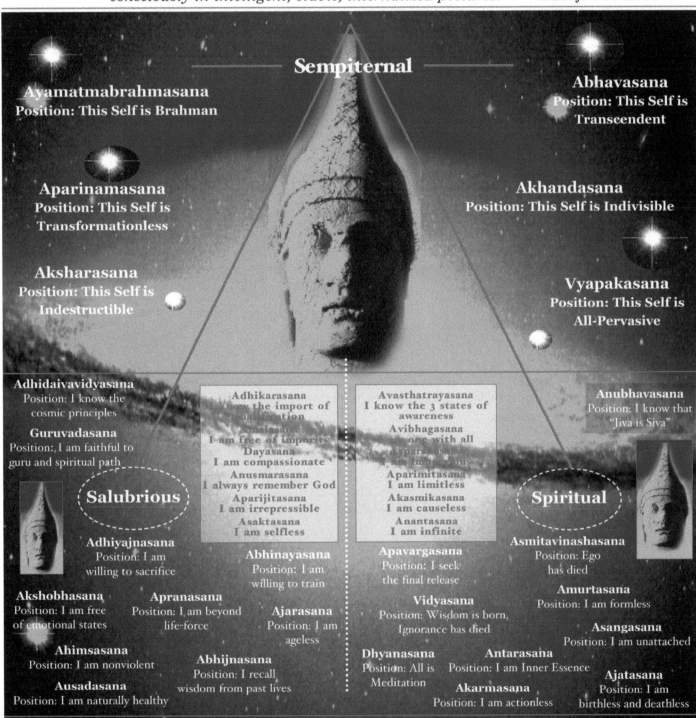

Sempiternal

Ayamatmabrahmasana
Position: This Self is Brahman

Abhavasana
Position: This Self is Transcendent

Aparinamasana
Position: This Self is Transformationless

Akhandasana
Position: This Self is Indivisible

Aksharasana
Position: This Self is Indestructible

Vyapakasana
Position: This Self is All-Pervasive

Adhidaivavidyasana
Position: I know the cosmic principles

Guruvadasana
Position: I am faithful to guru and spiritual path

Adhikarasana
I know the import of purification
Amalasana
I am free of impurity
Dayasana
I am compassionate
Anusmarasana
I always remember God
Aparijitasana
I am irrepressible
Asaktasana
I am selfless

Avasthatrayasana
I know the 3 states of awareness
Avibhagasana
I am one with all
Asparsasana
I am impervious
Aparimitasana
I am limitless
Akasmikasana
I am causeless
Anantasana
I am infinite

Anubhavasana
Position: I know that "Jiva is Siva"

Salubrious

Spiritual

Adhiyajnasana
Position: I am willing to sacrifice

Abhinayasana
Position: I am willing to train

Apavargasana
Position: I seek the final release

Asmitavinashasana
Position: Ego has died

Akshobhasana
Position: I am free of emotional states

Apranasana
Position: I am beyond life-force

Ajarasana
Position: I am ageless

Vidyasana
Position: Wisdom is born, Ignorance has died

Amurtasana
Position: I am formless

Asangasana
Position: I am unattached

Ahimsasana
Position: I am nonviolent

Abhijnasana
Position: I recall wisdom from past lives

Dhyanasana
Position: All is Meditation

Antarasana
Position: I am Inner Essence

Akarmasana
Position: I am actionless

Ajatasana
Position: I am birthless and deathless

Ausadasana
Position: I am naturally healthy

"Physical asanas are merely a matter of summoning up energy, but mental asanas are based within one's innate intelligence. After they are developed and honed in the salubrious atmosphere of mental purification, they are brought forth from previous lifetimes for purposes of peaceful, blissful, existence, and the natural benefit of all of humanity." — Babaji Bob Kindler

to curb it. Further, if lower *samadhi* is gained, and higher *samadhi* escapes the advanced practitioner due to fear of death, the posture of *Aksharasana* can be applied — for the Self, *Atman*, is indestructible. The reader is encouraged to study the book *Manasana, The Superlative Art of Mental Posture*, for more teachings concerning this powerful method of mental practice.

As was mentioned, the mind, as a subtle body, contains poisons just as the physical body does. This makes sense since the physical, or gross, has proceeded from the mental, or subtle. Our next chart up for review might not even belong in this chapter, but both as a reference point and a contrasting element, it can clarify certain matters for the practitioner.

It must be admitted that if there are beings who possess a marvelous ability of mind to remain positive, the opposite is also true — and in fact, a far greater percentage of living beings on earth today are under the influence of negativities which are too many to count, and too strong for them to overcome. From the spiritual standpoint, and according to the wisdom of beings who possess higher consciousness, or higher mind, the main blockages to thinking that proceeds via positivity, goodness, selflessness, compassion, and aspiration for higher goals — especially the Highest Goal — are both obvious and unnecessary.

Unfortunately, many beings holding these darksome impediments are doing so because they like such attitudes, and they despise those who would shed the Light of Awareness on earth in order to remove suffering and darkness. So many of the world's great luminaries have run up against the benighted souls who champion evil means and ill deeds. Steeped in delusion, the wayward thinker who has nothing but selfishness as the means suffers iniquitous postures in the mind that are inflexible, and which only further his or her fall into darkness. "Pleasure is what I seek"; "wealth is the goal of life"; "objects will make me happy"; and "I am this body which only lives once"; are some severely binding mental attitudes that stymie all possibility of true happiness.

Along with these, and of another caliber, are postures like "the world is real"; "religion is false"; "there is no soul"; and "God does not exist." Around these two main collections of pernicious mental *asanas* are sub-asanas that are both the cause of the latter, as well as seeds for more of the same in the near and distant future. The sense of superiority, the seeking of good only for oneself and not for others, clinging to ignorance, and seeking health and longevity via inferior modes of practice, are some of these.

The luminary has turned away from these flexuous modes of turpitude and embraced instead all the positive mental *asanas* that have been listed on the chart on page 719, plus more. To water the flowers and not the weeds, called *pratipakshabhavanam* in *Sanskrit*, is the idea, at least to begin with. After some control or mastery is gained, then the affirmation of these mental modes is to be followed up by deeper and deeper *sadhana*. The taking up of any given *manasana*, then, is a type of mental *sadhana*, but due to the way people's minds are in this day and age, the practice is apt to either go nowhere but a few minutes consideration, or not go deep enough due to surface affirmation only.

Of course, the test of the pudding is in the removal of the bad taste in ones mouth, i.e., if the problem that called for a mental *asana* to be taken up goes away with practice in due time. In the case of *Manasana*, it is an ingenious method which is perfectly suited for the next stage of humanity's spiritual evolution, as it were. Just simply practicing a few mental *asanas*, each for a time, may be enough to remove many problems that are plaguing the human mind at this juncture in time. Moreover, if the mind of the aspirant is already geared up for practice, having accomplished certain moral and spiritual disciplines leading up to this method, or in a past lifetime, then this qualification will lead to immediate success and its joyous results.

The subject of both positive and negative thoughts and mental conditionings infers the need for practice, or *sadhana*. The Self, *Atman*, is already and always perfect; it is the mind/ego complex that stands in the way of perceiving and living in this best of all states. For modern man, raised up as he has been in a thoroughly dualistic atmosphere, with its unforgiving accent upon morality and immorality, virtue opposite vice, good versus evil, etc., the nondual perspective of innate perfection

Mental Postures that Bind

Mental Perspectives that Stymie Spirituality

"To take up a posture (asana) in the mind (manas) in order to master one's awareness and attain to Yoga, union with Ultimate Reality, will bring about what has been called by luminaries every-where as balance of mind, steadiness of mind, equanimity of mind, purity of mind, equipoise — all leading to peace of mind, or, 'the Peace that passeth all understanding.'" Babaji Bob Kindler

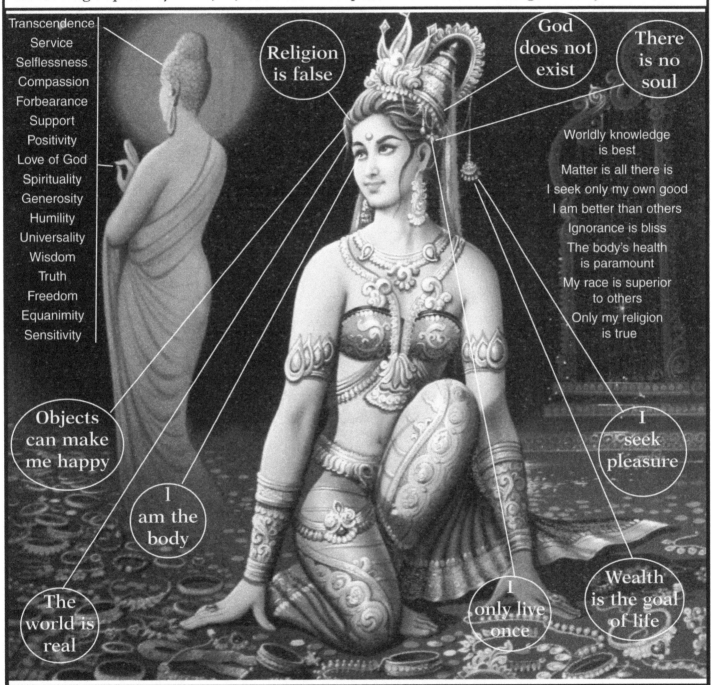

Transcendence
Service
Selflessness
Compassion
Forbearance
Support
Positivity
Love of God
Spirituality
Generosity
Humility
Universality
Wisdom
Truth
Freedom
Equanimity
Sensitivity

Religion is false

God does not exist

There is no soul

Worldly knowledge is best
Matter is all there is
I seek only my own good
I am better than others
Ignorance is bliss
The body's health is paramount
My race is superior to others
Only my religion is true

Objects can make me happy

I am the body

The world is real

I seek pleasure

I only live once

Wealth is the goal of life

"It is all a question of the mind; bondage and liberation are of the mind alone. If one holds false thoughts, then the world seems real and God disappears from sight. Further, it will not do to merely repeat, 'I am He, I am He!' Beings get free by following up affirmations with spiritual disciplines. In the case of the worldly, they never think about God even by accident. If they do find the right mental perspective, it lasts only about as long as a drop of water on a red-hot frying-pan." Sri Ramakrishna

has seldom been transmitted or received as a result — certainly not as a whole philosophy like in India. The downside of this is the emergence of guilt, shame, remorse, and a whole host of other, what to say, negative mental *asanas*. But the real message of Jesus, which should have also been Christianity's long range missive all along, is of the inherent perfection of the Soul and Its inseparable oneness with God. What Jesus realized as *"I and my Father are One,"* is truly a "sempiternal" *Manasana* which is meant to be realized by all beings, while negative *asanas* like "I am a sinner" or "I will burn in eternal hell-fires," are to be swiftly removed from the mind's thinking process as soon as humanly possible.

On the fresh chart on the facing page we see quotes from a few souls who were close to Jesus, showing that both their faith in His words, and the mental *asanas* they assumed as a result, were not only redeeming, but illuminating. Matthew, Luke, Timothy, and Mark were disciples who heard some of the nondual expressions of the Christ who, Himself, may have heard them from the dharmic source when He traveled to India in one period of His life, most likely. Whatever the case may be, these eternal verities speak to spiritual life rather than to a life of suffering, a life of worldliness, or one mere insouciance and jollification. This is shown clearly by Matthew's famous recalling of Jesus' words at the top of the chart, all around the need to love God more than family, and to follow His emissaries. This is true of those who quit mundane life as renunciates, i.e., *sannyasins,* as well as those who remain in the world yet seek to transcend it through seeking higher wisdom and performing selfless service.

The problem of attachment to money and the creature comforts that it buys was also understood by Christ's apostles. The five complacencies as regards to wealth (see chart on page 309) have long been known and observed closely in India, for they knew that to inherit a huge mass of wealth in the form of money, lands, and objects was a potentially wide open doorway to losing ones soul, as Luke states. Mark echoed these deep sentiments by bringing in the need for solitude, wisely utilized in order to gain distance from worldly beings who seek power as well. This was wise not only for this reason, but for taking the mind out of the atmosphere of idle chatter, as Timothy pointed out. Ones innate wisdom, as well as the knowledge that is being gleaned in this particular lifetime in order to awaken it more fully, is seriously at risk among the surface gossip and slander that always flows from the lips of the ignorant.

Then, there is the equally serious task of keeping what Lord Buddha called right-orientation (see chart on page 229) prominent, and in action. It is not just the giving up of the world and its enticements and allurements that constitutes mature renunciation, but doing so for the love of God. Wrong orientation means giving up the world out of hatred or aversion, amounting to immature detachment. Avoidance of wrong orientation actually leads the soul toward seeing God in everything, one of India's most mature statements on spiritual attainment. A mature orientation fuses the *yogas* of meditation and selfless service, or action and inaction, which is a rare combination to see fused in any living being.

Finally, the subject of death is also taken up. To recognize stubborn ignorance and give up *"strewing pearls before swine"* is to *"let the dead bury their dead,"* and follow the way of spirituality taught by the luminaries leading to freedom. Birthdays, marriages, and funerals are not for those who have realized God, nor for those who are seriously seeking God. Therefore, let the dead marry their own as well.

Nevertheless, mature renunciation, *tyaga* in *Sanskrit,* does not brook any compromises or initiations. The God-loving soul, whereas he/she does not literally hate the world, still sees through it as mutable, transitory, ephemeral, illusory, unreal, unsubstantial, and ultimately unfulfilling. It is not coveted or sought after for its own sake, for to try and possess the unreal is a fool's game, suffered by many. Religion's best aim and intention, if it be true to its calling, is to communicate such messages of nonattachment and transcendence to sincere seekers so that they can attain the "final beatitude" — Absolute Freedom *(moksha).*

The chart next up for examination follows in keeping with the universal teachings of Jesus,

✠ Christ the Sannyasin ✠
The Key Renunciation Teachings of Jesus of Nazareth

"Do not suppose that I have come to bring peace to the earth. I did not come to bring peace, but a sword. I have come to turn a man against his father, a daughter against her mother, a daughter-in-law against her mother-in-law. A man's enemies will be the members of his own household. Anyone who loves father or mother more than me is not worthy of me; anyone who loves their son or daughter more than me is not worthy of me. Whoever does not take up their cross and follow me is not worthy of me. Whoever finds their life will lose it, and whoever loses their life for my sake will find it."
Matthew 10:34-36

"None of you can be My disciple who does not give up all his own possessions."
Luke 14:33

"And the man said: 'Lord, first let me bury my father; then I will follow you.' But Jesus replied, 'Let the dead bury their dead; you come with me to proclaim the Kingdom of God.'"
Matthew 8:22

"Birds have nests and foxes have holes, but the son of man hath no place to lay his head." Matthew 8:18

"For, what will it profit a man, if he should gain the whole world but lose his soul?"
Luke 22:27

"And everyone who has left houses or brothers or sisters or father or mother or children or farms for My name's sake, will receive many times as much, and will inherit eternal life." Matthew 19:29

"Guard what has been entrusted to you, avoiding the world and its empty chatter and the opposing arguments of what is falsely called 'knowledge.'"
Timothy 6:20

"Seek ye first the kingdom of God, and his righteousness; and all things shall be added unto thee." Matt. 6:33

"Render unto Caesar what is Caesar's, but give unto the Lord what is the Lord's...."
Spiritual things, such as worship and obedience, give these to God; for these He demands from you as his right, and by so doing you will offend neither God nor Caesar." Mark 12:17

Wisdom Facets From The Garland of Universality

"Mankind ought to be taught that religions are but the varied expressions of The Religion which is Oneness, so that each may choose the path that suits him best."

Swami Vivekananda

"When ahimsa, the incapacity to harm others, and dharma, the inherent goodness dwelling in the heart, are fully developed in man, then he is said to have attained Enlightenment."

"Meditate deeply and reach the Great Source. Branching streams cannot compare to It. Then, sitting in utter silence, as the heavens turn and the earth is upset, you will not even wink."

"The two primal spirits, who reveal themselves in vision as twins, are the better and the bad, in thought, word, and action. Between these two the wise ones choose aright; the foolish, not so."

"A tall tree is at first a slender shoot. A tall tower is raised by placing a few stones atop one another. Journeys of many leagues begin with a single step. Be careful of your thoughts; they are the beginning of your deeds."

"I have fashioned a garland of the different religious traditions of the world, and have offered them all at the sacred Feet of the Mother of the Universe."

Sri Ramakrishna Paramahamsa

"Of old, heaven and earth were one, like an egg containing seeds. The pure part was drawn out to form heaven; the gross part became earth. Heaven formed first, earth thereafter. Divine beings were produced between them."

"Who is the wise man? Whosoever is constantly learning from others. Who is the rich man? Whosoever is contented with his lot. Who is the strong man? Whosoever is capable of self-mastery."

"Thou shalt hear what no ear has heard, thou shalt see what no eye has seen, and at last thou shalt come into that sacred Presence and thou shalt find only one sole Being in place of the world and its mortal creatures."

"And I turned within to behold wisdom, as well as madness and folly. Then I saw that wisdom excelled folly, as far as light excels darkness, and I invested myself with Her as a raiment of glory and put Her on my head as a crown of joy."

mainly that all authentic religion is true, and that God-men and God-women are coming to earth age after age to help souls breath the exhilarating "Air of Heights" spoken of by the *Upanisads* since the most ancient of times. Thus, eight of the world's major religions are represented in this fragrant garland of Universal Truth shown to the left. Swami Vivekananda's excellent quote on the subject tops the list, and gets the truth-fest started in fine fashion. True religion gets stamped out by narrowness and hypocrisy, so adopting the spirit of close brotherhood, members of all religious families come together to celebrate the "One God" Who is at the source of every world religion.

And Swami Vivekananda's great *Guru,* Sri Ramakrishna Paramahamsa, extends to us the centerpiece to this wide and catholic offering, being the one who practiced many paths and religions to experience nondual comprehension of this innate Oneness. He sites the Divine Mother of the Universe as the one Who wears this garland around Her lovely neck, weaving all faiths into a single, sententious and redolent vision.

Beginning with the quote from the religion of the Indian *rishis,* the point is made that nonviolence *(ahimsa)* is the main premise upon which true universality can be built. There can be no harboring of hatred, no hidden presence of jealousy, and no arrogant competition for supremacy or domination over others. Violence enters through the avenues of actions, words, and thoughts. Therefore the mind must be cleared of impurities so as to allow it to look upon others as children of God.

Moving to the right around this auspicious garland, Zoroastrianism is the next religion in view. Obviously it concurs with the principle of *ahimsa* in *Vedic* religion, as it, too, cites actions, words, and thoughts as the barometer by which to measure what is beneficial. These can also signal what is banal. The wise choose the former, letting the latter go completely.

Shintoism, in similar fashion, comes forward next to reveal the two worlds of what is negative and what is positive in order to indicate the presence of holy beings, or again, the wise. Earth and heaven are in everything, and the coming together of the two produces a grinding effect that polishes the diamond of human nature, turning it divine.

Following suit, Christianity gives out the teaching of folly and wisdom, side by side, in human doings, thinking, and vision. The wise, again, prevail, and seek out Wisdom as a "raiment" to place over these three bodies to clothe it and heal it. Then, the howling masses with their folly will not be able to harm or confuse the lover's of Divine Reality, nor dissuade them from seeking and attaining the highest station of peace and bliss.

Taking a definite turn towards the nondual, Islam puts on the raiment of silence to hear and see what no man hath ever heard or seen, leading the soul into chambers so interior that the many mysteriously become one. Even the world, so coveted by the masses, disappears There, and what is left over cannot be described. Like both Judaism and Christianity before it, realized seers of the Islamic tradition came to understand that God cannot be experienced with the gross senses. A much subtler set of senses, called "love eyes" and "love ears" by Sri Ramakrishna, must be gained.

And speaking of Judaism, the pathway leading towards such a pithy vision is paved with attainments that are of a special order by beings with voracious appetite for them. If one were to gain wisdom, true wealth, and strength — so coveted by luminaries of all the worlds religious traditions — then according to Judaism, open-mindedness, contentment with what is, and self-mastery must be among the foremost of qualities coveted.

And since a journey of a thousand miles begins with the first step, Taoism seems to concur with the need for patience and perseverance. It adds in the crucial point that everything — the journey, the wayfarer, and his movements — proceed from the mind, so keeping ones thoughts pure is essential to religious, philosophical and spiritual life, all.

Finally, and as a last look at the chart on page 724, the religion of *Buddhism* accents the fact that meditating on Ultimate Reality is necessary, and that the "branching streams" of other types of thoughts are inferior and potentially misleading. In the havoc of constant change, then, the meditator is to remain silent, still, and thereby remain untouched by the ongoing dangers always going forth in the realm of relativity.

In *Advaita Vedanta,* India's Great Master Nondualist, Gaudapada, concurs. His system called *Asparsha Yoga,* or the "Non-Touch *Yoga,"* confers exactly the kind of static stillness and crystal clarity required to remain free of the vagaries and vicissitudes of the worlds of name and form in time and space. The chart of the facing page explains this especial *Yoga* to us.

Is Nonduality a principle or a practice? It is both. *Advaita Vedanta Sadhana,* as the latter has been called, is simultaneously an observance of the perfection of the Soul/*Atman,* and an enforcing of incontrovertible spiritual laws that can become obscured as long as the embodied soul is associating with the limitations of name and form. The presence of root fear is the concern here, for the pressing in of relativity in the form of old age, disease, and death can make an impression on the mind in *maya.* Self-control, moderation of all appetites, and an ever-awake mind that prefers the "insomnia of *Yoga"* to the sleep of "blissful" ignorance, are earmarks here. Add to this a mind that has become stable, even in the midst of life's inevitable trials and tragedies, and the attainment of the Highest Goal *(nirvikalpa/nirvana/moksha)* is not only experienced, it is kept sacrosanct for all time. This is a simple recipe for nondual practice, though the subtitles of it are a bit more complex.

The wondrous results, or fruits of nondual practice, are then enjoyed, exquisitely, by the luminaries. Attributes such as refined knowledge come to the fore of consciousness. This possession keeps the Truth of Existence clear and shining eternally in the mind's eye. The *Avadhut,* in his own scripture, the *Avadhuta Gita,* tells of this shining verity that lies both at the root and the height of Awareness:

Transcending freedom and bondage, beyond life and matter,
outstripping all seeds and their respective origins, It just shines, eternally.
Its Light dissolves all divisions and barriers.
I am Pure Existence, Wisdom, and Bliss, as boundless as the sky, infinite like space.

Unoriginated, that Brahman is translucent Awareness.
Acreate, beyond all phenomena, It shines as incandescent Consciousness throughout Eternity.
Constant and imperishable, It knows not creation or destruction.
I am that Pure Existence, Wisdom, and Bliss, as boundless as the sky, infinite like space.

The presence of an unerring discernment, often termed spiritual discrimination, also becomes a readily available quality for the rare *asparsha yogi.* It is via this sterling quality that he is able to "shower beneficence" on all beings coming in contact with him. Thus it is that true happiness finally dawns, for helping others constitutes such an unalloyed and uninterrupted state. Others, by the millions, are busy running here and there trying to find that happiness for themselves, but their mistake is in not knowing that real happiness results in serving others. Once this lesson is learned, not only happiness comes, but also other pellucid qualities such as peace of mind and quiescence.

Due to the descent of such rare and lofty attributes, the *asparsha yogi* becomes "untouched" in another way as well. As the chart on the facing page reveals, argumentation and dispute die away, for he has found that which is unparalleled in spiritual life, in all of life — the rare and precious Truth. It renders him transcendentally taciturn. There is no need for disputation any more; he is supremely satisfied. Therefore he settles into that arrant and unmitigated state that is beyond both desire and nondesire. It is inexplicable, and in it is all rest, all refection, and all bliss.

The final result of the *Asparsha Yoga* "practice" holds itself in common with elements of both the *yogas* of Lord Vasishtha and of Lord Patanjali. All three have mentioned penultimate states wherein the soul's spiritually evolving process come to full fruition. All matters are settled, not only on earth in the body, but at the deepest level of freedom from rebirth, unmanifested nature, and the *gunas.* All these concerns, or *karmas,* or duties, or services — to all levels of living beings in all worlds — get themselves resolved completely in *Brahman,* like bubbles dissolving into water. Homogenous Awareness, which is all Bliss, all Knowledge, and all Existence, is all that is left. It was all there ever was.

Asparsha Yoga — The "Non-Touch" Yoga
◉ According to Gaudapada's Karika ◉

"I salute the best of beings, who with incomparable jnana has realized that all beings are unborn and infinite, like the sky. I salute him on bended knee, he who teaches the 'non-touch' yoga for the benefit of all beings, free of compromise, superior and unopposed." Gaudapada

Requisites of Non-Touch Yoga
The Practice of Nonduality

Freedom from fear
Self-control and perseverance
Moderate desire and enjoyment
Awaken mind and have samadhi
Stabilize the mind during unrest
Attain the Goal — Brahman

Results
of Non-touch Yoga

The Fruits of Nondual Practice
Secures right knowledge
Nonattachment via mature discernment
Showers benificence on all creatures
Realization of the highest happiness
Freedom from dispute and opposition
Transcendance of desire and nondesire
Culmination of processes in Brahman

"When there is no thought, when there is no taking up, no giving up, at that time Atmajnana is well set in itself, and nonoriginated, remaining equal. This is verily what is known as the non-touch yoga by name, very difficult of realization by ordinary yogis." Gaudapada

"The Province of the Enlightened"

The Three Types of Knowledge Samadhis in Advaita Vedanta

"The rare condition of knowing Brahman is spoken of as naturally calm and controlled because one's own nature is calm and controlled. Know this, then, and attain to calmness and control." Gaudapada

I.
Laukika Jnana

Knowledge when external objects are believed to exist.

"It is the Highest, and blazes forth with illumination on account of Its own Essential Nature."

II.
Shuddha Laukika Jnana

Knowledge when no objects exist, but perception of objects still exists.

III.
Lokottara Jnana

Knowledge when neither objects nor their perceptions exist, leading the seer to omniscience.

Descriptions of the Three Types of Samadhis

I. Duality with its objects and perceptions — "Practical"

II. Duality devoid of objects but with its perceptions — "Pure and Practical"

III. Duality without its objects and its perceptions — "Super-Practical"

The Agrayana's Process of Perception

Stage 1 — What is fit to be abandoned

Stage 2 — What is fit to be known

Stage 3 — What is fit to be secured

Stage 4 — What is specifically fit to be known (beyond perception)

"All entities are by nature calm and unoriginated from the very outset, of the nature of nirvana itself. But there is indeed no self-confidence in those who move about believing in an illusory world of differences. Those who hold to this doctrine descend into a world fraught with differences. They are traditionally known as 'nervous wrecks' and are very pitiable." Gaudapada

Further following along the *Advaita Vedanta* trajectory around Lord Gaudapada's teachings, the following chart on the opposite page lets us in on the three levels of knowers of *Brahman* in this system, and the three plateaus of *samadhi* that correlate with them. *Laukika Jnana, Shuddha Laukika Jnana,* and *Lokotara Jnana* are the three *samadhis* that are known by the Knowers, and their meanings all reflect the higher thinking that the Indian *rishis* have always championed, throughout time.

The first is a *samadhi* that is aware of objects. Since we are talking about spirituality here and not worldliness, this awareness is not concerned about or taken up with attachment to objects for the purposes of ownership and pleasure. In *Laukika Jnana Samadhi* the mind's thinking process is focused on the existence of the outer world and its elements, and since this purified mind has been stripped of overlays like desire and attachment, it is perceiving an entirely different realm than most beings have access to with the senses. All things, all objects, are offering up their secrets, as it were, and the relative freedom that dwells in the mind at this juncture is allowing it to extract essence from the external while being free of possessiveness and other unnatural impediments. This ability is what we notice in certain illumined souls who still maintain the body, and act in the world after Enlightenment has dawned. This state is akin to but not fully at-one with what is called *"...seeing Brahman in everything"* in the *Upanisads.*

When this natural and practical mind shifts levels of consciousness, much like an ordinary person shifts from dreaming into deep sleep, but more consciously, it then experiences the absence of objects while still keeping a very subtle memory of them. It is something like a runner running a race but forgetting that there is a track under his feet, or like a mother bird hatching her egg but forgetting the egg as she sits still upon it. Here, phenomena involving objects is fast fading away. The mind is, at this time, simultaneously practical, but also purer. Words begin to fail. As Lord Buddha has stated, *"When all phenomena are removed, all means of description are also removed."*

Both of these first two *samadhis* maintain a condition of relations with objects in the mind of the seer. It is not until *Lokotara Samadhi* visits that both the objects themselves and the perception that they exist, even when they are not seen, go away. "Omniscience" is the word applied to the result of this *samadhi,* for perception of Divine Reality, which is Formless, could not occur so long as any semblance of or belief in the presence of form was still occupying the mind. Therefore, as Gaudapada states, *"The condition of knowing Brahman to be calm and controlled is attained due to the meditator discovering that his own nature is calm and controlled."*

Back in the realm of objects, then, the *yogi* keeps his mind calm and controlled based upon having experienced these three states, in order. *Samadhi* begets more of *samadhi.* Additionally, the *yogi* found out that all objects were also calm by nature, peaceful at their core, and that it was only the mind out of control that perceived them differently, like with angst, fear, attraction, loathing, etc.

This seeker, *yogi,* meditator, or seer is called the *agrayana* in this fully realized system. The *Sanskrit* dictionaries define the word *agrahya* as meaning "that which is unfit to take." Ironically, it is both the world of objects and the nondual *Brahman* that are unfit to take, the latter simply because it cannot be grasped by the mind that is preoccupied with objects, as well as the thoughts of objects. Since this is a subtle process, even a causal one, the seekers and masters of *Advaita* give out the teaching that the Goal must be approached in four stages. The aforementioned discernment figures in here.

First, the aspirant must decide what is fit to be rejected, or what is unfit to keep. Less enlightened systems have seekers giving up all manner of things, but often in the wrong order and with the wrong method or attitude. As Gaudapada so astutely states in his famous *karika* on nonduality, since all beings and all things are unoriginated *(ajati)*, without inception, are pure and perfect in their own nature — *"are the nature of nirvana always"* — then why give things up for any other reason than the fact that they fall away from the mind naturally as it gains back its knowledge and approaches *Brahman*? And so the wise seeker approaches *Brahman* with the second stage in mind, and that is coming to know what is fit to be kept, at least temporarily. The mind itself is one of these principles, or *tattvas,* and elements of its thinking process (as in the knowledge of the presence of objects in their subtle and causal state) will be "secured" to be used in the third and fourth stages.

At a deeper stage of comprehension, which is getting beyond even the mind's thinking process, what was utilized in the previous stage is now placed under deeper inspection (see chart on page 303). Here is where facets of consciousness like the ego will lose their hold upon approaching Nondual Awareness, for they limit the limitless *Brahman* and are therefore unreal superimpositions. Only That which is *"specifically fit to be known"* and maintained will pass the acid test of highest *Samadhi*.

As an aid to all those who want to look into the singular and incomparable commentary of the ages on *Advaita Vedanta* by Lord Gaudapada, the chart on the facing page has been constructed and added into this book for ease of location and study. The actual commentary itself can usually be found accompanying any copy of the *Mandukhya Upanisad* with its twelve profound *slokas* that Gaudapada took up to do such final justice to for the *Advaita* system.

His commentary falls into four *prakaranas*, or chapters, each with their own set of subtitled sections. The first section *(agama prakarana)* is "AUM and the Three Stages of Existence" and takes up Gaudapada's unique explanation of the Supreme Being, or Divine Reality, as It comes to rest in *"three states of its own devising (avasthas)."* These are delineated into the three *matras* of AUM *(pranava)*, "A," "U," and "M," which are aligned with the waking, dreaming, and deep sleep states of mankind. The being moving among these three as the knower is given a name for each, as the knower of the gross *(vishva)*, of the rarefied *(taijasa)*, and of bliss *(prajna)*. The reader can look back at the chart on page 711 for descriptions of these three states (of ours). The balance of the first *prakarana* is given to the views of other schools. They are subjected to Gaudapada's scrutiny, and with fine contrast as well. Initial teachings on *Turiya*, the "fourth" state of Awareness, are also introduced.

In the second *prakarana*, we find *Vaitathya*, untruth, given room for explication. Basically, the assumption of the reality of the waking and dreaming states is taken to task. In these two states phenomena seems to shift from one location to another, but upon awakening the dreamer sees he has not moved at all. It has all taken place in his mind. This is where the teachings just given on the previous chart about approaching *Brahman* in four stages via three *samadhis* is helpful. Whatever the case, if the mind in not yet invested in deep introspection utilizing the tools of *yogic* practice *(sadhana)*, then at least he/she may become aware of the *"insubstantiality of both the waking and dreaming states."* Along the way of this *prakarana* the prime subjects of *Atman* and (its) *Maya* are introduced and explained.

The accent of prakarana three, titled *Advaita*, falls on the dual nature of creation, viewed side by side with the nondual principle of Reality. This point is brought out only after declaring that the *jivatman*, the embodied soul, is really nonseparate from the *Paramatman*, the Supreme Soul. Thus, the explanation of *Brahman* and *Atman*, together, are revealed. They are the same Reality. The latter simply has a possibility of taking on sheaths, or *koshas*.

The fourth and final *prakarana* is titled *alatashanti*, which translates as the "cessation of the firebrand." The waving of a burning stick at night creates the illusion of tracers and other imaginary appearances in the air. These cease when the motion stops. Similarly, when the motion of illusory bodies, worlds, etc., ceases, the still Essence of the backdrop comes forward and reveals Itself. This *prakarana* explains the rationale of Gaudapada's principle of Nonorigination, which proves to be superior to other theories about Existence and Consciousness, such as the ones involving creation, voidism, evolution, and transformation.

This *prakarana* also clears up the philosophical air around *Maya* and its superimpositions. Like Sri Ramakrishna much later, Gaudapada did not fall victim to calling the unreal, real, nor to posing *Maya* as an independent source. Nor did Krishna in early times. Gaudapada's student's student, Shankara, calls it "....neither real, unreal, nor a mixture of the two." Verily, it appears in *Brahman* like the image of a moon appears in a mud puddle. *Maya* belongs to *Brahman*, and *Atman* uses it for its own various posturings. According to Sri Ramakrishna, *maya* is in *Brahman* like poison in a snake, never harming the snake.

Guide to Gaudapada's Karika

"Gaudapada's famous Karika on the *Mandukyopanisad* consists of four sections, called prakaranas. The first is entitled *Pranava & Avasthas,* and concerns AUM and the three states of human awareness. The second, called *Vaitathya,* deals with mental and philosophical falsehood. The third, *Advaita,* takes up nonduality as its subject. The fourth, *Alatashanti,* which means *Cessation of the Firebrand,* brings in various effective ways of removing Maya and its evolutes from the mind." Babaji Bob Kindler

Prakarana 1
Supreme Being in Its Three States
Section a – 1 Reality, 3 States, sl. 1-5
Section b – Views of other Schools, sl. 6-18
Section c – 4 Quarters of Om, sl. 19-29

Prakarana 2
Insubstantiality of Waking & Dream
Section d – Jagrat & Svapna, sl. 1-10
Section e – Atman & Its Maya, sl. 11-38

Prakarana 4
Rationale of Nonorigination
Section i – Ajativada, sl. 1-46
Section j – Vivarta, sl. 47-100

Prakarana 3
Jivatman Is Paramatman
Section f – Nature of the Jiva, sl. 1-11
Section g – Creation is Duality, sl. 12-31
Section h – Brahman & Atman, sl. 32-48

"Prior to creation, what distinction between the Jiva and the Atman has ever been declared? It only pertains to a state yet to come. To regard this projected state of becoming as being the primary nature is irrational and unacceptable. The dualists may lay out their various conclusions, but these only contradict one another. In the truth-view, the Ajativada, there is no contradiction. It maintains no conflict with other views. Nonduality is the highest Reality. In those for whom duality exists, Advaita has no conflict." Gaudapada

❊ INSCRUTABLE EPITHETS OF BRAHMAN ❊

"Out of fear of Brahman the wind blows, the sun rises, Indra presides, death bows low, and the cosmic sets of fives carry out their respective functions. The individual soul only becomes fearless when it attains firm and peaceful ground in that Supreme Reality. Even a wise man falls victim to fear if he fails to reflect on Brahman." Taittiriya Upanisad

The Uncaused Cause

The Inactive Agent

The Unmoved Mover

The Unseen Seer

The Unstruck Sound

The Acreate Creator

The Unborn Procreator

The Unattached Lover

The Formless Refuge

The Unknowable Knower

The Impersonal Presence

The Inanimate Animator
∎

The Transcendent Pervader
∎

The Uninvolved Participant

The Immutable Transformer
∎

The Indivisible Multiplier
∎

"At times the snake sits still, at other times it wriggles across the ground, but it is all the same snake. Again, the snake contains poison within it, but it does not die because of that." Sri Ramakrishna

It is not only *maya* that is an enigma; *Brahman*, too, poses a conundrum for pondering souls. The chart opposite has listed many of the stultifying names that have been attributed to *Brahman*, so as to confer the idea of Its incomprehensibility. Should we conclude, then, that we are to give up the effort at knowing *Brahman?* If that were to be the case, then the *Upanisads* would not state, adamantly, *"Even a wise man falls victim to fear if he fails to reflect on Brahman."* Is *Brahman* knowable to the human mind? Not in its impure state, but when the mind becomes transparent, stripped of its conditionings and overlays, then it reveals nothing other than *Brahman*.

The first five epithets at the top of the chart on page 732 are fairly well known to seekers of Enlightenment via India's pathways. Nevertheless, to ponder them seriously is not given to many. Nonduality itself will offer up its shining treasure if one does. In the case of the "Inactive Agent," the luminary finds no trace of ego in *Brahman*. Agency is absent, thereby. Everyone from the Trinity on out and down to the human plane, with the gods in the middle, possess the sense of agency. It is therefore that *karma* comes to them, and that is why *Brahman* is called the "Uncaused Cause." Again, everything from The Trinity to the manifestation of the *Bhur Loka* is the result of a cause. That cause would be The Word, *AUM*. *Brahman* cannot be the cause of anything, which simply means that it is ever-present, or Eternal. Indian Philosophy does declare that everything is Eternal, but most of this "everything" falls into the category of the "changing Eternal," while *Brahman* alone is the authentic Unchanging Eternal.

It is also the "Unmoved Mover." This appellation explains why sensitive beings feel God in and through everything, and even intuit It working in the affairs of everyday life. But no one can find It or successfully seek it out in the realms of name and form. It is an underlying Substratum, or an all-pervasive Entity, but is not involved in the realms of cause and effect, of creation and destruction.

And in fact, it is the supersensitive beings, the seers, who declare this to be true. When they merge in highest *samadhi*, that *Brahman* becomes them. This is the "single-eye" experience that illumined beings have talked about. *Brahman* is the "Unseen Seer" among seers that truly see. Only by knowing *Brahman* do they become *Brahman*, states the *Upanisad*.

And finally, there is the "Unstruck Sound." While this epithet is usually assigned to The Word, it also applies very well to *Brahman*. This should be clear after studying the previous chart on Gaudapada's *Karika* on the *Mandukhya Upanisad*, whose twelve *slokas* are all on *AUM*. Being the word of *Brahman*, *AUM* is *Brahman's* gateway into Formlessness, and its exit back into form.

The remainder of the special epithets for *Brahman* listed on the chart each have something deep to communicate to us. *Brahman* is unborn, for certain, is the "Unborn Procreator," for without Its essential presence nothing else would see form at all. All of love that is in form is also in its creation, and that too is due to *Brahman's* presence. Being the "Impersonal Presence," however, It is called the "Unattached Lover." Itself, It is the "Acreate Creator," while all forms that virtually pour into creation do so at Its silent behest. And It knows all, but is unknown to others. Thus we call It the Unknown Knower." It is the refuge to all beings, but none about to go formless and take refuge in It can call it a place in space and time. Therefore It is called the "Formless Refuge."

The last five appelations that pertain to *Brahman* are various plays on words designed to entice the mind into trying to comprehend the incomprehensible. The poet-saint, Ramprasad, sings in one of his songs that we should strive to know the unknowable. He adds that we will never be able to do so, but that the attempt will purify our minds. With that pure mind we will finally see the Unseen Seer and hear the Unstruck Sound. The goal of attaining the "Transcendent Pervader" will also come to us, along with the knowledge of the still presence that causes all else to move in the "Inanimate Animator." And when we finally exit from the world stage, performing the last act of our lives in *maya*, perhaps we will catch a glimpse, even sidewise, of that "Uninvolved Participant" who has moved the body and limbs all along from a transcendent position. This will certainly be the case if the *Atman* is realized, but for that to be the case we may have to look for some epithets for It as well. *Atman* is *Brahman*, only with a slight case of association with cosmic coverings.

As we gaze upon the chart on the next page, however, we can see that *Atman* maintains sterling attributes all the while it associates with the *koshas*. It is *ajah*, unborn, so when the five sheaths of ego, intellect, mind, life-force, and body get born and die in nature, *Atman* remains free from such transitions and transformations. It is *sthanuh*, stable, and that stability is in Its constant and eternal nature. As Ashtavakra declares, ones eternal nature outlasts even the dissolution of the universe, which also means that every time the universes in space and time get reborn, *Atman* is the Witness, since It is anterior to the mind that projects the many interior and external worlds.

Nityah means eternal, or absolute. To meditate upon this Self as ones own, and as the essence of life and existence is to court freedom from all bondages. The *Upanisads* states that *Atman* is *"Nityo nityanam chetanas chetananam,"* It is the intelligence of the most intelligent beings and the Eternal among all noneternal things."

This is also due to the *Atman* being *puranah*, ancient. This really means timeless. It is ancient in the sense that no one can discover or remember a beginning to It; It is beyond phases of time. As Vivekananda states, *"When is the time that the soul will come and go, when all of time is in the soul?"* This confirms that the seers have found the unwinding of constant phases of time *(kalas)* existing as a cosmic law within their own minds, and within the Cosmic Mind as well. Knowing time to be nonexistent in Formless Awareness *(samadhi)* is tantamount to knowing it to be illusory in nature.

This transcendental *Atman* is also *achala*, immovable. As the *Upanisads* state, *"It outstrips all that run."* That is, since it is all-pervasive It does not need to move, being everywhere all at once. This is why, when the aspirant goes searching for It, or for God, that very Principle that is being searched after is already present within him/her. If every seeker were told this prior to their period of necessary *sadhana*, they would turn to look within in swifter fashion, thus take less time to remember their true nature.

As has been mentioned already, the *Atman* is *sanatanah*, or eternal. It is also called *avikaryah*, since, as Sri Krishna states, all actions really take place in nature, not in the Soul. Imagine the peace and bliss of that soul who realizes this, and refrains from taking credit, responsibility, or blame — all three — from all that transpires in nature. As was revealed in the previous chart, the sense of action would be absent in him, and no *karma*, or *karya*, would follow him from thenceforth.

The principle of immutability, or *aparinama*, is a key truism in the philosophy of Nonduality. This is also termed *shashvatah*, seeing that the *Atman* is immutable. The appearance of *parinama*, changefulness, is the thing to be taken to task here then, and the seeker does this armed with the truth of nontransformation in the face of apparent transformation. Rule of thumb predicates that all that changes cannot be *Brahman*, so by using this measure the sincere adept *"...separates the wheat from the chaff"* and finds the ever-present *Atman* at the foundation of all and everything, always.

The same measure is used for the appearance of form and formlessness as well, only pertinent to manifestation in the realms of name and form. The winsome characteristic of *avyaktah* states that *Atman* is always unmanifested, and this helps the aspirant further in perceiving the difference between the Real and the unreal. *Atman* may associate with coverings and overlays springing from *maya*, but it never identifies with them. To do so would be to lose memory of It — which is what most beings entering into the body in relativity have done.

The next characteristic of *Atman* is sweet indeed. It is inexhaustible, or *avyayam*, It is another way of saying boundless, or infinite. Though all the attributes mentioned previously on this chart describe It well, nonetheless it *"devours and It generates,"* say the *Upanisads*, cryptically. Cycles are in It, It is not in cycles. By knowing this the soul (mind) frees itself from false impressions as to the nature of Reality, and its own Self.

The indestructibility of the *Atman*, *avinashi*, is another of its winning facets. All else can come and go, get birthed and die, pass away in time and return again later, but the *Atman* remains present and constant. As the seers state, *"That which is present at the beginning, present at the end as well — though free of beginnings and endings — and is also there in the middle and throughout, that is the Atman. It does not suffer death at the end of cosmic cycles when all else disappears into pralaya."*

The Thirteen Inherent Characteristics of Atman

"It is not in the brain but in the heart that the Atman, possessed of knowledge, power and activity, has its seat. The chief nerve-center near the heart, called the sympathetic ganglia, is where the Atman has Its citadel." Swami Vivekananda

Sthanuh — Stable
"Adoration to my Self, impervious to decay, who outlasts even the dissolution of the universe, from Brahma down to a blade of grass." Astavakra

Ajah — Unborn
"Death nor fear, I have none, nor any distinction of caste; neither father nor mother, nor even a birth have I..." Shankaracharya

Nityah — Absolute "If you have known Atman as the one existence, and that nothing else exists, for whom, for what desire do you trouble yourself?" Vivekananda

Puranah — Ancient "To that timeless Brahman be thou devoted, through the primal and ancient Cause, Atman, the eternal Soul." Svetashvataropanisad

Achala — Immovable "The Self is unmoving, yet is faster than mind. Having preceded the mind, it transcends the senses. It outstrips all that runs." Isavasyopanisad

Sanatanah — Eternal "The wise do not grieve, having known the bodiless, all-pervading supreme Atman who dwells in all impermanent bodies." Kathopanisad

Avikaryah — Inactive "That one verily sees who sees that all actions are done by Prakrti alone, and that Atman is actionless." Sri Krishna

Shashvatah — Immutable "The 'I' and everything else is based in transformation. Only the Atman is immutable; wont of all change is Atman." Shankaracharya

Avyaktah — Unmanifested "Name, form, and function differ, but akasha, which holds them, remains unchanged. Similarly, Atman is unaffected by Its Maya-projections called individual souls. Who or what could possibly produce this Atman?" Gaudapada

Avyayam — Inexhaustible "With hands and feet everywhere; with eyes, heads, mouths, and ears everywhere, That exists, pervading everything." Svetashvataropanisad

Avinashi — Indestructible "That which, when name, space, time, substance, and causation are destroyed, dies not, is the Indestructible." Sarvopanisad

Sarvagatah — All-Pervading "Atman alone is; it is the all-full and blissful Consciousness pervading everything. It is the immaculate Jnana Itself, the all-pervading Akasha. The three worlds arise in It, yet they do not effect its true state." Vasishtha

Achintyah — Incomprehensible "Atman, hidden in all beings, reveals Itself not to all, but only to the seers via their honed and subtle intellect." Kathopanisad

"That which is Atman is unattached. Maya is in It. One cannot see Atman. Sugar mixed with water disappears. Just so, when Atman 'gets mixed' with the world, beings fail to notice It." Sri Ramakrishna

The Five Modes of the Divine Experiencer
And Their Five Corresponding Kanchukas

"The All-Experiencer, while enjoying the magnanimity of 'All This,' becomes proud of it and the idea of 'All this is mine' arises, followed by the thought, 'I am the author of all of this.' As this thought strengthens over time, he becomes fully absorbed in it and a feeling of identification duly settles into the mind. He thereby loses realization of his Divine Self and falls asleep in maya. The Experiencer in this state is called Purusha, wrapped in the five Kanchukas." Tantras

Nityatva
Principle of Eternity
↓
Kala
Limitation via Time

Purnatva
Principle of Perfection
↓
Kalas
Limitation via Activity

Vyapakatva
Principle of All-Pervasiveness
↓
Niyati
Limitation via Space

Sarva Kartrtva
Principle of Lordship
↓
Vidya
Limitation via Knowledge

Sarvajnatritva
Principle of All-Knowingness
↓
Raga
Limitation via Attachment

Five Principles of Universal Subject/Object

Shuddha vidya – Principle of Connections
Ishvara – The Principle of Identification
Sadasiva – The Principle of Being
Shakti – The Principle of Potential
Parama Siva – The Principle of pure "I" by Itself

"The entire process in terms of the manifestation of the Universe is in the experience of Parama Siva who is Awareness, pure and simple, as well as Revelation, revealing Itself as the One being experienced. The Kanchukas stick to all that is experienced." Sri Manoranjan Basu

Lord Vasishtha's quote under the next heading tells it all, and in all-comprehensive fashion. The *Atman* is *sarvagatah,* or all-pervasive. It is there within all things, but is not a thing in and of Itself. As Sri Ramakrishna has stated, *"It is like sweetness in sugar can juice, not seen but fully present all the same."* And therefore It is called *achintyah,* incomprehensible. In order to know It, It must be "tasted," as it were.

The truths of *Atman's* transcendence, as well as Its tendency to wrap Itself in sheaths, both have a correlative teaching in *Tantra,* which is helpful to explore and put side by side with *Vedanta's* view. The term in this *darshana* is *kanchuka.* It denotes a sheath under whose influence *"....you who are Almighty have become a little doer."* And so it is a limiting and constricting package that the limitless Soul has put on, much like a free-roaming snail who locates a shell and hides in it.

The chart on the facing page shows us about the five *kanchukas* in *Tantra.* All experience that the experiencer has "sticks" to the *kanchukas.* These five modes are taking on the limitations of time, space, knowledge, activity, and attachment. The *Purusha,* the experiencer, embroils itself in these five modes according to *Tantra.* It is a fairly advanced level of knowing in that the knower does finally find out that all and everything in the three worlds belongs to him. He is the author of the play he is participating in. But with this thought foremost in his mind he identifies more and more with the one having the experience and forgets his divine nature which is beyond experiences and experiencer.

The *Purusha* is really *Paramasiva,* whose nature is eternal *(niyatva)* and all-pervasive *(vyapakatva).* By identifying itself with time and space, instead of being satisfied with Its own ongoing pervasiveness, it wraps itself in time and space like a silkworm in a cocoon. It is the tendency of the mental complex *(antahkarana)* to do this. It is really the experience of life as an individual. All three — life, experiences during it, and the one having the experiences — are unsatisfying, especially next to the freedom of the unbound *Purusha.*

And it is not only time and space that foist constrictions on the soul, it is also knowledge and actions. The *Purusha* is Lord *(sarva kartrtva),* perfect and inactive through all phases of time *(purnatva),* but by taking on the limitations of knowership and doer-ship, it falls into the misconception that its knowledge and its activities are real and paramount. This position of lordship in both knowledge and actions causes the problem of spiritual ego, which places a sense of false "somethingness" over the actuality of the real "nothingness," so to speak.

Throughout the development of the four above mentioned *kanchukas,* the truth of the formless, actionless, transcendental Wisdom-knower, who witnesses all phases of time and the creation of worlds within it, remains unseen, unknown. The *Purusha* has a fourfold mask on, and begins to love its own hunkered down condition above all else. Its former All-knowingness *(sarva jnatrtva)* is being replaced by refined enjoyment, called *raga.* The attachment which springs from this tempered bliss is detrimental to the soul perceiving Its own glory. This problem, called subtle bliss, also appears in the *Yoga darshana* as one of the five impediments to *samadhi.* Love of being wrapped in limitation is the result, and *Tantra* thus explains this inexplicable tendency well. Eternal Life is forgotten for a life of the senses, or worldly life; terrestrial existence overcomes Transcendental Existence. As Sri Ramakrishna states, *"In this world, the power of avidya shakti (ignorance) is stronger than vidya shakti (wisdom)."*

The fivefold inset at the left hand bottom of the chart presently under study gives us the higher teaching on the intended relationship between Subject and Object. If separation is the name of the game for a deluded or deceived *Purusha,* then making connections with Divine Reality emerges as the real purpose for human life. If identification with all and sundry is the lost soul's penchant, then reidentification with the Divine Being, God with Form, or *Ishvara/Ishvari,* is the solution. If creating a false image and body are the work of the nefarious ego mechanism in *maya,* then seeking the pedestal of true Being and giving up the dream of becoming is the path back to bliss. If the wayward soul begins to strive for vaunted potential among unreal things, then seeking the Divine Mother power inherent in the soul, called *Shakti,* is the true fulfillment. Finally, learning to leave the

Essence, *Paramasiva*, alone, and merging with It, is the solution for the tendency to dream wistfully in the realms of name and form in time and space, and thereby suffering *karmic* accrual. Thus will the *Purusha* be what its name defines It as — the happy indweller in the city of nine gates.

To get a closer look at the *Purusha*, this time via the timeless eyes of the *Sankhya* philosophy, the next chart, on page 739, will help. To begin, a closer look at *Purusha's* partner, and Its potential undoing, is needed. *Prakriti*, according to the seers, is the eternal insentient principle, or material energy principle, that *Purusha* has a relationship with. The term, *Prakriti-samavaya*, defined here as "creative dependence," is meant to relate a heathy togetherness that the two are meant to enjoy. But for this to happen, as the Father of *Yoga*, Patanjali has stated, the Seer must remain in control of the seen. *Prakriti*, a host of compounded substances, are produced and projected by *Purusha* for Its own convenience and fulfillment. To think that the servant would be served by the master is unthinkable in India, particularly when the servant is an unconscious principle, say, a television set. The seer must master the seen and remain in control at all times. Besides being a teaching in proper orientation, this point also proves that there is a *Purusha* in existence, for Its overseership distinguishes It from changing and decaying matter.

Another proof of this fact of abiding Existence is the truth of *Sakshi-bhutam*, or Witness Consciousness. There is nature *(prakriti)* with its many modes, slimmed down to inertia, activity, and stasis (three *gunas*) (see charts on pages 221, 223, 307), then there is the mind and its thinking process *(chitta)*, and finally there is the seer looking on, the *Purusha*. Matter, energy, and thought must have an operator, and that is the witness of all phenomena involving these three, and the three *gunas* that underlie them. Thus say the seers who are the supreme Witnesses.

There is a proof of Existence that is obvious and undeniable. That is intelligence. It is not just a part of the mental complex, called *buddhi*. Consciousness Itself contains it in its purest form. It is termed *Sat-buddhi* by the seers. Nature/*Prakriti* and the *gunas* are mechanical and insentient. They need an operator. So besides being the Witness of all phenomena, Consciousness/*Purusha* is also the wise conductor of it all too. No matter how chaotic, confused, complicated, and convoluted matters get in the three worlds, pure, conscious Awareness stands aloof and sees through it all.

And it is not only an "on-high" Witness that knows all things, *Purusha* is also the underlying substratum, the *Kutashtanitya*. For, it is not only activity and its *karma* that needs seeing and sorting, it is living beings that need direction as well. All their many experiences in life and beyond always have a conscious and cohesive coordinator at the hub. It is that superconscious entity that awakens them from dreaming and deep sleep, transfering the ego from one level of awareness to the next. Presence and absence depend upon It.

As Lord Kapila has stated, the *Purusha* is *Shuddhabuddhamukta* — ever pure, ever aware, and ever-free. *Moksha*, or *mukti,* is then Its essential condition. Both the existence of bondage and the longing to be free imply Its existence, for there must be an entity to which these superimpositions occur, and the already perfect and preconscious condition of that entity proves that it is always free by nature. All beings that are wrapped in form, in limitation — as in the *koshas, upadhis, shariras,* or the *kanchukas* — feel the drive to be free due to the innate freedom of the Soul.

And just so, mind and matter in motion, along with the many laws of mutability in constant flux, infer an immutable backdrop. Relativity could not be that limitless collection of things in a series of ongoing movement with a stable backdrop upon which to move. Only something intrinsically still and static is capable of handling the infinite variety of movements that take place on the surface, like an ocean supporting trillions of waves. Therefore, if ones narrow mind, blunt intellect, erratic thoughts, and bloated ego need a good talking to about the true nature of Reality, the Six Proofs of *Purusha* has all that is needed and more to prove the superiority of nondual Awareness over matter, energy, and mind.

In another of Mother India's wonderful *darshanas,* namely *Buddhism,* the Underlying, All-wise, Eternally Stable, Ever-Liberated, Transcendent Onlooker has another noble name — that of *Tathagatagarbha*. It is an indeterminable mass of unconditioned, unbound Cognizance. It is pure

THE SIX PROOFS OF PURUSHA

"Purusha is Shuddhabuddhamukta — ever Pure, ever Aware, and ever Free." Kapila

1 ——— Creative Dependence (Prakrti-samavaya) ———

| Compounded Substances, Objects | → | Existence as Service | → | Eternal Subject, Purusha |

"Compounded substances, objects, exist to serve a sentient being, an Eternal Subject."

2 ——— Witness Consciousness (Sakshi-bhutam) ———

| The Three Gunas of Nature | → | Chitta — Mind-stuff, Cognization | → | The Seer, Purusha |

"Objects consist of the three gunas, and cognizing them via knowledge implies a Seer."

3 ——— Intelligent Existence (Sat-buddhi) ———

| Insentient Nature, Prakrti | → | Operative Laws of Karma & Gunas | → | Independent Agent, Purusha |

"Nature is nonintelligent; an intelligent agent must exist to experience its functionings."

4 ——— Cohesive Substratum (Kutasthanitya) ———

| Existence of Many Beings | → | Multifarious & Simultaneous Experiences | → | Coordinating Background, Purusha |

"Our various experiences occur simultaneously, which indicates a subtle Coordinator."

5 ——— Inherent Freedom (Moksha) ———

| The Bondage of Limited Existence | → | The Longing to be Free | → | The Ever-Free Reality, Purusha |

"The desire for freedom from bondage implies a Reality that is free by nature."

6 ——— Eternal Stability (Nitya-avasthana) ———

| Mind and Matter in Motion | → | Mutability and Flux | → | Immutable Reality, Purusha |

"Universal motion can be recognized only by that which is eternally stationary."

Tathagatagarbha / Atman — Transparency of the Self

akase'va sakuntanam gati tesham durannaya
"The actions of an Arhat are without trace, trackless — like birds flying through the sky."
Lord Buddha

Manjushri Nama Sangit

The Pervasive Self

The Supreme Self

Buddha Self

The Beginningless Self

Self that is the Source of All

The Diamond Self

The Self of Substance

Guardian Self of the Three Worlds

The Single Self

Self of Primordial Purity

Self of Thus-ness

The Holy Immovable Self

Subtle Indications of a Tathagagata

- No foundation for an individual self
- Free of conditioned phenomena
- Transcendent of men, gods, and mara
- Free of suffering and other burdens
- Free of mental projections and emotions
- Abandonment of the 5 Skandhas

"The root of all beings nothing else but one Se I am that place in w existence res

Samantrabadra, All-Creating

"Each sentient being contains the intrinsic indwelling potency for becoming a Buddha — fully awakened." Lord Buddha

The meaning of the word, Tathagatagarbha:
tatha – thus; gata – the Goal beyond coming and going; garbha – root, essence
"Tathagatagarbha is not 'I' or 'me,' is stationary and immovable though appearing and vanishing, transcends the human condition, is what really is – suchness – and is the ultimate Goal."

"The Universal Self sports through entities via Samadhi.
It performs deeds and works while stationed at one immovable post."
Guhya Samaja Tantra

Perception. The *Manjushri Nama Sangit*, which recalls the many divine names for the ultimate Self, applies to It ecstatic references such as pervasive, beginningless, supreme, singular, holy, immovable, and of primordial purity. It also confirms It as all-sustaining, of thus-ness, of diamond nature, and the Self of the three worlds. Like *Vedanta* and its blissful *Atman*, the Buddha states that this Self is in all beings, and that every soul (mind) has the potential for becoming a fully awakened Buddha.

In *Buddhism*, the negation of the nonself is paramount. There is no foundation for claiming the existence of the individual at all. Souls who appear as individuals are called *Tathagatas*. They have realized Buddha Nature by perceiving this essence beyond all lesser goals and thereby reached the Supreme Goal, or *Nirvana*. They have accomplished this by negating the sense of individuality that is called "I" and "me" by earth-bound beings. They are stable and immovable, like a realized *Purusha*, but they appear and vanish, and accomplish beneficial works from "one, stationary Post."

Other subtle indications of the presence of these illumined souls can be understood by the way they remain unaffected by changing phenomena and its many evils and sufferings, even though they are in and amidst phenomena. In the *Avadhuta Gita*, one such illumined soul states:

The six passions are like the sons and daughters of a barren woman to Brahman.
Supernatural agencies with their legerdemain over souls are a chimerical illusion to It.
What to speak of these, the physical world and its many blemishes cannot touch me.
For, I am Pure Existence, Wisdom, and Bliss, as boundless as the sky, infinite like space.

The chart on the facing page also declares that such beings are "beyond men, gods, and mara." The pure minds of these singular souls occupy the *"place where all of Existence resides,"* and do not anymore frequent *"the low-lying marshes and steamy wastelands of conventional thinking,"* as the Buddha stated. In the *Bhagavad Gita* Sri Krishna calls this *"...a distaste for the company of worldly beings"* and notes that *"...they prefer instead love of lonely study in sequestered places."* Again, the *Avadhut* has his own unique way of saying in this regard:

In the Supreme Brahman, all the gods have merged.
Therefore, all the many the worlds and lokas that the gods preside over
also melt away, soluble into That.
The three worlds are thus seen as a dreamlike projection.
I am Pure Existence, Wisdom, and Bliss, as boundless as the sky, infinite like space.

The subject of suffering also comes up for examination in terms of the *Tathagata*. Such a being is only slightly conscious of the body, so pains do not hamper him much. But he suffers for others, and strives to alleviate their unnecessary sufferings. The necessary sufferings he leaves alone, for they are beneficial. Forbearance is the default zone of the wise, as is said. The bliss that occurs beyond the body, only he and a small group of souls know about. One has to trade away the world to get that, and follow that renunciation up with intense spiritual disciplines.

All of this giving up is in the mind. Desires and the emotions that revolve around them, as well as mental projections that bespeak of expectations must all go. Peace of mind is penultimate to bliss, and the mind can never get this peace of mind if desires for the world and its objects and pleasures still muddy the waters of life. As Sri Ramakrishna was wont to say to both his householder and monastic disciples, *"Both monk and householder must renounce the world, the former entirely, inside and out, but the latter, only inside."*

In Zen *Buddhism*, all the same principles and practices apply as to other forms of *Buddhism*, but they are helped along here by the natural economy and ethic of the *Japan*ese mind and temperament. *Japan* was waiting for India's arrival on its shores for some 62 generations from the Buddha's advent in Mother India. Refined culture, controlled emotions, religious formality, and devout ritual were all a part of *Japan*'s swift development over centuries, but it took *Buddhism* to offer to this country its crown of philosophy towards spiritual maturity.

The chart on the facing page demonstrates how both *Japan's* quiet religious fervor and their love of language got easily ingested and complemented the wisdom of the Buddha. The quote from early Indian *Buddhism* at the top of the chart prefaces a list of advanced philosophical principles that were well comprehended and placed into practice in *Japa*n in both Chinese *Buddhism* and in Zen. For instance, *Ichinen-Fusho,* the natural keeping of thoughts from arising in the mind, is common to all meditation practices in the East, particularly to India. Further, *Hakushi,* "white paper," indicates the pure mind that receives no impressions upon it whatsoever, and is completely tranquil and empty.

Where nonduality is concerned, the terms *Shoso-Funi* and *Moku-Funi* point directly towards the presence of the nondual mind-set in Zen. The incomparable silence of the Self, or *Busho* in this case, is the condition of the luminary who courts and attains to nonduality. Similarly, and associated with that conditionless condition, the references of *Jakujo* and *Dai-Anjin* bespeak of a *"Peace that passeth all understanding,"* according to Jesus, or *Shanti* in *Sanskrit.*

Where the tradition of teacher and student is concerned, *Inshin-Denshin* in Zen reveals the presence of what we call "transmission" in today's spiritual circles. It is like *tejas* in the *Kundalini Yoga* tradition, wherein a deep power *(shakti)* of spiritual comprehension is transferred from *guru* to *shishya.* Other wisdom can be gotten from study of the scriptures, and practice, but this wonder is a gift of grace bestowed upon highly qualified practitioners who are already near the Goal in any given lifetime.

The tools and benefits of *karma yoga* are also not at all lost on Zen. Both *Fugyo-Nigyo* and *Mossosheki* reveal both the way of accomplishing works free of resultant *karmas,* and of doing so without leaving even the slightest trace of the ego behind for any sensitive soul to trip over. An advanced martial artist does not leave the slightest wrinkle on the rice paper he expertly walks across. Similarly, no wrinkle is left in time or space due to the luminary's presence in the body on earth. The story goes, that the gods *Yama* (death), *Karma* (cause and effect), and *Kama* (desire) went looking for a certain seer after his passing, but they could not find him. Then they consulted the goddess presiding over the register of births and deaths, and she had no record of his existence in relativity.

The sacred teaching of *Ishta-Nistha* in India has its mirror in Zen as well. This is called *Ishi-Injo,* or training by a single master. As Holy Mother, Sri Sarada Devi, has stated: *"All teachers hold the guru principle within them, but it is the mantri guru who initiates with the mantra who is the true guru."* In Zen, the presence of "Wild Fox" Zen and other immature tacts give rise to the phenomenon of thinking that one can go from teacher to teacher to get enlightenment, when the opposite is really the truth. Each master has a certain way of transmitting the Truth, and it may vary or even conflict somewhat with other teachers, and this will confuse the otherwise healthy student. If the student is to carry on the tradition under his master and become *Hassu,* it will be necessary to remain true to the path he walked. He gets a "one taste bowl" from this path, called *Ichimi-Shabyo* in Zen. No spiritual indigestion will then occur, and he can truly help others, having realized for himself.

Prajna and *boddhi* are *Sanskrit* words. In *Japanese,* the word *Hannya* is used to indicated spiritual wisdom in Zen. In Zen this wisdom is aligned specifically with meditation, and not so much with scriptural study or intellectual knowledge.

For the ever-pure mind in Zen, the words *Jisho-Shojo-Shin* are put together. This is *Chit-shuddhi* in *Sanskrit.* For simple everyday enlightenment, which is a profound state and teaching both in Zen, they call it *Bonpo-No-Joshiki.* In India, this is called *sahaja samadhi,* or natural Enlightenment. The reader is welcome to look back to the chart on page 651 to see some direct correlations between Zen *Buddhism* and *Advaita Vedanta.*

In the image on the chart on page 743, The Buddha is receiving arrows of hatred and dissent from the world, and sending back flowers of loving teachings in return. It is a famous story in *Buddhism.* All these profound designations can be meditated upon in order that they give the full flavor of the wonders of Zen.

Ri-Bi — Zen Buddhist Truth Principles

◯ The Moons and Flowers of Lord Buddha's Enlightenment

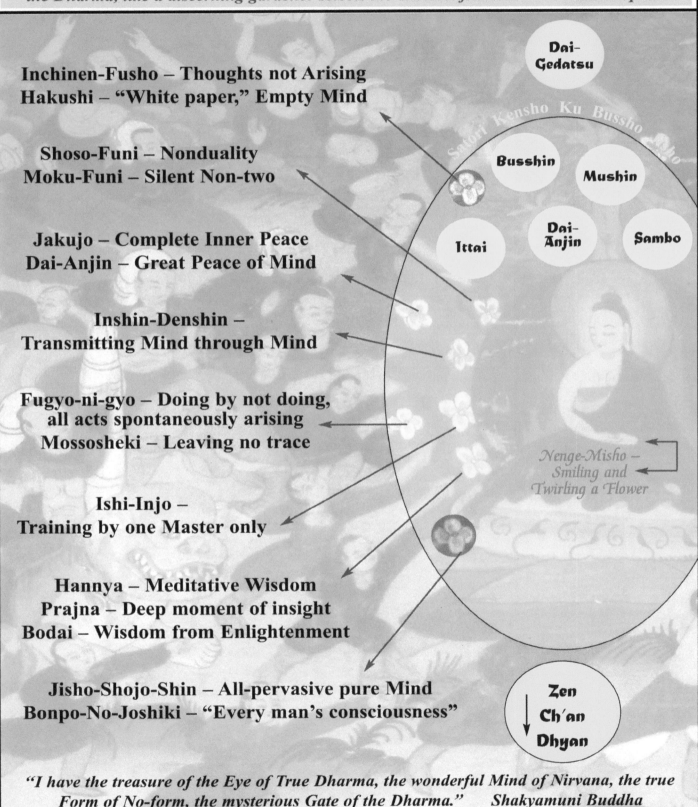

Inchinen-Fusho – Thoughts not Arising
Hakushi – "White paper," Empty Mind

Shoso-Funi – Nonduality
Moku-Funi – Silent Non-two

Jakujo – Complete Inner Peace
Dai-Anjin – Great Peace of Mind

Inshin-Denshin –
Transmitting Mind through Mind

Fugyo-ni-gyo – Doing by not doing,
all acts spontaneously arising
Mossosheki – Leaving no trace

Ishi-Injo –
Training by one Master only

Hannya – Meditative Wisdom
Prajna – Deep moment of insight
Bodai – Wisdom from Enlightenment

Jisho-Shojo-Shin – All-pervasive pure Mind
Bonpo-No-Joshiki – "Every man's consciousness"

Dai-Gedatsu

Satori Kensho Ku Bussho Sho

Busshin

Mushin

Ittai

Dai-Anjin

Sambo

*Nenge-Misho –
Smiling and
Twirling a Flower*

Zen
Ch'an
Dhyan

THE INCOMPARABLE VIEWS OF AN ADVAITA VEDANTIST
BEHOLDING THE TRUTH THROUGH THE MAZE OF MUNDANE HUMAN CONVENTION

"Nonduality is not a philosophy. It is the natural, transparent, and all-pervasive verity underlying all things, all phenomena, all beings, and everything that constantly undergoes change in cycles. Gaudapada has declared that It is the obvious and simple Truth, the Essence of Existence, uncontestable in all realms of the world's religions and philosophies." Babaji Bob Kindler

Denies Transformation, Accepts Nonorigination

Sees beyond Evolution & Involution into All-pervasive Stasis

Assigns name and form to Maya and realizes nameless, formless Essence

Observes time and space as relative laws that ultimately dissolve into Timeless Awareness

Three Pillars of the Advaita Vedanta

God/Brahman/Self

GOD DOES NOT CREATE WORLDS; THE MIND DOES THAT IN ITS INDIVIDUAL, COLLECTIVE, AND COSMIC FORMS VIA ITS INNATE POWERS OF COSMIC PROJECTION.

GOD DOES NOT BLESS OR CURSE ANYONE OR ANYTHING. THE LAW OF KARMA BRINGS ABOUT JUST FRUITS ACCORDINGLY; THAT IS ALL.

GOD DOES NOT HEAL OR CAUSE DISEASE. ALL ILLNESSES, THEIR CAUSES, AND THEIR CURES REST IN THE MIND, WITH THE INDIVIDUAL EGO.

GOD IS NOT RESPONSIBLE FOR FLOODS, FAMINE, AND PESTILENCE. SUCH CATASTROPHES ARE CAUSED BY NATURE, THE FIVE ELEMENTS, WEATHER, ETC. — ALL WHOSE CAUSES ARE TO BE FOUND IN THE MIND.

GOD, BRAHMAN, THE ABSOLUTE, CANNOT BE PRAYED TO, AS IT IS NOT AN INDIVIDUAL, BUT RATHER THE COHESIVE WHOLE. GOD WITH FORM CAN BE SUPPLICATED, BUT THAT GOD ABIDES IN THE MIND, AS DO HEAVENS/LOKAS.

GOD AND THE SOUL, ATMAN, ARE NONDIFFERENT. THUS, THE SOUL CANNOT BE CREATED — NEITHER FROM DUST, BY THE GODS, OR EVEN BY THE MIND. GOD/SOUL/SELF ARE IDENTICAL, UNDIVIDED, AND ACREATE.

GOOD AND EVIL ARE IN THE HUMAN MIND, NOT IN GOD. GOD DOES NOT TAKE SIDES IN WAR, NOR DOES GOD FASHION A DEVIL AND FIGHT EVIL. THE HUMAN MIND CAUSES ALL SUCH FOLLY, WHILE GOD REMAINS TRANSCENDENT, ALWAYS AND EVER ABIDING IN ETERNAL PEACE.

GOD, WHO IS ETERNAL LIFE, DOES NOT TAKE PART IN LIFE IN BODIES. — NEITHER IN HEAVEN, ON EARTH, OR IN HELL. GOD DOES NOT CAUSE DEATH, EITHER. THESE APPARENT ASSUMPTIONS AND MOVEMENTS ARE DREAMS IN THE COLLECTIVE MIND; GOD DOES NOT DREAM.

BRAHMAN, GOD, EXISTS BEYOND THE MIND AND ITS PROJECTING POWER. IT IS DESIRELESS, SO CAN ONLY BE UNITED WITH BY FULFILLING ALL DESIRES AND TRANSCENDING THE MIND.

TIME, SPACE, & CAUSE AND EFFECT (KARMA) OPERATE WHEN THE MIND IS PRESENT; THEY DO NOT FUNCTION IN THE BRAHMAN STATE. THEREFORE, EVENTS IN TIME, OBJECTS IN SPACE, AND THE HAPPINESS AND SUFFERING OF CAUSE AND EFFECT ARE NOT PRESENT IN BRAHMAN.

MIND, IN CONJUNCTION WITH NATURE, PRODUCES ALL THINGS, INCLUSIVE OF BODIES AND WORLDS. THIS AMOUNTS TO PROJECTION AND WITHDRAWAL OF CONCEPTS AND IDEAS IN CYCLES, RATHER THAN PRODUCTION AND EVOLUTION OF REAL OBJECTS WITH BEGINNINGS AND ENDINGS. MAN IS NOT AN ANIMAL; HE IS A SENTIENT, ETERNAL SOUL. HE HAS NOT EVOLVED FROM ANIMALS; ANIMALS AND ALL OTHER FORMS ARE ACTUALLY PROJECTED FROM HIS MIND.

Frees the small self from the dream of finitude and attains nontransmigration

Perceives birth, life, and death as mental dreams & becomes Ever-awake

Renders the functions and import of matter and life-force into the Devatmashakti

Realizes that activity, movement, and karma all take place in Nature, not in the Soul/Atman

Mind

COSMIC MIND AUTHORS THE 7 WORLDS; COLLECTIVE MIND FASHIONS THE HEAVENS; INDIVIDUAL MIND FORMS THE PHYSICAL UNIVERSE. GOD, THE UNDERLYING SUBSTRATUM BEYOND ALL WORLDS, REMAINS UNTOUCHED, UNTAINTED.

PURE MIND IS BRAHMAN; IT DOES NOT VIBRATE. IMPURE MIND, MANAS, INFECTS LIFE AND THE WORLDS WITH DUALITIES AND FILLS THEM WITH PLEASURE AND SUFFERING. PURE MIND REMAINS INDIFFERENT TO THESE.

MIND IS FOURFOLD: MANAS FOSTERS VARIETIES; CHITTA BROODS ON THESE; BUDDHI EXPANDS AND SPREADS THEM; EGO RUSHES TO OWN AND ENJOY THEM.

The World

THERE IS NO WORLD, OR WORLDS; THERE IS ONLY BRAHMAN. THOSE WHO CREATE A WORLD SEPARATE FROM BRAHMAN DO SO OUT OF FOLLY, AND TO THEIR OWN UNDOING.

THE WORLD, AS A WORLD, IS USEFUL FOR PURIFICATION OF THE MIND. BUT THE SOUL, THE TRUE SELF, IS EVER-PURE AND EVER-FREE. WHERE DOES THAT LEAVE THE WORLD?

SINCE THE WORLD IS A CONSTRUCT OF THE MIND, AND ITS OBJECTS ARE MERELY THOUGHT CONCRETIZED VIA DESIRES OF THE EGO — THEN MIND, EGO, THOUGHTS, WORLDS, AND OBJECTS SHOULD ALL BE DISSOLVED INTO THE FORMLESS BRAHMAN.

Reveals the truth of Spirituality & Enlightenment beyond the pale of social and religious conventions

Lifts sleeping souls out of lifetimes of ignorance with their ancestors

Prescribes sadhana, rather than works and wealth, as the solution for suffering, illness & death

Moves through work, duty, and dharma to the Goal of Nondual Wisdom & Love of God

"Sri Krishna called the world 'anityam asukham' — joyless and transient. Lord Buddha determined that the world was full of suffering. Jesus stated that the world was like shifting sands, and that man should never try to lay his head there. Sri Ramakrishna compared the world to a hole in the ground, and ignorant living beings like vipers therein. Considering testaments like these from such luminaries, should the world not be given up, post haste?" Babaji Bob Kindler

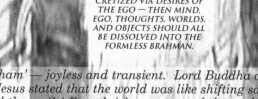

"I am a Vedantist; Satchitananda — Existence-Knowledge-Bliss Absolute — is my God. I scarcely find any other God than the majestic form of my own Self." Swami Vivekananda

Moving to our next offering, shown on the facing page, the accent shifts to the state of mind of the illumined soul, particularly with regards to his/her beliefs — or possibly better said, what he does not believe anymore. An *advaitist,* or nondualist, has given up not only the world as being separate from *Brahman,* but also all of the binding thought-forms that living beings entertain which keep them bound to the idea of a world of matter only.

The chart proceeds with statements of truth that the advaitist has come to realize, all placed upon/based upon three pillars — God, Mind, and the World. First of all, the appearances of change are denied, and only the changeless is accepted. Neither objects, worlds, events, nor living beings have any existence apart from Divine Reality. Since Divine Reality is Immutable, then the appearance of change within all four of these is a myth, an illusion, and only the changeless Essence in them is real. Therefore, that they are created or destroyed, blessed or cursed, sick or healed, threatened or saved, embodied or disembodied, etc. — as the many sidebars next to the pillars all explain — is all a matter of apparent transformation. Like the waves on the breast of an ocean, all appearing and disappearing continually, rising and sinking inexorably into the boundless expanse of water that their very forms consist of, objects, worlds, and living beings — all bodies — express a temporary showing of the Light of Consciousness that underlies them as Divine Reality. They are not real in and of themselves. As the *Upanisads* state,

> *There, in Brahman, the sun shines not, nor moon, nor stars, nor fire, nor lightning,*
> *much less the mortal frame and the prana that animates it.*
> *That one Light shining, all else shines; by Its Light all is made radiant.*

Much more could be stated about the singular nature of God/*Brahman*/*Atman.* Suffice to say that it transcends nature and all that issues from it, and is unaffected by all activities along with their multitudinous causes and effects. The second pillar on the chart deals with Mind. Mind dreams itself away from Nondual Reality. It projects the egos into endless bodies. It produces Nature via its shining intelligence and posits worlds of name and form there for enjoyment and suffering. That very Mind, when pure, stills all vibrations inherent in it and rests in highest *Samadhi.* As Sri Ramakrishna stated, and worth repeating, *"Mind is the gateway to heaven, but it is also the doorway to hell."* In its fourfold condition (*antahkarana,* or inner cause of everything), it *"....drags from birth to death and death to birth, the soul."* It is dual by nature. But rendered or kept in a nondual state, it is all Peace, Bliss, Wisdom, and Light. As Ramprasad Sen sings in one of his Wisdom songs:

> *Oh mind, you are just a small, shiny fish, sporting naively on the surface of the waters of relativity,*
> *where death is granted his fishing grounds.*
> *Quick! Before it is too late, dive deep into the Ocean of Immortality*
> *and escape death's painful net.*

The world is the third subject up for scrutiny under the *advaitist's* thorough and penetrating gaze. First, it is unreal, and even if it were real in any way, it would still be devoid of abiding substance and satisfaction. If it is a dream, then dreams vanish upon awakening; if it is created, creations cannot spring from nothing, but must have a "something" out of which they arise; and if it is projected, projections are temporary and are withdrawn into their Source, inevitably. Thus, the *advaitist* lives in the world like a mudfish lives at the bottom of a lake, impervious to the mud, with its scales still shining.

Speaking of pillars, though there are several key elements to the *Advaita* philosophy, two main pillars stand out on their own. The first is *Aparinama,* or Nontransformation. For teachings on that see the chart on page 265, and the chart just studied. The other is *Ajativada,* the "unoriginated" condition of all beings and all things — or the path of those who are never born and never die. Put obversely, these singular beings know that everything is eternal — God, Nature, Soul, even *Maya.* Living in this blissful, static eternity, they either watch the sport of playful mutability, or merge into transcendent Formlessness, as is their predilection.

Ajativada: Nonorigination

"Atman, the Indivisible Soul of mankind, is unborn. It does not pass in and out of existence; It is Existence! This truth is discovered in Consciousness as an eternal Verity. This is not a matter of going inside or outside; the Infinite Brahman can never be realized through the finite universe. Mind and matter are neither destructible nor indestructible. They are unoriginated." Swami Aseshananda

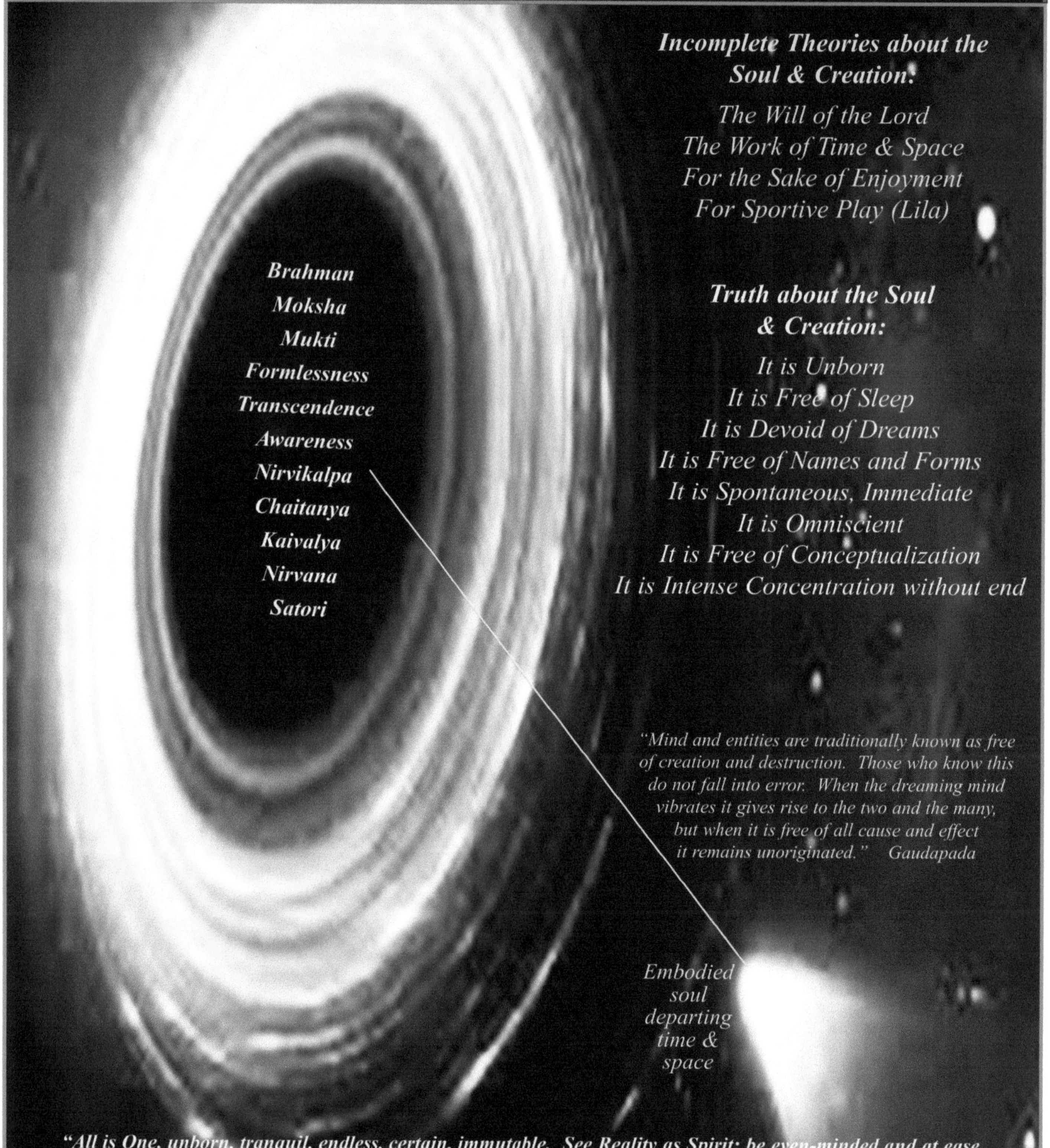

Incomplete Theories about the Soul & Creation:

The Will of the Lord
The Work of Time & Space
For the Sake of Enjoyment
For Sportive Play (Lila)

Truth about the Soul & Creation:

It is Unborn
It is Free of Sleep
It is Devoid of Dreams
It is Free of Names and Forms
It is Spontaneous, Immediate
It is Omniscient
It is Free of Conceptualization
It is Intense Concentration without end

Brahman
Moksha
Mukti
Formlessness
Transcendence
Awareness
Nirvikalpa
Chaitanya
Kaivalya
Nirvana
Satori

"Mind and entities are traditionally known as free of creation and destruction. Those who know this do not fall into error. When the dreaming mind vibrates it gives rise to the two and the many, but when it is free of all cause and effect it remains unoriginated." Gaudapada

Embodied
soul
departing
time &
space

"All is One, unborn, tranquil, endless, certain, immutable. See Reality as Spirit; be even-minded and at ease. This is the state through which you will become liberated, even while inhabiting a body."
Akshi Upanisad

The chart opposite cites profound facts and teachings about the principle of Nonorigination. Views that prefer origination are listed in contrast there. If one speaks about the "will of the Lord," and then cites God with form, or *Ishvara*, as being the originator of name and form in time and space, even still, it must be admitted that this very "Lord" Himself is unoriginated and unborn, for who would be his creator? Who gave Him birth? Truly, His very appearance is a matter of His own unoriginated Will. From Formlessness He arose, and to Formlessness He will return.

Further, is this rising and falling a matter of His divine play, or sport *(Lila)*? The scriptures call Him *"aphakial,"* free of desire, so why would He desire to sport? The *Upanisads* state about *Brahman,* *"That is partless, actionless, faultless, and divine."* Even being actionless alone, He would not want to sport. And creation for the sake of enjoyment? Bliss, *Ananda,* far outstrips enjoyment, and Bliss is His nature. As Sri Ramakrishna has stated, humorously, *"Once refined candy is tasted, one will not be satisfied anymore with mere treacle."*

Finally, there is the theory that creation is the work of time and space. Even aside from the fact that seers have seen that time and space are both illusory, both of them morphing and disappearing in the mind when it dreams and visits deep sleep, there is also the fact that everything, even insentient nature, follows patterns set down by an ever-present intelligence (see chart on page 739, *Proofs of Purusha*), and this intelligence is innate, both in mind and in Consciousness.

Looking deeper into the chart on page 746, the image depicts the soul — presently having dreamed itself away from its own Source — departing its various experiences in space and time and returning to merge in *Brahman*. Various profound words for this immersion in *Sanskrit*, like *moksha, mukti, kaivalya, nirvana, nirvikalpa,* and others reveal how widely known and highly courted this prime Goal is. In *Vedanta*, the *Atman,* having associated with the five sheaths in space and time, for reasons of helping souls out of suffering, or to get free of inordinate and habitual wandering and dreaming, is now sloughing off the coverings and giving up its own consciously assumed dream of finitude. As the *Avadhut* tells in his own song of highest revelation:

> *Do you really have any self, possess any names or forms — even to the extent of allusion?*
> *In an unending series of empty worlds, you are the only real Substance.*
> *Is there anything other than your Self in existence?*
> *Then why waste time grieving?*
> *You are Pure Existence, Wisdom, and Bliss, as boundless as the sky, infinite like space.*

Similar to the previous chart, this offering tells the truth about the Soul and creation; basically, that there is nothing other than the Self in Existence, and creation is its magical projection. Unborn, free of sleep, devoid of dreams, transcendent of names and forms, immediate, omniscient, and beyond conceptualization, It is perfect and one-pointed concentration without breaks or endings. As Swami Vivekananda has stated about It: *"Brahman is beyond both Ishvara and the world, and is not a state. It is the only unit not composed of many units. It is the principle which runs through all, from a cell to God, and without which nothing can exist. Whatever is real, is that principle, or Brahman. When I think 'I am Brahman,' then I alone exist. It is so also when you think so, and so on. Each is the whole of that principle."*

To finalize our study of the chart on the facing page, the quotes by certain luminaries are well worth contemplating. Mainly, the key point about *Ajativada* is that neither the Soul nor Matter are destructible; they are not indestructible either. They are unoriginated.

With all that has been said about the mind's powers of projection, called *sankalpa* in *Sanskrit*, a review of that principle on the cosmic level will be helpful here.

Since *Brahman* is beyond mind, its roving thought, its compartmentalized intelligence, its dualistic tendency, and its lean towards individualism, it is wise to leave That, Divine Reality, settled and undisturbed in all its original purity and blissful transcendence. This is where the word "Consciousness" has been borrowed in English, and "Awareness," for the mind's right to these terms, if it were granted, would stunt them. Consciousness in the mind as seen by contemporary thinkers is automatically routed along the senses and the nerve channels of the body, and Awareness is correlated to the brain and it functions. Consciousness as its own Entity, all-pervasive and exalted, is not admitted nor thought of, particularly in Western countries, and not even across the whole wide world — except in spiritual circles.

And it is in these spiritual circles, found in tiny pools of world religious thought, that the higher definition of Consciousness or Awareness is naturally mated up with greater intelligence and its wisdom. The mind also has a potential for courting and possessing this, but it cannot be allowed to stay in its ordinary condition, as cited just above. It must be opened so as to act like a huge bay that affords passage to the sea. Studying its blockages, then, is necessary (see chart on page 206).

In the spiritually oriented country of India, the "Mind Only" perspective took hold early on, which at once kept philosophy and its exponents away from assigning occurrences of thought, activity, and matter to God/*Brahman*, and also indicated clearly where the hub of such *karma*-bearing movements was located.

On the chart now up for study (page 749) the layout of the mind's strata is given in cosmic cross-sections, which also infer the mind's vast sphere of influence. A pumpkin patch has been selected to act as a microcosmic example of all that is contained in the mind — a mind that has Cosmic, Collective, and Individual manifestations (see charts on pages 161, 267, 453). It must be remembered that God/*Brahman* had no part in this massive projection; it is all mind's doing. The only "part" that *Brahman* might have is as the underlying backdrop, i.e., Consciousness/Awareness, like a stage for a dance troupe or soil for seeds and growth — although the mind could easily take credit (and blame) for this, too. *Brahman* might as well be envisioned as empty nothingness, a formless, amorphous mass of undifferentiated Awareness — but all Bliss! (see chart on page 732).

In the distance, beyond the pumpkin patch (or watermelon if one prefers), is the famed "Seedless" state, like *Nirbijam* in *Yoga*. Rows of barely seen pumpkins begin to emerge from that/That, symbolic of the hierarchy of cosmic beings, the higher and subservient gods and goddesses which are all powers in the mind. Less subtle than these are the next row of seed-bearing hosts, termed here the "celestials." Demigods and *asuras* would fall into this subdivision, which is a strata that is higher than the ancestor realms or lower heavens (within). Following the trend away from the involution process and towards evolution, the *prana* and ten senses appear next, all connecting the transmigrating soul to the body, which, ironically enough, given the pumpkin analogy, is described as a shell. The five elements form the field in which this body plays, being the outermost set of quintuplications (see chart on page 461). Everything from the gods (like the Trinity) on outwards consist of mind and its mentation, thought and its conception, intelligence and its knowledge, and the all-too pervasive ego with its insinuating possessiveness. It is this "complex complex" that is responsible for everything in the realms of name and form in time and space, based in cause and effect (*Maya*).

The inset box at the bottom left of the chart under study reveals the cosmic mind (*Mahat, Hiranyagarbha,* the Trinity) cut in half, as it were, revealing the presence of powerful seeds within it. Nature, worlds, bodies, objects, along with the different races and creatures, even the gods and the conception of God Itself, rest within the Great Mind. The substance that it all floats in is called *Ekarnava,* the ethereal ocean of primal matter, much like Unmanifested *Prakriti*. As was stated earlier, man's deep sleep state *(sushupti)* is when and where he connects with all of this, and perceives it all within him.

A read-through of Swami Vivekananda's quote at the bottom of the chart gives a short list of what the power of the mind is capable of, inclusive of all the many infernal objects but which, unfortunately, leaves out the Eternal Subject.

When beings take up the *Advaita* "philosophy," and pit it against the all-too-common world view of conventional thinking that opines the scientific Evolution idea and the 7-day Creation theory, nonduality begins to fade from their minds, being too hard to hold next to what is familiar and rooted deep in lifetimes of secular and dualistic thinking. This is why the teaching of *"vivarta"* (see

India's "Mind Only School" Perspective
Primal Seeds & The Seedless State

"The seers of India have realized that everything in form proceeds from the mind, and this is why they have revealed the singular way leading to its dissolution. Sri Ramakrishna has compared the mind's propensity for production to rice seed strewn across the ground before the rainy season sets in. A riot of growth is the result. But if these seeds are exposed to fire prior to their exposure to soil, their power of germination is destroyed. This fire is the practice of yoga which renders the mind's proclivity for desire-based expression nil and void, opening the gate to Samadhi. There are many types of seeded samadhis — of knowledge, of peace, of bliss, etc. But there is only one kind of Unseeded Samadhi." Babaji Bob Kindler

Asamprajnata Samadhi
Satori

The Seedless State

Nirvikalpa Samadhi
Nirvana

The Gods/Goddesses

The Celestials

The Ancestors

Senses & Prana

(vital force)

Physical Body
(outer shell)

Five Elements
(Primal Matter)

Internal Mind
(subtle body)

Mind Projects

Nature
Worlds
God
Bodies
Races
Objects
Gods

Ekarnava – Ocean of Ethereal Matter

"....and it is this Lord we are trying to realize from time without beginning in the objective, and in the attempt our minds throwing up such 'queer' creatures of our fancy as man, woman, child, body, brain, earth, sun, moon, stars, the world, love, hate, property, wealth, etc.; also ghosts, devils, angels and gods, God, etc."

Swami Vivekananda

chart on page 65) must be given to the mind, as a kind of antidote for the unwanted return of root ignorance *(mula-vidya)* and, as was just cited, the shortsightedness of the failure to take into account ones own, pristine Awareness *(chaitanya)*. The idea of false superimposition *(vivarta)* works on the disbelieving mind in two ways: either it sobers the mind by reminding it of the presence of the illusory nature of appearances and phenomena, or it brightens the mind by the reminder of the presence of *Brahman* in all things, everywhere.

This bright idea has been expressed in no better way than in Sri Ramakrishna's conversation with a deeper seeker after Truth while the Great Master was on earth in the body. Sitting one morning together, just about sunup, His devotee turned to the Master and asked Him how it could be that God/*Brahman* could exist in all beings and all things, and still be transcendent of name, form, and causality. Pointing to the many flowers and blades of grass lying on the temple grounds before them, the Master stated that just as the one sun shines in the dew drops collected on each of these expressions of nature, just so did God appear in all beings and all things while existing far above them, as the sun and its Light. *"This is how the indivisible One becomes the many."*

The chart opposite, then, like its companion on the previous page, gives us a list of some of the principles that receive the Light of Awareness, each depicted as a dewdrop sitting on the branch of *Brahman*, so to speak. *Brahma-jyoti*, the Light of pure, conscious Awareness, illumines the Great Mind, *Mahat*, as well as the Trinity, as seen prior, and the ultimate form of God called *Ishvara*. *Manas*, part of the collective and individual mind, also receives its light of lesser intelligence from that Divine Source of translucent Light. Trickling down and out to living beings, and the *lokas* they inhabit, the life-force that flows through them all, along with the senses and the subtle and gross elements. *"Light leaps through the nadis, as has been said."* As Shankara declares in his profound scripture, the *Vivekachudamani*:

Om mano na buddhih na shariram indriyam tanmatra-bhutani na-bhutapanchakam ahamkritis chapi viyat-svarupakam tam isham atmanam upaiti shashvatam

*That one realizes the Supreme, Eternal Self, who dissolves mind, intellect, body, senses,
the five subtle elements, and the five gross elements, into the Atman in meditation
along with time and space.*

And so, this is the astute philosophical explanation in India's "Mind Only" schools as to how God becomes all beings while remaining free of bodies; how God shines through all things while never becoming an object; how *Brahman* breathes in all forms while never being limited to or dependent upon a set of lungs; and how It permeates the entire set of worlds at all levels and in all dimensions without ever moving from Its ever-static, always stable, all-penetrating position. As Swami Vivekananda has put it: *"There is but One, seen by the ignorant as matter, by the wise as God. And the history of civilization is the progressive reading of spirit into matter. The ignorant see the person in the nonperson. The sage sees the nonperson in the person. Through pain and pleasure, joy and sorrow, this is the one lesson we are learning.* Further, he added:

"I fully believe that there are periodic ferments of religion in human society, and that such a period is now sweeping over the educated world. On planes physical, ethical, and spiritual, an ever-broadening generalization — leading up to a concept of Unity Eternal — is in the air; and this being so, all the movements of the time may be taken to represent, knowingly or unknowingly, the noblest philosophy of the unity of man ever had — the Advaita Vedanta."

In the ongoing study of profound principles such as *tathagatagarbha*, *ajativada*, *aparinama*, *vivarta*, and other high-minded facets of Truth, the simple mention of "light" has come up several times. In India, Light, or *Jyoti*, or *Bhati*, refers to radiance of an internal kind. And in fact, even the external light, say, of the sun, is seen as a manifestation of inner Light. This is the way of connections that has transported India into the forefront of religion and philosophy, entitling Her to be the Mother of all Religions.

Vivartopadana / Adhyasa Astitva

How the One Becomes the Many

"Just as the morning sun reflects its light in the many dew drops that settle on fields and flowers at dawn, so too does the one, Indivisible Brahman shine Its Light of pure Awareness through the world's many objects such as plants, animals, and human bodies — all without losing its homogenous nature in the least."
Sri Ramakrishna Paramahamsa

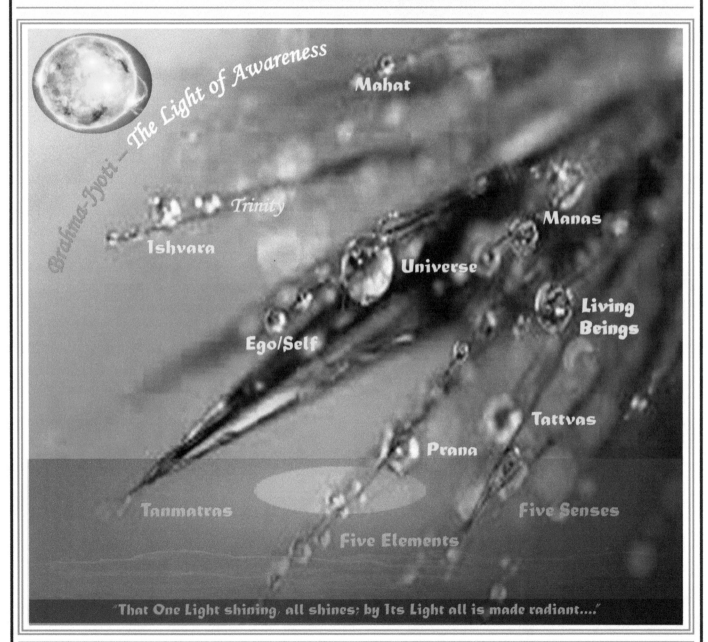

Brahma-Jyoti – The Light of Awareness

Mahat

Trinity

Ishvara

Manas

Universe

Living Beings

Ego/Self

Tattvas

Prana

Tanmatras

Five Senses

Five Elements

"That One Light shining, all shines; by Its Light all is made radiant...."

"Brahman is qualified by the universe and its living beings. At the beginning, while following the method of 'Not this, not this,' one has to eliminate the universe and its living beings. But as long as 'I-consciousness' remains, one cannot but feel that it is God Himself who has become everything. He alone has become the twenty-four cosmic principles."
Sri Ramakrishna Paramahamsa

All Hail, Surya Narayan!

"May we always
and ever meditate
on the radiant effulgence
of the Supreme Being,
abiding in our hearts
and minds,
eternally...."

brahman
sentiency
insight
wisdom
knowledge
physical light

mahashakti
pure consciousness
awareness
intelligence
mental comprehension
prana - life force
sensual perception

The Explorer of
Ethers.
The
Sky-Wanderer

Commander of the Armies of Light

Revealer of Darkness

Garland of Nature

Eternal
Flower
of Life

Staff of the Flood of Endless Days

There, within the inmost self
of every living being,
the sun does not shine,
nor the moon, nor stars,
nor fire, nor lightning —
much less this tiny mortal flame.
That one Light shining,
all else shines.
By Its Light all is made radiant.
May that one Light of pure,
conscious Awareness enter into us
and permeate us to the very core
of our being.
Om Peace, Peace, Peace."

Shining like burnished gold, highest and deepest,
the core intelligence of livings beings,
partless and indivisible,
ever pure and free of all taint,
the essence in everything that all beings seek,
either knowingly or unknowingly —
there shines Brahman.
It is that which the guru teaches,
it is that which the wise ones exult in.
Om Peace, Peace, Peace.

From the Light of Consciousness, to the God of Light, and on out to the billions of stars in the nocturnal sky, in India all light is a manifestation of Intelligence. Fire, on earth, is the grossest form of that, which is really why living beings have had a fascination with it from ancient times. When they behold it they are looking at their own power to burn away obstacles, such as ignorance. Activity, will power, discipline, and more — they all contain the force of fire which in turn represents Light. On earth, the ultimate fire is seen as the sun above in the ethers. Of sun-worshippers there are many here, and for different reasons, but in India the sun is a god called *Surya*, and His levels and manifestations go deep within.

In the *Katha Upanisad* where the young lad, *Nachiketas*, seeks out the god of death, *Yama*, similarly, in the *Akshi Upanisad*, the *rishi*, *Samkriti*, sought out the god of Light, *Surya*, to ask him about the most effective way to worship Light. The *Upanisad* states that *Samkriti "...repaired to the solar world"* in order to find Surya, which means that, in meditation, the *rishi* focused upon this deity by invoking the fire of psychic *prana*, then combining that with the light of concentration went within by these means to behold the Light of Consciousness. This Light, he knew, was within himself, and was his Self *(Atman)*.

Finding the Light of pure, conscious Awareness is both the Goal of life and reason for living. It is the Goal for those who, as yet, are not able to hold Awareness at the center of their being, and do so without gaps in their awareness even while inhabiting a physical form on the plane of matter. It is the reason for living to those who, after centering in the Light of the Self, turn to help others behold that selfsame Light within themselves — first as the ego in its disciplined, then ripened condition, and secondly as the only Reality — all in accord with the prime Subject of our recent set of charts in this chapter *(advaita)*.

On the chart on the opposite page, levels of this Light are cited, represented by the wisdom rays that are emanating off of the divine personage of Surya Narayan. At the fundamental level, the garland that drapes down from his shoulders is Nature itself; it is nothing more than light, both physically and spiritually. Its particles are the light of living, vibrating, whirling atoms and electrons, its forms are the light of the intelligence that fashioned it, originating from the Cosmic Mind (see recent chart on page 749). The staff *Surya* holds symbolizes the *"endless and veritable flood of days"* that he, as the expression of billions of suns, both mental and physical, lighting up the many worlds, bestows upon living beings. Surya also holds the *"Eternal Flower of Life,"* and that boon is granted to those who turn away from mundane, conventional life and living to embrace "Eternal Life," as Jesus advised.

The long, beautiful arms of *Surya* represent the twin play of light and darkness, the former being peopled by hosts of the armies of light that he commands, and the latter hiding secrets and mysteries untold from the curious and misguided gaze of stunted minds. At his heart is the appellation, *"The Sky Wanderer,"* a fitting moniker for the one who courses through the many ethers, bringing the Light of Consciousness in its various manifestations into all of them.

And it is from the heart on upwards towards his divinely shaped head that these manifestations are listed, across from one another but intrinsically connected. Sunlight and senses, knowledge and *prana*, mind and wisdom, insight and intelligence — finally reaching inwards to the transported echelons of nondual Awareness Itself, boundless and ever-free.

It has been mentioned that there are worshippers of the Sun-god everywhere, both conscious and unconscious of their love. India's devotion is unmistakable, as is instanced by the several "Light" *mantras* that have been placed on the chart presently under study (page 752). One of them is the sacred *Gayatri Mantra*, chanted by millions of souls daily here on the earth plane. Learning, studying, and memorizing them is tantamount to the best form of worship in India, for *Surya's* Light is Intelligence *(buddhi, prajna, jnanam, medha)* at its root and in its essence.

The mention of Lord Surya's "Armies of Light" helps to introduce the next chart up for study. It has to do with fighting hard for the existence of ones spiritual life in a world that is either ambivalent about such a life, or antagonistic against it. The scene on the chart on page 755, famous world round, is of Sri Krishna and Arjuna exchanging intense words on the battlefield of *Kurukshetra*. Though this war was a physical one, fought due to issues around power, domination, and wealth, like wars on earth are, the special implications of the *Kurukshetra* war have overtly spiritual connotations associated with them — as students and devotees of the *Bhagavad Gita* will attest to.

The two lists shown on each side of the battlefield, superimposed over each army, are meant to confer both warnings and encouragement to the soul striving to achieve growth in spiritual life, and to keep the *Atman* first and foremost in mind in the interim. Primarily, in spiritual life, true success is gained by getting distance from the conventional world and detachment from its various allurements. Therefore, the first sign of danger and pending failure would be noting a growing dependance in the mind upon the world and its objects and preoccupations. The discriminating soul would want to inquire as to whether any of these host of externals could grant lasting happiness and actual satisfaction of desires or, on the other hand, if a feeling of suspicion about them, accompanied by a sense of "world-weariness" was instead the case.

Secondly, attainment of getting what one seeks on the external level is always connected to work and activity. In a *rajasic*, materialistic society and world, the worker pays the cost of such pursuits with his or her time, energy, health, and even with ones sense of well-being or peace of mind. Due to the ongoing expenditure of these prime human commodities, exhaustion occurs. But the soul who scrutinizes the process from a witness level of awareness begins to pit work and wisdom, or activity and knowledge, against one another for comparison. The eventual supremacy of knowledge over action causes the wise soul to withdraw more and more from the world and focus all thought and energy on the source of Wisdom.

Turning away from success and failure, praise and blame, and other pairs of opposites, the now maturing soul, weaning himself off of the world and its pursuits, finds deeper and more lasting meaning in the testaments of illumined souls who have gone before, and takes recourse to awakened souls who now seem to come forward out of hiding to assist. Thus do signs of battle awaken qualified souls from the sleep of ignorance, yet escape the notice of those who are still steeped in the thick of the world's insipid pleasures and the confusion and depletion that they bring.

Poised between the two armies and their respective concerns, Sri Krishna gives Arjuna instructions for making ready for battle. The teachings will eventually help the soul transcend the world and its suffering, but in the meantime it is necessary to select between the type of suffering that only perpetuates itself continually in rounds, and a beneficial suffering that destroys *karmas* and trains and purifies the mind. The quote at the top of the chart by Sri Krishna explains this nicely.

In the four corners of the chart under study we see a quartet of wisdom sayings from Sri Sarada Devi, the Holy Mother, all of them unusual in their perspective. She states that God cannot be realized in the world, by the ordinary mind. It is the elevated mind that, having dissolved itself into higher Awareness, then perceives Divine Reality. She also points out that type of suffering that mimics and trades off with pleasure, which takes the mind away from thoughts of God and wallows in the mud and mire of lower mind. Again, She indicates the role of time in its many phases towards assisting in the fructification of positive attributes lying in the mind (see charts on pages 41 & 665).

Being the manifestation of the Divine Mother in this age, She states to us: *"I am your Guru; I know whether you are making progress or not. How can you understand it, but you will achieve everything. Most obstacles to worship are not external; they are internal. They will gradually fall off one after another by taking the Master's name and by meditation. Do your duty and keep the mind on God. Don't pay attention to whether the blemishes of the mind are persisting or not, for we are behind you. You all have come to me because you are all my own. If one is the "very own" of another, they remain inseparably connected in successive cycles of time. I have indeed taken your responsibility. Don't be afraid, have no fear — now you have been reborn. I am assuming the fruits of all the deeds of your past lives. Now you are pure, you are free of sin. I have taken charge of everything, good and bad. Can you understand everything I say? If you could it would lighten my burden immensely. I simply cannot put aside those whom I have accepted as my own."*

Signs of Battle
Maintaining Spiritual Life in the World

"What is sweet in the beginning is to be avoided, for it generally turns sour in the end; but that which is sour at the outset is to be forborne and purified, for it gradually transforms into the sweetness of true attainment."
Bhagavan Sri Krishna

"God is not realized in the world; He is realized in Spirit. Has God ever visited anyone who is devoid of ecstatic fervor?"
Sarada Devi

"Ordinary people are quite happy. They eat, drink, make merry, and forget God. Only the devotees know no end to real suffering, and that is because they do not see Him."
Sarada Devi

Indications of Forthcoming Success

Feeling a general dissatisfaction with the world

Performing disinterested works for a higher end

Considering the increase of knowledge and spiritual growth to be the point of life in the world

Treating the contrasting duality of praise and the blame equally

Taking seriously the words of illumined beings and following them

Indications of Pending Failure

Imagining that the world can grant all that one desires

Attachment to work, considering it everything in life

Thinking wealth and enjoyment of the sense objects to be the purpose of human existence

Getting elated by praise and honor and deflated by blame and criticism

Listening to conventional opinions only while turning away from wise counsel

INSTRUCTIONS IN MAKING READY FOR BATTLE

SUFFERING TO REMOVE KARMA & TRANSFORM ACTION INTO KNOWLEDGE

SUFFERING FOR THE SAKE OF PLEASURE & PAIN THAT CREATES MORE KARMA

TRANSCENDENCE OF WAR
Feet of Bliss

"The suffering of worldly beings pains me. But what can I do? They will not seek liberation. For sincere seekers, however, misery is the gift of God. It is a symbol of His compassion."
Sarada Devi

"When a favorable time dawns, man gets the desire to contemplate God. When unfavorable times come, he acquires the facilities for doing evil. Thus, one should constantly make oneself fit for the Grace of God."
Sarada Devi

"There are two tendencies in human nature: one to harmonize the ideal with the life, and the other to elevate the life to the ideal. It is a great thing to understand this, for the former tendency is the temptation of our lives." **Swami Vivekananda**

The Corrosion of Human Consciousness

"Lack of spiritual self-effort is the rust of households."

"Like nails left out in the rain in a bucket on a deserted construction site, gradually fusing with one another into lumps of rusty iron, similarly, the neglected and untrained mind forms complexes of residual karma, called samskaras, that impede spiritual progress and dictate the unhealthy condition of future births in ignorance."
Babaji Bob Kindler

Raja Yoga

Failure to meditate daily.

Failure to teach your children how to meditate.

Neglect of recitation and memorization of scripture.

Carelessness in implementing spiritual discrimination.

Jnana Yoga

Ignoring the need to contemplate the wisdom of the seers.

Forgetting to spread the precious dharma in the world.

"Negligence is the rust of the watchman, leading to calamity. Sloth is the rust of all good and beautiful things. Non-recitation of the wisdom scriptures is the rust of monasteries, and lack of spiritual self-effort is the rust of households." Lord Buddha, Dhammapada, Canto 18, sl. 241

Allowing worldly talk to replace talk of God.

Allowing money instead of service to become the main aim of earthly life.

Becoming complacent about reading out the bhakti sutras to family and children.

Failure to make use of the spiritual teacher, holy company, and recitation of the mantra in everyday life.

Leaving work undone, incomplete, or abandoned due to spiritual practice.

Bhakti Yoga

Karma Yoga

"Practice your breathing exercises, control the senses, study the dharma under a competent preceptor, and meditate upon divine Reality daily. In a mind that does all this, how can there be any lack of inner peace and abiding happiness?" Shankara

The chart just studied, plus the one on the facing page, are both placed in this chapter as protections against the loss of memory of the Self, or *Atman*. Transcendental Consciousness is always perfect, free of all conditionings, but the human mind easily falls away from such heights and then subjects itself to lives lived amidst ignoble circumstances. This is unfortunate, lamentable, and unnecessary. Therefore, "signs of battle" require being on vigil, for, whereas the *Atman*/Eternal Self of mankind is ever-pure and ever-perfect, the coverings that become imposed over It are not.

The image on the facing page are from a true story of a workman who, having to leave his work site due to hard, continual rains over the winter season, covered everything until his return. In his long absence, while it rained hard all day, the wind blew the canvas off of a bucket of nails and the bucket filled with water. Over time the nails began to rust, and soon fused together into a mass of rusty metal. This phenomenon is a fit and revealing analogy for the mind and how, while sitting in the waters of relativity and worldliness for extended periods of time, even lifetimes, it solidifies its contents into hard and fast impressions *(samskaras)*. Further activities performed under the presence and influence of these *samskaras* dictate its life and destiny — in this case, in unhealthy ways.

The chart and its teachings are placed upon the backdrop of the Four Yogas which, when combined and practiced under the tutelage of a master, are the "new religion of this age." Certain nails, or thoughts in the mind, are singled out under these four headings. The top half displays the yogas of meditation *(raja)* and wisdom *(jnanam)*. The rust of the thinking process here are such problems and oversights as forgetting to meditate daily, the failure to study the wisdom scriptures that tell of the indivisible Soul's perfection and the individual soul's relationship with God/*Brahman*. Add to this the very serious failure to teach ones family and children the *dharma* that saves all from the world and its sufferings, and the result is a fusing together of the many bad habits that arise as a result. Inside of the family setting, as Lord Buddha infers by his quote on this chart under study, this rust of households brings about failed relationships, wayward children, various troubles in the workplace, and betrayal of ones spiritual path and teacher.

All of this is further compounded by the other elements on the list's upper regions, like the stoppage of ones duty to spread the teachings of the *dharma* to the world, the advancing inability to contemplate the true meaning of the eternal words of the seers and, eventually, the unfortunate end to ones spiritual discrimination. When that *"viveka"* is lost, then peace of mind is also. Additionally, many beings never attained *viveka* in the first place due to the presence of those rusty nails in the bucket of their minds.

The bottom half of the chart lists a few of the problems that come on the level of devotion and activity. The yogas of *bhakti* and *karma,* kept fresh and constant, would disallow the formation of such corrosion in the mind's thinking and determinative process. One of the obvious detriments, so simple that it is hard to detect, is giving into worldly talk about mundane matters, and frequenting the company of the worldly-minded beings that engage in this habit. This has a doubly negative effect in that as one begins to prefer surface talk and preoccupations, the precious boon of holy company with the spiritual teacher and the *sangha* will be overlooked or cast aside. And as the previous chart (page 755) taught as well, the use of personal wealth and gain will begin to be frittered away on objects that increase enjoyment, so that soon the ego becomes convinced that the purpose of money is to spend it on material things for the sake of insouciance and jollification — as thousands of beings suffer from starvation, and *dharma* teachers and deserving spiritual organizations that can help them are left unsupported.

Under the heading of *karma yoga,* deserving of mention, is that *dharmic* works taken up in the world must be undergone and completed. This work is as much a part of ones spiritual practice as any other element in life. It is only that all must be done in the *dharma,* and one must come to know what the *dharma* is and consists of prior to the successful completion of this task. And so it is that Shankara states, in his *Bhaja Govindam* stotram: *"Practice your breathing exercises, control the senses, study the dharma under a competent preceptor, and meditate upon Divine Reality daily. In a mind that does all this, how can there be any lack of inner peace and abiding happiness?"* Additionally, if this practice is kept up, how can there be any rusty nails of complacency clogging up ones thinking process either, what to speak of any water of worldliness to cause mental corrosion in the first place?

On page 677 of this book, the chart entitled *"Mahavakyas of the World's Avatars"* was displayed. On the facing page here, we see the sequel to that *dharma* chart, the only real difference in the two being that the chart of page 759 is focused upon India's *avatars,* whereas the previous chart included great founders and luminaries of all the world's religious traditions. The "Signs of Battle" chart on page 755 shows Sri Krishna, one of the *Avatars* of India, giving instruction to His devotee, Arjuna. Divine Incarnations throughout the ages have been transmitting valuable teachings of the *dharma* for the highest good of seeking beings.

An *avatar* can be fully revealed, or hidden. He can even be partially revealed and, yes, can even be a She. Sri Sarada Devi is a example of that fact in recent times. She is a manifestation of Mother Kali, and Her husband, Sri Ramakrishna, was the *Avatar* of Kali, as well as an *Avatar* of Vishnu and Siva, combined. Their incomparable child and student was Swami Vivekananda, and fifteen other great souls incarnated with Them. A well-known *Sanskrit sloka* on all sixteen disciples of Sri Ramakrishna and Holy Mother was composed by a swami of a different order of monks about this:

Brahmanandam sivam shantam premarupam niranjanam
yogisham adbhutam nityam akhandadvaita lakshanam
vijnanam trigunatitam turiyabheda sangitam
subhodam saradam chaivam viveka shashi bhusanam

Swami Vivekananda also composed a *sloka* on the *Kali Avatar,* his own revered *guru:*

Om sthapakaya cha dharmasya
sarva dharma svarupine
avatara varishtaya
Ramakrishnayate namah
Om nama sri Bhagavate
Ramakrishnaya namo namah

This unprecedented downpouring of Divine Light was sorely required for this present age, being one of spiritual darkness. Three quotes assigned to this divine trio can be read and contemplated on the chart, opposite. Additionally, many books have been written on Them, including the classic *Gospel of Sri Ramakrishna,* now translated into many languages.

The divine incarnation, Sri Krishna, and the more recent manifestation of Him, Sri Chaitanya, are *avatars* of *Vishnu.* There are said to be ten *avatars* in this line, Sri Ramachandra being another one of these.

Among other great lights are Vedavyasa and Patanjali, the respective "fathers" of the orthodox *darshanas* of *Vedanta* and *Yoga.* Lord Kapila of earliest times, the father of the ingenious and long-lived *Sankhya Yoga* system, must also be included along with them.

Independent and unique, Lord Buddha must receive special mention here, even though the word *"avatar"* might not be of a philosophically sound usage among the later schools of *Buddhism.* Nevertheless, an *avatar* and a buddha have so many similarities, and a comparison of them, side by side, is sound enough.

The *darshana* of *Yoga,* just mentioned in relation to its founder, Patanjali, demands our attention next, keeping in mind and in conjunction with the chart just studied on the facing page. The next chart, on page 761, reveals how the *yogis* have penetrated through the main aspects of *maya,* with its covering and distorting powers, to find the Light of Consciousness *(Chaitanya/Jyoti)* within themselves and in everything. Six gateways to this realization are outlined.

Mahavakyas of the World's Avatars II

The tradition relates that there were 71 teachers from Kapila to Shankara, and from Shankara to the present day a lineage of 76 teachers has been enumerated. At approximately 1400 B.C. the Brhadaranyaka Upanisad enumerated 66 generations of teachers up to that time. Patanjali has stated that there are as many as 84 thousand rishis, custodians and conduits of a perennial wisdom which is revealed repeatedly in each cycle of creation.

Sri Ramakrishna

"Ah, the madness of Knowledge, the divine madness of Love! When dust is raised by a storm all things look alike. Just so, when these moods come upon me I see no difference between Brahman and the world"

Swami Vivekananda

"May the desire to realize the Eternal Brahman blaze up in you more and more until all your past karma is absolutely annihilated ."

Chaitanya

"One should be more tolerant than a tree, devoid of any and all sense of false prestige, and ready to offer sincere respect to others. With this pure state of mind one can chant the holy name of the Lord constantly."

"Seek enlightenment by prostrating, by questioning, and by service; the wise, the seers of Truth, will then initiate you into the esoteric wisdom path."

"If one is able to meditate upon the Guru and pray to God for even two minutes with full concentration, it is very good."

Vedavyasa

Buddha

Krishna

Sarada Devi

"Mind flows two ways: towards beatitude and towards evil. The former courses along the domain of discernment and merges in the reservoir of isolation. The latter enters the swamp of worldly transmigration."

"That one in whom is born a sublime longing for the Ineffable, whose mind is permeated by this deep yearning, such a one is called by the sages and seers 'one bound upstream.'"

"Unwavering illumination of discriminatory wisdom is the way of nullification of all negativities. They are eliminated via observance of the limbs of Yoga."

Patanjali

Kapila

"The union of the soul and nature has for its only object to give the soul the knowledge of nature and make it capable of eternal Freedom."

Maya has been defined well by Swami Vivekananda as name, form, space, time, and causation. To penetrate through it, then, would require the seeker to know not only its insinuations on the mind, but also these five cosmological elements. Knowing its evolutes would also fill out the picture (see chart on pages 240 & 279). When the *yogi* awakens the hidden powers of his mind, then that concentrated mechanism — now invested with higher consciousness, or deeper awareness — will perceive name and form as coverings, time and space as illusions, and causality as a kind of bondage that must be transcended. Other beings with minds do not go in this inward and transcendent direction, but sleep in time, brood and breed in space, and do so in endless cycles *(samsara)*. These cycles are a part of the mind's dreaming abilities *(sankalpa)*, so it is not just on the physical plane that these cycles occur. Evolution on earth can neither fully contain nor outlive nor outstrip these cycles *(kalas)*, nor explain them, for even the expanse and passage of time explained by the evolution theory is going on in the selfsame mind that projects it into manifestation. Thus life — all lives — is really a dream, and one is rowing the boat of the newly born body in it again and again. Reincarnation, as a relative law, must be examined anew in this day and age.

To begin to understand Reality and escape relativity, the intrepid individual will have to use rationale and take a scientific look at things. It will help immensely if this "look" possesses some sort of objectivity, or witness ability, some force of thinking that can separate itself from desire for matter steeped in pleasure, from emotions aligned with sentimentality and feelings, and from a thinking process that exists and operates on the intellectual frame of reference only.

The first gateway to deeper comprehension is the knowledge that everything in relative existence is based in vibration, what the Indian seers called *vrttis*. The source of all vibration is in the mind. The mind free of vibration is a mind that is free. The dead person's brain ceases to vibrate; the sleeping person's mind ceases to vibrate in deep sleep; the luminary in *samadhi* abandons all vibrations and reaches *Turiya*. While under the influence of relativity, the scientist discovers the secret that all vibrates by taking apart fragments of objects. Using a mind caught in time, he examines the object in time, over time, not knowing that his "Witness Consciousness" is perceiving everything from a timeless transcendence. To observe the movement of particles in accordance with the passage of time affords an advantage to the *yogi*, for he is already convinced that the mind is a limited mechanism for observing matter — that there is an Observer outside of space and time doing the observing. The mind is only a mechanism, a *tattva*. His meditation practice has afforded him this special knowledge.

Focusing on time, then, and opening the fourth gateway, the *yogi* does so in much the same way a scientist would attempt to find the makeup of an object, or a seeker of knowledge through languages would seek to find the meaning in words: they all look into increments, like small portions of particles. To do so with time would be to take it down to each second, for looking at minutes, hours, and days, etc., would lure the mind into the passage of time, and the *yogi* is looking to see through time. *"Enter into meditation and cut time down,"* sings Ramprasad in one of his wisdom songs.

By centering the mind in one moment, then, and taking it away from its apparent movement, the *yogi* freezes it in place and thereby gets a view of the presence of a static field of Infinity/Eternity that lies within the Great Self *(Atman)*. This field is boundless and boundary-less. When his mind shifts from the uninformed perspective of the passage of time, and posits its awareness in the field of timelessness, the *yogi* not only begins to see through the illusion of time, but also gets such boons as peace of mind, transcendent insight, and eventually, bliss.

Still, the idea of the passage of time comes dancing back, and the mind slides into the idea almost seamlessly. Further inspection of this nature causes the *yogi's* awareness to center on the timeless space which exists as the idea of one moment comes forth from the mind-field, passes, and then gives rise to the next moment. Expanding that timeless space between the mind's idea of two moments is what opens the gate of Infinity, or Eternity. This is also what beings experience in deep sleep, but devoid of their deeper awareness; their consciousness is not intact and accompanying them into these inner states.

The Six Esoteric Yogic Gateways

Yoga's Secret of Transcendence

"Each moment arises from Infinity. Each moment dissolves back into Infinity. The next moment also arises directly from Infinity. Concentration on what is between the dissolution of the prior moment and the arising of the subsequent moment opens the gates of Infinity. These subtle gateways, six in number, are the real powers of an illumined Yogi." Patanjala Yoga Commentaries

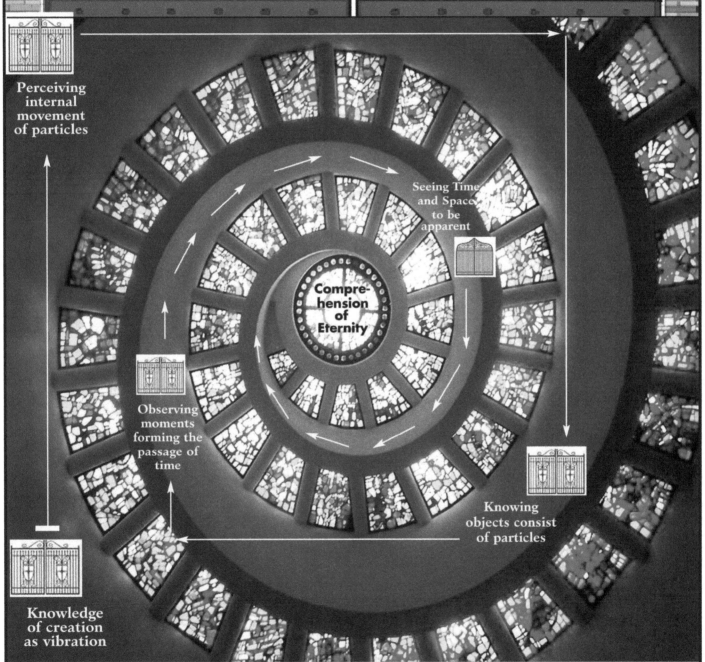

Perceiving internal movement of particles

Seeing Time and Space to be apparent

Comprehension of Eternity

Observing moments forming the passage of time

Knowing objects consist of particles

Knowledge of creation as vibration

"All of creation is made of vibrating particles. Each particle has an inner movement. Many particles together make up an object. Many moments following one upon another take up time. This cause and effect sequence in time and space is not literal – is only apparent. When this mental notion that time and space are real is transcended, Reality stands forth, revealed." Patanjala Yoga Commentaries

ॐ Cosmic Involution & Scientific Evolution ⏳

"Science and religion need not debate over whether life comes from a 'Big Bang' or a 'Heavenly Father.' The problem here is narrowness of outlook. Both views can and do coexist. It is only that evolution of embodied species from single-celled micro-organism to tadpole to four-legged creature to two-legged human takes place on the physical plane alone. Formless Awareness emanates through subtler levels of space that lie within consciousness — from God's Word to God's Mind to the realms of the gods to the life-heavens of the celestial beings and ancestors. 'The Kingdom of Heaven lies within.' 'My Father's Mansion has many chambers.'"

Babaji Bob Kindler

CHAITANYA Sagara

"Consciousness cannot be formulated. It neither originates nor speciates from matter; It is both the singular self-existent Entity, and the primal womb of all matter and all worlds." Babaji Bob Kindler

Divine Mother

Chidakasha

AUM — THE WORD

Jnanakasha

Wisdom Rays
Shakti Power

Chitakasha

Rounds of birth and death

Conceptual Rays
(Psychic Prana)

"People say that this is the age of the atom. I do not agree. It is the age of the Atman." Swami Aseshananda

Pranakasha

→ Ether
Air
Fire
Water
Earth

Birth
Growth
Disease
Old Age
Decay
Death

Heavenly Ascension

"Modern scientists are trying to convince us that if we want to see our ancestors, we have to go to the zoo." Swami Aseshananda

Rebirth in Matter

Solar Rays
(Gross Prana)

Bhutakasha

15 Million Year March of the Hominidae / Homo

Mammals
Tetrapods
Chordates
Primates
Eukaryotes

What really occurs that is unique to the conscious examiner is the giving up of the idea that time and space are real in and of themselves. They are apparent only, being constructs of the mind. Beings imprison themselves in this mind and its multifaceted processes, like Nature and the physical universe, and never know the Great Self, or timeless, deathless Awareness, that looks on, like with a "Single Eye." The expression "free your mind" takes on extra special meaning here, though that expression in America out of the 1960's was aligned with the taking of intoxicants. All things in the realm of matter, energy, and thought are intoxicants, from food to drugs to *prana* to knowledge. All of them lie in relativity, and therefore cannot grant one the superlative vision of Reality. *"One cannot get to the Infinite via the finite,"* as Swami Aseshanandaji Maharaj used to say. One must transcend the mind's projection of the finite, not use a drug from nature, i.e. *maya* (name, form, time, space, causation) that changes the mind's vibration and only adds in another vibration of its own, quite often an addled one based upon the lack of higher awareness in the one who is taking the intoxicant in the first place. Passage through the Six Esoteric Gateways are earned via spiritual qualification based on an individual seeker's *sadhana,* wherein pure, conscious Awareness is the only Bliss he will accept.

To explain the existence of others worlds, which are beyond the physical, all lying inside of the mind's infinite expanse of dream power, the chart on the facing page is given. The appearance on earth of eukaryotes, chordates, tetrapods, mammals, and primates, all leading up to the fifteen million year march of the hominidae — at least as the generally accepted scientific evolution theory would have it — has all taken place in what the seers call the *bhutakasha,* or physical world. They have seen and cited four other *akashas* (types of space) holding worlds of subtle energy (*prana/psychic prana*), worlds of desire-based thought, worlds of intelligent power, and ending or consummating in pure Consciousness, or "Spirit." The inward moving graph of this order lies on and up the left hand side of the chart under study.

Generally speaking, the *bhutakasha* holds the human and subhuman species, the *pranakasha* holds the ancestors and celestials, the *chitakasha* holds the gods and goddesses, or deities, the *jnanakasha* holds the luminaries and the Trinity, and the *Chidakasha* holds nothing whatsoever that partakes of form (or name, time, space, and causality, i.e., *maya*). The latter *akasha* is *Brahman,* All-Mighty Father, Allah, YHWH, *Tathagatagarbha, Chaitanya* — also called by other fine Names, often to sacred to utter. Every realm other than the last is a marvelous projection of thought and thinking at various levels of intensity (vibration/*vrttis*), a mass collective mental dream of the Mind (*Mahat*). If put into partitions, this dream occurs on cosmic, collective, and individual levels. These are the famous "Three Worlds" in *Vedic* philosophy. In the *Kundalini Yoga* system, these very realms are described in terms of seven *chakras,* as the forthcoming chart will reveal.

At the level of the *bhutakasha,* as shown on the bottom of the chart under scrutiny, it can be seen that all that comes forth there is born of solar rays. It is a sun-drenched projection, which is why the chart on page 752, revealing the sun-god, *Surya,* is interesting of note. The "heavenly ascension" that represents the next level of vibration is merely the soul's abandonment of the physical plane (of the mind) and the taking on of an etheric body that is suited for that "kingdom of heaven" that is under the sway of the *prana* rather than matter. The sun that supports life on earth has there taken on its etheric form as well, shining rays of sweet thought and conceptual happiness on the angelic beings who frequent that *akasha,* or *loka.*

But the next level of this grand dream projection, now falling more under the behest of *Shakti* rather than *prana,* has a sun that spreads wisdom rays throughout it. Souls there are divinely oriented, and accustomed to thought vibrations that have gotten refined into pure intelligence. Peace and Bliss are the foods ingested there, for these beings of Light can gaze upon with subtle senses internal wonders such as the *Mahat, Ishvara,* The Divine Couple *Siva* and *Shakti,* and The Word. All dreaming is fast coming to an end there, in the *Jnanakasha.* All desires except one have long since returned to the cosmic ignorance that birthed them, and the one aim for such beings who are still holding a tiny vestige of form is to "Go to God," dissolve into *Brahman.* The Peace that passeth all understanding and the Bliss that is unalloyed and uninterrupted is imminently accessible, and all beings fully present There only want to know, "I am That."

As the quote at the top of the chart just being concluded (page 762) states, argumentation about principles such as birth, death, creation, destruction, and the like — whether coming from dualistic religions or from contemporary science — are futile. When, as the Indian *rishis* have found, while setting down their sacred footsteps throughout all of the four exterior *akashas*, that Reality is Divine, is unoriginated *(ajati)*, is free of all transformations *(aparinama)*, is acreate *(asrsti)*, and is able to break Itself into distinctions and partitions via Its *Shakti* power without ever being touched or defiled *(asparsha)*, then why do such concerns occupy or bother the otherwise peaceful mind at all?

Earlier, in the chart on the Six Esoteric Gateways, a mention of the "Single Eye" was made. The chart back on page 553 allows the reader to receive teachings on this penultimate *"chakra,"* or *"Lotus."* The chart on the facing page will afford a richer look at all seven *chakras,* belonging to *Kundalini Shakti* Herself, Whose finest and best teachings will round out this book.

Pure Sentiency penetrates all levels of being, though It is hidden on the physical plane, *"...like oil in sesame seeds, or patina in copper,"* states the *Upanisads.* In the case of the *Kundalini Yoga* system this Sentiency collects like honey in what are refered to as *chakras.* As the quote on the top of the chart relates, mankind's inner sheaths, all made up of the *tattvas* that consist of the materials of unmanifested and manifested *prakriti,* provide grounds upon which these living, whirling spiritual vortexes lie and function, like seven splendid cities all sprawled out across vast desert sands, each one more and more refined than the last. Even the lowest, the *Muladhara,* connected with the physical realm, is divine, for Mother *Kundalini* has taken up secret residence there, awaiting Her time of rising for an auspicious moment, in inward ascension fashion. Mother's esoteric symbol of four red petals, connected by a seed *bijam,* and overseen by the Guardian deity, *Brahma,* provides an external sign of what lies deep within this lotus. Esoteric multi-dimensional diagrams with powerful letters mark the entrance into and existence of these subtle centers, seven in number — though the seventh is not really a center at all, but a *"....boundless expanse."*

The second lotus, *Svadhisthana,* with its mystic emblem the crescent moon, shines like glistening gold, and vibrates drunkenly with an orotund sound that signals the rising of primal awareness from its hidden abode below and within. The Divine Couple as *Vishnu* and *Rakini,* grace the region, and inspire the awakened *shakti* power to lift Itself, on subtle vital airs, to Her next purchase point in the *Manipura.* A downwards-facing *trikona* represents this center. The powerful masculine and feminine forces of *Rudra* and *Lakini* preside and are worshipped there.

At the heart, the *Anahata Chakra* gleams with its twelve shimmering green petals on a scarlet flame-like Lotus. This is where the "Ocean of Nectar" *(Ananda Sagara)* begins, states Sri Ramakrishna, the Great Master. The intrepid spiritual wayfarer who reaches this radiant realm, with its redolent Lotus, transcends the need for rebirth in any of the three lower worlds.

Continuing to rise, like a hot-air balloon into clear blue skies, the fifth Lotus is encountered, the *Vishuddha Chakra.* Its entrance is a beautiful silver crescent, surrounded by sixteen silver petals of scintillating smokey hue and quality. It is here where, in a secret chamber, the world of space and time dissolves for the deeply meditating *yogi* and *yogini.*

With the advent of dissolution the "show" is over, and the sixth center, the *Ajna Chakra,* illustrate this well. Two violet petals are suspended here, and the primal *bijam,* AUM, hums like a hive of huge, black bumble bees. When Consciousness reaches this inmost post of refuge, Its only wish is to look out on the play of life on all other levels as Witness. This is the "Single-Eye experience heard tell about by highest the seers.

Beyond that, in the *Sahasrara Chakra,* a "thousand" petals display themselves on the infinite flower of nondual Awareness. Colors there are none, and seeds disappear completely. *Paramasiva* and *Kundalini* Herself are There, for She has reached the Supreme Abode of Her Lord, Who is the fullness of All-Pervasive Awareness Itself. Gazing with single vision into this spaceless Space, countless illumined souls sing about Them, and That, with angelic voices choked with divine emotion:

The Kundalini Shakti and Her Chakras

Thou art the Primal Power, O Mother, She whose senses are controlled. The yogis meditate on Thee as Uma, great Himalaya's daughter. Thou who art the power of Siva, put to death my ceaseless cravings. Grant that I never fall again into the ocean of this world. Mother, Thou art the Primal Power, Thou, the five cosmic principles. Who can ever hope to know Thee, who art beyond all principles? Only for Thy bhakta's sake dost Thou assume Thy various forms. But when Thy devotee's five senses merge in the five subtle elements, Mother, it is Thyself alone that he beholds as formless Truth.

Sahasrara Chakra
Symbol: Lotus
Petals: Thousand
Seed: None
Deity: Siva
Shakti: Kundalini

Highest of all, within the head, the soul-enthralling center is where shines the thou-sand-petalled lotus, Mahadeva's dwelling place. Having ascended to His Throne, O Spouse of Siva, sit beside Him!

7

> *"Whirlpools of dynamic energy which congeal the potent spiritual awareness of Kundalini Shakti, the chakras permeate the etheric, subtle, and causal bodies of mankind which are made up of unmanifested prakriti/"*
> *Babaji Bob Kindler*

Ajna Chakra
Symbol: Triangle
Petals: Two Violet
Seed: Om
Deity: Siva/Shakti
Shakti: Hakini

6

And higher yet, between the eyebrows, blossoms the lotus of two petals, where the mind of man remains a prisoner and past controlling; from this flower one desires to watch the sportive play of life.

Vishuddha Chakra
Symbol: Silver Crescent
Petals: Sixteen Blue
Seed: Ham
Deity: Panchavakra Siva
Shakti: Shakini

Above, in the throat, is the sixteen-petalled lotus of smokey hue; there lies concealed a subtle space, transcending which one perceives the universe in space dissolve.

5

Anahata Chakra
Symbol: Circle
Petals: Twelve Green
Seed: Yam
Deity: Ishama Rudra
Shakti: Kakini

4

Beyond them lies the Lake of Nectar, in the region of the heart, where the twelve-petalled lotus flower enchants the eye with scarlet flame. When Thou dost open it, O Mother, touching it with Thy Lotus Feet, the age-long darkness of the heart instantly scat-ters at Thy sight.

Manipura Chakra
Symbol: Triangle
Petals: Ten Yellow
Seed: Ram
Deity: Rudra
Shakti: Lakini

3

At the navel is manipura, the blue ten-petalled lotus flower; through the pathway of Sushumna Thou dost ascend and enter there. O Lady of the lotuses, in lotus blos-soms Thou dost dwell.

Awakening

Longing

Knowledge

Worship

Svadhisthana Chakra
Symbol: Crescent Moon
Petals: 6 Orange
Seed: Vam
Deity: Vishnu
Shakti: Rakini

2

Above it lies the Svadhisthana where the four-petalled lotus blooms. There also Thou dost make Thy home. O mystic power of Kundalini, in the four petals of that flower and in Vajrasana's six petals.

Muladhara Chakra
Symbol: Yellow Square
Petals: 4 red
Seed: Lam
Deity: Brahma
Shakti: Dakini

1

Mother, in every living creature Thou dost have Thy dwelling-place. As Kundalini Thou dost live in the Lotus of the Muladhara.

Thy Name, I have heard, O Consort of Siva, is the destroyer of our fear. And so on Thee I cast my burden; Save me, O kindly Mother. Out of Thy Womb the world is born, and Thou it is who dost pervade it. Art thou Kali? Art Thou Radha? Who can rightly say?

Spiritual Transformation & The Goddess

"When everything melts away, it is then that pralaya comes. At that time I abide with Brahman, latent in It. When the worlds are projected again in a new cycle, I become Sri, Buddhi, Dhriti, Smriti, Shraddha, Medha, Daya, Lajja, Kshudha, Trishna, Kshama, Akshama, Nidra, Tandra, Jara, Ajara, Vidya, Avidya, Shakti, Ashakti, etc. It is I who become Para, Pashyanti, Madhyama, and Vaikari, and I flow through the 35 millions of nadis located in the sacred human form."

Bhagavati Durga Devi

Moksha

Kaivalya

Brahman

AUM   Atman   HRIM

Viveka

Vairagya

Ekagra

Amrita

Raga

Nirvikalpa (Asamprajnata)

Savikalpa (Samprajnata)

Jivatman

Mantra

Ajativada

Nirguna

Saguna

Gunas

Aparinama

Iccha

Shraddha

Jnana

Advaita   Vichara

Isvara   Avatar

Kriya

Dravya

Shishya

Satyam

Ahimsa

Brahma-Jnana

Prana

Prema-Bhakti

Astika

Nastika

Kripa

Sadhana

Pramana

Devi Padam

Kundalini Shakti & Chakras

Sharanagata

Prakasha Vikshepa Avarana

Dharma

Brahma   Vishnu

Nama   Rupa   Desha   Kala   Nimitta

Lokas   Puja   Siva   Bhajan   Lokas

Shatsampat

Purusharthas

Unmanifested Prakriti
Twenty-four Tattvas

Shabda

Yajna

Vidya

Manifested Prakriti
Panchakarana

Annam

Akasha

Pancha Indriyas/Bhutas

Is Goddess Kundalini merely the Consort of Shiva?
She alone flows through the six lotus centers of the precious human body,
guiding the mystical ascension of humanity.
Mother Kundalini is the Supreme Reality encountered in the thousand-petal lotus
at the culmination of the spiritual journey.
She is the sublime Warrior Goddess, the dynamic Truth
Who destroys countless forms of the Ego-Enemy as She stands naked, with strength and grace,
upon the Heart of Shiva, Who is the Awareness of Absolute Unity.
Gaze into Her dazzling Darkness; can you comprehend Her actions?
What conventional queen dances fiercely on the breast of her king?
This poet is bewildered and proclaims: "Mother's ecstatic Play is sheer Mystery.
Struggle to fathom Her, o mind, with every fiber of your energy.
Your intelligence will be purified, but you will never understand Her."

The final chart of this book lies on the facing page and, fittingly, is about the overall comprehensiveness of the *Mahashakti, Mahamaya.* Arranged cross Her august Form are many entries that make up a part of the Wisdom Teachings which She represents and transmits. So many of these, if not all of them, have been outlined and explained in the preceding chapters. Nevertheless, it would make for a fitting conclusion to mention all of them in the context of a kind of brief review which will also act as a reference guide for looking back to locate and reconsider both the charts and the many teachings themselves. For this we can start from the bottom of the chart on the facing page and work our way to the top.

All the *dharmic* entries here fall nicely into the three stages of Indian Philosophy (See chart on page 379), namely the dualistic (*dvaita*), the qualified nondualistic (*visishtha-advaita*), and the nondualistic (*advaita*). Really, the philosophies of every religious tradition of the world fall into one of these three subdivisions. This has always been the case for the objective-seeing seer, and as Swami Vivekananda put it in this day and age, during his most recent incarnation (1863-1902), *"Now I will tell you my discovery. All of religion is contained in the Vedanta, that is, in the three stages of Vedantic philosophy, the dvaita, vishishtadvaita and advaita; one comes after the other. These are the three stages of spiritual growth in mankind. Each one is necessary. This is the essential of religion. The Vedanta applied to the various customs and ethnic creeds of India, is Hinduism. The first stage, dvaita (dualism), applied to the ideas of the ethnic groups of Europe, is Christianity; as applied to the semitic groups, Mohammedanism. The advaita (nondualism) as applied in its yoga-perception form is Buddhism, etc. Now by religion is meant the Vedanta; the applications must vary according to the different needs, surroundings and other circumstances of different nations. Dualist, qualified monist, monist, shaiva, vaishnava, shakta, even the Buddhist and the Jain and others — whatever sects have arisen in India are all at one in this respect: that infinite power is latent in this jivatman (individualized soul); from the ant to the perfect man there is the same Atman in all, the difference being only in manifestation."*

With this stated and clarified, the chart on the facing page can offer up its beneficial aspects at all these three levels. At the lower left-hand corner, amongst all the *puja* articles, is seen the bell. It represents *shabda*, or divine sound. *Brahman* as sound, or vibration, is the emphasis here, and by vibration is meant not just the vibrations of atomic particles that underlie the constant change going on in the physical world, but subtler and subtler vibrations that cover the realms of life-force, mind and its thought, intelligence and its levels of knowledge, and especially higher Consciousness where all vibration ceases in *samadhi,* or *nirvana.* This path of *Shabda Brahman* epitomizes one of complete permeation, or saturation of all worlds by fully-conscious Awareness. Therefore, almost any teaching taken up in this book is fit to contemplate under Its comprehensive heading. To begin, all the charts on **mantra** (page, 131-143) can be reviewed and studied, as well as charts on thought as vibration — as in **samskaras** and general cause and effect (pages 167-172) — should be inspected. For more on this well-documented, highly-preferred path, many of them specific to **The Word** *(AUM)*,

Its seed words of power *(bijams)* that project or "create" worlds and objects, and the **prana** and subtle (psychic) *prana* that carries Its effects outwards, see the charts found on pages 33, 157, 323, 360, 421, 501, 503, 513, 533, 536-548, 595, 612, 624, 626, 630, 633, 652, 679, 749, and 761 — to name just a few that are more specific to the principle of vibration that is represented on the chart (presently under scrutiny) by the bell, *ghanta*.

Next to the bell is the water pot, a kind of *kosha*. It symbolizes space, or *akasha* in Sanskrit. Both time and space are ultimately illusory, as has been explained in many ways in this book, due to their being products of the mind, i.e., they do not exist and are never detected outside of the mind, beyond the mind. It is fitting that the *kosha* be placed right next to the bell, then, as the two have an intrinsic connection in *maya*, or in providing the foundation for the manifestation (mental projection) of names and forms (which are empty of substance but permeated by essence). As an important aside here, it can already be seen how important worship, or *puja*, is to Indian *dharma* and spirituality, in that every article, as well as the actions utilized in handling and making offerings to the deities, is not only fraught with significance, but actually represents Divine Reality appearing in form (by way of association). For charts on **akasha** and its important concomitants, both inner and outer — see pages 30, 190, 200, 267, 321, 327, 329, 349, 360, 363, 373, 375, 463, 529, 531, 548, 587, 595, 654, 716, 751.

Moving across the bottom of the reference chart (on page 766) we espy the five-flamed burner *(panch-arati puja* lamp) used in worship of the deities. Its higher designation is *vidya*, or knowledge. The light it sheds removes darkness and also connects with the higher wisdom present in the minds of the deities and illumined souls. From candle flame, to firefly, to campfire, to the moon, to the sun, light manifests more intensely by degrees. But we must not stop here if we want to become a knower of origins (so that we can reach the Originless *Brahma*n). From the sun, then, to billions of suns, then to the thoughts of the Great Ones which are all blazing suns of higher awareness that light up the inner worlds for perceiving — and finally to the Light of pure, conscious Awareness — all of this is stored, mystically, in the arati lamp. Since knowledge, *vidya*, is also the best purifier according to the seers, the charts on purification, *shuddhi*, will also be listed here. Overall, charts that indicate this profound principle are, again, to numerous to cite, but the ones most pertinent to the connections between *fire, thought, purification, and intelligence*, are to be found on pages 119, 125, 206, 225, 229, 231, 271, 272, 276, 293, 299, 333-339, 357, 381, 385, 419, 439, 495, 501, 513, 519, 550, 553, 564, 569, 595, 600, 635, 636, 647, 657, 670, 685, 719-21, 724, 728, 731, 744, 752, and 755.

The last *puja* item at the bottom of the chart under scrutiny is the sanctified rice offering, or *annabhoga*. It symbolically represents food to appease the ancestors, gods, and demigods, which takes no great leap of understanding, yet the many levels of food, and food's subtle significance overall, have escaped detection by most of the world's living beings over time. Even the organics movement of modern times has failed to see beyond the aspect of bodily health into the deeper causes and meanings, both positive and negative, of the principle of food. The first lesson is that all food must be offered, consciously, before it is taken. Food not offered on the physical plane retains its defects and contributes to illness, while food not offered in the knowledge of giving it to the inner deities cheats the same of their due in the life of the world, and worlds. The successive lessons on food, so well explained in India's scriptures, involve such indispensable education as the awakening of *Kundalini Shakti* at the root center *(muladhara)* at the base of the spine, and how She is drawn upwards utilizing spiritual practices performed by the energy *(prana)* gotten from sanctified food, or *prasad*. *Prana* has its own category to study, and so does Kundalini Shakti, but the charts that pertain to *food* specifically are to be found on pages 233, 235, 237, 423, 453, 493, 545, 581, and 584.

On the very bottom of the chart under study (page 766) are listed to *pancha* teachings of imminent import, they also being overlooked in the sense of being taken for granted by living beings. As the ground upon which all the aforementioned puja articles are sitting, the *pancha indriyas* and *pancha bhutas* are simply the five senses and the five elements of nature. These are two of the primal sets of quintuplications that life in bodies in the various worlds are based upon. Knowing them as causes and effects, i.e., their connections to one another, is what is missing in the world. That earth comes from smell, water from taste, fire from sight, air from touch, and ether from hearing is rare knowledge, even though not very deep knowledge to spiritually conscious beings. Meditating upon these supports (*alambanas*) opens up inner knowledge and inner realms, both. The charts pertinent to these ten lynch-pins of **triple world, triple body cosmology** can be viewed and studied on pages 151, 161, 164, 194, 349, 359, 417, and 519.

Another important article that sits on the floor of Mother's temple is the *yoni*. The *yoni* is the cosmic womb of shakti power within or upon which Lord Siva sits. Both Manifested *Prakriti* and Unmanifested *Prakriti* are designations assigned to it, and *yajna*, sacrifice, is also a fitting moniker as well. *Prakriti* is nature, of course. Since most beings are not aware of the existence of Unmanifested Nature, all systems of learning and knowledge in this world, except those singular Indian *darshanas*, stop dead in their tracks, remaining ever stuck on the external level of phenomena, both fascinated with appearances and devoid of any conclusive explanation for any of them. That a tree comes from a seed, and that tree produces more trees with more seeds, seems to be enough for limited thinkers to cogitate upon. This limited circular reasoning is widened considerably when the fact that both seed and tree come from a subtle seed is comprehended. This seed is called a thought. Objects are just thought made concretized. This is why the path of vibration is so important to study, and not only on a physical level, either. Those charts have been listed earlier. For teachings pertaining to **Prakriti** in its two forms, as well as on **yajna**, sacrifice, one can seek out the charts on pages 45, 47, 56, 321, 349, 451, 493, 495, 507, 511, 529, and 749.

Just above the *yoni*, but still on the floor of Divine Mother's temple, are a few fragrant flowers that have been offered. They have been titled *lokas*, which means worlds — whole collections of worlds. As usual with Mother India, worlds are not restricted to planets in outer space. Looking back on the charts just cited on *akasha*, which is space on many levels, we find that in the five *akashas*, also called the seven *vyahrtis*, there are many **lokas**. Thus, voluminous sets of worlds are strewn, like flowers, across divisions of space, both outer and inner. This expansive view of the many realms set in multidimensional space (all contained in the Great Mind) is best comprehended by viewing the charts on pages 30, 297, 327, 360, 363, 373, 375, 455, 457, 463, 507, 515, 529, 531, 548, 587, 595, 600, 617, 633, and 752.

Tracing our way up the middle of the main reference chart on page 766, we find the Goddess sitting on a raised dais. This platform has received its fivefold assignment in symbolic form. *Nama, rupa, desha, kala,* and *nimitta* are the main ingredients of *maya*, expressly, name, form, time, space, and cause & effect. These five constitute the main powers of Her enchanting projection. The individual soul, incarnating as it is in lower realms of matter, must penetrate this stultifying force of *maya* by coming to know, "from a distance," what its five veils consist of, and how they function. Then they can, as this chart reveals, move from these base, insentient stations to Her blissful, sentient Presence. The words, "from a distance," spoken by Sri Ramakrishna, indicate that embracing the worlds of matter and objects in ways that are based in enjoyment, via covetousnesss, with expectation, courting fulfillment of desires, or accompanied by attachment, will lead to bondage rather than liberation. To observe *maya* as a witness rather than a participant is the requirement for associating with it and being able to extract oneself from it after the experiences of life, which are "fleeting," as the seers state, are over. Much more can be written about this process of processes, but we can let the many illustrations and teachings in this book do the talking for us, using the charts on **maya/samsara** and its **gunas** on pages 41, 45, 56, 103, 116, 119, 197, 200, 221, 223, 240, 247, 249, 251, 275, 279, 294, 297, 307, 359-60, 441, 457-59, 513, 550, 569, 571-77, 600, 633, 636, 649, 652-62, 685, 721, 751, and 755.

Two, tall ghee-wick lamps stand in front of the Divine Mother's sacred platform, one labeled *puja* and the other, *bhajan*. These are sometimes called the "two alluring offerings," for they beckon Divine Mother and bring Her out of hiding. To do external worship, daily, is what the seers call the best austerity for the body, for it fuses the heart and mind and purifies the emotions. The participant in such joyful occasions will spontaneously voice their effects in sacred song, or *bhajan*. The charts referencing the two spiritual activities of **puja** and **bhajans** and their concomitants can be found on pages 103, 122, 357, 429, 471-79, 497, 559, 561, 675, and 737.

Next in order of ascension on the chart (page 766), though not necessarily philosophically speaking, is The Trinity, whose august names — *Brahma, Vishnu,* and *Siva* — form a *trikona* that straddles the base of Divine Mother's raised dais and intersects with the *yoni* wherein *Siva* finds his base. They cover *maya* in the respect that all of name and form originate in them, from the causal to the subtle to the gross realms. Their *maya* is *Mahamaya,* the Mother's own sweet and redolent realms of blissful play and highest *sattvic* purity. They are God in form, par excellence. Charts pertinent to **The Trinity** and Its offshoots and connections can be found on pages 41, 106, 227, 357, 359, 369, 371, 387, 431, 465-69, 473, 481, 485, 489-90, 497, 507, 526, 597, 600, 603, 617, 662, 675, 677, 701, 703, 715, 716, and 723-24.

Straight up from The Trinity's *trikona*, on the hem of the Divine Mother's garment, is the word *sharanagata*, which signifies sincere self-surrender. The idea is that the freedom-seeking soul may reach and attain very high heavens in its quest for liberation (*moksha*), but the most priceless spiritual attributes and principles may still remain far from his or her grasp without the full and complete surrender of the ego to the Divine. The assignment directly above *sharanagata*, namely *Devi-Padam*, the Feet of the Goddess — signifies the full refuge of the soul that will protect it from any further antics by the divisive mind/ego complex, whose potentially troublesome tendencies may still be lying unripe in the interior of the mind as hidden seeds. Charts pertinent to the important principles of **sharanagata** and **padam** are to be found and studied on pages 91, 271, 365-67, 443, 469-71, 475-76, 479, 509, and 555.

Coursing up the middle of the chart on page 766, and looking to the right of the entree just reviewed, titled *Devi Padam,* we see a conch shell sitting on one of the tall ghee-lamps, sporting the title of *dharma*. *Dharma* has a huge significance for today's world and its people, for it signifies the bounteous wealth of spiritual teachings from saints, sages, and seers, that are the only real solution to the pervasive ignorance of the contemporary mind, resulting in suffering. Morality and ethics, altruistic works and daily duties, singing and dancing, applying oneself to secular education, protesting injustices and working in political arenas, etc., none of these have the overall long-lasting and salubrious effect that *dharma* confers, once its content is thoroughly imbibed from an illumined preceptor. To be born into this world with parents who will teach one the *dharma* constitutes one of the greatest blessings possible in a human birth, for it will culminate in the freedom of the soul from all purposeless wandering and transmigration and set the soul once and for all in the firm foundation of peace and equanimity. Since enough has been said about *dharma* throughout the pages of this book, and almost every chart herein is either permeated with **dharma** or infers it, a review of the charts associated specifically with it and its import can be found on pages 109, 202-04, 315-17, 341-43, 357, 377, 435, 443, 445, 447, 481, 522, 524, 531, 575, 578, 603, 607, 609, 630, 665, 666, 670, 677-79, 680, 703, 709, 724, and 744.

The long, fragrant garland that encircles the Divine Mother of the Universe has several special assignments etched upon it. At the center, at Her navel, is one of exceptional import, again, to the people of this day and time. When Jesus stated that *"Man does not live by bread alone,"* He was not necessarily referring to either gross matter or the All-Mighty Spirit, but to *prana*. Unseen and unknown for the most part, it courses through, or causes to course through, all manner of energy on all levels of life and existence. In its gross form, again mostly unnoticed, it supports nature and the bodies of all beings, but its subtle form, as psychic *prana*, moves the thoughts of all minds, from Cosmic Mind down to the individuals that inhabit the inner and outer worlds. It has been called the web of Shakti, for through it the Divine Mother of the Universe can detect every movement, however slight, in every aspect of Her massive and marvelous projection. More charts that outline or heavily infer the presence of **prana** and its manifold functions are to be found on pages 19, 21, 172, 233-35, 237, 417, 423, 453, 459, 515, 529, 531, 536-545, 581, 583, 619-21, 624, 660, 715, and 752.

A further word on *prana,* as well as on the *tanmatras* (subtle elements which are the causes for the five elements), is that these two principle *tattvas* were proclaimed to be missing from all systems of Western thought, religion, and philosophy according to Swami Vivekananda when he arrived in America and inspected its knowledge bases. Even science and, unfortunately, medicine, have little to no concept of its presence other than by way of its outer effects only. Simply put, if *prana* were taken into account, then healing the body's and mind's many potential ills would be almost natural via conscious breathing. If the *tanmatras* were cognized and connected outside to nature and inside to the collective mind, then the inner realms would be perceived and the dream state of mankind could be seen as the kingdoms of heaven within. With these two fivefold, even ten-fold *tattvas* having gone missing in today's ideologies, embodied beings live only on the outside, in matter, their only recourse to any form of "inside" being examining the body (Western science and medicine) and conjecturing about the brain (Western psychology) while the vast and expansive interior fields of mind and intelligence — what to speak of the essential principle of pure, conscious Awareness, Existence Itself, — remain either undetected and unexplored, or flatly denied.

Coursing on in our conclusive inspection of this book's contents utilizing the chart on page 766, the two attributes on either side of *prana* are *kripa* and *sadhana,* grace and spiritual self-effort. It is fitting that these two lie close together, for it is taught in Vedantic circles that the soul will not awaken and begin the spiritual journey without the grace of the Divine. It may not seem this way at the outset, since people feel that it is by their own will or intuition that they suddenly get transported into realms of higher thinking, but later, when higher understanding dawns, they acknowledge this fact. Inner leanings from past lifetimes also play into this divine play, called good *karma,* and in alignment with what is termed auspicious timing by the seers. So, **grace** is most often a hidden facet of life and spiritual evolution. It is to be inferred by looking back, in most all cases. But spiritual self-effort, *sadhana,* is not so hidden, though it is often underestimated and under-utilized, to be sure. Charts on these two naturally coalesced attributes, particularly **sadhana,** are to be found on pages 41, 59, 65, 84, 103, 125, 135, 176, 197, 213, 271, 276, 339, 341-43, 345, 355, 357, 365-67, 383, 389-93, 396, 399-407, 411, 415, 417-21, 427-35, 439, 441, 443, 471, 473-76, 479, 481, 493-95, 497, 503, 505, 509, 511, 515, 519, 535, 545, 557, 559, 564, 571-72, 577, 578, 583, 584, 589, 595, 597-98, 609, 611, 614, 619-21, 622, 626, 636-38, 645, 657, 659-69, 685, 693, 715, 719, 751, and 755.

On the chart under study on page 766, directly above the principle of *prana* lies *shraddha,* at the Divine Mother's Heart, and directly above that, at Her Throat, lies *mantra.* These two, the sacred utterance and the faith it requires to fructify, are fittingly matched as well. For faith, all the charts in chapter eight (465-497) can be taken up, but it should be known, if it is not already obvious, that the Indian *rishis* had, and have, an intense fealty to *jnanam* as well. For the principle of **mantra,** its sacred seeds and syllables, additional charts on the following pages can be consulted: pages 131, 133, 135, 140, 142, 144, 146, 154, 157, 323, 533, 561, 584, 619-21, 624, 626, 629, 630, 633, 665, and 679.

Remaining at the center of the chart before taking up the principles on the sidelines, among the hosts of wisdom and devotional assignments we behold the Divine Mother's four arms, indicative of the four main powers of Shakti. The are *iccha, jnana, kriya,* and *dravya* — Divine Will, Supreme Wisdom, Spontaneous Activity, and Infinite Productivity. She has many sub-*shaktis,* or lesser powers, but these four cover the gamut of Her abilities most completely. For teachings on this, and on the **Mahashakti's Divine Forms** overall, we can refer to the charts on pages 293, 365-67, 369, 451, 463, 481, 483, 522, 548, 555-59, 619-21, 630-33, 645, 654, 680, and 683.

In the Divine Mother's hands She holds several divine objects, all having deep significances. First, on her shoulder sits a parrot, which represent the *jiva,* or embodied soul. In Her right and left upper hands She reveals a small shell that charms the parrot, and a container of divine elixir She feeds it on. Grasped in her two lower hands are seen a bouquet of flowers and a stalk of sugar cane, the former signifying the many souls that love Her, and the latter representing the seven worlds with their seven centers found in the *Kundalini Yoga* system of India — all laying within the very being of the precious human Soul. For charts laying out the esoteric wisdom of these principles, pertaining to devout or awakening souls, the attraction they feel for the Divine, the essence of Bliss that lies within them, and the ability to sport in the Seven Lotuses (**chakras**) that lie within them, refer to the charts on pages 47, 56, 164, 186, 293, 335-37, 359-63, 365-67, 369, 375, 463, 467, 469, 481, 483, 535, 555-59, 584, 587-93, 619-21, 633, 638, 645, 654, 680, 683-85, and 737.

At the *ajna chakra*, or "third eye" of the Blessed Goddess, is the word *ekagra*, signifying the one-pointedness of fully concentrated Mind. Above it, laid upon the two precious jewels in Her crown, are the assignments **viveka** and **vairagya**, the all-powerful aspects of authentic spiritual self-effort (*sadhana*) meaning discrimination between the Real and the unreal, and detachment from the latter. For charts specific to these valuable divine attributes of spiritual life coveted highly by the seers both in principle and in practice, see the charts on pages 19, 21, 65, 116, 125, 161, 172, 176, 180, 192, 221-23, 225, 227, 239, 231, 233-35, 237-40, 247-49, 251, 253, 255, 260-62, 267-69, 272, 276, 279, 293, 294, 297, 299, 303, 309, 333-37, 349, 351, 381, 383, 385, 389, 396, 411, 415, 417-19, 439, 441, 447, 451, 453, 455, 457, 459, 461, 503, 507, 509, 513, 519, 529, 545, 550, 553, 564, 569-77, 587, 593, 598, 600, 611, 614, 636-41, 649, 652, 654, 657, 660, 662, 666, 685, 686, 693, 698, 705, 712, 716, 719-21, 723, 728, 744, 749, 751, and 755.

Above the great principles of viveka and vairagya, at the crown of the Divine Mother's head, are the four principles of *AUM, Hrim, Brahman,* and *Atman*. The charts for *AUM* and *Hrim* have already been listed under the heading of Mantra and The Word. For *Brahman* and *Atman*, it will suffice to cover Them by taking up many of the assignments that lie on the two temple pillars on either side of Mother's raised dais.

The words, *shatsampat* and *purusharthas* appear at the very base of both of these pillars. *Shatsampat* means the Six Jewels which comprise one fourth of the *Sadhanachatustaya* that contains the Four Treasures of *Viveka* and *Vairagya* (just featured), and *Mumukshutvam*, the strong desire for Freedom. These six jewels, which are the third treasure of this system, are inner peace (*sama*), self-control (*dama*), contentedness (*uparati*), forbearance (*titiksha*), advanced meditation (*samadhana*), and faith (*shraddha*). The definitive chart for them is to be found on page 65. The **purusharthas** are the Four Boons of Spiritual Life, and the specific charts for them are to be found on pages 365 & 367.

The next teaching that appears near the lower part of the left hand pillar is the **three powers of maya**, *prakasha, vikshepa,* and *avarana*. They are singularly important because they veil Reality at different levels of density. *Avarana* completely covers, as in the case of form over formlessness. Beings do not perceive formlessness, neither formless nature nor formless Essence (Awareness), due to *avarana's* veiling power of form. It is the very dynamic of blindness and ignorance (*tamas*). As if that were not confusing enough, *vikshepa* is a power (*maya's* power in the mind) that distorts what should otherwise be clear. It takes what is and makes it seem other than it is. It is the very dynamic of delusion (*rajas*). *Prakasha* is lighter, being the revelatory power underlying all things, within all things. It is the very dynamic of understanding and comprehension. The chart that outlines this powerful dharmic teaching is to be found on page 293, and any of the charts pertaining to the three gunas can also be studied it the light of these three powers. They are a special gift of Indian philosophy, not found anywhere else in world religion and philosophy.

Above this triplefold assignment, and still lying next to the left-hand pillar, is the word *pramana*. It refers to the proof or proofs that Indian *darshanas* utilize to reveal the nature of Reality. For a list of several different systems that outline these proofs of existence, the reader can study the chart on the facing page.

As we continue to explore the chart on page 766, and reference the charts in this book, we can see next to *pramana*, and on the left-hand pillar, the word *astika*. Across the page, on the right-hand pillar, is the word *nastika*. **Astika** and **nastika** refer to the two divisions of philosophy in India, the former being of an orthodox leaning, and the latter being nonorthodox. More specifically, the orthodox systems, like *Vedanta*, utilize the *Vedas* and *Upanisads* as their prime authority, whereas systems like Jainism and Buddhism, for instance, though they may utilize the Vedas, do not hold them as their highest authority. A chart that reveals the details of this helpful division is to be seen on page 670.

❖ Six Proofs of Reality In Advaita Vedanta ❖

"Priests, pundits, and other knowers of the Vedas worship various gods. But the Maharishis say that just as the one Ganges manifests herself through many flowing channels, so too does the one Mahashakti express Herself in all deva and devi forms. To come to know this supreme Mahadevi, the best knowers of Truth advise utilizing the seven proofs of the existence of Brahman." Srimad Devi Bhagavatam

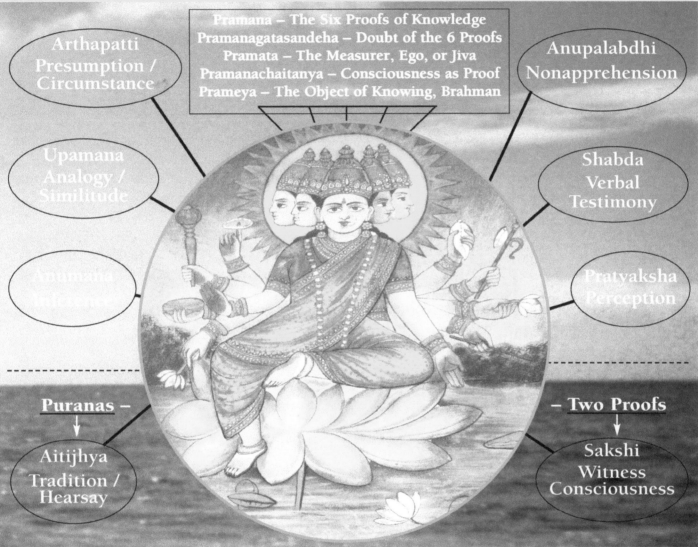

Arthapatti Presumption / Circumstance

Upamana Analogy / Similitude

Anumana Inference

Pramana – The Six Proofs of Knowledge
Pramanagatasandeha – Doubt of the 6 Proofs
Pramata – The Measurer, Ego, or Jiva
Pramanachaitanya – Consciousness as Proof
Prameya – The Object of Knowing, Brahman

Anupalabdhi Nonapprehension

Shabda Verbal Testimony

Pratyaksha Perception

Puranas –
↓
Aitijhya Tradition / Hearsay

– Two Proofs
↓
Sakshi Witness Consciousness

Perception — Direct, immediate cognition, external and internal, by the ten senses
Presumption — Assumption of a known fact in order to account for an unknown fact
Nonapprehension — Non-perception of a thing based upon the perception of the knower
Analogy — Attainment of knowledge by comparison and similarity
Verbal Testimony — Called apya-vakyas, or agama, it means uttered or written statements
Inference — Called "knowing after," it is a way of gaining knowledge from other knowledge

"Knowledge has come to the soul in two ways, i.e., through the instrumentality of the four inner faculties (antahkarana), and through the five states of consciousness (avasthas) that receive their source material from the five senses. Further, knowing is not a self-contained process, for it receives its initiative and its direction from God. God activates the soul and causes it to know in the same way as the soul activates the five organs of sense and causes them to know." Saiva-Siddhanta Darshana

On both sides of the Divine Mother's raised dais hang ghee-wick lamps which are labeled with the principles of *guru* and *shishya,* or teacher and disciple. Indian traditions are very big on this institution, for the fact is that few souls who seek Enlightenment ever find it without first taking recourse to an illumined preceptor. As Swami Vivekananda once wrote, *"Know for certain that without steady devotion for the guru, and unflinching patience and perseverance, nothing is to be achieved."* Further, many of the spiritual organizations in the West today are headed by spurious *gurus* who seek gain instead of God, enterprise instead of Enlightenment, commerce instead of Consciousness, and neither they nor the followers that flock to them in naive fashion or with similar intentions rightly represent the honorable institution of teacher and disciple whose main concern is authentic Spirituality. For charts related to the **guru/shishya principle**, see pages 59, 84, 88, 91, 103, 106, 545, and 675.

Above the ghee-wick lamp that reads *"guru,"* are seen the words *advaita* and *vichara.* Above the lamp on the right hand side that reads *"shishya"* are to be found the words *ishvara* and *avatar.* *Advaita,* nonduality, and *vichara,* intense inspection into Divine Reality, are well aligned with one another, for it is via deep scrutiny under the impulse of seeking freedom from the trammels of nature and form that the sincere soul (*shishya*) arrives at what is truly transcendent. On the other hand, those who are enamored of Divine Forms seek their liberation in God with Form, termed *Ishvara* and *Avatar.* These highest twin goals also appear on the chart under the two lamps, and are called *Brahmajnan* and *Premabhakti.* Charts that reveal **advaita** and **vichara** can be seen and studied on pages 109, 260-62, 265, 269, 271, 303, 335-37, 339, 341, 343, 345, 379, 381, 383-85, 389, 391, 411, 413, 45, 425, 427, 433, 439, 443, 503, 511, 513, 515, 526, 553, 564, 569-71, 578, 595, 597, 598, 600, 603, 604, 609, 622, 636, 638, 642, 647, 657, 665, 669, 686, 689, 691, 693, 701, 705-06, 709, 711-16, 719-21, 727-28, 733, 735, 739, 740-43, 744, 746, 749, 751, 760, and 762. Charts that relate to **Ishvara** and **Avatar** can be viewed and contemplated on pages 103, 106, 227, 371, 387, 465, 467, 469, 481, 483, 485, 489-90, 507, 555, 559, 575, 603, 607, 617, 633, 675, 677, 679, 683, 689, 701-03, 723, 724, 752, and 755.

Above the two upper ghee-wick lamps just studied, and attached to the two inner pillars of Divine Mother's raised dais, are the two assignments of **aparinama** and **ajativada.** These are the two main tenets of nonduality, namely nontransformation and nonorigination. Although they are inferred in several of the qualified nondualistic charts in this book, the main charts specific to these two are to be found on pages 265, 507, 680, 686, 727, 733, 743, 744, and 746.

Finally, and towards the top of the two outer pillars enclosing Divine Mother's raised dais, are the *samadhi* divisions of *nirvikalpa* and *savikalpa.* There can only be one ultimate *Samadhi,* but there are stages of *samadhi* leading to It. This answers the question in many seeker's minds about the attainment of Enlightenment and what it is and what it entails. The soul can be enlightened to a degree if the mind has been purified of root ignorance (*mula-vidya*), particularly about its assumed separation from Brahman. Beyond this freedom from ignorance lies the infinite expanse of pure, conscious Awareness which is inexplicable and must be experienced to be "understood" at the nondual level. As the Great Master, Sri Ramakrishna Paramahamsa, has stated, simply: *"Though a bird may soar high in the skies, there are always higher regions to explore."* Further, speaking about both lower and higher *samadhis,* He stated: *"Though a bird may soar high in the skies, it must eventually come to rest on the branches of a tree."* Charts pertinent to types of **samadhi** can be found on pages 413, 503, 511, 517, 545, 636, 645, 693, 697, 712, 727, and 728. In addition, a six-page list of all the charts is included at the end of the book as well, prior to the Sanskrit Glossary, placed in alphabetical order for ease of location and study.

It is with these handy reference guides to the many "Dharma Art Wisdom Charts" contained in this book that its pages can come to an apt conclusion. But the *dharma* of India is endless. It is also eternal. There can be no definitive or conclusive citing of chronological order for it, its systems, its teachings, or for its seers. Obviously, for the Indian seers, time is not a mere linear affair, but an ongoing series of mentally projected cycles that are stacked atop one another in endless fashion. To them, these illumined *rishis*, there are only two important facets of time to be kept foremost in mind: one, that all of its multi-directional reaches are contained in one eternal moment, no matter how otherwise it may seem; and two, that its existence, whether considered actual or not, is to be utilized for practicing sincere self-effort *(sadhana)* in order to enlighten the lazy and resistant human mind about the presence of Divine Reality and Its all-pervasive, blissful nature.

Viveka-pratyabhijna-sadhana may be a fitting expression for this exquisite spiritual procedure. Once recognizing the Divine Reality *(Brahman/Shakti)* underlying all phenomena, all things, the sincere seeker will draw it out of hiding utilizing the specialized tools of his or her religious path and training — as the dedicated worker will *"extract nutritious oil from sesame seeds."* Separating the wheat from the chaff in this manner, his recognition *(pratyabhijna)* will burgeon, opening the single eye of Wisdom *(jnana chakshu)* which is the unique internal portal into the Highest Reality.

This is beyond time, and transcendent of all practices — the only "practice" left to do for the spiritually awakened embodied soul is to remain aware of the *Sanatana Dharma* and spread it among sleeping humanity by divine example.

AUM Shanti, Shanti, Shantih — Peace, Peace, Peace.
May Peace be unto us, may Peace be unto all.

Charts in Alphabetical Order

	Page	Chapter
108 Upanisads, The	524	9
3 States, 7 Limbs, and 19 Mouths of the Individual	149	3
Advaita Vedanta's Pillar of Axioms	691	10
Ahimsa in Jainism	447	7
Ajativada: Nonorigination	746	10
Akasha — The Five Atmospheres	30	2
All Hail, Surya Narayan!	752	10
Ancient Chest of Consciousness, The	451	7
Aparinama — The Principle of Nontransformation	265	6
Appearance of the Puryastaka Body, The	194	4
Asana and Pranayama in Tantric Yoga	583	9
Asparsha Yoga — The "Non-touch" Yoga, According to Gaudapada's Karika	727	10
Astika & Nastika	670	9
Atmic and Mayic Sankalpa	269	6
Attainment of Rare Jnana, The	439	7
Binding and Liberating Nature of the Three Gunas of Prakriti, The	223	5
Brahmachakra — The Grand Vedic Wheel	457	7
Brahmapada: How Brahman, Divine Reality, Disports Itself	341	7
Causality, Origins, and Reincarnation	47	2
Cause and Effect in the Mind	172	4
Chain of Rebirth and its Twelve Links (Nidanas) in Buddhism, The	192	4
Chaturdasya Yoga — The Four Yogas	431	7
Chidabhasa — The Reflection of Brahman in the Cosmos	56	2
Chit Shuddhi, Kriya Shuddhi, and Dravya Shuddhi — The Three Kinds of Purity	122	3
Christ the Sannyasin: Key Renunciation Teachings of Jesus of Nazareth	723	10
Controlling the Chitta-vrttis in Yoga	421	7
Controlling the Five Senses in Yoga	417	7
Corrosion of Human Consciousness, The	756	10
Cosmic Involution and Scientific Evolution	762	10
Course of Atmic Realization, The	609	9
Curtain of Nescience/Cloud of Unknowing, The	550	9
Cutting Through Clouds of False Superimposition	657	9
Daigo-Tettei, Grounds of Satori	517	9
Daivi Vak — Divine Sayings	679	10
Dasabhumikas — The Ten Pure Lands	329	7
Desire, Karma, Sanskaras, and Rebirth	184	4
Destruction of Disease, The	235	5
Dharmashrama — The Four Stages of Life	204	4
Different Types of Diksha, Spiritual Initiation	626	9
Disappearance of Ignorance, The	569	9
Dissolved and Crystallized Mind	513	9
Dissolving the Mindstream	503	9
Divisions of the Atman, from the Sri Rama Hrydayam	716	10
Dynamics of Karma Yoga, The	213	4
Early Sankhya Acharyas	449	7
Echelons of Fire	635	9
Eight Devotional Aids of Narada, The	475	8
Eight Limbs of Patanjali's Yoga, The	69	3
Eight Subtle and Eight Visible Forms of Siva, The	371	7
Evolutes, Characteristics, and Limiting Factors of Maya, The	279	6
False Assumptions about the Atman	294	6
Fashioning a Pure and Buoyant Mind	519	9
Five Akashas of Vedanta Philosophy, The	327	7

Five Cosmic Bondages and Three Great Desires, The 240   5
Five Eternal & Essential Facts of Nondual Indian Philosophy................................709   10
Five Eternal Questions, The..116   3
Five Kinds & Twelves Types of Sacrifices, The 495   8
Five Koshas of the Adhara System, The 19   1
Five Modes of the Divine Experiencer (and Their Five Corresponding Kanchukas), The 737   10
Five Sheaths and their Properties, The..21   1
Five States of the Mind Field in Yoga, The..612   9
Five Types of Minds and Intellects in Action, The..353   7
Five Ways to Perfection According to Sri Ramakrishna, The..622   9
Fivefold Strata of Sacrifice (Yajna), The..^{Text}..493   8
Food and Brahman 581   9
Four Boons and The Four Fruits of Life, The..367   7
Four Celebrated Mystical Utterances, The 533   9
Four Clarities of Spiritual Life, The 423   7
Four Forms of Liberation & The Five Divine Moods, The..473   8
Four Levels of Brahman's Subtleties, The..705   10
Four Levels of Knowers of Brahman, The..88   3
Four Main Aspects of Kundalini Shakti 1, The 619   9
Four Main Aspects of Kundalini Shakti 2, The 621   9
Four Noble & Mighty Combats, The..662   9
Four Parts and Eight Glories of Ishvari/Ishvara, The..467   8
Four Plateaus for Approaching Brahman, The 597   9
Four Sensitivities, Four Beneficial Attitudes, & Four Perfections of the Heart, The..479   8
Four Sentinels and The Three Great Sources, The..345   7
Four Stages of Absorption & The Four Stages of Formlessness, The..712   10
Four Stages of Knowledge and Four Phases of the Word, The 154   3
Four Stages of Mantra Practice, The..140   3
Four States & The Vital Breath, The 539   9
Four States of Consciousness & Seven Attributes of Turiya, The 711   10
Four Treasures and Six Jewels, The..65   3
Four Types of Karma, The..210   4
Four Types of Love According to Sri Ramakrishna, The..469   8
Four Ways of Perceiving God in Indian Darshanas, The..703   10
Four Yogas and Their Synthesis, The 433   7
Fourfold Presence and Other Gita Teachings, The..387   7
Fourteen Qualities of a World Teacher..106   3
Fourteen Stages of Upper and Lower Knowledge, The..337   7
From Atomic to Atmic Particles..33   2
Fundamental Facts about the Mantra..131   3
Golden Rules for Sadhana and Transformation of Mind..125   3
Granthis —Knots in the Body/Mind Mechanism 206   4
Great Actor, The Great Enjoyer, and The Great Renouncer, The..641   9
Guide to Gaudapada's Karika..731   10
Hierarchy of Existence in Shavism, The..363   7
Illumination of the Jiva — How the Sharirin Informs the Sharira, The 638   9
Illusory Ego's Projection via Rebirth, The..200   4
Imminent and Transcendent Reality, The 465   8
Incomparable Views of an Advaita Vedantist, The..744   10
India's "Mind Only School" Perspective 749   10
India's Sanatana Dharma 317   7
Inner Meaning of the Mala, The..629   9
Inscrutable Epithets of Brahman..732   10
Insinuation of the Five Kleshas on Spiritual Life, The..419   7

Integral Constitution of the Luminaries, The 675   10
Inward Ascension of the Free Soul 535   9
Jnana Chakshu — The Wisdom Eye 553   9
Jnana Matra, Atom of Wisdom 501   9
Jugyu-No-Zu: The Ten Stages of Ox-Herding 669   9
Jujukai — The Ten Basic Precepts of Buddhism 445   7
Kalpa — The Concept of Time in Vedic Cosmology 39   2
Karma Yoga — The Philosophy of Work 216   4
King Janaka's Song of Victory 441   7
King Svotta's Sankalpa City 297   6
Knowledge, Knower, and That Which is to be Known 339   7
Kundalini Shakti and Her Chakras 765   10
Kundalini Yoga as Mahayoga 645   9
Lack of Spiritual Success & Its Causes 577   9
Lead Us from Lower Truth to Higher Truth 271   6
Lokas, Nadis, and the Transmigration of Souls 548   9
Lord Brahma's Universal Projection 617   9
Mahamudra — The Great Seal 647   9
Mahashakti — The Supporting Force 555   9
Mahavakyas of the World's Avatars 677   10
Mahavakyas of the World's Avatars II 759   10
Makeup of a Samskara and a Samskaraskandha, The 170   4
Manahpranasambandha, Connecting the Living Prana to the Luminous Mind 545   9
Manifested and Unmanifested Prakriti 321   7
Meaning of Maya, The 654   9
Meaning of Objects, The 652   9
Meaning of the Gayatri Mantra, The 630   9
Meditation and Prayer 509   9
Meditation on the Goddess 559   9
Mental Postures that Bind 721   10
Mighty River of the Manifest Brahman, The 459   7
Mind's Release from Rebirth, The 197   4
Mother India's Revealed Scriptures on Earth 522   9
Mother Kali, The Adyashakti 483   8
Narada's Eight Devotional Aids 476   8
Natural Renunciation in Four Phases 598   9
Natural Unity of Vedic Religion and Philosophy, The 315   7
Nine Complacencies and The Eight Great Accomplishments, The 309   6
Nine Limbs of Bhakti According to Sri Ram, The 497   8
Nine Obstacles (Vikshepas/Antarayas) to Yoga, The 255   5
Nine Step Process of Meditation on AUM 157   3
Nine Steps to Perfection, The 303   6
Nine Ways of Dealing with Desire, The 176   4
Nirguna and Saguna Brahman 507   9
Occult Powers & the Raincloud of Virtues, The 660   9
Ocean of Awareness and its Yogic Waves, The 435   7
Om and Hrim — The Two Great Bijas 144   3
Omkara — The Great Cause 323   7
Omkara: The Silent Call of the Hamsa 624   9
Origin and Perpetuation of Disease, The 233   5
Palace with Seven Gates, The 591   9
Palette of Conscious Future Lives, The 614   9
Pancha Bhava — The Five Worshipful Attitudes 471   8
Para & Aparavidya 600   9

Paravairagya & Aparavairagya..698　10
Patanjali's and Shankara's Yoga of the Mind...425　7
Patanjali's Kriya Yoga and the Three Treasures of Patanjala...407　7
Patanjali's Nine Levels of Awareness in Aspirants...409　7
Paths of Action and Inaction, The...427　7
Phases and Permutations of the All-Pervasive Prana..536　9
Phases of the Soul in Relativity..575　9
Points About Brahman According to the Upanisads..607　9
Prakasha Shakti — The Revealing Power..293　6
Prana and the Illusion of Death...543　9
Pratibha — The Power of Intelligence..272　6
Precepts, Points, Practice, and Process of the Vajrayana Path.......................................84　3
Precipitous Ascent into Higher Awareness, The..391　7
Preliminary Practices to Mantra and Meditation...561　9
Prescribed Pathways to Quiescence of Mind...443　7
Principles of Brahman According to the Upanisads..604　9
Process of Embodiment, The..164　4
Process of Neti Neti Leading to Nirvikalpa, The..636　9
Process of Samprajnata to Asamprajnata Samadhi,The...693　10
Progress Towards True Freedom..571　9
Province of the Enlightened: Three Types of Knowledge Samadhis in Advaita Vedanta, The.............728　10
Purusharthas — The Four Fruits of Life, The..365　7
Qualification is King..578　9
Quintessential Quintuplications...461　7
Rebirth and the Refinement of Consciousness..186　4
Ri-Bi — Zen Buddhist Truth Principles...743　10
Role of Food & Prana in Self-Realization, The...584　9
Sacred Bijas of Mantra Science...133　3
Sacred Doctrine of Conjunctions, The...531　9
Sadhana For Purification..564　9
Samskaras in the Human Mind..167　4
Sangai-Yui-Isshin — Three Worlds, One Mind..455　7
Seeded Samadhis of Patanjala, The...697　10
Seer, The Seen, The Unseen, & The Obscene, The...529　9
Seven Causes & Ten Impediments in Kundalini Yoga, The..589　9
Seven Centers & Planes of Awareness and Existence, The..587　9
Seven Descending Steps of Negligence of Brahman, The..253　5
Seven Earmarks of Self-Realization, The...701　10
Seven Great Universal Ideals, The..603　9
Seven Levels of Higher Knowledge in Those Fitted for the Brahman State, The........385　7
Seven Methods for Mastering Awareness, The...393　7
Seven Qualifications and Seven Victories of a Tantric Aspirant, The............................59　3
Seven Sat Chakras of Kundalini Yoga, The...593　9
Seven Spheres, Seven Worlds, Seven Chakras, and Five Koshas, The.........................375　7
Seven Stages of Knowledge in Yoga Vasishtha, The...335　7
Seven Stages of Spiritual Progress in Seven Systems, The..333　7
Seven Steps to Attainment of Kaivalya, The..413　7
Sevenfold Road to Ruination, The..189　4
Shaktadvaitavada — Divine Mother Nonduality...680　10
Shakti Mantra, Kamakala, and the Unity of Siva and Shakti...633　9
Shankara's Doorways to Yoga..415　7
Shankara's Vivekachudamani Siddhanta...526　9
Shuddha, Ashuddha, and Shuddhashuddha Tattvas..119　3
Signs of Battle: Maintaining Spiritual Life in the World..755　10

Singular Prana & Its Five Forms, The..541   9
Siva's Two Shaktis, Four Padas, and Five Functions 369   7
Six Complements & Ten Immutables of Paramatman, The 706   10
Six Esoteric Yogic Gateways: Yoga's Secret of Transcendence, The 761   10
Six Illusory Bodies, The...251   5
Six Passions, Six Transformations, Six Billows, and Eight Fetters, The..............247   5
Six Proofs of Purusha, The...739   10
Six Proofs of Reality in Advaita Vedanta, The....................................773   10
Six Treasures & Six Divine Powers of God, The....................................485   8
Six Ways of Attaining Brahmajnana in Tantra, The 595   9
Six-fold Process of Immersion in Brahman, The....................................715   10
Some Obstacles and Solutions in Spiritual Life 396   7
Spiritual Art of Mental Asana, The 719   10
Spiritual Awakening by Stages...572   9
Spiritual Transmission and the Goddess..766   10
Sri Ramachandra's Discourse of Divine Discontent 227   5
Sri Ramakrishna's Radiant Road to Self-Realization..............................103   3
Srsti Rahasya — Tantra's Secret of Creation......................................463   7
Stages of Dissolution of the Mind in Yoga 511   9
Stainless Cause of the Universe, The...45   2
State and Characteristics of a Jivanmukta, The...................................689   10
Supreme Pathway to the Eternal Moksha, The 343   7
Sword of Discrimination, The...276   6
Synchronicity of Iti Iti and Neti Neti, The.......................................383   7
Tantra's Siva and Shakti 683   10
Tathagatagarbha /Atman — Transparency of the Self 740   10
Teachings on the Bardo States...190   4
Ten Conditions of the Guru/Shishya Relationship, The............................91   3
Ten Divine Articles of Sri Durga, The...557   9
Ten Fundamental Tenets of Sankhya, The...351   7
Ten Major Knots in the Rope of Human Bondage, The 659   9
Thirteen Inherent Characteristics of Atman, The..................................735   10
Thirty-Six Cosmic Principles of Shaivism, The....................................359   7
Thirty-Two Points of the Immortal Dharma, The..................................357   7
Three Bodies and the Five Sheaths, The..453   7
Three Bodies Comprising the Nonself, The..161   4
Three Dispositions of Living Beings, The...237   5
Three Enemies of Reason, The Three Stupefactions, and The Four Deadly Traps, The......249   5
Three Eternal Gateways, The...377   7
Three Gunas of Maya According to Shankara, The.................................221   5
Three Gunas of Nature, The..307   6
Three Levels of Sankalpa/Vikalpa, The...267   6
Three Main Factors in the Attainment of Enlightenment, The......................665   9
Three Matras of AUM in the Mandukyopanisad, The 146   3
Three Pillars of Zen Practice, The 666   9
Three Stages of Indian Philosophy, The..379   7
Three Stages, Three Plateaus, and Three Obstacles, The..........................219   5
Three Types of Bondage and the Three Types of Liberation, The...................299   6
Threefold Fruits, Threefold Causes, and Five Incitements to Action in the Gita, The....355   7
Time and Enlightenment...41   2
Transcending the Six Billows and Six Transformations............................225   5
Transformation of Mind in Mantra Practice......................................142   3
Transmuting the Poison of Relativity Into the Nectar of Immortality..............685   10
Tree of Samsara, The 275   6

Triloka — The Three Worlds...373   7

Trividham Dukham — The Threefold Sorrows of Existence..............................231   5

True Meaning of Moksha/Mukti, The..686   10

True Meaning of Perfection — Siddhi, The..642   9

Truth of the Existence of Suffering (Four Noble Truths & Eightfold Path), The.......229   5

Twelve Higher Spandas of Shaivism, The..360   7

Twelve Levels of Vairagya, Detachment, The...389   7

Twenty Yamas and Niyamas of Tantra, The...403   7

Twenty-Four Cosmic Principles of Sankhya Philosophy, The..............................349   7

Twenty-one Points of Mantra Practice...135   3

Two Complementary Paths, The..429   7

Two Forms and Eight Main Types of Meditation..505   9

Two Main Forms of Desire, The...180   4

Two Yogas of the Matri Avatar, The...481   8

Unique Features of Sri Ramakrishna's Descent, Part 1, The...............................489   8

Unique Features of Sri Ramakrishna's Descent, Part 2, The...............................490   8

Varnashrama — The Four Castes of Life...202   4

Vedanta, Theology, and Science...262   6

Vedantic and Conventional Views of Birth and Death..260   6

Vedantic Secrets of the Scriptures...381   7

Vedic Triputis and Quintuplications...611   9

Vivartopadana /Adhyasa Astitva...751   10

Viveka, Vairagya, Abhyasa, and Sthiti...411   7

Walker of the Skies..515   9

Waves in the Ocean of Mature Universalism...109   3

Wisdom Facets from the Garland of Universality..724   10

Yamas and Niyamas of Patanjali's Yoga, The...399   7

Yogic Connections and Correlations in Meditation Practice................................151   3

Zen Buddhist and Advaita Vedanta Correlations..651   9

Zen Principles and Distractions..649   9

Sanskrit Glossary

Abhasa — Appearance; reflection, as in God/Brahman appearing in the Universe.

Abhava — Devoid of moods; negation; absence, nothingness other than Self.

Abavapadarthas — Examples of things that cannot exist, utilized in Vedanta to explain what is inexplicable – like maya – by way of inference, such as the horn of a hare, or a snake in a rope, etc.

Abhava Yoga — The highest state of Yoga reached by the knowers of nondual Reality.

Abhaya — Fearlessness.

Abhidya — Desire, in Buddhism, being one of the Five Hindrances (nivarana) of mind in its quest to attain meditational stages of absorption.

Abhijnas — In Buddhism, the powers of an illumined Buddha.

Abhinivesha — Fear of death/clinging to life, which is one of the five kleshas in Yoga. It is considered the lowest type of hell to fall into, since the Soul of mankind is birthless and deathless, i.e., Eternal.

Abhyasa Yoga — The path of constant and dedicated practice, well-defined by Lord Krishna in the Bhagavad Gita.

Acharyas — Teachers; preceptors who guide one in the study of the scriptures and spiritual life in general.

Achina — A mythical tree which none have been able to see, which is used as a metaphor for Ultimate Reality which cannot be perceived with the senses.

Adhibautika — One of the Threefold Miseries; dangers or sufferings arising from external forces proceeding from the presence of other living beings.

Adhidaivika — One of the Threefold Miseries; dangers or sufferings arising from cosmic forces or celestial beings.

Adhikara Vichara — The highest qualification granting spiritual life and practice.

Adhimatra — The ninth of the Twelve Levels of Detachment wherein dispassion becomes so intense that enjoyment of the world actually becomes a source of pain.

Adhyaropa — A mode of discrimination used by the jnanis which aids in the detection and removal of false superimposition and mental delusion.

Adhyasa — A superimposition or covering of one thing over another, philosophically speaking, like form over formlessness, or ignorance over knowledge.

Adhyatma-prasad — One of the Four Kinds of Clarities, relating to purity of heart and soul/spirit.

Adhyatma-vidya — The constant pursuit of the highest wisdom, leading to Truth.

Adhyatmika — One of the Threefold Miseries; dangers and sufferings arising within the individual in the twin modes of mental and physical imbalances.

Adishakti — A name for the Mother of the Universe as the first and foremost of all benign spiritual powers.

Adishankaracharya — An honorific name for Sri Shankaracharya, the great Advaitan.

Advaita — The Nondual Philosophy espoused by the ancient rishis of India, and more recently propounded by Gaudapada and Shankara, that is the foundation of all Hindu Scriptures; monism; direct perception of Brahman.

Advaitic — Referring to the supreme path or philosophy of Nonduality, Advaita Vedanta.

Advaitavada — The path of the Nondualists who comprehend the truth of non-origination, or non-evolution.

Advaitist — One who follows the way of Advaita Vedanta.

Advesta — Nonhating.

Agastya — A revered ancient rishi who caused the Vindhya mountains to fall and who taught the Dravidian tribes in South India; husband of the woman rishi, Lopamudra; a name for Shiva.

Agrayana — An adept practitioner of the nondual system of Asparsha Yoga, who renounces all that is unfit to be taken (agrahya) in life.

Ahaituka — Free of all motive power.

Aham Brahmasmi — "I am Brahman." One of the Four Mahavakyas or sacred declarations of the Upanisads.

Ahamkara — Egoism, or sense of individual I; one of the fourfold aspects of mind, the antahkarana.

Ahimsa — Nonviolence, or refraining from harming living things; one of the Ten Yamas and Niyamas of the Patanjala Yoga system.

Aishvarya — A rare type of spiritual wealth; riches on earth.

Ajanatah — Insensitivity, being one of the Three Stupefactions that rob one of both inherent spirituality, and the impetus to practice and realize it.

Ajati — Having no birth, applied to those rare souls who come into the body in full realization that they are really Atman, or Awareness.

Ajativada — The path or way of those who have come to know the birthless, deathless nature of all beings, all things.

Ajna chakra — The subtle spiritual vortex located at the third eye region, symbolically located in the middle of the forehead between the eyes.

Ajnana — Ignorance of one's true nature as pure, conscious Awareness; the antithesis of knowledge.

Ajnana-bhumikas — The Seven Lower Stages of Knowledge/Worlds.

Ajnani — One who is ignorant of one's true nature.

Akama — Freedom from desire.

Akamahata — One of the Four Qualifications of the Illumined Guru, namely freedom from any and all desires for the disciple other than he/she attain liberation.

Akarma — One of the three grades of karma based upon the subtle art of nonaccrual of karma, or what has been called "inaction" by the seers. It is attained via practice and gaining of the virtue of selflessness.

Akartrtvama — Moderation in all things in order to attain balance for spiritual practice.

Akasha — Subtle space, in any of its modes, such as consciousness space, intelligence space, thought space, energy space, material space (chidakasha, jnanakasha, chitakasha, pranakasha, bhutakasha); ether, one of the five elements of nature.

Akhanda Satchitananda — An incomparable Name for Divine Reality, meaning Indivisible Existence, Knowledge, and Bliss.

Aklista vrittis — Non pain-bearing thoughts of the mind that are beneficial, and which are meant to replace klista-vrittis in yoga practice.

Akshara Brahman — A name for Brahman, denoting Its indestructible nature.

Akshobha — Nonemotionalism, or emotional calm and balance.

Alabdhabhumikatva — Lack of assurance and the inability to muster any forward momentum in religious practice, being the eighth of The Nine Distractions in Spiritual Life cited by Patanjali in His Yoga Sutras.

Alambanas — The Twenty-four Tattvas, or cosmic principles of Sankhya, taken for stations of meditation rather than just philosophical study.

Alasya — Laziness, idleness, or mental inertia, often due to physical obesity, which is the fifth of Nine Distractions in Spiritual Life cited by Patanjali in his Yoga Sutras.

Amsa-Avatar — A partial incarnation of Gid.

Anadi — Without beginning; a term applied to the scriptures of Vedic Sanatana Dharma, which are of divine origin and not ascribable to human authorship.

Anahata chakra — The spiritual center, vortex, or "lotus," symbolically located at the heart region.

Anahata Dhvani — The subtle sound of AUM heard by the yogis in deep meditation.

Anandamayakosha — The sheath of bliss, or conceptual ego structure, the subtlest of The Five Sheaths of human existence as explained in the Adhara System of Vedanta.

Ananya-bhakti — The devotion of nonseparation espoused by Sri Krishna in the Bhagavad Gita, wherein devotion and wisdom are correctly conjoined; one-pointed concentration on any one of the various forms of God.

Anasakti — The sixth of Twelve Levels of Detachment that signals arrival at a foundational level of dispassion which is moderate and conducive towards higher attainment.

Anatma — The nonself, or what is insentient — like matter and ego.

Anava — The power of primal bondage; one of the Three Pasas, malas or limitations according to Tantra which bind in order to save. Anava represents connate impurity which deludes the soul and makes it a victim of samsara. Along with karmika and mayiya, anava binds certain kinds of evolving souls and veils from them their inherent nature as Shiva. Gaining initiation from a guru and attaining jnana, they can manage to get free.

Anavasthitatvani — Stagnation, instability, and the inability in spiritual life to attain higher levels of awareness, being the last of Nine Distractions in Spiritual Life cited by Patanjali in His Yoga Sutras.

Angamejayatva — Unsteadiness or shakiness of the body and limbs in meditation, which, according to Patanjala Yoga, is one of the Four Main Causes of Distraction.

Anima — One of the Eight Siddhis or Eight Occult Powers which enables the seeker of lower ideals to reduce physical matter to nothingness or to attain weightlessness.

Anishtam — Scattered results occurring due to actions done with an inattentive mind.

Anitya — Mutable; non-eternal; in Buddhism, transitoriness, being one of the Three Marks (trilakshana) wherein everything existing is assigned as impermanent.

Annamayakosha — The gross, physical, or apparent sheath of human existence, the body, as a part of the Adhara system explained by Vedanta science.

Annaprasada — Sacred food offering; one of the Four Clarities of Food; a Hindu rite celebrating the auspicious occasion of childbirth.

Annapurna — The Divine Mother of the universe who feeds and thus sustains all living beings.

Anoraniyan — The subtlest of the subtle, which is a descriptive word for Brahman.

Antah-jnana — Recognition of the fact that all knowledge lies within the Soul.

Antahkarana — The internal organ or fourfold mind. It consists of manas, the basic mind which considers; chitta, the mind's contents; buddhi, the intellect that determines; and ahamkara, the ego or sense of individuality.

Antaranga — The noble membership of the inner circle of devotees who gather around an Avatar, or true world teacher; also a name for the mind, or inner organ.

Antarayas — Obstacles; impediments; the chitta-vikshepas, sometimes called the Nine Distraction to Spiritual Life in Yoga.

Antaryami — The "Inner Ruler Immortal" seated in the heart, i.e., Atman.

Anubhava — True Being; the direct perception of Divinity which is the result of self-effort and Grace; after shruti, hearing the Truth, and yukti, contemplating the Truth, it is the third in this triputi of Vedantic practices which allows for the direct perception of Reality.

Anugraha — Grace.

Anya-samskara-pratibandhin — The willingness of the aspirant to dive deep into the mind in meditation to find what is obstructing its purification leading to Enlightenment.

Anupalabdhi — Nonapprehension, used as a proof of Reality in that the absence of a thing, being, or principle proves that it was once present and accounted for.

Ap, or Apah — The fourth element, water.

Apakvahamkara — The human ego, ahamkara, that has not yet become refined or matured, i.e., surrendered unto God, and is thus apakva — unripe.

Apana — Downwards/outwards moving prana.

Aparavidya — Lower or secondary knowledge, usually pertaining to secular or worldly subjects but sometimes even associated with mere scriptural knowledge as compared to the direct experience of Reality.

Aparigraha — One of the Five Yamas of Yoga, which tempers both the giving and receiving of goods and wealth based upon the danger of forgetting one's past lifetimes due to immediately engaging with all manner of material commerce at an early age.

Aparinama — The principle of nontransformation that, when seen as the truth of existence, reveals all worlds of name and form in time and space nonactual due to their constantly changing nature.

Aparokshanubhuti — Direct spiritual experience of the Truth gained by contact with holy company and studying the revealed scriptures under a competent guru.

Apaurasheya — Not of human authorship, used often in reference to the sacred scriptures of the Sanatana Dharma of India.

Apavada — A discriminatory power that, in conjunction with its partner, adhyaropa, recognizes and destroys delusions of the mind and false superimpositions over Reality.

Aradhana — Deep reverence.

Archa — Forms; objects of worship and their names; offerings made at the time of worship.

Archanam — Ritualistic worship; one of the Eight Devotional Aids, being adoration of the Lord, which is duly cited by Devarshi Narada in his Bhakti Sutras.

Arjuna — One of the five Pandava brothers who was a great devotee of Lord Krishna and who received the great Avatar's discourse and message of the Bhagavad Gita on the battlefield at Kurukshetra.

Arthavada — Eulogy and explanation; scriptural texts wherein convincing passages are given to induce the seeker to reject worldliness and commit to a path and go forward in spiritual life.

Arupaloka — In Zen, the realm of blessings and formless meditation.

Arya-Satya — The Four Noble Truths of Buddhism, i.e., there is suffering, a cause for suffering, a possible end to suffering, and a means to bring about an end to suffering (astangika-marga — the Eightfold Path).

Asamprajnata Samadhi — Described by Patanjali in Yoga Philosophy as a superconscious state of pure Awareness wherein all cognitive traces of the relative universe and the individual self are obliterated completely. It is generally synonymous with the Nirvikalpa Samadhi of the Vedanta school.

Asamvedana — A fully matured condition of mind that allows the luminary complete detachment from desires and impediments, which is really a special kind of nonreceptivity to them.

Asana — A physical seat used for formal meditation; third limb of Yoga concerned with basic and singular posture, recommended by Patanjali in his Raja Yoga system to facilitate a strong and steady foundation for the body so that it will remain stationary and still, allowing the mind to concentrate on Reality.

Ashani — Lord Siva in his all-powerful aspect.

Ashrama — One of the four divisions of living beings, according to their station in life; a physical location where the student meets with the guru to study dharma and meditate.

Asrsti — That which is beyond creation, or can never be subject to beginnings or inception, i.e., Consciousness/Brahman.

Ashtavakra — An enigmatic holy man, great sage, and rishi of the Vedic period, who was born deformed due to a curse from his father while in the womb, but who later saved his father's life and thus had the curse reversed. He is the author of the famed revealed nondual scripture, Ashtavakra Samhita.

Ashtavakra Samhita — A Sanskrit text concentrating on Nondual Wisdom that is one of the finest scriptures of Advaita Vedanta.

Ashuddha — What is impure.

Asparsha Yoga — The "Nontouch" Yoga transmitted by the great nondualist, Gaudapada, to his qualified students.

Asaucha — Impurity, as opposed to saucha which is one of the Niyamas or daily practices of Yoga; ritualistic observance of a period of purification due to the death of a relative or loved one.

Asta Siddhas — The Eight Occult Powers, proclaimed by enlightened beings to be detrimental sidetracks along the path of spiritual realization.

Ashtanga Yoga — The Eight-limbed Yoga of Patanjali, also called Patanjala and Raja Yoga, it focuses upon meditation and samadhi as the goal of life but also treats preliminary exercises and disciplines leading up it.

Asmita — Egoism, which is one of the Five Kleshas of Yoga.

Astabala Siddhis — The eight occult powers, which act as impediments on the road to Enlightenment.

Astamurti — The eight invisible forms of Lord Siva.

Astangika Marga — The Eightfold Path of Buddhism, one of Thirty-seven Limbs of Enlightenment, consisting of clear view, firm resolve, ennobling speech, dharmic conduct, right livelihood, pure aspiration, mindfulness, and perfect concentration.

Asteya — One of the Yamas of Yoga's first limb, which requires non-coveting of the goods and belongings of other beings and countries.

Asti — Growth, which is another of the false transformations over the immutable Soul, Atman.

Astika — Orthodox, referring to the traditional darshanas of India.

Astikya — Reliance upon the words of the illumined souls in spiritual life.

Ashuddha — Impure, referring to tattvas such as the five elements and active senses, called such not due to things vile and evil, but due to their being far away from their source, i.e., Brahman.

Asukham — Devoid of all true and abiding happiness, referring to the physical world.

Asuras — Powerful beings and demonic forces who vie with the gods for supremacy; negative forces or demons.

Asuric — Having to do with the influences of the asuras,

Asvattha — The banyan tree.

Atma Bodha — Self-knowledge; a sacred advaitic scripture of Sri Shankara dealing with the principles of Atman, Brahman, Maya, and Vedantic Philosophy in general.

Atma jnana or Atmajnan — Absolute Knowledge of the Immortal Self, the highest knowledge knowable to the human mind, actually beyond its scope, and by knowing which the soul will be led to spiritual realization.

Atman — The eternal Soul residing within every being and permeating creation, though indivisible and non-material in nature, which is birthless, deathless, pure, and perfect.

Atmarama — A name for Siva in his all-pervasive form, as the Atman in all beings.

Atma tripti — The three requisites for receiving the highest wisdom, namely sankalpa-vinashana, upekshanam,and brahmakaravritti.

Atma-vichara — The classic way of proceeding in advanced spiritual life by inquiring into the nature of Reality by analysing the self/Self. The question "Who am I" is pertinent here, but it must be accompanied by inspecting all that the Soul/Self is not, i.e., matter, nature, tattvas, etc.

Audasinya — An intense degree of detachment; the tenth plateau of the Twelve Levels of Dispassion wherein there is complete indifference to the objects and concerns of relativity.

Aum or Om — The primal vibration which is the sound symbol for Brahman, Ultimate Reality, and which is an essential element in all systems of Hindu Philosophy. From this primal sound come all aspects of the creation, yet being beyond the manifest universe it is the bija or sacred symbol for formless Reality Itself.

Autsuka-puraka — Possessing a ready store of inspiration for spiritual life, and for attaining Enlightenment.

Avadhut — A wandering ascetic belonging to the class of Avadhuts who represent a high state of sannyasi.

Avadhuta Gita — A sacred scripture focusing on Nondual Wisdom which, besides addressing the nature of Reality, also describes the condition and philosophy of the Avadhut, a wandering ascetic.

Avarana Shakti — A power of Shakti which seems to veil Reality; one of the two obscuring forces of Maya, the other being vikshepa, which appears to distort Reality.

Avasthas — States, stages, or levels of spiritual growth.

Avataravada — The sacred pathway of those who focus upon and involve themselves with the Divine Incarnation as He takes birth in the world of name and form throughout the span of human evolution.

Avatar — One who descends; the appearance of Divinity in human form; an incarnation of God.

Avidhi — Rites and rituals performed for inferior reasons.

Avirati — Non-abstention, as opposed to uparati, wherein the seeker fails to subordinate worldly life to the spiritual path; over-indulgence in sensual appetites, being the sixth of Nine Distractions in Spiritual Life, called antarayas or vikshepas according to Yoga.

Avisheshas — Aspects of the human being, finer than the visheshas, such as the tanmatras and the ego.

Avrijina — One of four necessary qualifications of the authentic guru which shows him/her to be one who lives a simple and unostentatious life, attended by qualities of detachment and equanimity.

Avyaktam — Unmanifest; invisible, like the three gunas prior to breaking into differentiation.

Ayamatma Brahma — "This self is Brahman." One of the four great declarations (Mahavakyas), or nondualistic mantras.

Ayodhya — The city of King Dasaratha where the young Prince Ram had his childhood, youth and home-life.

Bahirmukhavritti — The outward-going vibrations of the mind that bind the soul to external phenomena and its consequences.

Bahutva Marga — The path of religious convention that beings who only dabble in religion follow from life-time to lifetime.

Bandha — Bondage, which in Vedic philosophy is mainly associated with nature, livelihood, and family/ancestors.

Bhagavad Gita — The quintessential sacred scripture of the Hindus containing the comprehensive message of Lord Krishna.

Bhagavan — An especially sacred name for God which implies the Supreme Being who is endowed with the Six Treasures of the Godhead: power, virtue, fame, glory, detachment and freedom.

Bhagavati — A sacred name for the Divine Mother of the Universe; the Supreme Being in feminine form.

Bhairavi — A female ascetic, usually strong, independent, and fiercesome in character; a worshiper of Shiva and a Tantric aspirant or adept.

Bhajanam — Heartfelt devotions to and worship of the Lord; one of the Eight Devotional Aids according to Devarshi Narada.

Bhakta — A devotee of the God, of the Lord and Mother of the Universe; a follower of the path of bhakti.

Bhakti — Love and devotion for God.

Bhati — That which shines; Consciousness.

Bhavas — Devotional moods or spiritual feelings associated with the awakening of God-Consciousness.

Bhaya — Fear.

Bhedabheda — Difference in nondifference, indicating a philosophical perspective that interprets the soul as being both independent of and one with Supreme Reality.

Bhogamarga — The path of superficial enjoyment that worldly societies and living beings fall into, life after life, into dalliance with material objects and wealth alone.

Bhrantidarshana — False perception, or distorted perspective, being the seventh of Nine Distractions in Spiritual Life (antarayas) cited by Patanajli in His Yoga Sutras.

Bhumikatva — Stages or steps.

Bhumis/Bhumikas — Lands or grounds; in Buddhism, one of ten higher ascending lands that a bodhisattva passes through in order to attain full buddhahood.

Bhur Loka — The earth plane.

Bhuvarloka — The intermediary plane just above (further within the mind)) earth.

Bhushandhi — A crow mentioned in stories in the Vedic Itihasa or mythology.

Bhutas — Beings occupying the physical plane, along with its astral planes.

Bhutakasha — The earthly plane; the gross, physical atmosphere where bodies and forms exist.

Bhuvanas — Planes of existence within the Great Mind.

Bibhishana or Vibhishana — The brother of Ravana who, having gained Brahma's boon of never committing an unrighteous act, betrayed Ravana and, upon Shiva's advice, allied himself with Sri Ram.

Bijams — Subtle seed words of power which are the impetus for all of creation/projection, and which are found in slokas, sutras, and mantrams for the purification and enlightenment of the mind.

Bindu — The point of the Light of Consciousness from which all comes into manifestation, connected deeply with The Word.

Boddhamanah — Transformation of ordinary mind by the illumined intellect.

Bodhisattva — In Buddhism, an illumined soul who has attained freedom from ignorance, and who returns to the embodied condition for purposes of helping to free others.

Brahmacharya — Practice of celibacy in the young aspirant, it is one of the five yamas of Yoga.

Brahm'advitiye — One without a second, being a word describing Brahman.

Brahmagranthi — According to Vedanta and Tantra, a knot or barrier at the lowest of the seven chakras that keeps embodied beings from rising to higher centers of Awareness.

Brahma-nistha — One-pointed devotion to God; one of the Seven Qualifications of a Tantric Aspirant.

Brahmapadesha — Receiving the Feet of Brahman, i.e., taking mantra-diksha, or initiation.

Brahma-parayana — Taking full refuge in God; one of the Seven Qualifications of a Tantric Aspirant.

Brahmaikya-upadesha-vakya — Statements in the scriptures which concern themselves only with the knowledge of Brahman, especially through the vakyas, or great declarations.

Brahmajnana — The knowledge of Brahman, used in the sense of that which is to be known about Ultimate Reality, through direct experience.

Brahmakaravrittidhyan — The subtlemost act of dissolving all the vibrations of the mind into Brahman.

Brahmaloka — The highest of the seven realms lying in Consciousness, also called Satyaloka.

Brahman — The Absolute; the Ultimate Reality; formless Essence; pure Consciousness.

Brahmanas — The first of four sections of the Vedas; a sage of higher Wisdom; a word for Brahmin priests; one of the four castes of the Hindu social order.

Brahman satya, jagad mithya — One of the famous sayings in Vedanta meaning, Brahma is real, the world is unreal.

Brahmapada — How Brahman, Absolute Reality, disports Itself in the realms of name and form, usually described as appearing in the waking, dreaming, and deep sleep states of humanity.

Brahmasvarupa-nirupana-vakya — Statements on the nature of Brahman, direct and indirect, which indicate both the characteristics and inherent properties of Reality.

Brahmavadi — The path to Brahman alone; one of the Seven Qualifications of a Tantric Aspirant.

Brahmavid — A knower of God; the fourth qualification of the authentic spiritual teacher according to Shankaracharya; the first in a class of the Four Divisions of Knowers of Brahman who has attained mastery over the first four of the Seven Stages of Higher Wisdom.

Brahmavidvan — See Brahmavid.

Brahmavidvara — The second in a class of the Four Divisions of Knowers of Brahman who has attained mastery over the first five of the Seven Stages of Higher Wisdom.

Brahmavidvarishtha — The fourth in a class of the Four Divisions of Knowers of Brahman, who has attained mastery over all of the Seven Stages of Higher Wisdom.

Brahmavidvariya — The third in a class of the Four Divisions of Knowers of Brahman, who has attained mastery over the first six of the Seven Stages of Higher Wisdom.

Brahmetara-nirakarana — Statements in the scriptures of the neti-neti perspective which differentiate Brahman from everything that is not Brahman.

Brhadaranyaka Upanisad — Literally, "Great Scripture from the forest"; a lengthy and profound Upanisad from the White Yajur Veda containing many teachings of the rishi, Yajnavalkya, on Brahman and Atman.

Buddha — An enlightened being, considered to be an Avatar by the Hindus, and the founder of the religion that bears His name.

Buddhehparatah — The ability in the spiritual aspirant to transcend the relative plane of reference and gain intuitive wisdom of what lies within Consciousness at higher levels.

Buddhi — Intelligence; one of the four parts of Antahkarana, the mental sheath or thinking mind according to Samkhya and Vedanta.

Chaitanya — Consciousness fully aware of Itself; a great God-man of 14th-century Bengal, considered by some to be a divine incarnation of Radha and Krishna conjoined.

Chakra — A subtle center or vortex of spiritual energy, sometimes referred to as a lotus, through which Kundalini Shakti flows on its ascent to the crown of the head. There are said to be seven such lotuses from the base of the spine to the crown of the head and twelve more in the brain.

Chandala — An outcaste; a member of the untouchable caste.

Chandhi — One of the two great Mother scriptures of India, also known as Sri Durga Saptasati.

Chatak Bird — A mystical bird often characterized in the scriptures and stories of India to explain certain teachings and their inner meanings.

Chetana Samadhi — A class of samadhi, rare and special, which leaves the experiencer in a state of remembrance of all that occurred to it in that state, even after returning to the embodied condition.

Chidabhasa — The reflected Consciousness or Intelligence of the Supreme Brahman into the worlds of name and form in time and space, which when understood as just a reflection, assists the seeker of Truth in both separating Reality from nonreality ("wheat from the chaff" "God from Mammon"), and further to arrive safely and correctly at the Great Statement, "All Is Brahman."

Chidakasha — The boundless space of pure Spirit which is a realmless realm occupied by nothing other than pure Conscious Awareness, timeless, deathless and unlimited.

Chinmatra — Intelligence particles of Consciousness; Consciousness Itself.

Chitta — The "stuff" of the mind, such as thought, conception, ideation, etc.; one of the four conditions of the antahkarana

Chitta-bhati — The thoughts of the mind that remain illumined, always contemplating divine reality.

Chitta-chinta — The thoughts of the mind which tend towards heaviness, causing the mind to form habits of unnecessary brooding.

Chitta-lochana — The thoughts of the mind that tend towards aspiration and higher thinking.

Chitta-nirodha — The destruction of thought waves in the mind, leading to formless samadhi.

Chittaprasad — Purity or purification of the mind's thoughts, which is one of the Four Clarities.

Chit-shuddhi — Purity of mind; the third of the Three Kinds of Purity, which is hardest of attainment, the other two being Dravya Shuddhi and Kriya Shuddhi, purity of atmosphere and purity of action.

Chittakasha — The subtlest space of mind containing the infinite potential for thoughts, ideas, concepts, etc.

Chittavrttis — The vibrations or waves of the mind, i.e., the thoughts.

Chowrie — A fan used for ritualistic worship, usually made out of a yak's tail.

Daiva — Divine; the god who controls the destiny of living beings; one of three classifications of a seeker in Tantra, after pasu (animalistic) and virya (heroic), signifying a being who has reached the stage of identification with the inner Self.

Daivi-maya — The divine maya of the Universal Mother, as opposed to ordinary or deluding maya.

Daksha — Intelligent; able; one of the Seven Qualifications of a Tantric Aspirant.

Dakshinabandha — The bondage to conventional life, thereby stripped of dharma and higher attainments.

Dakshineswar — The temple where Sri Ramakrishna Paramahamsa served as priest in His youth, and where He performed His twelve-year world-transforming sadhana and gained the vision of Mother Kali.

Dama — Self-control, one of the Six Jewels, Shatsampatti, which bestows upon an aspirant the ability to control the mind and senses easily and naturally.

Danam — Charity and giving of alms in the right state of mind.

Dhammapada — The original scripture of Buddhism, being a compilation of all of Lord Buddha's sayings that were remembered by His students (Arhats) after he had passed from this world.

Dharmi — One who lives life in observance and practice of the dharma.

Darpa — Pride; pride of good conduct, which is one of the Eight Fetters.

Darshan — Literally, to see clearly; referring to the Six Darshanas, which when studied under an authentic teacher, enable the aspirant to be free from bondage and limitation and behold inherent divinity; direct association with a divine being.

Darshanas — The six orthodox systems of Vedic Philosophy, namely, Samhkya, Patanjala (or Yoga), Uttara Mimamsa (or Vedanta), Purva Mimamsa, Nyaya, and Vaisheshika — whose main proponents were Kapila, Patanjali, Vedavyasa, Jaimini, Gautama, and Kanada, respectively.

Dasabalas — The ten powers of a Buddha.

Dasabhumikas — In Buddhism, the Ten Pure Lands of Bodhisatvahood.

Dasya Bhava — Servant; one of the Five Divine Moods for Worshipping God found in Vaishnavism.

Dehadhyasahamkara — The primal mistake of the ego in superimposing the body over the Soul

Deh'anuvartanam — One of the three great desires of living beings, which is to inhabit bodies in order to enjoy the worlds of name and form.

Devavak — A name given to the Sanskrit language, meaning "divine speech."

Devayana — The Path of the Gods, beyond the ancestor regions, but short of Absolute Reality.

Dharmashrama — The system of the four orders of dharmic living, namely the renunciate, the forest dweller, the householder, and the celibate student.

Dhatus — Various elements of the physical body

Daurmanasya — Sorrow; despair; one of the Four Causes of Distraction according to Yoga.

Daya — Compassion, especially associated with the removal of suffering and specifically the ignorance which causes it.

Deha — The physical body.

Dehadhyasahamkara — One of the Three Types of Ego; the lowest and basest type of egotism which reflects in the mind as the actual belief that one is one's body.

Deha-samatva — Stationary position of the body in meditation, free from the desire to shift about — either out of discomfort, or due to the desire for hatha-yoga asanas.

Desha — Physical space; subtle space; locale.

Devabhasya — "The language of the Gods," a title assigned to the Sanskrit language, through which a cross section of an entire race (India) gained final liberation (moksha) from bondage to maya/nature.

Devas — The gods, like Indra and his pantheon, who oversee the affairs of celestials, ancestors, and mortals.

Devi — A name for the Goddess, often used as a suffix to Her many names.

Dhairya — Patience that serves one along the spiritual path, in anticipation of reaching the highest goal.

Dhananjaya — The master of wealth, which is a name for Arjuna in the Bhagavad Gita.

Dharana — Concentration; the sixth limb in the eight-limbed system of Patanjali's Yoga, which when mastered allows the aspirant to access deeper states of meditation.

Dharma — Proper and balanced living and thinking according to the scriptures; righteousness; virtue; one of the Four Fruits of Life (Purusharthas) granted by the Divine Mother of the Universe.

Dharmakaya — One of the three bodies of the Buddha, being the transcendental body.

Dharma-megha-samadhi — The "raincloud of virtues" state of mind, wherein all qualities come out of the mind and manifest themselves in the awakened human being.

Dharmic — Having to do with or pertaining to righteous thought and action.

Dhriti — Patience.

Dhyana — Meditation; the seventh limb in the eight-limbed system of Patanjali's Yoga which leads to Samadhi.

Diksha — Spiritual initiation, the conferring of mantra-diksha upon the ready aspirant.

Dik shakti — The Divine Mother's power of illusion or projection, especially in accordance with Her ability to produce space or atmospheres.

Dirgha-pranava — Uttering AUM once, with one long breath.

Dirghasvapna — An extensive dream, usually referring to life and the march of terrestrial and human evolution over millions of years.

Doshadristhi — Fault-finding; the inability to see perfection while always focusing on apparent imperfections.

Dravya — Substance, as in the five elements or other materials of creation.

Dravya Shakti — An aspect of the Divine Mother Shakti who aids in the creation of the phenomenal universe; the producer of substances.

Dravya Shuddhi — Purity, or purification of place and object.

Driti — Firmness, steadiness, like resolve to realize the highest Goal.

Duhka or Duhkha — Suffering; pain, misery; one of the Four Causes of Distraction in Yoga.

Durga — The Divine Mother of the Universe; the ten-armed Goddess who is the essence of all gods and goddesses; the first and foremost of Five Main Aspects of the Universal Mother (Prakriti Panchaka) according to the Srimad Devi Bhagavatam.

Dvaita — One of the three levels of philosophy in India, along with Visishtadvaita and Advaita.

Dvaitahina — An adherent of the nondual path; one of the Seven Qualifications of the Tantric Aspirant.

Dvaitist — Followers of dualism, which centers upon worship of God with form.

Dvandva-mohena — Delusion arising from the incorrect view which accepts multiplicity and diversity to be real and which fails to perceive Unity in everything; the infinite sets of pairs of opposites in relativity.

Dvapara Yuga — The third of four divisions of time, coming after the Satya and Treta Yugas, wherein living beings are in possession of one third of their inherent spiritual knowledge. In the present age, the fourth, called Kali Yuga, most living beings have lost touch with all spiritual sensibilities.

Dvesha — Aversion; hatred, dislike; one of the Five Obstacles to Yoga; one of the Eight Fetters according to Vedanta.

Ekam — One.

Ekam sat viprah bahudha vadanti — "Truth is One, seers refer to it in multiple divine ways," which is the oldest testament in writing as to the true nature of Existence, found in the Rig Veda.

Ekangi — One of Four Types of Love mentioned in Vaishnava scripture, called "one-sided," wherein there is no reciprocation forthcoming from the one who is loved.

Ekarnava — The boundless ocean of etheric waters upon which rests the deities at the time of pralaya.

Ekasana — The single-pointed position of the body that allows for meditation, representing the best of all asanas and their transcendence as well.

Eshanatrayam — The triple bondage of spouse, children, and wealth according to Tantra and Vedanta, which becomes a frightful bond when human life is not utilized for gaining spirituality and is instead given to the search for pleasure, superficial pursuits, and amassing fortune; one of the Sixteen Evolutes of Maya.

Ganapati — The elephant-headed god who grants success and good fortune.

Ganapatya — The path or sect of those who worship Ganapati, or Ganesha.

Ganesha — Another name for Ganapati, the elephant-headed god of the Hindu pantheon.

Gangasagar — A holy location where the sacred river Ganga meets with the waters of the ocean.

Gaudapada — An illumined rishi who was a major exponent of the Advaita Vedanta. He is said to have been the guru of Shankara or possibly the guru of Shankara's guru.

Gauna-bhakti — Fundamental devotional practice, sometimes called Vaidhi-bhakti, which is followed by Raga bhakti and Prema bhakti as the devotee matures.

Gauri — Fair; brilliant; beautiful; the Divine Mother of the Universe, consort of Shiva, and manifestation of Parvati; another name for the earth.

Gautama Buddha — An honorific name for Lord Buddha.

Ghanta — The sacred bell used for worship in puja and at temples

Ghat — Any of a series of landings along a lake or a river where boats put in and people bathe.

Giridhara — Holder of the mountain; a name for Sri Krishna associated with the tale of His lifting of Mt. Govardhan to use it as an umbrella of protection for the village of Vrindaban during a deluge caused by Indra's wrath.

Golakdham — A game.

Gopala — Protector of cows; a name for the baby Krishna.

Gopaniyata — Secretiveness; one of the Eight Fetters.

Gopi — Any one of the young cow-herd maidens who loved Sri Krishna.

Gotra — Pride of lineage; one of the Eight Fetters.

Govardhan — A mountain lifted by Sri Krishna to protect Vrindaban from a deluge of rain.

Govinda — Master of the mountain; knower of creation, referring to Sri Krishna as the master of the earth and the senses.

Granthi — Knot, or knots, or blockages in body, life-force, mind, and thought, that impede progress along the natural course of both earthly and divine life.

Grihastha — The second stage of life, wherein the individual marries, rears children, makes a living — all ideally while practicing dharma in spiritual life.

Guna — A trait or traits, attributes of nature; qualities born of nature of which there are three, sattva, rajas and tamas, balance, frenetic activity, and inertia.

Guru — Satchitananda or Ultimate Reality appearing as the Atman or true nature of every living being; the revered spiritual preceptor who is the provisional guru.

Guru-anushasana — The requirement of an illumined preceptor in spiritual life and practice, to be combined with Vidya-shastra and Aparokshanubhuti — deep study of the revealed scriptures and gaining one's own direct experience of Enlightenment. The three together are know as The Three Pillars of Advaita Vedanta, and/or the Three Great Sources.

Guru Nanak — The Founder of Sikhism and the first of its standing line of ten gurus.

Guru Parampara — The succession of a line of gurus and disciples through which the transmission of precious spiritual teachings passes from generation to generation.

Guru-Shishya Dashangika — The system of the Ten Conditions of the Guru/Disciple relationship.

Guruyoga — The path of union with God through following the illumined preceptor and his instructions with one-pointed devotion.

Hardwar — A holy city in India.

Hari — A special name for God associated with Lord Vishnu.

Harsha — Joy, bliss, exhilaration.

Hatha Yoga — A stage of Kundalini Yoga associated with natural and spontaneous expression of asana, mudra, pranayam, and kriyas; a system of body postures undergone for health of the body, longevity, and the attainment of occult powers, the practice of which is often detrimental to spirituality.

Himalayas —The wondrous mountain range which runs through Northern India and which is considered sacred to the Hindus.

Himsa — Violence, the opposite of ahimsa.

Hiranyagarbha — Literally, a "mass of Light," containing all the worlds, gross subtle, and causal, that lay inside of it like the contents of a "Cosmic Egg." It is often associated or likened to Cosmic Intelligence itself as it appears as The Trinity, The Word, and other profound principles.

Hiranyaksha — The demon who was slayed by Vishnu in His incarnation as a boar.

Homa — A ritualistic ceremony wherein offerings are made into the sacred fire, accompanied with recitation of slokas and mudras.

Homa Bird — A mythological bird who lays her eggs miles high in the sky so that they hatch in midair before touching the earth. It is used as a metaphor for the illumined being who is not really born of matter and only briefly sojourns on earth with the purpose of helping others realize their divine nature.

Hrdaya — The heart, specifically the heart center, also called anahata chakra.

Hrdayaguha — The secret subtle chamber of the heart where the yogis and spiritual practitioners meditate.

Hri — Modesty; one of the Twenty Yamas and Niyamas of Tantra listed in the Srimad Devi Bhagavatam; when defined as shame, it is one of the Eight Fetters.

Hrilleka Mantra — The mantra for Sri Durga, containing Her power bijam, Hrim.

Hrim — A powerful bija or seed syllable representing the power of purification, transformation, beauty, and Grace.

Iccha — Will; desire; one of the four main shakti powers of Divine Mother.

Iccha Shakti — The power of indomitable will inherent in the Divine Mother by which She accomplishes all manifestation, all action and all conceptualization; Dravya, Kriya and Jnana Shakti; Divine Will.

Indra — The Lord of all the Gods.

Indraloka — The inner world where Indra presides.

Indriyas — The ten senses, five active and five cognitive.

Isha — A word meaning Lord; a name that the Hindus have given to Jesus.

Ishana — Siva appearing as the Sovereign Lord.

Ishitva — One of the Eight Occult Powers by which those attracted to lower ideals attain domination over beings and situations.

Ishtam — One's chosen Ideal.

Ishta-nistha — One-pointed devotion to a single ideal.

Ishvara — The supreme and most comprehensive aspect of Divinity presiding over the three worlds who oversees its various lesser powers and their functions; God with form; Saguna Brahman.

Ishvarakoti — A class of illumined beings who are perfected in spiritual life, and who usually attend on a Divine Incarnation when such a being embodies.

Ishvara-pranidhana — One of the five niyamas of Yoga which encourages the worship of God with form as an aid towards self-realization.

Ishvari — The Divine Mother as Ishvara; the supreme power of the universe manifesting through a feminine aspect.

Ishvariya — One of the Four Points of View as to the Origin of the Scriptures, this one being that they were created by Ishvara.

Itihasa — Spiritual history and mythology of India, especially reflected in the Mahabharata, Ramayana, and other famous texts.

Iti-iti — "All this, all this," which is the conclusion that the mature practitioner comes to after practicing the discipline of neti-neti, "not this, not this."

Jagannath — The Lord of the Worlds; the deity worshiped primarily in Bengal, whose famous temple, visited by thousands of pilgrims, lies in Puri in the state of Orissa.

Jagat — The world; universe.

Jagrat — The waking state of the human being.

Jai — Victory.

Jayati — Birth, listed as one of the false transformations over the unborn Soul, Atman.

Jal — The Bengali word for water.

Janaka — A famous king, the father of Sita, who attained both lordship and enlightenment. The famous rishi, Yajnavalkya, was his court priest and guru.

Janaloka — The fifth of seven worlds within Consciousness, lying below Taparloka and Satyaloka.

Japa — The efficacious practice of silently reciting the sacred mantra or names of God while turning the holy beads (mala).

Japam — The same as japa.

Jara — Old Age, which is among the six transformations belonging to the body, not the Soul, Atman.

Jitendriya — Controller of the senses; one of the Seven Qualifications of a Tantric Aspirant.

Jivanmukta — An illumined being who is liberated while living, enlightened while still residing in the body.

Jivanmukti — The state of liberation attained by fully illumined beings.

Jivas — Embodied beings of the earth plane.

Jivatman — The Atman dwelling inside the embodied soul, unbeknownst to it.

Jnana — Special knowledge, more like wisdom, that centers around philosophy and spirituality and which, when acquired, easily takes the soul out of bondage and towards Freedom.

Jnanabhumikas — The seven higher stages of knowledge/worlds.

Jnana-chakshu — The "Third Eye," being the sixth and penultimate center (ajna) of the Kundalini system.

Jnanamatras — Particles of intelligence, extremely close to Consciousness and aligned with The Word.

Jnana Shakti — A power of the Divine Mother used for sustaining knowledge and wisdom; force of intelligence.

Jnana-vakyas — One of three groups or classifications of knowledge having to do with statements in the scriptures pertaining to the nature of Brahman.

Jnanakasha — The subtle space which supports intelligence and wisdom, and where illumined souls keep their subtle bodies in order to help the outer worlds.

Jnanamarga — The path of wisdom that leads the soul out of bondage via higher knowledge, as contrasted to the bhogamarga that embroils one into attachment to pleasure and its resultant suffering.

Jnanendriyas — The five cognitive senses, namely smelling, tasting, seeing, touching, and hearing.

Jnanis — Practitioners of the path of Jnana Yoga; one who has spiritual knowledge.

Jnano-daya Yoga — The rare path of giving out the noble dharmic teachings with the aim of compassionately removing the suffering of living beings. This yoga has seen a re-emergence in present times due to Sri Sarada Devi's presence on the world scene.

Kailas — The Holy Mountain sacred to Lord Shiva, said to be His abode.

Kaivalya — Spiritual emancipation; absolute independence or transcendence synonymous with the terms moksha or mukti, used particularly by Patanjali in his Yoga system.

Kaivalya-prag-bhara — Liberation stream; one of the Two Directions of the Mind-Stream after death mentioned by Patanjali and Vedavyasa. One stream of souls moves towards liberation, and the others towards bondage and rebirth in ignorance (samsara-prag-bhara).

Kala Shakti — Power of time; the shakti of Lord Shiva.

Kala — Time; a name for Yama, the god of death; a name for Shiva.

Kalachakra — The wheel of birth and death into which unawakened beings are born, experiencing various dualities such as good and bad, pleasure and pain, etc., according to their karmas until enlightenment dawns.

Kalas — Phases of time; one of the twelve higher tattvas in Shaivism.

Kali — The Divine Mother of the Universe in Her four-armed form, worshiped by Sri Ramakrishna Paramahamsa; the consort of Lord Shiva from the Tantric viewpoint.

Kalmi creeper — A plant which grows in water and covers the surface.

Kalpa — A phase of time consisting of many yugas.

Kalpanika — Imagings of the mind in time which, like seeds, will produce life and its dream-like experiences.

Kama — One of the Four Fruits of Life (Purusharthas) granted by the Divine Mother wherein one gets fulfillment of all legitimate desires; desire.

Kamadhatu — In Zen, one of the three worlds, being the world of desires, or earth.

Kama-vasayita — One of the Eight Occult Powers which allow those who seek lower ideals to thoroughly enjoy all desires which come to mind.

Kamarpukur — The small village in Bengal where Sri Ramakrishna took His birth in this incarnation, which has now become a scared pilgrimage place.

Kamakala — In Tantra, a designation that denotes Siva and Shakti in deepest Union.

Kanchukas — Limiting adjuncts; sheaths that constrict or seemingly modify Consciousness, causing It to think in terms of a finite being.

Kapila — Revered rishi who was the main proponent of the Sankhya System of Philosophy.

Kapilavastu — The birthplace of Lord Kapila, which several millennia later was also the birthplace of Lord Buddha.

Karanas — Causes of the external worlds and their objects, i.e., the senses connected to the mind.

Karana Sharira — Of the human being's three bodies, it is the causal body consisting of powerful seeds held in abeyance. Both the subtle and gross bodies, as well as the worlds, are drawn from these seeds.

Karanavairagya — The fourth of the Twelve Levels of Dispassion which comes about due to outer circumstances like the death of a loved one, but which does not last and gives way eventually to further attachment to the world.

Karika — A commentary on a scripture.

Karma Shakti — That power of the Divine Mother of the Universe Who over-sees all action and compels beings to action.

Karmendriyas — The five active senses, as in speaking, handling, moving, procreating, and excreting.

Karmika — Limiting cognitive power; one of the three pasas, malas or limitations according to Tantra which bind in order to save. Karmika blinds beings to subtle truths by fastening their minds upon the accrual of merit and demerit. Along with mayiya and anava, karmika binds certain kinds of evolving souls and veils from them their inherent nature as Shiva. Gaining initiation from a guru and attaining jnana, they can manage to get free.

Kartikeya — One of the sons of Lord Shiva, often called Skanda or Subrahmanya.

Kartritva-abhimana — The mistaken notion the Brahman/Atman is somehow the agent of actions, when it is really the ego-mind complex.

Karya Maya — One of the twelve cosmic principles of Shaivism citing the overall power of the Mahashakti to provide all and everything for the benefit of the entire creation.

Katha Upanisad — An Upanisad sacred to the Vedic tradition in which Nachiketas, a young man, journeys to the realm of Yama, the god of death, to uncover what lies beyond death and learn what is the essence of life.

Kavirajis — Members of a sect in India.

Kauravas — The greedy clan of brothers who strove to take away the kingdom of the Pandavas by deceit and war, as described in the Mahabharata, setting the stage for the acts/yogas of the Bhagavad Gita.

Kenopanisad — A short but powerful scripture that concentrates upon the transcendent and all-pervasive Atman and which includes a story about the gods and their encounter with the Absolute Brahman. In this Upanisad, the Divine Mother of the Universe also makes a rare appearance.

Keshava — A name for Lord Krishna meaning "long-haired; slayer of Keshi."

Khyati — Clarity of mind, most highly valued by all the luminaries.

Kileshas — Same as kleshas in Yoga, which in Buddhism are the various impediments to Nirvana.

King Janaka — A famous king of old India who gained both all that the world had to offer, plus spiritual

Enlightenment.

Kirtan — Dancing and singing in adoration of the Lord.

Kirtanam — Singing and dancing in devotion to the Lord; one of the Eight Devotional Aids according to Devarshi Narada.

Kleshas — The five impediments to freedom in Yoga, namely ignorance, egoism, attachment, aversion, and clinging to life/fear of death; kileshas in Buddhism.

Klistha-vrttis — Pain-bearing thoughts in the mind that bring about havoc in life.

Kosha — Sheath or covering. The term is used in Vedanta to indicate those aspects of creation — namely body, life-force, mind, intelligence, and ego — which obscure or apparently condition pure Consciousness called Brahman; a small metal container used for water offerings in sacred puja.

Krama Mukti — The gradual way or path to Enlightenment taken by awakening devotees who proceed from birth in the lower realms to those in higher realms, and finally into Brahman.

Kriya — To act; in Tantra, spontaneous divinely-oriented action; the internal rising of Kundalini Shakti which produces certain external effects on the body and mind; practice aimed at higher understanding with regards to spirituality.

Kriyamani — As in kriyamani karma, which is unexpected karma arising inscrutibly that surfaces in life while the aspiring jiva is attempting to work out other karmas and attain a balanced existence.

Kriya Shakti — That power of the Divine Mother which infuses beings with the energy to act and think, and pours life-force into the gross and subtle creations, permeating all worlds and realms with vitalizing power. Not only is She responsible for the activating force, She also acts in and through that which She animates.

Kriya Shuddhi — Purity of action.

Kriyayoga — According to Vedavyasa, that revitalizing aspect of Yoga which powerfully combines austerity (tapas), study of scripture (svadhyaya), and devotion to God (Ishvara-pranidhana), the three essential niyamas of Yoga, into a consummate method for realization.

Krodha — Anger; one of the Six Passions.

Kshama — Forgiveness; graciousness.

Kshara — Decay, one of the six transformations falsely imputed over the imperishable Soul, Atman.

Kshipta — Disturbed state of mind; the first and most difficult of the Five States of the Mind Field in Yoga, which makes the unfortunate sufferer unfit for both terrestrial and spiritual life.

Kubir or Kabir — A famous poet/songwriter of the Fifteenth Century who, as a boy, was adopted by poor Muslim and Hindu parents of a low caste, and whose collection of songs, called Bijak, are sung to this day by Hindus and Muslims alike.

Kumbhaka — The breathless state of suspended animation; retention and suspension of breath.

Kundalini — Coiled-up spiritual force; the powerful yet subtle spiritual power, that when awakened, brings illumination to all levels of one's being.

Kundalini Shakti — The wielder of the primal power of Kundalini.

Kurukshetra — A famous location in India where the great war spoken of in the Mahabharata took place and upon whose field Sri Krishna gave His inspirational discourse on Yoga and the Atman to a confused and dejected Arjuna.

Kutastha — Eternal underlying substratum which is changeless, as in pure, conscious Awareness.

Kutichakas — A class of roaming ascetics who are spiritual adepts that are steadily fixed in their realization.

Laghima — One of the Eight Occult Powers by which those who seek lesser attainments become weightless and are said to defy gravity.

Lakshmana — Literally, "bearing auspicious marks"; the devoted and illumined half-brother of Sri Ramachandra and husband of Sita's sister.

Lama — A teacher and guide in Tibetan Buddhism.

Laya — Dissolution; immersion.

Loka — Literally, world or realm; world of names and forms.

Lok'anuvartanam — One of the three primary desires of living beings, which is the desire to visit and abide in the various worlds of name and form in time and space..

Lokayatika Marga — The path of following the gross material world only.

Lopamudra — Literally, "of extremely subtle form." The illustrious wife of the renowned sage and rishi, Agastya, she was the authoress of a portion of the Rig Veda.

Mada — Vanity; one of the Six Passions; one of the Seven Malas of Maya.

Madhava — The Sweet One, being a name for the Lord, Sri Krishna.

Madhura Bhava — The love of the lover for the Beloved; one of the Five Divine Moods for Worshiping God, in Vaishnavism.

Madhyama — The third phase of the manifestation of pure knowledge from the primal sound vibration wherein thought and meaning are formed and fused; subtle sound.

Madhyavairagya — A mild and moderate level of detachment; the third of Twelve Levels of Dispassion noted in Vedanta Philosophy.

Mahabhutas — Great principles, tattvas; the Five Element: ether, air, fire, water, and earth.

Mahadeva — Literally, "Great God," which is a name for Lord Shiva.

Mahalila — The great play or sport of Consciousness; the cosmic theater with all beings as actors and actresses and the Divine Being as the writer, producer, and director; the divine sport of an Avatar.

Mahamaya — The grand illusion; the superimposition of the universe and its constituents over Brahman; the One who conjures up the grand illusion, the Divine Mother, the Mahashakti.

Mahamudra — In Tibetan Buddhism, one of the foremost of all practices, termed "The Great Seal" since it recognizes that all things bear the steadfast seal of spontaneous emptiness and luminosity.

Mahanarayana Upanisad — A fine Upanisad dealing with the religious life of Vedic culture in general, said to be transmitted by the revered rishi, Yajnatma Narayan.

Mahaprakriti — A name for the Divine Mother of the Universe, under whose auspice and control all of prakriti, nature, operates.

Mahapralaya — The withdrawal of all worlds of name, form, and concept back into their primal Essence at the time of universal dissolution.

Maharloka — The fourth of seven worlds within Consciousness, finer than svarloka but short of janaloka.

Mahasamadhi — An explanatory abd distinctive term utilized to describe the merging of an illumined soul into Brahman after its passing from the body and the physical realm.

Mahasamhitas — Great cosmic connections which are primal in their inception, they are eternally present in the Mind of God.

Mahashakti — The Supreme power inherent in Ultimate Reality which causes the powers of creation, preservation, and dissolution to formulate and activate the worlds of name and form.

Mahat — Cosmic Intelligence; the first principle of creation according to the Sankhya Philosophy of Kapila.

Mahatattva — Great principle, like the Bindu.

Mahat-seva — Service of the great ones, like the sages, seers, rishis, and the guru.

Mahavakyas — The four divine declarations of nondual experience; Tat Tvamasi, Aham Brahmasmi, Prajnanam Brahma, and Ayamatma Brahma.

Mahayoga — The fullest expression of Yoga, including all paths and philosophies within it.

Mahayuga — The collection of all four yugas, satya, treta, dvapara, and kali, as a very long phase of cyclical time.

Maheshvara — A powerful name for Divine Reality appearing as Lord Siva.

Mahima — Greatness, glory; one of the Eight Occult Powers which bestow upon those who seek lower pursuits the ability to become radiant, impressive or suffused with light.

Mahut — Elephant driver.

Maitrah — Friendliness.

Malas — Limitations; imperfections; negative tendencies in the mind which, according to Tantra, are ripened and transcended via spiritual practice. (These are not to be confused with a mala, which is a set of holy beads, like a rosary, used for mantra practice.)

Malaya breeze — The mythical, mystical wind blowing from the direction of Malaysia that was supposed to transform all trees into Sandalwood, an analogy used to illustrate the fact that when the wind of God's grace is blowing, all worthy beings realize their inherent divinity.

Mallika — A fragrant flower prized for its use in worshiping God in puja.

Mamakara — Strong sense of ownership; possessiveness; one of the Sixteen Evolutes of Maya.

Mamatva — The sense of I, me, and mine.

Manahpranasambandha — Literally, connecting oneself to the luminous mind via the purified prana, the idea being that most beings have not found and awakened their prana, so their subtle body (mind) remains unreachable to them. Thus, their consciousness remains only in the brain, or physical body.

Manasa-japa — Reciting the mantra silently, in the mind.

Manasana — The art of mental postures which, when assumed, heal, spiritualize, and perfect the mind.

Manasika — Having to do with the mental faculty.

Mandukyopanisad — A major upanisad made all the more important by Gaudapada's karika or commentary on it. Its teachings explain the four quarters of the sacred bija Aum and transmit the essence of nonduality called Advaita Vedanta.

Manipura — The chakra, "lotus," or spiritual center, third in succession, located at the navel.

Mano-buddhi Yoga — The rare yoga of focusing on the mind with purificatory disciplines designed to remove limitations and sufferings at their source. This yoga has seen a re-emergence in this day and time due to the influence of Sri Sarada Devi's presence on earth.

Manojavittvam — Acquiring mastery of the speed of the mind's thoughts, which is one of the victories of the Tantra tradition.

Manomayakosha — The sheath of the mind; the mental body as a covering over Reality.

Mantra — A powerful formula consisting of seed syllables and Holy Names that the initiate uses to purify the mind and invoke the presence of God.

Mantra Diksha — Initiation by a spiritual teacher into religious life.

Mantreshvaras — In Shaivism, a cross section of beings who still have a trace of desire left for the worlds of name and form, but whose minds vibrate with a subtler intelligence than most embodied beings.

Mantri Guru — That aspect or type of guru that facilitates and confers initiation into spiritual life.

Manus yatvam — A human birth, which is one of the three great boons needed in order to gain enlightenment.

Manvantara — An extended period of time consisting of 71 celestial yugas, and over which Manu rules.

Mara — In Buddhism, an enemy or demon; passion; desire; destroyer; a name for Siva.

Matras — Particles, or units, often used in the sense of the three sections/letters (matras) of The Word, AUM.

Matrika — Alphabets, words, letters, all in conjunction with their innate power to formulate worlds of name and form in time and space.

Matrika-shakti — The power of the Divine Mother inherent in all words, statements.

Matsarya — Jealousy; one of the Six Passions.

Mauna — Silence; a vow of silence taken by those who are striving for spirituality.

Maya — The deluding power that posits form over Formless Essence, and that consists mainly of name, form, time, space, and causality — all assumed to be real due to its stultifying influence.

Mayahamkara — Worship of the ego in maya by worldly and ignorant beings.

Mayic — Having to do with maya and its ever-changing effects.

Mayika — Projecting, deluding power; one of the three pasas, malas or limitations according to Tantra which bind in order to save. Mayika provides beings with the psycho/physical being and the many worlds and embroils them in enjoyment of the objects of pleasure. Along with karmika and anava, mayika binds certain kinds of evolving souls and veils from them their inherent nature as Shiva. Gaining initiation from a guru and attaining jnana, they can manage to get free.

Medhakendra — The knowledge of the heart.

Milarepa — A luminary of the Mahasiddha lineage of Tibet who was a fine songwriter and an uncommon and unique teacher. He was a student of Marpa who brought the yoga-based teachings of the Mahasiddhas to Tibet from India. His songs communicate the essence of enlightenment and are a living transmission even today.

Mirabai — North Indian princess of the Fifteenth century whose passionate collections of devotional songs of surrender to Lord Krishna, called Padavali, are popular all over India and abroad.

Mishtram — Mixed results, borne via works done with half-hearted attention.

Mithya — False, illusory.

Mithyajnan — Knowledge thought to be true, which is actually false.

Mithyajnan Marga — The path of delusion that ignorant beings fall into, life after life.

Moha — Delusion; false identification; infatuation; one of the Seven Malas of Maya; one of the Six Passions listed in Vedanta.

Mrduvairagya — Meek or exceedingly mild detachment, which has little or no lasting or beneficial effect on life; the second of the Twelve Levels of Dispassion of Vedanta Philosophy.

Mudha — Foolish; slothful; the second of the Five States of Mind in Yoga which conduces only to laziness and inadvertence and makes the aspirant unfit for spiritual realization.

Mudhavastha — One of Five States of Mind wherein one is completely forgetful of one's true nature; one of the Sixteen Evolutes of Maya.

Mudita — Unbridled joy, felt by the devotee upon communion with the Lord.

Mukhya Prana — The prana gotten from eating pure food, that must be transformed into refined energy for doing sadhana.

Mula — Root, as in the basis of a thing — like root ignorance, or mulashrama.

Muladhara Chakra — The root chakra located at the base of the spine where Kundalini Shakti lies coiled up until it is awakened by spiritual disciplines.

Mula-trikona — The "Primal Triangle," involved intricately with the conception of the first form.

Mulavidya — Root ignorance or primal ignorance. It is the same as mulajnana in that all potentialities, positive and negative, spring from it.

Mumukshutvam — A strong desire or longing for liberation; the fourth of the Four Jewels of Vedanta sadhana and spiritual attainment.

Mundakopanisad — Literally, the "cutting edge of a razor," this Upanisad gives teachings designed to cut away ignorance from the mind. Its profound authority comes from the fact that its wisdom, a direct transmission from the god Brahma, is given by the great rishi Angiras to the famed disciple Saunaka.

Muni — A wise person or sage, often one that observes mauna, silence.

Murti — Form; an idol to be worshipped.

Mussalman — An adherent and follower of the Muslim religion.

Nadis — Subtle channels, similar to the nervous system in the physical body, but permeating the subtle body and beyond. It is through these subtle nerves that prana, psychic prana, and shakti power course in the awakened aspirant and adept.

Nagas — A class of beings that inhabit the intermediate regions between earth and lower heaven, often seen in reptile form.

Namarupa — A cover-all term for name and form, applying to the world of created things that are transitory and impermanent.

Nandi — The sacred bull who acts as Shiva's mount and companion.

Narada — A luminary who wrote the Narada Bhakti Sutras which are definitive texts of Bhakti Yoga. Sage Narada appears throughout the many scriptures of Hinduism where he is privileged to have the darshan of Lord Vishnu and many other gods and goddesses. Sri Ramakrishna mentions him as a holy man of the highest order.

Narayan — A name for God; God manifest in mankind.

Nastika — Unorthodox, in reference to those darshanas or systems of philosophy that do not base their authority on the Vedas (i.e,. Buddhism, Jainism, etc.), as compared to Astika (i.e., Yoga, Vedanta, Sankhya, etc.), which do.

Nataraj — A name for Siva as the purifier of all impurities, and remover of limitations.

Natmandir — A music or lecture hall adjoining the temple precincts, usually used for devotional song and dance.

Neti-neti — "Not this, not this." A Vedantic practice of the Jnana Yoga school which proceeds by negating all phenomenal things until the Ultimate Reality stands revealed. The practice culminates in iti-iti, "all this, all this," which declares that all is indeed Brahman.

Nidanas — In Buddhism, the twelve links that bind the body into the cycle of rebirth by conditioning the mind into forms of bondage over several lifetimes.

Nididhyasana — Realizing the Truth after completing the steps of shravana and manana.

Nidra — Deep sleep; a type of samadhi wherein everything merges into formlessness.

Nimitta — Causality; one of the five aspects of maya, as in name, form, time, space, and causation.

Nirguna — Having no gunas, or qualities, thus formless and free of all conditionings.

Nilkantha — The blue-throated one, which is a name for Lord Siva.

Nirmamo — Freedom from egotism.

Nirmanakaya — One of the three bodies of the Buddha, being the body of transformation.

Nirodha — The end of all the mind's activities, culminating in nirvana or samadhi.

Nirvana — Literally, "Free of desire," it is the direct experience of freedom uninhibited by any condition or limitation; spiritual emancipation.

Nirvashana — The extinction of desires.

Nirvikalpa Samadhi — Direct nondual experience of the impersonal or egoless type; the highest Samadhi; immersion into formless essence.

Nischaya-dardhyam — The full inward resolve that "Existence Is."

Nistha — Firmly established; one-pointedness, as in Ishta-nistha, devotion to a single ideal; or Atma-nistha, dedication to Realization of the Atman; or Brahma-nistha.

Niskama karma — Work or actions performed without any desire for personal gain or recompense. It is the kind of activity, transcendent of any karmic residue, that enlightened beings engage in.

Nishtam — One-pointedness, like in works done for the Lord dwelling in living beings.

Nitai — An affectionate nickname for Chaitanya's beloved disciple, Nityananda.

Nitya — The Eternal, referring to Brahman, or pure, conscious Awareness.

Nityanitya-vastu-viveka — Exacting and noncompromising discrimination between the Real and the unreal, the changing and the Unchanging, which is an indispensable mainstay and often overlooked requisite for spiritual life and its aim of Self-realization.

Nitya-shuddha-bodha-rupa — The very nature of eternal purity and supreme intelligence.

Nityasiddha — A class of ever-free beings who are always aware of their inherent perfection.

Nivrittijnana — Higher knowledge that is based upon renunciation of the world, as contrasted to pravritti which follows the path of the world.

Nivrittimarga — The path of higher knowledge leading to the renunciation of the world.

Niyamas — Five practices in Yoga which constitute the second limb of Patanjala which, along with the five yamas, prepare the practitioner for encountering the six higher limbs in order.

Niyati — The principle of cosmic laws, which is one of the twelve higher tattvas in Shavism.

Ojas — Subtle internal power gathered from spiritual practices involving the ingestion of pure food, control of prana, striving for scriptural knowledge, etc., — all sublimated and brought inwards for purposes of purification leading to Enlightenment.

Omkaravrittidhyan — The dissolution of all the mind's thought-waves into The Word, AUM.

Pada — The formulation of letters and words into profound statements that illumine awareness; a principle that is taught and maintained, as in the Four Padas of Lord Siva.

Padartha Bhavana — The sixth of seven states of Higher Knowledge, a level of Consciousness that is penultimate to the highest realization, i.e., Turiya.

Pakvahamkara — The human ego, ahamkara, that through spiritual disciplines and self-surrender, has become refined or matured, i.e., surrendered unto God, and is thus pakva, ripe.

Panchakarana — The original ancient wisdom of the fivefold cause, which lists and traces the origin of all forms and worlds based upon the sets of fives, i.e., five elements, five senses, five pranas, etc.

Panchakosha — The classical five sheaths of Vedanta, listed as coverings over Reality, namely body, energy, mind, intellect, and ego.

Panchamahabhutas — The great five elements, namely earth, water, fire, air, and ether.

Pancha-yajna — The five sacrifices performed by dharmic beings, namely, to the rishis, the deities, the ancestors, the sub-species, and mankind.

Pandavas — The righteous clan of Arjuna and his brothers and family who fought for justice against the evil Kaurava clan in the sacred scripture of the Bhagavad Gita, contained in the Mahabharata.

Pani — Water.

Para — Supreme; the first stage of manifestation of highest knowledge through the primal sound vibration. It is an undifferentiated state where no concepts, thoughts, meanings or words are yet manifest.

Parabrahma — The Ultimate Reality or Supreme Being as formless essence or Pure Consciousness.

Paragatam — The supreme Goal; Nirvana.

Parama-drk — Clear grasp of the Supreme View.

Paramahamkara — One of the Three Kinds of Ego referred to in Vedanta scriptures, two positive and one negative, mainly Paramahamkara, Sakshahamkara, and Dehadhyasahmakara. The first is the most refined, subtle, and allows for the advent of spiritual Consciousness into the body/mind mechanism.

Paramahamsa — Literally, "Great Swan." A title referring to the highest class of sanyasins, as in the authentic Paramahamsa of this day and time, Sri Ramakrishna Paramahamsa.

Paramasiva — The Transcendental Siva, or Siva in His whole Essence as Formless Reality.

Paramatman — The Supreme Soul.

Paramukti — Absolute liberation.

Paraprakasha — The supreme space of nondual Awareness.

Parashakti — The highest aspect of shakti.

Parasparadhyasa — A stolid delusion in the human mind that perceives and enforces the idea of the physical body as the indwelling Self, and the indwelling Self as the body; one of the Sixteen Evolutes of Maya.

Paravairagya — Supreme detachment, being the highest station of dispassion possible; the final stage of the

Twelve Levels of Dispassion.

Paravidya — Supreme knowledge associated with the direct experience of Brahman; sometimes used to indicate the distinction between knowledge of the truths of the scriptures as opposed to secular knowledge.

Parigraha — The habitual exchanging of gifts and wealth among the peoples of the world, which takes attention away from the Goal of Life — to realize God.

Parigraha Shaktis — Lord Siva's two auspicious dynamic powers, through which he accomplishes the work of His four padas.

Parikarmas — Four types of beneficial attitudes to adopt in spiritual life in accordance with different kinds of beings one meets, namely friendliness, compassion, reverence, and indifference.

Parinama — The illusory phenomena of change; the appearance of transformation when there can be none — since all is unoriginated.

Partha — A name for Arjuna, the son of Priti.

Pasas — In Tantra, limitations or temporary imperfections that bind embodied souls to the sense of karma, relativity, and duality.

Pasyanti — The second stage of manifested knowledge through the primal sound vibration where undifferentiated Wisdom begins to condense and form in order to manifest as conceptualized thought on the cosmic level.

Pashupati — A name for Lord Siva, which is one of the most ancient appelations given to him.

Pasu — Animalistic, referring to the Three Designations of Aspirants in Tantra Philosophy, divine, heroic, and animalistic. The aspirant at the pasu level is still attached to the body and the senses and has gained little detachment from the world and its pleasures/sufferings as a result.

Patala — Nether region; the seventh and lowest of the hell realms.

Patanjala Yoga — Called Raja Yoga and Ashtanga Yoga, it is the classic yogic pathway with eight progressive but interconnected practices, namely: yamas, niyamas, asana, pranayama, pratyahara, dharana, dhyana, and samadhi. It bears little resemblance to, nor should it be mistaken for what passes for Yoga in present times, which is often just Hatha Yoga, a series of body postures practiced merely for gaining health, longevity and the occult powers, which are potentially detrimental to the attainment of true spirituality.

Patanjali — The founder of the Patanjala Yoga system and author of the Yoga Sutras.

Paurusheya — Of human authorship, used often in reference to the sacred scriptures of the Sanatana Dharma of India.

Phalaharini Devi — An aspect of the Divine Mother of the Universe in Her capacity of granting the fruits of actions, positive, negative, and mixed, to living beings.

Phalgu — An river in North India which over the course of time went underground and flows under a bed of sand.

Pitriyana — The Path of the Fathers, or the ancestors, wherein beings return to earth after heaven.

Pradhana Jaya — One of the seven victories of the Tantric aspirant wherein he/she gains control over the initial creative principle, i.e., Prakriti.

Prahlada — A sage written of in the Puranas, who though born of a demon King, and tortured as a boy for his purity, nevertheless became a great devotee of Vishnu.

Prajnanam Brahma — "Brahman is Pure Consciousness"; one of the four Mahavakyas or divine declarations of Advaita Vedanta.

Prajnaparam — A powerful Name for Brahman, declaring It as Supreme Intelligence.

Prajnaparamita — The Mother of the Buddhas; a set of sutras of great import in Mahayana Buddhism.

Prakamya — One of the Eight Occult Powers which allows those who pursue lower ideals to become free willed with regards to fulfilling any desire or wish.

Prakarana — A section or a chapter of a scripture or commentary.

Prakasha Shakti — The Divine Mother's power of revelation.

Prakriti — Nature; causal matter; the universe of name and form and those ingredients which comprise it; the pradhana of Samkhya which corresponds to the Maya of Vedanta with these main distinctions; it exists independent of Spirit, Purusha, and it is considered real.

Pralaya — The dissolution of all worlds and forms at the end of a cosmic cycle, to be followed by another cosmic projection of worlds thereafter.

Pralaya-kalas — In Shaivism, a cross section of subtle beings who are still bound by maya, but who gain liberation at the time of pralaya.

Pramachchadika — One of the five cosmic bondages, being attachment to nature, or gross form.

Pramada — Inattentiveness; negligence; one of the Nine Distractions to Spiritual Life listed in the Yoga Sutras by Patanjali.

Pramoda — Actual enjoyment of an object, used in conjunction with the Three States of Enjoyment of Objects: priya, joy of seeing the object; moda, approaching and gaining the object; and pramoda, the actual enjoyment of said object. The "object" in question here can be material in nature, but refers also to the joy of darshan with Ishvara, or realization of Brahman as well.

Pramuchadaka-prakriti-bandha — Attachment to insentient matter as if it were the only Reality.

Prana — The life-force running through all of nature, and all bodies, which though unseen, both animates and helps connect all of existence back to its Source.

Pranakasha — The space of subtle energy, prana, wherein the ancestors dwell; lower heaven.

Pranam — The act of bowing down in reverence before a divine image or an illumined soul.

Pranamayakosha — The vital sheath; life-force as a covering over Reality.

Pranas — The five types of the singular prana that operate to facilitate flow and health on the physical plane. These five have a fivefold counterpart on the subtle plane, or dream-state, which assume a psychic nature in order to move thoughts through different levels of consciousness.

Pranava — Another name for the sacred Word, AUM.

Pranayam — Breathing exercises designed to awaken subtle energy in both body and mind, it occupies the position of the fourth limb of Yoga's Eight-limbed system (ashtanga).

Pranic — Having to do with the prana.

Prarabdha — As in prarabdha karma, which is karma from previous existences that is taken up in the present lifetime for working out.

Prasad — Clarity, often connected to purification of food prior to its ingestion.

Prastanatraya — The three great landmarks is scriptural history, namely The Brahma Sutras, the Bhagavad Gita, and the Upanisads.

Pratibha — The flint-like intelligence that cuts through maya and its various overlays.

Pratibhandaka — The presence of obstructions and impediments potential in everything.

Pratibhandakabhava — The underlying power of subtle intelligence lying in every mind, every situation that, when accessed, provides thorough solutions for life's problems.

Pratibhasikasatta — The overall dream projection by the mind in its three phases, cosmic, collective, and individual.

Pratika — An object of sacred atmosphere utilized in early meditation to aid the mind's concentration.

Pratima — Similar to pratika, usually made of a physical substance like wood, metal, etc.

Pratipakshabhavana — The helpful mood or attitude wherein the aspirant causes the mind to raise an opposite wave in order to do away with negative or habitual thoughts.

Pratistha — Steadiness.

Prati-tantra siddhanta — The way of arriving at a religious or philosophical conclusion based upon contrasting one path, way, or religion, against another.

Pratitya Samutpada — "Conditioned Arising," enumerating the Twelve Nidanas, or links that bind the soul to the reincarnation process.

Pravrittijnana — Lower knowledge that focuses upon action to assist earthly existence.

Pravrittimarga — The path of lower knowledge that beings who desire the world of objects and pleasures walk, life to life.

Pratyagatman — A word that pertains to the supreme Self, or Atman as Brahman.

Pratyahara — Freeing the mind from attachment to senses objects, which is the fifth limb of Yoga falling after control of the prana, and before actual concentration.

Prema — Ecstatic Love for God; one of the Four Perfections of the Heart.

Prema-bhakti — The highest kind of devotion, beyond Vaidya and Raga Bhakti, which involve ritualistic devotion and the various devotional moods. To paraphrase Sri Ramakrishna, Prema Bhakti is that purest of Love which makes one forget personal considerations, even the body that is usually so dear to human beings.

Pretas — A cross section of lost beings who are bound to lower realms, or patalas.

Priya moda pramoda — With regards to the Lord, the bhakta loves to see, approach, and enjoy bliss.

Puja — Ceremonial worship attended by offerings, mudras, mantras, and devotional music.

Pujari — The officiating priest at a puja ceremony.

Puraka — The indrawn breath, in conjunction with suspended breath, kumbhaka, and the exhaled breath, rechaka.

Purna — Fullness; completeness.

Purna Brahma — A name for Divine Mother in Her role as the identity of Brahman.

Purnahanta — The real "I," in fullness.

Purusha — The Sentient Soul, different from prakriti, matter; The Supreme Soul, as in Paramapurusha.

Purushanyathatakhyati — Knowing the Divine Self to be completely unique and different from all created things; the highest or deepest of the Seven Victories of Involution in Tantra Philosophy.

Purusharthas — The Four Fruits/Ideals of life as granted by the Divine Mother of the Universe, namely dharma, artha, karma, and moksha.

Purva — View, or perspective.

Purva Mimamsa — One of the six orthodox philosophies, or darshanas, of India.

Puryastaka — The eight-fold body, deha, consisting of the five senses and a three-fold mind.

Pushkar Dvipa — The subtlest of all realms, often correlated with Brahmaloka.

Rabindranath Tagore — A great poet and philosopher of modern India.

Radhakrishna — The conjoining of Radha and Krishna.

Raga — Attachment, which is one of the seven malas of maya; a higher tattva in Shaivism which is the attracting power present in all of creation.

Raga bhakti — The second stage of bhakti's development wherein what was worshipped externally (in the vaidhi bhakti stage) begins to show up as devotion in the heart, internally.

Ragadveshau — The troublesome combination of two of the five kleshas in Patanjali's Yoga teachings, namely attachment and aversion.

Rahasya — Secret, as in Sristhi Rahasya, wherein the secret of all things is traced back to The Word.

Rajas — Rajo guna, the mode of Prakriti that, on a cosmic level, places all things in motion, and on an individual level, induces beings into all manner of activity, usually of a frenetic variety.

Rajasic — Influenced by the guna of rajas.

Ram — The Divine Incarnation of the Treta Yuga whose heroic actions and superior teachings appear in the *Adhyatma Ramayana* and other scriptures.

Ramachandra — The full name of Sri Ram, the Avatar of the treta yuga.

Ramakrishna — The great God-intoxicated holy man of nineteenth-century Bengal who was the guru of Swami Vivekananda and the husband of Sri Sarada Devi. Accepted by many as the Kali Avatar, the Divine Incarnation of this age, He came with a host of Ishvarakotis and illumined followers who founded the Order named after Him and whose followers sustain it in the present day. His advent has been responsible for the reemergence of the Divine Mother path and other beneficial blessings.

Ramana Maharshi — A fully realized seer of India who lived recently, in contemporary times, and who, among other things, brought the ancient nondual wisdom of Atma Vichara to practitioners of this era.

Ramanuja — The father and representative of qualified nondualism, contrasted to Madhva as the representative of dualism, and Shankara as the representative of nondualism.

Ramprasad — The well-loved poet/saint of eighteenth-century Bengal whose wisdom songs to Mother Kali, the Divine Mother of the Universe, inspired a nation and are still inspiring the world today.

Rasas — Fluid essences of the physical body.

Ravana — A powerful and arrogant rakshasa who abducted Sita and was finally destroyed by Sri Ramachandra.

Rechaka — The expelled breath.

Rishis — Illumined beings from ancient Vedic times who practiced extreme austerities in order to receive the truths contained in the Vedas and Upanishads. Most were married, of both sexes, and passed their wisdom to their children.

Roshi — A revered teacher in Zen Buddhism.

Rudra — Lord Siva in his wrathful or purificatory form.

Rudragranthi — A subtle knot or barrier at very high levels of Awareness, that nevertheless keeps souls from reaching the highest Formless Reality.

Rudraksha — A seed that is used to creat a special mala, considered extra auspicious for recitation of the mantra.

Rupaloka — In Zen, the realm of desireless form, being one of the three worlds.

Sadakhya — One of the twelve higher cosmic principles in Shaivism; an incredible teaching system that employs six higher principles in order to explain the appearance of all the worlds of name and form in time and space.

Sadasat — Being both real and unreal, simultaneously, which is a description of the world-bewitching maya.

Sadasiva — One of the twelve higher spandas of Shaivism; a name for the highest aspect of Lord Siva.

Sadguru — A rare world teacher of outstanding realization.

Sadhana — Spiritual disciplines undertaken to realize God.

Sadhanachatushtaya — The Four Treasures and the Six Jewels of Vedanta, the third treasure containing the six jewels. If there is any type of "practice" present in the Vedanta — it being all a statement of Truth — it is this system, which is really a stance of higher mind maintaining itself in nonduality amidst the vagaries of the world and maya. Thus it can be named Advaita Vedanta Sadhana, well-deserved.

Sadharani — An ordinary love that seeks its own good and ends first, regardless of the good of the beloved; one of the Four Categories of Love.

Sadhika — One who practices sadhana, or spiritual disciplines.

Sadurmi — The six waves, or transformations, in Vedanta, namely grief, delusion, hunger, thirst, decay, and death.

Sagara — Ocean, primarily used to describe the ocean of suffering (samsara sagara) and the ocean of bliss (bhava sagara).

Saguna — Invested with gunas and qualities, thus having to operate under their influence.

Saguna Brahman — God with attributes; Reality with name, form, and qualities.

Sahaja-tantra siddhanta — The way of arriving at a religious or philosophical conclusion based upon knowing the natural synthesis of all religions and pathways, all of them sourced and centered in Divine Reality.

Saham — "I am She," a nondualistic statement of the Divine Mother worshipper.

Sahasa — Courage, not just of the physical kind, but rather the courage to maintain spiritual life in the face of obstacles.

Sahashrara chakra — The highest center of awareness, called the crown chakra, located at the top of the head.

Sakalas — In Shaivism, a cross section of subtle beings who, though they have Siva's grace, are still bound by several malas of maya.

Sakama — With desire, as in actions done in selfishness.

Sakhya Bhava — A mood or attitude assumed by a devotee which looks upon God as friend or companion; one of the Five Divine Moods for Worshiping God.

Sakshi — A word referring to Witness Consciousness, which oversees all phenomena without getting involved in it or affected by it.

Sakshahamkara — One of the Three Kinds of Ego referred to in Vedanta scriptures, two of them positive and one negative, mainly Paramahamkara, Sakshahamkara, and Dehadhyasahamakara. It is the kind of ego that is the detached witness (sakshi) of all phenomena.

Salokya — Abiding in the same plane, realm, or world with the Lord.

Sama — Inner peace, one of the Six Jewels, Shatsampatti, being a state of calm and silent mental balance requisite to attaining deeper spiritual qualities of spiritual life and enlightenment.

Samadhana — One of the Six Jewels, Shatsampatti, which is a special type of concentration which naturally restricts the mind from falling back from higher states of meditation.

Samadarshitvam — Same-sightedness, looking upon all equally.

Samadhi — Literally, "to make immovable," steady and impervious to external conditions. Any of the various kinds of spiritual moods or states of Consciousness brought about by meditation upon Reality, either with form or without form.

Samana — The digestive, distributive prana.

Samanjasa — Love that seeks the good of the beloved, but whose motive is based upon its own good as well; one of the Four Categories of Love.

Samanya — Common, or ordinary; the second category of causes of diseases that are purely physical.

Samapati — Abiding equanimity of mind, which is one of the three treasures of Yoga.

Samartha — The highest type of love which seeks only to fulfill the needs of the beloved; one of the Four Categories of Love.

Samasti — The collective whole rather than the individual, the macrocosm as compared to the microcosm.

Samatva — Abiding calm and steadiness, throughout.

Sambhogakaya — One of the three bodies of the Buddha, being the blissful enlightenment body.

Samhitas — One of the primary sections of the Vedas containing hymns and sacred formulas.

Samipya — Exceedingly dear to the Lord while enjoying God's direct presence.

Samittis — In Jainism, the six types of conduct that ensure nonviolent action and lifestyle.

Sampradaya — A sect or religious organization.

Samprajnata Samadhi — A high state of Awareness mentioned by Patanjali in the Yoga Sutras which is still accompanied by traces of individualized consciousness. In it, an awareness of the triad of meditator, meditation and that which is meditated upon still remains. It is generally synonymous with Savikalpa Samadhi in the Vedanta school.

Samprasad — One of the four prasads or clarities, wherein the peaceful mood is attained and maintained.

Samsara — The wheel of birth and death in suffering caused by ignorance.

Samsaric — Referring to what involves samsara.

Samsaris — Beings caught in samsara.

Samsara-prag-bhara — Bondage stream; one of the Two Directions of the Mind-Stream after death mentioned by Patanjali and Vedavyasa. One stream of souls moves towards liberation (kaivalya-prag-bhara), and the other towards bondage and rebirth in ignorance.

Samshaya — Doubt; one of the Nine Distractions to Spiritual Life according to Yoga Philosophy.

Samskaras — Positive and negative latent impressions in the subconscious and unconscious mind that shape human character and which are caused by repetitious actions through many lifetimes.

Samskaraskandhas — Collections of samskaras that form subtle and impeding complexes in the mind.

Samvit — A word for Absolute Reality, nondual Awareness.

Samyama — The combination of dharana, dhyana, and samadhi, the final three stages of Patanjala Yoga, which enables the yogi to attain anything desired.

Sananda Samadhi — One of the four seeded samadhi's of Patanjala Yoga.

Sanatana Dharma —The Eternal Religion of the ancient Vedic culture; which is Eternal Truth, which is transcendent of conception by the human mind, and is ever-existent. All of the many pathways, religions, and darshanas of India make up this Eternal Truth. Sri Ramakrishna has stated that "...the Sanatana Dharma of India has always existed, and will always exist."

Sanchita — As in sanchita karma, it is the collected karma of many past lifetimes, a portion of which is taken up to be worked on each new lifetime.

Sandhya — Daily ritual of purification for the devout Hindu consisting of ablutions and prayer.

Sandilya-vidya — Proper orientation in spiritual life, which aids with right view.

Sanga — Literally, "in good company," the term is used to denote holy company, particularly with regards to the spiritual family of seekers with which the devotee associates.

Sankalpa — Mental projection, usually done out of desire for forms, worlds, wealth, and objects, it, along with its desire, are responsible for the appearance of the worlds of name and form in time and space.

Sankhya — One of six orthodox systems of philosophy in Vedic culture which astutely outlines the various principles that comprise the universe. Its widespread acceptance is noted in both Yoga and Vedanta.

Sanyasin — One who takes a vow of renunciation of the world and enters spiritual life, following the fourth and final station of the dharmashrama.

Santosha — One of the five niyamas of Yoga that is a blissful contentment.

Sarada Devi — The Divine Mother in human form manifesting in this age, also known as the Holy Mother, the spiritual consort of Sri Ramakrishna Paramahamsa. She lived from 1853 to 1920 and was the inspiration and spiritual leader of the Ramakrishna Order after the Great Master's Mahasamadhi, initiating hundreds of devotees into spiritual life.

Sarasvati — The Goddess of art and learning who is listed as one of the Five Main Aspects of the Universal Mother (Prakriti Panchaka) in the *Srimad Devi Bhagavatam*.

Sarupya — Being of the same form as God

Sarva-tantra siddhanta — The way of arriving at a religious or philosophical conclusion based upon accepting the beliefs of all paths, ways, and religions.

Sarvahimsa Vinirmukta — Complete nonviolence towards all beings; one of the Seven Qualifications of a Tantric Aspirant.

Sarvamukti — The totally emancipated state wherein all and everything is liberated.

Sarvam Khalvidam Brahman — "All This Is Brahman."

Sarva vyakatva shakti — The all-pervasive power of Divine Mother.

Sasmita Samadhi — One of the four "seeded" samadhis of Yoga, wherein the ripe ego enjoys subtle bliss.

Satatam — Steady in meditation.

Satchitananda — Pure Being, pure Consciousness, pure Bliss Absolute; a name for the formless Brahman.

Sati — The ancient practice of offering the body into fire as sacrifice

Satguru — A world teacher such as Krishna, Christ, Buddha, Mohammed or Sri Ramakrishna and other founders of the world's great religious traditions.

Satsang — Gathering in holy company to hear about, reflect, and question about the Truth.

Satta-samanya — Homogenous Existence, Absolute.

Sattva — Sattva guna. The mode of Prakriti that, on a cosmic level, fills the universe with peace and unity and, on an individual level, induces balance and equilibrium in human action and behavior.

Sattva Purusha Nyatakhyati — The ultimate Victory of the seven Tantric victories wherein the now illumined soul espies the Atman as the only Reality, and sees It existing on its own, in its own self-effulgent Light.

Sattvic — Being in a balanced and positive condition where sattva guna is predominant.

Satyaloka — Same as Brahmaloka.

Satyam — Truth; truthfulness in thought, word, and deed. It is one of the ten yamas and niyamas of Patanjala Yoga and a mainstay of spiritual life in general.

Saucha — Purity; one of the five niyamas of Yoga's second limb.

Savichara — Deliberate inquiry; inPatanjala, a type of seeded samadhi.

Savikalpa Samadhi — A very high state of Consciousness wherein Brahman with attributes is experienced through the refined mechanism of the detached and ripened ego/mind complex.

Savitarka — Explanation utilizing logic and argumentation; in Patanjala, a type of seeded samadhi.

Sayujya — Attaining oneness with Divine Reality; one of the Four Kinds of Liberations in form.

Seva — Selfless service rendered unto the guru, the ashrama, and the devotees.

Sevanam — Serving all beings as God; one of the Eight Devotional Aids according to Devarshi Narada.

Siddhantavakyashravana — Coming to the right conclusion about the nature of Divine Reality via counsel of the preceptor and study of the scriptures.

Shabda — The sound Brahman; God as subtle vibration.

Shaiva Agamas — Tantric Scriptures having to do with the worship of Shiva and His Shakti.

Shaivite — A worshipper of Lord Siva, follower of Shaivism.

Shaktadvaitavada — A superlative path that combines nonduality with Divine Mother worship.

Shakti — The creative force of the universe that is the active principle of Brahman yet identical with It. Shakti is different and more subtle than prana, which is a force that it uses to create. As the Mahashakti or Universal Mother, It is also the wielder of the forces of Maya and Prakriti.

Shakti Agamas — Tantric scriptures having to do with the worship of the Divine Mother of the Universe in Her many forms.

Shaktiman — The wielder of Shakti; Divine Mother.

Shamata — The "calm-abiding" practice, path, and meditation.

Shankara — The great exponent of Advaita Vedanta who brought it into prominence and spread it broadcast throughout India and the world. He authored such important texts as the Vivekachudamani and Atma Bodha among others; a name for Lord Shiva.

Shankaracharya — Shankara's name reflecting his guru status.

Shanta Bhava — One of the five devotional moods adopted by the bhakta, being the peaceful mood.

Shanti — Peace, particularly of mind.

Sharanagata — Taking refuge in God and spiritual life.

Sharanam — Taking whole-hearted refuge in the Lord; one of the Eight Devotional Aids according to Devarshi Narada.

Sharira — A sheath, or covering over Reality, like the body and mind.

Shastr'anuvartanam — One of the three great desires of living beings, which is to perform various rites and rituals — not to extract knowledge or higher purpose from them, but simply to be engaged in conventional religious activities and their ordinary fruits.

Shastras — The sacred scriptures.

Shatavadana — Doing a thousand things at once; one of the Sixteen Evolutes of Maya.

Shatsampatti — The third of the Four Treasures of Vedanta, consisting of six jewels, namely, inner peace, self-control, forbearance, contentment, concentration, and faith.

Shishya — An initiated disciple of a guru.

Shoka — Grief; one of the Eight Fetters.

Shraddha — Faith, one of the Six Jewels, Shatsampatti, signaling a firm and unshakable realization of the existence of Divine Reality.

Shravana — Hearing the Truth from an illumined preceptor, which along with its two concomitants, Manana and Nididhasana — contemplating and realizing the Truth — comprise the Three Great Practices of Advaita Vedanta.

Srimad Devi Bhagavatam — One of two Divine Mother scriptures in the world, very important to our day and time, wherein the Goddess teaches all beings in various ways through over 1000 pages of Wisdom.

Shravanam — Hearing the scriptures; listening to God's glories daily; one of the Eight Devotional Aids according to Narada along with smaranam, archanam, kirtanam, vandanam, sevanam, bhajanam and sharanam – remembering the Lord, adoring Him, singing His glories, worshipping Him, serving Him and His devotees, fostering devotion to Him and taking complete refuge in Him.

Shrotriya — One of the four classic qualifications of the guru wherein he/she possesses the ability to transmit the essence of the teachings unto the disciple.

Shruti — Hearing the Truth, to be followed by contemplating (manana) and realizing It ((nididhyasana).

Shuchi — Pure, untainted; one of the Seven Qualifications of a Tantric Aspirant.

Shuddha — Pure and untainted.

Shuddhabuddhamukta — Ever pure, ever aware, ever free, which is an assignment befitting the true Self, or Atman/Purusha, of mankind.

Shuddha Vidya — One of the twelve higher spandas of Shaivism, revealing the purest of wisdom.

Shuddhashuddha — A mixture of the pure and the impure, as in the middle grade tattvas like mind, and ego.

Shvasaprashvasah — Unevenness of breathing; one of the Four Causes of Distraction to Meditation and Spiritual Life in Yoga according to Patanjali.

Shunya or Shunyata — Emptiness, referring to the insubstantial nature of all things.

Siddhanta — An established tenet or philosophy; definitive conclusion around a philosophical perspective.

Siddhas — A class of perfected beings; a class of beings attracted to the attainment of limited occult powers.

Sita — The Divine Mother of the Universe in Her aspect of immaculate Purity who manifested in the Treta Yuga as the divine consort of Sri Ramchandra.

Sivakala —A name for Lord Siva in his role as the overseer of all phases of time.

Skandha — A collection of subtle residues in the mind that form into samskaras, mental impressions, and which, in turn, can form a collection of samskaras as well.

Slokas — Verses found in scriptures, written there by the seers, which are studied, memorized, and recited by the sincere spiritual aspirant.

Smaranam — Continual remembrance of God; one of the Eight Devotional Aids according to Devarshi Narada.

Smritihetu — Original memory, or the source of all memory, which is stored in the mind throughout its cycles of transmigrations. Accessing it brings knowledge of one's past incarnations to the fore.

Smriti-shuddha — Purity of mind and memory.

Spandas — Vibrating spheres of consciousness within the Great Mind, as in Akashas, Lokas, Fields of the Lord, or Kingdoms of Heaven within.

Sphota — The primal manifester, i.e., The Word, which bursts forth spontaneously.

Sri Aurobindo — A seer and luminary of contemporary India, and the author of numerous books on the Vedic and Yogic Path.

Sristi — Creation, which in Indian philosophy is used to explain the apparent beginning of things and cycles of time, all of which are really unoriginated, thus eternal.

Sristi Rahasya — The Secret of Creation.

Sthiti — Preservation, or sustenance, existing as the middle stage between sristhi and laya.

Sthiti Prajnasya — An elevated state of steady wisdom, covered by the luminaries.

Stula Sharira — Of the human being's three bodies, it is the gross body consisting of five elements, the five active senses, and the body.

Sthulavairagya — Immature detachment; a rudimentary to moderate type of detachment; the seventh stage of the Twelve Levels of Dispassion cited in Vedanta Philosophy.

Sthiramatih — Steady-mindedness.

Stotram — A classic Vedic hymn consisting of Sanskrit slokas set in musical form.

Styana — Incapacity; one of the Nine Distractions in Spiritual Life cited in Yoga Philosophy by Patanjali, wherein the aspirant can muster little or no ability to remain focused on the path and the practice.

Sukadev — A great rishi, son of Vedavyasa.

Sukshma Sarira — Of the human being's three bodies, it is the subtle body consisting of the prana, the five senses of knowledge, the five subtle elements, the fourfold mind, and kama and karma.

Shukracharya — Illumined guru of the invincible asura, Bali.

Suresha — Lord of the gods; another name for Shiva.

Surya — The God of the Sun, used as an epithet in both a physical and a cosmic sense.

Sushumna — The subtle spiritual canal which carries the Kundalini Shakti through the ascending lotuses to the Sahashrara Chakra in the crown of pure mind. Indicated as the central nadi, Kundalini power rises when She is awakened by yogic practices. This "lotus" and all lotuses lie within Consciousness, and the physical spine is an external facsimile of it.

Sushupti — Deep sleep, which is one of the three states of Consciousness in living beings. It is represented by the "M" of The Word, AUM, and is where all the seeds to manifestation are contained in potential prior to the dreaming and waking states to follow.

Sutra — A Sanskrit phrase, sentence or verse with profound meaning.

Sutratman — The Self within, which intrinsically connects to everything else due to its subtle and thread-like essence; the cosmic Self, or Hiranyagarbha; the sum total of all selves in existence.

Svadharma — One's highest path or way, the ultimate dharma of one's lifetimes.

Svadhisthana — The second chakra, located symbolically at the organs of sex and voiding.

Svadhyaya — The act of engrossing oneself in an in-depth study of the scriptures, particularly the Srutis, with a view towards comprehending Truth. If this prerequisite, one of the ten niyamas of Patanjala, is not satisfied, no appreciable success in yoga is possible.

Svajatiyavrittipravaha — The concentration of the mind on one's Divine Nature, only.

Svapna — The dreaming state of the human being.

Svapnamayasvarupa — The entire gamut or body of imagined or illusory phenomena perceived as real, as in a dream.

Svara — The segment of the written word, AUM, not connected to the rest of the word, and that represents transcendental Awareness, or Turiya.

Svarupa — Essence, used in relation to the Essence of Consciousness or the highest aspect of pure Spirit.

Svarupanyathabhava — The condition of being either totally unaware of or completely in denial of one's true inner nature as pure conscious Awareness; one of the Sixteen Evolutes of Maya of Neo-Vedanta.

Svarupapratistha — The state of being fully ensconced and established in the Atman, one's true nature.

Svatantriya — Unbounded, spontaneous freedom.

Svati — The star Arcturus, used in Hindu Itihasa and story to represent an auspicious period.

Svayamjyoti — Literally, shining by its own light; a name used to describe the Atman.

Svetasvataropanisad — One of the less ancient of the Upanisads which gives salient teachings ranging from dualism to Advaita. It is found as a portion of the Black Yajur Veda.

Swami Aseshananda — The last living direct monastic disciple of Holy Mother, Sri Sarada Devi, until his passing into Mahasamadhi in 1996.

Swami Vivekananda — The foremost disciple of Sri Ramakrishna Paramahamsa, he lived from 1863 to 1902. Considered to be an emanation of Lord Shiva, he was also the first to bring the spiritual teachings of Vedanta and establish them in the West. He is also credited, along with the monastic order He helped found, with giving lucid contemporary interpretations to many ancient scriptures. His auspicious appearance and august presence at the Parliament of Religions in Chicago in 1893 is a major spiritual event in the history of the Western hemisphere, holding profound significance.

Swami Brahmananda — One of Sri Ramakrishna's 16 direct disciples, often called His "spiritual son," who was considered a world teacher (jagad-guru) and who was the first President of the Ramakrishna Order and was a close brother monk of Swami Vivekananda.

Taijasa — A name for the individual as he abides in the dreaming state, the "U" of AUM.

Tamas — Tamo guna; the mode of Prakriti that induces slothfulness and inertia.

Tamasic — Being of the condition of tamas, slothful and dull.

Tandava — The cosmic dance of Siva Nataraj which sends all into a formless state.

Tanmatras — The elements in a rudimentary state, prior to the quintuplication process.

Tanmishra — Darkness, as in deep ignorance.

Tantra — Scriptures concentrating upon living a divine life in the world through the balancing of the Shiva and Shakti energies within the human being. Though they are considered by the orthodoxy as secondary scriptures, there is reason to believe that they are as old and as important as the Vedas since many of the Rishis were Tantric practitioners. Also, the worship of Shiva and Divine Mother Shakti probably predates the Vedas which suggests that the Tantric stream is extremely ancient.

Tantracist — One who practices Tantra.

Tantric — Having to do with Tantra, the ancient philosophy which stresses direct experience of spirituality while living in the world.

Tapana — To heat, the word usually being used in correlation with the word tapas, spiritual austerities, that heat up and purify the body/mind mechanism in yogic practice.

Taparloka — The sixth of seven inner realms lying in Consciousness, the realm of the mature ascetics.

Tapasvin — A yogic practitioner who uses intense austerities to purify all elements of life.

Tapatraya — The three types of sufferings as noted in the Vedanta philosophy and other darshanas.

Tara — A name for the Divine Mother of the Universe in Her compassionate aspect.

Tarkika-buddhi — The tendency of the mind and intellect towards argumentation, which later on becomes a huge problem when higher wisdom comes through the guru and the student merely argues it.

Tat tvam asi — Literally, "That thou art" in reference to the individual soul and its connection to the Supreme Soul.

Tatastha-lakshana — One of three groups of knowledge classification noted by Advaita Vedanta concerned with indirect statements that point to characteristics of Brahman, which are, nevertheless, not necessarily Its intrinsic qualities.

Tathagatagarbha — True inner being; the transcendent conscious Awareness that is the true nature of all things, all beings.

Tattva Samasa Sutras — One, if not the only, of a rare few scriptures from the time of Lord Kapila and his ingenious Sankhya Yoga system.

Tattva Shuddha — Purification of principles, referring to the crucial mental practices which, when accomplished, render the mind free of misconceptions as to the nature of relativity and the essence of Reality.

Tattvajnana — Knowledge principle, or knowledge of Reality, similar to Brahmajnana.

Tattvas — Cosmic principles; in Sankhya Philosophy, a term for twenty-four constituents of Prakriti which make up the universe of name and form.

Tattvavichara — A state of being fully qualified in knowledge of cosmic principles.

Tavaivaham — A devotional saying, mantra, and Tantric Vakya among the Tantric adepts meaning, "I am Thine alone," stated in regard to the devotee's self-surrender and immersion in the Divine Mother of the Universe.

Tejas — The light of fully sublimated ojas that luminaries utilize for transmitting wisdom and Truth to devotess and aspirants.

Tirodhana — Self-limitation; one of the Pancha-krityas of the Tattva Prakasha School of Tantra, which form the Five Essential Functions of Shiva with regard to His appearance aspect as opposed to His Consciousness aspect. They are: Sristhi (creation), Sthiti (sustenance), Samhara (dissolution), Tirodhana (self-limitation), and Anugraha (expression-grace).

Tirthankaras — In Jainism, the twenty-four illumined souls who have held and have taught the precious teachings of Jainism over the ages, the most recent being the great soul, Mahavir.

Tiryanmarga — The path of living beings who constantly take lower births from life to life.

Titiksha — Forbearance, one of the Six Jewels, Shatsampatti, allowing the aspirant to patiently endure and eventually transcend the various dualities such as heat and cold, pleasure and pain.

Tivyavairagya — The penultimate stage of detachment which is said to be of a very intense nature, and only just short of Paravairagya, Supreme Detachment; the eleventh of the Twelve Levels of Dispassion cited in Vedanta Philosophy.

Treta Yuga — The second of four phases of time within a Mahayuga, where living beings are said to lose one third of their remembrance of their divine nature.

Trigunatita — The state of being transcendent of the three gunas of tamas, rajas, and sattva.

Triloka — An expression citing the Three Worlds of Bhur, Bhuvah, & Svar, or sometimes designating the three partitions of worlds in general, as in gross, subtle, and causal, or imminent, transcendent, and absolute.

Trimargabhedam — The threefold pathways taken by the three types of beings, the divinities, the human beings, and the demonic.

Triputis — Any of a set of three principles which have an intrinsic connection and profound meaning such as the seer, what is seen, and the ability to see, or the knower, what is known, and the act of knowing.

Tulku — A teacher and guide in Tibetan Buddhism.

Tulsi — A sacred leaf used in the worship of Sri Krishna; a name for the Goddess; a short name for the poet-sage, Tulsidas.

Tulsidas — A famous devotional poet/saint of India who was a great devotee of Sri Ram and wrote many divine songs.

Turiya — Literally, "the fourth," referring to the fourth and highest state of Consciousness beyond waking, dreaming and deep sleep.

Tushti — Contentment.

Tyaga — Renunciation of the world for the sake of Enlightenment.

Udana — The upward moving prana.

Uddhava — Literally, "one who uplifts"; a member of the Yadava clan who was a great devotee of Sri Krishna.

Uddhava Gita — The Song of Uddhava, being a portion of a scripture excerpted from the Bhagavata Purana, the eleventh chapter, which constitutes Sri Krishna's final teachings to His disciple, Uddhava.

Ugra — Siva appearing as the undefeatable one.

Unmana Samadhi — A samadhi that takes one beyond the mind, manas.

Upadhis — Limiting adjuncts; body; vehicle; a subtle veil that obscures the true nature of a thing.

Upaguru — A preliminary teacher, through whose aid the aspirant is often brought in contact with the Guru.

Upalabdhi — Inner perception combined with spiritual attainment.

Upanisads — The Brahmakanda portion of the Vedas dealing with the knowledge that confirms the Truth of Brahman and reveals the Atman.

Uparamavairagya — The fifth of the Twelve Levels of Detachment which comes about due to satiety with the things of the world and experiences of earthly life. It signals the beginning of true detachment.

Uparati — Self-settledness or contentment, one of the Six Treasures (Shatsampatti) of Vedanta practice (sama, dama, uparati, titiksha, samadhana, and shraddha) which keeps the mind from drifting back to old habits and actions.

Upasana — Contemplation of God with form in meditation.

Upeksha — Equanimity; detachment; indifference.

Upeksha-ananyata — Absolute equanimity, even in the face of hard trials.

Urdhvaretoyogi — The luminary in whom the sexual energy has been controlled, refined, and sublimated and is flowing upwards to the crown of the head, emanating an abundance of qualities and boons upon life and living beings as a natural matter of course along the way.

Utpatti — The study of origins, based on inward examination to find the source for all that is external.

Utpaya Pratyaya — A helpful aid gained by the sincere practitioner which allows him/her to always move towards the highest Goal, and not settle for lower attainments.

Utsaha — Enthusiasm, as found in the most intrepid and forward moving devotees and aspirants of the Lord.

Vachaka — The pervading presence.

Vachya — The thing or object pervaded; that which can be denoted by speech.

Vahudakas — A class of roaming ascetics who are still seeking Self-realization and peace of mind.

Vaichitra — Varieties; one of the Seven Malas of Maya that distract the mind by spreading its attention over a wide range of objects and considerations.

Vaidhi bhakti — Rudimentary devotion utilizing the practice of rites and rituals before the shrine and altar.

Vaikhari — The external form of sound, worlds, bodies, and objects as a gross vibrational level of manifestation; one of the Four Manifestations of the Word, after Para, Pashyanti, and Madhyama.

Vaikuntha — The celestial city which is the subtle abode of Lord Vishnu.

Vandhyaputra — "Son of a barren woman," which is an example of an abhavapadartha.

Vairagya Shatakam — The Six Verses on Detachment composed by Shankara.

Vairagya — Detachment. Also defined as dispassion, it is one of the Four Jewels of Vedanta practice. After discrimination is applied revealing what is Real and what is unreal, detachment supplies the necessary power to withdraw from what is unreal.

Vaishikara — An intense level of detachment called "the lower level of the highest dispassion"; the eighth stage of the Twelve Levels of Dispassion cited in Vedanta Philosophy.

Vaishnavas — Followers of Vishnu; devotees of Krishna and Ram; those who follow Vaishnavism.

Vaishvanara — A name for the individual while he abides in the waking state, the "A" of AUM.

Vaishya — One of the four castes of Hindu society, or the merchant caste.

Vajrayana — The "Diamond Vehicle," referring to Tibetan Buddhism.

Vak — The Word, speech, language.

Vakdevi — Goddess of the Word; a name for Sarasvati, the Goddess of knowledge and learning. It is She who connects the thought, the sound, the word, and its meaning together, and it is She who is inherent in all four as the very power of comprehension.

Vaichika — The method of reciting the mantra out loud, as compared to muttering it or repeating it inaudibly.

Vaishesika — One of the six orthodox philosophies, or darshanas, of India.

Vaitrsnyamukti — The force of complete detachment which insures liberation from all manifest things.

Valmiki — Best known as the author of the Ramayana, he is also credited with writing the Yoga Vasishtha. Venerated as a sage, he was not always so. It was he, in his life as a thief, who attempted to rob Narada, but Narada reasoned with him and Valmiki repented. Entering spiritual life, Valmiki is said to have remained so long in meditation that an anthill (valmiki) rose up around him — thus, his name.

Vanaprastin — The third stage of dharmic living, wherein the husband and wife retire to the forest, away from society, to practice austerities, study, and meditate.

Vandanam — Devout worship of the Lord; one of the Eight Devotional Aids according to Devarshi Narada.

Vardhate — Disease, which is one in a list of six transformations superimposed over the ever-healthy Atman.

Varna — Caste; a form of the word; one of the six ways (sadakhya) in which to realize Brahman.

Vasanas — Desires, which when obsessed with and repeated, form subtle complexes in the mind and lead to rebirth in ignorance.

Vashitva — One of the Eight Occult Powers which allows those in pursuit of lower ideals to draw others to them.

Vasishtha — The great rishi, one of the seven great original Rishis according to Manu, who is said to be the author of the Rig Veda. The Yoga Vasishtha of Valmiki consists of instructions given to Rama by this great sage, for he was also the family priest of Ram's father, King Dasaratha.

Vastu — The difference between one substance or object and another.

Vatsalya Bhava — The relationship of parent and child; one of the Five Divine Moods for Worshiping God according to Vaishnavism.

Vedanta — One of the six orthodox darshanas, or paths of clear seeing, among India's host of high-minded philosophies.

Vedanta Dindima — The apt and final conclusion of the Vedanta, i.e., that "All is Brahman."

Vedavyasa — A name for Vyasa, the sage who gathered the Vedas into a collection, thereby preserving them for our times.

Vibhu — The all-pervading.

Vibhuti — Divine glory in manifestation; a special expression of God who reflects mastery over one power or area of spirituality.

Vichara — Inquiry into the nature of any aspect of Reality, such as the Atman, or a Mahavakya.

Vichikirsa — The indomitable Will of the Divine Being.

Vichikitsa — Perplexing; variegated; in Buddhism, the tendency towards skepticism that impedes the acceptance of spiritual truths.

Videhamukti — Freedom from all bodies, or ever taking birth in a body again out of ignorance.

Vidvan — A knower of Reality, applied specifically to those who are conscious of their inner divine nature.

Vidyadharas — A class of high-minded beings who are holders of the Eternal Wisdom, Dharma.

Vidyeshvaras/Vidyas — In Shaivism, two classes of higher beings who, though they still maintain a slight sense of separation from Siva, nevertheless have accomplished transcendence of maya's ill effects.

Vijnana — Highest knowledge denoting supreme intelligence, its acquisition is based on Self-realization.

Vijnana-kalas — In Shaivism, a cross section of subtle beings who possess wisdom during their lives and gain liberation at the time of pralaya.

Vijnanamayakosha — The sheath of the intellect; the intellectual body as a covering over Reality.

Vijnani — One who has gone beyond the duality of knowledge and ignorance. To paraphrase Sri Ramakrishna, in a spiritual context, an ajnani is ignorant that there is fire potential in wood; a jnani knows that there is fire potential in wood; but a vijnani knows how to kindle that fire in wood and can therefore cook his meal and receive nourishment. This demonstrates the difference between a worldly person, a wisdom seeker and an enlightened being.

Vikalpas — Creative imaginings; projections of the vibrating mind, usually based in desire, but used in the cosmic sense to reflect the initial power of the original creative urge.

Vikara — Modification, change, or transformation.

Vikarma — One of the three grades of karma arising from evil or ill-considered actions

Vikarana Bhava — One of the seven victories of the Tantric aspirant wherein he/she comes to know with certainty of the existence of Consciousness/God beyond the embodied condition.

Vikshepa — A power of Shakti that seemingly distorts Reality; one of the two obscuring forces of Maya, the other being avarana, which appears to veil Reality.

Vikshepas — Another name for the nine antarayas, the "despoilers," in Yoga.

Vikshipta — Distracted; not collected; one of the Five States of the Mind Field according to Yoga wherein the mind continually vacillates from calm to erratic in turns.

Vilva — A sacred leaf used in worship, especially auspicious for Lord Shiva.

Vimoha — Freedom from delusion.

Vina — A very ancient Indian stringed instrument associated with Sarasvati, the Goddess of art and learning.

Vinasha — Destruction.

Vinashini — An epithet for the Divine Mother in Her capacity for destroying ignorance in the minds of the devotees.

Viparita-bhavana — A particularly deluding evolute of maya which causes even intelligent beings to suppose that the physical world is the only reality, or that, obversely, nothing else exists but it.

Viseshas — Aspects of the human being that have special qualifications, such as the mind and the senses.

Viratrupa — The Lord in His form as the manifested universe.

Virochana — A king of the asuras who was the son of Prahlada.

Virya — Heroic; one of the Three Designations of Aspirants in Tantra Philosophy.

Visamvada-bhrama — Maya's power that causes beings to mistake one thing for another, like Consciousness for matter, etc.

Vishada — Depression; sorrow; listed as one of the Four Deadly Traps in Vedanta and one of the Seven Malas of Maya in Tantra Philosophy.

Vishalakshi — A name for a deadly whirlpool in a river in India; a name for the Divine Mother of the Universe.

Vishaya — An object of attraction.

Vishayashakti — One of the sixteen evolutes of maya that attracts the mind of the worldly person to enjoyment of the five senses only.

Visheshas — Attributes, like senses and elements of special quality.

Vishnu — The second deity in the Hindu Trinity; the God of preservation and the one from whom the Avatars emerge.

Vishnu Agamas — Tantric scripture having to do with the worship of Vishnu.

Vishuddha chakra — The spiritual vortex or chakra which is the fifth center of Kundalini Yoga Science, described as the "throat" chakra.

Vishnugranthi — A knot or barrier above the three lower chakras that must be penetrated before the soul can arrive at the heart chakra, thus go beyond rebirth in the lower worlds.

Vivarta — False superimposition; a term Vedanta teachers use to indicate the often unexplainable phenomena of the appearance of the unreal over the real, the apparent over the actual, of falsehood over Truth.

Visvamitra — An illumined Indian rishi.

Vishvarupa — The Cosmic Form; a being having all forms, like Lord Vishnu.

Viveka — Discrimination, of the type that allows one to see through all personal and collective delusions and penetrate the coverings over Reality.

Vivekachudamani — Crest Jewel of Discrimination; a profound text by Shankaracharya citing the value of spiritual life and containing deep philosophical teachings.

Vivekajnan — Special wisdom gained from the maturation of discrimination in the mind.

Vivekananda — See Swami Vivekananda.

Viveka-khyati — A special type of discrimination in Yoga that reveals to the aspirant the distinction between the buddhi, intelligence, and the Purusha.

Vrata — Vow

Vrindavan — The holy city in India associated with the life of Lord Krishna.

Vrittijnan — The subtle power of maya which causes beings to think that knowledge gotten from the world, from the senses, and from the ordinary mind is absolute knowledge.

Vrittis — Mental vibrations or thought forms.

Vyadhi — Disease of the body; one of the Nine Distractions to Spiritual Life according to Yoga Philosophy.

Vyahrtis — Bhur, Bhuvah, and Svah, eternal words for the Three Worlds.

Vyana — The all-pervading prana.

Vyapi — The all-pervading one.

Vyapti — One of the Eight Occult Powers which allow those who are attracted to lower ideals to increase in size and weight or appear bigger.

Vyasti — The individual rather than the whole, the microcosm rather than the macrocosm.

Vyavaharika — life and activity lived only in the phenomenal world, devoid of dharmic knowledge and spiritual realization.

Vyutthana-chitta — The worldly mind; worldliness; one of the Three Stupefactions of Neo-Vedanta.

Yahweh — A name for God in the Jewish religion.

Yajnavalkya — An ancient rishi of great repute who authored portions of the Upanisads, and who was the founder of the school of the White Yajur Veda. His discourse to Maitreyi, one of his two wives, forms an important part of the Brhadaranyaka Upanisad.

Yama — The Lord of Death.

Yamas — Five exercises in Yoga which constitute the first limb of eight in Patanjala, and which the practitioner should practice and accomplish before moving on to the successive seven limbs.

Yashodara — The wife of Lord Buddha

Yatamana — Control of mind based upon self-effort; one of the Four Steps to Fundamental Detachment.

Yogi — A practitioner and master of the path of Yoga.

Yogini — A woman who succeeds in the path of Yoga.

Yugas — One of four ages or divisions of time, called Satya, Treta, Dvapara, and Kali, each consisting of thousands of years, which together make up a Mahayuga or Chaturyuga.

Yukti — Reasoning about the Truth, to be utilized in connection with first hearing It, Shruti, and thereafter gaining personal experience of It, Anubhava.

SRV Associations

Other Books by Babaji Bob Kindler

- Twenty-Four Aspects of Mother Kali *
    (Kindle edition e-book available)
- The Ten Divine Articles of Sri Durga *
    (Kindle edition e-book available)
- The Avadhut and His Twenty-Four Teachers in Nature
- Sri Sarada Vijnanagita
- An Extensive Anthology of Sri Ramakrishna's Stories
- Swami Vivekananda Vijnanagita
- A Quintessential Yoga Vasishtha
- Reclaiming Kundalini Yoga *
- Dissolving the Mindstream *
- Jnana Matra – The Wisdom Particle *
- Manasana – The Superlative Art of Mental Posture
- Cosmic Quintuplications – The Secret of Panchakarana

Mini Series

- We Are Atman All-Abiding *
- Strike Off Thy Fetters! *
- Hasta-Amalaka Stotram *

(All three of the above books are soon to be published in one volume, entitled Triple Gem.

(* Kindle versions available)

Planned Future Releases

- Atmic Testament on Yoga
- Teachings of the Matri Avatar
- The Nine Limbs of Bhakti of Sri Ram
- Guru Yoga in Contemporary Times
- White Crane, White Swan: The Commonality of Zen and Advaita Vedanta

Further inquiries at:
SRV Associations
P.O. Box 1364
Honoka'a, Hawaii 96727
website: www.srv.org
email: srvinfo@srv.org

To purchase full-size charts appearing in *Footfalls of the Indian Rishis* and other works, visit:
www.dharmaartwisdomcharts.com

CPSIA information can be obtained
at www.ICGtesting.com
Printed in the USA
LVHW070953010222
709948LV00005B/9